The Complete
Encyclopedia of
Motorcars
1885 to
the Present

Edited by
G.N. Georgano

CONTRIBUTORS
Thorkil Ry Andersen
Glenn Baechler
Oluf Berrum
Gordon Brooks
Hugh Conway
Hugh Durnford
Bill Emery
David Filsell
H. A. Fitzpatrick

Eddie L. Ford
G. N. Georgano
G. L. Hartner
Peter Hull
Roland Jerry
Richard M.
　Langworth
Lucien Loreille
Keith Marvin
Court Myers

G. Marshall Naul
Hans-Otto Neubauer
T. R. Nicholson
Doug Nye
Cyril Posthumus
Michael Sedgwick
José Rodriguez–Viña
Michael Worthington-
　Williams
Aldo Zucchi

The Complete Encyclopedia of
Motorcars
1885 to the Present

E. P. Dutton and Company Inc., New York

This book was designed and produced by
George Rainbird Ltd,
Marble Arch House, 44 Edgware Road, London W2
for E. P. Dutton & Co Inc,
201 Park Avenue South, New York, N.Y. 10003

© George Rainbird Ltd, 1968, 1973

First edition 1968
Reprinted 1969 (twice), 1970, 1971, 1972
Second edition 1973

Library of Congress Catalog Card Number: 68–22674

ISBN: 0–525–08351–0

House Editor: Peter Coxhead

The text was filmset and printed by
Butler & Tanner Ltd, Frome.
The Color plates and jacket were printed by
C. J. Mason & Sons Ltd, Bristol.
The book was bound by
Webb, Son & Co, London.

PRINTED IN GREAT BRITAIN

To the memory of
George Ralph Doyle and John Pollitt

G. R. Doyle (1890–1961) was the first man to compile a worldwide address list of car manufacturers. *The World's Automobiles*, first published privately in 1932, stimulated the interest of countless enthusiasts. Without Doyle's pioneer work, the compilation of this encyclopedia would have been a near impossibility.

John Pollitt (1892–1958) was one of the most painstaking of researchers into motoring history. After his retirement from the Rover company in 1945, he devoted his entire time to investigations and correspondence on the subject, the fruits of which he wrote up in twenty-eight files, running to several million words. These files (generously lent by Dennis C. Field) have been among the most important cornerstones of the encyclopedia.

Acknowledgments

First of all, I would like to thank all the contributors, who have been unfailingly helpful, prompt in delivery of copy, and worked right up to the last minute in checking the more obscure points. Especially I must thank Michael Sedgwick, who has not only written one quarter of the book, but also made many valuable suggestions in general. He has been a tireless and painstaking collaborator. Particular thanks are also due to my friends David Filsell and Bill Emery, for whom this book has been the realization of a long-cherished ambition, and who have given much time and thought to the work.

For valuable help in many different ways, the contributors would like to thank the following people:

A. L. Abbott
Robert W. Ainsworth
Dr Giancarlo Amari
Harold Angel
Angelo Tito Anselmi
Alvin J. Arnheim
Miss Daphne Arnott
Ing Adolf Babuška
Pierre Badre
R. Baillie
Glenn M. Beach
Geoffroy de Beauffort
Doug Bell
Randolph P. Bellman
Jim Benjaminson
Tony Bird
Al Bloemker
Albert R. Bochroch
John Bolster
Brian Bolton
C. A. Bottoms
Tom Brahmer
E. S. Brown
Homer D. Brown
Dave Brownell
A. S. E. Browning
P. de Bruyn
E. W. Buis
John S. Burnham
Dick Caesar
W. Cameron
Michael Cannon
Sid Church
Matthew Clark
G. P. Clemons
John A. Conde
John Crosslé
John Davy
Edward du Cros
Paul Emery
Michael Erskine
Richard Evans
Dennis Field
Kevin Field
S. L. Fulker
Joaquín Ciuró Gabarró
Edward W. Gaylord
Yves Giraud-Cabantous
Dr Henry Goldhann
David Goode
Bryan K. Goodman
Randall Gould

Max Gregory
R. C. Harris
Colin Hilton
E. R. Holden
José Nestor Hopf
H. C. Hopkins
Roger Hurst
E. E. Husting
Robert Jaeger
David K. James
Stan James
Lytton P. Jarman
W. S. Jaro
Horton Johnson
Robert R. Johnson
Lars Kile
Miss Beverly Rae Kimes
Shotaro Kobayashi
Jacques Kupélian
Frank Kurtis
Margus-Hans Kuuse
N. A. Lawson
David Lazenby
Ian Leschallas
Harry Lester
Dr Alfred S. Lewerenz
William J. Lewis
H. B. Light
Ivor Linsdell
Brian Lister
Hector Mackenzie-Wintle
Ivan Mahy
Arthur Mallock
D. R. Manning
Thomas Maylone
F. Wilson McComb
Hector A. Mendizabal
David O. Millard
Warren K. Miller
David L. Morse
N. Barrington Needham
John Noble
C. E. Noel-Storr
Desmond Peacock
John M. Peckham
C. Poel Jr
Serge Pozzoli
A. James Price
Harry Pulfer
Daryl M. Quimby
Petr Rada

Peter A. Readyhough
E. T. Reynolds
Arthur Rippey
A. R. Ronald
G. Rosekilly
Michael Rosen
Miss Nancy Rott
J. Rousseau
Andrzej Rusinek
John Sawyer
Martin Schacht
J. D. Scheel
Wolfgang Schnieber
Robert Scoon
Robert Sexé
R. G. Shattock
J. A. Shaw
Bob Shepherd
T. L. Sherred
Miss Georgia Shovlain
Dave Skinner
Frank T. Snyder Jr
Horacio Speratti
R. C. Sprague
Charles Stowell
Lord Strathcarron
Marian Šuman-Hreblay
E. R. Tarnowsky
Alvaro C. Tatlock
David Thirlby
Brian Thomas
Eric Thompson
John Tojeiro
Erwin Tragatsch
Franklin B. Tucker
Robert N. Tuthill
Roger van Bolt
José B. Vazeilles
William Watson
C. R. Weaver
Wayne Weihermiller
Bernard J. Weis
John A. Weiszer
Joe H. Whitney
Andrew Whyte
Michael Wilby
Max Williamson
Andrew Wilson
Jonathan Wood
Bob Wyatt
Dr Percy Young

All photographs have been credited in their captions, but I would like to make special acknowledgment to the following, who have lent generously from their private collections:

Thorkil Ry Andersen
Ing Adolf Babuška
Comte Geoffroy de Beauffort
David Filsell
Maurice Harrison
G. L. Hartner
Gili de Heredia
Shotaro Kobayashi
Jacques Kupélian
Dr Alfred S. Lewerenz
Lucien Loreille
Ivan Mahy

Keith Marvin
T. A. S. O. Mathieson
Hans-Otto Neubauer
C. Poel Jr
José Rodriguez-Viña
Bernard Sanders
David Scott
Kenneth Stauffer
David Burgess Wise
Michael Worthington-Williams
Aldo Zucchi

I would also like to thank the following museums, journals, and libraries for their generous help in searching out and lending many rare photographs:

Antique Automobile: William S. Jackson, (formerly) Editor
Autocar, London: Maurice A. Smith, DFC, (formerly) Editor
        Bill Banks
        Mrs K. Maynard
        Miss Hazel Dumayne
Automobielmuseum, Driebergen: G. Riemer
Automobile Manufacturers' Association, Detroit: Peter B. Teeley
Automotive History Collection, Detroit Public Library: James J. Bradley
Autosport, London: Miss Peggie O'Mahony
        Michael Hollingshead
Gilltrap's Museum, Coolangatta, Queensland: Mrs K. Gilltrap
Glasgow Museum of Transport: A. S. E. Browning
Harrah's Automobile Collection, Reno: E. R. Tarnowsky
Henry Ford Museum, Dearborn, Mich.: Leslie R. Henry
Herbert Art Gallery & Museum, Coventry: Cyril J. Scott
Indianapolis Motor Speedway Museum: Karl Kizer
Long Island Automotive Museum, Glen Cove, L.I.: Henry Austin Clark Jr
Motor, London: Mrs E. Welch
Motor Sport, London: Laurence A. Morton
Musée de l'Automobile, Le Mans: Comte Bernard de Lassée
Musée de l'Automobile, Rochetaillée-sur-Saone: Henri Malartre
Museo dell'Automobile, Turin: Dr Giancarlo Amari
National Motor Museum, Beaulieu, Hants: Lord Montagu of Beaulieu
        Michael Ware
        Derek Maidment
Philadelphia Free Library, Miss Mary M. Cattie
The Raben Collection, Nysted: Baron J. O. Raben-Levetzau
Swiss Museum of Transport & Communications, Lucerne: Alfred Waldis
        Jacob Mösli
The Veteran Car Club of Great Britain, London: Dennis C. Field, Librarian
        Brian Dinsley, Librarian
        Mrs Joan Das, Secretary

G. N. GEORGANO

Contents

Introduction

When The Complete Encyclopedia of Motorcars was first mooted, there arose immediately the problem of its scope. Some people would question the temerity of using the word 'complete'; the humblest make of car can rate 1,000 words if all its history be recorded, while, as many excellent one-make histories have shown, for an important make 60,000 words is by no means too much. It was soon decided that the encyclopedia should not run to more than one volume, and that in order to allow ample room for photographic coverage, the text should not extend to more than 400,000 words. Within this limit we have tried to give balanced biographies of over 4,000 makes of car that have been offered for sale over the past eighty odd years.

The authors of sports and racing car books often begin by defining their subject. In our case this might seem unnecessary: the word 'complete' should mean every car ever made. However there have to be some limitations, the chief of which are as follows:

(1) In order to exclude the hundreds of one-off specials, we insist that there must be reasonable evidence of intention to manufacture cars for sale to the public. We are well aware that this is not a water-tight limitation, for to establish 'intention to manufacture' one would have to read the minds of car builders long dead. In the early days of the industry hundreds of amateur mechanics thought they could do as well as Louis Renault or Adolphe Clément, and took a small stand at the Paris Salon on which to exhibit their hastily-assembled prototype. If no interested customers appeared, this was often the end of the make, and sometimes the builder never even formed a company. The formation of a company, the announcement of a price, the issue of a catalog, are all fairly safe indications of intention to manufacture, and yet there have been stock promotion schemes which did all these things and yet had no aim beyond that of selling bogus shares, and never made a car. These are not included, although there are borderline cases which rate an entry, where at least one car was built. Every rule brings forth exceptions, and some people might question the allocation of nearly 500 words to the Owen from Comeragh Road, London, whose 36-year history on paper does not seem to have brought forth even one car. However this is such a persistent phantom, and involves so many 'makes', that it deserves a mention. Cars built by an organization for their own use, and not for sale, are not included; the most significant example of this is the B.R.M. racing car. Also excluded are the pioneer cars by such inventors as Lenoir and Markus, for, interesting though they were, they were in no sense even would-be production cars. Our starting date of 1885 is justified by two vehicles – the Amedée Bollée steam coach ordered by the Marquis de Broc, which although not a production car, was built for sale, and the first Benz three-wheeler. This was not sold to the public, but was the first of a line of cars which were very definitely on sale a few years later.

(2) As this is an encyclopedia of motorcars and not of commercial vehicles, only those cars which were built for private use as passenger-carrying vehicles are included. Estate cars and station wagons are mentioned where relevant, but mobile caravans built on goods vehicle chassis, although normally used by private individuals, are not included.

(3) Motorcycles are obviously excluded, but a few fully-bodied two-wheeled cars, such as the Atlantic, Moore (v), and Whitwood Monocar, are listed. A more difficult problem is posed by the distinction between a tricycle and a three-wheeled car. Early tricycles, such as the De Dion Bouton, were obviously of the motorcycle family, but from about 1903 a race of vehicles appeared using the frame, saddle, engine and final drive of a motorcycle, with two wheels in front and a seat, often of wickerwork, for

a passenger. Known as tri-cars, they were still of motorcycle descent, but gradually the driver's saddle became a seat, the handlebars were replaced by a steering wheel, and they took on the appearance of a tandem car on three wheels. With makes such as Riley it is almost impossible to decide at what point they became cars. The more car-like vehicles, such as the Bat, are included in the encyclopedia, while the many makes which never progressed beyond saddle, handlebars, and wickerwork, are not.

Adherence to these principles will explain the absence from the encyclopedia of a number of makes which have appeared in other lists. A surprising number of garages, coachbuilders, and cycle makers who never made a car, listed themselves hopefully as motor manufacturers in such works as Porter's Motor Trade Directory. In fact the ambitions of car builders knew no bounds: James & Browne of Hammersmith announced in January 1902 that they were to 'carry on the business of automobile, flying machine, and submarine manufacturers', while the Hungerford brothers of Elmira, N.Y. (whose car is not in the book; it is illustrated on the front end paper) described themselves as makers of 'Solar and Interstellar, Rocket Motors for Automobiles, Airplanes and Gliders'.

Having established which makes were to be included, the next problem was to determine the treatment each make should receive. It is obviously impossible to list every model made by each firm, and no attempt has been made to do so. For example, the English Daimler company offered 23 models in one year (1927), and to enumerate them all would be tedious and wasteful of space. However we have indicated the broad line of development, mentioning any technical features which were distinctive for the period. In pioneer days when wheel or tiller steering were used, each system is mentioned, but after 1900 it may be assumed that steering was by wheel unless stated otherwise. On makes with a long history we have indicated the introduction of such features as shaft drive, electric starting and lighting, front wheel brakes, and so on. The expression 'a thoroughly conventional car' may seem annoyingly vague to some readers, but it cannot be denied that by about 1910 car design had settled down to a pattern embracing a front-mounted in-line, water-cooled engine, driving via a three or four speed sliding pinion gearbox and propeller shaft to bevel-geared rear axle. Any deviations from this pattern such as V-engine layout, air-cooling, epicyclic gearbox or belt drive, are mentioned. Wherever possible we have given the horsepower rating (see Glossary) or cubic capacity, and number of cylinders.

Sporting activities are mentioned where they are relevant, and whenever cars were built for Grand Prix or other racing. Admittedly such cars may not always have been for sale to outsiders, but in the case of firms like Ferrari they form such an important part of the company's history that they cannot be omitted.

The dating of cars, especially in the captions to illustrations, may cause confusion because of the discrepancy between the model year and the calendar year. Normally the date given is the year in which the car was made (this follows the practice of the Dating Committee of the Veteran Car Club of Great Britain). However an exception has to be made for those cars announced as (for example) 1968 models, even though they were made during the last quarter of 1967. This is especially important with American cars, where the next season's models are almost always announced in September or October. The Mercury was introduced in November 1938 (hence a starting date of 1938 in our entry) but even the first cars made were always thought of as 1939 models, and are thus described in the caption. The only known example of a two year discrepancy is that of the Palmer-Singer company, who announced late in 1913 their 1915 models, in a frantic attempt to capture the public's attention.

The nationality of a car is indicated by the letter(s) used by the International Conventions of 1926 and 1949 (see page 18), and refer to the country where the parent firm was situated. Production under licence in other countries is mentioned in the text, but not in the heading or the address. Dual nationality may arise in two ways:

(1) Cars like the Belgian/Italian Hermes or H.I.S.A. which issued from factories in different countries at the same time, or used engines from one country and

chassis frames from another. These are indicated as follows: (B/I)

(2) Cars whose nationality changed for political reasons. The most familiar cases are the provinces of the Austro-Hungarian Empire which after 1918 became Czechoslovakia, and the provinces of Alsace and Lorraine, German to 1918 and French thereafter. Dual nationality of this nature is indicated by (A;CS), or (D;F).

The makes are listed in alphabetical order, but the following points should be noted:

(1) Makes having Christian names as part of their make-up are classified under the Christian name—eg: Georges Irat, not Irat, Georges.

(2) Makes beginning with Mc are listed between M.C.C. and Méan, not at the beginning of the letter 'M'.

(3) Makes beginning with De are classified under the letter 'D'. Thus De Lavaud is found in D, not L.

(4) Makes beginning with Le or La are classified under the letter 'L'. Thus La Salle is found in L, not S.

(5) Makes using initial letters joined by 'and', such as S. and M. Simplex, or S. and S., are classified as if they were spelt Sand . . .

(6) Names with modified letters (eg: ü or ø) are treated alphabetically as if they had unmodified letters.

(7) Romanization of Chinese characters. There are three systems of romanization in common use, Wade-Giles, Pinyin, and Yale. The name Hong-Chi, commonly used in Western circles for the Red Flag car, is in fact incorrect by any of the systems. It has to be one of the following:

HUNG-CH'I   (Wade-Giles)
HONG-QI   (Pinyin)
HUNG-CHI   (Yale)

In the encyclopedia we are using both Pinyin (p) and Wade-Giles (wg) systems, the makes being listed alphabetically under the former. The Wade-Giles form, and the English name, are given in cross-references.

We are very grateful to the producers for such a generous allocation of photographs, but even so, many have had to be left out, and we apologize to readers whose favourite model has been omitted. It has been impossible to find a satisfactory photograph of some interesting cars that we would like to have illustrated, despite the generous co-operation of many collectors. We are well aware that the quality of some photographs leaves much to be desired, but where nothing better was obtainable, we felt that readers would rather see an indifferent photograph than none at all.

Any corrections or additions which readers may think desirable for future editions will be very welcome. They should be sent to the Editor, c/o Rainbird Reference Books Ltd, Marble Arch House, 44 Edgware Road, London W2, England.

This new edition continues the original aim of listing every make of passenger car offered for sale to the public. Entries, whether of old or current makes, have been revised where necessary and, in some cases, rewritten. Current makes have been brought up-to-date to the end of 1972 and there are entries for the new makes that have appeared since the publication of the first edition. Earlier makes, brought to light as a result of further research and much valued correspondence from readers, are now added.

The careful reader will notice that a few makes have been deleted. These fall into two categories:

1. A very small number were found to be ineligible, because the manufacturers never built passenger cars.

2. Dune buggies and all-terrain vehicles. These have proliferated to such an extent since the publication of the first edition that to have included all the makes would have made impossible demands on the space available. The basic similarity in design of dune buggies, and the fact that they are not primarily road vehicles, makes them of minimal interest to readers of this encyclopedia. For the sake of consistency, the few makes which were originally included, such as the Empi and the Con-Ferr Cougar, have now been omitted.

Color Plates

Color Plates

1 1893 BENZ 5hp victoria. Owned by Museo dell'Automobile, Turin. Photograph by Josip Ciganovic.

2 1897 LÉON BOLLÉE 3hp voiturette. Owned for 38 years by S. C. H. Davis and now owned by Indianapolis Speedway Museum. Photograph by Charles Robinson.

3 1900 BENZ 'Comfortable' 3½hp vis-à-vis. Owned by Bryan K. Goodman. Photograph by Charles Robinson.

4 1901 DE DION-BOUTON 4½hp voiturette. Owned by Baron J. A. Raben-Levetzau. Photograph by Bernard.

5 1902 RAMBLER 8hp two-seater. Owned by Baron J. A. Raben-Levetzau. Photograph by Bernard.

6 c. 1902 HOLSMAN 8hp motor buggy. Owned by Baron J. A. Raben-Levetzau. Photograph by Bernard.

7 c.1904 DELAUGÈRE 24hp roadster. Owned by Baron J. A. Raben-Levetzau. Photograph by Raben.

8 1903 F.I.A.T. 16/24hp tonneau. Owned by Museo dell'Automobile, Turin, Photograph by Josip Ciganovic.

9 1904 CADILLAC 8½hp limousine. Owned by Mrs M. E. Bowden. Photograph by Derrick E. Witty.

10 1909 FORD Model T 20hp tourer. Owned by Baron J. A. Raben-Levetzau. Photograph by Bernard.

11 1907 SIZAIRE ET NAUDIN 8hp roadster. Owned by Museo dell' Automobile, Turin. Photograph by Josip Ciganovic.

12 1910 DELAUNAY-BELLEVILLE 25hp tourer. Owned by Baron J. A. Raben-Levetzau. Photograph by J. Bache.

13 1912 CLÉMENT-BAYARD 20hp tourer. Owned by Baron J. A. Raben-Levetzau. Photograph by J. Bache.

14 1912 HISPANO-SUIZA Alfonso 3.6-litre sports car. Owned by The Montagu Motor Museum. Photograph by Charles Robinson.

15 1913 MERCER Type 35 Raceabout. Owned by Dr Samuel Scher. Photograph copyright Henry Austin Clark Jr, Glen Cove, New York

16 1913 PEUGEOT 24hp tourer. Owned by Baron J. A. Raben-Levetzau. Photograph by Bernard.

17 1913 ZÜST 25/35hp tourer. Owned by R. A. Collings. Photograph by Derrick E. Witty.

18 1914 LOCOMOBILE 48hp roadster. Owned by Baron J. A. Raben-Levetzau. Photograph by Raben.

19 1912 AUSTRIAN DAIMLER Prince Henry 27/80hp tourer. Owned by C. J. Bendall. Photograph by Charles Pocklington.

20 1919 FIAT Tipo 501 1½-litre tourer. Owned by Museo dell'Automobile, Turin. Photograph by Josip Ciganovic.

21 1920 DETROIT ELECTRIC coupé. Owned by Baron J. A. Raben-Levetzau. Photograph by Bernard.

22 1922 PIERCE ARROW 38hp roadster. Owned by Baron J. A. Raben-Levetzau. Photograph by J. Bache.

23 1922 WILLS SAINTE CLAIRE V-8 roadster. Photograph copyright Wm A. C. Pettit III.

24 1923 CITROËN 5CV two-seater. Owned by Museo dell'Automobile, Turin. Photograph by Josip Ciganovic.

25 1925 MERCEDES-BENZ Model K 6.6-litre landaulette. Coachwork by Erdmann & Rossi. Owned by Baron J. A. Raben-Levetzau. Photograph by Raben.

26 1922 MARMON Model 34 speedster. Owned by J. K. Lilly III. Photograph by Spooner Studio, Falmouth, Mass.

27 1925 FRAZER NASH 1½-litre sports car. Owned by Geoffrey Hare. Photograph by John R. Price.

28 1926 LANCIA Lambda Sixth Series 2.1-litre tourer. Loaned by E. F. S. Seal to The Montagu Motor Museum. Photograph by Charles Robinson.

29 1926 BENTLEY 3-litre Red Label tourer. Owned by A. Edgell Baxter. Photograph by Charles Pocklington.

Continued on page 65

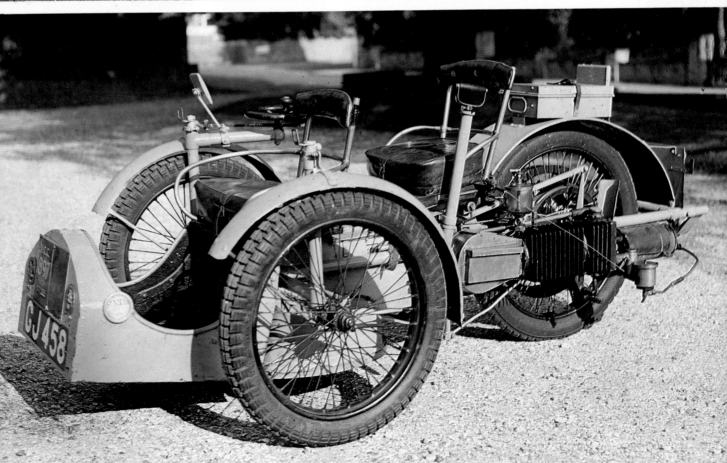

1. 1893 BENZ

2. 1897 LÉON BOLLÉE

3. 1900 BENZ

4. 1901 DE DION-BOUTON

5. 1902 RAMBLER

6. *c.*1902 HOLSMAN

7. *c.*1904 DELAUGÈRE

8. 1903 F.I.A.T.

9. 1904 CADILLAC

10. 1909 FORD

11. 1907 SIZAIRE ET NAUDIN

12. 1910 DELAUNAY-BELLEVILLE

13. 1912 CLÉMENT-BAYARD

14. 1912 HISPANO-SUIZA

15. 1913 MERCER

16. 1913 PEUGEOT

17. 1913 ZÜST

18. 1914 LOCOMOBILE

19. 1912 AUSTRIAN DAIMLER

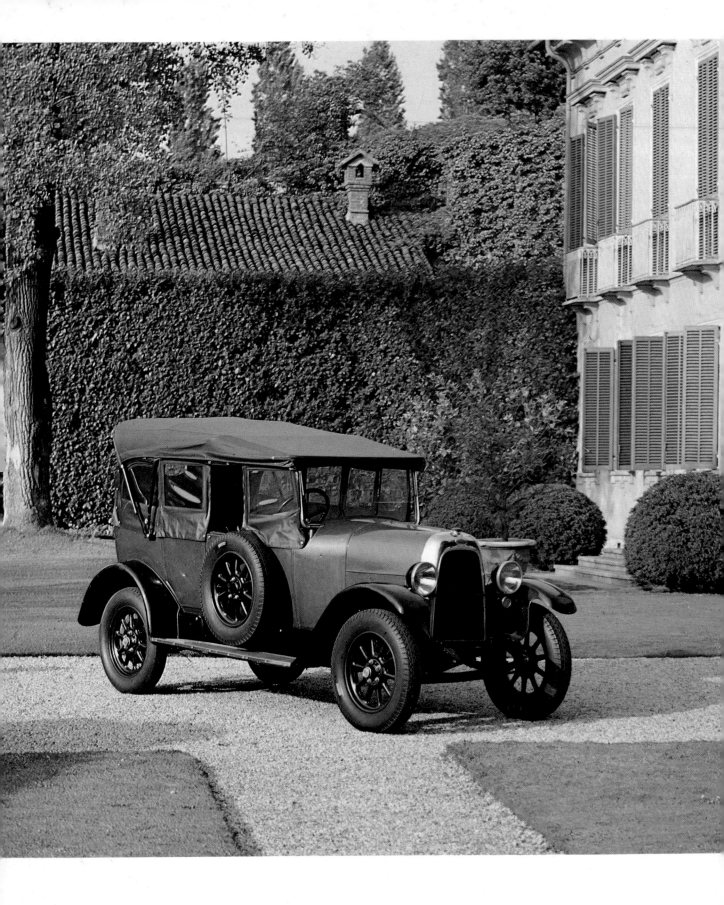

20. 1919 FIAT

21. 1920 DETROIT ELECTRIC

22. 1922 PIERCE ARROW
23. 1922 WILLS SAINTE CLAIRE

25. 1925 MERCEDES-BENZ

26. 1922 MARMON

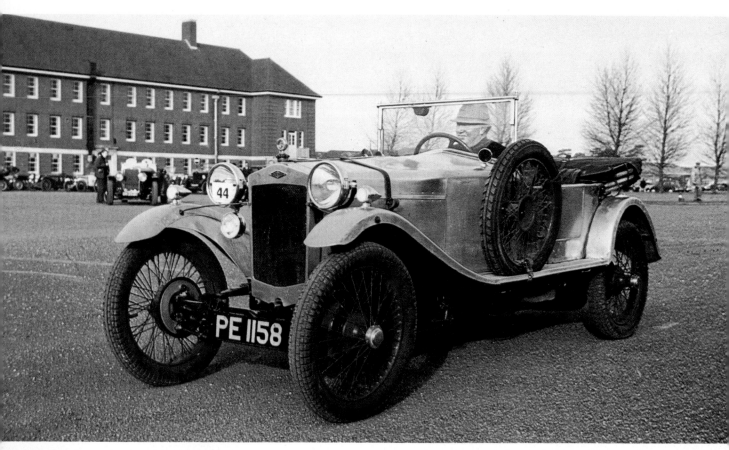

27. 1925 FRAZER NASH
28. 1926 LANCIA

29. 1926 BENTLEY

30. 1925 AMILCAR ITALIANA; 1930 AMILCAR

31. 1927 PACKARD

32. 1930 DUESENBERG

33. 1933 MORGAN

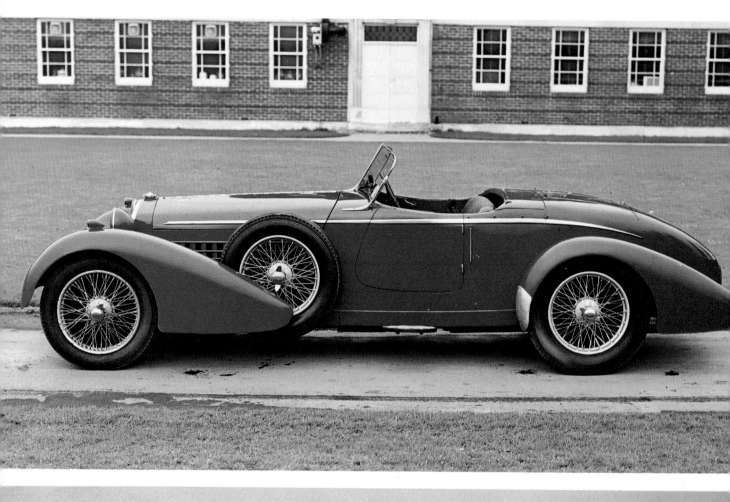

34. 1933 ALFA ROMEO
35. 1936 CORD

36. 1935 AUBURN
37. 1935 FIAT

38. 1927 BUGATTI; 1937 BUGATTI

39. 1936 VAUXHALL

40. 1937 WOLSELEY

41. 1940 LINCOLN

42. 1948 TUCKER

43. 1947 TRIUMPH

44. 1948 CISITALIA

45. 1950 JAGUAR

46. 1951 FERRARI

47. 1953 JOWETT

48. 1961 AUSTIN
49. 1959 B.M.W.

50. 1956 B.M.W.-ISETTA

51. 1964 VOLVO

52. 1960 CHEVROLET
53. 1965 RENAULT

54. 1969 PORSCHE

55. 1968 ASTON MARTIN

56. 1970 FORD

57. 1968 ROLLS-ROYCE

58. 1972 HONDA

59. 1973 VOLKSWAGEN

60. 1973 OLDSMOBILE

30 (*Left*) 1925 AMILCAR ITALIANA
Model CGSs 8.9hp sports car;
(*right*) 1930 AMILCAR CS8 2.3-litre
four-seater sports car. Owned by Bryan
K. Goodman. Photograph by Charles
Robinson.

31 1927 PACKARD 39.2hp saloon.
Owned by Baron J. A. Raben-
Levetzau. Photograph by Raben.

32 1929 DUESENBERG Model J 6.9-litre
sedanca de ville. Coachwork by
Barker. Owned by James E. Dougherty.
Photograph by John R. Price.

33 1933 MORGAN Super Sports 11hp
3-wheeler. Loaned by I. T. G. Pullar
to The Montagu Motor Museum.
Photograph by Charles Robinson.

34 1933 ALFA ROMEO Tipo 8C 2.3-
litre sports car. Owned by Mrs Angela
Cherrett. Photograph by Derrick E.
Witty.

35 1936 CORD Model 812 4.7-litre
convertible. Owned by James Leasor.
Photograph by Charles Pocklington.

36 1935 AUBURN Type 851 4.6-litre
speedster. Loaned by Vintage Tyre
Supplies Ltd to The Montagu Motor
Museum.

37 1935 FIAT Tipo 508S Balilla 995cc
sports car. Owned by the Hon Lady
Montagu of Beaulieu. Photograph by
Charles Robinson.

38 (*Left*) 1927 BUGATTI Type 43 2.3-
litre four-seater sports car; (*right*) 1937
BUGATTI Type 57S 3.3-litre drophead
coupé. Owned by T. A. Roberts.
Photograph by Charles Pocklington.

39 1936 VAUXHALL Model DX 14hp
drophead coupé. Coachwork by
Whittingham & Mitchel. Owned by
Mrs Gwen Bryant. Photograph by
Derrick E. Witty.

40 1937 WOLSELEY Super Six 25hp
drophead coupé. Built for Lord
Nuffield. Owned by The Montagu
Motor Museum. Photograph by
Charles Robinson.

41 1940 LINCOLN Continental 4.8-litre
cabriolet. Owned by H. T. C. Angel.
Photograph by Lee Heiland.

42 1948 TUCKER 5.4-litre sedan. Photograph copyright Wm A. C. Pettit III.

43 1947 TRIUMPH 1800 1.8-litre
roadster. Owned by H. W. Harold.
Photograph by Derrick E. Witty.

44 1948 CISITALIA 1090cc coupé.
Coachwork by Pininfarina. Owned by
Museo dell'Automobile, Turin.
Photograph by Josip Ciganovic.

45 1950 JAGUAR XK120 3½-litre sports
car. Loaned by Jaguar Cars Ltd to
The Montagu Motor Museum. Photograph by Charles Robinson.

46 1951 FERRARI 212 Export 2½-litre
sports car. Owned by Basil Panzer.
Photograph copyright Henry Austin
Clark Jr, Glen Cove, New York.

47 1953 JOWETT Javelin 1½-litre saloon.
Owned by Brian Street. Photograph by
Derrick E. Witty.

48 1961 AUSTIN Mini 848cc saloon.
Photograph copyright British Motor
Corporation Ltd.

49 1959 B.M.W. Typ 507 3.2-litre sports
car. Owned by C. W. P. Hampton.
Photograph by Charles Pocklington.

50 1956 B.M.W-ISETTA 248cc coupé
Photograph copyright Bayerische
Motoren-Werke AG.

51 1964 VOLVO 121 1.8-litre saloon.
Photograph copyright Volvo Concessionaires Ltd.

52 1960 CHEVROLET Corvair 2.3-litre
sedan. Photograph copyright General
Motors Corporation.

53 1965 RENAULT R16 1½-litre saloon.
Photograph copyright Renault Ltd.

54 1969 PORSCHE 912 1.6-litre coupé.
Owned and photographed by Josip
Ciganovic.

55 1968 ASTON MARTIN DBS 4-litre
GT coupé. Photograph copyright
Aston Martin Lagonda Ltd.

56 1970 FORD Escort TC 1.8-litre
saloon, winner of the World Cup
Rally. Photograph copyright Ford
Motor Co Ltd.

57 1968 ROLLS-ROYCE Silver-Shadow
6.2-litre convertible. Coachwork by
H. J. Mulliner, Park Ward Ltd.
Photograph copyright Rolls-Royce Ltd.

58 1972 HONDA Z coupé. Photograph
copyright Honda (UK) Ltd.

59 1973 VOLKSWAGEN 1303 saloon.
Photograph copyright Volkswagen
Werk AG.

60 1973 OLDSMOBILE Omega Hatchback coupé. Photograph copyright
General Motors Corporation.

INTERNATIONAL REGISTRATION LETTERS

The country of manufacture has been indicated in the text by the International Registration Letters (as established by the International Conventions of 1926 and 1949 and as notified to the United Nations). The letters printed in **bold** in the complete list (reproduced by courtesy of World Touring and Automobile Organisations) are those of the manufacturing countries:

A	Austria	**GBA**	Alderney	
ADN	Southern Yemen (formerly Aden)	**GBG**	Guernsey	(Channel Islands)
AL	Albania	GBJ	Jersey	
AND	Andorra	**GBM**	Isle of Man	
AUS	Australia (including Papua and New Guinea)	GBZ	Gibraltar	
		GCA	Guatemala	
		GH	Ghana	
B	Belgium	**GR**	Greece	
BDS	Barbados			
BG	Bulgaria	**H**	Hungary	
BH	British Honduras	HK	Hong Kong	
BR	Brazil	HKJ	Jordan	
BRG	Guyana (formerly British Guiana)			
BRN[1]	Bahrain	**I**	Italy	
BRU	Brunei	**IL**	Israel	
BS	Bahamas	**IND**	India	
BUR	Burma	IR	Iran	
		IRL	Ireland	
C	Cuba	IRQ	Iraq	
CDN	Canada	IS	Iceland	
CGO	Congo (Kinshasa)			
CH	Switzerland	**J**	Japan	
CHI[2]	China (People's Republic)	JA	Jamaica	
CI	Ivory Coast			
CL	Sri Lanka (formerly Ceylon)	K	Cambodia	
CO	Colombia	KWT[1]	Kuwait	
CR	Costa Rica			
CS	Czechoslovakia	L	Luxemburg	
CY	Cyprus	LAO	Laos	
		LB[1]	Liberia	
D	Germany	LS	Lesotho (formerly Basutoland)	
DK	Denmark (including the Faröe Islands and Greenland)			
		M	Malta	
DOM	Dominican Republic	MA	Morocco	
DY	Dahomey	MC	Monaco	
DZ	Algeria	**MEX**	Mexico	
		MS	Mauritius	
E	Spain (including Spanish Sahara and Spanish Guinea)	MW	Malawi (formerly Nyasaland)	
EAK	Kenya	**N**	Norway	
EAT	Tanganyika (Tanzania)	NA	Netherlands Antilles	
EAU	Uganda	NIC	Nicaragua	
EAZ	Zanzibar (Tanzania)	NIG	Niger	
EC	Ecuador	**NL**	Netherlands	
ET	United Arab Republic (Egypt)	**NZ**	New Zealand	
F	France (including French overseas departments and overseas territories)	**P**	Portugal (including the overseas territories of Angola, Cape Verde Islands, Mozambique, Portuguese Guinea, Portuguese Timor and São Tomé and Principe)	
FL	Liechtenstein			
GB	Great Britain and Northern Ireland			

PA   Panama
PAK   Pakistan
PE   Peru
PI   Philippines
PL   Poland
PTM   Malaysia
PY   Paraguay

R   Rumania
RA   Argentina
RB   Botswana (formerly
            Bechuanaland)
RC   Taiwan (Formosa)
RCA   Central African Republic
RCB   Congo (Brazzaville)
RCH   Chile
RH   Haiti
RI   Indonesia
RIM   Mauretania
RL   Lebanon
RM   Malagasy Republic (formerly
            Madagascar)
RMM   Mali
RNR[4]   Zambia (formerly Northern
            Rhodesia)
RSM   San Marino
RSR   Rhodesia
RU[1]   Burundi
RWA   Rwanda

S   Sweden
SD   Swaziland
SF   Finland
SGP   Singapore

SME   Surinam (Dutch Guiana)
SN   Senegal
SU[3] Union of Soviet Socialist
            Republics
SUD[1]   Sudan
SWA[5]   South West Africa
SY   Seychelles
SYR   Syria

T   Thailand
TG   Togo
TN   Tunisia
TR   Turkey
TT   Trinidad and Tobago

U   Uruguay
USA[6] United States of America

V   Vatican City
VN   Vietnam

WAG   Gambia
WAL   Sierra Leone
WAN   Nigeria
WD[1]   Dominica (Windward Islands)
WG   Grenada (Windward Islands)
WL   St Lucia (Windward Islands)
WS   Western Samoa
WV   St Vincent (Windward Islands)

YU   Yugoslavia
YV   Venezuela

ZA   South Africa

[1] not notified to the United Nations
[2] only used in this book
[3] also used in this book to indicate pre-revolution makes

[4] Z also used, although not established
[5] ZA also used
[6] **US** has been used in this book

EUROPEAN COMPANY NOMENCLATURE
The following abbreviations have been used in the names of European companies:

AB (aktiebolag(et)) *Swed*: joint-stock company; limited-liability company

AG (Aktiengesellschaft) *Germ*: joint-stock company

Akc. Spol. (akciova spolecnost) *Czech*: joint-stock company

Ans Ets (anciens établissements) *Fr*: former

AS (aksjeselskap(et) *Norw*; aktieselskab(et)) *Dan*: limited-liability company; joint-stock company

Cia (compagnia) *Ital*: company; (compañia) *Sp*: company

Cie (compagnie) *Fr*: company

GmbH (Gesellschaft mit beschränkter Haftung) *Germ*: limited-liability company

KG (Kommanditgesellschaft) *Germ*: partnership with limited liability; company in which one partner has limited liability

Mij (maatschappij) *Dutch*: company

np (národni podnik) *Czech*: national corporation

NV (naamloze vennootschap) *Dutch*: limited-liability company

SA (società anonima) *Ital*; (société anonyme) *Fr*; (sociedad anónima) *Sp*: limited-liability company

sarl, srl (società a responsibilità limitata) *Ital*: private or proprietary company; partnership with limited liability

S. en C. (société en commandite) *Fr*; (sociedad en comandita) *Sp*; limited partnership

SpA (società par azioni) *Ital*: joint-stock company

spa (société per actions) *Fr*: joint-stock company

srl (société à responsabilité limitée) *Fr*: partnership with limited liability

sta (società) *Ital*: company

sté (société) *Fr*: company

Tow. Akc. (towarzystwo akcyjne) *Pol*: joint-stock company

vorm. (vormalig) *Germ*: former(ly)

TECHNICAL

The following abbreviations have been used in the text for frequently repeated terms:

aiv	automatic inlet valve(s)		**kg**	kilogramme(s)
bhp	brake horsepower		**lb**	pound(s)
cc	cubic centimetre(s)		**lt**	low tension
ci	cubic inch(es)		**lwb**	long wheelbase
CV	cheveaux-vapeur		**mm**	millimetre(s)
dh	drophead		**moiv**	mechanically operated inlet valve(s)
dohc	double overhead camshaft(s)		**mpg**	miles per gallon
ft	foot (feet)		**mph**	miles per hour
fwb	four-wheel brakes		**ohc**	overhead camshaft(s)
fwd	front-wheel drive		**ohv**	overhead valve(s)
GP	Grand Prix		**oiv**	overhead inlet valve(s)
GT	Gran Turismo		**PS**	Pferdestärke
hp	horsepower		**psi**	pounds per square inch
hr	hour(s)		**rpm**	revolutions per minute
ifs	independent front suspension		**sec**	second(s)
in	inch(es)		**sv**	side valve(s)
ioe	inlet over exhaust		**swb**	short wheelbase
irs	independent rear suspension		**TT**	Tourist Trophy
km	kilometre(s)			

Anglo-American Terminology

Throughout the book technical and other terms are described according to current English usage. For the convenience of American readers we give below a short list of the more frequently-used terms whose meaning differs in American usage.

English	American
bonnet	hood
boot	trunk
capacity (of engine)	displacement
coupé de ville	town car
dickey	rumble seat
engine	motor
epicyclic (gears)	planetary (gears)
estate car	station wagon
gearbox	transmission
hood	top
mudguard	fender
paraffin	kerosene
petrol	gasoline
saloon	sedan
sedanca de ville	town car
shooting-brake	station wagon
silencer	muffler
track	tread
two-stroke	two-cycle
windscreen	windshield
wing	fender

Contributors

with a guide to their entries

THORKIL RY ANDERSEN (TRA)
Danish

GLENN BAECHLER (GB)
Canadian

OLUF BERRUM (OB)
Norwegian and Swedish

GORDON BROOKS (GB)
British (Lincolnshire and Bedford-shire cars)

HUGH CONWAY (HGC)
Bugatti and Hermes

HUGH DURNFORD (HD)
Canadian

BILL EMERY (BE)
USA, South American, Japanese, Russian, Polish, Chinese

DAVID FILSELL (DF)
British and some German, Italian and USA racing and sports cars

DR H. A. FITZPATRICK (HAF)
Lagonda and Rapier

EDDIE L. FORD (ELF)
Australian

G. N. GEORGANO (GNG)
British, French, USA, Italian, Swiss, etc.

G. L. HARTNER (GLH)
Hungarian

PETER HULL (PMAH)
Alfa-Romeo

ROLAND JERRY (RJ)
Canadian

RICHARD M. LANGWORTH (RML)
Kaiser, Frazer and associated makes

LUCIEN LOREILLE (LL)
French

KEITH MARVIN (KM)
USA and Canadian

COURT MYERS (CM)
Dort

G. MARSHALL NAUL (GMN)
USA

HANS-OTTO NEUBAUER (HON)
German, Austrian, Czechoslovak

T. R. NICHOLSON (TRN)
British, French, Italian, USA, Swiss, etc.

DOUG NYE (DCN)
French, Italian, German competition cars

CYRIL POSTHUMUS (CP)
Italian

MICHAEL SEDGWICK (MCS)
British, French, Italian, USA, etc.

JOSÉ RODRIGUEZ-VIÑA (JRV)
Spanish

MICHAEL WORTHINGTON-WILLIAMS (MJWW)
British and USA

ALDO ZUCCHI (AZ)
Italian

A

A.A. (i) (D) *1919–1922*

G für Akkumulatoren- und Automobilbau, Berlin N 65; Driesen-Vordamm

The firm produced electric cars, vans and lorries; later it was known as Electric. or petrol cars *see* Alfi. HON

A.A. (ii) (F) *1920*

teliers d'Automobile et d'Aviation, Paris

Mainly builders of electric trucks, this company made a few large, four-door ectric saloons. GNG

A.G. (D) *1900–1901*

llgemeine Automobil-Gesellschaft Berlin GmbH, Berlin

The company made voiturettes with single-cylinder 5PS engines designed by rofessor Klingenberg, which were typified by the *Kapselmotor* (engine unit, gearbox d differential fixed to the rear driving axle). In 1901 the design was acquired by e electrical concern A.E.G. to start car production. HON

BADAL (E) *1912–1914; 1930*

S. Abadal y Cía, Barcelona

Francisco Abadal was Hispano-Suiza's Madrid agent from 1904 to 1912, extend- g his activities to Barcelona in 1908. In 1912 he started to market cars under s own name, the 4-cylinder models being closely based on the contemporary His- ano-Suiza, especially a long-stroke T-head 3.6-litre almost identical to the Alfonso, ough it wore a handsome V-radiator. Cylinder blocks and chassis frames were ocured from Belgium, and Abadal received some assistance from the Imperia ompany. Also in the range was a 4½-litre six, something that neither Hispano-Suiza r Imperia offered. Production ceased at the outbreak of World War 1, when badal concentrated on special bodywork and (between 1919 and 1923) on tuned d modified versions of the 6-cylinder Buicks he had been selling since 1916. here were no more Spanish Abadals in the immediate post-war period, though oth 4-cylinder models were taken up by Imperia in 1919, and some 170 made—as gainst less than 90 before the war. Abadal did, however, have another brief fling 1930, when he announced an American-type sedan powered by a 3½-litre 6- ylinder sv Continental engine. Concessions to the European idiom were the 4-speed earbox and detachable disc wheels. MCS

.B.A.M. *see* KRIÉGER

ABARTH (I) *1950–1971*

barth & Co, Turin

Carlo Abarth, formerly associated with Cisitalia, launched out on his own in 950, concentrating at first on tuning equipment for Fiat and other makes, though few Fiat-based 1000cc sports coupés were made with Porsche trailing-arm inde- endent front suspension. Serious car manufacture started in 1955 with the 66bhp oano-bodied Tipo 207/A Spyder, still using a front-mounted engine and *Mille- ento* mechanical components. This was rapidly followed by the first of his Fiat 00-based rear-engined sports cars, a 39bhp open two-seater. Fiat components ere used mainly until 1962, though there was a 1-litre 88bhp coupé based on lfa-Romeo's Giulietta in 1958, and some special coupé bodies were built for orsche in 1960. The make arrived on the map with a series of attacks on long- istance International Class Records which started in 1956, using rear-engined treamliners with 500, 750 and 1,100cc power units. A '750' averaged 111.92mph or 72 hours in July 1957.

Production Abarths followed two lines of development: the first of these used he hulls and basic components of Fiat 500 and 600 *berline,* but the Abarth reatment included stiffer crankshafts, reinforced clutches, lowered suspensions, nd (from 1961) front disc brakes. Parallel with these were the true Abarths, 00-based coupés with bodywork by Allemano and Zagato, sold initially with ither a 747cc push-rod unit (in which form it did 95mph and sold for £2,248 in ngland in 1959) or with a fully-Abarthized twin-camshaft *bialbero* engine of 50cc. Bigger coupés and cabriolets with four wheel disc brakes and 2.2-litre iat-based 6-cylinder engines appeared in 1960, but they did not last long, and ere the last of the front-engined cars. The marque won the Nürburgring 1,000- ilometre sports-car race five years in succession (1960–64), taking 2nd place 1965. An unsuccessful design for Le Mans in 1961 saw the abandonment of wing-axle rear suspension and the introduction of a frontal radiator on the hotter' versions.

1913 ABADAL 15.9hp sporting tourer. Coachwork by Alin et Liautard. *Autocar*

1960 ABARTH 2.2-litre coupé. Coachwork by Elena. *Autosport*

1965 ABARTH OT 1300, 1.3-litre coupé. *Aldo Zucchi*

A year later the introduction of Simca's 1000 model sparked off anoth family of Abarth derivatives ranging from a warmed-up and lowered 1,100c 55bhp saloon to the usual aerodynamic coupés. 1964 developments included 995cc twin-camshaft Formula 2 racer, and a formidable *berlina* using a twin-car 1.6-litre Abarth engine in the new Fiat 850 hull; its top speed was 137mph. Th year 1966 marked a closer association with Fiat and the end of the Abarth Simca – though some of these were purchased by the company's British concessionaire Radbourne Racing, and marketed with tuned 75bhp Fiat 124 engines in 196 An immensely complicated range of Fiat derivatives, however, covered everythir from a lightly tuned 27bhp 500 berlina up to fully-tuned versions of the 850 coup and spyder with frontal radiators, 5-speed gearboxes, and all-disc brakes, even tl 1,946cc 147bhp unit being available. In 1967 an Abarth took 4th place in tl European Hill-climb Championship, and there was a 1-2-3 victory in the 196 Nürburgring 500 Kilometres, but latter-day competition activities never quite can off. A 600bhp 6-litre V-12 sports racer planned for 1968 had to be abandone in the face of revised international regulations, and though Abarth raced rea engined sports models with their own 2,968cc V-8 engine, a Formula 1 car wi this unit never reached a circuit. The 2-litre Group 5 4-cylinder was more succes ful, taking the first three places in the 1970 Circuit of Mugello, but towards tl end of 1971 the company went into liquidation. The last new touring Abarth wa the Scorpione of 1970; this was a rear-engined, wedge-shaped sports coupé wi retractable headlamps, powered by a 75bhp 1,280cc push-rod engine.   MC

1969 ABARTH 2000 2-litre sports car.
Abarth & C. Spa

ABBEY (GB) *1922*
Abbey Auto Engineering Co Ltd, London S.W.
This was a typical assembled car with a 4-cylinder 10.8hp engine by Coventry Simplex, Marles steering, and friction drive. The two-seater sold for £315.   GN

ABBOTT and ABBOTT-DETROIT (US) *1909–1918*
(1) Abbott Motor Car Co, Detroit, Mich. *1909–1915*
(2) Consolidated Car Co, Detroit, Mich. *1916*
(3) The Abbott Corp, Cleveland, Ohio *1916–1918*
The Abbott-Detroit was a conventional car using 4- and 6-cylinder Continenta and 8-cylinder Herschell-Spillman engines. By 1916 production was running a 15–20 units per day, and it was to improve on this figure that the company move to a larger factory at Cleveland. However, they over-reached themselves, and i April 1918 they were declared bankrupt. The Cleveland-built cars were generall known simply as Abbott.   GN

1911 ABBOTT-DETROIT 30hp tourer. *The Veteran Car Club of Great Britain*

A.B.C. (i) (US) *1906–1910*
(1) Autobuggy Manufacturing Co, St Louis, Mo. *1906–1908*
(2) A.B.C. Motor Vehicle Manufacturing Co, St Louis, Mo. *1908–1910*
Originally known as the Autobuggy, this car was a typical high-wheel moto buggy whose excellent ground clearance made it popular in rural America Powered by a 10/12hp 2-cylinder engine, it used a system of friction transmissio by cone and two bevel wheels, one for forward movement, one for reverse. Thi gave a maximum speed of 30mph in either direction. Later models included mor conventional roadsters with 2- or 4-cylinder air- or water-cooled engines. The com pany name was derived from the initials of the designer, A.B. Cole.   GN

A.B.C. (ii) (GB) *1920–1929*
A.B.C. Motors Ltd, Hersham, Surrey
A.B.C. engines for cyclecars (and also complete motor cycles) had been mad before the war. The first production cars employed castings, stampings and forging supplied by Harper Bean Ltd, and were fitted with a 24bhp air-cooled, flat-twir overhead-valve engine of 1203cc designed by Granville Bradshaw. Unfortunatel this unit, built down to a cost, was noisy, hard to start, inefficiently lubricate and liable to breakages, especially of the very long, exposed push-rods. Howeve in conjunction with the car's low weight, it made the A.B.C. exceptionally fas for its size, being capable of over 60mph with very good acceleration. The A.B.C handled well, too. By 1925 the engine was quieter and more reliable, having bee given more positive lubrication, and stronger valve gear and castings. One drawbac remained: because the fuel tank filler was on top of the 'radiator', the tank wa liable to be topped up with water by garage hands who did not recognize an ai cooled car. About 1,500 A.B.C.'s were made. To the end, both electric starter and four wheel brakes were extra.   TR

ABEILLE *see* A.M.

ABERDONIA (GB) *1911–1915*
Aberdonia Cars Ltd, Shepherds Bush, London W.; Park Royal, London N.W.
A conventional 4-cylinder car with a 3.2 litre side valve monobloc engine, the Aberdonia was a product of the coachbuilders Brown, Hughes and Strachan, ir whose Park Royal work the bodies were made, the chassis coming from Shepherd Bush. At Olympia in 1911 there was exhibited on the Brown, Hughes and Strachar stand an extraordinary 'Park Royal town landau', with barouche style coach work, the driver being located in a forward position with the engine out of sigh

1912 ABERDONIA 15.9hp Park Royal town landau. *Autocar*

between the driver's seat and the front portion of the barouche. It was almost certainly a one-off.

GNG

ABINGDON (i) (GB) *1902–1903*

John Child Meredith Ltd, Birmingham

Two models were made by this company, who were mainly makers of ignition equipment and accessories. They were a 9hp 2-cylinder tonneau usually known as the Meredith, and a 3½hp single-cylinder voiturette with two speeds and chain drive. This was known as the Abingdon because retail sales were in the hands of the firm of Coxeter & Sons of Abingdon, Berks.

GNG

ABINGDON (ii) (GB) *1922–1923*

Abingdon Works Ltd, Tyseley, Birmingham

Better known as makers of motor cycles, tools and the 'King Dick' spanner, Abingdon Works Ltd announced a conventional component-built light car with a Dorman 4MV 11.9hp engine. At £340 for a two-seater with dickey it was expensive and few were sold.

GNG

ABLE (F) *1920–1925*

(1) Paul Toulouse, Orgon, Bouches-du-Rhône
(2) Paul Toulouse, Avignon, Vaucluse

The Able was a conventional 4-cylinder light car offered with various proprietary engines such as Chapuis-Dornier, S.C.A.P., and C.I.M.E., ranging from 1100cc to 1500cc capacity.

GNG

ABLE EIGHT *see* VERNON

A.C. (GB) *1908 to date*

(1) Autocars and Accessories Ltd, West Norwood, London S.E. *1908–1911*
(2) Autocarriers (1911) Ltd, Thames Ditton, Surrey *1911–1922*
(3) A.C. Cars Ltd, Thames Ditton, Surrey *1922 to date*

This make succeeded the Weller and was a John Weller design developed from a commercial 3-wheeler, the Autocarrier (hence the initials) with a single-cylinder rear-mounted moiv engine, 2-speed epicyclic gear and tiller steering. These side-by-side two-seater A.C. Sociables were made up to World War 1 and sold for less than £100, but in 1913 the company brought out a 10hp 4-cylinder light car with a 3-speed gearbox in the rear axle; the engine was a 1,100cc Fivet. A modernized version with electrics and a disc transmission brake appeared with the 1½-litre side valve Anzani engine in 1919, this giving way to A.C.'s own power unit in 1925 – the fours were dropped at the end of 1928. Also at the 1919 London show was Weller's famous 1,991cc single ohc wet-liner six, an advanced power unit for its day. It did not get into production until 1922, but it remained in the catalogue until 1963, by which time output had gone up from around 35bhp to 103bhp. Under the aegis of S.F. Edge, the company's director from 1921 to 1929, A.C.'s were raced, though their main interest was long-distance record work. A 4-cylinder car took 57 records at Brooklands Track in 1921; J.A. Joyce's 16-valve ohc 1500cc single-seater covered 100 miles in the hour from a standing start in 1922; and Gillett broke the World's 24-hour Record at Montlhéry in 1925 on a 2-litre six. The 6-cylinder car of the Hon. Victor Bruce and W.J. Brunell became the first British entry to win the Monte Carlo Rally in 1926. In 1925 4-cylinder cars sold from £300, the cheapest six being £90 dearer, 4-wheel brakes were an optional extra, being standard on the 2-litre by 1927. All these cars retained the rear-axle gearbox, though the disc transmission brake did not last long.

Financial difficulties supervened in 1929, and virtually no cars were made for a couple of seasons, though the 1930 Magna series boasted hydraulic brakes. The Hurlock brothers bought the company in 1930, and the 2-litre emerged in 1933 as a sporting machine with mechanical brakes and a conventionally-mounted 4-speed gearbox, in 56bhp and 66bhp versions. These cars were made on a bespoke basis, prices starting at around £435. Pre-selector boxes were available from 1934 and standard 1935 versions had synchromesh, while cars sold in 1936 had engines of 60 and 70bhp with an 80bhp sports engine available in a special short-chassis two-seater model. A 90bhp super-charged engine was listed in 1939.

A.C. resumed car production in 1947 with a saloon in the modern idiom. This had a 74bhp engine, and hydro-mechanical (full hydraulic from 1950) brakes, but retained its semi-elliptical springing up to the end of production in 1957. Some 3-wheeled monocars for invalids were made with 250cc B.S.A. motor cycle engines, and in 1953 came the Petite, a 3-wheeler roll-top convertible with rear-mounted 350cc Villiers power unit; despite a price of under £400, this never really became popular and was dropped in 1958. 1954 saw the advent of the Ace sports two-seater, a tubular-framed machine with all-independent suspension designed by John Tojeiro. With an 85bhp A.C. engine it could top the 100mph mark, and was later made also with 2-litre and 2.2-litre Bristol (ii) and 2.6-litre Dagenham Ford engines. Front disc brakes were standardized in 1960. In 1963 this car was developed into the Cobra (inspired by the American, Carroll Shelby) with disc brakes all round and a 4.7-litre oversquare American Ford V-8 engine developing 330bhp.

1910 A.C. Sociable, 5/6hp 3-wheeler. *A.C. Cars Ltd*

1927 A.C. 2-litre two-seater. *A.C. Cars Ltd*

1966 A.C. 428, 7-litre convertible. *A.C. Cars Ltd*

1901 ACCLES-TURRELL 10/15hp tonneau. *The Veteran Car Club of Great Britain*

1903 ACHILLES 8hp two-seater. *Douglas Fitzpatrick*

1910 ACME(i) 50hp tourer. *Automotive History Collection, Detroit Public Library*

A Cobra finished 4th at Le Mans in 1964, but between 1965 and 1968 Shelby American Inc were responsible for the marketing of the 7-litre type, all Cobra production being abandoned in the latter year. From 1966, however, A.C. offered a luxury convertible or hardtop with Frua bodywork and a 7-litre Ford V-8 engine, available with a 4-speed manual or an automatic gearbox. This 428 series was continued into 1973 at a price of £7,010. A.C. also made a special single-seater 3-wheeler for invalids with single-gear automatic transmission, wheel or handlebar steering, and fibreglass coupé body, powered by a 500cc 4-stroke twin engine.   MCS

ACADEMY (GB) 1906–1908
E.J. West & Co Ltd, Foleshill, Coventry, Warwickshire

These cars were made by West for the Motor Academy, Notting Hill Gate, London and were fitted with duplicate clutch and brake controls. Otherwise they followed the usual West design, using a 14/20hp White & Poppe engine and shaft drive. Although built to the order of the Motor Academy, they were listed in *The Autocar Buyers Guide to the Cars of 1907* and one was entered in the 1906 T.T. race. It retired after 3 laps.   GNG

ACADIA (US) 1904
Ernest R. Kelly, Wilmington, Del.

This was a very small two-seater runabout with the engine under the seat. It was steered by wheel, had a single chain-drive and wire wheels.   GMN

ACADIAN (CDN) 1962-1971
General Motors Corp. of Canada, Oshawa, Ont.

Acadian and Beaumont were the brand names of General Motors cars sold in Canada. The original Acadian was based on the Chevy II and known as the Acadian Canso. In 1963 a larger model became available with the Chevelle body, known as the Acadian Beaumont. From 1966 to 1969 it was known simply as the Beaumont, and for 1970 was replaced in Pontiac showrooms by the Pontiac Tempest and Le Mans. (Although based on Chevrolet designs, Acadians were marketed by Pontiac in Canada.) From 1968 Acadians were imported from Michigan as a reduction in tariffs had reduced the necessity to make cars in Canada.   GNG

ACCLES-TURRELL (GB) 1900–1902
(1) Accles-Turrell Autocars Ltd, Perry Bar, Birmingham *1900–1901*
(2) Pollock Engineering Co Ltd, Ashton-under-Lyne, Lancs *1901–1902*

Accles Ltd was a general engineering firm when Charles McRobie Turrell, one of the organizers of the 1896 Emancipation Run, joined it in 1900. They began to make a car with a 10/15hp flat-twin engine designed by F.H. de Veuille mounted under the front seat. It also had a constant-mesh 2-speed gearbox. In 1901 the Pollock Engineering Co acquired the design and sold it as the Turrell car, with some improvements, notably a much larger radiator. However, Pollock soon joined Accles to form the well-known tube manufacturing firm of Accles & Pollock Ltd, and the car was made by the Autocar Construction Co as the Hermes (i).   GNG

ACCUMULATOR INDUSTRIES (GB) 1902–c.1903
Accumulator Industries Ltd, Woking, Surrey

As well as a heavy electric coach with a range of 80 miles, this company made a number of light electric two seater stanhopes. These were generally similar to contemporary vehicles such as the Riker and Columbia, but had solid tyres. Two $2\frac{1}{2}$hp Lundell motors were used.   GNG

ACE (i) (AUS) 1904
Holding & Overall, Drummoyne, N.S.W.

The second make of car to appear in New South Wales, the Ace was a light two-seater using a 10hp engine.   GNG

ACE (ii) (GB) 1912–1914
Salmon Motor Co Ltd, Burton-on-Trent, Staffs.

This was a light car with a very small monobloc 4-cylinder engine, 2-speed gearbox and chain drive, selling in two-seater form for £100. The company made larger cars under the names of Salmon and Baguley from 1911 to 1914.   GNG

ACE (iii) (US) 1920–1922
Apex Motor Corp, Ypsilanti, Mich.

An assembled car which used at various periods, a Gray-Bell 4-cylinder and Herschell-Spillman and Continental 6-cylinder engines. The Ace differed from other cars of its time because of the 'traditional' squared lines of its coachwork. The make was absorbed into the American Motor Truck Co of Newark, Ohio.   KM

ACE (iv) see FRONTENAC

ACHENBACH see HEXE

ACHILLES (GB) 1903–1908
B. Thompson and Co Ltd, Frome, Somerset

1906 ADAMS(ii) 35/40hp V-8 tourer. *Autocar*

The early production Achilles was a typical assembled car, with 6hp De Dion engine, tubular Lacoste et Battmann chassis, Malicet et Blin gears, and so on. In 1904 they announced that only steel castings would in future be brought out, though the engines were still 'of De Dion pattern', in 6, 8 and 9hp single-cylinder sizes, and 12hp twins. Some later cars may have been powered by White and Poppe. Certainly the firm possessed a foundry, for they cast some well-known statues, but much doubt remains as to the extent to which this was used in the motor business. The cars were cheap, lively, reliable and locally popular.

DF

ACME (i) (US) *1903–1910*
Acme Motor Car Co, Reading, Pa.

Acme was an outgrowth of the Reber Manufacturing Co which made the Reber car. The Acme was available in at least nine different models during its existence. Early models had 2- or 4-cylinder engines. Later cars were much larger, with 6-cylinder engines and ball-bearing transmission; they cost $3–5,000. The car was sold with an optimistic 'perpetual guarantee'.

GMN

ACME (ii) (US) *1908–1909*
Acme Motor Buggy Manufacturing Co, Minneapolis, Minn.

This car was a short-lived high-wheel motor buggy.

GMN

ACME (iii) (CDN) *1910–1911*
Acme Motor Carriage and Machinery Co Ltd, Hamilton, Ont.

This firm was organized to manufacture touring cars, taxicabs and commercial vehicles with bodies built in Hamilton and mechanical parts imported from the United States. A 30hp touring car was made.

GB

ADAMS (i) (GB) *1903–1906*
Adams & Co, Tunbridge Wells, Kent

H. Adams' first offering was a conversion set for turning horse-drawn carriages into motor vehicles. The engine was mounted on a swivelling fore-carriage, and steering was by wheel and vertical column. Other vehicles to use this system were the Scottish Madelvic and the American Cantono (electric) and Tractobile (steam). In 1905 Adams made a small 2-cylinder car sold under the name 'One of the Best'.

GNG

ADAMS (ii) (GB) *1905–1914*
Adams Manufacturing Co Ltd, Bedford

The early Adams cars, known as Adams-Hewitts until January 1907, were designed by Hewitt (see Hewitt Motor Co of New York). They used single- and 2-cylinder horizontal engines mounted under the front seat, and 2-speed pedal-operated epicyclic gears, which gave rise to the company's slogan, 'Pedals to Push – That's All'. Most of these cars had a short bonnet, despite the engine position, but some were forward-control town landaulettes.

In 1906 a range of 2- and 4-cylinder cars with vertical front-mounted engines was introduced, and also a short-lived 32hp V-8. This engine was the French Antoinette built under licence, and the only apparent difference between the English and French versions was that the former used mechanically operated inlet valves and the latter automatic. The single cylinder model was dropped in 1909 and replaced by a 10hp twin called the Varsity, and the range became more conventional in 1912 when the pedals-to-push system was abandoned. A new light car appeared in 1913 which reverted to the old horizontal underfloor position for the 8hp 2-cylinder engine. It even revived the epicyclic gear and single chain drive, but found few buyers at £130. World War 1 saw the end of all Adams production.

GNG

1906 ADAMS-FARWELL 40/45hp tourer.
Harrah's Automobile Collection

ADAMS (iii) (US) *1911*
Adams Bros Co, Findlay, Ohio

The Adams Model C, had a 4-cylinder, 4-stroke engine of 25/30hp. This was a five-seater touring model, but the main interest of this manufacturer was in commercial vehicles.

GMN

ADAMS-FARWELL (US) *1904–1913*
The Adams Co, Dubuque, Iowa

After six years of experiments, the Adams-Farwell with a 20hp 3-cylinder radial rotary engine was put on the market in 1904, followed by a 40/45hp 5-cylinder model in 1906. The cylinders and crankcase revolved in a horizontal plane about a fixed shaft, power being transmitted by bevel gears to a 4-speed gearbox (3 speeds after 1908), and thence by single chain to the rear axle. The engine was mounted under the rear seat ahead of the axle. The rotating mass of the engine acted as a flywheel and gave excellent cooling.

The 1904 models included a convertible brougham in which the driver's seat in front could be closed up, and control devices transferred inside for driving from the rear seat. The 40hp model had a short bonnet, and the general appearance of a conventional car. After 1908 the forward control model was dropped, but no new models appeared and only small changes were made to the existing range for the rest of the make's life. Prices reached $3,500 for the 40hp tourer by 1912.

GNG

ADAMS PROBE *see* PROBE

1914 ADAMSON 8hp cyclecar. *David Filsell Collection*

1902 ADER 8hp limousine. *Geoffroy de Beauffort Collection*

1900 ADLER 3½hp voiturette. *Adler Werke AG*

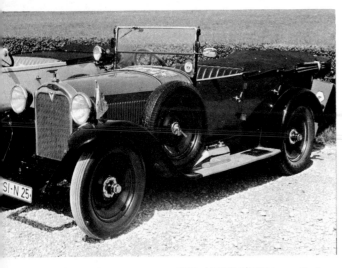

1925 ADLER 6/25PS tourer. *Neubauer Collection*

ADAMSON (GB) *1912–1924*

R. Barton Adamson & Co Ltd, Enfield Highway, Middlesex

R. Barton Adamson were well-known transport contractors, who built a number of cyclecars with 2-cylinder Alpha engines, 3 speeds and belt final drive. An underslung frame gave the cars a low build. Post-war cars also used Alpha engines, 2- and 4-cylinder models.   GNG

ADELPHIA (US) *1920*

Winfield Barnes Co, Philadelphia, Pa.

This medium-sized car had a wheelbase of 9ft 6in and right-hand drive. It was built for export only. The 4-cylinder engine was by Herschell-Spillman. This make probably never got beyond the prototype stage.   GMN

ADEM (I) *1912*

This was an Italian-built car placed on the British market by A. De Martini, after he had left the Martini company. It had a 17.9hp 4-cylinder monobloc engine of 2.9-litres capacity, and a 4 speed gearbox. Cooling was by fan blades on the flywheel. Few, if any, were actually sold in England.   GNG

ADER (F) *1900–1907*

(1) Sté Industrielle des Téléphones-Voitures Automobiles système Ader, Levallois-Perret, Seine *1900–1904*
(2) Sté Ader, Levallois-Perret, Seine *1904–1907*

The designer of these cars, Clément Ader, was a telephone engineer who is said to have installed the first telephone lines in France. He also built a number of unsuccessful steam-powered aircraft in the 1890s. The first Ader car used a 900cc V-twin engine of 8hp which was followed by a 12hp V-twin in 1902. Two of these cars, which used chain drive, ran in the 1902 Paris–Vienna race, but without great success. In 1903 a 16hp V-4 was added to the range, and the company fielded no less than seven cars in the Paris–Madrid race, one V-twin, three V-4s and three V-8s of 32hp, the latter engine being the result of coupling two of the V-4s together. All seven reached Bordeaux where the race was terminated.

For 1905 the V layout was abandoned for all but the smallest model, and a range of conventional vertical fours introduced of 16, 20 and 25hp, using chain or shaft drive for the smaller models and chain only for the 25hp. By 1906 there were no V-engined models at all, and this loss of individuality seems to have caused the disappearance of the make.   GNG

A.D.K. (B) *1924–1931*

SA des Automobiles de Kuyper, Brussels

This concern made well-designed cars with engines of their own construction, but in very small numbers. Their first car with a 4-cylinder 2-litre engine developing 42bhp, used Perrot front-wheel-brakes. In 1928 a 2.2-litre ohv straight-eight was announced, but only a few examples were made.   GNG

ADLER (D) *1900–1939*

(1) Adler Fahrradwerke vorm. Heinrich Kleyer AG *1900–1906*
(2) Adlerwerke vorm. Heinrich Kleyer AG, Frankfurt/Main *1906–1939*

This well-known bicycle and typewriter firm had already built components for Benz as well as a few De Dion tricycles when their first car appeared in 1900. This closely resembled the contemporary Renault, with tubular frame, shaft drive, and front-mounted 400cc single-cylinder De Dion engine; suspension was full-elliptic all round and steering was by tiller, but both these archaisms had gone by 1901 when a bigger 510cc power unit was standardized. By 1902 the company were making their own engines, an 850cc single and a 1.7-litre twin, there were four forward speeds, and the lateral radiators continued the Renault idiom.

With the arrival of Edmund Rumpler in 1903 the Adler idiom crystallized, even if his experimental swing-axle suspension did not pass beyond the prototype stage. Characteristics of the new models were side valves in an L-head, dual ignition, pressed-steel frames, and rectangular radiators. Four cylinders were preferred, though singles were still offered in 1905, and twins as late as 1909. By 1905 there were 4-cylinder cars of 2.8 litres, 4 litres, and 7.4 litres, this last figuring in Adler's Herkomer Trophy entry, and attracting an order from Kaiser Wilhelm II in 1907. If the 1906 Kleinwagen, a 1,032cc aiv V-twin with water cooling and steel artillery wheels, marked a retrograde step, by 1907 the company had adopted the unit gearbox, and were experimenting with ioe engines, achieving a 3rd place in the Prince Henry Trials. There were also some modest short-stroke fours. A 2-litre 8/15PS was followed a year later by the successful 1,555cc 7/15. This developed into the 1.8-litre 7/15, popular in England as the 12hp. These small Adlers had dual ignition, but foot accelerators were found only on the bigger cars as late as 1913. There was a fast 5.2-litre 76bhp ioe model for the 1910 Prince Henry Trials, and a smaller 3.2-litre version was offered to the public. It evolved into the 15/40 of 1913, with 3.8 litres and 69bhp, used as the basis for Adler's unsuccessful 1914 T.T. racers. Their Knight-engined 1911 cars did not progress beyond the prototype stage, but very attractive was that year's new model, the 1.3-litre K voiturette, initially with pair-cast cylinders, but offered in 1913 with monobloc engine and a choice of side-by-side or tandem seats. Rear suspension was full-elliptic. It did 50mph and 38mpg, and was well received by Britons, who bought it under the name of Morgan-Adler Carette. There were also some large sv fours, the 4.8-litre 19/45 appearing in 1911, followed in 1912 by a 7.8-litre 30/70, and in 1914 by a V-radiatored 9.1-litre monster, top of a nine-model range. Also new was an enlarged K, the 1,552cc KL with four-seater bodywork and semi-elliptic rear springs.

A selection of the more popular 1914 types reappeared in 1919, and even in 1922 a replacement for the KL, the 6/22PS, retained a fixed head and reverted to a separate gearbox. Adler's first sixes came in 1925, these boasting alloy pistons, detachable heads, and fwb. The 10/50 had a 2.6-litre monobloc engine, but the 4.7-litre 18/80 was of biblock type. Also new was an essay in the American idiom, Becker's 1,550cc 4-cylinder Favorit. Three years later it had been joined by a 2.9-litre six and a 3.9-litre straight-8, both with hydraulic brakes, these being offered on an enlarged and modernized Favorit in 1929.

At the Geneva Show of 1932 Adler presented their new 1.5-litre Trumpf with front-wheel drive and independent wheel suspension, a design of H.G. Röhr (qv). This first front-driven car was followed by the 1-litre Trumpf Junior, the 1.7-litre Trumpf and the 2-litre model. The competition versions of these models – very often fitted with aerodynamic bodies – were very successful in the years from their appearance to the outbreak of World War 2. Streamlined Trumpf and Trumpf Junior cars gained 22 international records in 1935 and 1936 on the Avus and the Darmstadt Autobahn. A win in the Leinster Trophy Race of 1934, a Team Prize at Spa in 1936 in the 2-litre class, a 2-litre class win and 6th place overall at Le Mans in 1937 were only a few of the victories. In 1937 Adler introduced a rear-wheel driven model again, the 2.5-litre with 6-cylinder 50bhp engine, aerodynamic body and swing axles. The sports version of this type developed 80bhp.

Production of private cars ceased in 1939. Some prototypes of the Trumpf Junior were produced after the war and were on show at the Hanover Fair 1948, but production was not taken up. Instead of this, production of motorcycles was resumed, lasting until 1957.   HON

ADRIA (US) 1921–1922
Adria Motor Car Corp, Batavia, N.Y.

The Adria appeared briefly on the automotive lists, offered as an assembled car with a 4-cylinder Supreme motor.   KM

ADVANCE (US) 1909–1911
Advance Motor Vehicle Co, Miamisburg, Ohio

This company took over the business of Hatfield Motor Car Co of Miamisburg which had made the Hatfield (i). The Advance was a typical motor buggy with large diameter wheels and solid rubber tyres.   GMN

A.E.C. (or ANGER) (US) 1913–1914
Anger Engineering Co, Milwaukee, Wisc.

The two models of the A.E.C. used 6-cylinder engines. One was a T-head of 6.9-litres, and the other, of 6-litres was an L-head. The larger car with a 4 speed transmission cost $2,500. The smaller $2,000 model had a 3 speed transmission.   GMN

A.É.M. (F) 1926–1927
At a time when the electric private car had practically vanished from the roads, this company launched an electric town car with front-wheel drive. It used the same chassis as the company's light van. In 1927 they introduced an electric cyclecar called the Electrocyclette but cannot have sold many.   GNG

A.E.R. see B.N.C.

AERIC see CORRE (i)

AERO (CS) 1929–1947
Tovarna letadel Aero Dr Kabes, Prague

The original Aero light car was said to be Czechoslovakia's smallest car, and was derived from the D.I.S.K. and Enka cyclecars of the 1920s designed by Novotny. The 1929 Aero Type 500 used a single-cylinder 2-stroke engine of 499cc developing 10bhp at 2,500rpm. It was developed into the 2-cylinder Types 20 and 30 (660 and 995cc) and finally in 1937 the 4-cylinder Type 50 which in twin-carburettor sports form developed 50bhp. Later Aeros were really handsome cars, especially in drophead coupé and open four-seater sports form. They all used 2-stroke engines and, from 1934, front-wheel drive. The Type 30 was revived after the war, now with a pointed radiator grille, and made until 1947.   HON

AEROCAR (i) (US) 1906–1908
(1) The Aerocar Co, Detroit, Mich. 1906–1907
(2) Aerocar Motor Co, Detroit, Mich. 1907–1908

The Aerocar was an ambitious venture by Alexander Malcolmson, a former partner of Henry Ford, available in five different models, both air-cooled and water-cooled. The Model F, a touring car offered in 1907 and 1908, was on a 9ft 7in wheelbase, powered by a 4-cylinder engine with 5in bore and stroke; standard colours were royal blue with cream trim.   GMN

1938 ADLER Trumpf Junior 1.1-litre saloon.
G.N. Georgano

1938 ADLER 2½-litre drophead coupé.
Jockisch Collection

1932 AERO Type 30 995cc two-seater. *Neubauer Collection*

1937 AERO Type 30 995cc drophead coupé.
Václav Petřík Collection

1946 AERO MINOR 615cc saloon. *Czechoslovak News Agency*

1924 AGA 1½-litre Targa Florio sports car. *Autocar*

AERO CAR (ii) (GB) *1919–1920*

Aero Car Engineering Co, Upper Clapton, London N.

This was a cyclecar using a 5/7hp air-cooled flat-twin Blackburne engine and Sturmey-Archer gearbox. GNG

AERO CAR (iii) (US) *1921*

Sheldon F. Reese Co, Huron, S.Dak.

This was the name applied to a tiny propeller-driven two-seater roadster that was to sell for $160. It had a track of 2ft 6in with wheelbase of 5ft and with a 6hp, 2-cylinder engine weighed about 150lb. GMN

AÉROCARÈNE (F) *1947*

This was a streamlined 3-wheeled coupé in which the complete hood slid back to give access to the seats, there being no doors. The front wheels were enclosed in spats, in the top part of which were mounted the headlamps which thus followed the direction of the wheels. With a 684cc vertical-twin engine, the claimed maximum speed was 82 mph. GNG

AEROFORD (GB) *1920–1925*

Aeroford Cars, Bayswater, London W.2

The Aeroford was one of many attempts to make the famous Model T Ford more attractive to customers by disguising its too familiar appearance with a special bonnet and radiator grille. GNG

AÉROLITHE *see* COADOU-FLEURY

AERO MINOR (CS) *1946–1952*

Letecke Zavody n.p., Jinonice

The Aero Minor was not in fact connected with the pre-war Aero, but was derived from the Jawa Minor, Jawa engineers having worked on it in secret during the German occupation. It used a 2-cylinder 2-stroke engine of 615cc and carried rather heavy-looking saloon and station-wagon bodies, although a sports version ran at Le Mans in 1949. Like its Jawa ancestor, the Aero Minor used front-wheel drive. HON

AERO-TYPE *see* PAGÉ

A.F. (i) *see* AUSTRO-FIAT

A.F. (ii) (GB) *1971–1972*

(1) Antique Automobiles Ltd, Baston, Peterborough, Northamptonshire *1971*

(2) A. T. Fraser, Aslackby, Sleaford, Lincs. *1971–1972*

Conceived by Alexander Fraser and Colin Crabbe, the little A.F. Spider was an attempt to recapture the allure of vintage Morgan 3-wheeler motoring with the advantage of modern standards of performance. The body-cum-chassis was a marine-ply monocoque with hardwood frame, the resultant all-up weight of only 952lb endowing the machine with startling acceleration, to a degree dependent on the specification of the tranverse Mini engine driving the front wheels. DF

A.F.A. (E) *1943*

This was a small electric cabriolet powered by a 5hp motor. GNG

A.G. (I) *1925–1927*

Istituto Feltrinelli, Milan

Giuseppe Alfieri's small sports cars featured all-round independent suspension and 1,100cc engines by Chapuis-Dornier and S.C.A.P. A Cozette-blown model was tried in 1927, but there was no serious production. MCS

AGA (D) *1919–1928*

(1) AG für Automobilbau, Berlin–Lichtenberg *1919–1926*

(2) Aga-Fahrzeugwerke, Berlin–Lichtenberg *1926–1928*

The first model was the 6/16PS based on the 6PS F.N. of 1914; it was not successful. In 1921 the 6/20PS model with 1420cc engine appeared. This model sold in greater numbers, and in 1926 AGA took over the Dinos works, which belonged like AGA to the Stinnes concern, to extend their production capacity. A two-seater sports version was introduced as the 6/30PS Targa Florio model which took part in the 1924 Targa Florio, gaining a 2nd and 3rd place in the 1–1½-litre class. A 6-cylinder 10/45PS also appeared in small numbers before AGA was forced to close down as a result of financial difficulties in 1926. The production rights were sold and the type 6/20PS was continued until 1928 in the original factory. Agas were also built under licence in Sweden by Thulin. HON

AGÉRON (F) *1908–1910*

Constructions d'Automobiles Agéron et Cie, Lyons

The Agéron works produced a small number of conventional cars with 4-cylinder 10/12hp engines, and chain drive. Their only unusual feature was a compressed air starter. GNG

A.G.R. (GB) *1911–1912*

Ariel & General Repairs Ltd, Camberwell, London S.E.5

This company were agents for Hurtu, and the car sold under the name A.G.R. was in most respects identical to the 12hp Hurtu. At £315 it was £50 more expensive; other differences were that it was slightly longer and had larger tyres. An open four-seater was the only available model. GNG

AIGLON *see* ALLIANCE

AILLOUD; AILLOUD & DUMOND (F) *1897–1904*

(1) Automobiles Ailloud, Lyons *1897–1900*
(2) Automobiles Ailloud et Dumond, Lyons *1900–1904*

Claude Ailloud was a bicycle maker who built a light car with an air-cooled engine in 1897, for which he was awarded a Silver Medal at the first Lyons Motor Show. In 1900 he was joined by Francisque Dumond, and they made about 5 cars with 5hp 2-cylinder vertical engines. In 1904 they produced one 14hp 4-cylinder car, but thereafter confined themselves to sales and repairs. GNG

AILSA *see* KENNEDY (ii)

AILSA CRAIG *see* CRAIG-DORWALD

AIREDALE (GB) *1919–1924*

(1) Nanson, Barker & Co, Esholt, Yorkshire *1919–1922*
(2) Airedale Cars Ltd, Esholt, Yorkshire *1922–1924*

Founded in 1911, Nanson, Barker & Co, built the Tiny cyclecar before the war. Their post-war product was a more substantial car using a 12/24hp 4-cylinder Dorman engine, a 4-speed gearbox and spiral bevel drive. In four-seater coupé form, it sold for £425 in 1922. GNG

AIREX *see* REX

AIROMOBILE *see* LEWIS AIROMOBILE

AIRPHIBIAN (US) *1950–1956*

Continental Inc, Danbury, Conn.

This was an aircraft-cum-automobile combination, powered by a 165bhp engine that gave an air speed of 120mph and a road speed of 55mph. The four small wheels were independently sprung. Unlike most such vehicles, the Airphibian passed the prototype stage, was fully licensed by the Federal Aviation Agency, and offered for sale. GNG

AIRWAY (US) *1949–1950*

T.P. Hall Engineering Co, San Diego, Calif.

The Airway was one of the many post-war minicars that failed to get into large-scale production. It carried two passengers and weighed 775lb. Its air-cooled engine gave 45 mpg. It was to sell for $500. GMN

AJAMS (F) *1919–1920*

The Ajams cyclecar used a 6/8cv 4-cylinder engine, and had independent suspension of all four wheels. The patents were sold to Sizaire-Naudin in March 1920. GNG

AJAX (i) (US) *1901–1903*

Ajax Motor Vehicle Co, New York City, N.Y.

The Ajax was a typical light electric runabout with an open two-seater body, spindly bicycle-type wheels and optional mudguards. GNG

AJAX (ii) (CH) *1906–1910*

(1) Dr G. Aigner Automobilfabrik, Zürich *1906–1907*
(2) Ajax AG, Zürich *1907–1910*

The first Ajax used a 4-cylinder 20/27hp monobloc engine, a 4-speed gearbox and double chain drive. In 1907 a range of three models was introduced, 16 and 24hp fours, and a 24hp six. The 16hp used shaft drive and chains were optional on the larger models. The cars had a mechanical self-starter operated from the running board.

Two chain-drive 6-cylinder Ajaxes ran in the 1907 Targa Florio. A large number of 16hp cars were used as taxicabs and one of these survives today in the Swiss Transport Museum at Lucerne. GNG

AJAX (iii) (F) *1913–1914*

Briscoe Frères, Neuilly, Seine

After resigning from the U.S. Motor Corp, Benjamin and Frank Briscoe went to France where they planned to make the Ajax cyclecar on a large scale. The car had a 12hp 4-cylinder engine and friction drive, and sold for the low sum of £78. When World War 1 interfered with their plans, the Briscoes returned to America and made the Argo cyclecar. This was similar to the Ajax, but used a conventional transmission. GNG

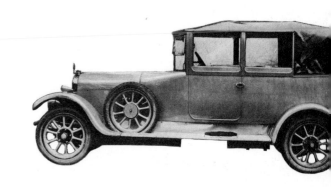

1921 AIREDALE 11.9hp all-weather tourer. Coachwork by Dixon of West Bromwich. *Autocar*

1908 AJAX(ii) 16hp landaulette. *Swiss Museum of Transport & Communication, Lucerne*

1925 AJAX(v) 3-litre sedan, with C.W. Nash. *American Motors Corporation*

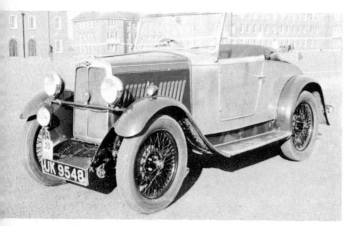

1930 A.J.S. Nine, two-seater. *G.N. Georgano*

1924 ALAN 6/30PS tourer. *G.L. Hartner*

1921 ALBA 10CV two-seater coupé. *Autocar*

AJAX (iv) (US) *1914–1915*

Ajax Motors Co, Seattle, Wash.

This Ajax company offered a car in three wheelbase lengths with a 6-cylinde engine available in sleeve-valve or conventional poppet valve form, 'changeab from one to the other at comparatively little expense'.
GN

AJAX (v) (US) *1925–1926*

Ajax Motors Co, Racine, Wisc.

The Ajax Company was a subsidiary of Nash and the 6-cylinder cars they bui were a form of Nash in everything except name. Manufacturing operations were i the former Mitchell factory acquired by Nash interests in 1924. The car was not success and was continued as the Nash Light Six in 1926
K

A.J.S. (GB) *1930–1933*

(1) A.J. Stevens Ltd, Wolverhampton, Staffs. *1930–1931*
(2) Willys-Overland-Crossley Ltd, Stockport, Cheshire *1931–1933*

The well-known motorcycle firm of A.J.S. had been making commercial vehicle for three years when they turned to the light car field in 1930. It has been claime that the A.J.S. car was based on the Clyno Nine, but although A.J. Stevens ma have bought a number of Clyno patents there was really very little resemblance be tween the two cars. The A.J.S. used a 1,018cc 4-cylinder sv engine by Coventry Climax, with 3-bearing crankshaft, and carried open two-seater, or four-seater 4-door saloon coachwork. Prices ranged from £210 to £240, which was expensiv for the type of car offered. After the parent firm's collapse in 1931, the desig was taken over by Willys-Overland-Crossley Ltd who marketed a 4-spee version. A 1½-litre ohv model at £325 got no further than the 1932 Olympi Show.
TR

ALAN (D) *1923–1925*

J. Mayer, Bamberg

This was a small 6/30PS car with a Siemens & Halske proprietary engine.
HO

ALAND (US) *1916–1917*

Aland Motor Car Co, Detroit, Mich.

This car had a very advanced 4-cylinder engine of 2.5-litres. It used four over head valves per cylinder, with a single camshaft. Aluminium alloy pistons were standard. The chassis was fitted with very early internal expanding brakes on al four wheels. The wheelbase was 10ft 2in and the two-seater and five-seater model cost $1,500 with Rudge-Whitworth wire wheels.
GM

ALATAC (B) *1913–1914*

Automobiles Catala, Braine-le-Comte

This company made two models of a conventional 4-cylinder car, a 9/12CV and a 12/16CV, both with side-valve monobloc Chapuis-Dornier engines. They had a conventional Malicet et Blin chassis, detachable wire wheels and a handsome V-radiator.
GNG

ALBA (i) (A) *1906–1908*

Automobil-werk 'Alba' AG, Trieste

Made in the former Austrian, now Italian, port of Trieste, the Alba was produced in two 4-cylinder models, a 25hp and a 45hp.
HON

ALBA (ii) (F) *1913–1928*

Constructions Métallurgiques, Suresnes, Seine

The Alba was a conventional light car made in various 4-cylinder versions with proprietary engines, mainly by Ballot. In 1926 there was a sports model with ohv engine, Cozette supercharger and Dewandre servo 4-wheel brakes.
GNG

ALBANI (AUS) *1921–1922*

Albani Motor Construction Pty Ltd, Melbourne, Victoria

The Albani Six was powered by a 25hp 6-cylinder engine, and had a five/six-seater tourer body. The name was sometimes erroneously listed as Albany.
GNG

ALBANY (i) (GB) *1903–1905*

Albany Manufacturing Co Ltd, Willesden, London N.W.

This company made both petrol and steam cars, the latter being designed by Frederick Lamplough who had built a shaft-driven steamer in 1896. Generally known as the Lamplough-Albany, it had a pair of engines coupled by cranks at right angles, and a super-heated coil-type generator. Steering was by wheel or tiller and the general appearance was that of a petrol car. It was only offered for one year, 1903, whereas the petrol cars, a 10hp single-cylinder and 16hp 2-cylinder, lasted for three seasons.

After mid-1905 Albany concentrated on selling Talbots and manufacturing radiators and other components.
GNG

ALBANY (ii) (US) *1907–1908*

Albany Automobile Co, Albany, Ind.

The Albany models, surrey and runabout, were rather crude vehicles, with false hoods and solid rubber tyres. The single or 2-cylinder air-cooled engines were of 6/7hp and 18/20hp respectively. GMN

ALBANY (iii) (GB) *1971 to date*
Albany Motor Carriage Co, Christchurch, Hampshire

The prototype Albany, designed and built by Brian Shepherd, used Ford E93A mechanical parts. The two-seater body styling was inspired by early Edwardian runabouts, with a high and exposed driving position. The production version favoured Morris Minor 1,098cc running gear, governed to 40mph in the interests of low insurance costs and the occupants' well-being, and was priced at £1,987. Later models used the Triumph Spitfire engine. DF

ALBATROS (i) (F) *1912*
Henri Billouin, Paris

This company made mainly cycles and motorcycles, but offered a light 4-cylinder car in 1902. Their advertisement spoke of '91 victories in 92 races', but this presumably referred to the 2-wheelers. GNG

ALBATROS (ii) (GB) *1923–1924*
Albatros Motors Ltd, Coventry, Warwickshire

The Coventry-built Albatros was a very conventional light car made in 8hp and 10hp versions with Coventry-Climax engines. The chief difference between them was that the smaller car was not fitted with a differential. Bodies were open two- and four-seaters. GNG

ALBERT (GB) *1920–1924*
(1) Adam Grimaldi & Co Ltd, Vauxhall, London *1920*
(2) Gwynne's Engineering Co Ltd, Chiswick, London *1920–1924*

The Albert was one of a crop of worthy, unremarkable light cars that appeared after World War 1 to cater for the boom in popular motoring. Designed by A.O. Lord, later designer of the Loyd-Lord, and propelled by a proprietary 4-cylinder, 12hp 1½-litre ohv engine, it was a solidly-built machine with the rather unusual feature, in a small car, of a 4-speed gearbox. Most of its appeal lay in its bodywork which, being made of aluminium, was both roomy and weatherproof, and light for its type. Adam Grimaldi & Co were taken over by Gwynne, who had made their engines, in 1920. The last few cars, called the Gwynne-Albert, had a slightly larger 14hp engine. TRN

ALBERTI (I) *1906*
Giuseppe Alberti, Florence

Signor Alberti was a car dealer who tried to make a large car on Florentia lines, but could not get sufficient capital and produced only one example. GNG

ALBION (GB) *1900–1913*
Albion Motor Car Co Ltd, Scotstoun, Glasgow

Still active as truck manufacturers within the Leyland Group, Albion was founded at the end of 1899 by T. Blackwood Murray and Norman Fulton, late of Arrol-Johnston and their early products were dogcarts with varnished-wood bodywork much in the Arrol-Johnston idiom, with 2-cylinder opposed-piston underfloor engines, low tension magneto ignition, and Murray's patent governor. Wheel steering replaced the tiller in 1902, and a year later Albion began production of a 16hp vertical-twin which was made for many years, usually with solid tyres, and often with shooting-brake bodywork. 'Cars for country houses', especially Scottish ones, were a speciality of the house, though rather less rustic was a side-valve 5.6-litre chain-driven four introduced in 1906. This 24hp model had a seven-year production run. The last Albion passenger car was a 15hp monobloc four with side valves in a T-head and worm drive, which sold for £475 in 1912. At the end of 1913 Albion elected to concentrate on commercial vehicles, though large shooting brakes using the 15hp engine continued to be made. MCS

ALBRUNA (GB) *1908–1912*
Brown Bros Ltd, London

This was a 1.4-litre light car announced by Brown Bros in November 1908. Its specification was conventional, with a 4-cylinder monobloc side-valve engine, 3-speed gearbox and shaft drive; a two-seater sold for £240. From 1910 models had a capacity of 1.6 litres, but after 1912 they ceased to market complete cars, concentrating on their business as motor factors. MCS

ALCO (US) *1905–1913*
(1) American Locomotive Automobile Co, Providence, R.I. *1905–1908*
(2) American Locomotive Co, Providence, R.I. *1908–1913*

The Alco was a high quality car built by a subsidiary of a well-known locomotive manufacturing firm. The cars were built under Berliet licence, and were more often called American Berliets up to 1908. The first models were chain-driven 4-cylinder machines, of 24 and 40hp, but shaft drive was introduced in 1907 on a 16hp 4-cylinder car mainly used for taxicab work. A 60hp 6-cylinder car appeared in

1903 LAMPLOUGH-ALBANY 12hp steam tonneau. *National Motor Museum*

1972 ALBANY(iii) replica roadster. *Albany Motor Carriage Co.*

1921 ALBERT 11.9hp tourer. Coachwork by James Young. *Autocar*

1906 ALBION 24/30hp tourer. *Albion Motors Ltd*

1911 ALCO 60hp tourer. *Alco Products Inc*

1912 ALCYON 3-litre racing car. Page at the wheel. *Veteran Car Club of Great Britain*

1921 ALDA 18/35hp tourer. *Autocar*

1966 ALEXIS-DAF Formula Junior racing car. *Autosport*

1908. The latter was the most famous Alco model, and was made with expensi open and closed bodywork priced at $6,000 to $7,250. In 1909 and 1910 Al cars won the Vanderbilt Cup.
GN

ALCYON (F) *1906–1928*
(1) Edmond Gentil, Neuilly, Seine *1906–1912*
(2) Edmond Gentil, Courbevoie, Seine *1912–1914*
(3) Automobiles Alcyon, Courbevoie, Seine *1914–1928*

This famous factory, established in 1902, has always been primarily concern with motorcycles, though they entered the car market with a brace of conventior voiturettes in 1906. These had thermo-syphon cooling, low-tension magneto ig tion, shaft drive and 3-speed gearboxes; in addition to the inevitable 950cc sing there was a small 1.4-litre 4-cylinder selling at £235. A wider range was availab in 1907, the 725cc and 1-litre single-cylinder cars having coil ignition, while a hig tension magneto was standard on the 2.7-litre L-head 4-cylinder model. Twin-cyl der Alcyons competed in the 1907 and 1908 Coupes des Voiturettes. In 1909 1.9-litre car with Zürcher engine was sold. As late as 1910 singles and twins we catalogued, but in 1911 an altogether more ambitious 3-litre ohv car ran in the Cou de L'Auto and a 16-valve engine was used in the 1912 race. The smaller touri Alcyons of the immediate pre-1914 era had T-head engines, though the bigg model, of 2.6-litres' capacity, had a single camshaft.

After 1918 motorcycles once again predominated, though an obscure 2-li model was made in the immediate post-war period and Giroux, the firm's Lyc agent, did quite well in local events with a tuned version which he sold as Alcyon-G.L. The last Alcyon cars were, however, identical with the contempora 500cc 2-stroke Sima-Violets. An even simpler single-cylinder cyclecar was a offered.
M

ALDA (F) *1912–1922*
(1) Fernand Charron, Courbevoie, Seine *1912–1920*
(2) Automobiles Farman, Billancourt, Seine *1920–1922*

After leaving the C.G.V. company, Fernand Charron acquired the old E.N works at Courbevoie and the patents of the Henriod rotary-valve engine. T equipped he began to make 15 and 25hp 4-cylinder cars with either rotary or pop valves, and dashboard radiators. The cars were originally to be called F. Charr but the name Alda (Ah, la Delicieuse Automobile) was chosen to avoid confus with the Charron cars still being made by C.G.V. In 1913 and 1914 only the 15 car was available, and the rotary-valve engine had been dropped.

During World War 1 M. Charron imported Federal trucks, and the post-v 20.1hp 3½-litre car was made in the Farman factory. It survived until 1922.
G

ALDO (US) *1910–1911*
Albaugh-Dover Co, Chicago, Ill.

The Aldo was a motor buggy for two passengers. Its engine was an air-cool opposed 2-cylinder type. It had planetary transmission with double chain dr and tiller steering.
G

ALDON (GB) *1971 to date*
(1) Aldon Automotive, Halesowen, Worcs. *1971–1972*
(2) Aldon Automotive, Brierley Hill, Staffs. *1972 to date*

Produced by Alan Goodwin and Don Loughlin, the first Aldon was an a minium monocoque sports car conceived for Group 6 racing but used in 19 for F100 events. The second model, the space-framed AL5, was designed for C sports racing, and buyers were offered a choice of either model in 1972.

ALES (J) *1921*
Hakuyosha Ironworks, Ltd, Tokyo

Designed by engineer Junya Toyokawa, the Ales experimental touring cars led the development of the commercially marketed Otomo of 1924. One prototype w powered by a water-cooled four cylinder side valve engine of 1,610cc, the other an air-cooled four cylinder power plant of 780cc. Toyokawa was also the inven of a gyro-compass for controlling aircraft and boats.

ALESBURY (GB) *1907–1908*
Alesbury Bros, Edenderry, King's County, Ireland

The Alesbury was a light car powered by an 8/10hp 2-cylinder Stevens eng and exhibited at the Dublin Motor Show in 1907. The 4-seater was construc 'entirely of Irish wood' and the car used solid rubber tyres.
G

ALEX (GB) *1908*
Alexander & Co, Edinburgh

The prototype Alex used a 14/18hp 4-cylinder Gnome engine and Rubery Ov chassis. It was found that the cost of production would be too great, and only car was made.
G

ALEXANDRA (GB) *1905–1906*
Phoenix Carriage Co, Birmingham

This company made an electric brougham with an all-wood body. The design included a safety device used in hansom cabs to prevent the passengers falling out in the event of a sudden halt. A petrol-engined version was also listed.   GNG

ALEXIS (GB) *1961 to date*

(1) Alexis Cars Ltd, Birmingham *1961–1970*
(2) Alexis Cars Ltd, Whitacre, Coleshill, Warwickshire *1970 to date*

The first products of Alec Francis and Bill Harris were front-engined Formula Juniors and trials specials. Later Junior machines, in the hands of David Prophet and others, were quite successful. A model suitable for either Formula 2 or 3 was then developed, similarly based on a tubular space-frame with coil spring-damper units, and accepting behind the driver such popular power units as the Cosworth-Ford. Production, to order, averaged only a handful annually. In 1965 the trials cars were dropped; Harris left at this time, and development was taken over by Alan Taylor and J. Russell. Late in 1967 came the Formula Ford Russell-Alexis. This was followed by a succession of Formula Ford designs, the Marks 14 (1968), 15 (1969), 18 (1970) and 22 (1973). Other models included Formula 3 versions such as the Marks 17, 19 and 23 of 1969, 1970 and 1973 respectively. The Formula Atlantic Mark 20 of 1972 was the firm's first monocoque, and the Mark 21 Clubman's car, with all-independent suspension, was raced successfully by M. Jackson. This car marked a return to two-seaters, forsaken since an unsuccessful foray into Formula F100.

The greater part of production has always been exported to North America, but the name has continued to appear regularly in British race reports, examples being the 18 victories of Dick Barker with a Mark 15 in 1969, and the Formula 4 Championship gained by Mike Greenwood with a Mark 12 in 1971.   DF

1972 ALEXIS Formula Ford racing car.
Alexis Cars Ltd

ALFA (I) *1907*

Anonima Lombarda Fabbricazione Automobile, Novara

Unrelated to the Alfa Romeo's precursor, the Novarese Alfa was a steam car with a 4-cylinder double-acting engine mounted vertically at the front, and shaft drive. The prototype was built in Milan by Olivari and Duse, but there is no record of any Alfas reaching the public.   MCS

ALFA-LEGIA *see* AUSTRO-DAIMLER

ALFA ROMEO (I) *1910 to date*

(1) A.L.F.A. (Anonima Lombardo Fabbrica Automobili), Milan *1910–1914*
(2) SA Italiana Ing. Nicola Romeo & C, Milan *1914–1930*
(3) SA Alfa Romeo, Milan *1930–1942*
(4) Alfa Romeo SpA, Milan *1942 to date*
(5) Alfa Romeo SpA, Pomigliano d'Arco, Naples *1971 to date*

A.L.F.A. (The Lombardy Motor Manufacturing Co) was founded in 1909 by Cav. Ugo Stella, formerly managing director of the Società Italiana Automobili Darracq, to manufacture a completely new range of Italian cars at Portello on the outskirts of Milan where, since 1906, small French Darracq cars had been assembled.

By 1910 the last Darracq had left the factory, and production commenced of a sturdy range of Alfa cars designed from scratch by Cav. Giuseppe Merosi, a native of Piacenza, who had been Chief Technician with Bianchi in Milan.

The first Alfas were a 24hp 4.1-litre car, later known as the 20/30hp, and a 12hp 2.4-litre, which became the 15/20hp. Both were well made, with side-valve 4-cylinder monobloc engines and shaft drive. In 1913 the sports 6.1-litre 40/60hp appeared with push-rod overhead valves operated by two camshafts in the crankcase. A one-off 4½-litre Grand Prix car was built in 1914 with a 4-cylinder twin ohc engine, but it never ran in international races.

In 1915 the factory was taken over by the industrialist Nicola Romeo, and after World War 1 the pre-war models were marketed as Alfa Romeos. The 20/30 ES Sport of 1921–22 was successful in Italian races, as was a special racing 40/60 driven by Campari, which scored the firm's first victory at Mugello in 1920.

A 6-cylinder luxury side-valve car called the G1 was not a success, but Merosi's best remembered designs followed it; the 3-litre 6-cylinder push-rod ohv touring, sports and racing RL series cars which first appeared in 1921 and went into production in 1922. A racing version won the 1923 Targa Florio. The similar 4-cylinder 2-litre type RM was marketed in 1923–26, but the pointed radiator sports 22/90hp RLSS and the touring 21/70hp RLT, which had a flat radiator, were sold until 1927.

In 1924 Alfa Romeo won the very first Grande Epreuve they ever entered, an unparalleled achievement, when Campari was victorious in the 1924 French Grand Prix at Lyons in the new straight-eight supercharged P2 car, designed by Vittorio Jano, who came from Fiat. In 1925 Alfa Romeo were declared World Champions.

Jano took over from Merosi in 1926 and his first touring and sports car designs soon became world famous, these having single and twin overhead camshaft 6-cylinder engines, first in 1500cc and then in 1750cc form. When supercharged, these cars won all the great sports car races in the period 1928–30, with the exception of Le Mans.

This latter omission was rectified from 1931 to 1934 when victory at Le Mans

1925 ALFA ROMEO RLSS. 3-litre drophead coupé. *Alfa-Romeo SpA*

1930 ALFA ROMEO GS 1750 Gran Sport two-seater. Coachwork by Zagato. *P.M.A. Hull*

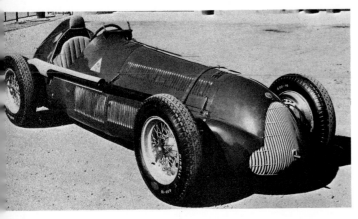

1939 ALFA ROMEO Tipo 158 1½-litre racing car. *Alfa Romeo SpA*

1947 ALFA ROMEO 6C 2500 Sport 2½-litre convertible. *Lucien Loreille Collection*

1966 ALFA ROMEO Giulia TI 1.6-litre saloon. *Alfa Romeo SpA*

1972 ALFA ROMEO Alfetta 1.8-litre saloon. *Alfa Romeo SpA*

each year went to Jano's next sports car design, which had a 2.3-litre straig eight supercharged engine with a central drive to the overhead camshafts. T engine also powered the successful Grand Prix Alfa Romeo of 1931, known as 'Monza' model and raced for the factory by Scuderia Ferrari. In 1932 this eng in 2.65-litre form, powered the Type B P3 Monoposto G.P. car, which pro virtually unbeatable and bore affinities with the Type A racing car of 1931 powe by two 1750cc engines side by side. In 1933 Alfa Romeo came under State own ship and the Monopostos were withdrawn from racing until right at the end the season. Ferrari continued G.P. racing with Monzas enlarged to 2.6 litres.

The Monopostos in 2.9-litre form were not powerful enough against the Merce and Auto Unions, although Chiron won the 1934 French G.P. for Alfa Rom whilst Nuvolari quite unexpectedly won the 1935 German G.P. in a 3.8-l Monoposto fitted with Dubonnet ifs. From 1936 to 1939 Alfa Romeo field independently sprung straight-eight, V-12, and V-16 cars in G.P. racing, against the German cars only isolated victories in smaller races were attair usually through the skill of Nuvolari. In 1935 Ferrari built two big *bi-mo* racing cars, with one P3 engine under the bonnet and another in the tail.

Some 2.9 P3 engines were put into all-independently sprung chassis in 1937- to make expensive but exceedingly fast prestige sports cars. In sports car rac Alfa Romeos won every Mille Miglia from 1928 to 1938 inclusive, except in 19

In 1934 Jano's unsupercharged 6-cylinder twin ohc 2.3-litre car replaced the 1 and 8C 2300, and, developed by Bruno Treviso, it later became the 2500 of 1 and the early post-war years. It was replaced in 1950 by the 4-cylinder 1900. T marked an important change in Alfa Romeo policy. Previously the touring A had been expensive and semi-bespoke machines, whereas the 1900 and its success were unitary construction saloons whose production has risen to about 30,000 u per annum at the present time. In 1954 was introduced the famous 1300cc Giule designed by Orazio Satta. From it were derived the successful 1600 Giulia and 6-cylinder 2600, introduced in 1962. For 1968 the 1600s were replaced by the 1 series, actually 1,779cc, available as a saloon (Berlina), coupé (1750 GT Veloce open sports (1750 Spider Veloce).

The remarkable Colombo-designed supercharged 1½-litre 8-cylinder Monopo known as the '158' was introduced in 1938 for voiturette racing. After the wa was eligible for the Grand Prix formula, and by remaining unbeaten in Gran Epreuves in 1946–48 and 1950 until mid-1951, it set up a record unequalled by other G.P. design. In 1946 it took the first three places in the G.P. des Nation Geneva, and repeated this finishing order in 1947 in the Italian G.P., the C d'Europe at Spa and the Swiss G.P. In 1948 a similar clean sweep was attaine the French G.P. and the Monza G.P. The most successful drivers during these ye were Jean-Pierre Wimille, Achille Varzi and Count Felice Trossi, but the dea of all three took place before the 1949 season and Alfa Romeo withdrew from rac as they had done in 1933. The 158s returned to the tracks in 1950 with Giuse Farina and Juan Manuel Fangio as their star drivers, and after victories in ev race the cars ran in, Farina was declared World Champion. In 1951 Fangio World Champion on the 400bhp Type 159, though the cars had to concede t first defeat, by an unblown 4½-litre Ferrari.

At the end of the season Alfa Romeo withdrew from G.P. racing, and altho the works Disco Volante sports racing 2½- and 3-litre cars of 1952–53 w generally unlucky in racing, the Giulias have had G.T. successes in recent year

Competition activities were resumed in 1967 with the T33, a rear-engined 2- 4ohc V-8 with hemispherical combustion chambers, fuel injection, alternator i tion, and a 6-speed all-synchromesh gearbox. Until 1969 a tubular trellis fr was used, replaced for 1970 by an orthodox platform, and the disc brakes mounted inboard. It was catalogued at 9,750,000 lire but was primarily used the Autodelta racing team; later cars had 2½-litre and 3-litre engines. In 1971 Romeos won the BOAC 1,000 Kilometres, the Targa Florio and the Watkins G 6 Hours, but in 1972 they were powerless against the all-conquering Ferraris the touring-car range, the six disappeared in 1969, and in 1970 the fuel-injec dry-sump 2.6-litre V-8 engine was applied to a conventional front-engined co the Montreal.

Other new 1972 models were the 2000, an updated 1750, and the 1750cc Alf saloon with 122bhp engine, a 5-speed De Dion transaxle, double wishbone ifs, inboard disc brakes. It has the angular rear-end treatment of Alfa Romeo's economy saloon. The Alfasud, made in the Naples factory opened during 1 This car had a 1186cc flat-4 engine with cogged-belt drive for its twin overh camshafts, hypoid bevel drive to the front wheels, all-disc brakes, and forward speeds PN

ALFI (i) (D) *1922–1924*

Automobil- und Akkumulatoren-Bau-GmbH, Berlin N 65; Driesen-Vordamm

Originally production was of electric cars (*see* A.A.A. and ELEKTRIC), petrol-driven cars designated 4/14, 5/20 and 7/35PS were offered, which competed at race meetings.

ALFI (ii) (D) *1927–1928*

'Alfi' – Automobile GmbH, Berlin N 39

Small cars were built under this name by another company in which A

scher – the designer – was a shareholder. In 1927 Fischer founded his own com-
~~ny,~~ producing small vans and private cars. There was a 3-wheeled vehicle with a
~~gle~~ front wheel, to which a DKW motorcycle engine was fitted and which could
turned around through 180 degrees for reverse drive. The 4-wheeled Alfi Sport
~~th~~ 2/10PS engine, an open or coupé two-seater, was produced in small numbers.

HON

~~A~~LLARD (i) (GB) *1899–1902*
~~A~~lard and Co Ltd, Coventry, Warwickshire

The original Allard Cycle Co was formed in 1891. In 1899 they began to
~~in~~terest themselves in motors, building a De Dion-based tricycle and a Benz-
~~de~~rivative known as the Express. Their 2½hp and 3hp voiturettes, however, used
~~sin~~gle-cylinder 500cc engines clearly based on De Dion practice. Tubular frames
~~an~~d belt drive featured in the specification, and the cars could be had with electric
~~or~~ tube ignition. An oddity was a narrow little *vis-à-vis* for two people only. Late
~~in~~ 1900 the firm undertook to build the belt-driven Charette in series for Inter-
~~na~~tional (i). In 1902 an entirely new 9hp single-cylinder Allard made its appearance.
~~Th~~is had a flitch-plate frame and live axle. In June of that year Allard joined forces
~~wi~~th the Birmingham Motor Manufacturing and Supply Co; the latter's Birmingham
~~fa~~ctory was sold, and the Coventry firm changed its name to Rex (i). Though there
~~was~~ no connection between Allard (i) and Allard (ii), Mr Fred Allard, son of the
~~he~~ad of the Coventry concern, was later chief designer of Armstrong-Siddeley
~~M~~otors Ltd.

MCS

~~A~~LLARD (ii) (GB) *1937–1960*
~~(1~~) Adlards Motors Ltd, Putney, London S.W.15 *1937–1945*
~~(2~~) Allard Motor Co Ltd, Clapham, London S.W.4 *1946–1960*

The Allard stemmed from a 'trials special' evolved by Sydney Allard out of a
~~19~~34 Ford V-8; this first car had a body from a G.P. Bugatti and divided-axle ifs,
~~an~~d its excellent record on the 'mud' resulted in a demand for replicas. These were
~~m~~ade in very small numbers, mostly with stark bodywork, up to World War 2.
~~So~~me cars had the 4.4-litre 12-cylinder Lincoln Zephyr engine. In 1946 the Allard
~~re~~appeared on the market with a lowered chassis, more civilized bodywork, and a
~~st~~riking radiator grille, still using the 3.6-litre sv Ford V-8 engine; prices of the
~~K~~ (two-seater), L (four-seater) and M (drophead coupé) ranged from £1,125 up.
~~Co~~il-spring ifs and hydraulic brakes appeared in 1949, followed shortly afterward
~~by~~ the light and accelerative J2 two-seater with a De Dion rear axle; home-market
~~m~~odels used the 3.9-litre ohv Ardun-Mercury conversion, but for cars sold in the
~~U~~.S.A. power came from big V-8s, such as the 5.4-litre Cadillac and Chrysler, and
~~O~~ldsmobile's Rocket. Sydney Allard won the 1952 Monte Carlo Rally on a P-type
~~sa~~loon in 1952, but Jaguar were already cutting hard into the specialist market, and
~~th~~e new 1953 models did not prosper; these were the big Monte Carlo saloon and
~~Sa~~fari station wagon with V-8 engines and De Dion axles, and a pair of smaller
~~ro~~adsters, the Palm Beach series with 1½-litre 4-cylinder and 2.3-litre 6-cylinder
~~D~~agenham Ford engines. Nor were American enthusiasts over-eager to buy the new
~~C~~adillac-engined JR sports-racer at $8,500. There was a brief flirtation with a
~~3~~46cc 3-wheeler, the Clipper, in 1955, and in 1956 the old Ford V-8 was at last
~~d~~ropped in favour of twin ohc Jaguar power units. Cars were now made to special
~~o~~rder only, and the last new design was a G.T. coupé introduced for 1958. Allard
~~th~~en made special modifications for Ford's 105E-type Anglia.

MCS

~~A~~LLARD-LATOUR (F) *1899–1902*
~~R~~. Allard-Latour, Lyons

M. Allard-Latour was a mechanical engineer who made a small number of belt-
~~o~~r chain-driven cars in his workshop. They never sold outside the Lyons area. GNG

~~A~~LL-BRITISH (GB) *1906–1908*
~~A~~ll-British Car Co, Bridgeton, Glasgow

The All-British Co was founded by George Johnston, formerly with Arrol-
~~J~~ohnston. Plants were made to produce 75 cars per annum as well as commercials,
~~b~~ut the company was liquidated before a dozen vehicles were made. The car was a
~~l~~arge, complex vehicle with a horizontal 8-cylinder engine.

GNG

~~A~~LLDAYS (GB) *1898–1918*
~~A~~lldays and Onions Pneumatic Engineering Co Ltd, Birmingham

The firm's first car was the Traveller, a wheel-steered quadricycle made in
~~p~~rivate and commercial forms. The rear end was unsprung, and power was provided
~~b~~y a 4hp De Dion single-cylinder engine. A shaft-driven light car, also single-
~~c~~ylindered, followed in 1903, but the company really made its name with the 1.6-
~~l~~itre vertical-twin side valve 10/12 which lasted from 1905 to 1913. This car was
~~p~~opular with commercial travellers and also did well in formula events at the hill-
~~c~~limbs of the period. A 16hp 4-cylinder car joined the range in 1906, and in 1908 the
~~E~~nfield Autocar Co was acquired.

Thereafter the range was rationalized; most models were sold under both brand-
~~n~~ames, the Alldays contribution being the well-established twin and fours of 14 and
~~2~~0hp, all shaft-driven. A 30/35hp six was listed from 1911 to 1914, compressed-air
~~s~~tarters were optional in 1911, and in 1913 came the 990cc V twin Midget cyclecar
~~w~~ith air cooling and shaft drive, at £138 10s. An 1100cc 4-cylinder version with

1948 ALLARD(ii) Model K 3.6-litre sports
car. *Autocar*

1957 ALLARD(ii) 3.4-litre GT coupé. *Allard
Motor Co Ltd*

1912 ALLDAYS 30/35hp limousine. *Autocar*

1920 ALLEN(ii) 3.1-litre tourer. *William S. Jackson*

1928 ALMA Six 1.6-litre coupé. *Musée de l'Automobile, Le Mans*

1929 ALPHI 1½-litre 6-cylinder racing car. *Musée de l'Automobile, Le Mans*

bullnose radiator appeared in 1914 and was popular at £175. Pair-cast side valve fours rated at 12/14, 16/20 and 25/30hp completed the immediate pre-war range. A further phase of rationalization after World War 1 resulted in the Enfield-Allday cars.

MC

ALLEN (i) (US) *1913–1914*
Allen Iron & Steel Co, Philadelphia, Pa.

The first models of the Allen used a 2-cylinder air-cooled engine. In 1914, these two-seaters had a 4-cylinder water-cooled engine, friction transmission and shaft drive. With a 9ft wheelbase and a 3ft 8in track, these cost $450.

GMN

ALLEN (ii) (US) *1914–1922*
Allen Motor Co, Fostoria, Bucyrus, Columbus, Ohio

The Allen was a popular and well-known 4-cylinder car. In its nine years of production, an estimated 20,000 units in both open and closed models were sold. The engine was a 3.1-litre side valve unit.

KM

ALLEN-KINGSTON (US) *1907–1909*
Allen-Kingston Motor Car Co, Kingston, N.Y.

This was a large car with 48hp T-head engine. The four-seater Gunboat had a very early boat-tailed body and runningboard-mounted spare tyres.

GMN

ALLIANCE (i) (D) *1904–1905*
Automobil- und Motorwerke Alliance Fischer & Abele, Berlin N 55

These were 2- and 4-cylinder cars. Chassis and engines were also supplied to other factories as proprietary components.

HON

ALLIANCE (ii) (F) *1905–1908*
Alliance Automobiles B. Baud, Paris

Also listed under the name Aiglon (in 1905), this car used Tony Huber engines of 10/12hp (2-cylinder), and 12/14 or 18hp (4-cylinder) and shaft drive. It was sold in England by the Alliance Manufacturing Co of Holborn.

GNG

ALLRIGHT (ALLREIT) (D) *1908–1911*
Köln-Lindenthaler Metallwerke AG, Cologne-Lindenthal

Two voiturette-type models were produced with 1-litre 2-cylinder engines, chain and cardan drive. They were marketed under the name 'Vindec' outside Germany.

HON

ALLSTATE (US) *1952–1953*
Kaiser-Frazer Corporation, Willow Run, Mich.

The Allstate was built by Kaiser-Frazer for Sears Roebuck, for sale by mail order or at Sears retail outlets. Its only significant exterior difference from the contemporary Henry J was in its grille and heraldry, and it used the same 4- and 6-cylinder Willys engines. Allstates carried a 90-day guarantee; the Sears tyres were guaranteed for 18 months and the battery for two years. Allstate prices bracketed Henry J prices both above and below. Only 1,566 were built for 1952 and 797 for 1953.

RML

ALL-STEEL (US) *1915–1916*
All-Steel Motor Car Co, St Louis, Mo.

The All-Steel, or Alstel, had a conventional 4-cylinder engine, but was unusual in having a narrow platform backbone frame which enclosed the propeller shaft and gearbox. The electrically welded body was attached to this frame and rear axle at only three points and could easily be removed. The price was only $465.

GNG

ALLWIN (GB) *c.1920*
Allwin Cyclecars, Bournemouth, Hampshire

This concern manufactured a few cyclecars. They followed the general pattern of the day, having a narrow body, air-cooled engine and drive by chain or belt to a differential-less back axle.

MJWW

ALMA (F) *1926–1929*
Etablissements Alma, Courbevoie, Seine

The Alma was a high quality small car using a 1600cc 6-cylinder Vaslin engine. This employed two inlet valves per cylinder but, except at high speeds, only one was used. The engine was so flexible that a 2-speed gearbox was used.

GNG

A.L.P. (B) *1919–1921*
SA des Automobiles Lerous-Pisart, Brussels

The A.L.P. was a light car using a 4-cylinder sv Decolonge engine of 1850cc. In 1921 the firm introduced the more advanced Somea.

GNG

ALPENA (ALPENA FLYER) (US) *1910–1914*
Alpena Motor Car Co, Alpena, Mich.

The Alpena was a light and inexpensive car, using a water-cooled 4-cylinder engine rated at 34hp. The two open models had 3-speed transmissions.

GMN

ALPHI (F) 1929–1931

Sté Alphi, Paris

Only four examples of the Paris-built Alphi were made, presumably to special order. The first two had the 6-cylinder 1,485cc C.I.M.E. engine; they were a two-seater sports car which raced at Le Mans in 1929 and a supercharged racing car which was built for the 1929 French Grand Prix, but was not ready in time. It was too heavy for the power available and never took part in a race. The other Alphis were both touring cars, powered by 6-cylinder and 8-cylinder Continental engines of 2.6 litres and 5 litres respectively. They had independent rear suspension by transverse springs and swing axles, but rigid front axles. Of the four Alphis made, two survive, the super-charged racing car and the 2.6-litre Continental-engined drophead coupé.   GNG

ALPINE (F) 1955 to date

Automobiles Alpine srl, Dieppe

This is one of the more successful French sports cars based on the rear-engined Renault, though production has been limited; 350 were built in 1964. The first model was the Mille Miles (so named because of its successful début in the hands of its sponsor, M. Redélé, in the 1955 Mille Miglia), which used Renault 4CV mech-anical components welded to two/four-seater fibreglass coupé bodywork. It won its class in the 1956 Mille Miglia, and by 1957 buyers had the choice of two-seater coupé or cabriolet bodies as well as more powerful engines; the 845cc Dauphine or a bored-out 904cc development. 103mph was now claimed from the more sporting types and the 1959 export price was $3,300. The Alpine's technical specification followed Renault evolution, and 1961 saw two new body styles: a '2 plus 2' GT coupé and an aerodynamic berlinette. Power output also went up: 77bhp from 998cc in 1961 and 87bhp from the Gordini-tuned 1,100cc unit available in 1964, when twin-camshaft and hemi-head variants were introduced, plus some single-seater racing versions, evolved in consultation with Ron Tauranac of the Brabham organization. Both For-mula 2 and Formula 3 Alpines had 5-speed gearboxes and disc brakes all round, but a twin-cam Gordini-Renault unit powered the former and a 996cc push-rod engine the latter. The Formula 3 model was quite successful, winning the Prix de Paris race, and gaining Henri Grandsire the French Formula 3 championship in 1964. The sports Alpines scored a class win in the Tour de France, as well as winning the Index of Thermal Efficiency at Le Mans, and 1965 brought them a Coupé des Alpes in the Alpine Rally and victory in the Nürburgring 500-Kilometre event. The 'hottest' version on general sale now offered 115bhp and 127mph from 1.3-litres. Disc brakes all round were introduced for all 1967 Alpines and 4-speed all-synchromesh gear-boxes made standard, a 5-speed box costing 950 francs extra. The biggest engine listed was a 1,296cc unit developing 120bhp, but 1968 saw the adoption of the 1,470cc 16. Meanwhile Alpine was assuming the role of Renault's competition department, with energetic support for F3, and the introduction of a rear-engined sports car with tubular frame and 3-litre V-8 power unit designed by Gordini. This was first seen in the 1967 1,000 Kilometres of Paris, and finished 8th at Le Mans in 1968, in which year the smaller Alpines won the Index of Performance.

Alpine repeated this feat in 1969, but thereafter the company concentrated on rallying, having already won the Alpine and Czech events in 1968, and the Alpine and the Three Cities in 1969. The 1970 score was headed by victories in the Italian and Acropolis rallies. The marque reached its zenith in 1971, with a 1-2-3 victory in the Monte Carlo, a second win in the Acropolis, and the manufacturers' cham-pionship. In addition the French national rally (J.P. Nicolas) and F3 (P. Depailler) champions won their titles in Alpines. A new touring model for 1971 was the A310 2+2 coupé with 140bhp 1,605cc engine, 5-speed gearbox, and servo-assisted discs all round. This continued into 1972, along with the two-seater Tour de France Alpines, powered by 1,289cc and 1,565cc units. Alpines are assembled abroad by Renault affiliates in Bulgaria, Brazil, Mexico and Spain. Interestingly, these overseas Alpines accounted for more cars in 1970 than the parent factory at Dieppe—1,640 as against 360.   MCS

ALSACE (US) 1920–1921

Automotive Products Co, New York

The short-lived Alsace was a small assembled car built by Piedmont Motor Co for Automotive Products, produced with right-hand drive for export only. It differed from the standard Piedmont only in its Rolls-Royce type radiator and right-hand drive. The engine was a 3.1-litre Herschell-Spillman 4-cylinder unit.   KM

ALSTEL see ALL STEEL

ALTA (i) (GB) 1931–1954

Alta Car and Engineering Co, Kingston-upon-Thames, Surrey

Geoffrey Taylor commenced building cars in his father's stables in 1928, choosing the name as a contraction of Alberta, a place which he liked the sound of. Most am-bitiously, laboriously and ingeniously, he fabricated his own engine, with aluminium block, and shaft-driven twin camshafts over a hemispherical head. An A.B.C. frame was used, and production frames were obtained from Rubery Owen. Leaf suspension was by Jonas Woodhead. 85mph could be achieved, or 110mph with a Roots-type 'blower' and attendant fits of temperament. The cars were run in trials, sprints and races – the class record for the Brooklands Mountain circuit was broken in 1934. Side-

1966 ALPINE Berlinette 1300 coupé. *Alpine Srl*

1972 ALPINE A.310 1.6-litre coupé. *Alpine Srl*

1920 ALSACE 19.6hp saloon. *Autocar*

c.1938 ALTA(i) 2-litre sports car. *Autosport*

1951 ALTA(i) 2-litre racing car. *National Motor Museum*

1920 ALVIS 10/30 two-seater. *Alvis Ltd*

1925 ALVIS 12/50 tourer. *Alvis Ltd*

lines, such as Austin Seven aluminium cylinder heads, helped the finances. In 1935 the 1,074cc model was augmented by versions in 1,496cc and 1,961cc, with chain-driven camshafts. For 1937 independent coil suspension was adopted, and weight considerably reduced. A supercharged 2-litre could churn out 180bhp, and many competition successes were gained. Well-known exponents of this period included G. Abecassis, Beadle, R. Cowell, R. Eccles, S.C.H. Davis, G. Hartwell, H. Hunter, R. Jackson, C. Mortimer, Miss D. Stanley-Turner, J. Wakefield and E. Winterbottom.

In World War 2 the firm manufactured aeroplane components and did prototype work. In 1945 a brave engine design was announced for the 'G.P.' model, using a Meehanite block casting, with light alloy crankcase and head, the whole tied together with long studs. The chassis was rubber suspended. The car's debut was inauspiciously delayed until 1948. Although George Abecassis in particular tried very hard, there were constant minor troubles, sometimes attributable to the two-stage supercharging. The 2-litre version of this engine, however, especially when running un-blown in Heath's Formula 2 H.W.M. team, was a model of reliability.

In 1951 Alta issued their own Formula 2 car, using the G.P. chassis, which though lightened and improved for 1952, never really made a mark. In 1954 this car was developed further to 2½-litres, for the new Formula 1, but the only car completed stayed in the works. The engine, however, was used in various other models, including the Connaught, which gave Tony Brooks the first all-British Grand Prix win in 1955 since Segrave in the 1920s.

Road cars never really interested the firm, although a saloon 2-litre was offered briefly after the war. In entering the monoposto lists, the tiny company was always fighting an uphill battle against those with greater resources, and eventually they concentrated more and more on specialized engineering work.   DF

ALTA (ii) (GR) 1968–1970
Alta Inc, Athens

This was yet another version of the German Fuldamobil 3-wheeler, with 198cc ohv single-cylinder engine and 4-speed gearbox.   MCS

ALTENA (NL) 1904–1907
(1) NV Haarlemsche Automobiel-en Motorrijwielfabriek, voorheen A. van Altena, Haarlem *1904–1906*
(2) A. van Altena, Haarlem *1906–1907*

Altena were motorcycle makers who progressed to cars, their 1905 range including an 8hp twin, and fours of 12/15hp, 24/28hp, and 40hp, this last model being capable of 60mph. The motorcycles were discontinued, but resumed soon afterward in 1906, when the largest Altena car was a 12/14 2-cylinder. A bankruptcy led to a factory auction later in the year, but Van Altena himself was the purchaser, and 8hp and 12hp models were offered briefly in 1907. Some 40 or 50 cars of all types were made.   MCS

ALTER (US) 1914–1917
Alter Motor Car Co, Grand Haven, Mich.

The 1914 Alter used a 4-cylinder engine of 22hp. In 1916 a five-seater with a 3.3-litre 6-cylinder engine was built in a chassis of 9ft 8in wheelbase. In 1917 this new policy was reversed with two sizes of Lycoming 4-cylinder engines being used.   GMN

ALTMANN (D) 1905–1907
Kraftfahrzeug-Werke GmbH, Brandenburg/Havel

Altmann was one of the few German makes of steam cars, and was quite an advanced design. In his use of a valve-timing engine Altmann followed the Gardner-Serpollet principle, although his engine differed from this design in other aspects. It had three cylinders and was capable of 15/25bhp. The use of a condensation system and consequently low water consumption gave the vehicle an effective range of about 125 miles on one tankful of water. Because of the death of Adolf Altmann production was never started on a large scale. Electric cars were later built by this firm.   HON

ALVA (F) 1913–1923
Automobiles Alva, Courbevoie, Seine

Alva made a considerable range of 4-cylinder cars with engines by S.C.A.P. and others from 1½-litre to 2.2-litre capacity. They used 4-wheel brakes as early as 1921, and some models used an ohc engine.   GNG

ALVECHURCH (GB) 1911
Alvechurch Light Car Co, Alvechurch, Birmingham

The Alvechurch was an attempt by Dunkleys, makers of prams and a coal gas powered car, to tap the cyclecar market. It used an air-cooled Matchless 2-cylinder engine and belt drive which slipped badly. Only two were made.   GNG

ALVIS (GB) 1920–1967
(1) T.G. John Ltd, Coventry, Warwickshire *1919–1921*
(2) Alvis Car & Engineering Co Ltd, Coventry, Warwickshire *1921–1937*
(3) Alvis Ltd, Coventry, Warwickshire *1937–1967*

From its beginnings, the name of Alvis has connoted high quality, long life and better-than-average performance. The first production Alvis set the trend. Those responsible for it were T.G. John, formerly of Siddeley-Deasy, and G.P.H. de Freville, who had worked for D.F.P. and had designed aluminium pistons bearing the name of Alvis for them. Their 10/30hp light car, current until 1922, used an extremely efficient 4-cylinder sv engine of 1460cc made by Alvis, a 4-speed gearbox and attractive aluminium bodies by Morgan or Charlesworth. It was available in two-seater, four-seater or Super Sports form. The last-named was the first Alvis to have the famous 'duck's back' body. Though noisy and expensive, the '10/30' was immensely popular among sporting motorists. In 1921, 322 examples were sold and by the following year the company employed 350 people. At the end of 1919, the newborn company had undertaken to deliver 1,000 cars, but the moulders' strike which crippled so many small manufacturers prevented Alvis from meeting the demand. For a brief spell during this period, the company made the Buckingham cyclecar.

In 1922, an engine of 1,598cc with a bigger bore and rated at 12/40hp was introduced in Alvis cars designed more for touring. Captain G.T. Smith-Clarke became chief engineer in 1923. He was responsible for the push-rod ohv 12/50hp engine, which was quieter and more powerful than its predecessors and at the same time extremely strong and long-lasting. It was first seen, in modified form, in the Alvis that won the Brooklands 200-Mile Race of 1923. The touring models were provided with 1598cc engines, but the Super Sports had a shorter stroke giving 1496cc and was more highly-tuned. The former were usually capable of about 60–65mph, but the latter would exceed 70mph comfortably. Handling qualities of all models were excellent, while bodies were by Cross & Ellis. During 1924 all cars went over to the new engine. At first, the firm's survival was doubtful. Although 963 units of the older models had been sold in 1923, a receiver had to be appointed in the following year, because of lack of the capital needed for production on a scale to meet demand. More money was forthcoming, however, and the new 12/50 restored the company's fortunes. Prices were reduced for 1926, and all models were given front-wheel brakes. The chassis was stiffened by doing away with the separate subframe that had carried the engine and gearbox, and the engine was rubber-mounted. The downward-sloping 'beetle-back' tail was now the Super Sports style. By 1928, 6,000 Alvises were on the road, and production was running at about 900 chassis per annum.

In that year, Alvis introduced a new type that was also to be a great success. Following fashion, it was a small six of 1870cc. Similar in design to the old four, it was smoother, more flexible and quieter. Bodies were roomier and gearing was lower. This 14.75hp was superseded by the Silver Eagle in 1929, a car with a bigger bore that gave 2148cc. Needless to say, a tuned sports version was added. Also in 1928, Alvis made a mistake. They put into production a sports machine that had front-wheel drive — the first instance of this type of drive in a British catalogued car — and independent suspension by four quarter-elliptic springs at the front and swing axles with quarter-elliptics at the rear. The 4-cylinder, 1482cc, single ohc engine utilized many 12/50 parts, and could be had with a Roots-type supercharger. Helped by a low centre of gravity, the roadholding was very fine, and so were the brakes. During 1928 this model finished 6th and 9th at Le Mans, and 2nd in the Ulster Tourist Trophy race. In the following year an 8-cylinder version, still of 1½-litres was added. Unfortunately, the fwd cars had a very specialized, limited appeal, being complicated, unconventional, temperamental and hard to work on. However, Alvis were so confident in them and in the new six that they announced suspension of the production of the 12/50 in 1929. It was hurriedly reinstated when the six, popular though it was, proved insufficient to keep the company going alone. It was listed until 1932, alongside a new sporting variant, the 12/60hp.

This was the company's last out and out sports car, but its reputation for high-performance vehicles was sustained by the introduction of another new line in 1932. The Speed Twenty was an exceptionally low-built, handsome fast tourer of modern appearance that combined the refinement of a medium-sized (2,511cc) six with speed, excellent roadholding and brakes, stamina and a reasonable price. This car, and the types which succeeded it were a great success. The engine was a slightly tuned version of the largest option available in the Silver Eagle, and the chassis, too, was basically similar to that of the earlier model, which was retained. The power output was about 87bhp, permitting the better examples of the Vanden Plas open tourer to attain 90mph, in spite of the car's weight, which was an equally traditional Alvis feature. The bodies were all coachbuilt.

With the introduction of this Alvis, the character of Alvis policy in the 1930s was set: the Speed Twenty and its developments provided the glamour, while an assortment of 'bread-and-butter' fours and sixes backed it up. All had push-rod ohv engines. The old '12/50' and '12/60' were replaced for 1933 by the heavier Firefly in the 1½-litre, 4-cylinder range. Much of the extra weight was added by the optional Wilson preselector gearbox, which could also be had on its development, the Firebird of 1935. This car, however, had an 1842cc engine, in an attempt to cope with the avoirdupois. The Silver Eagle was joined early in 1933 by the 2511cc Crested Eagle, which also had a Wilson gearbox. This was a chassis intended to carry heavier bodies, and was important because it was the first Alvis touring car to have independent front suspension, which was by a single transverse leaf. This feature, together with an all-synchromesh gearbox, was seen on the 1934 Speed Twenty. The latter model, which was also growing heavier with increasing public demand for comfort rather than sporting pretensions, was given a bigger engine of 2762cc in 1935 by lengthening the stroke.

For the same reason, the 3½-litre also made its bow. It was basically similar to the Speed Twenty, which it supplemented, but had a smoother, quieter engine with a bigger bore, providing 3571cc and was designed to accommodate more comfortable,

1930 ALVIS 16/95 Silver Eagle saloon. Coachwork by Weymann. *National Motor Museum*

1938 ALVIS 4·3-litre short-chassis saloon. Coachwork by Charlesworth. *Autocar*

1946 ALVIS TA14 saloon. *National Motor Museum*

1965 ALVIS TE21 saloon. *Alvis Ltd*

1922 AMBASSADOR(i) Model R 34hp tourer.
Keith Marvin Collection

1885 AMÉDÉE BOLLÉE steam mail coach for
the Marquis de Broc. *National Motor Museum*

less sporting bodies. The 3½-litre was, however, a more powerful car than the Spe
Twenty, with 110bhp. It was a short and logical step to replace the Speed Twenty w
a new car for 1936 that combined the virtues of both models. This was the fine Spe
Twenty-five, which used the 3571cc engine. Capable of a smooth and silent 95mph
saloon form, it was what many people still regard as the best Alvis ever built. At t
same time, a car that was originally envisaged as a replacement for the short-liv
3½-litre was announced. This 4.3-litre had the same engine, bored out to a capacity
4387cc and providing 123bhp. With the introduction of the short-chassis spo
tourer version for 1938, the 4.3-litre became the most exciting Alvis in the range,
it could easily exceed 100mph, with acceleration to match. Some consider that it w
not quite as good-looking as the Speed Twenty-five, nor equally refined.

A new four to replace the Firebird was listed for 1938. This was the 12/70hp,
George Lanchester design, with an 80mph performance in spite of its weight. T
engine size was unaltered. The Silver Eagle had been dropped in 1936, but the Crest
Eagle became available in a number of versions with the 2762cc and the 3571
engines as these appeared, in less highly-tuned forms. The Silver Crest, another c
in which George Lanchester had a hand, was also brought in for 1938 alongside th
12/70hp. It was intended to carry bodies of the more formal sort, and was power
by the 2762cc engine, among others. It, too, had independent front suspension.

An aero engine works had been opened as early as 1937. The car factory at Hol
head Road, Coventry was completely destroyed by bombing in 1940, but the compa
continued to make aero engines – Rolls-Royce Merlins – at eighteen shadow factori
After World War 2, Alvis made their own Leonides unit and car production was
started in 1946. A one-model policy, tailored to meet conditions of austerity, w
adopted. Quality was still the main characteristic of the new TA14, which, in Alv
tradition, used a 4-cylinder push-rod ohv engine, now of 1,892cc. This car was th
direct descendant of the 12/70hp. An ugly sporting model appeared briefly in 194
The TA14 was dropped during 1950 and the TA21, a big six, substituted. This was th
first entirely new post-war Alvis. Its 2993cc engine developed 90bhp, and this car
though not its sports roadster variant the TB21 – was a slower car than the Spee
Twenty-five. Not so its development, the TC21/100, listed for 1954 and 1955. Thi
after attention from Alec Issigonis, had a tuned engine providing 100bhp and a high
axle ratio, and carried a 100mph guarantee. Issigonis also designed an advanced V-
saloon which was never put into production. The TC21/100 did not last long, for
1955 there appeared one of the handsomest cars Alvis ever made, the Grabe
designed saloon on what was virtually the TC21/100 chassis. Few were built unt
1959, when this car was given a modified engine delivering 120bhp and renamed th
TD21. It acquired disc brakes as standard fittings on all four wheels for 1962. Fo
1964, it was replaced by the TE21, with 130bhp and five forward speeds. Automati
transmission was optional. In 1965 Rover acquired a controlling interest in th
firm; production of private cars ceased in the summer of 1967.   TR

A.M. (F) 1906–1915
Ateliers Veuve A. de Mesmay, St Quentin, Aisne

Known as makers of the Abeille proprietary engines (as used in Brush (i)) an
also of a light agricultural tractor in 1912, the de Mesmay company's status a
builders of complete cars depends almost exclusively on listings in directories.
1906 they were reported as marketing two 4-cylinder models rated at 12 and 20hp
as well as a 2-cylinder 12hp 'Abeille' car.   MC

AMALGAMATED (US) 1917–1919
Amalgamated Machinery Corp, Chicago, Ill.

The Amalgamated Six used a special engine in which the poppet valves were close
as well as opened positively. Instead of disc cams which lifted only, grooved cylindri
cal cams of the type familiar in machine tools and other machinery were used. KN

AMAZON (GB) 1921–1922
Amazon Cars Ltd, London E.C.3

The Amazon light car had a 6/9hp Coventry-Victor flat-twin engine, Juckes 3
speed gearbox and chain drive. Although the engine was mounted at the rear, the ca
had a bonnet and a dummy radiator.   GN

AMBASSADOR (i) (US) 1922–1926
Yellow Cab Manufacturing Co, Chicago, Ill.

The large Ambassador cars of 1922 and 1923 were simply leftover Shaw car
with a new emblem and a Continental engine, Yellow Cab having taken Shaw
(i) over in 1922. The 'Drive-Yourself' smaller cars, known as the Model D-1
appeared in mid-1924 and were marketed under the Ambassador name until 1926
when the name was changed to Hertz.   KN

AMBASSADOR (ii) see AMERICAN MOTORS

AMCO (US) 1919–1920
American Motors Inc, New York, N.Y.

The Amco used a 4-cylinder G.B. & S. engine and could be had either with left
or right-hand drive. The radiator was especially designed for tropical climates and
most of the cars were marketed in beige.   KN

AMÉDÉE BOLLÉE (F) 1885–1922
Amédée Bollée fils, Le Mans, Sarthe

The Bollée family were bell-founders of Le Mans, and Amédée père had made a number of experimental steam carriages and tractors from 1873 onwards. Young Amédée's first design, in which he was helped by his father, was a large steam mail coach built to the order of the Marquis de Broc in 1885, which cost the vast sum of 30,000 francs (equivalent then to £1,180). The same year Amédée built a small steam car of entirely his own design, but soon afterwards turned to the petrol engine. Years of experiment led to the first production car in 1896, a vis-à-vis with a 6hp 2-cylinder horizontal engine, and belt drive. One of these cars ran in the Paris-Marseilles-Paris race, but crashed into a tree. A few cars were made for sale in 1896, in which year de Dietrich took a licence for manufacture in Germany. Shortly afterwards Leesdorfer did the same in Austria. In 1898 a racing car was built with a streamlined body, probably the first use of streamlining for racing. Driven by Giraud, one of these was 3rd in the Paris-Amsterdam race, while Loysel won the Bordeaux-Biarritz race.

In 1899 a 20hp 4-cylinder racing car was made, with much lower lines. Production cars of this period had 10 or 12hp 2-cylinder engines, and large curved gilled-tube radiators. Vertical 4-cylinder engines appeared in about 1904, and steering-column gear change in 1906. Up to 1914 Amédée Bollée made cars in very small numbers, not more than 30 to 40 per year. They were bought by a largely aristocratic clientèle, including the Marquis de Broc who was evidently sufficiently pleased with his steam coach to order seven Bollée cars in all. The 1914 range consisted of two 4-cylinder cars, both chain-driven, a 16hp and a 30hp, the latter of 6333cc. A few cars were assembled after the war from pre-war parts, and a 20cv 6-cylinder model was announced in 1922.　　　　GNG

AMERICA (i) (US) 1911
Motor Car Co of America, New York, N.Y.

The America was available in five models, all with an L-head 4-cylinder engine of 40hp. The torpedo, for two passengers, had a long, low silhouette and rounded aft-section. An unusual feature of these cars was an auxiliary 1½ gallon fuel tank. It is claimed that this company was later associated with McIntyre.　　GMN

AMERICA (ii) (E) 1917–1922
America Autos SA, Barcelona

The America light cars were designed by the talented engineer Manuel Pazos who held a number of patents in the fields of valveless engines and internally sprung wheels. The Type A employed the valveless engine, but the most famous model was the 6/8hp Type B, a 4-cylinder 760cc light car. Often fitted with sporting bodywork, the Type B competed in races and hill-climbs where its chief rivals were the David and Diaz y Grillo cars. The Type C was sold in sports and single-seater racing form, and won the Gold Medal of the Royal Motorcycle Club of Catalonia in 1921.　　JRV

AMERICAN (i) (US) 1902–1903
American Motor Carriage Co, Cleveland, Ohio

This company made a light runabout powered by a 5hp single-cylinder engine, mounted under the seat. Steering was by tiller and the car used single chain drive. The price was $1,000, rather high for such a simple vehicle.　　GNG

AMERICAN (ii) (US) 1904
American Mfg Co, Alexandria, Va.

This company bought up promising patents from inventors and then manufactured the patented goods at their Alexandria works. They were simultaneously offering fire extinguishers, French fry potato cutters, and the American automobile in runabout and touring form. This was a conventional four-seater with shaft drive from a front-mounted engine.　　MJWW

AMERICAN (iii) (US) 1914
American Cyclecar Co, Detroit, Mich.

This car had a 4-cylinder water-cooled engine of 1.2 litres, and was built with a friction transmission and chain drive. The headlamps were inserted into the mudguards, a design which was later a distinctive feature of the Pierce-Arrow. This make was succeeded by the Trumbull.　　GMN

AMERICAN (iv) (US) 1914
American Cyclecar Co, Seattle, Wash.

The prototype American cyclecar had a 3-cylinder, 2-stroke engine with a friction transmission and chain drive to the front wheels. With a wheelbase of 7ft 6in and a track of 3ft 4in it weighed about 650lb. It was proposed to sell this car for $350.　　GMN

AMERICAN (v) (US) 1916–1920
American Motor Vehicle Co, Lafayette, Ind.

Also known as the American Junior, this was an ultra-light two-seater car with a single-cylinder engine, intended mainly for children. The makers also hoped to compete with rickshaws in China and to build electric invalid cars.　　GNG

1898 AMÉDÉE BOLLÉE 8hp Paris-Amsterdam racing car. *National Motor Museum*

1912 AMÉDÉE BOLLÉE 30hp tourer. *Musée de l'Automobile, Le Mans*

1933 AMERICAN AUSTIN Series 2-75 roadster.
Harrah's Automobile Collection

1938 (AMERICAN) BANTAM roadster.
G.N. Georgano

1971 AMERICAN MOTORS Gremlin coupé.
American Motors Corporation

1973 AMERICAN MOTORS Hornet 2-door sedan.
American Motors Corporation

AMERICAN (vi) (US) *1916–1924*

(1) American Motors Corp, Plainfield, N.J.

(2) Bessemer-American Motor-Corp, Plainfield, N.J.

The American, an assembled car using Amco, Rutenber, or Herschell-Spillman engines, was never common, although production reached 1,500 units in 1920. The American became amalgamated with the Bessemer Truck Corp, early in 1923 and in October the car and truck interests combined to form Amalgamated Motors which included Winther and Northway truck companies. Production of passenger cars ceased early in 1924. KM

AMERICAN AUSTIN; BANTAM (US) *1930–1941*

(1) American Austin Car Co Inc, Butler, Pa. *1930–1934*

(2) American Bantam Car Co, Butler, Pa. *1935–1941*

This was a licence-produced Austin Seven with mirror-image engine, Chevrolet-like styling, and fixed disc wheels with detachable rims, selling in sedan form at $445. Unfortunately Americans have never been keen on sub-compacts, and rumoured orders for 180,000 cars boiled down to a trickle of sales. The make's first year was its best, and even then only 8,558 were sold. There were receiverships in 1932 and 1934, and no cars at all were produced in 1935 or 1936. In 1937 the American Austin was renamed the Bantam, with styling by Alexis de Sakhnoffski, a new horizontal-barred grille, pressure lubrication, mechanical pump feed, and synchromesh. The 1940 models had enlarged 800cc engines with 3-bearing crankshafts, and the range now included a four-seater convertible as well as roadsters, tourings, station wagons and light commercials, but few found buyers. In the same year the company produced the first successful Jeep prototype with 4-cylinder Continental engine for the US Army. Though the big contracts went to Willys and Ford, Bantam not only rescued themselves but abandoned car manufacture for good. MCS

AMERICAN BERLIET see ALCO

AMERICAN EAGLE see EAGLE (vi)

AMERICAN ELECTRIC (US) *1899–1902*

(1) American Electric Vehicle Co, Chicago, Ill. *1899–1902*

(2) American Electric Vehicle Co, Hoboken, N.J. *1902*

This company made a rather high, ungainly-looking electric carriage, some with *dos-à-dos* four-seater bodies. They moved to New Jersey 'to find more wealthy buyers', according to the company's statement, but failed the same year. GNG

AMERICAN JUNIOR see AMERICAN (iv)

AMERICAN JUVENILE ELECTRIC (US) *1907*

American Metal Wheel & Auto Co, Toledo, Ohio

As the name implies this was an electrically-powered car, with seats for two children. The wheelbase was only 3ft 5in, but was complete with 'lights, bells, etc.' and tiller steering for $800. GMN

AMERICAN MERCEDES (US) *1904–1907*

Daimler Mfg Co, Long Island City, N.Y.

These cars were built as exact copies of Mercedes, under exclusive U.S. licence. Some commercial vehicles, such as ambulances, were also made. American Mercedes were in direct competition with Mercedes Import Co of New York, which handled the imported Mercedes for the whole of the United States, at least in 1906. GMN

AMERICAN MORS see STANDARD (iv)

AMERICAN MOTORS (US) *1968 to date*

American Motors Corp, Detroit, Mich.

American Motors was founded in 1954 as a result of the merger between Nash and Hudson interests. Their products were marketed under Nash and Hudson names until the 1958 season when they became Ramblers. In 1968 there appeared the first A.M.C. product to drop the Rambler name; this was the Javelin, a four-seater sport coupé to challenge Ford's Mustang and Chevrolet's Camaro. It was available with V-8 engines of 4.8, 5.6 and 6.4 litres, as well as a 3.8-litre six. The Javelin was supplemented by the shorter wheelbase two-seater AMX coupé, using the same V-8 engines; this model was withdrawn in 1971. The Rambler name was still used for the compact 440 and Rogue sedans, while other cars in the American Motors line-up were the medium-sized Rebel and the full-sized Ambassador sedans. In the summer of 1969 appeared the Hornet, a compact sedan available with 6-cylinder engines of 3.2 or 3.8 litres, or a 4.9-litre V-8. The Ambassador AMX, Javelin and Rebel continued in the 1970 range, but the Rambler name was dropped except in export markets where it was used for the Hornet. Even smaller than the Hornet was the sub-compact Gremlin introduced in mid-1970; this had an 8ft wheelbase and came with two 6-cylinder engines, 3.2 or 3.8 litres. For 1971 the Rebel became the Matador with three body styles and six engine options, from a 3.8-litre six to a 5.4-litre V-8.

For 1972 American Motors merged the worlds of couture and automobiles with the Gucci Hornet Sportabout and Cardin Javelin, using interior trim inspired by the well-known fashion designers, and continued this theme into 1973 with the Levi's Gremlin. Three engine options were available in the 1973 Gremlin: 3.8 or 4.2-litre sixes and a 5-litre V-8. Hornet, Matador, Javelin and Ambassador models were continued for 1973, with engine choices of two sixes and four V-8s, the largest a 6.6-litre unit developing 255bhp.   GNG

AMERICAN MOTOR SLEIGH (US) 1905

American Motor Sleigh Co

This vehicle was designed for travel on snow with a single-cylinder engine which drove a pronged wheel, and runners in the place of conventional wheels.   GMN

AMERICAN POPULAIRE (US) 1904

American Automobile Power Co, Lawrence, Mass.

The American Populaire was a four-seater tonneau powered by a 12hp 2-cylinder engine. Final drive was by single chain.   GNG

AMERICAN SIMPLEX (US) 1906–1910

Simplex Motor Car Co, Mishawaka, Ind.

This make used 4-cylinder, 2-stroke engines, initially of 40hp. These were later increased to 6.8 litres and rated at 50hp. For 1910, three open models and two closed versions were offered, ranging in price up to $5,400. The name was changed to Amplex in 1910 to avoid confusion with the better-known Simplex of New York. This change coincided with a company reorganization.   GMN

AMERICAN STEAM CAR (US) 1929–c.1931

American Steam Automobile Co, West Newton, Mass.

The American Steam Car was built by Thomas S. Derr, a former faculty member at the Massachusetts Institute of Technology. Derr, while specializing in modifications and improvements of the Stanley boiler and servicing and rebuilding Stanley cars, marketed a number of cars under the American Steam Car emblem. These used basic Hudson components, chassis and bodies. The condenser emblem and hubcaps, however, carried the American name.   KM

AMERICAN STEAMER (US) 1922–1924

The American Steam Truck Co, Chicago, Ill.; Elgin, Ill.

Only 16 of these cars were built in 1922, an additional cheaper model being unsuccessfully added to the line a year later. The car featured a 2-cylinder compound double-acting motor and was capable of a speed in excess of 60mph. The prototype of this car was tested as early as 1918 but neither the exhaustive testing nor the Lincoln-appearing condenser saved it from bankruptcy. A touring-car, roadster, coupé and sedan were available.   KM

AMERICAN TRI-CAR (US) 1912

Tri-car Co of America, Denver, Co.

This was a 3-wheeler with drive to the single rear wheel, which was also the only braked wheel. It had a 2-cylinder, 13hp air-cooled engine. A planetary transmission was used. This two-seater car had a wheelbase of 6ft 10in.   GMN

AMERICAN UNDERSLUNG (US) 1906–1914

American Motor Car Co, Indianapolis, Ind.

This make achieved its fame from the underslung models, so-called because the frame was slung below the axles, which gave a low appearance and centre of gravity, but did not sacrifice good ground clearance. In fact this design was not introduced until 1907, earlier cars having conventional chassis and 35/40hp engines. 1908 models used 40 and 50hp 4-cylinder T-head Teetor-Hartley engines. The most rakish models were the roadsters, originally only a two-seater, but supplemented in 1909 by a long-wheelbase four-seater. For 1912 a smaller car, the 22hp L-head American Scout was introduced, and the 60hp 6-cylinder Model 644 came in 1913.   GNG

AMERICAN VOITURETTE (US) 1913

American Voiturette Co, Detroit, Mich.

This was a light car powered by a 4-cylinder sv engine behind a V-radiator. The wheelbase was 8ft 4in, and the car came in roadster, tandem two-seater and four-seater versions.   GNG

AMERICAN WALTHAM (US) 1898–1899

American Waltham Mfg Co, Waltham, Mass.

This was a typical light steam buggy with a 2-cylinder engine under the seat, tiller steering and cycle-type wheels. It was the product of a bicycle firm, and must not be confused with the more famous Waltham or Waltham Orient steamer, made by another bicycle firm at the same time.   GNG

AMES (US) 1910–1915

(1) Carriage Woodstock Co, Owensboro, Ky. 1910–1911

1910 AMERICAN SIMPLEX 50hp tourer.
Automotive History Collection, Detroit Public Library

1922 AMERICAN STEAMER tourer. *Keith Marvin Collection*

1914 AMERICAN UNDERSLUNG Model 644 tourer. *Harrah's Automobile Collection*

1912 AMHERST 40, showing demountable rear seat. *Glenn Baechler Collection*

1925 AMILCAR Type CGS 9hp coupé. *Autocar*

1930 AMILCAR 2-litre straight-8 drophead coupé. *G.N. Georgano*

1936 AMILCAR Pégase 14CV drophead coupé. *G.N. Georgano*

(2) Ames Motor Car Co, Owensboro, Ky. *1912–1915*

Early Ames models had 4-cylinder engines with a choice of five-seater touri car or gentleman's roadster body styles. Later models with 2-stroke, 4-cylind engines of 45hp had friction transmissions and double chain drive. At $850 for t roadster, this was an extremely cheap car for its size.   GM

A.M.G. (S) *1903*
AB Motorfabriken, Gothenburg

This firm had produced paraffin-fuelled engines for several years before th turned to car manufacture. Their car used a German-made 2-cylinder engine ar carburettor, but all other parts were Swedish, including the handsome wooc body which was the product of a local carpenter. Only nine cars were made, b one was in regular use until 1928.

AMHERST 40 (CDN) *1911–1912*
Two in One Co, Amherstburg, Ont.

Designed in Detroit, the Amherst 40 was a tourer with a demountable re seat converting it quickly to a pick-up truck. Only three were constructed.

AMILCAR (F) *1921–1939*
(1) Sté Nouvelle pour l'Automobile Amilcar, St Denis *1921–1937*
(2) Sté Financière pour l'Automobile, Boulogne-sur-Seine *1937–1939*

Of all the sporting voiturettes that proliferated in France after World War 1, t Amilcar was the most famous and successful. Its name was an anagram of those its protagonists, Messrs Lamy, who had been concerned with the design of the l Zèbre before the war, and Akar, who financed it. The Amilcar's designer wa Edmond Moyet. The Type CC and its developments the CS and 4C all had 4-cylind sv engines of about 1-litre capacity, three forward speeds and quarter-elliptic sprin ing. They differed little, therefore, from hosts of their competitors. The CGS (Grand Sport of 1924 was a different and more serious proposition. It had a 1074c engine with full pressure lubrication, front-wheel brakes and front half-elliptic spring It was developed into the more powerful, lowered CGSS (Surbaisse) model in 192t Various touring cars of between one and two litres were also made, all with fou cylinders and side valves, but it was the CGS and CGSS that made the company reputation throughout the world.

Even so, the C6 Course, one of the very few pure racing cars ever to be pu into production, was still more exciting. Introduced in 1926, it dominated th 1100cc voiturette racing class. Its twin overhead camshaft, 6-cylinder engin developed 83hp and used roller bearings in works form. These cars were capabl of 118mph. A small touring straight-8 joined the range in 1928, as was the fashio then. This low-built C8 was another excellent machine, with good roadholding an and a creditable maximum speed of almost 80mph in spite of its considerabl weight. The 2-litre engine had a single overhead camshaft.

By 1930, the company was concentrating on touring cars; sports cars in France as elsewhere with the onset of the Depression, were in decline. The C8 was there enlarged to two litres. The 1¼-litre Type M, a sedate small four which had arrive in 1928, survived until 1935 as the M2, M3 and M4; latterly with a 1.7-litre engine Meanwhile, 1933 had brought Moyet's new 5CV, the Type C, current until 1935 i various forms, and the disappearance of the C8. From 1934 to 1937 the 12CV was offered, which used a Delahaye engine, and there was also the 14CV G36. Th last Amilcars, made by Hotchkiss, were far more interesting. These 'Compounds of 1938–39 had independent suspension front and rear, front-wheel drive on J.A Grégoire Tracta patents, and the Alpax unit construction of body and chassis tha incorporated much aluminium. The engine was an 1185cc four.   TR

AMIOT-PENEAU (F) *1898–1902*
l'Avant-Train Amiot et Peneau, Asnières, Seine

This vehicle originally appeared in 1897 as the Amiot, a very crude 4-wheele *avant-train* which could be attached to a 2-wheeled horse-drawn carriage. The Amiot et Peneau was a slightly more sophisticated two-wheeled *avant-train* whic was fitted to a variety of brakes and broughams as well as to commercial vehicles Both petrol and electric versions were made, the former with Augé engines, the latter with Patin motors.   GN

AMO (SU) *1927*
Amo Works, Moscow

The Amo light truck was the first vehicle to be completely designed and built ir the Soviet Union, and first appeared in 1924. A few heavy-looking touring cars were built on this chassis, which was powered by a 35bhp 4-cylinder engine.   GNG

AMOR (D) *1924–1925*
Amor Automobilbau GmbH, Cologne

This was a 4/16PS 4-cylinder small car with proprietary engine.   HON

AMPÈRE (F) *1906–1909*
Sté des Etablissements Ampère, Billancourt, Seine

The Ampère used a 10/16hp 4-cylinder engine driving the gearbox through an

ctrically operated clutch. It was shown at the 1908 Paris Salon, but few of these
rs were actually produced. GNG

MPHICAR (D) *1961–1968*
Deutsche Industrie-Werke, Lübeck-Schlutup *1961–1962*
Deutsche Waggons- und Maschinenfabriken GmbH, Berlin 52 *1962 to date*
The only amphibian car for private use on the world market was designed by
ns Trippel. A chassis-less cabriolet steel body with electric welded joints is used.
e engine is a 4-cylinder 1,147cc Triumph mounted in the rear. Only the rear
eels are driven. Two propellers for water cruising are mounted under the back
the car and are driven by a special gear. On the road the car is capable of about
mph, on water about 6½ knots. Normal steering is used in the water. In 1962 an
nphicar crossed the Channel from France to England. HON

MPLEX (US) *1910–1915*
Amplex Motor Car Co, Mishawaka, Ind.
Amplex Mfg Co, Mishawaka, Ind.
Amplex was a continuation of American Simplex. Both 40hp and 50hp models
re produced, with 2-stroke engines. These were expensive, a limousine costing
much as $5,600. This firm clung too long to the obsolete 2-stroke engine,
hough a 4-stroke design was used unsuccessfully in 1913. Gilette Motor Co
ok over the manufacturing facilities in 1916, perpetuating this aversion to
rmal engine-valving by manufacturing a rotary sleeve-valve power unit. There
no evidence of their having been any more successful than their predecessors.
GMN

M.S. (I) *1969 to date*
trezzature Meccaniche Speciali, Bologna
Dr Ing. Tancredi Simonetti was a graduate aerodynamics engineer who submit-
d body design studies to A.T.S. as an independent before joining them to design
eir F1 and later Tipo 1000 sports car, after a spell at OSI, Turin. He founded
M.S. Autoracing in February 1969 at Casalecchio di Reno and moved to the
rrent works in 1971. The first car was a 1,000cc Cosworth SCA-engined 1000SP
orts car with tubular frame, and this was accompanied in 1969 by a single Fiat-
gined Formula 850 car. In 1970 two 1000SPs were built with Novamotor-Ford
gines, Hewland gearboxes and tubular space-frame chassis, and two more 850s
d an Alfa Romeo GTAj-powered, Colotti-transmitted 1300SP were also pro-
ced.
Eleven cars were produced during 1971, three Novamotor 1000SPs, a single
0 and 1300SP (this with a Fiat 128 engine modified by Trivellato) and three
vanced 1790cc Cosworth FVC-powered semi-monocoque 2000SPs. In 1972 pro-
action was running at two cars per month, including 1971-style 1000 and 2000SPs
r home sale, a special-bodied Lamborghini Miura and a Group 5/Group 7 Cos-
orth-Ford BDE-powered sports-racing car. A.M.S. successes include 26 first
aces in national races during 1971, and Italian national racing and hill-climb
ampionships in their classes. DCN

MS-STERLING *see* STERLING (iii)

MX *see* AMERICAN MOTORS

.N. (F) *c.1921–c.1923*
llain et Niguet, Kremlin-Bicêtre, Seine
This was a 2-cylinder cyclecar of which few details are known. GNG

NADOL (TR) *1966 to date*
tosan Otomobil Sanayii AS, Istanbul
The first car designed for manufacture in Turkey, the Anadol was engineered
y Reliant and known at first as the Reliant FW 5. It was powered by a 1,198cc
ord Anglia Super engine, and had a separate chassis, four/five-seater fibreglass
aloon coachwork, and front disc brakes. Initially, the local content was 50%, but
is has been steadily increased. By the end of 1970, 10,000 Anadols had been
ade. Since 1969 1,300cc Ford engines have been used, and in 1972 a 4-door
aloon joined the range. GNG

NASAGASTI (RA) *1911–1915*
oracio Anasagasti & Cía, Buenos Aires
Horacio Anasagasti started by importing Isotta Fraschinis into Argentina. He
en branched out into the manufacture of automobile components, and progressed
cars built up from French components: engines were 12hp and 15hp 4-cylinder
allots and frames came from Malicet et Blin. Casting problems frustrated Anasa-
asti's plans for Argentinian-built engines, and in 1912 he adopted T-head Picker-
anvier units of 2,982cc and 3,610cc. He also campaigned with his cars energeti-
ally in France, with a good performance in the 1913 Tour de France and a less
ood one in the Coupe de l'Auto, where d'Avaray finished 7th and last. World
Var 1 made it impossible for the firm to get any more components from Europe,
nd the factory closed after only about 30 cars had been built. MCS

1939 AMILCAR Compound 1,185cc saloon.
G.N. Georgano

1908 AMPÈRE 10/16hp tourer. *Lucien Loreille Collection*

1966 AMPHICAR 1.2-litre amphibious cabriolet.
Deutsche Waggon und Maschinenfabrik GmbH

1972 ANADOL 1.3-litre saloon.
Otosan

1919 ANDERSON(ii) 25.3hp tourer. *Autocar*

1933 ANDRÉ 6hp sports car. *Autocar*

c.1908 ANGLO-DANE 2-cylinder landaulette.
Thorkil Ry Andersen

ANCHOR (US) *1910–1911*
(1) Anchor Motor Car Co, Cincinnati, Ohio
(2) Anchor Buggy Co, Cincinnati, Ohio
   This motor buggy, made by a branch of Anchor Carriage Co, while m
attractive in appearance than most, was not a financial success.   G

ANDERHEGGEN (NL) *1901–1902*
Ferdinand Anderheggen, Amsterdam.
   The Anderheggen was a light *vis-à-vis* four-seater powered by a 4hp wat
cooled Abeille engine. Transmission was by flat belt from the engine to a syst
of fast and loose pulleys giving two speeds. It was intended that the cars should
produced by a firm at Swalmen, Limburg, but in fact only 5 or 6 cars were ma
in Anderheggen's works in Amsterdam.   G

ANDERSON (i) (US) *1907–1909*
Anderson Carriage Mfg Co, Anderson, Ind.
   This Anderson was a typical high-wheeler with 2-cylinder air-cooled engi
solid tyres and transverse front suspension.   G

ANDERSON (ii) (US) *1916–1926*
The Anderson Motor Co, Rock Hill, S.C.
   This car, built by a former carriage works, was the most successful of all mak
built in the southern United States. Utilizing 6-cylinder Continental motors
various sorts, production reached nearly 2,000 units in 1923. Andersons appear
in a large variety of body styles and in unusual colour combinations and we
particularly highly regarded in the southern states, although they were so
throughout the country.   K

ANDINO (RA) *1967 to date*
Automotores 9 de Julio S.A., Buenos Aires
   This is a rear-engined GT coupé with fibreglass coachwork on an all-indepe
dently sprung backbone frame. Four-cylinder Renault engines are used, the origi
845cc type being replaced by a 58bhp 1,118cc unit in 1971.   M

ANDRÉ (GB) *1933–1934*
T.B. André, London, W.11
   The André V6 was a light two-seater sports car powered by a 728cc V-twin o
J.A.P. engine developing 28bhp at 4,500rpm. The front wheels were independent
sprung by a single transverse leaf spring, while the body floor acted as a chass
Only six of these promising little sports cars were made.   GN

ANDREAS (D) *1900–1902*
Sächsische Accumulatoren-Werke AG, Dresden
   These were electric cars constructed by Dr Ernst Andreas.   HC

ANDRÉ PY (F) *1899*
Cie des Automobiles du Sud Ouest
   The André Py voiturette was a Léon Bollée-like 3-wheeler with *dos-à-dos* seatir
for two, and a 3½hp horizontal single-cylinder engine. It had the unusual feature
front-wheel-drive and rear-wheel-steering.   GN

ANGELI (F) *1926–1927*
Automobiles Angeli, Neuilly-Plaisance, Seine
   The Angeli was a small saloon with a 7hp 4-cylinder engine. It never real
emerged from the prototype stage.   GN

ANGER *see* A.E.C.

ANGLADA (E) *c.1904–1907*
Anglada y Cía, Puerto de Santa Maria, Cadiz
   Francisco Anglada Gallardo was a cycle maker who experimented with cars fro
1902 and went into small-scale production in about 1904. In this year a 24h
4-cylinder car was supplied to King Alfonso XIII. A wide range of cars wa
listed in 1905, from 6 to 36hp and 1 to 4 cylinders, but it is unlikely that thes
were actually built.   GN

ANGLO-DANE (DK) *1902–1917*
H.C. Fredericksen, Copenhagen
   These cars derived their name from the fact that Fredericksen had original
built bicycles containing some English parts. There was nothing English abo
the Anglo-Dane cars, which were friction-driven vehicles powered originally by
single-cylinder Kelecom engine. Later cars had a single-cylinder 4½hp engine
Fredericksen's own design, and a double friction disc giving 12 speeds. 2-cylinde
engines were also used in later vehicles, but these were mostly trucks. In fact, of th
70 to 80 vehicles made up to 1917 the majority were trucks. The firm was the
merged with Jan and Thrige, the new company making Triangel commercial vehicle
up to 1945.   TR

ANGLO-FRENCH *see* ROGER

ANGLO-SPHINX *see* SPHINX

ANGUS *see* FULLER (i)

ANGUS-SANDERSON (GB) *1919–1927*

1) Sir William Angus, Sanderson & Co, Birtley, Co Durham *1919–1921*

2) Angus-Sanderson (1921) Ltd, Hendon, Middlesex *1921–1927*

The Angus-Sanderson was one of several early British attempts to mass-produce a medium-sized car, using some of the principles which had recently proved so successful in America. It was an assembled vehicle, its promoters lacking the capital for mass manufacture; indeed, they made fewer of their own parts than any other British car maker at the time. The engine was a 4-cylinder, 14.3hp of 2.3 litres made by Tylor, who also manufactured lavatory cisterns. Wrigley provided the 3-speed gearbox, Woodhead the suspension, and Goodyear the curious, polished-aluminium disc wheels. The bodies were very good-looking. Unfortunately delivery delays, and the rising cost of labour and materials, killed the Angus-Sanderson as they did other under-financed makes. Only a handful were ever made, and prices stayed high – £575 in 1920. An 8hp light car appeared in 1923, but nobody wanted it. Another brief revival in 1925 met the same fate. TRN

ANHUT (US) *1909–1910*

Anhut Motor Car Co, Detroit, Mich.

The Anhut used 6-cylinder ohv engines of 3.7 litres. Two- and four-seater open models were made, on a common chassis. In 1910, the company was succeeded by Barnes Automobile Co which failed a month later. GMN

ANKER (D) *1918–1920*

Anker Automobilfabrik Paul Griebert, Berlin-Tempelhof

Cars of this make were available with different bodies but all based on one standard type of chassis. It was not produced on a large scale. HON

ANNA (US) *1912*

Anna Motor Car Co, Anna, Ill.

The Anna was a two-seater, with what was termed a 'Democrat' body on an 8ft 4in wheelbase. Its water-cooled 2-cylinder engine was of 2.8 litres. GMN

ANN ARBOR (US) *1911–1912*

Huron River Mfg Co, Ann Arbor, Mich.

This was designed as a dual-purpose vehicle which could be converted from a private car to a small pick-up truck as required. GMN

ANSALDO (I) *1919–1936*

1) SA Ansaldo Automobili, Turin *1919–1932*

2) Costruzione e Vendita Automobili Ansaldo, Turin *1932–1934*

3) Ansaldo-Ceva SA, Turin *1934–1936*

One of Italy's biggest engineering groups, Ansaldo turned their idle aero-engine works over to car manufacture in 1919, their Soria-designed range being intended for volume production in competition with FIAT. The advanced 4-cylinder ohc engines contrasted with the 3-speed gearboxes, central change, wooden wheels, and austere, Chevrolet-like tourer bodywork, but even the basic 1,847cc 4A was capable of 55mph, and by 1922 it had been joined by the 2-litre 4CS that managed 70mph on an output of 48bhp. FIAT, however, were making five times as many cars. In 1923 there came both four-wheel brakes and a six, the 2-litre 6A with coil ignition. In 1926 there was even a cheap 1½-litre, the 10 with transverse front suspension. The 1927 sixes had 2.2-litre engines and four forward speeds; the latter, along with coil ignition, were found on the bigger fours by 1928. Unfortunately Soria's resignation in 1927 left Ansaldo with no new ideas, though his final efforts reached the market in 1929 and were the company's staples after 1930. The 18 was merely an enlarged 2.8-litre six, but the 22 was a large and luxurious 3½-litre pushrod straight-8 on an 11ft 2in wheelbase, distinguished by its disc wheels with quick-detachable rims. These were a product of Ruotificio Italiano, an Ansaldo subsidiary. In 1932 the CEVA concern was organized to take over the stock of 300 unsold 18 and 22 chassis, and these were still available, with restyled bodywork, as late as 1936. MCS

ANSBACH (D) *1910*

Fahrzeugfabrik Ansbach GmbH, Ansbach

This factory was founded to make commercial vehicles, but in 1910 a small private car known as the Kauz was produced with a 4-cylinder 6/14PS engine. HON

ANSTED (US) *1926–1927*

Ansted Motors, Connersville, Ind.

The Ansted car was in reality the Lexington with substituted radiator emblem and hubcaps. A few Lexingtons were changed in this way and these were marketed in the Chicago area. KM

1920 ANGUS-SANDERSON 14hp two-seater.
National Motor Museum

1923 ANSALDO 4C 1.7-litre tourer.
National Motor Museum

1931 ANSALDO 3½-litre 8-cylinder saloon.
Coachwork by Freestone & Webb.
Autocar

1901 ANTOINE 4hp tonneau. *Automobiel-museum, Driebergen*

1924 APOLLO(ii) 4/20PS sports car. *Neubauer Collection*

1920 APPERSON 33.8hp V-8 tourer. *Autocar*

ANTOINE (B) *1900–c.1902*
V. Antoine Fils et Cie, Liège

This firm were mainly makers of engines, but a few voiturettes were built. These used a 4hp single-cylinder Kelecom engine mounted at the front and a 2-speed gearbox.
GNG

ANTOINETTE (F) *1906*
Sté Antoinette, Puteaux, Seine

More celebrated for aero engines and aircraft, Antoinette showed a car powered by a 32hp V-8 engine at the 1906 Paris Salon. Two hydraulic clutches with variable slip were said to eliminate the need for a gearbox or differential. In 1907 they were offering a 16hp and 30hp car, the larger with V-8 engine, but most of their business was concerned with aircraft. A V-8 engine of Antoinette pattern was used in the 1906 Adams.
GNG

ANZANI (I) *1923–1924*
Motocicli e Motori Anzani, Milan

During World War 1, Anzani produced many aero engines, and after 1919 they became one of Europe's most famous producers of proprietary engines for use in motor cycles, cyclecars and boats. A factory was opened in France, and Anzani engines were also made in England by the British Anzani Company. The Anzani car had a much shorter existence than the engines; it was a fast, light cyclecar with twin-cylinder, air-cooled ohv engine, which appeared in 1923. One was raced at Monza in 750cc form that year, being beaten by the new baby Austin Seven in the Cyclecar Grand Prix. Alessandro Anzani himself settled in France, near Caen, and although no Anzani car appeared after 1924, proprietary engines bearing the name were produced until the 1930s, and after World War 2 in England.
C

A.P.A.L. (B) *1964–1969*
A.P.A.L. S.a.r.l., Blegny-Trembleur, Liège

This company made a two-seater GT coupé powered by a 1296cc Volkswagen engine. This 50bhp Okrasa-tuned unit was later replaced by a 1,565cc Renault 16TS unit developing 95bhp. Also offered was an open Jeep-type vehicle based on the Renault 4.
GNG

APOLLO (i) (US) *1906–1907*
Chicago Recording Scale Co, Waukegan, Ill.

The only model by this manufacturer was a five-seater with a *Roi-des-Belges* body. Power was provided by a 4-cylinder, water-cooled engine by way of a 3-speed transmission and shaft drive.
GMN

APOLLO (ii) (D) *1910–1926*
(1) A. Ruppe & Sohn AG, Apolda *1910–1912*
(2) Apollo-Werke AG, Apolda *1912–1926*

After 1910 Piccolo cars were sold under the name Piccolo-Apollo. In 1912 the firm was renamed Apollo-Werke. Karl Slevogt, who had worked as engineer for Laurin & Klement and Puch, was engaged by Apollo. Among the popular types he designed were some successful sports cars. These were the B 4/12PS 960cc and a tuned version developing 20bhp, and the F 8/28PS 2,040cc which was also available in special competition version. They were frequently in successful competition with Bugattis in pre-war events, often driven by Slevogt himself.

After World War 1 the sports car model 4/20PS was carried on until 1925. From 1920 it was the first production car in Germany to have a front swing axle. At the 1924 Avus race Apollo appeared with a streamlined car following Jaray design. Production cars were also available with Jaray bodies. A 1921 prototype with a V-8 engine was not put into production.
HON

APOLLO (iii) (US) *1962–1964*
(1) International Motorcars Inc, Oakland, Calif. *1962*
(2) Apollo International Corp, Pasadena, Calif. *1963–1964*

The Apollo was a small-production sports car powered by 3½-litre or 5-litre V-8 Buick engines. The sports two-seater or GT coupé bodies were hand-made in Italy. The name was changed to Vetta Ventura in 1964, and manufacture shifted to Dallas, Texas, where it lasted at least into 1966. About 90 Apollos were made.

APPERSON (US) *1902–1926*
(1) Apperson Bros Automobile Co, Kokomo, Ind. *1902–1924*
(2) Apperson Automobile Co, Kokomo, Ind. *1924–1926*

After the brothers Elmer and Edgar Apperson withdrew from the Haynes-Apperson concern, they introduced a front-engined car powered by a 16hp horizontally-opposed twin engine. A 4-cylinder model with horizontal engine followed in 1903, and for the 1904 season the company turned to a conventional vertical 4-cylinder layout. These were 25 and 40hp cars with double chain drive, although a 20/24hp horizontal twin was still made. They were expensive cars, the twin costing $3,500, and the larger four $5,000. By 1907 there were three fours, 24/30hp, 40hp and 50hp, the latter costing $7,500 for a limousine. In this year

eared the Jackrabbit, a 60hp two-seater speedster with flared wings, capable
5mph and costing $5,000. Later, the name Jackrabbit was applied to touring
ersons as well.

number of lower-priced models appeared in the next few years, the cheapest
g a 26hp four at only $1,350 in 1915. In 1914 a 29hp six and a 31hp V-8
e introduced; these had V-radiators, a feature which was continued until 1918.
5 was the company's peak production year, with 2,000 units sold. In 1917
eared the Silver-Apperson, an eight with styling by C.T. Silver the New
k dealer who later applied his styling talents to Kissel cars. The Silver-Apperson
an oval radiator, bullet-shaped headlamps and very clean, modern body lines.
name Silver-Apperson was dropped in 1919, but the design was continued
l 1923, when a new line with cycle-type wings was introduced. A proprietary
ne was now used, in the shape of a 3.2-litre Falls Six, although the 5.4-litre
was still Apperson's own make. These models, together with a range of
oming-engined straight-8s, introduced in 1925, were continued until the end of
luction. In 1924 there was a rumour of a refusion with the Haynes company,
this came to nothing. Front-wheel brakes were introduced on the 1926 models,
production ended in the summer of that year.   GNG

LE (US) *1917–1918*

. Apple Motor Car Co, Dayton, Ohio

he Apple 8 was a conventional-looking touring car with a pointed radiator
er like that of the contemporary Paige. It was priced at $1,150.   GNG

UILA *see* MAILLARD

UILA ITALIANA (I) *1906–1917*

brica Italiana d'Automobili Aquila, Turin

he Aquila (eagle) or Aquila Italiana, designed by Giulio Cesare Cappa, was
markably advanced vehicle in its time. Cappa's first cars, made in 1906, had
nes with 4 or 6 cylinders cast *en bloc*, a very early instance of this construction.
y were the first car engines known to use aluminium pistons. The inlet valves
e overhead, and the exhaust valves at the side. The crankshaft ran in ball
rings. This engine and the gearbox were carried on a common tray – a form of
construction. The last two features were extremely advanced for their day.
y gave some trouble, but in 1907 there were two fours and two sixes in the
e, all of the same design. The final drive was by a live axle.

ar production ceased for three years following the death of the company's
noter, but recommenced in 1909. The three 1912 models culminated in the
5hp six of 4.2-litres, with dual ignition. This engine developed 60bhp at the
high speed (for the time) of 3,600rpm. The other cars were fours. The range
tinued unaltered until 1917, the company's last year of production. An Aquila
ana ran in the 1914 French Grand Prix. It was a still more sophisticated
gn than its forerunners, having inclined all-overhead valves operated by two
camshafts via short push-rods. Giulio Cesare Cappa later worked for Fiat
Itala.   TRN

AB (GB) *1926–1928*

b Motors, Letchworth, Herts.

he Arab was one of the few out-and-out sports cars made in Britain during the
0s; although its life was short and few were made, its connections were
emely distinguished and its specification both interesting and advanced. Its
gner was said to be Reid Railton, later to be associated with the Brooklands
y Nine, and the Railton itself. The 4-cylinder, 1960cc engine of the Arab used
ined overhead valves operated by an overhead camshaft. Camshaft, dynamo,
oil and water pumps were all driven by a single chain, as in the case of the Stutz.
ve springs were of transverse leaf type, like those of the Marlborough-Thomas.
e sources say that J.G. Parry Thomas had a hand in the design of the Arab. The
tric fuel pump was a novel feature in Britain at the time. The two-seater sports
a maximum speed of 80mph, but the Super Sports was good for 90.   TRN

ABIAN (US) *c.1917*

iam Galloway Co, Waterloo, Iowa

his light car was a continuation of the Galloway and like its predecessor was
Argo (ii) built under licence. A two-seater and a four-seater were offered at
5 and $435 respectively. A 4-cylinder, water-cooled engine of 17.5hp was used.
drive system featured a Bailey transmission that drove each rear wheel separa-
                                                                      GMN

BEE (GB) *1904*

ers Bros, New Kent Road, London S.E.

he Arbee was a 6hp two-seater light car with tubular frame and two-speed
rbox, made for a short time by a firm of bicycle makers.   GNG

BEL (F) *1957*

omobiles François Arbel, Paris 17e

he Arbel was a modern attempt at making a petrol-electric car, which never

1913 AQUILA ITALIANA 12hp two-seater.
National Motor Museum

1927 ARAB 2-litre coupé. *National
Motor Museum*

1913 ARDEN 10hp two-seater. *M.R.J. Edwards*

1916 ARGO(ii) 22hp tourer. *Keith Marvin Collection*

1918 ARGONNE prototype roadster. *G. Marshall Naul Collection*

left the prototype stage. It used a rear-mounted petrol engine to drive [e]lectric motors, one in each wheel, and was the culmination of several year[s of] experiment.

ARBENZ (US) 1911–1918
(1) Scioto Car Co, Chillicothe, Ohio *1911–1912*
(2) ArBenz Car Co, Chillicothe, Ohio *1912–1918*

The prototypes of this car were known as Scioto after the Scioto River wh[ich] runs through Chillicothe. Production cars were always called ArBenz afte[r a] defunct furniture company whose plant was used for manufacture. Originally [the] ArBenz was a medium-large touring car with 48hp 4-cylinder engine, price[d at] $1,885. By 1917 ArBenz was offering a small touring car powered by a 2[0hp] 4-cylinder Lycoming engine, priced at $750.

ARCHER (GB) 1920
Designed by M. Archer, the inventor of the trench mortar, the Archer was fi[tted] with a two-seater tandem body and 2-cylinder 8/10hp engine.　　MJ[WW]

ARDEN (GB) 1912–1916
Arden Motor Co Ltd, Balsall Heath, Coventry, Warwickshire

Although it appeared at the time of the cyclecar boom, the Arden was more [a] substantial light car. It was originally offered with a choice of 2-cylinder engi[nes,] air-cooled by J.A.P., or water-cooled by Alpha, the former being a V-tw[in,] the latter a vertical twin. In 1914 a 4-cylinder water-cooled Alpha engine w[as] introduced, and a clover-leaf three-seater body supplemented the two-seat[er.] All Ardens had a three-speed and reverse gearbox, and shaft drive.　　　[GNG]

ARDENT (F) 1900–1901
Caron et Cie, Paris

The Caron company used their own make of 5hp V-twin air-cooled engine [in] their four-seater *vis-à-vis* light car. An unusual feature was that the body w[as] suspended on a frame, but the engine was in front of the frame and was unsuspend[ed.] The car was called a 'victoriette'.　　　　[GNG]

ARDITA (I) 1918
Costruzioni Automobili Ing. A. Gallanzi, Milan

Alfredo Gallanzi was a garage proprietor who acquired Antonio Chiribiri's [left] over stock of parts from 1914, and tried to market conventional sv 4-cylin[der] light cars with 1,100cc and 1,300cc engines. Credited with 'all the latest impro[ve]ments', they did not last long.　　　　[MS]

ARDSLEY (US) 1905–1906
Ardsley Motor Car Co, Yonkers, N.Y.

This fairly large and expensive car was designed by W.S. Howard, who [had] been previously connected with Howard Automobile Co also of Yonkers, N[Y.] It had a 30/35hp 4-cylinder engine and shaft drive.　　　[GMN]

ARGEO (D) 1925
Argeo Fahrzeugwerk Georg Kulitzky, Berlin S 14

This was a three wheeled cyclecar with two rear wheels, driven by a 2-str[oke] 123cc engine.　　　　[HON]

ARGO (i) (US) 1912–1914
Argo Electric Vehicle Co, Saginaw, Mich.

Argo electrics used a 60-volt system with Westinghouse motors. These w[ere] claimed to be capable of 20mph. Both four- and five-seaters, in open and clo[sed] versions, were made. All models used wheel steering.　　　[GMN]

ARGO (ii) (US) 1914–1916
Argo Motor Co, Jackson, Mich.

The Argo was originally a cyclecar based on the Ajax (ii) built by the Bris[coe] brothers in France. It had a 4-cylinder 12hp engine and differed from the A[jax] only in not using friction drive. Few cyclecars sold well in America, and in 191[5 it] was replaced by a conventional 22hp assembled touring car. In 1916 the na[me] was changed to Hackett and the company moved to Grand Rapids.　　[GMN]

ARGON (GB) 1908
Grannaway Engineering Co, Earls Court, London S.W.

The Argon was a fairly large touring car using a 25hp 6-cylinder Coven[try] Simplex engine, and was priced at £750. In 1905 the company was said to [be] planning a car to be called the Grannaway.　　　[GNG]

ARGONAUT (US) 1959–1963
Argonaut Motor Machine Corp, Cleveland, Ohio

One of the most ambitious attempts to market the 'super car', the first plan[ned] models of the make were to have been called the 'Argonaut State Limousine'. [The] first prototype was built on a Chrysler chassis, and one Argonaut is know[n] have reached private hands. Price listings were quoted from $26,800 to $36,000 and these behemoths were to have been built of stainless and special steels, magnesium, titanium and dural, and to feature a 12-cylinder ohc aluminium air-cooled engine developing 1,020hp. Argonauts were to carry a four-year guarantee. In the concern's elaborate illustrated catalogue both closed and open models were shown, the Smoke and Raceway open styles having a claimed maximum speed of 240mph.   KM

ARGONNE (US) *1918–1920*
Jersey City Machine Co, Jersey City, N.J.
The Argonne was an attractive two-seater, a prototype of which was made in 1918. For 1919 and 1920, a 3.7-litre 4-cylinder Buda engine was used. With this was used a 4-speed transmission with direct drive in third gear, this combination giving a guaranteed 70mph. Only 24 Argonnes were built, the last two modified to accept a Duesenberg 4-cylinder engine.   GMN

ARGUS (D) *1902–1910*
(1) Internationale Automobilzentrale KG Jeannin & Co *1902–1904*
(2) Argus Motoren-Gesellschaft Jeannin & Co KG, Berlin-Reinickendorf *1904–1910*
Early models were fitted with Panhard-Levassor engines, but after about 1904 the firm produced its own engines. Production models were in 2-, 4- and 6-cylinder versions. This make was not very widely sold, but it was of remarkable quality and counted among the best. The firm later made marine and aero engines, and were responsible for the straight-8 Horch engines of 1926–9.   HON

ARGYLL (GB) *1899–1932*
(1) Hozier Engineering Co Ltd, Bridgeton, Glasgow *1899–1905*
(2) Argyll Motors Ltd, Bridgeton, Glasgow *1905–1906; 1914–1932*
(3) Argyll Motors Ltd, Alexandria by Glasgow *1906–1914*
The first Argyll production model was the brainchild of Alex Govan and was based on the contemporary Renault. It was a voiturette or light car with a single-cylinder, 2¾hp, quarter-litre engine of De Dion type, shaft drive, and a tubular frame. A bigger 5hp engine was substituted in 1901, and one of 8hp a year later. There were four forward speeds – an unusual feature in so small a car – but the gear-change was not easy to operate. By now, 2- and 4-cylinder cars were also sold. By 1904 business was booming, and Argyll was already Scotland's leading make. Intensive competition in trials and record-breaking did much to keep the name before the public. Engines were by De Dion and by Argyll themselves (including a 3-cylinder), but most were made under Aster licence.
The business expanded and a huge and pretentious new factory was built at Alexandria, near Glasgow, but in 1907 Govan died and much impetus was lost. However, the name Govan had made for them kept them on an increasingly prosperous course for a while. A 6-cylinder model, and also a new 15hp, the famous 'Flying Fifteen', were added to the range in 1909. By this time, too, the gear-change was easier. One of the 1911 models had Rubury front-wheel brakes. The 1912 cars included one with Burt-McCollum single-sleeve-valves and by mid-1914 all Argyll engines were so furnished. These were excellent and popular cars, helping to make Argyll at one time the fifth biggest motor manufacturer in Britain, but the Alexandria factory was designed for production on a scale the company never attained, and expensive litigation over patents for the sleeve-valve engines further undermined its financial position. It passed into other hands in 1914. One of the pre-war models, the 2.6-litre 15.9hp was revived in 1920 and a new car, the 1½-litre Twelve was introduced for 1922, but neither could restore the earlier glories of the make and few were made.   TRN

ARIANE (F) *1907*
Automobiles Ariane, Suresnes, Seine
This was a small friction-drive two-seater using a single-cylinder 6hp engine. The friction discs were mounted at the rear axle.   GNG

ARIEL (i) (GB) *1898–1915; 1922–1925*
1) Ariel Motor Co Ltd, Birmingham *1898–1906*
2) Ariel Motors Ltd, Birmingham *1906–1915*
3) Ordnance Works Ltd, Coventry, Warwickshire *1922–1925*
The earliest Ariel road vehicles were motor quadricycles and tricycles. By 1902 the first Ariel car was being offered; a 10hp twin with automatic inlet valves. From about 1904 until World War 1, Ariel Motors concentrated on large, solid, conventional, 4-cylinder machines based on a variety of Continental makes, mainly Mercédès. The latter were known as Ariel-Simplex. Some big sixes were also built. In about 1909, a few Ariels were fitted with Alford & Alder front-wheel brakes. A 1.3-litre light car was announced in 1915, but the war killed it.
After the war, the company's efforts were devoted principally to motorcycles, but in 1923 they tried to cash in on the small-car boom with the Ariel Nine. This was a simple three-seater powered by an air-cooled flat-twin engine of a little less than 1-litre capacity. It was noisy and vibrated badly, but an improvement was offered in 1924 in the shape of a 1,100cc 4-cylinder water-cooled engine of 10hp.   TRN

1905 ARGYLL 16/20hp tourer. *Miss B. Wright*

1911 ARGYLL 15hp tourer. *M.A. Harrison Collection*

1906 ARIEL(i) 35hp tourer. *National Motor Museum*

1905 ARIÈS 30hp tourer. Baron Charles Petiet at the wheel. *Autocar*

1934 ARIÈS 9CV saloon. *Automobielmuseum, Driebergen*

1956 ARISTA(ii) Passy 848cc coupé. *Autosport*

1930 ARMSTRONG SIDDELEY 12hp two-seater. *Bristol Siddeley Ltd*

ARIEL (ii) (US) *1905–1907*

The Ariel Co, Boston, Mass.; Bridgeport, Conn.

Ariels were available with either air-cooled or water-cooled engines of 30hp using a single overhead camshaft. Radiators were oval in shape, reminiscent of the Delaunay-Belleville, giving rise to their slogan 'Look for the Oval Front'. In 1907 the make name was changed to Maryland (ii). GMN

ARIÈS (F) *1903–1938*

SA Ariès, Courbevoie, Seine

The first Ariès motor vehicle was the delivery truck of 1903, which was powered by an Aster 2-cylinder engine. The Paris Salon of that year saw the first Ariès car, which was also Aster-powered. It was designed by Baron Charles Petiet. These were unremarkable machines, except for the feature of De Dion-type drive, the rear wheels being driven by shafts above a 'dead' axle. Not all Ariès were so furnished: some models were available with the choice of live axle or chain drive. By 1905, 4-cylinder cars as well as a twin were listed. Engines were still by Aster. 1908 brought a six and a narrow V-4 engine of 60mm × 100mm, so compact that it was mistaken for a single and in 1910 Ariès catalogued the smallest 6-cylinder car in the world. All models had De Dion-type drive. The production of commercial vehicles took precedence over passenger cars towards the end of the decade. One of the 1913 range, following the fashion, used a Knight double sleeve-valve engine.

After making Hispano-Suiza engines during World War 1, Ariès went back to cars, but still in a small way. Among the longest-lived models were the 15CV and its close relative the 12CV, touring cars using a 4-cylinder sv engine with a cubic capacity of around three litres, and a 4-speed gearbox. From 1922 there was a Sport model with overhead camshaft and front wheel brakes. The smallest Ariès, the 5CV Type CC2 was worthy of more attention. It had a single overhead-camshaft engine of 1085cc and (from 1924) four forward speeds. The 1929 CC4S sports model, with two plugs per cylinder, was a fast car. The 15CV was still there, but by the end of 1930 both it and the CC4S had gone, making way for the 1½-litre CB4 and its successor the slightly bigger CC4B, current until 1934. The 4-cylinder, 10CV Super of 1934–38 boasted a 2-speed rear axle. TRN

ARIMOFA (D) *1921–1922*

Ari-Motorfahrzeugbau GmbH, Plauen

A small 4/12PS assembled two-seater of simple design. HON

ARISTA (i) (F) *1912–1915*

Etablissements Ruffier, Paris

The Arista was offered in no less than seven different models in one year, a very complex range for a small firm. The smallest was a 6hp single cylinder of 720cc, while the others were all fours from 8 to 12hp. Friction drive or conventional gearbox were available. GNG

ARISTA (ii) (F) *1956–1963*

Automobiles Arista, Paris 16e

The Arista was a sports coupé with fibreglass body based on Dyna-Panhard components. Models included the Passy two/four-seater with an ordinary 42bhp engine and the Sport two-seater with a Tigre 50bhp engine. GNG

ARMAC (US) *1905*

Armac Motor Co, Chicago, Ill.

The only car model produced under this name was a light roadster. GMN

ARMADALE (GB) *1906–1907*

(1) Armadale Motors Ltd, Northwood, Middlesex *1906*
(2) Northwood Motor & Engineering Works, Northwood, Middlesex *1907*

Known at first as the Toboggan, the Armadale Tri-car was a light 3-wheeler using either a single cylinder Aster or a 2-cylinder Fafnir engine. In 1906 the company also listed a conventional 4-wheeled car with a 16hp 4-cylinder engine. GNG

ARMOR (F) *1925–1928*

The Armor was a diminutive cyclecar using a single-cylinder engine of 98cc or a 2-cylinder of 496cc. GNG

ARMSTRONG see INTERNATIONAL (i)

ARMSTRONG (GB) *1913–1914*

Armstrong Motor Co, Birmingham

The Armstrong cyclecar was offered in two models, both with 8hp 2-cylinder Precision engines. The cheaper model (95 guineas) had an air-cooled engine and used belt drive, while the 100 guinea model was water-cooled and used shaft drive. GNG

ARMSTRONG SIDDELEY (GB) *1919–1960*

Armstrong Siddeley Motors Ltd, Coventry, Warwickshire

This firm came into being through the fusion of Armstrong-Whitworth's car making activities with Siddeley-Deasy of Coventry. Apart from the abortive Stoneleigh light car of 1922, their products were always solidly-built family vehicles emphasizing good workmanship, comfort and ease of driving rather than high performance. Up to 1939 they were readily identifiable by their massive V-radiators (except on certain smaller and cheaper versions), multi-stud disc wheels (though wire was also used in the 1930s) and Sphinx mascots. Their first design was a 5-litre ohv bi-block six of 30hp. This was joined by a smaller but equally massive 2.3-litre '18' in 1922, and by a 2-litre 4-cylinder '14' – also ohv, but with the first of the flat radiators – late in 1923: this was quite cheap at £360. Front-wheel brakes were available on the 6-cylinder cars in 1924, and these also had monobloc engines by 1926. In 1928 a sv 1.9-litre 15hp six was introduced, followed by an even smaller one of 12hp and 1236cc in 1929. Also in 1929 the Wilson preselective gearbox (already tried by Vauxhall) made its debut, first as an optional extra adding £35–£50 to the price, but as standard equipment on all types from 1933 on. The 1930 range consisted of the '12', the '15', a 2.9-litre '20' in owner- and chauffeur-driven versions from £485, and the big '30', now listed with formal coachwork only at £1,450.

1935 SIDDELEY SPECIAL 30hp sedanca de ville. Coachwork by Lancefield. *Autocar*

Armstrong Siddeley production was always on a modest scale, running at about 1,000 a year: one of the best seasons was 1932, at the height of the Depression! An interesting departure for 1933 was the sporting 5-litre Siddeley Special with hiduminium alloy engine. This 90mph machine was catalogued from £950 upward, and some 140 were sold over the next four seasons, while in 1934 there was a handsome sports coupé on the later (1.4-litre) 12hp chassis for 'daughters of gentlemen'. After the '12' was dropped at the end of 1936, all Armstrong Siddeleys were ohv sixes and in 1939 these came in 1.7-litre, 2-litre, 2.4-litre, 2.9-litre and 3.7-litre sizes, generally with formal saloon or limousine bodywork. Despite the 'unsporting' character of the cars, the company's preselector boxes found many applications on competition machines, noted users being E.R.A., H.W.M. and Connaught. The last Burney Streamlines of 1932–33 used the 20hp Armstrong Siddeley engine.

Armstrong Siddeley were among the first makers to announce a programme after World War 2. These cars used the pre-war 16hp 2-litre (enlarged to 2.3 litres in 1949) engine in a new ifs chassis with advanced and attractive styling. For the first time in many years a sliding-type gearbox (with synchromesh) was available as an alternative to the Wilson. The various models were named after famous aircraft produced during the war by the parent Hawker Siddeley Group: Hurricane, Lancaster, Typhoon and, from 1949–50, the Whitley. In 1953 the firm went over to a square 3.4-litre engine with hemispherical head, the result being the Sapphire with a choice of synchromesh or electrically-selected preselector. A twin-carburettor 100mph version followed in 1954, automatic transmission was optional on the 1955 models and power-assisted steering in 1956 when the range was extended by a brace of smaller models. These were the '234' with a 4-cylinder 2.3-litre engine based on the Sapphire, and the '236' using the old long-stroke six of similar capacity. Neither sold (or looked) well and they lasted only a couple of seasons. Last of all came the 4-litre Star Sapphire, made only with automatic gearbox, though like the later 3.4-litre cars, it was offered as a limousine as well as a saloon. In the meantime, Hawker Siddeley had amalgamated with another aircraft group, Bristol (ii). The Bristol cars were taken over by an independent company, but Armstrong Siddeley were less fortunate and the last Sapphire left the works in the summer of 1960.   MCS

1952 ARMSTRONG SIDDELEY Hurricane 2.3-litre drophead coupé. *Bristol Siddeley Ltd*

ARMSTRONG-WHITWORTH (GB) 1906–1915

Sir W.G. Armstrong, Whitworth and Co Ltd, Newcastle-upon-Tyne

This famous North Country engineering firm had previously manufactured the Wilson-Pilcher car, which was still being made in 1904–5. The first Armstrong-Whitworth as such appeared in 1906, with T-headed oversquare 4-cylinder engines, low-tension magneto ignition, 4-speed gearboxes and shaft drive. By 1908 production was concentrated on a solid 7.7-litre 40 costing £798 in chassis form, this being joined a year later by a smaller 18/22 of 3.4-litres' capacity with a 5-bearing crankshaft. Pressure lubrication and a monobloc engine were features of the company's 1910 2.4-litre model and the five types listed in 1912 ranged from a 2.7-litre 15/20 up to a big 5.1-litre six with 4-speed gearbox, dual magneto ignition, a power tyre pump and optional electric lighting – the chassis cost £950. At the outbreak of World War 1 Armstrong-Whitworth were marketing three L-head fours, the biggest of which was a 3.8-litre 30/40 with a 10ft 6in wheelbase, as well as an enlarged 5.7-litre version of their 6-cylinder 30/50. Their solid reputation and workmanship was transferred after the war to the Armstrong Siddeleys produced as a result of the merger with Siddeley-Deasy of Coventry, though no more cars were built at the Newcastle factory.   MCS

1960 ARMSTRONG SIDDELEY Star Sapphire 4-litre saloon. *David Goode*

ARNO (GB) 1908

Arno Motor Co, Coventry, Warwickshire

The Arno was a short-lived car using a 35hp 4-cylinder engine by White & Poppe and shaft drive.   GNG

ARNOLD (GB) 1896–1898

Arnold Motor Carriage Co, East Peckham, Kent

1913 ARMSTRONG-WHITWORTH 30/40hp limousine. *Autocar*

1955 ARNOLT-BRISTOL 2-litre coupé. *Bristol Cars Ltd*

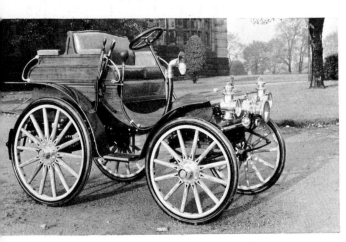

1955 ARNOTT 1,100cc sports car. *N.W. Norman*

1901 ARROL-JOHNSTON 10hp dog cart. *Museum of Transport, Glasgow*

1929 ARROL-ASTER 23/70hp saloon. *Autocar*

William Arnold & Sons were agricultural engineers who imported a 1½hp Benz in 1895, and made about twelve cars of Benz design, but fitted with their own engines. One Arnold was fitted with the Benz's first self-starter; a dynamotor coupled to the flywheel which was supposed to assist the car on hills, as well as to start it.
GNG

ARNOLT (US) 1953–c. 1964
S.H. Arnolt Inc, Chicago, Ill.

The first Arnolts used an M.G. chassis, but the best-known cars were the Arnolt-Bristols which had the 1,971cc Bristol engine and chassis with Bertone body. Competition, touring and GT coupé models were made, and the prices were from $6,000 up. Arnolt-Bristols achieved a number of sporting successes.
BE

ARNOTT (GB) 1951–1957
Arnott's Garages (Harlesden) Ltd, London N.W.10

Miss Daphne Arnott commenced production with a Formula 3 car devised by G. Thornton, using a tubular ladder frame with torsion bar suspension. This model achieved successes both in racing and in breaking Class I records at Montlhéry in 1953. A supercharged Austin A30-engined sports car was offered from 1954, and a 1098cc Coventry-Climax model was introduced in time for the 1955 Le Mans race. This machine employed spring damper units operated by lengthy wishbones from the wheels on the opposite side. Fibreglass bodies were fitted to most of the approximately 25 cars produced.
DF

ARO (R) 1971 to date
Uzina Mecanica Muscel, Brasov

The Aro is a 4-wheel-drive cross-country car based on the Russian GAZ-69. It is powered by a 2½-litre 4-cylinder ohv engine developing 75bhp and was displayed at the 1972 New York Show.
MC

ARROLL-JOHNSTON, ARROL-ASTER (GB) 1897–1931
(1) The Mo-Car Syndicate Ltd, Bluevale, Camlachie, Glasgow 1897–1906
(2) The New Arrol-Johnston Car Co Ltd, Paisley, Renfrewshire 1906–1913
(3) Arrol-Johnston Ltd, Heathhall, Dumfries 1913–1927
(4) Arrol-Johnston & Aster Eng Co Ltd, Heathhall, Dumfries 1927–1931

Arrol-Johnston was one of the famous makes of Scotland. It was born when George Johnston, Sir William Arrol (the civil engineer) and others, produced their first Dogcart, a strong reliable vehicle with an underfloor flat-twin, opposed piston engine and chain drive. Its high-wheeled, solid-tyred, horse-carriage type of body was retained well into the 1900s, a more modern 12hp machine was introduced alongside the Dogcart in 1905, with a front-mounted 3-cylinder engine and unit construction of engine and gearbox, but even the Dogcart outlived this one. The make received a new lease of life, however, with the arrival of J.S. Napier as chief engineer and the formation of a new company under Sir William Beardmore. Napier won the first Tourist Trophy Race in 1905 with an 18hp car of his own design. By 1908 it was making conventional cars only – three 4-cylinder models. T.C. Pullinger became general manager in 1909 and the company's most popular pre-war model, the 2½-litre 15.9hp appeared. It, too, was normal, except for its dashboard radiator and Allen-Liversidge front-wheel brakes. The latter were unsatisfactory, and lasted only until 1912. By that year, there were also a smaller four and a big six in the range. Experiments were made with an electric car, the Arrol-Johnston-Edison.

Arrol-Johnston planned to impress the post-war market with their advanced Victory model, designed by G.W.A. Brown. The single ohc engine, developed 40bhp from 2.6 litres. However, the car was too expensive and insufficiently developed. It broke down when on a Royal tour of the West of England, so that the publicity attending its début was not of the kind it needed. Hurriedly Arrol-Johnston resuscitated the old 15.9hp. It was cheaper, but this was at the cost of such unpopular American cost-cutting expedients as a black-painted radiator and fixed ignition. All the same, it saved the company for the time being, and a more modern version, the 20hp, was introduced alongside the 15.9hp in 1922. It had a monobloc engine with a detachable head. In 1926 overhead valves and front wheel brakes were added.

In 1927 Arrol-Johnston were merged with Aster and complication set in. The 15.9hp was retained. So were the two current Asters. Both the latter were given Burt-McCollum single sleeve-valve engines in the interests of silence, but the 21/60hp Aster was also available in its original ohv form, renamed the Arrol-Aster. Another completely new Arrol-Aster was the 2½-litre 6-cylinder 17/50hp with sleeve valves. The 21/60hp Arrol-Aster and the 15.9hp Arrol-Johnston were dropped for 1929, and a straight-8 Arrol-Aster substituted. It had a 3.3-litre sleeve-valve engine consisting of the 17/50 unit with two extra cylinders and was available in supercharged form. This was a fast car intended as a sports model, but unlike the French sleeve-valve designs it could not produce high outputs as revolutions were limited.
TR

ARROS (F) 1906
F. Couillens et Fils, Plaisance du Gers

This company made a short-lived 6hp two-seater voiturette. GNG

ARROW (i) (US) *1914*

National United Service Co, Detroit, Mich.

This was a 4-cylinder friction drive cyclecar selling at $395. GNG

ARROW (ii) (US) *1914*

M.C. Whitmore Co, Dayton, Ohio

This was a two-seater, belt-driven vehicle with a water-cooled, 4-cylinder, 1½-litre engine. It was priced at $395. GMN

ARROWBILE (US) *1937–1938*

Waterman Arrowplane Corp, Santa Monica, Calif.

One of the few flying cars to be offered for sale, the Arrowbile was a 3-wheeler powered by a Studebaker Commander Six engine driving a pusher propeller. It was to have been sold by selected Studebaker dealers for $3,000, but Waldo Waterman found that costs were much higher than expected, and only five Arrowbiles were built. In 1958 he built another flying car, this time powered by a Franklin flat-6 engine and christened the Aerobile, but only one was made. GNG

ARTÈS (E) *1966 to date*

José Artès de Arcos, Barcelona

This firm began production of Formula 4 racing cars under the name Guepardo in 1966, and the following year announced a rear-engined GT coupé with fibreglass body, in the style of the Ford GT 40. The prototype used an 1,100cc Gordini engine, but production models were powered by the Spanish-built Seat 1500 engine, tuned to give 140bhp. GNG

ARZAC (F) *1927*

The Arzac cyclecar boasted independent suspension and front-wheel drive. It used a 2-cylinder engine of 545cc. GNG

A.S. (i) (F) *1924–1928*

1) Voiturettes Automobiles A.S., Courbevoie, Seine *1924–1926*

2) Voiturettes Automobiles A.S., La Garenne-Colombes, Seine *1926–1928*

Although it was an attractive design of sporting light car, the A.S. was not produced in any numbers. One model used a twin ohc engine of 1,100cc and proprietary Chapuis-Dornier or C.I.M.E. engines were also used. GNG

A.S. (ii) (PL) *1927–1930*

Tow. Budowy Samachodow AS, Warsaw

The Jan Laski Organization and Alexander Liberman designed and built two versions of this car, the S-1 and S-2, in touring, taxi and delivery van styles using 4-cylinder Chapuis-Dornier and C.I.M.E. engines. BE

A.S.A. (I) *1962–1967*

Autocostruzioni S.p.A., Milan

This is one of the small Italian firms financed by well-to-do industrialists (in this case the de Nora family, with electro-chemical interests). The A.S.A. is a Bizzarini design based on an experimental Ferrarina (baby Ferrari) laid down in 1958 and in essence a scaled-down Testa Rossa. It was first shown at Turin in 1961 and was powered by a square (69 × 69mm) 1000cc light alloy single ohc cylinder unit developing 91bhp. Its specification included a 4-speed all-synchromesh gearbox with dual overdrive, servo-assisted 4-wheel disc brakes, and tubular chassis. It had a GT coupé body style. It would do 113mph, but was very expensive, and in 1964 only 52 cars were delivered. Financial difficulties were reported in the latter part of 1966, but for 1967 A.S.A. came out with an additional model, the Rollbar GT Spyder; this had fibreglass bodywork, and was offered on the home market with a tiny 1.3-litre 6-cylinder unit based on the original Mille, and for export with a bigger oversquare four of 1754cc giving 140bhp. MCS

ASAHI (J) *1937–c.1939*

Miyata Works Ltd, Tokyo

The Asahi was a light car powered by a 730cc 2-cylinder engine driving the front wheels. It had a two-seater body and independent suspension all round. GNG

ASARDO (US) *1958*

The Asardo Company, North Bergen, N.J.

This was a sports coupé powered by an Alfa Romeo Giulia engine and using Alfa Romeo transmission in a tubular space-frame with fibreglass body and aluminium underpan. GNG

ASCORT (AUS) *1959–1969*

Continental Coachwork Co, Sydney, N.S.W.

The Ascort was a two-seater GT coupé based on the Volkswagen, though Porsche Chevrolet Corvair engines were also available. GNG

1925 A.S.(i) 1,100cc racing car. *Fotocar*

1937 ASAHI 730cc two-seater. *Autocar*

1930 ASCOT(ii) 18/50hp fabric saloon. *National Motor Museum*

1961 ASHLEY Sportiva 1,172cc coupé. *G.N. Georgano*

1923 ASHTON-EVANS 11/16hp two-seater. *Autocar*

ASCOT (i) (F) *1914–1915*
Société Buchet, Levallois-Perret, Seine

The Ascot was an Anglo-French product, as the chassis was built by Buchet for the Hollingdrake Automobile Co of Stockport, who fitted their own bodies (mainly two-seaters and coupés). The engine was a 10hp side-valve with the gearbox in unit with it. The price was £195.   GNG

ASCOT (ii) (GB) *1928–1930*
Ascot Motor & Manufacturing Co, Letchworth, Herts.

The Ascot was the ambitious brainchild of a man better known for the Ascot-Pullin motor cycle – Cyril Pullin. The 10hp version, based on the Fejes from Hungary, was put together from welded steel pressings, castings being eschewed in the interests of cheapness. At £130 it was intended to compete with the mass-producers. At this figure it would have been Britain's second cheapest light car. No one without great reserves of capital could hope to attack the big producers on their own ground, and the 10hp was never put into production. A limited number of a bigger car, the 2¼-litre sv 6-cylinder known as the Gold Cup model were made from 1929.   TRN

ASDOMOBIL (D) *1913*
Alfred Schwefringhaus, Düsseldorf

A 3-wheeled vehicle of which no further details are known.   HON

ASHBY *see* SHORT-ASHBY

ASHEVILLE (US) *1914–1915*
Asheville Light Car Co, Asheville, N.Car.

This cyclecar used a 7hp Indian air-cooled engine, with drive through a friction transmission and belts to the rear wheels.   GM

ASHLEY (GB) *c.1958–c.1961*
(1) Ashley Laminates Ltd, Loughton, Essex
(2) Ashley Laminates Ltd, Harlow, Essex

Principally producers of fibreglass body shells and equipment. Ashley also marketed a few kit models. The 1958 Regent chassis was advertised as suited for B.M.C. 'A', B.M.C. 'B' and Ford 100E series engines; a complete kit suitable for Ford components was offered in 1961, with a 4-seater GT saloon body. When a recession in the kit-built car trade set in, Ashley concentrated on hardtop conversions and similar work.   D

ASHTON-EVANS (GB) *1919–1928*
Ashton-Evans Motors Ltd, Birmingham

The Ashton-Evans was one of the more unusual products of the post-war boom in popular motoring. The 1½-litre 4-cylinder engine, made by Coventry-Simplex, was normal enough, as were the three forward speeds. However, these were of constant-mesh type, engaged by dog clutches. At first, the rear wheels were only 8in apart – to avoid the expense of a differential. From 1920, the rear track was normal. A tubular chassis was used, carried on transverse springs at front and rear.   TR

A.S.P.A. *see* STELKA

ASQUITH (GB) *1901–1902*
William Asquith Ltd, Halifax, Yorks.

Well-known to the present day as makers of machine tools, William Asquith Ltd built a prototype car in 1901. It had a single cylinder De Dion engine, belt drive (later replaced by shaft) and a four-seater tonneau body.   GNG

A.S.S. (F) *1919–1920*
Automobiles Sans Soupapes, Lyons

This firm planned to produce light cars with 1,240cc 2-cylinder 2-stroke Thomas engines, but very few were made. The founder, P.Schmitt, afterwards joined Becard, another Lyons firm.   GNG

ASTAHL (D) *1907*
Two models were built by this firm, a single-cylinder De Dion-engined 6hp and a 4-cylinder 10hp with Helbe engine.   HON

ASTATIC (F) *1920–1922*
Automobiles Astatic, St Ouen, Seine

The Astatic was a light car using a sv S.C.A.P. engine of 894cc. Its only unusual feature was that it used coil suspension on all four wheels.   GNG

ASTER (i) (F) *1900–1910*
Ateliers de Construction Mécanique l'Aster, Saint-Denis, Seine

It is doubtful if this famous manufacturer of proprietary engines ever marketed a complete car, though they made gearboxes and chassis as well as power units and were undoubtedly equipped to do so. Their engines enjoyed wide currency among Aster's better-known customers were Gladiator and Ariès in France, a

Argyll, Singer, Swift and Dennis in Britain. From time to time, 'Aster' cars appeared at the Shows. The company displayed a 3½hp motor quadricycle with their own engine at the 1900 Paris Salon and a 12hp car was exhibited at the Crystal Palace in 1903; this was, however, credited with a British-made chassis. The 'Asters' marketed by the firm's English offshoot in the 1905–7 period were certainly Aster-engined Ariès. Other vehicles loosely referred to as Asters on the English side of the Channel are likely to have been products of Aster's obscurer customers such as Whitlock of London or West of Coventry. Even these had vanished by 1910, and it is almost certain that the only cars which can legitimately bear the name are the all-British Asters (ii) launched at the 1922 London Show. MCS

ASTER (ii) (GB) *1922–1930*
(1) Aster Engineering Co Ltd, Wembley, Middlesex *1922–1927*
(2) Arrol-Johnston Ltd, and Aster Engineering Co Heathhall, Dumfries *1927–1930*

The first Aster car was a finely constructed, expensive machine of modern design, made in limited numbers. Rated at 18/50hp, the 2618cc engine had push-rod overhead valves and coil ignition. Its main attraction was the bodywork, which was notably handsome and comfortable. In 1924 the bore was enlarged, dual ignition became optional, front-wheel brakes were standardized and the new model was named the 20/55. The Duke of York became the firm's most distinguished customer in 1925, but this did not save it from amalgamation with Arrol-Johnston two years later. Enlarged again the car became a 3-litre 21/60hp model in 1926. The 1927 models, the last true Asters, were the 21/60hp and the new 3½-litre 24/70hp, with single-sleeve valve engine. Designations and engine sizes were unchanged for 1928, but now both cars had Burt-McCollum single sleeve valve engines. The 1930 models were the last. TRN

ASTON (US) *1908–1909*
Aston Motor Car Co, Bridgeport, Conn.

'The Aston built to your order' is the information contained in the only advertisement traced for this car. At least one model in 1908 was rated at 25hp and one in 1909 at 40hp. No other data are available. GMN

ASTON MARTIN (GB) *1922 to date*
(1) Bamford and Martin Ltd, London, W.8 *1922–1925*
(2) Aston Martin Motors Ltd, Feltham, Middlesex *1926–1929*
(3) Aston Martin Ltd, Feltham, Middlesex *1929–1957*
(4) Aston Martin Lagonda Ltd, Newport Pagnell, Bucks. *1958 to date*

The Aston Martin's reputation has always far transcended its small-scale production. The first prototype was evolved by Lionel Martin and Robert Bamford in 1914, the Aston part of the name deriving from the Aston Clinton hill-climb. It used a 1.4-litre side-valve Coventry-Simplex engine in an Isotta-Fraschini voiturette chassis, and was followed by a second prototype in 1919. Production started in 1922 with a larger 1½-litre side-valve engine in a chassis with 4-speed gearbox and semi-elliptic springs all round. A complete car cost £850, and about 60 were made up to 1925. Successes included 2nd place in the 1922 200-Mile Race at Brooklands, and the collection of a number of world records in the same year. Front-wheel brakes were standard from 1923, and several overhead-camshaft engines were evolved for racing, initially of single-cam type, but later in 16-valve (1922) and 8-valve (1924) twin-cam forms, the former developing 54bhp. These were generally less successful than the production side-valves. The company exhibited at Olympia in 1925, but was wound up a few weeks later.

A comeback was staged in 1926, the new machine being an ohc 1½-litre designed by A.C. Bertelli. This was tested in an Enfield-Allday racing chassis and went into production at Feltham in 1927 in 50bhp form, with 4-speed separate gearbox, dash-mounted steering box, and David Brown worm final drive. Bodies were the work of Bertelli's brother Enrico, and early sports models weighed only 2,128lb complete. A 63bhp dry-sump competition engine was made in 1928, and two dozen cars had been delivered by 1929. The dry-sump engine was standardized in 1930 and the model had a long and distinguished competition history: 6th in the 'Double-12' at Brooklands in 1931, the award of the Biennial Cup at Le Mans in 1932, 5th at Le Mans in 1933 and 3rd in 1935, in which year a class win was recorded in the Mille Miglia. In 1938, two years after the 1½-litre had gone out of production, Polledry took 2nd place in the Bol d'Or 24-Hour Race, and a similar car was actually 5th as late as 1951.

Finance was always a problem; there was a brief marketing link with Frazer Nash in 1931 and in 1933 the firm came under the direction of R.G. Sutherland, who retained control until after World War 2. In 1932 the 1½-litre acquired bevel drive and a unit gearbox of Moss make, being sold in 55bhp touring and 70bhp sports versions, while the handsome MkII of 1934–36, though it now weighed 2,576lb, was capable of 85mph and sold for £610. Aston Martin's best sales year was 1933 with 105 cars delivered. The 80bhp Ulster model of 1935 could exceed 100mph. A 2-litre model, still with ohc was prepared for the cancelled 1936 Le Mans race and replaced the 1½-litre the following season, with wet-sump lubrication, synchromesh gearbox and Girling brakes at £575; a dry-sump Speed Model version was still available for £200 more. Prices were slashed to £495 in 1939, in which year the Speed Model was sold with aerodynamic bodywork and the Cross rotary-valve

1923 ASTON MARTIN 1½-litre sports car.
Autocar

1931 ASTON MARTIN 1½-litre saloon.
G.N. Georgano

1937 ASTON-MARTIN 2-litre tourer.
G.N. Georgano

1953 ASTON MARTIN DB3 Le Mans sports car. *G.N. Georgano*

1957 ASTON MARTIN DB2/4 Mark III
2.9-litre saloon. *Aston Martin Lagonda Ltd*

1968 ASTON MARTIN DBS 4-litre saloon.
Aston Martin Lagonda Ltd

1973 ASTON MARTIN V-8 5.3-litre saloon.
Aston Martin Lagonda Ltd

engine was tried, but not adopted. There were also wartime experiments with the Atom saloon with tubular chassis-body structure and Cotal gearbox, but the first post-war Aston Martin, a Claude Hill design, featured a short-stroke push rod 2-litre engine, independent front suspension, a hypoid back axle, hydraulic brakes and, for the first time, coil ignition. One of these cars won at Spa in 1948 but very few were made, even after the acquisition of the company by David Brown group in 1947.

In 1949 the 2.6-litre twin ohc 6-cylinder engine designed by W.O. Bentley for Lagonda (also part of the David Brown empire) was installed in an aerodynamic coupé using a space-frame with square-section tubes. It ran at Le Mans, reaching production status in 1950 as the DB2 available in 107bhp and 123bhp Vantage forms at a price of £1,915. These cars did well at Le Mans in 1950 and 1951 as well as winning their class in the 1951 Mille Miglia: they led to some all-out-and-out sports-racing machines, the DB3 (1952), with Eberhorst-designed structure and 5-speed gearbox, and the 2.9-litre DB3S (1953), which developed 210bhp and reverted to four forward speeds. Three wins in the Goodwood 9-Hour Sports-Car Race, and place at Sebring and 5th in the Mille Miglia in 1953, and two successive 2nd places at Le Mans (1955 and 1956) made the David Brown Astons a powerful force in international racing. The touring DB2 acquired rather occasional rear seats in 1954 and a 140bhp 2.9-litre engine in 1955.

1956 saw the first of two unsuccessful forays into Formula I (the second was in 1959), and the début of the DBR series of sports-racers with space frames and De Dion rear axles, the first Aston Martins to have disc brakes. These were raced in 2.5-, 2.9- and 3.7-litre forms and scored three successive wins in the Nürburgring 1,000-Kilometre race, a win at Spa in 1957, a 1-2-3 victory in the 1958 T.T., and finished 1st and 2nd at Le Mans in 1959. Also in 1959 Aston Martin became the first and only British makers to win the Sports Car Constructors' Championship. The MkIII version of the DB2/4 (1957) had front disc brakes, and could be had with overdrive or automatic gearbox – factory options which are found on all later Aston Martins. Manufacture was transferred to the former Tickford body works (which had made the N.P. car in the 1920s) at Newport Pagnell in 1958. 1959 saw a detuned 240bhp version of the 3.7-litre DBR engine installed in the DB4, an Italian-styled sports saloon with platform frame, trailing-link and coil rear suspension and all-round disc brakes. A 302bhp short-chassis GT version capable of 170mph followed in 1960. A 255bhp Vantage engine was an option on the standard chassis in 1962, and the 4-litre DB5 of 1964 had alternator ignition a diaphragm clutch and the new transmission option of five forward speeds. The 5-speed box was standard in the 282bhp DB6 which sold in 1966 for £5,084. A 325bhp Vantage version was also available. An additional 1967 model had coupé bodywork by Superleggera Touring of Italy – a return to two-seaters after a lapse of several years. In December 1966 it was announced that the company was developing a 5-litre V-8 racing engine to be installed in a Lola chassis. New for 1968 was the DBS coupé with four headlamps and De Dion rear axle, and in 1970 Mk 2 versions of the DB6 had power steering as standard and fuel injection as a regular option. A new DBS was powered by Aston Martin's V-8, a 4ohc 5.4-litre unit developing 375bhp; transmission options were a 5-speed ZF gearbox or Chrysler Torqueflite automatic. In 1972 Ogle produced their Karen-styled version of this car with 22 rear lamps, Sundym glass and headlamp washers. Aston Martin changed hands in April of that year, and the 6-cylinder cars were discontinued.

ASTRA (i) (F) 1922
E. Pasquet, Paris

This was a cyclecar with a 496cc 2-cylinder, 2-stroke engine and friction drive.

GNG

ASTRA (ii) (R) 1922–1924
Prima Fabrica Romana de Vagoarne si Motoare, Arad

Astra cars and commercial vehicles were made in the former Marta factory in Arad, which became a Rumanian town after World War 1. The bulk of production was given over to trucks and buses, but a few large cars with 45/60hp cylinder Bayer engines of 8-litre capacity were made.

GNG

ASTRA (iii) (B) 1930
Automobiles Astra, Liège

The Astra was one of the more blatant examples of pirating car design, as its 1,100cc S.C.A.P.-engined car which appeared at the 1930 Brussels Motor Show was an almost exact copy of the Tracta. Few were made, and the projected 6- and 8-cylinder versions were probably never built.

GNG

ASTRA (iv) (GB) 1956–1959
Astra Car Co Ltd, Hampton Hill, Middlesex

Made by a subsidiary of the British Anzani Company, the Astra was a small utility car which used a 322cc 2-cylinder 2-stroke Anzani engine and four-wheel independent suspension by swing axles. It was a two-seater with space for 250lb of goods. It was originally called the Jarc and there was a later two-seater coupé version known as the Gill Getabout.

GNG

ASTRA (v) *see* NATHAN

ASTRAL (GB) *1923–1924*
Hertford Engineering Co Ltd, Barking, Essex
The Astral was a short-lived make, but the car had several advanced features. The engine was a 1,720cc 4-cylinder unit with single overhead camshaft, and the car was equipped with 4-wheel brakes.   GNG

ATALANTA (i) *see* OWEN (i)

ATALANTA (ii) (GB) *1916–1917*
Atalanta Light Cars Ltd, Greenwich, London S.E.
Although a number of light car firms continued to turn out vehicles during World War 1, few started as late as Atalanta, who launched their 9hp 4-cylinder car in the middle of 1916. They were out of business by February 1917.   GNG

ATALANTA (iii) (GB) *1937–1939*
Atalanta Motors Ltd, Staines, Middlesex
The first Atalanta cars used Gough-designed engines of 1½-litre and 2-litre capacity. They were 4-cylinder single ohc units employing 3 valves per cylinder and developing 78 and 98bhp. This figure could be increased by the use of an Arnott supercharger which was available on both models. A tubular chassis was used, and suspension was independent all round by coil springs. In 1938 the car became available with the 4.3-litre Lincoln-Zephyr V-12 engine which gave increased performance at a lower rpm, with little increase in cost; in fact the most expensive 2-litre model was £37 more than the lwb V-12 saloon which cost only £750. Body styles were a 2-door saloon and drophead coupé, and a sports car with cycle-type wings, or full running boards.   GNG

ATHMAC (GB) *1913*
Athmac Motor Co, Leyton, Essex
The Athmac cyclecar used a 10/12hp 4-cylinder ohc engine with friction transmission and final drive by long belts to the rear axle.   GNG

ATHOLL (GB) *1907–1908*
Angus Murray & Sons, Glasgow
The Atholl was a conventional touring car with a 25hp 4-cylinder engine and shaft drive. Very few were made.   GNG

ATKINSON & PHILIPSON (GB) *1896*
Atkinson & Philipson, Northumberland Coach Factory, Newcastle-on-Tyne
The Northumberland Coach Factory had been in business since 1774, making mail coaches and then railway carriages for George Stephenson. In 1896 they made a crude-looking steam brake with iron-shod wheels which they advertised in the motor papers, but it is unlikely that many were sold.   GNG

A.T.L.A. (F) *1958*
This was a small fibreglass coupé with gull-wing doors like those of the Mercedes-Benz 300SL, which could be fitted with either Renault 4CV, Dauphine, or Dyna-Panhard engines.   GNG

ATLANTIC (D) *1921–1923*
Atlantic AG für Automobilbau, Berlin W.8
A single track car with two auxiliary side wheels and two-seater tandem body. An air-cooled 2-cylinder 1.8/6.5PS engine was used.   HON

ATLAS (i) (US) *1907–1911*
Atlas Motor Car Co, Springfield, Mass.
This was a subsidiary venture of the Knox Motor Truck Co, headed by Harry A. Knox. All models, both 2- and 4-cylinder, were two-strokes. The Atlas was more successful as a taxi than as a private car, although one Atlas was entered in the 1909 Vanderbilt race. The design was replaced by the Atlas-Knight.   GMN

ATLAS (ii) (F) *1951*
Sté Industrielle de Livry, Paris 15
Originally known as La Coccinelle, the Atlas minicar used a single-cylinder engine of only 175cc capacity. The fibreglass body seated two.   GNG

ATLAS-KNIGHT (US) *1911–1913*
Atlas Motor Car Co, Springfield, Mass.
This car was a continuation of Atlas (i) using the Knight engine to replace the obsolete 2-stroke engine of its predecessor. For 1912 the Atlas-Knight was available as either a five- or seven-seater touring car, the latter selling for $3,750. All cars carried a one-year guarantee.   GMN

ATOMETTE (GB) *1922*
Allan Thomas Ltd, Wolverhampton, Staffs.

1923 ASTRAL 12hp sporting four-seater. *Autocar*

1937 ATALANTA 1½-litre supercharged sports car. *National Motor Museum*

1923 ATLANTIC 6.5PS 2-wheel car. *Autocar*

1964 A.T.S. 2½-litre V-8 GT coupé. *National Motor Museum*

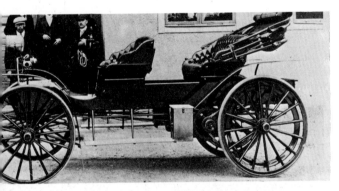

1910 ATVIDABERG 2-cylinder motor buggy. *Oluf Berrum*

1929 AUBURN(i) 6-80 3.1-litre coupé. *G.N. Georgano*

1934 AUBURN(i) 4½-litre straight-8 phaeton. *Kenneth Stauffer*

This was a very light three-wheeler, with a 2½hp Villiers engine driving the single rear wheel. The maximum speed was 30mph which cannot have attracted many buyers, even at the price of 90 guineas. GNG

ATOMO (I) *1947–1948*
S.A.M.C.A., Parma
One of many post-war minicars, the Atomo was a 3-wheeler powered by a 250cc engine. The open body seated two and the single wheel was at the rear. GNG

A.T.S. (I) *1962–1964*
(1) Scuderia Serenissima, Modena *1962*
(2) Automobil Turismo Sport, Bologna *1963–1964*
This expensive Italian venture was backed by the Scuderia Serenissima, an Italian racing stable financed by Count Volpi (who withdrew at the end of 1962) and Jaime Ortiz-Patino. The designer was Carlo Chiti, formerly of Ferrari. The first A.T.S. was a Formula 1 Grand Prix car on the usual rear-engined lines with 6-speed gearbox and Dunlop disc brakes (inboard at the rear). The 90-degree V-8 engine developed 190bhp. Though Phil Hill, Baghetti and Jack Fairman were retained to drive these cars, they achieved very little; their best place in 1963 was 12th in the Italian G.P. and in 1964, sponsored by V.W. Derrington and prepared by Alf Francis, the marque ran only once and retired on that occasion. During 1963 A.T.S. produced a sports coupé powered by a twin ohc V-8 engine mounted amidships, ahead of the gearbox. This could be had in 210bhp GT and 245bhp competition forms, with four Weber carburetters or Lucas fuel injection. A 5-speed all-indirect gearbox was used; two cars ran in the 1964 Targa Florio and both retired. By the end of 1964 A.T.S. was finished though Count Volpi later tried to revive the sports coupé under the name of Serenissima. MCS

ATTERBURY (US) *1911*
Atterbury Motor Car Co, Buffalo, N.Y.
This firm was well known as a truck builder, but in 1911 a few chain-driven passenger cars were made. Truck production lasted until about 1935. MJWW

ATTICA *see* FULDAMOBIL *and* SABRA

ATTILA (D) *1900–1901*
Attila Fahrradwerke AG vorm. Kretzschmar & Co, Dresden-Löbtau
A two-seater 3-wheeled vehicle with a 2½hp Aster engine. HON

ÅTVIDABERG (S) *1910*
Åtvidabergs Vagnfabrik, Åtvidaberg
Designed by Martin Eriksson, the Åtvidaberg was an old-fashioned looking vehicle on the lines of the American motor buggy. The horizontally-opposed 2-cylinder engine could be moved forward and backward to engage reverse gear. The electric lights were made to turn with the front wheels. Only twelve Åtvidabergs were manufactured. OB

AUBURN (i) (US) *1900–1937*
Auburn Automobile Co, Auburn, Ind.
One of the most famous of all American cars, the Auburn first appeared in 1900 when Frank and Morris Eckhart of the Eckhart Carriage Co, in Auburn, Ind., began experimenting with hand-built cars, selling them in and around Auburn. The first production car appeared in 1903 as a single-cylinder chain-driven runabout with the engine under the body and the fuel tank under the bonnet. A touring model was added in 1904 and in 1905, 2-cylinder cars were introduced and continued until 1910, in which year a 4-cylinder type with a Mercedes-shaped radiator and a Rutenber engine was introduced. Both open and closed bodies were available on this larger chassis. In 1911 Auburn bought the Zimmerman Manufacturing Co, which had been producing high wheelers under that name, and continued to manufacture them. Auburn introduced a 6-cylinder car with electric lights as standard equipment in 1912. Right- or left-hand steering was optional in 1914, and from 1914 to 1919, 4- and 6-cylinder cars were available with Teetor, Rutenber and Continental engines. In 1919, the company introduced its Beauty Six model featuring streamlined bodies with bevelled edges on the sides. In 1921 this became the 6-51 sports model with cycle-type mudguards, step-plates instead of running-boards, disc wheels and a small luggage compartment behind the front bumper. Nickel trim was also featured, as well as leather upholstery and an abundance of bright colour schemes. The Auburns of 1923 were powered by a Continental engine for the 6-43 or a Weidely ohv six for the larger model 6-63, or Supreme. In 1924, balloon low-pressure tyres were available on Auburns at extra cost. Up to now production figures had seldom exceeded 4,000 units per year.
In 1924 E.L. Cord bought the Auburn company and from that point on, the Auburn took a leading position in the American automobile business. Cord had the entire range redesigned by J.M. Crawford, and the 1925 line consisted of 4-, 6- and 8-cylinder models. The new cars had two-tone colour schemes and a novel belt moulding which extended at the cowl over the top of the bonnet with its apex at the radiator cap. The cars were handsome and well built, although some of the

larger models had ugly 6-spoked iron wheels more suited to truck design. These were soon discontinued and normal spoke or wire wheels became standard. The basic lines of the 1925 model were so advanced that the design remained practically the same until 1930. The 4-cylinder car was dropped in 1927 and sales climbed steadily. The 1931 Auburn was perhaps the sleekest car in the company's history and sales reached a peak of 28,103 that year. The 1931 Straight-Eight was augmented in 1932 with a new 6.4-litre V12, both cars being equipped with a Columbia dual-ratio rear axle. This V-12 was the first 12-cylinder car to sell under $1,000, and probably the only one, too. These lines were continued in 1933. In 1934 a new design replaced the basic 1931 type and a six was added to the range. In 1935 a new and handsome sports design was announced and a supercharged line of Auburns augmented the 653 six and 851 eight. The pointed-tail 150bhp speedster models were guaranteed to have been test driven at more than 100mph. The cars remained unchanged for 1936 and although a new range of Auburns had been planned for 1937, no cars were produced. KM

AUBURN (ii) (US) *1967 to date*
Auburn-Cord-Duesenberg Co, Tulsa, Okla.
   After building a small number of Cord replicas, Glenn Pray turned to the 1936 Auburn Speedster. His replica of this, known as the Auburn 866, uses a 7-litre Ford V-8 engine giving a top speed of 135mph. GNG

AUBURN-MOORE *see* MOORE (ii)

AUDAX (F) *1914*
Lenefait et Cie, Rouen
   The Audax was a 4-cylinder light car of conventional design. The makers were still listed in 1920, but were probably not producing cars after World War 1. GNG

AUDI (D) *1910–1939; 1965 to date*
(1) Audi Automobilwerke GmbH, Zwickau/Sachsen 1910–1939
(2) Auto Union GmbH, Ingolstadt 1965–1969
(3) Audi N.S.U. Auto Union AG, Ingolstadt 1969 to date
   After leaving the firm A. Horch (*see* Horch), which he had founded, August Horch started a new company in 1909 which he at first named August Horch Automobilwerke GmbH, also in Zwickau. He was not allowed to use his own name for the new company, however, so he chose the name 'Audi' which is the latinized form of Horch. The first Audi was the B 10/28PS with a 2,612cc engine which appeared in 1910, and was an immediate success. In the Austrian Alpine Trials in 1911 Horch himself drove one of these cars without incurring any penalty points. He was also successful with the same type in the same event in 1912. In 1912 the Type C 14/35PS appeared. In a short-wheelbase version, it became a very well-known competition car and was called the Alpensieger because of its successes in the Austrian Alpine Trials of 1913 and 1914. Other pre-World War 1 models were the D 18/45PS and the E 22/50PS. After the war the G 8/28PS appeared as a new model and types C, D and E were carried on. The 1922 ohv type K succeeded the C, the 3.5-litre engine developing 50bhp. With the type M 18/70PS ohc 6-cylinder of 1924 Audi started a range of 6- and 8-cylinder cars. The 1928 type R or Imperator 8-cylinder model with a 4,872cc 100bhp engine was the last true Audi; all the following models were to some extent assembled cars.
   J.S. Rasmussen (*see* D.K.W.) became the main shareholder of Audi in 1928. He had acquired Rickenbacker machinery lines from the U.S.A. and engines of Rickenbacker type were fitted to the Zwickau (8-cylinder 4,371cc and 5,130cc) and Dresden (6-cylinder 3,838cc) models. In 1931 a small Audi with 4-cylinder 1.1-litre Peugeot engine and D.K.W. chassis appeared. In 1932 Audi became a member of the Auto Union together with Wanderer, Horch and D.K.W. Two front-driven models (UW and 225) followed with 6-cylinder Wanderer engines. The last pre-war Audi was the Type 920, rear-driven again and with 6-cylinder 3281cc engine.
   The Audi factory and the other Auto Union production plants were nationalized in 1945. The Auto Union was re-established in Düsseldorf in 1949. In 1956 Mercedes-Benz became the main shareholder, but in 1964 the Volkswagen works obtained a majority. The Audi name was revived in 1965 on a new medium-sized saloon. An inclined 1.7-litre 4-cylinder ohc engine drove the front wheels, and features of the design were disc front brakes, ifs, and a beam rear axle. By the end of 1966 it was the staple Auto Union product, but two years later the range was quite extensive, including station wagons, a smaller 1½-litre 60, and a 1.8-litre Super 90. The 1969 merger with N.S.U. led to more models. In 1970 a 2+2 fastback coupé, the 115 bhp 100S, was added, and automatic transmission became a factory option. New for 1973 was a smaller type, the 80. This differed from earlier Audis in its all-coil suspension, belt instead of chain drive for the camshaft, and a patent steering stabilizator. It was available with 1,300cc or 1,500cc engines, the more powerful variant offering 98bhp and 105 mph. HON

AUDIBERT-LAVIROTTE (F) *1894–1901*
Sté Anon des Anciens Etablissements Audibert et Lavirotte, Lyons
   Maurice Audibert and Emile Lavirotte were among the first car makers in Lyons, their early designs being based, like many contemporary cars, on the Benz. They

1912 AUDI Type C 14/35PS Alpine Trial sporting tourer. *Deutsches Museum, Munich*

1928 AUDI 4.8-litre cabriolet. Coachwork by Neuss. *Autocar*

1937 AUDI Type 225 Front 2.2-litre drophead coupé. *Neubauer Collection*

1973 AUDI 80 1½-litre saloon. *Audi N.S.U.*

made their own 2- and 4-cylinder engines and carburettors, and from 1900 onwards, engines were mounted in front, with a 4-speed sliding gearbox and final drive by chains. About fifty cars were made in all; one survives in the Henri Malartre collection at Rochetailleé-sur-Saône.   GNG

AUDINEAU (F) 1897

The Parisian coachbuilder Paul Audineau built a voiturette with rear-mounted Pygmée engine.   GNG

AUGÉ (F) 1898–c.1901
Daniel Augé et Cie, Levallois-Perret, Seine

Augé cars were powered by the Cyclope engine, so called because the original models used hot-tube ignition, the platinum tubes being heated with one lamp. From 1899 electric ignition was used for the 4hp horizontal 2-cylinder engine. Transmission was by belts to a countershaft and final drive was by chain. Later models used engines of 5, 7 or 8hp, both horizontal and vertical. Body styles included a three-seater known as the troika. Sometimes the cars were listed under the name Cyclope.   GNG

1901 AUGÉ Cyclope 4½hp *dos-à-dos*. *Autocar*

AULTMAN (US) 1901–1902
The Aultman Co, Canton, Ohio

The Aultman was a typical light steam buggy of the period with two-seater body and tiller steering. The firm also experimented with a 4-wheel-drive steam truck.   GNG

AUREA (I) 1920–1933
(1) Società Italiana Ferrotaie, Turin *1920–1922*
(2) Fabbrica Anonima Torinese Automobili, Turin *1922–1933*

The Aurea was a conventional 1½-litre family tourer with side valves, magneto ignition, 3-speed gearbox, and wood artillery wheels. Output was 22bhp, though 30–35bhp were extracted from sports engines. Four-wheel brakes and 4 speeds arrived in 1925, as well as an improved 4000 series with 1,497cc ohv engine. This and its companion sv version, the 600, were the staple Aureas after 1928. Giovanni Ceirano acquired the company in 1932, car production ceasing shortly afterward in favour of subcontract work for Alfa Romeo, among others.   MCS

AURORA (i) (US) 1906–1908
Aurora Motor Co, Aurora, Ill.

This make was represented by 30hp touring cars and runabouts at a price under $1,000. The manufacturer is given variously as Aurora Motor Works, and Aurora Automobile Co. Production may have been resumed in 1909.   GMN

AURORA (ii) (US) 1958
Father Alfred Juliano, Branford, Conn.

A 'safety car' designed by a Catholic priest, the Aurora had one of the most unusual 4-door sedan bodies ever seen. Sculptured wings flowing from back to front gave the impression that the car was being driven in reverse. The driver sat behind a bulbous windscreen, and the general layout was distinctive if little else. A choice of Cadillac, Lincoln or Chrysler engines was offered, and the car could be bought for $15,000.   BE

1923 AUREA 10/15hp two/four-seater. *Autocar*

AURORA 8 *see* FUSI FERRO

AURORE *see* DECKERT

AUSFOD (GB) 1947–1948
Ausfod Motor Engineering Co Ltd, Chorlton-on-Medlock, Manchester 1

The Ausfod was one of the few trials specials which was actually offered for sale to the public. It used a Ford Ten engine in an Austin Seven chassis, with LMB trials front axle, and remote control gearbox. An aerodynamic sports car was advertised as well as the trials car, but it is not known if any of these were made.   GNG

AUSONIA (I) 1903–1906
Camone, Giussani Turrinelli e Cia, Milan

This firm marketed electric cars credited with a range of 90 miles at 15mph. Vehicle production ceased after a reorganization in 1906.   MCS

AUSPER (GB) 1960–c.1962
The Ausper started as a conventional Formula Junior car, with a rear-mounted engine set in a tubular space frame. The original model was based on the Tomahawk, a design by the Australian Tom Hawkes that was intended for export to his homeland. The 1962 version used a horizontal engine layout, and B.M.C. Mini suspension units.   DF

AUSTIN (i) (US) 1901–1921
Austin Automobile Co, Grand Rapids, Mich.

The Austin was known as The Highway King. Despite an output of 50 or less units per year, it was something of a pioneer in a number of ways. The 1902 2-cylinder models were much larger than most contemporary makes and for several

1958 AURORA(ii) safety sedan. *Image International*

years, although colours were optional, most of these big cars were painted either white with tan trim or light brown. By 1911, the cars were equipped with electric lights and left-hand steering. Two years later, Austins featured a highly successful two-speed axle, with wheel-base up to 11ft 10in. After 1915, the company attempted to market smaller and cheaper cars and also introduced a 12-cylinder model in 1917 which was produced until the firm ceased operations. About 1000 cars were made altogether.   KM

AUSTIN (ii) (GB) *1906 to date*

(1) Austin Motor Co Ltd, Longbridge, Birmingham *1906–1970*
(2) Austin-Morris Division, British Leyland Motor Corporation Ltd, Longbridge, Birmingham *1970 to date*

Herbert Austin resigned from the general managership of Wolseley in 1905, and formed his own company. He did not, however, pursue the development of the horizontal engine, but switched to more conventional designs using sv in-line units with T-heads, separately-cast cylinders and chain drive, first supplemented and then supplanted by shaft-driven cars. Most Austins of the pre-1914 period were fours, though sixes were marketed from 1908 to 1913, the 60hp being a really big machine of 9.7 litres' capacity. There was also an 1,100cc single in the 1909–11 period, but this was really a Swift distinguishable only from the Coventry company's version by its radiator. In 1909 Austin marketed a 15hp 4-cylinder town carriage with cab-over-engine layout at £475; at this time they were also making Gladiators for the British market. In 1910 a 1.6-litre 4-cylinder Ten was made for export only, being introduced to the home market the following year. In 1914, when Austin became a public company, three 4-cylinder models were listed, the largest, a 30 of nearly 6-litres' capacity, having electric lighting and starting.

After World War 1, Austin tried a one-model policy with a 3.6-litre monobloc sv 4-cylinder Twenty; the price had to be raised from £495 to £695 during the first year of production, which landed Austin in the hands of the official receiver, though the car proved a great success and was made until 1929. Despite financial troubles, however, the company came up in 1921 with their second great vintage design, the 1661cc Twelve, one of the hardest-wearing machines of all time. Enlarged to 1.9-litres in 1927, it remained in the catalogue, always with magneto ignition, right up to 1936, and survived in production as a taxicab into the 1940s. Finally, 1922 saw the Seven, one of the greatest of all baby cars; it gave 13bhp from 747cc, killed the cyclecar and boasted 4-wheel brakes, though these were not coupled until late 1930. The pedal worked the front ones and the lever the rear. By 1929, a supercharged sports version had 32bhp, still with a 2-bearing crankshaft: the 3-bearing crankshaft came out with the 1937 models. The Seven was extensively raced by the works; among its countless successes were a third place in the 1929 TT. and a win in the 1930 B.R.D.C. 500-Mile Race at Brooklands. Its descendants were legion; it was made in Germany by Dixi and their successors B.M.W.; in France by Rosengart; in Japan by Datsun and in the U.S.A. by the American Austin Co. Even after production ceased at Longbridge at the end of 1938, manufacture of the engine was taken over by Reliant and continued up to 1962.

6-cylinder cars reappeared in the range in 1927 with a 3.4-litre Twenty usually found with limousine bodywork, followed by a 2½-litre coil-ignition Sixteen in 1928. A less successful 1½-litre Six was introduced in 1931, but Austin found another winner in the 1.1-litre Ten of 1932, which was made until 1947. In 1934 the company offered a choice of over 50 models – the Seven, the Ten, a 1½-litre Light 12/4, the old Twelve and five Sixes from 1,496cc to 3,400cc – not to mention semi-sports versions of some of the smaller cars. Synchromesh was now standard, with the option of the American Hayes automatic gearbox on 16 and 18hp models only. In 1936 the company sponsored a team of three short-stroke twin ohc 750cc supercharged racing cars designed by Murray Jamieson, which had nothing in common with the ordinary Seven except for the transverse-leaf front suspension. Their engines developed 116bhp at 9,000rpm and they were raced until the outbreak of World War 2.

Austin styling received a face-lift in 1937, and again in 1939 when alligator bonnets came in with the 900cc 8hp which replaced the Seven, but the image remained the same – stolid and well-furnished cars of great durability appealing to the more conservative type of owner. Girling mechanical brakes were used. The first sign of a more progressive attitude came in 1945, when a 2.2-litre ohv 4-cylinder Sixteen came out using the chassis and body of the 1940 Twelve; this proved quite as durable as the famous Austins of the 1920s, and the engine was still being used in taxis and the 4 × 4 Gipsy in 1967. Coil and wishbone independent front suspension appeared in 1947 on the luxurious and traditionally-styled ohv 4-litre 6-cylinder Sheerline and Princess, and these were followed by the 1.2-litre A40 Dorset and Devon saloons with overhead valves and independently sprung at the front, which did well in America and helped Austin to sell over 85,000 cars in 1948. A further bid for dollar exports came with the big 4-cylinder A90 power-top convertible – successful long-distance record work at Indianapolis failed to attract many buyers, though the engine had a long run in the first Austin-Healeys.

Austin merged with Morris to form the British Motor Corporation in 1952, when there appeared their first unitary-construction car, the 803cc A30. The Healey sports car (q.v.) came under Austin's aegis that year, and in 1954 they started to make the little Metropolitan coupés and convertibles for Nash. In style these were

1914 AUSTIN(i) '66' 48hp tourer. *The Veteran Car Club of Great Britain*

1906 AUSTIN(ii) 25/30hp Longbridge limousine. *John Hardwick*

1922 AUSTIN(ii) Twelve/Four tourer. *R.J. Wyatt*

1929 AUSTIN(ii) Seven fabric saloon. *Motor*

1937 AUSTIN(ii) Cambridge Ten saloon.
British Motor Corporation

1966 AUSTIN(ii) Mini 848cc saloon. *British Motor Corporation*

1973 AUSTIN(ii) Maxi 1,750cc saloon.
British Leyland Motor Corporation

1959 AUSTIN-HEALEY Sprite 948cc sports car.
British Motor Corporation

Nash Airflytes in miniature, with 3-speed gearboxes. They were powered initially by the A40 engine and later by the 1½-litre A50. Production continued until 1961. From 1955 onwards all Austins save the 4-litre models had unitary construction, new models that year being the Cambridge with A40 or A50 engines, and the 2.6-litre 6-cylinder Westminster. The big Princess saloon went over to automatic transmission in 1957, and these Vanden Plas-bodied models subsequently (in 1960) became a make in their own right, under the name of Vanden Plas Princess. In 1959 the 948cc A40 appeared with Farina styling; this was later made in Italy under licence by Innocenti and paved the way to a rationalized range of 1½-litre saloons in the Farina idiom, made in Morris, M.G., Wolseley, and Riley forms as well as the basic Austin Cambridge.

1960 saw a new Austin Seven, the first of Alec Issigonis's Minis, which Morris sold as the Mini-Minor. It had an 848cc ohv 4-cylinder engine mounted transversely and driving the front wheels, the 4-speed gearbox lived in the sump, all wheels were independently sprung by rubber in torsion, and it had an unmistakable box-like silhouette. The name Mini was soon applied to all versions, Austin as well as Morris, and the car not only became a best-seller, but distinguished itself in competition as well, with numerous rally wins to its credit. Mini-Cooper versions joined the range in 1962, the hottest standard version in 1968 being the 1,275cc Cooper S with 76bhp and front disc brakes; later developments include a 4 × 4 Mini-Moke for off-the-road travel. Logical developments were the 4-door 1100 saloon with interlinked Hydrolastic suspension (introduced as a Morris in 1963, with an Austin version listed in 1964), and the bigger 1800 of 1965. Minis acquired Hydrolastic suspension in 1965, and all the smaller fwd cars were available with an automatic gearbox in 1967. Both the Mini and the 1100 are made for the Italian market by Innocenti.

Improvements in 1968 included all-synchromesh gearboxes for Minis and an alternative 1,275cc engine for the 1100. A special 'federalized' version of this 1300, the 2-door Austin America with automatic transmission, went on sale in the U.S.A. At the same time the 6-cylinder A110 gave way to a new 3-litre, combining the 1800's hull design and Hydrolastic suspension with the existing engine and conventional rear-wheel drive. This one, however, coincided with the merger of B.M.C. and Leyland interests in January 1968; it was slow into production, never caught on, and was discontinued in 1971. Later in the year came Mk II versions of the 1800 with 86bhp engines and optional power steering, made as Morrises and Wolseleys as well as Austins. An A60 replacement came in 1969: the 1½-litre Maxi in the Issigonis tradition with fwd and transverse engine. New were the 5-bearing engine with chain-driven ohc, the 5-speed all-synchromesh gearbox, and the 5-door semi-estate car body; by 1971 it had acquired a more satisfactory rod-operated gearchange and the option of a 1,748cc power unit.

In 1970 rationalization led to the replacement of the M.G. 1300 by the Austin 1300GT, and that August the former Austin and Nuffield elements in the British Leyland empire (Austin, M.G., Morris, Vanden Plas and Wolseley) were merged to form the Austin–Morris Division. Already at the 1969 Earls Court Show the Mini had been made a marque in its own right, and by early 1971 basic versions of the 1100/1300 theme were sold as Austins only, Morris variants being dropped. The 3-litre six's replacement appeared in 1972. This ADO 17 was based on the X6 already announced by British Leyland's Australian branch, and was in essence an enlarged Maxi on which the transversely-mounted ohc 2,227cc engine drove the front wheels. Basic price was £1,246. With the 1100/1300, the Maxi and the 1800 making up the 1973 range, Austin now offered only fwd cars, a far cry from the conservatism of pre-World War 2 days. Automatic and high-performance variants were also added in 1973.   MCS

AUSTIN (iii) (AUS) *1959 to date*
(1) British Motor Corporation (Australia), Zetland, N.S.W. *1959–1968*
(2) British Leyland Motor Corporation (Australia), Zetland, N.S.W. *1968 to date*

Austin cars of British design were assembled in Australia from 1948, but in 1959 specifically Australian variants were introduced in the form of the Austin A95 (and Morris Marshall) 6-cylinder saloons, and the Austin Lancer (and Morris Major) 4-cylinder saloons that were based on the Wolseley 1500. These were replaced in 1962 by the 2.4 litre Austin Freeway Six and Wolseley 24/80 that were almost completely built in Australia. Austin Mini 850, 1100 and 1500 cars were also built, and eventually the Freeway Six was dropped in favour of the Austin 1800. This did not compete successfully against Holden and Ford opposition, and was extensively modified during 1970 to result in the Tasman and Kimberly models with 2.25-litre 6-cylinder transverse ohc engines developing 102 and 115bhp respectively.   EL

AUSTIN-HEALEY (GB) *1953–1971*
(1) Austin Motor Co Ltd, Longbridge, Birmingham *1953–1970*
(2) Austin-Morris Division, British Leyland Motor Corporation Ltd, Abingdon, Berks. *1970–1971*

This make was the outcome of a simple and efficient sports two-seater evolved by Healey using the 2.7-litre ohv 4-cylinder Austin A90 engine, coil-and-wishbone ifs and optional overdrive; the British Motor Corporation took over its series production, and made it in large numbers until 1956, thus providing themselves with

114

big, tough sporting machine to compete with Triumph's TR series. The first of a
ries of 'streamliners' built for long-distance record work (later ones were based
 the smaller Sprite) was timed at over 180mph in 1954. A 132bhp version of the
iginal '100' with disc brakes was marketed in 1955, and for 1957 there was a new
00-6' with Austin's 2.6-litre 6-cylinder engine, the output of which had been
osted to 117bhp by the end of the season. New for 1958 was the Sprite, a small
orts car with a 948cc B.M.C. ohv engine, which weighed 11¾cwt (1,316lb) and did
er 80mph on 43bhp; the quarter-elliptic rear suspension was an unusual feature,
d subsequently an M.G. (q.v.) variant was offered under the name of 'Midget'.
 1960 the 6-cylinder cars had more power, front disc brakes and 2.9-litre engines,
d in this form they did extremely well in rallies, among their victories being the
61 and 1962 Alpines, the G.T. class of the 1964 Tulip, and the Austrian Alpine
d the Spa-Sofia-Liège in the same year.

Latterly Austin-Healeys were assembled in the M.G. factory at Abingdon. The
00 was discontinued in 1968, a victim of tougher American regulations, but the
rite outlived it by another three years; the final version, Mk IV, had a 1,275cc
bhp engine. After Donald Healey's departure to Jensen, the make's discon-
uation was only a matter of time, though the parallel M.G. Midget remained
 the B.L.M.C. range.   MCS

USTRALIAN SIX (AUS) *1919–1924*
) F.H. Gordon & Co, Rushcutters Bay, N.S.W. *1919*
) Australian Motors Ltd, Ashfield, N.S.W. *1920–1924*
) Harkness & Hillier, Sydney, N.S.W. *1924*

The Australian Six was intended to be a mass-produced assembled car, powered
 a 6-cylinder Rutenber engine. The first twelve cars had rounded radiators, but
 subsequent models wore a Rolls-Royce type radiator. Body styles included
urer, two-seater, cloverleaf and sedan, although only one of the last-mentioned
as made. Poor quality of the original Rutenber engines damaged the firm's
ances irreparably, and in December 1923 they were in the hands of creditors.
roduction was taken over by the hire-car company Harkness & Hillier, who made
out seven cars with Ansted engines.   GNG

USTRALIS (AUS) *1901–1906*
ustralis Motors, Leichardt, N.S.W.

This firm built a De Dion-powered quadricycle in 1897 and a tricycle powered by
 engine of their own make in 1898. Only two cars are known to have been built by
em, a single-cylinder 3hp two-seater in 1901 and a 7hp 2-cylinder tonneau in 1906.
                                                                        GNG

USTRO (A) *1913–1914*
The Austro was one of the few cyclecars made in Central Europe. It was powered
 a 6hp N.S.U. engine, had a 4-speed gearbox and double chain final drive. Front
spension was independent, by sliding pillars on the lines of the Morgan. Austro
clecars did well in mountain trials and in the Semmering Hill Climbs.   GNG

USTRO-DAIMLER (A) *1899–1936*
) Österreichische Daimler Motoren AG, Wiener-Neustadt *1899–1934*
) Steyr-Daimler-Puch AG, Wiener-Neustadt *1934–1936*

Austria's most famous motor car was born when Daimler of Cannstatt established
 factory in Vienna for the manufacture of about 100 of its cars annually. The
ustrian Daimler was a copy of its German parent. In 1906 the Austrian concern
ecame a separate financial entity, and a year earlier, Ferdinand Porsche had replaced
aul Daimler at Wiener-Neustadt as director. A new era began, for Porsche was a
esigner with original ideas. He did not exercise them at once; the two 1909 models
ere large well-made fours with side valves in a T-head and a choice of chain or
ve-axle drive. World-wide fame came to the company with their 1910 models,
specially the 22/80PS model originally designed to win the Prince Henry Tour
f that year. It accomplished this very convincingly. The five large valves per
ylinder – one inlet, four exhaust – were actuated by a single overhead camshaft.
 combination of well-shaped combustion chambers and light reciprocating parts
ade for an engine of an efficiency never before seen in a catalogued, non-racing car.
ts 5.7-litres produced 95bhp. Even Porsche, however, felt that so much power could
ot be safely transmitted by a live axle, and chain drive was used initially. The
2/80's small brother, the 16/18PS, had a side-valve L-head engine. After it had
wept the board in the Austrian Alpine Tour of 1911, the 16/25PS Alpine variant
as also listed. In 1914 the range consisted of these three cars, the sv 20/30PS,
nd the luxurious 35/60PS also with side valves. Both Austro-Daimler and Daimler
old the Lohner-Porsche, the name given to the electric and petrol-electric cars
esigned by Porsche before he went to Wiener-Neustadt. The Vienna firm was
ustria's largest manufacturer of motor cars.

Immediately after World War 1 a few cars were assembled in Liège from pre-war
ustro-Daimler parts by M. Klinkenhammers, and sold under the name Alfa-Legia.
n their home ground the company returned to high-grade fast tourers. As well as
e old '16/18' and '20/30', they made the new AD617, a 6-cylinder car of 4.4-litres
ith a single overhead camshaft, that was succeeded in 1923 by its development,
e ADV17/60PS, which was the same but for its front wheel brakes. Four years
arlier, Porsche had maintained his reputation for really exciting design by

1918 AUSTRALIAN SIX tourer.
Gilltrap's Auto Museum

1903 AUSTRO-DAIMLER Type PD tourer.
Steyr-Daimler-Puch AG

1912 AUSTRO-DAIMLER Prince Henry tourer.
Steyr-Daimler-Puch AG

1920 AUSTRO-DAIMLER ADV 4.4-litre town car.
National Motor Museum

1932 AUSTRO-DAIMLER ADR8 4.6-litre
drophead coupé. *Steyr-Daimler-Puch AG*

c.1922 AUSTRO-FIAT Type C1 9/24PS tourer.
The Veteran Car Club of Great Britain

1952 AUTOAR 2.2-litre saloon. *Autocar*

producing the Sascha-type Austro-Daimler, a 1,100cc – later 1½-litre – racing voiturette. Its four cylinders, like the six of the AD617, were of aluminium, with detachable steel liners. There were two overhead camshafts, however, and dry sump lubrication. The power output was 50bhp. Four-wheel brakes were, of course, fitted.

Although Porsche left Vienna in 1923 to return to Daimler, he was mainly responsible for the new ADM type, which was offered alongside the ADV17/60 from that year. The ADM1 was basically similar, but had a smaller engine of 2½-litres, and its rounded radiator was a departure from the hitherto traditional Austro-Daimler V-shape. It was sold in sports form in 1925 as the ADMII. After 1926, the old ADV17/60 was dropped and the ADM engine was enlarged to three litres by increasing the bore. This ADMIII in sports form developed 100bhp at 400rpm, and could do more than 100mph. Porsche's successor, Karl Rabe, designed the even more advanced ADR type. Its tubular backbone chassis and swing-axle independent rear suspension so resembled that of the Tatra that legal action was taken against Austro-Daimler. The ADR was available in sports or normal form. At first, the ADR used the old ADMIII engine, but the ADR6 Bergmeister of 1929, one of the most glamorous Austro-Daimlers built, had a new 3.6-litre power unit providing 120bhp. This car was made until production ceased shortly after the Steyr-Daimler-Puch amalgamation in 1934. The ADR8, the firm's first and last 8-cylinder car, designed for more formal bodies, had disappeared in 1933 after a life of three years.   TRN

AUSTRO-FIAT (A) 1921–1936
Österreichische Fiat Werke AG, Vienna

This firm was founded in 1907, but actual production of FIAT cars for the Austrian market did not start until 1912 and it was not until 1921 that vehicles of Austrian origin were offered, these being known as 'A.F.' for short. The standard private-car model, Type C.1, had a straightforward sv 2.5-litre 4-cylinder engine with 4-speed separate gearbox, magneto ignition and front-wheel brakes, but this gave way in 1928 to a 1.3-litre light car with Steyr-type swing axle independent rear suspension. In 1925 a separate company took over sales of Italian FIAT cars and Austro-FIAT became associated with Austro-Daimler and Puch. The last private cars, Type 1001A, differed from the earlier Type 1001 in having 34bhp engine and conventional rear axles. After 1936, Austro-FIAT concentrated on commercial vehicles, these being sold since 1947 under the name 'O.A.F.'.   MCS

AUSTRO-RUMPLER (A) 1920–1922
Austro-Rumpler-Werke, Vienna

This firm produced a single-seater cyclecar with a 3/10PS engine. There was no connection with the German Rumpler company.   HON

AUTOAR (RA) 1950–1962
Automotores Argentinos, Tigre, Buenos Aires

The Autoar project was sponsored by the Cisitalia engineer Piero Dusio who spent some years in Argentina. Production began in 1950 of a Jeep-engined utility vehicle, and by the end of 1951 a new saloon appeared using the same 2,199cc Jeep engine and transmission, with quite a handsome 2-door saloon body. It was fitted with an overdrive to counteract the low axle ratio of the Jeep. In 1952 a new ohv 3-litre six was announced, but apparently never went into production. At this time Dusio returned to Italy. During the 1950s production was sporadic and included a station wagon with Jeep-type 1,901cc engine and licenced manufacture of the German NSU Prinz.   B

AUTOBIANCHI see BIANCHI

AUTOBLEU (F) 1955–1958
Automobiles Autobleu, Paris 17e

This was a small car with de luxe Chapron bodywork on the Renault 4CV chassis. The stress was on luxurious coachwork rather than on performance, and the 4CV engine was not modified in any way. Convertible and closed coupé models were offered. A larger model used the Frégate chassis.   GN

AUTO-BUG (US) 1909–1910
Auto-Bug Co, Norwalk, Ohio

The Auto-Bug had large-diameter wheels and solid rubber tyres. It was built in two- and four-seater models. The drive was by double chains from a 22hp 2-cylinder engine and steering was by wheel.   GM

AUTOBUGGY see A.B.C. (i)

AUTOCAR (US) 1897–1911
(1) Pittsburg Motor Vehicle Co, Pittsburg, Pa, 1897–1899
(2) The Autocar Co, Ardmore, Pa. 1900–1911

The first products of this company were largely experimental and included single-cylinder tricycle and light 4-wheeler buggy (1898). Twenty-seven cars were made in 1900, by which date the company had moved to their new Ardmore factory, and in 1901 there appeared a 3½hp 2-cylinder car with shaft drive, the first multi-cylinder shaft-driven car in America. By 1905 large 2- and 4-cylinder cars were being made with gear change, clutch, spark and throttle all controlled from the steering column. Trucks were introduced in 1907, and after 1911 became the only products of the firm. Autocar still makes trucks. GMN

AUTOCRAT (GB) 1913–1926
Autocrat Light Car Co, Birmingham

The Autocrat light car was initially offered either in 9hp, twin-cylinder, 1,099cc form, or as a 1½-litre four, otherwise identical. Both cars had three speeds. The post-war Autocrat was a completely conventional assembled machine using only a 4-cylinder, sv Dorman engine of 12hp and 1½-litres. The coupé model of 1919 was available with a detachable hard top; its only striking feature. Five years later, a new model was added, the 10/12hp that had a push-rod ohv engine by Meadows. TRN

AUTOCYCLE (US) 1907
Vandergrift Automobile Co, Philadelphia, Pa.

This curious vehicle had four wire wheels arranged in a diamond pattern. It was steered by wheel, which turned the front wheel as well as the middle pair. The rear wheel was chain-driven from a 6hp air-cooled engine. GMN

AUTODYNAMICS (US) 1964 to date
Autodynamics, Inc, Marblehead, Mass.

Headed by Ray Caldwell, Autodynamics is America's largest builder of racing cars, and up to the middle of 1970 had produced over 1,000 competition cars. Most of these have been Formula Vee racing cars, but Caldwell has also built a Can-Am car, the D-7, and a number of Hustler VW-engined fibreglass sports cars. These are available in kit form or as complete cars. Autodynamics are also experimenting with an electric car and van to be introduced in 1974. GNG

AUTOETTE (i) (US) 1910–1913
Manistee Motor Car Co, Manistee, Mich.

The Autoette was one of the first American cyclecars, with single-cylinder 5hp engine of only 400cc capacity. It had friction transmission, final drive by V-belts, and small diameter wire wheels. The only body style was a two-seater road-ster which cost $300. From 1912 the car was also known as the Manistee. GMN

AUTOETTE (ii) (US) 1913
Autoette Co, Chrisman, Ill.

This was a short-lived cyclecar with a 9hp air-cooled engine, two speeds and reverse, and shaft drive. GNG

AUTOETTE (iii) (US) to date
Autoette Electric Car Co, Long Beach, Calif.

This is a small electric used for running errands. This type of car is relatively inexpensive and popular in Long Beach where many retired people live. BE

AUTOGEAR (i) (GB) 1922
Foster Engineering Co Ltd, Letchworth, Herts.

Sometimes known as the Foster, this light car used a 7hp flat-twin engine and friction drive. The price was £185. GNG

AUTOGEAR (ii) (GB) 1922–1923
Autogears, Leeds, Yorks.

The second car to carry the name Autogear appeared a few months after the Letchworth light car, but there is no known connection between the two makes. The Leeds Autogear was, in fact, very similar to the Stanhope 3-wheeler, with belt drive to the front wheel, but used a Blackburne V-twin engine. In 1923 the Stanhope design re-appeared under the name Bramham, while the Autogear was supposed to be made in Ireland under the name Leprechan. The exact connection between these marques is uncertain, but while Stanhope and Bramham were made in the same factory, the Autogear was made in another part of Leeds. GNG

AUTOGNOM (D) 1907
Deutsche Motorfahrzeugfabrik GmbH, Berlin

This make appeared at the Berlin Show and Paris Salon in 1907. HON

AUTO LÉGER (F) 1904–1907
Autos Léger V. Crepet, Lyons

Three Auto Léger cars were made, the most unusual being a 9hp 2-cylinder two-seater whose bonnet and mudguards were shaped as the head and wings of a dragon. The other two cars, a shaft-driven four-seater sold to a doctor, and a chain-driven two-seater, had conventional bonnets. GNG

AUTOLETTE (NL) 1905–1906
S. Bingham & Co, Rotterdam

This company built bicycles and motorcycles under the name Eenhoorn (unicorn),

1906 AUTOCAR 12hp two-seater. *Kenneth St*

1924 AUTOCRAT 10/12hp two-seater. *Autocar*

1972 AUTODYNAMICS Caldwell D-9B Formula Ford racing car. *Autodynamics Inc*

1921 AUTOMATIC(ii) electric light car. *Autocar*

1913 AUTOMOBILETTE 1-litre cyclecar. *The Veteran Car Club of Great Britain*

1904 AUTOMOTO 24hp tonneau. *G.N. Georgano Collection*

followed by a tricar which they renamed Autolette in March 1905. It had a 4hp single-cylinder engine, and was joined in 1906 by a 4-wheeler voiturette with 5½hp single, or 7hp 2-cylinder engine, and a larger 12hp 2-cylinder car sold under the name Bingham. All these cars had double chain drive. GNG

AUTO-LUX (I) *1937*

This light electric 3-wheeler was the combined effort of a group of electrical firms and was planned to beat the motor-fuel shortage then prevailing in Italy. It got no further than the 1937 Milan Show. MCS

AUTOMATIC (i) *see* STURTEVANT

AUTOMATIC (ii) (US) *1921*
Automatic Electric Transmission Co, Buffalo, N.Y.

The Automatic Electric was a very small two-seater with a wheelbase of only 5ft 5ins. It had a speed of 25mph, and a creditable range of 60 miles per charge, but the price of $1,200 was very expensive for so small a car. GNG

AUTO-MIXTE (B) *1906–1912*
SA Auto-Mixte, Herstal, Liège

These cars used the Pieper system of petrol-electric drive, although they were not built by Pieper. Most Auto-Mixte vehicles were commercials, although a 24hp 4-cylinder car chassis was shown regularly at motor shows in Belgium. A 1910 car used a Knight sleeve valve engine. GNG

AUTOMOBILETTE (F) *1911–1924*
(1) Cognet et Ducruzel, Billancourt, Seine
(2) Constructions Automobiles de Bellevue, Bellevue, Seine-et-Oise

The Automobilette was, with the Bedelia, one of the first French cyclecars. Early models had 6/8hp 2-cylinder engines of Automobilette's own manufacture, belt final drive and tandem seating with driver at the rear. A monocar was also offered. For 1914 a 6hp Anzani engine was available and also a 10hp 4-cylinder Automobilette engine; these models still used belt drive, but shortly before the outbreak of World War 1 a true light car was produced, using the 4-cylinder engine, shaft drive and side-by-side seating. Post-war Automobilettes used proprietary engines, the ohv 1,095cc Ruby or the sv 1,243cc Altos. GNG

AUTOMOBILE VOITURETTE *see* GASMOBILE

AUTOMOTETTE (F) *1898–1899*
Compagnie Française des Cycles Automobiles, Paris

This was a very light 3-wheeler (not unlike a Léon Bollée in appearance) with a 3½hp engine driving the single rear wheel by belt. It was sold by the Automobile Association Ltd of Holland Park, London, who listed it as a British car. The company also made a four-seater with single horizontal-cylinder engine in 1899. GNG

AUTOMOTO (F) *1901–1907*
(1) Chavanet, Gros, Pichard et Cie, St Etienne, Loire
(2) SA de Constructions Mécaniques de la Loire, St Etienne, Loire

This firm started as motor cycle makers, and their first car was a voiturette with a 4½hp vertical single-cylinder engine. This was available in England, in kit form, a year later for £97 10s. By 1903 they were making 4-cylinder cars, and their subsequent range included models of 12, 20, 30 and 40hp. They were solidly built and of conventional design. Some of these later cars were sold in England under the name Automotor. GNG

AUTOMOTOR (US) *1901–1904*
Automotor Co, Springfield, Mass.

Automotor's final model had a *Roi-des-Belges* five-seater body, with a 4-cylinder 16/20hp engine. The purchaser had a choice of planetary or sliding-gear transmission. This 1,700lb car was claimed to be capable of 45mph. GMN

AUTO PRATIQUE (F) *1912–1913*
Sté l'Auto Pratique, Paris

This was a cyclecar with 5hp single-cylinder engine and shaft drive – an unusual feature for so small a vehicle. GNG

AUTO RED BUG *see* RED BUG

AUTORETTE (F) *1913–1914*
Guerry et Bourguignon, Paris

A cyclecar with an 1,100cc 2-cylinder engine. GNG

AUTO SANDAL (J) *1954*
Japan Auto Sandal Motors, Tokyo

This was a two-seater minicar with a single-cylinder 5½hp air-cooled engine in the rear. It had 3-speed transmission and suspension was by leaf springs. BE

AUTO-TRI *see* KELSEY (i)

AUTO TRI-CAR (US) *1914*
A.E. Osborn, New York, N.Y.

This was a 3-wheeled vehicle, classed as a cyclecar. It used a single-cylinder engine with slide valves. This drove the single front wheel through a planetary transmission and a roller-chain. The steering was by tiller. Two models were offered with wheelbases of 8ft and 9ft respectively. The cost was $350.　　GMN

AUTOTRIX (GB) *1913*
Edmunds & Wadden, Weybridge, Surrey

The Autotrix was a 3-wheeler offered in two models. The larger used a 9hp 2-cylinder J.A.P. engine, Chater-Lea gearbox and chain drive, while the smaller used a 4hp single-cylinder J.A.P. and belt drive.　　GNG

AUTO UNION (D) *1958–1962*
A combine formed by Horch, Audi, Wanderer and D.K.W. in 1932.

Racing cars were produced and raced under this name, but private cars were also marketed under the four original names. All four factories were nationalized in 1945 (*see* IFA) and the headquarters of the Auto Union were transferred to Düsseldorf, later to Ingolstadt, where in 1950 production of D.K.W. cars was started again. The D.K.W. '1000' was marketed under the name Auto Union only. This model was produced during the years 1958–62 with a 3-cylinder 2-stroke engine of 981cc capacity. In 1965 the name Audi was also revived.　　HON

AUTOVIA (GB) *1937–1938*
Autovia Cars Ltd, Coventry, Warwickshire

This was an abortive luxury-car venture by Riley, using a 2.8-litre, 100bhp V-8 engine made up of two Riley 1½-litre blocks. The frame was underslung at the rear, and other features were a preselector gearbox, worm final drive, and a long (10ft 9in) wheelbase. At £975 there were few takers.　　MCS

AUTRAM (F) *1924*
The Autram was a conventional car powered by a large 4-cylinder engine of 2,951cc. It had a 4-speed gearbox and front-wheel brakes.　　GNG

A.V. (GB) *1919–1926*
(1) Ward & Avey Ltd, Teddington, Middlesex *1919–1923*
(2) A.V. Motors Ltd, Teddington, Middlesex *1923–1926*

The A.V. was one of the cruder and more conventional – but one of the most popular – of the cyclecar breed that proliferated in Britain after World War 1. Initially, it was little different from the pre-war Carden, except for its use of a V-twin engine. The A.V. started life as a single-seater monocar, but became available as a tandem 'bicar', and then in normal, side-by-side two-seater form. The power units, air-cooled motor-cycle type engines usually of 1,100cc, were made by J.A.P. or Blackburne and were mounted at the rear.　　TRN

AVANTI II (US) *1965 to date*
Avanti Motor Co, South Bend, Ind.

A new lease of life was given this sports car when several South Bend businessmen took over the dies and plant from Studebaker and rejuvenated the marque with some face-lifting and a 5.3-litre Corvette engine for power. In 1972 it had a 5.7-litre engine developing 270bhp, and a price of $8,145 compared with the $5,167 asked for a standard Chevrolet Corvette.　　BE

AVERAGE MAN'S RUNABOUT (US) *1907–1908*
Adams Automobile Co, Hiawatha, Kans.

This high-wheeler had a 14hp air-cooled engine mounted beneath the body. Wheelbase was 6ft 2in, and steering was by tiller.　　GMN

AVERIES (GB) *1911–1915*
Averies-Ponette Ltd, Englefield Green, Surrey

John Averies imported the single-cylinder La Ponette into England from the end of 1911 and this car was sometimes known as the Averies-Ponette. The Averies light car appeared early in 1913 and used an 8/10hp 4-cylinder engine. It had a 3-speed gearbox and shaft drive, but no differential. The design was based on that of the Rolling light car made by Paul Dupressoir of Maubeuge, France.　　GNG

AVERLY (F) *1899–1901*
G. Averly, Lyons

The Averly was a light electric car built in small numbers.　　GNG

AVIA (i) (CS) *1956–1957*
Only prototypes of this Prague-built make appeared. It had a centrally placed single front seat and steering column, two rear seats, a sliding cabin for access and a rear-mounted 2-cylinder 350cc Jawa motor-cycle engine. The same layout was used for the Moravan car, built at Oktrokovice.　　HON

1961 AUTO UNION Type 1000SP 981cc coupé. *Auto Union GmbH*

1938 AUTOVIA 2.8-litre V-8 saloon. *G.E. Weaver*

1920 A.V. Bi-car 8hp two-seater. *Autocar*

1967 AVANTI II 5.3-litre coupé. *National Motor Museum*

1913 AVERIES 8/10hp two-seater. *Mrs Constance Payne*

1956 MORAVAN 350cc saloon. (*left*);
1956 AVIA(i) 350cc saloon (*right*). *Ing Adolf Babuška*

1925 AVIS 4/20PS coupé de ville. *Technisches Museum, Vienna*

1919 AVRO 10hp tourer. *Autocar*

AVIA (ii) (GB) *1961*
Armat Ltd, West Kingsdown, Sevenoaks, Kent

The Avia was a fibreglass 2 + 2 coupé using the Triumph Herald engine and chassis. The price was to have been £655 ex works, but it never went into production.
GNG

AVIETTE (GB) *1914–1916*
Hurlin & Co Ltd, Hackney, London E.

The Aviette was a very light cyclecar sold either as a monocar or as a two-seater. The former used a 4hp single-cylinder J.A.P. engine and a boat-shaped body made of hickory. Transmission was by chain to a variable pulley on the countershaft, and thence by single belt to the offside rear wheel. It had a centrally pivoted front axle (which was outmoded in 1900) and coil springing and cost £55. The two-seater had a 6hp Blumfield engine and cost £65. Hurlin and Company also made the more substantial Hurlincar.
GNG

AVIONETTE *see* GAUTHIER

AVIS (A) *1925–1927*
Avis-Werke, Vienna

As their first model this firm produced a small car with a 2-cylinder 4/20PS engine. A 4-cylinder model of 1927 appeared only in limited numbers.
HON

AVOLETTE (F) *1956–1957*
Air Tourist, Paris 8e

The Avolette was a 3-wheeler using Ydral, Sachs or Maico motor cycle engines from 125 to 250cc capacity. Like the Mochet, the smallest model could be used by those who had not passed a driving test. All models used single-cylinder engines and final drive by chain.
GNG

AVON (GB) *1903–c.1912*
Avon Motor Manufacturing Co, Keynsham, Bristol

The Avon Trimobile was a tubular-framed 3-wheeler, with chain drive from a single-cylinder rear engine to a springless live rear axle – the body was sprung on the chassis frame. The initial model was of 4hp, and priced at 80 guineas. A 4-wheeler 5hp version was offered from 1905.
DF

AVRO (GB) *1919–1920*
A.V. Roe & Co Ltd, Manchester

This light car began to be made by the famous aircraft manufacturers after Crossley Motors Ltd acquired a controlling interest in the firm in 1920. It differed from the many other ephemerals in its class in its original mode of construction. This reflected the vehicle's aero ancestry, consisting of an integral body and chassis of light timber covered in aluminium. Power units varied. During the car's short life, there were Avros powered by a 1,330cc water-cooled 4-cylinder engine, driving through 3-speed epicyclic transmission, and others that apparently used engines as different as a single-cylinder 2-stroke and a 5-cylinder radial. It was even said that the Ford Model T engine was fitted.
TRN

A.W. (PL) *1939*
Antoni Wieckowski, Zakladow Blacharskich 'Bielany', Warsaw

Designed to compete with the Polish Fiat 508 sedan, the A.W. never went into production because of the outbreak of World War 2. The car used a 32hp, 4-cylinder engine of 1.3-litres and was being road tested at the time of the German invasion.
BE

A.W.E. *see* E.M.W.

A.W.S. (i) (D) *1949–1951*
Autowerke Salzgitter, Salzgitter

These were station wagons produced mainly from Jeep components. In 1951 a very interesting station wagon appeared with a 4-cylinder, 2-stroke radial diesel engine designed by Ludwig Elsbett, but only a few prototypes were produced.
HON

A.W.S. (ii) (D) *1971 to date*
A.W.S. – Auto-Teile GmbH, Ober Bessingen

The Piccolo, a small city car, features a new principle of construction. The body consists of a skeleton of square steel tubes, connected by special angular brackets. This framework is covered with plasticized sheet-metal panels. A Goggomobil 247cc 2-stroke rear engine is used.
HON

A.W.Z. *see* ZWICKAU

B

BABCOCK (i) (US) *1906–1912*

Babcock Electric Carriage Co, Buffalo, N.Y.

The company was formed by F.A. Babcock who built his first electric car in 1903. The Babcock did not differ greatly from the Buffalo (ii) which it succeeded. In turn it was superseded in 1912 by the Buffalo Electric Vehicle Co, which was formed from Clark Motor Co, Buffalo Automobile Station Co, and Babcock.　　GMN

BABCOCK (ii) (US) *1909–1913*

H.H. Babcock Co, Watertown, N.Y.

The Babcock line included a motor buggy with a 2-cylinder engine, as well as conventional cars with larger 4-cylinder engines rated at 35/40hp. The five-seater touring car was on a 9ft 6in wheelbase and weighed 2,500lb.　　GMN

BABY *see* FOURNIER (ii)

BABY BLAKE (GB) *1922*

E.G. Blake, Croydon, Surrey

The Baby Blake was a friction-driven cyclecar, but with a difference. It was fitted with *two* 2-stroke engines, the flywheels of which were replaced by discs running in opposite directions, and also had a third movable disc running between the other two, providing an infinitely variable gear. The car was exhibited at Crystal Palace, London, and sold for £150.　　MJWW

B.A.C. (GB) *1921–1923*

British Automotive Co Ltd, Chelsea, London S.W.

The B.A.C. was a light car which used a 9.5hp sv Peters engine and a 4-speed gearbox, though the first cars had been Mathis-based. Mostly two-seater bodies were fitted, and the radiator was a handsome design. Four cars were entered for the 1921 200-Mile Race at Brooklands but did not start.　　GNG

BACHELLE (US) *1901–1902*

Otto Bachelle, Chicago, Ill.

The Bachelle was a two-seater electric with tiller steering. The rear wheels were individually driven by separate motors. Total weight was 800lb and a full battery charge was sufficient for 35 miles, the manufacturer claimed.　　GMN

BADENIA (D) *1925*

Badenia Automobilwerke AG, Hamburg; Ladenburg-am-Neckar

This was a short-lived car powered by a 2-litre 6-cylinder engine.　　GNG

BADGER (i) (US) *1909–1912*

(1) Badger Four Wheel Drive Auto Co, Clintonville, Wisc. *1909*

(2) Four Wheel Drive Auto Co, Clintonville, Wisc. *1909–1912*

Otto Zadow and William Besserdich built a prototype 4-wheel-drive steam car in 1908, but the first car to be named Badger appeared in 1909. It had a 45hp Continental petrol engine. Production cars, of which only ten were made, used 4-cylinder T-head Wisconsin engines. Zadow and Besserdich turned to truck manufacture in 1912, and their F.W.D. company is still in business today.　　GNG

BADGER (ii) (US) *1910–1912*

Badger Motor Car Co, Columbus, Wisc.

This Badger had a 30hp 4-cylinder engine and Bosch dual ignition. Tourer and roadster models were made, priced at $1,600. Total production of Badger cars was 237.　　GMN

BADMINTON (F/GB) *1907–1908*

Badminton Motors Ltd, Willesden, London N.W.

The first Badminton chassis were built in France, and bodies in England, although there were plans to make the complete car at the Willesden factory. Two models were listed, a 14/20 and a 30hp, both with 4-cylinder engines and shaft drive. At least two cars were said to have been sold to China.　　GNG

BAER (D) *1921–1924*

Paul Baer Motorenfabrik GmbH, Berlin N 39

The firm was founded in 1908 for the production of petrol engines. After World War 1 they also began to produce small cars with 2-cylinder 2-stroke engines of 770cc developing 18bhp.　　HON

1909 BABCOCK(i) two-seater electric car. *Automotive History Collection, Detroit Public Library*

1921 B.A.C. 9.5hp tourer. Coachwork by W. & F. Thorn Ltd. *Autocar*

1914 BAGULEY 15/20hp Trent limousine. *The Veteran Car Club of Great Britain*

1913 BAILEY(ii) two-seater electric runabout.
Henry Ford Museum, Dearborn, Mich.

1908 BAILLEAU 8hp racing voiturette. *Jacques
Kupélian Collection*

1910 BAKER(i) two-seater electric phaeton.
Kenneth Stauffer

BAGULEY (GB) 1911–1921
Baguley Cars Ltd, Burton-upon-Trent, Staffs.

Made by the same company as the Ace and the Salmon, the Baguley was a solid 4-cylinder car using a 15/20hp engine with a 4-speed gearbox and worm drive. It was based on the 1910 B.S.A. which had been designed by Colonel Baguley. The company pursued a one-model policy for most of its life, but made a 1913 Colonial chassis with added ground clearance. In 1919 a 21.4hp model with enlarged bore, the Model AE, was introduced, but only four were built. Total production of Baguley private cars was 88.   GNG

BAILEY (i) (US) 1907–1910
Bailey Automobile Co, Springfield, Mass.

This car used a 4-cylinder rotary engine of 20/24hp, and of 4.2-litres capacity. It had a 2-speed selective transmission, shaft drive, and was on a wheelbase of 8ft 4in. The bonnet had a rounded cross-section and the five-seater body had a peculiar high appearance. There is no known connection with Bailey (ii), also of Massachusetts. Car and company were sometimes listed as Bailey-Perkins.   GMN

BAILEY (ii) (US) 1907–1915
S.R. Bailey & Co, Amesbury, Mass.

In 1911 the Bailey electric was available as a Victoria Phaeton with wheel-steering at a price of $2,600. For 1913, there was a chain-driven runabout with very advanced styling.   GMN

BAILEY & LAMBERT (GB) 1903–1905
Bailey & Lambert Ltd, London S.W.

This company sold a light car with 6½hp De Dion-Bouton engine. In 1903 it was called the B & L Wonder, and thereafter the Pelham.   GNG

BAILLEAU (F) 1901–c. 1914
A. Bailleau, Longjumeau, Seine-et-Oise

Bailleau's first car was a very light voiturette powered by a De Dion 2¾hp engine with air or water cooling, and single chain drive. The engine was under the seat, and the dummy bonnet was used as a tool chest. He also converted quadricycles to voiturettes of this type. By 1904 the cars had front-mounted De Dion engines of 6 or 9hp, and shaft drive. A 16hp 4-cylinder car appeared in 1906, and like most French voiturette makers, Bailleau entered a single-cylinder machine in the Coupe des Voiturettes races of 1907 and 1908. In 1911 the range consisted of a 6hp single, 6hp twin, and 10/12hp four.   GNG

BAILLE-LEMAIRE (F) 1898–1902
Constructeurs Baille-Lemaire, Crosnes, Seine-et-Oise

Baille-Lemaire were makers of steel tubes, headlamps and opera glasses, who made a few cars and entered one in the 1898 Paris–Amsterdam race. They had 8hp 2-cylinder vertical engines with air-cooled cylinders and water-cooled heads, and final drive by belt.   GNG

BAILLEREAU (F) 1908
A voiturette using a large single-cylinder engine and shaft drive.   GNG

BAILLEUL (F) 1904–1905
Louis Bailleul, Leballois-Perret, Seine

This was a short-lived medium-sized car using a 14/16hp 4-cylinder engine.
GNG

BAINES (GB) 1900
Baines Ltd, Gainsborough, Lincs.

Bicycle makers since 1886, Baines Ltd made a light 'cycle-built car' with a 2½hp De Dion-Bouton engine, belt drive and a frame of steel tubing. It was intended to sell this car for £100, but production never started.   GNG

BAJA (A) 1920–1924
Baja Cyclecar Co, Vienna

This firm produced single-seater cyclecars which were available either with single-cylinder 580cc, or V-twin 790cc engines. These were mounted in the rear and transmission was by chain to one of the rear wheels.   HON

BAKER (i) (US) 1899–1916
Baker Motor Vehicle Co, Baker, Rauch & Lang Co, Cleveland, Ohio

Early Bakers had one ¾hp motor with a maximum speed of 17mph and a 50-mile range on a full battery charge. Later models, such as the 1910 limousine, had a false bonnet holding batteries, steering-wheel controls and a speed of 30mph, all for $3,000. A Baker-built Torpedo established a 1km speed record in 1902. The company absorbed the R.M. Owen Co, makers of the Owen Magnetic, in 1915. Baker electric car production was among the most important in the US. GMN

BAKER (ii) (US) 1917–1924
Baker Steam Motor Car & Mfg Co, Pueblo and Denver, Colo.

This American steam car was more fancy than fact, although roadster and touring models, and also a truck, were produced about 1921. Baker boilers, designed by Dr H.O. Baker, were used successfully, however, as replacements on Stanley cars.

KM

BAKER (iii) *see* NIKE

BAKER-BELL (US) *1913*
Baker-Bell Motor Co, Philadelphia, Pa.
Hummingbird was the model designated for this obscure make of car. This two-seater roadster was driven by a 4-cylinder 22.5hp engine and cost $675. GMN

BAKER & DALE (GB) *1913*
Baker & Dale Ltd, Southbourne, Hampshire
This was a 2-cylinder cyclecar which used a long belt drive and a semi-circular steering wheel. GNG

BALBOA (US) *1925*
Balboa Motors Corp, Fullerton, Calif.
The Balboa had a supercharged rotary valve ohc engine of its own design and sleek, streamlined bodywork. A five-seater tourer, a sedan and a sports brougham were produced but the make lasted only one year. KM

BALDNER (US) *1901–1903*
Baldner Motor Vehicle Co, Xenia, Ohio
This company made a runabout with a 12hp engine, and a 20hp touring car.
GMN

BALDWIN (US) *1899–1902*
Baldwin Automobile Manufacturing Co, Connellsville, Pa.
The Baldwin steamer had a 2-cylinder double-acting vertical engine, with condenser mounted in front on the dash. The body was a two-seater, and final drive was by single chain. GNG

BALL (US) *1902*
Miami Cycle & Mfg Co, Middletown, Ohio
The Ball was one of the most luxurious and expensive steam cars made in America. Its engine developed a claimed 60hp, and, complete with seven-seater body, the weight was over 2 tons. It carried 24 gallons of petrol and 68 gallons of water, and was good for 40mph for long stretches at a time. Three were laid down, but only one was completed. Designed by C.A. Ball, it was also known as the Rama-paugh, after an Indian tribe. GNG

BALLOT (F) *1919–1932*
Etablissements Ballot, Paris
One of the most interesting of the new makes that sprang up in such numbers in France after World War 1 was the Ballot. Previously, Ernest Ballot had made well-known proprietary engines for other car manufacturers, including Delage and Mass. The first of his own cars were the 4.9-litre 8-cylinder racing machines built for the Indianapolis 500-Mile Race of 1919. They were designed by Henry, famous for his racing Peugeots of 1912 to 1914, and had twin overhead camshaft engines with four valves per cylinder, like that designer's earlier productions. The regulations of the 1921 French Grand Prix demanded 3-litre engines, so a smaller version followed. It was fitted with Hallot front wheel brakes. At the same time, Ballot made a 2-litre 4-cylinder racing car.
Ballot's first production car was based on this machine. Introduced in 1921, it was of the same design as the 2-litre racing car. Its performance was something extraordinary, but only about 50 were made. During the same year, a more practical fast tourer, of what was to become a characteristic French type, was offered. This 2LT Ballot was also a four, of the same bore and stroke, but with a single overhead camshaft. Even so, there were few cars like it in France in 1921, with its advanced engine design, high performance and front wheel brakes combined with touring car characteristics. The 2LT was developed into the 2LTS, a tuned version, in 1924; and in 1927 they were joined by a six of the same engine design and size. This was followed by the 2.6-litre RH, which was Ballot's first straight-8 since the 1921 Grand Prix cars, and was developed in 1930 into the 3-litre RH3. By now Ballot had been taken over by Hispano-Suiza, and the 1931 Hispano 'Junior' was built in the Ballot works. TRN

BALZER (US) *1894–c.1900*
1) Stephen M. Balzer, Bronx, New York City, N.Y. *1894–1898*
2) Balzer Motor Carriage Co, Bronx, New York City, N.Y. *1898–1900*
The Balzer car used a 10hp 3-cylinder rotary engine, probably the first application of such a design to a road vehicle. Unlike the later Adams-Farwell, the Balzer's engine was mounted vertically, revolving round a horizontal crankshaft, and driving the rear wheel by gearing. Several cars were made, and the 1894 prototype still exists in the Smithsonian Institution in Washington, D.C. The 1906 Carey used a 5-cylinder engine of Balzer design. GNG

1922 BALLOT 2-litre brougham. Coachwork by Saoutchik. *Autocar*

1926 BALLOT 2 LTS 2-litre cabriolet. Coachwork by Figoni. *Automobielmuseum, Driebergen*

1930 BALLOT RH-3 3-litre saloon. *Lucien Loreille Collection*

1956 BANDINI 750cc sports racing car.
Autosport

1933 BARCLAY 10hp saloon. *Autocar*

BAMBI (E) *1952*

Manufacturas Mecánicas Aleu SA, Barcelona

The short-lived product of a motorcycle firm, the Bambi was a very light wheeler with an open two-seater body, powered by a 125cc engine.　　GI

BAMBINO (NL) *1955–1956*

NV Alweco, Veghel

The Bambino was a light 3-wheeler closely resembling the Fuldamobil coup although an open two-seater was also made. The engine was a single-cylinder of 197cc which drove the rear wheel by chain. Maximum speed was 55mph. GN

BANDINI (I) *1947–1956*

Autocostruzione Bandini, Forli

Yet another product of the Italian post-war specialist constructors utilizing t ubiquitous Fiat engine, transmission and suspension as a basis was the Bandini 75 built by Ilario Bandini. Beginning with a special ohv head on a strengthened Fi block and twin Dell'Orto carburettors, it evolved into a beautiful little twin-o light alloy engined car which was a strong contender in Italian national 750cc spor racing events in the 1952–55 period, driven by Bandini himself and Massimo Bone in competition with Giaur, Stanguellini and other marques.

BANKER (US) *1905*

A.C. Banker Co, Chicago, Ill.

The Banker had a 4.6-litre 4-cylinder, sv engine which was water-cooled. T chassis had a tubular front axle and an 8ft 4in wheelbase. The five-seater sid entrance tonneau was priced at $2,250 with wooden body, or $2,500 with al minium one. A limousine was available at $3,000.　　GN

BANKER JUVENILE ELECTRIC (US) *1905*

Banker Brothers Co, Pittsburgh, Pa.

A small two-seater electric roadster intended for use by children.　　GM

BANNER BOY BUCKBOARD (US) *1958*

Banner Welder Inc, Milwaukee, Wis.

This car was similar to the Briggs-Stratton Flyer, and in fact used a Brigg Stratton 2¾hp single-cylinder air-cooled unit. However, instead of the fifth whe drive of the original, the Banner Boy transmitted its power to the right re wheel via a centrifugal clutch and V-belt.　　MJW

BANTAM (i) (GB) *1913*

Slack & Harrison Ltd, Kegworth, Leics.

The Bantam was one of the crowd of cyclecars that appeared in Britain betwee 1912 and 1914, and differed little from the norm. An 8hp V-twin Precision engir drove through belts and variable pulleys to a chain final drive.　　TR

BANTAM (ii) (US) *1914*

Bantam Motor Co, Boston, Mass.

The first American car of this name (not to be confused with the later, bette known small car from Pennsylvania), was a short-lived cyclecar with an air-coole V-twin engine and friction and chain transmission, costing $385.　　TR

BANTAM (iii) *see* AMERICAN AUSTIN

BARADAT-ESTEVE (E) *1922*

Cortina Baradat y Esteve, Barcelona

This was a revolutionary car introduced at the 1922 Barcelona Show. It use a four piston Torus engine with only 22 moving parts, originally designed fc aircraft. This engine could run up to 16,000rpm, and the greatest problem the designer was to find a metal capable of standing up to this speed. Suspensic was by longitudinal coils running parallel with the chassis frame, on the line of the modern Citroen 2CV. Only 12 Baradat-Esteve cars were made.　　JR

BARBARINO (US) *1924–1925*

Barbarino Motor Car Corp, New York, N.Y.; Port Jefferson, L.I., N.Y.

Salvatore Barbarino was an automobile designer and engineer who took ove the assets of the defunct Richelieu company in 1923 and set out to market a sma car embodying his own design. The Barbarino, of which about 10 were made, wa a high-grade product, including a 4-cylinder Le Roi engine of Barbarino's desig 4-wheel brakes, a high-rounded radiator, wheelbase of 9ft 2in and bodies built t the customer's own order by Chupurdy Auto Coach, New York City.　　K

BARCAR (GB) *1904–1906*

Phoenix Motor Co, Southport, Lancs.

The name Barcar was derived from the names of the two sponsors, Dr W.H Barrett and Mr C.C. Cardell, who had previously made the Phoenix (ii). Wherea the latter was closely based on the Hudlass, the Barcar was a new design wit a vertical 10hp 3-cylinder engine enclosed with clutch and transmission in a aluminium base casting bolted to the chassis. The company later moved to Altrincham and concentrated on motor boat engines.   GNG

BARCLAY (GB) 1933
Barclay Motors Ltd, Aston, Birmingham

The Barclay project was unusual in that the makers planned to make a conventional family saloon at a time when such cars were already the preserve of the big mass production firms. It was an assembled car, using a 10hp Coventry-Climax engine, Moss gearbox and E.N.V. spiral bevel rear axle. The gearbox was a 4-speed synchromesh, and a preselector could be had at extra cost. The only model was a 4-door saloon which was priced at £320.   GNG

BARDON (F) 1899–1903
Automobiles Bardon, Puteaux, Seine

The Bardon cars used horizontal opposed-piston engines of Gobbron-Brillié type, with 2 pistons per cylinder. These drove 2 crankshafts which meshed with a transverse shaft. This engaged with a differential shaft to provide 3 speeds, and final drive was by double chain. The first Bardon had a 4/5hp single-cylinder engine, which was supplemented by a 10hp twin in 1901. The single-cylinder engines were mounted under the floor, and the twins under a low bonnet. Shaft drive replaced chains in 1902, but at the 1903 Paris Salon only commercial vehicles were shown. The factory was later taken over by Georges Richard for the manufacture of the Unic.   GNG

1902 BARDON 7hp tonneau. *The Veteran Car Club of Great Britain*

BARISON (I) 1923–1925
Fabbrica Automobili Barison e Cia, Livorno

Designed by Silvio Barison, this car had a 2½-litre 4-cylinder valveless engine. Only 25 were made before financial troubles forced the firm to close down.   GNG

BARLEY (US) 1922–1924
Barley Motor Car Co, Kalamazoo, Mich.

This automobile was named after Albert Barley who headed the firm and who had also started the Roamer car; the Barley company was actually a subsidiary of Roamer. With a Continental 6-cylinder engine and standard components, Barleys were available as sedans, touring cars and taxis. Early in 1925, the name was dropped and the Barley became the Roamer '6-50', except for the taxicabs which were continued through the year under their old name of Pennant.   KM

BARNARD (i) (GB) 1921–1922
A. Ward, St Mark's Engineering Co, London E.

The Barnard sports car used a modified Henderson 4-cylinder motor-cycle engine, with four separately cast air-cooled cylinders in line. Final drive was by chain and steering by a duplicate wire and bobbin arrangement. The gearbox had three forward speeds but no reverse. Disc wheels were used, and with a two-seater body of sheet aluminium the car cost £188.   GNG

BARNARD (ii) (GB) 1966 to date
(1) Barnard Racing Ltd, Sittingbourne, Kent 1966–1971
(2) Berry, Ede & White Ltd, Rochester, Kent 1971 to date

Tom Barnard built his first 'Formula 6' car in 1965. The next year the tiny monocoque racer was available to suit three categories: 75cc, 110cc and unlimited. A complete kit, to build a car devoid of suspension, gears or footbrake, could be bought for £150. 'Sports' versions with enclosed wheels were also made, and in 1972 a vintage replica based on the Mercer Raceabout was to be added.   DF

1967 BARNARD(ii) 'Formula Six' racing car. *Barnard Racing Ltd*

BARNES (i) (GB) 1904–1906
(1) George A. Barnes, Lewisham, London S.E. 1904–1905
(2) George A. Barnes, Deptford, London S.E. 1905–1906

The Barnes was a tri-car with the unusual layout of a 5hp engine mounted in front of the front wheels, driving the rear wheel by a long V-belt. The price was 58 guineas. In January 1906 a 4-cylinder 12hp light car was announced, available in two- or four-seater form.   GNG

BARNES (ii) (US) 1910–1912
Barnes Mfg Co, Sandusky, Ohio

Barnes Mfg Co succeeded Anhut Motor Co in 1910, and produced both the Barnes and the Anhut. The Barnes was a 4-cylinder air-cooled roadster.   GMN

BARNEY (GB) 1971 to date
Mike Barney Competition Developments, Chessington, Surrey

Responsible for chassis construction for the Huron Company, Barney continued on his own account with production of Formula Ford cars when Hurons ceased. A projected Formula 3 machine was not developed, but Barney also assisted with Alain de Cadenet's Duckhams-Ford special that ran well at Le Mans in 1972.   DF

BARNHART (US) 1905
Warren Automobile Co, Warren, Pa.

1902 BARRÉ 8hp tonneau. *The Veteran Car Club of Great Britain*

1924 BARRÉ 10/12hp tourer. *National Motor Museum*

1932 BARRINGTON 782cc two-seater, with Amy Johnson. *David Filsell Collection*

The only known model of the Barnhart had a 44hp, 4-cylinder engine with an automatic control 'by which one or more cylinders can be cut out'. The touring car on a 9ft 2in wheelbase cost $3,500.
GM

BAROSSO (I) 1923–1924
Officine Barosso, Novara

This company built a few cyclecars of patented design, with foot gear change giving two speeds forward and two in reverse. The engine was a 495cc sv single and final drive was by chain.
MC

BARRÉ (F) 1900–1930
(1) G. Barré et Cie, Niort, 2-Sèvres *1900–1923*
(2) Barré et Lamberthon, Niort, 2-Sèvres *1923–1927*
(3) SA des Automobiles Barré, Niort, 2-Sèvres *1927–1930*

The Barré was a typical example of a regional French make which had a steady, if small, output through the years, but was not widely known outside its own district. Early models used 4½hp single-cylinder De Dion-Bouton engines for the voiturette or 8hp Aster or Buchet 2-cylinder engines for the tonneau. Bonnets and radiator were either of De Dion or Panhard pattern. Shaft drive was always used and by the outbreak of World War 1 the range consisted of seven models, from an 8/10hp to a 24/30hp, all with 4-cylinder monobloc engines. The firm produced all their own coachwork.

In the vintage period Barré used mainly Ballot side-valve engines of up to 2 litres capacity, but one model used a push-rod ohv S.C.A.P. of 1,614cc. Front-wheel brakes were used on the later models, but like many regional firms, Barré did not survive the Depression.
GNG

BARRIE see BELL (ii)

BARRINGTON (GB) 1932–1936
Barrington Motors Ltd, Sheffield, Yorks.

A former Scott motorcycle enthusiast, Barrington Budd tried for many years to find a marketing outlet for his own 3-cylinder water-cooled 2-stroke engines. A 782cc unit, used for some time previously in an Austin Seven Chummy, was transferred in 1932 to a two-seater of Budd's own design and construction. This car covered a considerable test mileage, and was followed in 1935 by a 9hp chassis of similar design. This was supposed to be the prototype for a production saloon model with Holbrook coachwork, but inadequate sponsorship caused the project to be shelved the following year.
DF

BARRIQUAND ET SCHMITT (F) 1905
This Neuilly-based company made a large 4-cylinder car with 4-litre ohv engine and semi-floating rear axle.
GNG

BARRON-VIALLE (F) 1923–1929
(1) Fabrique Alsacienne de Moteurs et Automobiles, Strasbourg *1923*
(2) Barron, Vialle et Cie, Lyons *1924–1929*

This car originally appeared as the Six made at Strasbourg, and only acquired the name Barron-Vialle when manufacture was taken over by the Lyons firm, who had been making commercial vehicles since 1914. Sixes and Straight-Eights were made with the same cylinder dimensions, 70×90mm, giving 2.1 and 2.7 litres respectively. The single ohc engine was designed by M. Gadoux who was also responsible for the Omega Six. In 1928 and 1929, engine sizes were increased to 2.4 and 3.2 litres.
GNG

BARROWS (US) 1897–1898
Barrow's Vehicle Co, Willimantic, Conn.

The Barrows was a two-seater electric 3-wheeler, with the drive through the single front wheel. It bore some resemblance to the French Mildé et Mondos.
GNG

BARTHOLOMEW see GLIDE

BARTLETT (CDN) 1914–1917
Canadian Bartlett Automobile Co, Ltd, Toronto and Stratford, Ont.

Named after its inventor, R.C. Bartlett, these cars were equipped with thin, solid rubber tyres, designed supposedly to last the life of the car. Suspension was entirely dependent upon pneumatic rubber cushions located between the frame and axles instead of conventional springs. Approximately 600 tourers and roadsters and trucks were constructed by this firm before shortages of parts ended production during World War 1. The first seven cars had Northway engines, the balance Le Roi. Bartlett was also responsible for the first 4-wheel-brake cars in Canada.
GB

BARTON (US) c. 1903
Barton Boiler Co, Chicago, Ill.

Though primarily a boiler manufacturer, Barton offered 'special steam tonneau cars' built to order. These used the Barton flash boiler, Burnell paraffin burner, and Mason 2-cylinder side-valve engine.
GNG

BASSETT (GB) *1899–1901*

Bassett Motor Syndicate, London W.C.

The Bassett light car used a 4hp Schwanemeyer motor-cycle engine mounted under the rear seat, driving a 2-speed constant mesh gearbox.　　GNG

BASSON'S STAR (US) *1956*

Basson's Industries Corp., Bronx, N.Y.

This was an ephemeral minicar with three wheels, fibreglass body, and 2-stroke single-cylinder German J.L.O. engine. The price was $999.　　GNG

BASTIN (B) *1908–1909*

Ateliers Bastin, Liège

This company made a limited number of cars using a small 4-cylinder engine and shaft drive. They featured a round radiator.　　GNG

BAT (GB) *1904–1909*

Bat Motor Manufacturing Co Ltd, Penge, Surrey

The Bat was one of the better-known tri-cars, and was more car-like than most, with a chair-type seat for the driver instead of the usual saddle, and a semi-enclosed wooden body for the passenger who sat in front. In 1909 the company introduced their 'Carcycle' which resembled a motor-cycle and sidecar, but had four wheels, the steering being by handlebar. The name came from the original maker, Samuel Robert Batson.　　GNG

BATES (US) *1903–1905*

Bates Automobile Co, Lansing, Mich.

The Bates car used an 18/20hp 3-cylinder engine, and had 3 forward speeds and shaft drive. With a four-seater tourer body, it cost $2,000. The company's optimistic slogan was 'Buy a Bates and Keep Your Dates'.　　GNG

BATEUP (AUS) *1939*

The Australian Car Syndicate, Adelaide, S.A.

This concern, headed by George Bateup, planned to make a light 4-cylinder car in the class of the Willys Four. One prototype was built, with a 15hp engine designed and made in Adelaide, but World War 2 put an end to the project.　　GNG

BATTEN (GB) *1935–1938*

Beckenham Motor Co Ltd, Beckenham, Kent

The Batten was a stark sports car based on a cut-down Ford V-8 chassis of the 1932/33 period with the later V-8 engine boosted to give 97bhp. With a very simple two-seater body the overall weight was only 2,184lb which gave excellent acceleration, and a maximum speed of 120mph. Most Battens used Ford-type suspension, but one or two were made with ifs. The price was £325. From 1936 a four-seater sports and dh coupé were also offered.　　GNG

BAUCHET (F) *1901–1903*

SA des Moteurs H. Bauchet, Rethel, Ardennes

The Bauchet was a light car powered by a 5/7hp vertical 2-cylinder engine. It was mounted at the front, and drove via a 4-speed gearbox and propeller shaft. A four-seater tonneau body was provided.　　GNG

BAUDIER (F) *1900–1901*

G. Baudier, Paris 17e

The Baudier was a voiturette with the general appearance of the contemporary Renault, powered by a 3hp water-cooled De Dion engine. It used shaft drive, and had a three-seater 'spider' body.　　GNG

BAUDOUIN *see* DECHAMPS

BAUDUIN-RADIA *see* L'AUTOMOTRICE

BAUGHAN (GB) *1920–1929*

1) Baughan Motors, Harrow, Middlesex *1920–1921*
2) Baughan Motors, Stroud, Gloucestershire *1921–1929*

As a sideline from their main motor-cycle and general engineering businesses, Baughan turned out cyclecars in small numbers. Motor-cycle gearboxes and chain final drive were used, with either J.A.P. or Blackburne front-mounted V-twin engines. Body styles were normal two-seater, or monocar with dickey.　　DF

B.A.W. *see* SCHURICHT

BAYARD, BAYARD-CLÉMENT *see* CLÉMENT-BAYARD

BAYLEY *see* LIPSCOMB

BAYLISS-THOMAS (GB) *1922–1929*

Excelsior Motor Co Ltd, Tyseley, Birmingham

1915 BARTLETT tourer. *Glenn Baechler Collection*

1935 BATTEN Special 3.6-litre sports car. *Autocar*

1925 BAYLISS-THOMAS 13/30hp two-seater. *Autocar*

1966 BEACH Formula Vee racing car
Autosport

1913 BEACON Mark VI 10hp two-seater.
Lytton Jarman

c.1922 BEAN 11.9hp two-seater. *Jonathan Wood*

1927 BEAN 18/50hp saloon. *Jonathan Wood*

The Bayliss-Thomas was a typical example of the assembled light car so comm
in Britain in the 1920s; in this case a 1½-litre Coventry-Simplex engine was ma
to a Wrigley gearbox. This car had no differential, unlike its smaller brot
with an 1,100cc ohv engine by Meadows, that joined it in 1923. Both models w
available with long-tailed sports bodies, which was also usual practice. By 19
four models, all with different engines of different sizes, could be had, but
many were made at any time, particularly after 1925. The company were be
known for their Excelsior bicycles and motor cycles.
T

BAY STATE (i) (US) *1906–1907*
Bay State Automobile Co, Boston, Mass.
The Bay State Forty was a large seven-seater vehicle with a 5.8-litre 4-cylin
engine. It had a 3-speed selective transmission, and final drive was by shaft.   G

BAY STATE (ii) (US) *1922–1924*
R.H. Long Co, Framingham, Mass.
In three years of production approximately 2,500 units of this assembled
left the factory. Powered by a Continental 6-cylinder engine, the Bay State w
designed by a former Winton technician, which accounts for the similarity
radiator appearance.

B.C.K. *see* KLINE KAR

B.D.A.C. *see* BUCKMOBILE

BEACH (US) *1962 to date*
Competition Components Inc, Clearwater, Fla.
Eugene Beach was one of the most prolific of the Formula Vee produce
surpassing the 200 mark for kits completed from the commencement of the Formu
up to mid-1967. Square-section tubular frames were supplied, with glassfib
bodies and other components as necessary.

BEACON (GB) *1912–1914*
(1) Beacon Hill Motor Works, Hindhead, Surrey *1912*
(2) Beacon Engineering Co, Hindhead, Surrey *1912–1913*
(3) Beacon Motors Ltd, Liphook, Surrey *1913–1914*
The Beacon cyclecar was chiefly notable for the fact that an ultra-light cane bo
was available as an alternative to the coachbuilt one. Experimental models us
J.A.P. V-twin engines and chain or friction drive, although one model was propelle
driven. The production model of 1913–1914 used a Griffon V-twin air-cool
engine and shaft drive to a 3-speed gearbox mounted on the rear axle.   GN

BEAN (GB) *1919–1929*
(1) A. Harper, Sons & Bean Ltd, Tipton, Dudley, Staffs. *1919–1926*
(2) Bean Cars Ltd, Tipton, Dudley, Staffs. *1926–1929*
The Bean was a remodelling of the Perry light car, whose manufacturers were take
over by Harper Sons & Bean, motor components makers, after World War 1. Th
Bean was to be mass-produced, in one 11.9hp model only. Its makers were membe
of a consortium of firms, including the famous, old-established names of Swift an
Vulcan, Hadfields, the engineers of Sheffield, Gallay Radiators and Marles Steerin
that was intended to achieve efficient quantity production by rationalization of part
In fact, Bean carried cost cutting too far with this car. Its 4-cylinder, side-valv
1,794cc engine was rough, the gear change difficult and the suspension harsh. Th
four-seater open body cost only £80. However, 1922 customers were car-starved an
undiscriminating, and 80 cars a week were made that year, even if the first targe
of 50,000 per annum remained a dream. The bigger, 2.3-litre Fourteen introduced fo
1924 was more modern machine, with its unit construction of engine and gearbo
Hadfields took over Bean early in 1926. For 1927, the company followed fashic
by introducing a six, the '18/50'. Its 2.7-litre, overhead-valve engine was made b
Meadows, and a rather square radiator replaced the well-known rounded Bean shap
Also new in 1927 was the Imperial Six, the first Bean designed specifically for expor
Unlike the 18/50 this had a Bean-built engine of 3.8 litres with a Ricardo cylinde
head. The Australian explorer Francis Birtles drove a disintegrating prototype fro
England to India, and in fact the Imperial Six was never put into production. Fro
1927 all cars were called Hadfield-Beans. The 2.3-litre 14/40 Hadfield-Bean, whic
joined the range in 1928, was no better, with its unreliable engine and overhead-wor
drive rear axle, bad brakes and difficult clutch and gear-change. It was also ol
fashioned in that it used a fairly large, long-stroke, side-valve 4-cylinder engine. Th
latter was economical, and the 14/40 Hadfield-Bean was cheap, but cost cuttin
presumably dictated the fitting of quarter-elliptic rear springs, which cannot hav
improved comfort. There was a 14/70hp sports version, which had better brakes
with Dewandre vacuum servo assistance, but the only good car in the range, th
old Fourteen, was desperately out-dated and no Hadfield-Beans at all were mad
after 1929.
TR

BEARDMORE (GB) *1920–1928*
Beardmore Motors Ltd, Glasgow

Beardmore, a new make in 1920, started life in what might be called the traditional ...ts manner as far as cars are concerned – with extremely strong, solid, reliable, ...er expensive motor cars, notably only for the fact that the three models were ...de in three different towns – Glasgow, Paisley (in a former Arrol-Johnston works) ...l Coatbridge – and for their forward-tilting radiator fillers. The 1,656cc Eleven, ...2,413cc Fifteen (designed mainly as a taxi) and the 4-litre Thirty were all 4-...nder, side-valve machines. The first and last were virtually unknown outside ...tland. However, in 1922 there arrived a new model of the Eleven which combined ...Beardmore's existing virtues with technical interest and high performance. It now ...l a bigger bore providing 1,860cc, and overhead camshaft, and four forward ...eds. A sports version, the most famous, used a 2-litre engine and aluminium ...ons, so that although, like all the breed, it was a heavy car, it could exceed ...nph. A highly-modified version took the course record at the Shelsley Walsh hill-...nb in 1925. After that, the car was superseded by the obscure side-valve Sixteen, ...l little was seen of the name except on taxicabs, though Beardmore remained ...ous in other fields of engineering. TRN

...ARDSLEY (US) 1915–1917
...rdsley Electric Co, Los Angeles, Calif.
...The Beardsley electric was offered in as many as twelve models, simultaneously. ...vas claimed that the lightest model was capable of 28mph. The common wheel-...e was 7ft 8in and the price range was $1,285 to $2,650. Most models were ...ipped with wire wheels. GMN

...ATRIX (F) 1907
...Tisserand, Paris
...The Béatrix car was powered by a 6-cylinder monobloc engine, an unusually ...vanced feature at a time when the six was still comparatively rare, and most such ...s had their cylinders cast in pairs. Models made included cars of 15/18, 24/30 ...l 30/40hp. GNG

...ATTIE (GB) 1969 to date
...Chas. Beattie Projects, Hanworth Air Park, Feltham, Middlesex 1969–1971
...Chassiscraft, London W.8 1971 to date
...Ex-racing mechanic Charles Beattie designed and advertised cars for FF, FB ...l F100 racing. Some success attended the space-framed Formula Ford machines, ...h conventional suspension and fibreglass bodies, and one-offs included a mono-...que sports car in 1972. DF

...AU-CHAMBERLAIN see HUDSON (i)

...AUFORT (D) 1901–1906
...aufort Motor Co, Baden
...The Beaufort company was capitalized and registered in England, but the cars ...re largely, if not entirely, German Arguses. They were sold in England from ...mises off Baker St, London and some may have been assembled there. The first ...r had an 8hp single-cylinder Bergmann engine and belt drive, but this was re-...ced by shaft drive in 1902. In the same year 2-cylinder cars of 12 and 18hp were ...roduced, joined by 14 and 24hp fours in 1903. All were conventional cars with ...aft drive. Later models ranged up to a 28/32hp four, and a 30hp six. GNG

...AUMONT (i) (F) 1913
...The Paris-built Beaumont was made in two models, both with 4-cylinder engines. ...ey were a 10hp 1,726cc, and a 13.9 2,722cc. GNG

...AUMONT (ii) see ACADIAN

...AVER (US) 1916–1923
...aver State Motor Co, Gresham, Oreg.
...Named after Oregon, the Beaver State, this was an assembled car with a 6-cylinder ...gine and worm drive. Very few were made. GMN

...E.B. (D) 1922–1923
...sse Elektromobil-Bau KG, Magdeburg
...is was a small electric-driven two-seater cyclecar, produced in limited numbers. HON

...ÉCHEREAU (F) 1924–1925
...uis Béchereau, Paris
...The Béchereau was a light car using a 1,100cc twin-cam Salmson engine with an ...vanced streamlined body and Lancia-type independent front suspension. Few ...re made. GNG

...ECK (F) 1920–1922
...utomobiles Beck, Lyons
...The Beck light car used a 1½-litre 4-cylinder engine in a chassis which had 4-wheel ...dependent suspension by coil. The 3-speed gearbox was mounted on the rear axle. ...odies were semi-streamlined and the cars had a handsome curved radiator. GNG

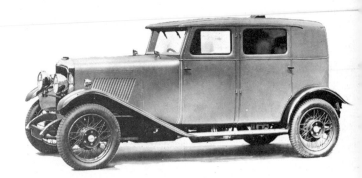

1929 HADFIELD-BEAN 14/70 saloon. *Autocar*

1923 BEARDMORE Type D 12.8hp tourer.
Th. van Wyk

1907 BEATRIX 6-cylinder tourer. *Lucien Loreille Collection*

1921 BECK 10hp chassis. *Autocar*

1904 BECKMANN 24PS tonneau-limousine.
Neubauer Collection

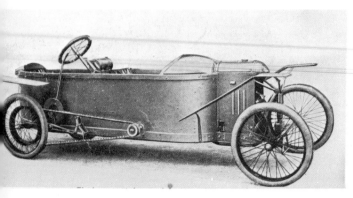

1913 BÉDÉLIA 8/10hp cyclecar. *David Filsell Collection*

BECKMANN (D) *1900–1926*

Otto Beckmann & Cie, Erste Schlesische Velociped- und Automobil-Fabrik, Bres

Beckmann produced bicycles before car production was taken up in 1900, at t with a voiturette using a single-cylinder De Dion engine. This model was built, w improvements, until about 1905. Beginning in 1901 2- and 4-cylinder models w also produced using French proprietary engines. After 1904 Beckmann's o engines were installed. Beckmann offered a great variety of different models with 4- and 6-cylinder engines ranging from 10 to 50PS. Beckmann cars took part in Herkomer Trials in 1906 and 1907. The make was not widely distributed but wa some local importance in Eastern Germany, as well as in Eastern Europe.

After World War 1 only small-scale production was carried on. The last mo of 8/32PS, used a Basse and Selve engine. In 1926 production ceased and works were taken over by Opel.

H

BÉDÉLIA (F) *1910–1925*

(1) Bourbeau et Devaux, Paris *1910–1916*
(2) Mahieux et Cie, Levallois-Perret *1920–1925*

The Bédélia of 1910 was the first of the French cyclecars. Low-built and v light, unlike earlier attempts to provide a truly popular car, it could carry t passengers in tandem. The rear passenger controlled the steering, which was the crude centre-pivot variety, and at first he also changed speed. The power u was a single-cylinder in any one of three sizes from $3\frac{1}{2}$ to $5\frac{1}{2}$hp, or else a V-t of 10hp. Transmission was by belts, providing two forward speeds. Cyclecars wa in popularity after World War 1, giving way to the light car, or miniature car, but the Bédélia was longer-lived than most. Postwar models had normal sea arrangements and three forward speeds, but the choice of a single or 2-cylin engine was still available. In 1920 the founders, Henri Bourbeau and Rob Devaux, sold the business to one of their agents, M. Binet, who had the car b for him by L. Mahieux et Cie.

T

BEDFORD (GB) *1904*

Wilson Bros, Bedford

Wilson Bros were electrical engineers who exhibited a range of three cars at t 1904 Crystal Palace Show: a 6hp single-cylinder two-seater with solid tyres, a 10 and 16hp 2- and 4-cylinder cars with pneumatic tyres. The latter carried a *R des-Belges* body by Vedrine of Paris, but the cars did not survive the year of th introduction.

G

BEDFORD-BUICK *see* BUICK

BEEBE (US) *1906*

Western Motor Truck & Vehicle Works, Chicago, Ill.

This obscure car used a 2-cylinder, two-stroke engine of 30hp connected to a fr tion transmission. Two models were offered with wheelbases of 6ft 8in and of 8ft 4 It has been claimed that these cars had push-button starting.

GM

BEESTON (GB) *1899*

Beeston Motor Cycle Co, Coventry, Warwickshire

These well-known makers of motor tricycles and quads showed a light car at t 1899 National Cycle Show. It had a $3\frac{1}{2}$hp engine under the seat, and spur-gear driv

GM

B.E.F. (D) *1907–1913*

Berliner Electromobilfabrik GmbH, Berlin SW

An electric 3-wheeler with an interesting front-wheel drive designed by Vict Harborn. Harborn founded Geha after leaving B.E.F.

HC

BEGGS (US) *1918–1923*

Beggs Motor Car Co, Kansas City, Mo.

A typical assembled car, the Beggs used standard components throughout. It w powered by a Continental 6-cylinder motor.

K

BÉGOT ET MAZURIÉ; BÉGOT ET CAIL (F) *1900–1902*

Bégot et Mazurié, Reims

Bégot et Mazurié were general engineers who made a few voiturettes with 4 single-cylinder engines of oversquare dimensions (100mm × 95mm). They we front-mounted, and final drive was by double chains. In 1901 two light ca appeared under the name Bégot et Cail. One had a 5hp single-cylinder De Dio engine, and the other a 7hp V-twin of their own make.

GM

BEISEL (US) *1914*

Beisel Motorette Co, Monroe, Mich.

This short-lived cyclecar used a 4-cylinder water-cooled Prugh engine of $1\frac{1}{2}$ litre A friction transmission was used, and this was connected to the rear wheels by dri belts. The wheelbase was 8ft, the tread 3ft 4in, and its cost was $385.

GM

BEKKA (F) *1907*

Barclay et Knudsen, Paris

The Bekka derived its name from the initials of the makers (B.K.). Two 4-cylinder models were listed, both with chain drive, a 12/16 and an 18/24hp.　　GNG

B.E.L. (US) *1921*
Consolidated Motor Car Co, New London, Conn.
　A small car of severely limited production, the B.E.L. was built by the company which had earlier produced the Sterling. The B.E.L. was mounted on an 8ft 5in wheelbase and powered by a 4-cylinder engine of its own design.　　KM

BELCAR *see* BRÜTSCH

BELDEN (US) *1908–1911*
Belden Motor Car Co, Pittsburg, Pa.
　Few of these cars were made. The company issued a catalogue in 1907 showing 6-cylinder cars, but in September 1909 admitted that it had just completed its first car.　　GMN

BELGA (B) *1920–1921*
Automobiles Belga, Marchienne-Zone
　The Belga was a light car using a 10hp Ballot engine. Its only unconventional feature was a friction transmission giving 10 forward speeds.　　GNG

BELGA RISE *see* SIZAIRE FRÈRES

BELGICA (B) *1902–1909*
Sté des Automobiles Belgica, Brussels
　The Belgica was made by a cycle company established in 1885. The first models were an 8hp single-cylinder with shaft drive, and two chain-drive models, a 12hp twin and a 20hp four. A 40hp racing car was also made, but was probably a one-off. A 24hp 4-cylinder shaft drive car was introduced in 1905, and remained in production until the company's demise in 1909. In this year a 58hp 6-cylinder car was listed. The factory was later acquired by Excelsior.　　GNG

BELL (i) (GB) *1905–1914*
Bell Brothers, Ravensthorpe, Yorks.
　The Bell was a solidly-built Yorkshire car which never achieved a great deal of fame outside its own district. The first model was an 8/10hp 2-cylinder car described as 'heavier than usual for this class of vehicle'. It was followed by 4-cylinder cars of 16, 20, 24 and 30hp, of which the 16hp was popular as a taxicab. Production ceased during World War 1 and in 1919 the works were acquired by the Co-operative Wholesale Society who planned to sell the 16, 24 and 30hp cars under the name C.W.S., as well as making a cyclecar. No cars appeared, although lorries of Bell design were made by C.W.S. at their Manchester works for a few years. The 16 and 25hp Bells were listed in Buyers Guides until 1926, and were presumably available if anyone wished to order one.　　GNG

BELL (ii) (US) *1915–1921*
Bell Motor Car Co, York, Pa.
　A small, inexpensive car (the Model 16 tourer of 1916 sold for $775) on a 9ft 4in wheelbase, which used G.B. & S. and Continental engines at first, and Herschell-Spillmans from 1919. Although made in limited numbers, at least one example still exists.　　GMN

BELL (iii) (CDN) *1916–1918*
The Barrie Carriage Co, Barrie, Ont.
　About 20 of these light touring cars were built, powered by a 4-cylinder Lycoming engine and using mainly imported parts secured from the U.S. Bell company.　　GB

BELL (iv) (GB) *1920*
W.G. Bell, Rochester, Kent
　The Bell was a 3-wheeled cyclecar steered by the front wheel only. Fitted with a J.A.P. Precision engine it was to be sold at £120–£150.　　MJWW

BELL (v) (F) *1924–1925*
Cyclecars Bell, Choisy-le-Roi, Seine
　Despite the company's name, the Bell deserved the title of light car rather than cyclecar, for it used a 4-cylinder engine and shaft drive. The engine was an ohv air-cooled flat-four of 1095cc, and it was planned to sell the car in Britain at a price of £95, but nothing came of the idea. In the English press the car was referred to as the Bellais.　　GNG

BELLANGER (F) *1912–1925*
Sté des Automobiles Bellanger Frères, Neuilly-sur-Seine
　Pre-World War 1 Bellangers used Daimler (ii) 4-cylinder sleeve-valve engines, and were made in 2-litre, 2.6-litre, 3-litre and 6.3-litre forms. All had cone clutches, Riley detachable wheels and bullnose radiators, and all except the 3-litre 20hp had worm drive. Side-valve Briscoe engines of American manufacture were adopted after

1908 B.E.F. two-seater electric car. *Neubauer Collection*

1910 BELL(i) 16hp landaulette. *Bell Bros*

1920 BELLANGER 3.2-litre tourer. *Jacques Kupélian Collection*

1901 BELLE 6/8hp tonneau. *National Motor Museum*

1900 (BELSIZE) MARSHALL 4½hp *vis-à-vis. Hull Transport Museum*

1913 BELSIZE 18/22 cabriolet. Coachwork by Salmons. *Autocar*

the War and unit 3-speed gearboxes, left-hand drive and disc wheels featured in the specification. The range embraced 3.2-litre and 4.25-litre fours and a large V-8 of 6.4-litre capacity with cantilever rear suspension. The last of the fours, made in 1922–1923, had coil ignition and wood wheels, and sold for £565 in England. The factory at Neuilly was later used by Peugeot and subsequently Rosengart, and in 1928 an attempt was made to boost De Dion-Bouton sales by fitting Bellanger radiators and marketing them under the latter name. This lasted only a very short while.   MCS

BELLE (CH/GB) *1901–1903*
E.J. Coles & Co, Upper Holloway, London N.

The origin of the Belle is doubtful as E.J. coles claimed that the car was designed and built entirely by him, although there are strong indications that it was imported from Switzerland. It had a front-mounted 6hp single-cylinder inclined engine, and belt drive to a countershaft which meshed with an intermediate shaft to give gear changes. From there final drive was by double chains. Pneumatic or solid tyres could be fitted. In 1904 Coles was agent for the Wyss or Berna car, which has led to a suggestion that the Belle was also built by Berna, but there is no evidence of this.   GNG

BELLEFONTAINE (US) *1908*
Bellefontaine Automobile Co, Bellefontaine, Ohio

The Bellefontaine Model B-8 had a five-seater *Roi-des-Belges* body. The engine was a 35hp, L-head, with four cylinders of 4.8 litres capacity. It had a selective transmission and was priced at $2,500.   GMN

BELMOBILE (US) *1912*
Bell Motor Car Co, Detroit, Mich.

This make was available only as a two-seater roadster on an 8ft 4in wheelbase. Its 20hp engine drove through a 3-speed transmission. Full elliptical springs were used in the rear, semi-elliptical in front. There is no known connection with the later Bell automobile.   GMN

BELMONT (i) (US) *1909–1912*
(1) Belmont Motor Car Co, New Haven, Conn.
(2) Belmont Motor Vehicle Co, Castleton-on-Hudson, N.Y.

The Belmont 30hp tourer had a complex history, certainly out of proportion to the few vehicles which could have been built between reorganizations. One of the originators was Dr C. Baxter Tiley, who was also connected with Tiley-Pratt. GMN

BELMONT (ii) (US) *1916*
Belmont Electric Auto Co, Wyandotte, Mich.

This car was somewhat unusual for an electric, as only four- and six-seater limousines were offered for sale. The company also produced commercial electric cars.
     GMN

BELSIZE (GB) *1897–1925*
(1) Marshall & Co, Manchester *1897–1902*
(2) Belsize Motor & Engineering Co Ltd, Manchester *1902–1906*
(3) Belsize Motors Ltd, Manchester *1906–1925*

The ancestor of the Belsize was the Marshall, put together by a former bicycle manufacturer at a time when all 'British' designs except one (Lanchester) were copies or adaptations of foreign cars. The Marshall was a modification of the French Hurtu, with a radiator added, which was in turn the German Benz, a small car with a single-cylinder horizontal engine and belt-and-chain transmission. The first cars to bear the Belsize name appeared in 1901. Most were of modern design, including the best known, a small 12hp with shaft drive and a 2-cylinder engine by Buchet that had mechanical inlet valves and was efficient for its day. Chain drive was still considered appropriate for big cars, like the 20hp Belsize, which also had a 3-cylinder engine and a dashboard radiator. At the 1906 Olympia Show, a fine shaft-driven six with overhead valves was exhibited. However, the firm gained most of its repute from its conventional, smaller cars, which came to use 4-cylinder, side-valve engines with a notably good power output, unit construction of engine and gearbox, and worm final drive. Commercial vehicles, including taxis, were also made.

The staple model by 1920 was the Fifteen, of 2.8 litres; but in 1921, a true light car was introduced, the Belsize-Bradshaw. This used a 1094cc, ohv V-twin engine with oil cooling, designed by Granville Bradshaw, that was quieter-running than most conventional twins. Granville Bradshaw also made similar and smaller oil-cooled engines, some flat-twins, for installation in motor cycles and other manufacturers' cars, as well as his famous air-cooled flat-twin (ABC). However, that in the Belsize-Bradshaw was unreliable and frail, and undistinguished water-cooled fours replaced it in the light car range. All the same, by 1924 all cars were called Belsize-Bradshaws. The firm's last fling was into multi-cylinderism on a miniature scale, with a 1696cc six in 1924, and, for 1925, a 2½-litre straight-8, both with overhead valves. The company was in the official receiver's hands before many of either could be made.
     TRN

BENDIX (US) *1907–1910*
The Bendix Co, Chicago, Ill.; Logansport, Ind.

The Bendix Co was the successor to the Triumph Motor Car Co who built the Triumph (ii). The Bendix '30' was a motor buggy with a 4-cylinder water-cooled engine of 30hp, selling for $1,500. Distinguishing features were large-diameter with solid tyres, and a minute bonnet. For 1910 a standard-size bonnet was used. The designer, Vincent Bendix, later became famous as a manufacturer of hydraulic brakes, and in 1934 his Bendix Aviation Corp built a purely experimental fwd streamlined sedan.

GMN

BENHAM (US) *1914–1917*
Benham Mfg Co, Detroit, Mich.

Successors to S. & M. (Strobel & Martin), Benham produced approximately 60 units. The Benham had a Continental engine and other standard components and was attractively streamlined for its time.

KM

BEN HUR (US) *1916–1918*
Ben Hur Motor Co, Willoughby, Ohio

The Ben Hur used a 5-litre 6-cylinder Buda engine, and had a wheelbase of 10ft 6in. Only open models were built, sporty two-passenger roadsters being typical.

GMN

BENJAMIN; BENOVA (F) *1921–1931*
Maurice Jeanson, Asnières, Seine

The Benjamin was a typical attempt to build a 4-cylinder light car and still stay below the statutory French weight limit for cyclecars (350kg). Features were a 750cc sv engine and a 3-speed transaxle with no differential, and suspension followed Austin Seven lines: transverse at the front and quarter-elliptic at the rear. By 1923 this engine was giving 14bhp, long-chassis four-seater versions were catalogued, and an ohc sports model was capable of 60mph. Unfortunately in 1924 there was an attempt at a true cyclecar in the shape of a tiny staggered two-seater selling for 5,500fr. This had a 525cc air-cooled vertical twin 2-stroke engine and 2-speed gearbox mounted at the rear of a crude boat-shaped perimeter frame. There was also a similar 3-cylinder 9CV model. Although Benjamin tried again with a rear-engined lightweight in 1925, this time with a 630cc 4-stroke motor, their regular offerings were now conventional machines powered by 945cc and 1,100cc Chapuis-Dornier 4-cylinder engines, the latter available with ohv. These had quarter-elliptic springing all round and worm drive. Four-wheel brakes were seen on the 1926 Paris Salon cars: these were the last Benjamins, though a year later the marque reappeared under the Benova name. The fours were continued, along with a small straight-8 using the new S.C.A.P. 1,500cc ohv proprietary unit. The Benova was still quoted in 1931, when four 4-cylinder models were offered, capacities ranging from 945cc to 2.1 litres.

MCS

BENNER (US) *1908–1910*
Benner Motor Car Co, New York, N.Y.

This car was powered by a 6-cylinder, 25/30hp ohv Brownell engine. The tourer was priced at $1,750. Nearly 200 were made.

GMN

BENOIS ET DAMAS (F) *1903–1904*
Benois et Damas, Neuilly, Seine

This company made a small number of cars with 8hp 2-clinder and 12hp 4-cylinder engines, both models using shaft drive.

GNG

BENTALL (GB) *1906–1913*
E.H. Bentall & Co Ltd, Maldon, Essex

Made by a firm of agricultural engineers who had been in business since 1792 (and still are today) the first Bentall cars appeared in 1906. There were two 2-cylinder models, 8 and 11hp, and a 4-cylinder 16/20hp. The company made a feature of over-square engines: the 16/20, the most popular Bentall, with its bore of 100mm was taxed at 24.8hp. Nearly all the engine and chassis parts were made in the works, bodies coming mostly from the local firms of Munnions of Chelmsford, and Adams of Colchester. About 100 Bentalls were made, one of which survives today.

GNG

BENTLEY (GB) *1920 to date*
1) Bentley Motors Ltd, Cricklewood, London N.W.2. *1920–1931*
2) Bentley Motors (1931) Ltd, Derby *1933–1945*
3) Bentley Motors (1931) Ltd, Crewe, Cheshire *1946 to date*

W.O. Bentley was already well-known as the importer of the D.F.P. car, a pioneer of aluminium pistons and a designer of successful rotary aircraft engines when his first 3-litre car appeared at the 1919 London Show. This model, indelibly imprinted in the layman's mind as the archetype of the Vintage sports car, had a long-stroke (80 × 149mm) single ohc engine with fixed head and dual magneto ignition developing about 70bhp in its early form. It was at its best in long-distance events; a team of 3-litres with flat radiators (the only instance of this apart from the same year's Indianapolis car) finished 2nd, 3rd and 5th in the 1922 T.T., and the model accounted for the first two of the marque's Le Mans wins, those of Duff/Clement in 1924 and Davis/Benjafield in 1927 on the badly damaged 'Old No. 7' – one of the legends of motor-racing history. Up to 1929 1,630 3-litres were made. 1924 saw the introduction of front wheel brakes and also the famous sports four-seater 'Speed Model' by Vanden Plas. Bentleys are popularly known by the colours of the enamel on their radiator badges – 'Red Label' signifying a Speed Model short-chassis 3-litre, 'Blue Label'

1921 BENJAMIN 8hp coupé. *Autocar*

1908 BENTALL 16/20hp tourer. *Bentall & Co Ltd*

1925 BENTLEY 3-litre Speed Model boat-tail two-seater. Coachwork by Mulliner. *Mrs Elizabeth Nagle-Turnbull*

1928 BENTLEY 6½-litre saloon. Coachwork by Harrison.
National Motor Museum

1930 BENTLEY 4½-litre saloon. Coachwork by
Weymann. *National Motor Museum*

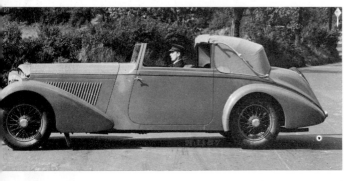

1936 BENTLEY 4¼-litre sedanca coupé.
Coachwork by Hooper. *National Motor Museum*

1968 BENTLEY T Series 6.2-litre 2-door saloon.
Coachwork by H.J. Mulliner, Park Ward.
Rolls-Royce Ltd

the early short, and long chassis which could and sometimes did carry limousine coachwork, and 'Green Label', a special short 100mph type made in very small numbers.

In 1926 the company made a bid for the carriage trade with a big 6½-litre six on similar lines. A chassis cost £1,450, but the Bentley image made no impression in this market. However, the model was developed into the 180bhp 'Speed 6' of 1929, considered by many to be the best of the old-school Bentleys, and responsible for the firm's last two Le Mans wins – Barnato/Clement in 1929, and Barnato/Kidston in 1930. In 1927 the 3-litre was developed into the 4½-litre, still with four cylinders, but with a 100bhp engine which was giving 130bhp by the time production ended. This admirable car could exceed 90mph in standard form, and was used by Barnato and Rubin to win Le Mans in 1928. A supercharged version was listed in 1930; it had 182bhp, and did not have the approval of Bentley himself, but it was an excellent if thirsty road car, and won Sir Henry Birkin an unexpected 2nd place in the *formule libre* French G.P. of 1930. Bentley finances were always shaky, and even Woolf Barnato's aid of 1927 did not last long; the company went down in the early summer of 1931 to the accompaniment of a splendid gesture – a 220bhp ohc 8-litre six, made in two wheelbase lengths, 12ft and 13ft. Only 100 of these were made, plus 50 examples of a rather uninspired inlet over exhaust valve 4-litre car.

Napier made an unsuccessful bid for the assets of the company, but were beaten by Rolls-Royce, who introduced their version of the Bentley at Olympia in 1933. This was an entirely different type, based on Derby's contemporary 3.7-litre ohv push-rod '20–25'. It had a 4-speed synchromesh gearbox, Rolls-Royce servo brakes, and sold for £1,460 with saloon bodywork. In this form, it could reach 90mph and merited its slogan 'The Silent Sports Car'. It was not raced, of course, apart from E.R. Hall's three consecutive second places in the T.T. (1934, 1935 and 1936). By 1936 it had grown into a 4¼-litre, the increase of capacity being necessitated by the rising weight of bespoke coachwork. An overdrive gearbox was standardized in 1939, and the 1940 Mk V had independent front suspension, though only a handful were made because of the war. The Derby car's swansong was a creditable 6th place by H.S.F. Hay at Le Mans in 1949, on a ten-year-old machine with 60,000 road miles behind it. Cylinder capacity was unchanged at 4,257cc in 1946, but ifs was standard, and Bentley, like Rolls-Royce, had gone over to inlet over exhaust valves. Prices rose from £2,997 to £4,474 in 1951 for the standard steel saloon, the first Rolls-royce product to have a regular series-produced factory body.

Thereafter the Rolls-Royce and Bentley identities merged, though in 1952 there was a special 'Continental' version of the latter with fastback 2-door saloon body by H.J. Mulliner which gave 120mph on a 3.077 : 1 top gear. Capacity went up to 4.6 litres in 1952 and 4.9 litres in 1955. Automatic transmissions, already optional, became standard that year; power-assisted steering and air conditioning followed in 1957, and for 1960 the old six at long last gave way to a 6.2-litre V-8 with full overhead valves, by which time only the radiator style distinguished one make from the other. The 'Continental' with separate chassis was discontinued at the end of 1966; 1972 Bentleys were the 6,745cc T saloon and the Corniche 2-door saloon and convertible. Even the price differential between the two sister makes was now a thing of the past, the T series selling for the same £10,455 as the Rolls-Royce Silver Shadow.

MCS

BENZ (D) 1885–1926

(1) Benz & Co, Rheinische Gasmotorenfabrik, Mannheim *1885–1899*
(2) Benz & Cie, Rheinische Gasmotorenfabrik AG, Mannheim *1899–1911*
(3) Benz & Cie, Rheinische Automobil- und Motorenfabrik AG, Mannheim *1911–1926*

Karl Benz is honoured throughout the world as the man who designed and built the first workable motor car driven by an internal combustion engine. It is established that in 1885 his first car was ready and made its first trials. Benz's ideas were concentrated from the beginning on a car as an organic unit of chassis and engine, not on motorization of existing vehicles. The first car was a three-wheeler with two driven rear wheels. The engine was a horizontal single-cylinder with a vertical crankshaft which had a horizontal flywheel. It developed ¾hp and a speed of 8mph is recorded for one of the first trial runs. This prototype Benz car had some features which are still very extensively used in automobile construction: the water-cooled engine, electric ignition, mechanically operated inlet valve, and a differential gear. This first car still exists and belongs to the Deutsches Museum, Munich, to which it was presented by its inventor. Several replicas were built and are now in different museums.

Only a few cars were produced in the following years. At the Munich Exhibition of 1888 Benz had the opportunity of showing his improved car to a wider public. Instead of the wire wheels of the first car the later models had wooden-spoked wheels. Engine output was increased to 2hp. Sales of Benz' stationary gas engines were quite satisfactory, while interest in motor cars was very limited and it was not until 1890 that Benz started a real, if small, 'to order' production. This was partly a result of exhibiting his car at the Paris World Fair in 1889 which led to increasing sales by his French agent Emile Roger, who already sold Benz stationary engines. The other important factor was that Benz was joined by two new partners in 1890. These two men who possibly saved Benz from the fate of numerous other inventors, driven aground by financial difficulties, were Friedrich von Fischer and Julius Ganss. Fischer took over internal administration and Ganss became responsible for sales. Benz himself was free for further developments on the technical side of the business.

ich made sound progress. 1893 saw the production of the first 4-wheeled Benz car, the Victoria. This model was also the basis for the first van and bus in 1895; its technical conception was also adopted for the Velo of 1894. This model has a place in the history of motoring as the world's first production car. Production figures for 1885 to 1893 were 69 cars. 67 cars left the factory in 1894, mainly Velos. These figures increased to 135 cars in 1895 and 181 in 1896.

In 1896 the first Benz Kontra-Motor appeared, an engine with two horizontally opposed cylinders. The first Benz lorry was produced in the same year. In 1898 pneumatic tyres were adopted for the Benz Comfortable. Production in 1899 was 572 cars, which brought Benz into the first rank of car producers. This number was surpassed in the following year with a production of 603 units. The first Benz racing car appeared in 1899 and was the start of numerous racing successes.

After 1901 sales of Benz cars declined as Benz stuck to his now outdated designs. Mercedes' successes led him to evolve new concepts of construction; the result was the 2-cylinder front-engined Parsifal presented in 1903, available with cardan or chain drive and various engine outputs. In the same year a new 4-cylinder engine appeared and was used in all subsequent models. A 1903 racing car developed 60hp and participated in the Paris-Madrid race. Karl Benz himself left the company in 1903 although he rejoined shortly afterwards. In 1906 he joined his sons in the firm of C. Benz Söhne. 1906 saw Benz gaining a second place in the Herkomer Trial while in the same event in 1907 a 5hp Benz finished first. Second and third place in the Coppa Florio, 1907, first place in the Florida 100-Miles Race, 1908, second and third place in the French Grand Prix, 1908, and second and fourth place in the American Grand Prix, 1908, led to the world records which were set with 150 and 200hp Benz cars by Bruce-Brown, Robertson, Oldfield and Hémery. With the 200hp Blitzen Benz Hörner covered a mile in 25.4 seconds from a flying start at Daytona Beach in 1911. This was a speed of 140.8mph, but was not recognized internationally as a Land Speed Record.

In 1910 Benz acquired the Süddeutsche Automobil-Fabrik of Gaggenau (see Gaggenau and Liliput). Production of private cars in this factory was given up and in the following years Benz concentrated on commercial vehicles there.

A wide range of cars was marketed in the 1910–1914 period, ranging from the 2-litre 8/20PS up to really big machines like the 10.1-litre 39/100PS, all with side valve engines and shaft drive. However, the 22-litre 200hp (which cost £1,800 in England in 1912, and must have been the largest-engined private car to go on the market) had ohv and final drive by side chains. Benz were successful in the Austrian Alpine Trials, the Tatra-Adria Trial and various trials in Russia, to name only a few. The great promoter of German motoring, Prince Henry of Prussia, used only Benz cars.

The first Benz 6-cylinder car was produced in 1914 with the type 25/65PS 6.5 litre. In 1918 the 6/18PS 4-cylinder 1540cc appeared, a type developed during the war. A very important Benz development was the precombustion chamber diesel engine. It was first used in 1922 for Benz Sendling agricultural tractors, and the first diesel-engined lorry by Benz appeared in 1924. These were steps towards later Mercedes-Benz diesel-engined cars. Another idea introduced by Benz which also appeared in later Mercedes-Benz cars was the swing axle. It was one feature of the 2-litre 6-cylinder Benz 'teardrop' racing car designed on Rumpler principles. However, this car was not a great success either in its racing or in its sports version. In the Grand Prix of Italy in 1923 they gained fourth and fifth place. In 1924 Benz and Mercedes began to combine their interests, amalgamating in 1926. For further models see Mercedes-Benz.   HON

BENZ SÖHNE (D) 1906–1926
C. Benz Söhne, Ladenburg/Neckar

When Karl Benz left the firm he had founded he built a new factory together with his sons Eugen and Richard. Until 1908 only a few cars were produced. Their 4-cylinder 10/22PS 2,608cc model became quite popular, and a 14/42PS 3,565cc model was built until 1920. Experiments were made in 1913 with Henriod engines, but they were not successful and production was not started. Car production was carried on until 1926, with the 8/25PS model as the last type.   HON

BÉRARD (F) 1900–1901
Bérard et Cie, Marseilles

Bérard was an engineer who made about 20 cars with 2-cylinder engines of his own design.   GNG

BERG (US) 1902–1905
(1) Berg Automobile Co, Cleveland, Ohio 1902–1904
(2) Worthington Automobile Co, New York, N.Y. 1905

The original Berg car was made for the Berg company by the Cleveland Machine Screw Co. It had a 4-litre 4-cylinder engine said to develop 15 to 20hp, a sloping gilled tube radiator and double chain drive. The 1903 model was basically similar, but for 1904 the company introduced a smaller car with 3.2-litre 15/18hp engine, vertical honeycomb radiator and shaft drive. The following year they merged with the Worthington Automobile Co of New York, who were also concerned with the Worthington-Bollée and Meteor (iv) cars. The larger, chain driven car was still made, now of 24hp.   GNG

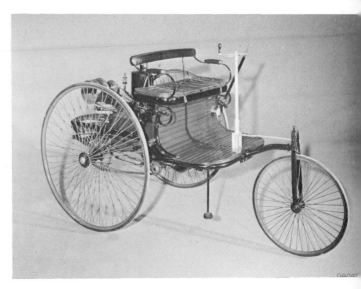

1885 BENZ 0.9PS 3-wheeler. *Daimler-Benz AG*

1903 BENZ Parsifal 10/12PS tonneau.
Daimler-Benz AG

1912 BENZ 25/55PS limousine. *Daimler-Benz AG*

1910 BERGDOLL 30hp tourer. *Kenneth Stauffer*

1959 BERKELEY 692cc sports car. *National Motor Museum*

1911 BERKSHIRE Model E roadster. *G. Marshall Naul*

1906 BERLIET 60hp roadster. *The Veteran Car Club of Great Britain*

BERGANTIN (RA) 1960–1962
Industrias Kaiser Argentina, Santa Isabel
This was an interesting combination of the Alfa Romeo 1900 sedan body and Willys Jeep engine, made for several years prior to IKA Rambler manufacture.

BERGDOLL (US) 1908–1913
Louis J. Bergdoll Motor Co, Philadelphia, Pa.
The Bergdoll Thirty was the model produced during most of the lifetime of t make. In 1911, five different models of 4-cylinder cars were available, from a touri car at $1,500 to a limousine at $2,500. This was one of the outstanding makes of t period from the standpoint of quality.　GM

BERGÉ (F) 1923
M. Caillat, Pré St Gervais, Seine
The Bergé was a conventional light car powered by a 7/10 or 10/12CV Fiv engine, or a 12CV Janvier. Body styles were open two-, three- or four-seaters, a a sporting model had a pointed tail. Wire or disc wheels were available.　G

BERGER (D) 1901–1902
Chemnitzer Motorwagen-Fabrik Bruno Berger & Co, Chemnitz
Cars built on Benz principles which were of only minor importance.　HC

BERGMANN see LILIPUT *and* ORIENT EXPRESS

BERGMANN; BERGMANN-MÉTALLURGIQUE (D) 1907–1922
Bergmann Elektrizitätswerke AG, Berlin-Reinickendorf-Rosenthal; Berli Halensee
The Bergmann Electric concern started production of both private and co mercial electric vehicles in 1907. After 1908 they were also sold under the name Fulgura. In 1908 their first petrol-driven car was produced. Of greater importan was the production of Métallurgique cars under licence from 1909. They we marketed as 'Bergmann-Métallurgique'. In the first years many original Méta lurgique components were used and the bodies were by Vanden Plas; later mode used German components, including the bodies.
After World War 1 2.6-litre 4-cylinder cars were marketed under the name Bergmann only untiil production of private petrol-driven cars ceased in 192 Until World War 2, Bergmann specialized in electric vans which were extensive used by the German Post Office.　HC

BERKELEY (GB) 1956–1961
Berkeley Cars Ltd, Biggleswade, Beds.
A Laurie Bond design, made by a firm of caravan manufacturers, its fro wheels were chain-driven in the manner of the Bond (ii) of 1948. The hull w a 3-piece affair of fibreglass, and the car was independently sprung all roun with swing axles at the rear. Engine and gearbox were of motor cycle type, pow units used being the 322cc British Anzani and 328cc Excelsior 2-stroke twin the 492cc 2-stroke 3-cylinder Excelsior, and the 692cc 4-stroke Royal Enfield. T most highly tuned version of the 692cc Berkeley was good for 90mph. A 328 3-wheeler version was also made, but the cars never really caught on, and a mo conventional design using the 997cc 4-cylinder Dagenham Ford 105E engine cam too late to save the venture.　M

BERKSHIRE (US) 1905–1913
(1) Berkshire Automobile Co, Pittsfield, Mass. *1905–1908*
(2) Berkshire Motor Car Co, Pittsfield, Mass. *1908–1909*
(3) Berkshire Auto-Car Co, Pittsfield, Mass. *1909–1912*
(4) Berkshire Motors Co, Cambridge, Mass. *1912*
(5) Belcher Engineering Co, Cambridge, Mass. *1912–1913*
The pilot model of this make was built as early as 1903. 4-cylinder Herschel Spillman engines were fitted in 1905 and 1906 Berkshires; later the company bui their own 35hp 4-cylinder units of 6.2 litres capacity. An early patented transmissio designed to prevent stripping was not successful. In the period 1907–9 a fe rakish speedsters were built.
After the Berkshire Motors Company was sold, Belcher Engineering bought u all spare parts and assembled three more Berkshires from these, bringing tot production of this make to an estimated 150 cars.　GM

BERLIET (F) 1895–1939
Automobiles M. Berliet, Lyons
Marius Berliet started modestly in 1895 in a small workshop, his first car having rear-mounted horizontal engines (easily removable as complete units 4-speed gearboxes, and left-hand drive with wheel steering. Even in 1899 annu output was only six cars. 1.2-litre horizontal-twin engines were being used 1900. The following year Berliet took over the firm of Audibert-Lavirotte, M Lavirotte continuing as commercial director. 2- and 4-cylinder cars with fror vertical aiv engines, side chain drive, and armoured wood frames were made, th 4-cylinder design being adopted by T.C. Pullinger as the basis for the 12h

unbeam made at Wolverhampton. 1902 brought the emergence of a new type of ~~B~~erliet on Mercedes lines, with mechanically-operated inlet valves, honeycomb ~~r~~diator, and pressed-steel frame, and this theme was pursued for several years. ~~Q~~uite big cars were produced, among them an 8.6-litre 60 and 80hp of over 11 ~~lit~~res' capacity, and some models had overhead inlet valves in place of the more ~~u~~sual T-head configuration. In 1906 Bablot's Berliet took 2nd place in the Tourist ~~T~~rophy, and the American Locomotive Company started to built Berliets under ~~li~~cence under the name of Alco – hence the locomotive emblem introduced in 1909, ~~a~~nd still found on present-day Berliet trucks.

The smallest model listed in 1907 was a 2.4-litre 14, but new that year were ~~a~~ 4-cylinder shaft-driven taxicab chassis and a 60hp 6-cylinder on accepted lines. ~~1~~908 saw an odd Berliet-Mixte, also a six with compressed-air starting and trans~~m~~ission, and shaft drive was now optional on both the 14 and the 3.8-litre 22. ~~T~~he big 60 in 4-cylinder guise had overhead valves. The 4-cylinder T.T. cars had ~~p~~ressure lubrication, which was catalogued in 1909, along with three small L-head ~~m~~odels, an 8hp twin and two small fours of 1½ litres' and 2.4 litres' capacity. ~~6~~-cylinder Berliets had conventional gearboxes once more, and in 1911 the 6.3-litre ~~6~~-cylinder model was catalogued with shaft drive at £795. Shaft drive, thermo~~s~~yphon cooling, and 4-speed gearboxes were universal in 1911, when a new L-head ~~2~~.4-litre 20/25 made its appearance, and in 1912 both this and the 15hp car could ~~b~~e had with either monobloc or pair-cast cylinders. The 6-cylinder cars were ~~a~~vailable only to special order, and by 1914 only monobloc fours were listed. The ~~r~~ange consisted of the 1½-litre 12, the 2.4-litre 15, the 3.6-litre 18, the 25, and ~~t~~he big 6.3-litre 40 (types U and R). De luxe models of the two latter types came ~~w~~ith electric lighting and starting as standard.

If the 1914 cars were conventional, their post-war equivalents were dull, ~~a~~nd the new 3.3-litre Type VB followed American lines, with sv 4-cylinder engine ~~i~~n unit 3-speed gearbox, fixed disc wheels, and detachable rims. It sold in ~~E~~ngland for £755, and was followed by a very similar 2.6-litre 12CV car. Front ~~w~~heel brakes were available in 1923, and the sv cars were still being made ~~i~~n 1925, though 1924 produced two new models with ohv engines, front-wheel ~~b~~rakes, 4-speed gearboxes, and detachable wire wheels: the 1.2-litre 10/20, ~~a~~nd the big 23/70hp 4-litre Type VIG. The company also experimented with ~~c~~ross-country cars, and with Imbert gas-producer plants, a line of development ~~w~~hich was pursued until 1938. A 2½-litre ohv car with central change appeared ~~i~~n 1925, and in 1927 there came a small six, the 14/40hp of 1.8 litres' capacity; ~~t~~his had side valves, pump cooling, a 4-bearing crankshaft, coil ignition, single~~p~~late clutch, 3-speed gearbox and wooden wheels; there were also a bigger 4.1-litre ~~6~~-cylinder and a straightforward sv 4-cylinder 1½-litre, rated at 12/25hp. The 14/40 ~~g~~rew up into a 2-litre in 1929, but no 6-cylinder cars were made after 1932; there ~~w~~as, however, a large sv 3.3-litre 4-cylinder.

In 1933 came the Type 944, a more advanced design with X-braced frame, ~~4~~-speed silent 3rd gearbox, and a choice of cylinder capacities (1.6 litres and ~~2~~ litres). De luxe versions had transverse independent front suspension. A saloon ~~c~~ost 24,900fr, and both ohv and sv versions were available, though only the ~~f~~ormer type was listed by 1936. Last of the line was the 2-litre Dauphine with ~~i~~ndependent front suspension, rack-and-pinion steering, and synchromesh; towards ~~t~~he end it used the same saloon body as Peugeot's 402. Private car production was ~~n~~ot resumed after World War 2, though Berliet acquired another Lyons firm, Rochet-~~S~~chneider, and in 1964 they announced the appointment of Alvis Ltd as United ~~K~~ingdom concessionaires for their all-wheel-drive military vehicles. The company ~~c~~ame under Citroën ownership in July, 1967.   MCS

BERNA (CH) *1902–1907*
(1) Joseph Wyss, Berne *1902–1904*
(2) J. Wyss, Schweizer Automobilfabrik Berna, Olten *1904–1906*
(3) Motorwerke Berna AG, Olten *1906–1907*

The first Berna cars used a 5½hp vertical single-cylinder engine mounted at the ~~r~~ear, a 2-speed gearbox, and De Dion rear axle. They had light *vis-à-vis* bodies. ~~I~~n 1903 an 8hp front-mounted engine was used, and in 1904 a few examples of the ~~U~~nicum model with a 5hp unit were made. A range of 2 ton lorries was introduced ~~i~~n 1905, and private cars were neglected for two years. 1907 saw a brief return ~~t~~o cars, with a modern design of 4-cylinder monobloc engine and shaft drive. ~~H~~owever, only six of these were made, after which Berna concentrated on com~~m~~ercial vehicles, which they still manufacture today.   GNG

BERNARDET (F) *1946–1950*
Automobiles Bernardet, Châtillon-sous-Bagneux, Seine

The Bernardet was one of many light cars to appear in France after World ~~W~~ar 2. It used a 4-cylinder 4-stroke engine originally of oversquare dimensions ~~(~~64 × 62mm) giving 800cc, increased in 1947 to 848cc (60 × 75mm). In 1949 a ~~7~~50cc air-cooled 2-stroke engine was adopted. This engine was mounted transversely ~~a~~nd drove the front wheels in the manner of B.M.C. Minis. Convertible and saloon ~~b~~odies were made.   GNG

BERNARDI (I) *1899–1901*
Società Italiana Bernardi, Padua

1923 BERLIET Type VL 16CV tourer.
Automobiles M. Berliet

1932 BERLIET 9CV coupé. *Lucien Loreille Collection*

1902 BERNA Ideal 785cc *vis-à-vis. Swiss Museum of Transport & Communications, Lucerne*

1947 BERNARDET 5CV 800cc two-seater. *Lucien Loreille Collection*

1924 BEVERLEY-BARNES 24/80 convertible saloon. Coachwork by James Young. *C.E. Noel-Storr*

1900 B.G.S. electric car. Holder of electric long distance record (262km). *Autocar*

1916 BIANCHI 42/70hp sporting tourer. *Autocar*

Successors to Miari e Giusti (which see), this company made light 3- and 4-wheelers to Enrico Bernardi's designs. Cars of 2½hp, 4½hp, and 6hp were listed, but the concern was wound up in June 1901. MC

BERRET (F) 1899–1903
Sté Cannoise d'Automobiles, Cannes, Alpes-Maritimes
Berret's prototype 3-cylinder car was built in 1895, and between 1899 and 1903 he produced a further seven cars, all with 3-cylinder engines. GN

BERSEY (GB) 1895–1899
W.C. Bersey, London
Although he made an electric omnibus as early as 1888, W.C. Bersey's first cars were not made until 1895. They featured twin motors, a 2-speed gear with clutch, chain final drive, and steering by a small wheel mounted in a fore-and-aft plane. With Arthur Mulliner bodies in horse-carriage style, the cars were capable of 9mph. Two Berseys took part in the Emancipation Run of 1896, though whether they ran the whole way from London to Brighton under their own power is problematic. From 1897 to 1899 Bersey operated a number of electric cabs in London; they were not a success, although the Prince of Wales rode in one from Marlborough House to Buckingham Palace and back in November 1897. After the end of manufacture Bersey turned to the sale of imported cars, while the Compagnie Générale de Voitures à Paris took out a licence for the manufacture of Bersey vehicles in France, and made, or imported, a quantity of this type. MC

BERTA (RA) 1967 to date
Oreste Berta SA, Córdoba
Oreste Berta began in business modifying Renault engines for national racing and this work continues today. He built his first prototype sports car in 1967, a space-frame design using the home-produced 4-litre Tornado 6-cylinder engine. Early in 1970 a Formula 1 Cosworth-Ford DFV V-8 engine was acquired to fit a new Berta space-frame, and this raced in Europe during the season. Tornado-powered variants have been sold to Argentine entrants, and Berta has developed his own V-8 based loosely on the Cosworth engine. The company has also built single-seater cars. DCF

BERTHIER see LA BUIRE

BERTOLDO see MARCA

BERTOLET (US) 1908–1912
(1) Dr J.M. Bertolet, Reading, Pa. 1908–1909
(2) Bertolet Motor Car Co, Reading, Pa. 1909–1912
The original Bertolet was available with interchangeable bodies, one a two-seater roadster, the other a five-seater touring type. Both bodies, with chassis, cost $2,400. Later models were rated at 40hp and had conventional water-cooled 4-cylinder engines. CMN

BERTRAND (F) 1901–1902
Bertrand et Cie, Paris
Two voiturette models were offered by the Bertrand company, with 4½hp De Dion-Bouton or 6hp Aster engines. Final drive was by single chain, and two- and four-seater bodies were available. In July 1901 a 6hp Bertrand won its class in the Moscow-St Petersburg Trial. GNG

BERWICK (US) 1904
Berwick Auto Car Co, Grand Rapids, Mich.
The Berwick was a two-seater electric runabout for which its manufacturers did not claim more than 15mph. It had three speed positions, was tiller-operated and had an abundance of brasswork, all for $750. GMN

BESST (AUS) 1926–1927
May's Motor Works, Adelaide, S.A.
The Besst was a conventional assembled touring car powered by a 19.6hp 4-cylinder Continental engine. Only five were made, of which one survives today. GNG

BEST (i) (US) 1899
Best Mfg Co, San Leandro, Calif.
The Best company were primarily known for their vast steam traction engines, but in 1899 they built a prototype seven-passenger car with 7hp horizontally-opposed 2-cylinder engine, friction clutch transmission and chain drive. MJWW

BEST (ii) (F) 1921
Built at Courbevoie, Seine, the Best was a conventional touring car powered by a 4-cylinder 2-litre Janvier engine. GNG

BEVERLEY-BARNES (GB) 1924–1931
(1) Lenaerts & Dolphens, Barnes, London S.W.13 1924–1928
(2) Beverley Works Ltd, Barnes, London S.W.13 1928–1931

Lenaerts & Dolphens made components for other manufacturers before going
to car production themselves. They should, perhaps, have stuck to their last,
for the Beverley-Barnes (made in the Beverley works at Barnes) was not a very
good car, though an ambitious one. It was always a straight-8 – a novelty in 1924
at the beginning of its career – with initially a single overhead camshaft, and
a luxury chassis designed to sell at a lower price than those of competitors. In
fact, their 1924, 4-litre, 24/80hp model, though intended to sell at £750, cost £1,150
in chassis form. The bodies offered were always handsome and of good quality,
but the chassis were not of the same standard. The engines which grew to 5 litres
and then shrank to 2½ litres, were rough, noisy and unreliable, and the brakes were
poor. This is surprising in view of the maker's Belgian affiliations – reflected in the
fact that early models had Vanden Plas bodies – which in theory should have
guaranteed the best workmanship. The last cars had twin ohc units, also fitted in
the Burney Streamline. In 1931 the company was assembling Invictas under
sub-contract. Total production did not exceed 15 cars.   TRN

BEVERLY *see* UPTON

B.F. (D) *1922–1926*
Bolle-Fiedler Automobilwerk GmbH, Berlin-Charlottenberg
A 3-cylinder 2-stroke engine of 1,026cc was used for this car. B.F. cars parti-
cipated successfully in various national race events.   HON

B.G.S. (F) *1899–1906*
Sté de la voiture Bouquet, Garcin et Schivre, Neuilly, Seine
The B.G.S. concern made a wide range of electric vehicles including dogcarts,
phaetons and family buses as well as commercial vehicles. Their most powerful
machines had a range of nearly 180 miles per charge, and one competed in the
Paris-Ostend race of 1899. The company was somewhat unusual in making their
own accumulators, and they also made some vehicles for sale by other firms such
as Créanche. From about 1904 they were generally known as Garcin or Garcin-
Renault. These had front-mounted motors, shaft drive and the appearance of
petrol engined cars.   GNG

BIANCHI; AUTOBIANCHI (I) *1899–1939; 1957 to date*
(i) Edoardo Bianchi, Milan *1899–1905*
(ii) Fabbrica Automobili e Velocipedi Edoardo Bianchi, Milan *1905–1939*
(iii) Autobianchi SpA, Milan *1957–1968*
(iv) Fiat SpA (Sezione Autobianchi), Milan *1968 to date*
Edoardo Bianchi was a cycle manufacturer who graduated to cars via the inevitable motor tricycle, his earliest efforts being in the De Dion-Bouton idiom with
single-cylinder De Dion engines and tubular frame. A 942cc unit featured in his
1903 models, but serious manufacture dates from the company reorganization of
1905. Inevitably large and expensive machines in the classical Italian idiom were
produced, with 4-cylinder engines (Bianchi never made a six, apart from a few staff
cars built for the Italian army in the late 1930s), side valves in a T-head, lt magneto
ignition, multi-disc clutches, 4-speed gearboxes and side-chain drive. Capacities of
the first types were 4½ litres and 7.4 litres respectively. However, the company's
bid for honours in the 1907 Kaiserpreis led to some more sporting models, such
as the enormous 11.4-litre 70hp E-type with ht ignition, standardized on the smaller
Bianchis by 1908; they were also available with shaft drive. New for 1908 was
a modern L-head monobloc four; initially this Tipo G had three forward speeds,
the extra ratio being added in 1910, when Bianchi delivered 450 cars. Further
monobloc fours followed, with 2.1-litre and 4.4-litre engines, though alongside these
was a traditional chain-driven sports model, the ohv 8-litre 60/75hp that survived
until 1915. A remarkable development for an Italian manufacturer was the Tipo
E of 1914, an inexpensive 1,244cc 3-speed affair available in only one body style
and one colour. Electrics were an optional extra, but were standard on Bianchi's
wartime newcomer, the orthodox 3.3-litre B type of 1915. The S was enlarged
to 1,460cc in 1916, but disappeared shortly after the end of World War 1 in favour
of a one-model policy based on the 1,693cc Tipo 12.
Vintage Bianchis typified the more conservative strain in Italian design, with
little sporting flavour, if an abortive contender for the 2-litre GP formula laid down
in 1922 is excepted. Its dohc 4-cylinder engine had dual magneto ignition and 90bhp
was claimed. By 1923 Tipo 12 had given way to Tipo 16 with detachable cylinder
head, and at the same time the company marketed the 2-litre pushrod Tipo 18,
a stolid family machine popular with British specialist coachbuilders of the period.
Four-wheel brakes arrived in 1924 on the 2.3-litre Tipo 20 with 59bhp engine:
so did the Rolls-Royce style of radiator, used by the firm until 1931. In 1925
came Bianchi's answer to the Fiat 509, the 1.3-litre ohv S4 with four-wheel brakes
and 4-speed gearbox; this sold steadily for nine years, acquiring coil ignition in
its S5 version (1928), and growing up to 1,452cc and 40bhp in 1932. Less fortunate
was a medium-sized luxury straight-8 unveiled in 1928; initially of 2.7 litres' capacity, it was enlarged to 2.9 litres in 1930. Wheelbase was 10ft 10in and features
of the pushrod engine were mechanical pump feed and dry-sump lubrication; a
short-wheelbase sports version, the S8bis of 1933, was said to do 85mph.
In 1934 Bianchi reverted to a one-model programme with the S9, a pretty little

1933 BIANCHI S8bis 2.9-litre sports saloon.
Lucien Loreille Collection

1965 BIANCHINA 500cc cabriolet. *Autobianchi SA*

1971 AUTOBIANCHI A112 900cc saloon.
SA André Citroën

1918 BIDDLE Model K 7-litre roadster.
Autosport

1920 BIGNAN 17CV 3½-litre sports car. *Autocar*

1½-litre sports saloon with 5-bearing crankshaft. Brakes were still mechanical, b[
by 1936 this successor to the S5 had acquired hydraulics and synchromesh, thou[
unusually for a cheap Italian car it rode on beam axles all round and wore Rud[
type wire wheels. A six/seven-seater long-wheelbase version did duty as a taxica[
in Italy. Production was on a modest scale and had petered out (in favour [
trucks and motorcycles) by the time Italy entered World War 2 in 1940.

These engaged Bianchi's attention in the immediate post-war years, a project[
S9 replacement only reaching the prototype stage in 1950. The revival of private-c[
production resulted from an infusion of Fiat and Pirelli capital in 1955, and wh[
the Autobianchi Bianchina appeared at the 1957 Turin Show it was revealed [
a de luxe rolltop convertible edition of Fiat's new 2-cylinder air-cooled 500. B[
1963 quite a wide range of bodies was available on the Bianchina chassis, b[
Fiat were now in sole command, and henceforward Autobianchi's role was to [
that of a forcing house for new Fiat ideas.

A sports convertible development of the 600, the Stellina of 1964, made litt[
impression, but the Primula introduced later that year anticipated Fiat's own 12[
with its transversely mounted 1,221cc 1100D engine driving the front wheels. Oth[
features were cooling assisted by an electric fan and all-disc brakes. A 1,352[
sports coupé followed in 1965, and Fiat 124 engines were standardized on 19[
models. In March 1968 the company was finally integrated into Fiat, and thou[
a rear-engined sports coupé of OSI design got no further than the Turin Sho[
the way was paved for the Fiat 127 in 1969 with the A112, a boxy little fw[
saloon using the 903cc 850 coupé engine. Autobianchi also took over the produ[
tion of Fiat 500 station wagons, which henceforward assumed their name. In 197[
130,000 cars were made, four times as many as in 1964. The original Bianchin[
were phased out, though in their place came an extension of the basic fwd them[
the A111 on 128 lines, but with 1,438cc pushrod engine. New for 1972 was [
'Abarthized' A112 with 58bhp, 982cc engine. MC[

BI-AUTOGO see SCRIPPS-BOOTH

BIDDLE (US) 1915–1923
Biddle Motor Car Co, Philadelphia, Pa.

A small luxury car, the Biddle featured exquisite coachwork and a wide variet[
of body variations with an optional choice of either Duesenberg horizontal valv[
or Buda 4-cylinder engines. Biddle cars were never common, and few were bui[
after 1921. Their design embodied a V-type radiator. K[

BIELKA A-50 'Squirrel' (SU) 1956
IMZ-NAMI, Motor Cycle Works, Sverdlovsk

Displayed in two styles, a sedan and a utility vehicle, this small car never g[
much beyond the prototype stage. Planned by the Automobile and Motor Scientifi[
Institute (NAMI) in Moscow, it was to have been manufactured in Sverdlovsk. I[
sedan form it was driven by a 2-cylinder, 4-stroke engine giving 22hp at 5,000rpm[
B[

BIENE (D) 1923
M.F.C. Zimmermann, Berlin, W 30

A friction-driven cyclecar using a B.M.W. 2-cylinder proprietary engine. HO[

BIFORT (GB) 1914–1915
Bifort Motor Co, Fareham, Hampshire

The Bifort light car used a 10½hp engine imported from Brussels, and a chassi[
from Maubeuge. Bodies, however, were English and were made at the works. The[
could be thought of as the first Duple bodies, as Mr White of Bifort afterward[
formed Duple Motor Bodies Ltd of Hendon. Biforts were said to be popular wit[
Royal Navy officers, but the company was killed by World War 1 before man[
cars had been made. GN[

BIGNAN (F) 1918–1930
Automobiles Bignan, Courbevoie, Seine

Jacques Bignan's products were a mixture of sophisticated competition machi[
nery with Causan-designed engines, and pedestrian assembled vehicles aimed a[
customers who wanted a famous radiator without a high purchase price or mechani[
cal complication. His original 17CV was a big and orthodox fast tourer mad[
in the Grégoire (i) works. It used a de la Fournaise chassis frame, a 2-bearin[
3½-litre sv 4-cylinder engine, and rear-wheel brakes only; by 1921 a 50bhp 3-litr[
unit had been adopted. It was marketed in England as the Grégoire-Campbell an[
persisted until 1923. Already, however, Bignan was racing, entering a 1,400cc T[
head four he had designed in 1914 in the 1920 G.P. des Voiturettes; the car[
finished 2nd and 3rd. For 1921 he built (but did not market) a Causan-designe[
96bhp 16-valve 3-litre ohc four that Guyot used to win the Corsican G.P.

A year later came the 75×112mm 2-litre, the company's mainstay for the[
rest of its life. Standard 11CV touring versions had orthodox 50bhp sohc engine[
4-speed gearboxes, and Hallot servo brakes on the front wheels only, in th[
Chenard-Walcker style. However, the first competition versions wore streamline[
four-seater bodies and their *desmodromique* engines developed 70bhp. This mode[
was catalogued, but a 3rd in the Belgian G.P. was its best showing, and by 192[

positively closed valves had given way to more orthodox, and more powerful -valve units. These cars were also more successful, with victories in the 1923 d 1924 Spanish Touring Car Grands Prix, and the 1924 Belgian 24 Hours, com- nsating for the failure of a promising 124bhp dohc six tried in the latter year. eanwhile lesser Bignans had made their appearance. The 10CV started in 1921 ith a 1,600cc sv Ballot unit, later acquiring a 1.7-litre ohc S.C.A.P. The 1.2-litre CV, also S.C.A.P-powered, was an E.H.P. with Bignan radiator. Even less original as the small 1,100cc sports car, which was an AL23 Salmson with the St ndrews' Cross removed from the radiator, though later a Bignan one was substi- ted. Meanwhile a touring 2-litre had won the 1924 Monte Carlo Rally, and in 926 the car was redesigned with an 8-valve engine incorporating twin oil pumps. his gave 60bhp and was offered on 10ft and 11ft wheelbases, rendering it suitable r elegant closed coachwork. The cars continued to race, lowered chassis, super- argers and tank bodies featuring on later competition versions, but a 3rd place the 1927 Spanish Touring Car G.P. was in fact their last effort. Jacques Bignan imself won the 1928 Monte Carlo Rally, but he did so in a Fiat. The last Bignans ere the 11CV 2-litre and a pair of S.C.A.P.-engined pushrod straight-8s with capa- ties of 1.8 and 2.3 litres. These had acquired 4-speed gearboxes by 1929.   MCS

1924 BIGNAN 11CV 2-litre saloon. *Autocar*

IJOU (GB) *1901–1904*
rotector Lamp & Lighting Co Ltd, Eccles, Manchester
The Bijou had a 5hp single-cylinder horizontal engine and a 2-speed gear change perated by internally expanding clutches; two clutch pedals were required, one for ach speed, and there was no reverse. The engine could be started by a handle om the driver's seat.   GNG

IJ 'T VUUR (NL) *1902–1905*
. Bij 't Vuur, Arnhem
The Bij 't Vuur car used a 6½hp 2-cylinder Aster engine, and had a four-seater onneau body with De Dion-Bouton type bonnet and radiator. Later cars had 9 nd 12hp 2-cylinder engines, and Mr C. Bij 't Vuur planned to make his own -cylinder engine. However, an ill-advised venture into the manufacture of buses he made only three) led to bankruptcy.   GNG

ILLARD (F) *1922–1925*
. Billard, Villeneuve-le-Guyard, Yonne
Billard cyclecars were very small machines, one with a 2½hp engine and single- eater body, the other a 4hp two-seater.   GNG

ILLIKEN (US) *1914*
Milwaukee Cycle Car Co, Milwaukee, Wisc.
The single model of this cyclecar was a two-seater with side-by-side arrangement. t was driven by a water-cooled 4-cylinder engine of 1.6 litres. It had an epicyclic earbox and shaft drive. The track was 4ft and the wheelbase 8ft.   GMN

ILLINGS (GB) *1900*
.D. Billings, Coventry, Warwickshire
Billings's voiturette had a 2¼hp De Dion engine mounted at the front of the ar out in the open, with no bonnet. Shaft drive and tiller steering were used, nd the body was a light open two-seater. The car was sometimes known as the urns, as it was to have been sold by J. Burns in London.   GNG

IMEL *see* ELCO

INGHAM *see* AUTOLETTE

INNEY-BURNHAM (US) *1901–1902*
inney & Burnham, Boston, Mass.
This was a steam car available in two- and four-seater versions, the latter with orward-facing, folding front seat, the driver being at the rear. The engine had two cylinders, and steam was supplied at a pressure of 150psi.   GNG

1969 BIOTA Mark 1 sports car.
Houghton Caldwell Ltd

BIOTA (GB) *1968 to date*
1) Houghton Coldwell Ltd, Thurcroft, Yorks. *1968–1970*
2) Biota Products Ltd, Dinnington, Yorks. *1970 to date*
Advertised as the Mini Sportscar Extraordinary, the Mark I Biota was designed rimarily as a road-going car utilizing B.M.C. Mini parts. The body was an unstressed fibreglass open two-seater, the chassis a triangulated tubular space-frame. The car, characteristically, was available as a complete kit priced at £650, or as body/chassis only. Some 25 were sold. The Mark II for 1973 was planned as a GT coupé, based like its predecessor on prototypes proven in competition, in this case a hill-climb special very successful during the 1972 season.   DF

BIRCH (US) *1917–1923*
Birch Motor Cars Inc, Chicago, Ill.
The Birch was a car which was sold exclusively by mail order, largely through magazine advertisements. Both 4- and 6-cylinder models were available with

1922 BIRMINGHAM 6-cylinder tourer.
Automotive History Collection, Detroit Public Library

1925 BISHOP 22.4hp trials car.
M. Worthington-Williams

1966 BIZZARRINI 5300 GT 5.3-litre coupé. *Aldo Zucchi*

1918 BJERRING V-4 cyclecar. *Norsk Tecnisk Museum, Oslo*

Herschell-Spillman, Lycoming and Le Roi engines of various ratings. Both open and closed body styles were available. K

BIRMINGHAM (US) 1921–1922
Birmingham No-Axle Motor Corp, Jamestown, N.Y.

The Birmingham car featured independent suspension by transverse semi-elliptic springs, while the fabric-covered bodies were a departure from normal American practices. A Continental 6-cylinder motor supplied power. About 20 cars were built, the first few being made in Detroit. Plans were laid to produce the design in Canada under the name of Parker. KM

BISCUTER (E) 1951–1958
Autonacional SA, Barcelona

Designed by Gabriel Voisin, the Biscuter was the most popular Spanish-built car during the great car shortage in Spain during the early 1950s. It used a 197cc single-cylinder Hispano-Villiers 2-stroke engine driving the front wheels, and the body was a very simple open two-seater. In 1956 a fibreglass sports coupé inspired by Pegaso designs was introduced, but was not a great success. About 5,000 Biscuters were made before growing prosperity reduced the demand for this type of car. JR

BISHOP (GB) c.1925
Bishop's Garages (Brighton) Ltd, Brighton, Sussex

The Bishop was an early example of a trials special, of which about five were built. They were based on the Model T Ford, but had underslung suspension, White-head fwb and ohv engines. The body was a two-seater with flared wings and a radiator reminiscent of the contemporary A.C. MJWW

BIZZARRINI (I) 1965–1969
Prototipi Bizzarrini Srl, Livorno

This company was established in 1962, but until 1965 it was engaged on prototype work, Bizzarrini being responsible for the design of Iso's A3C Grifo GT coupé. When he severed his connection with the Bresso firm, the GT Strada 5300 was produced, which followed closely the lines of the Iso with a 365bhp, 5,354cc V-8 Chevrolet engine, 4-speed all-synchromesh gearbox, 4-wheel servo-assisted disc brakes, and De Dion back axle. Over 160mph was claimed. 1966 saw a smaller Bizzarrini based on the Fiat 1500: this had all-round independent suspension, front disc brakes, and fibreglass bodywork, and had grown up a year later into the 1,900cc, 128mph 'GT Europa'. MCS

BJERING (N) 1918–1920
(1) H.C. Bjering, Gjøvik
(2) A/S Raufoss Ammunisjonsfabrikker, Raufoss

H.C. Bjering's cars were specially designed for narrow country roads and employed tandem seating, with the driver in the rear. The first five cars had wooden bodies and an air-cooled V-4 engine mounted between the seats. These cars were used by the country police, the arrested man being placed in the front seat where the policeman driving could keep an eye on him. Later Bjerings, of which not more than two were made, had metal bodies and an in-line 4-cylinder engine mounted at the rear of the car, behind the back wheels. OB

BLACK (US) 1903–1909
Black Mfg Co, Chicago, Ill.

The Black company made mainly high wheelers powered by 10hp 2-cylinder air-cooled engines, and using chain drive and solid rubber tyres. In 1909 they sold a number of the 4-cylinder cars made by the Crow Motor Car Company under the name Black Crow. GMN

BLACKBURN (GB) 1919–1925
Blackburn Aeroplane & Motor Co Ltd, Leeds, Yorks.

This famous Yorkshire aircraft firm, like so many others, ventured into motor manufacture after World War 1, when war-time contracts ended and the aircraft market virtually disappeared. Rather surprisingly, however, they produced a very conservative car when other aircraft manufacturers were adapting aviation experience to the road. The engine of the Blackburn was a big 4-cylinder Coventry Simplex of 3,160cc, its cylinders cast in pairs, although a monobloc was introduced for 1922, the gearbox separate. A cone clutch was used. The radiator was a copy of that of the Rolls-Royce, a common practice at the time. Like other aircraft manufacturers, Blackburn also made bodies for other car makers. TRN

BLACK DIAMOND see BUCKMOBILE

BLACKHAWK (US) 1902–1903
Clark Manufacturing Co, Moline, Ill.

The Blackhawk was a light two-seater phaeton with tiller steering and chain drive, priced at $750.
(Note: the name Black Hawk was used for the cheaper line of Stutz from 1930 to 1931, and is sometimes listed as a make in its own right). GNG

BLACK PRINCE (GB) *1920*

Black Prince Motors Ltd, Barnard Castle, Co Durham

The Black Prince was a very light cyclecar powered by a 2¾hp Union air-cooled 2-stroke engine. It had a 2-speed belt transmission and was made mostly of wood, both body and chassis. A version with two coupled engines was also made. At least two Black Princes survive today. GNG

BLAKE (GB) *1900–1903*

(1) F.C. Blake & Co, Hammersmith, London W. *1900–1901*

(2) F.C. Blake & Co, Kew, Surrey *1901–1903*

Blake was a maker of proprietary engines for other car firms (such as Pritchett & Gold), as well as marine engines. A number of cars were made, including a vis-à-vis with a 7hp 4-cylinder horizontal engine in 1900; another model was a tonneau with two 4hp 2-cylinder engines mounted under a long bonnet on top of which was a large, almost horizontal radiator. After 1903 the firm concentrated on making engines for light locomotives and launches. GNG

1920 BLACKBURN 20hp tourer. *Autocar*

BLAKESLEE *see* DE MARS

BLEICHERT (D) *1936–1939*

Bleichert Transportanlagen GmbH, Leipzig

A late manifestation of its type in Germany, this electric car had a small two-seater body. It was more extensively used as a commercial than as a private vehicle. HON

BLÉRIOT (F) *1921–1922*

Blériot Aéronautique, Suresnes, Seine

The Blériot cyclecar had an 8/10hp 2-cylinder 2-stroke engine, and shaft drive. It was called 'the French edition of the Bleriot Whippet' by *The Autocar*, but had little save size in common with its English namesake. GNG

1901 BLAKE tonneau; two 4hp engines. *Autocar*

BLERIOT-WHIPPET (GB) *1920–1927*

Air Navigation & Engineering Co Ltd, Addlestone, Surrey

The Bleriot-Whippet was unusual only in its transmission. This was infinitely-variable, by pulley and belt on Zenith-Gradua lines. The power unit was a centrally-mounted, air-cooled V-twin Blackburne. In 1922, like other cyclecar designs, the Bleriot-Whippet began to develop, in competition with the increasing popularity of the light car proper. Chain drive with a reverse gear were now featured, and a year later shaft drive and a conventional gearbox. One survives in the National Motor Museum at Beaulieu. TRN

BLISS (i) (US) *1901*

Bliss Chainless Automobile Co, Attleborough, Mass.

This company made an experimental steam car with drive by spur gearing to the rear axle, instead of the more usual chain drive. GNG

BLISS (ii) (US) *1906*

E.W. Bliss Co, Brooklyn, N.Y.

The Bliss had a 4-cylinder T-head engine of 6.2 litres. The flywheel and fan were integral. Final drive was by double chain. The only standard body was a five-seater tonneau, priced at $5,000; other bodies were built to order. The Bliss was advertised as 'The Finest American Motor Car'. GMN

1921 BLERIOT-WHIPPET 8.9hp two-seater.
National Motor Museum

B.L.M. (US) *1906–1907*

Breese, Lawrence & Moulton Motor Car & Equipment Co, Brooklyn, N.Y.

S.S. Breese and Chas. L. Lawrence were of school age when they built their first 12hp racer in 1905. The above company was formed to manufacture the Pirate, a racing runabout similar in appearance to the T-head Mercer, with a 24hp French-built engine. This was probably the first U.S. manufacturer to offer what is now known as a sports car. Despite their slogan 'The Greatest Runabout in the World', the company became bankrupt later in 1907. GMN

BLOMSTROM (US) *1907–1909*

Blomstrom Mfg Co, Detroit, Mich.

A five-seater touring car and a three-seater runabout made up the complete Blomstrom line. They had 4-stroke 4-cylinder engines developing 30hp. Final drive was by shaft. This manufacturer also built the Gyroscope. GMN

BLOOD (US) *1903–1905*

Blood Brothers Auto & Machine Co, Kalamazoo, Mich.

The last model of this car was a five-seater tonneau with a 2-cylinder opposed engine under the bonnet. The drive system had a 4-speed transmission and shaft to the rear axle. The wheelbase was 7ft 8in and cost $1,800. This company later built the Cornelian Cyclecar. GMN

B.M.A. HAZELCAR (GB) *1952–1957*

(1) Battery Manufacturing Association, Hove, Sussex *1952*

(2) B.M.A. & Electrical Equipment Co, Hove, in conjunction with Hazeldine

1952 B.M.A. HAZELCAR two-seater electric
car. *M.J. Worthington-Williams*

1932 B.M.W. 3/20PS tourer. *Neubauer Collection*

1935 B.M.W. Type 315 1½-litre cabriolet.
Bayerische Motoren-Werke AG

1937 B.M.W. Type 328 drophead coupé.
G.N. Georgano

1965 B.M.W. 2000CS 2-litre coupé. *Bayerische
Motoren-Werke AG*

Motors, Telscombe Cliffs, Sussex *1952–1953*
(3) Gates & Pearson Ltd, Hove, Sussex *1952–1953*
(4) Electric Motors (Hove) Ltd, Hove, Sussex *1954–1957*

The B.M.A. Hazelcar was a light electric two-seater sponsored by G.B. Gates an R.E. Hazeldine. The bodywork was of aluminium panels, and power was provided b a specially designed 1½hp electric motor which gave 18 to 20mph. Final driv was by enclosed double reduction duplex chain. The range was 50–60 miles pe charge. The high price of £535 and customer resistance to the idea of electric car prevented it from being a commercial success, and only six were made. A sevent was fitted with a Ford Eight engine, but did not go into production. Theoreticall the cars were available up to 1957, but it is unlikely that any were built afte 1954.

MJWV

BMC SPORTS (US) *1952*
British Motor Car Co, San Francisco, Calif.

The BMC Sports was a British Singer 1500 chassis fitted with an American-mad fibreglass sports body and a Simca grille.

B

B.M.F. (D) *1904–1907*
Berliner Motorwagen-Fabrik GmbH, Berlin-Tempelhof

This firm developed in 1901 out of the Gottschalk concern and until 1904 buil only commercial vehicles, which were used, among other purposes, for mail delivery In 1904 production of private cars was started. These cars had friction drive o Erdmann principles and as taxicabs many were built. After 1907 the firm's cars wer marketed as Oryxes and friction drive was abandoned. B.M.F. cars were also know under the name Tempelhof.

HON

B.M.W. (i) (D) *1928 to date*
(1) Bayerische Motoren-Werke, Eisenach; Munich *1928–1939*
(2) Bayerische Motoren-Werke AG, Munich *1952 to date*

This firm developed from the Bayerische Flugzeug-Werke, Munich, founded in 1916 for the production of aero engines. In 1922 the name was changed to Bayerische Motoren-Werke, and production of engines for boats, lorries and motor cycles began. In 1923 the first B.M.W. motor cycle appeared. In 1928 the Eisenach Dixi works were acquired and car production began with the BMW-Dixi, an Austin Seven built under licence. Car production was carried on in Eisenach, while production of motor cycles remained in Munich. The BMW-Dixi was succeeded in 1932 by the 800cc 3/20PS model with tubular backbone chassis and independent suspension.

In 1933 came the first 6-cylinder model (303). The range of sixes continued with the '315' (1,490cc, 34 and 40bhp) and '319' (1,911cc, 45 and 55bhp). The triple-carburettor sports versions of these laid the foundation for the famous B.M.W. sports cars, noted for their speed and appearance. The engine of the '326' (1,971cc, 50bhp) became the basis for the '327' and '328'. The '327' used the 55bhp engine, while the most successful '328' developed 80bhp. Two of this model's most remarkable successes amongst many in races, rallies and trials were a class win at Le Mans and the winning of the 1940 abbreviated Mille Miglia. The '327/328' used an 80bhp engine in the '327' longer wheelbase chassis and was also very successful in competitions. The last pre-World War 2 model was the '335' with a 3,485cc 90bhp engine. It was intended for the British market and only a few hundred were built. From 1935 to 1939 BMW's were imported into the United Kingdom and marketed under the name of Frazer Nash-BMW.

The Eisenach factory was lost through nationalization in 1945 (*see* E.M.W.). Production of motor cycles was taken up again in the Munich factory and facilities for car production were prepared. The first Munich-built car appeared in 1952, the '501' with a 6-cylinder 1,971cc engine, based on the last pre-war designs. This started the range of 6- and 8-cylinder prestige cars. The last of this range was the '3200' CS 2-door coupé with 3.2-litre 160bhp engine. In 1955 B.M.W. started production of the Isetta bubble car under licence, and this was followed in 1957 by the BMW '600' 4-seater based on it. In 1960 the '700' appeared with a 697cc air-cooled opposed twin-cylinder engine mounted in the rear. In 1962 B.M.W. began to produce medium sized cars again, bringing out the 4-cylinder '1500' (80bhp), which was developed into the '1800' (90bhp). The '1800' TI and the '1800' TI/SA were tuned versions developing 110 and 130bhp respectively. In 1965 the '2000' C (100bhp) and the '2000' CS (120bhp) coupés appeared. In 1966 the '1600' (83bhp), the '2000' (100bhp) and the '2000' TI (120bhp) with 4-cylinder in-line engines of 1,573cc and 1,990cc capacity were added to the range. In 1967 the Frazer Nash-BMW name was revived for a special luxury model of the '2000' TI, selling in England for £1,830. New for 1968 were the 2002, combining the 135bhp 2-litre engine with the 1600 chassis, and the 1600GT, which used the body of the former Glas 1700, a result of the B.M.W.-Glas merger of 1967. In 1969 the company produced their first six since 1958, the 2500. Mechanically this derived from the existing fours, but was powered by a 170bhp 2,494cc 7-bearing engine. A bigger 2.8-litre version was also available. By 1971 B.M.W. were offering a 2,985cc version with either twin carburettors or Bosch fuel injection; in the latter form it gave 200bhp. Also new in 1971 was a semi-estate car, the Touring, available in 1600, 1800, or 2000 guise. B.M.W. ran a Formula 2 team in 1969, using special 1.6-litre engines in British Lola chassis, but though there were several victories in 1970, the company retired from this branch of the sport after two seasons. The 1973 range embraced the 1600, 1800, 2000, and the sixes, as well as a new ohc 520 with 1,990cc 4-cylinder engine, wishbone and trailing-link front suspension, and saloon bodywork in the 2500 idiom. Options included 115bhp twin-carburettor or 130bhp fuel-injection models, and a choice of 4- and 5-speed manual and automatic transmissions. A 200bhp derivative of this unit powered a prototype mid-engined coupé, the Turbo, with all-disc brakes.

HON

1972 B.M.W. 2000 tii touring saloon.
Bayerische Motoren-Werke AG

B.M.W. (ii) (US) *c.1949 to date*
Boulevard Machine Works, Los Angeles, Calif.

This company produced electric minicars and golfmobiles for a number of years, and in 1966 introduced a larger electric roadster with two motors and eight 3-cell batteries giving a claimed maximum speed of 70mph.

BE

B.M.W. (iii) (ZA) *1968 to date*
Euro Republic Automobile Distributors Pty Ltd, Pretoria

The South African B.M.W. is peculiar to that country, combining the chassis/body structure of the defunct Glas 1700 with the ohc 1800 and 2000 B.M.W. 4-cylinder engines.

MCS

B.N. (I) *1924–1925*
Bianchi e Negro, Turin

A light car with 960cc ohv 4-cylinder engine and 4-speed gearbox of which touring and sports models were made. The latter was credited with 4,000rpm and 65mph. Appearance was reminiscent of the contemporary Lancia Lambda. MCS

B.N.C. (F) *1923–1931*
Bollack, Netter et Cie, Levallois-Perret, Seine

Developed from the Jacques Muller cyclecar, the B.N.C. was one of the better-known French sporting voiturettes. The first models had 4-cylinder sv engines by S.C.A.P. in the touring cars and Ruby in the sports versions. In 1925 more serious sports cars appeared, powered by 1,100cc S.C.A.P., 1,088cc Ruby DS or 1,097cc Ruby K engines. The latter developed 60bhp and gave a maximum speed of 100mph. At the end of 1925 a vertically-mounted Cozette supercharger was catalogued on sports B.N.C.s — probably the first supercharged French cars to be sold to the public. The supercharged short-chassis model became known as the Montlhéry, the unsupercharged short-chassis as the Monza, and the long-chassis as the Miramas. For 1927 a sloping radiator was introduced, and was found on almost all sporting B.N.C.s henceforth, an exception being the 1½-litre Meadows-engined model of which one ran at Le Mans in 1929, and a few were sold to the public. Ruby-engined B.N.C.s were very successful in competitions, finishing 1st and 2nd in the 1927 Bol d'Or. In 1929 B.N.C. took over the stock of Lombard parts and assembled a few cars which they sold under their own name, using their own radiator.

Towards the end of the firm's life B.N.C. tried to enter the luxury market with the Aigle, a large saloon with Delaunay-Belleville-built chassis and a choice of 4 or 5-litre sv straight-8 Continental engines. A.E.R. pneumatic suspension was tried on the Aigle, but few of these cars were made. A coupé with 2-litre engine, sometimes called the A.E.R., was seen on the B.N.C. stand at the 1930 Paris Salon, but did not go into production. B.N.C.s ceased to be made in 1931, but the Garage Siréjols assembled a few sports cars later, and the marque was raced at Le Mans as late as 1935.

GNG

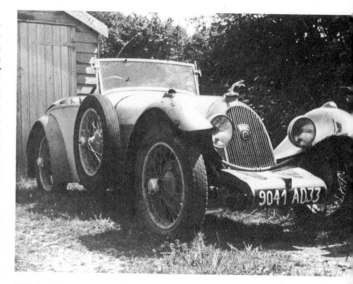

1927 B.N.C. Type St Hubert 1,100cc sports car.
Mrs R.A. Pilkington

BOB (D) *1920–1925*
(1) Bob Automobil-Gesellschaft Carpzow & Wachsmann, Berlin-Charlottenburg *1920–1921*
(2) Bob Automobil-Gesellschaft mbH, Berlin-Charlottenburg *1921–1922*
(3) Bob Automobil AG, Berlin SW 29 *1922–1925*

Bob was a small make using mainly Siemens & Halske engines. A 5/25hp sports and racing car took part in several national races.

HON

BOBBI-KAR (US) *1945–1947*
1) Bobbi Motor Car Corp, San Diego, Calif. *1945–1946*
2) Bobbi Motor Car Corp (Dixie Motor Car Corp), Birmingham, Ala. *1947*

One of the more promising minicars that failed to attain production, the Bobbi-Kar was shown in several plastic bodied prototype forms, variously powered by rear-mounted air-cooled and water-cooled engines. All four wheels were independently sprung. It was succeeded by the Keller in 1948.

BE

BOBBY-ALBA (F) *c.1920–c.1924*
Lucien Bollack, Paris

A product of Lucien Bollack, who later made the B.N.C. as well as cars under his own name, the Bobby-Alba was a conventional light car powered by a 1,131cc Ballot sv 4-cylinder engine.

GNG

BOBSY (US) *1962 to date*
C.W. Smith Engineering Co, Medina, Ohio

Small sports-racing cars, with engines by Ford, Osca, Porsche, SAAB or Alfa-

1920 BOBBY-ALBA 6CV coupé. *Musée de l'Automobile, Le Mans*

1899 BOLIDE 18hp racing car. Léon Lefébvre at the tiller. *Geoffroy de Beaufort Collection*

1972 BOHANNA STABLES 1½-litre coupé.
Bohanna Stables

1973 BOLWELL Nagari sports car.
Bolwell Cars Pty Ltd

Romeo driving through Hewland 5-speed gearboxes, achieved numerous cla successes in S.C.C.A. races. Single-seaters, with Volkswagen mechanical parts conform with Formula V, also figured in the range.

BOCAR (US) *1958–c.1960*
Bocar Mfg Co, Denver, Colo.

Bob Carnes built and tested a number of experimental sports cars before th first XP-4 was marketed. This two-seater was available with Chevrolet or Ponti power, Girling brakes and Jaguar wire wheels. In 1959 the XP-5 appeared wi a 7ft 6in wheelbase and strengthened V-W suspension. The further refined XP that followed was on a longer wheelbase and used a blown Chevrolet Corvet engine modified to produce 400hp at 6,200rpm. Body structure was of tubing a fibreglass, the brakes were by Buick and suspension was by rigid axles with pair trailing arms and torsion bars. Kerb weight with a full tank of fuel was 2,290l Acceleration was extremely good. A standing quarter mile was achieved 14.6 seconds with a speed of 112mph; 120mph was clocked in 16.0 seconds.

BOCK & HOLLENDER (A) *1899–1910*
Bock & Hollender, Vienna III

This firm of motor cycle manufacturers began car production in 1899 with 2-cylinder voiturette. A 4-cylinder car with a 16hp engine followed in 1902. 24 and 40hp models were also produced. In 1910 the factory was taken over by W.A. Bock & Hollender cars were also sold under the name of Regent.   HC

BOES (D) *1903–1906*
Jacob Boes & Co, Berlin-Charlottenburg

Several 2- and 4-cylinder models were made, and quite a number of Boes ca served as taxis in Berlin. A 24hp racing car appeared in 1905.   HC

BOHANNA STABLES (GB) *1972 to date*
R. Stables, Cadmore End, High Wycombe, Bucks.

This interesting design featured a British Leyland Maxi engine at the rear a tubular space-frame, incorporating a built-in roll bar. The fibreglass two-seat body had a detachable roof panel. It was intended not to aim for an ambitio performance, but rather to put the car in production at a reasonable price f such an advanced design. The prototype model was known as the Diablo, a was the work of Peter Bohanna and Robin Stables.

BOISSAYE (F) *1904*
Automobiles Boissaye, Paris

The Boissaye had a 12/15hp Mutel engine and shaft-drive.   GN

BOTEL (F) *1938–1949*
Automobiles Boitel, Paris 12e

The Boitel minicar began life with a 2-cylinder 400cc engine which was replace in 1948 with a 589cc D.K.W. unit. Engines were rear-mounted, and the body wa an open two-seater. Very few were sold to the public.   GN

BOLER (GB) *1971 to date*
Boler Engineering Ltd, Oldham, Lancs.

David Boler's 'T-Bone' was a fun car using Ford components, the exiguo bodywork of which was claimed to have been inspired by the early Ford Mod T. Exact specification was to customers' requirements, the basic price being £970

BOLIDE (i) (F) *1899–1907*
(1) Léon Lefebvre et Cie, Paris 17e *1899–1905*
(2) Sté l'Auto-Réparation, Paris 17e *1905–1907*

The original and most characteristic Bolide cars had large horizontal engines 8hp, 2-cylinder, 16hp, 2-cylinder and 40hp, 4-cylinder, the latter with dimensions 155mm × 155mm giving a capacity of 11,692cc. Drive was originally by a wide bel replaced in 1901 by a chain. These early Bolides were made at Ensival, Belgiu under the name Snoeck. 1902 Bolides had De Dion, Aster or Tony Huber engine and had lost most of their individuality. Léon Lefebvre, their designer, left th firm in about 1905 to make the Prima car. The last Bolides were made in four mode a 12hp monobloc four, a 22hp four, and a 35hp six, all with shaft drive.   GN

BOLIDE (ii) (US) *1969 to date*
Bolide Motor Car Corp, Long Island, N.Y.

The Bolide Can-Am 2 is a mid-engined sports coupé powered by a 5.8-litr Ford V-8 engine. The prototype Can-Am 1 appeared at the 1969 New York Au Show, and production of the Can-Am 2 was scheduled for 1971.   GN

BOLSOVER (GB) *1907–1909*
Bolsover Bros, Eaglescliffe, Co Durham

The Bolsover steam car used a 3-cylinder single acting engine, and a semi-flas boiler of Bolsover's own design. Very few cars were made.   GN

BOLTE (US) *1901*

.H. Bolte, Kearney, Neb.

This 4hp car was claimed to attain 20mph with two passengers. Full elliptical ⁣rings were used all round and final drive was by double chains. Steering was y tiller and the vehicle was priced at $600. GMN

BOLWELL (AUS) *1963 to date*

⁣olwell Cars Pty Ltd, Mordialloc, Victoria

Built by Campbell and Graeme Bolwell, this make began as a kit car with space-⁣ame chassis designed to take the Ford Cortina engine. This was followed by Holden-based model, and in 1968 came the first complete car, the Nagari coupé. ⁣his was a two-seater GT powered by a 4.9-litre Ford V-8 engine, which has ⁣nce been joined by an open sports model. The Nagari is sold in kit form as ⁣ell as complete, and is built under licence in South Africa. GNG

ON-CAR (GB) *1905–1907*

⁣dinburgh & Leith Engineering Co, Leith

Also known as the Bonne-Car, this was a steam car built in very small numbers. GNG

OND (i) (GB) *1922–1928*

⁣.W. Bond & Co, Brighouse, Yorks.

Several attempts were made in Britain in the 1920s to share in the success of ⁣merican imports by producing an American-type assembled car (*see* Cubitt, Brock-⁣bank, Ruston-Hornsby). The original 1922 Bond had a 14.3hp Tylor 4-cylinder ⁣ngine, but from 1923 a 6-cylinder Continental unit was used. Other American ⁣omponents were incorporated, and front-wheel brakes were a feature. In 1927 ⁣he Bond tourers were replaced by a sports car using an Anzani 1½-litre engine ⁣ the prototype, and Meadows 4EDs in the few production models that appeared. ⁣hese could be had with superchargers. The Bond company were also responsible ⁣or the design of the Australian Chic. At least one Bond, a Meadows-engined ⁣ports model, survives today. TRN

BOND (ii) (GB) *1948; 1961*

⁣ond Aircraft & Engineering Co (Blackpool) Ltd, Longridge, Lancs.

One of the 500cc pioneers, Laurie Bond's first tiny car upset many purists by its ⁣ack of amenities and by its agility. The Type C production version was similarly ⁣ront-engined, but had the refinement of a suspension system, incorporating friction ⁣iscs and rubber couplings. Another front-wheel drive single-seater was offered ⁣hen Formula Junior was fashionable. DF

BOND (iii) (GB) *1949 to date*

1) Sharps Commercials Ltd, Preston, Lancs. *1949–1964*
2) Bond Cars Ltd, Preston, Lancs. *1965–1970*
3) Reliant Motor Co Ltd, Tamworth, Staffs. *1971 to date*

This ingenious 3-wheeler was designed by Laurie Bond (*see also* Berkeley) and ⁣eatured a 122cc single-cylinder 2-stroke Villiers engine (later replaced by a similar ⁣97cc unit), 3-speed motor cycle-type gearbox, unitary construction, and a chain-⁣riven front wheel. Front springing was by vertical coil, rear suspension depending ⁣n the tyres! While most post-war cyclecars faded away, the Bond grew up, with ⁣ptional electric starter in 1952, front wheel brake and bonded-rubber rear suspen-⁣ion in 1953, and a reverse gear in 1957. Four-seater versions were listed from 1954, ⁣nd increasing use of fibreglass was made in the car's construction. A 246cc 4-speed ⁣ersion, still Villiers-powered, was listed in 1959, and this engine was standardized for ⁣he 1960 models. The Minicar was still going strong as late as 1965, but in 1963 Bond ⁣ad moved into the full-sized car market with a little G.T. coupé based on Triumph's ⁣ll-independently-sprung 1,147cc Herald, and in 1965 they offered a bigger rear-⁣ngined 3-wheeler using the mechanical components of the 875cc 4-cylinder Hillman ⁣mp. An additional model for 1968 was the Equipe 2-litre GT, a coupé powered by the ⁣-cylinder Triumph Vitesse engine. However, Reliant bought the company in 1969, ⁣losed the Preston works and abandoned the existing range in favour of the Bug, ⁣ sporty 3-wheeler with single front wheel and swing-up cockpit canopy, powered ⁣y Reliant's 700cc die-cast ohv 4-cylinder engine in 29bhp and 31bhp forms. Its ⁣apacity was increased to 750cc for 1973. MCS

BONIQUET *see* J.B.R.

BONNEVILLE (F) *1897–c.1900*

⁣. Bonneville, Toulouse

Bonneville was a bicycle maker who also had factories at Biarritz and Villeneuve-⁣ur-Lot. He made a small number of cars with rear-mounted De Dion engines, ⁣ubular frames and tiller steering. GNG

BORBEIN (US) *1903–1907*

1) H.F. Borbein & Co, St Louis, Mo.
2) Borbein Automobile Co, St Louis, Mo.

Borbein was the successor to Brecht. It was available as a four-seater car but ⁣ithout engine which had to be supplied and installed by purchaser. GMN

1923 BOND(i) 23.4hp all-weather tourer. *Autocar*

1951 BOND(iii) 197cc 3-wheeler. *Autosport*

1967 BOND(iii) Equipe 2-litre GT coupé. *Bond Cars Ltd*

1970 BOND(iii) Bug 700ES coupé.
Reliant Motor Co Ltd

1905 BORDEREL-CAIL (GROS) 15/18hp limousine. *Jacques Kupélian Collection*

1951 BORGWARD Hansa 1½-litre cabriolet.
Autocar

1953 BORGWARD 1500 Rennsport sports coupé.
Borgward-Werke AG

BORCHARDING (D) *1925*

Borcharding & Co, GmbH, Berlin

A two-seater cyclecar which was produced in small series.　　　HO

BORDEREL-CAIL (F) *1905–c.1908*

Sté Cail, Denain, Nord

The Société Cail were famous locomotive builders who made one of the first locomotives in Northern France in 1846. Their road vehicle activities began with the construction of the 6-wheel car designed by F. Gros. This was an ungainly-looking vehicle in which the centre pair of wheels drove, and front and rear pairs both steered. It had a 15/18hp 4-cylinder engine and solid tyres. In 1906 a similar car appeared at the Paris Salon, powered by a 25/30hp engine. A convenient 4-wheeled car with a 30hp monobloc 4-cylinder engine was made in 1907.　　　GN

BORGWARD (i) (D) *1939–1961*

(1) Carl F.W. Borgward Automobil- und Motoren-Werke, Bremen 11 *1939–1949*
(2) Carl F.W. Borgward GmbH, Bremen 11 *1949–1961*
(3) Borgward-Werke AG, Bremen 11 *1961*

Carl F.W. Borgward was the owner of the Hansa, Hansa-Lloyd and Goliath works. The production of the Hansa 1100 was carried on until July 1939, and a new 6-cylinder model, the 2300, based on Hansa's 1700 appeared under the name Borgward. After World War 2 the names Goliath and Lloyd reappeared on smaller cars made by the Borgward group.

The first post-war Borgward was the Hansa 1500 which appeared in 1949 at the Geneva Salon. With its all-enveloping body it was a real sensation, being the first German post-war car with this style. The production models which followed the '1500' were the '1800' (also available with Diesel engine), and the 6-cylinder '2400'. In 1954 the '1800' was developed into the unitary-construction Isabella. It proved a very successful model, and was available also in a TS (Touring Sport) version, developing 75bhp. From the Hansa 1500 and Isabella some very successful racing versions with push-rod as well as twin ohc units were derived, with output of up to 140bhp. In 1958 Borgward retired from racing. The last Borgward model was the 100bhp 6-cylinder 2.3-litre limousine, with optional air suspension, which was manufactured for only about 10 months before the collapse of the Borgward group.

The Lloyd Arabella de Luxe was marketed under the Borgward name in 1960 and 1961, however, and the Isabella was still available in 1966 from a small firm which obtained large stocks of original Borgward parts.　　　HON

BORGWARD (ii) (MEX) *1967 to date*

Fabrica Nacional de Automóviles S.A., Monterrey

This concern took over the manufacturing rights of the 2,238cc Grosse Borgward, the last new model to emanate from the defunct Bremen concern. In Mexican guise it differs only from its German prototype by virtue of the conventional coil rear springing in place of the previous pneumatic arrangements.　　　MCS

BORITTIER (F) *1899*

Built at Mayet, Sarthe, the Borittier was a two-seater voiturette powered by a rear-mounted De Dion engine and using belt drive.　　　GNG

BORLAND (US) *1903–1916*

(1) Borland-Grannis Co, Chicago, Ill. *1903–1914*
(2) Borland-Grannis Co, Saginaw, Mich. *1914–1916*

Also known as Borland-Grannis, these cars were electrically powered by General Electric motors. The Borland used shaft drive in place of the chain drive then usual for electrics. The last line of cars included one open model and three closed ones including a limousine at a price of $5,500. The maximum speed claimed was 22mph. In 1914 Borland merged with Argo (i) and Broc.　　　GMN

BOSS (US) *1903–1907*

Boss Knitting Machine Works, Reading, Pa.

The Boss steamer was sometimes referred to as Eck after its designer, James L. Eck. The car had a 2-cylinder 7/8hp engine, and was tiller-steered. It weighed 1,400lb and had a separate unsprung underframe for the running-gear. The price was $1,000. (There were two projected cars named Boss, one in 1904, the other in 1911, but neither is known to be connected with this steam car).　　　GMN

BOSTON (US) *1906–1907*

Concord Motor Car Co, Boston, Mass.

This electric car was scheduled for exhibition at the 1907 Boston Auto Show but did not make it. Further details are lacking.　　　GMN

BOSTON & AMESBURY (US) *1904*

Boston & Amesbury Manufacturing Co, Amesbury, Mass.

The only model built by this manufacturer was a two-seater roadster powered by a 2-cylinder water-cooled engine. This had an exposed coil radiator in front and was fitted with an early example of left-hand wheel steering.　　　GMN

BOSTON HIGH WHEEL (US) *1907*

Boston High Wheel Auto Mfg Co, Boston, Mass.

This vehicle had wheels of 44 and 48in diameter and solid rubber tyres. It was driven by a 2-cylinder air-cooled engine of 12hp. The transmission utilized an expanding/contracting sheave system with belts. GMN

BOTY'S (F) *1907*

The Boty's was a light voiturette with a single-cylinder 6.2hp engine. One was entered in the 1907 Coupe des Voiturettes, and finished 16th in a field of 31. GNG

BOUHEY (F) *1898–c.1902*

Sté des Usines Bouhey, Paris

A Bouhey electric phaeton was among the entrants in the Concours de Fiacres in Paris in 1898, and the company was making 10/12hp 2-cylinder petrol cars in 1901, although it is not certain if these were sold under the Bouhey name or not. GNG

BOULET (F) *1902–1903*

Boulet et Cie, Paris

The Boulet was a quadricycle with a single-cylinder 4, 6, or 9hp Aster engine mounted behind the back axle, driving by belts. One competed in the Paris-Madrid race but failed to finish. GNG

BOUND (GB) *1920*

Bound Brothers, Southampton

The Bound was a small monocar (outside width only 26in) fitted with a 3½hp Precision engine and friction drive. MJWW

BOURASSA (CDN) *1899–1926*

Montreal, Que.

H.E. Bourassa was a mechanical genius from rural Quebec who built the first car ever made in Montreal, a one-off runabout with the engine under the seat, in 1899. For several years after that he built much larger cars to special order, each one different. His goal was to form a regular production company, and in the mid-1920s he put an engine of his own design into a Rickenbacker chassis, which was to be the Bourassa 6 prototype. However, he could not raise enough capital and finally destroyed the car. HD

BOUR-DAVIS (US) *1915–1922*

1) Bour Davis Motor Car Co, Detroit, Mich. *1915–1917*
2) Louisiana Motor Car Co, Shreveport, La. *1919–1922*

The Bour-Davis was a conventional assembled car powered by a 6-cylinder Continental engine. After the failure of the first company, about 25 cars of Bour-Davis design were made by Shadburne Brothers of Frankfort, Ind., under the name Shad-Wyck from 1917 to 1918. In 1919 a new company recommenced manufacture under the Bour-Davis name, and this was continued until 1922 when the name was changed to Ponder. GNG

BOURGEOIS-MAGNIN (F) *1920*

Bourgeois et Magnin, Macon, Saône-et-Loire

This was a short-lived car made in 6 and 12hp versions, seating capacity varying between two and six passengers. GNG

BOURGUIGNONNE (F) *1899–1901*

Chesnay, de Falletans et Cie, Dijon

The chief interest of the Bourguignonne voiturette lay in its cooling. The vertical single-cylinder Gaillardet engine was nominally air-cooled, but when this proved insufficient, an auxiliary spray of water could be brought into use on the cooling fins. The car had wheel steering, and four speeds operated by fast and loose pulleys. GNG

BOURSAUD (F) *1897–1899*

Usines Boursaud, Baignes, Charente

These were small rear-engined cars with *vis-à-vis* coachwork, powered by 402cc single-cylinder water-cooled De Dion units. Two-speed Bozier gearboxes without reverse were used. Only three cars were made. MCS

BOVY (B) *c.1908–c.1914*

Ateliers de Construction Albert Bovy, Brussels

Bovy was a well-known maker of commercial vehicles from 1902 to 1930 who made a very limited number of cars in the pre-war period. They were mostly landaulets on a 2-cylinder chassis which could be used for taxi work, and in 1906 there was a voiturette similar in appearance to the De Dion Populaire. GNG

BOWEN (i) (GB) *1905–1906*

J. Bowen, Didsbury, Manchester

In 1903 James Bowen began experiments with a light car which he built to specifications set out by the Motor Trade Association, but the car was not completed until 1905 and was first shown to the public at the Manchester Show in February 1906. It

1957 BORGWARD Isabella TS 1½-litre coupé.
G.N. Georgano

1960 BORGWARD 2.3-litre limousine.
G.N. Georgano

c.1908 BOVY 2-cylinder landaulette. *Ivan Mahy Collection*

1906 BOWEN(ii) 9hp two-seater. *M.A. Harrison Collection*

1922 BOW-V-CAR 10hp two-seater. *Autocar*

1902 BOYER 12hp double phaeton. *The Veteran Car Club of Great Britain*

had a single-cylinder 6hp engine, a 3-speed gearbox and shaft drive. The price was £150 but few were sold and Mr Bowen moved to Edinburgh. The company afterwards made bicycles and motor bicycles named Ladas. GNC

BOWEN (ii) (GB) *1906–1908*
Bowen & Co, London W.C.

The London-built Bowen was made by a brass-foundry established in 1808 which is still in business today. The car used a 9hp vertical twin engine which, like the rest of the vehicle, was entirely made in the firm's Mount Pleasant factory. A 3-speed gearbox and shaft drive were employed and several body styles were offered, including a delivery van. The two-seater cost £175. GNC

BOWIN (AUS) *1968 to date*

The first Sydney-built Bowin was a Formula 2 racing car powered by a Cosworth FVA 1.6-litre engine. Only three F2 cars were made, two monocoques and one space-frame design, and since 1969 designer John Joyce has concentrated on Formula Ford cars, with space-frames based on those of the last F2 car. GNC

BOWMAN (US) *1921–1922*
Bowman Motor Car Co, Covington, Ky.

The Bowman, a short-lived car, was produced primarily if not exclusively as a roadster. This small car used an engine of its own manufacture. KM

BOWSER (GB) *1922–1923*
E. Bowser, Leeds, Yorks.

The Bowser was a conventional light car using a 9hp flat-twin Koh-i-Noor engine of 1,018cc, a 3-speed gearbox and shaft drive. The price was £300. GNC

BOW-V-CAR (GB) *1922–1923*
(1) The Plycar Co Ltd, Upper Norwood, London S.E.19 *1922*
(2) The Plycar Co Ltd, Luton, Beds. *1922–1923*

The Bow-V-Car used a 10hp V-twin Precision engine and unit construction of body and chassis. Final drive was by chain, and the car could be started by lever from the seat. GNG

BOYER (F) *1898–1906*
Boyer et Cie, Suresnes, Seine; Puteaux, Seine

This company was initially associated with Phébus motor tricycles powered by De Dion or Aster engines, and these were still being made in 1901, though a car of unspecified type competed in the Paris-Rambouillet-Paris Race in 1899. By 1901, the Boyer had emerged as a conventional voiturette with tubular frame and side-chain transmission. The frontal radiator was fed from a tank at the rear, and single-cylinder Aster or twin-cylinder Buchet engines were usually installed, though some cars used De Dion and Météore units. The cars sold in England under the name of York, the 1902 model 6hp selling for £190; imports were discontinued during the year owing to a drop in manufacturing standards. Also in 1902 a 4-cylinder Boyer appeared at the Gaillon hill-climb. In 1903 some larger touring cars were offered, with chain drive, armoured-wood frame, and mechanically-operated side valves in an L-head. The biggest model was rated at 24hp. Latterly the firm was associated with Prunel, and the cars were made in that company's factory at Puteaux. In 1906 there were three 4-cylinder models, all with steel frames, ht magneto ignition, and the more conventional T-head configuration favoured by Prunel. MCS

BOZIER (F) *1906–1920*
Voiturettes Bozier, Puteaux

This firm exhibited some motor tricycles at the 1901 Paris Salon, and in 1902 were making change-speed gears for tricycles and quadricycles. By 1906 they were making a curious little 4½hp voiturette with a single-cylinder De Dion engine, on which the crankshaft was set at 45 degrees to the front axle, the crown wheel was offset and there was no differential. It also went under the name of Mistral. Despite the firm's title a 24 4-cylinder car was also made. More conventional cars with single and twin-cylinder De Dion engines (the former with automatic inlet valves) were listed in 1908, while the big four was also available, as well as a 1.3-litre 2-cylinder car with a monobloc engine of Bozier manufacture and a neat dash tank. A 763cc single-cylinder survived in the 1910 range, but the company were also making something far more advanced in the shape of a 1.8-litre ohc 4-cylinder with full pressure lubrication; cooling was by thermo-syphon and a 3-speed gearbox was used. Four 4-cylinder cars were listed in 1912, the smallest having a 1100cc engine. Overhead valves were still used in 1913, but by 1914, Boziers were once again straightforward L-head types, though still with pressure lubrication. All brakes were on the rear wheels, and the cars were made in 2-litre, 2.4-litre and 3.6-litre forms, the two bigger models with four forward speeds. A 1.7-litre version was listed once again in 1915, but though Bozier were quoted as car manufacturers again in 1920, there is no evidence that production was resumed after World War 1. MCS

B.P.D. (GB) *1913*
Brown, Paine and Dowland Ltd, Shoreham, Sussex

The B.P.D. was a belt-driven cyclecar powered by an 8hp J.A.P. V-twin engine. Priced at 95 guineas, it had no unusual features. GNG

BRABHAM (GB) 1962 to date

1) Brabham Racing Developments Ltd, New Haw, Weybridge, Surrey 1962–1966
2) Motor Racing Developments Ltd, New Haw, Weybridge, Surrey 1966 to date

The meteoric rise and continued ascendancy of the Brabham was one of the most marked features of racing in the mid-sixties. Jack Brabham's world championships for Cooper in 1959 and 1960 were underlined by a further triumph in his own car in 1966, and by his driver Hulme in 1967. Advertising less power than their rivals, the Brabham scored on reliability, achieved by steady, logical development. For the 1½-litre Formula 1, Coventry-Climax V-8 engines were used, the great American driver Dan Gurney scoring two victories in the 1964 'grandes épreuves'. For the new formula a sohc. V-8, developed by Brabham's partner R. Tauranac from a quick design, was produced in conjunction with the Australian Repco concern. As in all Brabhams, a small-diameter tubular steel space-frame was retained, in an era when other contenders were following the monocoque fashion set by Lotus.

Success attended Brabham in whatever class he entered, the last year of Formula Junior (1963) being dominated by his products, usually driven by F. Gardner or D. Hulme, whilst Hulme sensationally won the 1965 Tourist Trophy in a BT8 sports car, with Coventry-Climax engine of only 2 litres. The record in the junior formulae was equally impressive, mastery of the Formula 3 class being achieved by 1965. In Formula 2 the marque won the majority of races in 1964, and the Honda-engined model completely swept the board in 1966.

The model numbering had reached BT21 by the beginning of 1967, this being a typically Brabham F3 car with Cosworth-Ford engine, Hewland Mark VI gearbox, tubular space frame, and three-piece glassfibre body. Total production passed the 500 mark during 1967.

The 1968 and 1969 seasons were less fruitful for Brabham, despite a developed version of the Repco engine and eventual adoption of the Cosworth unit in Formula 1. Some consolidation was achieved in increasing sales of single-seaters, noted for their handling qualities, in the lesser formulae. The firm's first monocoque was for Indianapolis in 1968, but others did not appear until 1970, when the BT33 Formula 1 cars had some success, and Tony Trimmer took the Formula 3 Shell Championship with a BT28 space-framed machine. Its successor, the BT35, had as much success in hill-climbs as on the circuits.

During 1971 and 1972 the quasi-works Rondel Racing (who included ex-World Champion Graham Hill) and other Formula 2 teams did quite well with the BT36 space-framed cars. Carlos Reutemann started 1972 by earning pole position in his first Grand Prix, but this was not fully followed up. He used a 'lobster-claw' BT34 with separate frontal radiators, and similar rear suspension to the earlier BT33.

The BT38 Formula 2, 3, B or Atlantic car of 1972 was the first Tauranac-designed 'for sale' monocoque, though shortly afterwards Ron Tauranac followed Brabham's lead in leaving the firm, and control passed to a group headed by financier Bernard Ecclestone. A further 'lobster-claw' Formula 1 model, the BT39, was developed from this design for the V-12 Weslake engine. New production models for 1973 were the BT40 (F2), BT40B (F Atlantic) and BT41 (F3). DF

BRADBURY (GB) 1901–1902

Bradbury Bros, Croydon, Surrey

The Bradbury company specialized in selling electrical equipment and accumulators, but they were also agents for Pinart engines and made a few voiturettes with ½hp single-cylinder front-mounted engines and chain drive. GNG

BRADLEY (US) 1920–1921

Bradley Motor Car Co, Cicero, Ill.

The short-lived Bradley was built in limited numbers, a five-seater touring car being its only model. Lycoming engines were used, a 4-cylinder type for the Model K of 1920 and 1921 and a six for Model F in the final year of production. The wheelbase was 9ft 8in and wooden artillery wheels were used throughout. KM

BRADWELL (GB) 1914

Bradwell & Co, Folkestone, Kent

The Bradwell Monocar was a very light single-seater cycle-car with a 3½hp engine, belt drive and starting operated from the seat. The price was £65. GNG

BRAMHAM see STANHOPE

BRAMWELL (US) 1902–1904

1) Bramwell Motor Co, Boston, Mass.
2) Springfield Automobile Co, Springfield, Ohio

The Bramwell had a two-seater body on a wooden frame and a 2-cylinder engine. The only unusual feature was a single head-lamp. GMN

BRAMWELL-ROBINSON (US) 1899–1901

John T. Robinson & Co, Hyde Park, Mass.

1963 BRABHAM Formula 1 Grand Prix racing car. *Autosport*

1964 BRABHAM BT8 2-litre sports/racing car. *Motor Sport*

1972 BRABHAM BT38 Formula 2 racing car. *Motor Racing Developments Ltd*

1948 BRANDT 985cc saloon. *Autocar*

This company were makers of paper box machinery who also made some notab[cars. The Bramwell-Robinson was a 3-wheeler powered by a horizontal 3hp sing cylinder engine which drove the single rear wheel by chain. It had tiller steerin W.C. Bramwell left to make cars under his own name, while Robinson made a line expensive cars, powered first by rear-mounted 2-cylinder, and later by from mounted 4-cylinder engines. From 1902 they were called Pope-Robinson.   GN

BRANDT (F) 1948

The Brandt was one of the most unconventional cars of the post-World War period, and it is hardly surprising that it never went into production. The 985 horizontal engine had 4 working cylinders containing 2 opposed pistons each, and al 4 charging cylinders. It had an epicyclic gearbox and front-wheel drive. Doors we at front and rear, and the four passengers sat either side of a gangway.   GN

BRASIE (US) 1914–1917

Brasie Motor Car Co, Minneapolis, Minn.

The Brasie was a light roadster powered by a 12hp 4-cylinder engine, with cha drive. The two- or four-seater open bodies had no doors. Known as the Bras Packet, the car sold for $450. From 1916 car and company name were changed Packet.   GN

BRASIER (F) 1897–1930

(Incl. Georges Richard, 1897–1903; Richard-Brasier, 1903–1904; Chaignea Brasier, 1927–1930.)
(1) Société des Anciens Etablissements Georges Richard, Ivry-Port 1897–1905
(2) Société des Automobiles Brasier, Ivry-Port 1905–1926
(3) Société Chaigneau-Brasier, Ivry-Port 1926–1930

The first car made by Georges Richard was a frail machine on Benz lines, wi belt drive and three forward speeds. By 1900, Richard was offering the Vivinus fro Belgium under his own name – another voiturette, but a quieter, smoother-runnin one with a fair turn of speed. It was powered by a 6hp 2-cylinder engine, and it to was belt-driven. However, the 7½hp Georges Richard of 1901 had shaft drive, in th approved modern fashion of Darracq and Renault. With the arrival of the designe Brasier, who had worked for Mors, Georges Richard gradually ceased to be asse ciated with voiturettes, but gained little originality. There were four new models 1902, all called Richard-Brasiers, rated at between 10 and 40hp but they were Panhard type in most respects. The smaller cars still had tubular chassis and not a models had chain drive, but all types had steel frames by 1904. In that year the were two twins and three fours, only the biggest of which, the 40hp, was chai driven. In 1904 and 1905, Brasier's cars won the Gordon Bennett Trophy for Franc bringing worldwide fame to the name.

In 1905 Georges Richard left to make the Unic at Puteaux, and Brasier continue to offer his cars, now known simply as Brasiers. They remained conservative design until 1912, with exposed valve gear and cylinders cast in pairs. In that yea a modern light car was introduced, with a 4-cylinder engine cast en bloc. Ivry-Po went on listing solid, unenterprising, relatively expensive fours until 1927. They wer brought up to date in 1923 by means of front wheel brakes and ohv engines, but th had become common practice, Brasier, in fact, was another famous old make whos popularity slowly declined, like so many in France at this time.

Reorganization in 1926 at first brought no important innovations, apart from change of name to Chaigneau-Brasier, and the introduction of a modern orthodo light car in the shape of the 9CV. Then, in 1928, the new company revealed th outcome of its rethinking. This had been over- instead of under-enterprising, fo the new car was a 3-litre, overhead-camshaft straight-8 with front wheel drive. Wi this car, and even more with the bigger Type DG8 of similar design that followed 1930, Chaigneau-Brasier committed the double error of plunging into the luxur market at a time of economic depression, and offering an unconventional design to public that distrusted such things. Chaigneau-Brasier were not the only French fir to make the same simultaneous, and fatal, mistakes, and they paid the same pric   TR

1901 GEORGES RICHARD 9hp enclosed tonneau. *The Veteran Car Club of Great Britain*

BRASINCA *see* UIRAPURU

BRAUN (A) 1899–1910

(1) August Braun, Erste Österreichische Motorfahrzeugfabrik, Vienna XVII 1899 1901
(2) August Braun & Co, Vienna XVII 1901–1910

Braun ranks among the Austrian pioneer car manufacturers. In 1899 he built hi first voiturette with a French air-cooled 3½hp engine and front drive. This wa based on the Victoria Combination, made by the Société Parisienne. Later produc tion models ranged up to 20hp; all of them were built in limited numbers only Willy Stift – later associated with Celeritas and Gräf & Stift – sponsored Braun initial efforts.   HO

BRAVO (i) (F) 1900

N.H. Bravo, Clichy, Seine

The Bravo was a six-seater waggonette powered by 5 or 8hp engines of Bravo own manufacture.   GN

c.1905 BRASIER 16hp tourer. *The Veteran Car Club of Great Britain*

BRAVO (ii) (D) *1921*

Union Kleinauto-Werke, Mannheim

During World War 1 this firm started manufacturing lorries. In 1921 a small 2-cylinder 4/10PS private car was introduced and later a 4-cylinder engine was used. The firm was also concerned with the production of the Rabag-Bugatti and the building of bodies for other firms.   HON

BRAZIER (US) *1902–1904*

H. Bartol Brazier, Philadelphia, Pa.

Brazier was a Frenchman who made a small number of cars to special order. They were mostly heavy-looking vehicles with waggonette bodies and double chain drive. Engines were 18hp 2-cylinders.   GNG

BRECHT (US) *1901–1903*

Brecht Automobile Co, St Louis, Mo.

Original models, powered by 2-cylinder non-condensing steam engines, were available in four body styles as well as a delivery wagon. Later, electrically-powered cars were built. In 1903 cars were marketed 'ready for power', in other words, engineless. This would indicate some indecision on the part of the manufacturer.

Brecht also built the Rushmobile and was succeeded by Borbein, another manufacturer who disdained to furnish ready-powered cars.   GMN

BREESE (F) *1911*

Robert Breese, Paris

Built by an American in Paris, the Breese was a light sporting car powered by 4-cylinder engines of Ballot or Fivet manufacture. About 65 were made, of which one survives today in the United States.   GNG

BRÉGUET (F) *1907; 1942*

(1) Ateliers Bréguet, Paris *1907*
(2) Sté des Ateliers d'Aviation Louis Bréguet, Paris 16e; Toulouse *1942*

The Bréguet works made two models of large 6-cylinder cars, a 30 and a 50hp. Very few were made, although the firm later became one of France's leading aircraft manufacturers. In 1942 the firm built a two-seater electric coupé, the Bréguet. The chassis consisted of a central frame, at the rear of which was mounted the Paris-Rhône motor, the body being mounted on outriggers. Range per charge was 65 miles, and maximum speed 30mph.   GNG

BREMAC (US) *1932*

Bremac Motor Car Corp, Sidney, Ohio

An experimental automobile, the Bremac featured an 80hp 8-cylinder engine mounted at the rear of the chassis. A five-seater sedan was the only body style planned. The Bremac differed from other experimental cars of the era in having no chassis frame or propeller shaft. The car was a failure.   KM

BREMS (DK) *1900–1907*

A.L. Brems, Viborg

The Brems works were founded in 1851, producing iron mountings, safe boxes and later bicycles. In 1899 two sons, Aage and Jacob, worked in Eisenach, where the Wartburg car was produced. Returning home they designed and built a 2-cylinder air-cooled car, very much on the lines of the Wartburg. The Brems car was introduced in Viborg in June 1900 and later in Copenhagen, and was the first Danish car to be produced for sale. The engine was a 3.8hp with surface carburettor situated under the driver's seat, the transmission being by friction clutch with 2 forward gears and no reverse. The first car was a small *vis-à-vis* with unsprung rear wheels, while later cars were all different in appearance, each car being an entirely new model. Eight cars only were produced, the first and the last being 2-cylinder models and the others of single-cylinder type.   TRA

BRENNABOR (D) *1908–1934*

Gebr. Reichstein Brennabor-Werke, Brandenburg

Cycles and motor cycles were already in production when Brennabor started car manufacture in 1908 with the Brennaborette, a 3-wheeler with a Fafnir engine and chain drive. Shaft drive was used later. In the same year appeared the first 4-wheel car, also with a Fafnir 2-cylinder engine. In 1909 followed the first car with a 4-cylinder engine of Brennabor's own design, though some engines were supplied by Stoewer. During the years before World War 1 further models came on to the market which were very popular although not of special technical interest. Brennabor cars were known for their durability and reliability, which they proved in several Long Distance Trials, such as the Russian Czar Nicholas Reliability Trial, St Petersburg-Sevastopol, of 1911. In 1910 and 1911 Brennabor also entered the pages of Brooklands history with some successes. In the United Kingdom Brennabor cars were marketed under the name Brenna in the pre-war years. In 1914 a small car was brought out, the three-seater 3/15PS 1½-litre. In the mid-1920s Brennabor introduced line production with a daily output of up to 120 cars. Following the trend of that time 6-cylinder (2½ and 3-litre) and 8-cylinder (3.4-litre) models were also produced by Brennabor including one 6-cylinder front-driven model (the Juwel 6

1911 BRASIER 11hp coupé. *Geoffroy de Beaufort Collection*

1927 CHAIGNEAU-BRASIER TD-4 9CV saloon. *Autocar*

1911 BRENNABOR 10hp two-seater. *Neubauer Collection*

1931 BRENNABOR Juwel 6 Front saloon. *Jaeger Collection*

1919 BREWSTER 26hp town car. *Antique Automobile*

1920 BRIGGS & STRATTON Flyer 2½hp buckboard. *Harrah's Automobile Collection*

1915 BRISCOE 2½-litre roadster. *Kenneth Stauffer*

Front, 2,460cc, 45bhp) in 1930/31. The last Brennabor was the type D, 1-litre, car production ceasing in 1934. HON

BRENNAN (US) *1907–1908*
Brennan Motor Manufacturing Co, Syracuse, N.Y.

Brennan were engine makers who supplied power units to several manufacturers, including Selden, and made a very few medium-sized 4-cylinder cars. GNG

BRESCIANA *see S.M.B.*

BREW-HATCHER (US) *1904–1905*
The Brew & Hatcher Co, Cleveland, Ohio

Sometimes known as the B & H, this car was powered by a 16hp horizontally-opposed 2-cylinder engine mounted at the front under a bonnet. It had 3 forward speeds (direct drive on top) and shaft drive. With a four-seater rear-entrance tonneau body, the price was $1,750. GNG

BREWSTER (US) *1915-1925; 1934-1936*
(1) Brewster & Co, Long Island City; New York, N.Y. *1915–1925*
(2) Springfield Mfg Co, Springfield, Mass. *1934–1936*

Between 1915 and 1925, the venerable firm of Brewster & Co, carriage builders and makers of custom-built car bodies, produced an expensive and meticulously-built automobile in a variety of open and closed models. Powered by a 4-cylinder Knight sleeve-valve engine, these compact town-carriage types of cars were widely sought after by the wealthy who did not want the ostentation of a larger custom-built car. Production of the initial Brewsters ceased shortly before the company was absorbed by Rolls-Royce of America, Inc.

The Brewster name re-appeared in 1934 in a series of open and closed Brewster bodies mounted on Ford, Buick and other standard chassis. Approximately 300 of the later Brewsters were built, the cars carrying the Brewster name and costing $3,500 KM

BRIDGWATER (GB) *1904–1906*
Bridgwater Motor Co, Eastover, Bridgwater, Somerset

The Bridgwater was an assembled car using either a 14hp White & Poppe or a 16/20hp Ballot engine. Gearboxes and axles were by M.A.B., while the bodies were built by the Bridgwater firm, Raworth & Co. Six cars of each model were made, and although larger cars of 18 and 24hp were listed in *The Autocar* and elsewhere, it is unlikely that they were built. GNG

BRIERRE (F) *1900–1901*
E.J. Brierre, Paris

The original Brierre car was a light voiturette powered by a 3½hp Morisse single-cylinder horizontal engine. In 1901 Brierre became the Paris agent for Cottereau; one model was said to be made by him under Cotterau licence, but other cars sold under the name Brierre were, in fact, made in the Cotterau factory. GNG

BRIEST-ARMAND (F) *1897–1898*
Eugène Briest et Frères, Nantes

Eugène Briest's first vehicle was a steam tricycle, but the cars used single-cylinder horizontal petrol engines. They were made in two, four- or six-seater models. In 1898 Briest made a twelve-seater bus. GNG

BRIGGS & STRATTON (US) *1919–1924*
Briggs & Stratton Co, Milwaukee, Wis.

To the comfort-loving American motorist, the cyclecar was a bad joke, and the Briggs & Stratton was one of the worst. The buckboard of 1919 resembled nothing so much as a child's soapbox racer, except that it had rather less bodywork. Two bucket seats sat on a frame with a pram wheel at each corner, while a fifth trailing wheel carried a single-cylinder air-cooled engine that also powered lawn-mowers. In the United States, rough country roads were highly unsatisfactory for the cyclecar which was even less of a commercial success in America than in Europe. Briggs & Stratton went on to make outboard motors, pumps and generators. An alternative name for the buckboard was Red Bug, or Auto Red Bug, coined by the American Motor Vehicle Company of Lafayette, Ind., who originated the design in 1916, then sold the licence to the A.O. Smith Company of Milwaukee, who sold it to Briggs of Stratton in 1919. The names were continued by the Automobile Electric Service Co of Newark, N.J., who made petrol and electric models. TRN

BRIGGS-DETROITER *see DETROITER*

BRIHAM (GB) *1966-1968*
Briham Ltd, London S.E.15

Brian Hampsheir's interesting Formula 4 single-seater featured a full monocoque construction, combining a Mallite alloy/wood sandwich with bonded fibreglass, and with inboard suspension units. A Group 6 sports model was also designed, but only six Formula 4 cars were actually made. The Hampsheir brothers later recommenced manufacture under the name Elden. DF

BRILLIÉ (F) 1904–1907

Société des Automobiles Eugène Brillié, Le Creusot; Le Havre

Eugène Brillié parted company with Gustave Gobron in 1903 and formed his own company in Paris. His speciality was commercial vehicles and he was responsible for the French capital's omnibuses. Production of Brillié vehicles was undertaken by the Schneider armaments firm, which built one or two experimental cars in the 1903–04 period. Interestingly enough Brillié abandoned the opposed-piston engine for which the Gobron-Brillié partnership had become famous, and both cars and trucks used ioe units. A cab-over-engine layout was also found on early vehicles, which included 4-cylinder shaft-driven taxis rated at 18/24hp and designed to run on either petrol or alcohol. By 1906 a big 35/45hp model, also shaft-driven, was listed and a smaller ioe 16/20hp was made with shaft drive, ht magneto ignition, and 4-speed gearbox. Two 4-cylinder types were still catalogued in 1907. In February 1908, Eugène Brillié's company went into liquidation. MCS

BRISCOE (US) 1914–1921

Briscoe Motor Corp, Jackson, Mich.

The Briscoe car, originally designed in France, was manufactured by Benjamin Briscoe, formerly head of Maxwell. Several thousand of the 4-cylinder cars, using a 3-litre engine of his own make, left the factory in nearly eight years of production. There was also an ohv V-8 in 1916. The early cars featured a single or 'cyclops' headlamp which was built directly into the radiator cowling. In the autumn of 1921, the car became the Earl, which was outwardly similar to its predecessor. KM

BRISTOL (i) (GB) 1902–1908

(1) Bristol Motor Co, Bristol 1902–1904
(2) Bristol Motor Co Ltd, Bristol 1904–1908

The first Bristols were 10hp 2-cylinder cars of Daimler layout. In 1905 a 4-cylinder 15/20 model of 3,053cc was introduced, with steel cylinder liners. Castings were obtained locally, and the entire chassis was built in the works. Nearby coachbuilders supplied bodies to customers' requirements. Up to 1908 only some 24 cars had been made — the proprietor (W.H. Appleton) was becoming increasingly concerned in experimental work, and the manager (A.E. Johnson) was developing agencies for more popular makes. DF

BRISTOL (ii) (GB) 1947 to date

(1) Bristol Aeroplane Co Ltd, Filton, Bristol 1947–1960
(2) Bristol Cars Ltd, Filton, Bristol 1960 to date

The first Bristol 400 was an anglicized version of the well-liked German 2-litre B.M.W. featuring a 6-cylinder ohv push-rod engine developing 85bhp in standard form, transverse ifs, rack and pinion steering, and centralized chassis lubrication. It was expensive at £2,375, and was supplemented by the '401' saloon and '402' cabriolet with Italian styling. Bristols were strictly fast touring cars, and a '400' took 3rd place in the 1949 Monte Carlo Rally, though a team of aerodynamic coupés ran in the 1953 and 1954 Le Mans 24 Hour Races. The engines, however, were supplied to Frazer-Nash, A.C. and Cooper (iii) as well as numerous smaller specialist constructors, while the American Arnolt was a sporting version produced for a Chicago importer. By 1955 the Bristol had grown into a 4-door saloon with battery and spare wheel housed in the front wings, and overdrive as standard; this model, the '405', acquired disc brakes in 1958. Its successor, the '406' had a 2.2-litre engine, and was even more expensive (£4,493 as against £3,189 for the '405'); production was down to a trickle. The old 6-cylinder unit finally gave way in 1962 to a 250bhp ohv Chrysler V-8 and Torqueflite automatic gearbox, and by 1968 this 407 had evolved into the 410 with minor styling improvements and a gear selector on the floor in place of the older push buttons. Since 1970 Bristol have made the 6,277cc 411 on similar lines; in 1973 form it offered 335bhp and 138mph, with such refinements as dual-circuit disc brakes, power-assisted steering, and through-flow ventilation. MCS

BRIT (GB) 1902–1905

1) Hunt's Steam Sawmills and Carriage Accessories, Bridport, Dorset
2) E.A. Chard & Co, Bridport, Dorset

The first Brit was a modified Daimler, with a replacement engine designed by John Hunt. A few further cars were built and sold entirely locally, before the firm (as the Brit Engineering Works Ltd) concentrated on the development of boat engines. DF

BRITANNIA (i) (GB)

1) Britannia Electric Carriage Syndicate Ltd, Colchester, Essex 1896–1899
2) Britannia Engineering Co Ltd, Colchester, Essex 1906–1908

Both Britannia companies were branches of the Britannia Lathe & Oil Engine Co Ltd, which had been founded in 1871. The electric cars bore a close resemblance to horse-drawn vehicles, body styles being landaus or barouches with flowing lines. During their second phase of manufacture, Britannia made conventional petrol-engined cars with 12/18hp and 24/40hp 4-cylinder engines, and one 6-cylinder model, with a 30/45hp engine. GNG

BRITANNIA (ii) (GB) 1913–1914

Britannia Engineering Co, Ltd, Nottingham

1902 BRISTOL(i) 10hp tonneau. *The Veteran Car Club of Great Britain*

1947 BRISTOL(ii) 400 2-litre coupé. *Bristol Cars Ltd*

1973 BRISTOL(ii) 411 6.3-litre saloon. *Bristol Cars Ltd*

1907 BRITANNIA(i) 24/40hp limousine. *National Motor Museum*

1921 BRITISH ENSIGN 38.4hp tourer. *Autocar*

1934 BRITISH SALMSON 12/70 sports car.
G.N. Georgano

1939 BRITISH SALMSON 20/90 drophead
coupé. *Owen Moulding*

The Britannia cyclecar was listed with a 2-cylinder air-cooled 2-stroke engine, but other engines could be fitted to the customer's choice. Four speeds were provided, and final drive was by belt. The price was £85. GNG

BRITANNIA (iii) (GB) 1957–1961
(1) Britannia Cars Ltd, Ashwell, Herts.
(2) Tojeiro Automotive Developments Ltd, Barkway, Royston, Herts.

This was an ambitious glassfibre-bodied GT car using a Ford Zephyr engine, disc brakes, and independent suspension all round. Very few were made. Designer John Tojeiro took over the remains, developing a Formula Junior car for export, and briefly offering an improved GT machine with a Chevrolet Corvette engine. DF

BRITISH (GB) 1905–1907
British Motor and Engineering Co Ltd, London; Caversham, Reading, Berks.

Two models of the British were marketed, with ioe Fafnir engines, and (until 1907) tubular chassis. Model A was a 6hp, 2-cylinder two-seater; Model B a 10/12hp, 4-cylinder, four-seater. Constant-mesh gearboxes were used, with a steering-column change to operate on the dogs. Engine sizes were increased in 1906. A noteworthy feature was the dash-operated starting handle, connected by a slender chain to the back of the crankshaft. DF

BRITISH EAGLE see HODGSON

BRITISH ENSIGN (GB) 1913–1923
Ensign Motors Ltd, Willesden, London N.W. 10

Ensign Motors devoted most of their efforts to commercial vehicles, like Guy Maudslay and Leyland, who also ventured into the luxury car field after World War 1, none of them making more than a handful of private cars. Unlike their products, however, the British Ensign appeared in many forms under many names. Before 1914, it was a normal, medium-sized four. In 1919 there appeared an assembled light car that survived for five years, but its stablemate, the luxury six, was better known. The 6.7-litre engine was of the most modern type, with an overhead camshaft and aluminium cylinders with steel liners.

In 1921, J.L. Crown, the American who had acquired rights in the Entz magnetic transmission (Owen Magnetic, Crown Magnetic), offered the bigger British Ensign, with Entz transmission, from premises in Chelsea, first as the Crown Magnetic, then as the Crown-Ensign. The last car produced by the firm was the completely different 4-cylinder, £100 Gillett runabout of 1926. TRN

BRITISH LION (GB) 1903–1904
British Lion Co, Leicester

This company supplied chassis frames, artillery wheels, bucket-seat bodies, bonnets, gear-boxes and axles; everything, in fact, except engines. They advertised that these components were for sale in large quantities, so they were presumably suppliers to the trade rather than to the do-it-yourself owner. GNG

BRITISH SALMSON (GB) 1934–1939
British Salmson Aero Engines Ltd, Raynes Park, London S.W.20

The first cars were 1½-litre 4-cylinder twin ohc fast tourers based on the French Salmson S.4C model. A later and less sporting 14hp model (1937–8) had independent front suspension. The '20–90' was an entirely British 2.6-litre twin ohc sports car with ifs, made in very small numbers from 1936 onwards. In 1939 this was the only model offered, British Salmson otherwise acting as importers of the parent company's 4-cylinder machines. MCS

BRITOMOBILE – American steam car imported into GB, probably Locomobile.

BRITON (GB) 1908–1928
(1) Star Cycle Co, Ltd, Wolverhampton, Staffs. 1908–1909
(2) British Motor Co, Ltd, Wolverhampton, Staffs. 1909–1928

The Briton was successor to the Starling which had been made by the Star Cycle Co. However, a new company, run by Edward Lisle Jr, was formed in 1909 to build this high-quality but low-priced light car. At first, a 10hp twin and 14hp 4-cylinder machine were listed, but the small car was far more successful and well-known. For 1913, it acquired four cylinders and 1,750cc but retained its 10hp rating. A two-model policy was pursued after World War 1, but the 9.8hp Briton was the principal offering. It used an ohv 1,373cc engine and worm final drive, and a sports version was obtainable.

The larger, more expensive Star car was made by the Star Engineering Company, a separate concern run by Joseph Lisle. TRN

BRIXIA-ZÜST see ZÜST

BROADWAY (GB) 1913
Broadway Cyclecar Co, Coventry, Warwickshire

The Broadway was a typical cyclecar powered by an 8hp air-cooled Fafnir engine with final drive by V-belts. The price was £80. GNG

ROC (US) 1909–1916
Roc Carriage & Wagon Co, Cleveland, Ohio; Saginaw, Mich.
The electric Broc offered three or four models each year. The earlier models had hp series motors, with five speed settings, and either shaft drive or double-chain drive. Later models were claimed to reach speeds up to 24mph.   GMN

BROCKLEBANK (GB) 1927–1929
Brocklebank & Richards Ltd, Birmingham
The Brocklebank was an attempt to rival the popularity of American cars in Britain by offering a similar type of car. A 2-litre, 6-cylinder engine with overhead valves was built in unit with a 3-speed, central-change gearbox. The gear change was easy, the suspension was soft, while Lockheed hydraulic brakes were fitted. The Brocklebank saloon was roomy and inexpensive at £395. It sold quite well in Australasia. However, its appearance was against it, being high and square when even American cars were acquiring rounded corners and lower lines.   TRN

BROCK SIX (CDN) 1921
Brock Motors Ltd, Amherstburg, Ont.
Originally incorporated as Stansell Motors Ltd, the company changed its name to Brock in January 1921. It planned to build 1,000 units per year of the Brock Six, a five-seater touring car with 55bhp Continental Red Seal engine, but only one car was completed.   GNG

BROCKVILLE 30 see BROCKVILLE ATLAS

BROCKVILLE-ATLAS (CDN) 1911–1914
Brockville Atlas Auto Company Limited, Brockville, Ont.
This company's first product was called the Brockville 30, and was really an Everitt assembled from parts supplied by Tudhope in Orillia. A conventional 4-cylinder design, the Brockville-Atlas model A replaced it for 1912. Electric lighting, metal bodies and a six had been added by 1914.   HD

BROGAN (US) 1946–1948
B and B Specialty Co, Rossmoyne, Ohio
A two-passenger, 3-wheeled clutchless machine with an air-cooled, rear-mounted engine of 10hp.   BE

BROMPTON (GB) 1921
The Brompton cyclecar was powered by a water-cooled MAG V-twin engine, but differed from the majority of its kind in that this power unit drove the front wheels, and all the wheels were independently suspended by coil springs.   TRN

BROOKE (GB) 1901–1913
J.W. Brooke & Co Ltd, Lowestoft, Suffolk
The Brooke company were originally millwrights, boilermakers, and iron and brass founders, and were also celebrated for marine engines. Their first car was tested during 1901 and put on the market early in 1902. It was of somewhat unusual design, with a 10hp 3-cylinder vertical engine mounted transversely under a very small bonnet; this drove by chain to an all-chain gearbox, and final drive was also by chains. In 1903 a new car with a longitudinal 14hp 3-cylinder engine appeared, although the transverse-engine model was still made. The longitudinal engines drove by shaft to the gearbox, which was still of the chain variety, but in 1905 came a range of more conventional cars with 15/20hp and 35hp 4-cylinder engines, and ordinary sliding gears. At this time cars accounted for 75% of Brooke's business, the rest being devoted to marine engines. In the summer of 1906 a 6-cylinder car appeared of 25/30hp, with pair-cast cylinders and, for the first time, shaft drive. A 40hp six supplemented it in 1907, and thereafter no more fours were made. However Brooke's best period was over by 1908, after which they no longer had a stand at Olympia. *The Autocar* listed the sixes until 1910, and some other lists carried the name on to 1913, but the company was mainly concerned with marine engines by this time.   GNG

BROOKE-SPACKE (US) 1919–1921
Spacke Machine & Tool Co, Indianapolis, Ind.
The cyclecar in its European form was altogether too crude, draughty, noisy, cramped and uncomfortable for the vast majority of American motorists. By 1916 most of the short-lived makers of these machines in the United States were finished and the survivors did not last long thereafter. The Brooke-Spacke was actually a new arrival, even though the market of dedicated enthusiasts was minute and rapidly diminishing. Like most of its breed it had a 2-cylinder air-cooled engine, which was used by many other cyclecar makers, but it catered for American taste with electric lighting and starting, and three forward speeds. Later cars reverted to cyclecar tradition by using 2-speed epicyclic transmission.   TRN

BROOKS (i) (GB) 1902
Brooks Motor Co Ltd, Foleshill, Coventry, Warwickshire
The Brooks light car used 8 or 12hp Pinart engines mounted in front, with shaft drive. Two- and four-seater bodies were available.   GNG

1910 BRITON 10hp two-seater. *The Veteran Car Club of Great Britain*

1927 BROCKLEBANK 15hp saloon. *National Motor Museum*

1921 BROOKE-SPACKE cyclecar. *Autocar*

1905 BROTHERHOOD 20hp tourer. Percy
Richardson at the wheel. *Autocar*

1935 BROUGH SUPERIOR 4.2-litre drophead
coupé. *Railton Owners Club*

*c.*1908 BROUHOT 10hp two-seater. *David
Filsell Collection*

BROOKS (ii) (CDN) *1923–1926*

Brooks Steam Motors Ltd, Stratford, Ont.

The Brooks Steam Car was second in popularity to the Stanley in the Americas
the 1920s, more than 300 units being delivered in the car's relatively short existence
It used a 2-cylinder steam engine of Brooks design, and only one body style, a 4-door
five-seater closed model, was available.   K

BROOKS AND WOOLLAN (GB) *1907–1910*

Brooks and Woollan, Reading, Berks.

This car was also known as the Doru (the Greek word for 'spear'), an allusion
their slogan 'Swift and silent as the spear'. Financed by Brooks, S.W. Woollan ha
many years of experience to put behind the few cars he assembled from proprieta
components, to the customer's requirements. A typical production was a 15.9
White & Poppe-engined car, with Malicet et Blin chassis parts, which ran at Broo
lands. Production ceased when a De Dion-Bouton agency was developed, and t
shop facilities became fully occupied in body-building.

BROTHERHOOD (GB) *1904–1907*

(1) Brotherhood-Crocker Motors Ltd, West Norwood, London S.E. *1904–1906*
(2) Brotherhood-Crocker Motors Ltd, Tinsley, Sheffield, Yorks. *1906–1907*

The Brotherhood car was designed by Percy Richardson who had formerly be
with Daimler, the engines being made by the London engineering firm of Pet
Brotherhood. The first model was a 12/16hp 4-cylinder, with pair-cast cylinders a
double chain drive. Later, 20 and 40hp models, all with 4-cylinder engines were mad
The Yorkshire landowner Earl Fitzwilliam had been on the board from the start, a
in 1906 production was transferred to his factory at Sheffield. The following year t
name of the car was changed to Sheffield-Simplex, and new models introduced.   GN

BROUGH (GB) *c.1899–1908; 1913*

W.E. Brough, Basford, Nottingham

W.E. Brough built a De Dion engined belt-drive car in 1899, and a large tonnea
in 1908, but they were only experimental. In 1913 he made a V-twin cyclecar. H
son George Brough built the Brough Superior in the 1930s.   GN

BROUGH SUPERIOR (GB) *1935–1939*

Brough Superior Cars Ltd, Nottingham

Built by George Brough, maker of 'the Rolls-Royce of motor cycles', the Broug
Superior was one of several British makes of the 1930s using American engines wi
British chassis and bodywork. In Brough's case the engine was a Hudson Six
Straight-8, although the 1932 prototype had used a Dorman engine. Originally t
only body available was a four-seater drophead by Atcherly of Birmingham, but
1936 a 4-door saloon and a stark two-seater sports called the Alpine Grand Sport wi
the 6-cylinder engine appeared. The latter was intended to be a competitor to t
Railton Light Sports, but even with a Centric or Shorrock supercharger it was not
fast, being heavier and less powerful. The last Brough model, appearing in 193
was the Type XII, a handsome 4-door saloon with Charlesworth body and a Lincol
Zephyr V-12 engine. Three of these were laid down, but only one completed.   GN

BROUHOT (F) *1898–1910*

Brouhot et Cie, Vierzon, Cher

The first Brouhot had a rear-mounted 2-cylinder horizontal engine, constant mes
gears (4 speeds), and spur gear transmission to the rear axle. For 1903 vertical engine
and chain drive were adopted, the models being a 10hp twin, and 15 and 20hp four
Later Brouhots were of thoroughly conventional design, with 4-cylinder T-hea
engines of 10 to 60hp. An 8hp twin was made up to 1906, in which year shaft driv
appeared on the smaller models. At least one model was sold in England in 1908 unde
the name Club. The only break with tradition towards the end of the Brouhot's li
was the appearance of a 9hp car with belt drive, made from 1908 to 1910.   GN

BROWN (i) (GB) *1901–1911*

Brown Bros Ltd, London

This well-known firm of factors were marketing motor tricycles and the Whitne
(i) steam car in 1899. Two years later they offered complete vehicles under their ow
brandname, but both the origins and true nationality of these remain in doubt, thoug
some were certainly made by Star of Wolverhampton, and bodies were by Salmons
Initially they were straightforward shaft-driven light cars with 3-speed gearboxe
and automatic inlet valve Aster engines, in 6hp single-cylinder and 8hp 2-cylinde
forms. The latter cost £275 with tonneau body in 1902 when 'almost any type o
engine can be fitted' and buyers could have shaft or chain drive. A surviving 190
18/20hp Brown has a Brotherhood-Crocker engine, but Brown did not normally us
this make of engine. Mercedes-style honeycomb radiators were available in 1904
when a 6hp two-seater with armoured wood frame and chain transmission could b
bought for £175, and a Forman-engined 12/16hp 4-cylinder was also made. Mech
anically operated valves came in 1905, when the range included a small 1.8-litr
4-cylinder rather optimistically rated at 14hp. A big 3.8-litre '20/22' of 1906 had
pressed-steel frame. Other models available included a fully-enclosed doctor's coup
at £280, and a large solid-tyred brake with chain drive at £450; both these cars use

cylinder engines. Though twins were still catalogued in 1908, the trend was thence-forward in the direction of bigger vehicles, still modestly priced. The '20/22' was st supplemented and then supplanted by a very similar T-headed 4.1-litre '25/30' th gate change and a foot-operated accelerator. From 1907 to 1909 there was a 1-litre shaft-driven six with separately-cast cylinders, 4-speed gearbox, and twin rburettors, at £775. Late in 1908 the firm resumed its interest in small cars, sold der the name of Albruna; no Brown cars were listed after 1911. MCS

ROWN (ii) (US) 1914
rown Cyclecar Co, Asbury Park, N.J.
The Brown cyclecar had a track of 3ft 8in and a wheelbase of 8ft. It was driven y a 2-cylinder Spacke engine, with V-belts to the rear axle. GMN

ROWNIE (US) 1916–1917
O. Carter, Hannibal, Mo.
The Brownie was a light car powered by a 4-cylinder engine of 38bhp. The price as $735. GNG

ROWNIEKAR (US) 1908–1910
mar Motor Co, Newark, N.Y.
This was an ultra-light two-seater with a 3hp single-cylinder engine and belt rive. It cost only $150, and was intended mainly for children, the advertisement aiming that it could be operated by any intelligent child of 8 years or more. It was esigned by W.H. Birdsall, chief engineer of the Mora Motor Car Company, ho also made the Browniekar, Omar being a convenient anagram of Mora. GNG

RUBAKER (US) 1972 to date
he Brubaker Industries, Los Angeles, Calif.
The Brubaker Box is a new concept of car combining the advantages of conven-onal sedan and panel delivery truck. It uses a Volkswagen 1600 engine and hassis, and has a bonnetless single-door body which seats five, the rear seat being -shaped. It sells complete for $3,995. GNG

RULÉ-PONSARD (F) 1900–1901
. Brulé et Cie, Paris
The Brulé-Ponsard was an *avant-train* unit which could be fitted to existing horse-rawn vehicles. It was powered by a 4½hp Rozer et Mazurier 3-cylinder engine, in hich the exhaust gases from the two cylinders actuated the third or 'hot air cylin-er'. As with most *avant-train* attachments, drive was to the front wheels. GNG

RUNAU (CH) 1907
runau, Weidmann & Co, Brunau, Zürich
J. Weidmann was mainly a maker of chassis for commercial vehicles. However, *coupé de ville* and a limousine with 4-cylinder monobloc engines of 14/18 and 0/24hp respectively were shown at the Zürich Show in 1907, and possibly a few ther private cars were built as well. GNG

RUNNER (US) 1909–1910
runner Motor Car Co, Buffalo, N.Y.
The Brunner company concentrated on light delivery trucks. They also built very small number of cars on the truck chassis, employing 16hp horizontally-pposed 2-cylinder engines driving through 2-speed gearboxes to enclosed shaft rive. MJWW

RUNSWICK (US) 1916
runswick Motor Car Co, Newark, N.J.
This was a conventional assembled car powered by a 4-cylinder Wisconsin ngine. GNG

RUSH (i) (GB) 1902–1904
1) Brush Electrical Engineering Co Ltd, London S.E. *1902–1904*
2) Brush Electrical Engineering Co Ltd, Loughborough, Leics. *1904*
The first Brush car appeared on the market in March 1902. It was powered by 10hp 2-cylinder Abeille engine, and had a Sage 3-speed gearbox and double chain rive. For 1903 it was joined by 4-cylinder cars of 12, 16 and 20hp, also using Abeille ngines and chain drive. For part of 1904 these cars were still made in London, but t the same time a completely different design known as the Brushmobile was made t Brush's other factory at Loughborough. This had a 5 or 6hp single-cylinder hori-ontal engine, single chain drive and coil suspension. It was identical in design, though ot in appearance, to the 6hp Vauxhall, and all but the last six Brushmobiles made ere, in fact, built in the Vauxhall factory. GNG

RUSH (ii) (US) 1907–1913
1) Brush Motor Car Co, Detroit, Mich.
2) Brush Runabout Co, Detroit, Mich.
The Brush was a popular two-seater runabout with coil springs all round, and wooden frame and axles. The initial model had a single-cylinder, 12hp engine,

1905 BROWN(i) 18/20hp tourer. *Brown Brothers Ltd*

1972 BRUBAKER Box. *Brubaker Industries*

1903 BRUSH(i) 10hp tonneau. *G.N. Georgano Collection*

1910 BRUSH(ii) 10hp two-seater. *The Veteran Car Club of Great Britain*

1957 BRUTSCH Mopetta 49cc 3-wheeler.
Autosport

1922 B.S.A.(i) 10hp two-seater coupé. *The
Daimler Co Ltd*

1935 B.S.A.(i) Light Six coupé. *Autocar*

1935 B.S.A.(ii) Scout 9hp sports car. *M.J.
Worthington-Williams*

with chain-drive and solid tyres, priced at $780. By the end of 1907 the pri‹
was down to $500, and in 1912, a stripped version, the Liberty-Brush, sold f‹
only $350. Brush chassis with an abbreviated landaulette body were marketed ‹
1912 for taxicab use under the name Titan. Later models used a larger engi‹
and pneumatic tyres, but the basic design of the car remained unchanged. T‹
car was designed by Alanson P. Brush, and the company was formed by Fra‹
Briscoe. Later, Brush became a division of U.S. Motors Co and ceased producti‹
with the collapse of this combine in 1913.   GM

BRÜTSCH (D) 1951–1957
Egon Brütsch Fahrzeugbau, Stuttgart

A range of prototypes was developed by Brütsch, but production was nev‹
started. The range comprised 3- and 4-wheeled vehicles with single-, two- or fou‹
seater fibreglass bodies. The Brütsch 1200 was based on the Ford Taunus 12M, wi‹
a body of Brütsch design. The 3-wheeled Mopetta of 1956, with a 49cc engine, on‹
driven front wheel and single seat was possibly the smallest car ever built. It wa‹
5ft 7in long, 2ft 11in wide and had a weight of 134lb. In 1957 it appeared as th‹
Opelit Mopetta; Georg von Opel — formerly of the Opel company — acquired ‹
licence but did not succeed in putting the car into production. The Swiss Belcar an‹
the French Avolette were built under Brütsch licences.   HO

BRYAN (US) 1918–1923
Bryan Steam Motors, Peru, Ind.

The Bryan steam car was a handsome vehicle, its outward appearance close‹
resembling that of the Apperson. Six of these 4,500lb touring cars were produce‹
in six years of business.   K

B.S.A. (i) (GB) 1907–1926; 1933–1936
Birmingham Small Arms Co Ltd, Sparkbrook, Birmingham; Coventry

In 1907 the famous Midlands arms manufacturers began to make cars as a sid‹
line. They were not entirely new to the field, having made parts for the Roots in 189‹
Neither then nor later did they show much originality. E.E. Baguley, formerly ‹
Ryknield, was in charge, and later produced, in 1908, a copy of the successful 40h‹
Itala from Italy. Other conventional, medium-sized fours followed in small quant‹
ties. The major change that followed in 1911, after the company's takeover ‹
Daimler, was the adoption of Knight double sleeve-valve engines, as used by th‹
latter concern, in B.S.A. cars. These differed from Daimlers in being general‹
smaller and lighter. The first, the Twelve of about two litres, weighed only 1,232‹
in chassis form. Open bodies were of pressed steel from 1912: a single, importa‹
innovation that went largely unregarded. B.S.A. also made the Stoneleigh, whic‹
was a B.S.A. except for name and radiator, from then until 1914. It should not b‹
confused with the better-known Stoneleigh light car of the 1920s.

The first post-war B.S.A. was a light car — an attempt to cash in on the boo‹
in popular motoring, but superior to a great many. The Ten of 1921 was powered b‹
an air-cooled V-twin engine of modern design, with overhead valves, coil ignitio‹
aluminium crankcase, and aluminium pistons in iron liners. It developed 18bhp fro‹
a cubic capacity of 1,080cc, and was made by Hotchkiss of Coventry. This powe‹
unit was smooth and though, like all of its kind, it was noisy, it was eventuall‹
made quieter by improvements. The rear axle with its underslung worm drive o‹
Lanchester patents, was always silent. This uncharacteristic quality helped to se‹
the Ten well until it was dropped in 1924. The next B.S.A.'s were in fact sma‹
Daimlers, with 6-cylinder Knight double-sleeve-valve engines of under two litre‹
They were discontinued in 1926. From 1933 to 1936, this policy was resumed. I‹
1931, B.S.A. had taken over Lanchester and introduced a line of completely ne‹
Lanchesters as cheap Daimlers. In turn, a still cheaper range christened B.S.A.‹
followed from 1933, consisting of a machine basically similar to the Lanchester: ‹
Ten but with a side-valve engine, and a Light Six identical to its Lanchester opposit‹
number. These cars were made in the Daimler factory at Coventry. After 1936, n‹
more cars came from the motor car division of B.S.A.   TR‹

B.S.A. (ii) (GB) 1929–1940
B.S.A. Cycles Ltd, Small Heath, Birmingham

In 1924 Hotchkiss, makers of proprietary engines for other car firms, were take‹
over by their main customer, William Morris. They had also made an excelle‹
1,100cc, V-twin, air-cooled engine with overhead valves for the Birmingham Smal‹
Arms Company, for use in that company's B.S.A. light car. (This engine als‹
powered the short-lived Hotchkiss light car itself.) B.S.A. Cycles Ltd (the motor cycl‹
division of B.S.A.) acquired manufacturing rights in the engine to drive, in 1-litr‹
form, the front wheels of a 3-wheeler of very modern conception with independen‹
front suspension. This, the famous Beeza, first appeared in 1929, ready for the 193‹
season. In 1933 flexibility was added to the B.S.A.'s virtues when a water-coole‹
1,100cc 4-cylinder sv engine became available. In the previous year, the manufac‹
turers had already tried to attract a wider market by adding a solid axle and anothe‹
wheel at the rear. This became the Nine in 1933. The front wheel drive 4-wheele‹
was dropped for a season, but reappeared as the 9hp Scout in 1935. From 1936 t‹
1940 the Scout in 1,200cc Ten form was the only B.S.A. sold, the 2- and 4-cylinde‹
3-wheelers having been dropped in the former year. There was talk in the early 1950‹

resuming production of a small car with a 2-cylinder air-cooled engine, but it came
nothing.   TRN

UAT (F) *1901–1906*
Automobiles Léon Buat, Senlis, Oise
The original Buat used a 3½hp single-cylinder De Dion-Bouton engine, but by
1903 they were using Aster engines in their range of five cars, 6½hp and 9hp single-
cylinders, a 12hp 2-cylinder and 16hp and 24hp 4-cylinders. The smaller cars had
De Dion-type bonnets while the 4-cylinder models generally resembled Peugeots.
By 1905 the range had been enlarged to six cars, from 8hp to 30hp.   GNG

BUC, BUCCIALI (F) *1923–1933*
Bucciali Frères, Courbevoie, Seine
A spate of very unconventional designs, all of them too far ahead of their time,
appeared in France towards the end of the 1920s. The Buc or Bucciali, incorporating
features that did not become common until the 1960s, was one of these. The Bucs
of 1923 to 1924 were Violet-inspired 2-strokes, a twin followed by a V-4. In 1925
came the conventional AB 4/5 with 1.6-litre ohc S.C.A.P. engine, followed by a
90bhp AB6 6-cylinder. Of these, only the AB 4/5 was made in series. The TAN
of 1928 was completely unconventional, except for its power unit, which was a
medium-sized sv engine available in 6- or 8-cylinder form. It served only as a means
of propulsion for the assembly of novelties which made up the rest of the car: front-
wheel drive, independent suspension on rubber to all 4 wheels, and Sensaud de
Lavaud infinitely-variable automatic transmission. The most exotic Bucciali was
built in 1931 to 1932, and is said never to have run under its own power, although
the chassis survives today. This was the Double Huit, powered by two 3.8-litre
Continental straight-8 cylinder blocks mounted side-by-side on an aluminium
crankcase. Two crankshafts geared together, and two radiators were used. After this,
the last Bucciali model seemed something of an anticlimax, fine car though it was.
This was the TAV-12, a front-wheel-drive machine powered by a V-12 Voisin
engine. Only two were made. In all 151 Bucs or Bucciali were made, of which 38
were front-wheel-drive models.   TRN

BUCHET (F) *1911–1929*
(1) Société Buchet, Levallois-Perret, Seine *1911–1918*
(2) Gaston Sailly, Moteurs et Automobiles Buchet, Billancourt, Seine *1919–1929*
In the first decade of the present century, Buchet were active competitors of
De Dion and Aster, supplying proprietary engines to numerous motor cycle and
car makers. Reyrol was among the latter. Though their productions included a
monstrous 4,245cc racing tricycle in 1902 and a V-8 aero-engine as early as 1906,
they did not offer a complete 4-wheeler (a taxi) until 1910 and their first private
car did not follow until a year later. The 12/20hp Buchet was a conventional sv
monobloc 4-cylinder of 2.2-litre capacity with pump-and-trough lubrication,
magneto ignition, 3-speed gearbox and bevel drive, selling in England for £275
complete. This was followed by an equally ordinary 6CV of 1,100cc, sold as the
Ascot (i) in England which had grown up by 1920 into a 1½-litre car with a 4-speed
gearbox, full electrics and wire wheels. The first post-war models retained the pedal-
operated transmission brake. With 1551cc engine and modernized braking arrangements it could be bought in England for £420 in 1922 and by 1924 versions were
being sold with ohv and front-wheel brakes. The smaller 6CV had acquired the
typically French arrangement of front-wheel and transmission brakes by 1926, and
the two 4-cylinder types survived until the end of production. They were joined in
1928 by an unremarkable sv 1.7-litre 6-cylinder with magneto ignition and a 4-speed
gearbox, for which 40bhp was claimed.   MCS

BUCKAROO (US) *1957*
The Buckaroo is reported to have been a small air-cooled cyclecar, built in Cleveland, Ohio, with a speed of 18mph and a price of $400.   BE

BUCKEYE *see* LAMBERT (i)

BUCKINGHAM (i) (GB) *1913–1923*
(1) Buckingham Engine Works, Coventry, Warwickshire *1913–1915*
(2) Buckingham Engineering Co Ltd, Coventry, Warwickshire *1922–1923*
The cyclecar designed by J.F. Buckingham was originally sold under the name
Chota. The first model had an 8hp single-cylinder air-cooled engine of Buckingham's
own design and manufacture, and this was supplemented by a 12hp V-twin. The cars
had two forward speeds and final drive was by belts. In September 1913 the name
was changed to Buckingham and a water-cooled single-cylinder model added to the
range. The Buckingham achieved some competition successes in pre-war days, and
fifteen cars a week were being made early in 1914. After World War 1 the Buckingham was made in the Alvis works in Holyhead Road, Coventry and offered with one
engine only, a 10hp V-twin similar to the pre-war design, although there was now a
conventional 3-speed gearbox and bevel drive. However, the new Buckingham was
too expensive and much heavier than the pre-war one. None of the models sold well,
and production ended by 1923. J.F. Buckingham himself was more famous for his
wartime incendiary bullet.   TRN

1922 BUC 1.3-litre 2-cylinder racing car.
Autosport

1929 BUCCIALI TAV-30 coupé. *Autocar*

1913 BUCHET 12/20hp two-seater. *Autocar*

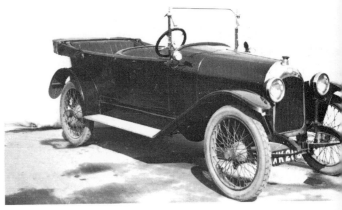
1922 BUCHET 10/18hp tourer. *Autocar*

1955 BUCKLER Mark X sports car. *Lucien Loreille Collection*

1904 BUFFUM flat-8 racing car. *Autocar*

1910 BUGATTI Type 13 1,327cc two-seater.
The Veteran Car Club of Great Britain

1924 BUGATTI Type 35 2-litre racing car.
Autosport

BUCKINGHAM (ii) (AUS) *1933–1934*
Buckingham Ward Motors (Australia) Ltd, Footscray, Victoria
   The Buckingham differed from most of its Australian counterparts in that it was powered by a 4-cylinder 21.7hp engine of the firm's own manufacture. At least two Buckingham Sixtys were made, a sedan and a coupé. Although the company was called Buckingham Ward, the cars were always known as Buckinghams, Ward being the name of a projected truck by the same firm.   GNG

BUCKLE (AUS) *1957–1960*
Buckle Motors, Sydney, N.S.W.
   The Buckle was an attractive fibreglass coupé powered by a Ford Zephyr engine, mostly with full Raymond Mays conversion; 20 cars were made. The Buckle company also made saloon and coupé bodies for the Goggomobil, to the standard German design, and a two-seater sports Goggomobil derivative of their own design, known as the Dart.   GNG

BUCKLER (GB) *1947–1962*
(1) Bucklers, Reading, Berks. *1947–1954*
(2) Buckler Cars Ltd, Reading, Berks. *1954–1958*
(3) Buckler Cars, Reading, Berks.; Crowthorne, Berks. *1958–1961*
(4) Buckler Engineering Ltd, Crowthorne, Berks. *1961–1962*
   Production Bucklers started with the Mark V, based on a multi-tubular space-frame. Ford 10 mechanical parts were fitted, incorporating already recognized Buckler modifications, such as independent front suspension and close-ratio gears. A long-wheelbase version, the Mark VI, was obtainable in two- or four-seater guise. Marks XV and XVI accepted various B.M.C. components, and were supplemented by the 90, a very successful 1,172 Formula car. The DD1 was designed for the FWA 1,098cc Coventry-Climax engine, and used a De Dion type rear axle. The DD2 was sprung at all corners by coil/damper units, and was advertised to take any engine up to 2 litres. A backbone-chassis model was also made, but the car side of the business was sold due to Derek Buckler's ill health, and the new company produced only the established designs. During the heyday of the kit-built car, Buckler's reputation was high, and numerous competition successes were achieved, in races, trials, sprints and hill-climbs alike. About 500 chassis were sold, including a large number of special order one-offs to accept all manner of unusual engines.   DF

BUCKLES (US) *1914*
T.E. Buckles, Manchester, Okla.
   This was a two-seater cyclecar with a 2-cylinder, air-cooled Spacke engine, a friction transmission, and belt drive.   GMN

BUCKMOBILE (US) *1903–1905*
(1) Buckmobile Co, Utica, N.Y. *1903–1904*
(2) Black Diamond Automobile Co, Utica, N.Y. *1904–1905*
   Buckmobile was a small two-seater roadster with a 15hp 2-cylinder engine (either air- or water-cooled) mounted under the seat. In 1904 Black Diamond Automobile Co (B.D.A.C.) bought Buckmobile Co and the plant of Remington Automobile & Motor Co; they continued the manufacture of Buckmobiles, but there is no evidence of a Black Diamond car.   GMN

BUFFALO (i) (US) *1900–1902*
Buffalo Automobile & Auto-Bi Co, Buffalo, N.Y.
   This was a light runabout with 7hp single-cylinder engine which became the Thomas in 1902, and thus can be considered as the ancestor of the great Thomas Flyer, winner of the 1908 New York to Paris Race.   GNG

BUFFALO (ii) (US) *1901–1906*
Buffalo Electric Carriage Co, Buffalo, N.Y.
   This company built a wide range of electric vehicles, from typical light runabouts to some exceptionally large and expensive cars. The 1903 four-seater tourer had wheel steering and a small front bonnet under which some of the batteries were housed, the others being beneath the body. It had a range of 75 miles per charge. 1904 models ranged from a two-seater runabout at $1,650 to a six-seater tourer at $5,000. After 1906 the cars were renamed Babcock (i). Other cars which bore the Buffalo name include: (a) experimental cars by the Buffalo Gasolene Motor Co, who made engines for the later Selden cars; (b) the 1908 de Schaum. There were also several firms making petrol and electric commercial vehicles under the name Buffalo.   GNG

BUFFALO (iii) (US) *1912–1915*
Buffalo Electric Vehicle Co, Buffalo, N.Y.
   This car was merely a revival of the Buffalo (ii) and the immediate successor to the Babcock (i), and was formed from Clark Motor Co, Buffalo Automobile Station Co, and Babcock (i).   GMN

BUFFAUD (F) *c.1900–c.1902*
Buffaud et Robatel, Lyons
   Buffaud et Robatel were general engineers who made a number of experimental

hicles, some of which they sold, although they were never really in business as
r manufacturers. They made a steam carriage in the 1890s, and experimented
th compressed air cars at the turn of the century. Later they made a few steam
ries for sale.   GNG

UFFUM (US) *1901–1907*

.H. Buffum & Co, Abington, Mass.

This company was a pioneer of the flat engine and of multi-cylinders. In 1902
ey offered a 16hp horizontally opposed 4-cylinder car, and in 1904 a racing car
th horizontal 8-cylinder engine and coil springs all round. From 1905 to 1907
ey made a V-8 with the same dimensions as the V-8 Hewitt.   GMN

UGATTI (D:F) *1909–1918; 1918–1956*

utomobiles E. Bugatti, Molsheim, Bas-Rhin

Ettore Bugatti was perhaps the greatest maker of racing cars until his fellow
alian Ferrari began to dominate the scene in recent years. Born into an artistic
mily in Milan, Bugatti soon found that the graphic arts were not to his liking and
rned to the mechanical. Drawn by speed and racing, at the age of 18 he attracted
tention in early motor cycle and tricycle races in Northern Italy, inevitably apply-
g his mechanical talent to the improvement and alteration of the machines.

1925 BUGATTI Type 23 Brescia Modifié saloon.
Coachwork by Freestone & Webb. *Monty Bowers*

In 1900, at the age of 19, he embarked on the design and production of his own
cylinder, 90 × 120mm car with the help of Count Gulinelli, and won a medal for
at the Milan exhibition in 1901. Baron de Dietrich who was attracted by the
achine and who was searching Europe for designs to produce at his Niederbronn
orks, signed an agreement with Bugatti to design for him. Bugatti moved to Nieder-
onn in 1902 to produce in the next two or three years a basic design of 4-cylinder,
4 × 130mm chain-driven chassis with variations, sold commercially as the De
ietrich-Bugatti, or in England as the Burlington, and occasionally raced by
ugatti himself. Engine dimensions varied, as was customary in those days, and
rger engines were also listed.

De Dietrich was offering other designs at the same time, particularly the Turcat-
éry, and Bugatti's car was not a commercial success; the arrangement came to an
d around 1904, and Bugatti teamed up with Mathis, moving to Strasbourg, the
strict where he was to remain for the rest of his active career.

The Mathis collaboration produced the Hermes car, which bore a strong resem-
lance to the earlier De Dietrich design, certainly in conception – 4 large cylinders,
-speed gearbox, chain drive, semi-elliptic springs – but by now it had a modern type
f radiator with a surrounding shell to replace the earlier exposed film type.

In 1906 Bugatti and Mathis fell out and separated, Bugatti going to the
eutz factory at Cologne to design and produce cars for them. Two chassis were
roduced, the first another typical 4-cylinder layout with an engine of 145 or
50×150mm and chain drive, and later a smaller 92×120mm car with, for the first
me in Bugatti's designs, a shaft drive.

1929 BUGATTI Type 44 3-litre saloon.
Lord Cholmondeley

During this period (about 1908) Bugatti produced at his own expense (and, it
said, in the cellar of his home at Cologne) the miniature chassis, with a 4-
ylinder, 60×100mm engine, and shaft drive which founded the thoroughbred
ne of his designs and enabled him later to produce his own car. This prototype
Type 10 in the Bugatti series) is still in existence.

There is at least some evidence that the creation of this car owes something
o the 1908 Coupe des Voiturettes Isotta Fraschini; it is more than likely that
ugatti saw and was inspired by these beautiful little cars. There is certainly
o evidence that the Isotta Fraschini cars owe anything to Bugatti, and their
esigner Cattaneo has denied the suggestion. The overall conceptual similarity is,
owever, striking.

Whatever the origins of his thoroughbred, Ettore Bugatti found a backer who
ould help him to start up production of his own car at the end of 1909, in a disused
ye works at Molsheim a few miles west of Strasbourg. Here production was started
f the real Bugatti car, with 4 cylinders, 65×100mm, (1,327cc) and 2 valves per
ylinder operated from an overhead camshaft with curved, sliding tappets and three
hassis lengths; Type 13 with a 6ft 6¾in wheelbase, Type 15, 7ft 10½in, and Type
7, 8ft 4½in and reinforced back springs for heavy bodywork.

1930 BUGATTI Type 46 5.3-litre
saloon. *G.N. Georgano*

Output was a few cars in 1910, but the car caused a great deal of favourable
omment at the 1910 Paris Salon, and in the early speed events it was entered in;
ommercial success, in spite of a high price, came immediately and several hundred
ars had been produced by 1914. During this period Bugatti also sold a licence to
eugeot for an 850cc Baby car, and kept his interest in large cars by producing a
ew chassis with a 4-cylinder 5-litre (100×160mm) ohc engine and reverting again
o chain drive, for racing. The first chassis went to the aviator Roland Garros and
urvives as the famous Black Bess (Hampton collection). Others competed un-
uccessfully at Indianapolis in the 500 mile race in 1914 and 1915.

The early 8-valve chassis had conventional semi-elliptic springs and radiators
f squarish, 5-sided shape. At the end of 1913, Bugatti introduced his reversed quarter
lliptic springs on the two long-length chassis, probably to simplify the fitting of
he body: many of Bugatti's design features show more originality than essential
ogic. This spring feature was to remain on all Bugatti's chassis designs produced
fterwards. At this time he also introduced his design of oval radiator, pear-
haped, but later more like an inverted horse shoe.

1931 BUGATTI Type 40A 1½-litre two-seater.
Conway Collection

1939 BUGATTI Type 57 3.3-litre coupé.
Coachwork by Graber. *G.N. Georgano*

1909 BUICK 18hp roadster. *Don McCray*

1920 BUICK 27hp two-seater (English-bodied
Bedford-Buick). *G.N. Georgano*

Just before World War 1 he produced a modified engine for voiturette racing, with 4 valves per cylinder (2 inlet, 2 exhaust), and an enlarged bore (66mm initially, later 68–69mm) giving more power, but the war prevented its use. Molsheim was soon occupied by the Germans and Bugatti found himself spending the next years in Paris working on aero engines.

In 1919 he reoccupied the factory himself, finding it happily undamaged, and resumed production of the 8-valve chassis and then the new 16-valve version. Wins at Le Mans in 1920 and at Brescia (1921) in voiturette races once more established his reputation and regular production of the car, now known as the Brescia, followed steadily. The long-wheelbase chassis were now known as Type 22 (7ft 10½in) and Type 23 (8ft 4½in) was retained for the short racing model. Improvements followed such as a crankshaft carried on ball bearings, better crank lubrication, a prettier radiator, and eventually 4-wheel brakes: in spite of these changes the similarity between the last chassis in 1926 and the first in 1910 is striking.

In 1922 Bugatti produced his first 8-cylinder production model, the Type 30, with a 2-litre 60 × 88mm engine, an overhead camshaft and 2 inlet and 1 exhaust valve per cylinder. This 3-valve layout had been seen on the pre-war Garros car and the aero engines. Racing versions were entered in the 1922 French Grand Prix at Strasbourg, Friderich, Bugatti's faithful mechanic, finishing 2nd. Production continued for the next few years of the 4-cylinder and 8-cylinder cars; an abortive attempt to produce a successful streamlined 'tank' with the 2-litre engine was made for the French GP at Tours in 1923 and then for 1924 Bugatti made the successful effort to produce a racing car which combined performance with aesthetic quality – the Type 35 was the result.

The new 1924 car had the Type 30 engine with its plain bearing crank replaced with a full ball and roller bearing, built-up unit, and a completely new chassis of fine lines carrying a handsome body, and first class brakes inside cast aluminium wheels. Tyre trouble prevented success in its first outing but soon success followed success, culminating in the world championship in 1926.

Although reluctant at first to fit a supercharger as his competitors had, Bugatti eventually in 1926 added one to the car to produce the Type 35C (2-litre, 60 × 88mm), Type 35B (2.3-litre, 60 × 100mm) and Type 39 (1.5-litre, 60 × 66mm). A sports car version (Type 35A) used the touring engine, and in 1926 a 4-cylinder (69 × 100mm, 1.5-litre) engine appeared, similar in layout to the 8-cylinder engine, but with a 5-(plain) bearing crankshaft, which when fitted to the GP chassis became the main sports car version (Type 37). Later this too had a blower fitted and became very potent (Type 37A).

In the period 1926–29 a profusion of models was listed: racing types 35, 35B, 35C, 39; sports versions Types 35A, 37, 37A; the touring model Type 30 replaced with a similar Type 38, later itself replaced by the 3-litre 8-cylinder Type 44 (69 × 100mm); Type 40 using the 4-cylinder engine from the Type 37; a splendid Type 43GP sport four-seater using the Type 35B engine in a long-wheelbase chassis and catalogued as the fastest sports car in the world (110mph) which it was; and to crown all the Royale.

The Royale (Type 41) was to be Bugatti's car of kings. It had a 12.7-litre (125 × 130mm) 8-cylinder engine of typical Bugatti layout producing over 250hp, fitted in an enormous chassis, intended to carry the works of the world's finest coachbuilders. Although a batch of 25 was projected only six were built and indeed only three were sold (in 1932–33), the financial crisis of 1929 intervening to spoil Bugatti's plans.

Around 1930 Bugatti continued to produce fine cars mixed with oddities. The Type 44 3-litre touring car became the Type 49 with the bore increased from 69 to 72mm, one of the best models. The Type 46 5.3-litre with a 3-speed gearbox in the back axle was introduced as a small size Royale and several hundred were produced. A racing 16-cylinder (Type 45, 47) was made, having some success in hillclimbs, and later an unsuccessful 4-wheel drive Type 53. The de luxe 5.3-litre had a new twin ohc engine fitted to become the Type 50 of 4.9 litres, very exciting and exotic but rather too powerful to be safe, even in the racing version, the Type 54.

The GP type 35 had a new engine with twin overhead camshafts fitted in 1931 to become the Type 51, a very successful and fine-looking car which was perhaps the most effective racing model Bugatti ever produced, but the search for power and the competition demanded a larger car. Thus in 1933 Bugatti produced the Type 59 3.3-litre racing car which was his last racing production except for specialized single-seaters. Meanwhile a sports version of the Type 51, the Type 55, had appeared usually with a roadster body among the handsomest ever fitted to a car.

The touring equivalent of the Type 59, the Type 57, was the last Molsheim model to go into production; about 800 were produced between 1934 and 1939. This had a twin-ohc 72 × 100mm, 3.3-litre engine, integral 4-speed gearbox, and a conventional Bugatti chassis with semi-elliptic springs at the front and reversed quarter-elliptic at the rear. Later supercharged versions (Type 57C) and sports versions (Type 57S, 57SC) were produced.

Production was interrupted by the war, and only sporadic and half-hearted attempts were made (a few Type 101 models were produced) to resume car manufacture after Ettore Bugatti's death in 1947. In 1956 two Formula 1 GP cars were built. Known as the Type 251, they had 2½-litre straight-8 engines mounted transversely behind the driver in a space frame. One was driven by Trintignant in the 1956 French GP at Reims, but retired, and the cars were never heard of again. HGC

BUGATTI-GULINELLI (I) *1901-1903*

Officine Gulinelli, Ferrara

This company was founded by Count Gulinelli and Ettore Bugatti to build a
4-cylinder high-performance car to the latter's design. It had a 3,054cc engine and
side-chain drive, but the Ferrara venture closed down when Bugatti departed to
work for De Dietrich at Niederbronn, and it is probable that only one Bugatti-
Gulinelli was made. MCS

BUGETTA (US) *1969 to date*

Bugetta, Inc, Costa Mesa, Calif.

In addition to their well-known off-road vehicles, Bugetta offer a sports car for
two or four passengers, powered by a mid-mounted Ford 4.9-litre engine. It has
a one-piece fibreglass body and optional top in either fibreglass or cloth. The price
is $3,695. GNG

BUGGYCAR (US) *1907–1909*

Buggy-Car Co, Cincinnati, Ohio

This was a two-seater buggy-type car with solid rubber tyres. It had an opposed
2-cylinder air-cooled engine under the seat. The final drive to the rear axle was by
cable. GMN

BUGMOBILE (US) *1909*

Bugmobile Co of America, Chicago, Ill.

The Bugmobile was a tiller-steered two-seater high-wheeler with a 2-cylinder,
2-stroke 15hp engine. The final drive was by belts to the rear wheels. This car was
devoid of mudguards. GMN

BUICK (US) *1903 to date*

(1) Buick Motor Car Co, Detroit. Mich, *1903*

(2) Buick Motor Car Co, Flint, Mich. *1904 to date*

David Buick's first car followed conventional American design in having a
flat-twin engine mounted amidships under the floor, a two-speed planetary transmission, and final drive by chain – but unusual were its mechanically-operated full
overhead valves, a feature of all cars bearing the name of Buick to the present
day, apart from fours of the 1906–9 period, which had side-valves in T-heads.
Capacity was 2.6 litres, and it sold for $1,250. Developments of this original model
were selling in England for £294 in 1907, but there was already a companion
2-litre four with front-mounted engine, and 1908 saw a 'square' four
(95.2 × 95.2mm) with planetary transmission added to the range. In 1908 W.C.
Durant formed General Motors, Buick being one of the original members of the
group. In 1909 Bob Burman drove a Buick to victory in the first race ever held
at Indianapolis Speedway. Sales had exceeded 30,000 cars by 1910. For the next
few years Buicks with English bodywork were sold in Britain first as 'all British
Bedfords', and then as 'Bedford-Buicks'. By 1912 planetary transmission had been
dropped and 4-cylinder cars were available in 2.7-litre, 3.3-litre and 5.2-litre sizes,
still with rhd, but with the brake and gear levers faired into the driver's door. Delco
electric lighting and starting were standard on all models by 1914, in which year
Buick marketed their first six, the B-55. Nearly 126,000 cars were sold in 1916,
and the company entered the post-World War 1 era with a 2.8-litre four and a
3.9-litre six, cars which brought Buick into fourth position in U.S. sales, behind
Ford, Dodge, and Chevrolet, all far cheaper vehicles; a Buick Six tourer cost
$1,795 in 1921.

Drastic change came in 1924. The cars acquired front wheel brakes as standard
equipment, while cylinder heads were now detachable, and the rounded radiator
shell gave way to an angular, Packard-like outline that was to continue until 1928.
Prices of fours started at $935, and the cheapest six was listed at $1,565. The 6-
cylinder cars became the staple in 1925 and the 'back-to-front' gear shift pattern
shared with Dodge was discarded in 1927. The cars were completely re-styled in 1929,
when hydraulic shock absorbers were added, and the capacities of the two basic
models were increased to 3.8 litres and 5.1 litres respectively. Prices ran from $1,195
to $2,145, but for Buick customers with slenderer pockets there was the Marquette
(q.v.). Buick went over to an all-straight-8 programme, still with overhead valves,
in 1931. Expanding brakes were now standard at front and rear. Synchromesh was
standardized on the more expensive models and available as an extra on all, and
was standardized throughout the range in 1932.

Buick's evolution up to World War 2 followed General Motors policy: cruciform-
braced frame and no-draught ventilation in 1933, Dubonnet-type ifs in 1934, and
turret-top styling, down-draught carburation and hydraulic brakes in 1936 with
the DA-series – one example of which became famous when it took Mrs Ernest
Simpson into exile at the time of the British Abdication crisis. Despite Buick's
upper middle-class position in the G.M. sales picture, the 1937 range of 4.1-litre and
5.2-litre eights covered everything from a sedan on a 10ft 2in wheelbase at $855
up to a seven-seater C090 limousine at $2,095; prices in Britain, where the cars
were consistently well received between the Wars, were £500 and £865 respectively.
1938 Buicks had coil springing all round, and that year the Division produced
G.M's first 'dream car', a two-seater convertible coupé styled by Harley Earl on a
Roadmaster chassis. Buicks used the same engines up to 1952, though they came out

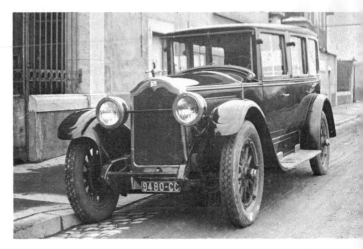

1926 BUICK Model 50 4.4-litre sedan. *Lucien
Loreille Collection*

1932 BUICK Light Eight 3.8-litre sedan.
G.N. Georgano

1961 BUICK Special 3½-litre sedan. *G.N.
Georgano*

1968 BUICK Riviera 7-litre coupé. *General
Motors Corp*

1973 BUICK Century Luxus coupé.
General Motors Corp

1928 BURNEY Streamline saloon. The prototype
with 12/75 Alvis engine. *National Motor Museum*

with a 2-speed Dynaflow automatic transmission in 1948. In 1948 they pioneered the now popular hardtop convertible body with their Riviera. The smaller engines were, however, enlarged to 4.3 litres in 1952, and the following year the Division's first ohv V-8 unit appeared; its capacity was 5.3 litres, and its output 188bhp. All 1954 Buicks used this type of engine.

Sales dropped in 1958, but the 1959 cars were style leaders with the delta tail and fins. Buick's first effort at a compact car in 1961 was the Special with an all-aluminium 155bhp, 3½-litres V-8 engine, replaced the following year by a cast-iron V-6, used also by Oldsmobile. The demand for cars with a sporting flavour resulted in the handsome Riviera sports coupé of 1963, which by 1966 was giving 340bhp from 7 litres, and was capable of 120mph. Automatic transmission was, of course, standard. The 1966 Buick range had a more sporting atmosphere than in the past, and embraced the Special with a 9ft 7in wheelbase and a choice of V-6 or 4.9-litre V-8 engines; the Skylark with the same chassis dimensions and a 6.6-litre V-8 engine; and the bigger Buicks in the shape of the 5½-litre Le Sabre, the 6.6-litre Wildcat, the Electra and the top-line Riviera. These models continued without basic change until 1971, though concealed screenwipers (found on other GM cars of that year) and the option of front disc brakes came in 1967, and cylinder capacities were increased: the biggest V-8 ran to 7,046cc in that year, to 7,456cc in 1970. The small 3½-litre V-8 abandoned by Buick in 1963 was taken up by Rover of England in 1968 and was subsequently supplied by them to Morgan. The 1971 Buick station wagons featured glide-away tailgates. By 1972 all but the economy Skylarks had front disc brakes as regular equipment. Engine outputs were reduced (from 370bhp to 250bhp in the case of the most potent V-8), and the Riviera was restyled in the Chevrolet Corvette hardtop idiom. Only V-8s, of 5,736cc and 7,456cc, were offered in 1973; the Skylark gave way to a new car with an old Buick name, the Century, that reverted to the single-headlamp layout.   MCS

BULLOCK (AUS) 1901
Bullock Cycle Works, Adelaide, S.A.
A few voiturettes with water-cooled engines and chain drive were made by this cycle works.   GNC

BULLY (D) 1933
Bully Fahrzeugbau, Berlin SO 16
The Bully was a 3-wheeled two-seater coupé, powered by a 200cc single-cylinder 2-stroke engine driving the rear wheel by chain. A 600cc engine was also available.   GNC

BURDICK (US) 1909–1910
Burdick Motor Co, Eau Claire, Wisc.
The Burdick was a very large car, with an 11ft 10in wheelbase. The 6-cylinder engine of 9.7 litres was linked with a 4-speed transmission and shaft drive to the rear axle. The Model C eight-seater touring car was listed at $7,000.   GMN

BURG (US) 1910–1913
L. Burg Carriage Co, Dallas City, Ill.
Early Burg cars had 4-cylinder engines. There were five-seater tourer, two-seater roadster and runabout versions. The Burg range was later extended to larger cars with 6-cylinder engines developing 40hp.   GMN

BURGERS (NL) 1898–1900
Eerste Nederlandsche Rijwielenfabriek, Deventer
A few light cars with De Dion engines were made by this company, who also produced light goods vehicles and motor tricycles.   GNC

BURKE (GB) 1906–1907
Burke Engineering Co Ltd, Clonmel, Tipperary
The Burke used a 24/30hp 4-cylinder engine of French manufacture, although the firm made their own chassis and gearbox. Final drive was by side chains.   GNC

BURLAT (F) 1904–1905
Burlat Frères Constructions de Moteurs Rotatifs et Chassis Automobiles, Lyons
The four Burlat brothers made a limited number of cars powered by horizontal rotary engines. A 20hp car was shown at the 1905 Paris Salon, but production was sporadic, and in 1906 a new firm was founded to make lorries only, under the name C.A.R.   GN

BURNEY (GB) 1930–1933
Streamline Cars Ltd, Maidenhead, Berks.
This creation of the airship designer Sir Dennistoun Burney had an aeroplane-type of body with all seven seats within the wheelbase, all wheels independently sprung, and the engine at the rear, flanked by twin lateral radiators. The prototype was built up on a front-wheel-drive Alvis chassis turned back to front, but the twelve production cars made in the famous 'Jam Factory' at Maidenhead, home of G.W.K. and Marendaz had 3-litre twin ohc Beverley Straight-8, Lycoming and 20hp Armstrong-Siddeley power units. Although one of the Beverley-powered cars was supplied to H.R.H. the Prince of Wales in 1931, the Burney at £1,500

was not a viable proposition in the Depression years, and the design was taken up in 1933 by Crossley.   MCS

BURNS *see* BILLINGS

BURNS (US) *1908–1911*
Burns Bros, Havre de Grace, Md.
This was one of the few makes of high-wheelers built east of the Allegheny Mountains. During its career the Burns used a 2-cylinder air-cooled engine with friction transmission and double-chain drive. Steering was by wheel.   GMN

BURROWES (US) *1905–1908*
E.T. Burrowes Co, Portland, Maine
An early model, with the engine under the seat, single-chain drive and tiller steering, had wire wheels and full-elliptical springs. The model E, made in 1908, had a 4-cylinder L-head engine of 30hp and wheelbase of 9ft 9in. Probably fewer than a dozen Burrowes were built, two of which still exist.   GMN

BURROWS (US) *1914*
Burrows Cyclecar Co, Ripley, N.Y.
This tandem two-seater cyclecar had a wheelbase of 8ft 10in, and a track of 3ft. Its 2-cylinder engine was air-cooled and rated at 9hp. It drove the 715lb car through a friction transmission. The headlamps were mounted above the level of the body.   GMN

BUSH (US) *1916–1924*
Bush Motor Co, Chicago, Ill.
Like the Birch, the Bush was a mail-order car. Lycoming and Continental units were used for both the 4- and 6-cylinder versions of these vehicles.   KM

BUSSON (F) *1907–1908*
Voiturettes Busson, Paris
This company began by selling the Nagant 30hp 6-cylinder under the name Busson-Dedyn, but made a number of 7/9hp 2-cylinder voiturettes of their own 1908. They also sold the small 6-cylinder de Bazelaire as the Busson-Bazelaire.   GNG

BUTTERFIELD (GB) *1961–1963*
Butterfield Engineering Co, Nazeing, Essex
A B.M.C. Mini-based kit-built car, the Butterfield Musketeer was available either with the standard 848cc or the 997cc Cooper engine. The rather inelegant body was a glassfibre 2-seater GT type, which was fitted on a tubular chassis.   DF

BUTTEROSI (F) *1919–1924*
Sté Nouvelle des Automobiles Butterosi, Boulogne-sur-Seine
The Butterosi was a conventional light car with a 4-cylinder side-valve engine of 1,327cc. Disc wheels were standardized, and a heavy-looking 6-light saloon was shown at the first post-war Olympia Show in London in 1919.   GNG

BUTZ (D) *1934*
Bungartz & Co, Munich
A small two-seater car with a 2-cylinder 400cc 12bhp rear engine and independent wheel suspension. It could be supplied with a 2-wheel trailer in matching colours or luggage.   HON

BYRIDER (US) *1908–1909*
Byrider Electric Auto Co, Cleveland, Ohio
The Byrider electrics were all small two-seater cars. The only model for 1909 was on a wheelbase of 6ft 9in with a track of only 4ft. This vehicle was advertised to sell for $1,800.   GMN

B.Z. (D) *1924–1925*
Bootswerft Zeppelinhafen GmbH, Potsdam-Wildpark
A two-seater cyclecar using the opposed-twin B.M.W. motorcycle engine of 494cc. The body was made of aluminium. In spite of its sturdy construction this make was forced to close down as a result of financial troubles.   HON

B-Z-T (US) *1914*
B-Z-T Cyclecar Co, Owego, N.Y.
This cyclecar had a full set of mudguards and a V-twin engine of 12/15hp. It used a friction transmission and final drive was by chain. The only model made was a two-seater which was priced at $385.   GMN

1919 BUTTEROSI 12hp saloon. *Autocar*

1934 BUTZ 400cc two-seater coupé. *Neubauer Collection*

1929 CABAN 6CV cabriolet. *Yves Giraud-Cabantous*

1906 CADILLAC 8hp three-seater. *Western Reserve Museum, Cleveland, Ohio*

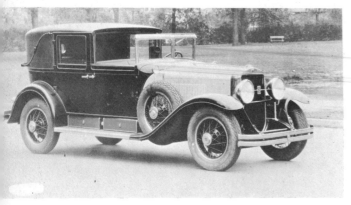

1928 CADILLAC Series 341 5.5-litre town car. *General Motors Corporation*

CABAN (F) 1926–1932

Yves Giraud-Cabantous, Boulogne-sur-Seine

Caban cars were built by the racing driver Yves Giraud-Cabantous, using vario models of 4-cylinder Ruby engine in chassis of Cabantous' own construction. T earliest models had the 30bhp Ruby Type OC engine, but from 1928 onwar the 38bhp Type OS was employed. Some cars of 1931 and 1932 employed t still more powerful Type K developing 43bhp, and one or two racing Cabans us the K engine with supercharger, giving 60bhp and 105mph. Capacity of all the engines was 1,097cc. Total production of Cabans was only 28 cars, of which were sports or racing models, 6 were saloons, and 3 cabriolets. The marque's m notable sporting success was Giraud-Cabantous' victory in the 1930 Bol d' (Cabans took the first four places in the 1,100cc class), but they also won t 1931 Circuit de Torvilliers, and came 2nd in class at Le Mans in 1931. GM

CADILLAC (US) 1903 to date

(1) Cadillac Automobile Co, Detroit, Mich. *1903–1905*
(2) Cadillac Motor Car Co, Detroit, Mich. *1905 to date*

The 'Standard of the World' started humbly as a single-cylinder car selling f $750. Henry M. Leland, its creator, had been associated with Henry Ford and ha also built engines for Oldsmobile. The Model-A Cadillac was markedly similar the early Fords in having a horizontal underfloor engine, 2-speed planetary tran mission and central chain drive via a spur-type differential, but Cadillac's 1½-lit inlet over exhaust power unit had one cylinder where Ford used two. There was n bonnet on the early models. This very successful design remained in productic until 1908, later improvements including rack-and-pinion steering, transverse fro suspension and a dummy bonnet. The marque was introduced to Britain by F. Bennett, who in 1908 conducted a 'standardization test' at Brooklands. Thre single-cylinder cars were dismantled and the parts mixed up — they were the reassembled and the vehicles run on the track. The R.A.C. awarded Cadillac t Dewar Trophy for this achievement.

A 30hp 4-cylinder car with separate cylinders and copper water jackets w announced for 1906 and 75,000 of this type were sold before it was discontinue in 1914. The original planetary transmission gave way first to a convention 3-speed box, and finally in 1914 to a 3-speed box with 2-speed back axle. Cadilla was one of the firms organized into the General Motors group in 1909 by W.C Durant, and in 1910, when a 4-cylinder tourer could be bought for $1,600, th company was claiming that tolerance on 112 parts of the car were accurate t one-thousandth of an inch. 1912 saw a most important innovation: the standardiza tion of the Delco system of electric lighting and starting on the Cadillac, now c 5½-litres capacity and capable of 60mph. The first left-hand drive Cadillac of 191 was also the first of the company's V-8s, to become as much a hallmark of th breed as were Buick's overhead valves. Inspired by the De Dion-Bouton of 191 it had a 5.1-litre engine and sold for $2,700. 13,000 were sold in the first year c production and the model was widely used by the U.S. Army in World War Cylinder heads were detachable from 1917 on, and 1924 versions had Duc cellulose finish and front wheel brakes.

In 1927, when 47,000 cars were sold, a less expensive companion make, L Salle appeared, and the cars were restyled in 1928. The synchromesh gearbo made its world debut with the 1929 models, which also featured chromium platin and safety glass, with a price range from $3,295 to $5,995. 1930 saw the advent c the ohv V-16 of 7.4 litres, which gave 185bhp and had a wheelbase of 12ft 4in. Th sold at an average rate of 500 a year for eight seasons in the $6,000–$9,0C price bracket. It was joined in 1931 by an equally impressive ohv 6-litre V-1: Improvements over the next few years included power brakes (1931), ride contr (1932), no-draught ventilation (1933), Dubonnet type ifs (1934) and 'turret-to all-steel bodies (1935). 1938 models had column change as standard, a year ahea of other G.M. products, while the V-12 and V-16 were dropped in favour of side-valve short-stroke 16-cylinder model which was made until 1940. Another ne model for 1938, the 8-cylinder Sixty Special, anticipated G.M.'s 1940 styling wit its absence of running boards and 4-light sedan bodywork. 5.7-litre side-valve V-8 in three wheelbase lengths made up the 1941 range, on which Hydramatic transmis sion was optional for the first time.

The post-war era was to see Cadillac outstrip all its competitors in the top-pric class and become an international symbol of wealth. Sales climbed from 66,0C in 1941 to 103,857 in 1950, and to a new record of 165,959 in 1964. Tail fins mad their first appearance on the company's 1948 fastback coupé, and in 1949 Cadilla along with Oldsmobile, adopted overhead valves and oversquare cylinder dimen sions, their new 5.4-litre engine developing 160bhp. Cadillacs were raced at Le Mans in 1950 by Briggs Cunningham and the engine was also used in export editions of Britain's J.2. Allard. Power output increased steadily: 190bhp in 1952 (by which time manual transmission was no longer offered), 210bhp in 1953 (when a 12-volt electric system was standardized), and 230bhp in 1954, the year when panoramic wrap-around windscreens and power-assisted steering became standard.

The expensive Eldorado Brougham of 1957 (it cost over $13,000) was the first car to have air suspension (dropped after a few seasons) as standard equipment, while Cadillac, along with Lincoln, started the fashion for four headlamps, that later became universal in the U.S.A. 1966 Cadillacs featured G.M.'s perimeter-type chassis frame, a 340bhp 7-litre engine, variable-rate power steering, full air conditioning, electric door locks and seat controls, a time switch for the headlamps and a six-position steering wheel. Prices started at $4,650. In 1967 Cadillac set a new sales record of 213,161 cars, bettered in 1969 with 266,798. They introduced a fwd car on Oldsmobile Toronado lines, the Fleetwood Eldorado with torsion-bar ifs, self-levelling suspension, and front disc brakes, these last being applied to the more expensive Fleetwoods with conventional drive, and to all the 1969 range. Capacity of the V-8 engine was increased — to 7,735cc in 1968 and to 8.2 litres in 1970, but otherwise there were no major changes. In 1973 Cadillac were one of the few firms offering a nine-seater limousine: the 75 with a wheelbase of 12ft 7½in and an overall length of 20ft 8in.　　　　MCS

1935 CADILLAC V-12 6-litre town car. *G.N. Georgano*

CADIX (F) *1920–1923*
Automobiles Jean Jannel, Cadix-Martinville, Vosges

The Cadix was a medium-sized car using Ballot engines of 1½-litres or 2.3-litres capacity. Two- and four-seater open bodywork was offered.　　　　GNG

CAESAR *see* SCACCHI

CAFFORT (F) *1920–1922*
Sté des Anciens Etablissements Caffort, Paris

The Caffort company had been in existence since well before World War 1 making marine and industrial engines at Marseilles, but the cars were made in Paris. They used air-cooled flat-twin 1-litre engines mounted over the front wheels which they drove through bevel gears. The front wheels were so close together that the Caffort had the superficial appearance of a three-wheeler. Commercial models were also made, and a number were used as taxicabs in Paris.　　　　GNG

1953 CADILLAC Eldorado 5.4-litre convertible. *General Motors Corporation*

CAIL-BORDEREL *see* BORDEREL-CAIL

CALCOTT (GB) *1913–1926*
Calcott Bros Ltd, Coventry, Warwickshire

The Calcott was typical of the makes which sprang to life at the start of the boom in 'motoring for the masses' and faded away in competition with more efficient producers. It was made by a firm of bicycle and motor cycle manufacturers. Calcott radiators copied a more successful make — Standard — and the cars provided roomy, reliable transport at a moderate price. All had side-valve engines. Some 2,500 were made altogether. They grew up from a light car, the well-known Ten of 1914, current to the end of car production, to the less familiar 2-litre Twelve and 6-cylinder, 2½-litre Sixteen, both of which had four forward speeds. The last-named was a 60mph vehicle with a seven-bearing crankshaft, intended for the more prosperous owner. Few were sold and in 1926 Singer acquired the company.　　　　TRN

1973 CADILLAC Fleetwood Brougham 7.7-litre sedan. *General Motors Corp*

CALDWELL VALE (AUS) *1913*
Caldwell Vale Truck & Bus Co, Auburn, N.S.W.

This company was better known for large 4-wheel-drive road tractors, but it also made a 30hp touring car with 4-wheel-drive and steering.　　　　GNG

CALEDONIAN (GB) *1899–1906*
Caledonian Motor Car & Cycle Co, Aberdeen

This company assembled a small number of cars to special order, using De Dion engines for the voiturettes, and Daimler engines for larger cars. A later make also called Caledonian made a few taxicabs at Granton from 1912 to 1914.　　　　GNG

CALIFORNIA (i) (US) *1900–1902*
California Automobile Co, San Francisco, Calif.

This company offered petrol, steam and electric cars ranging in price from $500 to $3,000. It is not certain how many of any type were actually built. The petrol cars were also offered under the name Calimobile.　　　　MJWW

CALIFORNIA (ii) (US) *1913*
California Cycle Car Co, Los Angeles, Calif.

This cyclecar used a 2-cylinder air-cooled engine of 1.1 litre. It had a friction transmission with belt drive and an underslung frame.　　　　GMN

CALIFORNIAN (US) *1920–1921*
California Motor Car Corp, Los Angeles, Calif.

1913 CALCOTT 10.5hp two-seater. *G.N. Georgano*

1910 CALTHORPE 12/14hp tourer. *Autocar*

1915 CALTHORPE 10hp sporting two-seater.
David Burgess Wise

1900 CAMBIER 8hp 'petit omnibus'. *The
Veteran Car Club of Great Britain*

The Californian was an assembled car with 6-cylinder Beaver engine which wa
first shown in May 1920 in the showrooms of the Gates-Kelly Automotive C
of Los Angeles. The car was advertised as having been designed for the require
ments of the Western motorist, but this short-lived concern had failed by 1921. KM

CALIMOBILE *see* CALIFORNIA (i)

CALL (US) *c.1911*
Call Motor Car Co, New York, NY
   This car appeared in four models with engines of 30 and 36hp.   GM

CALORIC (US) *1904*
Chicago Caloric Engine Co, Chicago, Ill.
   The single model of this car was a closed coupé with a height equal to its length
It was driven by a 3-cylinder, 9hp engine with hot-tube ignition, and a 3-spee
transmission.   GMN

CALTHORPE (GB) *1904–1932*
Calthorpe Motor Co Ltd, Birmingham
   In 1904 G.W. Hands, a bicycle manufacturer, introduced the first Calthorpe car
It was a small, low-priced, 10hp 4-cylinder machine with shaft drive, continued as
a 12/14hp. Bigger Calthorpes were made, of which the best-known was the 16/20
announced for 1907. The really large 28/40hp of that year was short-lived: light
cars remained the company's forte. Generally, they were powered by White & Poppe
engines. Works teams of Calthorpe cars, based on the 12/14hp and its successor
the 13.9hp, entered the Coupe de l'Auto races in France more consistently than any
other British make, but with no success.
   The car which made the firm's name more than any other before World War 1
was the little Calthorpe Minor, a beautifully-made 10hp light car current from
1913 to 1915. Like all Calthorpes, it was a conventional machine, with a 4-cylinder
side-valve engine and 3-speed gearbox. Hands left the company after the war to
make the Hands light car, but the 10hp was continued. It was a notably good-
looking and well-finished machine with a good performance, but the handsomest
Calthorpes were its two- and four-seater sports variants, with polished aluminium
bodies by Mulliner, a subsidiary company. Their alloy reciprocating parts were
drilled for extra lightness and balance, permitting higher engine revolutions. These
sports cars were good for over 60mph. A new Calthorpe, the Twelve, followed
in 1923, which was more refined but heavier and less attractive. An obscure
15hp six with overhead camshaft, which had been the last Hands model, was the
company's last new car. It was introduced in 1925, by which time G.W. Hands had
returned to the firm. Very few cars were made after 1927, though motor cycle
manufacture continued. The car factory was reopened in the same year as
the Colmore Depot Ltd's Morris service centre.   TRN

CALVERT (US) *1927*
Calvert Motor Associates, Baltimore, Md.
   A low-priced small car using a 6-cylinder engine of the firm's own manufacture.
Calverts were available in three open models only, or as a chassis at $550.   KM

CAMBER (GB) *1966–1969*
(1) Checkpoint Engineering Ltd, Rye, Sussex *1966–1967*
(2) W. West (Engineers) Ltd, Rye, Sussex *1967-1969*
   In the manufacturers' words, this was a 'constructor's car'. Designed to incorporate B.M.C. Mini sub-frames and components, the glass-fibre body was mounted
on a tubular frame, with steel roof reinforcement. These features enabled greater
safety to be claimed than was usual with this class of vehicle. The name was
changed to Maya GT in 1967, but few cars were sold.   DF

CAMBIER (F) *1897–1905*
Etablissements Cambier, Lille, Nord
   Before making cars the Cambier company were specialists in air-compressing
equipment. Their first cars were rear-engined machines on Benz lines (some of
these were made under licence in Belgium) but in 1897 they made a diligence
for Algeria with a 3-cylinder horizontal engine of 30hp. Their 1900 car used an
8hp 2-cylinder horizontal engine and it was stated that single-, 3- and 4-cylinder
models were also available. The latter were probably commercial vehicles, for the
company soon made a name for themselves in lorries, buses and fire engines. 1901
cars were made under Mathieu patents, the range consisting of a 6hp belt-drive
voiturette and 8 and 12hp chain-driven cars. In 1902 they went over to shaft drive
and front-mounted engines under a bonnet. Cars of 8 and 12hp were made until
the end of production two or three years later.   GNG

CAMBRO (GB) *1920*
Central Aircraft Co Ltd, Northolt, Middlesex
   At a price of 79 guineas, the Cambro was advertised as 'the cheapest car in the
world'. It had a 2-cylinder Economic engine of only 192cc mounted directly over
the single rear wheel, and only one speed. The single-seater body looked exactly

like a child's pedal car, and the whole contraption weighed only 165lb. Fuel consumption of 100mpg was claimed. GNG

CAMERON (US) 1902–1921
1) United Motor Co, Pawtucket, R.I. 1902–1903
2) James Brown Machine Corp, Pawtucket, R.I. 1903–1904
3) Cameron Car Co, Brockton, Mass.; New London, Conn. 1905–1908
4) Cameron Car Co, Beverly, Mass.; New London, Conn. 1908–1912
5) Cameron Motor Co, West Haven, Conn. 1912–1913
6) Cameron Motor Co, New Haven, Conn. 1914–1916
7) Cameron Motors Corp, Norwalk, Conn. 1917–1918
8) Cameron Motors Corp, Stamford, Conn. 1917–1921

Few cars can have had so many changes of address and company organization as the Cameron. It began life as a light two-seater powered by a 6hp single-cylinder air-cooled engine, and using shaft drive. This lasted during the Pawtucket period, but with the formation of the Cameron Car Co. at Brockton larger cars with 2- or 3-cylinder engines of up to 12hp were made. They had the gearbox mounted on the rear axle, a feature that was retained until the end of Cameron production. In 1908 a 20hp 4-cylinder car was introduced, still with air-cooling and a round bonnet rather like that of the contemporary Franklin. A six was made for a short time in the New London factory, and in 1913 came the first cars with water-cooled engines. Apart from the position of the gearbox the later Camerons were conventional cars, though the 1917 models had adjustable cantilever suspension. The Stamford factory was bought in 1917, and a 6-cylinder car was built in small numbers until 1921. GNG

1904 CAMERON 9hp two-seater. *Michael Ware*

CAMPBELL (i) (AUS) 1901
A.M. Campbell, Hobart, Tasmania

The Campbell was a steamer with two single-cylinder engines on each side of the body, developing 7hp between them. It had tiller steering and a *dos-à-dos* four-seater body. GNG

CAMPBELL (ii) (US) 1918–1919
Campbell Motor Car Co, Kingston, N.Y.

This was a 4-cylinder car built in small numbers and in tourer form only. KM

CAMPION (GB) 1913–1914
Campion Cycle Co, Ltd, Nottingham

The Campion cyclecar made by a well-known motorcycle firm used an 8hp J.A.P. air-cooled engine, friction transmission and belt final drive. GNG

CANADA CARS see GALT

CANADIAN (CDN) 1921
Colonial Motors Ltd, Walkerville, Ont.

Designed by E.G. Gunn, formerly of Packard, this car had independent front suspension consisting of two semi-elliptic transverse springs linked by short king-pin support arms at the outer ends. The touring version was designed to sell at $2,600 and at least one was built. Advertised as the 'all-Canadian' car, it had a low V-type radiator and curiously flared front wings, and was powered by a Continental engine. RJ

1922 CANADIAN Six tourer.
Glenn Baechler Collection

CANADIAN BABY CAR (CDN) 1914
Montreal, Que.

A cyclecar, known as the C.B.C., which offered a choice of J.A.P., De Luxe or Wizard engines, all 2-cylinder air-cooled units. Two-speed planetary transmission and drive through V-belts to the rear wheels were standard, as were a 7ft wheelbase, 3ft track and wire wheels. The cost was $495. HD

CANADIAN MOTORS (CDN) 1900–1902
Canadian Motors Ltd, Toronto, Ont.

This was a rather ambitious attempt to revive the Still Motor Co, and almost all its products were like those of its predecessor. They were powerful and well built but the company failed and was bought by Canada Cycle & Motor Co. HD

CANADIAN MOTOR SYNDICATE (CDN) c.1895–1899
Canadian Motor Syndicate, Toronto, Ont.

This informal organization produced an electric delivery tricycle in 1898, an electric passenger tricycle in 1899 using designs of William Still, and also experimented with a petrol engine. It was absorbed by the Still Motor Co in 1899. HD

CANADIAN STANDARD (CDN) 1912–1913
Canadian Standard Auto and Tractor Company, Moose Jaw, Sask.

A number of conventional 4-cylinder tourers were assembled in a plant promoted by an American named A.R. Walton. They were put on display but company officials apparently disappeared before production could begin. HD

1962 CANNON(ii) trials car. *Motor Sport*

1904 CANTERBURY 8hp two-seater. *M.J. Worthington-Williams*

1900 CAPEL 4hp voiturette. *The Veteran Car Club of Great Britain*

C. & H. (GB) *1913*
Corfield & Hurle Ltd, Stamford Hill, London N.

The C. & H. cyclecar was made in two models, with a 6hp Fafnir engine or an 8hp Precision. Both models had 3 speeds and chain final drive. Prices were £99.15.0 and £105 respectively. GNG

CANNON (i) (US) *1902–1906*
Burtt Mfg Co, Kalamazoo, Mich.

This maker built several different tonneau models. Both 2- and 4-cylinder engines were used of up to 6.5 litres capacity. Smaller models used a friction transmission, larger ones a sliding-gear type. Both shaft and chain drive were used. This make is shown by most compilers as a steamer, but this is apparently due to confusion with a home-built steam racing car. GMN

CANNON (ii) (GB) *1953 to date*
M.R.B. Cannon, Gover Hill, Tonbridge, Kent

Entirely single-handed, Mike Cannon had constructed about 120 cars by the end of 1966. Nearly all were trials machines, using Ford Ten mechanical constituents, and the price (in component form) seldom exceeded £300. In the hands of such protagonists as Rex Chappell, the robust and simple Cannons practically monopolized British mud-plugging trials for longer than most people cared to remember. From 1967 onwards vehicles were built only to special order, one or two per year: the market was saturated, the cars not inclined to wear out, and rising production costs reduced profitability. DF

CANSTELL (AUS) *1971 to date*
Specialized Fibreglass Mouldings Pty Ltd, Taren Point, NSW.

The Canstell is a two-seater sports car similar to the Lotus Seven, available with a choice of Ford Anglia 105E, Cortina, or Consul Mark 2 engines. GNG

CANTERBURY (GB) *1903–1906*
Canterbury Motor Co, Canterbury, Kent

This was one of many companies who assembled cars, mainly from foreign components. In 1903 there was a light car with a 6hp De Dion-Bouton engine and a larger machine with a 12hp Aster engine, four-seater tonneau body and chain drive. In their last year, a few cars were made using the 16/20hp White & Poppe 4-cylinder engine. GNG

CANTONO (i) (I) *1900–1905*
CANTONO (ii) (US) *1904–1907*
F.R.A.M. (I) *1905–1911*
(1) E. Cantono, Rome *1900–1905*
(2) Cantono Electric Tractor Co, Canton, Ohio *1904–1907*
(3) Società Anonima F.R.A.M., Rome *1905–1906*; Genoa *1906–1911*

Cantono, like Kriéger in France and Kühlstein-Vollmer in Germany, sought to convert existing horse-drawn vehicles by replacing the front wheels with a self-contained 'power pack'. In the Cantono system the batteries were mounted over the axle and electric motors provided an independent gear drive to each wheel; in other words, there were rudimentary power brakes and steering. The after part was also modified to take mechanical band brakes on the rear wheels. Cantono had a rear-wheel-drive trolleybus running in 1905. His vehicles were sold in France from 1902 by the Compagnie des Voitures Electriques of St Ouen (Seine). Despite the conveniently euphonious Cantono Electric Tractor Co, Canton, Ohio, the American Cantono was merely the Italian design built under licence from 1904–1906. In 1906, operations of the parent firm were transferred from Rome to Genoa, and the name was also changed to F.R.A.M. (Fabbrica Rotabili Avantreni Motori).

The range consisted of Tipo-A, a Private-car conversion kit, Tipo-B, an omnibus conversion kit, and Tipo *Turismo,* in which case the coachwork and after chassis were supplied complete with the tractive unit. The use of conventional wheel steering together with the 'bonnet' covering the electric motors and batteries, gave the F.R.A.M. landaulet a more conventional appearance than might have been expected. A 2-cylinder petrol-driven F.R.A.M. was reported in 1906, and in 1908 a licence for Eugenio Cantono's designs was taken out by the Deutsche Elektromobil GmbH of Düsseldorf. The make was no longer quoted in Italy after 1911 and all Cantono's commercial ventures were defunct by 1914. MCS

CAP (B) *1914*
The Cap light car was said to have been designed in England, but built entirely in Belgium. It had a tandem two-seater body, and a J.A.P. air-cooled V-twin engine. GNG

CAPEL (GB) *1900–1901*
Creek Street Engineering Co Ltd, Deptford, London S.E.

The Capel light car was designed by Herbert Capel, of the Clarkson & Capel Steam Car Syndicate (*see* Clarkson). He died before the car was completed and manufacture was taken up by the Creek Street Engineering Co. The car had a 4hp 2-cylinder engine and carried a three-seater *vis-à-vis* body.

CAPITOL (US) *1902*

Capitol Auto Co, Washington, D.C.

The Capitol steam car used a 6hp 2-cylinder engine and cost $1,200. Solid tyres were used, and the body had more opulent curves than most light steamers of the period　　　　　　GNG

CAPRONI *see* CEMSA

CAPS (US) *1905*

Caps Bros Mfg Co, Kansas City, Mo.

The Caps was built as a two-seater runabout and as a side-entrance tonneau. Both were powered by a 14hp engine. Production had hardly started when the company was taken over by Kansas City Motor Car Co.　　　　　　GMN

C.A.R. (i) (I) *1906*

Cantieri Automobilistici Riuniti, Palermo, Sicily

This company was formed to manufacture touring and racing cars, light cars, voiturettes, goods vehicles and omnibuses, but little is known about the actual machines made. Apart from the even more shadowy Olivieri, the C.A.R. is the only known car firm in Sicily.　　　　　　GNG

C.A.R. (ii) *see* COSMOS

C.A.R. (iii) (I) *1927–1929*

Costruzioni Automobili Riuniti, Milan

The second Italian C.A.R. was built under French G.A.R. licence, with 961cc or 1,095cc ohv Chapuis-Dornier engines. Open tourer and taxicab versions were offered.　　　　　　MCS

CARCANO (I) *1898–1901*

This Milanese maker of motorcycle engines displayed a 3hp voiturette at the 1901 Milan Show. Carlo Maserati had a hand in its design.　　　　　　MCS

CAR DE LUXE (DE LUXE) (US) *1906–1910*

(1) De Luxe Motor Car Co, Detroit, Mich. *1906*
(2) De Luxe Motor Car Co, Toledo, Ohio *1906–1910*

The company combined with C.H. Blomstrom Motor Car Co in 1906 and moved to Toledo where they produced the Queen as well as the Car De Luxe. The latter was a 60hp 4-cylinder car with expensive features, such as roller-bearings on the crankshaft. The seven-seater touring car was priced at $4,750.　　　　　　GMN

CARDEN: NEW CARDEN (GB) *1913–1925*

(1) Carden Engineering Co Ltd, Teddington, Middlesex *1913–1920*
(2) Carden Engineering Co Ltd, Ascot, Berks. *1920–1922*
(3) Arnott & Harrison Ltd, Willesden, London N.W.10 *1923–1925*

The Carden cyclecar was one of the odder examples of its breed, being at first a single-seater with a rear-mounted single-cylinder engine. In 1919, it reappeared as a two-seater powered by a 2-stroke, flat-twin engine of only 707cc. This was in unit with the rear axle, driving direct through reduction gearing (instead of by chain, as in the earlier model) and there were two forward speeds – in fact, the whole engine and transmission were in one unit. In 1922 a hinged rigid top was offered. In the following year the Carden, now renamed the New Carden, was given normal two- and two/four-seater open bodies. In spite of its peculiarities, the Carden was popular in the car-starved conditions of the early 1920s, mainly because it was cheap. A more expensive three-seater tourer (£130 compared with £90) was sold in 1924 and 1925 under the name Sheret. At the peak of the Carden's popularity over 40 per week were being turned out.　　　　　　TRN

CARDINET (F) *1900–1906*

Compagnie Française des Voitures Electromobiles, Paris 17e

Cardinet electric cars originally carried their batteries slung under the vehicle, but by 1901 they were mounted out of sight within the body. The usual range of open and closed town carriages were made, including a hansom cab with two motors driving the rear wheels, and a front-wheel-drive landaulette.　　　　　　GNG

CARDWAY (US) *1923–1925*

Frederick Cardway, New York, N.Y.

This was an assembled car, using a Continental 6-cylinder engine. A total of six cars, all touring models, were built by Colonel Cardway, of which one was fitted with right-hand drive and exported to Australia.　　　　　　KM

CAREY (US) *1906*

Carey Motor Co, New York, N.Y.

This car used a Balzer type, front-mounted air-cooled 5-cylinder rotary engine and was exhibited at the A.C.A. Show in 1906. It had no known connection with either the Carey Mfg Co of Fairmount, Ind. (1904) or the later Carey Motor Car Co of Detroit (1910).　　　　　　GMN

1913 CARDEN 4hp monocar. *David Burgess Wise*

1920 CARDEN 7hp two-seater. *National Motor Museum*

1903 CARDINET electric landaulette. *The Veteran Car Club of Great Britain*

1900 CARON 5hp *vis-à-vis*. *The Veteran Car Club of Great Britain*

1921 CARROW 11.9hp two-seater. *Autocar*

CARHARTT (US) *1910–1911*
Carhartt Automobile Co, Detroit, Mich.

Carhartt offered a choice of two models, the '25–30' and the '30–35' with runabout or tourer bodies, at prices ranging from $1,100 to $2,250. The make was launched with massive coast-to-coast publicity, including a sales office in New York's Plaza Hotel, but lasted less than two years. Cars were announced for 1912 but probably never produced. GMN

CARLETTE (GB) *1913*
Holstein Garage, Weybridge, Surrey

The Carlette cyclecar used an 8hp J.A.P. V-twin for power, which was taken to a countershaft by belt. The countershaft could be swung to and fro to give a variable gear, and final drive was also by belt to one rear wheel only. The weight was only 280lb, and a tuned model was said to be capable of 60mph. GNG

CARLTON (i) (GB) *1901–1902*
Carlton Motor Co, Coventry, Warwickshire

Three models of the Carlton were listed, a 6hp single, a 12hp twin and a 24hp 4-cylinder car. All used Aster engines. GNG

CARLTON (ii) (NZ) *1928*
Carlton Car Co, Gisborne, North Island

This was a small 4-cylinder car of about the same size as the Austin Seven. It was designed by John North Birch who had previously designed the Marlborough (ii) cars. Only one prototype was built. GNG

CARNATION (CAR-NATION) (US) *1912–1914*
American Voiturette Co, Detroit, Mich.

This was a cyclecar weighing 700lb, powered by a 4-cylinder air-cooled engine. It had a 3-speed transmission and cost $495. The American Voiturette Co was also the last owner of the Keeton make. GMN

CAROLUS; CAROLETTE *see* KNÖLLNER

CARON (F) *1900–1901*
Caron et Cie, Paris 17e

The Caron voiturette used a 5hp 2-cylinder air-cooled engine, mounted at the front of the car. Transmission was via a 3-speed gearbox and propeller shaft to the rear axle. GNG

CARPEVIAM (GB) *1903-c.1905*
Charles Peacock & Co Ltd, London E.C.

The origin of the Carpeviam is uncertain, as Charles Peacock & Co were selling agents rather than manufacturers. The car was a light 3-wheeler with a 3½hp single-cylinder engine driving the single rear wheel by chain. Construction was on tricar lines, but the two seats were side-by-side; optional equipment included a canopy for hot weather. The price was from £99, with 70 shillings extra for the canopy. GNG

CARRIAGE-MOBILE *see* SUMMIT (i)

CARRICO (US) *1909*
Carrico Motor Co, Cincinnati, Ohio

This was not a complete car, but a chassis ready for mounting a body. It was complete with a 2-cylinder air-cooled, 2-litre engine. The chassis layout was typical of the motor buggy. GMN

CARROLL (i) (US) *1912–1920*
Carroll Motor Car Co, Strasburg, Pa.

The Carroll cars featured a 4-cylinder engine with a 126mm × 126mm bore and stroke. Later cars with a 6-cylinder engine augmented the 4-cylinder line. The Carroll never sold in large numbers. KM

CARROLL (ii) (US) *1920–1922*
Carroll Automobile Co, Lorraine, Ohio

Few Carrolls were built and all were open models. Although a Duesenburg 4-cylinder engine was announced as the power unit, in fact the cars used a Beaver 6. The cars were distinctive in appearance, fitted with disc wheels and a radiator which was set back behind the front axle. KM

CARROW (GB) *1919–1923*
(1) Whitley Bay Motor Co, Newcastle-on-Tyne *1919–1921*
(2) Carrow Cars Ltd, Hanwell, Middlesex *1921–1923*

The Carrow light car was a conventional machine using an 11.9hp 4-cylinder Dorman engine, 3-speed gearbox and shaft drive. An electric starter was available and there were three body styles: two-seater, three-seater (clover-leaf) and four-seater tourer. From 1921 a Peters engine, also of 11.9hp, but with a capacity of 1,795cc, was fitted. GNG

CARTER (GB) *1913*

. Carter, Selly Oak, Birmingham

The Carter cyclecar used a very small 4-cylinder engine of 6.2hp and shaft rive.   GNG

CARTERCAR (US) *1906–1916*

1) The Motor Car Co, Pontiac, Mich. *1906–1908*

2) The Cartercar Co, Pontiac, Mich. *1908–1916*

This firm employed friction-drive transmission on all models, using a 2-cylinder ngine in one model as late as 1909. The Model R for 1912 was a 4-cylinder car, sing single chain drive to the rear axle. The Motor Car Co combined with the Pontiac Spring and Wagon Co in 1908 to form the Cartercar Co, which also made he Pontiac (i). They became part of the General Motors Corporation in 1909.

GMN

CARTERET (F) *1922*

Automobiles Carteret, Courbevoie, Seine

Like many other light French cars, the Carteret used a small 4-cylinder Ruby ngine of 904cc. Four speeds were available through cone friction transmission nd the final drive was by bevel gear.   GNG

CARTERMOBILE (US) *1924–1925*

Carter Motor Car Co, Washington, D.C.

An unsuccessful assembled car powered by a 4-cylinder Herschell-Spillman engine. Open and closed body styles were available.   KM

CARTER TWIN-ENGINE (US) *1907–1908*

Carter Motor Car Co, Washington, D.C.: Hyattsville, Md.

The Carter Twin-Engine was an early attempt at complete reliability as it was owered by two independent systems. The car could operate on either of its 24hp 4-cylinder engines singly or on both together. The separate systems were extended o individual radiators, ignition and exhausts. This shaft-driven five-seater touring car cost $5,000. The same company built the Washington (ii). The Carter Twin-Engine appears to have been preceded by Carter, built at least in 1904 by American Mfg Co of Alexandria, Va.   GMN

C.A.S. (CS) *1920*

Česka Automobilová Společnost, Prague

This firm built one of the very early scooters before introducing a cyclecar in 1920, with a Walter or 650cc Coventry-Victor engine. Production was limited.

HON

CASE (i) (CDN) *1907*

Lethbridge Motor Car Co, Lethbridge, Alt.

The Case Model A had a 20/24hp 4-cylinder air-cooled engine, friction drive, and what were described as 'Fawkes airless tyres'. The price was $2,000.   GNG

CASE (ii) (US) *1910–1927*

The J.I. Case Threshing Machine Co, Racine, Wisc.

The Case was a conventional car made by one of America's best-known makers of threshing machines, steam traction engines and agricultural tractors. The cars were mainly sold through the farm equipment dealers. At first 4-cylinder cars only were made, the 1914 range consisting of a '25', '35', and '40', but a Continental-engined six was offered for 1918. This was available in three body styles, a touring, a sedan, and a 'sport', which was a close-coupled open four-seater. The engine was rated at 29.4hp (3.9-litres), and this was gradually increased to 31.5hp (5.3-litres) by 1923. These 6-cylinder engines were all by Continental, and usually only one size was offered each year, although in some years (such as 1923) an overlap between models made two sizes available. From 1924 a smaller six of 4-litres was made, but in decreasing quantities, and in 1927 car production ceased. The company is still active and well-known in the field of agricultural tractors and other farm equipment. These, like the cars, carry the eagle emblem modelled on 'Old Abe', the famous mascot of the 8th Wisconsin Regiment from 1861 to 1881.   GNG

CASSELL (GB) *1900–1903*

Central Motor Co, Glasgow

The Cassell was an assembled car using 2- or 4-cylinder engines by Aster or De Dion-Bouton.   GNG

CASTLE THREE (GB) *1919–1922*

Castle Motor Co Ltd, Kidderminster, Worcestershire

Apart from the Morgan, and later the B.S.A., 3-wheeled cars did not catch on in Britain, but several attempts were made to popularize them in times of car shortage or economic crisis. The Castle Three tried to get away from the breed's spidery cyclecar image by providing a 'proper' car engine in the shape of a water-cooled, 4-cylinder side-valve unit, initially a 1,094cc Dorman, and later a 1,207cc Peters, steel artillery-type wheels instead of wire or wooden discs and shaft drive. It still featured the 2-speed epicycle gears which were associated with minimal motoring. A prototype 4-wheeler, the Castle Four was made in 1922.   TRN

1909 CARTERCAR 22hp three-seater roadster.
Henry Ford Museum, Dearborn, Mich.

1914 CASE(ii) 30hp tourer. *National Motor Museum*

1920 CASTLE THREE 10hp 3-wheeler. *Autocar*

1903 CASTRO 14hp tonneau. *J. Rodriguez-Viña*

1925 CEIRANO(ii) S.150 10.4hp tourer. *G.N.
Georgano*

1925 CEIRANO(ii) S.150 10.4hp saloon. *Autocar*

CASTRO (E) *1901–1904*

(1) J. Castro Sociedad en Comandita, Barcelona *1901–1904*
(2) Fabrica La Hispano-Suiza de Automoviles, Barcelona *1904*

Castro was the most important creditor of the La Cuadra concern, and in reorganizing that firm he continued to use the services of Marc Birkigt. The first Castro cars followed the design of the 4½hp chain-driven La Cuadra, but in 1902 a 10hp 2-cylinder shaft-driven car appeared, followed in 1903 by a 14hp 4-cylinder model. Strikes caused further financial difficulties, and in 1904 the company was taken over by a group of businessmen who formed a new company, La Hispano-Suiza Fabrica de Automoviles, in June 1904. Though relatively unsuccessful himself, Sr Castro helped to bring about one of the most famous names in the history of fine cars.   JRV

C.A.T. (F) *1911*

Construction Automobiles Tarnaise, Rabastens, Tarn

The C.A.T. was a light two-seater made in open and coupé form, powered by an 8hp 4-cylinder engine. No claims for high speed were made, and the catalogue stated that the car's 30mph maximum would avoid excessive tyre consumption.   GNG

CAUSAN (F) *1923–1924*

Automobiles Causan, Levallois-Perret, Seine

The Causan cyclecar used a single-cylinder 2-stroke engine of 350cc, a 2-speed gearbox and, unusually for so simple a machine, shaft drive. In 1924 the name was changed to d'Aux and production transferred to Reims.   GNG

CAVAC (US) *1910*

Small Motor Car Co, Detroit, Mich.

The Cavac was built only as a two-seater roadster, with a 4-cylinder water-cooled engine. Its crankshaft was fitted with two ball-bearings, while the chassis was slung below the axles in the same manner as that of the larger American Underslung.   GMN

C.B. (US) *1917–1918*

Carter Brothers Motor Co, Hyattsville, Md.

The C.B. was offered in three models, a 28hp four, a 35hp eight, and a 65hp twelve. The latter was priced at only $2,500, a low price for a 12-cylinder car. The name C.B. was also applied to a model of Downing-Detroit, which has been confused with the Maryland car.   GNG

C.C.C. (GB) *1906–1907*

Chassis Construction Co Ltd, Taunton, Somerset

With the idea of attracting coachbuilders and assemblers, this company presented a range of Ballot-engined types, from 8hp, single-cylinder to 24/30hp, 4-cylinder (4,942cc) models. The largest model was chain-driven. Most chassis components were from Malicet et Blin, but the 'assembled' stigma was countered by the claim that the vehicles were an amalgamation of the best features of various makes. A Metropolitan-type taxicab was also offered, but was not developed.   DF

C. DE L. (US) *1913*

C. de L. Engineering Works, Nutley, N.J.

This was made in two models, one with 20–40hp engine and the other designated as 30–60hp. These had capacities of 3.2 and 7 litres respectively. The pistons were either single- or double-acting 'at the pleasure of the operator'. The smaller chassis had a 9ft 10in wheelbase, and the larger was 11ft 8in. Prices ranged from $1,500 to $2,800.   GMN

CEGGA (CH) *1960–1967*

Etablissements Cegga, Aigle

The brothers Claude and Georges Gachnang made modified cars to special order, concentrating on modifications to chassis and suspension, using engines from well-known makers. Their first car was the Cegga-Bristol coupé which finished 22nd at Le Mans in 1960. This was followed by Cegga-Ferrari sports and Formula 1 cars, and the Cegga-Maserati Formula 1. Their cars have been more successful in hill-climbs than in races, a 2-litre Cegga-Maserati taking the record for the Lens-Crans hill in 1964. A sports coupé with 3-litre Ferrari V-12 engine was under development in 1967, but this was the make's last appearance.   GNG

CEIRANO (i) (I) *1901–1904*

(1) Fratelli Ceirano, Turin *1901–1903*
(2) G.G. Fratelli Ceirano, Turin *1903–1904*
(3) Ceirano & Cia, Turin *1904*

The first car to bear the Ceirano name was Renault-based, with single-cylinder engine by Aster or De Dion, four forward speeds, and shaft drive, but in 1903 Aristide Faccioli (late of F.I.A.T.) designed a 16hp four, also shaft-driven. Initially the brothers Giovanni Battista and Matteo were in partnership, but after Matteo's resignation Giovanni the younger took his place, and the firm concentrated on De

Dion-engined light cars. In 1904 Giovanni set up on his own as manufacturer of the Junior (i) car, and shortly afterwards Giovanni Battista reorganized the company as S.T.A.R. (Rapid).

MCS

CEIRANO (ii) (I) *1919–1931*

(1) Giovanni Ceirano Fabbrica Automobili, Turin *1919–1924*
(2) Società Ceirano Automobili Torino, Turin *1924–1931*

Giovanni Ceirano and his son Ernesto sold their S.C.A.T. interests in 1917, but two years later they were back with a new make, obviously inspired by 1914 S.C.A.T. models. Early Ceiranos had sv fixed-head 4-cylinder engines, the 16/20 hp C.1 having a capacity of 2.3 litres. The bored-out 2,950cc Corsa was credited with a mere 35bhp, in spite of which it had a successful career in national sporting events. Like S.C.A.T., Ceirano tried their luck with a six, this time an ohv 3-litre, Tipo 30. However, when Ceirano repurchased S.C.A.T. and closed down his own works, all these models were dropped to be replaced by a modern 1½-litre, the 150, with 4-wheel brakes, a 4-speed gearbox, and tourer bodywork in Lancia Lambda style – though Ceirano, unlike Lancia, favoured a conventional chassis frame. The 150 Normale had side valves and was capable of 55–60mph on 30bhp, but the ohv 150S wore wire wheels and was good for 65mph: Newton & Bennett sold it in England as the Newton-Ceirano. In 1926 there was a short-lived ohv 2.3-litre, the 250, but latterly Ceirano concentrated on lorries that were marketed by the Consortium FIAT selling group. The last 150S variant, announced for 1930, had independently-sprung front wheels and resembled a scaled-down Lancia Artena saloon, but very few of these were made and in 1931 Ceirano sold out to S.P.A., by now a wholly-owned subsidiary of FIAT.

MCS

CELER (GB) *1904*

The Celer Motor Car Co, Nottingham

The only evidence for this company's existence lies in a surviving car, which carries the maker's plate on the engine. It had an 8hp vertical-twin engine with automatic inlet valves, a 3-speed gearbox and shaft drive.

GNG

CELERITAS (A) *1901–1903*

Automobilfabrik Celeritas, Vienna

Willy Stift founded this firm after backing August Braun's projects. In a small factory he built voiturettes with 2-cylinder Buchet engines. Later he joined the Gräf brothers in setting up the Gräf & Stift concern.

HON

CELTIC (i) (GB) *1904–1908*

(1) Bradford Motor Car Co, Bradford, Yorks. *1904–1907*
(2) Thornton Engineering Co, Bradford, Yorks. *1907–1908*

These cars were of conventional 4-cylinder shaft-drive design and were entirely hand-made, only 8 cars leaving the works in 5 years. Engines were Aster (first 4 cars), Mutel (1 car), and White & Poppe (3 cars), and the vehicles enjoyed a good local reputation. The Thornton Engineering Co later sold the Teco car which was an imported Bailleul.

GNG

CELTIC (ii) (F) *1908–1913*

Marcel Caplet, Le Havre, Seine-Inférieure

Before commencing car manufacture, Marcel Caplet had made 3-cylinder engines called Triplex, but his cars seem to have used only 4-cylinder engines. They were conventional shaft-drive machines of 12hp.

GNG

CELTIC (iii) (F) *1927–1929*

Compagnie Générale des Voitures à Paris, Paris 1er

The small, conventional Celtic had an sv 4-cylinder engine of 700cc, increased in 1927 to 1,086cc. A larger car made by the firm was the Classic (ii).

GNG

CEMSA (I) *1946–1950*

Caproni Elettromeccanica Saronno, Cameri

The CEMSA or Cemsa derived its name from the manufacturing organization Caproni Elettromeccanica Saronno, and was an interesting prototype produced after World War 2 by a major aircraft concern looking for something else to make in its factories. Type-numbered the FM and first appearing in the 1947 Paris Show, where it caused a sensation, the Cemsa had a horizontally opposed, water-cooled 4-cylinder 1,100cc engine mounted ahead of the driven front wheels, a pressed steel platform-type chassis, and independent suspension all around. The same car reappeared at Turin in 1949, but plans to put it into production never materialized; Minerva took up the design, equally abortively in 1953. Its advanced design was far from abortive however, for ten years later it formed the basis of the highly successful 1½-litre front-drive, flat-four Lancia Flavia of 1960.

CP

CENTAUR (i) (GB) *1900–1901*

Centaur Cycle Co Ltd, Coventry, Warwickshire

The Centaur was a four-seater *dos-à-dos* dogcart with a 4½hp single-cylinder engine mounted at the front. Transmission was via a Benz-type system of fast and loose pulleys.

GNG

1904 CELER 8hp two-seater. *G.N. Georgano*

1947 CEMSA Caproni F11 1.1-litre saloon.
Lucien Loreille Collection

1904 CENTURY(i) 8/10hp two-seater. *G.N. Georgano*

1923 C.E.Y.C. 792cc three-seater light car. *J. Rodriguez-Viña*

CENTAUR (ii) (US) *1903*
Centaur Motor Vehicle Co, Buffalo, N.Y.

This was a light two-seater electric runabout priced at $850.　GNG

CENTAUR (iii) (GB) *1965 to date*
Centaur Engineering, Halesworth, Suffolk

Richard Scott's first Centaur was a space-framed special for the 1172 formula, and this was followed by a couple of slender single-seaters for Formula 3 and the 'monoposto' class. A Clubman car with inclined engine and all-independent suspension came next; the Mark 5 was a simpler and more conventional version. The 750 Formula was sampled with the Mark 6 and the Mark 7 of 1968 was a successful lhd midget racer for the oval tracks. A Formula 1200 kit car followed and the Mark 9 was allotted to a wide-track Formula Ford model built in 1969. The next all-independent Clubman car, with disc brakes, was offered at £588 for 1970, and the Mark 11 was another Formula 750 model, supplied in kit form. The 1971 Mark 12 was a further Formula 1200 car, and the Mark 14, the basic kit for which cost £175 in 1972, was a Formula 1200 or Clubman car. By then approximately 20 cars had been constructed in all.　DF

CENTRAL (US) *1905–1906*
Central Automobile Co, Providence, R.I.

This car used a rotary steam engine, an unusual design for a steamer.　GMN

CENTRON (GB) *1970 to date*
G.P. Speed Shop Ltd, Hanworth Air Park, Feltham, Middlesex

Mainly producers of Beach Buggies, this firm offered also a GT coupé for Volkswagen parts. The basic kit cost £600; the fibreglass body had a lift-up centre section for access. A version with conventional doors was planned for late 1972.　DF

CENTURY (i) (GB) *1899–1907*
(1) Century Engineering & Motor Co Ltd, Altrincham, Cheshire *1899–1901*
(2) Century Engineering & Motor Co Ltd, Willesden, London N.W. *1901–1904*
(3) Century Engineering Co Ltd, Willesden, London N.W. *1904–1907*

Ralph Jackson of Altrincham, a bicycle maker since 1885, began vehicle manufacture with the Century Tandem, a two-seater tricar with 2¼hp single-cylinder engine and wheel steering which sold for £115. After the move to London, the company was taken over by Sydney Begbie who had introduced Aster engines to England. He extended the range of tandems to three; they used engines by De Dion (3½hp), Aster and M.M.C. (both 5hp). In 1903 he introduced the Century car with 8 and 12hp Aster 2-cylinder engines and 22hp Mutel 4-cylinder engines and english chassis and bodies. 1905 saw a range of improved tandems with 2-cylinder engines and two radiators, one on each side of the rear wheel. In 1906 the company was making Princess cars with 4-cylinder 16hp engines.　GNG

CENTURY (ii) (US) *1899–1903*
Century Motor Vehicle Co, Syracuse, N.Y.

The first car produced by the Century company was a light steamer powered by a 4¾hp 2-cylinder vertical engine. Final drive was by bevel gear instead of the more usual single chain. This model was made until 1903 when it was succeeded by the petrol-engined Century Tourist. This was also a tiller-steered two seater, but had a single-cylinder engine and chain drive.　GNG

CENTURY (iii) (US) *1911–1915*
(1) Century Motor Co, Detroit, Mich. *1911–1913*
(2) Century Electric Car Co, Detroit, Mich. *1913–1915*

The Century was an electric car with an underslung chassis. It was tiller-operated, and the customer had a choice of solid or pneumatic tyres. The speed controller gave a choice of six speeds, and the series-wound Westinghouse motor was geared directly to the rear axle.　GMN

CENTURY (iv) (GB) *1928–1929*
Century Cars Ltd, London N.W.1

The Century light car was one of several attempts in the late 1920s to make a £100 car. It used a 2-stroke engine of the same dimensions as the Austin Seven and had a light open two-seater body on a chassis of 7ft 3in wheelbase.　GNG

CERTUS (i) (GB) *1908*
Certus Gearless Co Ltd, London

The Certus was a conventional car apart from its friction transmission. It used an Aster 4-cylinder engine of 3-litres capacity and was built mainly to test the principle of friction drive. Few, if any, were marketed.　GNG

CERTUS (ii) (D) *1928–1929*
Diercks & Wroblewski, Offenburg

This coach-building firm started to produce their own cars in 1928. S.C.A.P. engines were fitted to chassis and bodies of their own production. Engines available were 7/32, 8/45, 6/60 and 8/80PS.　HON

CÉSAR (F) *1906*

David, Boudène & Cie, Paris

The César was made in two models, one using a 7hp single-cylinder, the other a 12hp 4-cylinder engine. The cars were made for David, Boudène & Cie by Doriot-Flandrin who also made the D.F.P. GNG

C.E.Y.C. (E) *1922–1926*

Centro Electrotecnico y Comunicaciones, Ministero de la Guerra, Madrid

This car was unusual in that it was designed and built by the Spanish War Ministry, and no cars were sold new to the public, although a number reached the market second hand. It was a light car designed for military communications, and used a 4-cylinder 792cc 2-stroke engine with only two combustion chambers. Later models were capable of nearly 70mph. Total production was about 1,000 cars. At least one C.E.Y.C. survives today. JRV

C.F. *see* CORNISH-FRIEDBERG

C.F.B. (GB) *1920–1921*

C.F.B. Car Syndicate Ltd, Upper Norwood, London S.E.

The C.F.B. light car used an 8hp air-cooled V-twin engine and a complicated transmission system. This involved a friction disc which drove a countershaft on which were mounted two pulleys from which drive was taken to the rear wheels by rubber belts. The frame was of reinforced ash and the provisional price was £250. GNG

C.F.L. (GB) *1913*

F. Clayton & Co, Blackheath, London S.E.

The C.F.L. was a simple cyclecar using an air-cooled flat-twin engine and belt drive. The price was £105. GNG

C.G. (F) *1967 to date*

Carrosserie Chappe Frères et Gessalin, Brie-Comte-Robert, Seine-et-Marne

This small firm stands in much the same relation to Simca as Alpine does to Renault; fibreglass-bodied rear-engined roadsters and coupés are built up from Simca 1000 mechanical elements. Initially the basic 944cc engine was used, but since 1969 C.G.s have been marketed with the 85bhp 1,204cc unit from the Simca 1200S coupé. Blown and unblown 1,300cc units are also available, and production is modest—about 40 cars per year. MCS

C.G.E. (F) *1941–1946*

Compagnie Générale Electrique, Paris

The C.G.E. was one of several makes of electric car which appeared in France during the acute wartime shortage of petrol. It used a cast aluminium frame designed by Jean Grégoire and an open two-seater body. Range on one charge was 56 miles and maximum speed 36mph. It appeared at one post-war Salon with the option of a closed coupé body. GNG

C.G.V.; CHARRON (F) *1901–1930*

(1) Charron, Girardot et Voigt *1901–1906*

(2) Automobiles Charron Ltd, Puteaux, Seine *1906–1930*

All three original partners in this concern had raced Panhards; Charron won the first Gordon Bennett Cup Race in 1900, while Girardot, who had been associated with him in a Parisian Panhard agency since 1897, enjoyed the reputation of being 'the Eternal Second'. Thus it is not surprising that C.G.V.'s first cars reflected Panhard influence with their flitch-plate frames, 4-cylinder automatic inlet valve engines, 4-speed gearboxes and side-chain drive. Their capacity was 3.3 litres. Girardot drove a 9.9-litre racing machine in the 1902 Gordon Bennett Cup, but retired, though the touring models rapidly established a sound reputation and were made under licence in the U.S.A. by Smith and Mabley, later to be responsible for Simplex (ii). In 1903 C.G.V. built one of the world's first straight-8s, a racing 7.2-litre machine with no gearbox. In the same year they also made an *auto-mitrailleuse* based on their private-car chassis, a line of development they were still exploring in 1906. Mechanically-operated inlet valves featured on their bigger models, though there was also an 8hp automatic inlet valve twin in addition to the original '15'. By 1905 automatic inlet valves had been dropped altogether and the firm were turning out big 4-cylinder cars of 4.9-litre, 6.2-litre and 9.8-litre capacity, all T-headed and still with flitch-plate frames, but now with high-tension magneto ignition and swivelling acetylene head-lights. C.G.V.s had Renault-type bonnets, but adhered to pump cooling and under-slung frontal radiators. The biggest model cost £1,200 for a bare chassis in England. Girardot's entry of a twin-radiatored car for the French Gordon Bennett Eliminating Trials was written off in a crash. The company never raced again. Shaft drive was found on a 14/18hp model in 1906, while at the other end of the range there was an immense 12.9-litre chain-driven 75/90hp with geared-down starting handle; one huge *berline de voyage* with built-in lavatory was shipped to an American client! In this year the firm became a British limited liability company and Girardot left to sponsor the G.E.M. petrol-electric. By 1912, Fernand Charron was also engaged on a venture of his own, the Alda.

From 1907 the cars were known as Charrons, and the 14/18hp had acquired a

1903 C.G.V. 40hp tonneau. Coachwork by Muhlbacher. *The Veteran Car Club of Great Britain*

1914 CHARRONETTE 10hp two-seater. *G.N. Georgano*

1920 CHARRON 18/24hp landaulette. Coachwork by Gurney Nutting. *Autocar*

179

1903 CHABOCHE 12hp steam double phaeton.
The Veteran Car Club of Great Britain.

1907 CHADWICK Great Six tourer. *Kenneth Stauffer*

1901 CHAINLESS 16hp tonneau. *The Veteran Car Club of Great Britain*

monobloc engine, while shaft drive was available a year later on the 4.9-litre '20/2[
The smaller models appeared on the home market with left-hand drive. 1909 saw t[
advent of a new line which was to continue with little change up to 1914. The
Charrons had L-head engines, thermo-syphon cooling and dashboard radiators livir
uncomfortably near their petrol tanks. They were made in 1.2-litre 2-cylinder, 2.
litre and 3.7-litre 4-cylinder, and 3.9-litre 6-cylinder versions, the two bigger typ[
having 4-speed gearboxes. The twins were dropped at the end of 1912, and the six
a season later. At the same time the bigger models continued unchanged, with flit[
plate frames, and chain drive, the latter being still listed as an option as late as 191
The make was used widely as a taxicab in London and some cars were tried wi
Lentz hydraulic transmissions in 1913. Just before World War 1 came a baby
cylinder, the 845cc Charronette with 3-speed gearbox and detachable wood whee[
which offered a 40mph performance for £214. Other models listed in 1914 we
monobloc fours of 2.4-litres (the well-known '15') and 3.4-litres.

The larger post-war Charrons were uninteresting cars, differing from their 19[
forebears in having pump cooling, conventional frontal radiators, and full electric
equipment. The 3.4-litre '18/24' with sv and fixed head cost £1,525 in England
1920, but alongside this was developed a new Charonette with 1,057cc sv engin[
2-bearing crankshaft, thermo-syphon cooling, frontal radiator, trough-and-dipp[
lubrication and a central vertical gate change for the 3-speed separate gearbox.
had little affinity with the British-made Charron-Laycock made in Sheffield fro[
1920, but the latter's presence kept it off the English market until 1922, when
was listed at £325. Charrons were not made with front-wheel brakes until 1925, whe
a 1½-litre ohv 10CV on conventional lines was announced. Like many a Frenchmake
Automobiles Charron departed from the scene with an undistinguished small six. I[
capacity was 2.8 litres, the valves were overhead and cooling was by pump. A small[
1.8-litre version was listed in 1929, but this marked the end of the make.   MC

CHABOCHE (F) *1901–1906*
E. Chaboche, Paris

The Chaboche steam car was originally made in two models. The smaller was
vis-à-vis with rear-mounted boiler and 6hp horizontal engine mounted in the centr[
of the chassis, while the larger had a six-seater brake body, 12hp engine, and boil[
mounted in front in the style of a steam lorry. This was later developed into a lin
of commercial vehicles, while the private cars acquired engines of 12 or 20hp fc
1903, and a range of limousine and coupé-de-ville coachwork. Chaboche entered tw[
30hp racing cars in the Paris-Madrid race of 1903, but neither reached Bordeau[
Apart from Serpollet, he was the only French manufacturer to race steamers. 190[
Chaboche cars had a 30hp vertical engine mounted under a bonnet, but the followin[
year they abandoned the production of private cars, in order to concentrate o[
heavy steam lorries.   GN

CHADWICK (US) *1904–1916*
(1) L.S. Chadwick, Chester, Pa. *1904–1906*
(2) Fairmount Engineering Co, Philadelphia, Pa. *1906–1907*
(3) Chadwick Engineering Works, Pottstown, Pa. *1907–1916*

The Chadwick was the first high-performance car of U.S. manufacture to achiev[
volume production and recognition. The first Chadwick model had a 4-cylind[
engine and double chain drive. In 1905 and 1906 this car had 4-speed progressiv[
transmission. With the introduction in 1907 of the Great Chadwick Six with its larg[
11.2-litre engine, the make began competing successfully in racing events. Th[
engine, designated Type 19, had overhead valves and copper water-jackets. By 191[
the wheelbase had expanded to 11ft 1in, and the five-seater tonneau model co[
$5,500. The 1908 racing cars entered in the Vanderbilt Cup and Savannah Gran[
Prize employed supercharging, the first recorded instance of this method [
increasing power. It was not offered on production Chadwicks.   GM

CHAIKA (GAZ M-13) 'SEAGULL' (SU) *1958–1965*
Zavod Imieni Molotova (Gorky Auto Works), Gorky

Looking not unlike the 1955 Packard Patrician, this medium-sized sedan wa[
introduced as a replacement for the Zim (Gaz M-12) which had become somewha[
outdated. A step below the Zil in prestige it was not commonly available to th[
Soviet motorist for it served, like the Zil, as transportation for various officia[
and important professional men. Powered by a 195hp 5.5-litre V-8 motor, it wa[
equipped with electrically operated windows, push-button automatic transmissio[
5-band radio and two collapsible bucket seats.   B

CHAINLESS (F) *1900–1903*
SA des Voitures Légères 'Chainless', Paris

The Chainless, which derived its name from the fact that all models used shaf[
drive, was described by its makers as a high-powered voiturette. Bucket engines wer[
used, at first of 8 and 12hp, then in 1903 a 24hp model was added. The cars wer[
unusually low in build, and even the 8hp model was good for over 40mph. In 1900–0[
the firm also made chain driven cars under the name Knowles-Chain.   GN[

CHALFANT (US) *1906–1912*
Chalfant Motor Car Co, Lenover, Pa.

The Chalfant was built as a five-seater touring car. Its water-cooled engine was a horizontally opposed 22hp 2-cylinder type. A planetary transmission and double chain drive were used. The 1907 Model C sold at $1,300. GMN

CHALLENGE *see* MARCUS

CHALMERS; CHALMERS-DETROIT (US) *1908–1924*
Chalmers Motor Car Co, Detroit, Mich.

The Chalmers was one of the most popular automobiles made in the United States for more than a decade. It was the successor to the Thomas-Detroit which was built by a company which had been founded in 1906 by E.R. Thomas (builder of the Thomas car in Buffalo, N.Y.) Roy D. Chapin and Howard Earle Coffin; the two latter had previously served at Oldsmobile. The Thomas-Detroit of which some 500 were sold during the first year of production, was marketed through the parent firm in Buffalo which manufactured a larger line of cars under the Thomas emblem. The Thomas-Detroit was a medium priced four-cylinder car which had been designed by Coffin. In 1907, Hugh Chalmers, vice president of the National Cash Register Co and a noted salesman, entered the firm. Shortly after, he bought a half of E.R. Thomas' stock and became president of the company which became the Chalmers-Detroit Motor Company. The Thomas-Detroit became the Chalmers-Detroit in 1908 and in 1910, the Chalmers. Open and closed models in two lines comprised the Chalmers four-cylinder cars, with self-starters appearing in 1912. Chalmers (as Chalmers-Detroit) had distinguished itself in road races as early as 1908 when W.R. Burns won the Motor Parkway Sweepstakes at Jericho, N.Y., averaging 48.7mph in the six-lap 240.76 mile run.

In 1913, the Chalmers brought out its first 6-cylinder model, as well as the four and apart from small mechanical and design changes, continued both until 1914. The four was dropped from the 1915 line, however, and sixes were to be used exclusively until the ending of manufacture. By 1915, some 20,000 cars per year were coming off the Chalmers production line and would even exceed that figure before the advent of World War 1. In 1917, an L-head motor replaced the earlier overhead-valve type and on August 4th, Chalmers again headed racing news when Joe Dawson won the 24-hour Stock Car Endurance Run at Sheepshead Bay, N.Y. Sales flagged following the end of the war and Hugh Chalmers, always the salesman, and with the realization that a competitor, Maxwell, wasn't faring well either, arranged to lease his plants to Maxwell, using his salesmanship to promote the two concerns and getting the benefit of Maxwell tooling and manufacturing equipment. By the early 1920s, however, many makes of cars were in financial difficulties due to over-expansion and recession, and Walter P. Chrysler was called in to try and reorganize Maxwell. Chrysler was at this time planning his own corporation and in 1922 Chalmers was taken over by Maxwell which had become a Chrysler subsidiary. The last Chalmers cars were equipped with Lockheed hydraulic brakes but 1923 was the last year of production with some 9,000 units leaving the factories. The Maxwell survived until 1925 when it became the Chrysler Four. KM

CHAMBERS (GB) *1904–1925*
Chambers Motors Ltd, Belfast, Northern Ireland

The Chambers was the most significant of the handful of cars made in Ireland. Robert Chambers began by making a machine for wiring corks onto soda-water bottles and turned to cars in 1904. His brother J.A. Chambers had worked for Vauxhall. The first car was powered by a 7hp flat-twin engine. Its 3-speed epicyclic transmission was housed in the rear axle, and there was worm final drive. By 1910, a vertical 4-cylinder engine was standard; the transmission was of the normal sliding-pinion variety.

The Chambers of the post World War 1 years, like its predecessors, was a very strong, long-lived machine. There were two standard offerings; both assembled cars powered by 4-cylinder, side-valve engines, with the same stroke but differing bores, giving 2 and 2.4 litres. Each had three forward speeds in a normal Meadows gearbox, but there was still worm final drive. The bigger machine was the old 12/16hp, current since at least 1912, in revamped form. Two 75mm × 120mm cars replaced them, the larger with six cylinders. In the make's last years, only the latter was listed. In fact, only a few hundred Chambers of any type were made – none at all after 1925 – as the company was perennially short of capital. It finally failed in 1929. TRN

CHAMBON (F) *1912–1914*
Auguste Chambon, Lyons

The Chambon was a medium-sized touring car powered by a 4-cylinder 3-litre engine, probably of Luc Court manufacture. The 4-speed gearbox was mounted on the rear axle. About 20 were made, together with one car specially built for a local doctor. This had two engines mounted side by side, and with a six-seater tourer body was capable of over 70mph. GNG

CHAMEROY (F) *1907–1911*
Automobiles Chameroy, Le Vésinet, Seine-et-Oise

Chameroy were makers of non-skid tyres who made a small number of light cars and voiturettes using single, 2- and 4-cylinder engines. They used variable belt drive and dispensed with gearbox and differential. GNG

1909 CHALMERS 30hp roadster. *J. Price*

1923 CHALMERS 25hp sedan. *Chrysler Corporation*

1908 CHAMBERS 6/7hp tourer. *Belfast Museum & Art Gallery*

1920 CHAMBERS 12/16hp tourer. *J.A. Chambers*

1956 (MAICO) CHAMPION Type 400 coupé.
Neubauer Collection

1927 CHANDLER 33hp 8-cylinder saloon.
Autocar

1940 CHAPEAUX electric coupé.
Lucien Loreille Collection

CHAMPION (i) (US) *1908–1909*
Famous Mfg Co, East Chicago, Ill.

This vehicle was a high-wheeler with front wheels of 36in and rear wheels of 42i.
A 10/12hp 2-cylinder engine was located under the seat. The two-seater roadster ha solid rubber tyres.   GM

CHAMPION (ii) (US) *1916–1917*
Champion Auto Equipment Co, Wabash, Ind.

This car was very similar in appearance to the contemporary Ford. It used 3-litre, 4-cylinder L-head engine. A two-seater roadster was produced.   GM

CHAMPION (iii) (US) *1917–1923*
(1) Direct Drive Motor Co, Pottstown, Pa.
(2) Champion Motors Corp, Philadelphia, Pa.

Originally sold under the name Direct Drive, early models drove through gearin mounted on the rear wheel rims. Later cars had conventional drive. Two near identical versions were available, the Tourist with a Lycoming 4-cylinder engin and the Special with a 4-cylinder Herschell-Spillman. The only external differen was in the radiator shape, the Tourist carrying a Packard or Paterson type whi the Special had one resembling the Rolls-Royce. A 6-cylinder Falls engine wa used in the 1919 Model C-6. Prices ranged from $1,050 to $1,195.   K

CHAMPION (iv) (D) *1947–1954*
(1) Hermann Holbein, Herrlingen *1947–1950*
(2) Champion Automobil GmbH, Paderborn *1950–1952*
(3) Rheinische Automobilfabrik Hennhöfer & Co, Ludwigshafen *1952–1954*
(4) Rheinische Automobilwerke Thorndal & Co, Ludwigshafen *1954*

These were small two-seater cars with 250cc rear-mounted T.W.N. and later 400c Ilo and 450cc Heinkel engines. In 1955 this make was taken over by Maico.   HO

CHAMPROBERT (F) *1902–1905*
De Champrobert & Cie, Levallois-Perret, Seine

The Champrobert used an 8hp De Dion engine and a petrol-electric drive givin five forward speeds and one reverse. From 1903 onwards the car was known a the Electrogénia. The Electrogénias of 1904–1905 used a 12hp De Dion or 16h Aster engine.   GN

CHANDLER (US) *1913–1929*
Chandler Motor Car Co, Cleveland, Ohio

A highly esteemed independent make of American car, the Chandler reached i greatest production in 1920, with an output of approximately 20,000 cars. Design wa generally conventional, but the make was noted for its Traffic Transmission, a con stant-mesh gear-change introduced in 1924, and for all-round lubrication effected b the pull of a lever, adopted two years later. Engines were sixes of Chandler's ow make, joined in 1928 by two eights. Sales tapered off towards the end of the 1920 and the company was absorbed by Hupmobile in 1929. Although at least one proto type of the 1930s line was built, the Chandler name ended with the 1929 models. cheaper line was the Cleveland six, made from 1919 to 1925.   K

CHANNON (GB) *1903–1907*
E. Channon and Sons, Dorchester, Dorset

Edward Channon advertised cars under his own name from his coachbuildin firm. It is likely that proprietary mechanical components were used. The 1905 10h 2-cylinder model was advertised with automatic advance and retard of th ignition.   D

CHAPEAUX (F) *1940–1941*
Voitures E. Chapeaux, Lyons

Emile Chapeaux designed a small two-seater electric car with a maximum spee of 40mph, but only four cars were built, because of shortage of raw material The cars were made in the Ultima motorcycle factory.   GN

CHAPMAN (US) *1899–1901*
Belknap Motor Co, Portland, Maine

The Chapman was a light electric car weighing 360lb designed by W.H. Chapmar who was an electrician employed by the Belknap company. It was also known a the Electromobile.   GN

CHAPUIS-DORNIER (F) *1919–1921*
This well-known proprietary engine maker exhibited a car at the 1919 and 192 Paris Salons, but production never started. It had a 4-cylinder 3-litre engine.   GN

CHARENTAISE (F) *1899*
Pougnaud et Brothier, Ruffec, Charente

A two-seater voiturette powered by a front-mounted 2¼hp single-cylinder engine   GN

CHARETTE *see* INTERNATIONAL

CHARLES RICHARD (F) *1901–1902*

Sté des Moteurs et Autos Charles Richard, Troyes, Aube

The Charles Richard was a belt-driven light car powered by either a 4hp single cylinder or an 8hp 2-cylinder horizontal engine. Cars and light lorries of this make competed in the Northern Alcohol Trials of 1901 and 1902.   GNG

CHARLES TOWN-ABOUT (US) *1958–1959*

Stinson Aircraft Tool and Engineering Corp, San Diego, Calif.

Named after its sponsor Dr Charles H. Graves, the Town-About was an attempt at electric vehicle manufacture. Prototypes resembled the VW-Karmann Ghia in appearance, the experimental layout varying with each car. Several of them had fibreglass bodies and two batteries powering motors adjacent to the rear wheels.   BE

CHARLON (F) *1905–1906*

Sté des Automobiles Charlon, Argenteuil, Seine-et-Oise

Although short-lived, the Charlon company offered a wide range of cars: a single-cylinder 6hp and 9hp with belt drive, a 12hp 2-cylinder, and three 4-cylinder models, from 16/20 to 40/50hp. They were conventional in most respects, the largest model using chain drive, the other 4-cylinder models shaft drive.   GNG

CHARRON *see C.G.V.*

CHARRON-LAYCOCK (GB) *1920–1926*

W.S. Laycock Ltd, Millhouses, Sheffield, Yorks.

The name of the Charron-Laycock was misleading, for it was not a car of French origin. Charron Ltd of London, who imported the Charron from France, had acquired a controlling interest in W.S. Laycock of Sheffield, the railway equipment manufacturers, in order to begin making cars in England. W.S. Laycock had in fact announced in 1919 that they would be building the 3-litre Charron, but the product bearing their name, when it appeared, was a light car of British type, sold only in Britain, even if it included 'features of French design'. The Charron-Laycock was a beautifully-finished, extremely expensive (£425 to £525 in 1925) solid little machine with a side-valve 4-cylinder engine of 1,460cc and 10hp rating. From 1923 it had a 4-speed gearbox. This car should not be confused with the even smaller Charronette, which was imported from Puteaux and sold in Britain.   TRN

CHARTER (US) *1903*

James A. Charter, Chicago, Ill.

The Charter Mixed Vapor car was supposed to run on a half-and-half mixture of petrol and water, which was injected into the combustion chamber in atomized form. The petrol exploded in the normal way and the water was converted into superheated steam, which was said to result in a longer and softer explosion. A four-seater rear-entrance tonneau body was fitted to the car.   GNG

CHARTER OAK (US) *1916–1917*

Eastern Motors Syndicate, New Britain, Conn.

Named after the famous tree where the 1662 Charter was hidden, the Charter Oak was an old-fashioned car powered by a 6-cylinder Herschell-Spillman T-head engine. The original factory was at New Britain, but the makers intended to move to Hartford or Waterbury during 1917.   GNG

CHASE (US) *1907–1912*

Chase Motor Truck Co, Syracuse, N.Y.

Chase built a 'Business Runabout' or Surrey which could be converted from a four-seater, high-wheeled car to a light truck. It was powered by an air-cooled 2-cylinder engine with chain drive and solid rubber tyres. The main product of this company was commercial vehicles.   GMN

CHATEL-JEANNIN (D) *1902–1903*

Cie de Construction d'Automobiles Chatel-Jeannin, Mulhouse, Alsace

The smaller model of Chatel-Jeannin was a most unusual car: it had a 6½hp single-cylinder engine which, together with the flywheel, gearbox and rear axle were all enclosed in a casing from which no mechanical parts showed. A panel in the casing could be removed for maintenance. The 12hp 2-cylinder car was more conventional, with a centrally-mounted engine and double chain drive.   GNG

CHATER-LEA (GB) *1907; 1913–1922*

Chater-Lea Ltd, London E.C.

Chater-Lea were well-known motor cycle and component makers who had two phases of car manufacture. The first was in 1907 when they made a light car with a 2-cylinder air-cooled engine mounted on the offside of the body, mid-way between front and rear wheels. This was hardly more than a prototype, but in 1913 they started to build a conventional light car using an 8hp 4-cylinder engine and shaft drive. Nearly all parts were made in the company's new nine-story factory in Banner Lane and the cars were sold in some numbers. A few were made after World War 1, but the company decided to concentrate on motor cycles, continuing to manufacture them until 1935 in their Letchworth factory.   GNG

1921 CHARRON-LAYCOCK 10.5hp two-seater. *G.N. Georgano*

1902 CHATEL-JEANNIN 6½hp two-seater. *Neubauer Collection*

1913 CHATER-LEA 8hp two-seater. *Autocar*

1966 CHECKER Marathon sedan. *Checker Motors Corporation*

1922 CHELSEA(iii) electric coupé. *National Motor Museum*

c.1913 CHENARD-WALCKER 12/18 or 16/20hp coupé. *National Motor Museum*

CHATHAM (CDN) *1907–1908*

Chatham Motor Car Co, Chatham, Ont.

Originally a 2-cylinder light tourer of 22hp and shaft drive, the Chatham ha limited production. Following reorganization in early 1908, it became a large, fanc bodied touring car with a choice of either a 4-cylinder water-cooled or 4-cylind Reeves air-cooled engine. Wood bodies were built by Wm Gray & Sons Ltd, w later built the Gray-Dort.

CHAUSSON *see* C.H.S.

CHAUTAUQUA (US) *1913–1914*

Chautauqua Cyclecar Co, Jamestown, N.Y.

This cyclecar had a steering column gear change. The only model was a tw seater driven by a 2-cylinder air-cooled engine of 12hp.   GM

CHAVANET *see* AUTOMOTO

CHECKER (US) *1959 to date*

Checker Motors Corp, Kalamazoo, Mich.

Although the Checker company has existed since 1923 as a maker of taxicab it is only in recent years that private cars have been made. The standard ca was offered as a 'pleasure car' in catalogues from 1948 onwards, but official private car production dates from 1959. Two models were made, the Superba an the Marathon, both differing from the cabs in relatively small ways. High doo allowed easy access, and with the two auxiliary seats, the cars could accommoda eight persons. Until 1965 engines were 3.7-litre Continental sixes, as had bee used in Checker cabs for years, but since then these have been replaced by Chevrol six (3.7-litre) or V-8 (4.6 and 5.3-litre). Styling has remained practically unchange since 1959. The cars are extremely well built, and mileages of more than 400,000 hav been reported. The price of the 10ft-wheelbase sedan is $3,871; that of the long wheelbase 10ft 9in limousine $4,528. Also offered are a station wagon and a 8-door twelve-passenger Aerobus for hotel or airport work. All 1973 models com with automatic transmission as standard, engine options being a 4.1-litre six c a 5.7-litre V-8.   K

CHELMSFORD *see* CLARKSON

CHELSEA (i) *see* WELCH

CHELSEA (ii) (US) *1914*

Chelsea Mfg Co, Newark, N.J.

This car was classed as a cyclecar despite its standard track of 4ft 8in. Its 4-cylind engine was water-cooled and developed 12hp. Shaft drive was used. The side-by-sid two-seater was priced at $390.   GM

CHELSEA (iii) (GB) *1922*

Wandsworth Engineering Works, Wandsworth, London S.W.18

The Chelsea Electric Coupé had a two-seater body, and conventional bonne giving it the appearance of a petrol-engined car. The batteries of 44 cells wer mounted partly under the bonnet, and partly over the rear axle. The B.T.H. moto was mounted just ahead of the rear axle. Catalogues were issued, and a price o £700 fixed, but it is doubtful if many were sold.   GN

CHENARD-WALCKER (F) *1901–1946*

(1) Chenard, Walcker et Cie, Asnières, Seine *1901–1907*

(2) SA des Anciens Établissements Chenard et Walcker, Gennevilliers, Seine *1907– 1946*

This company was founded in 1899 and made tricycles before exhibiting it first car at the 1901 Paris Salon. It was a 1,160cc twin with mechanically operate side valves in a T-head, coil ignition, four forward speeds, and a flitchplate frame The most interesting feature was, however, the 'double' back axle with the driv taken by two cardan shafts independently of a second, dead axle beam. This wa to be a feature of the make until the middle 1920s, though at first a cheape 10hp car was offered with conventional drive, and there was also a short-live 12hp twin with side-chain transmission in 1904. A 4.1-litre 4-cylinder with lt mag neto ignition followed in 1903, and by 1905 only fours were made, the smalles model catalogued on the home market being a 3,021cc 14/16, though a paralle short-stroke 2.6-litre was made exclusively for export to Britain. By 1906 the car had the classic radiator with round core. In 1907 Chenard-Walckers had pressed steel chassis, twin transmission brakes, and no hand throttle. New during 1908 was a 9/10hp single that had a 4-speed gearbox, though neither this nor its com panion twin was quoted after 1910, by which time L-head engines had arrive on the 2.1-litre P-type. From 1912 to 1914 the cars had monobloc power unit with full-pressure lubrication. Friction dampers were standard, and capacities o the fours were 1.6 litres and 3 litres. A big six joined the range in 1913.

The staple 1919 Chenard-Walcker was the usual uprated 1914 design, the 3-litr UU, still with separate 4-speed gearbox and foot transmission brake; it was joine by a 2,651cc 12CV in 1920, and by a 2-litre, the TT, in 1921, and a 3-speed 1½-litre, Type Y, appeared in 1923, these old-fashioned machines persisting for several years. New in 1922, however, was the Touté-designed 3-litre, an ohc four with dry-sump lubrication that gave close on 90bhp, and had the unusual Hallot servo brakes on front wheels and transmission only. These cars finished 1st and 2nd in the first Le Mans 24-Hour Race of 1923, as well as winning the 1924 Circuit des Routes Pavées. A 2-litre edition followed soon afterwards, these sports Chenards being made until 1927. From 1925 there were also parallel sv touring editions with similar chassis and plug covers giving the appearance of ohv units.

In 1924 and 1925 the company raced a bi-block straight-8 which in its final form had brakes on all four wheels, and achieved nearly 110mph on 130bhp. But it was never reliable though it was catalogued, at 84,525 francs for a tourer. Much more successful were the 1,100cc 'tanks' with 55bhp 2-bearing pushrod engines and differential-less back axles that had two successful racing seasons (1925 and 1926) and even staged a comeback in 1937, when two examples finished 1st and 2nd in the Bol d'Or. For 1927 the company introduced the 8CV Z2, a tough little family car with 1,300cc sv short-stroke engine, magneto ignition, 4-speed gearbox, conventional rear axle, and fabric bodywork; it sold for 24,000 francs. That year, however, an association with Delahaye, which lasted until 1932, led to the rationalization of both companies' ranges, and it became difficult to tell the two makes apart. A production edition of the 'tank' came out in 1928 with a 1½-litre ioe engine, but this was the last Chenard with any sporting potential; the range now consisted of pedestrian sv fours, plus a couple of Delahaye-like ioe sixes with capacities of 2½ litres and 2.9 litres. The smaller of these, the 14CV, was still being made in 1934. In 1932 the T11 appeared, a new 12CV four on the usual lines with a free-wheel as standard equipment. Then in 1934 Chenards, now free of Delahaye influence, adopted transverse ifs. They also offered a 3,560cc sv V-8, the Aigle 8, which used their own engine, in effect a double T11 unit. In 1935 the cars had torsion-bar front suspension and the option of a Cotal gearbox, and ohv engines became available; the range consisted of two fours and the eight. A 4-cylinder fwd car did not go into production.

From 1937 onwards Chenard-Walckers slowly lost their individuality. Their bodies were replaced by Chausson coachwork identical to that of the Matford, and only one model retained the 2,180cc ohv Chenard-Walcker engine. The others had 1,911cc 4-cylinder Citroën and 3,622cc Matford units. Finally Citroën and Matford chassis were adopted as well and the Chenard engine dropped, the only 'native' components of the cars being their back axles — though the cabriolets were quite handsome, being of Vutotal type with no screen pillars. A few 11CV and 21CV cars were made after World War 2, but from 1947 the staple Chenard-Walcker product was a forward-control light van, the development of which was continued by Peugeot after that company took over in 1951.　　　　MCS

CHENHALL (GB) 1902–1906
(1) Chenhalls Motor Car Ltd, Plymouth, Devon 1902
(2) St Andrews Cycle and Electrical Co, Plymouth, Devon 1903–1906
　　It is believed that J.S. Chenhalls constructed a few cars for sale locally, but no details appeared in the contemporary motoring press.　　　　DF

CHENU (F) c.1903–c.1907
Automobiles Chenu, Paris
　　1903 Chenu cars were made in several sizes including a 9hp single and 12hp twin, both with shaft drive, and 12, 20, 30 and 40hp 4-cylinder chain-drive cars. Two 20hp cars, one driven by M. Chenu, competed in the Paris-Madrid race. De Dion engines were used in a number of models. The company later made aero engines.　　GNG

CHESWOLD (GB) 1911–1915
E.W. Jackson & Son Ltd, French Gate, Doncaster, Yorks.
　　This car, which took its name from a local stream, was designed by M.C. Inman-Hunter, who had formerly been chief designer for Adams-Hewitt. During five years of production only one model was made, a 15.9hp 4-cylinder car with four speeds and worm drive. The cylinders were separately cast and the radiator was mounted behind the engine, Renault-fashion. The company made their own engine and gearbox, the rear axle being by Wrigley. The price of the five-seater tourer was £440.　　GNG

CHEVROLET (i) (US) 1911 to date
Chevrolet Motor Co, Detroit, Mich.
　　Chevrolet, General Motors' least expensive American car and the world's best-seller, was actually started by W.C. Durant at a time when he did not control G.M. In association with racing driver Louis Chevrolet he brought out a 4.9-litre six with side valves in a T-head, selling for $2,150. This was followed by a smaller 6-cylinder model, but the marque's first big impact came with the 4-cylinder overhead-valve Baby Grand touring car at $875, and its companion roadster model, the Royal Mail. Electrics were an optional extra on Chevrolets until 1917, but in the meantime the company had come right to the fore with the 2.7-litre 4-cylinder 490, also an ohv, in 1916. The type designation indicated its original list price in dollars, and sales went up from 13,600 to 70,701.

1928 CHENARD-WALCKER 1½-litre 'tank' coupé. *Autocar*

1933 CHENARD-WALCKER Aigle-4 2.2-litre saloon. *Jacques Kupélian Collection*

1939 CHENARD-WALCKER Aigle 8 3.6-litre drophead coupé. *Lucien Loreille Collection*

1912 CHESWOLD 15.9hp tourer. *Autocar*

1912 CHEVROLET(i) Classic Six 30hp tourer.
General Motors Corporation

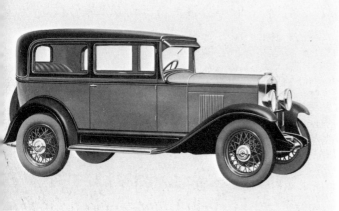

1930 CHEVROLET(i) Model AD 26hp sedan.
General Motors Corporation

1935 CHEVROLET(i) Master EC 3.3-litre coupé.
G.N. Georgano Collection

1968 CHEVROLET(i) Corvette 5.3-litre sports car.
General Motors Corporation

General Motors acquired Chevrolet in 1917, and by 1920 the marque was ousted in the United States only by Ford and Dodge. A one-model policy was pursued in 1923, but before this there had been other types of Chevrolet including the FA and FB fours, and a short-lived V-8 with a Mason engine at $1,100. There was also an abortive air-cooled car using the regular chassis and body styles in 1923. The 1925 Superior coach with disc wheels and Duco cellulose finish sold for $650, and two years later Chevrolet outsold Ford for the first time, though this was hardly a fair comparison since Ford was shut down for a good part of the year during the change-over from the Model T to the Model A. Chevrolet did not have front-wheel brakes until 1928, the last year of the 4-cylinder cars. In 1929 came the 'Cast Iron Wonder', the 3.2-litre ohv International 6 with an 8ft 11in wheelbase and detachable disc wheels. More than a million were sold during its first season at $595, and the engine was progressively developed up to 1953.

In 1931 Chevrolet finally went ahead of Ford and stayed there apart from three seasons. 1932 cars resembled scaled-down Buicks or Oldsmobiles and featured rubber engine mountings, synchromesh and a free wheel, all for $495. In 1933 a V-grille was adopted, and capacity went up to 3.4 litres. G.M.'s Dubonnet-type ifs was fitted on the 1934 cars – in that year the ten millionth Chevrolet was delivered. Turret top styling followed in 1935 and hydraulic brakes in 1936. Engine capacity was increased slightly again in 1937. 1939 was the year of the fifteen millionth car; station wagons were catalogued, column-shift was optional, and prices ranged from $628 upwards. In 1940 Chevrolet was offering a power-top convertible in the low-price field, and Juan Manuel Fangio scored his first big victory in a long-distance race in Argentina at the wheel of one of that year's coupés. Fastback coupés were listed in 1942, but along with most other American makes, the cars were little altered when they reappeared on the market after World War 2.

Extensive restyling and lowering took place in 1949, when a sedan cost $1,460, but in 1950 Chevrolet offered the option of a 2-speed Powerglide fully-automatic transmission, as well as a now-fashionable hardtop coupé style. A new sports car, the Corvette, with fibreglass bodywork, featured in the 1953 programme with a 160bhp version of the regular 6-cylinder engine.

Chevrolet's lead over Ford was down to a narrow 20,000 margin by 1954. In 1955 they came out with a 4.3-litre ohv V-8 on conventional lines, giving 162bhp with an 180bhp 'power pack' available at extra cost. The capacity of the companion six was now 3.9 litres. By 1957 the Corvette had acquired the 8-cylinder engine, and special SS versions were being tried with 360bhp power units and 4-speed all-synchromesh boxes listed as a factory option. 1958 V-8 Chevrolets had 5.7-litre engines and air suspension was available, though the idea was soon discarded.

A new departure was the Division's 1960 compact car, the Corvair, a 2.3-litre air-cooled flat-6 with engine at the rear, unitary construction of chassis and body and all wheels independently sprung. It proved a little too advanced for the market at which it was aimed, but by 1966 had entered upon a new lease of life as a specialist semi-sporting machine available with such options as a 4-speed box and 180bhp turbosupercharged engine.

The evolution of subsequent Chevrolets reveals the need of the modern American mass-producer to offer a diversity of products, rather than to concentrate on a single basic model and ring the changes on body styles. In 1963 the company started to bridge the gap between the Corvair and the inexpensive, but by no means small Impala, Bel Air and Biscayne series (that year's versions were 17ft 6in long!) with a 'semi-compact', the Chevy II. This had integral construction, a 9ft 2in wheelbase and the choice of two engines of modest dimensions, a 2½-litre four and a 3.2-litre six. The slightly bigger Chevelle of 1964 was the first Chevrolet to use G.M.'s perimeter-type chassis frame (standardized on the big cars in 1965) and was available either with the Chevy II six or a 4.6-litre V-8. Another new model in 1964 was the Corvette Stingray sports car with retractable headlamps, giving 145mph from 360bhp: the following season it had disc brakes as standard equipment. 1966 coverage of the market was comprehensive. Besides the specialized Corvair and Corvette there was the Chevy II in three series, the Chevelle with a wide choice of power units and five different types of full-sized Chevrolet from the inexpensive Biscayne up to the luxurious Caprice. Prices ranged from $2,028 for the simplest Chevy II with 90bhp 4-cylinder engine up to the Caprice custom station wagon at $3,347. Chevrolet engines were used by Checker, Avanti, the revived 8/10 Cord, Excalibur, the last Canadian-built Studebakers, the Anglo-American Gordon-Keeble and the Italo-American Iso and Bizzarini. They were also used in the smallest Oldsmobiles in 6-cylinder form and in Canadian-built Pontiacs and the Acadian, an all-Canadian G.M. product. They are also found in the biggest 8-cylinder Opels. For 1967 the company added to its range a sports coupé model, the V-8, 5.7-litre Camaro with 295bhp and front disc brakes, a belated answer to Ford's Mustang.

Meanwhile Corvette-powered cars were dominating Can-Am racing, continuing to do so until 1971. Chevrolet's sixth two-million year came in 1968 (the others had been 1962-66 inclusive), the tenth successive season in which they had outsold Ford. Camaros were now available with 6½-litre engines, and the Corvette was completely restyled. Then 1969 brought the demise of the Corvair, the final season's sales being a low 2,359 as against its 1961 peak of 316,000. A further gap in the range was filled by the Blazer, a 4 × 4 jeep-type vehicle offered with 6-cylinder or V-8 engine. Sporting and prestige images were combined in the Monte Carlo of 1970, a coupé on the Chevelle chassis with front disc brakes and a choice of five V-8 units, the biggest having 7.4 litres and 360bhp. This was the last year of 4-cylinder engines in the Chevy II line, and Camaro sales came within 20,000 of the Ford Mustang's. The major news of 1971 was a sub-compact, the unitary-construction Vega with coil rear suspension, offered in hatchback coupé, 2-door sedan and station wagon styles, and powered by a new 2.3-litre 4-cylinder engine with alloy block and cogged belt drive for its overhead camshaft. Transmission options included a 3-speed semi-automatic and front disc brakes were standard. The 1973 line was one of the biggest in the U.S.A., embracing the Vega, Chevy II Nova and Chevelle in the compact and intermediate markets, the Bel Air, Impala and Caprice with 10ft 1½in wheelbase in the full-size group; the Camaro and Monte Carlo coupés; the Corvette sports car; and such specialist semi-utility types as the Blazer, the Suburban station wagon on a light-truck chassis, the forward-control twelve-seater Sportvan station wagon, and the El Camino, a car-based coupé-utility in the Australian idiom. All passenger-car types with the exception of the Nova had front disc brakes as standard equipment, while innovations were a Nova hatchback coupé and a restyled and lowered Monte Carlo available with V-8s of 5,736cc or 7,440cc. Power-assisted steering was standard on Camaros, big Chevrolets were now offered only with automatic transmissions, and energy-absorbing front bumpers were found on all types.

In the summer of 1972 Chevrolet announced plans for a Wankel-powered Vega to be available by 1975.   MCS

1971 CHEVROLET(i) Vega 2.3-litre coupé.
General Motors Corp

CHEVROLET (ii) (RA) *1962 to date*
G.M. Argentina S.A., Buenos Aires

This company manufactures a local version of the Chevy II with 6-cylinder pushrod engine. Early ones had a capacity of 3.8 litres, later increased to 4.1 litres. Four-speed ZF gearboxes appeared in 1971, and were standard on the 1972 Chevy Super Sport, a 4-door sedan on a 9ft 2in wheelbase.   MCS

CHEVROLET (iii) (BR) *1964 to date*
G.M. do Brasil S.A., São Caetano do Sul

The first true Brazilian Chevrolet was the C-141, a station wagon with a high ground clearance suitable for bad roads. Its 4.3-litre 6-cylinder engine was a direct descendant of the original 1929 cast-iron Chevrolet 6, and the last of this series to be made anywhere. 1969 saw the Opala series of sedans and coupés of mixed Chevrolet and Opel Rekord lineage; engines were Chevrolet, either 2½-litre fours or 3.8-litre sixes. The latter was enlarged to 4.1 litres and 140bhp for 1972.   MCS

1973 CHEVROLET(i) Caprice Classic sedan.
General Motors Corp

CHEVRON (GB) *1961 to date*
A.D. Bennett and Co, Salford 6, Lancs.

Derek Bennett built specials for the 750 and 1172 formulae and Formula Junior before introducing the first Chevron as a 2-seater for Club racing, with Holbay-Ford 1½-litre dry-sump engine. A run of successes was achieved by this model, in the hands of Bennett, Robert Ashcroft and others. In 1966 a G.T. appeared. The tubular chassis was fitted with Armstrong coil/damper units, and wore a metal body, with hinged sections at front and rear. As sold, rear-mounted B.M.W. 2-litre or Cosworth-Ford 1,600cc engines drove through Hewland HD5 gearboxes, but two of the seven cars completed before the end of the year embraced B.R.M. V-8 and Coventry-Climax engines respectively. 1967 developments included a Formula 3 single-seater, and a 3-litre Martin V-8-engined Group 6 sports car.

The B6/B8 GT model was homologated for Group 4 racing in 1968, and 90 were made in all. The B9 was a successful derivative of the 1967 Formula 3 model, and the B10 a Formula 2 version. B12 was a Repco V-8-engined sports car (there was no B11 or B13). B14 was the 1968 Formula B car, and B15 the 1969 Formula 3/B machine that achieved many successes. Nevertheless these were overshadowed by the Groups 5 and 6 2-litre sports-racing cars: the tubular-framed B16 GT of 1969, the B19 spyder of 1969 and its successor the B21 of 1972; these achieved a remarkable record of class victories and championships. The B17, B18 and B20 were the single-seater models for 1970, 1971 and 1972 for Formulae 2, 3, B and (later) A. The B18 broke new ground for Chevron in adopting a central-tub monocoque construction. The B23 was the 1973 2-litre sports-racing car, B24 a Formula 5000 design which proved promising in 1972 in the hands of Brian Redman, and B25 a similar pure monocoque design for Formula 2.   DF

1966 CHEVRON GT coupé. *A.D. Bennett and Co*

CHIC (AUS) *1923–1929*
Chic Cars Ltd, Adelaide, S.A.

The Chic was designed by the firm who made the Bond (i), and like the later Bonds it used an ohv 14/40hp 4-cylinder Meadows engine. Most other components were also of British origin. About 50 cars were made.   GNG

CHICAGO (i) (US) *1905–1907*
Chicago Automobile Manufacturing Co, Chicago, Ill.

This was a steamer with an unusual V-4 engine, 2-speed transmission and shaft drive, with a wooden *Roi-des-Belges* body. The price was $2,500.   GMN

CHICAGO (ii) (US) *1915–1916*
Chicago Electric Motor Co, Chicago, Ill.

1973 CHEVRON B23 2-litre sports/racing car.
Derek Bennett Engineering Ltd

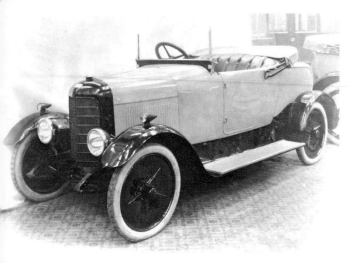

1920 CHIRIBIRI 12hp two-seater. *Autocar*

1925 CHIRIBIRI Tipo Milano 10.4hp saloon.
G.N. Georgano Collection

1905 CHRISTIE 50hp tourer. Coachwork by
Healey. *Keith Marvin Collection*

Chicago electric cars were primarily enclosed coupés for four or five passengers, which could be operated from either the front or rear seats. The doors were arched at the top for easier entrance and exit. The speed controls gave five positions, up to 23mph.
GMN

CHICAGOAN (US) *1952–1954*
Triplex Industries Ltd, Blue Island, Ill.
The Chicagoan sports car used a 6-cylinder Willys engine and had a two-seater fibreglass body. Not more than 15 were made.
GNG

CHICAGO MOTOR BUGGY (US) *1908*
Chicago Motor Buggy Co, Chicago, Ill.
This was a typical high-wheeler with a 14hp air-cooled engine. The price was $550.
GNG

CHILTERN (GB) *1919–1920*
Vulcan Motor & Engineering Co Ltd, Dunstable, Beds.
By using the well-tried Dorman engine, the makers of the Chiltern were able to produce a vehicle of a semi-sporting nature during 1919. An unusual feature of this car was the method by which the gearbox was mounted; a similar system had been used on the Vulcan car of 1914 so it is possible that there was a link with the Stockport firm of the same name.
GB

CHINGKANGSHAN see JINGKANGSHAN

CHIRIBIRI (I) *1913–1927*
Chiribiri & Co, Turin
Antonio Chiribiri was one of the lavish crop of gifted engineers produced by Italy around the turn of the century. He worked for Isotta-Fraschini among other firms, then went into business on his own, his first cars being called S.I.V.A. He began with an 8/10hp light car with four cylinders cast monobloc, alloy pistons, worm drive and sporting pretensions. It was given a bigger bore in 1915, as the 1,300cc 10/12hp. In this period he also built an air-cooled cyclecar. These machines were little-known. Chiribiri's name only became famous in the 1920s. He was one of the makers to concentrate on fast touring cars while ensuring a steady return with a line of less exciting family machines and other engineering products – in his case, aero engines. All Chiribiris were small, however, and in this he was unusual. His 'utility' range consisted of the 12/16hp Normale, a side-valve four of 1,600cc current until 1921, which was replaced by the Roma, Monza and Milano 1½-litre cars. Their engines were of the same dimensions as those of Chiribiri's two current sports models, the Monza Normale and Monza Speciale. Both had twin overhead camshafts. The Monza Corsa, which was supercharged, developed 93bhp. The company's racing cars won it renown in Italy, starting with an ohv racing car based on the 12/16bhp in 1921.
TRN

CHIYODA (J) *c.1932–1935*
Tokyo Gas and Electric Engineering Co, Tokyo
Trucks built by Tokyo Gas and Electric had been in production since 1918 and were named Chiyoda in 1931. It was in that year that a T.G.E. truck was purchased by Kunaisho (Dept. of The Imperial Household) and in honour of that event the line was renamed for Chiyoda, the place where the Imperial Household is situated.
Due to military needs, Chiyoda products were built for the Japanese government and some staff and command cars were assembled from about 1932–1935. Model HF was a 4-door, seven-seater touring car; Model H was a four door sedan with grille similar to the 1935 Pontiac, and Model HS was a 6-wheel, seven-seater.
BE

CHOTA see BUCKINGHAM

CHRISTCHURCH-CAMPBELL (GB) *1922*
J. Campbell Ltd, Christchurch, Hampshire
About six Christchurch-Campbells were made, using 10.8hp Coventry-Simplex engines and Meadows gearboxes. The last car was powered by a tuned 11.9hp Dorman engine.

CHRISTIANE HUIT (F) *1928–1929*
A. Andrieux, Rennes, Ille-et-Vilaine
The Christiane was an advanced sports car using a 2-litre straight-8 engine with single ohc. The depression killed any chance of successful sales.
GNG

CHRISTIE (US) *1904–1910*
(1) Christie Iron Works, New York City, N.Y.
(2) Direct Action Motor Car Co, Hoboken, N.J.
J. Walter Christie was the first serious proponent of front-wheel drive cars in the United States. He brought his principle before the public eye with racing cars, the first of which appeared on the race track in January 1904. It had a 30hp 4-cylinder engine mounted transversely, the crankshaft taking the place of the front axle.
Six racers were built in all, of which one had two 60hp engines, one at each end of the car, while the machine entered in the 1907 Grand Prix had a V-4 engine of

,618cc, making it the largest car ever to take part in a Grand Prix. Two or three ~~t~~uring cars were built in 1905, and a later (1909) Christie vehicle was a taxicab ~~w~~ith a 4-cylinder transverse engine. Christie subsequently made front-wheel-drive ~~tr~~actor conversions for fire engines, and tanks. KM

~~C~~HRITON (GB) 1904

~~C~~hriton Automobile Co, Saltburn-by-the-Sea, Yorks.

This company made a 10hp 4-cylinder shaft-driven light car selling at £195. They ~~al~~so advertised a 24hp 4-cylinder and 30hp 6-cylinder car, and 'higher powered cars ~~to~~ order'. However, it is unlikely that any but the 10hp models were made. GNG

~~C~~HRYSLER (i) (US) 1923 to date

~~C~~hrysler Corporation, Detroit, Mich.

Walter P. Chrysler, formerly of Buick and Willys, acquired Maxwell-Chalmers ~~in~~ 1923, and the first car to bear his name, the 6-cylinder '70' of 1924, was something ~~o~~f a sensation with its 4-wheel contracting hydraulic brakes and 70mph performance. ~~A~~t $1,645 for a sedan, 43,000 were sold in 1925. The 1926 range was widened to ~~in~~clude a 3-litre 4-cylinder '58' to replace the Maxwell and the expensive 4.7-litre ~~6~~-cylinder Imperial, selling for $3,095. The 6-cylinder roadsters offered an excellent ~~ro~~ad performance for a modest price, as was shown by their 3rd and 4th places at ~~L~~e Mans in 1928, behind a Bentley and a Stutz. The 1929 models had internal-~~ex~~panding brakes and their body styling and ribbon-type radiator shells were widely ~~im~~itated in Europe over the next few years.

Meanwhile Chrysler had laid the foundations for a motor empire to rival General ~~M~~otors and Ford by taking over Dodge and launching two new makes, the Plymouth ~~fo~~ur in the lowest price sector and the De Soto Six in a slightly higher bracket – all ~~th~~is in 1928. Chrysler sold 98,000 cars in 1929. The 1931 cars featured the long, low ~~lo~~ok inspired by the Cord of 1929; 4-speed gearboxes were offered for a short while ~~a~~nd for the first time a brace of straight-8s featured in the range – the medium-priced ~~C~~D, and the 6.3-litre CG-type Imperial for the carriage trade, often with bodies by ~~L~~e Baron. 1932 saw fully flexible rubber engine mountings ('Floating Power'), ~~au~~tomatic clutches and free wheels. Synchromesh followed a year later. Automatic ~~ov~~erdrive was available in 1934, and regular equipment by 1936. The Chrysler line ~~fo~~r 1934 was spearheaded by the revolutionary CU-type 8-cylinder Airflow, with ~~w~~elded unitary construction of chassis and body, all seats within the wheelbase, ~~h~~eadlamps mounted flush in the wings, a full aerodynamic shape and concealed ~~l~~uggage accommodation. At $1,345 it was a commercial failure, though it was ~~c~~ontinued till 1937. Chrysler hurriedly brought out the more conventionally styled ~~A~~irstream line in 1935, and for the next twenty years the company's styling policy ~~w~~as cautious, though technical progress is represented by the adoption of independ-~~e~~nt front suspension and hypoid rear axles (1937), steering-column gear-change ~~(1~~939) and optional fluid drive from 1939 onward.

The 1942 cars, generally competitive with G.M.'s Buick, embraced two 4.1-litre ~~si~~xes and three 5.3-litre eights, all side-valve, with prices from $1,295 for the ~~W~~indsor to $3,965 for the Crown Imperial limousine on the 12ft 1½in wheelbase.

Early post-war design followed the 1942 models closely, apart from some inter-~~e~~sting 'Town and Country' bodies, basically standard sedans and convertibles with ~~w~~ooden exterior trim in station-wagon style. In 1951, however, Chrysler broke new ~~g~~round with a 5.4-litre overhead valve oversquare V-8 with hemispherical heads, ~~a~~ fully automatic transmission and the option of hydraulic power-assisted steering. ~~T~~his was at the time America's most powerful car and engines were fitted and raced ~~b~~y Allard (ii) and Cunningham (ii). Caliper disc brakes were optional, but were ~~d~~ropped after a few years, while another individual feature of Chrysler Corporation ~~p~~roducts was the push-button layout of controls for the automatic transmission, ~~fo~~und on cars made between 1956 and 1965. Chrysler's lag in styling was painfully ~~a~~pparent by 1954, when the group lay a bad third behind G.M. and Ford, and 1955 ~~n~~ot only saw the retirement of the old side-valve six in favour of a 4.9-litre 188bhp ~~V~~-8, but also new, lower 'Flight Sweep' lines which put the cars well back in the ~~r~~unning. A new range of '300' coupés and convertibles gave Chrysler a 'personal ~~c~~ar' competitive with Ford's Thunderbird and the 6¼-litre V-8s used in the 1957 ~~C~~hryslers developed more bhp than any of their rivals. Alternator ignition and ~~u~~nitary construction of chassis and body were adopted in 1960, while Chrysler, who ~~h~~ad had a gas-turbine car running experimentally in 1954, built a series of fifty ~~v~~ehicles using Plymouth running gear in 1964 which were supplied to selected ~~c~~ustomers for evaluation.

The 1960s also saw the corporation extend its motor-car interests into Europe ~~b~~y the acquisition of majority interests in Simca of France and the Rootes Group ~~o~~f Great Britain. Another overseas venture was Chrysler Australia Ltd of Adelaide ~~(~~see Chrysler (ii)). Chrysler's V-8 engine was also used by Facel Vega in France, ~~a~~nd by Bristol and Jensen in Britain. Chrysler's 1968 cars were all V-8s in the ~~$~~3,300–$4,600 price class, with 6.3-litre or 7.2-litre engines. Automatic transmis-~~s~~ion was standard on the more expensive New Yorkers and the 350bhp 300 coupé. ~~T~~here were no major changes in subsequent years, though the general derating ~~o~~f American power units was reflected by the standardization of 5.9-litre, 6.6-litre ~~a~~nd 7.2-litre V-8 in 1972 and 1973, with outputs ranging from 175bhp to 245bhp. ~~B~~etween 1955 and 1967 a handful of special-bodied Chryslers, Dodges and Ply-~~m~~ouths with Ghia coachwork were sold under the Dual-Ghia name. MCS

1931 CHRYSLER(i) Imperial CG 6.3-litre sedan.
National Motor Museum

1934 CHRYSLER(i) Airflow CU 4.4-litre sedan.
Chrysler Corporation

1946 CHRYSLER(i) Town & Country 5.3-litre
sedan. *Chrysler Corporation*

1973 CHRYSLER(i) New Yorker Brougham.
Chrysler Corporation

1972 CHRYSLER(ii) CH 2-door hardtop.
Chrysler Australia Ltd.

1948 CISITALIA 1,090cc coupé. Coachwork
by Pinin Farina. *Museo dell'Automobile, Turin*

1961 CISITALIA 750cc coupé. *Cisitalia SpA*

CHRYSLER (ii) (AUS) *1928 to date*
Chrysler Australia Ltd, Adelaide, S.A.

Before World War 2 Australian Chryslers used imported chassis and engin
with locally-made Richards bodies. In the early 1950s Plymouth, Dodge and D
Soto models were built with 120bhp 6-cylinder engines. The first 'genuine' Austr
lian Chrysler was the Royal built from 1956 to 1963; this used 6- and 8-cylind
engines in what was basically a 1954 Plymouth body but with front and re
bumpers of later style. With the introduction of the Valiant in 1961 the Roy
was gradually phased out, and the Valiant, which has become increasingly Austr
lian in content and styling, has been the staple product of the Adelaide plant ev
since. The 145bhp slant-6 engine was supplemented by a V-8 in 1964, and in 196
a new body based on the Dodge Dart was introduced. New models with Australi
styled bodies were introduced in 1971, and were available on three wheelbas
and with a choice of three sixes and one V-8 engine. The most powerful, althoug
not the largest, was the 280bhp RT Charger coupé. Other Chrysler produc
assembled in Australia include the Hillman Hunter and Dodge Phoenix.   EI

CHRYSLER (iii) (F) *1970 to date*
Chrysler France S.A., Poissy, Seine-et-Oise

Originally a Rootes design, the French Chrysler was unveiled at the 1970 Par
Salon and was built in the Simca factory. Features of the design were a 5-bearin
ohc 4-cylinder engine, a 4-speed all-syncromesh gearbox, rack and pinion steerin
McPherson strut ifs and coil rear suspension. The standard 1,639cc model ha
disc brakes on the front only, all-disc brakes being used on the 1.8-litre version
Wheelbase was 8ft 9in and only saloons were offered. The 1972 prices starte
at 14,795 francs, or 1,500 francs more than the standard 1301 Simca.   MC

C.H.S. (F) *1948*
SA des Usines Chausson, Asnières, Seine

The C.H.S. was a light car planned by the Chausson bus manufacturing company
but it never went into production. It used a 330cc single-cylinder 2-stroke engin
driving the front wheels, independent suspension and a very light open two-seate
body. It was also to have been made in England by L.T. Delaney & Sons Ltd c
Cricklewood.   GN

CHURCH-FIELD (US) *1912–1913*
Church-Field Motor Co, Sibley, Mich.

This was an unusual electric car with an underslung chassis. It used 2-spee
planetary transmission which, combined with ten electrical selector positions, gav
a total choice of twenty speed ranges.   GMI

CHURCHILL *see* **HALLAMSHIRE**

C.I.D. (F) *1912–1914*
Constructions Industrielles Dijonaises, Dijon

C.I.D. cars were made by the company who had previously been responsible fo
the Cottereau. The best-known C.I.D. was the Baby, a light car with a single
cylinder 8hp Buchet engine and 4-speed friction transmission. Front suspension wa
by single transverse spring. The same basic design was also sold as the Emeraude
although in this case front suspension was by ordinary semi-elliptics. Larger C.I.D
cars had 4-cylinder sleeve-valve engines of 14, 16 and 22hp.   GNC

C.I.E.M. (CH) *1904–1906*
Compagnie d'Industrie Electrique et Mécanique, Geneva

This company made petrol-electric cars and commercial vehicles. In 1904 a
8hp V-twin and a 16hp V-4 engine were used to provide power. For normal runnin
the petrol engine was used, but the cars could travel up to 30 miles on the batterie
alone. For 1905 an 8hp vertical-twin and a 16/24 vertical-four engine were used
From 1906 onwards the cars made by C.I.E.M. were called Stella, and the petrol
electric system was abandoned.   GNC

CINCINNATI (US) *1903–c.1905*
Cincinnati Automobile Co, Cincinnati, Ohio

The Cincinnati was a two-seater which did not differ greatly from the many othe
steamers of the time, although it had a rather lower build. The 2-cylinder engine
was under the seat, final drive was by chain, and steering by tiller.   GNC

CINO (US) *1909–1913*
Haberer & Co, Cincinnati, Ohio

The Cino had a 4-cylinder engine with overhead valves. The wheel hubs and
hub-caps were similar to those of the Packard. Beginning with five body types,
the line was reduced at the last to a five-seater touring car and a roadster.   GMN

C.I.P. (I) *1922–1924*
Cyclecar Italiana Petromilli, Turin

The C.I.P. was a 1,075cc ohv 4-cylinder light car designed and built by Constan
tino Petromilli.   GNC

SITALIA (I) *1946–1965*

italia SpA, Turin

Piero Dusio's brainchild was the Italian equivalent of Amedée Gordini's
cial Simcas in that it made use of Fiat 1100 mechanical components. The first
s were single-seaters with multi-tubular space frames, transverse leaf ifs, torsion
and coil rear suspension, magneto ignition and 3-speed gearbox. With 60bhp
ilable, 110mph were claimed and some 40 of these were sold in 1946 at the
uivalent of £1,000.

Special races were staged for these cars, not only in Italy but also in Egypt.
volari drove a sports version into 2nd place in the 1947 Mille Miglia. Touring
sions carried elegant coupé bodies – foreshadowing Italian preeminence in
post-war G.T. field – semi-elliptic rear springs and a choice of 50bhp or
bhp engines.

In 1948–49 a talented team – Ferry Porsche, Carlo Abarth and Hruschka – evolved
ingenious 4 × 4 1½-litre car for Formula 1. The 4 ohc, 300bhp flat-12 engine was
r-mounted, tankage was lateral as on later G.P. Lancias, and there was a 5-speed
arbox. However, Cisitalia ran out of money before the G.P. car had run under
own power, and in 1949 Dusio transferred his entire operation to Argentina.
ough the Autoar produced in that country wore a Cisitalia badge, its basis was
llys Jeep and in 1950 it was announced that production of the basic 1,100cc
sitalia coupés was to be resumed in Italy under new sponsorship. Though cars
re made intermittently until 1965, the firm never recovered its former position.
1952 a bigger coupé model was announced, with a 2.8-litre 4-cylinder ohc B.P.M.
rine engine and gearbox in unit with a De Dion back axle; 160bhp and 137mph
re claimed, but this made little impression, any more than did a transformation
the Fiat 1900 with sports saloon bodywork and an ugly 'waterfall' grille. In
54 the principal offering was a 70bhp version of the '1100' with wire wheels and
erdrive, of which about a hundred were made. This had evolved by 1957 into the
248cc Volo Radente, but no cars were produced between 1958 and 1961 and the
t Cisitalias, known as Coupé Tourism Specials, were only 750cc and 850cc
rivatives of the rear-engined Fiat 600 and not outstanding in any way. MCS

TO (D) *1905–1909*

) Cito Fahrradwerke AG, Cologne-Klettenburg *1905–1907*
) Cito-Werke AG, Cologne-Klettenburg *1907–1909*

Cito was already a producer of bicycles and motor cycles when car production
s started in 1905 with Omnimobil components. The first model was called the
tomobil. In 1906 four new types appeared with 2-cylinder Aster and 4-cylinder
fnir engines. Proprietary engines from these firms were also used for the 4-cylinder
dels 10/16PS and 18/20PS of 1908. HON

TROËN (F) *1919 to date*

) SA André Citroën, Paris *1919–1968*
) Citroën SA, Paris *1968 to date*

André Citroën, a former chief engineer of Mors, started his own gear-making
m in 1913, a fact commemorated by the 'herring-bone bevel' emblem used on all
troën cars. He put his knowledge of American mass-production methods to good
ect in 1919, when, in association with Jules Salomon (already responsible for Le
bre and later to be behind the Rosengart), he evolved two designs. The bigger
these, a sleeve-valve 4-litre, was taken over by Gabriel Voisin, but the 1.3-litre
cylinder Type-A was put into production in a factory previously used by Mors.
his was a straghtforward sv machine with disc wheels, cone clutch, full electrical
uipment, left hand drive and central change for the 3-speed gearbox. By the
d of 1919 it was selling for 7,950fr in France and £500 in England. 10,000 cars
ere made in 1921.

The need for expansion was soon to lead to the acquisition of Clément-Bayard.
t this time, Citroën was developing the half-track system evolved by M. Kégresse,
rmer manager of Tsar Nicholas II's garage. This was mainly applied to com-
ercial and military vehicles, but the smaller Kégresse versions were adaptations of
itroën's private-car chassis, and among their exploits was the first successful
ossing of the Sahara by motor car in 1922–23. The 1922 Citroën range included
improved Type-B of 1½-litres, and the 856cc 5CV with cloverleaf bodywork,
etachable head, quarter-elliptic springing all round, a foot transmission brake
d coil ignition. Though neither a brisk goer nor a brisk stopper, it was indestructible
d remained in production until 1925, in which year Noel Westwood used one to
ive all round Australia. 15,000 Citroëns had been sold by 1924, when 250 cars
day were being turned out and Opel were marketing what amounted to a copy of
e 5CV under the name of Laubfrosch. 1925 saw the advent of cheap all-steel
loon bodies made under Budd patents; this angular *tout acier* model sold in
ngland for £325, or only £100 more than the standard tourer. Though a modernized
erivative of the 5CV was to reappear in 1929 as the Sima-Standard, Citroën
emselves concentrated in 1926 on the 12hp type, now enlarged to over 1½ litres,
d given a flat radiator, 4-wheel brakes, and semi-elliptic springs. Cars were also
eing assembled outside France. The British factory at Slough was opened in 1926
d was followed by others in Italy and Germany. In 1934 Gräf u. Stift of
ienna also built cars under Citroën licence. Of these only Slough survived the
930s, British-built Citroëns continuing to appear until 1965.

1919 CITROËN Type A 10hp tourer.
SA André Citroën

1924 CITROËN 5CV town coupé. *Autocar*

1930 CITROËN C-6 20hp saloon. Coachwork by
Weymann. *National Motor Museum*

1934 CITROËN 7CV Traction Avant saloon.
SA André Citroën

1955 CITROËN 2CV saloon. *SA André Citroën*

1967 CITROËN DS21 Pallas saloon. *SA André Citroën*

1972 CITROËN GS 1.2-litre saloon. *SA André Citroën*

The company was now firmly established with Peugeot and Renault as one France's 'big three'. In 1928 the saloons became more streamlined – they w also cheaper, the 12/24hp costing £220. Production in 1929 was 100,000 vehicl new for that season was the 2.4-litre 6-cylinder C6, a conventional sv mach with 3-speed box, coil ignition, servo brakes and gravity feed. The 4-cylin cars were enlarged to 1.6 litres and had a similar specification. These two ba types were continued to 1932, when the company offered a new 1½-litre Ten alo with the bigger Four and the Six. These cars had low-pressure tyres, box-secti frames, 'Floating Power' engine mountings under Chrysler licence and synchrome gearboxes. The Ten cost £198 and the bigger cars were available in long-wheelb form with seven-seater coachwork. Under the sponsorship of the Yacco Oil compa the 10hp Citroën 'Petite Rosalie' successfully undertook a herculean program of long-distance record work, in the course of which 187,500 miles were cover at 58mph and 128 International Class and 43 World Records were acquired. Th models formed part of the range until 1936, acquiring four forward speeds in 19 but they were overshadowed by yet another Citroën revolution, the first 7C *traction avant* which appeared in that year. This had front-wheel drive, an o wet-liner engine, unitary construction of chassis and body, and all-round torsi bar independent suspension. The 3-speed synchromesh gearbox had dashbo change and production engines had a capacity of 1.6 litres. This design formed backbone of Citroën's range until 1955, and was not withdrawn until July 1957, which time 708,339 4-cylinder fwd cars had been built and the car's appeal w largely founded on its now 'traditional' styling.

A 3.8-litre fwd V-8 was shown at the 1934 Paris Salon, but early the followi year André Citroën found himself in serious financial difficulties and was forc to sell out to the Michelin interests. Meanwhile an alternative 1.9-litre engine h been applied to the *traction avant* and by mid-1935 three additional types we available: the 11 légère (Sports 12 or Light 15) which shared a hull with the 7C and the 11 *normale* (Big 15), made in two wheelbase lengths, 10ft 1½in and 1 9in, the latter for seven-seaters. In 1936 Francois Lecot drove a 7CV 400,0 kilometres in 12 months. The 1937 fwd Citroëns had rack-and-pinion steering, re wheel drive cars were still made with the 11CV engine and (for a short while) option of a diesel power unit. The 1939 range was rounded out with a 2.9-li 15CV 6-cylinder fwd car on regular lines, which sold in England for £328 and j before World War 2 downdraught carburettors were standardized. 1939 models Georges Irat, Rosengart, and smaller Chenard-Walckers used 11CV mechani components as a basis for their cars, to be followed in 1947 by D.B.

After the war the 7CV was dropped, but production of the other fwd mode was resumed, cars for the French market being supplied only in matt black. 1949, however, the fruits of ten years of experimentation were seen in anoth revolutionary Citroën, the Boulanger-designed 2CV. Like its bigger sisters, had fwd and unitary construction, but it also had interlinked coil suspension, 4-speed all-synchromesh and all-indirect gearbox with geared-up top and qui detachable bonnet, doors and front wings for easy maintenance. Power came fro a 375cc 9bhp ohv flat-twin and the corrugated grey finish attracted unkind co parisons with garden sheds. Supply, however, never caught up with demand: Citro production jumped from 48,177 in 1950 to 78,199 in 1951 as the 2CV got into stride. 1955 cars had 425cc, 12bhp, and centrifugal clutches, and in 1958 came *tous terrains* model with twin engines and 4-wheel drive. The Slough factory offer the Bijou variant in 1960 with a fibreglass coupé body, but at £695 it was hard competitive. By July, 1966, 2,574,642 2CVs had been sold.

The full-sized Citroëns of 1953 came with built-out boots and heaters standard equipment, and a year later the Six was available with self-levelli hydropneumatic suspension. This led to the DS19 introduced at the 1955 show on which the only old features were the fwd and the long-stroke 4-cylinder engin now up-rated to 65bhp. The self-levelling suspension was joined by power assistan for the brakes (disc front and drum rear), steering and gear-change. There we 4 forward speeds, the roof section was of reinforced plastic, and the single-spo steering wheel found on Humbers of half a century before was revived. It w expensive (£1,726 in England) and complicated, and a year later a simplified ID version retained the advanced springing but eliminated the power assistance. cost £140 less than the DS in France and Citroën sales rose to 206,138 cars. 19 had seen the first association between the company and Panhard, which was to le to a full integration within the next decade, while Cooper (iii) in England use Citroën gearboxes on their racing cars from 1956 onward. A Citroën won t 1959 Monte Carlo Rally.

A development of the 2CV was the Ami-6 flat-twin of 1961, a curious-looki little 4-door saloon which took some time to find acceptance. In 1965 shor stroke engines were at long last adopted for the more expensive 4-cylinder car though it was not until 1967 that the basic 1934–35 unit was dropped from the I The most expensive 1967 model was the 2.2-litre 108bhp DS21; it acquired swivelling 4-headlamp installation in 1968 and could be had with fuel injectie in 1971. The Dyane of 1968 filled a gap in the range: it was a more refine 2CV available either with the latter's uprated 435cc unit or with the 602cc Ar motor. An open jeep-type version, the Méhari, arrived a year later. But meanwh during 1968 Citroën had acquired Italian affiliations, first entering into an agre ment with Maserati and then negotiating (against General de Gaulle's wishes) wi

...t. As a result the Italian giant acquired a 15 per cent stake in the company ...d their new French ally undertook the distribution of Autobianchi products in ...ance. In 1969 there was an experimental batch of 500 M35 coupés using 49bhp ...ankel engines in Ami-type structures, but a year later came the result of the ...aserati alliance, in the shape of the SM sports coupé, powered by a 2.7-litre ...hc V-6 engine developing 170bhp. This, of course, drove the front wheels via ...5-speed all-synchromesh gearbox; other features were power steering and disc ...akes, and a 6-headlamp layout. With a price of 51,800 francs and a top speed ...137mph it was the fastest and most expensive Citroën ever, and it helped boost ...e marque's flagging reputation in rallies. Their only major performance (a near ...ss in the 1968 London–Sydney Marathon apart) had been a 1-2-3 victory in ...e 1969 Moroccan event, but the SM won again in Morocco in 1971.

For 1971 another gap was bridged with an answer to Peugeot and Renault: ...e 1,015cc GS. This had an air-cooled ohv light-alloy flat-4 engine, and all-disc ...akes, those at the front being inboard. A station wagon followed in 1972, when ...ly automatic gearboxes and fuel injection were available on the big 4-cylinder ...loons, and the twins continued in 2CV Dyane, Méhari and Ami forms. Even more ...werful DS Citroëns were offered in 1973, outputs of the new 2.3-litre engines being ...5bhp in carburettor form, or 130bhp with fuel injection: the latter was standard-...d on the SM. At the same time the GS was made available with automatic ...ansmission, and the option of a 1,200cc engine. The 2-cylinder Citroëns were ...sembled or manufactured in eight countries, and D-series models produced in ...uth Africa and Yugoslavia. In the latter country Citroëns are marketed under ...e Tomos name.   MCS

1972 CITROËN SM 2.7-litre coupé.
S.A. André Citroën

...TY & SUBURBAN (GB) *1901–1905*

...ty & Suburban Electric Carriage Co Ltd, London

This firm operated from the 'Niagara', a converted skating-rink in Westminster, ...t though they supplied a two-seater victoriette to Queen Alexandra in 1901, ...ost of the electric cars that bore their name were Columbias (i) of American ...anufacture with G.E.C. motors, rear-mounted batteries, spur gear drive and ...ritish bodywork. A pneumatic-tyred runabout for doctors, the Niagara, could be ...ought in 1903 for £250, and bigger vehicles included landaulettes and shooting-...akes. Early in 1903 a petrol-electric prototype was exhibited, but this was merely ...old-type Coventry-Daimler with a 5½hp 2-cylinder engine arranged to drive ...ectric motors in the rear wheels. A 12hp development was announced, but never ...parently made. The last City and Suburban landaulettes of 1904–05 were of a ...fferent type, with wheel steering and the load of batteries distributed evenly ...etween front and rear.   MCS

1902 CITY & SUBURBAN electric victoria.
G.N. Georgano Collection

...IVELLI DE BOSCH (F) *1907–1909*

...ivelli de Bosch et Cie, Paris

This company made three models, an 8/10hp 2-cylinder, a 16/25hp 4-cylinder ...nd a 40/50hp 6-cylinder. All used shaft drive.   GNG

...LAN (GB) *1971 to date*

...lan Motor Co Ltd, Washington, Co Durham

The Clan Crusader project was started in Norwich in 1969 by Lotus employee ...aul Haussauer. The body shape of the rear-engined fibreglass two-seater coupé ...as the concept of Lotus stylist John Frayling. In 1971, when series production ...tarted, the car soon earned an excellent reputation in its class for handling and ...erformance. Weight was only 1,344lb with all Sunbeam Imp mechanical parts, ...e model being designed for development with alternative engines at a later date. ...was available either complete or as a kit car, the latter priced at £1,118, and ...ales passed 100 in mid-1972. The Crusader has been rallied with some success, and ...was hoped that it could be homolgated for Group 4 racing.   DF

...LARENDON (GB) *1902–1903*

...larendon Motor Car & Bicycle Co Ltd, Earlsdon, Coventry, Warwickshire

The Clarendon was a typical two-seater voiturette using a 7hp single-cylinder ...ngine and shaft drive.   GNG

1972 CLAN Crusader 875cc coupé.
Clan Motor Car Co Ltd

...LARIN MUSTAD (N/F) *1916–1917; 1935*

1) Mustad & Son, Oslo, Norway *1916–1917; 1935*

2) Clarin Mustad, Duclair, Seine-Inférieure, France *1917*

The Clarin Mustad was one of the rare 6-wheeler private cars. The rear four ...wheels were driven. The car was built as a limousine, although an open tourer ...vas also planned. Originally a 4-cylinder engine was used, replaced in 1917 by ...a 7-litre 6-cylinder unit developing 85bhp and giving the heavy car a speed of ...ver 60mph. Both engines were built in Mustad's workshops; the Oslo firm of ...O. Sørensen produced the bodies. After initial development work in Norway, opera-...ions were transferred to Duclair, but plans to build more cars together with ambu-...ances, lorries and buses were never realized. Mustad made various other experi-...ental vehicles, including in 1935 a neat-looking single-seater coupé using some ...Fiat components. The prototype 6-wheeler, rebodied and re-engined in 1927, was ...used in the evacuation of Oslo in 1940. It survives today in the Norsk Teknisk ...Museum, Oslo.   MJWW

1899 CLARKSON & CAPEL steam barouche.
Autocar

1927 CLAVEAU 4CV two-seater. *Photo Omnia,
Lucien Loreille Collection*

1901 CLÉMENT-PANHARD 4½hp dog cart.
National Motor Museum

CLARK (i) (US) 1900–1909
Edward S. Clark Steam Automobiles, Dorchester, Mass.

After several years of experimental work at Boston, Edward Clark began manufacture of steam cars at Dorchester. These were of advanced design, using horizontally-opposed 4-cylinder engines of 20hp. These were mounted amidships, with the flash boiler under the bonnet. Final drive was by shaft. Earlier models were expensive ($5,000 in 1904), but by 1909 the price had been reduced to $2,500. However, this was still over $1,000 more than the price asked for a comparable Stanley Steamer, and very few Clarks were sold.
GN

CLARK (ii) (GB) 1901
Charles Clark & Sons, Retford, Notts.

This Clark was a voiturette with a 2¾hp De Dion engine, converted from a De Dion tricycle. Production was intended, but never started.
GN

CLARK (iii) (US) 1910–1912
Clark Motor Car Co, Shelbyville, Ind.

The design of the Clark car was typical for these years, with a 4-stroke water-cooled 4-cylinder engine of 30/40hp. Shaft drive was used, with selective transmission at the axle. This car became the Meteor (v).
GM

CLARK (iv) (US) 1910–1912
Clark & Co, Lansing, Mich.

This Clark was a 3-seater high-wheeler with solid rubber tyres and wheel steering. Its 2-cylinder opposed engine was air-cooled and developed 14hp. Full elleptical springs were used.
GM

CLARKE-CARTER see CUTTING

CLARK-HATFIELD (US) 1908–1909
Clark-Hatfield Auto Co, Oshkosh, Wisc.

This car was a typical high-wheeler with an air-cooled 2-cylinder horizontally opposed engine of 16hp. This 4-stroke power unit was mounted cross-wise behind the two-passenger seat. No mudguards were fitted.
GM

CLARKMOBILE (US) 1903–1906
(1) Clarkmobile Co, Lansing, Mich. 1903–1906
(2) Deere-Clark Motor Car Co, Moline, Ill. 1906

The 1903 Clarkmobile was a two-seater roadster, shaft-driven from a single-cylinder, 7hp engine, with steering by wheel. Its cost was $750. In 1906 the car became the Deere-Clark, in turn succeeded by the Deere.
GM

CLARKSON (GB) 1899–1902
(1) Clarkson & Capel Steam Car Syndicate Ltd, London S.E. 1899–1902
(2) Clarkson Ltd, Chelmsford, Essex 1902

Well-known as manufacturers of steam commercial vehicles, Clarksons produced several highly individual private cars, although very few were sold. At the Automobile Club Show at Richmond in 1899 they exhibited a massive six-seater steam barouche whose body was suspended by C-springs on an underframe which carried all the machinery. The engine was a compound paraffin-fuelled unit, as employed in the firm's lorries, and was mounted at the extreme rear of the vehicle under the driver's seat. The condenser was at the front. At the same show was a small steam-driven two-seater victoria which had been converted from a horse-drawn vehicle.

To celebrate the move to Essex, Clarkson next produced a 12hp 2-cylinder car called the Chelmsford. This had a curious swan-neck curved condenser at the front and carried closed bodywork of the station bus variety with side-facing seats. Later Clarkson built large steam buses and lorries.
GN

CLASSIC (i) (US) 1916–1917
Classic Motor Car Corp, Chicago, Ill.

Both four-seater and five-seater touring models of the Classic were offered at $885. The common chassis had a wheelbase of 9ft 6in. The car was powered by a four-cylinder Lycoming engine of 3.2 litres. Both models had early slanted windscreens.
GMN

CLASSIC (ii) (F) 1925–1929
Cie Générale des Voitures à Paris, Paris 1er

The Classic was a conventional medium-sized car powered by a 2,116cc Sergant engine, although a 1½-litre sleeve-valve unit was also available. Tourer and saloon bodies were made, but most Classics were built as taxicabs.
GN

CLAUDE DELAGE (F) 1926
Claude Delage, Clichy, Seine

No connection with the cars of Louis Delage, the Claude Delage was a conventional car powered by a 1,843cc sv Sergant engine. It had a 4-speed gearbox and touring bodies.
GNC

CLAVEAU (F) *1926–1934; 1946–1950*
Automobiles Claveau, Paris

In practice if not in intention, Emile Claveau was an experimenter rather than a manufacturer, for although his strange cars were offered to the public from time to time, few were sold. His first design of 1926 was an open two-seater powered by an 1,100cc flat-four engine mounted just ahead of the rear axle, and in 1927 the capacity was enlarged to 1½ litres and a five-seater saloon added. All these cars had monocoque construction and all-independent suspension. Claveau's 1928 offering was the 4CV, an open three-seater powered by a 498cc vertical-twin engine, but this was replaced in 1930 by a front-engined fwd car with 750cc 2-stroke engine. Other fwd designs followed up to 1934, powered by proprietary engines as well as Claveau's own, but there was then a gap in Claveau's activities until the appearance in 1946 of the Descartes. This was a monocoque five-seater saloon powered by an 2.3-litre twin ohc V-8 engine driving the front wheels via a 5-speed all-synchromesh gearbox.   TRN

C.L.C. (F) *1911–1913*
Cockborne, Lehucher et da Costa, Paris

This company introduced a small car with a 6hp single-cylinder 2-stroke engine in 1911, and in 1912 a 10hp 4-cylinder car, also a 2-stroke.   GNG

CLECO (GB) *1936–1940*
Cleco Electric Industries, Ltd, Leicester

The Cleco firm specialized in light battery-electric vans, but made a small number of electric saloon cars on a 6ft 6in wheelbase.   GNG

CLEM (F) *1912–1914*
(1) Cie Lyonnaise d'Etudes Mécaniques, Lyons *1912–1914*
(2) Sté des Voiturettes Clem, G. Gineste-Lacaze et Cie, Lyons *1914*

The Clem light car was designed by Gaston Bouvier, chief tester for La Buire. It was an assembled machine, using a 7hp 1,130cc 4-cylinder Fondu engine, and a Dupressoir chassis, while the bodies were made by a Lyons firm. Open and closed two-seater coachwork was usually fitted. In 1914 a larger model with an 8/10hp 1,320cc engine was added to the range.   GNG

CLÉMENT (i); CLÉMENT-BAYARD (F) *1899–1922*
(1) Clément et Cie, Levallois-Perret, Seine *1899–1903*
(2) SA des Ets Clément-Bayard, Levallois-Perret, Seine; Mézières *1903–1922*

Adolphe Clément was one of the more notable company promoters of the early motoring world and had already made a fortune in the allied fields of bicycles and pneumatic tyres when he began car manufacture. The first car firm in which he had an interest was Gladiator; early cars were known as Clément-Gladiators as well as plain Cléments. After 1903, when the Bayard name was added to the cars built by Adolphe Clément, all plain Cléments were in fact built in the Gladiator factory. In 1899 tricycles and quads were being made and by 1900 two distinct cars bore the Clément name. One was a light rear-engined voiturette powered by a 2¼hp De Dion engine geared to the rear axle. It was presumably one of these cars that Tart drove into second place in the 1900 Paris-Rouen-Paris race, this being Clément's first competition entry. The other design was the Clément-Panhard which had been designed by Commandant Krebs of Panhard-Levassor (of which company Adolphe Clément was a director) but never produced by them. It had a rear-mounted 3½hp single-cylinder inclined engine, automatic inlet valve and hot tube ignition. The first models had no reverse gear, but the most archaic feature was the centrally-pivoted steering, in which the whole front axle turned with the steering. Open two- and three-seater bodies were usually fitted. The design was made under licence in Scotland as the Stirling-Panhard or Clément-Stirling by Stirlings of Edinburgh, who fitted some pill-box-like closed coupé bodies. Also in 1900 Clément was listed as a maker of electric vehicles, but these were apparently l'Electromotion cars which were at that time imported Columbias.

By the end of 1901 Clément were making front-engined light cars designed by Marius Barbarou; these had 7hp single-cylinder engines, or 12hp twins, and shaft drive. Two 12hp cars were driven in that year's Paris-Berlin race, while for the 1902 Paris-Vienna race, Clément entered no less than seven 20hp 4-cylinder cars, one of which was driven by D.M. Weigel who later imported Cléments into England and was one of the founders of the Clément-Talbot company. The 1903 Clément range consisted of 9, 12 and 16hp cars, the latter two having 4-cylinder engines with mechanical overhead inlet valves. At this time Cléments and Gladiators were being made in the same factory; the main difference was that Cléments had shaft drive while the Gladiators still used chains. In October 1903 Adolphe Clément parted from the Clément-Gladiator concern and gave up the right to call his cars Cléments; instead he chose the name Clément-Bayard, after the 16th-century hero the Chevalier Bayard who had saved the town of Mezières, where Clément had a factory, from the Duc de Nassau in 1521. Known as 'le Chevalier sans peur et sans reproche', he was greatly admired by Clément, who later officially changed his surname to Clément-Bayard.

The new make was handled in England by the British Automobile Commercial

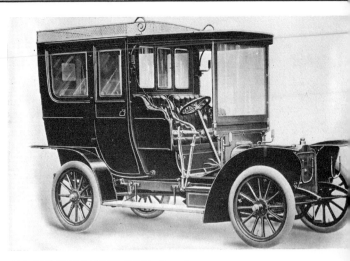
1906 CLÉMENT-BAYARD 20/24hp limousine.
Lucien Loreille Collection

1913 CLÉMENT-BAYARD 8hp two-seater.
G.N. Georgano

1921 CLÉMENT-BAYARD LM-4 8hp two-seater. *Autocar*

1913 CLEMENT(ii) 16/20hp all-weather tourer.
Autocar

1900 CLEVELAND(i) electric stanhope. *Hull Transport Museum*

1924 CLEVELAND(iv) 6-cylinder tourer.
Keith Marvin Collection

Syndicate, financed by the Earl of Shrewsbury and Talbot, and headed by D.M. Weigel. A factory was built at Ladbroke Grove in West London and the cars known as Clement-Talbots, being practically identical to the French product. At the same time Gladiator-built Cléments were being imported by E.H. Lancaster, who continued to do so until 1908 when Clements, i.e. Clement (ii)s, began to be built in Coventry.

1904 Clément-Bayards were made in five models, all with shaft drive; a 6hp single, a 7hp twin and 4-cylinder cars of 14, 20 and 27hp. For the 1904 Gordon Bennett Eliminating Race, Clément entered two vast cars of 80 and 100hp. The latter had an engine of 16,286cc capacity and chain drive. They were not chosen to represent France and despite regular efforts up to 1911, Clément was never really successful in racing. His best performances were 3rd in the 1906 Grand Prix (his son Albert driving), and 4th in the 1908 Grand Prix. Driven by Rigal, this car had a 13,693cc monobloc 4-cylinder engine with inclined overhead valves operated by a single overhead camshaft.

By 1907, production Clément-Bayards ranged from an 8/10hp twin to a 50/60hp four, the larger models having chain drive. A pointer to the future was a new 10/12hp with a monobloc 4-cylinder engine and dashboard radiator, a feature which characterized the smaller Clément-Bayards up to 1914. 1911 was the last year of the big 35/45 and 50/60hp chain-drive cars and thereafter all models had shaft drive and dashboard radiators. Three models of 6-cylinder car were available in 1911, a 15, 20 and 30hp, while a new 7hp twin was introduced in 1912. They were now sufficiently different from the English Talbot to make it worth while importing them and they were re-introduced to the British market in 1911, being sold by Clement-Talbots. At the outbreak of World War 1, 12 models were being made, from the 7hp twin to the 30hp six, one car using a 20hp 4-cylinder Knight engine.

A new 8hp 4-cylinder light car with a front-mounted radiator was listed for 1915 and 1916, but few can have been made. It was re-introduced after the war and, together with a 17.9hp (12CV) of 2.6 litres, was made until 1922. In this year the Levallois-Perret factory was taken over by Citroën (the Mezières factory, which was smaller, had been given up some time before). The post-war cars were no longer sold in England by Clement-Talbot, but by Bayard Cars of Great Portland Street. However, as a postscript, it was announced in December 1923 that Bayard Cars Ltd had transferred their activities to Clement-Talbot Ltd; by this time only spares were being sold.

Adolphe Clément-Bayard retired from his company in 1914.　　GNG

CLEMENT (ii) (GB) 1908–1914
Clement Motor Co Ltd, Coventry, Warwickshire

After Clement-Talbot Ltd had been formed to manufacture cars of Clement Bayard design in England (*see* Clément (i)), Gladiator-built Clément cars continued to be sold in England by E.H. Lancaster. In 1907, however, the name of the selling company was changed to the Clement All British Motor Company, and sale of these all-British Clements began in 1908. They were built in the Swift factory at Coventry, and were almost identical to Swifts, except for slightly longer wheelbases, higher prices, and Talbot-like radiators. Models were a 10/12hp twin, 14/18 and 18/28hp fours. In addition there were two larger models, a 25/35 and a 35/45hp, whose specification was identical to those of the equivalent Gladiator models, and these were presumably imported French cars. For 1909 and 1910 the range was similar, all Olympia Show cars in 1910 having coachwork by Salmons. All 'British Clements' for 1911 were Swift-built, the large 35/40hp model being described as a French Clement, i.e. Gladiator. By 1913 the twin had been dropped, and two 4-cylinder cars made up the Clement range; a 12/14 and a 14/18hp, being almost identical to the 12 and 15hp Swifts respectively. For 1914 a new 16/20hp car was introduced which did not correspond exactly with any Swift model, but was generally similar in design.　　GNG

CLÉMENT-ROCHELLE (F) 1927–1930
Clément et Rochelle, Clamart, Seine

The Clément-Rochelle was a light car using a 1,100cc Ruby engine. It had four-wheel independent suspension, and was available as a saloon, fixed or drop-head coupé, and doorless two-seater sports car.　　GNG

CLEMENT-TALBOT *see* TALBOT

CLESSE (F) 1907–1908
Clesse et Cie, Levallois-Perret, Seine

The first Clesse was a friction-driven voiturette powered by a 6.2hp single-cylinder engine, but in 1908 the company made a 2.8-litre 4-cylinder car.　　GNG

CLEVELAND (i) (US) 1899–1901
Cleveland Machine Screw Co, Cleveland, Ohio

The first make to bear the name Cleveland was a light electric two-seater with solid rubber tyres. In its last year of production it was known as the Sperry.　　GNG

CLEVELAND (ii) (F) 1904–1909
Cleveland Motor Car Co, Cleveland, Ohio

The second make to bear the name Cleveland was a conventional touring car with a 4-cylinder 18hp engine, priced at $2,800. Later, a larger car costing $4,000 was introduced, this model being responsible for the company's closure as it was too expensive in comparison with other cars of its kind. The only unusual feature of the Cleveland was that the rear axle half shafts could be slid out simply by removing the hub caps.   GNG

CLEVELAND (iii) (US) 1914
Cleveland Cyclecar Co, Cleveland, Ohio

The Cleveland was advertised as 'The Aristocrat of Cyclecars'. It seated two passengers, side-by-side, and it had a water-cooled 4-cylinder *en bloc* engine. GMN

CLEVELAND (iv) (US) 1919–1926
Cleveland Automobile Co, Cleveland, Ohio

This car was really a smaller version of the Chandler, produced in a separate factory. It was powered with the firm's own 6-cylinder ohv engine.   KM

CLIFT see SINCLAIR

CLIMAX (GB) 1905–1907
Climax Motor Co, Coventry, Warwickshire

The Climax was an assembled car using either Aster or White & Poppe engines, 3-speed gearboxes and shaft drive. 1905 models used a 10/12 Aster twin, a 15hp White & Poppe 3-cylinder, or 16 and 20hp Aster fours. For 1906 only fours were made, a 14hp W & P and a 22hp Aster. A 20hp W & P 6-cylinder model was made in 1907. Early Climaxes had Rolls-Royce type radiators, but from 1906 they were flat-topped.   GNG

1958 CLUA 497cc sports coupé. *G.N. Georgano*

CLIMBER (US) 1919–1923
Climber Motor Corp, Little Rock, Ark.

This car was available in both 4- and 6-cylinder models, all open, with Herschell-Spillman engines. The Climber Corporation built several hundred cars in its few years of production. Ten distribution agencies, most of them in Arkansas, handled the make.   KM

CLINTON (CDN) 1912
Clinton Motor Car Co Ltd, Clinton, Ont.

Mainly builders of trucks, the Clinton company exhibited a 4-cylinder touring car and a combination car convertible to a light truck at the 1912 Toronto Auto Show.   GNG

CLIPPER (US) 1955–1956
Studebaker-Packard Corp, Detroit, Mich.

The former Packard Clipper was marketed as a separate make for the 1956 season only, in an attempt to establish the 'senior' Packards as a luxury make more expensive and exclusive than the medium-priced Clippers. They came in three models, DeLuxe, Super DeLuxe, and Custom, all using 5.8-litre V-8 engines developing 240bhp (275bhp in the Custom model). Wheelbase was 10ft 2in, and prices ranged from $2,731 to $3,069. For the 1957 season the Clipper was re-absorbed into the Packard range, and in fact used a Studebaker body shell.   GNG

1923 CLUB(ii) 5/18PS two-seater. *Neubauer Collection*

CLOUGHLEY (US) 1902–1903
Cloughley Motor Vehicle Co, Parsons, Kans.

The Cloughley company had made an experimental steamer at Cherryvale, Kansas as early as 1896, but their production cars did not appear until 1902. They used an 8hp 2-cylinder engine, front-mounted and driving the rear axle by chain. Steam was provided at 175psi from a 19in water tube boiler. The only body style was a four-seater surrey. This car was also available with a 2-cylinder petrol engine.   GNG

CLOUMOBIL (D) 1906–1908
Automobilbauerei 'Clou' Alfred Karfunkel, Berlin-Charlottenburg

This firm produced a 4-cylinder voiturette as well as an electric 3-wheeler with one driven front wheel.   HON

CLOYD (US) 1911
Cloyd Auto Co, Nashville, Tenn.

The Cloyd used a 4-cylinder 40hp water-cooled engine. Wheelbase was 10ft 3in for the five-seater touring cars and 9ft 10in for the runabout and roadster.   GMN

CLUA (E) 1958–1959
Construcciones Metálicas Clua, Barcelona

A short-lived product of a motor-cycle manufacturer, the Clua was a small car powered by a 497cc 2-cylinder 4-stroke engine, with a fibreglass two-seater body. About 100 were made.   JRV

CLUB see BROUHOT

1923 CLULEY 10.4hp tourer. *Mrs Mary Field*

1908 CLYDE 12/14hp tourer. *G.N. Georgano*

1924 CLYDE 8hp two-seater.
G.N. Georgano Collection

1927 CLYNO 10.8hp tourer.
David Burgess Wise

CLUB (i) **(CLUB CAR)** (US) *1910–1911*

Club Car Co, New York, N.Y.

The Club Car Co, was a unique co-operative organization formed to furnis cars for its members. The cars were actually built by Merchant & Evans Co. Philadelphia, with 4-cylinder 40/50hp engines from the American & British M Co. of Bridgeport, Conn. Body styles included a limousine, a seven-seater tourin car, a torpedo and a club runabout, all made by Biddle & Smart of Amesbury, Mas Prices to members ranged from $2,800 to $3,750.   GM

CLUB (ii) (D) *1922–1924*

Club Automobilfabrik GmbH, Berlin-Charlottenburg

A small assembled car with a 4-cylinder 1.3-litre Atos engine.   HO

CLULEY (GB) *1922–1928*

Clarke, Cluley & Co, Coventry, Warwickshire

The Cluley in its best-known form was a typical light car of the early 1920 using proprietary 4-cylinder, side-valve engines of 10 and 11.9hp. A 6-cylinde car followed in 1924 and a 14/50hp 4-cylinder car with overhead valves wa announced for 1928, but few, if any, of either were made. Earlier, the firm ha made bicycles, and a tri-car, known as the Globe Cymocar, in 1904.   TR

CLYDE (GB) *1901–1930*

(1) Clyde Cycle & Motor Car Co Ltd, Leicester *1901–1904*
(2) G.H. Wait, Leicester *1905–1907*
(3) G.H. Wait & Co Ltd, Leicester *1908–1930*

G.H. Wait was a bicycle maker who also manufactured cars and motor cycle over a considerable period, but in small quantities. Not more than 260 cars an commercial vehicles left the factory in 30 years, compared with 470 motor cycle and over 4,000 bicycles. The first car had a front-mounted 3½hp Simms engine, an belt drive to a countershaft which was geared to the rear axle. For 1902 a 5h Aster or 6hp De Dion engine was used, and by 1905 8hp White & Poppe or 12h Aster twins were being used. For 1906 3-cylinder 12/14hp W & P and 4-cylinde 24/30hp Aster engines were used and most Clydes made up to 1914 had engines o these two makes. Very few Clyde cars were made after the war, although an 8h twin and an 11.9hp four were listed up to 1930 and in some lists to 1932.   GN

CLYMER (US) *1908*

Durable Motor Car Co, St Louis, Mo.

The only product was a two-seater motor buggy with a 12hp engine and a one year guarantee. This period was longer than the Clymer was produced.   GMM

CLYNO (GB) *1922–1930*

(1) Clyno Engineering Co (1922) Ltd, Wolverhampton, Staffs. *1922–1929*
(2) R. H. Collier and Co Ltd, Birmingham *1929–1930*

The Clyno car was a nine years' wonder on the British market. Deriving from a moribund motor cycle business, the marque rose to pre-eminence in the marke in 1926, and as swiftly declined. The name originated with the inclined motor cycle belt pulleys which had been the Smith cousins' first commercial venture The early cars used a 1,368cc sv 4-cylinder Coventry-Climax engine, with two ball-race main bearings. A 3-speed gearbox was fitted on the end of the torque tube, and pivoted to a chassis cross-member. Aided by light weight, pleasant steer ing, sprightly performance and utter reliability, sales quickly outstripped other assembled marques. Improvements included the adoption of plain main bearings in 1925, and half-elliptic front suspension, with 4-wheel brakes of efficient design as standard instead of as an optional extra, in 1926. Various styles were available, including a few sports versions and de luxe models known as Royals. Of the many component suppliers, it was perhaps only to the makers of the economical Cox Atmos carburettors that the Clyno concern remained faithful for all models.

Successfully rivalling the Morris Cowley, Clyno also made several efforts to establish a larger model to challenge the Oxford sales. In 1927 the old 10.8hp was lengthened, and the 3-bearing 12/28 version boosted. Generally, bodies were heavier, and the transmission was not immediately upgraded to match the added weight and power. Moreover, under the stress of expansion, production tolerances and inspection standards became a little lax. After a while the early reputation for reliability started to fade – just as a larger factory was coming into use.

In 1928 the main distributors and exporting agents, the Rootes organization, decided to concentrate on Hillmans and the like, and the early successes of the heavier Colonial models brought no lasting recompense. For 1928 the attractive radiator was changed, and the Nine was introduced. Bodies were skimped, and the 8.3hp engine breathed less freely than the public might have wished. A very spartan version, the Century, was intended to sell at not much over £100, but merely succeeded in giving a disastrous image to a basically sound little car that stopped and handled in true Clyno fashion. Bodies on the larger cars, by now also mostly fabric, tended to become too expensive – with the 12/35 Olympic saloon the firm sought to reach well above their customary market. When, in 1929, the 10.8hp was finally pensioned off, the last links with the policies of 1926, when sales of this model alone passed 11,000, appeared to have been severed.

In 1929 the firm was still experimenting with larger cars, and a straight 8-
[cyl]inder prototype was made. All these factors, combining with the trade recession,
[ca]used the fall of the always under-capitalized company. Inevitably a few cars
[192]2/35) were assembled by the successors. A.J.S. also took over some copyrights,
[an]d although their Nine bore no similarity with actual Clyno models, it was said
[to] have been derived from these patents – certainly A.G. Booth had been concerned
[wi]th both design teams. A Birmingham engineering firm perpetuated the name of
[Cl]yno on various products for several years.   DF

1928 CLYNO Nine de Luxe saloon.
G.N. Georgano

C.M. (F) *1924–1930*
[C]harles Mochet, Saint-Ouen, Seine

Charles Mochet's principal line of business, and one which he pursued through-
[ou]t the 1930s, was the Velocar. This was a pedal-propelled 4-wheeler, of which a
[po]wered version with 142cc engine was offered in 1929. The C.M. was, however, a
[tr]ue cyclecar, with rear-mounted 350cc 2-stroke single-cylinder engine, 3-speed-
[an]d reverse gearbox and chain drive. A kick-starter was fitted and the boat-shaped
[bo]dywork was made of plywood. It offered a 30mph performance for 4,995fr.
[C]yclecar manufacture was not resumed until 1951, when the machines were known
[as] Mochets.   MCS

C.M.N. (I) *1919–1923*
[C]ostruzioni Meccaniche Nazionali SA, Milan-Pontedera.

C.M.N. was one of many concerns which switched from aviation and engineering
[w]ork to car manufacture after World War 1. The marque's main claim to fame
[no]wadays seems to be that it served as a stepping stone in the career of Enzo
[Fe]rrari, who joined the factory at Pontedera in 1919 as a tester and driver, and
[re]mained until 1920, when he joined Alfa Romeo. He raced a C.M.N. in local hill-
[cl]imbs and in the 1919 Targa Florio, in which he retired, while Sivocci in another
[C.]M.N. finished 7th. The production C.M.N. was a conventional, rather dated,
[hi]gh-built design with 2.3-litre 4-cylinder and 2.9-litre 6-cylinder sv engines, though
[a 2]-litre ohv Tipo 7 Sport appeared in 1922.   CP

C.M.V. (E) *1944–1946*
[C]onstrucciones Moviles de Valencia, Valencia

The C.M.V. was a small electric car made at a time when the Spanish government
[w]as trying to encourage electric vehicles in order to save petrol. They showed
[a] car at the Government-sponsored Electric Motor Show in Madrid in 1946.
                                                                                  JRV

COADOU-FLEURY (F) *1921–c.1935*
[M]arcel Coadou, Trébeurden, C.-du-N.

The original Coadou-Fleury was a cyclecar of monocoque construction powered
[b]y a 850cc 4-cylinder Ruby engine, with 2-speed epicyclic gearbox and shaft drive.
[T]he aluminium monocoque frame made the car much more expensive than the
[co]nventional cyclecar, and Coadou could not find a backer to put his car into
[pr]oduction. He built several successive versions while carrying on his profession
[a]s a military flying instructor. The 1927 model had a B2 Citroën engine converted
[to] ohv, and later cars had coupé bodies. The final model, known as the Aérolithe,
[h]ad an ingenious sliding cockpit for ease of entry, and an aerodynamic tail. This
[c]ar survives today.   GNG

1900 COCHOT 2½-hp tandem voiturette.
Neubauer Collection

COATES-GOSHEN (US) *1908–1910*
[C]oates-Goshen Automobile Co, Goshen, N.Y.

This car had 4-cylinder Rutenber engines of 25 or 32hp and appears to have
[be]en a pioneer of the modern dropped frame. A fire in the plant contributed to
[th]e early demise of this make after only 32 cars had been made. Later Coates
[C]ommercial Car Co (1912–1914) attempted a 3-wheeled parcel van.   GMN

COATS (US) *1922–1923*
[C]oats Steam Car Co, Columbus, Ohio

Despite wide publicity, few Coats Steamers were marketed. The car was powered
[b]y a 3-cylinder engine of Coats design, and, unusually for a steam car, it had
[a] two-speed and reverse gear with floor change. A tourer was the only model
[a]vailable. A few cars were built in 1923 by the Y.F. Stewart Motor Mfg Co,
[a]nd sold under the name Stewart-Coats.   KM

COCHOT (F) *1899–1901*
[G]. Cochot, Paris

Cochot made voiturettes in two models, a tandem two-seater steered from the
[re]ar seat, and a side-by-side two-seater. Both were powered by a 2½hp engine of
[C]ochot's own construction geared to the rear axle. Cochot later made a 4-cylinder
[c]ar called the Lutèce.   GNG

COEY (US) *1913–1917*
[C]oey Motor Co, Chicago, Ill.

The Coey was available in two versions, the Bear, which was a cyclecar, or
[a] full-sized model, the Flyer. The Flyer had a 6-cylinder engine of 6.3 litres capa-

1913 COEY Flyer Model A tourer. *Harrah's
Automobile Collection*

1913 COGNET DE SEYNES 1,124cc tourer.
Lucien Loreille Collection

1965 COLANI 1.2-litre sports car. *Neubauer
Collection*

1921 COLE Aero Eight 39.2hp tourer. *Automotive
History Collection, Detroit Public Library*

city, but the 1917 model was a smaller car with 22hp engine. Subsequent manufacture was limited to commercial vehicles and the company was absorbed by t
Wonder Motor Truck Co in 1916.   GN

COGGSWELL (US) *1911*
Coggswell Motor Co, Grand Rapids, Mich.

This firm built at least some pilot models as five-seater touring cars which ha
a wheelbase of 9ft 4in. The 4-cylinder, 3.7-litre engine had a single overhead ca
shaft with valves at 45° to the head. It was provided with dual ignition.   GN

COGNET DE SEYNES (F) *1912–1926*
Automobiles Cognet de Seynes, Lyons

The staple Cognet de Seynes was a small 4-cylinder 6/10hp car. The 1,124
sv monobloc engine was of their own design, and was mounted in unit with t
3-speed central-change gearbox, propellor shaft, and rear axle. Post-1918 versio
had a longer wheelbase and full electrics. During the early 1920s production r
at 25–30 chassis a year, mostly sold locally. A 6-cylinder model planned in 19
never progressed beyond the drawing board.   M

COHENDET (F) *1898–1914*
A. Cohendet et Cie, Paris

Like Malicet et Blin, Cohendet were principally makers of components f
the industry – Decauville was among their clients – and trucks bulked larger
their Quai de Jemmapes factory than private cars. As early as 1898 they we
listed as manufacturers, both a 3hp quad and a 2-cylinder air-cooled light c
being reported. Two years later they were announcing their intention of bringin
out steam and electric as well as petrol-driven vehicles, and a proprietary 700
single-cylinder light car engine was on the market in 1901. Contempora
advertisements, however, showed medium-sized tonneaux on conventional line
and both 2- and 4-cylinder Cohendets were exhibited at the 1903 Salon. All the
1904 models had 3-speed gearboxes and shaft drive. A 2½-litre 4-cylinder model wi
mechanically operated inlet valves was the biggest Cohendet. A 12hp was st
being listed in 1905, but thereafter the company concentrated on sub-contract wo
until 1910/11 when the Americaine voiturette appeared under the sponsorship
C.R. Goodwin, an American resident in Paris. This featured a 703cc single-cylind
engine and friction drive and sold for the equivalent of £104. This was offere
until 1914, being joined in the last year of peace by a 1½-litre 4-cylinder machin
also with friction drive.   MC

COLANI (D) *1964–1968*
Lutz Colani, Berlin 15

The only German do-it-yourself kit was offered under this name. It was a tw
seater streamlined sports body, available in roadster or coupé form, designed
use the Volkswagen chassis and mechanical parts.   HO

COLBURN (US) *1906–1911*
Colburn Automobile Co, Denver, Colo.

Early models were roadsters and racers, the 1909 model advertised as havir
a top speed of over 70mph. Their 4-cylinder engines were rated at 40hp and th
cars weighed 2,600lb. Colburn also built large touring cars with radiators behin
the engine, and a sloping bonnet similar to early Renaults.   GM

COLBY (US) *1911–1914*
Colby Motor Car Co, Mason City, Iowa

With a 40hp L-head engine, the Colby five-seater 'foredoor' model sold fo
$1,750. Its selective transmission gave three forward speeds.   GM

COLDA (F) *1921–1922*
Automobiles Colda, Paris 17e

The Colda was a short-lived medium-sized car using a 1.8-litre 4-cylinde
Sergant engine.   GN

COLDWELL (GB) *1967 to date*
Coldwell Engineering and Racing Ltd, Sheffield, Yorks.

The rear-engined Mini-powered Coldwell GT, of which some half-dozen wer
made, was seen both on the road and in competition and provided a basis fo
the series of 2-litre sports-racing cars quietly developed from 1970 onwards b
designer Bill Needham. The C14 Cosworth FVC-powered long-distance model c
1972 was raced with some success in many countries.   D

COLE (US) *1909–1925*
(1) Cole Carriage Co, Indianapolis, Ind.
(2) Cole Motor Car Co, Indianapolis, Ind.

The first Coles were typical high-wheelers powered by oversquare 14hp ai
cooled flat-twin engines, but in 1910 the company turned to a straightforward in-lin
four of 30hp, with pair-cast cylinders, dual ignition, a cone clutch, a 3-speed gea
box, and a shaft drive, retailing at $1,500. Electric lights and a starter were sta

ardized in 1913, when a big 7.3-litre six was added to the range. Cole-built engines were still used in 1914, coil ignition and left-hand steering now featured, and the four ran to 4.8 litres. Both this and the 6-60 survived into 1916, although for the last two years Northway were responsible for the 6-cylinder engines. They also provided engines for the 1915 new model, a 5.4-litre V-8 destined to be the staple type from 1917 onwards. This unit had detachable heads and semi-pressure lubrication, and wheelbase was 10ft 7in. Price rose from $1,595 in 1916 to $2,395 in 1918, in spite of which Cole managed to sell 5,000 cars in 1919, their best performance. Coles of the early 1920s were noted for their unusual closed bodies (octagonal rear quarter windows were a feature), and nomenclature was also peculiar ('tourosine', 'brouette'). The company claimed to be pioneers of balloon tyres, which they adopted in 1924, but though the cars also wore Westinghouse air springs, 4-wheel brakes were never factory equipment. To the end the Cole Aero Eight retained a cone clutch.   MCS

COLEMAN (US) *1933*
Coleman Motors, Littleton, Colo.
  The Coleman was an unsuccessful attempt to interest the public in a low-priced car with straight body sides and without wing mudguards, rather in the manner of 1960s design. The engine was mounted under the sharply-arched front axle. The closed model, the only one offered by the company, was listed to sell at less than $1,000.   KM

COLE-WIEDEMAN (GB) *1905–1906*
William Cole & Co Ltd, Hammersmith, London W.
  This was a short-lived tourer powered by a 14hp White & Poppe 4-cylinder engine, and using shaft drive. A bigger four and a 20/24hp six were also listed.   GNG

COLIBRI (D) *1908–1911*
Norddeutsche Automobilwerke GmbH, Hameln/Weser
  The Norddeutsche Automobilwerke produced the Colibri and Sperber cars during their existence and they were known under these names, not the name of the factory, although sometimes the abbreviation N.A.W. was used. The first Colibri of 1908 had a 2-cylinder 860cc engine developing 8bhp. After 1910 a 4-cylinder 1,320cc 10bhp engine was used.   HON

COLIN (F) *1934*
Automobiles Colin, Gennevilliers, Seine
  The Colin minicar used a 500cc 2-cylinder engine and a 4-speed gearbox. Open and saloon models were offered.   GNG

COLLINET (US) *1921*
Collinet Motor Co, Garden City, Long Island, N.Y.
  This car was displayed in chassis form at the 16th Auto Salon in New York. Despite a chassis price of $5,500, it had a 4-cylinder Wisconsin engine. It is not known whether this make ever got into production.   GMN

COLLINS (US) *1920*
Collins Motors Inc, Huntington, Long Island, N.Y.
  The Collins Country Club Six used a 29hp 6-cylinder engine, and was made in two wheelbases. Very few were sold under the name Collins, but it has been suggested that the design was sponsored or taken over by Peerless, who made it as the Peerless Six.   GNG

COLLIOT (F) *1900–1901*
Deliry et Fils, Soissons, Aisne
  This was a light car powered by a 4hp V-twin engine, and using a 4-speed gearbox and chain final drive. It had a neat appearance, rather like the contemporary Renault.   GNG

COLOMBE (F) *1920–1925*
Automobiles Colombe, Colombes, Seine
  The first Colombe was an assembled car using the Model T Ford engine and transmission, but in 1923 the company introduced a 3-wheeler with a tiny single-cylinder 345cc engine driving the front wheel by chain. These competed in the Bol d'Or races and a single-seater version took three World Records for the 350cc class at Arpajon in 1924.   GNG

COLOMBO (I) *1922–1924*
Officine Mecchaniche Colombo, Milan
  The first Colombos were commercial 3-wheelers, but this aero-engine factory also made a few light cars with 1,300cc ohc 4-cylinder engines.   MCS

COLONIAL (i) (US) *1912*
Colonial Electric Car Co, Detroit, Mich.
  This electric car was built as a five-seater closed model and as a two-seater roadster. The steering was by tiller. It was claimed that the top speed was

1908 COLIBRI 860cc two-seater. *Neubauer Collection*

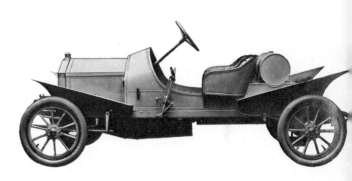

1910 COLIBRI 12/14hp roadster. *Autocar*

1922 COLONIAL(v) 29hp roadster. *Keith Marvin Collection*

1901 COLUMBIA(i) electric dog cart. *The Veteran Car Club of Great Britain*

25mph and that it could travel 75 miles on a single charging. The wheelbase was 7ft 9in. The closed models included a cut-glass flower vase. GMN

COLONIAL (ii) (US) *1917–1921*
Colonial Automobile Co, Indianapolis, Ind.

Few of these assembled cars were produced in the four years during which they were presumably manufactured. The cars, mostly touring models, were powered by a 6-cylinder overhead-valve engine. The wheelbase was 9ft 8in and prices started at $995. KM

COLONIAL (iii) (US) *1920*
Mechanical Development Corp, San Francisco, Calif.

Although only one of the West Coast Colonial cars was built, it is important as being presumably the first car built, at least in the United States, with four-wheel hydraulic brakes, appearing even before the similarly equipped Duesenberg and Kenworthy. The car had a straight-8 engine with a bore and stroke of 63mm × 114mm which developed 60bhp. Besides a unique hard-top touring body, readily convertible into a closed car, it featured disc wheels with two side-mounted spares. The prototype probably cost $30,000 to construct, but production models were to have sold for $1,800. KM

COLONIAL (iv) *see* SHAW (i)

COLONIAL (v) (US) *1921–1922*
Colonial Motors Co, Boston, Mass.

The Colonial was a disc-wheeled, attractive sporting-type of car which the prospectuses claimed would be produced 'in excess of 100' units in its first year of production. Probably no more than ten units – if that – ever got on the road. With a high, rounded radiator and a 130-inch wheelbase, the Colonial was powered with a 6-cylinder Beaver engine with a 88mm × 133mm bore and stroke. Five body styles were offered but probably only the open models were ever made. KM

COLT (i) (US) *1907*
Colt Runabout Co, Yonkers, N.Y.

This car was built only as a two-seater runabout, using a 40hp 6-cylinder engine, and sold for $1,500. With a weight of 1800lb their 'Mile-a-Minute' slogan was probably realistic. GMN

COLT (ii) (US) *1958*

Advertised as 'Built in America by Americans' the Colt was a two-seater fibre-glass minicar with a single-cylinder air-cooled engine. BE

COLTMAN (GB) *1907–1913*
H. Coltman & Sons, Loughborough, Leics.

The Coltman was a conventional car with a 20hp 4-cylinder engine, shaft drive and furnished mainly with side-entrance touring bodies. GNG

COLUMBIA (i) (US) *1897–1913*
(1) Pope Manufacturing Co, Hartford, Conn. *1897–1899*
(2) Columbia Automobile Co, Hartford, Conn. *1899*
(3) Columbia & Electric Vehicle Co, Hartford, Conn. *1900*
(4) Electric Vehicle Co, Hartford, Conn. *1901–1909*
(5) Columbia Motor Car Co, Hartford, Conn. *1909–1913*

The detailed organizational history of this make is complex, and its ancestry includes such pioneers as Riker and Morris & Salom. The initial models were electrically powered and this source was used until at least 1907. They were sold in England under the name City and Suburban, and in France as l'Electromotion. Petrol models were introduced in 1899, known then as the Pope-Columbia, and were designed by Hiram Maxim. These petrol cars were advanced for their time, with left-hand steering wheel, full elliptical springs, a coil radiator in front, and a 2-cylinder engine. The 1903 Type XLI showed definite European influence, with a sloping bonnet, double chain drive, and its 14hp engine drove it at 45mph.

In 1907, an electric transmission was introduced, giving 7 forward speeds, with a 4-cylinder engine of 48hp. In 1911 a Knight sleeve-valve engine was used in one model known as the Columbia-Knight. This had a 6.3-litre engine, and was continued to 1913.

The Columbia Motor Car Co was absorbed by United States Motor Co in 1910, and the make ended when this company collapsed in 1913. GMN

COLUMBIA (ii) (US) *1914*
Seattle, Wash.

This was a side-by-side two-seater cyclecar. It used a 2-cylinder engine with overhead valves, combined with a friction transmission and belt drive. Its wheelbase was 8ft, with a track of 3ft 4in. The name of the manufacturer is not known. GMN

COLUMBIA (iii) (US) *1914–1918*
Columbia Electric Vehicle Co, Detroit, Mich.

This electric car was made in open two-seater, three-seater 'coupelette', and four-seater brougham form and was furnished with wire wheels. The price-range of this model, with various options, was $785 to $985. Soon after its introduction, the name was changed to Columbian.

GMN

COLUMBIA (iv) (US) 1916–1924
Columbia Motors Co, Detroit, Mich.

The Columbia was a well thought of assembled car of its era and its low price attracted a considerable number of buyers. Two basic models were offered, both sixes and both powered by Continental engines. As many as 6,000 units were sold in 1923, principally the roadster at $995 (disc wheels were extra). Planning to expand its manufacturing activities, Columbia purchased the Liberty in 1923, but both makes failed a year later. Noteworthy was Columbia's use of thermostatically-controlled radiator shutters as early as 1920 which opened as radiator temperature increased. This was one of the first automobiles to use this device and doubtless it aided Columbia sales.

KM

COLUMBUS see IMPERIAL (ii)

COLUMBUS (US) 1903–1913
Columbus Buggy Co, Columbus, Ohio

The Columbus cars were either electric or gasoline powered, and it appears that they were not always offered simultaneously. 4-cylinder, 4-stroke engines, with three-speed transmissions in chassis of 9ft 2in were built in 1909, with one open electric car. For 1913, large 6-cylinder cars were built. Also for 1913, four closed electric models were made with General Electric motors, and six speed ranges.

GMN

COMET (i) (US) 1906–1908
Hall Auto Repair Co, San Francisco, Calif.

This car had a 25hp 4-cylinder engine with square dimensions (4 × 4in) and overhead valves. The two-seater runabout had a wheelbase of 8ft 6in, and the few cars made did well in West Coast races. Probably not more than five cars were made. Mr Hall achieved greater fame subsequently with the manufacture of Hall-Scott engines used in railcars, trucks, buses and aircraft.

GNG

COMET (ii) (CDN) 1907–1908
Comet Motor Company, Montreal, Que.

The Comet was the first car to reach production in Montreal and was undoubtedly the most successful. It was backed by a number of Quebec businessmen, and probably reached the height of its fame when a Comet was used to drive the Prince of Wales during a visit to Quebec.

The Comet was well-promoted and production is believed to have been at least 100 units and possibly as high as 200. Bodies were made locally, but most of the mechanical components were imported from Europe – a majority from France. Fours and sixes were planned but most if not all production was of fours. Engine castings were bought from Clément-Bayard and the clutch was a Hele-Shaw. Shaft drive was used. Doors were fitted only to the tonneau and the wooden body was covered with fabric. When the company found itself unable to expand it ceased car production and turned to selling other makes, eventually the Packard.

HD

COMET (iii) (US) 1914–1915
(1) Economy Cyclecar Co, Indianapolis, Ind. 1914
(2) Comet Cyclecar Co, Indianapolis, Ind. 1915

The Comet cyclecar was a tandem two-seater with an air-cooled 2-cylinder engine and final drive by belt.

GNG

COMET (iv) (US) 1914
Continental Motors Corp, Buffalo, N.Y.

The information on this make is sparse. The two models, a roadster and a five-seater touring car, were listed at $750 and $950 respectively. These were both powered by a 4-cylinder 25hp engine.

GMN

COMET (v) (US) 1917–1922
Comet Automobile Co, Decatur, Ill.

An assembled car using initially Lewis and then Continental 6-cylinder engines, the Comet sold in small but consistent numbers. Open models as well as closed cars were available but sales were generally restricted to the area of manufacture.

KM

COMET (vi) (GB) 1921
Preston Autocar Co Ltd, London W.C.1

Described as a light sporting car, the Comet used a 10hp 4-cylinder engine, 4-speed gearbox and shaft drive. It was priced at £600 for a two-seater, but few, if any, reached the public.

GNG

COMET (vii) (GB) 1935–1937
Comet Car & Engineering Co Ltd, Croydon, Surrey

1919 COLUMBIA(iv) Six tourer. *Keith Marvin Collection*

1908 COMET(i) 25hp roadster. *Warren K. Miller*

1921 COMET(vi) 10hp sports car. *Autocar*

This was a high performance light car with comfortable coachwork which nev[er] progressed beyond the prototype stage. It had a 1.2-litre 4-cylinder ohv engi[ne] developing 46bhp at 5,500rpm, a 4-speed gearbox and independent front suspe[n]sion. Four body styles were listed, two- and four-seater sports, saloon and drophe[ad] coupé, the latter two by Abbott. Prices were in the range of £435 to £465.   GN

COMET (viii) (US) 1946–1948
General Development Co, Ridgewood, Long Island, N.Y.

Weighing 175lb, this 3-wheeler had a 4½hp air-cooled engine in the rear. Th[e] plastic body was mounted on a tubular frame and Comet claimed a fuel consum[p]tion of 100mpg. An odd aspect of the Comet distributing plan was that the compan[y] asked potential dealers to produce their Marvel delivery car on a royalty basis [of] no less than one hundred units per year.

COMMERCE (US) 1924
Commerce Motor Truck Co, Detroit, Mich.

This well-known truck manufacturer offered briefly a Model 20 De Luxe seda[n] powered by a 4-cylinder engine.   GN

COMMONWEALTH (i) (US) 1903–1904
Coburn & Co, Boston, Mass.

The Commonwealth was offered in both two- and four-seater models, powere[d] by a vertical single-cylinder engine mounted in front under a Renault-style bonne[t.] Final drive was in most cases by chain, but chainless systems were available [at] customer's choice.   MJW

1920 COMMONWEALTH(ii) 20hp tourer. *Autocar*

COMMONWEALTH (ii) (US) 1917–1922
Commonwealth Motors Co, Joliet, Ill.

Formerly the Partin-Palmer, this typical assembled car used a 4-cylinder engin[e] throughout its existence except for a Victory Six model in 1919. Commonwealth['s] Checker taxicab model ultimately became the famous Checker taxi.   K[M]

COMPOUND (US) 1904–1908
Eisenhuth Horseless Vehicle Co, Middletown, Conn.

The Eisenhuth company gained its name from a Mr Eisenhuth who built a[n] experimental car in San Francisco in 1896. The company later moved to Ne[w] Jersey where they experimented with cars using the Graham-Fox compound engin[e.] This was a 3-cylinder unit in which the centre cylinder ran solely on the pressur[e] of exhaust gases from the other two. It was claimed to be very smooth-runnin[g] and silent. A Graham-Fox 60hp car was shown at the Madison Square Garden Show in 1903, but the first cars to be put into production were made at Middletow[n] and called Compounds. Their 3-cylinder engines were of 12/15hp and 24/28hp, an[d] they were of conventional design apart from their power units.   GN

CONDOR (i) (CH) 1922
Condor SA, Courfaivre

Condor are one of Europe's oldest motor cycle makers – they started in 190[1] and are still in business today. Their venture into a car building was very brie[f,] only five vehicles being made. They had an 1,130cc 4-cylinder MAG engine, shaf[t] drive and a two-seater body.   GN[C]

1906 COMPOUND 16hp tourer. *Harrah's Automobile Collection*

CONDOR (ii) (GB) 1960
Condor Motorcar Co Ltd, Guildford, Surrey

The first production specification of this unsuccessful Formula Junior ca[r] embraced a front-mounted Triumph Herald engine and gearbox, B.M.C. differentia[l,] inboard rear brakes, and a square-section tubular space-frame fitted with aluminiu[m] bodywork. Condor wheels were popular with other constructors.   D[?]

CONE (GB) 1914
Cone Car Co Ltd, Leyton, Essex

The Cone cyclecar derived its name from the fact that it used a system o[f] friction drive by cones. The engine was a 4½hp single-cylinder air-cooled uni[t.]   GN[?]

CONNAUGHT (GB) 1949–1957
(1) Continental Cars Ltd, Send, Surrey 1949–1951
(2) Connaught Engineering Ltd, Send, Surrey 1951–1957

The original L2 Connaught was the work of Rodney Clarke and Kenneth Mc[c] Alpine; its name derived from Continental Cars Ltd and the word automobile[.] The 1949 version was based on the 14hp sports Lea-Francis and retained tha[t] type's beam front axle, though power was boosted to 102bhp and it had aerodynami[c] two-seater coachwork and a lift-up bonnet in the manner of the David Brown Asto[n] Martins. The price was £1,275. A lighter and faster L3 model with independentl[y] sprung front wheels followed, but the firm's name was made with its racing cars[,] the first of which was the 2-litre Type A for Formula 2. This had the Lea-Franci[s] engine (now giving 135bhp), a preselector gearbox and all-independent suspension[;] it was tried with fuel injection. The Type B of 1954 onwards was a 2½-litre G.[P] car using the twin ohc 4-cylinder Alta power unit; all-enveloping bodywork wa[s]

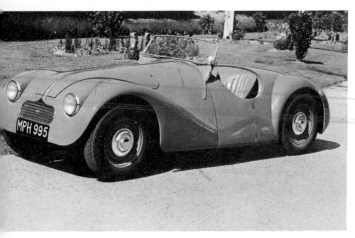

1949 CONNAUGHT L-Series 1,767cc sports car. *Autocar*

...ed though it was the unstreamlined version that was responsible for the marque's ...incipal success, Tony Brooks's win in the 1955 Syracuse G.P. A 115bhp 1½-...re sports car ran unsuccessfully at Le Mans in 1955, but the cost of running a ...cing team was too much for the little company and the works were sold up in ...57. Not more than 30 sports cars were made, together with 9 A and 7 B types.

MCS

1953 CONNAUGHT A-Series Formula 2 racing car. *Charles Dunn*

ONOVER (US) *1906–1908*
...onover Motor Co, Paterson, N.J.
This was a massive-looking car, available as a five-seater tonneau or runabout. It ...as powered by a 4-cylinder 35/40hp engine. The transmission was of the sliding-...ar type, with three forward speeds, and drive to rear axle was by shaft. GMN

ONRAD (US) *1900–1904*
...) Conrad Motor Carriage Co, Buffalo, N.Y. *1900–1903*
...) Lackawanna Motor Co, Buffalo, N.Y. *1904*
The Conrad company made mainly steam cars, light 2-cylinder vehicles with ...de-tiller steering and single chain drive. In 1903 they introduced two petrol-...ngined cars of 8 and 12hp, both with 2-cylinder engines, 3 speeds and single ...hain drive. They were out of business by the end of 1903, but one of their petrol-...ngined models was exhibited by the Lackawanna Motor Company at the 1904 ...ew York Show. However, this latter company concentrated mainly on engines.

GNG

ONRERO (I) *1953–1960*
...irgilio Conrero, Moncaliere, Turin
This well-known Turin tuning establishment offered a front-engined Formula ...unior, with coil/damper suspension units, and sleek bodies styled by Michelotti. ...lternative engines were the 1,100cc Fiat or a linered Peugeot 203. At least one ...T Coupé with Alfa Romeo 1,900 engine was made in 1953. DF

CONSTANTINESCO (F) *1926–1928*
...i. Constantinesco, Paris
Georges Constantinesco was a gifted engineer who had provided the Allied air ...orces of World War 1 with a synchronizing gear which enabled a machine-gun to ...e fired through the propeller arc of an aircraft. A Roumanian by birth and a ...aturalized Briton, he produced his car, or rather the vehicle for his ideas on ...ansmission, in Paris. At the 1926 Salon he showed a 5CV voiturette powered by ...½-litre, 2-stroke engine that drove to the nearside rear wheel via a variable-torque ...ransmission. The torque converter was in a housing between the two cylinders. ...onstantinesco believed that his transmission enabled a really small engine ...o propel a car of normal size effortlessly under all conditions. It was seen as ...n answer to the gear-changing difficulties which were the principal bogy of the ...verage driver. In fact the car was underpowered beyond redemption. TRN

CONTESSA *see* HINO

CONTINENTAL (i) (US) *1907*
...continental Motor Car Co, Chicago, Ill.
This was a two-seater roadster with an oval bonnet, on a wheelbase of 7ft 6in. ...t was equipped with a 2-cylinder, 12hp engine, with a choice of air- or water-...ooling. A planetary transmission and shaft drive were used. GMN

1926 CONSTANTINESCO 5CV two-seater. *National Motor Museum*

CONTINENTAL (ii) (US) *1907–1909*
...) University Automobile Co, New Haven, Conn.
...) Continental Automobile Mfg Co, New Haven, Conn.
This make was available in the form of a three-seater runabout, or a six-seater ...ouring car. Both used a 4-cylinder engine with Apple ignition. The transmission ...ad four forward speeds. GMN

CONTINENTAL (iii) (US) *1909–1914*
...ndiana Motor & Mfg Co, Franklin, Ind.
A touch of elegance was added to this car by a mahogany dash panel. The only ...model available was a five-seater touring car weighing 2,200lb. Power was furnished ...by a 4-cylinder L-head engine of 4.4 litres. GMN

CONTINENTAL (iv) (US) *1914*
...continental Engine Mfg Co, Minneapolis, Minn.
The power for this cyclecar was furnished by an air-cooled T-head engine of ...4-cylinders and of 1.1 litres capacity. This engine was of their own manufacture. ...The final drive was a choice of belt or chain. The track was unusually narrow ...at 2ft 8in, with a wheelbase of 7ft 8in. The price was $360 for the two-seater ...tandem model. GMN

CONTINENTAL (v) *see* MOOSE JAW STANDARD

CONTINENTAL (vi) (US) *1933–1934*
...continental Automobile Co, Detroit, Mich.
Sold in one 4- and two 6-cylinder models, the Continental was an unsuccessful ...attempt by the famous engine-building concern to market the defunct De Vaux

1933 CONTINENTAL(vi) Beacon roadster. *Keith Marvin Collection*

1956 CONTINENTAL(vii) Mark II 6-litre coupé.
G.N. Georgano

1911 COOPER(i) 20hp limousine. Coachwork
by Sanders of Hitchin. *Autocar*

1923 COOPER(ii) 11hp two-seater. *Autocar*

under the Continental name. Prices started as low as $335. The car was also sol
in Canada under the Frontenac emblem.   K

CONTINENTAL (vii) (US) *1955–1957; 1968 to date*
Ford Motor Co, Continental Division, Detroit, Mich.

The Continental Mark II was introduced for the 1956 season as a luxury ca
which would be a spiritual descendant of the much-prized Lincoln Continental
of 1940–48, and a rival to the best imported automobiles. It was a four-seate
coupé powered by Lincoln's 6-litre V-8 engine, and cost $8,800 compared wit
$4.064 for the Lincoln Premiere. The Continental Mark II remained basicall
unchanged during its 20-month life, although a convertible was listed for the 195
season, and prices were increased that year to $9,695. Production was discontinue
in June 1957 after 3,012 Continentals had been built. The name Continental wa
continued for a model of Lincoln after 1957, but in early 1968 it was revive
once more for a separate range, known as the Continental Mark III. This use
Lincoln's 7½-litre V-8 engine in an individually-styled coupé body. The price wa
$6,800. As with the Mark II, annual changes were not envisaged for the Mar
III, and 1973 models are similar, except for small details, to the 1968 cars.   GN

CONVAIR (GB) *1958–1959*
Convair Developments, Leytonstone, London E.

This was a typical, but not especially popular, kit-built car, with a twin-tub
chassis frame, B.M.C. A series mechanical constituents and a fibreglass body
                                                                        D

CONVAIRCAR (US) *1947*
The Consolidated-Vultee Aircraft Corp, San Diego, Calif.

The Convaircar was an interesting project that combined a car with an air
craft. The wings and engine assembly were built as an entirely separate unit tha
could be attached to a small Crosley-powered 2-door sedan of Convair design
Flight and road tests were conducted but the plan was later abandoned.   B

CONY (J) *1952–1967*
Aichi Machine Industry Co, Ltd, Nagoya

A 4-wheeled companion to the Giant series of 3-wheelers, the Cony began a
a range of commercial vehicles and developed into private cars as the Japanes
motor industry expanded. The Cony 360 series included a small 2-door sedan an
a station wagon, powered by an amidships-mounted 354cc 2-cylinder engine whic
developed 18.6bhp at 5,500rpm.   B

COOK (I) *1900*
Officine Pastore e Racca, Turin

A small car designed by Advocato Marcello Racca, the Cook had a 3½hp single
cylinder Aster engine, two speeds, belt drive, and bar steering. It took success
fully in local competitions.   MCS

COOPER (i) (GB) *1909–1911*
Cooper Steam Digger Co Ltd, Kings Lynn, Norfolk

Made by a firm of traction engine builders, the Cooper used a 22hp 4-cylinder
piston-valve 2-stroke engine designed and made by the company. The cars used a
3-speed gearbox and 2-speed rear axle, giving six forward speeds and two reverse.
Only six cars were made, and all were supplied to directors of the company or to
their friends. One car, a tourer, survives today.   GNG

COOPER (ii) (GB) *1919–1923*
(1) Cooper Car Co, Bedford *1919–1920*
(2) Cooper Car Co, Ltd, Coventry, Warwickshire *1922–1923*

The original Cooper used a vertical 3-cylinder air-cooled engine of 11hp, but
only a prototype was made. Later Coventry-built Coopers were conventional light
cars using Coventry-Climax engine and a Moss gearbox. They had long, rakish
bonnets and German silver radiators. The company also made the 1½-litre Janvier-
engined Warwick racing car, entered for the 1923 Brooklands 200 Miles Race.
                                                                        GNG

COOPER (iii) (GB) *1948–1969*
Cooper Car Co Ltd, Surbiton, Surrey *1948–1969*; Byfleet, Surrey *1966–1969*

John Cooper, with his father Charles, commenced car construction with 500cc
single-seaters. Two were built in 1946, using Fiat Topolino parts and Speedway
J.A.P engines, for himself and Eric Brandon. These proving successful in 1947,
commercial production was commenced with the Mark II version the following
year. Amongst the first drivers were Sir Francis Samuelson, R.M. Dryden, and an
unknown youth called Stirling Moss, who drew attention to the marque and to
himself by notching 11 wins in his first season. A sports car was built using a J.A.P.
engine, but the first production 2-seater type was the 1,442cc Vauxhall-engined
model of 1949, using a '500' type chassis but front engine location. The M.G.-engined
versions, especially that of Cliff Davis, were successful in racing.

The 500cc cars were developed at the rate of approximately a Mark per year
up to the end of the old Formula 3 in 1958. From 1950 to 1953 there were serious
threats from Kieft and J.B.S., but apart from some interference from Staride,

rnott and some specials on isolated occasions, Cooper otherwise dominated the
~~ass~~ for its entire life-span. The standard specification embraced independent
~~suspension~~ by transverse leaf springs, and at first a box-section frame. The 1952
~~M~~ark VI employed a multi-tubular chassis, and another new frame was seen in the
~~M~~ark VIII of 1954. Disc brakes appeared with the Mark IX the following year. By
~~1~~956 some 360 had been made in all, but thereafter interest in the class tailed
~~o~~ff. In the latter years the 'double-knocker' twin overhead camshaft Norton engine
~~w~~as almost ubiquitous, though some races were held especially for J.A.P.-engined
~~m~~achines.

Spike Rhiando in 1948 was the first to put a 1,000cc J.A.P. V-twin in a Cooper.
~~S~~uch machines, when driven with care, made their presence felt in the shorter
~~F~~ormula 2 races, but it was in hill-climbs that they became quite invincible. They
~~d~~ominated the British Championships for many years from 1951, in the hands of
~~W~~harton, Boshier-Jones, Marsh and most other serious contenders. In the record-
reaking field, Formula 3-based cars achieved 56 class records between 1951 and
~~1~~956, mostly at Montlhéry and Monza.

In 1952 the Mark V chassis was modified, with a front-mounted 2-litre Bristol
~~e~~ngine, tuned at first to 135bhp and ultimately to over 150bhp. Mike Hawthorn's
~~p~~henomenal achievements in one of the first of these cars earned him recognition as
~~a~~ top-flight driver, and a place in the Ferrari works team. The 1953 version used a
~~t~~ubular frame, and alternative engines used by private owners included Alta, E.R.A.
~~a~~nd Maserati. A sports model was also made, retaining the earlier box-section chassis,
~~b~~ut with 141bhp for a weight of 1,316lb. The last front-engined sports models were
~~t~~he multi-tubular space-framed cars designed for P.N. Whitehead in 1954 with 'C'-
~~t~~ype Jaguar engine, and the following year's Mark II version with 'D'-type
~~e~~ngine.

The real milestone was the 1,098cc Coventry-Climax-engined sports model,
~~w~~ith rear engine and central driving position. A space-frame was used, retaining
~~t~~ransverse leaf suspension, transmission being via a reversed Citroën gearbox. The
~~a~~luminium all-enveloping body pioneered the 'shovel-snout–Kamm tail' profile that
~~b~~ecame almost universal amongst sports-racing cars of the 1960's. The dozen made
~~i~~n 1955 achieved immediate success in their class, and in the class above. One of these
~~m~~odels, fitted with a full-width single-seater body and BS4 Bristol engine, provided a
~~B~~ritish Grand Prix entry for Jack Brabham. Cars finished at Le Mans that year and in
~~1~~956, in which year the 1,460cc FWB Coventry-Climax engine was adopted.

The next step was the introduction of a Formula 2 version, which achieved
~~s~~ome success, mainly because it appeared earlier than its rivals. The 1957 model
~~e~~mployed the 1,475cc FPF engine with dohc, and in 1958 coil front suspension at
~~l~~ast replaced the traditional leaf spring. Ten out of thirteen Formula 2 races were
won that year, achieving the class Championship. Meanwhile, the engine had been
stretched to $2\frac{1}{4}$ litres, and Moss and Trintignant pointed to the future by winning a
Grand Prix each.

In 1958, too, the Cooper Monaco was introduced – a rear-engined catalogued
sports car which, designed for Coventry-Climax engines of $1\frac{1}{2}$ or 2 litres, achieved a
remarkable run of successes. Some 30 were made up to 1964, including the American
V8-engined Shelby King Cobra versions.

In 1959 the Formula 1 engine had grown to 2,462cc, developing 236bhp, providing
Cooper and Jack Brabham with their first World Championships. This marked a
turning-point in Grand Prix design, all other marques subsequently following
Cooper's lead in situating the engine at the rear. In Formula 2, Borgward engines
were used with success. The 1960 G.P. machine was lower, adopted coil rear
suspension and a 5-speed gearbox, and retained the honours. Formula Juniors Marks
1 and 2 appeared, with B.M.C. engines, and gave John Surtees his first racing on
four wheels.

1961 brought the new $1\frac{1}{2}$ litre formula, but no Coventry-Climax engines
sufficiently powerful to stave off the Ferraris. Brabham, however, showed a portent
of things to come by finishing 9th at Indianapolis with only $2\frac{3}{4}$ litres in his offset,
modified Formula 1 car. Meanwhile, the Coopers had been busy on 'Minis', and in
1961 B.M.C. announced the 'Mini-Cooper' sports saloon, with engine stretched to
997cc, two HS2 S.U. carburettors and disc front brakes. During the following years
there were a number of developments, of 970, 998, 1,071, 1,275 and 1,293cc, and
countless racing and rally successes, culminating in the European Rally Championships held by the incomparable B.M.C. team of Aaltonen, Hopkirk and Makinen.
Scarcely ever have Cooper themselves employed a less than outstanding driver, and
works racing exponents have included, in addition to those mentioned elsewhere,
Banks, Brown, Bueb, Fitzpatrick, Handley, Hill, Leston, Lewis-Evans, Love,
Rhodes, Rindt, Rodriguez, Russell and Sir John Whitmore.

By 1962 the Formula 1 V-8 Coventry-Climax was ready, and McLaren and
Coopers achieved a little success. A new car (the Type 66) with 6-speed gearbox
was made for 1963, but most success came in the sports class, headed by Salvadori.
B.M.C. 'hydrolastic' suspension was tried on the Formula Junior machines. For
1964 new tubular space-frames were re-inforced by 'semi-monocoque' bodies, but
it was only in Formula 3 – where Stewart's Type 72 won twelve of the seventeen
races – that success was found.

1965 saw suspension and other improvements, and for the 3-litre Formula 1 of
1966 onwards a new monocoque was designed by Robinson for the V-12 Maserati
engine.

1947 COOPER(iii) 500cc sports car. *Autocar*

1952 COOPER(iii) Mark VI Formula 3 racing
car. *Autosport*

1952 COOPER-BRISTOL 2-litre racing car.
National Motor Museum

1957 COOPER-CLIMAX 1,100cc sports car.
Charles Dunn

*c.*1910 CORBIN 32hp tourer. *Kenneth Stauffer*

1931 CORD L-29 4.9-litre sedanca de ville. Coachwork by Murphy. *National Motor Museum*

1937 CORD Model 812 Custom Beverly sedan. *G.N. Georgano*

1907 CORONA 9/11PS tonneau. *Neubauer Collection*

The company's financial standing was strengthened by backing from the Chipstead Motors group from 1965, and between 1964 and 1967 over 60 Formula 2 and Formula 3 monopostos were sold. From then on they suffered a further and fatal decline accelerated by misfortunes and bad engine choices in Formula 1. A final attempt was made to cash in on the new Formula 5000 with a modification of the Formula 1 car, but though the T90 was among the first vehicles built for this formula, its performance was quickly eclipsed by later designs. When British Leyland rationalized their Mini range for 1972, the Cooper name disappeared entirely from the manufacturers' catalogues.

DF

COQ (F) *1920*

Robert de Coquereamont, Rouen, Seine-Inférieure

The Coq was a small French cyclecar fitted with a 2-stroke engine driving through a 4-speed gearbox. The car had a torpedo body and also boasted the refinements of electric lighting and starting.

MJWW

CORBIN (US) *1903–1912*

Corbin Motor Vehicle Co, New Britain, Conn.

Early Corbins had 4-cylinder engines air-cooled by two fans set above the cylinders. Water cooling appeared in 1908, but air-cooling was continued as an alternative until 1910. The 1905 cars pioneered metal brake-shoes, but this feature was not continued. Later models, all with 4-cylinder engines, were rated at either 32 or 36hp. A distinctively peaked radiator shell and bonnet was a feature of all Corbins. The parent company (American Hardware Corp) is still in business. GMN

CORBITT (US) *1912–1913*

Corbitt Auto Co, Henderson, N.C.

The 4-cylinder Corbitt came in three body styles, on a chassis with 10ft wheelbase. Model A, a two-seater roadster cost $1.750 and Model C, a five-seater touring car cost $1,800. The name Corbitt lasted until 1958 on trucks. GMN

CORD (i) (US) *1929–1937*

Auburn Automobile Co, Auburn, Ind. *1929–1937*

The first American front-drive car to win popular approval, the Cord was one of a trio of distinctive cars (the others being the Auburn and the Duesenberg) that made up Erret Lobban Cord's empire. The first Cord was the Model L-29, powered by a 4,934cc straight 8 engine made by Lycoming, another Cord subsidiary. The L-29 was much lower than most contemporary American cars and was made in open and closed models, as well as being given special coachwork by such firms as Murphy, Hayes, and in England, Freestone & Webb. However, the price of over $3,000 was against the car in the Depression years, and production ended in 1932 after some 4,400 cars had been sold.

The name re-emerged later in 1935 with the strikingly modernistic Model 810. Designed by Gordon Buehrig, this car had originally been intended as a small model of Duesenberg. Like the L-29 the new car was front-driven and Lycoming-powered, although by a slightly smaller V-8 engine of 4,730cc. The body was of a very advanced design, and featured retractable headlamps and a wrap-around grille. Body styles were the Westchester and Beverly sedans (identical except for upholstery pattern), two-seater Sportsman and four-seater Phaeton convertibles. In 1937 the Model 812 series was introduced, featuring a long-wheelbase Custom berline with chauffeur division, while an optional supercharger boosted power to 195bhp. Prices ranged from $1,995 for the early models to $3,575 for the 1937 Supercharged Custom berline, and this drastically restricted sales. Only 2,320 examples of the 810 and 812 were made.

KM

CORD (ii) (US) *1964 to date*

(1) Auburn-Cord-Duesenberg Co, Tulsa, Okla. *1964–1967*
(2) Elfman Motors, Inc, Philadelphia, Pa. *1967–1968*
(3) S.A.M.C.O., Inc, Tulsa, Okla. *1968 to date*

By the mid-1960s the Model 810/812 Cords had become such popular classic cars that Glenn Pray put on the market a scaled-down 8/10ths version of the two-seater convertible using a Chevrolet Corvair engine and Royalex plastic bodywork. It was priced at $4,700, and about 85 cars were made. Like the original Cords, the 8/10 had front-wheel drive, but the next attempt at Cord revival turned to rear-wheel drive and Ford V-8 power and abandoned the retractable headlights that had been such a feature of the pre-war Cords. Cords for 1971 came in two models, the Warrior powered by a 5-litre Ford V-8 engine, and the Royale with 7.2-litre Chrysler Magnum V-8 engine. Prices were from $7,000 up. GNG

CORINTHIAN (US) *1922–1923*

Corinthian Motors Co, Philadelphia, Pa.

An assembled car of short duration, the Corinthian was available as a medium-priced car with a Herschell-Spillman 4-cylinder engine and a large and expensive version with a 4-cylinder Wisconsin T-head power plant. KM

CORMÉRY (F) *1901*

H. Corméry, Billancourt, Seine

The Cormèry was a light car with diamond pattern wheel arrangement, like that of the Sunbeam-Mabley. GNG

CORNELIAN (US) 1914–1915
Wood Bros Machine Co, Allegan, Mich.
The Cornelian cyclecar had a 4-cylinder Sterling engine and the unusual feature for the time of independent rear suspension. About 100 were made, after which the makers devoted themselves to producing universal joints. A racing version driven by Louis Chevrolet ran at Indianapolis in 1915. At 1.8 litres, its engine was the smallest of any Indy car at that time. GNG

CORNILLEAU (F) 1912–1914
Automobiles Cornilleau, Asnières, Seine
The Cornilleau company made a range of three models, an 8/10hp 2-cylinder, and 10 and 12hp 4-cylinder, all conventional cars using shaft drive. GNG

CORNILLEAU STE BEUVE (F) 1904–1909
Cornilleau et Ste Beuve, Paris 17e
Also known as the C.S.B., this car was made in two 4-cylinder models, a 14/18 and 20/30hp. They had variable lift inlet valves, an unconventional gearbox and shaft drive. In 1906 the 20/30, also known as a 25hp, was built for Straker-Squire, the same design later being made in England. GNG

CORNISH-FRIEDBERG (C.F.) (US) 1908–1909
Cornish-Friedberg Motor Car Co, Chicago, Ill.
A three-seater roadster and a five-seater touring car were built by this manufacturer. The engine used was a water-cooled, 4-cylinder one, developing 35hp at a speed of 1,000rpm. The final drive was by shaft, and both models were priced at $2,250. GMN

CORNU (F) 1906–1908
Paul Cornu, Lisieux, Calvados
The Cornu voiturette had a very light tubular frame, and was powered by 2 single cylinder Buchet engines, each driving a rear wheel independently by long belts. Maximum speed was nearly 50mph. The inventive M. Cornu also built a twin rotor helicopter powered by a 24hp Antoinette V-8 engine in 1907. GNG

CORONA (i) (D) 1904–1909
Corona Fahrradwerke und Metallindustrie AG, Brandenberg/Havel
When Corona started to develop their motor cycles into small cars, their first attempt in 1904 was the Coronamobil, a 3-wheeler with single-cylinder Fafnir engine. The first 4-wheel car, built in 1905, was a 6/8PS single-cylinder voiturette built under Maurer licence and using the Maurer engine. Another model was built under Maurer licence with a 2-cylinder 9/11PS engine. HON

CORONA (ii) (GB) 1920–1923
Meteor Manufacturing Co Ltd, London N.4
This was a light car using a Bovier 9hp flat-twin engine, a 3-speed gearbox and worm rear axle. A two-seater body was standard. In 1923 there was a 4-cylinder model with 9.8hp Coventry-Climax engine. GNG

CORONA (iii) (F) 1920
Automobiles Corona, Paris
The French Corona is something of a phantom make, for no evidence of its manufacture can be found, although specifications were issued. These showed it to be a large and advanced car with a 7.2-litre V-12 engine with overhead valves operated by twin camshafts mounted in the crankcase. If made, it would undoubtedly have been a very expensive vehicle. GNG

CORONET (i) (GB) 1904–1906
Coronet Motor Co Ltd, Coventry, Warwickshire
The Coronet company was founded in 1903 to build motor cycles and began car production the following year. The chief engineer was Walter Iden, son of George Iden of M.M.C. Two models were made at first, an 8hp single and a 16hp 4-cylinder car with the unusual firing order of 1-2-3-4. The radiator, ignition coil and springs were imported from France; all other parts were said to be British. A 12hp 2-cylinder model was added for 1905; like the 16hp it had shaft drive and a four-seater tonneau body. Early in 1906 the Coronet factory was taken over by Humber. GNG

CORONET (ii) (GB) 1957–1960
Coronet Cars Ltd, Denham, Bucks.
The Coronet 3-wheeler was similar in general design to the Powerdrive, but used a slightly modified body. The engine was a 328cc Anzani 2-cylinder 2-stroke, which drove the rear wheel by chain. GNG

CORRE (i); LA LICORNE (F) 1901–1950
Sté Française des Automobiles Corre, Courbevoie, Seine
J. Corre made motor tricycles and quads, as well as acting as an agent for De

1905 CORONET(i) 16hp tonneau. *G.N. Georgano Collection*

1957 CORONET(ii) 328cc 3-wheeler. *British Resin Products Ltd*

1906 CORRE 8/9hp tonneau. *The Veteran Car Club of Great Britain*

1909 (CORRE) LA LICORNE Model R 25hp landaulette. *Lucien Loreille Collection*

1924 (CORRE) LA LICORNE 10hp tourer.
Lucien Loreille Collection

1929 (CORRE) LA LICORNE 5CV Femina cabriolet.
Mrs Angela Cherrett

1939 (CORRE) LA LICORNE 6CV saloon.
Lucien Loreille Collection

Dion, Peugeot, and Renault in 1899. When he launched his first car in 1901 it was almost a carbon copy of the contemporary Renault, with a 3hp single-cylinder water-cooled De Dion engine at the front of a tubular frame, a 3-speed gearbox and shaft drive. Corres paralleled the Renault idiom until 1906: in 1904 the company offered an 8hp single and a 10hp twin, both De Dion-powered, as well as a big 16hp with the 3,163cc 4-cylinder Aster unit. A year later 4-cylinder models were available with Mutel or De Dion engines, and in 1905 Corre followed Renault by adopting dashboard radiators in place of the lateral arrangement. In 1906 the firm built a 10.6-litre racer for the French Grand Prix.

In 1907 not only were frontal radiators adopted but also the La Licorne name (generally applied after 1909). There was now a steadily widening range, headed in 1908 by a 4.9-litre 30. The company remained faithful to De Dion engines, which enabled them to field a freakish single-cylinder racing voiturette with cylinder dimensions of 100 × 300mm in 1909, and to offer an infinite variety of types in 1910, ranging from three singles of 763cc, 1,021cc, and 1,257cc up to a 35CV V-8, Type V, though it is unlikely that this reached the public. Also in the catalogue were two different sv monobloc fours rated at 10CV, and a 2-litre DX-type with their own 4-cylinder engine. The bigger La Licornes now had 4-speed gearboxes, but the singles were dropped at the end of 1912, and the fours included some medium-sized types powered by ioe units of Chapuis-Dornier manufacture. The 1914 catalogue ranged from a 1,244cc sv two-seater with sv Chapuis-Dornier engine and 3-speed gearbox and curious stepped-quadrant change up to the 4.4-litre S-type. The company was at this time planning to re-enter racing with a 1,400cc pushrod light car designed by Causan. This was in fact campaigned by Collomb between 1920 and 1923.

The 7CV was the staple 1919 La Licorne, and early post-World War 1 models used sv units by Chapuis-Dornier and Ballot with capacities of 1,327cc and 1,593cc, 3-speed gearboxes, cone clutches, and accelerator pedal linkages attached to their steering columns. V-shaped stoneguards lent distinction to the radiators, but hand starting and acetylene lighting were standard until 1921, and as late as 1925 the cheapest Licornes still lacked electrics. A bigger model, the 1,692cc 9/12CV, was introduced in 1923 and until 1927 a wide range was offered. The largest model ran to 2.3 litres, ohv and four-wheel brakes made their appearance on a sports 9/12CV in 1925, and in the same year a 7-bearing 1,500cc six with ohc competed in the Tour de France, but it never went into production.

Though some of these traditional types were still available on paper as late as 1931, there was a change of direction at the 1927 Paris Salon in the shape of the 900cc 5CV with 2-bearing sv engine, full-pressure lubrication, magneto ignition, and quarter-elliptic rear springing. This was the French equivalent of cars like the Triumph Super Seven, and it set the tone for the firm's subsequent products, all of which were modestly rated small saloons of superior elegance. By 1930 the 5CV was available with 4-door saloon coachwork, and coil ignition appeared on a bigger development, the 1,125cc 6/8CV, in 1931. The same short-stroke sv theme persisted on the 1,451cc 8CV of 1932, and at the top of the range was a 2.2-litre machine, the DR4. The 5CV had disappeared in 1932, but a 935cc replacement appeared in 1934; at the same time the more expensive Licornes fell into line with prevailing trends, with ifs, synchromesh, and ohv, though there were still quarter-elliptics at the rear, and the 2-bearing sv units persisted until 1937, in which year the company started to buy bodies from Citroën. The 1938 11CV was in fact 90 per cent Citroën – ohv *traction* power unit turned back to front to drive the rear wheels, and a Citroën body mated to a La Licorne radiator and bonnet. New for 1939 were the 6CV and 7CV, advanced small saloons with forked backbone frames, ifs, and Michelin Pilote wheels, plus, inevitably, quarter-elliptics at the rear. The smaller car had a 1,125cc ohv Licorne engine, but the 1,628cc Citroën unit was used in the 7CV. Electric conversions of these two types were marketed under the Aéric name during World War 2 and a few 6CVs were made between 1946 and 1948. La Licorne attempted a comeback at the 1949 Paris Salon with a 14CV six, but this never reached production.   MCS

CORRE (ii) (F) 1908–1914

(1) J. Corre, Rueil, Seine-et-Oise
(2) Corre et Cie, Rueil, Seine-et-Oise

Like a number of manufacturers including Karl Benz, August Horch and R.E. Olds, Corre left the firm which he had founded successfully (Corre-La Licorne) and began to make cars under the name Corre, Le Cor or J.C. They were small 4-cylinder machines, not unlike the Licornes which were being made at the same time, although the range was smaller, and they tended to have shorter stroke engines. They were made in 8, 10 and 12hp sizes.   GNG

CORREJA (US) 1908–1915

Vandewater & Co, Iselin, Elizabeth, N.J.

The chief model was a 'speed runabout' for which was claimed a speed of more than 60mph. This car used a 35hp engine and 3-speed transmission and sold for $1,450. Manufacture may have begun before 1908.   GMN

C.O.S. (D) 1907

Carl Oskar Schlobach, Breslau

This small firm is reported to have produced 4-cylinder 14PS and 6-cylinder 20PS models. Further details are not known. HON

COSMOPOLITAN (HAYDOCK) (US) 1907–1910
D.W. Haydock Automobile Mfg Co, St Louis, Mo.

The Cosmopolitan was a spindly high-wheeler with a single-cylinder, air cooled engine mounted in front of the body. The car had wheel steering and double-chain drive. It lacked mudguards and was priced at $350. GMN

COSMOS; C.A.R. (GB) 1919–1920
Cosmos Engineering Co Ltd, Bristol

The Cosmos of 1919 was the creation of A.H.R. Fedden, who had designed the pre-World War 1 Straker-Squire, but unlike the latter, the Cosmos was a highly unconventional light car. The power unit was an air-cooled, 3-cylinder radial engine of exactly 'square' dimensions (75mm × 75mm), with a roller-bearing crankshaft. There were three forward speeds and no differential. The front and rear suspension was of AFS type, using bell crank levers with a lateral coil spring. The total weight was a mere 672lb. The Cosmos was of fairly normal outward appearance, in spite of its hidden peculiarities, and might well have succeeded, but only prototypes were made. The C.A.R., which was a version with an engine of 5mm greater bore and stroke, was developed, but before it could be put into production financial troubles forced the company into the arms of the Bristol Aeroplane Company, which was not interested in cars at that time. TRN

COSTIN (GB) 1971–1972
Costin Automotive Racing Products Ltd, Little Staughton, Beds.

Frank Costin was well known for his work on Lotus, Vanwall, Marcos, Nathan, Protos and Johnny Walker cars before producing a GT two-seater under his own name. This, the Amigo, retained the gaboon plywood chassis he always favoured, with a notably aerodynamic fibreglass body. Some prototypes were built in North Wales, including one sprinted successfully by Costin's partner Paul Pycroft. For the production car a works was obtained not far from Luton, where the main mechanical parts were produced by Vauxhall. With 2.3-litre ohc engine the top speed was quoted at 135mph, and the price of £3,326 embraced a very comprehensive specification. DF

COSTIN-NATHAN see NATHAN

COTAY (US) 1920–1921
Coffyn-Taylor Motor Co, New York, N.Y.

The Cotay designers attempted a compromise between the cyclecar and the full-sized car. A 4-cylinder, in-line engine (albeit air-cooled) by Cameron, coil ignition, unit construction of engine and 3-speed sliding-pinion gearbox, shaft drive, cantilever rear springs and electric lighting and starting were combined with the 'cyclecar' features of a wooden frame integral with a wood and aluminium body, and wooden disc wheels. The weight was 1,512lb. E.S. Cameron, the designer and manufacturer of the engine, which had horizontal over head valves, was in fact a member of the company. The Cotay was offered in England; a classic case of coals to Newcastle. TRN

COTE (F) 1900; 1908–1913
(1) Sté des Automobiles et Moteurs Côte, Saint-Dizier, Haute-Marne 1900
(2) Sté des Automobiles et Moteurs Côte, Pantin, Seine 1908–1913

The original Côte was a 3hp voiturette with spur gear drive and handlebar steering. Its twin-cylinder engine was water-cooled and horizontally mounted. Thereafter the name disappeared until 1908, when the firm submitted a vertical 4-cylinder 2-stroke engine for test to the A.C.F. 2-stroke Côtes were marketed in 2- and 4-cylinder form, 1912 prices ranging from 6,500fr to 12,000fr. The firm also competed in the *Coupe de L'Auto* races of 1911 and 1912; their 3-litre racing cars had 4-speed overdrive gears, Riley detachable wire wheels, and rounded radiators reminiscent of the contemporary racing Delages. De Vere's Côte finished last in the latter event. In 1913, the last year of production, a 1.1-litre 8/17CV and a 2.1-litre 16/28CV were listed. Apart from the engines, they were conventional. MCS

COTTA (US) 1901–1903
(1) Cotta Automobile Co, Lanark, Ill. 1901–1902
(2) Cotta Automobile Co, Rochford, Ill. 1902–1903

In appearance the Cotta was similar to many other light steam cars of the period, but it was the only one to feature four-wheel drive and steering. The 6hp 2-cylinder engine was mounted exactly in the centre of the chassis and power was transmitted to all four wheels by compensating chain gear. GNG

COTTEREAU (F) 1898–1910
Cottereau et Cie, Dijon

The first Cottereau was a 1-litre air-cooled V-twin with coil ignition, tubular frame, 3-speed gearbox, central chain drive to a differential back axle and handlebar steering. Wheel steering was an option in 1900, when the enlarged engines had

1920 COTAY 11hp two-seater. *Autocar*

1900 CÔTE 3hp voiturette. *Neubauer Collection*

1903 COTTEREAU 5hp tonneau. *Musée de l'Automobile, Rochetaillée-sur-Saone*

1911 COTTIN-DESGOUTTES 40hp tourer.
Bernard Sanders

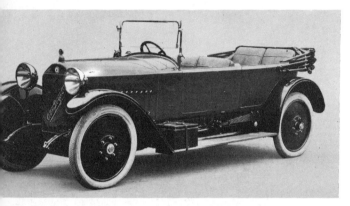

1920 COTTIN-DESGOUTTES 14CV tourer.
Automobielmuseum, Driebergen

1927 COTTIN-DESGOUTTES Sans Secousses
12CV saloon. *Lucien Loreille Collection*

water-cooled heads. A 3½hp vehicle of Benz type was also made in that year. Cottereau ran a 1.4-litre 2-cylinder machine in the Paris-Toulouse-Paris Race, and a 10hp 4-cylinder *voiture de course* in Nice-Draguignan. A still bigger 4-cylinder racer of 20hp was made in 1901, when the production twins were sold under the charming name of *voiturines*.

Several types were marketed in 1903, of which the 5hp Populaire single, selling for £195 in England, had mechanically-operated inlet valves and, surprisingly, steel artillery wheels; a reverse gear was extra. The V-twins came in a variety of guises and with a camshaft brake, Rover style. Smaller models had side-chain drive and there was a 1½-litre with full water cooling and shaft drive. At the top of the range was a chain-driven 16hp 4-cylinder with 4-speed gearbox and the choice of either automatic or mechanically-operated inlet valves. This complexity was typical of Cottereau's offerings and 1904 saw the firm's first 3-cylinder model, a T-headed 2½-litre with honeycomb radiator. In 1905 the firm were employing 350 people, and making everything themselves, bodies included.

Two singles, a twin, two 3-cylinder cars (the 2.5-litre and a smaller 1.8-litre '12/14') and a brace of fours made up the 1906 programme; the single cylinder 8hp could be had with shaft, side-chain, or central chain drive, and with pressed steel or tubular frame, but the latter was available only when a single-chain layout was specified. An enormous 18.3-litre 6-cylinder chain-driven racer with high-tension magneto and Mercedes-like appearance was on display at the 1906 Salon, but not, apparently, anywhere else, for the largest of the later Cottereaus with their round radiators, though still made in a vast variety of types (eight models in 1908) was a 4-cylinder 22/26hp of 4.2 litres. There were still 3-cylinder cars, and both shaft and chain drive remained available. The latter was usually found on the bigger cars – and confined to them in 1907. But as late as 1910 a 9hp single-cylinder voiturette was available with side chains at the equivalent of £172. Already, however, the firm was experimenting with 4- and 6-cylinder rotary-valve units, and in 1911 the make had a new identity as the C.I.D.   MCS

COTTIN-DESGOUTTES (F) *1905–1933*
Cottin et Desgouttes, Lyons

While Paris tended to concentrate on small cars, the area round Lyons was always better known for fast, expensive, beautifully-made machines. In this, the Cottin-Desgouttes was a typical product of its region. Originally known simply as Desgouttes, the 24/40hp which made its bow at the 1905 Paris Salon was on the popular Mercedes lines, with four cylinders, mechanical inlet valves, pressed-steel chassis, gate gear-change and honeycomb radiator. By 1908, two sixes had been added to the range. Conventional design was the rule until 1923, when the 12CV arrived. This car had three overhead valves per cylinder and was sold in several bore dimensions. The 3-litre, a fast tourer of typical French *panache*, was the best known. It achieved fame in touring-car races, and a production model, the GP, was offered for sale. A six of the same bore and stroke was listed. In 1927 Cottin et Desgouttes departed further from the norm with their Sans Secousse version of the 12CV, which had independent suspension of all wheels by transverse springs, in-board rear brakes and steering arms to each front wheel. By 1930, all Cottins were sixes and all had independent suspension. Production ended in 1931, but cars assembled from stock were available up to 1933.   TRN

COTTON (GB) *1911*
Rennie & Prosser Ltd, Glasgow

A small number of cars (at least 7, probably 12 to 15) were specially built for the Australian outback. They had a ground clearance of 15in and a winch for pulling the car out of soft ground. The engine was a 24hp 4-cylinder ohv White & Poppe. GNG

COUDERT *see* LURQUIN-COUDERT

COUGAR (GB) *1972 to date*

Peter Harrington offered for sale replicas of his extremely successful Formula Ford single-seater during the 1972 season.   DF

COUNTRY CLUB (US) *1904*
Country Club Car Co, Boston, Mass.

The Country Club was distinguished by a 3-speed sliding-gear transmission operated by compressed air. Its horizontal 2-cylinder engine produced 16hp and had a Longuemare carburettor.   GMN

COUNTY (GB) *1907*
Halifax Motor Car Co, Halifax, Yorks.

The County was a medium-sized 4-cylinder car made in very small numbers by a well-known firm of retailers.   GNG

COURIER (i) (US) *1904*
Sandusky Automobile Co, Sandusky, Ohio

The Courier was a light open two-seater, powered by a single-cylinder engine with 117mm bore and 146mm stroke. A sliding-gear transmission was used with a single chain for final drive.   GMN

COURIER (ii) (F) *1906–1908*
Euston Motor Co Ltd, London N.W.

This Courier was assembled from French components, including engines by Gnome and Mutel, and some of the cars may well have been imported already assembled. Models included an 8/10hp 2-cylinder, 18/24 and 24/30hp 4-cylinders, and in 1908 a 25hp 6-cylinder. Coventry-Simplex engines were also used, and the same company were responsible for the Wasp (i).   GNG

COURIER (iii) (US) *1909–1912*
(1) Courier Car Co, Dayton, Ohio
(2) United States Motor Co, Dayton, Ohio

Made by a subsidiary of Stoddard-Dayton, the Courier was similar in design to the product of the parent company, but a cheaper and smaller car. Originally a 25hp 4-cylinder engine of 3.2 litres capacity was used, followed in 1912 by a 30hp of 3.7 litres. Roadsters and tourers were made, 1912 models being known as Courier-Clermont. When Stoddard-Dayton was acquired by the United States Motor Company, Courier was naturally included in the combine, and the name disappeared with the failure of the U.S. Motor Company.   GMN

COURIER (iv) (US) *1922–1924*
Courier Motor Co, Sandusky, Ohio

Successor to the Maibohm, the Courier had a 6-cylinder Falls engine with full-pressure lubrication.   KM

COUVERCHEL *see C.V.R.*

COVENTRY-PREMIER (GB) *1919–1923*
Coventry-Premier Ltd, Coventry, Warwickshire

Coventry-Premier Ltd made bicycles and motor cycles until 1913, when they engaged G.W.A. Brown, formerly of Clement-Talbot, to produce a small car. When it appeared six years later the Coventry-Premier was basically a cyclecar with three wheels instead of the more normal four. The power unit, a water-cooled V-twin, was in character, but although early models were chain-driven, an attempt was soon made to give the little machine at least one 'big-car' characteristic by providing a 3-speed and reverse sliding-pinion gearbox and shaft drive. In fact, it grew up very quickly, for after being taken over by Singer in 1920, it reappeared with four wheels, still under its own name. By the following year it had a 4-cylinder Singer engine with push-rod ohv and was a cheap version of the Singer Ten.   TRN

COVENTRY-VICTOR (GB) *1926–1938*
Coventry-Victor Motor Co Ltd, Coventry, Warwickshire

The name of Coventry-Victor was most familiar in the 1920s on small proprietary engines, but the company also made its own car. It was a 3-wheeled cyclecar, which arrived at a time when (except for Morgan) other makers of the type had either been driven out of business by the light car, the 'big car in miniature', or else had gone over to the latter type. The Coventry-Victor family model was powered by a water-cooled, side-valve flat-twin engine of 688cc which, enlarged to 749cc for competition purposes, was used in the Sports model. Transmission was by chain and there was no self-starter. The Beauvais-styled 'Luxury Sports' with starter appeared in 1932, though the austere Midget could still be bought for £75. The Luxury versions were made until 1937 with 850cc, 900cc and 1,000cc engines. In 1949 several prototypes of a small saloon with a 747cc flat-4 engine were made, code-named 'Venus', but they did not go into production.   TRN

COVERT (US) *1901–1907*
(1) Byron V. Covert & Co, Lockport, N.Y. *1901–1904*
(2) Covert Motor Vehicle Co, Lockport, N.Y. *1904–1907*

The 1901 Covert range consisted of a light steam runabout with 2-cylinder engine and chain drive, and a 3hp petrol car that weighed only 350lb. Later shaft-driven Coverts used petrol engines of 6½hp single-cylinder (Model A) and 24hp 4-cylinder (Model B).   GMN

COWEY (GB) *1913–1915*
Cowey Engineering Co Ltd, Kew Gardens, Surrey

The speciality of the Cowey company was their pneumatic suspension in which the weight of the car was carried on four cylinders of compressed air. The system incorporated automatic levelling as on the Citroën DS 19. Two experimental cars with De Dion engines and solid tyres were shown at Olympia in 1910.

The production Cowey was a light car with a 10hp Chapuis-Dornier engine. In addition to the pneumatic suspension it used a friction drive in which a flywheel with conical facing acted as the driving disc. In production from 1913 to 1915, it sold for £300.   GNG

COX *see G.T.M.*

COYOTE (US) *1909–1910*
Redondo Beach Car Works, Redondo Beach, Calif.

1921 COVENTRY-PREMIER 8hp 200 Mile Race Car. *W.J. Brunell*

1904 COVERT 6½hp two-seater. *Henry Ford Museum, Dearborn, Mich.*

1914 COWEY 10/12hp two-seater. *Autocar*

1903 CRAIG-DÖRWALD 16hp traveller's car.
Robert Kisch

1915 CRANE-SIMPLEX Model 5 46hp tourer.
Don McCray

1922 CRAWFORD Six tourer. *Robert H. Kohl*

A two-seater roadster which was apparently powered by a 50hp engine of eight cylinders. It had very rakish mudguards, presumably to denote speed.　　　GMN

C.P.T. (US) 1906
Chicago Pneumatic Tool Co, Chicago, Ill.
　Although they made vans for some years, the only private car venture of the C.P.T. company was a 22hp runabout with solid tyres which they built for the use of their travellers.　　　GNG

CRAIG-DÖRWALD (GB) 1902–1912
Putney Motor Co, Putney, London S.W.
　Craig-Dörwald cars were made in very small numbers, mainly to special order, and were of individual design, most parts being made on the premises. A 5hp single-cylinder single-speed light car was made in 1902, and a 10hp 2-cylinder commercial traveller's car in 1903. Later 'standard' Craig-Dörwalds included an 8hp single, 18hp twin and 36hp four, while the largest car made was a 50hp 4-cylinder with a sumptuous barouche body by Hamshaw of Leicester. Built to the order of the Earl of Norbury, it had worm drive and only one speed. Not more than 12 cars were made in all, the company being more famous for their marine engines. In this field they made the world's first V-12 engine, a 150hp unit, in 1904.　　　GNG

CRAIG-TOLEDO (US) 1906–1907
Craig-Toledo Motor Co, Dundee, Mich,; Toledo, Ohio
　This company offered a three-seater runabout for 1907 at $4,000. The company was still in existence in 1909 but there is no evidence of manufacture after 1907.　　　GMN

CRAMPIN-SCOTT (GB) 1900–1901
Crampin, Scott & Co, London W.C.
　The Crampin-Scott used a horizontal single-cylinder 6hp engine and a gearbox providing two forward speeds. Reverse was an optional extra. Maximum speed was said to be 12mph.　　　GNG

CRANE (US) 1912–1915
(1) Crane Motor Co, Bayonne, N.J. *1912–1915*
(2) Crane Motor Co, New Brunswick, N.J. *1915*
　The Crane Motor Car Co was a successor to Crane & Whitman Automobile Works of Bayonne, N.J. which went out of existence in 1908 after building several experimental cars. The Crane had a 4-cylinder engine of 9.2 litres rated at 46hp. It had a four-speed transmission and its wheelbase was 11ft 1in. The chassis was priced at $8,000. The Crane became the Crane-Simplex when the Simplex Automobile Co took over the company.　　　GMN

CRANE & BREED (US) 1912–1917
Crane & Breed Mfg Co, Cincinnati, Ohio
　For 1912 this company listed a 48hp 6-cylinder car with six body styles, at prices from $3,000 to $4,500. However, most of their subsequent production was devoted to ambulances and hearses.　　　GNG

CRANE-SIMPLEX (US) 1915–1924
Simplex Automobile Co, New Brunswick, N.J.; Long Island City, N.Y.
　One of America's outstanding prestige cars of any time, the Crane-Simplex (or Simplex, Crane Model No. 5), with its $10,000 chassis, succeeded the earlier Simplex after Henry M. Crane had taken control of operations. It was powered by a 6-cylinder engine of over 9 litres capacity designed by the firm, and was sold in many body styles with coachwork by a variety of America's finest custom builders, including Holbrook. In 1922, after the purchase of Crane-Simplex by Hare's Motors, who already owned Locomobile, a new Simplex was announced with 4-litre single-ohc 6-cylinder engine. It was to be built in the Locomobile factory at Bridgeport, Conn.　　　KM

CRAWFORD (US) 1905–1923
Crawford Automobile Co, Hagerstown, Md.
　This car was built under the aegis of M.P. Möller, a successful builder of pipe organs. Only limited numbers were built, chain drive being used up to 1907, with transaxles on 1911–1914 models. Later models featured disc-covered artillery wheels and were powered by Continental 6-cylinder engines in 60 and 70bhp forms. The company afterwards made the Dagmar car.　　　KM

CRAWSHAY-WILLIAMS (GB) 1904–1906
Crawshay-Williams Ltd, Ashtead, Surrey
　This company made two models of 4-cylinder car, with 14/16 and 20/24hp Simms engines. They used chain drive and were generally similar to Mercedes in appearance.　　　GNG

CRÉANCHE (F) 1899–1906
Sté L. Créanche, Courbevoie, Seine
　The original Créanche voiturette had a 4hp De Dion engine mounted on a mov-

ble fore-train. This could be moved forward or backward to give variable tension to a belt that connected the engine to a countershaft at the rear of the car. They also sold under their own name light electric cars made for them by B.G.S. Later Créanches were more conventional, with 8hp De Dion engines, and shaft drive. In 1905 they listed a range of five cars, from 10 to 30hp, and in 1906 four models, from 6 to 16hp. At least one Créanche survives today, a 1900 4hp, in a Swiss collection. GNG

CREMORNE (GB) 1903–1904

Cremorne Motor Manufacturing Co Ltd, Chelsea, London S.W.

The Cremorne steam car was made in two forms using 6½ or 12hp 2-cylinder vertical engines with steam generated at 220psi. Chain drive was used and open and closed bodywork was offered. The company also made larger engines of 18 and 24hp, but these were apparently not fitted into vehicles. GNG

CRESCENT (i) (US) 1907

Crescent Motor Car Co, Detroit, Mich.

This firm was said to be building a large factory to carry on the touring car business of the Reliance Motor Car Company, and the runabout business of the Marvel Car Company, but they probably never actually turned out cars. GNG

CRESCENT (ii) (GB) 1911–1915

1) Crescent Motors Ltd, Walsall, Staffs. 1911–1913
2) Crescent Motors Ltd, Birmingham 1913–1915

The Crescent cyclecar had a more car-like appearance than many of the breed, but used a 7/9hp air-cooled 2-cylinder engine and belt drive. After the move to Birmingham, a change was made to a water-cooled Blumfield V-twin engine and chain drive. GNG

CRESCENT (iii) (US) 1913–1914

Crescent Motor Co, Cincinnati, Ohio

Two models of this make were advertised, the Ohio and the Royal. The former was a continuation of Ohio (iii) and was the smaller of the two, with a 4.4-litre 4-cylinder engine, on a chassis of 9ft 8in wheelbase. This was built as a five-seater. The Royal model, with a wheelbase of 11ft used a 6-cylinder engine of 7.4 litres. This manufacturer may have moved to St Louis, Mo. late in 1914. GMN

CRESPELLE (F) 1906–1923

F. Crespelle, Paris 12e

The original Crespelles were sporting cars which made a feature of long-stroke single-cylinder engines, including Aster (106 × 192mm) and De Dion 100mm × 80mm). They were very successful at hill climbs, winning their class at Gaillon five times between 1906 and 1912 and entered in races such as the 1909 Coupe des Voiturettes, the 1910 Catalan Cup and even the 1912 French Grand Prix. In races, however, they were much less successful than hill climbs. By 1913 they were using 4-cylinder engines, still with long strokes, such as the 3-litre 78mm × 156mm Janvier, and a range of six models was offered. The 3-litre model actually led the field for the first five laps of the 1913 Coupe de la Sarthe.

After World War 1 Crespelles were less interesting, and used mainly the 4-cylinder Sergant engine in models ranging from 1.3 to 2.4 litres capacity. Three- and four-speed gearboxes were available. GNG

CRESTMOBILE (US) 1900–1905

Crest Manufacturing Co, Cambridge, Mass.

The first cars made by this company were called simply Crest, and had a De Dion engine mounted in front of a straight dash, with no bonnet. Final drive was by single chain. By 1903 the engine was enclosed in a neat bonnet, and four-seaters were being made as well as two-seaters. The 1904 Crestmobile had an 8hp air-cooled engine of the company's own manufacture, epicyclic gearbox, and shaft drive. It was sold in England by O'Halloran Brothers under the name OHB, the cheapest model costing only 100gns. GNG

CREWFORD (GB) 1920–1921

Crewford Garage, London N.7

The Crewford used an underslung Ford Model T chassis with standard Model T engine and transmission. Two- and four-seater polished aluminium bodies, with either bullnose or Rolls-Royce-type radiators, gave the cars a distinctive appearance. GNG

CRICKET (US) 1914

Cricket Cyclecar Co, Detroit, Mich.

A small cyclecar driven by a 2-cylinder engine with 2-speed transmission which cost $385. This company combined late in 1914 with the Motor Products Co, manufacturers of motor cycles. GMN

CRIPPS (GB) 1913

Cripps Cycle Co, Forest Gate, London N.

1904 CREMORNE 12hp steam limousine. *Autocar*

1902 CRESTMOBILE 8hp two-seater. *National Motor Museum*

1949 CROSLEY Super Sports 750cc sports car.
Autosport

1965 CROSSLÉ 4.2-litre sports/racing car.
Autosport

1912 CROSSLEY 15hp coupé. *National
Motor Museum*

The Cripps cyclecar used a 7hp J.A.P. V-twin engine, a 3-speed gearbox, and chain final drive. It was fitted with a dashboard-operated chain starter, and wa priced at £95. GN

CRITCHLEY-NORRIS (GB) *1906–1908*

Critchley Norris Motor Co Ltd, Bamber Bridge, Lancs.

This company was mainly a producer of bus chassis, but a few cars were mad with 40hp Crossley 4-cylinder engines, 4-speed gearboxes and double chain drive They were also responsible for the fwd Pullcar. GN

CROESUS JR (US) *1907*

(1) Croesus Motor Co, Kansas City, Mo.
(2) W.L. Bell, Kansas City, Mo.

This very obscure make was represented by both a two-seater roadster and seven-seater touring car. The latter had a wheelbase of 9ft and was powered by a 4.8-litre 4-cylinder engine. Final drive was by shaft. GM

CROFTON (US) *1959–1961*

Crofton Marine Engine Co, San Diego, Calif.

This company built small vehicles including the Bug, a 4-wheeled utility machin using a 35bhp 4-cylinder, overhead cam engine based on the Crosley Cobra. B

CROISSANT (F) *1920–1922*

Sté Anon des Anciens Etablissements V. Couverchel, H. Croissant et Cie, Paris 8

This company began by making simple cyclecars, but soon turned to a larger ca with a 4-cylinder 1.6-litre single ohc S.C.A.P. engine. They also advertised car with an 8-cylinder engine which may well have been two of the 4-cylinde units coupled together, as the dimensions (70mm × 110mm) were the same, an S.C.A.P. did not make a straight-8 as large as this. GN

CROMPTON (i) (US) *1903–1905*

Crompton Motor Carriage Co, Worcester, Mass.

The Crompton steam car used 24 separate fire-tube boilers mounted in two group on each side of the 4-cylinder horizontal engine. Drive was by vertical shaft t the rear axle. A two-seater body with curved dash in the style of the Oldsmobil was fitted, but steering was by wheel. GN

CROMPTON (ii) (GB) *1914*

Crompton Engineering Co, Hendon, Middlesex

Designed by T.D. Crompton, this cyclecar was sometimes known as the T.D.C It was available as a monocar or as a two-seater, J.A.P. engines of 5/6hp or 8h being available in either model. A welded steel body was used, which gave the ca a very clean appearance as no joints were visible. GN

CROSLEY (US) *1939–1952*

(1) Crosley Motors Inc, Richmond, Ind. *1939–1941*
(2) Crosley Motors Inc, Marion, Ind. *1945–1952*

The radio pioneer Powel Crosley developed this small car and succeeded i competing on the American market where few other cars of this type had. Althoug not as inspired in appearance as many of its overseas contemporaries, soun engineering did go into its production; its post-war water-cooled engine wa particularly notable.

Before World War 2 the Crosley had used an air-cooled Waukesha 580cc twin but the opportunity to power the vehicle with the 722cc ohc 4-cylinder Cobr engine presented itself when production was resumed. This engine was the resul of a U.S. Navy project. The block was originally made of oven-brazed coppe and sheet steel with a fixed cylinder head. Later this was replaced by the CIBA engine which was of cast iron for greater economy and strength. Pistons, pumps intake manifold and bell housing were of aluminium and the crankshaft ran i five main bearings. The CIBA engine developed 26.5hp at 5,400rpm and was use in Crosley sports cars with great success.

At the peak of its post-war boom Crosley was making a wide range of vehicle including sedans, station wagons, delivery vans and several sports models. The Hot shot was a doorless two-seater; the otherwise similar Super Sports had small doors. BE

CROSSLÉ (GB) *1959 to date*

(1) John L. Crosslé, Drumreagh, Belfast
(2) Crosslé Car Co, Holywood, Belfast

In the days of the 1172 Formula Crosslé's specials were so successful in loca events that other enthusiasts, such as C. Eyre-Maunsell, persuaded him into produc tion. One or two Formula Junior machines, with a similar conventional space-frame layout, were also made. Subsequent single-seaters included monocoque models with all-independent suspension, using a 4.7-litre Ford V8 engine in 1965 and th double ohc 1,598cc Ford in 1967. From 1964 a number of Group 7 sports cars wer also made, with tubular frames and partly stressed body panels. Various engine were used, notably the ubiquitous Ford in Irish events, and the 2-litre B.M.W. i international contests. By 1967 some three dozen cars had been sold in all, an

roduction continued at a steady rate thereafter, cars being available for virtually
ll the single-seater classes. There was a scheme in 1969 for the 16F Formula
ord model to be marketed through C.T. Wooler Ltd, but subsequently Crosslé
everted to handling his own sales. A 1968 12F driven by R. Barr won the U.S.
ormula B Championship, and the 14F and 18F models that superseded it were
lmost as successful. A 16F was used by Gerry Birrell to become European Formula Ford Champion in 1969 and the 20F that succeeded this model was raced
otably in Britain by John Trevelyan and by Jay Pollock in Ireland. The designation
7F was applied to a Formula 3 car, 21F and 24F to Formula Super Vee models,
s used in Britain by the very successful Brian Henton and exported in numbers
o the U.S.A. In the unlimited class Irish racing in 1972 was almost monopolized
y the 22F Formula 2 cars of Brian Nelson and Ken Fildes, still following orthodox
acing-car design principles. Then 23F was allocated to another F3 design, but
ressure of sales on other models precluded production.   DF

1920 CROSSLEY 25/30hp tourer. *National Motor Museum*

CROSSLEY (GB) 1904–1937
1) Crossley Brothers Ltd, Gorton, Manchester *1904–1910*
2) Crossley Motors Ltd, Gorton, Manchester *1910–1937*

The name of Crossley was famous on engines before it was famous on cars; n
fact the company was the first in Britain to make 4-stroke internal combustion
engines on the Otto principle. Later, Daimler engines were made under licence.
The first Crossley car, a chain-driven 22hp 4-cylinder, appeared for the 1904 season.
A 28hp and 40hp followed, all three cars being of normal design and foreign
nspiration. Their designer was J.S. Critchley, formerly of Daimler. Shaft drive
ppeared in 1906, and late in 1909, some were fitted with Allen-Liversedge front-
wheel brakes, but Crossleys, though excellent machines, made little impression
until after 1910. The 4-litre 20hp which then made its bow was a well-constructed,
durable and very popular car. Designed by A.W. Reeves, it lived on in modified
form until 1925. Its finest hour came in World War 1, when, as the 20/25hp it
achieved fame as a staff car in the Royal Flying Corps, and as an ambulance and
ight truck. The model was extremely popular with the British Royal Family after
he war in its 25/30hp version. In its early years, however, it was rivalled by the
15hp. The efficiency of the latter's otherwise conventional engine, a side-valve
four like the rest, gave it a better performance than most cars in its class and
encouraged the makers to offer a special sporting variant, the Shelsley.

1934 CROSSLEY-BURNEY 2-litre saloon.
National Motor Museum

The Fifteen was discontinued after 1914, but a new Crossley arrived for 1921.
This 19.6hp was a rather more modern design, having a detachable cylinder head,
and it was cheaper and lighter on fuel than its 25/30hp companion. The performance
was about the same. It was also made in sporting form as the 20/70hp, but this
model was heavy, like the '19.6' itself, and the brakes were not good enough for
the 75mph that was available. Crossley did not make a serious attempt to invade
the middle-class market until 1923, when the 12/14hp, later called the Fourteen,
was introduced. Like its brothers, this was a simple side-valve four, in this case of
2.4 litres, but was more modern, with its unit construction of engine and gearbox
and central gear-change. The Fourteen was a very successful model, being flexible
and, thanks to its light weight, both roomy and economical. It survived until 1927.
By this time the two bigger Crossleys were giving way to a much more up-to-date
car; the company's first six and its first overhead-valve machine. This 18/50hp model
was a spacious, heavy 2.6-litre car with good brakes but somewhat lacking in power.
Its engine was enlarged to 3.2 litres and 20.9hp for 1928. At the same time a new
small Crossley of similar design, the 2-litre 15.7hp was introduced, to which a
sporting alternative reviving the Shelsley name was added in 1929. Lagonda's
16/80 model used this engine later. The 6-cylinder 15.7hp continued until 1934 and
the 20.9hp until 1937. Wilson pre-selector gearboxes were fitted from 1934.

1936 CROSSLEY Regis Ten saloon.
Autocar

In 1932, the company had introduced a light car, the Ten. This was an assembled
vehicle powered by an 1,100cc Coventry-Climax engine with overhead inlet valves.
It was too heavy (a drawback compounded by the pre-selector gearbox), it was very
low-geared and its brakes were mediocre. Another mistake was Crossley's attempt
to market the Burney rear-engined car with all-independent suspension. It was
given a 15.7hp Crossley engine and a Wilson box, but it was too unconventional
in appearance and handling. Very few were made. In 1935, Crossley introduced
its new Regis range of small cars with handsome bodies styled by C.F. Beauvais.
They consisted of the Ten and a new 1½-litre six of the same design also powered
by Coventry-Climax, both with a new lowered frame. Both cars, together with the
last 20.9s, disappeared after 1937.

Crossley assembled other people's cars as well as making their own, beginning
with the Willys-Overland Model 4 in 1920. The Gorton-produced Willys came to
include more and more British-made parts, such as a Morris Oxford engine. A less
likely diversion was an attempt in 1921 to make the Type 22 Bugatti in England,
but only a handful of these Crossley-Bugattis appeared. In 1932–33 the factory
made the AJS as well.   TRN

CROSVILLE (GB) 1906–1908
Crosville Motor Co Ltd, Chester

Only five Crosville cars were made, all different, but designed by the Frenchman
Georges Ville whose cars were built by Morane of Paris. Three of the Crosvilles
were, in fact, made in France, two 20hp 4-cylinder tourers and a coupé de ville,

1901 CROUAN 5hp voiturette. *The Veteran
Car Club of Great Britain*

1912 CROUCH(ii) Carette 8hp three-wheeler.
Herbert Art Gallery & Museum, Coventry

1910 CROWDY 20/30hp tourer. A.E. Crowdy
at the wheel. *Autocar*

1916 CROW-ELKHART 15/20hp two-seater.
Autocar

while only one car, a 50hp 4-cylinder with round Hotchkiss-type radiator, was completely English-built. The company later turned to coach operation, in which field they are still celebrated today.　　　　GNG

CROUAN (F) *1897–1904*
Sté des Automobiles Crouan, Paris 16e.

　The first Crouan had a 10hp 2-cylinder engine, and by 1900 two models were being made with several advanced features. The 16hp 2-cylinder car had automatic advance and retard of ignition, and a pneumatic transmission, while the 5hp single-cylinder voiturette had the automatic ignition but an ordinary gearbox. For 1902 Crouans had 5 forward speeds; the models this year were a 6hp twin and a 16hp four, both with front-mounted horizontally-opposed engines.　　　GNG

CROUCH (i) (US) *1897–1900*
Crouch Automobile Manufacturing & Transportation Co, New Brighton, Pa.

　The Crouch was a conventional-looking steam carriage with an 8hp V-twin engine and a boiler providing super-heated steam at a working pressure of 275psi.　GNG

CROUCH (ii) (GB) *1912–1928*
Crouch Cars Ltd, Coventry, Warwickshire

　The Crouch started life as the Carette, a 3-wheeled cyclecar, but from 1913 was offered as a 4-wheeler. Its snub-nosed appearance was due to the fact that the Coventry-Simplex engine, a water-cooled V-twin of 1-litre capacity, was centrally-housed. There were three forward speeds and chain drive. In 1922, a more normal car was substituted, with a front-mounted engine, still a V-twin, and shaft drive. The twins ran in the 1922 and 1923 200 Mile Race at Brooklands and in 1923 a model with a 4-cylinder Anzani power unit was added. It could be had in expensive but very fast Super Sports form, guaranteed to attain 90mph. At the end of its career, the Crouch had lost all resemblance to a cyclecar, only small 4-cylinder light cars being made.　　　TRN

CROW (CDN) *1915–1918*
Canadian Crow Motor Co Ltd, Mount Brydges, Ont.

　Though allied with the U.S. Crow-Elkhart Motor Car Co, this firm was mainly backed by local residents in an agricultural community. Most parts were imported from the American company but some were Canadian, and all bodies were built in the firm's factory. About 100 open cars were built before the concern went bankrupt.　　　GR

CROWDEN (GB) *1898–1901*
Charles T. Crowden, Leamington Spa

　Crowden's vehicles were mainly experimental and included a steam brake and a 10hp petrol-engined dog-cart made to test the relative merits of the two systems. Presumably he considered petrol to be the best, for his 1900 model had a single-cylinder 5hp horizontal engine and three speeds by belts and pulleys. In 1901 he made a petrol-engined fire engine using a steam pumper.　　　GNG

CROWDUS (US) *1901–1903*
Crowdus Automobile Co, Chicago, Ill.

　The Crowdus was a light electric runabout with a tubular frame. The steering tiller also operated speed changing and braking. The car had a range of 50 miles per charge.　　　GNG

CROWDY (GB) *1909–1912*
(1) Crowdy Ltd, Latimer Road, London W *1909–1911*
(2) Crowdy Ltd, Birmingham *1911–1912*

　In October 1909 the newly-formed Crowdy company (A.E. Crowdy had formerly managed the Lancashire business of Wolseleys) acquired the assets of Weigel Motors Ltd and a month later they showed three models at Olympia. Two of these were conventional cars of the Weigel type with 4-cylinder engines of 20/30 and 30/40hp, but the third used a 12/24hp Hewitt piston valve engine and sported a dashboard radiator. The following year three models were again available, a 19 and a 39hp 4-cylinder, and a 29hp 6-cylinder, all with the piston-valve engine, but with the radiator in the normal position. All models had pressure lubrication, leather clutch and worm or bevel drive. The company moved to Birmingham in August 1911, but this overstrained their resources and the newly acquired works were sold by auction in May 1912.　　　GNG

CROW-ELKHART (US) *1909–1924*
Crow-Elkhart Motor Car Co, Elkhart, Ind.

　The Crow-Elkhart was a conventional car made originally as a 30hp 4-cylinder tourer, although by 1911 no less than ten different body styles were available, including closed models. Production reached its peak in about 1915, when prices were at their lowest, the 25hp tourer or coupé costing only $725. On the whole Crow-Elkhart styling was angular and uninteresting, but the 1918 Clover-Leaf Tourer and Roadster featured V-radiators and dual-tone colour schemes. In 1919 6-cylinder cars were available as well as the fours, but had been dropped y 1922 when the company was standardizing on one 4-cylinder model with a Herschell-Spillman engine. Also in 1919 they built the prototype of a car intended for export to Great Britain, to be called the Morriss-London. This was later made by a new company, Century Motors Co, but few Morris-Londons were actually built.   GNG

CROWN (i) (GB) *1903*
Crown Car Co Ltd, London W.C.

This company made, or possibly only sold, a very light 3-wheeler with a 5hp engine mounted over the front wheel. The whole machine weighed only 224lb and was sold at the modest price of £80.   GNG

CROWN (ii) (US) *1905*
Detroit Auto Vehicle Co, Detroit, Mich.

The Crown was a side-entrance five-seater with wheelbase of 8ft 2in. The engine was a 4-stroke, 4-cylinder one of 3.4 litres, with overhead valves. The final drive was through a friction transmission and shaft.   GMN

CROWN (iii) (US) *1907–1910*
1) Crown Motor Vehicle Co, Amesbury, Mass. *1907–1909*
2) Graves & Congdon Co, Amesbury, Mass. *1909–1910*

The Crown two-seater high-wheeler had tiller-steering and air-cooled 2-cylinder 12hp engine, mounted cross-wise under the seat. The chassis had a 'reach' frame and platform springs. Double chains drove the rear wheels.   GMN

CROWN (iv) (US) *1913–1914*
1) Crown Motor Car Co, Louisville, Ky. *1913–1914*
2) Hercules Motor Car Co, New Albany, Ind. *1914*

The Crown cyclecar was a two-seater, priced at $385. It had a 4-cylinder engine of 1.7 litres and a friction transmission. Its wheelbase was 7ft 6in. This make was succeeded by the Hercules (iii).   GMN

CROWN ENSIGN, CROWN-MAGNETIC see BRITISH ENSIGN

CROWTHER; CROWTHER-DURYEA (US) *1915–1916*
Crowther Motors Co, Rochester, N.Y.

This was a light car, powered by a 4-cylinder engine of 3.1 litres. The two-seater was on a wheelbase of 9ft 4in and sold for $450.   GMN

CROXTED (GB) *1904–1905*
Croxted Motor & Engineering Co Ltd, Herne Hill, London S.E.

The original Croxted had an 8hp 2-cylinder engine and a De Dion-type bonnet. In 1905 two 4-cylinder models were listed, a 14 and a 20hp, both with conventional honeycomb radiators.   GNG

CROXTON (US) *1911–1914*
1) Croxton Motor Co, Massilon, Ohio *1911*
2) Croxton Motor Co, Cleveland, Ohio *1911–1912*
3) Croxton Motors Co, Washington, Pa. *1912–1914*

In 1911 F.M. Keeton left the Croxton-Keeton company to return to Detroit where he took up again manufacture of the Keeton car. The conventional Croxton-Keeton with 40hp 4-cylinder Rutenber engine was continued, known in 1912 as the 'German 45' and in that year it was joined by cars of Renault origin. These had dashboard radiators, and were known as the French Six, and 'French 30', with 6- and 4-cylinder engines respectively. In 1911 H.A. Croxton merged his company with Royal Tourist of Cleveland, but in less than a year this merger was dissolved and a new company was formed to make the cars at Washington, Pa. The same designs were made in small numbers, and a new six was added. In 1914 the company foundered in an attempt to launch a $475 cyclecar.   GMN

CROXTON-KEETON (US) *1909–1910*
Croxton-Keeton Motor Co, Massilon, Ohio

H.A. Croxton who had made the Jewel (i) joined forces with F.M. Keeton of Detroit to make the Croxton-Keeton car. Two models were listed, the 'German type' which was based on the Rutenber-engined Jewel 40, and the 'French type' which sported a dashboard radiator and all seating between the axles. In 1910 the two partners separated, and made cars under their own names.   GNG

C.R.S. (GB) *1960–1961*
C.R.S. Auto Engineers Ltd, Footscray, Kent

A box-section chassis for E93A Ford parts was offered by this firm. Bodies were mostly the E.B. Debonair, the same as those used by L.M.B.   DF

CRUISER (US) *1917–1919*
Cruiser Motor Car Co, Madison, Wisc.

This was an attempt to sell a car and camping outfit as a single package, the roadster model carrying such gear as bed, chairs, ice-box, tent, stove and cooking

1904 CROXTED 8/10hp two-seater. *G.N. Georgano Collection*

1910 CROXTON-KEETON 40hp tourer. *Keith Marvin Collection*

1922 CUBITT 16/20hp tourer. *Autocar*

1901 CUDELL 3.5PS voiturette, built for
the Sultan of Turkey. *G.N. Georgano
Collection*

1905 CUDELL Phönix 35/40PS limousine.
Neubauer Collection

utensils. There was also portable plumbing in the form of a water closet and ho
and cold running water in four large storage compartments, two on each runnin
board. Prices were from $1,175. Several of the Cruisers were used experimentall
by the U.S. Army.   KN

CRYPTO (GB) *1904–1905*
Crypto Engineering Co, London E.C.
    This company made a very small number of assembled cars using a 2-cylinde
Tony Huber engine in a Dupressoir chassis.   GN

CRYSTAL CITY (US) *1914*
Troll & Manning, Corning, N.Y.
    The Crystal City, named after the famous American glass centre, was a sma
2-seater car with 4-cylinder water-cooled engine, and 3-speed selective transmissio
                                                                                                                        GM

C.S.C. (GB) *1955*
Gainsborough Engineering Co Ltd, Middleton, Lancs.
    This was a lightweight 2-seater with Austin A30 mechanical parts and a Rochdal
fibreglass body.   D

CSONKA (H) *1906–1912*
Janos Csonka Automobile Works, Budapest
    Originally this company built tricycles and quadricycles for the Hungarian Pos
Office, but in 1906 production began of cars with single-cylinder 4hp engines and
later, 4-cylinder engines of 8/9hp, 12/14hp, 16hp, 20/25hp and 24/28hp, with 3-spee
gearboxes and shaft drive. A few 40hp cars were also made. Stephen Röck drov
one of the 16hp cars in the 1909 Prince Henry Trial, and came through withou
a fault. More than 150 Csonka cars were built.   GL

CUB (US) *1914*
Szekely Cyclecar Co, Richmond, Va.
    The Cub was a cyclecar with a tubular frame and a 2-cylinder De Luxe V-typ
air-cooled engine. The drive to the rear axle was by belt. The weight of the vehic
was 550lb and its price $350.   GM

CUBITT (GB) *1920–1925*
Cubitt's Engineering Co Ltd, Aylesbury, Bucks.
    The manufacturers of the Cubitt were among several firms (Angus-Sanderso
Bean, Ruston-Hornsby, etc.) to adopt certain mass-production techniques in orde
to compete with the post-1918 flood of American imports, but were unfashionabl
in that they admitted that theirs was an American-type car. Their single mode
the 16/20hp, was a simple, cheap, rugged machine. Its 4-cylinder, 2.8-litre engin
used coil ignition and was made in unit with the 4-speed gearbox, which had a centra
gear lever. Final drive was by overhead worm. Its body cost only £20 to make
It was a high, heavy car, and it rolled. Unfortunately manufacturing difficultie
common to the whole industry beset the Cubitt and it never achieved the 5,00
units a year planned or low price. In its last years, J.S. Napier and S.F. Edg
were both directors and late in 1924 Cubitts were making A.C. engines unde
licence. The Cubitt was lowered and its engine was made smoother and give
lighter reciprocating parts, but it died.   TR

CUBSTER (US) *1949*
Osborn Wheel Co, Doylestown, Pa.
    This was a home assembled 6.6hp chain-driven car, also available as a chassi
assembly only.   B

CUDELL (D) *1898–1908*
(1) Cudell & Co, Motoren- und Motorfahrzeug-Fabrik, Aachen *1898–1900*
(2) AG für Motor- und Fahrzeugbau vorm. Cudell, Aachen *1900–1902*
(3) Cudell Motor-Compagnie mbH, Aachen *1902–1905*
(4) Cudell Motoren-Gesellschaft mbH, Berlin N 65 *1905–1908*
    Max Cudell, the founder of the Cudell works, is to be counted among the
pioneers of car manufacture in Germany. He obtained licences for De Dion engine
and vehicles and in addition to engines in 1897 started to build 3-wheelers o
De Dion principles, which were followed in 1899 by the 3.5PS voiturette, als
under De Dion licence. Cudell followed De Dion principles until 1904 when h
started to build cars to his own designs. In 1905 the Phönix, designed by Slevog
appeared at the Berlin Motor Show and was a technical sensation. However, thi
advanced model (with a 5-bearing crankshaft and overhead valves) was not pro
duced on a great scale as the firm left the scene a few months after its debut. Th
Berlin branch of Cudell built cars in small numbers until 1908.   HO

CULVER (i) (US) *1905*
Practical Automobile Co, Aurora, Ill.
    This typical high-wheeler had wheel-steering, with a tilting column for ease o
entry. The 2-seater had an under-the-seat, 2-cylinder air-cooled engine. A planetar
transmission and double chains completed the power system.   GM

CULVER (ii) (US) 1916

Culver Mfg Co, Culver City, Calif.

This vehicle was a youth's car selling for $225. The single-cylinder engine was built by Culver and was air-cooled. The wheelbase was 5ft 6in.　　GMN

CUMBRIA (GB) 1913–1914

Cumbria Motors Ltd, Cockermouth, Cumberland

The only known car maker in Cumberland, Cumbria Motors were also among the relatively few to make a single-seater cyclecar. This used a 6/8hp air-cooled twin J.A.P engine and belt drive, while its companion 2-seater used an 8/10hp engine, also by J.A.P., and chain drive. In 1914 a 4-cylinder shaft drive light car was introduced.　　GNG

CUMMIKAR *see* RONTEIX

CUNDALL (GB) 1902

Cundall & Sons Ltd, Shipley, Yorks.

This firm were makers of stationary oil engines, who announced in January 1902 that they would make a car using one of their 2-cylinder horizontal engines. It developed 7bhp at 850rpm, but very few were made.　　GNG

CUNNINGHAM (i) (US) 1907–1936

James Cunningham Son & Co Inc, Rochester, N.Y.

The first Cunningham cars were made in 1907 by an old-established manufacturer of carriages. At first they were assembled vehicles. Before World War 1, Cunninghams were powered by 4- and 6-cylinder engines made by Buffalo and Continental, and by a 40hp four of Cunningham's own manufacture. The first completely Cunningham-built car appeared in 1910. Until 1915 carriages continued to be made alongside the cars, but from that year cars only were offered, in a single model. This V-8 Cunningham was one of the handsomest cars to come out of America in its period and in 1916, its first production year, it was of extraordinarily modern lines. Mechanically, it was generally conventional, although the V-8 engine was one of the early examples of its type. This 6-litre power unit gave around 100bhp at 2400rpm. The Cunningham was a finely-made luxury car, built a few at a time, and selling at up to $9,000 in open touring form. Owners included Marshal Field (the store tycoon), William Randolph Hearst, Mary Pickford and Harold Lloyd. It was still being offered as late as 1933. From then until 1935 only bodies were made for other manufacturers' cars) and also ambulances and hearses on the original chassis. Like Brewster, they offered a town car version of the Ford V-8.　　TRN

CUNNINGHAM (ii) (US) 1951–1955

B.S. Cunningham Co, West Palm Beach, Fla.

The racing and sports car driver Briggs Cunningham set out to produce an American sports car that would surpass European machines of the same class, but though his cars scored some successes in American events he was never able to achieve his goal of victory at Le Mans. Six different models were made beginning with the C-1, containing stock Cadillac and Chrysler engines in a tubular chassis. The C-2 was nearly identical in appearance but was powered by a 180hp Chrysler unit. It came in 18th at Le Mans and 1st at Watkins Glen in 1951. The C-3 was a Vignale-bodied coupé of Michelotti design with an automatic transmission and a 220hp Chrysler engine. The C-4 was available as a coupé or roadster with 200hp. C-5s with a 310hp engine and a SIATA gearbox finished 3rd, 5th and 10th at the 1954 Le Mans. The final model, the C-6, was driven by a 16-valve, 4-cylinder Offenhauser engine of 260hp but lacked the speed of previous machines.

The cars sold in small numbers and were costly to produce but they represented a valiant attempt in the field of sophisticated motor-car design.　　BE

CURTIS (US) 1921

Curtis Motor Car Co, Little Rock, Ark.

The Curtis (sometimes listed as Curtiss) was a minor assembled car which used a 4-cylinder Herschell-Spillman engine.　　KM

CURTISS (US) 1920–1921

Curtiss Motor Car Co, Hammondsport, N.Y.

The Curtiss was a custom-built car designed and built by Miles Harold Carpenter on a Phianna chassis and utilizing the Curtiss OX-5 aircraft engine. These were built on special order for Glenn Hammond Curtiss (born in Hammondsport) and his friends. They were long-wheelbase high-performance cars. Charlie Kirkham, the original designer and chief engineer of the Curtiss Aeroplane Co, was brought in to modify these engines for automobile use; he was already producing Kirkham proprietary engines for other assembled-car manufacturers and had also made the engines for the famous Curtiss motorcycles (and for Marvel motorcycles, also built in 1912 at Hammondsport). The Curtiss company did not survive the 1921 slump.　　MJWW

CUSTOKA (A) 1971 to date

Custoka Kunststoffkarosserien, Leoben

The Custoka is a Volkswagen-based GT coupé with fibreglass coachwork and

1912 CUNNINGHAM(i) 40hp limousine. *Keith Marvin Collection*

1928 CUNNINGHAM(i) 6-litre V-8 sedan. *Harrah's Automobile Collection*

1951 CUNNINGHAM(ii) 5.3-litre sports car. *B.S. Cunningham Co*

1972 CUSTOKA Hurrycane coupé. *Custoka Kunstoffkarosserien*

1910 CUTTING Model A-40 roadster.
William S. Jackson

1904 CYKLONETTE 3-wheeler. *Neubauer*
Collection

1926 CYKLON (SCHEBERA) 5/18P
two-seater. *G.L. Hartner*

a recessed 4-headlamp layout. It uses either a 1,584cc VW or 1,679cc VW-Porsche 4-cylinder engine. The firm also makes a beach buggy, the Amigo.　　M

CUTTING (US) *1909–1912*
(1) Clarke-Carter Automobile Co, Jackson, Mich. *1909–1911*
(2) Cutting Motor Car Co, Jackson, Mich. *1911–1912*
　　The Cutting was a powerful, good-quality car using engines by Milwaukee, Model or Wisconsin of 30, 40, 50 and 60hp. Cuttings were entered at Indianapolis in 1911 and 1912, their best performance being 10th place in the 1911 event. Prices were modest, ranging from $1,200 to $1,500. The company failed in 1912 because of insufficient capital.　　GM

C.V.I. (or C.VI) (US) *1907–1908*
C.V.I. Motor Car Co, Jackson, Mich.
　　The C.V.I. was built as either a touring car or a roadster with a common chassis. A 4-cylinder 4.2-litre engine was used in this car. With 3-speed selective transmission and shaft drive, these cars sold for $4,000.　　GM

C.V.R. (F) *1906–1907*
Automobiles C.V.R., Boulogne-sur-Seine, Seine
　　Previously Automobiles Couverchel at Neuilly, the C.V.R. company made a range of six models, ranging from 12/16hp to 40/50hp, the latter a 6-cylinder. Several models used Mutel engines. 4-speed gearboxes were standardized.　　GN

C.W.S. (PL) *c.1922–1929*
Centrale Warsztaty Samochodowe, Warsaw
　　Made under Berliet licence, the C.W.S. was the first car built completely in Poland. The C.W.S. T-1 had a 3-litre, 4-cylinder, 4-stroke engine of 61hp at 3,000rpm and a gearbox that could be locked. It was fitted with 4-wheel brakes with extra large drums, and vertical coil suspension. Simple construction assisted repair. An unusual aspect of its design was that all screws used in construction were of the same size, namely M-10. The range eventually included touring cars, sedans, sports cars, ambulances and commercials. In 1929 two prototypes were tested: the 4-cylinder, 1.5-litre T-4 and the 8-cylinder, 3-litre T-8. As Fiat and other cars interests started to enter Poland, the manufacture of the C.W.S. was terminated.　　E

CYCLAUTO (F) *1919–1923*
Sté Française du Cyclauto, Suresnes, Seine
　　This was a 3-wheeler which began with a 496cc 2-cylinder engine, replaced by a 4-cylinder 904cc Ruby or C.I.M.E., an unusual refinement in a 3-wheeler, as was the bevel drive. The 2-cylinder model used belt drive.　　GN

CYCLEPLANE (US) *1914–1915*
The Cycleplane Co, Westerly, R.I.
　　A bridge type frame and body support (used much later by Maserati) was one feature of this cyclecar. Its appearance was distinguished by the use of a one-piece horizontal mudguard running the full length of the bonnet and body (except at the single entrance). Three models used single- and 2-cylinder Deluxe engines.　　GM

CYCLOMOBILE (US) *1920*
Cyclomobile Mfg Co, Toledo, Ohio
　　This lightweight automobile with a 7ft 6in wheelbase was available either as a two-seater roadster or a light-delivery truck. It was powered by a 2-cylinder air-cooled V-type Spacke engine of 1,120cc. It used friction drive, power being transmitted to the rear axle by a heavy chain.　　K

CYCLOPE see AUGÉ

CYKLON (D) *1902–1929*
(1) Cyklon Maschinenfabrik GmbH, Berlin O *1902–1922*
(2) Cyklon Automobilwerke AG, Berlin-Charlottenburg; Mylau *1922–1929*
　　Cyklon motor cycles were characterized by engines mounted above the front wheel which was chain driven. The principle of one driven front wheel was also employed in a 3-wheeled vehicle, which first appeared at the Leipzig Motor Show in 1902 and, after 1904, was known as the Cyklonette. It developed from a single-cylinder 3.5PS 450cc 2-seater into a 2-cylinder 10PS 1,290cc 4-seater and was very popular as a private car as well as a van. It was built until 1922 to the same basic design, although with minor improvements. After World War 1 Cyklon became a part of the Schapiro concern which controlled several German car factories. From 1923 a 5/20PS 1.3-litre type was produced exclusively for Schebera. The Cyklon 9/40PS 6-cylinder was identical with the 9/40PS Dixi. The 7/40PS 1.8-litre type D was built under Zedel licence.　　HO

CYRANO (F) *1899–1900*
　　The first Cyrano voiturette used a single-cylinder horizontal engine, replaced in 1900 by a 2-cylinder unit, with belt and pulley transmission. Final drive was by spur gearing to the rear axle. Two- or four-seater *vis-à-vis* bodies were fitted.　　GN

D.A.C. (US) *1922–1923*

Detroit Air-Cooled Car Co, Detroit, Mich.

This air-cooled V-6 was first shown to the public in late 1922, but only a few touring cars were actually produced. KM

D.A.F. (NL) *1958 to date*

Van Doornes Automobielfabriek NV, Eindhoven

The first serious entry by the Netherlands into private-car manufacture since the demise of the Spyker in 1925, the D.A.F. was the product of a firm which had been making commercial trailers since 1928 and built a military 4 × 4 in 1940. They began to make commercial vehicles in 1950, this venture reaching proportions that warranted the opening of a German assembly plant in 1961. The D.A.F. car was announced early in 1958, and went into production a year later. It incorporated the ingenious and jerk-free Variomatic transmission, a fully automatic system using a centrifugal clutch and V-velt drive with a limited-slip differential. All four wheels were independently suspended, and power came from a front-mounted 600cc ohv air-cooled 22bhp flat-twin.

With only a simple forward-and-reverse lever the D.A.F. is one of the easiest cars to drive, and its appeal was widened in 1962 with the introduction of the 750 and the Daffodil with 30bhp and 750cc, in which forms maximum speed was boosted from 52 to 64mph. By 1962 60,000 had been sold, and two years later production was running at 20,000 units a year. During 1965 the transmission was adapted to a light military 4 × 4 and to a Formula 3 racing car. D.A.F. have done well in rallies, their successes including a team prize in the 1966 Marathon de la Route. The basic model was still in production in 1967, but was joined by the Type 44, a roomier and more powerful design also with a flat-twin engine and Variomatic drive. Styling was by Michelotti, and with 40bhp available from 844cc, the bigger D.A.F. was capable of over 75mph. The 55 with 1,100cc 4-cylinder Renault engine was introduced in 1968, a sports coupé version following a year later. Group 6 variations on the latter were offered in 1970, the 1,440cc type with twin dual-choke carburettors giving 115mph on 140bhp. The fastest D.A.F. listed in 1972 was the 63bhp Marathon 55 coupé.

For 1973 the 55 was replaced by the 66, still with Renault engine, but with a new centrifugal clutch incorporated in the Variomatic transmission, and a De Dion back axle. MCS

DAGMAR (US) *1922–1927*

Crawford Automobile Co, M.P. Möller Car Co, Hagerstown, Md.

The Dagmar, one of the most distinctive sporting cars in the United States, first appeared in 1922 in both open and closed models which featured straight-line fenders and all-brass trim instead of the then-conventional nickel. The Dagmars were actually the basic Crawford car with sport treatment and were named for the daughter of M.P. Möller, a Hagerstown pipe organ manufacturer who had many cars before acquired the Crawford Automobile Co. Powered by a Continental 6-cylinder engine, additional body styles were added in 1923 and a year later, conventional fenders were available as an alternative to the straight type. By 1925, a smaller Dagmar was placed on the market, also powered by Continental, of smaller specifications.

The final year for general production was 1926 and the last car built, an enormous 7-passenger sedan, was made in 1927 for Mr Möller when he returned for a visit to his native Denmark with his family. Although only a few hundred Dagmars were built over a six-year period, the Möller interests also produced the Crawford and Standish cars as well as the Paramount, Luxor, Astor, Five Boro, 20th Century and Möller taxicabs. KM

DAGSA (E) *1951–1952*

Defensa Antigas SA, Segovia

The Dagsa light car was built by a firm who specialized in making military equipment. It had a 500cc 4-cylinder engine, and was available as a four-seater saloon or as a van. About 50 were made. JRV

DAIHATSU (J) *1954 to date*

Daihatsu Kogyo Co Ltd, Ikeda City, Osaka Pref.

The parent firm of Daihatsu was founded in 1907 to make internal combustion engines, and the first complete vehicles were 3-wheeled vans which appeared in 1930. In the early 1950s came the first passenger car, the Bee 3-wheeler which had

1966 D.A.F. Daffodil 746cc saloon. *Van Doornes Automobielfabriek*

1973 D.A.F. 66 1.1-litre saloon. *Van Doornes Automobielfabriek*

1924 DAGMAR 6-70 34hp petite sedan. *Keith Marvin Collection*

1966 DAIHATSU Compagno Berlina 800 saloon.
Daihatsu

1973 DAIHATSU Fellow Max GHL 356cc coupé.
Daihatsu

1893 DAIMLER(i) 4PS two-seater. *The Veteran Car Club of Great Britain*

1897 DAIMLER(i) 4/9PS victoria.
Daimler-Benz AG

a rear-mounted 540cc ohv air-cooled 2-cylinder engine, and a four-door saloon body. Many were used as taxis.

In 1963 the Compagno line of 4-wheelers appeared, including saloon sports cars and station wagons with 797cc 4-cylinder engines. The 1966 catalogue listed a 958cc version available with front disc brakes and fuel injection; output was 65bhp. That year the Daihatsu became the first Japanese make to be marketed in Britain. In 1967 there was, briefly, a Group 6 racing prototype powered by a 1,261cc dohc fuel-injected 4-cylinder engine, as well as a return to the minicar field with the Fellow, an all-independently sprung four-seater saloon of conventional specification, apart from the water cooling for its 2-stroke twin-cylinder 356cc engine. Tuned versions were claiming as much as 40bhp by 1972. However, in 1968 Toyota absorbed Daihatsu and their subsequent 4-cylinder models followed Toyota practice. The Compagno power unit was listed as late as 1970, but subsequent Consortes were little more than thinly disguised Toyota Corollas. Saloon and station wagon versions of the Fellow were the principal 1973 offerings, the saloon in 33 and 40bhp forms.

B

DAIMLER (i) (D) *1886–1902*

(1) Gottlieb Daimler, Bad Cannstatt *1886–1890*
(2) Daimler Motoren-Gesellschaft, Bad Cannstatt *1890–1902*

Gottlieb Daimler was employed until 1882 as technical director at the Gasmotorenfabrik Deutz, where he worked on internal combustion engines. Wilhelm Maybach was also engaged by Daimler at the Deutz works. Daimler held shares in the Deutz company and the income from these gave him some financial support when he left Deutz. He moved to Bad Cannstatt near Stuttgart where he started a small workshop for research and experimentation and brought in Maybach to work for him. Daimler's plans were to develop a high-speed internal combustion engine which could be fitted into road and rail vehicles as well as into boats. In 1883 high-speed prototype petrol engines with hot-tube ignition were built. This was the first time that petrol was used for an internal combustion engine. The next step was the construction in 1885 of the world's first motor cycle, which was also the last one ever built by Daimler or later companies bearing his name. Next, trials were made with a motorized boat and sleigh before Daimler and Maybach fitted an engine to an ordinary horse-drawn carriage, modified for the purpose. The car was ready in 1886 and made its first trial runs around Cannstatt. The engine was an air-cooled vertical single-cylinder or 1.5hp with tube ignition. Further trials with Daimler engines in boats, trams and fire-engines followed.

For some time Maybach had tried to convince Daimler that they should build a vehicle designed from the start as a motor car. Daimler opposed the idea for a long time but he at last agreed to build a prototype. It was a two-seated 4-wheeled vehicle with a rear-mounted V-twin engine. The chassis was a tubular steel frame and the steel wire wheels gave the car its name of 'Stahlradwagen'. The car was sent to the Paris World Fair of 1889. Panhard-Levassor and Peugeot took a great interest in this car, and both firms started car production with Daimler engines and laid the foundation of the French motor car industry.

In 1890 the Daimler Motoren-Gesellschaft was founded but soon differences arose between Daimler and his new partners. This led to Daimler's separation from the company in 1893. He and Maybach started an experimental workshop in the Hotel Hermann; this can be regarded as an independent Daimler enterprise which also built cars. Daimler successfully continued his efforts to develop a high speed engine for motor cars. The very important invention of the atomizing carburettor was also made in the Hotel Hermann. In 1895 an agreement was reached and Daimler and Maybach returned to the Daimler company. The cars produced were of the belt-driven 2-cylinder type, the first Daimler car manufactured in any numbers. It was succeeded in 1897 by the Phönix, the first type with front engine. 1899 saw the first 4-cylinder engines. A car with a 28hp engine was entered by its owner, Emile Jellinek for the Nice Week, 1899; it was called the Mercedes after his eldest daughter.

Jellinek was a successful business man and Consul-General of the Austro-Hungarian empire in Nice, taking a great interest in motoring and especially Daimler cars. He acted as an unofficial agent selling cars to his wealthy friends. But he was not satisfied with their performance and suggested that the Daimler company should build a high-performance car of an entirely new conception. The result was the 35hp 4-cylinder model which became known as the first Mercedes car. It was designed by Maybach, incorporating some of the principles of the P.D. Car designed by Paul Daimler, a son of Gottlieb Daimler. It made a very successful debut at the Nice Week, 1901. Jellinek had a seat on the Daimlers' board of directors since 1900. He now obtained the sole agency for France, Belgium, Austro-Hungary and the United States of America. He sold the cars under the name of Mercedes – which formerly had been only his pseudonym – to counter possible legal proceedings by Panhard-Levassor, who owned licences for Daimler cars under an earlier agreement with Gottlieb Daimler himself. As a result of the great successes of Mercedes cars Daimlers decided in 1902 to accept this as new brand name for all subsequent private cars. Commercial vehicles continued to be marketed under the name Daimler, and this name was also applied to the cars built in 1901 by the breakaway M.M.B. company in Berlin.

HON

DAIMLER (ii) (GB) 1896 to date

Daimler Motor Syndicate Ltd, Coventry, Warwickshire 1896–1904
Daimler Motor Co (1904) Ltd, Coventry, Warwickshire 1904–1910
Daimler Co Ltd, Coventry, Warwickshire 1910 to date

The Daimler Motor Syndicate was formed in England in 1893 by F.R. Simms to exploit Gottlieb Daimler's motor patents, but it was not until 1896 that the Coventry factory became active as part of H.J. Lawson's empire. Though Daimler himself was a director until 1898, the English and German concerns pursued their separate ways. In the first two years cars were mostly imported, and early English Daimlers were 2-cylinder machines, largely on Panhard lines, with automatic inlet valves, tiller steering, tube ignition, 4-speed and reverse gearboxes, chain drive and solid tyres. Prices ranged from £368 for a phaeton up to £418 for a 'private omnibus'. 1899 saw the first 4-cylinder car, a 3-litre machine rated at 12hp; it had wheel steering, and the Hon. John Scott-Montagu became the first British driver to compete in a continental race on a vehicle of British construction when he drove one in the Paris-Ostend that year. King Edward VII, while still Prince of Wales, took delivery of his first Daimler in 1900, thus forging a connection between the company and the reigning house which lasted until the 1950s. Design policy was very uncertain for the next few seasons, but in 1902 there was a chain-driven 1.8-litre twin, as well as fours of 3.4 and 4½ litres' capacity with tubular, Panhard-like radiators. These cars retained stand-by tube ignition. The fluted radiator and 3-piece bonnet, both to become Daimler hallmarks, were introduced in 1904, the year in which the company went over to large and powerful chain-driven fours with mechanically-operated side valves and coil ignition, which ran in such events as the Herkomer Trophy Trials. The 9¼ litre '35' was typical, but there were even bigger versions of over 10½ litres, and Daimler advertising made much of sprint wins on the Continent and in the U.S.A. as well as at home. Some of these cars were made under licence in Italy as the De Luca.

1909 saw a complete volte face with the adoption of Charles Yale Knight's double-sleeve valve engine and underslung worm drive, and the Daimlers of the next 23 years were smooth, and silent, but not capable of high performance. They also changed little in appearance, since Daimler, unlike most luxury-car makers, built their own bodywork. Poppet valves were dropped altogether after 1909. By 1914 the company's range extended from a 4-cylinder 3.3-litre '20' with rear-axle gearbox at £430 for a chassis up to a very large 7.4-litre 6-cylinder '45'. Electric lighting and starting were standard on the bigger cars. The purchase of Daimler by B.S.A. in 1910 made no difference to the cars, though the B.S.A. itself became merely a cheap Daimler.

After World War 1, 4-cylinder cars were dropped (apart from a short-lived '20' in 1922) and the same solid conservative machines were offered in a range of fearsome complexity. There was a 1½-litre six in 1923 and front wheel brakes arrived with the 35hp model in 1924, becoming universal late in 1925, when light steel sleeves were adopted and outputs went up. The immense and stately 12-cylinder 7.1-litre Double Six was introduced in 1927; 12-cylinder Daimlers were used by the Royal Family and persisted in a variety of capacities from 3.7 litres until 1938, the last ones using poppet valves. In 1927 the company offered 23 separate models (exclusive of body styles), using five engines from 1.9 litres to 7.1 litres, and twelve wheelbase lengths from the 9ft 9in of the owner-driver '16-55' up to the 13ft 7in of the Royal model of the Double-Six, which cost £1,950 for a chassis alone. In 1930 Daimler pioneered the fluid-flywheel transmission with column selector which was used on all models from 1932 to 1956. The Lanchester company was acquired in 1931 and the make downgraded into another species of inexpensive Daimler. In 1933 the influence of Laurence Pomeroy Sr was reflected in a 1.8-litre 6-cylinder '15' with overhead valves for the owner-driver at £450, and this was followed by a series of ohv sixes and straight-8s, some of them with fixed cylinder heads. Independent front suspension appeared on 1938 versions of the '15'. In 1939 there were three sixes and two eights, the top of the range being the 4½-litre 32hp limousine.

After World War 2 the 2½-litre DB.18 (descended from the '15') was revived and there were two limousine models with hypoid final drive, a 4-litre six and a 5½-litre eight. A certain lack of direction punctuated the early 1950s, which saw the short-stroke 2½-litre 'Conquest' saloon and its 100mph variant, the 'Conquest Century', and also a sports two-seater. The company was reorganized in 1956, in which year automatic transmission was available as an alternative to the fluid-flywheel gearbox. The 3.8-litre 6-cylinder 'Majestic' of 1958 had automatic transmission and disc brakes as standard equipment and a year later came the Turner-designed V-8 2½-litre SP.250 sports car, a 120mph machine which broke away from traditional Daimler appearance and sold for £1,395. A synchromesh gearbox was standard. A pair of 4.6-litre V-8s with traditional bodywork joined it in 1960, in which year the company was bought by Jaguar. A 2½-litre saloon using the small V-8 Daimler engine in a Mk II Jaguar body was introduced for 1963, and gradually Jaguar influences took over. The 8-cylinder Majestic Major saloon was replaced in 1967 by the Sovereign, a Jaguar 420 down to its dohc 6-cylinder engine, and a year later there was a new Jaguar-based limousine using the 4,235cc power unit and a Vanden Plas body. The last V-8 Daimlers were made in 1969, and inevitably the 1973 season brought a Daimler version of the 5.3-litre V-12 XJ6 Jaguar, designated the Double Six; a long-chassis version had trim by Vanden Plas   MCS

1897 DAIMLER(ii) Crawford 4hp wagonette.
The Veteran Car Club of Great Britain

1904 DAIMLER(ii) 28hp landaulette.
Daimler Co Ltd

1930 DAIMLER(ii) 25/85hp sports saloon.
Coachwork by Weymann. *National Motor Museum*

1973 DAIMLER(ii) 4.2-litre limousine.
Daimler Co Ltd

1906 DALHOUSIE tourer. *Anderson-Grice Co*

1908 DANA 6hp cyclecar. *Thorkil Ry Andersen*

1920 DANIELS 39.2hp Submarine Speedster. *National Motor Museum*

DAINO (I) *1923–1924*
Fabbrica Automobili Daino, Cremona

Like more than one other Italian factory, Daino built a 4-cylinder light car c 65 × 110mm (1,460cc). Despite pushrod-operated ohv, its output was a mode 16bhp.   MC

DAINOTTI (I) *1922–1923*
Fabbrica Automobili Dainotti, Pavia

The Dainotti was an oddity, being powered by 8-cylinder engines of mode capacity. Standard versions were 1½-litre 60 × 66mm, 2-stroke in-line affairs retai ing at 20,000 lire, but there was also a 2-litre 4-stroke sports model credited wit 75mph.   MC

DALAT (VN) *1971 to date*
South Vietnam's first private car, made in Saigon, is an open jeep-type vehic based on Citroën's 602cc Mehari and using Citroën mechanical elements. Bodywor is of metal, and production had reached 13 units a day by the end of 1971.   MC

DALGLEISH-GULLANE (GB) *1907–1908*
Haddington Motor Engineering Co, Haddington, East Lothian

This light car was powered by an 8hp single-cylinder De Dion engine with shaf drive. About ten two-seaters were made, of which one survives.   GN

DALHOUSIE (GB) *1906–1910*
The Anderson-Grice Co Ltd, Carnoustie, Forfar

Makers of foundry equipment since 1860 and cranes since 1885, this compan (which is still very active) entered the motor industry in 1906. One or two two seater cars were constructed utilizing a 4-cylinder engine designed and built in th works (the cylinders were each separately cast) but in 1907–8 more serious produc tion of a four-seater was undertaken. The cars, named after the Marquess of Dal housie, a past Viceroy of India, were designed by A.G. Grice and John William and were distinguished by stylish bodies with sharply raked radiators – this lin being perpetuated in the angle of the bonnet louvres and the dash. Economic pres sures dictated the closure of the department in 1910 and remaining cars and spare were purchased by James Law, a motor engineer of Arbroath, who may hav assembled a few more.   MJW

DALILA (F) *1922–1923*
Bouquet et Cie, France

The most interesting feature of the Dalila light car was its suspension which was by quarter elliptic springs extended forward and backward from the frame and interconnected. The engine was a 6.9 or 7.5hp 4-cylinder Ruby and the ca had shaft drive.   GNC

DALLISON (GB) *1913*
Dallison Gearing and Motor Co Ltd, Birmingham

The Dallison was a cyclecar using a Precision air- or water-cooled engine and shaft drive.   GNC

DALTON (US) *1911–1912*
Dalton Motor Car Co, Flint, Mich.

Hubert K. Dalton, former manager of the Whiting Motor Car Co, planned to build a car basically similar to the Whiting under his own name. It had a 20hp 4-cylinder engine and an 8ft wheelbase. Only three were made.   GNC

DANA (DK) *c.1908–1914*
Hakon Olsen, Maskinfabriken Dana, Copenhagen

Hakon Olsen used 6hp Peugeot air-cooled engines for his 260kg cyclecars. The car had 2 forward speeds and reverse. The price in 1913 was 2,400 kroner. It had some success when cars of more than 450kg were forbidden on Danish side roads but the abolition of this law forced the Dana out of the market.   TRA

D & V (US) *1903*
DeVigne & Van Sickle, Paterson, N.J.

The only known model of this car was a tonneau of 'simplified French type'. The engine was claimed to deliver 16hp from the three cylinders of 3.7 litre capa city.   GMN

DANDY (GB) *1922–1925*
James Summer & Sons, Southport, Lancs.

The Dandy was a light car using an 8.9hp 2-cylinder engine. Although a price of £220 was fixed, the Dandy barely progressed beyond the prototype stage.   GNG

DANGEL (F) *1969 to date*
Henri Dangel, Mulhouse, Haut-Rhin

The Dangel was a very low two-seater sports car powered by a rear-mounted Renault 1,255cc engine. It had a 5-speed gearbox, and independent suspension all round. An unusual feature was that the cooling water circulated in the tubes of the frame from the front-mounted radiator to the rear engine. The fibreglass body was by Gangloff of Colmar, formerly famous for their work on Bugattis. Several Dangel cars have done well in hill-climbs. LL

DANIELS (US) 1915–1924

(1) Daniels Motor Car Co, Reading, Pa.
(2) Levene Motor Co, Philadelphia, Pa. 1923–1924

G.E. Daniels had been President of Oakland before turning to manufacture on his own account. The Daniels was a big, expensive and short-lived luxury car made in very small quantities, mostly to order, and best-known in its powerful speedster form. All were powered by side-valve V-8 engines. The Herschell-Spillman was used up to 1919, giving way to their own 6.4-litre unit. The Submarine Roadster and the starker Submarine Speedster of 1919 were extremely handsome sports cars. In 1923 Daniels' assets were sold to the Levene Motor Company of Philadelphia, who assembled a few cars and sold them at the inflated price of $10,000, more than $2,500 above the price of the 'genuine' Daniels. Daniels cars carried no identification apart from the letter 'D' on the hubcaps. About 2,000 were made in all. TRN

DANSK (CHRISTIANSEN; DANSK FABRIKAT) (DK) 1901–1908

(1) Dansk Automobil & Cyclefabrik, Copenhagen 1901–1903
(2) Dansk Automobilfabrik, Copenhagen 1903–1908

H.C. Christiansen started a cycle repair shop in 1896. Three years later he began building 3-wheelers with Cudell engines. A prototype 4-wheeler which he built in 1899 still exists. In 1901 he formed the Dansk Automobil & Cyclefabrik together with the wealthy Fonnesbech-Wulff. Nine cars ranging from 2 to 6hp were exhibited in Tivoli in 1902. The cars were rather primitive, with 2 forward speeds and no reverse, the transmission being a metal clutch with a central chain for each gear. Ignition was by trembler coil and there was no differential. Christiansen delivered Copenhagen's first motor taxi, but it was found too noisy by the authorities and Oldsmobile engines were used for later cabs. In 1903 the name of the firm was changed to Dansk Automobilfabrik, and a year later it produced the first Danish motor bus, possibly with an Oldsmobile engine. Engines were still single- or 2-cylinder, even for buses. 1905 saw a 12/16hp 4-cylinder governed engines with leather cone clutch, 3 forward speeds and shaft drive. These cars were sometimes marketed under the names Christiansen or Dansk Fabrikat. For motor buses a 4-cylinder engine of 25hp was now adopted. Production figures are not known. TRA

D'AOUST (B) 1912–1927

Automobiles J. D'Aoust, Anderlecht; Berchem Ste Agathe

The D'Aoust was typical of Belgian makes in that it was always strong and beautifully made, but differed in that it was best known for small to medium-sized cars. At first it seems that D'Aousts were powered by Aster and Chapuis-Dornier proprietary engines, among others, but the best-known of them was the 10/14CV of 1912, which had a 4-cylinder, long-stroke side-valve engine of a little under 2 litres' capacity, made by d'Aoust. This was an efficient power unit in a chassis that afforded good roadholding, so when the 10/14CV was continued after World War 1, it is not surprising to find a 2-litre sports model with a slightly bigger bore and four forward speeds alongside it. A 3-litre model was listed in 1921. From 1924, front-wheel brakes were fitted. The long-lived 10/14 was listed until 1927, together with two light cars, the 6CV with three forward speeds and the 8CV with four, both with front-wheel brakes and both also available in sports form. Probably the most famous D'Aoust was a specially-built racing car powered by a 9.4-litre Hispano-Suiza V-8 aero engine, driven by Arthur Duray in 1924. TRN

DARBY (US) 1909–1910

Darby Motor Car Co, St Louis, Mo.

The Darby high-wheeler used solid rubber tyres. The steering was by wheel and power came from a 2-stroke 2-cylinder engine somewhat optimistically rated at 20hp. The four-seater model was available for $800. GMN

DAREN (GB) 1968 to date

Daren Cars, Leighton Buzzard, Beds.

John Green's Daren GT cars were successful in competition right from their debut, with Vegantune Ford 1600 engine in a light space-frame. Eight of the Mark 2 monocoque model were built in 1969 and 1970, and campaigned particularly successfully by Martin Raymond. One had a 3-litre Martin V-8 engine. Palliser assembled four of the six Mark 3s of 1971 under an agreement, and a couple went to Italy. The 1972 Mark 4 was an FVC-powered car for the European long-distance races, and the Mark 5 was designed primarily for the BDA engine for the US 1300 class and featured a rear radiator and pontoon petrol tanks. DF

DARLING (US) 1917

Darling Motor Co, Dayton, Ohio

The Darling was built as a five-seater touring model of pleasing lines. It was powered by a 6-cylinder Continental engine of 5 litres. The wheelbase was 10ft 10in and wire wheels were standard equipment. GMN

1922 DANIELS 39.2hp sedan. *Keith Marvin Collection*

1902 DANSK 6hp four-seater *vis-à-vis. Thorkil Ry Andersen*

1970 DAREN Mark 2 Group 6 sports car. Jeremy Richardson at the wheel. *Autosport*

1937 DARMONT Junior 1,100cc sports car.
G.N. Georgano

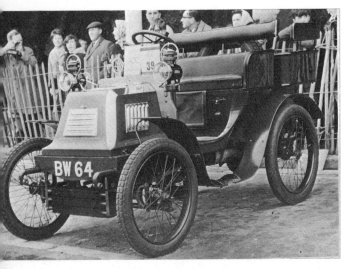

1900 DARRACQ 6½hp tonneau. *G.N. Georgano*

1907 DARRACQ 8hp two-seater. *The Veteran
Car Club of Great Britain*

DARMONT (F) 1924–1939

R. Darmont, Courbevoie, Seine

The Darmont 3-wheeler was closely based on the contemporary Morgan, being almost indistinguishable in appearance. Two sv models were made, the air-cooled Etoile de France, and a water-cooled version. The most powerful was the ohv Darmont Spéciale which could be had in supercharged form when it was capable of nearly 100mph. The engines were French-built versions of the Blackburne. In 1936 Darmont introduced a light sporting 4-wheeler, the V-Junior, powered by a 1,100cc V-twin engine. Like the 3-wheelers, it had Morgan-type independent front suspension. GNG

DARNVAL (F) 1972 to date

Sté Darnval, Le Havre, Seine-Maritime

The Darnval sports coupé has a ladder-type frame, Renault engine and suspension by the British Lenham company. LL

DARRACQ; TALBOT (ii) (F) 1896–1959

(1) Société A. Darracq, Suresnes *1896–1905*
(2) A. Darracq & Co (1905) Ltd, Suresnes *1905–1920*
(3) Automobiles Talbot, Suresnes *1920–1959*

An immense complexity of nomenclature surrounds these two makes. While the cars themselves were always designed and built in France, the company was financed in England during its golden period and after (1905–1935), then merged with a French concern which had been formed to make Italian cars, and subsequently acquired American affiliations! Alexandre Darracq founded the Gladiator cycle company in 1891, selling out to British interests five years later. He then turned briefly to the manufacture of electric carriages, exhibiting a coupé at the 1896 Paris Salon. In 1898, however, he acquired (for £10,000) the manufacturing rights of Léon Bollée's 4-wheeler voiturette, a belt-driven 5hp machine with a single-cylinder air-cooled horizontal engine, tube ignition and steering-column gear-change. It was not a success, though column change was to persist on some of Darracq's own designs until 1910.

The idea of a small and inexpensive runabout persisted, and in 1900 came the first real Darracq: its 785cc front-mounted vertical single-cylinder engine had automatic inlet valves, coil ignition, a cone clutch and shaft drive – Alexandre Darracq, like Louis Renault, never marketed a chain-driven car. It could be bought in England for £250 in 1901, in which year the Société Darracq took up racing with a 1.9-litre 2-cylinder machine driven by Henry Farman. Though only 'singles' were offered to the public in 1902, racing Darracqs were formidable voiturettes with 5.9-litre 4-cylinder engines and won the light-car category of the Concours du Ministre alcohol race, besides doing well in the Paris-Vienna. A manufacturing licence for Germany was taken out by Opel that year. Darracqs were raced until 1906, winning the light-car and voiturette categories of the Circuit des Ardennes. The company's *grandes voitures* were less successful: Darracq was determined to win the 1904 Gordon Bennett Cup and entered not only his own team of 11.3-litre machines for the French *éliminatoire*, but also sponsored three Opel-built cars in Germany, with another three cars specially built from scratch by Weir of Glasgow, to carry the British colours. Only von Opel's Opel-Darracq actually raced at Homburg and this failed to survive a single lap! Some very light 9.9-litre ohv cars were prepared for 1905, but it was not until the following season that a twofold success was achieved: Wagner's victory in the Vanderbilt Cup, and Algernon Lee Guinness's 117.66mph over the kilometre at Ostend on a special 22.5-litre ohv V-8 sprint car. Darracqs took 2nd and 3rd places in the 1908 T.T. but no more were raced until 1921.

Meanwhile the utility cars prospered. Single-, twin- and 4-cylinder models were marketed in 1903, all but the smallest having mechanically-operated side valves in a T-head, while the simplified 8hp Populaire sold for only 4,800fr in France. 1904 saw the introduction of steel frames pressed out of a single sheet of metal and also the advent of the rapid 3.1-litre 4-cylinder Flying 15 at £460. The new type of chassis was universal by 1905, when the company was reorganized under British registry, and some quite big cars were offered, though these were modestly priced, at the top of the regular range being a 5.9-litre 28hp with dual ignition and a 12ft 4in wheelbase at only £687. It was also possible to buy a 70hp sporting model based on the 1904 Gordon Bennett cars.

The 1907 1,100cc single sold for £159 and had mechanically-operated valves, but at the other end of the range there were the 4.7-litre '20/28', the 11½-litre ohv 'Vanderbilt Cup' type, and a 5.7-litre 4-speed six selling for £850. This had grown up to 8.1-litres with square cylinder dimensions a year later, though Darracqs still had a progressive gear change, and there was a short vogue for rear-axle-mounted gearboxes on a brace of new L-head monobloc fours with 2.3-litre and 3.1-litre engines. This transmission was dropped in 1909, the last year of 'singles', and the twins disappeared twelve months later. Gate change arrived in 1910. In 1911 there were seven Darracq models, the 15hp at £275 having overhead inlet valves. The 1912 programme, however, saw a catastrophic flirtation with the Henriod rotary-valve engine, installed in the 4.4-litre P12 4-cylinder with a 10ft 5in wheelbase, worm drive and dashboard radiator. A 2.6-litre rotary-valve model had conventional cooling arrangements, but profits faded away to almost nothing, and in the ensuing

heaval M. Darracq retired. Owen Clegg from Rover took over the management
[an]d the 1913 Darracqs were obviously inspired by his successful Rover Twelve.
[T]hey came in 2.1-litre and 2.9-litre sizes with L-head monobloc 4-cylinder engines
[an]d worm drive and very soon the firm was back on a sound footing. Additional to
[th]e 1914 range was a 4-litre '20/30' and the 16hp Darracq was sold with electric
[li]ghting and starting. This latter model went back into production in 1919 and was
[jo]ined shortly afterward by an advanced 4.6-litre sv V-8 with coil ignition and
[sp]iral bevel final drive, which had acquired 4-wheel brakes by the time it reached
[th]e production stage.

In June 1920 the British firms of Sunbeam and Talbot, who had joined forces in
[19]19, merged with Darracq and thenceforward nomenclature becomes complex.
[F]or the first few years after the amalgamation, the term 'Talbot-Darracq' was freely
[us]ed on both sides of the Channel, but strictly the cars were 'Talbot' (pronounced
[à] la Française) in Europe, and 'Darracq' in the British Commonwealth up to 1939.
[T]he new combine supported racing, though the very successful Henry-designed twin
[oh]c 4-cylinder differential-less voiturettes evolved in 1922 ran indiscriminately as
[T]albots and Darracqs. They and their descendants were, however, conceived and
[de]signed at Suresnes and victories included the 200-Mile Race at Brooklands (1922
[wi]nning unblown, 1924 and 1925 in supercharged form), the Coupe des Voiturettes
[19]22 and 1923), and the Penya Rhin race (1923). 1926 saw a team of advanced
[bl]own twin ohc 1½-litre straight-8s which never really proved themselves before
[Su]nbeam-Talbot-Darracq's precarious finances forced a withdrawal from racing
[in] 1927.

In the touring-car field, S.T.D. settled down to fifteen years of competing against
[th]emselves. A 3.2-litre sv 15hp Darracq with detachable head appeared in 1921, still
[w]ith worm drive, and this was followed a year later by a small ohv 970cc machine
[w]ith no differential and coil ignition, made also in England as the 8/18 Talbot, and
[th]e first of a line of 1½-litre ohv fours, the 10CV, selling at £595. Worm drive was
[d]ropped, and fwb had spread to the smaller Darracqs in 1924 with the 2.1-litre DS —
[in] sports form this was said to give 57bhp — but though the firm reverted to magneto
[ig]nition they retained wood wheels (still found on some cars as late as 1931) and
[3-]speed gearboxes. A year later the 1½-litre had grown up into the handsome '12/32'
[w]ith 4-wheel brakes and Weymann saloon bodywork; this theme was continued until
[1]928, by which time the car had a 1.7-litre engine and four forward speeds. Late in
[1]925 came the first of a long line of ohv push-rod sixes on conventional lines, with
[3-]speed gearboxes, single-plate clutches, magneto ignition and Perrot-type fwb:
[t]he 2.5-litre TLA gave 72bhp and sold for £800. Both an extra forward ratio and
[t]he option of a 2.9-litre unit came the following year. 1928 saw a real light six of
[3] litres' capacity with coil ignition, Talbot (i)'s bi-metal pistons and Bendix brakes.
[O]nly 6-cylinder cars were marketed in 1929, when 7-bearing crankshafts and central-
[iz]ed chassis lubrication made their appearance, while the inevitable straight-8 was
[li]sted for 1930: it featured a 3.8-litre 100bhp engine with a 9-bearing crank and
[ni]tralloy liners, and could be had on an 11ft 10in wheelbase. The next major face-
[l]ift came in 1933, with box-section frames and transverse ifs on the sixes and eights.
[O]nly one 6-cylinder model was catalogued in 1934, the year in which Darracq
[f]ollowed the lead of Roesch at Talbot (i) by adopting the Wilson preselective gear-
[b]ox which was retained until 1954.

After the collapse of S.T.D. Motors in 1935 the Suresnes factory came under
[t]he control of Major A.F. Lago, who had been well known in London for his L.A.P.
[oh]v conversions in the 1920s. Lago introduced a new line of 6-cylinder ohv cars
[re]taining the X-braced frames and ifs, while synchromesh gearboxes were available
[o]n the cheaper variants. The 2.7-litre 15CV and 3-litre 17CV were pleasant but not
[p]articularly lively tourers, but the 4-litre 23CV with 7-bearing crank disposed of
[1]65bhp in its Lago Special guise with cross-push-rod valve gear and hemispherical
[h]ead, and would comfortably exceed 100mph. A 1-2-3- victory in the 1937 French
[sp]orts-car Grand Prix at Montlhéry in 1937 was followed up by Comotti's win in
[t]he T.T. Under the 1938 G.P. formula the cars were less successful — stripped sports
[m]achines could do nothing against Mercedes-Benz and Auto-Union, while the low
[o]ffset 1939 4½-litre single-seaters were not much faster. A 3-litre blown V16 engine
[n]ever came to anything, any more than did a plan laid in 1937 to revive the Invicta
[(i]ii) name by building 3-litre and 4-litre Darracqs with Delage-style bodywork in
[L]ondon.

After World War 2, however, the 4½-litre racers (now 'Talbot' or 'Lago-Talbot',
[n]ever 'Darracq') came into their own. What they lacked in power they made up in
[m]odest fuel consumption, and could often go through a race without refuelling,
[a]n attribute not shared by blown 1½-litre machines. Chiron's win at Comminges in
[1]947 was a prelude to a career that spanned four seasons, and was backed by
[R]osier's 1950 Le Mans victory on a similar machine with sketchy road equipment.
[P]ierre Levegh would have repeated this in 1952, against Mercedes-Benz, had he
[n]ot attempted a single-handed drive for the 24 hours. Touring-car production was
[h]ampered by crippling taxation and uncertain finances: 433 cars were sold in 1950,
[b]ut only 80 in 1951. In spite of this M. Lago had a revised 4½-litre 170bhp Lago
[R]ecord sports car with hydraulic brakes in production in 1946, following it up
[w]ith a simpler and cheaper cross-pushrod four, the 2.7-litre Baby in 1950. This
[w]as said to have 118bhp, had hydraulic brakes and the choice of synchromesh
[o]r preselector, and was offered only with rhd; but it was not a particularly good
[c]ar, and its styling did not enhance it. By 1952 the range had been restyled, but

1914 DARRACQ 12/16hp two-seater. *G.N.
Georgano*

1924 DARRACQ 15/40hp sports car. Coachwork
by Grose. *Autocar*

1930 DARRACQ TL 20/98 saloon. *G.N.
Georgano*

1949 TALBOT-LAGO 4½-litre sports saloon.
Coachwork by Saoutchik. *Automobielmuseum,
Driebergen*

1955 TALBOT-LAGO 2½-litre coupé. *Lucien Loreille Collection*

1920 DAT Model 41 saloon. *Nissan Motor Co Ltd*

1938 DATSUN 7hp saloon. *Nissan Motor Co Ltd*

though Lago was extracting 247bhp from his Le Mans engines, he met with success, and henceforward the road lay downhill. Various engines were tried: 1955 there was a 5-bearing 2½-litre four on established Talbot lines, with a 4-spe ZF gearbox and handsome GT-style bodywork. In 1956 Maserati 250 engines we fitted in the Le Mans cars and in 1957, when two cars were still being turn out every week, a final attempt was made to earn dollars with the Lago Americ the 1955 chassis with a 2.6-litre B.M.W. V-8 power unit. By 1959 Simca we in control at Suresnes, and the Talbot coupé had yet another engine – the o sv V-8 motor inherited from Ford of France. Though an odd-looking coupé wi Simca Aronde engine was shown on the Talbot stand at the 1960 Paris Salo no more cars have been made. It is ironic to note that the three partners in th S.T.D. venture were re-united once more as a result of the Rootes-Chrysler de in 1965, Chrysler already having a substantial stake in Simca.   MC

DARRIN (US) 1946; 1953–1958
(1) Howard A. Darrin Automotive Design, Los Angeles, Calif. 1946; 1955–1958
(2) Kaiser-Frazer Corporation, Willow Run, Mich. 1953
(3) Kaiser-Willys Sales Corporation, Toledo, Ohio 1954

The famed coachbuilder and Kaiser-Frazer designer produced several cars und his own name, including a one-off convertible in 1946 – one of the first fibreglas bodied cars, with a forward-hinged complete body section ahead of the firewa and hydraulic controls for jacking, bonnet lifting, etc. In 1952–3 Darrin designe and built 62 prototype (split-windscreen) sports cars for Kaiser-Frazer, and 43 production versions were produced for 1954 by its successor, Kaiser-Willys. Aft the demise of Kaiser-Willys cars Darrin marketed several conversions of 1954 Da rins using supercharged Willys engines or Cadillac V-8s, and in 1958 he designe the Flintridge-Darrin D.K.W. fibreglass sports body on D.K.W. convertible chassi of which only about 25 were ultimately built.   RM

DARROW (US) 1902–1903
Darrow Motor Vehicle Co, Owego, N.Y.

The Darrow light runabout used a 3½hp Thomas engine, and in two-seater form cost $550.   GNG

DART (i) (US) 1914
Automatic Registering Machine Co, Jamestown, N.Y.

The Dart two-seater cyclecar, built by the world's biggest voting machine maker had a 2-cylinder engine. Its wheels had Bugatti-style slab spokes.   GM

DART (ii) (CDN) 1914
Dart Cyclecar Co, Toronto, Ont.

This typical cyclecar, based on the U.S. Scripps-Booth, was assembled unde licence for a short time. All parts were made in Detroit. The company later becam body builders.   G

DART (iii) see MARTIN (iv)

DASSE (B) 1894–1924
Automobiles Gérard Dasse, Verviers

The first Dasse car was a 3-wheeler powered by a horizontal single-cylinder engine with hot-tube ignition. It had belt drive and tiller steering to the single front wheel. In 1895 car the wheel layout was reversed, and in 1896 came the first 4-wheeler. This had a 2-cylinder engine with electric ignition, a 3-speed belt transmission and chain final drive. It was the first model to be built for sale. Later development of Dasse cars followed conventional lines, with shaft drive coming in about 1902. A 1904 model had a flexible propeller shaft made up of a bundle of thin rods. By 1914 a wide range of 4-cylinder cars was being made, from an 8hp to a 24/30hp, all with shaft drive. The 8 and 14hp models had monobloc engines, the others having their cylinders cast in pairs.

At the 1922 Brussels Salon, Dasse showed two car chassis, a 12/14hp and a 30hp, both with 4-cylinder ohv engines, and handsome pointed radiators. However, few post-war cars were made, and in 1924 the company abandoned private cars in order to concentrate on commercial and military vehicles.   GNG

DASTLE (GB) 1967 to date
Dastle Mfg Co, Ripley, Surrey

Designer Geoffrey Rumble had been connected with a Gemini Formula Junior model and had built a couple of specials before offering his first production car, the space-framed Type 3 midget racer, available in kit form from only £350. Subsequent models were variations on this most successful design, with the exception of the Type 6 Formula Ford car. In 1972 the firm broke new ground with the Type 9 Formula 3 machines, raced by Steve Thompson and James Hunt under Lord Hasketh's sponsorship. Type 10 was an improved version of this model.   DF

DAT; DATSON; DATSUN (J) 1912–1930; 1931; 1932 to date
DAT 1912–1930
(1) Kwaishinsha Motor Car Works, Tokyo 1912–1918

Kwaishinsha Motor Car Co, Tokyo *1918–1925*
) DAT Motor Car Co, Tokyo *1925–1926*
) DAT Automobile Manufacturing Co, Osaka *1926–1930*
ATSON *1931*
AT Automobile Manufacturing Co, Osaka (becomes a division of the Tobata
nono Co) *1931*
ATSUN *1932 to date*
) DAT Automobile Manufacturing Co, Osaka *1932*
) Jidosha Seizo Co Ltd, Yokohama *1933–1934*
) Nissan Motor Co Ltd, Yokohama *1934–1944*
) Nissan Heavy Industries Corp, Yokohama *1947–1949*
) Nissan Motor Co Ltd, Yokohama *1949 to date*

One of the giants of the Japanese car industry, Datsun has a history commencing
1912 with an experimental car constructed by the Kwaishinsha Motor Car works.
his was not considered very successful, but by 1914 a second machine was com-
leted and the Dat name was adopted, derived from the partners' initials: K. *Den*,
. *A*oyama and A. *T*akeuchi. In 1915 the Model 31 was marketed followed by
odel 41 in 1916. Construction of cars and trucks continued in Tokyo until 1926,
hen the company merged with Jitsuyo Jidosha Seizo to form the Dat Automobile
anufacturing Co of Osaka. Jitsuyo Jidosha Seizo had been producing Lila cars,
ut manufacture of these and of the Dat automobile was given up and all facilities
ere devoted exclusively to trucks until 1930. In that year a Dat test car, Model
1, was built, and this led to a return to car manufacture in 1931 with the Datson
r son-of-Dat. In order to make use of the national rising sun emblem, the name
as finally altered to Datsun in 1932.

The new patron of the make, Tobata Imono Co, disposed of the Osaka plant
Ishikawajima in 1933 and established a fresh firm, Jidosha Seizo, in Yokohama.
atsun manufacture continued there, to be joined by a larger private car range
hen the company name was changed to Nissan. The little Datsuns of the 1930s
ere well-proportioned and attractive and were built in sedan, phaeton, coupé and
oadster forms. They were closely based on the British Austin Seven, but by the
te 1930s had acquired more flowing lines.

The evolution of the make can be traced through the DAT 41 of 1924, which
as a five-seater sedan with a 4-cylinder, water-cooled engine of 17hp and a top
peed of 30mph; the Datson phaeton of 1931, a two-seater with a 10hp, 4-cylinder
ngine and a 45mph speed; and the 1936 Datsun sedan with a 4-cylinder, 15hp
ngine driving it at 50mph.

Early post-war styling owed much to the American Crosley, though the 1952
ports model had a look of M.G. about it. It was not until 1958 that the old,
ustin-like sv engine disappeared, replaced by a 988cc 4-door saloon with 37bhp
-cylinder pushrod unit. Coil ifs did not arrive until the 310 series of 1959, which
ad 1,189cc engines and three forward speeds. A sports two/four-seater version
ad fibreglass coachwork. In 1960 the group replaced its licence-produced Austin
50s with the 1½-litre and 2-litre 4-cylinder Cedrics, invariably sold as Nissans
ntil 1966. By 1963 the sports Datsun Fairlady was a more serious proposition,
ith elegant open coachwork, 2LS front brakes, and a 1½-litre engine giving 71bhp.

In 1966 Nissan/Datsun offered an impressive range. Their small family saloon,
he Bluebird, had progressed to full unitary construction, alternator ignition, an
ll-synchromesh gearbox, and a 1,300cc pushrod engine, and the Fairlady had
rown up into the 1,600cc Silvia, with 96bhp 5-bearing unit and front disc brakes;
hardtop was available as well as the roadster. In addition to the standard pushrod
edrics there were a 2.2-litre diesel-engined four and an ohc 7-bearing 1,987cc
ix developing 123bhp; this was available with automatic transmission and could
each 100mph. Finally Nissan offered a prestige car, the President saloon on a
ft 4½in wheelbase, with a 3-litre 6-cylinder engine and manual gearbox, or a 4-litre
ushrod V-8 of American type and automatic. The absorption of the Prince con-
ern led to further complications, for though the marque disappeared there were
ow a host of 'ex-Princes' in the medium category sold under the Skyline and
Gloria names.

The main consequence was an increasing sophistication, especially in engines
nd suspensions. Transverse-leaf ifs came on the conventional 988cc ohv Sunny
aloon of 1967. The Bluebird was completely redesigned in 1968, emerging with
96bhp 5-bearing ohc slant four engine of 1.6 litres' capacity, and all-independent
pringing.

By 1969 Nissan/Datsun had pushed production to nearly 700,000 units a year,
s well as delivering their 5 millionth car. In 1970 896,748 cars were made. A
ompetition programme pursued since 1966, initially with Group 6 and Group 7
acers, was extending in the direction of international rallies: 1600s won the Team
rize in the 1969 R.A.C. event, and a year later a 1600SS was victorious in the
ast African Safari. Fastest of the 1970 big saloons was a 2.3-litre ohc six, and
he company also marketed two high-performance 6-cylinder coupés, both with
-speed all-synchromesh gearboxes, irs, and front disc brakes. The 240Z, widely
xported, used a 160bhp 2.4-litre sohc unit. The 2-litre Z432 had twin overhead
amshafts.

At the end of 1970 Datsun fell into line with the prevailing fwd idiom. Their
herry was a fastback saloon using a transversely-mounted 5-bearing pushrod
ngine in an all-independently-sprung unitary structure; 988cc and 1,171cc versions

1950 DATSUN 850cc saloon. *Nissan Motor
Co Ltd*

1967 DATSUN Bluebird 1600 saloon. *Nissan
Motor Co Ltd*

1967 DATSUN Fairlady 2000 2-litre sports car.
Nissan Motor Co Ltd

1973 DATSUN 200L 2-litre saloon.
Nissan Motor Co Ltd

1918 DAVID 8/10hp cyclecar. *G.N. Georgano*

1952 DAVID 345cc 3-wheeler. *G.N. Georgano*

1948 DAVIS(iv) 2.6-litre 3-wheeled coupé.
National Motor Museum

were offered, with outputs ranging up to 80bhp, as well as 3- or 4-speed gearbox
front disc brakes (though drums were standard), and coupé and station-wag
bodies. The 1972 Datsuns included the Cherry; the conventional 4-cylinder Sun
with 1.4-litre or 1.6-litre ohc engines; the similarly-engineered Bluebirds, of whi
the most powerful was the 1800SSS-E hardtop with 125bhp fuel-injection engin
the medium-sized Skyline and Laurel saloons and station wagons; the sohc a
dohc 6-cylinder sports cars; and the luxurious President series. Revised versio
of the Laurel and Bluebird were introduced during the year. Datsuns were a
made under licence by YLN in Taiwan.

D'AUX (F) *1924*
The d'Aux was a very small cyclecar powered by a 350cc single-cylinder Caus
engine, with final drive by variable belts. Maximum speed was 36mph. It was ma
by a firm of industrial belt manufactureres in Reims.
GN

DAVID (E) *1913–1922; 1950–1956*
David SA, Barcelona
The David must have had one of the strangest origins of any motor vehicle. Jo
Maria Armangué was interested in bob-sleighs. Annoyed on the occasion of a
important contest by the lack of snow, he devised a wheeled 'bob-sleigh'. The spo
that resulted must have had much in common with the 'soap-box Derby' so belove
of small boys of the time (c. 1909). Next, Armangué fitted a tiny motor-cycle engin
not to go faster downhill, but to get to the top of the hill under power. It was b
a short step to motorized transport proper. The original David was the best-know
of Spanish cyclecars, unusual among its breed for using a water-cooled, 4-cylind
engine. These were made by M.A.G., Ballot or Hispano-Suiza, and could be ha
with either side or overhead valves. The transmission was by variable pulleys an
belt, and there was independent front suspension by two transverse springs. Th
wooden frame carried two- and four-seater bodies. The sports model had front whe
brakes. Saloons and taxis were also made. Manufacture of this first David cease
in 1922.
A few electric cars were made during the Civil War (1936–1939) and a ne
David cyclecar appeared in 1950. It had three wheels and was powered by a singl
cylinder, 2-stroke engine of 345cc, driving the front wheel. There was independe
front suspension, as before, but now by a telescopic fork. The frame was of ste
tubes. The resurrected David was current until 1956.
TR

DAVIS (i) (US) *1908–1930*
George W. Davis Motor Car Co, Richmond, Ind.; Baltimore, Md.
George Davis, a builder of buggies and wagons, entered the automobile busine
with a successful 4-cylinder touring model and subsequently added a six, a twi
six and, in 1927, an eight. Most of these cars had Continental engines. Davis car
through the years were sold with a variety of body styles and two-tone colo
schemes at a time when the latter were unusual. Noteworthy were the Fleetawa
touring car and the Man-o'-War roadster of the early 1920s characterized b
sporting lines.
The company was acquired by the Automotive Corp. of America in 192
which continued the Davis Eight and the New York Six, both available with
patented Parkmobile device which lifted the cars into tight parking places. Afte
1930 the company's activities at Richmond were concentrated on the productio
of aircraft, lawn-mowers and power machinery.
K

DAVIS (ii) (US) *1914*
Davis Cyclecar Co, Detroit, Mich.
The Davis cyclecar used the familiar 2-cylinder, air-cooled Spacke engine. Th
was connected with a 3-speed selective transmission and a double chain drive. Th
tandem two-seater cost $425.
GM

DAVIS (iii) (CDN) *1923*
Davis Dry Dock Company, Kingston, Ont.
This was a luxury car project by an internationally famous builder of fine boat
A pilot model, powered by a Stearns-Knight engine, was completed but high cos
ended production hopes. The pilot model remained in use over 40 years.
H

DAVIS (iv) (US) *1947–1949*
Davis Motor Co, Van Nuys, Calif.
The Davis three-wheeler was one of the more spectacular attempts to produce
small car in America. The original model had an all-aluminium body, tubular fram
Kinmont disc brakes (all the designers were in some way connected with the aircra
industry), coil springing at the rear and a 2.2-litre 4-cylinder Hercules engin
Later cars (only seventeen were made altogether) were rather more conventiona
and used a channel frame, Bendix hydraulic brakes and semi-elliptic springs. Th
engine was a 2.6-litre 4-cylinder Continental as used in the contemporary Del Ma
The all-enveloping coupé body seated four abreast, not five as has been claime
The company advertised a speed of 100mph and fuel consumption of 35mpg, bu
the best that test cars could do was 75mph and 28mpg. In the 1960s Gary Davi
built an experimental jeep-based 3-wheeler.
GN

DAVRIAN (GB) *1967 to date*

Davrian Developments Ltd, London S.W.4

Designed and built by Adrian Evans, the Davrian Imp was based on a fibreglass monocoque body/chassis unit, development of which started in 1965. All mechanical constituents were Hillman Imp, the car being available as a bare shell or complete except for wheels and engine; 200 had been sold by August 1972, a number of them exported. Mini or VW engines were available in the 1973 coupés. A Formula Super Vee car, based on the Palliser, was raced successfully by Bob Jarvis.   DF

DAVY (GB) *1909–1911*

Davy Engineering Ltd, Hulme, Manchester

The Davy car appeared at Olympia on the same stand as the Crowdy with which it shared the Hewitt piston valve engine made under licence from Hewitt Engines Ltd. As used in the Davy it was a 15/20hp 4-cylinder engine, and the car carried a striking 'Canadian canoe' body.   GNG

DAWSON (i) (GB) *1897–1900*

1) The Dawson Gas Engines Syndicate Ltd, Clapham, London S.W. *1897–1900*
2) H.T. Dawson & Son, Canterbury, Kent *1900*

Henry Thomas Dawson was a successful marine artist who was also interested in engineering. Originally he built stationary gas engines, and in conjunction with Paris Singer he built various engines of 1-, 2-, and 3-cylinder layout. Before a complete car was produced, however, he quarrelled with Singer who formed his own company to make the Paris Singer car. Dawson and his son moved to Canterbury where he built various experimental cars. In 1903 Henry Dawson junior joined Henry Pavillet to make the Canterbury car.   MJWW

DAWSON (ii) (US) *1900–1902*

Dawson Manufacturing Co, Basic City, Va.

The Dawson was a typical tiller-steered steam runabout with a 2-cylinder engine and single chain drive.   GNG

DAWSON (iii) (US) *1904–1905*

J.H. Dawson Machinery Co, Chicago, Ill.

This car was built only as a four-seater touring car. Its power came from a 2-cylinder, 16hp engine. It had a peculiar 2-speed transmission and a very long single chain drive to the rear axle.   GMN

DAWSON (iv) (GB) *1919–1921*

Dawson Car Co Ltd, Coventry, Warwickshire

Designed by A.J. Dawson, formerly works manager of Hillmans, the Dawson was a quality light car which was unusual in that it was a manufactured and not merely an assembled car. It used a 1,795cc 4-cylinder engine with a single overhead camshaft and carried open and closed bodies by Charlesworth. However, it was high priced even for 1919 (£750 to £995); after about 65 had been made production ceased and the Triumph Cycle Co acquired the factory for their new car.   GNG

DAY-LEEDS (GB) *1913–1924*

Job Day & Sons Ltd, Leeds, Yorks.

Well-known as makers of automatic tea-packaging machinery, Job Day & Sons began to make motor cycles in 1912, and a 2-cylinder cyclecar in 1913. This was soon replaced by a 4-cylinder shaft-drive light car, originally with a Turner engine, but later mainly with 1,286cc engines of Day's own design. It was a reliable machine carrying well-built open 2-seater and coupé bodies by Lockwood & Clarkson of Leeds. Little change was made in the cars after World War 1, but the price had risen from £195 in 1915 to £500 in 1920.   GNG

DAYTON (i) (US) *1909–1911*

W.D. Dayton Automobile Co, Chicago, Ill.

The Dayton was a high-wheeler with a water-cooled ohv 2-cylinder engine. The steering was by wheel, and the car had solid tyres and full mudguards.   GMN

DAYTON (ii) (US) *1911–1915*

Dayton Electric Car Co, Dayton, Ohio

This company made electric cars in small numbers, although they listed as many as six different models each year. Prices ranged from $2,000 to $3,000.   GNG

DAYTON (iii) (US) *1913–1915*

(1) Dayton Cyclecar Co, Joliet, Ill. *1913–1914*
(2) Crusader Motor Car Co, Joliet, Ill. *1914–1915*

This was a cyclecar available in either side-by-side or tandem arrangement for two passengers. The frame was of ash, and the engine was a 2-cylinder air-cooled Spacke of 9/13hp. The price was $375.   GMN

DAYTON (iv) (GB) *1922*

Charles Day Manufacturing Co Ltd, London W.10

1970 DAVRIAN 875 coupé. *Davrian Cars Ltd*

1920 DAWSON(iv) 11.9hp saloon. *Autocar*

1920 DAY-LEEDS 10hp coupé. *Job Day & Sons Ltd*

1952 D.B. 750cc coupé. *Autosport*

1908 DEASY 35hp cabriolet. *Autocar*

1907 DE BAZELAIRE 10/14hp racing voiturette.
Lucien Loreille Collection

This was an extremely small and simple cyclecar using a 4hp single-cylind
engine, and costing £115.
GN

DAYTONA (US) *1956*
Randall Products, Hampton, N.H.
The $495 Daytona minicar was an ultra-light two-seater with no doors
weather protection, powered by a 2hp Briggs & Stratton engine. The make
claimed that the rear-mounted engine could be used as a 1,000-watt pow
generator, or for scores of jobs about the house.
GN

DAY UTILITY (US) *1911–1914*
Day Automobile Co, Detroit, Mich.
The Day utility car used a conventional 4-cylinder engine and shaft drive, b
was unusual in offering a body which could be converted from five-seater tour
to light truck in one minute. There should have been a wide market for such
vehicle among farmers and small tradesmen, but even so, the Day only lasted fo
three years.
GN

D.B. (F) *1938–1961*
Automobiles D.B., Champigny-sur-Marne, Seine
Deutsch and Bonnet were building 'specials' based on 11CV *traction ava*
Citroëns in 1938. In 1947 limited production began again, the first D.Bs bein
competition machines largely built up from reconditioned components, using 1
litre and 2-litre engines and 4-speed gearboxes. A new car based on the Dyn
Panhard ran at Montlhéry in 1948, while in 1949 the company produced a 500c
single-seater version for Formula III, with the Panhard engine mounted in th
nose, and independent swing-axle rear suspension. Some 100mph Citroën-base
convertibles were also made, but after 1950 D.B. devoted all their energies t
Panhard derivatives. Though never a major force in Formula III, the cars gaine
numerous International Class Records and won the Index of Performance at L
Mans five times (1954, 1956, 1959, 1960 and 1961). Also Laureau's D.B. won th
1954 T.T. outright. An attempt to contest the 2½-litre G.P. Formula of 1954 wit
the alternative permitted size of 750cc supercharged was a fiasco, and little cam
of the curious Monomills (the same cars with blowers removed) with which Deutsc
and Bonnet tried to popularize one-class racing in France. Equally abortive wer
experiments with twin engines and 4-wheel drive (1952) and with rear-mounte
Renault engines and 5-speed gearboxes (1953). The production D.B. sports coup
used regular Panhard mechanical components allied to light alloy bodywor
(fibreglass from 1955) and were marketed in various engine capacities from 610c
(30bhp) to 1,300cc (65bhp). M.A.G. low-pressure superchargers were listed from
1954, and disc brakes were an option a year later. The standard 1958 model wa
the Rallye coupé with a 55bhp 850cc engine. D.B. remained faithful to Panhar
until the partnership was dissolved in 1961. René Bonnet continued the manufactur
of cars in the Champigny works under his own name.
MC

DEAL (US) *1905–1911*
Deal Motor Vehicle Co, Jonesville, Mich.
This was a small four-seater motor buggy, with solid rubber tyres, but it ha
wheel steering even in 1905.
GMN

DEASY (GB) *1906–1911*
Deasy Motor Car Manufacturing Co Ltd, Coventry, Warwickshire
Sponsored by Captain H.H.P. Deasy, the English importer of Martini cars, anc
designed by E.W. Lewis, formerly of Rover, the original Deasy was a 4½-litre 4-
cylinder machine with some unusual features. These included a side-valve monobloc
power unit, transverse rear suspension, pressure lubrication, an armoured-wood
frame, both sets of brakes working in enormous drums on the rear wheels, and a
camshaft brake inherited from Rover. Transmission brakes had been adopted by
1908, when the company was offering a big 8.6-litre '35' and an enormous over-
square-engined 12-litre '45'. A smaller 2.9-litre '15' appeared in 1909, which sold
for £425, complete with speedometer, but when J.D. Siddeley moved in from
Wolseley that season a change of policy was at once apparent, though the old-type
3-litre and 4.9-litre Deasys continued into 1910. The new models had pressed-steel
frames and their 4-cylinder thermo-syphon-cooled engines were housed under coffin-
shaped bonnets with dashboard radiators. Two engine sizes — 2.9-litres and 4.1-
litres — were available, and there were four wheelbase lengths ranging from 9ft 5in
to 10ft 7in. Chassis prices started at £365 and only the new 'J.D.S.' cars were
listed in 1911, the existing '14/20' and '18/28' being joined by a 1,944cc '12' with
a choice of three or four forward speeds. Shortly afterwards the name was changed
to Siddeley-Deasy.
MCS

DE BAZELAIRE (F) *1907–1928*
F. de Bazelaire SA, Paris
The entry of a team of 1,100cc 2-cylinder racers for the 1907 Coupe des Voiturettes was De Bazelaire's debut. As the French press was describing them as 'new'
manufacturers in 1908, it is logical to assume that series production had only just
started. 1908 models used L-head engines with magneto ignition and were noted

r their back-axle gearboxes: models listed were the 1,100cc 8/9hp and 1.7-litre 2/14hp, both twins, and a 2-litre 4-cylinder. Overhead inlet valves were adopted 1910, when a 2.5-litre 6-cylinder model was listed, and 1911 cars had gate change. y 1914 De Bazelaire was offering five 4-cylinder models, still with the same basic ransmission: Ballot engines were used in the smaller cars, while the big ones (which ncluded an ultra-long-stroke 80mm × 180mm Type MM-Sport) used T-head nvier units. At the 1913 Paris Salon the company showed a six with the Fischer ide-valve engine – but like Delaugère-Clayette, who also toyed with this design, ey went no further with it. The first post-war De Bazelaires retained the old nvier engines – the 3.6-litre version was made until 1924 – but the last of the e were some conventional assembled machines with 4-speed gearboxes and 1.2- re and 2.1-litre 4-cylinder S.C.A.P. engines, the latter with ohc. MCS

E BOISSE (F) 1900–1904

de Boisse, Paris 11e.

The first De Boisse car was a 3-wheeler with a single-cylinder water-cooled engine ounted on the front wheel which it drove by chain. The car was an open two-seater nd steering was by a very long tiller. One was entered in the 1901 Paris-Bordeaux ace but failed to finish. The next De Boisse was a more conventional light car owered by a 6hp De Dion engine, and using shaft drive and De Dion rear axle. wo of these were entered in the 1903 Paris-Madrid race, and both finished. In 904 a larger car with a 12hp 2-cylinder De Dion engine was made. GNG

E BRUYNE (GB) 1968

e Bruyne Motor Car Co Ltd, Newmarket, Suffolk

Displayed at the 1968 New York Show, the de Bruyne was an attempt to revive e Gordon-Keeble, and two GT saloons were made on Keeble lines with 5,367cc hevrolet V-8 engines. There was also a prototype mid-engined coupé, also Chevro-t-powered, with power-assisted steering and 5-speed transaxle for which 180mph as claimed. There was no series production. MCS

ECAUVILLE (F) 1898–1910

té Decauville, Corbeil, Seine-et-Oise

This famous firm of locomotive manufacturers began their series of road vehicles y making the Guédon small car, which they renamed the Decauville. This first ecauville would have been called a voiturette, but for the fact that Léon Bollée ad already appropriated the word for his own little machine. Thus it was termed e Decauville Voiturelle. It had four wheels, unlike the Bollée, and was powered y a vertical twin-cylinder air-cooled engine of 3½hp, at first mounted at the rear. here were two forward speeds. However the remarkable feature of the Voiturelle as its front suspension, which was independent – the first known instance of this n a production petrol car. Suspension was by a transverse spring and sliding illars. There were no rear springs at all. The water-cooled 5hp model of about 1899 ad three forward speeds. On the 8hp model of 1900, the engine was moved to the ont, shaft transmission was used, and four speeds were supplied. The 1901 Decau-ille had a fully-floating axle, and direct drive on top gear. From 1903 onwards ecauvilles were conventional shaft-driven vehicles, with side valves in a T-head, oneycomb radiators, pressed-steel frames, and 3-speed gearboxes. However, the igger ones had dual ignition, the coil being backed by a ht magneto by 1905, nd the largest models were available with side-chain transmission. A 12/14hp twin as listed until 1905, but thereafter only 4-cylinder machines were catalogued. The ompany's peak year was probably 1904, with 350 units delivered. Five types were ataloged in 1906, with capacities of 2.7, 3.3, 4.8, 6.4, and 9.2 litres, and short trokes were favoured – the 24hp model was 'square' at 115 × 115mm. These hanged little in successive years. Though models from 12 to 60hp were still being dvertised in 1909, the Decauville lasted only another year. Both the rear-engined oiturelles and the later fours were made under licence in Germany and Italy, hough different firms handled the two varieties in each country. In 1898 the com-anies were Wartburg (Dixi) and Marchand; in 1906 Ehrhardt and Lux of Turin. TRN/MCS

DE CÉZAC (F) 1925–1927

utomobiles de Cézac, Perigueux, Dordogne

De Cézac cars were made largely to special order. Two models were listed, with ,200cc C.I.M.E. or 1,685cc Ballot engines. GNG

DECHAMPS (B) 1899–1906

Ateliers H. Dechamps, Brussels

The first Dechamps had a 6hp 2-cylinder engine, and a four-seater brake body which could be replaced by a van. In 1901 a 20hp 4-cylinder car ran in the Paris-Berlin race, and the following year no less than four 20hp Dechamps ran in the Paris-Vienna. As well as their 20hp, Dechamps were making a 7hp single and 9hp twin, all with front-mounted vertical engines and chain drive. From 1904 to 1906 wo 4-cylinder cars with single ohc engines of 15 and 25hp were sold under the ame Baudouin. GNG

DECKER (US) 1902–1903

Decker Automatic Telephone Exchange Co, Owego, N.Y.

1899 DECAUVILLE 3½hp 'voiturelle'.
Museo dell'Automobile, Turin

1909 DECAUVILLE 16/20hp tourer.
G.N. Georgano Collection

1902 DECHAMPS 9hp tonneau. *The Veteran Car Club of Great Britain*

1907 LORRAINE-DIETRICH 60hp two-seater. *Autocar*

1899 DE DIETRICH(ii) Petit Duc.
Neubauer Collection

1928 LORRAINE 15CV saloon. *Autocar*

1923 LORRAINE-DIETRICH 15CV tourer.
National Motor Museum

The Decker was a light roadster with a single-cylinder 7hp engine mounted
front driving the rear wheels by shaft. Radiator and bonnet were on the Rena
pattern.
GM

DECKERT (F) *1901–1906*
H. Deckert, Paris 17e
   Deckert cars were conventional machines made in four models, a 6hp sing
cylinder, 12 and 16hp 2-cylinders and 20hp 4-cylinder. One of the latter ran in t
1902 Circuit du Nord race for alcohol-fuelled cars, and a 12hp in the Circuit d
Ardennes of the same year, but neither distinguished itself.
GM

DECOLON (F) *1957*
   The Decolon was a two-seater 3-wheeler powered by a 200cc engine driving t
single rear wheel by chain.
GM

DE COSMO (B) *1903–1908*
De Cosmo et Cie, Liège
   J. de Cosmo was an Italian who designed the first F.N. cars. In 1903 he beg
to make cars of his own, powered by pair-cast 4-cylinder engines of 24/30hp an
30/35hp, both with 3-speed gearboxes and shaft drive. The 24/30 was to have bee
made in England by the Wilkinson Sword Company, but the few Wilkinsons whic
did appear were probably Belgian-built. In 1906 a 45/55hp 6-cylinder car wi
chain drive was made. Later de Cosmos had round radiators in the style of th
Delaunay-Belleville. However, they were uneconomic to turn out, and had gone o
of production by 1908.
GM

DE CROSS (US) *1913–1914*
De Cross Cyclecar Co, Cincinnati, Ohio
   The De Cross was a freakish cyclecar, with tandem arrangement and driver
controls in the rear seat. Its engine, of 1.1 litres, had two cylinders and ai
cooling. The final drive was by belts.
GM

DE DIETRICH (i); LORRAINE-DIETRICH; LORRAINE (F) *1897–1934*
(1) De Dietrich et Cie, Lunéville, Lorraine *1897–1905*
(2) Société Lorraine des Anciens Etablissements de Dietrich et Cie, Lunéville, Lo
raine; Argenteuil, Seine-et-Oise *1905–1934*
   This manufacturer of railway rolling stock entered the automobile industry b
the acquisition of a licence to build Amedée Bollée's horizontal-twins in 2.3-litr
and 3-litre sizes. These featured tube ignition and a complex transmission wit
primary belt and final drive by two sets of bevels; they persisted until 1902
although their poor showing in the Paris–Berlin event (1901) convinced the com
pany that something more modern was needed. In 1902 De Dietrich started t
make cars to Turcat-Méry designs, these being on Panhard lines with front-mounte
vertical aiv 2- and 4-cylinder engines, low-tension magneto ignition, tubular radia
tors, armoured wood frames, and side-chain drive. The 1903 range consisted o
fours of 3 litres, 4.1 litres and 5.4 litres. Moiv came in 1904, when racing version
ran to 12.8 litres and 100hp; overhead inlet valves were used briefly in 1905. A
reversion to the L-head layout came in 1906, the season's smallest model, the 3-litr
DH, having ht magneto ignition as well.
   Towards the end of 1905 the cars had been renamed Lorraine-Dietrich, the Cros
of Lorraine on their radiators emphasizing their French origins. From 1928 the
were known simply as Lorraines.
   A distinguished racing career (3rd in the 1903 Paris–Madrid, 2nd, 5th and 10t
in the 1905 Coppa Florio, and 3rds in the 1906 Vanderbilt Cup and the Circu
des Ardennes) led to a boom in sales which rose from 253 in 1902 to 650 i
1906. Lorraine-Dietrich went 'empire building' in 1907, acquiring Isotta Fraschi
of Italy and Ariel of England. Neither venture prospered: the Milanese firm soo
regained its independence, and it is unlikely that more than one 'British' Lorrain
was produced. In 1907 there were also a few 6-wheelers based on the 1905 Turca
Méry, and at the top of the range was an enormous 12.4-litre 60. Shaft driv
made its appearance on the smaller cars (which included a 3.6-litre six) in 1908
there was a small twin in the 1909 catalogue; and 1910 brought a modern s
monobloc four, the 2,121cc 12/15hp. Under the influence of a new designer, d
Groullard (also responsible for the company's last racer, the 15,095cc chain-drive
1912 GP machine), these features spread up the range, with a parallel 16CV i
1911 and an 8.3-litre 40 with pair-cast cylinders in 1913.
   During World War 1, Marius Barbarou joined the company to help with the
aero-engine programme, and though a long-stroke 6.1-litre sv six was introduced i
1919, along with a companion V-12 that never saw production, the staple Lorrain
of the 1920s was the 15CV, a 3.4-litre pushrod six on American lines with co
ignition, 3-speed unit gearbox and central change. A flexible machine that achieve
60mph on 40bhp, it evolved into an excellent sports car that won the 1925 an
1926 Le Mans 24-Hour Races. Four forward speeds were available from 1924
when front-wheel brakes were standardized, and in 1927 the valve gear wa
enclosed and 12-volt electrics made their appearance. Between 1923 and 1929 th
company also marketed a companion 12CV four. The 15 was made until 1932
in which year the last of the Lorraines was introduced. This was a 4.1-litre 20C

ith 7-bearing crankshaft and a radiator of Hispano-Suiza type; it was too heavy and expensive to sell well, and Lorraine's increasing involvement with aero-engines d them to close down their automobile department in 1934, though subsequently atra cross-country 6-wheelers were made under licence at Argenteuil.   MCS

E DIETRICH (ii) (D) *1897–1904*

De Dietrich et Cie, Niederbronn, Alsace

Until 1902 the German half of the De Dietrich empire built 2-cylinder Amedée ollées identical to their French counterparts, though a few Belgian Vivinus light ars were also made under licence at Niederbronn in 1899 and 1900. Then in 902 a new designer arrived, Ettore Bugatti, who created some advanced chain-riven fours with lt magneto and coil ignition and armoured wood frames. These ame in 5.4-litre and 7.3-litre sizes; unusual features were the pullrod ohv and e cylindrical water jackets entirely surrounding the pair-cast cylinders. Sold as urlingtons in England, these De Dietrichs proved expensive to make and the Ger-san company abandoned car manufacture late in 1904.   MCS

E DION-BOUTON (F) *1883–1932*

1) De Dion, Bouton et Trépardoux, Paris *1883–1894*
2) De Dion, Bouton et Cie, Paris *1894–1897*
3) De Dion, Bouton et Cie, Puteaux, Seine *1897–1932*

Count Albert de Dion went into partnership in 1883 with Georges Bouton and is brother-in-law Trépardoux. By 1887 one of their steam tricycles had attained 0mph, but most of the early production De Dions were heavy commercial vehicles, ke the brake which put up the fastest performance in the 1894 Paris–Rouen Trials. This line of business was pursued until 1904, but in 1893 the Count was experi-nenting with petrol engines, a step to which Trépardoux was so opposed that he esigned in 1894; though not before he had devised the De Dion axle, a system whereby the drive was transmitted by universally jointed halfshafts while the weight of the vehicle was taken by a tubular dead axle also carrying the wheels. The ext step was Bouton's high-speed engine of 1895, initially a 137cc air-cooled single with non-trembler coil ignition capable of 2,000rpm. It was fitted to large numbers f tricycles and quads produced by the firm in the 1896–1902 period, and was lso the leading proprietary unit for voiturettes of the era. Over 140 makes of ar used De Dion engines at one time or another, not to mention copies perpetrated y firms like Humber and Pierce-Arrow.

The first De Dion voiturette appeared in 1899, its 402cc water-cooled engine being set vertically at the rear of a simple tubular frame. The 2-speed expanding-clutch transmission dispensed with a conventional clutch pedal, steering was by ar, and though it was fairly expensive at £210, it was reliable, foolproof, and capable of 25mph. The earliest cars had no reverse gear or rear springing, but 1,500 had found buyers by April 1901, in which year an electric version was tried, ut soon abandoned. These rear-engined types persisted until 1903, but in 1902 here was a new line of front-engined, wheel-steered De Dions with underslung ubular radiators and 864cc or 942cc power units. These were joined a year later by the cheap 698cc Q on similar lines, retailing at £160 in France or £200 in England. These simple aiv lightweights were immensely popular and had a long un, the very similar AL surviving until 1910. In the meanwhile, however, bigger models appeared. In 1903 a 1.7-litre twin was introduced with three speeds and a primitive form of preselection, and De Dion (who did not usually race, though they produced racing engines for other factories) entered a team of 4-cylinder voi-turettes for the Paris–Madrid event. They used these as the basis for their first catalogued four, the 2,545cc AD with 3-speed sliding-type gearbox introduced dur-ng 1904 and followed two seasons later by a big car, the 4.4-litre AP that sold in England for £897.

Up to 1914 the range was wide and complex, but De Dion were falling into line with convention. All but the smallest cars had orthodox bonnets and radiators by 1906, and moiv was featured by 1907. The 1908 catalogue included a 1.8-litre L-head four with pair-cast cylinders, the BH, as well as some long-stroke sporting singles capable of 50mph, their engines based on the special Coupe des Voiturettes units. In 1910 there was actually a De Dion without the De Dion axle, the CD single. Only the AL retained the old expanding clutches, and the company moved into the luxury field with the world's first series production V-8, the 6.1-litre with dual-magneto ignition: ht magnetos were now standard equipment on De Dions. By 1914 there was a choice of four eights: a small 3½-litre; the 4.6-litre ES; the 7.8-litre EY-type 50 that offered 55mph from 69bhp; and the monstrous 14.8-litre EZ with twin rear tyres, probably only a prototype. The last singles had been made in 1912, and though the twins survived for another couple of seasons the standard small De Dion was now the 8hp EJ4, a little monobloc four with 3-speed unit gearbox and pull-on handbrake instead of the traditional push-on type, though the De Dion decelerator pedal was retained. Electric lighting and starting were standard equipment on the largest 1914 De Dions, and during the year the rounded V-radia-tor made its appearance.

De Dion never recovered from World War 1, lacking the resources to essay volume production, though they were back in 1919 with a 3-model range using their own Victrix magnetos, alloy pistons, 4-speed unit gearboxes, and full electrics. There was a 1,847cc four backed by a pair of V-8s, of which the smaller had

1900 DE DION BOUTON 3½hp voiturette.
National Motor Museum

1902 DE DION-BOUTON 8hp tourer. *The Veteran Car Club of Great Britain*

1914 DE DION-BOUTON 18hp limousine. Coachwork by Caversham Motor Co. Ltd. *J.R.S. Goulding*

1930 DE DION-BOUTON LA 11CV coupé. *Autocar*

1921 DEEMSTER 10hp entered for Brooklands
200 Mile Race. *National Motor Museum*

1923 DELAGE Type GL 40/50hp saloon.
Coachwork by Barker. *National Motor Museum*

1930 DELAGE D.8 4-litre drophead coupé.
Coachwork by Belvalette. *Lucien Loreille
Collection*

a capacity of only 2.3 litres. The last year of the eights came in 1923, but b
now the more expensive 4-cylinder cars came with detachable heads, ohv, an
4-wheel brakes. A truly luxurious 4-cylinder was introduced in 1924, the 4-lit
JK that cost £1,025 in England and was available with servo-assisted brakes b
1927. In 1926 came a cheap modern small car, the 1,328cc sv JP with alloy bloc
2-bearing crankshaft, and such styling features as a ribbon radiator shell and nick
eled hubcaps; but it arrived too late, and a year later the factory was forced t
close down. The subsequent revival was half-hearted, though it lasted until 193.
The principal model was a straightforward ohv 2-litre four of 11CV, the LA, bu
there was also a 2½-litre straight-8, the LB, enlarged to 3 litres by 1930. Commerci
vehicles were built in modest numbers until 1950.   MC

DEEMSTER (GB) 1914–1924
Ogston Motor Co Ltd, Acton, London, W.3
   The Ogston Motor Co, run by former Napier personnel, acquired the Wilkinso
T.M. Co of Acton, together with their projected light car, which was named th
Deemster. This was a conventional machine with three forward speeds, shaft driv
and their own 4-cylinder, 10hp, 1,100cc engine. This was a unit with good low-spee
pulling power, and as the car was light in weight it was fast and accelerativ
yet flexible and economical. Plans to make the Deemster in America fell through
in any case it could hardly have succeeded in a country where small cars wer
unsuitable and disliked. An Anzani-engined 12hp followed in 1922.   TR

DEEP SANDERSON (GB) 1960–1969
Lawrencetune Engines Ltd, London W.3
Chris Lawrence Racing, London S.W.7
   Chris Lawrence's tubular tetrahedron-framed formula Junior cars compounde
their name from the music of 'Deep Henderson', and Sanderson, the backer. Th
301 coupé, introduced in 1963, employed a backbone chassis, fibreglass body, inde
pendent suspension and a B.M.C. Mini engine. Detail specification varied, as the car
were built to order in limited numbers. From 1969 onwards the only cars mad
were experimental or prototype machines, either one-off or pre-production run
such as the Martin V-8-engined cars built as precursors to the Monica GT.   D

DEERE (US) 1906–1907
Deere-Clark Motor Car Co, Moline, Ill.
   Succeeding Clarkmobile and Deere-Clark, the Deere Type B for 1907 was a four
seater car driven by a 4-cylinder engine of 25/30hp. It cost $2,500.   GMN

DEERING MAGNETIC (US) 1918–1919
Magnetic Motors Corp, Chicago, Ill.
   Designed by Karl H. Martin, designer of Roamer and Kenworthy and late
builder of the Wasp automobile, the Deering Magnetic was a prestige motor car in
every sense of the word. It had a Dorris 6-cylinder engine and an Entz electri
transmission, which eliminated the functions of the electric starter, flywheel
clutch and gearbox. An 11ft wheelbase allowed for luxury coachwork and prices fo
the closed models approached $7,000.   KM

DEGUINGAND (F) 1927–1930
Sté des Nouveaux Ateliers A. Deguingand, Puteaux, Seine
   Violet, the famous French designer of small 2-stroke cars, designed a tiny
5CV for the Deguingand concern in 1928. It had a 735cc, 4-cylinder engine with
only two combustion chambers. The gearbox, integral with the rear axle, contained
two forward speeds and reverse, the latter being actuated by a separate lever
Front suspension was by a single transverse spring. The basic Deguingand design
reappeared in 1931, made by the Donnet company as their new, small model. The
Galba (1929) and Huascar (1931) were also close relations.   TRN

DEHN (D) 1924
H.C. Dehn, Hamburg
   A small two-seater with Dehn's own air-cooled 2½/8PS single-cylinder engine.
                                                                              HON

DELACOUR (F) 1914–1920
Sté des Automobiles Delacour, Paris
   The Delacour was a light car with a 10hp 4-cylinder engine and friction drive.
In 1920 Delacour announced two models, a 7hp and a 12hp.   GNC

DELAGE (F) 1905–1954
(1) Automobiles Delage, Courbevoie, Seine 1905–1935
(2) Automobiles Delage, Paris 1935–1954
   Louis Delage, a former employee of Turgan-Foy and Peugeot, started modestly
with a conventional shaft-driven single-cylinder 6½hp runabout with a De Dion
engine which was marketed in England as the Baby Friswell. As early as 1906
Delage showed an interest in racing, and the make's second place in that year's
Coupe des Voiturettes was followed in 1908 with an outright win on a single powered
by a Causan-designed engine. Meanwhile touring Delages continued to use De Dion
power units, and later 4-cylinder engines of modest capacity built by Ballot,

hough single-cylinder cars rated at 6, 8 and 9hp were still catalogued as late as 910. The 1.4-litre '12' of 1909 was a neat little machine with monobloc cylinders, -speed gearbox and fuel tank streamlined into the dashboard, which sold for 230 and was progressively developed up to 1914. It had a pressure-fed crankshaft n 1910 and was joined in 1911 by a 2.5-litre 30bhp six on similar lines: the footbrake, nusually, worked on the rear wheels. This model had acquired a 4-speed gearbox and lectrics by 1914, a version with 11ft wheelbase being listed for town-carriage work.

Delage also pursued his racing career to good purpose, winning the 1911 Coupe e l'Auto with a horizontal-valve 3-litre 4-cylinder which had a 5-speed gearbox vith overdrive top. These features were also found on the 6.3-litre cars which von both the 1913 G.P. du Mans and the 1914 Indianapolis 500-Mile Race, while for he 1914 Grand Prix his 4½-litre cars had twin ohc, desmodromic valves and 4-wheel rakes (but no handbrake). While producing munitions in World War 1, Delage ound time to develop a new long-stroke 4½-litre sv 6-cylinder (Type CO), which vent into production in 1919 with 4-wheel brakes, but still with a fixed cylinder ead. There was also a companion 3-litre 4-cylinder, and by 1921 the CO had leveloped into the CO2 with ohv, twin-plug head, dual magneto ignition and 8bhp. The 1920s saw a line of excellent fast tourers, while from 1922 to 1927 a ostly but very successful racing programme was pursued. Starting with the -cylinder Delage I and Delage II sprint cars, the company progressed to an ohv V-12 of 10.7 litres' capacity in 1923, with which René Thomas annexed the World's Land Speed Record at Arpajon in the following year with a speed of 143.31mph. The car subsequently had a long and distinguished racing career in England. For he 2-litre G.P. Formula in 1924 Planchon designed a four ohc V-12 of great com-lexity – in twin-supercharged 1925 form it gave 190bhp and won the French nd Spanish Grands Prix. Equally costly were the Lory-designed 1½-litre twin-am straight-8s of 1926–27, with 5-speed overdrive gearboxes and various types of upercharging. In their early days they had a bad name for overheating but they vere unbeatable in 1927, with five major Grands Prix to their credit. There was also R.J.B. Seaman's triumphal 1936 voiturette season, when the nine-year-old Delage trounced the E.R.A. and Maserati opposition.

Mainstay of the touring-car programme from 1924 onwards was the classic 2.1-itre 4-cylinder DI, with ohv, 4-wheel brakes, magneto ignition (coil on later cars), 4-speed gearbox and single-plate clutch. At £475 in England it was excellent value and sports versions with aluminium pistons were quite fast. At the same time the company offered the vast 6-litre Type-GL as competition for the Hispano-Suiza: unusual features of this ohc 6-cylinder were the clutched fan, twin oil pumps, X-braced frame and hydraulic servo brakes – it could be bought in England for £1,650 in 1925. The DI was only produced up to 1927. The DI had gone a year later, Delage turning to 6-cylinder cars of more modest capacity: the 3.2-litre ohv DM followed by a less successful sv DR, made in 2.2-litre and 2.5-litre forms. The 1929 Paris Salon saw the first of the big ohv long-stroke straight-8s, all with coil ignition, pump and fan cooling, and 4-speed gearboxes. Valve bounce was countered by making the springs operate separate rocker arms. It came in several wheelbase lengths from 10ft 10in to 11ft 11in, and carried superbly elegant if not always practical bodywork. In 1931 it was joined by a 3-litre D6 which was the same car with two less cylinders.

A super-sports D8 was available in 1932: though often overbodied it took its International class 12-hour record at 112mph. The range was further complicated in 1932 by the advent of a new series of short-stroke models, the first of which, the D6-11, had an almost square 2.1-litre 6-cylinder unit, with the D8's valve gear, independent transverse front suspension and a silent-third gearbox. Inexpensive pressed-steel saloon bodywork was used and the car sold for £595. By 1934 there was not only a companion straight-8 (the D8-15) of 2.7 litres, but also a 1½-litre 4-cylinder version. The big D8s were still listed. 1935 Delages featured synchromesh and hydraulic brakes and slightly undersquare 6- and 8-cylinder engines were used: all cars now had ifs. Louis Delage was, however, forced to sell out to Delahaye and thereafter the cars slowly evolved into more florid versions of that make, built in the same factory. The 4-cylinder cars died out with the obscure 2.2-litre mechani-cally-braked DI-12 of 1936, a badge-engineered Delahaye. There was an abortive plan to make Delages in England in 1937. Up to World War 2 the company's offerings were the 2.7-litre D6-70 and the 4.3-litre 8-cylinder D8-100 and D8-120. All had hydraulic brakes, Cotal gearboxes and ifs, and the D6-70 could be bought in England for £695. It was raced to some purpose, winning the 1938 T.T. and taking second place at Le Mans in 1939, in which year capacities of both engines were increased. The 3-litre 6-cylinder car appeared after the war, but only a few were made, and Louveau's and Jover's second place at Le Mans in 1949 was almost the last that was heard of the make. Along with Delahaye, Delage was absorbed by Hotchkiss in 1954.

MCS

1939 DELAGE D.8 120 4.7-litre drophead coupé. *Autocar*

1949 DELAGE D.6 3-litre saloon. *Autocar*

1900 DELAHAYE 6hp two-seater. *Automobielmuseum, Driebergen*

DELAHAYE (F) 1894–1954

(1) Emile Delahaye, Tours; Paris *1894–1898; 1898*
(2) L. Desmarais et Morane, Tours; Paris *1899–1902; 1902–1906*
(3) Automobiles Delahaye, Paris *1906–1954*

This firm was established in 1845 and initially produced brick-making machinery, later launching out into stationary engines. The first Delahayes were very much on Benz lines with slow-running, rear-mounted horizontal engines and belt

1925 DELAHAYE Type 87 1.8-litre saloon.
Musée de l'Automobile, Le Mans

1939 DELAHAYE Type 135 3½-litre drophead
coupé. *Automobielmuseum, Driebergen*

1951 DELAHAYE Type 235 3½-litre drophead
coupé. *Autosport*

transmission. Radiators and frames were tubular; Archdeacon and Delahaye himself took 4th and 6th places respectively in the Paris-Marseilles-Paris Race of 1896, though the firm took little interest in competition and their last appearance was in the Paris-Vienna (1902). By contrast, they were very interested in commercial vehicles, which made their debut in 1898 and bulked larger and larger in later years. In 1898 a 1.4-litre single and twins of 4½hp and 6hp were being made, the Paris works were opened, and Charles Weiffenbach joined the firm as Chief Engineer, a post he was to retain until after World War 2. By 1899, 600 Delahayes had been delivered, and production was running at 20 cars a month. Emile Delahaye himself retired in 1901, when wheel steering was standardized, though the old belt-driven designs were still catalogued as late as 1904, and there was even a short-lived 1902 model with front vertical engine and belt drive. More advanced was Type 10B, a 2.2-litre 4-cylinder, still with aiv, but with Panhard styling, final drive by side chains, and detachable cylinder heads; this was followed by a bigger 4.4-litre car said to develop 28bhp.

In 1904 detachable heads were found on both the 2.7-litre Type 15B twin at £420, and on a big 4.9-litre 4-cylinder car which also had a water-cooled exhaust system. T-head engines, gate change, and ht magneto ignition made their appearance in 1905, when the range included two twins and three 4-cylinder cars, the largest an 8-litre. The King of Spain bought one of these big Delahayes, with two hand and two foot brakes, and a foot-operated decompressor, in 1906. In 1907 licence-production of the make was undertaken in Germany by Presto, transverse rear suspension was featured, and the small 2-cylinder model acquired shaft drive. In the usual French tradition L-head monobloc engines appeared in 1908 on the 1.9-litre 12/16hp (Type 32), but the chain-driven cars were listed as late as 1911. An even smaller 1.2-litre 4-cylinder sold for £240 in 1909, and the new monobloc engines were used by White in America as the basis for their first petrol car, the 20/30. 1911 brought an interesting departure in the shape of the 3.2-litre Type 44, a blockcast V-6 with 4-speed gearbox. It sold for £470 in England, and was still being made in 1914. A 4-cylinder car was used for tests with the Parry Thomas electric transmission. Apart from such ingenious features as pressure lubrication to the spring shackles, the other 1914 Delahaye models were conventional monobloc 4-cylinder machines, available with detachable wheels and electric lighting. They came in 1.6-litre, 2.3-litre, 2.6-litre, 3-litre, 4-litre and 5.7-litre sizes, all but the smallest with 4-speed gearboxes.

After World War 1 the company settled down to 14 years of stodgy, dependable, and uninteresting cars, now with full electrical equipment and V-radiators, though at first the foot-operated transmission brake was retained. 4-cylinder models were sold with 2.6-litre and 3-litre sv engines, but there was also a 4.1-litre six (Type 82), with the unusual combination of detachable head and valve caps, which acquired front wheel brakes in 1921. All other Delahaye models were so equipped by 1925, but in the meanwhile the firm was ringing the changes on a complicated and dull range which included a 1.8-litre in sv and ohv versions, and two bigger inlet over exhaust fours, the 2.4-litre 15/35hp and the 2.9-litre 18/40hp. 4-speed gearboxes, pump cooling, and wooden wheels were regular features. In 1927 Delahaye formed a consortium with Chenard-Walcker, Donnet and (for a short while only) Unic, which was supposed to rationalize production, and did to the extent that it was hard to distinguish the 6-cylinder Delahaye from its Chenard-Walcker counterpart, though the former had full overhead valves and the latter inlet over exhaust. These sixes appeared in 1928, the Delahayes coming in 2.5-litre and 2.9-litre sixes, with magneto ignition up to 1929, and coil thereafter. 1929 was also the last year for the V-radiator, which gave way to an American-style ribbon-type. In 1930 there were also two 4-cylinder models, the smaller a straight-forward sv 1½-litre (Type 109), which was still listed in 1932. A bigger 6-cylinder (Type 126) pointed the way to better things, and in 1934 independent front suspension was offered on the 2,150cc Super 12 4-cylinder and on the 18CV Superlux, an ohv 6-cylinder which was also available with a Wilson gearbox.

In 1935 Delahaye bought the ailing Delage company, and in 1936 they were supplying 2.2-litre ohv 4-cylinder engines to Amilcar for installation in that firm's Pégase model. More important, they had come out with two exciting 6-cylinder sports models, both with ohv push-rod engines, independent front suspension, Bendix brakes, and synchromesh or Cotal gearboxes; the 3.2-litre Coupé des Alpes had 110bhp, and the 3.5-litre Type 135 120bhp. Both were capable of over 100mph in standard form, and the 135s proceeded to take 2nd, 3rd, 4th and 5th places in the 1936 French Sports Car Grand Prix, following this up by wins in 1937 and 1939 Monte Carlo Rallies, and at Le Mans in 1938. A Type 135 also won the controversial 'Fastest Sports Car Race' at Brooklands in 1939, where the opposition included a 2.9-litre Alfa-Romeo. There was a long-chassis version of Type 135, the Type 148, and in 1937 came the Jean François-designed Type 145, a short stroke 4½-litre ohv V-12 with Cotal gearbox and De Dion rear axle; its output was 238bhp, and the two-seater was capable of 165mph. Delahaye tried very hard with this car during the 1938 G.P. season, even beating Mercedes-Benz at Pau, as well as finishing 4th in the Mille Miglia – a remarkable double. It was outclassed, however, and even more so in 1939, despite the introduction of a single-seater version. A very few 'cooking' V-12s with conventional rear axles, hydraulic brakes, and exotic roadster coachwork were sold in 1939 at £1,485; though the 135 continued to do well.

During World War 2 Delahaye joined Baron Petiet's G.F.A. (Groupe Française ⌐utomobile) selling organization, these initials appearing on the radiator badges ⌐f all post-war cars, though the group ceased production in 1952. Production of the ⌐-cylinder 134 as well as the 135 was resumed in 1946, though the former did not ⌐ast long. Output of the sports cars was now 130bhp, and narrower, more ornate ⌐adiator grilles were used. In 1948 came the 4½-litre Type 175 series with hydraulic ⌐rakes; output was quoted as 185bhp, but they were not a success and were dropped ⌐rom the range in 1951. Penal taxation was in any case making life difficult for ⌐rance's quality-car makers, and combined Delahaye and Delage sales dropped ⌐rom 483 in 1950 to only 77 in 1951, in which year Delahaye won the Monte Carlo ⌐ally for the second and last time. It also marked the introduction of the company's ⌐ast new designs – a Jeep-type 4 × 4 with all-round independent suspension, and ⌐n improved 3½-litre, the Type 235 with aerodynamic bodywork, its output increased ⌐o 152bhp, and still with mechanical brakes. The marque was still exhibiting at the ⌐alon in 1953, but the following year they merged with Hotchkiss, and under ⌐he new management only trucks were made. After 1956 these too only bore the ⌐ame of Hotchkiss.   MCS

⌐E LA MYRE-MORY (F) *1911–1914*
⌐ts G. de la Myre-Mory, Neuilly, Seine

This company made 6-cylinder engines which could be fitted to other manu-⌐acturers' cars, and also one model of a complete car, a 4-cylinder 10hp with ⌐hree speeds and shaft drive, which was supplied with a four-seater torpedo ⌐ody.   GNG

⌐E LANSALUT (F) *1899*

The Paris-built de Lansalut was a voiturette powered by a 2½hp single-cylinder ⌐ir-cooled engine inclined at an angle of 45°. Transmission was by belts.   GNG

⌐ELAUGÈRE (F) *1901–1926*
⌐A des Etablissements Delaugère, Clayette, Frères et Cie, Orléans, Loiret

Regional makes are not peculiar to Great Britain and the U.S.A. The cars of ⌐elaugère-Clayette survived for a quarter of a century, little known even in their ⌐omeland. They were apparently never exported. Initially tricycles and quads ⌐ere marketed, as well as conventional single-cylinder runabouts of 475cc and ⌐00cc with 3-speed gearboxes, but by 1903 the company had progressed to bigger ⌐ehicles on Panhard lines with 2- and 4-cylinder automatic inlet valve engines ⌐nd side chain drive: the bigger 20hp had four forward speeds. Six models were ⌐isted in 1905, the top of the range being represented by an 8-litre 4-cylinder ⌐nd an even larger four of about 15 litres. 1906 models were still chain-driven, ⌐ut gate change was now featured, and a 16hp 4-cylinder could be bought for ⌐3,000 francs. A year later there were shaft-driven Delaugères as well: all had ⌐ow-tension magneto ignition, and there were a 1.8-litre twin, and two 4-cylinder ⌐ars of 4.4 and 8-litres. Monobloc engines came in with a 10cv 2.1-litre four in ⌐911. Twins were still catalogued in 1912, along with a 5.2-litre 6-cylinder Type ⌐N. At the 1913 Paris Salon the firm adopted a rear-axle gearbox on some models, ⌐while there were fours and sixes with the Fischer slide-valve power unit, also ⌐ried by De Bazelaire in France and Palmer-Singer in U.S.A.

After World War 1 there were no more departures from conventional design. ⌐n 1920 there were a 2.2-litre 4-cylinder and a 4.8-litre 6-cylinder, both electrically-⌐quipped: the latter was a big sv machine with fixed cylinder head and an 11ft 6in ⌐wheelbase which acquired fwb by 1923. Other models that year were sv 4-cylinders ⌐f 1.7-litres and 3.2-litres, with cone instead of multiplate clutches and rear-wheel ⌐rakes only, plus a 2.2-litre ohv car with detachable head. In 1926, the last year ⌐f manufacture, only 4-cylinder cars were made: they were ordinary to the end ⌐nd came in 1.7-litre, 2.1-litre, and 4.1-litre sizes.   MCS

⌐ELAUNAY-BELLEVILLE (F) *1904–1950*
⌐A des Automobiles Delaunay-Belleville, St Denis, Seine

The first cars made by this celebrated firm of locomotive and marine boiler ⌐makers appeared at the Paris Salon of 1904, when a beautifully-built, expensive ⌐machine was shown. It was designed by Marius Barbarou, formerly of Benz, and ⌐ater of Lorraine-Dietrich. Three 4-cylinder models were available for 1905, in 16, ⌐4, and 40hp sizes. They had separately-cast cylinders, T-head engines, full-pressure ⌐ubrication, 4-speed gearboxes and chain drive. The range of fours was extended to ⌐ive models between 10 and 40hp by 1907, when 15 and 40hp sixes were introduced. ⌐he larger models were chain-driven until 1910 when shaft drive was standardized ⌐n all models. In 1909 there was a small 10CV six of great refinement. The sixes ⌐ere both smoother and more reliable than other early examples, the very rigid ⌐rankshaft largely eliminating vibration.

Up to 1914 the Delaunay-Belleville was regarded by many as the best car in the ⌐world, and was favoured by buyers who valued quiet, unostentatious dignity. The ⌐ars were never entered in competitions and were usually chauffeur-driven. Among ⌐royal customers was Tsar Nicholas II of Russia who had a number of Delaunays, ⌐including the 70hp chain-driven six known as the model SMT (Sa Majesté le Tsar).

One of the features of the Delaunay was the round radiator and bonnet, and ⌐this was continued on the post-war cars, although in accordance with fashion

1912 DELAUNAY-BELLEVILLE Type SMT
70hp limousine, built for the Czar of Russia.
Autocar

1924 DELAUNAY-BELLEVILLE 15.9hp
drophead coupé. *Roger McDonald*

1928 DELAUNAY-BELLEVILLE 21hp
Greyhound saloon. *Autocar*

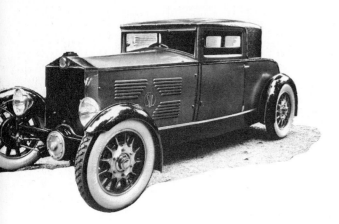

1927 DE LAVAUD 2.3-litre coupé. *Autocar*

1924 DELFOSSE 1½-litre sports car. *Oliver Herbosch*

the radiator was slightly pointed. The 1922 range consisted of a 10/12 and a 14/16hp four, and three sixes from a 14/16 to a massive 40/50 of 8-litres capacity and using dual ignition. The P.4B 2.6 litre of 1922 to 1929 had a single ohc engine, while from 1926 a range of push-rod ohv fours and sixes was offered. However the marque had lost its pre-war cachet, which had been taken over by Hispano Suiza and Rolls-Royce, and during the 1930s it lost its individuality as well. In 1931 Continental 4 or 4½-litre straight-8 engines from America were available in the 21CV 6-cylinder chassis. With greater and more silent power, they were cheaper than the French-engined cars. The eights were still theoretically available in 1936, but by that time the main Delaunay model was the 2.3-litre 6-cylinder R.16. This represented a further loss of individuality, as it closely resembled the Type 230 Mercedes Benz, although it had a longer stroke engine. It reappeared after World War 2 with a Cotal electric gearbox, and modernized 'waterfall' grille and was listed up to 1950. In the same early post-war years the factory which had made 70hp cars for the Tsar was turning out the 425cc Rovin minicar.   TRN

DELAUNÉ *see* LE ROLL

DE LAVAUD (F) *1927–1928*
E. Sensaud de Lavaud, Paris 16e

The main feature of the de Lavaud car was its automatic transmission, which had been tried out on a Voisin earlier. The propeller shaft drove a swash plate mounted near the rear axle; the variable angle of the plate gave an infinite variety of gear ratios. Another unusual feature of the car was the frame, which was made of a one-piece casting in Alpax, an alloy of aluminium and silicon. The cylinder head was also made of Alpax. The 2.3-litre 6-cylinder engine was steam-cooled, the radiator acting as a condenser. The low coupé body was only 5ft 1in in height. The de Lavaud was shown at the Paris Salon in 1927 and 1928, but few, if any, were sold to the public.   GNG

DELCAR (US) *1947–1949*
American Motors Inc, Troy, N.Y.

Although the short-lived Delcar was initially built as a delivery van, one, and possibly more station wagons were produced. With a 5ft wheelbase and a 4-cylinder engine located forward under the floor, it could seat six in relative comfort.   KM

DELECROIX (B) *1899*
The Delecroix was a light four-seater with a 3½hp single-cylinder vertical engine under the bonnet, and single chain drive.   GNG

DELFOSSE (F) *1922–1926*
Delfosse et Cie, Cambrai, Nord

The Delfosse was an attractive-looking small sports car using a variety of 4-cylinder engines by Altos or C.I.M.E., although a 2-cylinder engine was also available in 1922 and 1923. A feature of the Delfosse was the rear suspension which was by a combination of semi-elliptics and reversed quarter elliptics.   GNG

DELIN (B) *1899–1901*
Usines Delin, Louvain

The first Delin was a very light voiturette powered by a 2¼hp De Dion engine driving the front wheels in the style of the Victoria Combination. In 1901 a more conventional light car with a 3½hp engine driving the rear wheels by single chain was made. A few large cars of Daimler design were also made. In 1902 the factory was acquired by Mathieu.   GNG

DELLA FERRERA (I) *1924*
Fratelli Della Ferrera, Turin

This well-known motorcycle maker showed a prototype cyclecar in 1924. Its 707cc water-cooled 2-stroke engine sat well back in the frame, and had its four cylinders cast in pairs. The brake drums were integral with the wire wheels. It was never marketed.   MCS

DELLING (US) *1923–1927*
Delling Steam Motor Co, West Collingwood, N.J.; Philadelphia, Pa.

The Delling Steamer was developed by Eric H. Delling, who had designed Mercer cars and was later associated with Stanley. Both open and closed models were shown, powered by a 2-cylinder engine of Delling design mounted, together with the boiler, under a frontal bonnet. Few cars were produced.   KM

DELLOW (GB) *1949–1959*
(1) Dellow Motors Ltd, Alvechurch, Birmingham *1949–1956*
(2) Dellow Engineering Ltd, Oldbury, Birmingham *1956–1959*

The first production Dellows were evolved from a trials special built by K.C. Delingpole and R.C. Lowe. They used a Ford Ten engine in an A-shaped tubular chassis with a very simple two-seater body, which in the early models had no doors. Good acceleration and precise steering made the cars popular in rallies after they had been superseded in trials by more specialized vehicles. An optional extra was a Wade supercharger, while later improvements included a four-seater version (Mark III), and coil front suspension in place of the original transverse semi-elliptics (Mark V).

In 1956 a new company introduced the Mark VI, with all-enveloping fibreglass body and a longer wheelbase. In doing so, they sacrificed the originality which had made the earlier Dellows popular and few Mark VIs were sold. GNG

DEL MAR (US) *1949*
Del Mar Motors Inc, San Diego, Calif.

The Del Mar was an early post-war compact car, using a 2.6-litre 4-cylinder Continental engine developing 63bhp. It had a 3-speed Warner gearbox and the price was to be $1,200 for a 2-door five-seater sedan or convertible. There were ambitious plans to set up factories at Chicago, Philadelphia and Fort Worth, but only a few prototype cars were made. GNG

DELPEUCH (F) *1922–1925*
Automobiles Delpeuch, Neuilly, Seine

The Delpeuch was a medium-sized touring car powered by a 15CV 4-cylinder engine of 2,815cc capacity. The cylinders were cast in pairs. A five-seater open body was used, and the car had wire wheels. GNG

DELTA (i) (F) *1905–1915*
M. De Colange, Puteaux, Seine

The first Delta cars were advertised in 1905 in a wide range of 6, 8, 12, 14, 20 and 24hp models. It is not certain how many of these were made, and the next trace of Delta comes in 1913 when a single model of 10/12hp 4-cylinder light car was announced. It was usually made in two-seater form. GNG

DELTA (ii) (DK) *1918*
Mammen & Drescher, Jyderup

Twenty chassis were obtained from Reed & Glaser in 1917 and stored in New York until World War 1 was over. The engine used was a 4-cylinder unit of 8.6hp. TRA

DELTA (iii) (US) *c.1923–1925*

Of unknown origin, the Delta car was presumably a pilot model for a line of cars which never materialized. A 6-cylinder Continental engine and standard components were used. Whether more than a single car was built is not known. KM

DE LUCA (I) *1906–1910*
SA Fabbrica Automobili de Luca, Naples

De Luca was the name given to Italian-built Daimler cars. In 1903 a company had been formed at Milan called Motori Daimler for the manufacture and sale of cars, but no manufacture took place until the foundation of De Luca in 1906. A range of four cars was listed, a 16/24, 28/40, 32/55, and 42/65hp, all 4-cylinder models. How many of these were actually made in Italy is uncertain. In 1910 De Luca were said to be among the European firms taking out licences to build the Knight sleeve-valve engine; this was a separate licence from that of Daimler of Coventry. GNG

DE LUXE *see* CAR DE LUXE

DE MARÇAY (F) *1920–1921*
de Marçay et Cie, Paris 15e

The de Marçay cyclecar was powered by a 987cc Anzani air-cooled V-twin engine. It had a 3-speed gearbox, shaft drive and no differential. GNG

DE MARS (US) *1905–1906*
De Mars Electric Vehicle Co, Cleveland, Ohio

This was an electric car driven by a 1½hp motor. One distinguishing feature was a single electric headlamp. Final drive was by double chains. Changes of ownership resulted in the cars being called Blakeslee from 1906 to 1907, and Williams from 1907 to 1908. GMN

DEMATI (B) *1937–1939*
Defay, Matthys et Timberman, Brussels

Eugene Matthys was a coachbuilder with experience in making lightweight bodies since the 1920s, and the Demati prototypes used a special integral construction tubular frame. The first prototype had a 980cc J.A.P. V-twin engine driving the front wheels, and rear-wheel steering. The second car had normal front-wheel steering, and was powered by a 1,100cc 4-cylinder Ruby engine. The body was a 2-door saloon. GNG

DEMEESTER (F) *1906–1914*
Automobiles H. Demeester, Courbevoie, Seine

This was a light car made in 2- and 4-cylinder form. Demeesters were entered in voiturette races during the period 1908 to 1909, the cars in the latter Coupe des Voiturettes using a 4-cylinder ohv Sultan engine. By 1912 only 4-cylinder engines were being used, of 10, 12 and 16hp. The Sinpar light car was, at least towards the

1952 DELLOW Mark II 10hp sports car. *Autosport*

1913 DELTA(i) 10/12hp two-seater. *Autocar*

1906 DEMEESTER 1,104cc two-seater. *Museo dell'Automobile, Turin*

1912 DENNIS 24hp landaulette. *Dennis Bros Ltd*

1949 DENZEL 1,131cc sports car. *Dr Henry Goldhann*

end of its life, made by the same company, and the 1913/14 8hp 4-cylinder Sinpar was also included in the Demeester range, but sold under the name Demeester. GNG

DEMISSINE (B) *c.1901–c.1903*
O. de Ruyter Demissine, Brussels

Demissine light electric cars were shown at the 1902 Brussels Salon. GNG

DEMOCRATA (BR) *1963–1967*
Industria Brasileira de Auto, São Paulo

An elegant fibreglass coupé intended to use a front-mounted 2,498cc aluminium V-6 engine of Brazilian design and construction. It was planned to finance the company by public subscription. The only car ever seen used an American Chevrolet Corvair air-cooled unit. MCS

DEMOT (US) *1909–1911*
Demot Car Co, Detroit, Mich.

The Demot was a light (800lb) two-seater roadster with a 2-cylinder water-cooled engine. It was driven through a 2-speed planetary transmission. Brake-linings were of asbestos and camel's hair. GMN

DE MOTTE (US) *1904*
De Motte Motor Car Co, Valley Forge, Pa.

In one year of operation, De Motte offered a 10hp runabout and a 4-cylinder chain-driven touring car, as well as several models of commercial vehicles. GMN

DENNIS (i) (GB) *1899–1915*
Dennis Bros Ltd, Guildford, Surrey

John and Raymond Dennis made bicycles, motor cycles and tricycles under the name Speed King, and their first car also bore this name. It was a light two-seater with 3½hp De Dion engine at the rear, and tiller steering. It was shown at the National Cycle Show in November 1899, but was apparently not produced for sale. The next Dennis cars appeared in 1901, with an 8hp De Dion engine mounted in front under a De Dion-type bonnet. They had 3-speed gearboxes with direct drive on top, and shaft drive. A 10hp 2-cylinder model was also made. 1903 cars had ordinary bonnets with gilled-tube radiators; the small De Dion-engined cars were supplemented by 2- and 4-cylinder Aster-engined models of 12/14 and 16/20hp, while at least one 40hp 'Gordon Bennett type racer' was made with a Simms engine. In 1904 the famous overhead worm drive was introduced which was continued until the end of car production. Two stock 14hp tourers were entered in the 1905 T.T., finishing 16th and 18th, while in 1906 a Dennis performed so well in a 4,000 mile reliability trial that they were awarded the Dewar Trophy the following year.

In 1906 larger 30/35hp engines were used, made by White & Poppe of Coventry, and soon afterwards Dennis standardized on this make of engine, some being made specially to Dennis order. A wide range of reliable touring cars was made, from 15.9 to 60hp, the latter being a short-lived six made from 1910 to 1911 only. Dennis did not participate in racing, and gradually they found that goods vehicles and fire-engines were so much in demand that private car production had to be curtailed. The last models were 15.9 and 24hp fours, and after World War 1 cars were not re-introduced. Dennis are still well-known for their commercial vehicles today. GNG

DENNIS (ii) (GB) *1911*
John Dennis and Co, Harrow, Middlesex

The Dennis two-seater cyclecar had a big 1½-litre V-twin air-cooled engine; ignition was by magneto, and there was a conventional 2-speed gearbox and worm final drive. MCS

DENZEL (A) *1948–1960*
Wolfgang Denzel, Vienna VI

Denzel built two-seater sports cars using Volkswagen chassis and his own bodies. Porche 1.3- and 1½-litre engines were mainly used, and also Volkswagen units. During its early years the make was sold as the W.D. A Denzel, driven by its constructor, made best performance in the 1954 International Alpine Rally. HON

DE P (GB) *1914–1916*
(1) The Depford Co, Deptford, London S.E. *1914–1915*
(2) The Depford Co, New Cross, London S.E. *1915–1916*

The De P light car used a 10hp 4-cylinder Dorman engine and shaft drive. It was made by L.F. de Peyrecave, who had formerly been with the Duo cyclecar company, and was made in the Duo factory. In fact, some Duo-type cars with V-twin engines and belt drive were advertised under the name De P in late 1913. The company name Depford had no connection with the place of manufacture, but was formed from the names of the two sponsors, L.F. de Peyrecave and H.G. Burford. GNG

DERAIN (US) *1908–1911*
(1) Simplex Manufacturing Co, Cleveland, Ohio *1908–1910*
(2) Derain Motor Co, Cleveland, Ohio *1910–1911*

The Derain used 4-cylinder, two-stroke engines which were air-cooled. These, it was claimed, had a range of 100 to 2,000rpm. The larger models, for seven passengers, used a wheelbase of 10ft 5½in, and weighed up to 3,600lb. GMN

DERBY (i) (F) *1921–1936*
B. Montet, Courbevoie, Seine; Saint-Denis, Seine

The Derby started life as a typical French voiturette of its period. The American-made V-twin motor-cycle engine that powered it was soon replaced by a 4-cylinder, water-cooled Chapuis-Dornier unit of 900cc. Both models had three forward speeds. The Chapuis-Dornier versions' radiator was a copy of that of the successful 5CV Citröen. A variety of proprietary engines were fitted in the ensuing years, including Chapuis-Dornier, Ruby, and S.C.A.P. Several sports versions were built, the most potent being the Special. Its 1,100cc S.C.A.P. engine had three valves per cylinder, and was available with a Cozette supercharger. Though two touring 6-cylinder cars with side-valve engines were introduced in 1928, the make came to be associated primarily with sports cars. This was reinforced by the record-breaking activities of Miss Gwenda Stewart at Montlhéry track in her Derby-Miller, which started life in 1930 powered by a Miller racing engine, but came to include a majority of Derby-made components. The last Derbys were the most interesting. The L2 of 1931 had a small 6CV 4-cylinder engine that drove the front wheels, while the 11CV L8 of 1933, also with front-wheel drive, used a 2-litre V-8 engine. There was also a 1½-litre car with the Meadows 4 ED unit. The Derby was sold in England in the 1920s by Vernon Balls as the Vernon-Derby. TRN

DERBY (ii) (CDN) *1924–1927*
Derby Motor Cars Ltd, Winnipeg, Man., and Saskatoon, Sask.

With headquarters in Winnipeg, and an assembly plant in Saskatoon, the Derby was a copy of the U.S. Davis (i) and even shared that car's slogan, 'Built of the Best'. With a 6-cylinder Continental engine it sold for approximately $2,000. It is unlikely that sales reached 200 units. GB

DER DESSAUER (D) *1912–1913*
Anhaltische Automobil- und Motorenfabrik AG, Dessau

This firm followed the Motor-Werke Dessau (M.W.D.) and continued the M.W.D. 2.1-litre 8/22PS model, increasing the engine output to 24PS. A sports version was available with a 26PS engine. Although this model sold well, production had to cease in 1913 as a result of financial difficulties. HON

DEREK (GB) *1925–1926*
Derek Motors Ltd, West Norwood, London S.E.27

The Derek was a conventional light car available with 9/20hp sv or 10/25hp ohv Chapuis-Dornier engines. Two- or four-seater open bodywork was listed and prices ranged from £175 to £330. GNG

DE RIANCEY (F) *1899–c.1901*
Sté des Automobiles de Riancey, Levallois-Perret, Seine

The de Riancey had a 2-cylinder air-cooled engine mounted on a swivelling *avant-train*, drive being to the front wheels. Steering was by tiller, and the car had a light two-seater body. GNG

DE SALVERT (F) *1904–1906*
Perrier et Cie, Paris

The De Salvert was a conventional car using a 24/30hp engine with four separately-cast cylinders. Shaft drive was employed and the cars could carry roomy closed coachwork. GNG

DE SANCTIS (I) *1958–c.1966*
Automobili de Sanctis, Rome

The first car to bear the name of the de Sanctis family, who had a large Fiat dealership in Rome, was a rear-engined Formula Junior racing car powered by a Fiat 750 engine, in which Luciano de Sanctis had a number of successes during the 1958 season. It was later fitted with a Fiat 1100 engine, and replicas of this went into production in 1959. However, the advent of British engines in Formula Junior soon outclassed de Sanctis as it did other Italian FJ cars, and in the early 1960s de Sanctis turned to Ford-based units for their FJ and, later, Formula 3 cars. These achieved considerable national success, especially when driven by Jonathan Williams. GNG

DESBERON (US) *1903–1904*
Desberon Motor Car Co, New York, N.Y.

The 1903 model of this car used a 4-cylinder engine of 6.2 litres. It was a five-seater with left-hand drive, a 3-speed transmission and double-chain drive. In 1904, a smaller model with a 12hp engine was also built. GMN

DESCHAMPS (F) *1913*
Deschamps et Cie, Paris

Not to be confused with the Belgian Dechamps, the Deschamps was a cyclecar using a 6hp single-cylinder engine, a 3-speed gearbox and shaft drive. GNG

1925 DERBY(i) 8hp two-seater. *J.H. Noott*

1934 DERBY(i) V-8 2-litre two-seater. *Musée de l'Automobile, Rochetaillée-sur-Saone*

1931 DE SOTO(ii) Model SAX 3.2-litre sedan.
National Motor Museum

1932 DE SOTO(ii) Model SC 3.3-litre convertible.
Chrysler Corporation

1942 DE SOTO(ii) Model S-10 3.7-litre sedan.
Chrysler Corporation

1958 DE SOTO(ii) Fireflite convertible. *Chrysler Corporation*

DE SCHAUM (US) *1909*

De Schaum Motor Syndicate Co, Buffalo, N.Y.

The appearance of the De Schaum high-wheeler was somewhat more attractive than the majority of this type. The horizontal engine was of two cylinders and was air-cooled. The car had a friction transmission and double chain drive. **GMN**

DESGOUTTES *see* COTTIN ET DESGOUTTES

DESHAIS (F) *1950–1951*

Automobiles Deshais, Paris 11e

The Deshais was a minicar with a flat-twin 2-stroke engine and two-seater body. A speed of 50mph was claimed. **GNG**

DE SHAW (US) *1906–1909*

(1) Charles De Shaw, Brooklyn, N.Y. *1906–1907*

(2) De Shaw Motor Co, Evergreen, L.I., N.Y. *1907–1909*

This was essentially a built-to-order car. The engines used were 3-cylinder, 2-stroke types of 12/14hp. These were very light power units weighing only 119lb. A planetary transmission was used and the car had a distinctive oval bonnet. **GMN**

DESMOULINS (F) *1920–1923*

E. Desmoulins, Paris 11e

The Desmoulins was one of the very few cars to use two completely separate engines. They were Ballots, one of 1,131cc and one of 1,590cc, mounted side by side and driving through twin propeller shafts an underslung worm axle. This was called the sports model and used no gearbox, but a conventional single-engined touring model boasted no less than five speeds. **GNG**

DE SOTO (i) (US) *1913–1916*

De Soto Motor Car Co, Auburn, Ind.

The De Soto appears to have succeeded the Zimmerman. This was a large car with a 55hp, 6-cylinder engine, which was furnished with a compressed-air starter. The model Six-55 five-seater touring car sold for $2,185. **GMN**

DE SOTO (ii) (US) *1928–1960*

Chrysler Motors Corp, Detroit, Mich.

The De Soto was launched in 1928 as a 3.2-litre side valve six to compete with Oldsmobile, Pontiac and the cheaper Nashes. Styling and general design were in line with the 1929 Chryslers, and at $885 for a sedan (£340 in England) 90,000 were sold in the first twelve months. A 3.4-litre straight-8 on a 9ft 6in wheelbase was announced for 1930 as the world's cheapest 8-cylinder car. However, De Soto suffered badly in the Depression, and in 1932, when flexible rubber engine mountings and free wheels were made available, sales dropped to 26,000 cars.

The De Soto disappeared from the British market about this time, though certain 'Chrysler' models listed in England (the Mortlake, Croydon, and some of the Richmonds) were in fact De Sotos in all but name. A 6-cylinder version of Chrysler's advanced unitary-construction Airflow, the SE-type with a 4-litre engine, was brought out in 1934, but was as unsuccessful as its bigger sister. Later De Sotos followed regular Chrysler lines closely though in later years there was a tendency to move into a higher price class than Dodge; by 1952 De Sotos started $300 higher than the companion make.

By 1939 the cars were being made with independent front suspension, hypoid back axles and column change. There was a choice of two 6-cylinder engines and three wheelbase lengths, the longest of these being reserved for seven-seater bodywork – De Soto continued to offer a really roomy family car right up to 1954. A 4-speed semi-automatic Vacumatic transmission became an option in 1941, but De Soto's big post-war change of models did not take place until 1952, when the division followed Chrysler's lead in adopting the oversquare ohv V-8; their version was of 4½-litre capacity and developed 160bhp. With the advent of Chrysler's 'flight sweep' styling in 1955, the side-valve sixes were dropped and the standard engine was now a 4.8-litre eight, giving 185bhp in Firedome guise, and 200bhp in Fireflite form. Though this redesigning saved Chrysler sales generally, the slump in the medium-price class had an adverse effect on De Soto and in 1959 the division was merged with Plymouth. Last of the De Sotos were the 1961 models, unitary-construction cars with a choice of three engines: Plymouth's 145bhp ohv 'slant six' as used in the Valiant, and V-8s of 230 and 265bhp, the two former only in Canadian De Sotos. Production ceased in November 1960 after only a few had been delivered. **MCS**

DESSAVIA (D) *1907*

Anhaltische Fahrzeugfabrik Robert Krause, Dessau

A small two-seater car with friction drive was produced by this firm in limited numbers. **HON**

DE TAMBLE (US) *1908–1913*

(1) Speed Changing Pulley Co, Indianapolis, Ind. *1908–1909*

(2) De Tamble Motors Co, Anderson, Ind. *1909–1913*

The initial De Tamble model was a small runabout with a flat 2-cylinder engine

hich sold for $650. From 1909, larger conventional 4-cylinder cars were made. our body types were offered, the largest being Model K, a seven-seater touring ar with a 10ft wheelbase.
GMN

. et B. (F) *1896–1902*
ie des Automobiles David et Bourgeois, Paris 13e

D. et B. cars were large, heavy-looking vehicles with Daimler-type bonnets and rtillery wheels. The first model was powered by a 4-cylinder Pierre Gautier engine ounted in front, with a 4-speed gearbox and double chain drive. In 1900 a lighter hp 2-cylinder model was introduced, as well as the 16hp 4-cylinder model.
GNG

E TOMASO (I) *1959 to date*
e Tomaso Automobili SpA, Modena

After racing Oscas in Europe from 1956, Alejandro de Tomaso, an Argentinian nthusiast, turned manufacturer, starting with the Isis Formula Junior racer and ormula 2 machines. Fiat, Osca and Alfa-Romeo engines were used, and some ars were exported to America, though later competition models seldom progressed eyond the experimental stage. These included a Formula 1 flat-8 (1962), a 1963 ndianapolis contender on which the rear-mounted engine served as a structural nember and the frame was a light alloy casting; and a flat-4 for Formula 2 using development of the 1962 8-cylinder unit. None of these actually raced. De omaso then progressed to sports racers, also with rear engines, all-independent pringing and central backbone frames. The 1964 car used a 1.8-litre version of ne flat-8, but in 1965 De Tomaso adopted a 5-litre V-8. Also in 1965 he essayed road-going GT, the Vallelunga on classic De Tomaso lines, with GT coupé coach-work by Ghia and a 1,500cc British Ford Cortina engine. A companion open car, ne Pampero, followed in 1966, and a year later De Tomaso acquired the Ghia rm and exhibited the prototype Rowan electric city car at the Turin Show.

More serious was the Mangusta, a derivative of the Vallelunga powered by a 7-litre Ford V-8 engine, and incorporating a 5-speed ZF transaxle, servo-assisted -wheel Girling disc brakes, and a limited-slip differential. It was capable of 155mph nd went on sale in America in 1969 at $10,950, including air conditioning. It lso led to a closer association with Ford, who have since distributed De Tomasos the U.S.A., and a second coachbuilder, Vignale, joined the De Tomaso-Ford-Ghia alliance. In 1969 the company returned to racing with an unsuccessful F2 nachine using a Cosworth-Ford engine, and there was a new GT coupé, the Mus-ela. Little was heard of this car, which used a 2.9-litre British Ford V-6 engine onverted to ohc and fuel injection: its published output of 230bhp closely matched ne power developed by the Mangusta's V-8 in federalized form. In 1970 there vas a new Formula 1 car, also Cosworth-Ford-powered, and the company offered heir first front-engined touring model, the Deauville. This was a luxury 4-door ports saloon closely resembling the Jaguar XJ6 in appearance. Automatic ransmission was standard; engines were dohc American Ford conversions with apacities of 4.7 or 5.8 litres. The bigger engine, in 330bhp pushrod form, powered ne Pantera of 1971, a Mangusta development credited with 162mph, and a two-oor development of the Deauville, known as the Longchamp, was introduced for 973.
MCS

ETROIT (i) (US) *1899–1902*
Detroit Automobile Co, Detroit, Mich.

Although very few cars were made, this company is significant as it was the redecessor of the Cadillac Automobile Co, and because its chief engineer was Ienry Ford. Although formed in 1899, the company did not turn out any cars ntil 1901 when a Ford-designed car with 2-cylinder engine, epicyclic gears and ingle chain drive appeared. The engines were built by Henry M. Leland's company, eland & Faulconer, and in 1902 Leland took control of the Detroit Automobile Co. He changed the name to Cadillac, and the first Cadillac car to be made on production basis left the works in March 1903.
GNG

ETROIT (ii) (US) *1904*
Wheeler Manufacturing Co, Detroit, Mich.

This Detroit was a five-seater tonneau with rear entrance. Its 15hp opposed 2-ylinder engine was claimed to give 35mph. It was furnished with a removable vooden top, and the standard colours were red and green with yellow running-ear.
GMN

ETROIT (iii) (US) *1904–1908*
Detroit Auto Vehicle Co, Detroit, Romeo, Mich.

This car was built as a two-seater runabout, or a five-seater tourer. The final nodels of this make were shaft-driven and had 2-cylinder engines of 22/24hp. These ad a complex bonnet and radiator outline.
GMN

ETROIT (iv) (US) *1914*
Detroit Cyclecar Co, Detroit, Mich.

This was a cyclecar, at 850lb somewhat heavier than was normal for its type, which used a 4-cylinder water-cooled engine of 1½ litres' capacity. It was known as he Little Detroit.
GMN

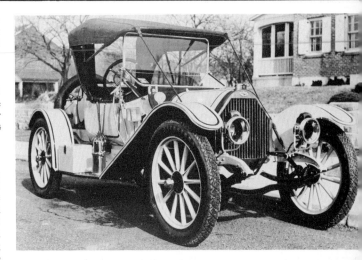

1909 DE TAMBLE 36hp roadster. *Automotive History Collection, Detroit Public Library*

1901 D. et B. 16hp six-seater. *The Veteran Car Club of Great Britain*

1965 DE TOMASO Vallelunga GT coupé. *Carrozzeria Ghia*

1973 DE TOMASO Pantera GTS coupé. *Automobili de Tomaso SpA*

1909 DETROIT ELECTRIC brougham. *The Veteran Car Club of Great Britain*

1914 DETROIT ELECTRIC brougham. *Gilltrap's Auto Museum*

1931 DE VAUX Model 6-75 coupé. *Keith Marvin*

DETROIT-DEARBORN (US) 1910–1911
Detroit-Dearborn Motor Car Co, Dearborn, Mich.

A touring torpedo, designated the Minerva model, and a roadster termed Nik were the two models of this make. They used a 4-cylinder engine of 35hp.　GM

DETROIT ELECTRIC (US) 1907–1938
(1) Anderson Carriage Co, Detroit, Mich. *1907–1910*
(2) Anderson Electric Car Co, Detroit, Mich. *1911–1918*
(3) Detroit Electric Car Co, Detroit, Mich. *1919–1938*

One of the best-known electric automobiles built in the United States as well a one of the most long-lived, the Detroit Electric car reached its peak in productio and sales between 1912 and 1920. Its success was largely due to the demand b women for a simple car for urban use. More than 1,000 units per year were sold u to World War 1, but production tapered off in the 1920s. A few Detroits wit Renault-type bonnets were made under licence by Arrol-Johnston in 1913/14. I 1920, the old-fashioned appearance of the cars was modified by the introduction c false front which made the Detroit look more like a conventional car. In the earl 1930s, production was cut to individual orders, and bodies for the more cor ventional-looking cars were obtained from Willys-Overland, complete with th horizontal bonnet louvres. The earlier design, however, with rounded batter covers, fore and aft, was also available. Only a handful of Detroit Electric car were produced annually after 1935. Some of the last cars used the Dodge bonne and grille.　K

DETROITER; BRIGGS-DETROITER (US) 1912–1917
Briggs-Detroiter Motor Car Co, Detroit, Mich.

The Detroiter was a popular light car sold in large quantities. The early model were powered by a 32hp, L-head engine. For 1915 a five-seater touring car was pro duced with a V-8 engine of 3.3 litres. This car weighed less than 2,300lb and sol for $1,295. In 1917 a Detroiter with 6-cylinder Continental engine was listed. GM

DETROIT-OXFORD; OXFORD (US) 1905–1906
Detroit-Oxford Mfg Co, Oxford, Mich.

This car used a 16hp 2-cylinder (opposed) engine with water cooling. It had sha drive and a doorless five-seater body.　GM

DETROIT STEAM CAR (US) 1922–1923
Detroit Steam Motors Corp, Detroit, Mich.

The Detroit Steamer initially appeared as the Trask-Detroit. Very few of thes touring cars were actually built. All of them had a 2-cylinder engine of their ow design. A handful of prototype models carrying the Windsor name were also buil for the company's projected sales in Canada.　KN

DEUTSCHLAND (D) 1904–1905
Motorfahrzeugfabrik Deutschland GmbH, Berlin NW

This company made steam cars designed by Peter Stoltz. The 4-cylinder stear engine developed about 40bhp. The Deutschland appeared at the Berlin Moto Show in 1903, but production was never started on a great scale.　HO

DEUTZ (D) 1907–1911
Gasmotorenfabrik Deutz AG, Cologne-Deutz

The firm of Gasmotorenfabrik Deutz were not pioneer car builders, but neverthe less they have an important place in the history of motoring. They produced the firs gas engines invented and designed by Nicolaus August Otto, and it was this whic to a great extent led to the use of such engines in cars. Daimler and Maybach wer employed at Deutz before Daimler started his own business in Bad Canstatt. Whe Deutz decided to establish an automobile department they engaged Ettore Bugat as chief designer. His first car appeared at the Berlin Motor Show of 1907, bu until 1909 only prototypes were produced. The layout of the engine showed som features which later appeared in Bugatti designs: for example, the detachable valv guide and seat, the quadrant and roller interposed between the camshaft and valv stems, and the use of a single block for the four cylinders with the lower part of th bore spigotted into the crank-case. The Deutz engine can therefore be considered a the prototype of all subsequent Bugatti engines and cars.

The models 8a, 8b and 9c were based on the same principles, all with 4-cylinde in-line monobloc engines. Bugatti also built a prototype of a small 1.3-litre ca which was raced at the Gaillon Hill Climb in 1908 and at a Frankfurt Race Meetin in 1909 under the Deutz emblem. This car did not go into production at Deutz bu was later developed into Bugatti's Type 13. After Bugatti founded his own factor in 1909 he still worked as consulting engineer for Deutz. The '21' of 1910 and tw subsequent models based on it were the last private cars made by Deutz. Productio ceased in 1911. The firm continue to turn out agricultural tractors, and Magirus Deutz lorries and buses are produced at Ulm.　HO

DE VAUX (US) 1931–1932
De Vaux-Hall Motor Corp, Oakland, Calif.; Grand Rapids, Mich.

The De Vaux was an economy car with a 6-cylinder engine and a full line of body styles which failed after 14 months in business. The 1931 cars were called the Model 6-75. By January 1932, sales were poor and the De Vaux was in financial trouble. Its assets were taken over by the Continental Motor Company of Detroit, Mich. and subsequent cars produced during 1932 were known as the De Vaux Model 80 or the De Vaux Continental. As Continentals they were sold until 1934.   KM

DE VECCHI (I) *1905–1917*
1) De Vecchi, Strada & Cia, Milan *1905–1908*
2) De Vecchi & Cia, Milan *1908–1917*

De Vecchi cars were conventional, well-built machines, mainly with 4-cylinder engines. In the early years there were 10/12 and 16hp versions, the latter with shaft drive. The firm also showed interest in racing, and De Vecchi himself won the 1908 Padua–Bovolenta Race. In the 1914 Targa Florio a 20/30hp De Vecchi driven by Gloria finished second, and the other car driven by Sivocci actually led the race for some time before an accident forced its withdrawal. The 1914 De Vecchi cars were made in three 4-cylinder models, a 15/20 monobloc, a 20/25 and a 25/30, both with pair-cast cylinders. All had shaft drive. Production dwindled during World War 1, and ceased altogether in 1917.   AZ

DE-VO (US) *1936*
De-Vo Motor Car Corp, Hagérstown, Md.

Norman De Vaux, builder of the De Vaux car in 1931 and 1932, set up a corporation in Maryland late in 1936 with the idea of manufacturing a 4-cylinder, full-size five-seater sedan for the export market. The prototype car was shown at the Waldorf-Astoria Hotel in New York City late in 1936 or early in 1937 with production scheduled for early 1937. It was displayed by the M.P. Möller Co of Hagerstown, Md., which had previously built the Crawford, Dagmar, Standish and other cars, and resembled the 1933/4 Continental with a 1935 Reo-style grille.   KM

D.E.W. (D) *1927*
Zschopauer Motorenwerke J.S. Rasmussen AG, Filiale Berlin, Berlin O17

Before Rasmussen started to build his D.K.W. cars he produced electric cars in his Berlin factory. The chassis-less wood-framed body which later became typical of the D.K.W. cars, was first used on these electric vehicles. This lightweight construction was very useful for electric cars which had formerly suffered from the great weight of their chassis, and D.E.W. cars were frequently used as taxicabs.   HON

DEWALD (F) *1902–1926*
Charles Dewald, Boulogne-sur-Seine

Very little is known of the work of this firm, which was in existence in Paris in 1896, though a 1902 directory listing of '*travaux pour amateurs*' suggests that they built prototypes to order rather than production vehicles for sale to the public. The first reference to Dewald cars as such comes in 1912, and in 1913–14 they were turning out three 4-cylinder models; of these the two smaller cars of 2.1 litres and 3.6 litres respectively had shaft drive, but side chains were used on the big 5.3-litre Type KA.

In 1919 a prototype 4.8-litre single-ohc straight-8 appeared, but although this was announced for production in 1924 and listed until 1926, most Dewalds sold were commercial vehicles.   MCS

DE WANDRE (B) *c.1922–1925*
Éts F. De Wandre, Brussels

Like its compatriot the Speedsport, the De Wandre was based on the Model T Ford. The makers said that while Americans wanted cars purely for transport, the European customer valued an attractive appearance, so the De Wandre carried a distinctive V-radiator, wore disc or wire wheels and came in four body styles, three-seater roadster, touring car, saloon and town landaulet. The chassis was lowered by 5½in and lengthened by 18in.   GNG

DEWCAR (GB) *1913–1914*
D.E.W. Engineering Co Ltd, Eynsford, Kent

Harold Dew was one of the earliest cyclecar builders and had made a number of ultra-light single-seaters for his own use before he began manufacture. His production cars used a single-cylinder Precision engine of 4½hp in the monocar, and an 8hp 2-cylinder Precision in the two-seater. Both cars used belt drive. In May 1914 the name of company and cars was changed to Victor and the company later moved to Ealing. Dew afterwards designed the D. Ultra cyclecar.   GNG

DEXTER (F) *1906–1909*
Constructions d'Automobiles Dexter, Lyons

Dexter cars were built in very small numbers by A. Faure, a former racing cyclist. They used very large 4- and 6-cylinder engines of 50/60hp, 72hp, and 100hp and chain drive.   GNG

DEY (US) *1917*
Dey Electric Corp, York, Pa.

This company made a short-lived three-seater electric runabout.   GNG

1927 D.E.W. electric saloon. *Neubauer Collection*

1913 DEWCAR 4hp monocar. *Motor*

1906 DEXTER 100hp racing car. *Lucien Loreille Collection*

1924 D.F.P. 12hp tourer. *Lucien Loreille Collection*

c.1921 DIABLE 1,096cc 3-wheeler. *Autocar*

1924 DIABOLO 1,100cc 3-wheeler. *Neubauer Collection*

DEY-GRISWOLD (US) 1895–1898

Dey-Griswold & Co, New York, N.Y.

Invented by Harry E. Dey, the Dey-Griswold was probably the only car to combine an electric motor with a fluid drive system whereby oil was forced through turbines attached to the rear wheels. After three years of experiments, the system was abandoned as there was too much slippage in the turbines for the limited power available.   GNG

D.F.P. (F) 1906–1926

Doriot, Flandrin et Parant, Courbevoie, Seine

Doriot and Flandrin had worked for Clément-Bayard and Peugeot, and their first products were straightforward shaft-driven single-cylinder voiturettes with transverse rear suspension, sold as Doriot-Flandrins until Parant arrived to complete the triumvirate. The singles were still being marketed with 1,100cc engines as late as 1910, but the 1908 range already included two 4-cylinder cars with sv Chapuis-Dornier engines of 2.4-litres and 2.8-litres capacity. By 1910 there was a small four, the very successful 10/12hp of 1.6 litres, with L-head monobloc engine, magneto ignition, thermo-syphon cooling, cone clutch and 3-speed gearbox. There was also a 25/30hp 6-cylinder car in 1911. In 1912 D.F.P. started to make their own engines, the '10/12' being joined by an excellent 2-litre '12/15' with pressure lubrication, 3-bearing crankshaft and 4-speed gearbox, capable of 2,500rpm and 55mph. Further, the British concession was acquired by the brothers W.O. and H.M. Bentley, who ran the '12/15' in competitions; by the end of 1913 a specially prepared example had been timed over the half-mile at 89.70mph. Nothing, however, could be done with the 16/22hp, a 2.8-litre (later 3-litre) machine with pair-cast cylinders and poor performance. In 1914 came the sporting 12/40hp with V-radiator and electrics: for this model the Bentleys persuaded D.F.P. to fit aluminium pistons, as a consequence of which a 65mph performance was available for only £320. W.O. Bentley finished 6th in that year's T.T., an excellent effort for a 2-litre car competing against specialized 3.3-litre machines.

D.F.P. never recovered fully from World War 1 and Bentley's decision to set up as a manufacturer in his own right meant that the company lost its best export market. A 12/15hp chassis now cost £675 as against £290 in 1914. Failing finances forced the company to use proprietary engines, Altos for the 2-litre models, and a Sergant in the '10/12', which went American in 1922 with central change and coil ignition, but reverted to a magneto in 1923. 1922 '12/40s' had 4-wheel brakes, and a year later this model was supplanted by an ohv 4-speed '13/50', once again with a D.F.P.-built engine. At the same time the company marketed the little D.F. Petite, a sporting machine in the Amilcar idiom, with an ohv 1,100cc engine, 3-speed gearbox, quarter-elliptic springing all round and a back axle without differential. This had front-wheel brakes by 1925, but a year later production had ceased, the factory being acquired by the Lafitte concern.   MCS

D.F.R. (F) 1924

Désert et de Font-Réault, Neuilly, Seine

This motorcycle company made a number of 3 and 6hp cyclecars.   GNG

DHUMBERT (F) c.1920–1930

Automobiles Dhumbert, Voiron, Isère

The Dhumbert appeared first as a 10hp 4-cylinder car, but in 1930 the firm announced that they were building 6- and 8-cylinder cars with independent suspension. They probably never built more than prototypes.   GNG

DIABLE (F) 1921–c.1924

The Paris-built Diable 3-wheeler was powered by a 1,096cc 2-cylinder engine, and had chain drive to the single rear wheel.   GNG

DIABLO see BOHANNA STABLES

DIABOLO (D) 1922–1927

Diabolo Kleinauto GmbH, Stuttgart

A small 3-wheeler car with a 1.1-litre Motosacoche engine, this car showed some resemblance to the Morgan 3-wheeler.   HON

DIAMANT (F) 1901–1906

(1) Hammond, Mouter et Cie, Paris 17e
(2) Sté La Française, Paris 17e

The Diamant was a conventional car powered by a 5 or 7hp single-cylinder engine, a 9 or 12hp twin, and from 1904 a 24hp 4-cylinder unit. The cars were also known as La Française, a name which was born by the firm's motor cycles which were better-known than the cars. In fact, as made by Alcyon, the name La Française-Diamant was found on motor cycles as late as 1959. Another car carrying the name La Française was made by Onfray in 1900/1901.   GNG

DIAMOND (US) 1910–1912

Diamond Automobile Co, South Bend, Ind.

The Diamond was a continuation of the Ricketts. The 50hp 6-cylinder Diamond

s produced in three body types, including the five-seater touring car at $2,200.
ring 1911 and 1912, this car was referred to as the R.A.C., apparently in
mory of the Ricketts Automobile Co.   GMN

AMOND T (US) 1905–1911
amond T Motor Car Co, Chicago, Ill.
Diamond Ts were all large cars with 4-cylinder engines of 4.7 to 7.1 litres with
ings up to 70hp. They were all equipped with sliding gear transmission and shaft
ve. As many as five body types were offered in one year. The name Diamond T
vives on large commercial vehicles to the present day.   GMN

ANA (i) (D) 1922–1923
ana Automobilwek GmbH, Munich
A cyclecar with tubular chassis and a 4-cylinder engine.   HON

ANA (ii) (US) 1925–1928
ana Motors Co, St Louis, Mo.
The Diana Company was a subsidiary of the Moon Motor Car Co. The cars,
wered by a 4-litre 8-cylinder Continental engine, carried a radiator which was an
nost exact copy of the Belgian Minerva and, on one model of sports roadster, was
ered in bronze instead of nickel, with bronzed wire wheels to match. Steel wind-
ield posts on the closed models afforded the driver increased visibility. Prices
Dianas ranged from $1,595 to $2,895 and a rarely seen town car was offered at
,000.   KM

ATTO (I) 1905–1927
Diatto-A. Clément Vetture Marca Torino, Turin 1905–1909
Società Officine Fonderie Fréjus Vetture Diatto, Turin 1909–1918
Fonderie Officine Fréjus Automobili Diatto, Turin 1918–1919
Automobili Diatto, Turin 1919–1923
Autocostruzioni Diatto, Turin 1924–1927
The Diatto railway engineering concern entered the automobile industry by ally-
g themselves with Adolphe Clément (who joined the board) to build Clément-
ayard cars under licence in Italy. Various 2- and 4-cylinder models were marketed
tween 1906 and 1910; all had T-head engines, ht magneto ignition, and shaft
ve, though latterly the largest Diatto, the 4.8-litre 28/35, could be had with side
ains as well, and in 1908 there was a short-lived 4.1-litre six. Clément's resigna-
n in 1909 coincided with the company's first monobloc engine, the 2.9-litre 16/20,
t this was still of T-head type. The L-head configuration did not arrive until
e 2-litre 12/15 of 1910 (sometimes known as the Fréjus); this evolved into the
ple pre-World War 1 Diatto, and grew up to 2.4 litres with a 4-speed gearbox
1915. In that year Scacchi and Newton were absorbed, and Diatto turned over
trucks and Bugatti aero engines, though new 2.7-litre and 4-litre fours were
nounced in 1916.
The firm made a few 1½-litre Bugatti Brescias in 1919 under the Tipo 30 designa-
n, but their own post-war programme consisted of a 2.7-litre 4-cylinder in the
aditional idiom, and Tipo 10, a simple light car with 1,018cc sv engine, 3-speed gear-
x, and plate clutch. This attempt to compete against Fiat had been abandoned
the end of 1922, in which year the company introduced their successful Tipo
, a 2-litre four with shaft-driven overhead camshaft, 4-speed gearbox, and the
ual Italian mock-Rolls-Royce radiator. Output, originally a modest 40bhp, was
rked up to around 70 by Diatto's development engineer, Alfieri Maserati. Com-
tition successes included three successive victories (1922, 1923 and 1924) in the
rcuit of Garda, as well as the 2-litre honours in the 1924 Gran Premio della
otte at Monza. The short-wheelbase high-performance 20S, as well as 4-wheel
akes, appeared in 1924 and at the end, in 1926–27, 2.6-litre (Tipo 26) and 3-litre
ipo 25 and 35) developments were listed, in addition to the basic model. Maserati
ilt a dohc supercharged straight-8 Diatto for the 2-litre Grand Prix formula in
25, but it made one brief and unsuccessful appearance. By 1926 it had been
designed, and was being raced as the first car to bear the Maserati name.   MCS

IAZ Y GRILLO (E) 1917–1922
iaz y Grillo SL, Barcelona
The Diaz y Grillo or D. y G. was a sporting light car in the same category as the
avid and the America, originally using 2-cylinder 2-stroke Blumfield engines, but
ter 4-cylinder 4-stroke MAG 1,100cc engine. Torsion bar suspension gave a com-
rtable ride on bad surfaces and helped the D. y G. to success in rallies.   JRV

ICKINSON MORETTE (GB) 1903–1905
E. Dickinson & Co, Birmingham
The Morette was a very light 3-wheeler with the choice of a 2½hp single-cylinder
a 4hp 2-cylinder engine driving the single front wheel by chain. The car could be
arted from the seat by a flexible cord fitted to a groove in the flywheel. The price
as from 70 to 80 guineas, according to the model.   GNG

IEBEL (US) 1901
iebel Cox Mfg Co, Philadelphia, Pa.

1926 DIANA(ii) 3.9-litre roadster. *Automobile Manufacturers Association*

1920 DIATTO 16hp tourer. *Autocar*

1903 DICKINSON MORETTE 2½hp 3-wheeler. *G.N. Georgano Collection*

1912 DIEDERICHS 10/12CV tourer.
H-O Neubauer

1965 DIVA 1.2-litre GT coupé. *Diva Cars Ltd*

The Diebel was a light runabout with a 7hp 2-cylinder engine which was a
cooled by toothed-edge fins projecting from the cylinders. The price was $650. G

DIEBLER & RUSSELL (US) 1908
Diebler & Russell Co., Berlin, Wisc.
Only three cars with this name were built. They used a 4-cylinder 40hp Ruten
engine. Further details are lacking. GM

DIEDERICHS (F) 1912–1914
Société des Automobiles Diederichs, Charpennes, Rhône
Charles Diederichs of the Bourgoin (Isère) textile-machinery family built a stea
tricycle at Bourgoin in 1878, and (in association with his brother Frédéric) o
or two prototype cars in the 1899–1901 period. The production cars were, howev
made at Charpennes in a separate factory, and were straightforward sv 4-cylind
machines rated at 10/12CV. 2,155cc Luc-Court engines of long-stroke type we
used, and not more than 60 were made. M

DIEHLMOBILE (US) 1962–1964
H.L. Diehl Co, South Willington, Conn.
A 'spare car' that folded to fit in the boot of a car. When assembled it was
3-wheeled conveyance with a 3hp Briggs and Stratton engine and a canopy to

DILE (US) 1914–1916
Dile Motor Car Co, Reading, Pa.
This make of light car appears to have been made only as a two-seater roadst
It had a 1.4-litre 4-cylinder engine, sliding-gear transmission and wire wheels. GM

DINARG (RA) 1959–1969
(1) Dinamica Industrial Argentina SA, Córdoba 1959–1966
(2) Stad Srl, Córdoba 1966–1969
The Dinarg minicar had a rear-mounted 191cc single-cylinder 2-stroke engine
4-speed gearbox and chain final drive. The body was a 2-door saloon not unlike th
of the early Goggomobil in appearance.

DINGFELDER (US) 1902–1903
Dingfelder Motor Co, Detroit, Mich.
The Dingfelder was a typical motor buggy with a horizontal water-cooled,
cylinder engine of 3.5hp. Price for this two-seater car was $500. GM

DININ (F) 1904
Alfred Dinin et Cie, Puteaux, Seine
Unlike most electric vehicles which were heavy town carriages, the Dinin wa
small, reasonably-priced two-seater with the batteries under a bonnet which gave
the general appearance of a petrol-engined car. 'Dinin cars' said a corresponde
'supersede the somewhat wanting look of the average electric car.'

DINOS (D) 1921–1926
Dinos Automobilwerke AG, Berlin W 57; Berlin-Hohenschönhausen; Berli
Tempelhof
Dinos followed the firm of Loeb. 4-cylinder 8/35PS and 6-cylinder 16-72
models were produced with ohc engines, the latter only in small numbers. Produ
tion of Dinos cars ceased in 1926 to make way for an additional production pla
for the AGA, which belonged to the same concern. HC

DIRECT (B) 1904–1905
Sté de Constructions Mécaniques et d'Automobiles, Brussels
The Direct car was so-called because it had no gearbox, drive being direct to
countershaft from which the rear wheels were driven by double chains. The lar
40/50hp 4-cylinder engine was said to be very flexible, and any necessary reducti
in gear ratio could be obtained by varying pressure of the clutch. M. Goldschmi
who designed the car later made steam wagons for use in the Congo. G

DIRECT DRIVE see CHAMPION (iii)

DISBROW (US) 1917–1918
Disbrow Motors Corp, Cleveland, Ohio
Louis Disbrow, a noted racing driver, designed this two-seater speedster from t
engine up. Its appearance was similar to the racing cars of the time, with the additi
of cycle-type mudguards. The car was fitted with wire wheels but no running boar
A choice of Wisconsin-built 7.9 or 9.9-litre 4-cylinder, T-head engines was availab
The larger engine would drive the car to 90mph, it was claimed. GM

DISK see ENKA

DISPATCH (US) 1911–1922
Dispatch Motor Co, Minneapolis, Minn.
The first Dispatch cars had 2-stroke engines, but these were replaced by a co

ntional sv Wisconsin unit of 23hp. Roadster, tourer and coupé models were made, prices from $935 to $1,210. An unusual feature of the cars was that they used ain drive until at least 1918. GNG

TELLA (RA) *1959–1966*

.A.M. (Sociedad Industrial Americana de Máquinas) di Tella Automotores SA, enos Aires

From humble beginnings in 1910 Torquato di Tella's industries grew to include tories producing steel pipes, electrical equipment, and motor vehicles, these last ng based on B.M.C.'s 55bhp 1½-litre Farina-styled saloons and station wagons Austin, Morris, MG or Riley forms. Price of Di Tella's MG Magnette was und £2,000 in 1966, when the factory was taken over by I.K.A. This latter ncern continued the manufacture of Di Tella types. MCS

VA (GB) *1962–1968*

Tunex Conversions Ltd, London S.E.5. *1962–1965*

Diva Cars Ltd, London S.E.5. *1966–1967*

Skodek Engineering, London S.W.7 *1967–1968*

The Diva GT, designed by A.J.D. Sim, utilized a multi-tubular space frame with lependent spring/damper units at front and rear. Any of the usual Ford-based gines could be fitted, the most common being the 105E. A run of class victories racing, particularly those achieved by Doug Mockford and John Miles in 1964 and 65, brought sufficient demand for production (mostly in kits) to exceed 50 in 1966, s qualifying for homologation as a Group 4 sports car. The mid-engined Valkyr s then introduced, built for Lotus-Cortina power or Coventry-Climax units of to 300bhp. A neat fibreglass coupé body was fitted to comply with International pendix J regulations. Hillman Imp engines have also been used in mid-engined upé versions. In 1967 manufacturing rights for all Diva cars were sold, but the w firm did not survive on the market for long. DF

XI (D) *1904–1928*

Fahrzeugfabrik Eisenach, Eisenach *1904–1920*

Dixi-Werke AG, Eisenach *1920–1928*

The Fahrzeugfabrik Eisenach produced motor cars from 1898 under the name of artburg, but after 1904 the name was changed to Dixi (literally 'I have spoken'; lloquially 'It is the last word'). The first models were the S 12 (shaft drive) and 17 (chain drive). They were followed by a wide range of models until World War 1. a result of their very solid construction and good quality finish they were very pular and appeared in large numbers. In Britain they were known as Leanders, in ance as Reginas. A small model, the B 1 with a 5/14PS 1,320cc engine, had its but in 1914 and was also built after the war. In 1920 the Dixi works were bought the Gothaer Waggonfabrik, builders of railway coaches. 1922 was the year of e second Avus Race – in its early years a national event only – and Dixi had a great ccess in gaining 1st, 2nd and 4th place with a racing version of their 6/24PS type. ixi mainly concentrated on this model. A 6-cylinder 13/60PS was produced in small mbers in 1927. The 6-cylinder 9/40PS of 1928 was identical with the Cyklon 40PS. The best known model built by Dixi was also their last. It was the 3/15PS, e Austin Seven built under licence. This small and reliable car became very pular in Germany. At first it appeared as a two-seater roadster, later also as casional four-seater. When the Dixi works were acquired by B.M.W. late in 1928 is model was continued under the name of BMW-Dixi. HON

XIE; DIXIE JR (US) *1908–1909*

outhern Motor Car Factory, Houston, Tex.

The Flier, the roadster model of the Dixie, had a 4-cylinder water-cooled engine 24hp with a 2-speed transmission and shaft drive. The Dixie Jr was a high-wheeler ith an air-cooled, 2-cylinder under-seat engine of 10/12hp, with friction trans-ission and double-chain drive. GMN

XIE FLYER (US) *1916–1923*

entucky Wagon Mfg Co, Vincennes, Ind., Louisville, Ky.

The Dixie Flyer was an assembled car which used various engines by Lycoming Herschell-Spillman at different times and was available in numerous body types. 1922, with the Jackson car, the Dixie Flyer was absorbed by National and came the National Model 6-31. KM

K.R. (DK) *1953–1954*

utofabriken D.K.R. AS, Roskilde

F. Gabrielsen, S.A. Mathiesen and Ahlmann-Ohlsen were concerned in this pro-ct to build a Danish plastic-bodied motor car. It had an all-enveloping plastic loon body and 1,100cc Heinkel flat-4 engine. However, the managers lacked capi-; they were unable to obtain help from the Danish government and the project iled. TRA

K.W. (D) *1928–1966*

) Zschopauer Motoren-Werke J.S. Rasmussen-Zschopau; Berlin-Spandau *1928–* 939

1905 DIXI 28/32PS tourer. *Deutsches Museum, Munich*

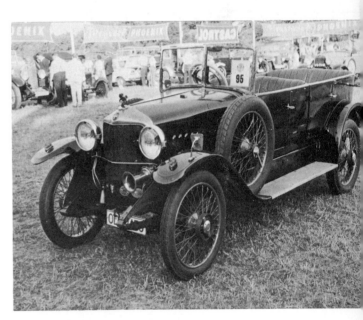

1924 DIXI 6/24PS tourer. *G.N. Georgano*

1932 D.K.W. Type F.1 490cc cabriolet. *Auto Union GmbH*

1937 D.K.W. Type F.7 Meisterklasse 684cc drophead coupé. *Neubauer Collection*

1953 D.K.W. Sonderklasse 896cc drophead coupé. *Auto Union GmbH*

(2) Auto Union GmbH, Düsseldorf; Ingolstadt *1950–1966*

D.K.W. was already a well-known producer of motor cycles when the firm's first car appeared in 1928 at the Leipzig Fair. It was produced in the former D-Wagen works in Berlin, which were taken over by D.K.W. This first model was characterized by its 2-stroke engine, a principle which D.K.W. used for their motor cycles and which they followed up to the end in 1966. The 584cc 2-cylinder engine developed 16.5bhp. The car was a chassis-less wood-framed construction by Slaby (S.B.). A very popular two-seater sports version with an 18bhp engine was developed from this model. In 1930 the '4/8' with a 780cc 22bhp engine appeared. 1931 saw the debut of D.K.W. front-driven cars, the F 1 with a 490cc and the F 2 with a 584cc engine. The front-wheel drive principle was adopted for several subsequent models. In 1932 D.K.W. became a member of the Auto Union Group. The 2-cylinder front-driven 589cc Reichsklasse and 684cc Meisterklasse and the V-4 rear-driven models 1,054cc Sonderklasse and Schwebeklasse were among the most popular German cars up to 1939.

In 1945 the D.K.W. works were nationalized together with all other Auto Union plants. Auto Union was re-established in 1949 in Düsseldorf and production of the first post-war D.K.W. started in 1950. It was a 2-cylinder 2-stroke 690cc model called the Meisterklasse F 89, mechanically based on the last pre-war model but with a new body. A range of Sonderklasse models followed with a 3-cylinder 896cc engine; these were also known by the designation '3/6' and were based on a 1940 prototype. The '1000' model (3-cylinder, 981cc) was not marketed under the name D.K.W., but only as the Auto Union, although it was a true D.K.W. The Junior and the F 11, F 12 and F 102 also had 3-cylinder 2-stroke engines but different bodies from the former models. All post-war models had front-drive.

In 1957/58 a sports version, the Monza, was produced by Fritz Wenk of Heidelberg. '3/6' 896cc, 40bhp and '1000' 981cc, 44bhp engines were used, the latter also in a tuned version developing 55bhp. Chassis were original D.K.W. while the bodies were specially made of fibreglass. This model gained five world records at the Monza circuit and also was successful in several international competitions. D.K.W. engines were available in several tuned versions and used for Formula Junior racing.

D.K.W. cars are built in Brazil under licence by DKW-Vemag. The nationalized East German factory also produced D.K.W.'s, in 2- and 3-cylinder form, until 1956. In 1966 production of D.K.W. cars was given up.   HON

D.L. (GB) *1913–1920*

(1) W. Guthrie & Co, Motherwell, Lanarks.
(2) D.L. Motor Mfg Co Ltd, Motherwell, Lanarks.

The D.L. was an attractive-looking light car with a V-radiator. It was available in two sizes, an 8hp and 10/12hp, both 4-cylinder cars, costing £150 and £16? respectively for a two-seater.   GNG

D.L.G. (US) *1906–1907*

St Louis Automobile & Supply Co, St Louis, Mo.

The initials of this car stood for Dyke, Leibert and Givens, the first named being A.L. Dyke who had sold cars for home assembly a few years earlier. The D.L.G. had a 4-cylinder 35hp engine with overhead inlet valves, and was sold as a two seater runabout.   GNG

D.M.C. (GB) *1913–1914*

Dukeries Motor Co Ltd, Worksop, Notts.

The D.M.C. 3-wheeler used a tiny 4½hp single-cylinder engine of the company's own manufacture, and belt or chain drive. The price was £85.   GN

DOBI (E) *1919–1920*

Autociclos Dobi, Madrid

The Dobi was a short-lived cyclecar using a Douglas engine and belt drive.   JRV

DOBLE (US) *1914–1931*

(1) Abner Doble Motor Vehicle Co, Waltham, Mass. *1914–1915*
(2) General Engineering Co, Detroit *1916–1918*
(3) Doble Steam Motors Corp, Emeryville, Calif. *1924–1931*

Steam as a means of propulsion for passenger cars persisted longer in America than elsewhere because of the degree of flexibility it afforded, and the finest by far of steam cars in America or anywhere else was the Doble. As far as the public was concerned, the major snag of steam cars was the time they took to start from cold, but in its final, 1923 form the Doble, the most sophisticated of the breed, got up steam automatically in less than one and a half minutes after the electric ignition switch lit the burner. There was also a really efficient condenser, which gave a range of up to 1,500 miles on 24 gallons of water. A horizontal 4-cylinder engine fed from a flash boiler developed something like 75bhp, providing acceleration and hill climbing ability out of the ordinary even among steamers. With all this went an elegance and luxury that was even rarer, a price of about $8,000 and a three-year guarantee.

After experimental vehicles had been made, the first Doble to be offered for sale appeared in 1917, and allegedly 11,000 orders were received, but war priorities stopped the project. Plans were made to restart production in 1924, 1,000 cars a year being the target. In addition, a line of cheaper steamers costing $2,000 was to be made. In fact Abner Doble was a perfectionist who could never produce on such a scale, and not more than 45 Dobles were ever made. These came from a succession of companies and factories. The General Engineering Company of Detroit was to have made the 1917 car as the Doble-Detroit. Then Doble moved west to California, where a big new factory at Emeryville was to have coped with the expansion of 1924, but this dream never became reality. TRN

DOCTORESSE (F) *1899–1902*
Sté Française d'Automobiles (Système Gaillardet), Paris

The Doctoresse cars were designed by Frédéric Gaillardet who afterwards became chief engineer of the Sté La Française, and then consultant to the Mildé company. The Doctoresse was made in two models, 6 or 12hp, both with front-mounted 2-cylinder engines and chain drive. A speed of 60 mph was claimed for the 12hp model. The 1899 Gaillardet was a 5hp 3-wheeler. GNG

DODDSMOBILE (CDN) *1947*
Only one prototype was built of the Doddsmobile 3-wheeler. It had a small air-cooled engine driving the rear wheel, open two-seater moulded plywood body, and automatic transmission. GNG

DODGE (i) (US) *1914 to date*
(1) Dodge Brothers, Detroit, Mich. *1914–1928*
(2) Chrysler Corp, Detroit, Mich. *1928 to date*

The brothers John and Horace Dodge, early Ford shareholders and builders of engines for the Ford Motor Co, produced their first car in November 1914. It was a conventional side valve monobloc four of 3½-litres, developing 25bhp. It was noted for its 12-volt electrics, and 'back-to-front' gear change, features that were not discarded until 1926. The tough Dodge 4 won early acceptance by the American army after being used in General Pershing's punitive expedition to Mexico in 1916, and the type was widely used in World War 1 as a staff car and ambulance. Also in 1916 Budd all-steel tourer bodywork was adopted; some saloons were also made in this year, using the same construction. The price of open cars was $785, and Dodge was fourth in overall U.S. sales in 1916 with 70,700 cars delivered, following this up with a second place in 1920. The four was still the staple product in 1924, when 1,000 cars were being made a day. A new departure for 1927 was a 3.7-litre side-valve six with internal-expanding hydraulic brakes.

In July 1928, Walter P. Chrysler paid $175,000,000 for the company. Discontinuation of the four, now developing 40bhp and fitted with front-wheel brakes, followed almost immediately, but for the next three years Dodges preserved their individual appearance. Though their cars were reckoned more expensive than De Sotos, Dodge offered a very cheap Standard 6 at $765 in 1929, their other models being the Victory at about $1,000, and a big Senior which paralleled Chrysler's 75 at $1,675. A straight-8 was listed from 1930 to 1933. Free wheels were among the regular Chrysler improvements which appeared on the scene in 1932, followed by synchromesh gearboxes in 1933. In this year Dodge again took fourth place in sales, with 86,062 cars delivered. There were no Dodge versions of the Chrysler Airflow, but 1935 cars had the Airstream styling and side-valve 6-cylinder engines of 3.6-litre capacity. Overdrive, hypoid rear axles and independent front suspension made their appearance in the later 1930s, and Dodges of the 1940s were hard to distinguish from De Sotos or the de luxe Plymouths.

The expected ohv V-8, publicized under the name Red Ram, materialized in 1952; it was a modest-sized 3.8-litre unit, and in 1955, when Chryslers were largely restyled, the cars were available both with the old 3.8-litre side-valve six and with V-8s in three ratings up to 193bhp. By 1959 – the last year of the sv 6-cylinder – the most powerful eight disposed of some 345bhp, from 6.3 litres. Dodge has continued to offer more potent alternatives to the regular sedans, with a brisk Charger fastback coupé available in 1966. A 'compact' car, the Lancer, was listed in 1961, but this was virtually indistinguishable from the Plymouth Valiant. Regular 1967 Dodges had Chrysler's unitary construction and alternator ignition introduced in 1960, and there were three basic ranges: the semi-compact Dart on a 9ft 3in wheelbase; the medium-sized Coronet; and the big Polara and Monaco on a wheelbase of 10ft 1in, with V-8 engines of up to 7.2 litres' capacity. The more sporting Charger coupé appeared in 1968, available with a 6,981cc hemi-head V-8 of 425bhp; concealed wipers came on the 1969 models; and in 1970 the Challenger filled the gap between Dart and Coronet: standard engines were a 3.7-litre six or a 5.2-litre V-8. There was a Dart sports coupé, the Demon, in 1971, but this was also the last year of the hemi-head engine and of convertibles in the Dodge range.

For 1973 there were the Dart on a 9ft wheelbase, the Challenger coupé, the Coronet and its sporting sister, the Charger, and the full-sized Polara and Monaco series. The Monaco had concealed headlamps. The biggest Dodges had V-8 engines, automatic transmissions and power steering as standard. Electronic ignition was standard on all models, and all but the basic Darts had front disc brakes. Engines available were sixes of 3,245cc and 3,688cc, and V-8s of 5.2, 5.6, 6 and 7.2 litres.

Since 1970 Dodge have been selling the Japanese Mitsubishi Colt as a small-car line in the U.S.A. MCS

1925 DOBLE Model E tourer. *Henry Ford Museum, Dearborn, Mich.*

1900 DOCTORESSE 6hp voiturette. *Neubauer Collection*

1915 DODGE(i) 3½-litre sedan. *Dodge Division, Chrysler Corporation*

1934 DODGE(i) Six 3½-litre sedan. *National Motor Museum*

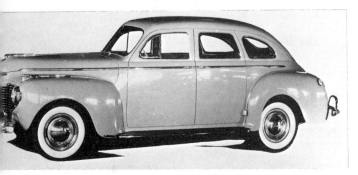

1941 DODGE(i) Custom 3.6-litre sedan. *Dodge Division, Chrysler Corporation*

1973 DODGE(i) Challenger hard top. *Dodge Division, Chrysler Corporation*

1948 DOLO JB-4 571cc coupé. *Autocar*

DODGE (ii) (US) 1914–1915
A.M. Dodge Co, Detroit, Mich.

This was considered a cyclecar despite its standard track and 102 in wheelbase. It had a 4-cylinder 25hp water-cooled engine, with a friction transmission, and was designed by George Wahl of Wahl Motor Co. The company was sued in 1915 by Dodge Bros who successfully claimed that their name had been infringed.　GMN

DODGESON (US) 1926
Dodgeson Motors, Detroit, Mich.

The Dodgeson was designed and engineered by John Duval Dodge, son of John F. Dodge, builder of the Dodge Brothers car. It had a straight-8 rotary valve engine with a 63mm × 127mm bore and stroke (3.2 litres) producing 72bhp at 3,000rpm. The engine was placed in a 4-point suspension position, being supported between a channel section of side rails by rubber shock insulators set in brackets. Only prototype models were built and series production was never started.　KM

DODO (US) 1912
Autoparts Mfg Co, Detroit, Mich.

This car, with tandem seating for two passengers, looked like a cyclecar, although it had standard tread of 4ft 8in with a wheelbase of 8ft 4in. It used front-wheel drive from a 2-cylinder air-cooled engine of 10-12hp. The brand name for this car was somewhat prophetic as it probably never got beyond the one prototype.　GMN

DODSON (GB) 1910–1914
Dodson Motors Ltd (David Brown & Sons Ltd), Huddersfield, Yorks.

Dodsons were made in two models, a 12/16hp and a 20/30hp. They were almost identical to the equivalent Renaults, except for a Zenith carburettor and modified lubrication and ignition system.　GNG

DOLLY (GB) 1920

The Dolly Light car was fitted with a 4-cylinder water-cooled engine, separate gearbox and underslung worm drive. The design was unusual in that the engine and transmission slanted rearwards so that there was no need for a universal joint on the drive shaft.　MJWW

DOLO (F) 1947–1948
Etablissements B.D.G., Pierrefitte, Seine

The Dolo was listed in two models, both using horizontally-opposed engines with oversquare dimensions (58mm × 54mm), a four of 571cc, and an eight of 1,142cc. The cars had 4-wheel independent suspension by torsion bars, and closed bodies with transparent Plexiglass roofs. The 4-cylinder car was shown at the Paris Salon, but it is not certain if the eight was ever built.　GNG

DOLORÈS (F) 1906
Dolorès et Cie, Paris

Dolorès cars were listed in 10, 16, 24 and 50hp models, for one year only. As with many ephemeral makes, the larger models were probably never built.　GNG

DOLPHIN (i) (GB) 1906–1909
The Two-Stroke Engine Co Ltd, Shoreham, Sussex 1908–1909

The Dolphin car was built by Ralph Ricardo's marine engine company and utilized the 28–30hp cylinder 2-stroke engine designed by his cousin (later Sir) Harry Ricardo. Initially, Lloyd & Plaister of Finchley Road, London, supplied engine and gearbox parts, but chassis came from Thorneycrofts who had family ties with another director, Michael Sassoon (brother of Siegfried, the poet). Total production was about twelve cars plus a 2-cylinder prototype of 15hp used by Harry Ricardo as personal transport until 1919. He sold the manufacturing rights to Lloyd & Plaister who used the design in single-cylinder form in their Vox cyclecar.　MJWW

DOLPHIN (ii) (US) 1961

This California-built space-framed vehicle, with a Ford 105E engine and fibreglass body, was offered to West Coast Formula Junior enthusiasts. The designer was John Crosthwaite, who had worked in Britain with Lotus and Cooper.　DF

DOLSON (US) 1904–1907
(1) J.L. Dolson & Sons, Charlotte, Mich.
(2) Dolson Automobile Co, Charlotte, Mich.

The Dolson was a large car with a 60hp engine. In 1907 a seven-seater touring model cost $3,250. There were also smaller chain- and shaft-driven 20hp flat-twins and a shaft-driven four of 28/30hp.　GMN

DOMINION (i) (CDN) 1911
New Dominion Motor Co, Windsor, Ont.

In 1910 Dominion Motors Ltd was organized to build engines and a car, styled after the U.S. Regal, to be known as the Royal Windsor. After a company reorganization the projected car was renamed the Dominion, but this effort failed and the firm was liquidated. In 1911 the assets were bought by Detroit ...ncipals who formed the New Dominion Motor Co and apparently did produce ...ne cars called Dominions.   GB

...OMINION (ii) (CDN) *1914*
...minion Motor Car Co, Coldbrook, N.B.
This firm was organized largely with U.S. capital to assemble a car of British ...sign near the ice-free port of Saint John. It bought machinery and land, and ...parently displayed some pilot models, but never started production.   HD

...OMMARTIN (F) *1949–1950*
...mpagnie des Moteurs Dommartin, Dommartin, Somme
The Dommartin company was formed to exploit and race the redesigned ...F.A.C. racing car, but after this plan failed they brought out a small car using ...800cc rear-mounted 2-cylinder engine, an open four-seater body and a 5-speed ...arbox. Few, if any, reached the market.   GNG

...ONG-FENG (p); TUNG-FENG (wg) (EAST WIND) (CHI) *1958 to date*
...1 Automobile Plant, Changchun, Kirin, Manchuria
The first Dong-Feng was a 4-door saloon powered by a 1½-litre 4-cylinder ohv ...gine driving through a 3-speed syncromesh gearbox. Despite attempts at export ...s model was short-lived, and was replaced on the production line by the Hong-Qi ...ousine.
The name Dong-Feng has survived on various Chinese cars and lorries, including ...3-wheeler of 1968 and a saloon with a 1,930cc 4-cylinder single-ohc engine and ..., announced in 1969.   BE

...ONNET; DONNET-ZÉDEL (F) *1924–1934*
...a des Automobiles Donnet, Nanterre, Seine; Neuilly, Seine; Pontarlier, Doubs.
After Zédel and Vinot et Deguingand ceased production, Donnet, a new company ...nstituted from them in 1924, offered two new cars called Donnet-Zédel. A light ...r was made, the 7CV Type G, which had a side-valve 4-cylinder engine of ...00cc and (unusual for so small a vehicle) a 4-speed gearbox. It was a solidly-built ...achine, and a sports model was listed. There was, in addition, a medium-sized ...ur of about 2¼ litres. From 1926, the firm came to concentrate upon a 2½-litre ..., also with side valves, which proved a popular car. Another, smaller six with ...3-litre (later 1.8-litre) Sainturat-designed engine was also offered. In the 1932 ...nge however, was a new small car in the shape of a 750cc 2-stroke. This, a Violet ...esign, had been sold as the Deguingand until 1930. A fwd 2-litre 6-cylinder shown ...the 1931 Paris Salon came to nothing. With the demise of Donnet, Simca took ...er the factory.   TRN

...ONOSTI (E) *1922–1923*
...araje Internacional, San Sebastian
The Donosti was an advanced design of sports car using a 3-litre 6-cylinder twin ...hc engine with four valves per cylinder. It was planned to enter three cars in the ...asarte circuit races, but they were not ready in time.
A 4-cylinder engine was also made, but only a few cars were completed, all to ...ecial order.   JRV

...ORA (I) *1905–1906*
...ta Industriale Dora, Genoa; Alpignano, Turin
This company intended to make electric vehicles for private and commercial use, ...ut after the production of a few prototypes, they turned to general electrical ...gineering.   GNG

...ORCHESTER (US) *1906–1907*
...ub Automobile Co, Boston, Mass.
The Dorchester was an obscure runabout, with a choice of single- or 2-cylinder ...ir-cooled engines. The engine was exposed and was mounted in front of the dash-...oard. The final drive was by chain and steering was by tiller.   GMN

...ORÉ (F) *c.1900*
...té G. Doré, Levallois-Perret, Seine
The Doré car used an electric *avant-train* unit, most of the bodies being taxicabs. ...petrol engine was also made by Doré, but it is not thought that there was ever a ...omplete Doré car.   GNG

...OREY (F) *1906–1907; 1912–1913*
...H. Dorey, Paris
W.H. Dorey was a French-Canadian factor and accessory merchant who assemb-...ed a few cars at different times. His first cars used the familiar single-cylinder De ...Dion engine for the voiturette, and 4-cylinder V.R. and Mutel engines for larger cars, ...ll of which used shaft drive. He apparently made no cars between 1907 and 1912, ...hen he produced a 2-cylinder air-cooled cyclecar.   GNG

...ORIOT-FLANDRIN see D.F.P.

1958 DONG FENG 1½-litre saloon. *David Scott*

1930 DONNET 7CV coupé. *Autocar*

1932 DONNET 11CV saloon. *G.N. Georgano*

1923 DONOSTI 3-litre sports car
J. Rodriguez-Viña

1906 DORRIS 30hp tourer. *Automotive History Collection, Detroit Public Library*

1923 DORRIS 38hp sedan. *Jacques Kupélian Collection*

DORMANDY (US) *1903–1905*
(1) United Shirt & Collar Co, Troy, N.Y.
(2) Troy Carriage Works, Troy, N.Y.

Four Dormandy automobiles were built, all of them powered by 4-cylinder cooled engines. In the last car, certain Frayer-Miller Components were used.

DORNER (D) *1927*
Dorner Ölmotoren AG, Hanover

The 'heavy oil engine' designed by Hermann Dorner was intended for use in sm private cars. The 3/10PS engines were arranged as single or V-twin units. Dor took up manufacture of the first diesel-engined private cars in the world, but finan difficulties prevented large-scale production. Licences for Dorner diesel engines w acquired by some American firms, such as Packard and I.H.C.

DORNIER DELTA *see* ZÜNDAPP

DORRIS (US) *1905–1926*
(1) St Louis Motor Carriage Co, St Louis, Mo. *1905–1906*
(2) Dorris Motor Car Co, St Louis, Mo. *1906–1926*

Cars built by George P. Dorris between 1897 and 1905 were known as St Lo automobiles; thereafter the Dorris name was used. The cars were of advanc design. The earlier 4-cylinder Dorris models gave place to sixes in 1916 and Do engines were used throughout production. Later cars were prestige vehicles w prices approaching $7,000 for closed models. The Pasadena phaeton with o engine was well thought of in the 1920s. The complete range of Dorris mod was available until the end of 1926, although production actually ceased in 1 1923.

DORT (US) *1915–1924*
Dort Motor Car Co, Flint, Mich.

Joshua Dallas Dort had been building carriages for many years when he decid to go over to car manufacture. His 1915 Model 5 was the first car he produced, a he went on to sell some 107,000 cars altogether. 1916–17 Dorts were similar to t Model 5, but there were 4 doors now instead of 3 on the five-seater tourer. fleur-de-lys roadster and a centre-door sedan were added and prices ranged fro $695 to $1,065. The engine, a 4-cylinder L-head 2.7-litre Lycoming, had therm syphon cooling and the axle was of the three-quarter-floating type. All Dorts we equipped with cantilever rear and semi-elliptic front springs.

Lycoming's famous 4-cylinder L-head Model K engine was adopted in 1918 capacity was 3.1 litres – but the old clutch and service brake controls were retaine both on the same pedal: the other pedal operated the 'emergency' brake. Open ca cost $865, the sedan and a coupé $1,265. A 'sedanette' was introduced at $1,00 this had removable sides. 1919 Dorts were similar but higher in price. 1920 broug such improvements as conventional pedal controls, a hand-brake lever, and the r moval of the petrol tank to the rear. Although prices had risen to $985–$1,535, th was probably the firm's most successful period and more than 30,000 cars were so

A new phase began in 1921, with Rolls-Royce-type radiators and longer bodie In 1922 an unusual 9-window sedan and a delivery van joined the range. Improv ments included a disc instead of cone clutch, spiral bevel gears, S.S. tyres an later, Lynite pistons which, with a heavy 2-bearing crankshaft, provided good torqu maximum rpm was 2,000 and engine rating was 19.6hp. Prices ranged from $8 to $1,445. Dorts were little changed in 1923, when sports models were given di wheels. A six with a Falls ohv power unit was added to the range. The popular Do fours were abandoned, surprisingly, in 1924. The six, a smooth, powerful car wi forced lubrication, was given new body styles, but retained its 2-wheel brakes. Do ceased production in this same year and another marque passed into history. Se also Gray Dort.
C

DOUGILL (GB) *1896–1899*
A.W. Dougill & Co Ltd, Leeds, Yorks.

From 1896 to 1898 Dougill made a number of experimental cars with horizont engines at the rear, belt drive to a counter-shaft, and chain final drive. In 1899 number of Lawson Motor Wheels were assembled at Dougill's factory. These wer self-contained power units, with road wheel, petrol tank and brake, which coul be fitted to any 2-wheel horse-drawn vehicle. From 1903 to 1905 the name Doug was sometimes given to the friction driven Frick cars.
GN

DOUGLAS (i) (GB) *1913–1922*
Douglas Bros Ltd, Kingswood, Bristol

A neat cyclecar with pressed steel frame, an air-cooled flat-twin engine of 1,070c shaft transmission and coil rear suspension was offered from 1913, in sports o everyday form. The post-war version was over 200lb heavier, and was upgraded t 1,224cc. In 1932 a revised edition with a 750cc engine and cantilever suspensio was announced but production remained devoted to motor cycles.
D

DOUGLAS (ii) (US) *1918–1922*
Douglas Motors Corp, Omaha, Nebr

Formerly the Drummond car, the Douglas (sometimes erroneously spelled Douglass') was announced in May 1918 'with the idea of supplying the Middle-West with a high-powered car at a reasonable price . . .' The Douglas, with an 8-cylinder Herschell-Spillman engine, was available in roadster and touring car forms at prices ranging from $2,000 to $2,150.   KM

DOWAGIAC *see* LINDSLEY

DOWNING (US) *1913–1915*
Downing Cycle Car Co, Cleveland, Ohio
   Despite the manufacturer's name, this was a light car with a 'standard' track of 4ft 8in and a wheelbase of 8ft 2 in. It was furnished with a 4-cylinder Farmer engine with overhead valves and a capacity of 1.6 litres.   GMN

DOWNING-DETROIT (US) *1913–1915*
Downing Motor Car Co, Detroit, Mich.
   This cyclecar was made in two models. One was driven by a conventional air-cooled V-twin engine of 13hp and carried two passengers in tandem. The more advanced model was akin to a light car with a water-cooled, 4-cylinder engine and a 3-speed transmission.   GMN

D.P.L. (GB) *1907–1910*
Dawfield, Phillips Ltd, West Ealing, Middlesex
   These cars were mainly sold as taxis, especially to Australia, but could be used privately for town use. The 12/15hp flat-twin engine was under the front seat, and final drive was by chain.   GNG

DRAGON (i) (US) *1906–1908*
(1) Dragon Automobile Co, Philadelphia, Pa. *1906–1907*
(2) Dragon Motor Co, Philadelphia, Pa. *1908*
   This car was built in two- and five-seater touring models with 25hp and 35hp 4-cylinder engines. These were all equipped with sliding-gear transmissions and shaft drive. The last models included a very sporty runabout on an 8ft wheelbase.   GMN

DRAGON (ii) (F) *1913*
P. Milhuet, Sancerre, Cher
   This company made two light car models, one with a 6hp single-cylinder engine and the other with a 10hp 4-cylinder engine.   GNG

DRAGON (iii) (US) *1921*
Dragon Motors Corp, Chicago, Ill.
   A short-lived and attractive car produced in very limited numbers. Featuring wire wheels, individual door steps and a high, pointed radiator quite similar to the ReVere, the Dragon was available as a speedster, and as four-seater and six-seater passenger touring models.   KM

DRAGSPORT (GB) *1971 to date*
Dragsport Autos, Upper Batley, Yorks.
   Following the fashion for Ford T-shaped fun cars, Graham Marshall's Dragsport used a tubular chassis and fibreglass tub body, with the usual options of Ford mechanical parts.   DF

DREXEL (US) *1916–1917*
Drexel Motor Car Co, Chicago, Ill.
   The Drexel succeeded the Farmack (1916). Two models were built. Model 5-40 was a five-seater touring car with a 4-cylinder Farmer overhead camshaft engine at a surprisingly low $985. Model 7-60 was available either as a four-seater roadster or as a seven-seater touring car. The '7-60' had a remarkable 3-litre, 4-cylinder engine with double overhead camshafts operating four valves per cylinder. This engine developed 65hp at 3,600rpm; a very high speed for that time.   GMN

DREYHAUPT (D) *1905*
Richard Dreyhaupt, Leipzig-Eutritzsch
   This was a small car with Omnimobil components, powered by a 4-cylinder 10PS engine.   HON

DRIGGS (US) *1921–1923*
Driggs Ordnance & Mfg Co, New Haven, Conn.; New York, N.Y.
   The Driggs was a small car with a 4-cylinder engine of its own design which, according to the company was 'Built With the Precision of Ordnance'. Driggs cars were relatively expensive for their size and production never exceeded a few units per day. Closed and open models were available.   KM

DRIGGS-SEABURY (US) *1915–1916*
Driggs-Seabury Ordnance Corp, Sharon, Pa.
   The initial model of this make was an open two-seater cyclecar, with underslung chassis and a water-cooled 4-cylinder engine. This model was succeeded by the

1918 DORT 3.2-litre tourer. *Court Myers*

1914 DOUGLAS(i) 10hp two-seater. *Motor Sport*

1922 DRIGGS 11hp sedan. *Floyd Clymer Publications*

1971 DRI SLEEVE Moon-Raker sports car. *Dri Sleeve Car Co Ltd*

1907 DRUMMOND(i) 14/16hp two-seater. *National Motor Museum*

1961 D.R.W.-FORD sports car. *Motor Sport*

Sharon late in 1915. Later Driggs-Seabury cars included both open and close models which were small but well-proportioned, with wire wheels. This manufacture was also involved in building Driggs, Ritz, Twombly (iii) and Vulcan (ii) cars.

GM

DRI SLEEVE MOON-RAKER (GB) *1971*
Dri Sleeve Car Co, Warminster, Wilts.

This was a close replica of the Bugatti Type 35, powered by a Ford 1600 G engine. It had a Ford rear axle, modified VW front axle and aluminium wheels The bonnet and side panels were in aluminium and the rear body section wa of fibreglass. Each car was supplied with a 'Dri Sleeve' to protect the driver's righ arm in bad weather while using the outside gear lever and handbrake. The Moon Raker was available both in kit form and fully assembled, but only five were sold.

GNG

DRUMMOND (i) (GB) *1905–1909*
North British Manufacturing Co Ltd, Dumfries

The first Drummond had a 20/24hp 4-cylinder engine, and was originally buil specially by D. McKay Drummond of the Dumfries Ironworks for his own use ir reliability trials. Later a number of 14/16hp and 20/24hp cars were produced fo sale.

GNG

DRUMMOND (ii) (US) *1915–1918*
Drummond Motor Car Co, Omaha, Nebr.

The Drummond was an assembled 4-cylinder car which sold in limited quantity with bodies ranging from a roadster and touring car at $1,095 to a 'town car with detachable top at $1,445. In 1917 a larger model was introduced, using a Herschell-Spillman V-8 engine which was claimed to develop 70bhp at 2,400rpm The next year the name of company and car was changed to Douglas.

KM

D.R.W. (GB) *1959 to date*
(1) D.R.W. Engineering, Kensington, London W8 *1959–1961*
(2) D.R.W. Motor and Engineering, Highgate, London N6 *1964–1969*
(3) D.R.W. Developments, Highgate, London N6 *1969 to date*

A handful of D.R.W. cars were built, based on the Lotus Seven, but with independent rear suspension. They were raced successfully in various sports classes according to the type of engine – usually of Ford origin – fitted. The Mark 6 hill-climb car built in 1965 used a rear-mounted Imp engine and was driven by Peter Voigt. Constructor David Warwick's partner Jack Murrell was still constructing Clubman cars for his own use in 1970, when other productions included the 8F Formula Ford car and the 9S Formula F100 priced at £1,350. Neither of these attracted further orders, and subsequent work was confined once more to Clubman sports-racing cars.

DF

D.S. *see* STOEWER

DS MALTERRE (F) *1955*
Éts Malterre Frères, Paris 12e

A prototype 3-wheeler minicar powered by an Ydral engine, built by a motor-cycle firm.

GNG

D.S.P.L. (F) *c.1910–1914*
Comte Pierre d'Hespel, Péranchies, Nord

Comte Pierre d'Hespel entered a 4-cylinder car in the 1910 Grand Prix des Voiturettes, and for 1912 and 1913 listed two 4-cylinder sporting cars: a 12/14 of 2,120cc and a 15hp of 2,815cc. At least one was shown at the Paris Salon.

GNG

D.S.R. (F) *1908–1909*
Sté d'Etude Dannadieu, Saussard et Robert, Paris

The D.S.R. was a light car powered by a 4-cylinder valveless air-cooled engine. Transmission was by an epicyclic gear combined with the differential.

GNG

DUAL E TURCONI (I) *1899–1901*
Dual e Turconi, Milan

A small workshop that made a few 3- and 4-wheeled voiturettes, mostly built up from imported parts. Their 3½hp Ideale had a front-mounted single-cylinder engine, two speeds and belt drive, and successfully made the journey from Milan to Paris and back.

MCS

DUAL-GHIA (US) *1955–1967*
Dual Motors Corp, Detroit, Mich.

The original Dual-Ghia Firebomb used a convertible body by the Italian coach-builders Ghia and a 5.2-litre Dodge V-8 engine in a Dodge chassis shortened to 9ft 7in. A total of 117 Firebombs were made between 1955 and 1958, at prices that reached $8,000 by the latter year. In 1962 a new model, the L6.4, with a 6.4-litre Chrysler engine and convertible or coupé bodies was announced. Assembly was completed in Italy, and the price was $15,000 when the cars reached the United States. Among the most prominent customers for Dual-Ghias was Frank Sinatra.

GNG

DUBONNET (F) *1933–1936*

André Dubonnet, Courbevoie, Seine

The aperitif millionaire and racing driver André Dubonnet built a few advanced cars. One used a 6-cylinder Hispano-Suiza engine, independent suspension all round and a low 4-door saloon body, while the 1936 car had a rear-mounted Ford V-8 engine and teardrop body, with no bonnet, and the front of the car well ahead of the front axle. It was not a production car. GNG

DUCOMMUN (D) *1903–1904*

Werkstätte für Maschinenbau vorm. Ducommun, Mulhouse, Alsace

Lorries and buses were a speciality of this company. For a short period private cars were also built. 2-cylinder 12PS or 4-cylinder 24PS models were offered. HON

DUCROISET (F) *1897–1900*

Ducroiset et Fils, Grenoble

The Ducroiset was a large car of heavy, solid appearance. It was powered by an 8hp 2-cylinder horizontal engine mounted at the front, with belt drive to a countershaft, and chain final drive. It was sold in England under the name Hercules. GNG

DUDLY; DUDLY BUG (US) *1913–1915*

Dudly Tool Co, Menominee, Mich.

This ash-framed cyclecar at first had a 2-cylinder air-cooled engine and final drive was by V-belts. A two-seater open model was the only type offered. The 1914 Dudly had a 4-cylinder engine of 1,570cc capacity. GMN

DUER (US) *1907–1908*

Chicago Coach & Carriage Co, Chicago, Ill.

The Duer was a two-seater high-wheeler. It was tiller-steered and the 1907 model had its 2-cylinder, 12/15hp engine under the seat. In 1908, the engine was moved to a bonnet in front. The final drive was by rope to the rear wheels. GMN

DUESENBERG (i) (US) *1920–1937; 1966*

(1) Duesenberg Motor Co, Indianapolis, Ind. *1920–1937*
(2) Duesenberg Corporation, Indianapolis, Ind. *1966*

Fred Duesenberg began by making bicycles and designed his first car, the Mason, in 1904. He and his brother August made engines with horizontal overhead valves for the 1912 Mason racing cars, and founded Duesenberg Motors in the following year in order to produce marine engines and complete racing cars bearing the Duesenberg name. The most famous of the latter appeared in 1920: a 3-litre Bugatti-inspired straight-8 with single overhead camshaft and three (vertical) valves per cylinder. It won the 1921 French Grand Prix. In the 1920s the racing cars were the great rivals of the Millers at Indianapolis, and victory was assured in 1924 by the adoption of a centrifugal blower. Though a two-stroke 1½-litre 8-cylinder racing engine capable of 7,000rpm was made in 1926, this was not proceeded with. The horizontal-valve Duesenberg engine was taken over in 1920 by the Rochester Motor Manufacturing Co Inc and was used in various sporting and luxury cars.

Meanwhile, at the end of 1920, the first Duesenberg production car made its debut. This Model A was an extremely expensive, if very advanced, luxury car, embodying an 8-cylinder in-line engine – the first to be seen in an American production car – of 4.2 litres, basically similar to the racing unit, but with only two valves per cylinder and developing about 100bhp. There were also hydraulically-operated front wheel brakes – another 'first' as far as America was concerned. The Model A was current until 1926. A handful of its little-altered successor, the Model X, was made in 1926–27, but in the former year E.L. Cord of Auburn acquired control of the company. He stipulated that Fred Duesenberg's next car should be completely new, and a quite exceptional machine. In fact, the Model J, which made its bow at the end of 1928, was the most remarkable automobile in America: bigger, faster, more elaborate and more expensive than any other, yet also superior to them in refinement and good looks. Its 6.9-litre, 8-cylinder engine, made by Lycoming (a firm which Cord had also bought), had two chain-driven overhead camshafts operating four valves per cylinder; a layout of racing type unique among American cars at the time and said to develop 265bhp at 4,250rpm – more than double the output of any rival. Although the complete car weighed more than 4,980lb, it was claimed to be capable of 116mph in top gear and 89mph in second. Only chassis were made for which $8,500 was asked in 1929. Immensely long and strong and low-built, Duesenbergs were very popular with all the leading coachbuilders. The company preferred to sell cars complete with bodies designed by them but made by approved builders, such as Murphy, Bohman & Schwartz, Judkins, Derham and Le Baron. In this form, catalogued models cost up to $17,950. The transmission – apart from the double dry-plate clutch – was conventional, as was the suspension by half-elliptic springs and hydraulic shock absorbers. The brakes, of course, were hydraulic, with vacuum servo assistance from late 1929.

In 1932 a supercharged version of the Model J, the SJ, was added. To cope with the 320bhp now alleged to be available, bearings, reciprocating parts and valve springs were strengthened. Usually, the shortest J chassis was used, with the highest axle ratio and stronger front springs. A maximum speed of 129mph was attributed to the SJ, with an acceleration figure of 0–100mph in 17 seconds.

1913 D.S.P.L. 15hp sporting tourer. *Autocar*

1932 DUBONNET 8-litre saloon. *Lucien Loreille Collection*

1898 DUCROISET 8hp wagonette. *David Filsell Collection*

*c.*1926 DUESENBERG(i) Model A roadster. *G. Marshall Naul*

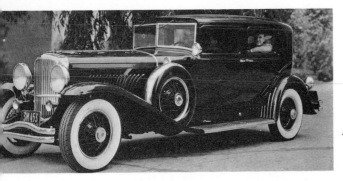

1933 DUESENBERG(i) Model J 6.9-litre sedan.
National Motor Museum

1933 DUESENBERG(i) Model J 6.9-litre roadster.
Kenneth Stauffer

1937 DUESENBERG(i) Model J 6.9-litre
convertible sedan. Coachwork by Rollston.
A.J. Hoe

1971 DUESENBERG(ii) Model SSJ replica roadster.
Duesenberg Motor Corp

Duesenberg survived the Depression, but died in the collapse of the Cord Corporation in 1937. Attempts to revive the name were made in 1947 and in 1966. The first was unsuccessful, and in 1966 only one car was actually made, powered by a 7-litre V-8 Chrysler engine with push-rod overhead valves, developing 431bhp at 5,000rpm. Transmission was automatic, front suspension was independent, and there were disc brakes. Body styling was by Ghia. This venture, too, collapsed.　　TRN

DUESENBERG (ii) (US) 1971 to date
Duesenberg Motor Corp, Gardena, Calif.

One of the most ambitious of the replicars, this is a full-size version, almost indistinguishable in external appearance, of the 1936 Duesenberg SSJ roadster, of which only two were built. It is powered by a modified 6.3-litre Chrysler V-8 engine in a chassis based on that of a Dodge truck, with semi-elliptic springs at front and rear. Transmission is either 4-speed manual or 3-speed automatic.　　GNG

DUFAUX (CH) 1904–1907
C.H. Dufaux et Cie, Les Acacias, Geneva

These cars were built by the brothers Charles and Frédéric Dufaux, Charles being responsible for the design, while Frédéric drove the cars in competitions. The first car was built in the Piccard-Pictet factory; it had a straight-8 engine with the cylinders cast in pairs, was described as a 70/90hp and had a capacity of 12,763cc. It was entered for the 1904 Gordon Bennett race, but did not start. In 1905 the brothers acquired a factory of their own and the first production touring cars were made, with 35hp 4-cylinder engines. The straight-8, now called an 80hp, was again entered for the Gordon Bennett race, and again did not start. Also in 1905 the 150hp 4-cylinder car was made with astonishing dimensions of 225mm × 166mm, and a capacity of 26,401cc. It had no conventional radiator, cooling surfaces being incorporated in the cylinder head.

The 1906 range consisted of the 'baby' 4-cylinder 16hp with a capacity of 4.1 litres, and the 40hp four, while at least one *berline de voyage* was made with the 80hp straight-8 engine. In 1907 the straight-8, now called a 120hp, ran in the Grand Prix, but lasted only six laps.

Despite the small numbers in which they were made, two Dufaux racing cars survive: a 70/90hp in the collection of Fritz Schlumpf of Malmerspach and the 120hp G.P. car at the Swiss Transport Museum, Lucerne.　　GNG

DUHANOT (F) 1907–1908
Sté des Automobiles Duhanot, Paris 11e

The Duhanot company began by listing a range of six different models, from 10 to 35hp, but in 1908 they cut this to three: the 8/10hp which was a 2-cylinder, and the 12/14 and 17hp which were 4-cylinders. The 8/10hp was often made in taxicab form and much of Duhanot's business was done in this field. At least one model had a radiator with revolving tubes, 'constituted after the fashion of a windmill's sails'.　　GNG

DULON (GB) 1967 to date
(1) Maxperenco Products Ltd, Kidlington, Oxon. 1967–1969
(2) Maxperenco Products Ltd, Didcot, Berks. 1969 to date

The name Dulon derived from the surnames of co-founders of the marque, Andrew Duncan and Bill Longley. Maxperenco was a contraction of Maximum Performance Engineering Components, denoting their wide interests. The first regular models were kit-built Formula Ford machines. During 1969 and 1970 a few sports-racing and road-going GT cars were made, as well as the LD8 Formula 5000 single-seater for Bob Miller. In 1972 the LD9 Formula Ford car of Ian Taylor kept the name on the map, besides appearances of two sports cars in International Group 6 events. Projected designs included a monocoque Formula Super Vee or Formula 3, and the firm also built chassis for Siva.　　DF

D. ULTRA (GB) 1914–1916
D.U. Manufacturing Co Ltd, Clapham, London S.W.

Designed by Harold E. Dew, the D. Ultra light car used an 8hp Chater-Lea 2-cylinder engine, friction transmission and final drive by chain. It cost £115.　　GNG

DUMAS (F) 1902–1903
M.A. Dumas fils, Champigny-sur-Marne, Seine

The Dumas was a low 3-wheeler powered by a 4½hp Buchet engine under a bonnet, driving the single front wheel by chain.　　GNG

DUMONT see SANTOS DUMONT

DUMONT (F) 1912–1913
Automobiles Dumont, Asnières, Seine

The Dumont was a light car with a large single-cylinder engine (100 × 170mm), and an unusual form of friction drive. The engine was mounted transversely and at each end of the crankshaft there revolved a steel disc across the face of which a friction disc moved. From each friction disc a long propeller shaft drove the rear wheels through bevel gears. The chassis took a four-seater body.　　GNG

JMORE (US) *1918*

American Motor Vehicle Co, Lafayette, Ind.

This was a late cyclecar and was built for a short time only. It appeared as a two-seater roadster selling for $410. The 4-cylinder engine had a capacity of 1,100cc and either a chain or belt drive. The manufacturer built the American Junior from 1916 to 1920.
KM

DUNALISTAIR (GB) *1925–1926*

Dunalistair Cars Ltd, Nottingham

The Dunalistair used a 14hp Meadows engine and gearbox, but 'imported' its chassis from Mechins of Glasgow. The four-seater tourer bodies were made in Nottingham, but only four cars were actually produced.
GNG

DUNAMIS (B) *1922–1924*

Automobiles Dunamis, Antwerp

Designed by Theo. Verellen, the Dunamis was a large luxury chassis with a straight-8 engine. Only two prototypes were built, assembled for Dunamis in the Hesse factory.
GNG

DUNKLEY (GB) *1896–c.1924*

Dunkleys, Birmingham

The first Dunkley car was a highly unusual vehicle in which the four wheels were arranged in diamond formation, the front and rear wheels being much smaller than those at the side. Seating was arranged in *dos-à-dos* pattern, and the vehicle could be steered from either end, the rear-facing passenger operating the brake. The engine was powered by coal gas, and it had a wicker body. *The Autocar* correspondent treated it with some degree of levity. Dunkleys also made a 3-wheeler on the lines of an invalid car. In 1901 there appeared a tandem two-seater, also powered by coal gas, which was apparently sold for a few years. Apart from the Alvecurch cyclecar which is dealt with separately, and a short-lived 3-wheeler of 1915, Dunkleys' next venture in powered vehicles was the Pramotor, or motorized pram, which appeared in 1922. This consisted of a scooter minus the front wheel, which could be attached to any perambulator, preferably a Dunkley as they were well-known pram manufacturers. Models listed were a 1hp and a 2¼hp, but few were sold because of the price (up to 135gns) and the law forbidding the use of powered vehicles on the pavement.
GNG

DUNN (US) *1914–1918*

Dunn Motor Works, Ogdensburg, N.Y.

This car maker persisted with the cyclecar design to a later date than most. The Dunn had a 2-speed transmission and shaft drive connecting its 4-cylinder engine to the rear wheels. With wire wheels, this two-seater model cost $295.
GMN

DUO (GB) *1912–1914*

(i) Duocars Ltd, Deptford, London S.E. *1912–1913*

(ii) Duo Cyclecars Ltd, Deptford, London S.E. *1913–1914*

The Duo was a belt-drive cyclecar which used a variety of engines during its two year lifespan, including a 6/8hp Buckingham single-cylinder, a 10hp Dorman 4-cylinder and a 10hp Chapuis-Dornier or Mathis 4-cylinder. In September 1913 F. de Peyrecave took over the Duo works and the following year began to sell his De P car which also used a Dorman engine. 1914 Duos were announced using shaft drive.
GNG

DUPLEX (i) (GB) *1906–c.1909*

Duplex Motor Engine Co, London

The first car of this name made in Britain was powered by an unusually large 2-stroke engine: a 4-cylinder unit rated at 30 and, later, 35hp. An early example used chain drive; later ones had shaft drive.
TRN

DUPLEX (ii) (US) *1909*

Duplex Motor Car Co, Chicago, Ill.

The Duplex was so named for its unusual drive system which consisted of two friction transmissions each with its own drive-shaft and separate differential on the rear axle. The transmissions were driven, one at each end of the crankshaft by a 2-cylinder 20hp engine mounted transversely.
GMN

DUPLEX (iii) (GB) *1919–1921*

British Commercial Lorry & Engineering Co Ltd, Trafford Park, Manchester

Apart from its engine, the Duplex was a conventional enough light car of its time. The 10hp 1½-litre power unit had eight cylinders in two parallel rows of four, cast monobloc – a very complex piece of workmanship. Each pair of cylinders had a common combustion chamber, with sleeve valves. This engine was dropped, and a normal 1½-litre four with Coventry-Simplex engine took its place.
TRN

DUPLEX (iv) (CDN) *1923*

United Iron Works Co, Montreal, Que.

The main feature of this car, built on a Hudson chassis, was its unique 4-

1905 DUFAUX 80hp 8-cylinder racing car. *Swiss Museum of Transport & Communications, Lucerne*

1906 DUFAUX 80/100hp limousine. *Jacques Kupélian Collection*

1902 DUMAS 4½hp 3-wheeler. *G.N. Georgano Collection*

1912 DUO 8hp cyclecar. *The Veteran Car Club of Great Britain*

1920 DUPLEX(iii) 10hp coupé. *Autocar*

1929 DU PONT(ii) Model G 5.2-litre speedster.
Don McCray

1929 DU PONT(ii) Model G 5.2-litre roadster.
National Motor Museum

cylinder engine with two pistons per cylinder. The company claimed a record f
petrol economy. The sedan was priced at $1,750.
H

DU PONT (i) *see* SPHINX (i)

DU PONT (ii) (US) *1920–1932*
(1) du Pont Motors Inc, Wilmington, Del. *1920–1923*
(2) du Pont Motors Inc, Moore, Pa. *1923–1932*
E. Paul du Pont's company built quality cars in limited numbers, total produc
tion being 537 vehicles of all types. First of the line was a 4.1-litre sv four wi
their own engine, selling for $2,600, but this gave way to proprietary-engined sixe
initially powered by Herschell-Spillman. The 1925 Model D had a 6-cylinder 5-lit
Wisconsin engine with overhead valves that developed 75bhp, a constant-mes
gearbox, and Lockheed hydraulic brakes to all four wheels. Its successor, the Mod
E. could be had with a supercharger, but the best-known, and best, du Pont w
the Model G speedster introduced in 1928. With its narrow straight wings copi
from the Amilcar, Woodlite headlamps and grille concealing the radiator, the la
a pioneering feature, the Model G was not a good-looking car, but it was a ve
effective one. Like all the du Pont speedsters it had four forward speeds. T
5.3-litre, sv straight-8 engine, by Continental, gave 114bhp at 3,600rpm wi
catalogued modifications. With the latter, 100mph was guaranteed. In the 1929 I
Mans 24 Hours Race the Model G proved itself faster than the other America
entries, Stutz and Chrysler. Touring bodywork was, of course, available, and
1931 came the long wheelbase (12ft 2in) Model H, built in a Stearns Knight fram
The later cars were assembled in the Indian motorcycle factory at Springfield, aft
E. Paul du Pont had acquired this concern.
TR

DUPRESSOIR (F) *1900–1914*
Paul Dupressoir, Maubeuge, Nord
The original Dupressoir cars were light voiturettes powered by De Dion or Aste
air- or water-cooled engines of $2\frac{1}{4}$ or 3hp. They were mounted under the sea
Dupressoir made chassis for other firms such as Crypto, these chassis being so
under the name Rolling. They included engines of 1, 2 and 4 cylinders, from
to 24hp. In 1912 a new Rolling range appeared. These were conventional ca
with 4-cylinder monobloc Chapuis-Dornier engines of 7, 9, 10 and 12hp. The 9
model was the basis of the English Averies light car of 1913 to 1914.
GN

DUQUESNE (i) (US) *1903–1906*
(1) Duquesne Motor Co, Buffalo, N.Y. *1903*
(2) Duquesne Motor Co, Jamestown, N.Y. *1903–1906*
The Duquesne was a medium-sized tourer powered by a 16/21hp 4-cylinder ai
cooled engine, with a circular bonnet in the Hotchkiss style. It featured a 'sel
starter' by foot-operated ratched mechanism operating on the flywheel, and a devic
whereby the rear doors opened when either of the front seats was tilted forwar
One car was made in Buffalo, and five in Jamestown.
GN

DUQUESNE (ii) (US) *1912–1913*
Duquesne Motor Car Co, Pittsburgh, Pa.
This Duquesne was made in two models; the smaller on a wheelbase of 10ft 4i
used a T-head 4-cylinder engine of 6.4 litres. The larger model had a 6-cylinde
6-litre engine and a longer wheelbase. Prices ranged from $2,600 to $2,700 fc
five-seater models.
GM

DURANT (US) *1921–1932*
Durant Motors Inc, New York, N.Y.; Lansing, Mich.; Muncie, Ind.; Oakland, Calif.
Elizabeth, N.J.; Long Island City, N.Y.; Toronto and Leaside, Ont.; Syracuse, N.Y
The Durant was, with the Star, Eagle, Flint, Princeton, Rugby and Locomobile
one of several makes comprising William C. Durant's automobile empire. It wa
introduced as a 4-cylinder car and used its own ohv engine. The first models i
1921 had disc or wooden spoke wheels and a five-seater touring car cost $850. I
1922, the peak year of production, 55,000 units were sold, the figure falling t
39,000 in 1923 and fluctuating thereafter. The 4-cylinder model remained basicall
the same through 1926 with various modifications added in keeping with the times
A car with a 6-cylinder Ansted engine was built in 1922 and 1923 at the Munci
plant. In 1927 Durant suspended production, but started again in 1928 with
completely redesigned line of 4- and 6-cylinder cars which were continued in 1929
Another new line was brought out in 1930 and the 4-cylinder car was dropped. Th
1930 range included two sixes, with wire wheels as standard equipment for th
larger of the two. The 1931 models were unchanged except for the engines whic
were Continentals. Sales had dropped severely, however; the 43,951 cars sold i
1928 dropped to 20,261 in 1930. In 1931, only 7,270 Durants were sold and ear
in 1932, the firm went out of business. The Canadian Durant cars were markete
under the name Frontenac from 1931 and were sold until 1933.
KM

DUREY-SOHY (F) *1899–1903*
Automobiles Durey-Sohy, Paris
This company began by making a voiturette with a vertical 2-cylinder engine

and an electric hansom cab. They continued the latter to 1903, and extended their petrol car range to two 2-cylinder models, of 8 and 12hp. In 1903 they took over the Hanzer range of cars and motor cycles, and marketed them under the Durey-Sohy name for a very short time.   GNG

DÜRKOPP (D) 1898–1927

(1) Bielefelder Maschinenfabrik vorm. Dürkopp & Co AG, Bielefeld *1898–1913*
(2) Dürkoppwerke AG, Bielefeld *1913–1927*

Dürkopp cars made their first public appearance in 1899. They had 2-cylinder engines and were based on Panhard-Levassor principles. After 1902 4-cylinder cars were also built, a 3-cylinder and a 6-cylinder model being added in 1903. Dürkopp had a branch factory in France and the cars were also known under the name Canello-Dürkopp. In the United Kingdom they were marketed as Watsonias.

Dürkopp was seldom active in sports events and specialized in heavy types of touring car. These were based on a racing car developed for the Kaiserpreis Race of 1907 with a 4-cylinder 7.2-litre engine developing 70bhp. The largest model DG43 with a 13-litre engine developed 100bhp. From 1908 small models were also built, later known under the name of Knipperdolling, of which the type EK6 continued in production after World War 1. Another post-war model was the P8 with a 2-litre 8/32PS engine. This model was also available as a sports car with a 40bhp engine and with a blown engine developing 60bhp. This latter version brought Hans Stuck his first racing successes.

Production of private cars ceased in 1927, while production of lorries, which had started early in the century, lasted until 1929. Motor cycles were built by Dürkopp from 1900 to 1914 and again from 1948, the best-known post-war product being the Diana scooter.   HON

DUROCAR (US) 1907–1909

Durocar Manufacturing, Co, Los Angeles, Calif.

This early Western car used a 2-cylinder water-cooled 4-stroke engine of 26hp, placed horizontally under the front seat. The drive to the rear axle was by 3-speed selective transmission and drive-shaft. Surrey, runabout and touring body types were offered.   GMN

DURSLEY-PEDERSEN (GB) 1912

Dursley-Pedersen Cycle Co, Dursley, Gloucestershire

This famous firm of bicycle makers announced a cyclecar with a 7hp 4-cylinder engine and shaft drive to sell for 100 guineas. It would have been extraordinarily good value, but there is no evidence that it was marketed.   GNG

DURYEA (i) (US) 1895–1913

(1) Duryea Motor Wagon Co, Springfield, Mass. *1895–1898*
(2) Duryea Mfg Co, Peoria, Ill. *1896–c.1898*
(3) Duryea Power Co, Reading, Pa. *1899–1908*
    (Licensees at Waterloo, Iowa; Coventry, England; and Liège, Belgium, during part of this period)
(4) Duryea Motor Co, Saginaw, Mich. *1908–1913*

These four firms represented the commercial endeavours of Charles E. Duryea, who with his brother Frank constructed one of America's very first cars in 1892–93. It was a powered horse buggy, with single-cylinder 4hp engine and friction drive. A second prototype was the work of Frank, who won America's first motor race, from Chicago to Evanston on Thanksgiving Day, 1895. There was only one other finisher, a Benz, and Frank Duryea took nine hours to cover the 50 miles. Charles Duryea had set up the first company formed in America expressly for the purpose of making petrol motor cars, and 13 vehicles were made with horizontal engines, 3-speed belt transmissions and low-tension ignition. Two of these took part in the original Emancipation Run from London to Brighton in November 1896. 3-wheelers were in production at Peoria in 1898, followed in 1900–01 by cars with transverse front suspension and flat-twin engines. By this time Frank was engaged in the development of the Stevens-Duryea car for the Stevens Arms and Tool Co, and all subsequent Duryeas were entirely Charles's work. In the 1902–06 period he made 3- and 4-wheeled vehicles powered by rear-mounted transverse 3-cylinder engines of square dimensions with water-jacketed heads, a two-speed crypto gear mounted in a 'power drum' alongside the engine and tiller steering. Much was made of the single-lever control whereby the tiller also served as gear selector and throttle. A Duryea could be bought for £275 in England in 1902, and shortly afterwards Henry Sturmey organized a British Duryea Co which made the cars under licence in Coventry; their engines were the work of Willans and Robinson, and they had moiv and high-tension ignition. In 1906 Charles Duryea listed a three-wheeler at $1,200, a 12/15hp 4-wheeler with similar mechanics at $1,300 and a big 25hp car, still with three cylinders, at $2,000. By this time the British Duryeas had faded out, the factory being used for the manufacture of the Lotis car but Charles Duryea made a 3-cylinder rotary-valve model in 1907, before turning his attention to the high-wheeler in 1908. His version, the Buggyaut, was powered by a 2-cylinder horizontally-opposed 2-stroke engine at the rear, drive being by twin grooved rollers on the crankshaft which engaged with the rims of the rear wheels. A centrally-mounted tiller enabled it to be controlled from either seat, and

1923 DURANT Four 24hp tourer.
National Motor Museum

1905 DÜRKOPP 18/32PS landaulette. *Neubauer Collection*

1896 DURYEA(i) 4hp motor buggy. *Kenneth Stauffer*

1911 DURYEA(i) Electa 12hp motor buggy.
Jackson Products

1916 DURYEA GEM 10hp 3-wheeler. *Automotive History Collection, Detroit Public Library*

1972 DUTTON B-type sports car.
Dutton Sports Ltd

1925 D'YRSAN 8hp sporting 3-wheeler. *National Motor Museum*

it cost $750, pneumatic tyres being extra. This car survived most of its competitors, as it was still listed in 1913.　　　　MCS

DURYEA (ii) (US) *1914–1915*
Cresson-Morris Co, Philadelphia, Pa.

This short-lived cyclecar was designed by Charles E. Duryea. It used the same rim drive as his Buggyaut car, had a 4-stroke flat-twin engine and side-by-side seating. The price was $400.　　　　MCS

DURYEA GEM (US) *1916*
Duryea Motors Inc, Philadelphia, Pa.

This 3-wheeler cyclecar with single front wheel used the same basic transmission as the Buggyaut and the Duryea (ii). It sold at $425 and was no more successful than Charles E. Duryea's other cyclecar venture.　　　　MCS

DUTTON (GB) *1969 to date*
Dutton Sports Ltd, Fontwell, Sussex

The Dutton P1, designed and built by Tim Woolley, was a light sports car in the Lotus Seven image based on the Mark 1 Sprite. When these became scarce the B type was produced, with Triumph suspension and transmission and choice of engines. Fixed-head and racing versions were also advertised, but most sold were open two-seater road cars, powered by B.M.C., Triumph, Ford or (in one case) Alfa-Romeo Giulia engines. The tubular space-frame incorporated an integral roll-over bar. A complete car could be had for no more than £500.　　　　DF

DUX (D) *1909–1926*
(1) Polyphon-Werke AG, Wahren bei Leipzig *1909–1916*
(2) Dux-Automobilwerke AG, Wahren bei Leipzig *1916–1926*

After 1909 the Polyphon works marketed their cars – which were formerly known as Polymobil – under the name Dux. The first Dux car was the E12 with a 6/12PS engine. Dux cars took part in many sporting events of the pre-World War 1 period with considerable success. The 6/18PS 1½-litre F6 type was also produced in an improved form after the war. A 4-cylinder 4,680cc and a 6-cylinder 4,520cc model developing 50 and 60bhp respectively were the post-war products.　　　　HON

D-WAGEN (D) *1924–1927*
(1) Deutsche Werke AG, Haselhorst bei Spandau, Berlin *1924–1925*
(2) Deutsche Kraftfahrzeugwerke AG, Berlin-Spandau *1925–1927*

This former arms and ammunition factory started production of motor cycles after World War 1 and in 1924 they exhibited a car at the Berlin Motor Show. This was a 5/20PS 1.3-litre 4-cylinder model of conventional design. After production ceased the factory was used for assembling American Durant cars for a short period before it was taken over by D.K.W.　　　　HON

DYKE (US) *1901–1904*
A.L. Dyke Auto Supply Co, St Louis, Mo.

The Dyke was one of the first kit cars sold in component form for home assembly. A variety of designs was offered, with engines from a 5hp single to a 12hp twin, two-, four- or five-seater bodies, and solid or pneumatic tyres. All components were available from A.L. Dyke, whose prices ranged from $700 to $1,000.　　　　GNG

DYMAXION (US) *1933–1934*

The Dymaxion was an experimental car in teardrop aerodynamic design conceived by Buckminster Fuller and initially tested by Capt. Al Williams, a stunt aviator. The three-wheeled car, with the single wheel at the rear, was largely constructed of balsa wood and duraluminum and built in the old Locomobile plant at Bridgeport, Conn. Power was supplied by a Ford V-8 engine. The 1,850lb. Dymaxion achieved 120 miles per hour when tested in July, 1933. A later crash killed two passengers. Two more Dymaxions were subsequently built.　　　　KM

DYNAMOBIL (D) *1906*
E.H. Geist Elektrizitäts AG, Cologne

This company announced a petrol-electric car with a 24hp petrol engine, and two 12hp electric motors. They were more concerned with lorry and bus chassis, and the private car was probably only a prototype.　　　　GNG

DYNA-VERITAS *see* VERITAS

D'YRSAN (F) *1923–1930*
Raymond Siran, Cyclecars d'Yrsan, Asnières, Seine

Three-wheeled cyclecars were even less popular in France than in England, and the only wholly home-grown product among them was the d'Yrsan. It was also the most sophisticated, using a 4-cylinder Ruby engine with a capacity of about 1 litre, three forward speeds, shaft drive and independent front suspension. Although heavier than tricycles of the Morgan type, a lowered racing model could exceed 80mph. Some 4-wheeler sports cars, also Ruby-engined, were listed from 1927 to 1930, and 3-wheelers were given up in 1928.　　　　TRN

EAGLE (i) (GB) 1901–1908

① Eagle Engineering & Motor Co Ltd, Altrincham, Cheshire *1901–1907*
② St George's Motor Car Co Ltd, Leeds, Yorks. *1907–1908*

Ralph Jackson made Eagle Tandems which were the same design as the Century
-cars. This situation lasted until 1904, the rival but identical machines occupying
different stands at the Motor Shows. In 1903 Eagle cars were introduced, a 9hp
cylinder and a 16hp 4-cylinder with epicyclic gears. The 3-wheeler range now
-luded a £100 single-seater runabout and the formidable 16hp New Eagle Racer,
single-seater said to be capable of 80mph.

In 1907 the Eagle Engineering Company was wound up, and Jackson started
-lling the cars New Eagle, assembling them at Broadheath Generating Station
d selling them through the St George's Motor Car Co. They were available in
/12, 24/30 and 35/45hp 4-cylinder models, but few were made. GNG

EAGLE (ii) (US) 1904–1905

ne Eagle Auto Co, Buffalo, N.Y.

Two models of this car were produced, both five-seater rear-entrance tonneaux.
ne smaller used an opposed 2-cylinder engine of 12hp, the larger model a 24hp,
cylinder unit. These were both air-cooled. Final drive was by roller-chain. GMN

EAGLE (iii) (US) 1905–1906

agle Automobile Co, Rahway, N.J.

The Eagle had a 4-cylinder air-cooled engine of 20/24hp and chain drive. A five-
-ater touring body was the only model offered. GMN

EAGLE (iv) (US) 1908

agle Motor Carriage Co, Elmira, N.Y.

The Eagle high-wheeler had solid tyres and a rope drive. The engine was a 4-stroke
pe with two opposed cylinders. Single cantilever springs were used on each side
f the body extending from front to rear axles. Steering was by a wheel. GMN

EAGLE (v) (US) 1909

agle Automobile Co, St Louis, Mo.

This roadster with solid rubber tyres sold for $650. It was powered by a 2-cylinder
ir-cooled 4-stroke engine of 14hp. GMN

EAGLE (vi) (GB) 1912–1914

①) Eagle Motor Manufacturing Co Ltd, Shepherds Bush, London W. *1912–1913*
②) Eagle Motor Manufacturing Co Ltd, Barnes, London S.W. *1913–1914*

The 1913 range of Eagle light cars consisted of two models, both using an 8/10hp
-twin engine of Eagle's own make, and worm drive. One model had a pressed-
-eel frame, and the other a tubular frame. For 1914 only one 4-cylinder 8hp car
as offered, and production came to an end early in that year. The works at Barnes
ere later occupied by the makers of the Beverley-Barnes car. GNG

EAGLE (vii) (US) 1914–1918

-agle-Macomber Motor Co, Sandusky, Ohio

This cyclecar was also known as the Eagle-Macomber. Macomber was the name
f its unusual air-cooled 5-cylinder engine, which was a West Coast product. The
-ve cylinders were mounted horizontally in a cylindrical pattern so that each operated
gainst a wobble-plate cum flywheel. This 1.3-litre engine developed about 13hp.
n 1918 a larger car was made, with 4.1-litre 5-cylinder radial engine. GMN

EAGLE (viii) (US) 1923–1924

Durant Motors Inc, New York, N.Y.

This Eagle was a 6-cylinder car produced by William C. Durant for a very short
me, ostensibly to fill a gap between the Star Four and Durant Four cars in the
Durant line. A Continental engine was used and the Eagles were priced at $820.
-ew were marketed and a tourer was the only model. KM

EAGLE (ix) (US/GB) 1966 to date

1) All-American Racers Inc, Santa Ana, Calif. *1966 to date*
2) Anglo-American Racers, Rye, Sussex *1966–1968*

Grand Prix driver Dan Gurney established two racing-car companies when he left
he Brabham team at the end of 1965. All-American Racers in the United States
ere to build Indianapolis and Formula A cars, while in England, Anglo-American

1901 EAGLE(i) 3½hp tandem tricar. *R.J. Wyatt*

1907 NEW EAGLE(i) 24/30hp tourer. *R.J. Wyatt*

1924 EAGLE(viii) 6-cylinder tourer.
McKean Collection, Free Library of Philadelphia

1968 EAGLE(ix) Indianapolis racing car. Bobby Unser at the wheel. *Indianapolis Motor Speedway*

1924 E.B.S. 3-wheeler. *The Veteran Car Club of Great Britain*

1907 ECLAIR(i) 20hp limousine. *Lucien Loreille Collection*

Racers in Rye, Sussex, were to build and race Weslake V-12-engined F1 car
All were to be known as Eagles, and Gurney was backed by Goodyear and Carro
Shelby of Cobra fame. The F1 project foundered in 1968 after the make wo
the 1967 Belgian GP, but the American AAR works was most successful, buildir
and selling Indy and Formula A cars in considerable numbers. Eagles won th
Indianapolis 500 in 1968 and took the Formula A Championship that same seaso
The 1972 track-racing Eagles designed by Roman Slobodynskij were the first t
lap Indianapolis at an average of more than 190mph. Complete engines and cylinde
heads have been supplied for Ford-powered sports cars and dragsters.   DC

EAGLET (GB) 1948
Silent Transport Ltd, Woking, Surrey

Introduced during the period when there was no basic petrol ration in Englan
the Eaglet was a light electric 3-wheeler coupé with a range of 25–30 miles per charg
and a speed of 30mph. The price was an expensive £412, and the makers did mor
business in the conversion to electricity of Opel Cadets and Fiat Topolinos.   GN

EARL (i) (US) 1907–1908
(1) Earl Motor Car Co, Milwaukee, Wisc. 1907–1908
(2) Earl Motor Car Co, Kenosha, Wisc. 1908

This was a light (1,200lb) roadster on an 8ft 4in wheelbase with an early 'rumble
or folding seat. The car was driven by a 2-cylinder engine of 15hp. Power to th
wheels was by friction transmission and chain drive. The Earl was succeeded b
the Petrel.   GM

EARL (ii) (US) 1921–1923
Earl Motors Inc, Jackson, Mich.

The Earl was the continuation of the Briscoe. Both open and closed models of th
4-cylinder car were available, and approximately 2,000 were produced.   K

EASTBOURNE (GB) 1905–1906
Eastbourne Motor Works, Eastbourne, Sussex

The only car made in the South Coast resort of Eastbourne, this was an assemble
vehicle using a 2-cylinder Aster engine, a 4-speed gearbox and shaft drive. It wa
priced at £300 for a four-seater tonneau.   GN

EAST GLOWS (CHI) c.1964 to date
Car Factory No. 1, Peking

One of the more recent designs to appear in China, the East Glows is a hand
built saloon with a 6-cylinder 150bhp engine.   B

EASTMAN (US) 1899–1902
Eastman Automobile Co, Cleveland, Ohio

The Eastman Electro Cycle was a 3-wheeler steered by a very long tiller to th
single front wheel. It had a single-seater body which was said to be the first all-stee
body in America, a tubular frame, and bicycle wheels.

The company later specialized in making steel bodies for other firms.   GN

EASTMEAD-BIGGS (GB) 1901–1904
Eastmead & Biggs, Frome, Somerset

Only three cars of this make were built, being assembled by T.J. Biggs at Frome
Eastmead was a lift manufacturer of Blackfriars who was to have sold the cars i
London. They used Simms or Aster engines and mainly French components. Bigg
afterwards went on to Raleigh's where he designed their first car.   GN

EAST WIND see DONG FENG

EATON (US) 1898
Eaton Electric Motor Carriage Co, Boston, Mass.

The Eaton company showed a light electric two-seater at the 1898 Boston Motor
cycle Show.   GN

E.B.M. (D) 1912
E.B.M. Maschinenfabrik

This little-known car had a 4-cylinder engine of 3.8 litres. Further details ar
not known.   GN

E.B.S. (D) 1924
Ernst Bauermeister & Söhne, Berlin-Baumschulenweg

This was a 3-wheeled vehicle with the front part – including the driver's seat –
derived from a motor cycle. The rear part of the vehicle had a two-seater cabin ove
the rear axle. Single-cylinder engines of 200, 250 and 350cc were used. Transmissio
was by chain to the gearbox and then by shaft to the rear axle.   HO

ÉCLAIR (i) (F) 1907–1908
SA des Constructions d'Automobiles l'Eclair, Paris

This company made a conventional car with 20hp 4-cylinder engine, and shaf ive. Open and closed bodies were available, and the firm was also listed as a maker of electric vehicles. GNG

CLAIR (ii) (F) *1920–1923*
Rebeau-Cordier, Courbevoie, Seine
This was a cyclecar with 7/9hp V-twin Anzani engine and shaft drive. GNG

ECLIPSE (i) (US) *1900–1903*
Eclipse Automobile Co, Boston, Mass.
The Eclipse steam runabout was powered by an 8hp 3-cylinder engine. Unlike the average chain-drive steamer, it used shaft drive to the rear axle. In other ways it was typical of its kind, with a two-seater body, tiller steering and wire wheels. GNG

ECLIPSE (ii) (GB) *1901–c.1904*
Eclipse Engineering & Motor Co, Wandsworth, London S.W.
This company made engines, and in 1901 announced that they were about to build a light car. Details are not known, but during the next few years they assembled a few cars from various components, using 2-cylinder 12hp and 4-cylinder 20/24hp engines. GNG

ECLIPSE (iii) (US) *1905*
Kreuger Mfg Co, Milwaukee, Wisc.
The small Eclipse had an attractive appearance and a single-cylinder engine of 7 litres. This was fitted with a planetary transmission and shaft drive. The single model, designated A, was a five-seater with rear entrance. This company also made a car called the Kreuger. GMN

ECO (AUS) *1923*
Eco Motors Co Ltd, Melbourne, Victoria
The Eco was an assembled car powered by a Lycoming engine. It was distinguished by a massive-looking egg-shaped radiator which was its chief identifying factor. KM

ECONOM (D) *1950*
Econom-Werk Hellmuth Butenuth, Berlin-Haselhorst
This small two-seater appeared only as a prototype. Butenuth was better known as a producer of commercial vehicles. HON

ECONOMIC (GB) *1921–1922*
Economic Motors, London W.1.
This was one of the lightest cars of the post-World War 1 cyclecar era. It was a 3-wheeler with a single front wheel and a simple two-seater body rather like that of the Briggs & Stratton Buckboard. No springs were fitted as it was claimed that the resilience of the ash frame absorbed all road shocks. The engine was a 2-stroke flat-twin of under 200cc capacity, the magneto was incorporated in the flywheel and final drive was by chain to the offside rear wheel. Unladen weight was only 150lb, maximum speed was 30mph and the price £60. GNG

ECONOMY (i) (US) *1914*
Economy Car Co, Indianapolis, Ind.
The Economy cyclecar used coil springs in front and quarter-elliptical springs in the rear. It had a 2-cylinder Spacke engine, a planetary transmission and chain drive. The two-seater sold for $375. GMN

ECONOMY (ii) (US) *1917–1921*
Economy Motor Co, Tiffin, Ohio
This was an assembled car, offered with either 4- or 8-cylinder engines on a standard chassis. Prices for roadsters and touring models ranged from $985 to $1,395. In 1920 a Continental-engined six was introduced. GMN

ECONOMYCAR (US) *1913–1914*
Economycar Co, Providence, R.I.
The Economycar was a two-seater tandem cyclecar with belt drive and a 2-cylinder air-cooled engine. The front axle was pivoted for steering by capstan cable. The address is sometimes given as New York City and Indianapolis, but the factory was at Rhode Island. GMN

ECONOOM (NL) *1912–1914*
Hautekeet & Van Asselt, Amsterdam
The Econoom appeared at the time of the cyclecar boom, but was more of a genuine light car. It used an 8/12hp Ballot 4-cylinder engine, M.A.B. chassis and shaft drive. About 85 were made before World War 1 stopped production. GNG

EDFORD (P) *1930–1938*
Ferreirinha et Irmao, Oporto
The only known Portuguese make of car, the Edford was a sports car based on Ford components. The first models were lowered versions of the Model A with two-seater roadster bodies and cycle-type wings, and in 1936 an attractive V-8-

1921 ECONOMIC 3-wheeler. *Autocar*

1917 ECONOMY(ii) tourer. *Kenneth Stauffer*

1937 EDFORD V-8 3.6-litre sports car.
G.L. Hartner Collection

based sports car was announced. This had an aluminium body weighing only 150k coil ifs and a tuned engine that gave the car a maximum speed of 110mph.　　GN

EDIS (E) *1919–1922*
Carlos Jaumandreu Martorell, Barcelona

The first Edis cars were powered by vertical-twin engines of 1,108cc capacit Four of these were built, followed by two 4-cylinder cars with 1,100cc engine Two- and four-seater bodies were available.　　GN

1919 EDIS 10hp two-seater.
Joaquín Ciuró Gabarró Collection

EDISMITH (GB) *1905*
Edwin Smith, Blackburn, Lancs.

Edwin Smith was a garage owner who exhibited a small car with a 9hp De Dic engine at the Manchester Show of 1905.　　GN

EDIT (I) *1924*
Armino Mezzo, Turin

The Edit was a more conventional 4-wheeled light car by the designer of th Motocor 3-wheeler. It had a 1-litre air-cooled vertical-twin engine and three forwa speeds, and was intended to sell for 13,850 lire.　　MC

EDITH (AUS) *1953*
Gray & Harper Pty, Melbourne

Of the enormous number of post-war 3-wheeled minicars, the Edith was o of the few to be built in Australia. It used a 197cc rear-mounted Villiers engine, 4-speed gearbox and independent suspension on all three wheels. The body w a low-slung aluminium two-seater. The makers claimed 58mph and 95mpg.　　GN

EDMOND (GB) *1920–1921*
Shand Motor & Engineering Co Ltd, Lee Green, London S.E.

This was a cyclecar using a 5/7hp 2-cylinder Coventry-Victor engine and sing chain drive. The two-seater cost £198.　　GN

1921 EDMOND 5/7hp cyclecar. *Autocar*

EDMUND (GB) *1920*
C. Edmund & Co (1920) Ltd, Chester

This was a firm of motor-cycle makers who built a small number of cycleca with 2-cylinder engines and shaft drive.　　GN

EDSEL (US) *1957–1959*
Ford Motor Co (Lincoln-Mercury-Edsel Division), Detroit, Mich.

The Edsel was introduced for the 1958 season by Ford's Lincoln-Mercury Divisic to fill the supposed gap between the Ford and Mercury lines. Despite vast sun spent on customer research and public relations, the project backfired. The gap di not exist, and only 35,000 Edsels found customers during the first six months production. The car itself was typical of its period, with coil-and-wishbone inde pendent front suspension, wrap-around windscreen, and a choice of two V-8 engine both oversquare ohv units with capacities of 5.9 litres and 6.7 litres. The small one offered 303bhp. The cheaper Ranger and Pacer series were available wit manual, overdrive or automatic transmission, but only push-button automatic wa listed on the costlier Corsair and Citation. A distinctive feature of the car was i curious, horse collar-shaped radiator grille. An attempt was made to widen th make's appeal with a low-cost ohv 3.6-litre 6-cylinder in 1959, but the Edse was dropped shortly after the announcement of the 1960 models.　　MC

1958 EDSEL Citation 6.7-litre hard top. *Ford Motor Co*

EDWARDS (i) (GB) *1913*
This was a cyclecar using an 8/10hp air-cooled Precision engine, friction trans mission and chain drive.　　GN

EDWARDS (ii) (US) *1953–1955*
E.H. Edwards Co, South San Francisco, Calif.

A Ford V-8-engined prototype appeared in 1949, but the production Edward sports car used a Lincoln engine in a cut-down Ford chassis with a fibregla body. The price was $4,995.　　B

EDWARDS-KNIGHT (US) *1912–1914*
Edwards Motor Co, New York, N.Y.

This car with a Knight engine became the Willys-Knight after 1914. It was fairly large car powered by a 4½-litre 4-cylinder engine rated at 25hp. The 4-spee transmission was direct in third gear, giving overdrive in fourth. Built as a five seater touring car, it cost $3,500.　　GM

E.E.C. (GB) *1952–1954*
Electrical Engineering Construction Co Ltd, Totnes, Devon

This 3-wheeled bubble car was of the front-opening variety, and was simply cor structed from single-curvature steel panels. An Excelsior 250cc 2-stroke twin pro vided adequate motive power for a dry weight of 588lb. James Elliott persisted wit his design for a couple of seasons, but found that he could not, without a sponso become a competitive manufacturer.　　D

1953 EFFYH 500cc racing car. *Autosport*

EFFYH (S/DK) *c.1950–c.1953*
Thorkil Grue, Copenhagen
   The first Effyh, designed by the Swedish brothers Håkansson, employed a very light tubular frame and all-independent suspension by quarter-elliptic springs. It competed in many 500cc races, particularly in the hands of Åke Johnsson, and achieved more consistent success than any other non-British contender in this class. Quite a number of these well-turned out machines were built, but the British retained their virtual stranglehold on International Formula 3 racing.   DF

EGAN SIX (AUS) *1935–1936*
W. Egan, Geelong, Victoria
   The Egan Six was a conventional medium-sized car using an 80bhp 6-cylinder Lycoming engine and a mainly Australian-built chassis and six-seater saloon body. It was priced at £A420 and had a maximum speed of 80mph. However, Egan did not have the mass-production facilities which were necessary for this sort of model and it could not compete with American cars.   GNG

EGG (CH) *1896–1900*
Automobilfabrik Egg & Egli, Zürich
   Rudolf Egg's first experimental 3-wheeler was made in 1893, and production began in 1896. The cars were Bollée-like 3-wheelers, but had side-by-side seating, a 3hp De Dion engine and belt drive. In 1898 a licence was sold to Bachtold of Steckborn, who made only six cars, and to Weber of Uster, who made over 50. In 1899 the design and all manufacturing rights were sold to the Züricher Patent Motor-wagen-Fabrik Rapid, who sold the car under the name Rapid. In 1900 Rudolf Egg made a number of 4-wheelers on the lines of the Benz Velo, while later designs of his were manufactured by Excelsior (ii), and Moser.   GNG

EGO (D) *1921–1926*
(1) Mercur Flugzeugbau GmbH, Berlin SO 36 *1921–1925*
(2) Hiller Automobilfabrik AG, Berlin SO 36 *1925–1926*
   Ego was a small firm which specialized in light cars. A sports version of the sv 4/14PS model developing 24bhp was raced by Rudolf Caracciola to his first victory in 1923 in the Berlin Stadium Race. Later cars had 1.3-litre ohv engines.   HON

E.H.P. (F) *1921–1929*
Ets H. Precloux, Courbevoie, Seine; La Garenne-Colombes, Seine
   In most respects the E.H.P. was a conventional French voiturette of its period, with a 4-cylinder, side-valve Ruby engine of 900cc (other units were also fitted), transverse front suspension and three forward speeds. It was unusual in that it was often produced with closed body-work, instead of the customary stark sporting two-seater style. Cantilever rear springs were fitted. Special cars were built for racing, among them the 1925 overhead-camshaft, 1½-litre machine with underslung chassis. Like some other voiturette manufacturers, E.H.P. went on to offer a small six when their original product became unfashionable; in their case the 1,300cc Type DU of 1928. The E.H.P. was made in Spain as the Loryc.   TRN

EHRHARDT (D) *1904–1922*
Heinrich Ehrhardt, Düsseldorf; Zella-St Blasii
   When Heinrich Ehrhardt left the Fahrzeugfabrik Eisenach which made Warburg and later Dixi cars, his son Gustav continued car production in the Ehrhardt works at Düsseldorf and Zella-St Blasii. The Wartburg cars were Decauvilles built under licence. From 1904 to 1906 Ehrhardt continued to produce cars based on Decauville designs, selling them as Ehrhardt-Decauvilles. The first car of his own design was the Fidelio, with a 2-cylinder 1,272cc engine, which appeared in 1905. After 1906 Ehrhardt built only cars of his own design, powered by sv 4-cylinder engines from 1909 on. A very exclusive model was the 31/50PS 8-litre derived from the Kaiserpreis racing car. This was the first German car to be fitted with 4-wheel brakes (1913). After World War 1 two types were produced before the amalgamation with Szawe.   HON

EHRHARDT-SZAWE (D) *1922–1924*
Ehrhardt-Szawe Automobilwerk AG, Berlin; Zella-St Blasii
   Ehrhardt and Szawe amalgamated in 1922 and Szawe cars were marketed under the name Ehrhardt-Szawe until 1924. Best-known was the 10/50PS model with a 6-cylinder 2.6-litre engine.   HON

E.H.V. *see* COMPOUND

EIA (I) *1928*
Società Lombarda Anonima Industriale Automobili
   This was a conventional 1-litre 4-cylinder machine with 3-speed gearbox that never reached series production.   MCS

EIBACH (D) *1924*
Eichler & Bachmann GmbH, Berlin NW 7
   This was a 3-wheeled vehicle with a single rear wheel. The driver sat behind a

1922 EGO 4/14PS two-seater. *Neubauer Collection*

1927 E.H.P. 8/9CV coupé. *Jacques Kupélian Collection*

1907 EHRHARDT 15/24PS tourer. *Neubauer Collection*

1924 EIBACH 200cc 3-wheeler. *The Veteran Car Club of Great Britain*

1925 ELCAR 20hp tourer. *Automotive History Collection, Detroit Public Library*

two-seater cabin. A single-cylinder 200cc D.K.W. engine drove the rear wheel.   HON

E.I.M. (US) *1915*
Eastern Motor Car Co, Richmond, Ind.

This was a very late entrant into the American cyclecar market. The single model had a two-seater body on an underslung chassis, with a 1½-litre 4-cylinder engine.

GMN

EINAUDI (F) *1926–1927*
Cyclecars Einaudi, Bois-Colombes, Seine

The Einaudi was a very small cyclecar using a 3½hp single-cylinder engine and a 4-speed gearbox. The price was 6,000 francs.

GNG

EISENACH (D) *1898–1903*
Fahrzeugfabrik Eisenach, Eisenach

The Fahrzeugfabrik Eisenach started production in 1898 with electric cars and a petrol-driven car using a 2-cylinder Benz engine. For the latter type no chains were used for transmission, which was by toothed wheels and universal joints. Electric cars were produced until about 1903 and were marketed under the name of Eisenach. Petrol-driven cars were built only in small numbers and were succeeded in the same year by the Wartburg cars.

HON

EISENHUTH *see* COMPOUND

EKAMOBIL (D) *1913–1914*
Ing. Erhard Brandis, Berlin N 58

A 3-wheeled vehicle which had a front-mounted engine of 6hp and transmission by shaft and chains to the rear axle.

HON

ÉLAN (F) *1899–1900*
Sté des Automobiles Elan, Paris

The Elan was a light voiturette using a 3hp De Dion engine and chain drive. A later model had two separate 3hp De Dion engines driving the rear wheels independently.

GNG

ELBERT (US) *1914*
Elbert Motor Car Co, Seattle, Wash.

For a cyclecar, this make had a very shapely body. The cross-section of this tandem two-seater was similar to an inverted bell. It had a 4-cylinder engine of 1.6 litres, a 2-speed transmission and what was called a 'gearless' differential. The price was very low at $295.

GMN

ELBURN-RUBY *see* RUBY

ELCAR (US) *1915–1931*
(1) Elkhart Carriage & Motor Car Co, Elkhart, Ind.
(2) Elcar Motor Co, Elkhart, Ind.

From 1909 to 1915 the products of the Elkhart Carriage & Motor Car Co were known as Sterlings, but for the 1916 season the car's name was changed to Elcar. The first model was a conventional car made in two- and five-seater versions, powered by a 20hp 4-cylinder Lycoming engine of 3 litres capacity. This engine was used until the mid-1920s, but the range was increased by a 6-cylinder car with 3.6-litre Continental engine in 1918. A conventional range of cars was built during the 1920s, all using the 4-cylinder Lycoming or 6-cylinder Continental engine, a number of the former being make as taxicabs. In 1925 the company branched out into the 8-cylinder field, with a car powered by a 4.8-litre straight-8 Lycoming engine. In its final form this engine developed 140bhp, making it the third most powerful car engine in America at the time. Production of Elcars was never large, reaching a peak in 1919 with 4,000 units sold. Experiments with the Powell Lever engine came to nothing, though a Lever-powered Elcar 6 with 8in stroke appeared at the 1930 New York show. In their last year, 1931, the Elcar factory was used for the construction of the revived Mercer, which used an Elcar chassis and a 140bhp Continental engine. Only two of these cars were made.

KM

ELCO (US) *1915–1916*
Bimel Buggy Co, Sidney, Ohio

The Elco 30 was fitted with a 4-cylinder Davis L-head engine of 1.8 litres. The only model was a five-seater touring car on a wheelbase of 8ft 6in. The weight was 1,750lb, the price $585, with speedometer $15 extra.

GMN

ELDEN (GB) *1969 to date*
Design Formula Elden, London S.E.15

Peter and Brian Hampsheir, who had previously built the Briham cars, embarked on a Formula Ford programme with their first Elden, featuring inboard front suspension. An F100 design was also produced, being developed later as the Sturdgess. Tony Brise won 22 races with the Mark 8 FF car in 1970 and 1971. This was succeeded by the Mark 9 for 1972, with Nike-built chassis and fibreglass body by Marchant and Rose. This model earned considerable success in Britain in the

ands of Buzz Buzaglo, Mike Catlow, Ian Grob, Johnny Gerber, R. Robarts, Chris
mith and Danny Sullivan. New for 1973 was the Mark 10 FF with new nose cone,
e Mark 11 sports car and the Mark 12 F3.   DF

LDIN ET LAGIER (F) *1898–1901*
din et Lagier, Lyons
    Eldin and Lagier were De Dion agents who assembled a small number of cars
oradically, but did not go in for series production. Their voiturette of 1899,
esigned by Capt. Barisien, used two front-mounted 1¾hp De Dion engines, while
1901 they made a large car with a 20hp 4-cylinder engine for King Leopold II
f Belgium. Alphonse Eldin was later sales director of Rochet-Schneider.   GNG

LDREDGE (US) *1903–1906*
ational Sewing Machine Co, Belvedere, Ill.
    The Eldredge was a light two-seater runabout, with an early example of left-hand
heel steering. It had an 8hp under-seat engine connected to the rear axle by
ackshaft and chain drive. From 1904 there was a larger tonneau with 16hp flat-4
ngine. The sales slogan of the Eldredge, 'Just what it ought to be', was not very
nformative.   GMN

LECTRA *see* FAURE

LECTRA (i) (D) *1899–1900*
. Krüger, Berlin
    A small 3-wheeled electric two-seater.   HON

LECTRA (ii) (US) *1913–1915*
torage Battery Power Co, Chicago, Ill.
    The Electra was driven by a 2½hp electric motor geared to the rear axle. It was
closed two-seater which weighed only 750lb.   GMN

LECTRA KING (US) *1961 to date*
and Z Electric Car Co, Long Beach, Calif.
    Small and of simple construction, this electric is built in 3- and 4-wheeled models
or running errands or for use by the handicapped. Four 6-volt batteries powered
he 1hp D.C. motor capable of operating up to 40 miles on a charge. The 4-wheeled
model was discontinued in 1967, but reintroduced in 1971.   BE

LECTRICAR (F) *1920–1924*
ouaillet, St Ouen, Seine
    This was a two-seater 3-wheeler powered by a 2½hp electric motor.   GNG

LECTRIC SHOPPER (US) *c.1964 to date*
lectric Shopper, Long Beach, Calif.
    A small 3-wheeled car similar to the Electra King with a plastic body which
s made for short local journeys.   BE

LECTROCICLO (E) *1945–1946*
Electrociclo SA, Barrio Chonta, Eibar, Guipuzcoa
    The only car to be made in the Basque province of Guipuzcoa, the Electrociclo
was a small two-seater electric car built for the Government-sponsored Electric
Motor Show in Madrid in 1946.   JR-V

LECTROCYCLETTE *see* A.E.M.

LECTROGÉNIA *see* CHAMPROBERT

LECTROLETTE (F) *1941–1943*
.A. André, Nice
    The Electrolette was a very light electric car made in open two-seater and
coupé forms. The 1½hp motor gave a speed of 20mph, and the cars had independent
suspension all round. During 1942 they were made at the rate of two per day.   GNG

LECTRO MASTER (US) *c.1962 to date*
Nepa Mfg Co, Pasadena, Calif.
    With a 40-mile driving range, the little Electro Master was built of steel and
ibreglass and weighed 680lb. A 2hp motor and six 6-volt batteries pushed it along
at 20mph.   BE

LECTROMOBILE (i) *see* CHAPMAN

LECTROMOBILE (ii) (GB) *1901–1920*
British Electromobile Co Ltd, London
    This company, whose earlier products also went by the names of B.E.C. and
Powerful, derived from the former British and Foreign Electrical Co which imported
the front-wheel drive Kriéger electric cars from France. By 1902, however,
Electromobiles had emerged as rear-wheel-driven vehicles with motors on the rear

1966 ELECTRA KING two-seater runabout.
B & Z Electric Car Co

1904 ELECTROMOBILE(ii) electric
victoria. *G.N. Georgano Collection*

1919 ELMO 8/12hp electric limousine.
Coachwork by Gill of Paddington. *Autocar*

1921 ELFE 2-cylinder cyclecar. *Autocar*

1918 ELGIN Six 21hp convertible sedan. *The Veteran Car Club of Great Britain*

1927 ELITE(ii) 12/50PS saloon. *Neubauer Collection*

wheels, inclined wheel steering and solid tyres. From 1903 their electric brougham were made on the Contal system : tyres were now pneumatic, the motor was mounted on the rear axle with double-reduction drive and the batteries were mounted under the floor. The market was limited and design changed little, though Electromobi ran a contract-maintenance service under which an annual payment of £32 covered everything except the driver's wages. For a short while the firm collaborate in the marketing of Napier's petrol broughams, later taking up the Opel concessic in England to supplement the sales of their own products which neither wore ou nor became obsolescent. Hire became more important than manufacture in th years just before World War 1, though an attempt was made to revive the marqu in 1919 with the Elmo landaulette, rated at 8/12hp, and differing in appearance fror earlier Electromobiles in having a short bonnet. Despite a compact wheelbase of 8 9in and a modest list price of £1,050, nothing came of this. MC

ÉLECTROMOTION (F) *1900–1909*
Sté l'Electromotion, Paris

This company made a wide range of electric town cars based on Columbi designs. GN

ELECTRONIC LA SAETTA (US) *1955*
Electronic Motor Car Corp, Salt Lake City, Utah

Referred to as a 'turbo-electric' car, the Electronic used an 80-cell batter system that was regenerated by a petrol or diesel turbogenerator. The fibreglas bodied La Saetta two-seater sports was exhibited in Salt Lake City in 195! Announced at the time, but not completed, were a sedan, station wagon, pane truck and children's La Saetta. After a promising start nothing came of thi interesting project. B

ELECTRONOMIC *see* HOOD

ÉLECTRO-RENARD (F) *c.1943–1946*
The Electro-Renard was a very small electric two-seater made at Lyons. A range of 45 miles per charge was claimed. GN

ELECTROSPORT (US) *1972 to date*
Electric Fuel Propulsion Inc, Ferndale, Mich.

The Electrosport is the first commercial offering of a company that has buil a number of experimental electric conversions of petrol-engined cars, including th Hornet-based E.F.P. that won the 1970 Clean Air Race. The Electrosport is base on the Hornet station wagon and is priced at $11,900. Top speed is 69mph an range at 40mph is 73 miles. B

ELEKTRIC (D) *1922–1924*
Automobil- und Akkumulatoren-Bau-GmbH, Berlin N 65; Driesen-Vordamm

Electric cars which succeeded the A.A.A. Private cars were produced only ii small numbers, vans and lorries being more popular. HON

ELFE (F) *1919–1922*
Ateliers Defrance Frères, Vierzon, Cher

The Elfe cyclecar first appeared as a monocar or tandem bicar with a front-mounted V-twin engine and V-belt drive to the rear wheels. The 1920 competition version had an 1,100cc V-twin Anzani engine at the rear, and final drive by chain It was also a tandem two-seater, in which driver and passenger sat on saddles; i the passenger became tired, he had nothing to lean on but the hot exhaust pipe. This machine, driven by Mauve, its designer, competed in the Cyclecar Grand Prix at Le Mans from 1920 to 1922 but never with any distinction, on one occasion lapping at only 19mph. It did, however, win its class at the Nice flying kilometre trials in 1921. In 1923 Mauve began to make a more conventional car under his own name. GNG

ELFIN (AUS) *1959 to date*
Elfin Sports Cars, Edwardstown, South Australia

The first Elfin was a Formula Junior racing car based on the Lotus 18, and was followed by a Formula 3 version and a Clubman-type sports car. A completely new monocoque chassis was introduced in 1965, available for 1,100cc or 1½-litre Ford engines for the current Australian Formulas 2 and 3. This car was also fitted with a 2½-litre Repco V-8 engine in 1969, and raced with great success by Elfin's founder Garrie Cooper. Other cars built by Elfin have included Formula Ford and Vee models, and a large Group 7 sports made in conjunction with Frank Matich. GNG

ELGÉ (B) *1912–1914*
Lambin et Gendebien, Houffalise

The Elgé was made in one model only, with a 4-cylinder monobloc 2.3-litre engine. An aluminium casing around the crankcase and gearbox gave the impression of unit engine and gearbox construction. Very few Elgés were made. GNG

ELGIN (i) (US) *1899–c.1901*
Elgin Automobile Co, Elgin, Ill.

This company made a very simple single-cylinder runabout with a 5hp engine. It was sometimes known as the Winner, but had no connection with the later car made under this name at St Louis. Elgin also made an electric runabout. GNG

ELGIN (ii) (US) *1916–1925*
(1) Elgin Motor Car Corp, Argo, Ill. *1916–1923*
(2) Elgin Motor Car Corp, Chicago, Ill. *1924–1925*
The Elgin was a conventional car built originally in 4-cylinder form, but using the 6-cylinder ohv Falls engine in 1918. The most interesting model was the six introduced in 1922, with Cutler-Hammer pre-selector, and double transverse rear springs. The body featured a built-in luggage boot which, although small in comparison with today's equivalents, was an advanced feature for its day. GNG

ELIESON (GB) *1897–1898*
Elieson Lamina Accumulator Syndicate Ltd, Camden Town, London N.
This company offered a light electric four-seater with very narrow front track, and chain drive. It was sometimes known as the Swan. They also made a taxicab and delivery van. Elieson supplied the batteries and the cars were constructed at the Reading works of John Warrick & Co Ltd. GNG

ELITE (i) (US) *1901*
D.B. Smith & Co, Utica, N.Y.
The Elite was a typical American light steam car, differing only from the general run by its ornate bodywork and profusion of brass on lamps, dash, hubs and steering tiller. It used a 2-cylinder engine, and a petrol car with similar body was also listed. GNG

ELITE (ii); **ELITE-DIAMANT** (D) *1920–1928*
(1) Elite Motorenwerke AG, Brand-Erbisdorf *1920–1922*
(2) Elitewerke AG, Brand-Erbisdorf *1922–1927*
(3) Elite-Diamant-Werke AG, Brand-Erbisdorf *1927–1928*
This firm was founded in 1914, but not originally to build cars. In 1917, however, the Geha works were taken over and after the end of World War 1 production of electric cars started. They continued the Geha electric 3-wheeler and also built a 4-wheeled car, which was mainly used as a taxicab. In 1920 the first petrol-driven car appeared. Best known were the 4-cylinder E 12/40PS of 3.1 litres and the 6-cylinder 18/70PS of 4.7 litres. The latter was also available in a sports version developing 90bhp. The 6-cylinder 10/50PS, 12/55PS and 14/60PS completed the range. After amalgamation in 1927 with Diamant the cars were also known as Elite-Diamant until production ceased in 1928. The company was then acquired by Opel. HON

ELITEWAGEN (D) *1921–1923*
Elitewagen AG, Ronneburg
The Rex Simplex make of cars was taken over by the Elitewerke in 1921. The Rex Simplex 13/40PS was continued under the name of Elitewagen, while the original Elite cars were built under that name in the plant at Brand-Erbisdorf. Production at Ronneburg ceased in 1923. HON

ELIZALDE (E) *1914–1928*
(1) Biada, Elizalde y Cía, Barcelona
(2) Fabrica Española de Automóviles Elizalde, Barcelona
The early history of this firm is obscure, and the first car of Arturo Elizalde of which details have survived was a 75mm × 130mm machine of 15/20hp. In 1919 it was known as the Type 26 and had front-wheel brakes. There were four forward speeds and cantilever springing was used front and rear. This was a very successful competition car. Rather larger models, the 16/20hp and 18/23hp (also with four wheel brakes) were made as well. From now on, however, Elizalde concentrated on making luxury cars for the export market, as did Hispano-Suiza. The 1920 range included four models, of which the 50/60hp Type 48 was the biggest. This was the largest car at the Paris Salon of 1921, its eight cylinders totalling over eight litres in capacity. Its front-wheel brakes were servo-assisted. However, Elizalde was forced to diversify and by 1922 a 3-litre eight, the 20/30hp, which survived until car production ended, had appeared alongside the monsters. By the following year two true light cars, the 6/8hp and the 8/10hp had joined them, and the latter, too, lived on until 1928. Thereafter the company made only aero engines. TRN

ELKHART (US) *1908–1909*
(1) Elkhart Carriage & Manufacturing Co, Elkhart, Ind. *1908*
(2) Elkhart Motor Car Co, Elkhart, Ind. *1908–1909*
The Elkhart was a medium-sized five-seater touring car which weighed 2,400lb. Its 4-cylinder 30/35hp engine had a capacity of 4.4 litres. GMN

ELLEMOBIL (DK) *1909–1913*
J.C. Ellehammer, Copenhagen
Ellehammer was a well known inventor. He offered a scooter from 1904 to 1914, and in 1906 he became world famous as the first aviator in Europe to construct and

1927 ELITE(ii) 18/70PS sports tourer.
Václav Petrík Collection

1922 ELIZALDE Tipo 20C 3-litre sports car
Gili de Heredia

1922 ELIZALDE Tipo 48 8-litre limousine.
Gili de Heredia

1909 ELLEMOBIL 2-cylinder cyclecar. *Thorkil Ry Andersen*

1904 ELMORE 5hp runabout. *Henry Ford Museum, Dearborn, Mich.*

1904 ELSWICK 20hp landaulette. *G.N. Georgano Collection*

fly a heavier-than-air machine. In 1909–10 he offered a 2-cylinder air-cooled car with friction transmission and belt drive. In 1913 a flat 3-cylinder 11hp, with his newly invented hydraulic clutch, was built into his experimental car. The weight of the car was only 300kg, but it never went into production. Once an invention of his had succeeded Ellehammer often lost interest in it. TRA

ELLIS *see* TRIUMPH (i)

ELLSWORTH (US) *1907*

J.M. Ellsworth, New York, N.Y.

This car offered a choice of shaft or double-chain drive. Its 4-cylinder engine had a single overhead camshaft operating T-head valves. The crankshaft journals were the same diameter as the crank throws. Twin ignition was used as well as a 4-speed transmission. GMN

ELMO *see* ELECTROMOBILE (ii)

ELMORE (US) *1900–1912*

Elmore Mfg Co, Clyde, Ohio

Elmore were the most persistent advocates of the 2-stroke engine in America, and never made a 4-stroke engined car. From 1900 to 1904 they made a light runabout with a 5hp single-cylinder engine under the seat, 3 speeds, single chain drive and tiller steering. The first models had vertical engines, but from about 1902 they were horizontal. In 1903 a 2-cylinder model was added, and in 1904 the larger car had a dummy bonnet, although the engine was still under the seat. For 1906 a completely new range was introduced, with front-mounted engines of 22/24hp (2-cylinder) and 32/35hp (4-cylinder), shaft drive and side-entrance tourer bodies. A 24hp 3-cylinder model appeared in 1907, and was made for several years. In 1909 the Elmore company was absorbed by General Motors, and production ended three years later. The last models were 4-cylinder cars of 30 and 50hp, still 2-strokes. GNG

ELSWICK (GB) *1903–c.1907*

Elswick Motor Co, Newcastle-upon-Tyne

The Elswick was an assembled car made in various sizes using 6hp De Dion, 20hp Brouhot or 24hp Mutel engines. In 1906 Elswick were offering two models under the name S.P.Q.R. (Speed, Power, Quietness, Reliability). They were a 15/20hp and a 26/30hp, both with 4-cylinder engines and shaft drive. GNG

ELVA (i) (F) *1907*

Voitures Elva, Paris

This was a short-lived make which was available in two models, a 6/8hp 2-cylinder two-seater, and a 12/14hp 4-cylinder four-seater double phaeton. GNG

ELVA (ii) (GB) *1955–1968*

(1) Elva Engineering Co, Bexhill and Hastings, Sussex *1955–1966*
(2) Elva Cars (1961) Ltd, Rye, Sussex *1961–1966*
(3) Elva Cars (1961) Ltd, Croydon, Surrey *1966–1968*
(4) Elva Cars Ltd, Shenley, Herts. *1967*

The original Elva was aimed to be a low-cost sports-racing car, with power unit to suit the customer's pocket. A simple tubular frame took Standard front suspension, and a Ford Anglia rear axle was modified to give a De Dion type layout. An ohv conversion for the 1,172cc Ford engine was devised by M. Witts and H. Weslake, and used with outstanding success in this model. Frank Nichols steadily developed his design, the Mark 4 of 1958, with 1,098cc Coventry-Climax engine, featuring a rear end based on the M.G., but with independent suspension and inboard brakes.

The Mark 5, with small-diameter tubular frame and coil suspension, formed the basis for the 1959 Formula Junior car. As this was at the time the only production car in the class, sales were spectacular, and the standard D.K.W.-engined models achieved considerable success until the advent of the rear-engined contenders in 1960. Elva countered with a rear-engined version of their own, but sales of the front-engined car continued into 1961, finally exceeding 150.

Meanwhile, the Courier road car had been introduced in 1958, based on a large-diameter steel tube ladder chassis, with M.G.A. engine and fibreglass body. Available as a kit, this car sold very well, and some 700 were made up to the end of 1961. The Mark 4 version, retaining the Triumph ifs and MGB mechanical components of the Mark 3, but with a box frame moulded into the body, was still offered in 1967, being chiefly purchased for racing circuit training in the U.S.A.

Other models had included the Mark 7 of 1963, with 1,588cc Ford engine, and the 1964GT '160' with dry-sump B.M.W. engine, the elegant body being designed by Fiore and made by Fissore of Turin. The design and manufacturing rights of the Courier had been taken over previously by Trojan Ltd, and in 1964 this firm took over the company entirely. The Courier only was produced for a period at Shenley before manufacture returned to Croydon. By then the only vestige of the racing models was in the name McLaren-Elva, and this too was dropped some time after Courier production ceased in 1968. DF

ELYSÉE (F) *1921–1925*

Automobiles Elysée, Paris

The Elysée was a light car available with either belt or shaft drive. The belt-drive vehicle used a 780cc engine, and the shaft-drive a 950cc, both 4-cylinder units. GNG

EMANCIPATOR (US) *1909*

Emancipator Automobile Co, Aurora, Ill.

The two models of the Emancipator (three- and five-seaters) had 2- and 4-cylinder opposed engines placed crosswise under the bonnet. Drive was by planetary transmission with shaft drive to the rear axle. GMN

EMBREE (US) *1910*

McLean Carriage Co, St Louis, Mo.

In 1910 the Embree had an engine rated at 35hp. Other details are lacking. GMN

E.M.C. *see R.F.*

EMERALD (GB) *1903–1904*

Douglas S. Cox & Co, West Norwood, London S.E.

The Emerald was a very light two-seater voiturette with a 4hp single-cylinder engine, 2-speed gearbox and a long belt drive to the rear axle. D.S. Cox later acquired the works of the Weller company, also at West Norwood, where he made a small number of Osterfield cars. GNG

EMERAUDE (F) *1913–1914*

The Emeraude cyclecar used a single-cylinder Buchet engine, friction transmission and chain final drive. Its most unusual feature was that two electric head-lamps were built into the top of the radiator shell. The car was made by Constructions Industrielles Dijonaises (C.I.D.). GNG

EMERSON (i) (US) *1907*

(1) V. L. Emerson, Cincinnati, Ohio

(2) American Auto Car Co, Cincinnati, Ohio

The short-lived Emerson 'Military' model was an $8,000 three-seater car weighing 1,500lb and with an 8ft wheelbase. Steering was described as being through 'toggle movement'. Its 6-cylinder 10.6-litre engine had rotary valves. It had only two forward speeds. Performance, though unknown, must have been unusual. GMN

EMERSON (ii) (US) *1916–1917*

Emerson Motors Co, Kingston, N.Y.

The Emerson was a conventional car with a 22hp 4-cylinder engine and five-seater touring body. It sold for $545 which was reduced to $395 for 1917. It was succeeded by the Campbell (ii), which was a similar design, also selling for $395. GNG

EMERY (GB) *1963–1966*

Paul Emery Cars Ltd, Fulham, London S.W.

In 1966 the tubular space-framed Emery GT, available with Ford or Hillman Imp engine, gained several class racing successes. Suspension was by conventional coil damper units, with anti-dive features, and total height of the fibreglass bodywork was 3ft 4in. Only four of these cars were built, the firm receiving more orders for their lowered and tuned Imp model, the Emery Imp GT. DF

EMERYSON (GB) *1949–1952; 1960–1961*

Emeryson Cars Ltd, Twickenham, Middlesex *1949–1952*

Connaught Cars Ltd, Send, Surrey *1960–1961*

Noteworthy for front-wheel drive, absence of differential, independent rubber suspension and rapid cornering, the first production Emeryson was a 500cc contender. Successes were few, and only eight were built, although for 1952 weight was reduced, and coil suspension adopted. For the next few years, only one-offs were made: Paul Emery, with his son, had constructed a Duesenberg-engined car for the first post-war Formula 1, and this was superseded by a car which successively used Aston-Martin, Alta and fuel-injected Jaguar 2.4-litre engines. For 1961, in conjunction with Connaught, a few Formula Junior Emerysons were made, of conventional design, and a team of Maserati-powered Formula 1 machines for the Equipe Nationale Belge. These cars had a somewhat erratic career, and were later re-hashed as the American-sponsored Sciroccos. DF

E.M.F. (US) *1908–1912*

Everitt-Metzger-Flanders Co, Detroit, Mich.

The E.M.F. was a slightly larger car than its companion make, the Flanders, both makes being marketed by Studebaker. Throughout its existence the E.M.F. used a 2.7-litre water-cooled, 4-cylinder engine. This was coupled with a 3-speed transmission and shaft drive. The wheelbase remained constant at 8ft 10in. Both runabout and touring models were built for sale in the range of $900 to $1,100. The name disappeared when Studebaker started to build as well as act as a selling organization. GMN

1957 ELVA(ii) 1,100cc sports car. *Autosport*

1965 ELVA(ii) Courier 1½-litre sports car. *Trojan Ltd*

1963 EMERY 875cc GT coupé. *Autosport*

1952 EMERYSON Formula 3 racing car. *Richmond Pike*

1912 E.M.F. 30hp tourer. *Kenneth Stauffer*

1914 EMPIRE(iii) Model 31 tourer. *Antique Automobile*

1952 E.M.W. Type 327 2-litre cabriolet. *G.N. Georgano*

EMMS (GB) *1922–1923*
Emms Motors Co, Coventry, Warwickshire

The Emms was a short-lived light car using the 9.8hp sv Coventry-Simplex engine, a 3-speed gearbox and worm drive. As well as a two-seater tourer, a pointed-tail sports and a closed coupé body were available.
GNG

E.M.P. (GB) *1897–1900*
Electric Motive Power Co, Balham, London S.W.

The first E.M.P. vehicle was an electric conversion of a horse-bus which appeared in 1896. The following year they made a four-seater electric victoria with a 2hp motor and solid tyres. Later they made a 5hp four-seater dogcart, and a 2hp 3-wheeler. Although exhibited at shows, they were little more than experimental vehicles.
GNG

EMPIRE (i) (US) *1901–1902*
Empire Mfg Co Inc., Sterling, Ill.

Also known as the Sterling Steamer, this was a typical light steam buggy in appearance, but was unusual in using a V-twin engine. A water-tube boiler produced superheated steam at a pressure of 400psi, and maximum speed of the two-seater was 30mph.
GNG

EMPIRE (ii) (US) *1904–1905*
William T. Terwilliger & Co, Amsterdam, N.Y.

This steamer had an opposed 2-cylinder engine of 15hp rating. This was 'hung pivotally from rear axle' and the 'cylinder end was suspended from boiler'. It had tubular steel wheels and its rear-entrance tonneau body carried five passengers.
GMN

EMPIRE (iii) (US) *1909–1919*
(1) Empire Motor Car Co, Indianapolis, Ind. *1909–1912*
(2) Greenville Metal Products, Greenville, Pa. *1912–1919*

A two-seater with a 4-cylinder, 20hp G.B.S. engine with pair-cast cylinders was produced with little change from 1909 to 1912. It was known as The Little Aristocrat and cost $950. In 1912 operations moved to Pennsylvania, and for one season the car was known as the Fay. Although sold by the Empire Automobile Co of Indianapolis, all subsequent cars were made in Greenville. After 1912, a large line of cars in two-, four-, and five-seater models was made, with wheelbases up to 10ft. These were powered by 4-cylinder Teetor and 6-cylinder Continental engines and prices ranged to $1,360.
GMN

EMPIRE STATE (US) *1900–1901*
Empire State Automobile Co, Rochester, N.Y.

This company made a light runabout with wire wheels, tiller steering, chain drive, and the engine under the seat. There was also an Empire State Motor Wagon Co, of Catskill, N.Y., who operated one of America's first used car lots, and may have made one or two light runabouts.
GNG

EMPRESS (GB) *1907–1910*
Empress Motor Co Ltd, Manchester

The Empress was quite an advanced design of car offered in four sizes: 16/20 and 20/24hp 4-cylinders, and 24/30 and 30/36hp 6-cylinders. All cars had shaft drive, and employed pressure lubrication and detachable cylinder heads. After 1910 Frank Smith, the man behind the car, turned his attention to aviation.
GNG

EMSCOTE (GB) *1920–1921*
Emscote Motor Co Ltd, Warwick

Two models of the Emscote light car were made, one with a 2-cylinder 8/10hp J.A.P. engine, and the other with an 11.9hp Alpha 4-cylinder engine. Drive was by shaft, and the design included frameless construction with front suspension by a single transverse semi-elliptic spring.
GNG

E.M.W. (D) *1945–1955*
Eisenacher Motoren-Werke, Eisenach

The Bayerische Motoren-Werke (B.M.W.) of Eisenach were nationalized in 1945. Production of pre-war B.M.W. cars was taken up again in 1945, under the management of a consortium called Awtovelo, mainly for export. The original B.M.W. emblem was used. In 1952 the factory was renamed the Eisenacher Motoren-Werke. The E.M.W. 321 was identical to, and the 327 only slightly different from, the pre-war 2-litre B.M.W. models. Model 340/2 was based on the 326, but had a new radiator grille. Some very successful sports and Formula 2 racing cars were developed by E.M.W., also based on earlier B.M.W. designs. These were known as A.W.E.s (Automobilwerk Eisenach) and the later versions (1954–55) had twin ohc engines. The name Automobilwerk Eisenach was officially adopted in 1955 and production of B.M.W.-based cars ceased.
HON

ENDURANCE (i) (GB) *1899–1901*
Endurance Motor Co Ltd, Coventry, Warwickshire

Endurance cars were closely based on Benz designs, with 4½ or 6hp horizontal ngle-cylinder engines, and 2-speed belt transmissions. One was entered in the 1900 000 Miles Trial, but retired.   GNG

NDURANCE (ii) (US) *1923–1924*

durance Steam Car Co, Los Angeles, Calif.

A short-lived steamer built on conventional lines, the Endurance was produced ly as a five-seater touring car. Disc wheels were standard equipment and the ice was $1,885.   KM

NFIELD (i) (GB) *1906–1915*

) Enfield Autocar Co Ltd, Redditch, Worcs. *1906–1908*

) Enfield Autocar Co Ltd, Birmingham *1908–1915*

The first products of the Enfield Co, after becoming independent of Royal nfield in 1906, were shaft-driven 4-cylinder cars with round radiators, made in 4.1- re and 5.9-litre forms at £420 and £525 respectively. The company found itself in ancial difficulties early in 1908 and was bought by Alldays who thereafter arketed more expensive versions of their own cars under the Enfield name. These ere all conventional side-valve machines and extended up to a large 6.1-litre four £450 in 1911, but though Alldays listed a six, Enfield never did. A single-cylinder ar-engined 3-wheeler with epicyclic gear, the Autorette, was offered for a short hile in 1912, but it gave way to versions of the Alldays Midget light car, of which e 1914 Enfield version was known as the Nimble Nine. Post-1918 products were ld under the name of Enfield-Allday.   MCS

NFIELD (ii) (GB) *1969 to date*

nfield Automotive, London, S.W.19

The Enfield 465 is a small electric saloon for city work, powered by a 4.65hp AV 48-volt motor, giving a speed of 40mph and a range of 30/40 miles per arge. The fibreglass body has two sliding doors. Several prototypes have been ilt, including an open four-seater beach car, and production is planned.   GNG

NFIELD-ALLDAY (GB) *1919–1925*

nfield-Allday Motors Ltd, Sparkbrook, Birmingham

The Enfield-Allday concern was the outcome of the fusion of two old-established anufacturers of small cars, the Enfield and the Alldays & Onions. Both names ad been borne by conventional family cars, so the Enfield-Allday Bullet which ppeared in 1919 was a radical break with tradition. Designed by A.W. Reeves and .C. Bertelli (the works manager), it was powered by an aero-type 5-cylinder, air- oled, sleeve-valve radial engine of 1½ litres. Its tubular backbone frame, with antilever springs front and rear, carried a three-seater body on outriggers. Only handful of these revolutionary little machines was built; they were too expensive make. A sleeve-valve 15hp six was listed, but does not seem to have been made. he company would have died but for another, completely orthodox car, the)/20hp, which Bertelli hurriedly introduced. With its 1½-litre, in-line, water- oled 4-cylinder engine, it was unusual only in being exceptionally well- nished, handsome and fast. In Bertelli's hands, a special 10/20 furnished with vo overhead inlet valves per cylinder and front-wheel brakes won its class in e 1922 Tourist Trophy race. 1923 saw the 12/30hp, with a bigger bore and a 4- eed gearbox, but all Enfield-Alldays were extremely expensive cars and only out a hundred were made. A.W. Reeves had gone on to make plans to produce e radial-engined car himself, as the Reeves Radial, while Bertelli, after an qually abortive attempt to make his own cars, became associated with Aston lartin Motors Ltd.   TRN

NGELHARDT (D) *1900–1902*

lermann Engelhardt Motoren- und Automobilfabrik, Berlin SW

A small firm which produced a 6.5PS car with an interchangeable passenger and an body.   HON

NGER (US) *1909–1917*

nger Motor Car Co, Cincinnati, Ohio

The first Enger was a 2-cylinder high-wheeler, but rapidly evolved through the 910 40hp model to the Twin Six of 1915. This engine was designed and built by nger and the car was one of the earliest 12-cylinder models in America. The 1916 odel had an overhead-valve engine which could be converted to work as a 6- ylinder unit, by operating a lever which stopped the flow of fuel and opened the alves of one bank of cylinders. This engine developed 55hp at 3,000rpm.   GMN

NGLER (US) *1914–1915*

V.B. Engler Cyclecar Co, Pontiac, Mich.

This two-seater cyclecar used a DeLuxe air-cooled, 2-cylinder engine of 2 litres, driving through friction transmission and belts. The price was $385.   GMN

NGLISH MECHANIC (GB) *1900–1905*

The English Mechanic was never a make in the ordinary sense of the word, for here was no company or factory of this name. In January 1900 the magazine 'The nglish Mechanic and World of Science and Art' began a series of articles entitled

1952 E.M.W. Type 340 2-litre saloon. *Eisenacher Motoren-Werke*

1907 ENFIELD(i) 15hp tourer. The designer, E.H. Lancaster, at the wheel. *Autocar*

1921 ENFIELD-ALLDAY 10/20hp saloon. *Autocar*

1904 ENGLISH MECHANIC 8hp tonneau. *Mrs D.J. Shawe*

1960 ENZMANN 506 1.3-litre sports car. *Garage Enzmann*

'a small car and how to build it'. Written by the engineer, T. Hyler White, th‑ articles gave detailed instructions and plans, and gave advice on where to b‑ those parts which the amateur mechanic did not feel up to making himself. Th‑ first car had a 3hp single-cylinder engine, and was very similar to the Benz desig‑ Later designs included a 2-cylinder double-acting steam car with front-mounte‑ condenser and chain drive, a light steam 3-wheeler with a 2-cylinder singl‑ acting engine and a slightly Bollée-like appearance, a petrol car with an 8hp ‑cylinder vertical engine and shaft drive, and finally a 5hp runabout on America‑ lines, with a single-cylinder engine under the seat, and single chain drive. When th‑ last car article had appeared in July 1905, the versatile Hyler White started a ne‑ series on how to make the English Mechanic piano player! At least two Englis‑ Mechanic cars survive, a 1900 Benz-type, and a 1904 8hp 2-cylinder tonnea‑

GN

ENGSTRÖM (S) *1900*
C.A. Engströms Vagnfabrik, Eskilstuna

The third petrol-engined car to be made in Sweden, the Engström used a singl‑ cylinder $3\frac{1}{2}$hp engine and single chain drive. The car had only one forward spee‑ and only a prototype was made.

G

ENKA (CS) *1925–1928*
F. Koland akc. spol., Prague

In 1924 the engineer Novotny designed a 2-stroke-engined light car called th‑ Disk. It appeared in modified form the next year as the Enka, and was made in ver‑ small numbers by Koland (The name is simply the phonetic sound of N.K., Novotn‑ & Koland). In 1929 the design was put into large-scale production by Aero. GN

ENSIGN (i) *see* BRITISH ENSIGN

ENSIGN (ii) (GB) *1971 to date*
(1) Ensign Cars Ltd, Cheslyn Hay, Staffs. *1971*
(2) Ensign Cars Ltd, Walsall, Staffs. *1971 to date*

Racing driver Maurice Nunn's Ensign design pioneered the use of side radiator‑ which became fashionable among single-seaters during 1971. A pair of Formul‑ Atlantics were made and an F2 machine for John Burton, but the firm really co‑ centrated during 1971 and 1972 on Formula 3, in which the dozen or so LNF‑ models were remarkably successful, particularly in the hands of Mike Walker, Coli‑ Vandervell, Bev Bond, Rikki von Opel, Steve Thompson, Dave Purley and Jerem‑ Gambs. The cars followed mainly conventional design principles, with fibregla‑ bodies by Specialised Mouldings.

D

ENTROP (NL) *1909*
De 's-Gravenmoersche Rijwielen- en Motorrijwielenfabriek, 's-Gravenmoer

Marinus Entrop had been building bicycles for three years when he turned ‑ motor manufacture with a tiller-steered 3-wheeler powered by either a single- ‑ 2-cylinder engine mounted behind the front wheel. Only four Entrop cars wer‑ made.

GN

E.N.V. (F) *1908*
E.N.V. Motors Ltd, Courbevoie, Seine

This was an English company with French works who were mainly known fo‑ aero engines. They obtained their name from the French 'en-V', meaning a V-layou‑ engine. At the 1908 Paris Salon they exhibited a car with a 40hp V-8 engine, 2-spee‑ gearbox and 2-speed rear axle, giving 4 forward speeds in all.

GN

ENVOY (GB) *1960*
Sewell and King Ltd, Chelmsford, Essex

This svelte little car was designer/driver Ian Raby's concept of a moderatel‑ priced Formula Junior contestant. A square-section ladder chassis, with coil sus‑ pension, accepted rear-mounted B.M.C. or Ford engines, and various proprietar‑ parts for transmission and controls. Light alloy and fibreglass bodies were fitted. D

ENZMANN (CH) *1957–1970*
Garage Enzmann, Schupfheim

The Enzmann sports car used a Volkswagen engine and frame on which wa‑ mounted an open two-seater fibreglass body without doors, made by Staempfli ‑ Grandson. Design changed little after the car's introduction, although the 1,192c‑ standard engine was supplemented by the 1,295cc Okrasa-modified unit givin‑ a maximum speed of over 100mph. About 100 cars had been made by the en‑ of 1966. Production ceased in 1968, but a final Enzmann was made in 1970. GN

ÉOLE (F) *1899–1901*
J.B. Clement et Cie, Paris

The original Éole voiturette used a front-mounted $2\frac{1}{2}$hp Aster engine, shaft driv‑ to a 3-speed gearbox, and final drive by chain. Like several contemporary manufac‑ turers they increased the power of their next model, not by enlarging the engine, bu‑ by simply adding another one. The resultant $4\frac{1}{2}$hp car was capable of 35mph. I‑ 1901 they used one 6hp Buchet engine.

GN

ÉOLIA *see* TRACTION AÉRIENNE

EOS (D) *1922–1923*
Rossineck & Co, Berlin N 39
A small car with a 3-cylinder 2-stroke 5/20PS engine. This car was earlier marketed under the name of Erco.   HON

ÉPALLE (F) *1910–1914*
Épalle et Cie, St Etienne, Loire
The Épalle company made a range of four cars: an 8/10hp 2-cylinder, and three 4-cylinder models, of 10/12, 12/16 and 14/20hp. They were of conventional layout with shaft drive.   GNG

E.R.A. (GB) *1934–1952*
(1) English Racing Automobiles Ltd, Bourne, Lincs. *1934–1945*
(2) English Racing Automobiles Ltd, Dunstable, Bedfordshire *1946–1952*
The E.R.A. was produced by Raymond Mays, Humphrey Cook and Peter Berthon as a challenger in the 1,500cc racing class. It used a conventional chassis, a 4-speed pre-selector gearbox and a highly-developed version of the blown 6-cylinder ohv Riley engine giving 165bhp. There were 1,100cc and 2-litre power units as alternatives, and with the D-series Porsche trailing-arm independent front suspension was introduced. Only 16 cars were made, but they dominated the voiturette class in the hands of such drivers as Mays, B. Bira, Seaman, Fairfield, Arthur Dobson and Earl Howe. Victories outside Britain included the Eifelrennen, the Coppa Acerbo, Berne and Masaryk in 1935; the Prince Rainier Cup and Albi in 1936; the Avus, Picardie, Albi and Berne in 1937; and Picardie again in 1938. They also dominated British road racing in their day and Raymond Mays achieved numerous fastest times at Shelsley Walsh with his 2-litre car. Fifteen cars still survive and are prominent in 'historic' racing. A sports-car project in 1937 came to nothing, but a new 240bhp short-stroke six, the E-type with torsion-bar ifs, a De Dion rear axle, synchromesh gearbox and streamlined body, appeared in 1939.
After World War 2 Mays and Berthon worked on the B.R.M. V16, while E.R.A., now under the control of Leslie Johnson, struggled on with the unsuccessful E-types until 1949. The company assisted in the design of Jowett's 1950 'Jupiter' sports car, but their last racing machine, the G-type, was designed for Formula 2, and had a 150bhp 6-cylinder Bristol engine and tubular frame to the designs of David Hodkin. This final product was sold to Bristol's for testing.   MCS

ERCO (D) *1921–1922*
Rossineck & Co, Berlin N 39
A small car with a 3-cylinder 2-stroke 5/20PS engine. Later marketed under the name Eos.   HON

ERDMANN (D) *1904–1908*
Friedrich Erdmann, Gera
Erdmann started production of cars in 1904. His friction-drive design was unusual as it was only used for moving off and for steep gradients. For normal drive the power was transmitted directly to the rear axle by cardan shaft. 2-cylinder Körting and Fafnir and 4-cylinder Fafnir and Horch engines were used for various models. From 1906 the name F.E.G. was also used. Production ceased in 1908. B.M.F. used the Erdmann friction drive under licence for some of their models.   HON

ERIC (GB) *1911–1914*
P. and C. Syndicate Ltd, Northampton
The Eric 3-wheeler was one of the earliest of the cyclecars that proliferated just before World War 1. It used a 6hp 2-cylinder engine, a 3-speed gearbox and chain final drive to the single rear wheel. The 1913 models used an 8hp Salmon 4-cylinder engine, and an unusual option for so light a machine was a closed coupé body.   GNG

ERIC-CAMPBELL (GB) *1919–1926*
(1) Eric, Campbell & Co Ltd, Cricklewood, London N.W.2. *1919–1922*
(2) Vulcan Iron & Metal Works Ltd, Southall, Middlesex *1922–1926*
The 'Eric' in Eric-Campbell came from the name of Hugh Eric Orr-Ewing who with Noel Campbell Macklin, later of Silver Hawk and Invicta, launched their new light car in 1919. Initially, it was untypical in that it was intended primarily not for the family man but for the sportsman. Its specially-tuned 1½-litre engine, a Coventry-Simplex, gave it a maximum speed of 65mph. One of them was driven in the Targa Florio race of 1919 by Jack Scales and Cyril Snipe. Initially it was made in the Handley-Page aircraft factory. However, the market for such a car was tiny and in its last years the Eric-Campbell had become a conventional, heavy little machine of 12/30hp with an Anzani engine.   TRN

ERIC-LONGDEN (GB) *1922–1927*
Air Navigation & Engineering Co Ltd, Addlestone, Surrey
The original Eric-Longdens were powered by V-twin J.A.P. engines, either 8hp sv, or 10hp ohv, the latter said to be capable of over 70mph. They had shaft

1936 E.R.A. B-type 1½-litre racing car. Douglas Hull at the wheel. *National Motor Museum*

1952 E.R.A. G-type 2-litre Formula 2 racing car. Stirling Moss at the wheel. *W.K. Henderson*

1920 ERIC-CAMPBELL 10hp two-seater. *National Motor Museum*

1922 ERIC-LONGDEN 9hp sports car. *F.H. Farley*

1928 ERSKINE Six Type 50 sedan. *G.N. Georgano*

1922 E.S.A. 4-cylinder town car. *Dr Henry Goldhann*

drive and polished aluminium bodies, not unlike those of the G.N. At the 1922 Olympia Show two 4-cylinder models appeared, with 9hp Alpha or 11hp Coventry-Simplex engines. The latter was available as a sports car or as a miniature saloon.   GNG

ERIDANO (I) *1911–1914*
Ditta Solavo, Turin

Eridanos were conventional light cars with 1,693cc 4-cylinder engines, cone clutches, and 4-speed gearboxes, selling for 5,500 lire complete.   MCS

ERIE (US) *1916–1919*
Erie Motor Co, Painesville, Ohio

The Erie was built in sedan, tourer and roadster models, designated Model 33 because the 4-cylinder engine developed 33hp.   GMN

ERNST (CH) *1905–1908*
Ateliers Gustave Ernst, Geneva

Gustave Ernst made a small number of assembled cars using Malicet et Blin chassis and Aster engines. These were 12hp 4-cylinder units at first, but from 1907 a larger 16hp engine was used. The cars had 3-speed gearboxes, and chain drive.   GNG

ERSKINE (US) *1926–1930*
Studebaker Corporation, South Bend, Ind.

This compact car by Studebaker was named after the company President, Albert R. Erskine. It had a 2.3-litre sv 6-cylinder engine, and prototypes exhibited in Europe in 1926 had two unusual features: fixed wire wheels with demountable rims and fuel feed by electric pump; both of these were discarded on production machines in favour of wood wheels and vacuum feed respectively. Though it sold well enough on the export market, the Erskine was never successful at home, even when restyled in 1929, in which form a sedan cost $945. In 1930, its last year, it had grown up into a 3.4-litre car with a 9ft 6in wheelbase and was nothing more than a small Studebaker.   MCS

E.S.A. (A) *1920–1926*
Egon Seilnacht, Atzgersdorf, Vienna

Although Seilnacht only had a small workshop he made nearly every part of the car on his premises. Two models of E.S.A. were made, a four and a six, both with sv engines. They were of conventional chassis design and, like most Austrian and German cars of the period, began with sharply pointed V-radiators, changing to a flat radiator in about 1922. Approximately 200 4-cylinder cars were made, and 30 to 40 sixes.   GNG

ESCULAPE (F) *1899*
Automobile Union, Paris

The Esculape voiturette had a 2¼hp De Dion engine, 2-speed gear and cycle-type wheels.   GNG

ESCULAPIUS *see* KNIGHT OF THE ROAD (i)

ESHELMAN SPORTABOUT (US) *1953–1960*
The Eshelman Co, Baltimore, Md.

With its top speed of 30mph and a fuel consumption of 50mpg, the tiny Sportabout was built for errand running and golf-course transport. An 8.4bhp air-cooled engine powered it. A snowplough attachment was optional. This design was abandoned after four units had been built but in 1960 a dozen fibreglass-bodied models were produced.   BE

ESPAÑA (E) *1917–1927*
Automóviles España, Barcelona

Founded by D. Felipe Battlo y Godo, a textile engineer and racing driver, this company produced well-made medium-sized cars with patent rear suspension by four cantilever springs. Although various racing prototypes were built, only two models were catalogued, the 1,593cc, 24bhp Tipo 2 and the 3,690cc, 58bhp Tipo 3. Financial difficulties, including the fact that old cars taken in part exchange for new Españas proved unsaleable, forced the company to close in 1927, but a new firm afterwards made the Ricart-España. One España, a Tipo 2, survives today.   JRV

ESPERIA (I) *1905–1909*
Società Automobili Lombarda, Bergamo

Also known as Lombarda or S.A.L., this car was made in two 4-cylinder models. The 20hp used a monobloc engine, while the 40hp had the cylinders cast in pairs. Chain drive was optional on the latter. The make was still listed in directories in 1910, but it is not certain if manufacture continued up to this date.   GNG

ESS EFF (US) *1912*
Ess Eff Silent Motor Co, Buffalo, N.Y.

This car was built only as a cheap ($350) two-seater runabout. It used a 2-stroke, cylinder, air-cooled engine of 1.4 litres and had a friction transmission and t-dated double-chain drive. GMN

ESSEX (i) (US) 1906

sex Motor Car Co, Boston Mass.

This was a steamer with a single-acting, 4-cylinder engine. Cylinders were of .5mm bore and 101.5mm stroke. Poppet valves were used. The side-entrance nneau was similar in appearance to the French Serpollet. GMN

ESSEX (ii) (US) 1918–1932

udson Motor Car Co, Detroit, Mich.

The Essex, introduced as a low-priced line at $1,595 by Hudson in 1918, featured 2.9-litre ioe 4-cylinder engine developing 55bhp, which gave it a top speed of mph in standard form. It was recognizable by its angular lines and radiator utters and the very cheap coach (2-door sedan) available at $1,295 in 1922 made a best-seller. In 1924 the rapid four was supplanted by a 2.1-litre side-valve k, later enlarged to 2.5 litres. This model pushed Hudson sales up to over 300,000 1929, in which year the company ranked third in the U.S.A. with 6.6 per cent total registrations. Four-wheel brakes were an optional extra in 1927, and andard in 1928. The Essex was equally popular in Britain as the cheapest form multi-cylinder motoring available – costing £250 from 1927 to 1929 and £235 1930, when the new 18.2hp Challenger with ribbon radiator and 60bhp engine as introduced. In 1931 it sold for a mere £185. In 1932 the Essex grew up into 3.2-litre car with V radiator, detachable wire wheels, free wheel and Startix tomatic starter, but it was supplanted the following season by the Terraplane. MCS

ESTONIA (SU) 1958 to date

stonia works, Tallinn

The only quantity-produced competition cars in the Soviet Union come from e former independent republic of Estonia. The first racing car was powered by rear-mounted 500cc motorcycle engine, and in 1959 there appeared the Estonia-3, so a 500cc machine, which went into small-scale production. The next phase Estonia development saw the introduction of the Wartburg 3-cylinder 2-stroke ngine, and 38 of these cars were produced between 1967 and 1969. Fibreglass odies were introduced with the Estonia-9 of 1967, and have been used on all stonias since. Special cars have used 2½-litre Volga and 5-litre Chaika engines, d in 1971 the range consisted of two models, the Estonia-15M with 347cc Jupiter otorcycle engine developing 23bhp at 5,500rpm, and the Estonia-16M with 480cc Moskvitch engine developing 85bhp at 7,000rpm. Karts have also been roduced in large numbers (800 between 1965 and 1969), and one sports/racing r similar to the Cooper-Monaco has been built. GNG

ETNYRE (US) 1910–1911

tnyre Motor Car Co, Oregon, Ill.

The Etnyre had a 4-cylinder 7.7-litre engine. The 4-speed selective transmission ave direct drive in third gear. A seven-seater touring car, a five-seater closed coupé d a four-seater roadster were the body styles built. GMN

EUCLID (i) (US) 1904

erg Automobile Co, Cleveland, Ohio

The Euclid had a 'domestic' appearance, while the Berg (by the same manu-cturer) had a 'European' flavour. The Euclid was a five-seater touring car, weighed ,650lb, cost $2,750 and was powered by a 4-cylinder 3.2-litre engine of 18hp. GMN

EUCLID (ii) (US) 1907–1908

uclid Automobile Co, Cleveland, Ohio

The 3-cylinder Euclid engine was a 2-stroke type, but with separate compression hamber, operated by the pistons, lower in the cylinder wall than the combustion hamber. It was air-cooled and was claimed to produce 20hp. A planetary trans-ission and double-chain drive were used. The models available were a roadster nd a light touring car. GMN

EUCLID (iii) (US) 1914

uclid Motor Car Co, Cleveland, Ohio

The manufacturer described the Euclid as a 'cycle-light car'. It used a 1.6-litre, cylinder air-cooled engine. The weight was 775lb and the price $445. GMN

EUCORT (E) 1946–1951

utomóviles Eugenio Cortés SA, Barcelona

Eucorts were basically similar to the pre-war D.K.W., using 2-cylinder 765cc nd 3-cylinder 990cc 2-stroke engines driving the front wheels, the latter giving 1bhp at 3,900rpm. Bodies were of entirely Spanish design and included saloons, abriolets, station wagons and taxis. During the period of their production the ucort factory was the most important car making firm in Spain, and over 1,500 ere built. Failure was caused by insufficient credit, and the impossibility of import-g essential machine tools. JRV

1918 ESPAÑA 6-cylinder tourer. *J. Rodriguez-Viña*

1921 ESSEX(ii) 2.9-litre roadster. *American Motors Corporation*

1929 ESSEX(ii) Super Six 2.6-litre coach. *G.N. Georgano*

1970 ESTONIA 16M racing car. *E. Pärnamets*

1949 EUCORT 1,034cc saloon. *G.N. Georgano*

1907 EUDELIN 14/16hp cab de ville. *Lucien Loreille Collection*

1966 EVAD 250cc Formula 4 racing car. *Evad Developments*

1912 EVERITT 38hp tourer. *The Veteran Car Club of Great Britain*

EUDELIN (F) *1905–c.1908*

M.A. Eudelin, Paris

The Eudelin was one of those cars whose makers advertised 'vehicles of : powers', but it is not certain how many actual models were made. They use Barriquand et Marre engines, though in 1908 Eudelin was experimenting with : 8hp 'constant power' engine with opposed pistons.　　　GN

EUREKA (i) (US) *1899*

Eureka Automobile & Transportation Co, San Francisco, Calif.

The Eureka four-seater surrey was powered by a horizontal 3-cylinder engir mounted under the rear seats. It had four forward speeds and reverse, and fin drive was by single chain. Plans were announced to make cars and trucks in 'a ve large factory', but apparently nothing came of this.　　　GN

EUREKA (ii) *see* PARISIENNE

EUREKA (iii) (F) *1906–1908*

Automobiles Mainetty, La Garenne-Colombes, Seine

The Eureka was a four-seater voiturette, which used a single-cylinder 6h De Dion engine, friction transmission, and belt final drive.　　　GN

EUREKA (iv) (US) *1907–1914*

Eureka Motor Buggy Co, St Louis, Mo.

This was a high-wheeled buggy with solid rubber tyres. It had wheel steerir and a 2-cylinder horizontally opposed air-cooled, 4-stroke engine. The wheelba of this two-seater vehicle was only 6ft 8in and the gross weight was 1,000lb.
　　　GM

EUREKA (v) (US) *1908–1909*

Eureka Motor Buggy Co, Beavertown, Pa.

This was yet another high-wheeled motor buggy with solid rubber tyres whic used a 2-cycle Speedwell engine of two cylinders, giving 10–20hp. The two-seat car had a wheelbase of 6ft 7in. This became the Kearns.　　　GM

EUREKA (vi) (US) *1909*

Eureka Co, Rock Falls, Ill.

This was a high-wheeler with 40 and 42in wheels and solid rubber tyres. Tl 2-cylinder engine was mounted under the bonnet. A planetary transmission cor nected with shaft drive and steering was by wheel.　　　GM

EURICAR (GB) *1930*

J.V. & E.G. Eurich, Manchester

The Euricar 3-wheeler was powered by a 980cc J.A.P. V-twin engine mounte over the rear wheel. Production was planned but never started.　　　GN

EUROPÉENNE (F) *1899–1903*

Sté Européenne d'Automobiles, Paris

The Société Européenne entered the market with two models of light steam ca a 3-wheeler with *dos-à-dos* tandem seating and steering by a long tiller to the fro wheel, and a four-seater 4-wheeler, also *dos-à-dos*, with wheel steering. In 190 they produced a 12hp internal combustion-engined car with four forward facir seats, and in 1903 a light four-seater tonneau with a 6hp De Dion engine, and 30hp racing car which competed in the Paris-Madrid race, but did not finish.　　GN

EUSKALDUNA (E) *1928*

Compania Euskalduna de Construccion y Reparacion de Buques SA, Madrid

This light car was made in the Madrid workshops of a famous Bilbao ship building firm. In design it was a slightly modernized version of the C.E.Y.C. Abou 200 were made in the one year 1928.　　　JR-

EVAD (GB) *1966–1968*

Evad Developments, Holcombe Rogus, Wellington, Somerset

A Formula 4 car announced in 1966, the Evad was offered to suit Classes (250cc), 2 (650cc) or 3 (875cc). Fibreglass bodies were fitted to light space frame with Armstrong coil spring/damper units at the corners. A Class 1 car, with Merlin rotary-valve engine, weighed less than 336lb. dry. Designer and builde David Brain sold about six kits before production ceased.　　　D

EVANSVILLE (US) *1907–1909*

Evansville Automobile Co, Evansville, Ind.

This make was available with either 20hp or 30/35hp 4-cylinder engines. A 3 speed selective transmission drove the rear wheels through double roller chains.
　　　GM

EVELYN (GB) *1913–1914*

This was a light car sold by a firm in Gt Portland St, London called the Carett Company. It used a 10hp 2-cylinder Dorman engine, a Wrigley 3-speed gearbo and shaft drive. On the eve of the outbreak of war a 4-cylinder model wa announced, but very few were made.　　　GN

EVERITT (US) *1909–1912*

Metzger Motor Car Co, Detroit, Mich.

This company was founded by Everitt and Metzger who had previously launched the Flanders and the E.M.F. The last model of the Everitt was a 6-cylinder, hp five-seater. This had a 'self-starting device' and sold for $1,850. In 1912 there was also a model with a 25.6hp 4-cylinder Continental engine.   GMN

EVERYBODY'S (US) *1907–1909*

Everybody's Motor Car Mfg Co, St Louis, Ill.; Alton, Ill.

This was a light runabout powered by an air-cooled flat-twin 10hp engine. The price was $400.   GNG

EVERY-DAY (CDN) *1910–1912*

Woodstock Automobile Mfg Co Ltd, Woodstock, Ont.

This shaft-driven high-wheeler was equipped with a low, rounded bonnet over a 2-cylinder engine. Fully equipped with bumpers, headlights, sidelights and top, it sold for $650. Companion production included a light delivery wagon called the Oxford.   GB

EXAU (F) *1922–1924*

Cyclecars Exau, Paris 17e

The Exau was a neat-looking small car with an 893cc 4-cylinder S.C.A.P. engine and shaft drive.   GNG

EXCALIBUR J (US) *1952–1953*

Brassie Engineering Co, Milwaukee, Wisc.

This sports car used a modified Henry J chassis and engine (although one prototype used an Alfa Romeo '1900') with an aluminium body designed by Brooks Stevens. Three prototypes were to be raced during the 1953 season to see if it was worth going into production, but apparently it was not. The intended price was $3,000.   GNG

EXCALIBUR SS (US) *1964 to date*

SS Automobiles Inc, Milwaukee, Wisc.

This Brooks Stevens design is externally a replica of the SSK Mercedes-Benz (even the catalogue uses period Daimler-Benz typography), but is built up from modern American components. The first cars used Studebaker's supercharged V-8 engine, but since that company's demise Chevrolet Corvette V-8 mechanical elements have featured in the Excalibur. On 1970 models the coil ifs was matched for the first time by irs, and capacity was 5,735cc; also new was the flexible-bag fuel tank. Three models were listed for 1973: the SS four-seater and roadster, and two-seater SSK. All had 325bhp 7,440cc V-8 engines, with a choice of 4-speed manual or Turbo-Hydramatic automatic transmissions. In 1968 the company distributed another short-lived Brooks Stevens effort, a mock-Bugatti built in Europe and based on Opel Commodore mechanical elements.   MCS

EXCEL (US) *1914*

Excel Distributing Co, Detroit, Mich.

At 1,000lb this two-seater cyclecar was heavier than most of its kind. It had a 1.5-litre water-cooled engine of four cylinders. The drive was by friction transmission and belts.   GMN

EXCELSIOR (i) (B) *1903–1932*

Compagnie National Excelsior, Brussels *1903–1907*

A. de Coninck et Cie, Brussels; Liège *1907–1911*

SA des Automobiles Excelsior, Saventhem *1911–1929*

SA des Automobiles Imperia-Excelsior, Saventhem; Nessonvaux-les-Liège *1929–1932*

With the Minerva, the Excelsior was the premier make of Belgium, a country noted for finely-engineered motorcars. It began modestly enough, however, and by 1905 a range of cars powered by French Aster engines with one, two or four cylinders was offered. The great days of the name began after 1907, when Arthur de Coninck's new model, the Type Adex, arrived. This was technically a conventional machine, seen mostly with a long-stroke, 9.1-litre, 6-cylinder side-valve engine, which served as the basis of the Grand Prix engine of 1912. The classic model was the 20/30hp introduced in 1911, with an 85mm × 130mm engine of 4 litres. There was also the 14/20hp 4-cylinder, 3-litre car with the same cylinder dimensions. Both were fast enough in normal form, but sports models with overhead exhaust valves were offered. An Excelsior team ran in the 1911 Coupe des Voitures Légères and in 1912 and 1913 the company fielded 6-cylinder racers, Christiaens taking 6th place in the 1912 Grand Prix. The old six was continued after World War 1, but a new and much more modern design supplanted it.

This was the new Type Adex, which had an 85mm × 140mm, 4,767cc engine with an overhead camshaft and a diagonally-compensated 4-wheel braking system also called Adex. This car was developed in 1922 into the most magnificent car the Belgian industry ever produced – the Albert I Excelsior, comparable with the contemporary H6B Hispano-Suiza from France. The engine was an efficient

1966 EXCALIBUR SS 5.4-litre sports car. *SS Automobiles Inc*

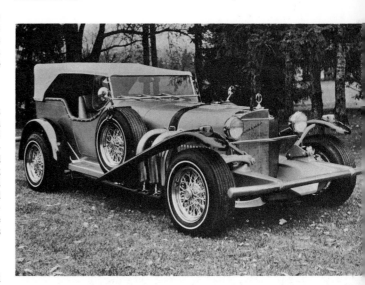

1973 EXCALIBUR SS 7.4-litre four-seater. *SS Automobiles Inc*

1914 EXCELSIOR(i) 14/20hp coupé. *The Veteran Car Club of Great Britain*

5,350cc six with overhead camshaft, large valves and lightweight pistons. A sporti version had three carburettors and could exceed 100mph. The Adex brakes of Albert I had Dewandre vacuum servo assistance. Rumours of an amalgamat with F.N. in 1927 came to nothing, but two years later the firm was absor by Imperia and the great car was no more.　　　　T

EXCELSIOR (ii) (CH) *1905–1907*
Motorwagenfabrik Excelsior, Wollishofen

Excelsior cars were designed by Rudolf Egg, who had previously been responsi for the 3-wheelers built by Egg & Egli, Bachtold, Weber and Rapid. The fi Excelsior was similar to the curved-dash Oldsmobile, with a 6hp single-cylin engine, single chain drive, and semi-elliptic springs extending from front axle rear. In 1906 a number of light cars were made with 4-cylinder Fafnir engir and shaft drive. The bodies were made by a firm in Lugano.　　　G

EXCELSIOR-MASCOT (D) *1910–1922*
Excelsior Werk, Fabrik für Feinmechanik mbH, Cologne-Nippes

This firm produced small cars with proprietary engines. Types 4/8PS (2-cylind 6/14PS and 8/18PS (4-cylinder) were produced.　　　H

EXOR (D) *1923*
Excelsior Maschinen-Gesellschaft mbH, Berlin

This company produced a small car with a 4-cylinder 5/16PS engine.　　H

EXPRESS (D) *1901–1910*
Express-Werke AG, Neumarkt

This firm had been making bicycles and motor cycles for a few years when th produced their first motor car in 1901. Electric cars were also included in range. Production of cars was only on a small scale and interrupted from ab 1905 until 1909, when another model with a 4-cylinder engine was brought o However, this did not last long either and in 1910 car production was discontinu altogether. A member of the Zweirad Union, the Express concern still produ motor cycles.　　　H

E.Y.M.E. (GB) *1913*

The E.Y.M.E. cyclecar was powered by a 964cc J.A.P. V-twin engine, h variable belt transmission and chain final drive.　　　G

EYSINK (NL) *1899–1920*
M. & A. Eysink, Amersfoort

The prototype Eysink voiturette which appeared in 1897 was powered by a 2 Benz engine, but the first production cars used a single-cylinder engine of Eysink brothers' own design. They had tubular frames, belt primary drive, and cha final drive. In 1901 or 1902 two new 2-cylinder cars appeared, of 10 and 12h These were shaft-driven, like all subsequent Eysink cars. Between 1902 and t outbreak of war in 1914 a range of three 4-cylinder cars was made, of 10/1 16/20 and 20/30hp, as well as a 30/40hp six. The latter had two Zenith carburetto an unusual feature for that time. In 1912 Eysink introduced a light car with 6/8hp 4-cylinder engine; the steering gear and axles were bought out from t French firm of Malicet et Blin. This light car had a troublesome form of pressu lubrication operated by the exhaust gases. It was re-introduced for a brief peri in 1919, now with a V-radiator and inboard handbrake, but few post-war Eysin were made. The earlier cars were exported to the Netherlands East Indi Denmark and Great Britain, where a number were used as taxicabs in Londc Eysink were always better known for their motor cycles, made until 1956.　　G

1921 EXCELSIOR(i) 30hp sporting tourer.
Autocar

1899 EYSINK single-cylinder light car. A.
Eysink at the wheel. *C. Poel Jr*

F.A.B. (B) 1912–1914
Fabrique Automobile Belge, Brussels

The F.A.B. was a product of the Ateliers Vivinus, and went into production just when the Vivinus cars ceased to be made. It was made in two models, a 2-litre 12/16hp, and a 3½-litre 20/28hp, both with 4-cylinder sv engines. A 2-litre car ran in the 1912 Belgian Grand Prix and the 1913 Coupe de l'Auto, and F.A.B.s participated in most of the local speed trials of the period.   GNG

FACCIOLI (I) 1905–1906
Società Ing. Aristide Faccioli, Turin

After his dismissal from F.I.A.T. in 1901 Aristide Faccioli set up shop in Turin as an engine manufacturer, progressing to complete cars and omnibuses in 1905. During 1906 two shaft-driven prototypes, a single-cylinder 9hp and a 12hp four, were built, but a reorganization later in the year led to the abandonment of this line of business in favour of components once more.   MCS

FACEL VEGA (F) 1954–1964
Facel SA, Pont-à-Mousson

This fast and costly Franco-American car was the product of a firm which had previously built bodies for Panhard, Simca and Ford (iv). The first cars used boxed frames, coil-and-wishbone ifs and hydraulic brakes. They were powered by 4.5-litre hemispherical-head V-8s of Chrysler manufacture, developing 180bhp. The elegant coupé bodies were welded to the frames and the instrumentation was reminiscent of a light aircraft. Facel Vegas were available with either Pont-à-Mousson 4-speed gearboxes or with automatic transmission. Later editions of the Chrysler engine brought capacity and output up to 5.8 litres and 325bhp respectively by 1958, and ultimately to 6.3 litres and 390bhp, giving a top speed of 135mph. Power-assisted steering was available from 1957, in which year the long-chassis Excellence 4-door saloon was introduced. From 1960 the big Facels had disc brakes. In 1960 came the smaller Facellia, also with disc brakes and powered by Facel's own twin ohc 120bhp 1.6-litre 4-cylinder engine. However, these units gave trouble and after financial difficulties in 1962 they were discarded in favour of a 1.8-litre push-rod Volvo engine giving 108bhp. The price of this model in England was £2,211. A version using the Austin-Healey 3000 engine was in preparation in 1964, but the firm went bankrupt before this could be made in series.   MCS

c.1960 FACEL VEGA 6.3-litre coupé. *Facel SA*

FADAG (D) 1921–1925
Fahrzeugfabrik Düsseldorf AG, Düsseldorf

The two models produced by this firm stood out from among the designs of the many other small firms of that period. Their 4-cylinder 2,020cc 8/35PS model had a 3-bearing crankshaft and detachable cylinder head. The 6-cylinder 2,560cc 10/50PS model had an overhead camshaft driven by spiral bevel gears.   HON

FADIN (I) 1924–1926
Fabbrica Automobili Officine Trubetzkoy, Milan

Fadins were French Derbys built under licence. Chapuis-Dornier engines were fitted, a 960cc sv unit in the case of the Normale, and an 1,100cc ohv type in the case of the 925 Sport.   MCS

FAFAG (D) 1921–1923
Fahrzeugfabrik AG, Darmstadt

A small car which had a 976cc 4/25PS ohc 4-cylinder engine. The sports version took part in several races.   HON

FAFNIR (D) 1908–1926
Aachener Stahlwarenfabrik, Fafnir Werke AG, Aachen

The Aachener Stahlwarenfabrik started production of engines for motor cycles and motor cars under the name of Fafnir, and these were used by firms in various countries. In 1904 Fafnir began manufacture of the Omnimobil kits. These kits were the basis for several makes of cars. However, Fafnir themselves did not produce cars under their own name until 1908, when a range of 4-cylinder models was introduced. The 1912 Fafnir 472, with a 1,924cc 8/22PS engine, had some very advanced ideas, such as interior gear lever, low centre of gravity and automatic lubrication. This and the 1910 '384' with a 2,496cc 10/25PS engine were continued after World War 1 in improved form. The '471' had a 1,950cc 50bhp engine which was also available in a supercharged version developing 80bhp. This latter model

1962 FACEL VEGA Facellia 1.6-litre cabriolet. *Sedgwick & Marshall Collection*

1922 FADAG 10/50PS tourer. *Neubauer Collection*

1922 FAFNIR Type 471 8/50PS sports car.
Neubauer Collection

1917 FAGEOL 13½-litre tourer. *The Veteran Car Club of Great Britain*

1956 FAIRTHORPE Atom coupé. *Motor*

1968 FAIRTHORPE TX-GT 2-litre coupé.
Technical Exponents (Fairthorpe) Ltd

was used in various racing events. Rudolf Caracciola drove it in his first race on the Berlin Avus Track in 1922. Car production ceased in 1926.　　HON

FAGEOL (US) *1916–1917*

Fageol Motors Co, Oakland, Calif.

The few private cars produced by this well-known bus and truck company were among the largest and most expensive ever built in America. An enormous 6-cylinder, 13½-litre Hall-Scott engine of 127mm × 178mm bore and stroke giving 125hp at 1,300rpm powered these cars, which had wheelbases measuring up to 12ft 1in. Closed and open models were available. Prices were from $9,500 for a chassis to $17,000 complete.　　KM

FAIRFAX (GB) *1906*

J.S. Fairfax & Co Ltd, Chiswick, London W.

The Fairfax tourer used a 7/9hp 2-cylinder White & Poppe engine and a very short bonnet in order to give a large amount of room for the body on a short wheelbase.　　GNG

FAIRLEY (GB) *1950*

Jas. Fairley & Sons Ltd, Sheffield, Yorks.

Fairley Number 1 was a 500 special, using an Austin Seven chassis with Ballamy suspension. Later, a Jowett Javelin motor was installed, and the car converted for trials. Thus inspired, its designer R. Phillips planned to market a tubular-framed car to accept Javelin mechanical components, in convertible five-seater and competition two-seater body styles. The project did not materialize, and subsequent Fairleys reverted to being one-off specials, mostly for sprints.　　DF

FAIRTHORPE (GB) *1954 to date*

(1) Fairthorpe Ltd, Chalfont St Peter, Bucks. *1954–1961*
(2) Fairthorpe Ltd, Gerrards Cross, Bucks. *1961–1964*
(3) Fairthorpe Ltd, Denham, Bucks. *1964 to date*

Air Vice-Marshal D.C.T. Bennett commenced motor manufacture with the Atom, a fibreglass-bodied two/four-seater saloon with all-independent suspension. This was available with rear-mounted B.S.A. engines of 250, 350 or 650cc. In 650cc form, performance was markedly above average for a minicar, but the model rather lacked comfort. It was superseded by the front-engined Atomota. In 1958 the Electron was introduced, with a simple tubular ladder frame, coil independent front suspension, and fibreglass bodywork. This was one of the smallest, lightest and cheapest cars available with the 1,098cc Coventry-Climax engine, but it was soon decided to market a yet cheaper model, the Electron Minor with a 948cc Standard engine. Production at times exceeded 20 a month, and the EM version with a Triumph Spitfire engine was still selling well nine years later. A saloon version, the Electrina, was also available, and other models included the Zeta, with Ford Zephyr power unit, and the Rockette, with the 1,596cc Triumph Vitesse, both being similar in layout to the Electron. A different style came out in 1965, when Torix Bennett developed the TX 1. This model had a distinctive suspension system, incorporating cross-linked irs to achieve negative camber under roll and Armstrong Selectaride damper units for all wheels. For 1968 the Electron Minor was given the Triumph Spitfire 1300 engine, while the TX 1 was developed into the TX GT, with Triumph GT 6 engine and new body, but retaining the TX 1's rear suspension. This model was supplemented later with the lighter and more luxurious TXS and TXSS. The latter was available from 1971 with Triumph 2.5PI engine at £1,700 in component form, but with the transverse-rod suspension system as an optional extra. The Electron Minor continued with the Triumph 1300 engine, reaching a Mark 6 version priced at £1,330 in 1972. The TX Tripper was marketed separately by Technical Exponents Ltd.　　DF

F.A.L. (US) *1909–1913*

(1) Fal Motor Co, Chicago, Ill. *1909–1913*
(2) Fal Auto Co, Chicago, Ill. *1913*

With a 4-cylinder, L-head engine of 4.6 litres, this medium-sized car was available in three body sizes: a two-seater, 'toy' tonneau and a seven-seater tourer. Selective transmission gave three forward speeds.　　GMN

FALCON (i) (US) *1909*

Falcon Engineering Co, Chicago, Ill.

This monster, with 12ft 4in wheelbase, was powered by a 6-cylinder engine of 90hp and 10½-litre capacity. The nine-seater touring model was priced at $12,500. The Falcon had two reverse speeds in addition to three forward ones.　　GMN

FALCON (ii) (US) *1914*

Falcon Cyclecar Co, Cleveland, Ohio

The Falcon was an attractive cyclecar with a typical air-cooled 2-cylinder engine rated at 10hp. The vehicle weighed only 325lb and its price was $385.　　GMN

FALCON (iii) (D) *1921–1926*

(1) Falcon Automobilwerke GmbH, Sontheim *1921–1922*

Falcon-Werke AG, Ober-Ramstadt *1922–1926*

Two Falcon models were built, one of 6/20PS (1,250cc) and the other of 6/36PS (₂496cc). The latter car was also available in a sports version. HON

ₐLCON (iv) (US) *1922*

ₐlladay Motor Car Co, Newark, Ohio

This Falcon was a high-quality small car built by a firm that also made larger ₛs under the name Halladay. Falcons were powered by two sizes of Turner & ₘore 4-cylinder engines, of 19.6hp and 22.5hp rating. They were distinguished ᵦ high, rounded radiators and beautifully appointed bodies by Healey & Company. KM

ₐLCON (v) (GB) *1958–1964*

Falcon Shells Ltd, Waltham Abbey, Essex *1958–1959*

Falcon Shells Ltd, Epping, Essex *1959–1961*

Falcon Cars Ltd, Epping, Essex *1961–1962*

Falcon Cars Ltd, Hatfield, Herts. *1962–1964*

Previously a purveyor of fibreglass body shells, Falcon initially offered a ₗin-tube chassis 2-seater for 100E Ford mechanical components. Space-frame ₐassis based on Len Terry's 1,172 Formula Terrier special were also used, and ₑr frames were built by the Progress Chassis Co, with coil suspension all ₐund, independent at the front. Basic bodies, available over several years, ₗcluded the Competition open 2-seater and the Caribbean GT coupé. Some 4-ₛₐters were sold, including the Bermuda saloon. By 1962 kits to suit five engines ₑre advertised – the 100E and 105E Fords, Coventry-Climax 1,098cc and 1,216cc, ₐd the M.G.A. In 1963 the '515' was exhibited, with a GT body styled by T. ₚhonyi, a Brazilian. This was bonded to the tubular frame, which was designed ₜ accept Ford Cortina major mechanical parts. DF

ₐLCON-KNIGHT (US) *1927–1928*

ₐlcon Motor Corp, Detroit, Mich.

Although the Falcon-Knight was theoretically an independent car, it was ₚₐced on the market by John North Willys as a companion car to the smaller ₜhippet Six and the Willys-Knight 70. Powered by a 6-cylinder Knight sleeve-ₐlve engine, the car had a 9ft 1½in wheelbase and was equipped with artillery ₙeels, although wire wheels were used in the Gray Ghost roadster. A complete ₗₑ of closed and open models constituted the catalogue, with prices from ₉95 for the coupé and brougham to $1,250 for the Gray Ghost Roadster. The ₐlcon-Knight was officially taken over by the Willys-Overland Corporation late ₗ 1928 and discontinued. KM

ₐLKE (D) *1899–1908*

ₐ) Fahrrad- und Automobilwerke Albert Falke & Co, Mönchen-Gladbach ₉07–1908

ₐ) Falke Motorfahrzeuge Albert Falke & Co, Mönchen-Gladbach *1907–1908*

ₐ Falke was a bicycle manufacturer who made 3-wheeled motor cycles before ₜurning to car manufacture in 1899. His first four-wheeled motor car showed some ₑₑsemblance to the Decauville Voiturelle. His second model of 1900 was already ₐaracterized by a front engine of his own design and cardan drive. Later models ₑre equipped with Fafnir and Breuer engines: 2-cylinder units of 700cc, 800cc ₙd 1,250cc and 4-cylinder units of 1,500cc and 1,600cc. Falke cars were not ₗdely distributed although they were of sound design and construction. HON

ₐMOUS (US) *1908–1909*

ₐmous Mfg Co, East Chicago, Ill.

The Famous had an air-cooled, overhead valve 2-cylinder opposed engine under ₑ seat. The rear wheels were larger than the front ones. There were several ₜwo-seater models ranging in price from $450 to $600. GMN

ₐNNING (US) *1902–1903*

ₜhe F. J. Fanning Mfg Co, Chicago, Ill.

The Fanning had a 9hp 2-cylinder vertical engine under a short bonnet, and ₛngle chain drive. A two-seater runabout was the standard body, but a four-seater ₜonneau was also available. An electric runabout was also made. GNG

ₐRMACK (US) *1915–1916*

ₐrmack Motor Car Co, Chicago, Ill.

The Farmack was available with a five-seater touring body, or in two-seater ₜoadster form for $885. The engine was a Farmer 4-cylinder with overhead camshaft. ₜhe Farmack was superseded by the Drexel. GMN

ₐRMAN (i) (F) *c.1902*

ₕ. Farman et Cie, Paris

Henry and Maurice Farman, who were Englishmen, were famous cyclists before ₜhey became even more widely known as racing drivers. Like others of their ₚrofession, they sold other people's cars, including Mors, Peugeot, and Panhard, ₜhen went on to make their own, which they hoped to sell on the strength of their ₙame. The first was a 12CV machine with two cylinders. The Farman brothers later

1963 FALCON(v) Type 515 1½-litre coupé. *G.N. Georgano*

1928 FALCON-KNIGHT 20hp Gray Ghost roadster. *Autocar*

1899 FALKE voiturette. *Neubauer Collection*

1925 FARMAN(ii) A6B 6.6-litre tourer. *National Motor Museum*

1930 FARMAN(ii) NF2 7½-litre sedanca de ville. Coachwork by Million-Guiet. *Lucien Loreille Collection*

1924 FAUN 6/24PS tourer. *H-O Neubauer*

made aircraft, but in 1920 they were involved in another car, the luxury Farman (

T.

FARMAN (ii) (F) 1920–1931
Automobiles Farman, Billancourt, Seine

Like the Hispano-Suiza, the post-World War 1 Farman was a luxury car ma by engineers with aero experience, and this was reflected in its design. The cylinders of the A6B Farman, totalling 6.6 litres, were at first of steel welded in a steel water jacket, and elsewhere there was much aluminium alloy. The valv were actuated by a single overhead camshaft. The curious suspension was by single transverse spring combined with two cantilever springs, at both front a rear. The Farman scored over the Hispano in having four forward speeds, and w just as fast, in its earlier form at least. In about 1927 the NF Farman joined A6B; it had a still larger engine, of 7½ litres, but was otherwise similar. By t time, the A6B had an aluminium block and crankcase, with steel cylinder line Both front wheels of the A6B and NF were now steered by means of duplicat mechanism. The Farman, like so many other cars of its kind, was killed by t Depression. Total production was about 120. There were plans for a revival of t make in the late 1930s, to be powered by a V8 engine, but these came to nothin

TH

FARMAN-MICOT (F) 1898
Farman, Micot et Cie, St Maurice, Seine

This was a light 3-seater car using a 2-cylinder Augé Cyclope engine.　　GN

FARNER (US) 1922–1923
Farner Motor Car Co, Streator, Ill.

A short-lived assembled car using a 6-cylinder Falls motor. Few were built.　K

FASCINATION (US) 1971 to date
Highway Aircraft Corp, Sidney, Neb.

Designed by Paul M. Lewis who made the pre-World War 2 Lewis Airomobil the Fascination is projected as a 3-wheeled, five-seater sedan with a steel-reinforce fibreglass body completely surrounded by bumpers. A 4-cylinder 70bhp Renau unit is to be used in the initial production, but a Lewis-designed boilerless stea engine is planned for later adaptation. The Egging Manufacturing Co of Gurle Nebraska, is to build the Fascination for Highway Aircraft Corp.

F.A.S.T. (I) 1919–1925
Fabbrica Automobili Sport Torino, Turin

The F.A.S.T. was a sports car with a 2.9-litre ohv 4-cylinder engine by Artur Concaris, a former aero-engine maker; it did well in local events, but financia troubles led to the purchase of the firm by Alberto Orasi in 1923. Under Orasi th cars appeared in touring and sports forms with four forward speeds instead of thre An F.A.S.T. engine was tried in one of the Invicta (iv) prototypes, but was rejecte on grounds of insufficient flexibility.　　MC

FASTO (F) 1926–1929
Ateliers Mécaniques de St Eloy, St Eloy-les-Mines, Puy-de-Dôme; St Ouen, Seine

The Fasto was an undistinguished family car using 4- and 6-cylinder sv engine in a thoroughly conventional chassis. The 4-cylinder engines had a capacity o 1.6 and 1.7 litres, and the six, 2.4-litres.　　GN

FAUBER (US) 1914
W.H. Fauber, New York, N.Y.

This two-seater cyclecar was priced at $285. It was powered by a 2-cylinder, 8h air-cooled engine, had a friction transmission and final drive by belts.　　GM

FAUGÈRE (F) 1898–c.1901
(1) Faugère, Ochin et Dangleterre, Corbeil, Somme
(2) Sté des Automobiles Légères, Paris

The Faugère had a 3hp 2-cylinder horizontal engine with two flywheels Transmission was by belts to a countershaft, with chain final drive. The engine could be started by a lever from the driver's seat. The make has been erroneously listed as Faugue et Dangleterre.　　GNC

FAULKNER-BLANCHARD (US) 1910
Faulkner-Blanchard Motor Car Co, Detroit, Mich.

This little-known make offered a five-seater touring car for $2,500 in 1910 It was powered by a 6-cylinder engine of 33hp.　　GMN

FAULTLESS (US) 1914

The Faultless was one of the many ephemeral cyclecars, and not even the name of the manufacturer is known. It was a 2-seater with staggered seats, on a wheelbas of 8ft 4½in. The 2-cylinder engine was air-cooled and drove through friction transmission.　　GMN

FAUN (D) 1924–1927
Faun-Werke AG, Nuremberg

Faun, a specialist builder of commercial and municipal vehicles, built a private car in 1910 called the Ansbach, from an earlier name of the company. Another private car was brought out in 1924 with a 6/24PS, 1,415cc engine. The engine output of later models was increased to 28bhp. A version with a larger bore and stroke was available in 1925–26 as well as a 1½-litre ohc sports car. Production of private cars was given up in 1927, but the firm has continued to build commercial vehicles up to the present day.   HON

FAURE (F) *1941–1947*
Pierre Faure, Paris
    The Faure was one of a number of small electric cars which achieved some sales during World War 2 in France, but could not compete when petrol returned. It was a 4-wheeled coupé with independent suspension on all wheels, a maximum speed of 28mph and a range on one charge of 43 miles. It made one appearance at a post-war show, the 1946 Paris Salon.   GNG

FAVEL (F) *1941–1944*
Ets Favel, Fabrication de Véhicules Automobiles Electriques Légers, Marseilles
    The Favel was a 2-door electric coupé with a streamlined five-seater body. Sales were almost entirely confined to the Marseilles area.   GNG

FAVORIT (D) *1908–1909*
Favorit Motorwagen-Fabrik Carl Hübscher, Berlin
    A 3-wheeled two-seater which was built on motor cycle lines but was fitted with conventional wheel steering and had two rear wheels driven by a cardan shaft.   HON

FAWCETT-FOWLER (GB) *1907–1909*
Fawcett, Preston & Co Ltd, Liverpool
    The Fawcett-Fowler was a steam car using a 4-cylinder opposed engine of 20/25hp under the bonnet, and a flash boiler over the rear axle. Final drive was by double chains, and the car carried a circular condenser which gave it the appearance of an internal combustion-engined car such as the Delaunay-Belleville. The range was 150 miles.   GNG

FAWICK (US) *1910–1912*
Fawick Motor Car Co, Sioux Falls, S. Dak.
    Thomas L. Fawick built two cars which he called Silent Sioux before going into production with his Fawick Flyer. This was a large tourer with a 40hp 4-cylinder Waukesha engine.   GNG

F.D. (i) (GB) *1911*
Vining Tractor & Motor Manufacturing Co, Shepherds Bush, London W.
    The initials of the F.D. simply stood for front drive, the car having a transverse 4-cylinder engine which drove by chain to a gearbox mounted in front of the engine, and thence by spur gearing to the front axle. The Vining company who handled it had previously made front-wheel drive cabs and small buses under the name V.H. or Vining-Hallett.   GNG

F.D. (ii) (B) *1921–1925*
Automobiles F.D., Roulers
    Made by Florent Depuydt, the Belgian F.D. was an assembled light car using various French proprietary engines. The smallest model had the 1,100cc ohv Ruby engine, while larger cars were powered by 1½-litre C.I.M.E. or 2-litre Altos units. Touring and sports models were offered, the latter said to be capable of 80mph. The F.D. was also made in France, at La Madeleine, Nord.   GNG

FEDELIA (US) *1913–1914*
J.H. Sizelan Co, East Cleveland, Ohio
    A boat-tailed body distinguished this cyclecar which was driven by a 1.1-litre De Luxe engine. It had a narrow track of 3ft 2in.   GMN

FEDERAL (i) (US) *1901–c.1903*
Federal Motor Vehicle Co, Brooklyn, N.Y.
    The Federal was a typical light steam buggy with a 10hp 2-cylinder engine, tiller steering and single chain drive.   GNG

FEDERAL (ii) (US) *1907*
Federal Motor Car Co, Chicago, Ill.
    This was a very crude-looking runabout with a 12hp 2-stroke engine, friction transmission and steering by wheel. No mudguards were supplied with this vehicle. It may have become the Federal (iii).   GMN

FEDERAL (iii) (US) *1907–1909*
(1) Federal Automobile Co, Chicago, Ill. *1907–1908*
(2) Rockford Automobile & Engine Co, Rockford, Ill. *1908–1909*
    The Federal was a typical motor buggy or high-wheeler of the period, designed

1926 FAUN 6/24PS tourer. *Neubauer Collection*

1941 FAURE Electra electric coupé. *Jacques Kupélian Collection*

1909 FEDERAL(iii) 14hp buggy. *The Veteran Car Club of Great Britain*

1926 FEJES 9hp chassis. *Autocar*

1923 FERBEDO 1.9PS cyclecar. *Jaeger Collection*

1921 FERGUS(i) 6-cylinder sedan. *Autocar*

for two passengers. Its engine was air-cooled and had two opposed cylinders giving 14hp. A friction transmission and belt drive were used.　GM

FEDERAL (iv) (AUS) 1925

The Federal Six was a conventional five-seater touring car with wire wheels priced at £A425.　GNG

F.E.G. see ERDMANN

FEJES (H) 1923–1928

Fejes Lemezmotor es Gepgyar, Budapest

The Fejes car was designed to be made cheaply by unskilled workmen. It was made of pressed and welded sheet-iron, so as to avoid the need for castings. Not even the 1,244cc 4-cylinder engine, which had overhead valves, embodied castings. It was of built-up construction. Light weight and therefore economy of running were by-products of these methods, but the resulting vehicle was crude and ugly. This hardly mattered in Hungary, where it was seen mainly as a military and postal machine, but nothing came of Cyril Pullin's plans to make the Fejes in England as the 10hp Ascot, even though steel and not iron was to be used.　TRN

FELBER (A) 1952–1953

A. Felber & Co, Vienna

The Felber was a small 3-wheeler with one driven rear wheel and a 398cc 2-stroke opposed twin Rotax engine. Production was limited.　HON

FELDAY (GB) 1966–1967

Felday Engineering Ltd, Dorking, Surrey

Peter Westbury had achieved many successes with his 4-wheel drive one-off Daimler V-8 powered cars, including the British Hill-Climb Championships in 1963 and 1964. Replicas of the 2-wheel drive tubular-framed Felday 6 were then offered, in either hill-climb or Formula Libre trim. A fibreglass body was fitted, with a 4.7-litre Ford V8 rear-mounted engine driving through a Hewland gearbox. No more customer cars were sold, despite a road-car project. Westbury concentrated thereafter on engine preparation and racing a Formula 3 Brabham himself.　DF

FELDMANN (D) 1905–1912

Westfälische Automobilgesellschaft B. Feldmann & Co, Soest

Feldmann started to produce a voiturette in 1905 with Omnimobil components. Known as the Nixe, it had a Fafnir 2-cylinder 6bhp engine. This model was built until 1908 and was followed by a 4-cylinder 10/25bhp tourer, as well as a sports car with a 40bhp ohv engine. Feldmann cars were produced only in small numbers and not widely sold. Car manufacture ceased in 1912.　HON

FEND (D) 1948–1953

Fend Kraftfahrzeug GmbH, Rosenheim

The small single-seater 3-wheeled Fend car was first introduced as an invalid car and was available either in a manually driven version or with 38cc Victoria or 98cc Sachs engines. The first model was fitted with bicycle wheels. These were replaced by small scooter wheels on a later version which was powered by a 100cc Riedel engine. The next improvement was the design of a 2-seater tandem version, taken over by Messerschmitt in 1953.　HON

FENG-HUANG (p) (wg) (PHOENIX) (CHI) 1958 to date

Shanghai Motor Vehicle Plant, Shanghai

The first models of this hand-built car showed Plymouth influence in their styling, and were powered by 4-cylinder 78bhp engines. Several revised versions, introduced during the 1960s, have been reported to have 6-cylinder 150bhp engines, integral construction and air conditioning. Said to have been designed with the help of West German engineers, the Phoenix was being made at the rate of one per week in 1965. Recent news from China has referred to this car as the Shanghai, and a production total of 500 units has been claimed for 1971.　BE

FENIX (E) 1901–1904

D. Domingo Tamaro y Roig, Barcelona

Tamaro worked with Marc Birkigt in the La Cuadra factory, and it is likely that it was he who first persuaded Birkigt to come to Spain. The Fenix car used a 2-cylinder engine with a chain-driven gearbox on the rear axle, and was in many ways similar to the La Cuadra. The factory made no more than 25 cars, and in 1905 Tamaro moved to Marseille to work for Turcat-Méry.　JRV

FENTON see SIGNET

FERBEDO (D) 1923–1925

Ferdinand Bethäuser, Nuremberg-Doos

This firm produced a unique cyclecar which was in fact a 4-wheeled motorcycle with saddles for one to three persons. A 1.9PS Breuer engine was used. In 1925 the car was renamed Tom.　HON

FERGUS (i); O.D. (GB and US) *1915–1922*
(1) J.B. Ferguson Ltd, Belfast *1915–1916*
(2) Fergus Motors of America, Newark, N.J. *1921–1922*
(3) O.D. Cars Ltd, Belfast *1921*

The Fergus was a remarkably advanced concept that emanated from the works of J.B. Ferguson, bodybuilder and machine-tool maker of Belfast, in 1915. A 4-cylinder 2.6-litre, single overhead-camshaft engine was installed in a rigid boxed frame that had cantilever springs at each corner; the modern combination of an efficient engine in a stiff frame with soft suspension. Furthermore, the engine was rubber-mounted, the earliest recorded instance of this anti-vibration practice. There was an engine-driven tyre inflator and fully automatic chassis lubrication to ease maintenance, and the standard of workmanship was very high. The designer was J.A. McKee. World War 1 prevented Ferguson from putting his car into production in Ireland, so its manufacture was transferred to the United States. However, wartime restrictions caught up with it there as well, and the Fergus appeared not in 1917, as planned, but in 1921. By then it had acquired the additional refinements of six cylinders (a modified Northway engine was used) and front-wheel brakes, but it was too expensive for a fairly small car. Just one was made in Ireland in 1921. Its new name was to be O.D., for owner-driver, stressing its ease of maintenance, but this third attempt to sell it also came to nothing.　　　TRN

FERGUS (ii) (US) *1949*
Fergus Motors Inc, New York City, N.Y.

The same company who developed the Fergus (i) built up a prototype sports car using Austin A40 components and an all-enveloping body not unlike that of the English Austin A40 sports. The Fergus did not go into production.　　　GNG

FERNA *see* H.H.

FERNANDEZ *see* La SIRÈNE

FEROLDI (I) *1912–1914*

A maker of carburettors in Turin, Feroldi offered only one car model, a 20/30hp four of 3.3-litre capacity with 4-speed gearbox, closely resembling contemporary Fiats, except for its pair-cast cylinders. Subsequently the firm built trucks in a new factory at Saluzzo.　　　MCS

FÉRON ET VIBERT (F) *c.1905–c.1907*
Féron et Vibert, Soissons, Aisne

This company made a small number of conventional touring cars with 4-cylinder engines and shaft drive.　　　GNG

FEROX (GB) *1914*
Ferox Light Car Co, Paisley

The Ferox was a conventional light car with a 1.3-litre 4-cylinder sv Ballot engine and shaft drive. A two-seater body was standard. Very few were sold.　　　GNG

FERRARI (I) *1940 to date*
(1) Auto Avio Costruzione, Modena *1940–1945*
(2) Auto Costruzione Ferrari, Modena *1946–1960*
(3) Società Esercizio Fabbriche Automobili e Corse Ferrari Maranello, Modena *1960 to date*

No Italian make of car commands such world-wide respect as the Ferrari, yet as a marque Ferrari has scarcely existed 25 years. Its founder, Enzo Ferrari, left the CMN concern to join Alfa Romeo as driver and tester in 1920, won several races, and in 1929 founded a unique racing stable, the Scuderia Ferrari, using as its escutcheon the prancing horse motif formerly used by a famous airman, Francesco Baracca, who died in World War 1.

Soon Enzo Ferrari was running the GP Alfas for the factory, scoring many great victories until, in 1938, the firm decided to race their cars themselves. Ferrari left to form his own company, and at short notice built two cars for the 923 mile Brescia sports car Grand Prix of 1940. These cars, entered as Auto Avio Costruzione products, were the first Ferraris. They were built in about three months around Fiat frames and suspension, and had straight-8 1½-litre engines developed by Massimino and Nardi, using modified Fiat heads on a light alloy block. Called Type 815, they led their class but retired.

War intruded on further development, and Ferrari switched to machine tool manufacture, but by 1946 his works at Maranello, near Modena, reverted to car design. This time the engine was a 1½-litre 60° single-ohc V-12, designed by Colombo propelling a light two-seater sports car through a 5-speed gearbox. A tubular frame carried independent front suspension and a live rear axle, with transverse leaf springs front and rear. Raced from 1947, these cars gained many successes, while road cars were also built and sold. These were the 2-litre Tipo 166 Inter, 2.3-litre Tipo 195 Sport, and the 2.5-litre Tipo 212 Inter and Export. They carried attractive bodies by Farina, Touring, and Ghia among other coachbuilders, but relatively few touring cars were made at this stage of Ferrari's history. Engine size of the sports cars was increased to 2 litres, and by 1949 Ferrari had won their first Le

1947 FERRARI 166 Inter 2-litre sports car.
SEFAC Ferrari

1949 FERRARI 166 2-litre saloon. *Autocar*

1949 FERRARI 125S 1½-litre racing car
Villoresi at the wheel. *Corrado Millanta*

1958 FERRARI 250GT 3-litre Tour de France
type coupé. *G.N. Georgano*

1964 FERRARI 275LM/P 3.3-litre coupé
Bandini at the wheel. *Motor Sport*

1966 FERRARI 330/GTC 3.9-litre coupé.
SEFAC Ferrari

1973 FERRARI 365/GTB4 Daytona 4.4-litre coupé.
Maranello Concessionaires

Mans victory with the Type 166. In the absence of the famous Type 158 Alfa Romeo that same year, Ferrari all-independently sprung single-seaters also dominate Formula 1 and 2 racing, with and without superchargers respectively.

Then Aurelio Lampredi developed the big unsupercharged 4½-litre Ferrari which broke Alfa Romeo's five-year grip on GP racing in 1951. Next, when races were switched to the 2-litre Formula 2 for 1952–53, Lampredi's new unblown 4-cylinder Ferraris dominated affairs, Alberto Ascari becoming World Champion in both years.

The new 2½-litre Formula 1 of 1954–60 brought strong opposition and less success for Ferrari at first, but meantime an even bigger sports car, the 4.9-litre V-12, had won Le Mans again in 1954. From 1951 onwards a series of large capacity V-12 touring cars was developed, primarily for the American market. Beginning with the 4.1-litre, 200bhp Tipo 342 America, capacity and power were increased to 4.5-litres and 300bhp in the Tipo 375 of 1953, and to 4.9-litres and 340bhp in 1955. Disc brakes were introduced in 1959, and the model remained in production as the Tipo 500 Superfast, until 1966. In its final form, the engine developed 400bhp, and the 2 + 2 coupé was the most expensive car on the British market, at £11,519.

When the Lancia concern ran into difficulties in 1955, their 2.5-litre V-8 GP cars were handed over to Ferrari to race. Improved for 1956, they won Fangio his fourth World Championship, while a V-6 derivative, named the Dino in memory of Ferrari's won Alfredino, made its mark in racing between 1958, when Mike Hawthorn won the Championship in a front-engined Ferrari, and 1961, when Phil Hill became Champion in a rear-engined model. In the meantime the Testa Rossa 3-litre V-12 sports car carried Ferrari's name to further glory, winning Le Mans and the World Sports Car Championship in 1958, 1960 and 1961.

By 1962 all competition Ferraris, single-seater and prototype sports, were rear engined; the sports type won Le Mans in 1962, 1963, 1964 and 1965. The touring V-12s, however, retained the front-engined layout. By 1967 these were being made in three forms: the 3,286cc 275, the 3,967cc 330 and the 4,390cc 365. Two years later this last was available as the GTB4, with a top speed of 174mph on 352bhp. It cost almost eight million lire. A prototype rear-engined sports model, the Dino 246, appeared in 1965. It went into production in 1967 and had a transversely mounted 1,987cc dohc V-6 unit, made for Ferrari by Fiat, and fitted in detuned form to Fiat's own front-engined Dino.

In the racing field Ferrari tried V-6, V-8 and V-12 units, but though John Surtees won the 1964 World Championship, 1966 brought a return to the classic 12-cylinder engines and a decline in the company's Grand Prix fortunes. There were, however, victories in the Belgian and Italian Grands Prix, and in 1967 sports Ferraris won at Daytona and in the Monza 1,000 Kilometres. In 1968 there was only one Formula 1 victory and none at all in 1969, when there were also sallies into Can-Am racing (with large 6.2-litre and 6.9-litre V-12s) and Formula 2 (with Dino-engined cars). In 1970 came a new flat-12-engined G.P. car, the 312B. It won the Austrian, Canadian, Italian and Mexican G.P.s for Ferrari, and the 5-litre 512 sports cars won at Sebring and Kyalami. The sports cars took 2nd place at Daytona and 3rd at Le Mans in 1971, but though the Formula 1 season started well with a victory in the South African G.P., a 2nd at Barcelona and five 3rds in other championship events were less inspiring. The 1972 season was no better, but in the Manufacturers' Sports Car Championship Ferrari achieved eleven consecutive victories from Buenos Aires in January to Watkins Glen in July.

By 1970 Fiat had a 50 per cent holding in Ferrari, and their own Dino (now enlarged, along with the Ferrari version, to 2.4 litres) was being made at Maranello. A Spyder version of the Ferrari Dino with semi-open body appeared during 1972, and a revised 365, the GT4 2+2, was announced for 1973. Also new that year was the company's first touring flat-12, the Berlinetta Boxer. This featured a mid-engine installation, all-independent suspension, a 5-speed transaxle, and retractable, swivelling headlamps. Output of the 4.4-litre oversquare unit was 360bhp.   CP

FERRIS (US) 1920–1922
Ohio Motor Vehicle Co, Cleveland, Ohio

The Ferris was an assembled car of high quality which used a Continental 6-cylinder engine and other standard components. The makers placed great emphasis on perfection of coachwork. Disc wheels were standard, and open and closed models were available. A high, rounded radiator was a distinguishing factor of this expensive car. Fewer than 1,000 were produced.   KM

FERRO (I) 1935
Autorimessa Ferro, Genoa

An aerodynamic 3-wheeler with 650cc 4-cylinder engine and 3-speed-and-reverse gearbox, said to be capable of 55 mph, the Ferro did not progress beyond the prototype stage.   MCS

FERT (I) 1905–1906
Antonietti e Ugolino, Turin

These cars used Fafnir engines in chassis assembled from imported parts. A 3.8-litre 4-cylinder model rated at 24hp was shown at Turin in 1906, but both this and the firm's agency for the French Pivot ceased shortly afterwards.   MCS

FERVES (I) *1968 to date*

Ferves Srl, Turin

The Ferves Ranger is a light four-seater Jeep-type vehicle powered by a Fiat ... engine. It is also made as a light truck, named the Ferves Cargo. GNG

F.I.A.L. (I) *1906–1908*

Fabbrica Italiana Automobili Legnano, Milan

Also known as the Legnano, the F.I.A.L. was a light car with an 8hp vertical ... engine and shaft drive. Few were made, but two examples survive, one at the ... Museo dell' Automobile in Turin, and one in Australia. A 10/12hp 4-cylinder car ... also listed. GNG

F.I.A.M. (I) *1924–1927*

Fabbrica Italiana Automobili Motori, Turin

This was a light car powered by a 2-cylinder 706cc 2-stroke engine. GNG

F.I.A.T. (I) *1899–1906*
FIAT (i) *1907 to date*

Fabbrica Italiana Automobili Torino (1899–1918): Fiat SpA (1918 to date)

Fiat is an industrial colossus whose ramifications include commercial vehicles (since 1903), ball bearings (Giovanni Agnelli of F.I.A.T. founded the RIV concern in 1905), ship-building (since 1905), aero engines (since 1908), large marine engines (since 1910), complete aircraft (since 1915) and railway rolling stock. Other car makers have been absorbed: S.P.A. in the mid-1920s, Ansaldo in 1929 and O.M. in 1933, while Fiat has a controlling interest in Autobianchi and has helped finance Ferrari's Grand Prix endeavours. The company's share of the Italian private-car market fluctuates between 70 and 90 per cent, and in 1962 795,504 of the 946,743 motor vehicles produced in Italy came from factories under the company's control.

The founders of the company were Giovanni Agnelli, di Bricherasio and Count Carlo Biscaretti Di Ruffia, who took over the small Ceirano factory, inheriting with it the services of two great future racing drivers, Felice Nazzaro and Vincenzo Lancia, and the Faccioli patents under which F.I.A.T's first car was made. This was a 679cc flat-twin with rear engine, cone clutch and chain drive, rated at 3½hp, but by 1901 the company were making a front-engined 1.2-litre vertical twin with central chain drive. An aiv 4-cylinder, the work of Ing. Enrico, appeared in 1902 and the firm soon came under the influence of Mércèdes, with pair-cast cylinders, mechanically-operated sv in a T-head, low-tension magneto ignition, gate gear change and honeycomb radiator. Though the 4.2-litre '16' and its companion 6.3-litre model still used armoured wood frames in 1903, the company adopted the pressed-steel type in 1904, as well as scroll instead of cone clutches and belt-driven lubricators. Water-cooled transmission brakes made their appearance in 1905, when the biggest model was a 10.2-litre '60'. 1907 novelties were the company's first six, a chain-driven 11-litre available with compressed-air starter, and the first shaft-driven Fiat (the full stops had been dropped at the end of 1906), a modest 14/16hp with the differential mounted directly behind the gearbox. In this year licence-production was also started in Vienna; the independently-designed Austro-Fiats did not make their appearance until 1921.

Meanwhile the company had been making its name in racing. A team of Mércèdes-like racers ran in the 1904 Gordon Bennett Cup, but far more successful were their 16.3-litre successors of 1905 with full ohv. F.I.A.T. had to content with second places in the Grand Prix and the Vanderbilt Cup in 1906, but 1907 was a great year for the company and Nazzaro alike, since he won the Kaiserpreis, the Targa Florio and the Grand Prix. Both ohv and ioe configurations were raced in 1908, in which year the formidable 18.2-litre Mephistopheles performed at Brooklands, while an even larger car, the S.76 was produced in 1911. It used a 28.3-litre 4-cylinder bibloc dirigible engine and was timed at 132.37mph at Ostend in 1913; it was also the first Fiat to have the pear-shaped radiator. Overhead camshafts were also found on the 10.5-litre S.61 of 1911 and the 14½-litre cars which contested the 1912 Grand Prix – virtually the last of the chain-driven giants. Fiat entered a team of 4½-litre 135bhp cars with front-wheel brakes for the 1914 Grand Prix, but they met with no success.

1908 saw the beginning of a new era in touring-car design with the 10/14hp Tipo b chassis, a real breakaway from Mercedes ideas. It had a 2-litre 4-cylinder T-head monobloc engine, high-tension magneto ignition, pump and fan cooling, a 3-speed gearbox, multi-plate clutch and bevel drive; 4-speed gearboxes were available by 1909, in which year the older designs also appeared with shaft drive. More important, the '10/14' formula had been extended right down the range by 1913. Models available were the Tipo Zero and Tipo 1 with 1.8-litre engines, the 2.8-litre Tipo 2, the 4.4-litre Tipo 3, the 5.7-litre Tipo 4 and the enormous 9-litre Tipo 5 with its chain drive counterpart the Tipo 6, all fours with 4-speed gearboxes. The larger ones had vaned flywheels to assist cooling and water-cooled transmission brakes. There was also a 3.9-litre 6-cylinder Tipo 57 version made only in 1911 and 1912. An independent Fiat Motor Co was formed in the U.S.A. in 1910 to build and market this range. Chain-driven sports cars were still made in limited numbers, a 10.1-litre ohc 75/90hp being introduced in 1911, while there was also a 4.8-litre (95mm × 170mm) variant with shaft drive. The pear-

1908 F.I.A.L. 6/8hp two-seater. *Museo dell' Automobile, Turin*

1901 F.I.A.T. 8hp 2-cylinder phaeton. *Museo dell' Automobile, Turin*

1903 F.I.A.T. 16/24hp tonneau. *Museo dell' Automobile, Turin*

1911 FIAT(i) 20/25hp State Car for the Makarao of Kota. *Autocar*

1921 FIAT(i) Tipo 501 1½-litre two-seater. Coachwork by Chalmer and Hoyer. *The Veteran Car Club of Great Britain.*

1921 FIAT(i) 6.8-litre V-12 coupé de ville. *Autocar*

1929 FIAT(i) Tipo 509A 990cc fabric saloon. *National Motor Museum*

shaped radiator was available by 1914, as were (on the larger models) wire whee and electric lighting and starting. During World War 1 the 15/20hp Tipo 2B w made in large numbers as a staff car.

In 1919 FIAT emerged as mass-producers with the sv 1½-litre Tipo 501, a c of great smoothness and durability which featured a detachable head, full electr and all brakes on the rear wheels — a surprising deviation from a firm who w still using a transmission parking brake on some models in the middle 196 It could be bought in England for £340 in 1925, when front-wheel brakes we optional and there were companion 2.3-litre 4-cylinder and 3.4-litre 6-cylin derivatives. The old tradition of luxury was carried on by a vast 6.8-litre o V-12 with front-wheel brakes, of which fewer than 10 were made in 1921–22, a by the smaller 4.8-litre Tipo 519, a 6-cylinder car with hydro-mechanical ser brakes which could be bought for less than £1,000 and was still catalogued in 192 Racing activities were resumed in 1921 with a 3-litre dohc straight-8, follow by the Bertarione-designed 2-litre 6-cylinder machine which won the French a Italian Grands Prix in 1922 and inspired the later 2-litre Sunbeams. The fi had supercharged racing cars — a 1½-litre 4-cylinder and a 2-litre 130bhp straight- in 1923, and won the European G.P. with the latter. After 1924 they dropped c of the *grandes épreuves*, though they experimented with an opposed-piston 2-stro engine and made a 175bhp 1½-litre twin-6 with crankshafts geared together whi won its only race — the 1927 Milan G.P. The old chain-driven Mephistopheles w re-engined by E.A.D. Eldridge in 1923 with a 21.7-litre 6-cylinder FIAT airsł engine and took the World Land Speed Record in 1924 at 146.01mph.

Flat radiators, already found on the V-12 and the '519', were seen on t advanced 990cc '509' of 1925, with an ohc engine, low-pressure tyres, fw thermo-syphon cooling and single-plate clutch. This was a best-seller (ov 90,000 sold between 1925 and 1929, at a time when only 172,000 private cars we registered in Italy) and could be bought in England for £195 in later years. Fla radiator, Ricardo-headed versions of the 1919 sv designs came in 1926, and a ye later the Tipo 520 marked the beginning of a long series of American-styled lor stroke 6-cylinder cars with coil ignition. Bigger models (the 2.5-litre '521' and t 3.7-litre '525') joined the range in 1928, the latter being the first Fiat to be fitt with hydraulic brakes, late in 1930. A companion straight-8 never went into pr duction, while the 1.4-litre 4-cylinder '514' which replaced the 509A in 1929 w a dull car and the nearest thing to a failure that Fiat has ever produced in serie Nonetheless, it marked the beginning of N.S.U.'s switch from their own desig to licence-produced Fiats, their staple car products until 1957. By 1931 the cylinder 522 offered a cruciform-braced frame and hydraulic brakes for only £33 and a year later came an advanced small car, the Tipo 508 Balilla with a 3-bearin short-stroke (65mm × 75mm) 995cc engine and hydraulic brakes. This had acquir synchromesh, a 4-speed gearbox and 4-door pillarless saloon bodywork by 193 when a brace of bigger short-stroke fours, the 1.7-litre and 1.9-litre '518' mode were also available. The ohv sports Balilla had a 36bhp engine and dominat the 1,100cc class in sports-car events for the next two years, though only a fe (about 1,000 out of 113,000 ordinary Balillas) were produced. It formed the bas for French licence-production of Fiats by Simca which started in 1935 and al for the Polski-Fiats made in Warsaw up to World War 2: 1938 Tipo 508Cs we produced later. The last long-stroke 6-cylinder machines (Tipo 527) were ma in 1936, in which year the revolutionary 6-cylinder short-stroke ohv 1,500 we into large-scale production. This had a backbone frame, Dubonnet-type ifs a aerodynamic saloon bodywork with recessed headlamps. It cost £298 in Engla and paved the way to even greater successes — the legendary 500 Topolir (late 1936) and the 508C Millecento (1937). The former had a tiny 570cc 4-cylinder engine mounted in front of its radiator, synchromesh, hydraul brakes, ifs and a 2-seater rolltop convertible body. The English price wa £120 and it offered 55mph and 55mpg at the cost of being difficult to maintai It continued with little change until 1948. The Millecento was a 1,089cc 4-do saloon on the same lines with ohv and 32bhp; superb handling was combine with 70mph and 35–40mpg. It was also made in long-chassis taxicab forr and as the 1100S aerodynamic coupé, a 90mph machine which cost £375 and led a whole series of Fiat-based sports cars in post-war Italy: among those who ha used Fiat components are Abarth, Cisitalia, Giannini, Moretti, Siata, Stanguell and (on the 1940 Tipo 815) Ferrari. In 1939 there was also a big 2.8-litre 6-cylind Fiat with seven-seater bodywork, of which only a few were made.

Fiat made a good recovery from World War 2, turning out an impressiv 75,000 vehicles in 1949. However, nothing new appeared for the first few yea apart from a 16.5bhp ohv version of the Topolino (1948) and revised '1100s' ar '1500s' with steering-column change (1949). The results of Marshall Aid we seen in 1950 with the oversquare (82mm × 66mm) 4-cylinder '1400', featurir push-rod ohv, unitary construction, hypoid final drive and coil-spring ifs. Abo 150,000 were made up to 1959. Its derivatives included a cross-country vehic with ifs, the Campagnola, a 1.9-litre diesel model and the luxury '1900' of 1953 wi a 5-speed gearbox which cost the equivalent of £1,060 and came complete with Tachimedion average-speed calculator. All-round independent suspension wa seen on the limited-production 2-litre V-8 sports car of 1952, which was capab of 120mph; the chassis was used for Fiat's experimental gas-turbine coupé of 195 In 1953 the '1100' went over to hypoid rear axle and unitary construction, t standard 35bhp berline being joined shortly afterwards by a 48bhp *turismo veloce* type. In 1955 the faithful old '500C' gave way to the advanced new '600', a 633cc rear-engined unitary-construction saloon with all-round independent suspension and 21.5bhp. By 1960 a million of these had been made and it was still listed in 1967 with a 767cc, 25bhp power unit. A real minicar was the Nuova 500 of 1957, a variation of the '600' theme with ohv air-cooled vertical-twin engine and 4-speed non-synchromesh gearbox. A slow seller at first, it formed the basis of Bianchi's return to private-car manufacture and was subsequently up-rated to 499cc and 22bhp. Station-wagon versions made from 1960 had the engine mounted horizontally under the floor. Some new thinking was seen in 1959 with a brace of 6-cylinder ohv saloons with 1.8-litre 75bhp and 2.1-litre 82bhp engines, torsion-bar ifs and all-synchromesh gearboxes. These acquired disc brakes in 1961 but, like their 4-cylinder derivatives, the '1300' and '1500' of the same year, they retained non-independent springing at the rear. A station-wagon-cum-taxi variant of the '600', the Multipla, had been introduced in 1956 and from 1959 onward limited-production sporting models reappeared. The first of these was the dohc '1500S' with an Osca-designed engine, which had grown up by 1962 into a disc-braked 1600cc, 85bhp model. This was followed by a 6-cylinder '2300S' capable of 120mph.

Fiat's role as a universal provider has resulted in a steadily widening range. In January 1967, the make was being manufactured or assembled in 18 different countries, not including the Spanish S.E.A.T, the Austrian Steyr-Puch and the German Neckar (by N.S.U. at Heilbronn) which rate as individual makes, or the agreement negotiated by Fiat with the Soviet Government in 1966 to build a car factory in the U.S.S.R. Another rear-engined model of 850cc joined the range in 1964. The '1100' was brought up to date in 1966 when the car acquired floor change and front disc brakes and lost its time-honoured transmission handbrake. For those requiring something between this and the roomy '1300', there was the 1.2-litre Tipo 124 with an all-synchromesh gearbox, disc brakes front and rear and a 5-bearing crankshaft. Early in 1967 the Idromatic semi-automatic transmission became available as an optional extra on the '850', while two new sports models were announced: the 124 Sport with twin ohc, cogged-belt camshaft drive and the option of a 5-speed gearbox, and the Ferrari-designed 2-litre 4ohc V-6 Dino with front-mounted engine (unlike its Maranello counterpart). Twin-ohc 4- and 5-speed 124 derivatives, the 1,600cc 125 saloons, followed soon afterwards.

Fiat made 1,346,000 private cars in 1968, and extended their interests acquiring a 50 per cent holding in Ferrari and 15 per cent in Citroën. At the same time Autobianchi was integrated into the parent company. Over the next 12 months new models were limited to a special version of the 850 saloon with front disc brakes; more powerful 903cc 850 spyders and coupés; a more powerful 124, the Special with 1,438cc pushrod engine and four headlamps; and a revised Dino with transistorized ignition. This last was given a 2.4-litre, 180bhp engine and strut-type irs in 1969, when Fiat acquired the Lancia company. But the most important news of the season was a long-awaited 1100 replacement, the fwd 128 saloon. This derived from the Autobianchi Primula and A112, and featured an 1,116cc 4-cylinder transverse engine with cogged-belt ohc, all-independent springing, and front disc brakes. It attained 88mph on 55bhp. By October 1971, 700,000 had been made. The range was widened with a station wagon, a 1,290cc Rallye version capable of 95mph, and a series of coupés with various engine options. Also new was the 130, Fiat's first true prestige car for many years, and their first to have an auto-matic gearbox as standard, though these had been available on the 6-cylinder 2300 as long ago as 1963. The 2,866cc dohc V-6 engine had almost square dimensions. Other features were alternator ignition, power steering, all-disc brakes, and indepen-dent suspension all round. It did not begin to appear in quantity until 1971, by which time there was an alternative coupé version, capacity was up to 3.2 litres, and buyers could specify a 5-speed ZF manual gearbox. The 600 and 1100 were finally phased out at Turin during 1970. A year later the 850 saloon had also departed, replaced by the fwd 127, a scaled-down 128 offered as a 2-door saloon or estate car. It had front disc brakes and the 903cc 850 coupé engine set trans-versely. Fastest of the 124s was now the 1.4-litre dohc Special T, and all but the basic 1,197cc variant were available with automatic.

Meanwhile Fiat had returned to competitions with a rally team of 124 Sports, scoring their first big victory in the 1972 Acropolis. During 1972 the 125 was replaced by the 132, a big saloon styled in the manner of the 130. New 1.6-litre and 1.8-litre dohc 4-cylinder engines were used, and the cars were available with three transmissions: 4- or 5-speed manual, or automatic. When the 124 was revised for 1973 these new engines were installed in both the Special T and the Sport versions of the family; spyders and coupés were available with the bigger unit in 118bhp form. Also new for 1973 were the 126, a four-seater saloon with rear-mounted 594cc air-cooled 2-cylinder engine, and the X1/9, the company's first mid-engined sports coupé, powered by a 75bhp 1.3-litre 128 unit.

The rest of the Italian Fiat range comprised the indestructible twin-cylinder 500, as well as the 127, 128, 130 and Dino families. Production was divided among the three major Turin plants (Mirafiori, Rivalta and Lingotto), the overflow handled by Autobianchi of Milan (some 500s), Naples (850 minibuses), and Ferrari (all Dinos). Fiats were also manufactured or assembled in some 25 countries, the major sub-species being Fiat-Concord (Argentina), Polski-Fiat (Poland), S.E.A.T. (Spain),

1936 FIAT(i) Tipo 500A 570cc coupé. *Museo dell' Automobile, Turin*

1952 FIAT(i) 8V 2-litre V-8 coupé. *Fiat SpA*

1953 FIAT(i) 1100/103 1.1-litre saloon. *Fiat SpA*

1972 FIAT(i) 132 1.8-litre saloon. *Fiat SpA*

1973 FIAT(i) 126 594cc saloon. *Fiat SpA*

1973 FIAT(i) X1/9 1.3-litre coupé. *Fiat SpA*

1915 FIAT(ii) Light 30 4.4-litre two-seater. *Michael Sedgwick*

Steyr-Puch (Austria), VAZ (Russia), and Zastava (Yugoslavia). Obsolete models produced outside Italy included the 600s and 850s of S.E.A.T., and 1963-type 1100 still made in India by Premier of Bombay. During 1973 Fiat (England) Ltd were importing S.E.A.T.-built 850s for the British market. MCS

FIAT (ii) (US) *1910–1918*
Fiat Motor Co, Poughkeepsie, N.Y.

This was an independent concern, formed with American capital to manufacture Fiat cars under licence. It handled only the bigger models of the '50' series with 4-cylinder L-head monobloc engines, shaft drive, multi-plate clutches and 4-speed gearboxes, starting in 1910 with the 5.7-litre Tipo 54. In 1914 came the big 9-litre Tipo 55 and later in the year the Light 30, which was in fact the short-chassis 4.4-litre Tipo 53, which cost $3,750 with full electrical equipment. Peculiar to America was the 8,553cc Tipo 56, a 6-cylinder machine on similar lines, but with all brakes on the rear wheels. It sold for $4,650. From 1914 onwards the later pear-shaped radiator was generally found on American FIATs. In 1917 a one-model policy was pursued with an improved Tipo 55, the E-17 on an 11ft 8in wheelbase. One of the last American cars to have right-hand drive, it sold for $5,500. Production ceased in March 1918, when the factory was sold to Rochester-Duesenberg for aero-engine manufacture. MCS

FIAT (iii) (RA) *1960 to date*
Fiat Concord SAIC, Buenos Aires

This company makes Fiat products for the Argentinian market, both the 600 and the 128 being offered during 1972. In addition it has built some local types with no exact Italian equivalent, among them a 1500 sports coupé and 797cc rear-engined coupés and spyders which combine the styling of the sports 850 with 600-type mechanical elements. In 1972 it was making the Sport 1600, a 2+2 fastback coupé powered by a 1,625cc 3-bearing 4-cylinder engine, and a saloon of 125 shape with the same unit. MCS

F.I.A.T.-ANSALDI (I) *1905–1906*
F.I.A.T.-Ansaldi SA, Turin

This concern was a joint venture by F.I.A.T. and machine-tool manufacturer Michele Ansaldi, which produced a small car designed by Cesare Momo. The 3,053cc 4-cylinder T-head engine of the 'Brevetti' followed standard F.I.A.T. practice, the ht magneto ignition apart, and the first cars had side-chain drive, though bevel drive was adopted at the beginning of 1906, and with it a 3-speed gearbox. Soon afterwards Ansaldi sold out in order to join Matteo Ceirano's new S.P.A. company, and F.I.A.T.-Ansaldi were integrated into the parent concern. Fiat made 'Brevettis' until 1912. MCS

FIDÉLIA (F) *1905–1906*
Voitures Fidélia, Angers, Maine-et-Loire

The Fidélia was one of a crop of short-lived steam cars which appeared in France at a time when the steamer was losing popularity everywhere. It had a vertical single-acting 4-cylinder engine, and the front-mounted condenser gave it very much the appearance of a petrol-engined car. GNG

FIDELIO *see* EHRHARDT

FIDES (I) *1905–1911*
(1) Fides Fabbrica Automobili, Marca Brasier, Turin *1905–1908*
(2) Fides Fabbrica Automobili Brevetti Enrico, Turin *1908–1911*

Initially the Fides was merely a licence-produced Brasier, but in 1906 ill-health forced Giovanni Enrico to resign as chief engineer at F.I.A.T., and after he came to Fides that company marketed a pair of sv fours to his design. The company also continued experiments with Enrico's oil-pressure-operated gear change, already tried on F.I.A.T.s. The firm went into liquidation in 1911, the factory being acquired by Lancia. MCS

FIEDLER (D) *1899–1900*
Berliner Electromobil- und Accumulatoren-Gesellschaft, Berlin

These were electric vehicles mainly built as vans, although quite a number of private cars were also produced. HON

F.I.F. (B) *c.1909–1914*
Automobiles F.I.F., Etterbeek, Brussels

The F.I.F. was a 4-cylinder car which the makers entered in a number of sporting events, though without any great success. In 1909 three cars with 1,858cc engines ran in the Coupe des Voiturettes, while for the 1911 Coupe de Voitures Légères a team of cars with push-rod ohv engines was specially prepared. The production cars of 1912 came in three models, all with 4-cylinder monobloc engines; an 8/10, a 12/14, and a 16/18hp. For 1913 a new range of smaller cars was introduced, a 7/12 and an 8/16hp. One of the 7/12s ran in the 1913 Cyclecar Grand Prix. It was driven by the company's managing director, Ferdinand Heck, and finished in 9th place. GNG

GARI (I) *1925–1926*

In 1925 Gian Vittorio Figari and Prof. Francesco Bonavoglia of the Milan Polytechnic tested an interesting prototype with 840cc supercharged 4-cylinder 2-stroke engine said to give 30bhp at 3,800rpm. It was planned to produce Figaris in a factory at Monza, but the necessary funds were not forthcoming.　　MCS

GINI (I) *1900–c.1907*

ta Luigi Figini & Cia, Milan

Another motorcycle firm that tried its luck briefly with cars, starting on singles d progressing to twins and fours. Figinis were never made in any quantity.　　MCS

LIPINETTI (CH) *1966–1967*

orges Filipinetti, Grandson

This car was conceived by Minister Georges Filipinetti, owner of the motor useum at the Château de Grandson. It was a GT coupé powered by a Volkswagen 00 engine, and had a fibreglass two-seater body, servo-assisted disc brakes at front, and a maximum speed of 116mph. The prototype appeared in 1966, d a small series production was planned for 1967.　　GNG

LOQUE (F) *1902*

oque père, Bourgtheroulde, Eure

This company advertised a 6/8hp voiturette and 4-cylinder cars of 10, 15 and hp. It is probable that the larger cars were never in fact made.　　GNG

LTZ (F) *c.1899–c.1903*

é des Moteurs et Voitures Automobiles Filtz, Neuilly, Seine

Filtz was mainly a maker of proprietary engines for use by other firms, notably argan-Foy, but he exhibited a light car under his own name in 1899, and made a cing car with 4-cylinder 30hp engine in 1902.　　GNG

MER (I) *1947–1949*

bbrica Italiana Motoveicoli e Rimorchi, Milan

The Fimer was a minicar with a rear-mounted 250cc 2-cylinder engine, an en two-seater body, and all-round independent suspension. A maximum speed 55mph was claimed.　　GNG

NA-SPORT (US) *1953–1955*

rry Fina, New York City, N.Y.

The Fina-Sport was a convertible with bodywork by Vignale, built on a modified rd chassis with a Cadillac engine and Hydramatic transmission.　　BE

NCH LIMITED *see* PUNGS-FINCH

NLAYSON (AUS) *1900–1908*

nlayson Bros & Co Pty Ltd, Devonport, Tasmania

The first Finlayson of 1900 was a 2-cylinder steam car built for George Finlayn's own use, but from 1907 to 1908 the company made a number of petrolgined vehicles to special order. These included a single-seater and a two-seater owered by Gnome engines, two eight-seaters for hire work and at least three ses.　　GNG

REBALL (GB) *1969 to date*

) J.B. Developments, Aldershot, Hampshire *1969-1971*
) F.J. Boyle, Aldershot, Hampshire *1971 to date*

The Fireball was a midget oval-track racing car designed specifically for the pedeworth formula. It featured a transverse rear-mounted Mini engine, a neat esign ensuring an exceptional power/weight ratio. The design was developed by rank Boyle who eventually set up on his own. In 1972 J.B. Developments were ontemplating production of a sports car.　　DF

REFLY (GB) *1902–1904*

irefly Motor & Engineering Co Ltd, Croydon, Surrey

The Firefly company made shaft-driven light cars powered by Aster or De Dion ngines of 6hp. These were supplemented in 1903 by chain-drive cars with 9 or 12 hp Ierald 2-cylinder engines, as well as bigger 4.6-litre 4-cylinder versions. More ireflys were sold as delivery vans than as private cars.　　GNG

FIRESTONE-COLUMBUS (US) *1907–1915*

Columbus Buggy Co, Columbus, Ohio

The Firestone-Columbus made in 1907 and 1908 was a high-wheeled buggy. For he years 1909–11, a 'Mechanical Greyhound' roadster was built as well as a fiveeater touring car. The two-seater roadster had a 26hp engine and an 8ft 10in wheelase. Some closed models were offered in 1913 and 1914.　　GMN

ISCHER (i) (D) *1902–1905*

ischer & Co, Pfälzische Motoren- und Automobilfabrik, Hassloch/Pfalz

Small vehicles produced only in limited numbers.　　HON

1970 FIREBALL 1,275cc racing car. *E. Setchell*

1902 FIREFLY 6hp tonneau. *National Motor Museum*

1908 FIRESTONE-COLUMBUS motor buggy. *Antique Automobile*

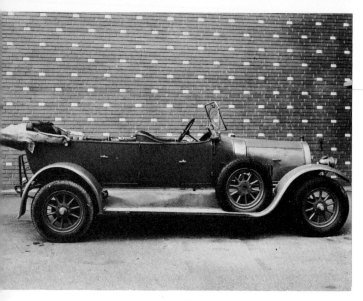

1913 FISCHER(ii) 16/22hp tourer. *Swiss Museum of Transport & Communications, Lucerne*

1966 FITCH PHOENIX 2.7-litre sports car. *Autocar*

FISCHER (ii) (CH) *1909–1919*
Fischer-Wagen AG, Zürich-Enge

After leaving the Turicum company in 1908, Martin Fischer formed his ow concern, and built a number of conventional 4-cylinder five/six-seater cars fro 1909 to 1910. For 1911 he introduced a single-sleeve-valve 4-cylinder monobl engine of 16/22hp. About 200 cars were made, one-third of the production bei exported, especially to South America. This design of engine was built under licer by Delaugère-Clayette in France, and by Mondex-Magic and Palmer-Singer America. A prototype 4.1-litre 6-cylinder on similar lines was ready for producti in 1914, and in 1919 Fischer tried again with a cyclecar using a friction transmissi and twin-cylinder M.A.G. engine. Nothing came of this.   GN

FISCHER (iii) (D) *1912–1913*
Westautohaus Alex Fischer & Co, Berlin

Electric private cars and light vans were manufactured by this company. Al Fischer was later connected with the production of A.A.A. and Alfi.   HO

FISCHER (iv) (US) *1914*
G.J. Fischer Co, Detroit, Mich.

This was a light car rather than a cyclecar, as it had standard track and an 8ft 8 wheelbase. It was built in two- and four-seater versions, including a sedan, power by Perkins 4-cylinder, water-cooled engines of 1.6 litres. It had a selective tran mission and shaft drive. The two-seater cost $525, the sedan $845.   GM

FISHER (CDN) *1914–1915*
Fisher Motor Car Company Limited, Walkerville, Ont.

This was an attempt to salvage the remains of the Tudhope Motor Compan and Fisher cars were Tudhopes in everything but name and were assembled Orillia. The company later built Yellow Cabs under licence for export.   H

FISSON (F) *1895–c.1898*
L. Fisson et Cie, Paris

The Fisson was one of a number of French cars closely based on the Ber design. Two-, four-, and six-seater cars were made.   GN

FITCH (US) *1949–1951; 1966*
(1) Sport and Utility Motors Inc, White Plains, N.Y. *1949–1951*
(2) John Fitch & Co Inc, Falls Village, Conn. *1966*

Racing driver John Fitch made two attempts at sports-car building. The fir used a Ford V-8-60 2.2-litre engine in a modified Fiat 1100 chassis, with a bod resembling that of the Crosley Hotshot. Fitch raced one with some success, comin 2nd in his class in the 1950 Watkins Glen G.P.; a price of $2,850 was quote although very few were made. His second attempt was the very handsome Fitc Phoenix of 1966, powered by a Chevrolet Corvair engine tuned to give 170bh Only one Phoenix was made.   GN

F.L. *see* OTTO (i)

FLAC (DK) *1915*
Mammen & Drescher, Jyderup

Only 25 of these cars were produced. They used 10hp 4-cylinder America engines of unknown origin, friction transmission with final drive by a chain runnin in an oilbath. The Flac weighed about 1,320lb.   TR

F.L.A.G. (I) *1905–1908*
Fabbrica Ligure Automobili Genova, Genoa

The F.L.A.G. was a solidly-built touring car made in several sizes. These include a 12/16 and a 16/24hp with shaft drive, and a 40hp with chain drive. All had cylinders cast in pairs. The F.L.A.G. company were the Italian agents fo Thornycroft, which gave rise to the suggestion that their own cars were copies o Thornycrofts, but they categorically denied this.   GNG

FLAGLER (US) *1914–1915*
Flagler Cyclecar Co, Sheboygan, Wisc.

The Flagler was one of the few cyclecars with a positive (geared) transmission and shaft drive, rather than a chain or belt. It was powered by a 4-stroke water cooled 4-cylinder engine. The weight of this car was 900lb and its price $450: very low cost-to-weight ratio, even for a cyclecar.   GM

FLAID (B) *1920*

The Flaid was a Belgian-built light car which was intended to be sold on the British market. It was of conventional design, and used a 4-cylinder 10/12hp engine A stand was taken for it at the 1920 White City Exhibition (shared with Th Schneider) but apparently it did not turn up.   GNG

FLANDERS (i) (US) *1909–1912*
Everitt-Metzger-Flanders Co, Detroit, Mich.

The Flanders 20 was a light car which was marketed by Studebaker and remained ~tually unchanged throughout its life. It used a 4-cylinder engine of 2½ litres. 1909, a 2-speed transmission was employed, but this was changed to one with ~ree forward speeds for the succeeding models. Two-seater and five-seater open ~odels were offered as well as a two-seater closed coupé. The E.M.F. was a ~mpanion make.   GMN

~ANDERS (ii) (US) *1912–1915*
~) Flanders Manufacturing Co, Pontiac, Mich. *1912–1913*
~) Tiffany Electric Co, Detroit, Mich. *1913–1914*
~) Flanders Electric Co, Pontiac, Mich. *1914–1915*
The Flanders Electric was a typical electric car made in open and closed form, ~th rather attractive flowing lines. From October 1913 to March 1914 only, the car ~as known as the Tiffany.   GNG

~ANDRIA (B) *1953*
This was a prototype minicar powered by a rear-mounted Ilo motorcycle engine.
                                                                 GNG

~EETBRIDGE (GB) *1904–1905*
~. Bentley, Blackfriars, London E.C.
The Fleetbridge was a very light tandem two-seater powered by a single-cylinder ~hp engine. It used single chain drive, a tubular frame and cycle wheels, and cost ~ly £70. If the driver wished to carry luggage instead of a passenger, the ~ar seat folded flat to make a luggage compartment. In 1905 an improved version ~th a 5hp Fafnir engine was available at 80gns. The Fleetbridge was also known ~ the Royal Fleetbridge or the Ludgate.   GNG

~ETCHER (GB) *1966–1967*
~orman Fletcher (Sales and Developments) Ltd, Walsall, Staffs.
~ Stemming from the Ogle SX 1000, the Fletcher GT was of similar design, with ~x-section chassis, fibreglass body and B.M.C. Mini mechanical parts. Prices in ~mponent form were identical in £ sterling with the capacity in cc of the various ~ini engines used, and not many were sold.   DF

~LINT (i) (US) *1902–1904*
~int Automobile Co, Flint, Mich.
The Flint was a light two-seater runabout with a rear-mounted single-cylinder ~gine and no mudguards. It was designed by A.B.C. Hardy who was later general ~anager of Marquette (i) and then Chevrolet. It is sometimes erroneously called ~e Hardy after the designer.   GNG

~LINT (ii) (US) *1923–1927*
~int Division, Locomobile Co of America, Long Island City, N.Y., *1923–1924*; ~izabeth, N.J., *1924–1927*; Flint, Mich., *1924–1926*
Fitted with a 7-bearing crankshaft and a steel tube for added reinforcement, the ~lint occupied an important niche in William C. Durant's car empire. With its 6-~ylinder Continental engine and a price of less than $2,000 for the closed models, it ~as popular in its class and as many as 3,000 were sold in a year. Lockheed hydraulic ~-wheel brakes came with the 1925 model, and during the company's last two years ~ere were two biggish sixes of 3.8 litres and 4½ litres, as well as the 2.8-litre 'Junior', ~ compact six with rear wheel brakes only.   KM

~LINT-LOMAX (US) *1905*
~int-Lomax Electric & Mfg Co, Denver, Colo.
This was a light five-seater touring car with side entrance. Its 14hp engine had ~ cylinders with 2.4 litres capacity and overhead valves. Along with this was a ~-speed transmission and shaft drive. Such a car was displayed at the 1905 Denver ~uto show, but further information is lacking.   GMN

~LINTRIDGE *see* DARRIN

~LIRT (I) *1913–1914*
~itta Ing. P. Pestalozza, Turin
The charming 'English' period name was in fact Latin, standing for *Fortis Levis ~ucunda Rapida Transeat*. Ing. Pestalozza's 20/30hp was exhibited at the 1913 Paris ~alon and had a brief success. Behind the pear-shaped radiator of Fiat, Züst, or ~sotta Fraschini pattern was a 2.7-litre 4-cylinder engine with side valves in a T-~ead. The marque lasted only one year.   MCS

~LORENTIA (I) *1903–1912*
~abbrica di Automobili Florentia, Florence
Though the Fabbrica Toscana di Automobili was formed in Florence in 1901, ~roduction did not get under way until the change of name two years later. Early ~lorentias were conventional 2-cylinder machines designed by Ing. Cattaneo (later ~f Isotta-Fraschini) assisted by Antonio Chiribiri, but from 1905 onward the ~ompany built Rochet-Schneiders under licence in 16hp and 24hp forms. These had ~-cylinder T-head engines, 4-speed gearboxes, honeycomb radiators and chain drive.

1904 FLEETBRIDGE 3½hp two-seater. *G.N. Georgano Collection*

1925 FLINT(ii) 24/40hp tourer. *National Motor Museum*

1912 F.N. Model 2700 2.7-litre limousine
Fabrique Nationale d'Armes de Guerre

1924 F.N. Model 1300 1.3-litre sporting four-
seater. *Fabrique Nationale d'Armes de Guerre*

1933 F.N. 3.2-litre straight-8 saloon. *Fabrique
Nationale d'Armes de Guerre*

1934 F.N. Prince Albert saloon. Coachwork
by Pritchard et Demoulin. *Fabrique Nationale
d'Armes de Guerre*

A shaft-driven 4.4-litre 18/22, also a Rochet-Schneider derivative, joined the range in 1906 and in 1907–1908 there were also some bigger chain-driven cars, the including a 9.9-litre 4-cylinder 40/50 and a 6-cylinder 6.6-litre type. With the purchase of the S.V.A.N. company of Venice in 1906, Florentia became increasingly interested in motor boats, which occupied most of their activity in later years. They were last quoted as car-makers in 1912.　　　　　　　　　　　　　M

FLORIO (I) *1912–1916*
Florio Automobili di G. Beccaria & Cia, Turin

Beccaria was a well-known metal-forging firm who supplied Fiat and Store with steel chassis. In collaboration with Cav. Vincenzo Florio they made a sm number of cars powered by 4-cylinder engines in 3- and 5-litre versions. They we of typical Italian appearance, with radiators like those of the Lancia or small Fiats. In 1914 the name of the cars was changed to Beccaria.　　　　GN

FLYER (US) *1913–1914*
Flyer Motor Car Co, Mt Clemens, Mich.

The Flyer had a monobloc 4-cylinder water-cooled engine with selective tran mission. It should be classed as a small car as it had standard track and a 8ft 4in wheelbase.　　　　　　　　　　　　　　　　GM

FLYING FEATHER FF-2 *see* SUMINOE

FLYING SCOTSMAN *see* SCOTSMAN (i)

FLYING STAR (F) *1906*
Voitures Flying Star, Lyons

A small number of conventional 10/12hp 4-cylinder cars were assembled und this name.　　　　　　　　　　　　　　　　　GN

F.M.R. *see* MESSERSCHMITT

F.N. (B) *1899–1935*
Fabrique Nationale d'Armes de Guerre, Liège

The F.N. was Belgium's longest-lived make and was made in greater numbe than any other Belgian car, even at the beginning of its career. In 1900, 10 examples of a 2-cylinder voiturette with a water-cooled (originally air-cooled) 3½h engine were made. It had two forward speeds, with belt primary and chain fin drive. This little car was well-made on conservative, well-tried lines, typical of F.N cars throughout their history. In 1906, they changed over from chain drive to a liv axle. By 1909, car production was running at three or four a day, rising to fiv by 1914. The 8/10hp of that year was a modern light car with a 60mm × 110mm 4-cylinder, side-valve 1,245cc engine. It was continued after World War 1 a the '1250', and developed in 1923 into the famous '1300', with a bigger bo providing the cubic capacity implied. This car also had push-rod overhea valves, unit construction of engine and gearbox, and front wheel brakes. Th open four-seater had light and elegant lines. With the bore again enlarged, th '1300' became the '1400', with four forward speeds for the first time. A twin carburettor sports model was also offered. The '1400' became the '1625', whic was listed until 1933. The 1300 F.N. and its successor were very successful i competitions, with a third place on General Classification in the 1925 Mont Carlo Rally, class wins in the Spa 24 Hours race in 1925, 1926, and 193 and a Coupe des Alpes for the works team of '1625s' in the 1931 Alpin Trial. In 1928, the 1300 F.N. had become the first normal wheeled vehicle t cross Africa from north to south. Although the small F.N.'s were always the bes known, larger cars were made, up to the '3800' luxury chassis of 1920. straight-8 3.2-litre model was current from 1930 to 1935, in conformity wit fashion. The last small F.N. vanished with the '1625' which was replaced by th new 2-litre Baudouin. This was now accompanied by the bigger Prince Alber model. Production ceased in 1935, though motorcycles and trucks have been mad since World War 2.　　　　　　　　　　　　TR

F.N.M. (BR) *1959 to date*
Fabrica Nacional de Motores SA, Rio de Janeiro

This firm has been making Alfa-Romeo commercial vehicles under licence sinc 1956, and in 1968 Alfa-Romeo acquired an 85 per cent holding. Their staple privat car is based on the Alfa-Romeo 2000 saloon of 1957, initially with the standar 1,975cc unit, but now with a 2,132cc engine developing 118bhp. A 5-speed gearbo was used, and an expensive coupé model known as the Onça was added to the rang in 1970.　　　　　　　　　　　　　　　　MC

F.O.D. (I) *1925–1927*
Fonderie Officine Debenedetti, Turin

The F.O.D. was a cyclecar unusual in that its body and chassis were of integra construction. It was powered by a water-cooled ohv 4-cylinder engine of only 565cc made principally of aluminium. The crankcase was extended to form th forward end of the frame.　　　　　　　　　　TR

FOGLIETTI (I) *1958–1960*
Automobili Foglietti, Milan

The Foglietti was one of the first Italian racing cars built for Formula Junior. The Fiat 1100 engine was mounted in the front of a tubular chassis, its position being offset to the right so that the propeller shaft passed to the right of the cockpit, itself offset to the left.   GNG

FOLGORE (I) *1900–1902*
Sebastiano Castagneri, Alessandri

These were light cars with 1¾hp engines, but no other details are available.   MCS

FOLLIS (F) *1968 to date*
Automobiles Follis Frères, Craponne, Rhône

M. Follis was a cycle and motor cycle maker who turned to the manufacture of karts in 1960. Known as Follkarts these earned an excellent reputation, and in 1968 his sons began manufacture of single-seater racing cars powered by 1,440cc Gordini engines. In 1971 they introduced a rear-engined two-seater sports car with fibreglass body that is built to special order.   LL

FONCK (F) *1920–1925*
Sté des Automobiles René Fonck, Fraisse-Unieux, Loire

The Fonck was a high-quality car built in 4-, 6-, and 8-cylinder models, the bore and stroke being the same at 80mm × 130mm. They had a single overhead camshaft and unit construction of engine and gearbox, while the 8-cylinder model had 4-wheel brakes. René Fonck was a well-known air ace of World War 1, and like the Hispano-Suiza, the Fonck cars bore the emblem of the Cigogne Volante. The car was built by a steel works who supplied many French manufacturers, and in the long run they found they preferred to keep their clients than to be their rivals. Not more than 12 Fonck cars were made.   GNG

FONDU (B) *1906–1912*
Automobiles Charles Fondu, Vilvorde, Brussels

The Fondu was a large, well-built car which in its first model used a 4-cylinder 24/30hp engine of 4.8 litres' capacity with pair-cast cylinders. This model was made for some years, and was supplemented by cars with smaller monobloc engines of 1.7 and 2.1 litres. In 1912 a genuine light car with a 1,131cc engine was made. Apart from use in their own cars, Fondu engines were used by S.A.V.A., Linon, Elgé, and F.I.F. in Belgium, and Mathis and Turner abroad. The 24/30hp Fondu was the basis for the first Russo-Baltic car.   GNG

FONLUPT (F) *1920–1921*
Etablissements Fonlupt, Levallois-Perret, Seine

The Fonlupt was a short-lived car made in 4- and 8-cylinder models using the same bore and stroke of 70mm × 140mm. Capacities were 2.1 litres and 4.2 litres respectively. The chassis design was thoroughly conventional.   GNG

FORD (i) (US) *1903 to date*
Ford Motor Co, Detroit, Mich.

Henry Ford built his first experimental car in a workshop behind his home in Bagley Avenue, Detroit, in 1896. It had a twin-cylinder engine with chain-cum-belt drive, and attained 20mph. A second car was made and tested in 1898. In 1899 he left his employment with Edison to help organize the Detroit Automobile Co. He was replaced there by H.M. Leland, and his third experimental machine had certain similarities with Leland's Cadillac, notably the basic layout, wheel steering, and planetary transmission. The first production Ford, the Model A of 1903, had a flat-twin underfloor-mounted engine, central chain drive, and rear-entrance tonneau bodywork, and sold for $850, or $100 more than the Cadillac. 1,708 were sold in the first season, and from the beginning Ford elected to fight both Selden's alleged master patent and the Association of Licensed Automobile Manufacturers set up by those makers who were willing to recognize the patent's validity. Ford and the other rebels were not finally vindicated until 1911. During these early years Ford built a number of experimental racing machines, of which the most famous was the 999, a vast 4-cylinder affair without clutch or gears, in which Henry himself recorded 91.4mph on the frozen Lake St Clair in 1904. That year the company offered Model C, a development of the original A with the now-mandatory dummy bonnet, and the first of their fours, Model B at $2,000. Both these models had the 2-speed planetary transmission, and this was applied in 1905 to a 6-litre six, the Model K, selling at $2,500. The transmission proved the big car's Achilles' heel, and no more 6-cylinder cars were marketed until 1941. In 1906 Ford undercut Oldsmobile with the 4-cylinder Model N runabout at $500, and this led logically to the immortal Model T announced in the 1909 season.

The Tin Lizzie put the world on wheels during its 18-year production run; for its day it was very advanced, with a 2.9-litre monobloc sv 4-cylinder engine, detachable head, a top speed of 40–45mph, and a fuel consumption of 25-30mpg. Original list price was $850, but this was progressively cut until a roadster could be bought for as little as $260 in 1925. The car retained Ford's pedal-controlled transmission with 2 forward speeds, and some American states were, as a result,

1968 FOLLIS 1.4-litre racing car.
Lucien Loreille Collection

1906 FORD(i) Model K 6-litre roadster. *The Veteran Car Club of Great Britain*

*c.*1913 FORD(i) Model T 2.9-litre tourer. Coachwork by Sanders of Hitchin. *Bernard Sanders*

1929 FORD(i) Model A 3.2-litre roadster. *Ford Motor Co*

1932 FORD(i) V-8 3.6-litre victoria.
G. Marshall Naul

1937 FORD(i) V-8 3.6-litre sedan. *Ford Motor Co*

1948 FORD(i) V-8 3.9-litre sedan. *Ford Motor Co*

1955 FORD(i) Thunderbird 4.8-litre sports car.
Ford Motor Co

to issue two categories of driving licence – one for ordinary cars, and others for planetary types, i.e. the Ford. More than 15 million were made between October 1908, and May 1927. It formed the basis for a farm tractor (1916) and a one-ton truck (1917), and in 1919 41 per cent of all motor vehicles registered in Great Britain were Fords. Production figures soared: more than 100,000 were made in 1913, the 300,000 mark was passed in 1914, and more than half a million left the works in 1916. The first 'million year' was 1922, and the Model T reached its production peak a year later, with more than two million cars delivered. A British factory was opened in Manchester in 1911, and subsequently French and German plants were to produce their own individual species of Ford. Black was the only colour offered from 1914 to 1925, and a painted black radiator shell replaced the original brass type in 1917; 4-wheel brakes were never available, but electric starters were, from 1920, though it was possible to buy an open car with hand starting only and magneto-driven headlamps as late as 1925.

With the demise of the Model T in 1927, the factory was idle for six months pending the changeover to the Model A, which turned out to be a conventional 3.3-litre 4-cylinder sv machine with 3-speed sliding-type gearbox, 4-wheel brakes, and pleasing lines inspired by the Lincoln (v) which had been under Ford control since 1922. The price was $450, and four-and-a-half million were sold in four seasons despite the Depression, Ford outselling Chevrolet two-to-one in the peak year, 1930. The Model A was also sold in station-wagon versions from 1929, the first large-scale production of a style of body that is now a *sine qua non* in an American manufacturer's range. In 1932 Ford again broke new ground with a mass-produced 3.6-litre V-8 offering 70bhp for $460. It used the 4-cylinder chassis, and as in roadster form it weighed only one ton, the performance was exciting and sometimes lethal. A revised four, the Model B, was made for a short while, but was dropped once V-8 production got into its stride. Inherited from both the T and the A was the all-round transverse-leaf suspension of the B and all V-8s up to 1948. The V-8's first million year was 1935. The Rumanians Zamfirescu and Cristea won the 1936 Monte Carlo Rally for Ford, a success repeated by the Dutchman Bakker Schut in 1938. A smaller companion V-8, the 2.2-litre Model 60, came out in 1936, but it was not a great success, and disappeared after 1940. V-8s acquired hydraulic brakes in 1939, and column change in 1940, and a companion 3.7-litre six was listed in 1941.

After World War 2 the 1942 Fords were continued for three seasons with little change, but the 1949 line, though it used the same power units, was entirely new, with a longer and lower silhouette, and coil-spring independent front suspension. Automatic transmission became available during 1950, and in 1952 a 'square' 3½-litre ohv six was introduced. Two years later the old sv V-8 at long last gave way to a new 130bhp ohv engine in the modern idiom, while another unusual departure was the sporting two-seater Thunderbird, described by its makers as a 'personal car'. Engine options were 4.8 or 5.1 litres, the latter giving a speed of 113mph, but by 1958 it had grown up into a bulky five-seater convertible with unitary construction. Fords were further restyled in 1955, and from 1957 to 1959 there was a fully-convertible hardtop, the Skyliner. In 1958 the most powerful V-8 engines developed 300bhp from 5.8 litres. The 50 millionth Ford was delivered in 1959 and along with G.M. and Chrysler the company had a compact ready for the 1960 season, in the shape of the ohv 6-cylinder 2.3-litre Falcon. A step towards the semi-compact was achieved in 1962, when the big Fairlane models were listed with two modest-sized engines, a 2.8-litre six and a short-stroke eight of 3,622cc, the exact capacity of the original 1932 V-8.

Since 1962 there has been an increasing emphasis on competition; the big Galaxies with 7-litre engines finally ousted the Jaguars from their domination of British saloon-car racing, while the adoption of the V-8 engine by A.C. Cars Ltd for their Cobra model brought Ford back into the sports car field as well. A team of Falcon Sprints was entered in the 1963 Monte Carlo Rally and dominated the big-car class. 1964 brought the Mustang, a compact semi-GT with close-coupled four-seater bodywork, sold for $2,480 with a 4.7-litre V-8 engine giving a top speed of over 110mph; a cheaper model used a 120bhp six. This car achieved a sensational success, with half a million sold in less than eighteen months, and the 1½ millionth delivered in June 1967. Even in 1970, when the effects of new American legislation were already being felt, the U.S.A. alone registered 165,415 new Mustangs. Works support for racing ceased at the end of 1967. For 1968 Ford offered their contribution to the popular intermediate class, the Torino on a 9ft 8in wheelbase. A 115bhp 3.3-litre six was standard, but V-8 options with outputs of up to 390bhp were also catalogued.

The first of a new generation of compacts, the Maverick, appeared in 1969. This had a 7ft 7in wheelbase and at 15ft overall was shorter than the original 1960 Falcon. Engines were 2.8-litre and 3.3-litre 6-cylinder. Other features were a platform frame and semi-elliptic rear springing. Initially it was sold only as a fastback coupé, but by 1971 a 4-door sedan on a longer chassis had joined the range, and the old Falcon had been discontinued, except by Ford of Australia. At the other end of the Ford spectrum were the high-performance Torino Cobra hardtop with 5.7-litre 285bhp V-8 engine and 4-speed manual gearbox, and the costly Thunderbird, with a 7-litre unit and front disc brakes as standard, and a price of $5,295.

More important, however, was 1971's novelty, the Pinto sub-compact introduced wards the end of 1970, when it helped Ford beat Chevrolet in the sales race. This had a sizeable European content. The German factory made the 3-speed gearboxes and buyers had a choice of two 4-cylinder engines, the British 1,600cc Cortina or the 86bhp 2-litre ohc model from Cologne. Drum brakes were standard. The expected swing away from manual transmissions and the sporting image came in 1972: Cobra units were derated to 266bhp, and Ford's biggest engine, the 7½-litre V-8 available as an option in the Thunderbird, gave only 212bhp. Front disc brakes were standardized on the Torino series, and halfway through the season came a station wagon version of the Pinto. The main 1973 improvements concerned safety energy-absorbing bumpers. However, the big Fords (Custom, Galaxie and LTD) on the 10ft 1in chassis were restyled, at the same time receiving front disc brakes as regular equipment. Six-cylinder and manual transmission options were discontinued on this series, as were all American Ford convertibles with the exception of the Mustang. In addition to the full-sized Fords and the intermediate Torino family, the range embraced the Pinto, Maverick, Mustang and Thunderbird. Like Chevrolet, Ford also offered several types on the borderline between private car and truck. These included campers; the 4 × 4 Bronco; the forward-control Econoline station wagon powered by a commercial-model 4.8-litre 6-cylinder engine; and the Ranchero, a coupé-utility on the car chassis which came with a 4.1-litre six as standard equipment.

MCS

1967 FORD(i) Mustang 4.7-litre coupé. *Ford Motor Co*

FORD (ii) (GB) *1911 to date*

1) Ford Motor Co Ltd, Trafford Park, Manchester *1911–1931*
2) Ford Motor Co Ltd, Dagenham, Essex *1932 to date*
3) Ford Advanced Vehicles Ltd, Slough, Bucks *1964–1966*

Until 1932, Ford of England made only rhd versions of the American Ford, Models T and A: the only exception was a small-bore (14.9 R.A.C. rating) version of the latter model known as the AF, designed to beat the British horsepower tax. The opening of the new Dagenham factory in 1932 produced the first true British Ford, the 8hp 933cc Model Y with side-valve engine and transverse springing at £120 (it was also made by Ford (iv) in Cologne). This was joined by the Model C Ten of 1,172cc in 1935, a car which was to supplant the Austin Seven as the favourite basis for British road-going and trials 'specials'. In October 1935 the price of the 2-door saloon Eight was reduced to £100, making it the first full-sized closed car sold at this figure in the U.K. The Eight and the Ten had developed into the Anglia and Prefect with more modern bodywork and pressed-steel wheels by 1939. British-made and assembled V-8s during this period were identical to their American counterparts with one exception: the 1937–39 version of the '60' model rated at 22hp selling for £220. This was very similar to the French Matford.

After World War 2 the small Dagenham Fords continued with little alteration until 1953, a companion V-8, known as the Pilot, being offered in the 1947–50 period with the pre-war 22hp styling, the 3.6-litre side-valve engine and column gear change. In 1951 came the Consul and Zephyr (a 1½-litre four and 2.3-litre six respectively) which featured independent front suspension, oversquare ohv power units, 12-volt electrics and slab-sided styling. Both cost less than £650. In 1954 a wide range was available, with convertible versions of the bigger models, a de luxe variant of the Zephyr known as the Zodiac, and new small cars (the 100E versions of the Anglia and Prefect) with the same basic chassis specification as the Consul and Zephyr, but retaining long-stroke side-valve power units and of course 3-speed gearboxes. At the bottom of the range, listed at only £391, was the Popular, a simplified version of the old Anglia with 1,172cc engine; this indestructible period piece was still being made in 1959, complete with 1935 side-valve engine, beam front axle and mechanical brakes! Restyled Consuls, Zephyrs and Zodiacs appeared in 1956, and a year later they were available with the now generally accepted options of overdrive and automatic transmission. A step towards greater efficiency came in 1960, when the 105E Anglia was introduced. Its layout was conventional, but the forward-sloped rear window gave it a distinctive appearance. A 4-speed gearbox was featured for the first time and an ultra-oversquare 4-cylinder 997cc (80.96m × 48.4mm) engine introduced the average British motorist to engine speeds of 5,500rpm and higher. The 1954 Anglia was given a few more seasons' life as the Popular. The 1.3-litre 4-headlight Classic of 1961 and its sports coupé version, the Capri, were less successful, but Ford did much better with an improved line of big cars: 4- and 6-cylinder Zephyrs and a 6-cylinder Zodiac with Dearborn-styled bodies and front disc brakes.

Ford's answer to the B.M.C. Minis came in 1963. It was a roomy and conventional saloon, the Cortina, powered by developments of the 105E engine in 1.2-litre and 1½-litre forms, giving 48 and 64bhp respectively. The Cortinas were followed shortly afterwards by a 1½-litre GT model with front disc brakes and 83bhp and a super-sporting 1,558cc twin ohc Lotus-Cortina developed with the assistance of Colin Chapman of Lotus and capable of over 100mph. In 1964 the Cortina range was extended by standard and G.T. versions of the Corsair, a full six-seater; 1965 versions were available with automatic gearbox and air conditioning. During the 1960s Ford had been doing increasingly well with the 105E engine in competitions, and this unit formed the basis of 'specials' in every category from road-going G.T.s with fibreglass bodies up to the rear-engined Formula Junior racers, in which category Ford had a virtual monopoly of success.

In 1967, the British Ford range covered every category except the ultra-small

1971 FORD(i) Pinto sedan. *Ford Motor Co*

1973 FORD(i) Thunderbird 7½-litre coupé. *Ford Motor Co*

1934 FORD(ii) Model Y 8hp saloon. *Ford Motor Co Ltd*

1951 FORD(ii) Consul 1½-litre saloon. *Ford Motor Co Ltd*

1965 FORD(ii) Anglia de Luxe 997cc saloon. *Ford Motor Co Ltd*

1969 FORD(ii) Escort GT 1.3-litre saloon. *Ford Motor Co Ltd*

and the super-luxury models. The Anglia was available in 997cc and 1.2-litre forms. The Cortinas, now all with front disc brakes, ranged from the basic 1.2-litre 2-door saloon at £648 up to the Lotus-Cortina at £1,010. The bigger cars had gone over to V-engines, starting with the 1.7-litre and 2-litre Corsairs in October 1965 and followed by the Zephyrs and Zodiacs in the spring of 1966. Ford's Advanced Vehicles Division also evolved a rear-engined G.T.40 coupé with the American-built V-8 engine, intended primarily for competitions; 50 were made of which about 30 were sold privately. This development programme on both sides of the Atlantic resulted in the first American victory at Le Mans in 1966, the car being a Ford 7-litre G.T. Mk 2 driven by McLaren and Amon. Ford repeated this success in 1967. However, the Advanced Vehicle Division at Slough had closed down at the end of 1966, and the 1967 Le Mans cars were made entirely in the USA, mainly by a Ford subsidiary known as Car Craft.

During 1967 the company experimented with the Comuta, a diminutive two-seater electric city car only 80in long and 49.5in high, but this project was shelved in 1971. Of greater interest to the car-buying public were the 1967 versions of the best-selling Cortina (over one million in four years), which was restyled on Corsair lines with the choice of 1.3-litre or 1½-litre 5-bearing engines; a year later the bigger engine was enlarged to 1.6 litres and crossflow heads were adopted. After a production run of 1,300,000 cars the 105E Anglia gave way in January 1968 to the Escort, featuring a Cologne-designed 4-speed all-synchromesh gearbox and rack and pinion steering, as well as crossflow 5-bearing engines of 1,098cc or 1,298cc. Both the GT and the 1,558cc twin-cam versions had front disc brakes; the model won Ford the 1968 and 1969 Rally Constructors' Championships and the 1970 World Cup Rally, successes reflected in the introduction early in 1970 of the RS1600 model with dohc 16-valve engine featuring cogged-belt camshaft drive. This was made in a new Advanced Vehicles plant at Aveley. Ford had also assumed the role of general provider to the racing-car industry, with its 4-cylinder Formula 2 and V-8 Formula 1 3-litre engines made to Cosworth designs. A new and successful 'poor man's' Formula (Formula Ford) was built up round the standard 1,600cc crossflow engine.

Meanwhile Ford's European operations were being rationalized. The Escort was made by Cologne as well as by Dagenham, and the same applied to the 2+2 Capri coupé introduced early in 1969 – though in this case British and German versions used different engines. The British version had sold over 800,000 by August 1972, and came initially with a wide choice of engine and trim options, the former ranging from the 1,300cc ohv in-line four up to the big 3-litre V-6 that developed 136bhp. Front suspension was of McPherson strut type and front disc brakes were standard. During 1970 the Corsair range was discontinued. There were victories in 1971 in the Circuit of Ireland and the Scottish Rally, as well as some interesting experiments such as a 4×4 Capri for Rallycross, and a mid-engined sports coupé prototype, the GT70 with 5-speed gearbox, all-independent suspension, and fibreglass bodywork. The engine was a German-built 3-litre V-6. In the same year the Cortina series was completely redesigned, emerging as bigger cars with double wishbone ifs, and sohc in-line fours of 1,593cc or 1,992cc as an alternative to the established crossflow units. Irs reached series-production Fords during 1972, when the ageing Zephyr IV family gave way to the Consul/Granada series (also shared with Cologne). V-engines (a 2-litre four or sixes of 2,500cc and 3,000cc) were used. The most expensive GXL Granada had a vinyl roof, power-assisted steering, and automatic transmission as standard. The Consul, Cortina and Granada were continued into 1973, along with a slightly revised Escort, and some improved Capris, which could be had for the first time with 1,600cc sohc engines giving 72bhp or 86bhp.   MCS

FORD (iii) (AUS) *1925 to date*
Ford Motor Company of Australia Ltd, Geelong; Broadmeadows, Victoria

Fords were first assembled in Australia in 1925 (Model T), and Model As had Australian-made bodies on American chassis. Australian Ford V-8s made from 1932 to 1960 had small body variations from their American counterparts, such as greater slope on the roof lines of the Tudor sedans of the late 1930s, making them similar to Holden's coupés on GM chassis such as Chevrolet, Pontiac and Vauxhall. The Broadmeadows plant was opened in 1960 to make the Falcon, with 6-cylinder engine up to 1966, when it was supplemented with a V-8. In 1967 the more expensive Fairlane V-8 was added to the Ford of Australia range, and in 1972 both Falcon and Fairlane were completely restyled so that they were quite distinct from American models of the same name. The 1973 range comprised three 6-cylinder engines and two V-8s.   ELF

FORD (iv) (D) *1931 to date*
Ford-Werke AG, Cologne

Ford started assembling the Model T in Berlin in 1925 and Model A in 1927. A new factory was built at Cologne and production began in 1931 with the Model B, later known as the Rheinland, with a 4-cylinder 3,285cc engine using many imported parts. The Köln was built in the new works to American designs, using a 933cc engine, and was almost identical to the English Ford 8, the first Dagenham-built Ford. The V-8 was imported at first, but after 1935 it was built entirely at Cologne. A very popular model was the Eifel (1,157cc) available as a sedan or a two-seater convertible. In 1939 the Taunus appeared with a 1,172cc 34bhp engine and streamlined body, but this type was only produced in small numbers as a result of the outbreak of World War 2. The Taunus was continued after the war in 1948 with the same 1,172cc engine. An engine with the same specification was used for the British Ford 10 and Prefect from 1935 for about 20 years. The name Taunus later came to be used for all German Fords, and the 12M, 15M and 17M were fitted with 4-cylinder 1.2-, 1.5- and 1.7-litre engines respectively. The 12M was offered with front drive in 1962, and was available with V-4 engines of 1.2 and 1.5 litres' capacity. The 17M also appeared with a V-4 engine in 1964, available in 1.5- and 1.7-litre sizes, but this car was rear-driven. The Taunus 20M was a 2-litre V-6 introduced in 1964. Sports tourer (TS) versions of the front-drive 12M, and the 17M and the 20M were also available. The most powerful car of the V-6 range was introduced for 1968; known as the 20M RS, it had a 108bhp 2.3-litre engine.

An increasing tendency to rationalize Ford's European programme became apparent when Dagenham and Cologne offered identical Escort ranges in 1968. In 1969 there were German as well as British Capri coupés, though engine options were different: V-4s of 1.3, 1.5, and 1.7 litres, and 2-litre and 2.3-litre V-6s, with outputs ranging from 63bhp to 123bhp. With this came an increasing interest in competitions; Glemser won the 1969 German Saloon Car Championship with an Escort, and the 1971 European Touring Car Challenge as well. The Taunus name, dropped in 1967, returned in 1971 on a replacement for the fwd 12M. This marked a reversion to conventional drive as well as new 5-bearing ohc in-line 4-cylinder engines of 1,300cc and 1,600cc, and coil-and-wishbone ifs in place of Ford's familiar McPherson struts. The bigger cars retained V-engines, and Ford of Cologne entered 1972 with a range extending from the basic 1,098cc Escort up to the 142bhp 26M six with 2,548cc engine and all-disc brakes. The most powerful catalogued Capri was the 150bhp RS2600, also with discs all round; a team of 2.9-litre versions took the first three places in the Spa 24-Hour Race that year. During the season the 17M and 26M were replaced by German versions of the British Consul-Granada saloons, with all-independent springing. These came with four different engines: a 1.7-litre V-4, a 2-litre ohc in-line four, a German-designed 2.3-litre V-6, and the 3-litre British Ford V-6.   HON

FORD (v) (F) 1947–1954
Ford S.A.F., Poissy, Seine-et-Oise

The post-war French Ford Vedette succeeded the Matfords, production of which had ceased at the outbreak of World War 2. Once again power was provided by the small 2.2-litre 63bhp V-8 introduced for 1936, installed in a chassis resembling that of the 1949 American Fords, with coil-and-wishbone ifs, hydraulic brakes and hypoid final drive. A fastback style of body was used and the basic model was continued with few changes until 1954. A Comète sports coupé with Facel bodywork and optional 4-speed Cotal gearbox was available from 1952. The 1953 cars had 'notch' backs and could be supplied with automatic transmission. A bigger sv V-8 of 3.9 litres was listed for 1954, when Comète versions were sold with 4-speed all-synchromesh boxes. The 1955 line featured unitary construction, Macpherson-strut ifs and two leading-shoe brakes. It used an 80bhp version of the small V-8. Simca acquired the company from Ford in November 1954 and production of these models was continued under the name of Simca Vedette.   MCS

FORD (vi) (BR) 1967 to date
Ford-Willys do Brasil S.A., São Bernardo do Campo

This company resulted from a 1967 merger between the Willys and Ford interests in Brazil, where Ford had been assembling since 1924. The resultant range was an extraordinary international mix-up, with Renault Dauphines being built alongside the 2.7-litre Aero-Willys 6-cylinder ioe sedan and its de luxe variant, the 3-litre Itamaraty, the Jeep-based Rural-Willys station wagons, and a local edition of the American Ford Galaxie with 4½-litre V-8 engine. There was also a long-chassis executive limousine Itamaraty. The 1969 Ford V-8s came with 4,752cc units, and power-assisted steering and air conditioning as standard, and there was also a new small 4-cylinder sedan, the Corcel, available in 1,289cc 68bhp standard and 1,400cc 80bhp GT types. Styling was by Ford's Roberto Araujo, but design was on Renault lines, with fwd, coil-and-wishbone ifs, and a rigid axle with coils at the rear. Body styles included a 4-door sedan, 2-door coupé in standard or GT forms, and a station wagon. The Rural, the Corcel and the big Fords were still being made in 1973, though the Willys-based sixes had been discontinued during the previous season.   MCS

FOREST (US) 1905–1906
Forest Motor Car Co, Boston, Mass.

The Forest five-seater tourer was powered by a 20hp flat-twin engine, and had a wheelbase of 7ft 2in.   GNG

FORMAN (GB) c.1904–c.1906
Forman Motor Mfg Co Ltd, Coventry, Warwickshire

Forman were well-known engine builders who supplied power units to a large number of firms. However, they did make a few cars using their 12/14hp 2-cylinder or 14hp 4-cylinder engine, and shaft drive.   GNG

1932 FORD(iv) 3.6-litre V-8 cabriolet. *Lucien Loreille Collection*

1938 FORD(iv) Eifel 1,172cc drophead coupé. *Ford-Werke AG*

1973 FORD(iv) Consul L coupé. *Ford-Werke AG*

1951 FORD(v) Comète 2.2-litre coupé. *Autocar*

1907 FOSSUM single-cylinder runabout.
Oluf Berrum Collection

1901 FOUILLARON 10hp tonneau. *The Veteran Car Club of Great Britain*

1902 FOUILLARON 10hp tonneau. *Geoffroy de Beauffort Collection*

FORREST (GB) 1907–1916
J.A. Wade & Co Ltd, Liverpool

The Forrest was a light car which made use of a friction transmission and shaft final drive. The original cars used an 8hp V-twin engine, which was supplemented by a small 4-cylinder unit. In the last few years of production, the company concentrated on light vans which, like the cars, were sold in London under the name Realm-Forrest.　　　　　　　　　GNG

FORSTER (i) (CDN) 1920
Forster Motor Car Mfg Co, Montreal, Que.

A big, streamlined, Herschell-Spillman-powered six with right-hand drive, the Forster almost certainly never entered production.　　　　HD

FORSTER (ii) (GB) 1922
Forster Light Cars Ltd, Richmond, Surrey

Derived from the Globe (ii), the Forster was one of the less successful of the many light car makes of the early 1920s. It used a 10hp 2-cylinder engine and cost £225, but hardly progressed beyond the prototype stage.　　　GNG

FORT PITT (US) 1908–1909
Fort Pitt Mfg Co, New Kensington, Pa.

The Fort Pitt had a 6-cylinder, 9.1-litre engine of 70hp. Three body models were available on a standard chassis with a 10ft 1in wheelbase. The cars were shaft-driven. After 1909 the cars were known as Pittsburghs.　　　GMN

FOSSUM (N) 1906–1907
Marcus Hansen Fossum, Oslo

Fossum's first car had a 2-cylinder air-cooled engine fitted in a vehicle of the buggy type. His second venture had a single-cylinder water-cooled engine and generally resembled the Curved-Dash Oldsmobile. However, lack of capital prevented either of these cars from going into production.　　　OB

FOSTER (US) 1900–1905
(1) Foster Automobile Co, Rochester, N.Y. *1900–1903*
(2) Artzberger Automobile Co, Allegheny, Pa. *1903–1905*

These steamers, of which there were three models, operated with boiler pressure of 250psi. The rear axle was chain-driven and the frame was of the 'reach' type. The manufacturer proudly claimed the 'best performance' in several endurance runs against internal combustion engines, but they also offered a short-lived petrol car from the Rochester factory in 1903.　　　GMN

FOSTLER (US) 1904–1905
Chicago Motorcycle Co, Chicago, Ill.

This was a flimsy two-seater with a single-cylinder water-cooled engine with radiator in the rear. Chain drive was used to the rear wheels, which were on a dead axle consisting of two lengths of angle-iron.　　　GMN

FOSTORIA (US) 1916–1917
Fostoria Light Car Co, Fostoria, Ohio

The Fostoria, a light four-seater car was powered by a Sterling overhead-valve 4-cylinder engine of 2.1 litres. It weighed 1,910lb and cost $675.　　　GMN

FOTH (D) 1906–1907
Carl Foth Maschinenfabrik, Dömitz

A friction-driven single-cylinder 8PS voiturette was the sole product of this firm. Only a few were built.　　　HON

FOUCHER ET DELACHANAL (F) 1897–c.1900
Foucher et Delachanal, Paris

This car had a 2-cylinder horizontal engine, with belt drive to pulleys on a countershaft behind the rear axle, and final drive by double chain. It had a three-seater body, and tiller steering.　　　GNG

FOUILLARON (F) 1900–1914
G. Fouillaron, Levallois-Perret, Seine

The Fouillaron's outstanding feature was its peculiar transmission: interestingly enough, it survived for fifteen years without major deviation from the original idea. Power was transmitted by belts running over expansible pulleys to a countershaft and side chains, giving an infinitely variable gear. The rest of the car was conventional in appearance and proprietary engines were used. The makers claimed that their car had been road-tested over 2,500 miles before going into production. By 1902 some quite large Fouillarons had been made with 20hp 4-cylinder Buchet motors, not to mention a 24hp version entered for the Paris-Madrid race in 1903. Catalogued models were, however, more modest, consisting of three singles and two twins with ratings from 6 to 12hp. Honeycomb radiators and Malicet et Blin steering gear featured in 1904, with mechanically-operated side valves on the bigger models. While the small cars had a lateral primary belt drive, the longitudinal drive line was retained on 4-cylinder versions, but with shaft final drive in place of the chains. Seven models, from 6 to 24hp, were available in 1905. From 1906 to 1908 Fouillaron supported voiturette racing, though without success, and they also adopted round radiators and a curious configuration involving not only a drive line which ran diagonally, but also an angled engine mounting. Cars were made with single-, 2-, 3- and 4-cylinder engines, the smaller ones with De Dion power units. By 1908 the round radiator had gone and among the types offered were two small fours with capacities of 1.6 and 1.8 litres. Nothing bigger than a 2.1-litre 4-cylinder was quoted in 1910, when shaft final drive was universal. To the end devotees of expansible-pulley transmission were always offered a diversity of engines and powers; the smallest Fouillaron was a 1-litre single (still listed in 1913–14) and the largest a 16/20hp 4-cylinder of 3.7 litres. In 1914 there was even a light six with a 15/18hp 2.8-litre engine.　　　MCS

FOURNIER (i) *see* SEARCHMONT

FOURNIER (ii) (F) *1913–1924*
SA Anciens Etablissements Fournier, Levallois-Perret, Seine
The original Fournier cars were made in two models, a single-cylinder 6/8hp, and a 4-cylinder 10hp, the latter using a Ballot engine. Like all Fourniers, they used friction transmission, and the pre-war cars were sold by V. Silvestre of Paris under the name Baby-Silvestre. Post-war cars used the V-twin Train engine or 4-cylinder units by Ballot or Ruby.　　　GNG

FOURNIER-MARCADIER (F) *1963 to date*
Fournier et Marcadier, Lyons *1963–1967*
Fournier et Marcadier, Mions, Rhône *1967 to date*
Marcel Fournier and André Marcadier went into business in 1960 with the manufacture of karts, and in 1963 built their first car, a two-seater with rear-mounted Renault R8 engine. From 1966 they built Renault Gordini-powered Formula France racing cars. These had a number of successes in hill-climbs and circuit racing. In 1967, in a new factory, production began of the Borzoi two-seater coupé with gull-wing doors and Renault-Gordini 1300 engine; this, with the Aral Formula France car, remains the firm's staple production. In 1971 one example of a B.M.W.-powered car was built, for Mmes Baronne and Marcadier to drive in the Paris–St Raphael Rallye Feminin. Since 1969 André Marcadier has been in sole charge of the company.　　　LL

FOX (i) (F) *1912–1914; 1919–1923*
(1) M.L. van der Eyken, Neuilly, Seine *1912–1914*
(2) M.L. van der Eyken, Puteaux, Seine *1919–1923*
The pre-war Fox was made in five models, all with 4-cylinder monobloc engines, ranging from 9hp to 18/20hp, the latter having a capacity of 3.6 litres. The post-war model used an 11.9hp 4-cylinder Chapuis-Dornier engine.　　　GNG

FOX (ii) (US) *1921–1923*
Fox Motor Co, Philadelphia, Pa.
The luxurious Fox provided the Franklin with its only serious competition among American air-cooled cars. It was bigger, both in dimensions and engine (4 litres against 3.3 litres), lower-built and better-looking. Like the Franklin, the Fox had overhead valves, but they were actuated by an overhead camshaft and there were aluminium pistons. With its 50bhp, this was the more efficient engine, making the Fox the faster car. Speed, combined with a comparative freedom from overheating, gave the Fox a certain vogue among bootleggers. The method of cooling was similar to that of the Franklin: six separately-cast cylinders cooled by a fan blower.　　　TRN

FOY-STEELE (GB) *1913–1916*
S.M.C. Syndicate Ltd, Willesden, London N.W.
The Foy-Steele was built by the company which had experimented with the Shave-Morse steam car and lorry. It was a conventional car with a 4-cylinder monobloc 14.3hp Coventry-Simplex engine, a 3-speed gearbox and shaft drive. Two- and four-seater open bodies were available, including a 'speed model' and a Colonial tourer with greater ground clearance. The name was taken from Foy steel, an alloy used in the car's universal joints and other components.　　　GNG

F.R. (F) *1927–1928*
Fehr & Rougouchin, Paris
The F.R. was a light 3-wheeler powered by a 500cc Hannisard 2-cylinder 2-stroke engine. It had vertical coil suspension for the two front wheels and the general appearance of a Morgan.　　　GNG

F.R.A.M. *see* CANTONO

FRAMO (D) *1932–1937*
Framo-Werke GmbH, Frankenberg/Saxony: Hainichen/Saxony
J.S. Rasmussen (of D.K.W.) was the owner of Framo-Werke which was not, however, affiliated to the Auto Union combine. The firm's first private car appeared

1921 FOURNIER 8hp coupé. *Autocar*

1922 FOX(ii) 4.4-litre sedan. *Kenneth Stauffer*

1933 FRAMO Stromer coupé. *VEB Barkas*

1922 FRANÇON 458cc two-seater. *Autocar*

1905 FRANKLIN 12hp two-seater. *Henry Ford Museum, Dearborn, Michigan*

1923 FRANKLIN 25hp sedan. *G.N. Georgano*

in 1932. The first model was a 3-wheeler combination car which could be converted to a light truck, the second was a 3-wheeled two-seater called the Piccolo. Both models had one driven front wheel with the engine mounted above it. D.K.W. 200cc engines with compressed-air cooling were used. In 1933 the Stromer was presented, also a 3-wheeler, but with two driven front wheels, using the D.K.W. transmission and D.K.W. engines of 200, 400 and 600cc capacity. The Stromer was built only for about two years. In the same year the 4-wheeled Piccolo was introduced with a 300cc rear-mounted D.K.W. power unit driving the rear axle. The engine capacity was reduced to 200cc in 1935. Production of private cars ceased in 1937, but vans were continued until 1939. The Framo works were nationalized in 1945 and have since produced light commercial vehicles. HON

FRANCO (I) *1907–1914*
Automobili Franco, Sesto San Giovanni, Milan

Little is known about the early Franco cars, and the make's chief claim to fame is the victory in the 1910 Targa Florio. The first Targa Florio entry was in 1908, when Cariolato's Franco retired, but two years later, again driven by Cariolato, a Franco won at an average speed of 29.1mph. The car had a large 4-cylinder engine of about 6.8 litres' capacity, 4 speeds and double chain drive. AZ

FRANÇON (F) *1922–1925*
(1) Truelle et Cie, Rueil-Malmaison, Seine-et-Oise *1922–1925*
(2) Truelle et Cie, St Ouen, Seine *1925*

Built by a firm who specialized in industrial and marine engines, the Françon was a light car with a 2-stroke engine, originally with 2 separate cylinders and a capacity of 458cc, later replaced by a monobloc unit of 664cc. The latter engine was designed by Chedru and used piston pumps à la Trojan. Transmission was by a 5-speed friction drive, and final drive was by chain. The original cars had wooden chassis, and body styles were similar to those of the 5CV Citroën. GNG

FRANKLIN (US) *1901–1934*
(1) H.H. Franklin Mfg Co, Syracuse, N.Y. *1901–1917*
(2) Franklin Automobile Co, Syracuse, N.Y. *1917–1934*

Probably the world's most successful air-cooled car before the advent of the Volkswagen, the Franklin inspired an intense make-loyalty. H.H. Franklin had founded a factory for the manufacture of die castings in 1895, and in 1901 he was introduced to John Wilkinson's air-cooled designs by Messrs Brown and Lipe, later well known as manufacturers of proprietary transmissions. The New York Motor Co had already made three prototypes before the first Franklins went on sale in 1902. These featured transversely-mounted 1.7-litre 4-cylinder air-cooled engines – the valves were overhead, with mechanically operated inlet valves from 1905 – float-feed carburettors, 2-speed planetary gearboxes, central change, full-elliptic suspension and the wooden frames which were to be standard on all Franklins up to the end of 1927. A push-on handbrake was used until 1906. Although a version with water-jacketed engine was projected, the company remained faithful to air-cooling until they closed down. Sales rose from 13 in 1902 to 184 in 1903, when wire wheels gave way to the wood artillery type, and in 1904 a Franklin broke the San Francisco–New York record. The transverse-engined cars were catalogued until the end of 1906, but from 1905 onwards new models with conventionally-located engines made their appearance. These had auxiliary exhaust valves, shaft drive, 3-speed sliding-type gearboxes and round bonnets modelled on the Delaunay-Belleville. A 4-cylinder sold for $1,800, but there was also a 6-cylinder Model H with a 7-bearing crankshaft and a 9ft 6in wheel-base for $4,000: all subsequent 6-cylinder Franklins had seven main bearings. A straight-8 appeared without success in the 1905 Vanderbilt Cup Eliminating Trials. Franklin's full-elliptic suspension was continued. This gave an excellent ride and resulted in tyre mileages in the region of 20,000: this is why the company was refusing to fit detachable rims as standard equipment as late as 1922! In 1907 an automatic advance-and-retard was fitted and in 1908 a gear-driven fan. The 1910 cars used a suction-driven sirocco fan incorporated in the flywheel. Smallest of the 1909 range was the 18hp Model G, a 2.3-litre 4-cylinder car with quadrant change sold at $1,850. Selective change was used on the bigger fours and sixes which had oversquare cylinder dimensions and cost $2,800 and $3,750 respectively. With the 1912 models came a Renault-type bonnet and full pressure lubrication, and a 4-cylinder was still available at $2,000, or $1,500 less than the big 38.4hp 6-cylinder.

In 1914 only a 6-cylinder car, the '6/30', was offered, and Franklin fell into line with the rest of the American industry by going over to left-hand drive, central change and full electrical equipment. A year later aluminium pistons were adopted. A stunt drive from Walla Walla, Washington, to San Francisco in bottom gear demonstrated the car's ability to keep cool. The 1917 models had electric chokes, while imitators arose in the industry to try and cash in on Franklin's success with air cooling. One of these firms, Holmes, was headed by a former vice-president of the Franklin Automobile Co. By the end of World War 1 a 6-cylinder Franklin could be bought for $2,050, reduced two years later to $2,000. 8,648 cars were sold in 1920. Late in 1922, came a redesigned car with a 'horse-collar' bonnet allegedly modelled on the Fiat, pressure air cooling with frontal blower, unit gearbox, single dry-plate clutch, 6-volt instead of 12-volt electrics and detachable rims. Sales rose to 11,000

nd the company which had pioneered series-production closed cars as early as 1913 as offering a sedan at $2,850. During 1925 the design was face-lifted once again nd the De Causse-styled Series 11 introduced. Cylinder capacity remained a modest 3 litres, but appearance was entirely changed with a 9ft 11in wheelbase and a ertical-barred 'radiator'. This revolutionary step so appalled John Wilkinson that he signed from the company forthwith! Some of the semi-custom body styles — specially the boat-tailed sports coupé at $3,150 — were remarkably attractive. ubsequently some excellent and expensive custom bodywork was designed for ranklin by such firms as Derham, Willoughby, Holbrook, and (especially) ietrich. Over 13,000 Series 11s were sold between mid-1925 and the end of 1926, mong those who favoured Franklins being Colonel Charles Lindbergh. Yet even e '11B' of 1927 retained the wooden frame, full-elliptic suspension and foot ansmission brake. Front-wheel brakes did not arrive until the introduction of e 1928 3.9-litre Airman, which boasted internal-expanding Lockheed hydraulics t a time when the contracting type was generally favoured in America. In 1928 long-hassis models were given steel frames, standardized in 1929, and a standard sedan old for £885 in England. All but the cheapest Franklins now had silent 2nd gear-oxes. This was the period in which Dietrich introduced their delightful speedster ctually a 4-door convertible sedan) and a 4½-litre 6-cylinder Franklin engine ctually took to the air in a Waco biplane. Prices were generally in the $2,200–3,500 range, with custom models running up to $7,200.

The 1930 Series 14 introduced a new radiator and side-blast cooling, and the egant Pirate models had concealed running-boards as well. The unconventional, owever, could no longer be sold in America, and only 2,851 Franklins were delivered in 931. In 1932 came synchromesh, free wheels and 'Startix' devices, as well as a agnificent Dietrich-styled 6.8-litre supercharged V-12 (Series 17) on a 12ft wheel-ase. Unfortunately this was re-engineered to incorporate proprietary axles and emi-elliptic suspension, and in production form it weighed nearer three tons than e two tons of the prototype. It combined elegance, 95mph, and 150bhp for $4,400, ut few were sold, though a drastic price cut to $2,885 was made for 1933. The last ew Franklin was the Olympic, an inexpensive 6-cylinder using a Franklin engine edded to a Reo chassis and body. The factory closed down in 1934. The patents ere, however, taken over by the Air-Cooled Motors Corporation (now Franklin ngine Co.), whose Syracuse factory has specialized in light horizontally-opposed ircraft engines: a 6-cylinder Franklin helicopter engine, converted to water cool-g, powered the Tucker of 1947. Two-, 4-, and 6-cylinder units of up to 5.7 litres' apacity were being produced in 1972.   MCS

RANTZ (US) 1901–1902

he Reverend H.A. Frantz, Cherryville, Pa.

In 1900 an announcement appeared in the English motoring press that 'The Revd. .A. Frantz of Cherryville, Pa. believes he has received a call to the motor trade, nd will henceforth make petrol cars in place of sermons.' No details of the cars ere given, and shortly afterwards a further notice said 'the Revd. H.A. Frantz, ho retired from the ministry to build automobiles, has resumed his former calling, n intimation the significance of which depends entirely upon your point of view.'   GNG

RANZ *see* WETZIKON

RASER (i) (GB) 1911

ouglas S. Fraser & Sons Ltd, Arbroath, Angus

The Fraser steam car was only built in three examples: two with 3-cylinder ngines, and one 4-cylinder model. They had single-acting poppet-valve engines ith coil-tube boilers.   GNG

RASER (ii) (GB) 1967–1968

lan Fraser Engineering Co, Hildenborough, Kent

A rear-engined GT car for Group 6 competition work, the Fraser was based on design by Tom Killeen, who had constructed many 'specials' on monocoque rinciples since the war. Some of the mechanical components were modified from illman Imp units, though the design was intended to be equally suitable for most ngines up to 2 litres.   DF

RAYER-MILLER (US) 1904–1910

scar-Lear Automobile Co, Springfield, Ohio; Columbus, Ohio

This make featured air cooling, via a rotary blower which forced air through luminium jackets surrounding the cylinders. In other respects, including appear-nce, the cars were conventional, with side valves in a T-head, cone clutch, 3-speed liding-type gear, and bevel drive. Front suspension was by transverse leaf spring. 24hp 4-cylinder sold for $2,500 in 1905, and the following year it was joined by 6½-litre six. Three 110hp 4-cylinder cars with oversquare engines and left hand rive were entered for the 1906 American Vanderbilt Cup Eliminating Trials, but nly Lawwell's was chosen to compete. It retired during the race.   MCS

RAZER (US) 1946–1951

aiser-Frazer Corp, Willow Run, Mich.

The Frazer was a more expensive, better fitted-out line mate to the Kaiser,

1928 FRANKLIN 26hp sedan. Formerly owned by Col Charles Lindbergh. *Henry Ford Museum, Dearborn, Michigan*

1967 FRASER(ii) 1,140cc GT coupé. *Alan Fraser Engineering Co*

1908 FRAYER-MILLER tourer. *Kenneth Stauffer*

1949 FRAZER Manhattan 3.7-litre 4-door convertible. *Kaizer Jeep Corporation*

1924 FRAZER NASH 1½-litre sports car. *David Thirlby Collection*

1932 FRAZER NASH TT Replica 1½-litre sports car. *David Thirlby Collection*

1954 FRAZER NASH Sebring 2-litre sports car. *National Motor Museum*

actually conceived before Henry Kaiser interests joined those of Joseph W. Fraze Original list price was $2,053, against $1,868 for the Kaiser, and specificatio was straightforward: box-section frame, coil-spring irs, 3-speed synchromesh gea box, 3.7-litre sv 6-cylinder Graham-Paige engine based on Continental's pre-wa Red Seal design, and straight-through wings created by Robert Cadwallader fro a much less slab-sided prototype designed in 1945 by Howard Darrin. Fraze Manhattan luxury model set new industry standards in coordination of colour an fabric, and with Kaiser introduced the first post-war four-door convertible for 194! For 1951 Kaiser interests, by then in firm control of the company, decided t phase out the Frazer, which received only a front-and-rear facelift and used u all left-over early series Kaiser-Frazer bodies, including Kaiser's utility Vagabon model. For 1952 Frazer's Manhattan name was transferred to Kaiser and the mar que was no more, but more than 100,000 cars had been produced in its five mode years.   RM

FRAZER NASH (GB) *1924–1960*

(1) Frazer Nash Ltd, Kingston on Thames, Surrey *1924–1925*
(2) William G. Thomas & Frazer Nash Ltd, Kingston on Thames, Surrey *1925–192*
(3) A.F.N. Ltd, Isleworth, Middlesex *1926–1960*

After Captain A. Frazer-Nash left G.N. Ltd, the company he had helped t found, he at first made orthodox family cars with shaft drive and water-coole 4-cylinder engines of Deemster extraction. However, only a handful of ligh cars were made before Frazer-Nash reverted to type. His new car of 1924 wa based largely on the G.N., retaining its dog-clutch gear-change, separate chain for each of the three forward speeds, solid rear axle, hard quarter-elliptic suspen sion and high ratio steering. After the Plus-Power engine, he adopted the s water-cooled 4-cylinder 1½-litre Anzani unit, giving 40bhp. Thus the G.N.' combination of simplicity, strength, modest price, low weight and high power wer combined in a still brisker sporting machine. The Frazer Nash, together with th Aston-Martin, was Britain's nearest answer to imported sports cars in the Bugat Brescia class. It was so popular that it remained in production, basically unchange for 15 years, even though dog clutches and chain drive had been outmoded when i was first introduced.

The principal alterations were to the power unit. A Meadows engine of the sam size, but with overhead valves, and giving 50bhp, supplemented and then replace the Anzani from 1929 and four forward speeds were provided. Alternatively avail able from 1934 was the 1½-litre single ohc Frazer Nash engine, known as the Goug after its designer. This unit normally delivered 60bhp, but was also availabl supercharged in the Shelsley or T.T. Replica chassis which had cantilever fron springs. The model names applied to the chassis, which could be fitted with an engine. Thus some Shelsleys were equipped with the twin ohc 1,657cc 6-cylinde Blackburne, which was a smoother, more flexible unit.

It was clear that such a fundamentally primitive design could not last for ever however efficient. H.J. Aldington, who had gained control of A.F.N. Ltd in 1929 sought an alternative by importing the German B.M.W. from 1934 – the B.M.W Type 319 engine was used in the chain-driven Frazer Nash chassis. The last Fraze Nash of the old pattern was made in 1939, but the name re-appeared 8 years late attached to a thoroughly up-to-date car. Its power unit was developed jointly b A.F.N. and Bristol, using the pre-war B.M.W. Type 328 engine modified for highe output. In the Frazer Nash the 2-litre cross-push-rod operated ohv unit develope from 75 to 135bhp, depending on the stage of tune required. It was installed i a tubular chassis with transverse leaf independent front suspension and torsio bar rear suspension. There was a normal synchromesh gearbox and live axle. Th car was light – the chassis weighed 1,176lb – and held the road extremely well The High Speed Model of 1948 was developed into the Le Mans Replica which gain ed a 3rd place in that race in 1949, as well as being the only British car to win th Targa Florio, in 1951. From 1953 a De Dion-type rear axle was used in some car including the Competition Model. When B.M.W. began making a 2.6-litre V-engine, this was put in the Competition Model and in a new two-seater coup the Continental. This was very expensive at £3,751. Only the B.M.W. unit wa available from 1957, increased to 3.2 litres in 1959. This was the last year at whic Frazer Nash cars were seen at the Earls Court Motor Show and production cease soon after that.   TRM

FREDERICKSON (US) *1914*

Frederickson Patents Co, Chicago, Ill.
This was a two-seater (tandem) cyclecar with an air-cooled 2-cylinder engine. I had friction transmission, weighed 650lb and cost $375.   GMN

FREDERIKSEN *see* ANGLO-DANE

FREDONIA (US) *1902–1904*

Fredonia Manufacturing Co, Youngstown, Ohio
The Fredonia was built in two- and five-seater versions. It used a single-cylinder engine of a hybrid type. An annular chamber was used to pre-compress the fuel mixture before introduction to the cylinder, an arrangement which dispensed with valves. The final drive was by a single chain.   GM

FREIA (D) *1922–1927*
(1) Kleinautobau AG, Greiz *1922–1923*
(2) Freia Automobil AG, Greiz *1923–1927*
    Production started in 1922 with a 5/14PS 1,320cc model. Engine output was later later increased to 20PS, while 6/30PS (1,472cc) and 7/35PS (1,807cc) models were also made. Freia-built engines as well as Steudel proprietary units were used. Freia cars had 3-speed gearboxes and shaft drive.   HON

FRÉJUS *see* DIATTO

FREMONT (US) *1921–1922*
Fremont Motors Corp, Fremont, Ohio
    The Fremont was a typical assembled car powered by a 6-cylinder Falls engine. The bodywork was attractive, with separate step plates and no running board.   GNG

FRENAY (B) *1914*
Automobiles Frenay, Liège
    The Frenay was a neat-looking two-seater with a pointed radiator rather like that of a Métallurgique. It had a 10/12hp 4-cylinder Ballot engine, and was intended to sell in England at £250, but as it was introduced only three months before the outbreak of World War 1, it never became established.   GNG

FRERA (I) *1905–1913*
Corrado Frera & Cia, Tradate
    The Frera motorcycle had a long and distinguished career, but the firm also made a few light cars with air-cooled twin engines which they called Piccolos, before turning to the licence-production of the Franco–Swiss Zédel. Even this activity had ceased by 1913.   MCS

FRICK (GB) *1904–1906*
A. Dougill & Co Ltd, Leeds
    The Frick used a system of friction drive incorporating two driven discs, final drive being by chain. The first model used a 7hp single-cylinder engine, but this was replaced by a 2-cylinder unit in 1906. A number of commercial vehicles were also made, and production of these continued for several years after 1906.   GNG

FRIEDMAN (US) *1900–1903*
Friedman Automobile Co, Chicago, Ill.
    The Friedman was a runabout powered by a 2-cylinder engine under the seat. It had single chain drive, tiller steering, and cost $750. There was also a Friedman steamer, but it was probably not a production car.   GNG

FRIEND (US) *1920–1921*
Friend Motors Corp, Pontiac, Mich.
    The Friend was built in limited numbers. It was equipped with artillery wooden wheels and its own make of 4-cylinder engine. The price of the five-seater touring car was $1,285.   KM

FRISKY (GB) *1957–1964*
(1) Henry Meadows (Vehicles) Ltd, Wolverhampton, Staffs. *1957–1958*
(2) Frisky Cars Ltd, Wolverhampton, Staffs. *1958–1959*
(3) Frisky Cars (1959) Ltd, Wolverhampton, Staffs. *1959–1961*
(4) Frisky Cars (1959) Ltd, Sandwich, Kent *1961–1962*
(5) Frisky Spares and Service Ltd, Queenborough, Kent *1963–1964*
    A chequered career distinguished this minicar, designed by Captain Raymond Flower for Meadows, the well-known manufacturers of proprietary engines — hence the name Meadows Frisky applied to early models. The basic specification included a separate chassis, chain drive and a narrow rear track which obviated the need for a differential. The 249cc 2-stroke air-cooled twin Villiers engine was mounted at the rear, there was a 4-speed motor-cycle type gearbox (with a reverse obtained by reversing the engine) and independent front suspension of Dubonnet type. The prototype appeared with Michelotti-styled coupé coachwork and gull-wing doors, but simpler fibreglass open and closed bodies, made in the nearby Guy commercial-vehicle factory, were found on the production machines which started to appear at the end of 1957. These also used 16.5bhp 328cc Villiers engines, and 65mph was claimed for £484. A more ambitious sports two-seater was introduced in 1959, the Friskysprint with swing-axle rear suspension, a differential and a 492cc 3-cylinder 2-stroke Excelsior engine developing 30bhp. This was never produced, and Frisky next tried a 3-wheeler to carry 2 adults and 2 children: this 'Family Three' used the 197cc Villiers 9E power unit and later the more powerful 250cc 2-cylinder Excelsior. After the move to Sandwich, production was concentrated on 3-wheelers and a bigger and roomier version, the Prince, was built with a 324cc engine (both Villiers and Excelsior units were offered). Cars were listed until 1964, but the firm's final title indicates the scope of latter-day operations.   MCS

1904 FREDONIA 9hp tonneau. *Keith Marvin Collection*

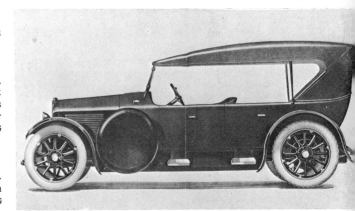
1922 FREMONT Six tourer. *Keith Marvin Collection*

1957 FRISKYSPORT 328cc two-seater. *Autosport*

1906 FRISWELL Baby 6½hp two-seater.
Autocar

1915 F.R.P. 4-cylinder tourer. Non-standard
radiator. *Keith Marvin Collection*

1957 FUJI CABIN 5.5hp coupé. *Matsubayashi
Photo: Lucien Loreille Collection*

FRISWELL (GB) *1906–1907*

Friswell (1906) Ltd, London N.W.

Friswells had made a speciality of selling the single-cylinder Baby Peugeot, and after production of this ceased they replaced it with a small car sold under their own name. It used a single-cylinder De Dion engine of 6½hp, a 3-speed gearbox and shaft drive, and owed its origin to Louis Delage who was just beginning car manufacture at this time.   GNG

FRITCHLE (US) *1904–1917*

Fritchle Auto & Battery Co, Denver, Colo.

The Fritchle company achieved some renown in 1908 when they challenged other makers of electric cars to a race from Lincoln, Nebraska to New York. No one took up the challenge, so the Fritchle made the journey alone, completing the 1,800 miles in 28 days. It was helped by lightweight batteries which gave it a range of over 100 miles per charge, a very high figure then, or now. Encouraged by this sporting success Fritchle included a two-seater roadster in their range for subsequent years, in addition to the usual coupés and broughams with prices up to $3,600. In 1916 Fritchle announced a petrol-electric car on the lines of the Woods Dual Power, with a 4-cylinder air-cooled engine. They sold very few of them, and the following year abandoned car production.   GNG

FRONT DRIVE (US) *1906*

Automobile Front Drive Mfg Co, St Louis, Mo.

This car was powered by a 16hp Streite engine driving by chain to the front axle. It had a crude-looking four-seater body, and solid tyres. The company invited inquiries for financing manufacture, but apparently the car did not go into production.   GNG

FRONTENAC (i) (US) *1906–1913*

Abendroth & Root Mfg Co, Newburgh, N.Y.

This car was built in several body types from a two-seater roadster to a seven-seater limousine. Chassis were large, none having less than a 10ft wheelbase. All models had selective transmission and shaft drive.   GMN

FRONTENAC (ii) (US) *1922*

Frontenac Motor Corp, Indianapolis, Ind.

This was an advanced touring car designed by Louis Chevrolet, who had built racing cars called Frontenac, and C.W. van Ranst. It was backed by Stutz officials, and was sometimes called the Stutz-Frontenac. The engine was a 3.2-litre single-ohc 4-cylinder unit with thermo-syphon cooling, unusual on an American high-performance car at this date. Because of financial troubles, production never started.   GNG

FRONTENAC (iii) (CDN) *1931–1933*

Dominion Motors Ltd, Leaside, Ont.

This was the last Canadian car built in any quantity. Durant Motors of Canada, the Canadian branch of Billy Durant's U.S. empire, did so well in the late 1920s that it became independent in 1931, changing its name to Dominion Motors. The first Frontenac, basically a more powerful and luxurious Durant six, was introduced in August, and a model based on the U.S. DeVaux was added for 1932. For 1933 the line-up was based on the U.S. Continental, with prices slashed and a four added. Despite the quality and value offered, however, the company succumbed to the Depression that year.   HD

FRONTENAC (iv) (CDN) *1959–1960*

Ford Motor Company of Canada Ltd, Windsor, Ont.

This was identical to the Falcon except for its special grille and trim. The Frontenac was sold only in Canada to widen Mercury-Lincoln agents' coverage of the market.   HD

FRONTMOBILE (US) *1917–1918*

(1) Bateman Mfg Co, Grenlock, N.J.

(2) Safety Motor Co, Camden, N.J.

As the name implies, this roadster had front-wheel drive. The transmission was placed between the 4-cylinder engine and the front axle, necessitating a complex mechanism for changing gear: it was accomplished by the use of two straight-line levers. Transverse springs were used and the frame dropped abruptly behind the engine to give a very low centre of gravity.   GMN

F.R.P. (US) *1914–1918*

The Finley-Robertson-Porter Co, Port Jefferson, Long Island, N.Y.

Finley Robertson Porter, designer of the T-head Mercer, constructed a handful of the revolutionary F.R.P. cars which featured a 170bhp engine and a chassis priced from $5,000. A V-shaped radiator distinguished the car and bodies were custom built by well-known coachbuilders.   KM

F-S (US) *1911–1912*

F-S Motors Co, Milwaukee, Wisc.

This car, by the makers of the Petrel, was offered with three different chassis. These were powered by 4-cylinder Beaver engines of 22hp, 30hp, and 40hp respectively. Friction transmission and double-chain drive were used.　　GMN

FUCHS (A) 1922

Herzerdorfer Industriewerke Hans Fuchs AG, Vienna III
This company produced a 5/15PS, 1,180cc sports car, and also a racing version which competed successfully in various national events.　　HON

FUJI CABIN (J) 1957–1958

Fuji Motors Corp, Tokyo
Eighty-five units of this plastic-bodied 3-wheeler were built. It used a single-cylinder 5.5hp air-cooled engine giving a top speed of 37mph.　　BE

FULDAMOBIL (D) 1950–1960

Elektromaschinenbau Fulda GmbH, Fulda
Nordwestdeutsche Fahrzeugbau GmbH, Wilhelmshaven, *1954–1955* only)
This was a three-wheeled car with one driven rear wheel, changed to twin rear wheels after 1955. The first model had an alloy panelled wood-framed body, but after 1953 an all-steel body was fitted. Single-cylinder engines of 250cc (Ilo) and 400cc (Sachs) were used at first, later models having a 200cc Ilo engine. During 1954–55 this car was built under licence by the Nordwestdeutsche Fahrzeugbau GmbH (NWF 200). A fibreglass body replaced the steel body in 1957. Production for the German market ended in 1960. The Fuldamobil was built under licence in Greece (the Attica), Chile (the Bambi), India (the Hans Vahaar) and Great Britain (the Nobel). It was available in various versions, as a closed or open two-seater, as a 3-wheeler or as a 4-wheeler. A pick-up was also built.　　HON

FULGURA *see* BERGMANN

FULLER (i) (US) 1907–1909

Angus Automobile Co, Angus, Neb.
This company built conventional touring cars in three models, two with 4-cylinder engines of 22/26hp and 35/40hp, and a 60hp six. The make has sometimes been listed under the name Angus.　　GMN

FULLER (ii) (US) 1909–1910

Fuller Buggy Co, Jackson, Mich.
The Fuller company offered high-wheelers as well as models of normal design. The high-wheeler had double-chain drive, while the others had shaft drive. The standard models used 4-cylinder water-cooled engines. Full-elliptical springs were used on all Fuller cars.　　GMN

FULMEN (E) 1921

Ernesto Rodriguez Iranzo, Barcelona
The Fulmen was an ephemeral cyclecar designed by an industrial engineer and author of a number of books, including *Enciclopedia del Automóvil*.　　GNG

FULMINA (D) 1913–1926

(1) Fulmina-Werk Carl Hofmann GmbH, Mannheim-Friedrichsfeld *1913–1921*
(2) Fulminawerk GmbH, Mannheim-Friedrichsfeld *1921–1926*
This firm did not produce many cars. Manufacture started in 1913 with two models which were continued after World War 1 until 1926, when the types 10/30PS (2,515cc) and B 17/55PS (4,390cc) were made.　　HON

FULTON (US) 1908

Connecticut Motor Works, New Haven, Conn.
The Fulton was a light car using a 10/12hp 2-cylinder air-cooled engine, which used a combination flywheel and fan. Had it appeared a few years later it would have been called a cyclecar, and might have proved more successful, but in fact never went into production.　　GMN

FUSI FERRO (I) 1948–1949

Società Fusi Ferro, Turin
Designed by the engineer M. Fusi, this was one of the more unusual post-war European prototypes. It had a 1,086cc sv straight-8 engine developing 60bhp, and all-round coil independent suspension. The body was an aerodynamic six-seater saloon, with central driving position, and an electrically operated blind below the transparent plexiglass roof. The car was also known as the Aurora 8.　　AZ

F.W.D. *see* BADGER (i)

1951 FULDAMOBIL coupé. *Autocar*

1910 FULLER(ii) 2-cylinder motor buggy.
National Motor Museum

1914 FULMINA 16/45PS limousine. *Neubauer
Collection*

1915 GADABOUT Model G 10hp two-seater.
The Veteran Car Club of Great Britain

1910 GAETH 30hp tourer. *Automobile Manufacturers' Association*

1907 GAGGENAU '60' 8.8-litre tourer.
Neubauer Collection

GABRIEL (F) *1912–1914*

Gabriel Campana, Paris 20e

Gabriel cars were conventional machines made in three 4-cylinder models of 9/1 13/18 and 20/30hp, the last of these having a capacity of 4½ litres. All models ha 4-speed gearboxes, and chassis layout was in no way out of the ordinary. GN

GADABOUT (US) *1915*

Gadabout Motor Corp, Newark, N.J.

The Gadabout was a two-seater cyclecar with a water-cooled 4-cylinder engin An unusual feature was its wickerwork body. This was claimed to excel in ridir comfort, but it cannot have been very durable. GM

GAETH (US) *1902–1911*

Gaeth Motor Car Co, Cleveland, Ohio

Paul Gaeth was a bicycle maker who added stationary engines to his busines and made an experimental steam car in 1898. His petrol cars were unusual in usir a large 3-cylinder horizontal engine of 25/30hp. Although the car had a dumm bonnet, the engine was mounted under the front seat, from where it drove by a epicyclic gearbox and chain final drive. This car, known as the Gaeth Triplex, wa made until about 1908, when a conventional car with a front-mounted vertic 4-cylinder engine was introduced. At $3,500 it was nearly $1,000 more expensi than the Triplex, and it did not sell well. In 1911 Gaeth's company was absorbe by Stuyvesant. GN

GAGGENAU (D) *1905–1911*

(1) Süddeutsche Automobil-Fabrik GmbH, Gaggenau *1905–1910*
(2) Benz-Werke Gaggenau GmbH vorm. Süddeutsche Automobilfabrik, Gaggena *1911*

The motor-car division of Bergmann's Industriewerke became independe under the name of Süddeutsche Automobil-Fabrik in 1905. The Bergmann Lilipu was continued until 1907. Other models were generally known as Gaggenaus, but th designations S.A.F. and Safe were also used. The Ga^genau 18/22PS and 24/36P were the first of the line. A very advanced engine design was used in '35' (4,700c and 55bhp) and '60' (8,830cc and 75bhp). Features of these engines were the fou cylinders cast in pairs, overhead valves and camshaft, 3-bearing crankshaft an vertical shaft drive for the camshaft. Gaggenau cars participated in many sportin events, such as the Herkomer and Prince Henry Trials and the Kaiserpreis rac Some smaller models were also produced up to 1910. A Gaggenau was the first ca to cross Africa from East to West (Dar-es-Salaam to Swakopmund) in 1907–09. Th journey took 630 days. After 1907 the Süddeutsche Automobilfabrik merged wit Benz and took a leading part in the manufacture of commercial vehicles. On 31s December 1910 Benz took over the factory, concentrating commercial vehicle pr duction there. The Gaggenau 35 and 60 continued in production for some month under Benz management. HO

GAINSBOROUGH (GB) *1902–1903*

Gainsborough Motor Engineering Co Ltd, Gainsborough, Lincs.

This car had a 16hp horizontal 4-cylinder engine mounted under the floor boards, and chain drive to a 2-speed gearbox, whence final drive was again b chain. It had a very early example of hard-top convertible body; an aluminium to changed the car from a tonneau to a closed brougham. GNC

GALBA; HUASCAR (F) *1929–1931*

(1) Sté Sylla, Courbevoie, Seine *1929–1930*
(2) Voiturettes Huascar, Courbevoie, Seine *1931*

The Galba and its descendant the Huascar were the last commercial ventures of Violet who had previously been associated with Violet-Bogey, Major, Mourre, Sima Violet and Deguingand cars. In its original form the Galba used a 564cc 2-strok vertical-twin engine, a 2-speed gearbox and shaft drive, together with transvers leaf suspension at the front, in the style of Violet's previous efforts. With a ver simple two-seater body the price was the equivalent of £75. In 1931 the name wa changed to Huascar, and engine size increased to 625cc. GNC

GALE (US) *1904–1910*

Western Tool Works, Galesburg, Ill.

The Gale car began as a light runabout with an 8hp single-cylinder horizonta engine mounted under the seat, epicyclic gearbox and shaft drive. In 1905 a 16h

316

cylinder model was added. Both these cars had bodies which were hinged at the [r]ar, so that the whole body could be lifted up when the engine needed attention. [Th]is was the best-known feature of Gale cars. In 1907 a 26hp 4-cylinder car was [a]dded to the range; in this car the engine was mounted vertically under a bonnet.

GNG

[G]ALILEO (I) *1904*

[Of]ficine Galileo, Florence

This company made a few electric cars, some of which they exported to the [Un]ited States.

MCS

[G]ALLET ET ITASSE (F) *1900–1901*

[G]allet et Itasse, Boulogne-sur-Seine

Also known as 'La Gazelle', the Gallet et Itasse voiturette used a 2¼hp De Dion [en]gine geared to the rear axle. The front wheels were carried between cycle-type [fo]rks, and front suspension was by vertical compressed-air plungers. The 1901 [m]odel used an Aster engine and chain drive.

GNG

[G]ALLIA *see* REGINA (i)

[G]ALLIOT (F) *1908*

[Soci]été d'Allumage Electrique et d'Accessoires, Paris

The Galliot was a tandem two-seater steered from the rear seat. The single-[cy]linder engine was mounted between the front and rear seats, with the radiator be-[hi]nd the engine, forming a dashboard for the rear seat. Drive was by single chain. A [m]ore powerful model was projected, with a 3-cylinder Anzani radial engine.

GNG

[G]ALLOWAY (i) (US) *1908–1910; 1915–1917*

[Th]e William Galloway Co, Waterloo, Iowa

This famous wagon-building firm made a number of vehicles which could do [do]uble duty, as load carriers on weekdays, and as private cars at weekends. They [ha]d 2-cylinder engines mounted under the seat, solid tyres and chain drive. In [19]15 Galloway advertised a 4-cylinder light car, made for them by the Argo Motor [C]o of Jackson, Mich., and apparently identical with Argo's own light roadster. [In] 1917 Galloway sold this car under the name Arabian.

GNG

[G]ALLOWAY (ii) (GB) *1921–1928*

[(1)] Galloway Motors Ltd, Tongland, Kirkcudbright *1921–1922*

[(2)] Galloway Motors Ltd, Heathhall, Dumfries *1923–1928*

The Galloway was the light-car line of the Arrol-Johnston concern. Designed [b]y T.C. Pullinger and inspired in part by the very successful Tipo 501 Fiat from [It]aly, the 10.5hp Galloway was a sound little car combining strength of construc-[ti]on with ease of maintenance. Design was modern and conventional – a 1,460cc [4-]cylinder, side-valve engine with a detachable head, made in unit with a 3-speed [ce]ntral-control gearbox. Late in 1925 the 10.5hp was withdrawn and a 12hp with [pu]sh-rod overhead valves substituted. The first works, at Tongland, was staffed [m]ainly by women, with Miss Dorothée Pullinger in charge.

TRN

[G]ALT (i) (CDN) *1911–1913*

[C]anadian Motors Ltd, Galt, Ont.

The 1911 models were based on the Alpena Motor Car Company's roadster [an]d touring and undoubtedly were imported from the U.S. for sale in Canada, [a]s the Canada Tourist and Canada Roadster. Galt production started later with [H]azard engines and other U.S. parts. The 30hp model found about 50 buyers. [T]he 1912 model had an electric starter which gave so much trouble that sales [w]ere reduced to the point of bankruptcy. The company ceased operation in 1913, [af]ter producing models with 45 and 50hp, on 9ft 10in chassis.

GB

[G]ALT (ii) (CDN) *1911–1935*

[G]alt Motor Company, Galt, Ont.

This firm's involvement with the motor car began with the development in 1911, [o]f a gas-electric power plant system. In 1913 the firm completed, from parts pur-[ch]ased from the defunct Canadian Motors Ltd, approximately ten Galt petrol-pow-[er]ed cars. The gas-electric car, announced in 1914, was powered by a 2-cylinder, [2]-stroke combustion engine that developed a constant 700rpm. This engine drove [th]e generator which provided energy to storage batteries and the electric motor [us]ed to drive the vehicle. The car had five speeds forward and three reverse, and [w]as controlled by a single lever. Two Galt gas-electrics were constructed. The [s]econd unit was used up until 1927 as an experimental and test chassis, with con-[st]ant attempts to arrange financing both in Canada and the U.S.

GB

[G]ALY (F) *1954–1957*

[A]utomobiles Galy, Forges et Ateliers de la Vence et de la Fournaise, Paris

The Galy was a small coupé rather like the early Goggomobil in layout, with [a] rear-mounted engine which was either a 175cc Ydral (11bhp), or a 280cc AMC [(1]8bhp). A maximum speed of over 60mph was claimed for the larger model, but [ve]ry few of either were sold. The 'Vistand' model had a rather Jeep-like open body, [w]hile the 'Vibel' was a coupé.

GNG

1904 GALE 8hp two-seater. *Herbert de Garis*

1924 GALLOWAY(ii) 10.5hp two-seater.
Museum of Transport, Glasgow

1928 GALLOWAY(ii) 12/30hp coupé. *Autocar*

1899 GARDNER(i) phaeton. *Geoffroy de Beaufort Collection*

1930 GARDNER(ii) roadster. *Kenneth Stauffer*

1908 GARFORD 40hp tourer. *Automotive History Collection, Detroit Public Library*

G.A.M. (F) *1930*
Etablissements G.A.M., St Etienne
    The G.A.M. was a cyclecar with tandem seating. It appeared at least ten yea too late for such a car to find favour with the public, and did not go into productic
GI

GAMAGE (GB) *1903–1904; 1914–1915*
A.W. Gamage Ltd, Holborn, London E.C.
    This famous department store did a lively trade in motor accessories, and it al sold complete cars under its own brand-name. These were single and twin-cylind vehicles with De Dion engines, made probably by Lacoste et Battmann, thou De Dion-Boutons and Renaults were also being handled in 1903. The 1914 Gama light car had a 1½-litre sv Chapuis-Dornier 4-cylinder engine and could be start *via* a cable linkage from the driver's seat. In 1920 Gamage's were importing t German Slaby-Beringer light electric car.
M

GAMMA (F) *1921–1922*
Sté des Automobiles Gamma, Courbevoie, Seine
    The Gamma was a conventional small car available with either a 1½-litre Ball or a 2-litre Altos engine. Both were 4-cylinder sv units. A handsome V-radiator ga more distinction to the looks of the Gamma than the car actually warrante
GI

GANZ *see* RAPID (iv)

G.A.R. (F) *1922–1931*
(1) Cyclecars G.A.R., Clichy, Seine
(2) Gardahaut et Cie, Asnières, Seine
    The first G.A.R. was a cyclecar with a 2-cylinder engine, but the bulk of t company's production was devoted to small sports cars which were often entere for races. They had engines by Chapuis-Dornier (961 and 1095cc), which we available in supercharged form, or S.C.A.P. (1,492 straight-8), and also used the own single ohc engines of 735cc 4-cylinder, or 1,375cc straight-8. Two 4-cylind models were built under licence in Italy, initially as G.A.R.s, then under the nar C.A.R.
GI

GARANZINI (I) *1924–1926*
Fabbrica Automobili Oreste Garanzini, Milan
    Oreste Garanzini was a former motor-cycle champion who built a few small car They had 1,200cc ohv 4-cylinder engines, independent suspension, and headligh which turned with the wheels.
A

GARBATY (D) *1924–1927*
Autowerk Garbaty, Mainz
A small car with a 5/25PS 1.2-litre 4-cylinder engine.
HC

GARCIN *see* B.G.S.

GARDNER (i) (F) *1898–1900*
Frank L. Gardner, Paris 20e
    Before sponsoring the steam cars designed by Léon Serpollet, the America company promoter Frank L. Gardner made a few petrol-engined cars at his larg works in the rue Stendhal. Designed by an Englishman, Charles W. James, they we conventional belt-driven voiturettes with single-cylinder horizontal engines. At lea one car, however, was a 12hp 2-cylinder streamlined racing car with a claime maximum speed of 40mph.
GN

GARDNER (ii) (US) *1919–1931*
Gardner Motor Co Inc, St Louis, Mo.
    Russell E. Gardner made the horse-drawn Banner Buggy before turning to mot cars in 1916. At first his works was the local assembly plant for Chevrolets an also made bodies for them. Then, in 1919, the first Gardner car appeared. It was a assembled, but well-made machine with a 4-cylinder, 3.4-litre, side-valve engir specially built for it by Lycoming, who supplied all the Gardner power units. T four was replaced by a 3.6-litre six and a 4½-litre straight-8 for 1924. Fro 1926 to 1929, only eights were offered. The largest came into the luxury categor with a price of $2,295. So far the Gardner had run true to American form, exce for its 'tailor-made' engines, but the new six of 1929 not only lost cylinders whe other makers were adding them — its hydraulic brakes were internal expanding, great rarity at the time in America. The make went out in a spectacular fashio with the exceptionally low-hung front-wheel-drive six of 1930.
TR

GARDNER-SERPOLLET *see* SERPOLLET

GAREAU (CDN) *1909–1910*
Gareau Motor Car Co Ltd, Montreal, Que.
    This well-built car featured a 4-cylinder engine of its own design and bodies bu by a local carriage-maker. Only three cars, all tourers, were built but they perform well. Inability to raise enough capital caused the firm to close down.
H

ARFORD (US) *1906–1912; 1916*

arford Mfg Co, Elyria, Ohio

The Garford was a large car made originally in 4-cylinder 40hp form, replaced ter by a 6-cylinder engine of 6½ litres' capacity. Some of the later models had single headlamp mounted in the top of the radiator, as on the Briscoe. As well their own cars, Garford made chassis for Studebaker from 1904 to 1911, when ey were acquired by Willys-Overland. They were also well-known makers of ucks. From 1913 to 1915 they built Willys-Knight cars, but for 1916 they again fered a range of cars under their own name.   GMN

ARRIGA (E) *1923*

uto Academia Garriga, Barcelona

José Garriga Albaret was a garage owner and driving instructor who built a nall sports car powered by a 1,100cc 4-cylinder S.C.A.P. engine. Few were made, ut they took part in competitions at least until 1926.   GNG

ARY (US) *1916–1917*

ary Automobile Manufacturing Co, Gary, Ind.

This company made a short-lived car with a 34hp 6-cylinder engine. It was made roadster and tourer form, and cost $2,300.   GNG

AS-AU-LEC (US) *1905–1906*

) Vaughn Machine Co, Peabody, Mass.

) Corwin Manufacturing Co, Peabody, Mass.

This was a petrol-electric vehicle with a 4-cylinder engine of over 7 litres pacity. The engine had electromagnetically operated valves whose timing could varied by the operator. The electric generator was directly connected to the gine. Storage batteries were used for reserve and for very slow speeds. This was lled 'The Simple Car'.   GMN

ASI (D) *1921*

asi-Motorradwagen-GmbH, Berlin-Dahlem

This firm produced a 3-wheeled cyclecar with one front and two rear wheels. The ody was a tandem two-seater, the back seat being for the driver. An air-cooled -cylinder engine was used. Transmission was by chain to an intermediate shaft and y two belts without differential to the rear wheels.   HON

ASLIGHT (US) *1960–c.1961*

aslight Motors Corp, Detroit, Mich.

One of several attempts to offer a replica veteran car, this time based on the 1902 ambler. Built on a 77in wheelbase and weighing 640lb, the Gaslight was powered y a modern air-cooled, single-cylinder engine of 4hp. The price of this replica was 1,495.   MJWW

GASMOBILE (US) *1900–1902*

utomobile Company of America, Marion, N.J.

This company began manufacture of cars and tricycles in 1899, under the name utomobile Voiturette, but the name Gasmobile was not applied until 1900. The ars originally had rear-mounted 3-cylinder horizontal engines, and chain drive. y 1902 two lines of design were being followed: the horizontal rear-engined models ade in 9 and 12hp form, and a front vertical-engined car with 20hp 4-cylinder engine hich was said to be a close copy of the Panhard. There was also listed a 35hp orizontally-opposed six, but whether this was actually made is uncertain.   GNG

GATSO (NL) *1948–1950*

M. Gatsonides, Heemstede

Sometimes known as the Gatford, this was a short-lived venture by the inter-ational rally driver Maurice Gatsonides. Ford mechanical components were used, he engine being a 3.9-litre Mercury (vi) sv V-8 with twin downdraught carburettors iving 120bhp. Brakes were hydro-mechanical and there was overdrive on all three ears. The duralumin-panelled body was of aircraft-fuselage type with a 'bubble' ockpit hood, and there were three headlights, the central one in the radiator rille. Buyers had the option of a 170bhp ohv engine, but only a few cars were nade.   MCS

GATTER (CS) *1929–1930*

ng. Gatter, Reichstadt

Gatter cars existed as prototypes only. In 1929 a four-seater car with central ubular frame, swing axles and a 4-cylinder engine was introduced. This version vas of outstanding technical quality and finish. In 1930 a two-seater cyclecar vith a 350cc single-cylinder Villiers engine appeared.   HON

GATTS (US) *1905*

lfred P. Gatts, Brown County, Ohio

Only five examples of this car were built, one of which survives in an Indiana ollection. These were powered by a single-cylinder air-cooled engine with integral lywheel and fan. Starting was by a crank in the rear of the body.   GMN

1923 GARRIGA 1,100cc racing car. *Joaquín Ciuró Gabarró Collection*

1921 GASI 2-cylinder 3-wheeler. *Neubauer Collection*

1948 GATSO 3.9-litre aero-coupé. *National Motor Museum*

1899 GAUTIER-WEHRLÉ 4½hp voiturette.
Neubauer Collection

1955 GAYLORD(ii) Gladiator V-8 coupé.
Lucien Loreille Collection

1938 GAZ M11-40 3.6-litre tourer. *Autocar*

GAUTHIER (F) 1904–1937
(1) Gauthier et Cie, La Garenne-Colombes *1904–1932*
(2) G. Gauthier, Blois, Loir-et-Cher *1933–1937*

More of an inventor than an industrialist, Gauthier's total production betwee
his first experimental cars of 1902 and his death in 1939 was only about 350. Mo
were lightweights of sundry configurations, such as the Auto-Plume Cabri and Aut
Fauteuil models introduced in 1927. Various air- and water-cooled single-cylind
engines were fitted, of 350, 400, 500 and 550cc. A light channel frame carried th
driver and engine amidships, and passengers could be carried over the back whe
and between the front wheels. A power take-off was available. Robust and reliabl
Gauthiers appealed to missionaries and indigent rural clergymen. In 1918 a V-tw
engined cyclecar was demonstrated to the army, and the performance over roug
ground earned the model the name Avionette. Patented suspension, inter-connecte
fore and aft, was featured. A 3-wheeler version was available up to 1927.   D

GAUTIER (F) 1902–1903
Charles Gautier et Cie, Courbevoie, Seine

Gautier, who had formerly been with the Gautier-Wehrlé company, made a wi
range of cars for a short period. He offered five models, a voiturette with a 6½hp I
Dion or Aster engine a 12hp twin and 16, 22 or 30hp 4-cylinder cars with engin
by Aster or Mutel. Shaft or chain drive was available on the two smaller model
while the fours all used chain drive.   GN

GAUTIER-WEHRLÉ (F) 1894–1896 (steam); 1896–1900 (petrol); 1898 (electri
(1) Rossel Gautier et Wehrlé, Paris *1894–1897*
(2) Société Continentale, Paris *1897–1900*

This pioneer firm started by manufacturing steam cars, one of which w
entered by Gautier in the 1894 Paris-Rouen event, in which it took 16th plac
An improved version, La Cigale, with Serpollet boiler and wheels of equal siz
was entered for the Paris-Bordeaux the following year, but failed to complete th
course. In 1896 the company was already advertising 'chainless and vibrationles
petrol vehicles with amidships-mounted engines and a year later these were th
staple product, though by this time the 8hp horizontal power units with tub
ignition were mounted under vestigial bonnets. Steering was by handlebars, but th
transmission arrangements were most advanced, drive being by shaft to a 3-spee
rear-axle-mounted gearbox. In 1898 the firm was not only offering 5hp and 12h
singles, but also a vertical-twin version, while electric cars were also bein
produced. They were also supplying bodies to outside firms as well as for their ow
chassis, and doing sub-contract work for Serpollet. Two models were listed in 189
a 4½hp dogcart costing 7,000fr, but after this production ceased.   MC

GAYLORD (i) (US) 1910–1913
Gaylord Motor Car Co, Gaylord, Mich.

The Gaylord was one of several makes of this era which was convertible fro
a four-seater private car to a utility vehicle, with rear space for packages; 4-cylinde
ohv engines of 20, 30, 35 and 40hp were used, the last in 1912–1913 only.   GM

GAYLORD (ii) (US) 1955–1956
Gaylord Cars Ltd, Chicago, Ill.

The Gaylord Gladiator was a luxury two-seater coupé with automatic retractabl
hard top. The prototypes used Chrysler engines, but production cars had a modifie
6-litre V-8 Cadillac unit. Two prototypes and three production cars were built. GN

GAZ (SU) 1932 to date
Zavod Imieni Molotova, Gorky

When the first four-seater touring car was driven from the Gorky Automobil
Works in 1932 it looked more than slightly like its American cousin, the Model
Ford, for the GAZ-A was built with considerable help from Ford engineers. Th
M-1, constructed in 1936, also bore a great likeness to the 1933–34 America
product, although Ford furnished no direct assistance on this or any further GA
designs. Ford influence continued to be felt, however, as was shown by the appear
ance of sedans turned out until the German invasion of 1941. Model M-11 (11–73
was built in 1940 as a further development of the M-1 sedan. It was a five-seate
version with a 6-cylinder, water-cooled engine of 76hp. A fuel consumption of 1
litres per 100km was obtained and maximum speed was about 70mph.

During the war years the plant manufactured the GAZ-67, a 4-cylinder utilit
vehicle for the armed services and produces the 'B' version of this even now.
GAZ 69 heavy-duty, 4-cylinder, 72hp, 4-wheel-drive utility is manufactured, wit
Gorky plant cooperation, at the Ulyanovsk Motor Works. Like the '67', it is use
by both civilians and the military.

All models originating from Gorky and its subsidiary plants are given a numbe
and may also be known by a more familiar 'brand' name. The GAZ M-20 seda
was better known as the Pobieda or Victory. The Volgas that replaced it wer
designated M-21, M-22 and M-25. The Zim limousine was the GAZ M-12, an
its successor the Chaika the M-13. The Gorky works were once the largest ca
plant in Europe, and further expansion is in hand to meet the growing deman
for private transport in the Soviet Union.   BE

G.B. (GB) *1922–1924*

George Baets, London S.W.1

The G.B. was an unusual 3-wheeler using a 5/7hp Coventry-Victor 2-cylinder engine driving the rear wheels, and unit construction of body and chassis. It was a two-seater with a very long bonnet between the driver and the single front wheel. George Baets planned to sell the car at £150, but very few were made.   GNG

G.C. (F) *1908*

Automobiles G.C., H. Guyot et Cie, Paris

This was a light car powered by a 9/12hp 4-cylinder Sultan engine of 1,940cc.   LL

G.E.A. (ORMEN LANGA) (S) *1905*

AB Gustav Ericssons Automobilfabrik, Stockholm

Better known for his lorries, Gustav L.M. Ericsson made one very large 6-cylinder car, the Ormen Langa or Long Serpent. It had a bonnet very like the Delaunay-Belleville and a two-seater roadster body.   OB

GEARLESS (i) (US) *1907–1909*

1) Gearless Transmission Co, Rochester, N.Y. *1907–1908*

2) Gearless Motor Car Co, Rochester, N.Y. *1908–1909*

The 1907 Gearless cars had large engines of 50hp (2-stroke), 60 and 75hp (4-stroke), friction transmission and double chain drive. In 1909 came the Gearless 35, a much cheaper car selling at $1,500 compared with the $3,500 to $4,000 of the larger cars. Also in the 1909 range was the Olympic 35 with a similar engine to the Gearless 35 but with a conventional transmission.   GNG

GEARLESS (ii) (US) *1921–1923*

Gearless Motor Corp, Pittsburgh, Pa.

The Gearless, produced as a roadster and touring car at $2,650 and $2,550 respectively, had two separate 2-cylinder double-acting side-valve steam engines for power, and was available with either wood or wire wheels. It was claimed that the use of two engines, each operating one rear wheel, avoided the necessity of a differential for the rear axle. Both engines were controlled by a single throttle. The company failed when four of its officials were charged with mail frauds and conspiring to sell more than $1,000,000-worth of company stock fraudulently.   KM

G.E.C. (US) *1898–1902*

1) General Electric Co, West Lynn, Mass. *1898*

2) General Electric Co, Schenectady, N.Y. *1902*

The only cars to be made by the vast General Electric Company were both experimental. The earlier was an electric carriage, while the later model was a petrol-electric car with a 4-cylinder engine. The Philadelphia-built General Electric car had no connection with G.E.C.   GNG

GEERING (GB) *1899*

T. Geering & Son, Rolvenden, Kent

This firm made stationary engines running on heavy oil, and built a prototype car powered by a rear-mounted 2-cylinder 3hp oil engine.   GNG

GEHA (D) *1910–1923*

1) Elektromobilfabrik Gebhardt & Harborn, Berlin-Schöneberg *1910–1917*

2) Elitewerke AG, Zweigniederlassung, Berlin-Schöneberg *1917–1923*

An electric 3-wheeler with one driven front wheel designed by Victor Harborn. The works were taken over by Elite in 1917 and continued as a branch factory. Geha cars were made until 1923. Electric 4-wheeled cars produced in Berlin were marketed under the name of Elite.   HON

GELRIA (NL) *1900–1902*

Gelria Machine- en Motorenfabriek, Arnhem

The first model made by the Gelria company used a large single-cylinder 4hp engine mounted at the front, a 2-speed gearbox and final drive by chain. Body styles were a four-seater tourer, a *dos-à-dos* and a Duc three-seater. In 1901 they produced an enclosed brake with solid tyres and a 2-cylinder 6hp engine. Production of these vehicles was only sporadic, and ended completely in 1902.   GNG

G.É.M. (F) *1907–1909*

Sté Générale d'Automobiles Electro-Mécaniques, Puteaux, Seine

The G.E.M. was a petrol-electric car designed by Léonce Girardot, formerly a partner of the C.G.V. company. Later models used a 4-cylinder Daimler-Knight sleeve-valve engine, but it was not a commercial success, and Girardot turned to the sale of Daimler cars in France. In 1912 Girardot built a car under his own name, powered by a sleeve-valve Panhard engine in a Charron chassis.   GNG

GEM (i) (US) *1917–1919*

Gem Motor Car Co, Jackson, Mich.; Grand Rapids, Mich.

The Gem was a light, assembled car using a 4-cylinder G.B. & S. engine. Only two models were made, a touring car, selling at $845, and a light delivery van.   KM

1940 GAZ M11-73 3.6-litre saloon. *NAMI, Moscow*

1900 GELRIA 4hp phaeton. *C. Poel Jr*

1908 G.E.M. 20CV sedanca de ville. *Lucien Loreille Collection*

1960 GEMINI Formula Junior racing car.
Autosport

1902 GENERAL(i) 40hp racing car. *National Motor Museum*

1926 GÉNESTIN 1½-litre sports car. *Jacques Kupélian Collection*

GEM (ii) (GB) 1968
Grantura Plastics Ltd, Blackpool, Lancs.

Designed by two ex-T.V.R. engineers, the Gem GT was a fibreglass two-seater coupé powered by a Ford V-6 3-litre engine, with all-independent suspension and disc brakes all round. Appearance was strongly reminiscent of the T.V.R.   GNG

GEMINI (GB) 1959–1963
Chequered Flag Engineering Ltd, Chiswick, London W.4

After some false starts Moorland Cars Ltd produced a promising Formula Junior machine, with a multi-tubular chassis and B.M.C. engine. Graham Warner then took both the car and the designer (L. Redmond) under his wing, and together they developed the Gemini — Warner's Zodiacal sign. Independent suspension all round was by Armstrong coil/damper units; alloy bodies were supplied by Williams and Pritchard. Most Geminis were Cosworth-Ford engined. The ascendancy of rear engines led to the Mark 3 in 1960. In 1961 and 1962 Marks 4 and 4A were developed, and total production exceeded 60. Raced by Warner, Geoff Duke, Tony Maggs, Mike Parkes and others, the Gemini was notably rapid for the money but could never quite vanquish all the Lotuses.   D

GENERAL (i) (GB) 1902–1905
(1) General Motor Car Co Ltd, Norbury, London S.W. *1902–1903*
(2) General Motor Car Co Ltd, Mitcham, Surrey *1903–1905*

This company was supposed to be building a 24hp racing car for the 1902 Bexhill Speed Trials, but it did not appear. However, at the end of 1902 a racing car was made, with a 40hp 4-cylinder Buchet engine. The bonnet came to a sharp point, and *The Autocar* remarked that it would certainly deter any police constable from physical obstruction to the progress of the car. In 1903 more practical cars were being made, powered by 6½hp and 12hp Aster or Buchet engines, and the company was supposed to be making light vans for G.P.O. work. The 1904 light car had a spiral radiator and shaft drive, and was said to be suitable for medical men. Some larger cars with 30hp Simms and 40hp Buchet engines were made towards the end of the company's life.   GNG

GENERAL (ii) (US) 1902–1903
General Automobile & Manufacturing Co, Cleveland, Ohio

This company succeeded the Hansen Automobile Company in September 1902 and announced a car similar to the Hansen, but with an 8hp 2-cylinder engine, choice of wheel or tiller steering, and detachable tonneau body. In October 1903 the General's plant was acquired by Studebaker.   GNG

GENERAL ELECTRIC (US) 1898–1899
General Electric Automobile Co, Philadelphia, Pa.

These cars had no connection with the famous G.E.C., but were a product of the Brill Company, makers of trams and electrical equipment. The cars were light runabouts with especially light batteries which permitted a long range per charge.   GNG

GENESEE (US) 1912
Genesee Motor Co, Batavia, N.Y.

This extremely large car, with a wheelbase of 12ft 4in, was driven by a 6-cylinder 11.1-litre engine. It featured electric lights, compressed-air starter, two spare tyres, clock, rear-view mirror and a gradometer. The eight-seater torpedo touring model cost $8,000 and a limousine was listed at $10,000.   GMN

GÉNESTIN (F) 1926–1929
P. Génestin, Fourmies, Nord

The Génestin was a light car which used a wide variety of engines. The touring models came in four sizes, from an 1,100cc 4-cylinder to a 1,681cc 6-cylinder, the engines being made by Chapuis-Dornier or C.I.M.E. The sports models used ohv S.C.A.P. engines, fours of 1,084 and 1,476cc, and a straight-8 of 1,808cc. The fours were available with a Cozette supercharger driven by bevels from the front of the engine. Génestins competed in a number of races, including Le Mans, and the Circuit des Routes Pavées.   GNG

GENEVA (i) (US) 1901–1904
Geneva Automobile & Mfg Co, Geneva, Ohio

This was a 2-cylinder steamer with its engine connected directly to the differential. The smaller of the two models produced was tiller-operated, while the larger one was steered by wheel. It is sometimes stated that Genevas were also built with internal-combustion engines.   GMN

GENEVA (ii) (US) 1916–1917
Schoeneck Co, Chicago, Ill.

This was a large car with a wheelbase of 11ft 7in. It used a 6.8-litre 6-cylinder engine by Herschell-Spillman. The two-seater speedster had a sporty appearance, with vents on top of the bonnet and cycle-type mudguards, with two spare tyres mounted flat on the tail of the body. There may be a connection with the elusive Owen Schoeneck car of 1915–16.   GMN

ENIE (US) *1959–1969*

British Motor Car Importers, San Francisco, Calif.

Rear-engined Formula Junior cars, with multi-tubular space frames designed by Huffaker, were the initial product of this firm. Later, sports-racing cars were assembled, using various American engines.   DF

GEORGES IRAT (F) *1921–1946*

1) Automobiles Georges Irat, SA, Chatou, Seine-et-Oise *1921–1929*
2) Automobiles Georges Irat, SA, Neuilly, Seine *1929–1934*
3) Automobiles Georges Irat, SA, Levallois-Perret, Seine *1935–1946*

The vintage Georges Irat was a well-built fast touring car rather than an out and out sports car, although it was entered in many races including Le Mans, and did particularly well in the Circuit des Routes Pavées, which it won in 1923, 1925, and 1927. The first model used a 4-cylinder 2-litre ohv engine of Georges Irat's own design and 4-wheel Dewandre vacuum servo brakes. This was succeeded in 1927 by a 3-litre six with the same cylinder dimensions (69 × 130mm). About 200 of these cars were sold per year right through the vintage period, but in 1929 the company moved to Neuilly where they tried to produce large luxury cars with 6- and 8-cylinder Lycoming engines and independent front suspension. Saoutchik built some very handsome bodies for these cars, but they were never produced in series.

In 1935 the firm moved again, to Levallois, and began to make a small sports car with an 1,100cc Ruby engine, and front-wheel drive. Although they were more sporting in appearance than performance, these cars became quite popular in France, and were made up to 1939 when another fwd car appeared, this time with the 11CV Citroën engine and rubber suspension. About 1,000 of the Ruby-engined cars were made. A number of minute electric cars were made during World War 2, and in 1946 Georges Irat showed a prototype with an 1,100cc flat twin engine, magnesium alloy body and strip headlamps on the front bumpers. This was never manufactured, and after experimenting with Diesel lorries, Georges Irat left the field of vehicle building to concentrate on engines.   GNG

GEORGES RICHARD *see* BRASIER

GEORGES ROY (F) *1906–1929*

Automobiles Georges Roy, Bordeaux

This was a regional French firm with a long record of unspectacular motor cars. In 1906 they offered an 1,100cc single, a very large twin of 2.9 litres' capacity and a 4.6-litre 4-cylinder, all with 3-speed gearboxes. The range was widened in 1907 to include a 10.2-litre 6-cylinder. The twins were still being made in 1908, when there were also 4-cylinder 2.9-litre, 3.8-litre and 5.9-litre models, and an 8.5-litre 6-cylinder car at 18,500fr for a chassis. Chain drive was optional on the two largest types, but in 1909 only fours were made. Two types, a four and a six, were listed in 1910, sharing the same cylinder dimensions of 80 × 110mm. By 1912 all Georges Roys had four speeds and shaft drive, the 20CV being a 3.6-litre 6-cylinder car. Radiators were round and a 1½-litre sv monobloc model on straightforward lines was added to the range in 1913. After World War 1 the Georges Roy appeared as a very conventional 3-litre sv long-stroke model with fixed head, pump cooling, 4-speed unit gearbox, cone clutch, bevel drive, disc wheels and a bull-nose radiator. This was joined a year later by the 1½-litre SBD type with thermo-syphon cooling and separate gearbox. The big OBD had acquired front-wheel brakes by 1923, but by 1926, when it had been discontinued, the smaller models still had brakes on the rear wheels only. These were not listed with fwb until 1928. Two years later the firm were making light commercials only, still on the same chassis.   MCS

GEORGES VILLE (F) *1904–c.1909*

Sté d'Industrie Mécanique, Paris 13e

Georges Ville's cars were mainly intended for town use, and some models had frames specially curved at the rear to allow for low-entrance brougham bodies. When introduced in 1904 they had 15 or 30hp 4-cylinder engines which were said to be so flexible that only 2 speeds were necessary. Reverse was by a separate epicyclic gear. Ville was a designer rather than a manufacturer, and many of his parts were made by other firms, mainly Morane. The English Crosville cars were designed by George Ville.   GNG

G.E.P. (F) *1913–1914*

Automobiles G.E.P., Gennevilliers, Seine

The G.E.P. used friction transmission and chain final drive on all models. It was available with an 8hp single-cylinder engine, a 10hp twin, and a 10hp four, the last engine being made by Ballot. It was announced that the make would be revived after the war, but nothing came of this.   GNG

GERALD (GB) *1920*

Gerald Cyclecar Co, Birmingham

The Gerald was fitted with an 8hp water-cooled J.A.P. engine, modified by D.G. Taylor, and arranged lengthways in the frame on two tubular cross members. Transmission was by chain to a countershaft and thence by central belt to a solid rear axle.   MJWW

1935 GEORGES IRAT 1,100cc sports car. *Autocar*

1920 GEORGES ROY 18hp tourer. *Autocar*

1904 GEORGES VILLE 30hp tonneau. *Geoffroy de Beauffort Collection*

1900 GERMAIN 10hp limousine. *G.N. Georgano*

1913 GERMAIN 20hp saloon. *Geoffroy de Beauffort Collection*

1972 GIANNINI Sirio 650cc two-seater.
Giannini Auto SpA

GÉRARD (F) *1927*

Automobiles Gérard, Clichy, Seine

The Gérard was a conventional light car powered by an sv 1½-litre S.C.A.
engine, and using a 4-speed gearbox.   GN

GERMAIN (B) *1897–1914*

SA des Ateliers Germain, Monceau-sur-Sambre

The first cars to emerge from the Germain factory were German Phoenix
Daimlers built under licence; hence their name Daimler-Belge. Up to 1903, 2- and 4-
cylinder models were offered, on Daimler and then on the very similar Panhard
lines; in fact the 1901 cars were now described as 'improved Panhards'. The first
home-grown design was the 15/18hp of 1903, which like all Germains to come was a
beautifully-made machine with above average performance. The L-head, 4-cylinder
engine had dual ignition and, unusual in Belgian cars at the time, a 4-speed gearbox.
The 1904 cars had pressed-steel chassis and in 1906 the shallow oval radiator
was adopted. The best-known Germain appeared in 1905: the 14/22hp Chainless,
so called because it had a live axle instead of chain drive. A fine 22hp six with
ball-bearing crankshaft was listed for 1907. The new cars for 1912 included a
20hp with a Knight double-sleeve-valve engine, and a most exciting 15hp with
chain-driven overhead camshaft neatly enclosed. All had full pressure lubrication.
World War 1 and occupation by the Germans stopped production, which was never
resumed.   TR

GERMAN-AMERICAN (US) *1902*

German-American Automobile Co, New York, N.Y.

This company announced a 24hp 4-cylinder car which, it was said, 'closely
followed the general lines of the Daimler (i.e.: Mercedes), but incorporated some
novel features to make the car more suitable for American roads'.   GN

GERONIMO (US) *1917–1920*

Geronimo Motor Co, Enid, Okla.

Named after the famous Red Indian chief, the Geronimo began its existence as
a 4-cylinder assembled car, but changed its power plant to a 6-cylinder Lycoming
engine in 1918. Less than 1,000 were built, and only open models were available.
                                                                          KM

GHENT (US) *1917–1918*

Ghent Motor Co, Ottawa, Ill.

This was an assembled car without distinguishing features, on a 10ft 5in wheelbase. The Model 6-60 was a five-seater with a 5-litre 6-cylinder engine.   GMN

GIANNINI (I) *1963 to date*

Giannini Automobili SpA, Rome

Established in 1920, Giannini have been selling tuned and customized Fiats on
a commercial scale since 1963, their 1972 programme embracing special 500s, 127s
and 128s: the fiercest version of this last offered 106mph from 82bhp. Alongside
these have been some more original creations. In 1963 there was a 600-based sports
coupé with 850cc 52bhp engine, replaced in 1965 by a Vignale-bodied 930cc 850-
derivative. In the same year they devised a 698cc flat-4 from two destroked 500
blocks and fitted it to a modified 500 berlina. The 1967 cars ranged from an experimental electric conversion of the 500 to a formidable power plant for 850s in
the shape of a small alloy V-8 offered in 985cc and 1,595cc sizes, the latter developing 170bhp. None of these reached production and a year later Giannini were
listing a 994cc 104bhp dohc in-line four of Abarth type. In 1972 there was the
Sirio, a 652cc, 500-based fibreglass sports cabriolet capable of 99mph.   MCS

GIAUR (I) *1950–1954*

Officina Meccanica Berardo Taraschi, Teramo

The Giaur, whose name derives from a combination of Giannini and Urania, was
one of the small-capacity Italian competition cars built around Fiat suspension and
engine parts. Domenico Giannini, an *amelioratore* of Fiats since the 1920s and a
noted engine expert, produced the 750cc ohv engine for the first Giaur, while the
chassis was based on that of the Urania 750cc car, successfully raced by Berardo
Taraschi of Teramo since 1947. The marque Giaur was particularly successful in
Italian national 750cc races, driven by Sesto Leonardi, who won the 750cc class
in the Mille Miglia four times. Giaur later built a 500cc single-seater racing
car for Formula 3, using a linered-down Fiat 570cc Topolino 4-cylinder water-
cooled engine, and shaft drive, but it could not match the pace of the simpler, lighter
nimbler British 500s with racing motor-cycle engines at the rear.   CP

GIBBONS (GB) *1921–1926*

Gibbons & Moore, Chadwell Heath, Essex

The Gibbons was one of that strange race of cars, which included the Cricket
and the Gordon (iii), which carried their engine on the offside of the body. In the
case of the Gibbons, three kinds of engine were offered: a 349cc Precision single-
cylinder, a 488cc Blackburne single-cylinder, or a 688cc Coventry-Victor 2-cylinder.
The last of these seems to have been the most popular on the few Gibbons sold.
There were two speeds and drive was by by belt – high ratio to the nearside rear

heel, low to the offside. The two-seater body (tandem on the smallest model) was made of three-ply wood.   GNG

GIBSON (US) *1899*
.D.P. Gibson, Jersey City, N.J.
The Gibson was powered by a horizontal 2-cylinder engine designed to run on arbonic acid gas which was stored in batteries at a pressure of 6,000psi. It was aid to develop 12bhp at 500rpm, and to have a maximum speed of 60mph, which ould have almost gained it the Land Speed Record in 1899! There were plans to orm a syndicate to manufacture it, but they came to nothing.   GNG

GIDEON (DK) *1913–1920*
. Kramper & Jørgensen, Horsens
Rudolf Kramper produced stationary engines from 1895. The Gideon cars were ntirely Danish except for the Bosch magneto. A 4-cylinder sv engine developing .7hp with each cylinder mounted separately on the aluminium crankcase, was used or private cars. For trucks and fire engines a 3.9-litre sv and a 5.5-litre ohv engine vere used, both of them fours having automatic carburettors. The total output was 29 vehicles. They were all very reliable and Gideon fire engines were in use until a ew years ago. The firm was liquidated in 1920, but a few years later it started up gain, going into tool production.   TRA

GIESBERGER (F) *1921*
The Giesberger was a gyroscope-balanced 2-wheeled car. It had a 4-cylinder ngine, 3-speed gearbox and double shaft drive. The radiator was a curious double arrangement mounted on each side of the front wheel. Although hardly a serious roduction car, the Giesberger was shown at the 1921 Paris Salon.   GNG

GIGNOUX (F) *1907*
. Gignoux, Lyons
Gignoux was a maker of motor cycles who assembled a few 4-cylinder cars, robably less than 10.   GNG

GILBERN (GB) *1959 to date*
Gilbern Sports Cars (Components) Ltd, Llantwit, Pontypridd, Glamorgan
In the early 1960s there was a gap in the British market for a moderately priced GT four-seater, into which the little Welsh car successfully insinuated itself. Giles mith and Bernard Friese had graduated from building specials to marketing omplete cars – frequently in kit form to beat the tax impost. A multi-tubular square ection chassis was employed, with B.M.C. running gear. An attractive fibreglass ody, of a higher standard than was then usual, helped sales. Engines at first were Coventry-Climax 1,098cc, B.M.C. 'A' or B.M.C. 'B' units. The M.G.A. (B.M.C. 'B') ngine was standardized for 1962, and from 1963 onwards the M.G.B. unit was used. rom 1966 a larger model, the Genie, was also offered, utilizing 2,495cc or 2,994cc ord V-6 engines, still with B.M.C. chassis components. Total production of the riginal model had by early 1966 exceeded 500.
In 1969 the much-improved Invader, still with V-6 Ford engine, replaced the Genie, and from 1971 the Mark 2 version became available also in estate-car form. The factory was expanded to meet the hoped-for demand for the wider and lower Mark 3, introduced in September 1972, incorporating a revised box-section frame, Cortina front suspension, Taunus rear axle and a 3-litre Ford engine developing 140bhp at a price of £2,493   DF

GILBERT (GB) *1901*
Ralph Gilbert & Son, Birmingham
The Gilbert used a single-cylinder horizontal engine of 3½hp and chain drive. The engine was a 2-stroke of Gilbert's own design, and could run on either paraffin or etrol.   GNG

GILBURT (GB) *1904–1906*
Gilburt Motor Car Co Ltd, West Kilburn, London N.W.
The Gilburt light car used a 6½hp 2-cylinder Fafnir engine mounted transversely, with chain drive to the gearbox and from there to the rear axle. A differential was mounted in the offside hub. Two- or three-seater bodies were available.   GNG

GILCHRIST (GB) *1920–1923*
Gilchrist Cars Ltd, Govan, Glasgow
The Gilchrist was a conventional light car using an ohv version of the 11.9hp Hotchkiss engine supplied to Morris. Open and closed bodies by Sims & Wilson of Cathcart were listed, but competition from Morris was too great, and only about 20 Gilchrists were made.   GNG

GILDA (RYCSA) (RA) *1957*
Rosati y Christoforo, Buenos Aires
A water-cooled V-4 engine of 57bhp at 3,900rpm drove this six-seater 2-door sedan at 70mph. Designed by Giovanni Rossi, who had been with Fiat, the car was assembled mainly from sub-contracted parts. It was also available as a pickup. BE

1952 GIAUR 750cc Mille Miglia sports car.
Associated Press Ltd

1964 GILBERN GT 1.8-litre coupé. *Gilbern Sports Cars Ltd*

1973 GILBERN Invader Mark III 3-litre coupé.
Gilbern Cars Ltd

1902 GILLET-FOREST 7hp two-seater.
G.N. Georgano

1926 GILLETT 8hp two-seater. *Autocar*

1962 GINETTA G4 997cc coupé. *Ginetta Cars Ltd*

GILL (GB) *1958*

Gill Getabout Cars Ltd, London W.1

The Gill Getabout was identical to the Astra (iv), except that it had a two-seate coupé body. A four-seater version was intended to be used as a taxi, but neithe progressed much beyond the prototype stage.   GN

GILLET-FOREST (F) *1900–1907*

Sté Gillet-Forest, St Cloud, Seine

Early Gillet-Forest cars could easily be recognized by the large, curved gilled tube radiator which looked rather like the condenser of a steam car. In fact it did ac as a condenser for the steam given off by the water jacket; this was perhaps the onl water-cooled car which was intended to boil! The condensed water returned to th cylinder head, while any surplus went to a tank at the rear of the car. The first Gille Forest had a horizontal single-cylinder engine of 5hp, and shaft drive. This wa supplemented in 1902 by a 9/10hp and a 12hp, still with a single-cylinder horizonta engine. For the 1905 season the cars became quite conventional. The horizonta engine was abandoned except for commercial vehicles, and instead a range of verti cal engines made under Métallurgique licence was offered. These were 8 and 12hp 2 cylinders, and 16, 24, 30 and 40hp 4-cylinders, with chain drive on the two larges models. The condenser radiator was replaced by an ordinary honeycomb type. GN

GILLETT (GB) *1926–1927*

British Ensign Motors Ltd, Willesden, London N.W.10

A product of the firm who had made the massive and old-fashioned British Ensig car, the Gillett was one of a crop of £100 cars which made a brief appearance at th end of the 1920s. It had an 8hp 4-cylinder ohv engine, shaft drive, electric lightin and starting, and accommodation for two adults and two children. Thus it was in n way a crude cyclecar, but it sold no better than the other £100 cars, the Century the Seaton-Petter or the rear-engined Waverley. Only 25 Gilletts were made.   GN

GILLETTE *see* AMPLEX

GILSON (CDN) *1921*

Gilson Mfg Co, Guelph, Ont.

The Gilson company were manufacturers of stationary engines, tractors and agri cultural machinery. Some of the tractor components were used in attempts at initia construction of three touring cars. Only two of the small 4-cylinder units wer ever completed.   G

GILYARD (GB) *1912–1916*

Barkerend Engineering Co, Bradford, Yorks.

The Gilyard cyclecar used an 8hp 2-cylinder Chater-Lea engine and chain drive The price was £100.   GN

GINETTA (GB) *1957 to date*

(1) Walklett Bros, Woodbridge, Suffolk *1957–1962*
(2) Ginetta Cars Ltd, Witham, Essex *1962–1972*
(3) Ennerdale Racing, Canterbury, Kent *1970–1971*
(4) Ginetta Cars Ltd, Sudbury, Suffolk *1972 to date*

The G2 was the initial Ginetta production model, based on a multi-tubular fram and offered as a kit for Ford components. In 1959 the G3 was introduced, and pro duction surpassed 100 in 1960. The G4 followed in 1961, with coil spring/dampe units, fibreglass GT body and a Ford 105E engine. This model achieved numerou competition successes, and some 350 had been sold by the end of 1966. Other model included the G10 and G11 fibreglass coupés, for Ford V-8 and M.G.B. engines re spectively, and the rear-engined G12 Competition GT, with a 5-speed Hewland gear box. This model gained many class successes on the circuits with Ford 105E-base engines. New for 1968 was the Hillman Imp-engined G15 coupé, and this mode became the company's mainstay. In the small Modsports racing category, Barr Wood took the 1972 Championship, and Brian Tavender gained the 1971 Sprin Championship. The G16 was a competition GT model, G17 a Formula 4 car an G18 the Formula Ford type later produced at Canterbury. It was hoped to begi production of the attractive G21 road coupé after a move to larger premises i 1972. This model was available with 1600 or 3-litre Ford or 1725 Rapier engine. DF

GIRARDOT *see* G.E.M.

GIRLING (GB) *1913–1914*

Girling Motor Ltd, Bedford

A 3-wheeled cyclecar with a continuously variable ratio gearbox was manufac tured in 1913–14. Other features, including a third seat over the rear wheel, detach able spare wheel and tiller steering, were fitted to make this an attractive car. I was powered by a 6hp single-cylinder air-cooled engine.   G

GITANE (GB) *1962*

G.F. Plant Ltd, Wolverhampton, Staffs.

An ambitious 2-seater GT with rear engine, the Gitane employed a square section tubular space frame. Disc brakes (on all wheels) were fitted inboard of the ub carriers. At one time there were plans to develop the Italian Giannini engine, ut in the event B.M.C. Mini components were predominant, and the price was too gh for any market impact. DF

.J.G. (US) *1909–1911*
.J.G. Motor Car Co, White Plains, N.Y.

The various models of the G.J.G. had imaginative names such as Scout, Pirate, omfort and Carryall. With 4-cylinder, 5.8-litre engines and 3-speed selective ansmissions, it was claimed these cars could attain 65mph. G.J.G. bonnets had peculiar 'cupola' running the full length. The designer was G.J. Grossman. GMN

GLADIATOR (F) *1896–1920*
1) Société Gladiator, Pré-St Gervais *1896–1909*
2) Société Gladiator, Puteaux, Seine *1910–1920*

The original Gladiator firm was founded by Aucoc and Darracq in 1891 to make ycles, but was bought out in 1896 by a British group with which Harvey Du Cros as concerned. This new group proceeded to amalgamate with Clément, from which oncern Adolphe Clément himself subsequently resigned in order to launch the lément-Bayard business; to complicate matters, the Clément-Gladiator combine lso made Clément cars which were of very similar design to their Gladiators. Gladiator's first car was a simple little voiturette of 4hp with a single-cylinder orizontal engine mounted in a tubular frame, cycle-type wire wheels, and handlebar teering, but by 1899 the firm were making $2\frac{1}{2}$ and $3\frac{1}{2}$hp Aster-engined machines with ansversely-mounted power units at the front, wheel steering, and pedal control for he 2-speed gear. Final drive was by chain, and the make was introduced to England y S.F. Edge's Motor Power Co, who marketed it at £118.15s in 1900. Edge con- nued to sponsor the Gladiator until his preoccupation with Napier affairs caused im to discard both this make and the Regent. A more conventional $6\frac{1}{2}$hp single, till Aster-powered, was available in 1901, in which year an 18hp 4-cylinder racing oiturette contested the Paris-Berlin: almost the last serious competition attempt y Gladiator, though a single-cylinder chain-driven voiturette ran in *L'Auto*'s first ght-car race in 1905, and cars also started in the early Tourist Trophies. Late in 901 came a conventional 12hp car with armoured wood frame, side-chain drive, and vertical-twin aiv Aster engine, selling for £395. A wide range, from a $3\frac{1}{2}$hp quad o 4-cylinder types, was available in 1902, and a Mercédès style of bonnet was ound on the 2.2-litre twin in 1903, though it still housed a tubular cooler. The ttle 6hp was rather expensive at £300 in England. 4-cylinder models were available oth in 2.1-litre and 2.7-litre forms, with engines said to be made by Gladiator hemselves: the bigger 16hp had mechanically-operated side valves and only a single amshaft. Mechanically-operated valves were found on all models save the 12hp win in 1904, and it was hard to sort out the Cléments from the Gladiators, though he former were turning to bevel drive while the latter adhered to chains. A 4-litre 8hp 4-cylinder with ht magneto was listed in 1905, but smaller cars, including nother four of 3 litres' capacity, continued to use Aster units, and at the bottom of he range was a very archaic 9hp 1.7-litre, still with automatic inlet valve, rear- mounted water tank, and sprag.

All the models of a very complicated 1906 range now had mechanically-operated alves, the 12/14hp 4-cylinder had shaft drive in conjunction with a 4-speed gearbox, nd frames could be of either armoured wood or pressed steel, though the latter ariant was found in the English catalogue, but not the French one! The largest four was of 4.8 litres, but during the year a chain-driven 5.5-litre 38bhp six made its ppearance. Magneto ignition was standard in 1907, and for 1908 it was announced hat certain Gladiator models were to be built in England by Austin (i). How many were actually made is problematic, but the 1908 and 1909 catalogues showed three nominally British types, the 18/24hp and 40hp 4-cylinder, and the 60hp 6-cylinder, which were uncommonly like their Austin counterparts. (Swift, in which Harvey du Cros had an interest as well, were making Cléments at the same time in Coventry!) On top of these variants, Pré-St Gervais offered 4-cylinder cars of 2.2, 3.7, 4.8, 5.8 and 6.3 litres. The smallest of these, rated at 12/14hp, marked a reversion to the L-head configuration and had shaft drive, but all the others were chain-driven T-headers on traditional lines. In 1909 Vinot et Deguingand acquired Gladiator, and production was transferred to Puteaux. All that in fact happened was that Gladiator now had another *alter ego*: the cars looked like Vinots, shared the Vinot's technical specification, and even their prices, though there were no 6-cylinder 'Vinot' Gladia- tors, chain drive was not offered after 1910 except on cars bearing the Vinot name, and it was announced in 1911 that Gladiators were not to share the vertical gate change. However, as a result of the new association the 1912 Type-AL Gladiator (a designation shared with Vinot) came out with a monobloc engine and pressure lubrication. 1914 models were, understandably, 4-cylinder machines with capacities of 1.7 litres, 2.2 litres, 2.7 litres, and 4.1 litres, and both the 12hp and the long- stroke 15/20hp were once again offered in 1919–20, the former costing £785 in England. After this, however, Vinot could no longer afford the luxury of a dual personality. MCS

GLAS (D) *1955–1968*
Hans Glas GmbH, Isaria Maschinenfabrik, Dingolfing

An old-established manufacturer of agricultural machinery, Glas started

1968 GINETTA G15 875cc coupé. *Ginetta Cars Ltd*

1900 GLADIATOR 3hp voiturette. *The Veteran Car Club of Great Britain*

1903 GLADIATOR 10hp tonneau. *National Motor Museum*

1957 GLAS Goggomobil 250 saloon. *Hans Glas GmbH*

1966 GLAS 2600 V-8 coupé. *Hans Glas GmbH*

1972 GLASSIC roadster. *Glassic Industries Inc.*

production of the Goggo, the German-designed scooter, in 1951. The Goggomob small cars were built from 1955 and were available with 250cc, 300cc and 400cc 2 cylinder 2-stroke engines, mounted in the rear. In 1958 the larger Isar model appeare with 600cc and 700cc front-mounted 2-cylinder 4-stroke engines. Since 1961 a rang of cars characterized by 4-cylinder 4-stroke engines with 5-bearing crankshafts an overhead camshafts with cogged belt-drive has been offered: the '1004' (993cc '1204' (1,189cc), '1304' (1,289cc) and '1700' (1,682cc), all available with differen engine outputs. Models 1300 GT and 1700 GT were two-seater sports versions wit twin-carburettor engines developing 75bhp and 100bhp respectively. In 1965 th '2600' was introduced with a 2.6-litre V-8 engine of 140bhp and a Frua-designe body.

The Goggomobils were phased out during 1966 after some 250,000 had bee built. B.M.W.'s acquisition of Glas in 1967 led at first to a rationalization (1700 and V-8s were sold under the B.M.W. name) and ultimately to the disappearanc of the marque.

From 1962 to 1966 Goggomobil saloons and commercial vehicles were built i Spain by Munguia Industrial SA of Bilbao.   HO

GLASSIC (US) *1966 to date*
Glassic Industries Inc, West Palm Beach, Fla.

Styled in the manner of 1931 Model A Ford roadsters or phaetons, Glassic use fibreglass coachwork and the chassis of the 4 × 2 International (iii) Scout Early versions had International's 93bhp 4-cylinder engine and 3-speed synchro mesh gearbox, but since 1972 the standard power unit has been a 4,950cc For V-8 with Ford-built manual or automatic transmission, and hypoid rear axle. Th 1973 list price was $6,995.   B

GLEASON (US) *1909–1914*
Kansas City Vehicle Co, Kansas City, Mo.

The Gleason, which succeeded the Kansas City (i), was a high-wheeler, althoug later models used pneumatic tyres. Two-cylinder, water-cooled engines were used and final drive was by shaft.   GM

GLEN (CDN) *1921*
Scarboro Beach, Ont.

The Glen was an odd-looking air-cooled 3-cylinder cyclecar that resembled scaled-down American Essex with a kennel-shaped bonnet and a Rolls-Royce styl of radiator. Passengers sat side by side in the plywood body.   R.

GLIDE (US) *1903–1920*
The Bartholomew Co, Peoria, Ill.

Also known as the Bartholomew, the first Glide had an 8hp single-cylinder engin mounted horizontally under the seat, and single chain drive. Similar to the earl Cadillac in appearance, it was made until 1907, by which time it had been joine by a 14hp 2-cylinder horizontal model, and a 30hp 4-cylinder vertical model wit shaft drive. The latter had a Rutenber engine, and this make was used in all 4- an 6-cylinder Glides until the end of production. Touring and roadster bodies wer available, including a four-seater roadster on a short wheelbase. From 1915 to th end of production, Glide used a 40hp 6-cylinder Rutenber engine, and was conventional design.   GN

GLISENTI (I) *1900*
Ditta Glisenti, Brescia

A well-known ordnance works which turned out a few 3hp light cars with Ber nardi engines.   MC

GLOBE (i) (GB) *1904–1907*
Hitchon Gear & Automobile Co Ltd, Accrington. Lancs.

This car is sometimes known as the Hitchon-Weller, as an original partner wa John Weller who had made the Weller car at West Norwood. Two models wer made, one with a 9hp single-cylinder engine designed by Alfred Hitchon whic incorporated a variable-lift inlet valve, and the other with a 12hp 4-cylinder Whit & Poppe engine. Both models used the Hitchon free-wheel, and a worm-drive back axle. About twelve examples of each model were made.   GN

GLOBE (ii) (GB) *1913–1916*
Tuke & Bell Ltd, Tottenham, London N.

The Globe cyclecar was designed by an Englishman, J.H. Forster, and built i France by F. Terrier et Cie (Sphinx-Globe), and in England by sanitary engineers Tuke & Bell Ltd. Anzani or Aster single-cylinder engines or J.A.P. 2-cylinde engines were used, and the cars had belt or chain final drive.   GN

GLOBE (iii) (US) *1921–1922*
Globe Motors Co, Cleveland, Ohio

The Globe was a conventional assembled car powered by an 18.2hp 4-cylinde Supreme engine, and using a Warren 3-speed gearbox. Body styles were a five seater tourer or two-seater roadster.   GN

GLORIETTE (A) *1932–1936*
Hans Pitzek, Vienna

The Gloriette was a small car of advanced design. The engine was a 2-cylinder 495cc unit developing 20bhp. Central tubular frame and swing axles were other features. Production was on a small scale only.   HON

GLOVER (i) (GB) *1912–1913*
Glover Bros, Coventry, Warwickshire

This was an ultra-light cyclecar with a 4¼hp single-cylinder Precision engine, belt drive and a wooden frame. Only nine were made.   GNG

GLOVER (ii) (GB/US) *1920–1921*
Glovers Motors Ltd, Leeds, Yorks.

Like the Alsace, Amco and others, the Glover was an American-assembled car intended for export to England. In this case the design also was English; it had a 15.7hp 4-cylinder engine, 3-speed gearbox and a two-seater body with a dickey seat. The radiator was of Rolls-Royce pattern, and the car was intended to sell at £550.   GNG

G.M. (F) *1924–1928*
Gendron et Cie, Paris 17e

The Gendron was a light car made in 1,100 and 1,500cc versions using C.I.M.E. engines. Sports models competed at Le Mans in 1925. The most unusual feature of the design was that the brakes operated on the front wheels and on the transmission, but not on the rear wheels. This system was also used on some Chenard-Walcker models.   GNG

GMUR (CH) *1914*
Gmur et Cie, Schänis

This company made a few heavy electric cars, using their own make of motor and chain final drive.   GNG

G.N. (i) (GB) *1910–1925*
(1) G.N. Ltd, Hendon, Middlesex *1910–1920*
(2) G.N. Motors Ltd, Wandsworth, London S.W. *1920–1923*
(3) G.N. Ltd, Wandsworth, London S.W. *1923–1925*

The G.N. was the best-known and longest-lived of the British cyclecars; the vehicles that provided the earliest form of motoring for the masses. H.R. Godfrey and A. Frazer-Nash installed air-cooled 1,100 V-twin engines of J.A.P. and Antoine manufacture in the prototypes. By 1911 G.N. were manufacturing their own 90° V-twin using in that year Peugeot cylinder barrels and in 1912 their own oe design cylinder heads. The pre-World War 1 cars used a variety of transmissions incorporating belts and chains. Production at Hendon was low, not exceeding two cars a week. After the war the British Grégoire works at Wandsworth were taken over, and the car was redesigned. A steel chassis replaced the original ash, a conventional steering box replaced the wire and bobbin, and the final drive was by chains rather than by belts. Though high-geared, the steering was extremely light, road-holding was excellent, and the complete car weighed very little – 6½cwt for the basic 2-seater Popular of 1920. In conjunction with reasonable power and good low-speed torque, this recipe gave a sporting performance, simplicity and economy, and attracted many sportsmen. These were catered for by the Légère, a tuned model, and the Vitesse, a still faster car with chain-driven ohc.

Some 50 G.N.s were being made per week in 1920 and 1921. Further developed, the Vitesse became a really powerful little racing car, with shaft-driven overhead camshafts operating very large inclined valves. In 1922 Godfrey and Frazer-Nash left the firm. By 1923 the family motorist had abandoned the cyclecar in favour of the comforts of the light car, so G.N. Ltd began to build this type alongside the old. Shaft-driven chassis were made, powered either by the twin, in smoother, quieter and less potent form, or by water-cooled 4-cylinder units; DFP, Chapuis-Dornier and Anzani were used. Very few were in fact produced. The cyclecar and the G.N. name disappeared, but G.N. carried on in theory until 1929; in 1926 the firm re-issued an instruction book. G.N. Ltd still survives as a Vauxhall agent in Balham.

G.N.s were made and sold in France by the Salmson aero engine company between 1919 and 1922.   TRN

G.N. (ii) (GB) *1912*
F.W. Berwick & Co Ltd, London W.

Little is known about this car, said to be 'of entirely British origin', and sold by F.W. Berwick & Company who afterwards were concerned in the Sizaire-Berwick. The G.N. had a large 4-cylinder engine of 3,308cc, front-mounted flywheel, 4-speed gearbox and overhead worm drive. The chassis was fully described in *The Autocar*, but there seems to be no subsequent trace. It may well have been an imported car with which Berwick did not proceed.   GNG

GNESUTTA (I) *1900*
Officine Meccaniche E.Gnesutta, Milan

The prototype Gnesutta was the work of Adolfo Schlegel. Its 2-cylinder Welleyes

1904 GLOBE(i) 12hp tourer. *National Motor Museum*

1924 G.M. 1.2-litre saloon. *Musée de l'Automobile. Le Mans*

1921 G.N.(i) Legère 1,100cc two-seater. *David Thirlby Collection*

1925 GNOME(ii) 343cc two-seater. *Autocar*

1904 GOBRON-BRILLIÉ 25hp tonneau. *G.N.*
Georgano Collection

1909 GOBRON 50hp roadster. *The Veteran Car*
Club of Great Britain

1913 GOBRON 20hp sporting tourer. Coachwork by Rothschild. *Autocar*

engine was designed by Aristide Faccioli and was virtually identical to that used in the original Tipo-A F.I.A.T. Production was planned, but it never materialized.

MC

G.N.L. *see* NEWEY

GNOM (CS) *1921*
Kleinautowerk Fritz Hückel, Nový Jičín

Hückel, who inspired the first 6-cylinder Nesselsdorf and raced Tatras as an amateur, started manufacture on his own account in 1921, producing his Gnom cyclecars in small numbers. They were successful in various national race events. In 1935 he introduced the Hückel Special, with a 6-cylinder Tatra engine, but it did not go into production.

HO

GNOME (i) *see* GRACILE

GNOME (ii): NOMAD (GB) *1925–1926*
(1) Gnome Cars, London S.W.6 *1925–1926*
(2) Nomad Cars Ltd, London S.W.6 *1926*

The weird little Gnome or Nomad was totally unsprung, the comfort of its passengers depending entirely upon balloon tyres at the very low pressure of 6lb per square inch. The body and chassis were of integral construction, in steel and plywood. The power unit was a Villiers single-cylinder air-cooled 2-stroke of a mere 343cc, with friction disc and single chain drive. The Gnome was a fatal reversion to the cyclecar of a few years before which had been too crude to survive the arrival of the good, cheap, comfortable light car, and it suffered the same fate.

TR

GNOME ET RHÔNE (F) *1919*
Sté des Moteurs Gnome et Rhône, Paris

This was a high-quality car built by the well-known firm of aircraft engine makers. It had a 40hp 6-cylinder single ohc engine and 4-wheel brakes, and had the makers continued with the project it might have rivalled the Hispano-Suiza. However, only three cars were made.

GNC

GOBRON-BRILLIÉ: GOBRON (F) *1898–1930*
(1) Sté Gobron-Brillié, Boulogne-sur-Seine *1898–1918*
(2) Automobiles Gobron, Levallois-Perret *1919–1930*

These cars should strictly be designated Gobron from 1903, when Eugene Brillié severed his connection with Gustave Gobron and went to work with the Ateliers Schneider at Havre, mainly on commercial vehicles. Generally speaking, however, they were known as Gobron-Brilliés up to World War 1, and (invariably) as Gobrons after 1918. The keynote of a design that claimed to be 'the first car driven by a petrol motor which is absolutely free from vibration' was the opposed-piston configuration. In this the cylinders were normally cast in pairs with four pistons per pair, the lower ones direct-coupled by normal connecting-rods to a common crankpin, and the upper ones coupled to a cross-head, from each end of which tubular connecting-rods gave motion to crank throws opposed at 180° to the rods actuated by the lower pistons. A similar idea was adopted by Arrol-Johnston in Scotland, while the layout was revived in the 1950s on the Commer TS3 2-stroke diesel engine. Gobrons continued to have two pistons per cylinder up to 1922. The earliest examples had 'square' vertical 2-cylinder engines developing 6bhp and mounted either amidships or at the rear of the tubular frame, with chain drive, wheel steering and solid tyres. An ingenious metering device consisting of 'an intermittently rotating cone with recesses each sufficient for fuel for each intake stroke of the engine' was used in place of a carburettor until 1903, and the Gobron-Brillié was claimed to be a multi-fuel unit. It certainly ran happily on alcohol, as witness its good performance in the Concours du Ministre of 1902, but there is no evidence to support the 1901 catalogue's assertion that it would perform with equal felicity on 'gin, brandy, or whisky'. Cars were sold in England in 1900 under the name of Teras. The Belgian Nagant company entered the motor industry *via* licence-production of the Gobron-Brillié, and the Nancéenne made at the turn of the century was really a Gobron under another name. By 1901 front-mounted engines and variable-ratio steering featured on some Gobron-Brillié models, which now gave 10hp and cost £272. There were two gear levers, one for forward-and-reverse and the other for selection of ratio. Bigger models retained the central engine location and 'chainless' types were also listed for a short while.

In 1901 a Gobron-Brillié took part in the Paris-Berlin race and the company's light cars did quite well in the Paris-Vienna the following year. By 1903 all cars were front-engined and 30hp 4-cylinder models were listed: buyers had the choice of ignition by low-tension magneto, coil, or even tube. A great step forward was taken with Rigolly's 110hp racer which did 83.47mph at Ostend that summer, raised this to 84.73mph at Dourdan in November and swept the board at the 1904 Nice Speed Trials. This car retained the tubular chassis, but the 13½-litre 4-cylinder engine had mechanically-operated side valves in an L-head and a conventional carburettor. Though it became the first car officially to exceed 100mph with a speed of 103.55mph in July, 1904, it never achieved much in circuit racing, this despite appearances in the 1904 and 1905 French Gordon Bennett Eliminating Trials, and in the Grands Prix of 1906 and 1907. However, it paved the way for improved touring Gobron-Brilliés

hich in 1904 had pressed-steel frames, T-head engines, spray carburettors, high-
nsion magneto ignition, single-lever change and Mercedes-type radiators. Tubular
olers were back again by 1906, but the single-camshaft had arrived for good
n the 7.6-litre '40/60', a chain-driven monster with gate change, double-cone
utch and twin transmission brakes, which cost £1,100 and could do 70mph. Both
ate change and L-head engines were standard practice in 1907. In 1908 came a
odest 15/20hp 4-cylinder and a 6-cylinder 70/90hp, a vehicle which is not quite
redible even when viewed in the metal. A chassis alone cost £1,600. A 2.3-litre
xicab chassis with shaft drive was listed in 1909, and a year later a 12/16hp 2-
ylinder model could be bought for £300. This was the smallest model available in
911. Others included a 2.7-litre 4-cylinder with pressure lubrication and 4-speed
earbox at £395, a bigger 20/30hp shaft-driven car and two large chain-driven fours,
he old '40/60' and a powerful ioe 50hp with 250mm stroke at £960. The smaller cars
till had simple cone clutches, but though worm drive was adopted in 1915, there
ere still some very large Gobrons listed with chain drive as late as 1914.

The Gobron story after 1918 is typical of many a French firm, though there was
ne final essay in the magnificent, the fearsome 25CV of 1922. This was the last of
he opposed-piston Gobrons and it had the additional complications of sleeve valves
nd a camshaft brake, and three carburettors. Fwb were provided, there was a
andsome V-radiator and the wheelbase was a fraction under 13ft. A year later all
his had been swept away in favour of a conventional 1½-litre car with ohv Chapuis-
Dornier engine, coil ignition, 4-speed gearbox, and a single-disc clutch which had
everted to a magneto by 1925. Sales were poor, even when the cars were also
marketed under the name of Stabilia (this company was also in trouble). Gobron,
owever, made a brave exit with the Type CA 4 'Turbo-Sport' of 1928. Largely the
ork of M. Chabreiron of E.H.P., this had an ordinary enough 1½-litre sv power
nit, but with the aid of a Cozette supercharger it was persuaded to give 88bhp and
06mph. Very few were made – reputedly only two out of a preliminary batch of
ix laid down.   MCS

1923 GOBRON 10hp tourer. *Ivan Mahy
Collection*

GODIVA (GB) 1900–1901
ayne & Bates Ltd, Coventry, Warwickshire
Payne & Bates were gas engine manufacturers who made a number of experimental cars, and a small series which they sold to R.M. Wright of Lincoln who
marketed them under the name Stonebow. These had a 9hp 2-cylinder front-
mounted engine, double chain drive, and a four-seater *dos-à-dos* body. The only
urviving Godiva car is similar to the Stonebows, but has artillery wheels in place
of the wire wheels of the latter. In 1901 Payne & Bates were advertising cars of
7, 9, 14 and 25hp, with 2- and 4-cylinder engines.   GNG

GOGGOMOBIL see GLAS

GOLDEN GATE (US) 1894–1895
A. Schilling & Sons, San Francisco, Calif.
This company was well known for its Golden Gate gas engines. In 1894 a 3-
wheeled, two-seater car with 2hp engine was sold to a customer in Santa Maria.
This was probably the first petrol car built for sale in California.   GNG

GOLDSCHMIDT-DIRECT see DIRECT

GOLIATH (D) 1931–1963
(1) Hansa-Lloyd & Goliath-Werke; Borgward & Tecklenborg; Bremen 1931–1933
(2) Goliath-Werke GmbH, Bremen 1950–1959
Though a 4-wheeled prototype cyclecar was built in 1924, the first Goliath motor
vehicles were 3- and 4-wheeled vans. In 1931 a 3-wheeled private car, the Pionier,
was introduced. It had two driven rear wheels, a two-seater body and a single-
cylinder 2-stroke 198cc Ilo engine. It was produced until 1933, after which Goliath
concentrated on vans again.
In 1950 a new private car appeared, the Goliath GP 700 with a 2-cylinder 2-stroke
688cc engine. It was followed by the 886cc GP 900 and both models were available with fuel injection. Two-seater sports coupé versions of these cars were also
offered but only built in small numbers. A 4-stroke flat-4 engine was used from 1957
in the '1100'. This model, like the earlier '700' and '900', had front-wheel drive.
After 1958 it was marketed as the Hansa 1100. It was available with a 40bhp engine
unit and also with a twin-carburettor engine of 55bhp. There were also some 4-wheel
drive *Jagdwagen* (Jeep-like vehicles) with both 2- and 4-stroke engines. Goliath
was affected by the failure in 1961 of the Borgward combine of which it formed
part. Production ceased, but cars were assembled in the original factory until
1963.   HON

GOODCHILD (GB) 1914–1915
F.B. Goodchild & Co Ltd, London S.W.
The light cars sold by F.B. Goodchild used 4-cylinder engines of 10.4 or 10.8hp.
They had two-seater bodies and neat, slightly pointed radiators.   GNG

GOODSPEED (US) 1922
Commonwealth Motors Co, Chicago, Ill.

1901 GODIVA 9hp *dos-à-dos. Herbert Museum
and Art Gallery, Coventry*

1933 GOLIATH Pionier 198cc coupé. *Borgward-
Werke AG*

1951 GOLIATH GP-700 845cc sports coupé.
Borgward-Werke AG

1952 GORDINI 2-litre Formula 2 racing car.
F. Taylor

1952 GORDINI 2.3-litre sports car. *Autosport*

1955 GORDINI 2½-litre Formula 1 racing car.
Autosport

1914 GORDON(ii) 9hp two-seater.
Gordon Armstrong

The Goodspeed was an abortive attempt to market a luxury car under th direction of Commonwealth Motors' personnel after production of the Commor wealth had ceased. Two of the aluminium-bodied sports phaetons carrying th Goodspeed name were built, with plans for subsequent production. The Two $5,40 open cars, however, constituted the entire Goodspeed output. They were shown a both the New York and Chicago Shows. K

GOODYEAR (GB) *1924*

American Auto Agency Ltd, Manchester

In the years immediately following World War 1, when reliable, comfortable and inexpensive light cars were in exceedingly short supply in Britain, some shor lived manufacturers tried to fill the gap with hybrids assembled from Model T Fore parts. The Goodyear's engine, transmission and axles were Ford, but in othe respects — longer, lower frame, sporting body, and equipment — it was British, an tried to look British rather than like the despised Model T. The 2.9-litre engine wa tuned, providing 2,000rpm instead of 1,800 and 50mph instead of 40. TR

GORDANO (GB) *1946–1950*

Gordano Motor Co Ltd, Clifton, Bristol

Some enthusiastic Bristolians, aided by the Fry family finances and abetted b designer Dick Caesar, projected a multi-purpose sports car with a 1,500cc engine The chassis was box section, with sliding pillar independent front suspension and a independent rear axle and gearbox of their own manufacture. A Cross rotary-valv engine was experimented with, though the test car ran with an M.G. VA engine The only other car completed used that well-tried stand-by of post-war builders the 1,767cc Lea-Francis unit. The car was named after a valley near Caesar' Somerset home. D

GORDINI (F) *1951–1957*

Automobiles Gordini, Paris

Amédée Gordini made his name in the 1930s as a successful tuner and driver o small sports cars, producing his own developments of the Simca-built Tipo 508 Fiat. In 1939 he won the Index of Performance at Le Mans with a special versior of the Simca-Huit (Fiat 508C) and from 1946 to 1950 he was responsible for a series of rapid if fragile single-seaters with 1,100cc and 1.4-litre engines, sponsorec by Simca and using Simca components in a tubular frame of Gordini design. These units were giving 84bhp in 1947, and supercharged sports and racing versions were made in 1950. The following year, however, Gordini parted company with Simca anc started to build competition machines in his own small works in Paris. For sever years the firm struggled on, always short of cash, a situation which precluded any sustained success. In 1952 came the 2-litre Formula 2 single-seater, with 'square twin-ohc 175bhp 6-cylinder engine, a parallel-tube frame, all-round independen suspension by wishbones and torsion bars, and hydraulic brakes. Jean Behra won a Rheims that year, and Robert Manzon put up an impressive performance in the Carrera Panamericana on a sports version. At the end of the season a 4-cylinder sports car on similar lines was announced, to sell at £2,500, and the firm exhibited at the Paris and New York Shows. There were Formula 2 victories at Cadours and Chimay, together with a 1½-litre class win at Le Mans in 1953. Gordini also produced a sports-racing 3-litre straight-8, with dry sump lubrication, 5-speed gearbox and central driving position, which finished 2nd at Agadir in 1954. After a brief and unsuccessful 1,100cc sports machine, Gordini developed his eight into a Formula 1 G.P. car for 1955: it had Messier disc brakes all round (inboard at the rear) and straight bevel drive, with quick-change spur gears in the back axle. Also offered were 6- and 8-cylinder sports models, and in 1956 Gordini announced a new 1½-litre Formula 2 racer on the usual lines. Output was quoted at 175bhp, but finances did not improve, and in 1957 Gordini accepted an offer from Renault to work on high-performance versions of their 850cc Dauphine. MCS

GORDON (i) (GB) *1903–1904*

Gordon Cycle & Motor Co Ltd, London N.

The Gordon Miniature was a voiturette using a 6hp single-cylinder engine, a 2-speed gearbox and single chain drive. The overall weight was less than 488lb and the price 125 guineas. For 1904 a 3-speed gearbox was available. GNG

GORDON (ii) (GB) *1912–1914*

East Riding Engineering Works, Beverley, Yorks.

The Gordon cyclecar was powered by a rear-mounted 9hp V-twin J.A.P. engine, with chain drive to the gearbox, and chain final drive as well. The design incorporated unit construction of body and chassis. Two- and four-seater bodies were made, the latter very unusual on cyclecars. One front-engined car was built, the prototype of a series intended for export to Australasia had not World War 1 intervened. This still exists in South Australia. GNG

GORDON (iii) (GB) *1954–1958*

Vernon Industries Ltd, Bidston, Cheshire

Built by a subsidiary of Vernons Pools, the Gordon was one of the simplest of the post-war British 3-wheelers. It used a 197cc single-cylinder Villiers 2-stroke engine which was mounted on the offside of the vehicle, and drove one rear wheel only, by chain. Suspension was by coil, and the open body seated two. At just over £300 it was the cheapest car on the English market, and this kept sales going until increasing affluence ended demand for almost all the 3-wheelers.　　　GNG

GORDON (iv); GORDON-KEEBLE (GB) *1960–1961; 1964–1967*
1) Gordon Automobile Co Ltd, Slough, Bucks. *1960–1961*
2) Gordon-Keeble Ltd, Eastleigh, Hampshire *1964–1965*
3) Keeble Cars Ltd, Southampton *1965–1967*

One of the new generation of Anglo-Americans aimed at offering a high-grade GT car combining a reasonable price and world-wide service facilities, the original Gordon was the work of John Gordon, formerly of Peerless (ii), and Jim Keeble. It appeared just as the Peerless was going out of production. It had much in common with this car, its specification including a space-frame, coil-and-wishbone ifs, a De Dion back axle and disc brakes all round, but power was provided by a 4.6-litre V-8 ohv Chevrolet engine mated to a 4-speed all-synchromesh gearbox, while Bertone was responsible for the all-steel four-seater saloon body. The price was £3,045 and the top speed 140mph. This never went into production, but in 1964 a new company was formed at Eastleigh Airport to market a revised version, the Gordon-Keeble with fibreglass body by Williams and Pritchard, and a bigger 5.4-litre Chevrolet unit. The list price of £2,798 was competitive rather than realistic, and in March 1965 the firm failed after only 93 cars had been made. Two months later new backing was furnished by Mr Harold Smith, a London motor trader, and limited production was resumed at Southampton. The 300bhp GK. 1 models sold for £4,058. Early in 1968 it was announced that production would restart at Newmarket of two- and four-seater cars to be sold in America under the name De Bruyne. Only two De Bruynes of Gordon-Keeble type were made, together with one mid-engined coupé.　　　MCS

GORHAM (J) *1920–1922*
Jitsuyo Jidosha Seizo Co, Osaka

An important design historically, the Gorham was originally constructed by the American William R. Gorham who came to Japan in 1918 to manufacture aircraft and engines. Although the aircraft venture failed because of the recession after World War 1, Gorham became interested in motor vehicles and in 1919 built an experimental truck in a factory at Kawasaki City and in addition devised a special three-wheeled vehicle for his plant manager, Mr Kusibiki, who suffered from a physical disability. The Jitsuyo Jidosha Seizo Co. was established to manufacture his tri-car.

The 1920 Gorham looked like a three-wheeled motor-cycle with a semi-enclosed cab, seating three. It was propelled by an air-cooled, 2-cylinder, 8hp engine with chain drive to the right rear wheel and attained a speed of 30mph. This vehicle influenced the fledgling Japanese car industry and many similar machines were, are still are, being built as commercial vehicles; these account for quite a high percentage of the total produced.

In 1921 a 4-wheeled version replaced the tri-car, because of performance problems, and horse power was increased to 10. Production of the Gorham ended in 1922 and in 1923 the more advanced Lila light car was marketed.　　　BE

GÖRICKE (D) *1907–1908*
Bielefelder Maschinen- und Fahrradfabrik August Göricke, Bielefeld

A three-wheeled two-seater derived from motor-cycle designs, the Göricke had two rear wheels driven by cardan shaft and used a conventional steering wheel.　　　HON

GÖRKE (D) *1921*
Fritz Görke Kleinautobau, Leipzig

This was a three-wheeled cyclecar with a side-mounted N.S.U. engine and chain drive to one of the two rear wheels. Two- and three-seater versions were available, but production was only on a small scale.　　　HON

GORM (DK) *1917*
Karl J. Smidt, Copenhagen

Gorm cars were light two- and four-seaters with 6½hp 4-cylinder engines believed to be of foreign origin. The cars had wire wheels and their weight was 1,113lb. Little more than twenty cars were produced.　　　TRA

GOTTSCHALK (D) *1900–1901*
Berliner Motorwagen-Fabrik Gottschalk & Co KG, Berlin W.

Small private cars and more particularly commercial vehicles were produced by this firm. After 1901 it was known as the Berliner Motorwagen-Fabrik (B.M.F.) and concentrated on commercials.　　　HON

GOUJON (F) *1896–1901*
E. Goujon, Neuilly-sur-Seine

The Goujon was a Benz-like 3½hp vehicle featuring a rear-mounted single-cylinder engine, three forward speeds, belt drive and, unlike the products of Mannheim, burner ignition. Bodywork was in the *vis-à-vis* style. 1901 versions had four speeds, but that year's Salon was the make's last appearance.　　　MCS

1956 GORDON(iii) 197cc 3-wheeler. *G.N. Georgano*

1965 GORDON-KEEBLE 5.4-litre GT coupé. *Keeble Cars Ltd*

1920 GORHAM 8hp 3-wheeler. *Shotaro Kobayashi Collection*

1924 GRADE Type F2 3/16PS two-seater.
Neubauer Collection

1921 GRÄF & STIFT SR-1 8-litre tourer.
Václav Petřík Collection

1936 GRÄF & STIFT SP-8 5.9-litre saloon.
Gräf & Stift Automobilfabrik AG

GOVE (US) *1921*

Gove Motor Truck Co, Detroit, Mich.

Gove trucks were manufactured from 1920 to 1922, and during this period th
company built a few prototypes of a small 4-cylinder car with an air-cooled engine
GN

G.R.A.C. (F) *1963 to date*

Groupe de Recherche de l'Automobile Compétition, Valence, Drôme

This company was founded by Serge Aziomanoff who has built and sold a varie
range of single-seater racing cars. His space-frame Formule France or Formul
Bleu cars have been successful; his Formula 3 models, such as the 1969 wedge
shaped MT8, have raced in international Formula 3, but with little success
A coupé was announced in 1972, known as the MT-15 after the racing drive
Maurice Trintignant, who supervised the design.
DCN

GRACIELA (RA) *1960–1961*

D.I.N.F.I.A. (formerly IAME), Cordoba, Camino San Roque

Built in a government-owned aircraft factory, the Graciela 2-door saloon wa
developed from the short-lived Justicialista of 1955. Body lines remained the sam
but the grille was changed and a 37hp, 3-cylinder East German Wartburg engine
was used to power the front wheels. Suspension was independent at the front, by
semi-elliptic springs at the rear. Top speed was about 70mph. Later models use
the Wartburg 900 4-door saloon body.
B

GRACILE (F) *1905–1907*

Gracile Motor Car Co Ltd, London

This company was formed as the Gnome Motor Car Co Ltd, but before the year
was out the name was changed to Gracile. They were not manufacturers but sol
cars of Prunel origin.
GN

GRADE (D) *1921–1926*

(1) Grade Automobilwerk AG, Bork bei Brück *1921–1925*
(2) Grade Automobil AG, Bork bei Brück *1925–1926*

Grade was well known for his aircraft. After World War 1 he designed ar
unconventional two-seater car with a boat-shaped body and no chassis. It had ar
air-cooled, 2-cylinder 2-stroke engine of 808cc capacity and final drive was by chain
to a rear axle without a differential. A four-seater version with a 980cc engine
was produced for a short time.
HON

GRÄF & STIFT (A) *1907–1938*

(1) Gräf & Stift, Vienna *1907–1908*
(2) Wiener Automobilfabrik AG vorm. Gräf & Stift, Vienna *1908–1938*

The three Gräf brothers, who had a bicycle business, built their first motor car
during the years 1895–97 to a design of Josef Kainz. Although no more of this model
were made, it had some interesting details. It used a single-cylinder De Dion
engine – placed in the front – and had front drive. This car can claim to be the first
in the world to follow this principle.

In 1902 the Gräf brothers founded the firm of Gräf & Stift with Willy Stift,
who had earlier built the Celeritas cars. They next built Spitz cars to the order
of Arnold Spitz. This cooperation ended in 1907, when Graf & Stift started production under their own name, specializing in the heavier type of private car. They
made T-head 4-cylinder types of 16/22PS and 4.2 litres, 18/32PS and 5.9 litres,
28/45PS and 7.3 litres and 35/65PS and 10 litres. De Dion rear axles were found on
some models from 1913. Gräf & Stift cars were used by the Austrian Imperial Court
and played a part in the last days of the monarchy. Archduke Franz Ferdinand was
assassinated in a car of this make in 1914; the vehicle is now in the Military Museum
in Vienna. The last Austrian Emperor went into Swiss exile in another Gräf & Stift
after World War 1.

The post-World War 1 models were the Graf & Stift VK (4-cylinder, 1,940cc),
SR 4 (6-cylinder, 7,745cc), SP 5 (6-cylinder, 3,895cc) and SP 8 (8-cylinder, 5,923cc).
The SP 8 with an in-line ohc engine headed the range and was known as the Austrian
Rolls-Royce. It was available with various bodies, chiefly as an open tourer, as a
4-door four-seater sports coupé, or as a six-seater saloon. These cars carried a
distinctive silver lion mascot. Two prototypes of 1938 marked the end of private-car
manufacture: the G36, a 4.7-litre single-ohc straight-8, and the C12, a 3.9-litre
sv V-12. Before World War 2 Gräf & Stift built the 6-cylinder Citroën and the
German Ford V8 (Gräfford) under licence. After the war the Czech Aero Minor
was produced under licence from 1949 to 1950, but only on a small scale. Gräf
& Stift still build trucks and buses today.
HON

GRAHAME-WHITE (GB) *1920–1924*

The Grahame-White Co Ltd, Hendon, Middlesex

Appropriately enough, Claude Grahame-White, the aviation pioneer, operated
from Hendon airport. Like other airmen, he turned to cars after World War 1,
when the market for aircraft almost vanished overnight. He made luxurious bodies
for expensive chassis such as Rolls-Royce, but his complete cars were at the other
extreme. The Grahame-White Buckboard was just that: a platform on spindly wire
wheels with a rudimentary bucket seat on top. The engine was a 3½hp, 348cc single-

ylinder unit, brought to life by a kick-starter. There were two forward speeds. A 7hp friction-driven car was also offered, and even what sounds like a normal light car, with a water-cooled, 4-cylinder, 1,100cc Dorman engine.　　　TRN

GRAHAM-FOX see COMPOUND

GRAHAM MOTORETTE (US) 1902–1903
Charles Sefrin & Co, Brooklyn, N.Y.
This car had a single-cylinder, 3hp air-cooled engine with a friction transmission. It was a two-seater with tiller steering. Final drive was by a single chain.　　　GMN

GRAHAM-PAIGE: GRAHAM (US) 1927–1941
Graham-Paige Motors Corp, Detroit, Mich.
The Graham brothers, Joseph, Robert and Ray, acquired the old Paige concern in 1927. Their Graham-Paiges were conventional machines noted for their internal-expanding hydraulic front wheel brakes and 4-speed 'twin-top' gearboxes, and 78,000 were sold in their first year of production. The range embraced three sixes and two eights, the biggest of these being the '835' with an 11ft 5in wheelbase and a 5.3-litre engine. One of these straight-8 Graham-Paiges won the last race ever held on the Brooklands Motor Course in August 1939. The name of the make was simplified to Graham for the 1931 season, though design underwent little alteration until the arrival of the 1932 Blue Streaks, headed by a 4-litre eight which introduced skirted front wings to the American market and was immortalized in the 'Tootsie Toys' found in many a nursery of the 1930s. 1934 8-cylinder cars were available with a centrifugal supercharger rotating at $5\frac{3}{4}$ times the engine speed, which gave them a top speed of 95mph. After 1935 only sixes were made, the $3\frac{1}{2}$-litre Cavalier being listed in 80bhp unblown and 112bhp blown versions, both with aluminium cylinder heads – this chassis formed the basis of the Anglo-American Lammas. Despite an attempt to compete in the lowest-priced field with the 2.8-litre Crusader at $595 (it cost less than £300 in England), Graham achieved little beyond three successive outright wins in the Gilmore-Yosemite Economy Run, though these small sixes were copied by Nissan of Japan. An ugly concave nose and spatted rear wheels characterized the 1938 and 1939 Grahams, which were $3\frac{1}{2}$-litre cars available with or without superchargers. The company's final fling was the 1940 Hollywood, which made use of the body dies from Cord's 810/812 series. Like Hupmobile's very similar Skylark, this was not a commercial success, and after World War 2 Graham-Paige joined forces with Henry J. Kaiser to build the Kaiser and Frazer cars: the latter were named after Graham-Paige's President Joseph W. Frazer.　　　MCS

GRAMM (CDN) 1913
Gramm Motor Truck Co, Walkerville, Ont.
Mainly known as a truck builder, Gramm made a few cyclecars with 2-cylinder air-cooled engines, tandem seating and belt drive.　　　GNG

GRAMME (F) 1901
Sté des Accumulateurs Compound, Levallois-Perret, Seine
This light car derived its name from the make of electric motor used. It was a three-wheeler in which the 3hp motor drove the single front wheel by belt.　　　GNG

GRANT (US) 1913–1922
Grant Motor Car Corp, Findlay, Ohio
The first Grant was a 12hp 4-cylinder light car made in two-seater form, and sold in England as the Whiting-Grant, by Whiting Ltd of Euston Rd, London. In 1915 the Grant company changed their policy and introduced a 44bhp 6-cylinder tourer. A 1917 model of this could be converted from tourer to sedan by the addition of a 'winter top'. In 1920 a smaller six was introduced, of 20hp. This also appeared on the British market, sold now by T.B. André.　　　GNG

GRANTA (GB) 1906
Granta Motor Co, London W
The Granta was sold from an address in Horseferry Rd, Westminster, and was probably an imported car. It had a 28/34hp 4-cylinder Ballot engine and double chain drive. The Westminster car was sold from the same address.　　　GNG

GRAVES & CONGDON see CROWN (iii)

GRAY (i) (US) 1920
Gray Light Car Corp, Longmont, and Denver, Colo.
This concern with a splendid-sounding title in fact only built two cars, both of them cyclecars of what sounds like a particularly spidery kind. One was powered by a single-cylinder motor-cycle engine and the other by a twin, both made by Harley-Davidson. Motor-cycle wheels were fitted.　　　TRN

GRAY (ii) (US) 1922–1926
Gray Motor Corp, Detroit, Mich.
During the 1920s, two new makes, Star and Gray, tried to win a share of the mass market dominated by the Ford Model T. The Gray was in fact made by former

1929 GRAHAM-PAIGE Model 621 4.7-litre tourer. *National Motor Museum*

1938 GRAHAM $3\frac{1}{2}$-litre supercharged sedan. *Autocar*

1920 GRAHAME-WHITE 7hp two-seater *National Motor Museum*

1922 GRAY-DORT 19.6hp tourer. *Hugh Durnford*

1972 G.R.D. 372 Formula 3 racing car. *Group Racing Developments Ltd*

1909 GREAT WESTERN 40hp two-seater. *Keith Marvin Collection*

employees of Ford, who included the head of the Gray Corporation, F.L. Klingen smith, and was similar to the Ford in several features of engine and chassis. A side valve, 4-cylinder, 2.7-litre engine was used. Unlike the Ford, the Gray's springing wa by conventional quarter-elliptics at front and rear. Front-wheel brakes were offered in 1926, but that year was its last. The company's grandiose plans, which include making nearly a quarter of a million cars in the first full year of production, at $49 for the touring car and $760 for the coach, were never fully realized. TR

GRAY-DORT (CDN) *1915–1925*
Gray-Dort Motors Ltd, Chatham, Ont.

The Gray-Dort was undoubtedly one of the most successful and popular car built by a Canadian company. Production was about 26,000 units, and at one tim the company outsold the much-cheaper Chevrolet in Ontario. The Gray-Dort wa based on the American Dort car, and the Canadian company only went out o business after the American firm closed down. The American Dort never matched th success that the Gray-Dort achieved in Canada.

The Canadian firm originated in a carriage and sleigh-making concern, Wm Gray-Sons-Campbell Ltd of Chatham. The 1915 Gray-Dorts were almost al American-built cars with such items as emblems and hub caps changed, or wer assembled in Chatham from American-made parts. Real production began in 191 with Canadian-made components. While the cars were similar to the America Dorts, the Canadian company did produce several de luxe sports models includin a 1922 Special which was claimed to have the industry's first automatic reversin light as standard equipment. A previous sports car, the 1918 Special, was so wel received that 200 of them were exported to America. The 4-cylinder Lycomin engine proved well-suited to the harsh Canadian climate and Gray-Dort kept it i production right until the end, although it was dropped in America shortly afte introduction of the six in 1923. Gray-Dort prices were in the medium range, bu generally increased over the years. The 1917 tourer cost $885 while closed cars i the 1920s were about $2,000. The company also imported the American Gray car for a very short time in the 1920s and continued selling 1924 Gray-Dorts into 1925 while winding up operations. HD

GRAZIOSA (A) *1899–1901*
Graziosa Fahrradwerke Benedict Albl & Co, Graz

This company built motor-tricycles and also one model of voiturette in limited numbers. HON

G.R.D. (GB) *1971 to date*
Group Racing Developments Ltd, Griston, Norfolk

Founded by ex-Lotus men Mike Warner, Derek Wild, Gordon Huckle and Dave Baldwin in conjunction with J. Stanton and J. Reynolds, G.R.D. aimed to emulate March in achieving overnight success as a racing-car manufacturer. They adopted a different approach, aiming first to conquer the lesser formulae where the sales prospects lay. Twenty-five of the purposeful side-radiator monocoques had been built by June 1972, and in Formula 3 Roger Williamson's 372 became the car to beat, ably backed by Andy Sutcliffe, Pierre-François Rousselot and others. Jo Mar quart's Formula 2 272 design was very similar and new models for 1973 included the B73 for F3/Atalantic, and the S73 2-litre sports car. DF

GREAT EAGLE (US) *1910–1918*
U.S. Carriage Co, Columbus, Ohio

These were big cars, mostly seven-seaters, with large wheels, and 5.8-litre 4-cylinder engines. The wheelbase on several models was greater than 11ft. GMN

GREAT SMITH *see* SMITH

GREAT SOUTHERN (US) *1910–1914*
Great Southern Automobile Co, Birmingham, Ala.

The Great Southern was made as a five-seater tourer or two-seater roadster. These were available with either 30hp or 50hp 4-cylinder engines. The 50hp models had engines of 8.6 litres. GMN

GREAT WESTERN (US) *1908–1916*
(1) Model Automobile Co, Peru, Ind. *1908–1909*
(2) Great Western Automobile Co, Peru, Ind. *1909–1916*

This make started out with a seven-seater touring car with a 50hp engine, and a smaller touring car with a 2-cylinder engine. In 1910 a 4-cylinder 40hp engine in a standard chassis of 9ft 6in wheelbase was adopted. As many as five models of this Great Western Forty were available. The Great Western had an elaborate radiator insignia, with a winged 'W'. GMN

GREELEY (US) *1903*
E.N. Miller, Greeley, Colo.

This was an unlikely location for the building of two-seater cars with 4-cylinder engines, epicyclic transmission and chain drive. The weight of this vehicle was put at 1,345lb, and it cost $1,150. GMN

GREENLEAF (US) *1902*

Greenleaf Cycle Co, Lansing, Mich.

The Greenleaf was a light surrey powered by a 2-cylinder horizontal engine developing 10hp at 700rpm. GNG

GRÉGOIRE (i) (F) *1903–1924*

(1) Grégoire et Cie, Poissy, Seine-et-Oise

(2) SA des Automobiles Grégoire, Poissy, Seine-et-Oise

Throughout their history, the Grégoires from Poissy were best known as fast, if conventional, small cars, though larger cars were also made. Their earliest range, for 1904, consisted of an 8CV single, a 12CV twin, and a 20CV four, but the first famous Grégoire appeared two seasons later, an 80 × 110mm twin. In 1908 it could be had in 4-cylinder form as well as a 2-litre 10CV. Both were modern L-head monobloc fours. In 1911 came the most celebrated Grégoire of all, the 16/24hp with the same bore but the remarkably long stroke of 160mm. This was a car of sporting performance that had originated as a racing voiturette, as the ultra-long stroke suggests. Both the 10CV and the 16/24 were listed in 1914, together with a new T-head sports model of 70 × 140mm, also with four cylinders. Its engine developed 38bhp at 2,500rpm, aided by light steel pistons and a short, stiff crankshaft. The 10CV was still in evidence after World War 1. Even at that stage in its career, its efficient, high-speed engine, enlarged to 2.3 litres in 1921 and given overhead valves, made it an exceptionally fast car, capable of over 60mph. The last car to bear the Grégoire name was an 1,100cc overhead-valve voiturette of normal type, with three forward speeds and transverse-spring front suspension. It was in fact made by Hinstin and sold under the name Little Greg in Britain. The Grégoire factory was also responsible for the assembly of the 3-litre Bignan. TRN

GRÉGOIRE (ii) (F) *1945–1962*

Automobiles Tracta SA, Asnières, Seine

J.A. Grégoire, associated in pre-1939 days with the Tracta front-wheel-drive cars and the Amilcar Compound, unveiled his ingenious ultra-light 600cc fwd saloon in 1945. This had a nearly square (72 × 73mm) 15bhp ohv flat-twin engine cooled by twin fans, hydro-mechanical brakes and all-round independent suspension. The use of Alpax for the platform-type frame and dash was inherited from the Amilcar of 1937, and this structure weighed only 100lb. It never saw production as the Grégoire, though it formed the basis for Panhard's successful Dyna series. Attempts were made to produce it in series in England as the Kendall (ii) and in Australia as the Hartnett. Grégoire, however, came up with a more ambitious design in 1947, this having a 64bhp 2-litre water-cooled flat-4 engine and 4-speed overdrive gearbox. It was made in limited numbers by Hotchkiss in the early 1950s. At the 1952 Paris Salon the S.O.C.E.M.A.-Grégoire turbocar was shown: its features included a 100bhp Cematurbo gas turbine engine mounted at the front, rear-wheel-drive, a Cotal gearbox and an electro-magnetic transmission brake. Nothing came of this project and in 1956 the inventor reverted to his 1947 theme with a supercharged 2.2-litre 130bhp derivative of the Hotchkiss-Grégoire. The handsome cabriolet bodies were the work of Henri Chapron. This was still being quoted with disc front brakes as late as 1961–2, but it is doubtful if it ever attained series production. MCS

GREGORY (i) (US) *1918–1922*

Front Drive Motor Co, Kansas City, Mo.

Ben F. Gregory built about 10 cars, all using fwd. Some were tourers, including one exhibited at the 1921 Kansas City Auto Show. He also built a few racing cars. His own demonstration racing car was powered first by a Curtiss OX-5 and later by a Hispano-Suiza aero engine. Some of Gregory's ideas were used by Harry Miller in his fwd racing cars. After World War 2 Gregory returned to car manufacture with the Gregory (ii). GNG

GREGORY (ii) (US) *1949; 1952*

Ben Gregory, Kansas City, Mo.

Ben Gregory exhibited a sedan in 1949 with a 40hp 4-cylinder Continental engine mounted in the rear, driving the front wheels. In 1952 he constructed a front-wheel-drive Porsche-engined sports car but neither of these prototypes entered production, and Gregory went on instead to success in designing military vehicles. BE

GREMLIN *see* AMERICAN MOTORS

GREUTER *see* HOLYOKE

GREYHOUND (US) *1914–1915*

Greyhound Cyclecar Co, Toledo, Ohio

This was a two-seater (tandem) cyclecar with driving controls in the rear seat. It had a sliding-gear transmission, shaft drive and electric starting. It was succeeded by the States. GMN

GRICE (GB) *1927*

G.W.K. Ltd, Maidenhead, Berks.

This was a light 3-wheeler with single front wheel that A.G. Grice hoped to

1910 GRÉGOIRE(i) 14CV berline. *Autocar*

1961 GRÉGOIRE(ii) 2.2-litre convertible. *Autocar*

1927 GRICE 3-wheeler. *National Motor Museum*

1907 GRIFFON 7hp voiturette. *The Veteran Car Club of Great Britain*

1927 GROFRI 1,100cc sports car. *Dr Henry Goldhann*

1901 GROUT 4hp steam runabout. *G.N. Georgano Collection*

market at £90. The rear-mounted 680cc air-cooled J.A.P. V-twin engine drove the rear wheels by a 3-speed gearbox, and not by the usual friction wheel; other features were all-coil suspension and 3-wheel brakes. It did not go into production.

MCS

GRIDI (D) 1923–1924
Gridi Kraftfahrbau GmbH, Saulgau/Württemberg

A small car with a single-cylinder 865cc engine.

HON

GRIFFITH-TVR: GRIFFITH (US) 1964–1966
(1) Griffith Motors, Syosset, Long Island, N.Y. *1964–1965*
(2) Griffith Motors, Plainview, Long Island, N.Y. *1965–1966*

The Griffith was originally a British TVR sports coupé with a Ford Fairlane 271hp engine. It sold well on its reputation for smart acceleration until the supply of bodies ceased with the failure of Grantura Engineering in 1965. The company moved to a large factory and acquired the rights to build the Apollo (iii) under the name Griffith-GT. Chrysler was to supply V-8 engines for the new model. Very few were made, but in 1966 the design, now Ford-engined again, was taken over by Steve Wilder and re-named Omega (vi).

BE

GRIFFON (F) 1906–1910; 1921–1924
SA des Cycles Griffon, Courbevoie, Seine

Griffon were well-known manufacturers of bicycles, motor-cycles and tri-cars. In 1906 they introduced a light two-seater voiturette powered by a 7hp single-cylinder engine. This was made for a few years, after which Griffon reverted to 2-wheeled machines. However the post-war cyclecar boom attracted them to cars again. Their cyclecars used a 984cc V-twin Anzani engine, and had chain drive to the gearbox, and belt drive to the rear wheels.

GNG

GRINNELL (US) 1910–1913
Grinnell Electric Car Co, Detroit, Mich.

The Grinnell electric was claimed to travel 90 miles per battery charge. The five-seater closed coupé was on a wheelbase of 8ft and cost $2,800. This make succeeded the Phipps-Grinnell.

GMN

GRISWOLD (US) 1907
Griswold Motor Car Co, Detroit, Mich.

This car was designed by the well-known J.P. La Vigne. It offered three different chassis, all with 2-cylinder water-cooled engines. These were of 10hp, 15hp and 20hp. The longest chassis had a wheelbase of 9ft 2in.

GMN

GROFRI (A) 1922–1927
Grofri-Werk AG, Atzgerdorf, nr Vienna

Grofri produced a 6-cylinder 12/45PS car before taking up production of an Amilcar-based model with a 4-cylinder 1.1-litre engine. It was capable of 20bhp, but supercharged versions with 40 and 50bhp were also available, the latter being good for about 85 mph. Two and four seaters were offered.

HON

GRONINGER (NL) 1898–1899
Groninger Motorrijtuigenfabriek, Groningen

The first Groninger was completed early in 1898, and at the 1899 Dutch Motor Show two heavy *dos-à-dos* cars were shown, with 2½hp and 4hp engines. The company also planned to make buses, but were out of business by the end of 1899.

GNG

GROPA see NOMAD

GROSE (GB) 1899–1900
Grose Ltd, Northampton

The Grose Company made a small number of voiturettes and dogcarts on Benz lines, with 4hp horizontal engines and belt drive. The company is still in existence as a well-known firm of distributors of Rolls-Royce, Bentley, Daimler, Jaguar and other cars.

GNG

GROUSSET (F) 1904–1905
Atelier de Mécanique et d'Automobiles Grousset et Fils, Firminy, Loire

Owners of a general engineering business, Paul Grousset and his sons made about twelve cars for local clients before concentrating on the manufacture of hexagonal screws, which is still the firm's business today.

LL

GROUT (US) 1899–1912
(1) Grout Bros, Orange, Mass. *1899–1903*
(2) Grout Bros Automobile Co, Orange, Mass. *1903–1908*
(3) Grout Automobile Co, Orange, Mass. *1909–1912*

The Grout company began manufacture with a typical light steam buggy with a 2-cylinder 4hp engine and single chain drive. An unusual model was the New Home Coupé, a completely enclosed coupé on a very short wheelbase which looked like a mobile sentry box. From about 1903 the steamers began to look more like ordinary cars, although the bonnet was circular and had a single headlamp mounted in the entre, locomotive style. One model continued the locomotive appearance with an enormous cow catcher to act as a bumper.

The last steamer, a 12hp 2-cylinder model, appeared in 1905, and a year earlier the company had introduced a petrol-engined car with a 30hp 4-cylinder engine and shaft drive. Few of these were made as the company was often in financial difficulties from 1905 onwards. The earlier steamers were sold in England under the name Weston.   GNG

G.R.P. (F) *1924–1928*

G. et R. Paul, Paris 15e

The brothers Georges and René Paul were mainly known as builders of taxicabs, but they did produce a small number of touring and sports cars with 4-cylinder ohv engines of 1,690cc, enlarged in 1926 to 1,890cc.   GNG

GRYFON; GRYPHON (GB) *1969 to date*

Beamond Engineering, Welwyn, Herts.

Stuart Rolt's first Gryfon was derived from a U2, modified to all-round wishbone suspension. For 1970 replicas with an original chassis were offered at £600. Production was then undertaken by Beamond Engineering under Andy Diamond, who constructed the very successful cars Noel Stanbury used in Clubman's racing during 1971 and 1972.   DF

G.S.M. (ZA/GB) *1958–1966*

(1) Glass Sports Motor Co Pty Ltd, Bottelary, Cape Town *1958–1962*

(2) G.S.M. Cars Ltd, West Malling, Kent *1960–1964*

(3) G.S.M. Pty Ltd, Paarden Eiland, C.P. *1963–1966*

The Dart model was known in Britain before Bob van Niekerk came to develop the Delta, with which he obtained prominence in the 1,000cc sports racing class. Transverse leaf independent front suspension, a Ford 100E rear axle on coil springs, and a Ford 105E engine were fitted to a tubular frame, with fibreglass two-seater or coupé bodywork. Many were sold in kit form. Van Niekerk returned to South Africa, to develop the Flamingo and other models. Though the original South African productions had Ford Ten sv engines, the later 2 + 2 coupé used the 1,498cc Cortina GT unit.   DF

G.T.M. (GB) *1966 to date*

(1) Cox & Co (Manchester) Ltd, Hazel Grove, Cheshire

(2) G.T.M. Kit Cars, Hazel Grove, Cheshire *1969 to date*

At the end of 1966 Cox & Co (Manchester) Ltd offered the first mid-engined car kit. This comprised a semi-monocoque steel chassis unit, fibreglass body and B.M.C. Mini mechanical components. The manufacturing rights were taken over later by Howard Heerey, who had achieved considerable racing success. In 1972 Ian Wilson entered one in Scottish Championship rallies.   DF

GUEPARDO *see* **ARTÈS**

GUERRAZ (F) *1900–1902*

Voitures Légères Louis Guerraz, Levallois-Perret, Seine

Guerraz light cars used a variety of engines: Bolide, Aster, Buchet and Soncin, all of between 5 and 7hp. They had 3-speed gearboxes and chain final drive.   GNG

GUILDFORD (GB) *1920*

Griffith's Engineering Works, Guildford, Surrey

The Guildford was a cyclecar using a Blackburne 8hp V-twin engine and chain drive. The makers stated that they were willing to dispose of the design to anyone willing to manufacture it in quantity. Apparently no-one was willing, and it was never put on the market.   GNG

GUILICK (F) *1914–1929*

G. Guilick et Cie, Maubeuge, Nord

The Guilick was one of a number of assembled cars made either at Maubeuge or Cons-la-Granville. Other makes in the group included Henou, Hinstin and S.U.P. Chassis design was generally similar and thoroughly conventional, and the makers used a variety of 4-cylinder engines by Altos, Ruby and C.I.M.E.   GNG

GUILLIERME (F) *1906–1910*

Automobiles Guillierme, Paris

The Guillierme used a 10/12hp 4-cylinder Ballot engine and shaft drive. After the initial appearance of the car, the makers concentrated more on commercial vehicles with the engine mounted under the seat.   GNG

GURGEL (BR) *1966 to date*

(1) Macan Ind e Com Ltda, São Paulo *1966–1968*

(2) Gurgel Veiculos, São Paulo *1969 to date*

The Gurgel is a doorless open four-seater with fibreglass coachwork, suitable for off-road use. Engines are by Volkswagen, with capacities of 1,300cc, 1,500cc or 1,600cc.   GNG

1960 G.S.M. 1.2-litre sports coupé.
Autosport

1901 GUERRAZ 7hp *vis-à-vis. The Veteran Car Club of Great Britain*

1950 GUTBROD Superior 600 coupé.
Autocar

*c.*1920 GUY(iii) 20hp V-8 tourer. *National
Motor Museum*

1926 GUYOT Spéciale 1½-litre racing car.
P.M. Kirkpatrick

GURLEY (US) 1901
T.W. Gurley, Meyersdale, Pa.

The Gurley was a typical two-seater motor buggy with a petrol engine, and a tubular reach frame. Bicycle-type wire wheels and tiller steering completed this undistinguished vehicle.　　　　　　　　GMN

GUTBROD (D) 1949–1954
Gutbrod Motorenbau GmbH, Plochingen; Calw

Wilhelm Gutbrod produced the Standard Superior cars before World War 2. In 1949 a new Gutbrod appeared: the Superior 600, a two-seater with a 2-cylinder 2-stroke 593cc engine. This was followed by the 663cc Superior 700. Both models were available with fuel injection. A sports roadster and a convertible were only produced in small numbers. The Superior 604 and 704 were four-seater versions with the same engine characteristics. Production ceased in 1954.　　　HON

GUY (i); LE GUI (F) 1904–1916
(1) H. Guillemin et Cie, Courbevoie, Seine 1904–1909
(2) E. Nicolas et Cie, Courbevoie, Seine 1909–1916

In the early years the two names assigned to this make were used indiscriminately and to complicate matters the car was also known in England as the Millard-Le Gui, after one of the importers who handled it. At their first showing in 1905, the cars had conventional shaft-driven chassis and round radiators, but also in the range was a short-lived 7hp air-cooled four with oversquare cylinder dimensions; this soon gave way to conventional voiturettes of 9hp and 11hp, priced at 5,400fr and 6,500fr respectively, the former with a 942cc Buchet engine. By 1908 the company was offering quite a wide range, all with proprietary power units (Barriquand et Marre in the bigger cars): 4-cylinder machines came in 1.8-litre, 2-litre, 3.1-litre and 5.5-litre sizes, the biggest ones having chain drive. A 1.3-litre 4-cylinder Le Gui ran in the 1908 Coupe des Voiturettes. Under Nicolas's control the firm concentrated increasingly on small cars with L-head monobloc 4-cylinder engines and 4-speed gearboxes: a 1.6-litre Ten sold for only £250 in England in 1910, and was credited with 35mph and 28mpg. There was also a larger 15hp with an ioe Chapuis-Dornier engine in a similar chassis. The same type and make of unit was fitted in the 1912 2.1-litre version. Later Le Guis were all Chapuis-Dornier-powered, the range including a very long-stroke (85 × 160mm) 3.6-litre four.　　　MCS

GUY (ii) (CDN) 1911
Mathew Guy Carriage and Automobile Co, Oshawa, Ont.

A 30hp tourer and a 1 ton truck were the basis of this carriage company's venture into car manufacture, but only a few were built.　　　GB

GUY (iii) (GB) 1919–1925
Guy Motors Ltd, Wolverhampton, Staffs.

Like other commercial-vehicle concerns (Leyland, Maudslay, British Ensign), Guy went into luxury-car manufacture in a small way after World War 1. The 1919 Guy was unusual in that its eight cylinders, which totalled just over four litres, were disposed in V-formation. France and America were already familiar with this new arrangement, but in Britain, only one Vulcan model had it. Rare anywhere was the Guy's automatic chassis lubrication, which was a surprising feature to find on a car that would be usually looked after by a chauffeur. The engine's detachable cylinder heads and inclined side valves, and the subframe that carried engine and gearbox, were characteristic of Guy commercial chassis. About 150 of the V-8 were made, but the medium-sized family cars that followed it from 1921, with 4-cylinder in-line engines of 2 and 2½ litres' capacity, appeared in far smaller numbers. All retained automatic chassis lubrication. After 1925, the Guy name appeared only on commercial, public service and military vehicles.　　　TRN

GUYOT SPÉCIALE (F) 1925–1931
Ets Albert Guyot et Cie, Clichy, Seine

Albert Guyot was one of the numerous racing drivers who tried, generally without success, to make and sell cars bearing their own names. A handful only of Guyot Spéciales appeared, in two types. One was a pure racing car to the 1926–27 Grand Prix formula, powered by a supercharged 1½-litre, 6-cylinder engine with the unusual feature of single-sleeve valves. This engine was made in England under Burt-McCollum patents and assembled in France. Three of these ran at Indianapolis in 1926; two entered by Albert Schmidt, under the name Schmidt Special, and the third entered and driven by Guyot himself. The other model was a touring car powered by a 6-cylinder 3½-litre Continental engine. Saloon and even *coupé de ville* bodies were fitted, and the radiator was a very close copy of the Alfa-Romeo. Few were made, and even fewer of the 1929 Super-Huit, which had a straight-8 Continental engine of 5.2 litres' capacity.　　　TRN

GUY VAUGHAN (US) 1910–1913
Vaughan Car Co, Kingston, N.Y.

This make was also known as the Vaughan and was apparently confined to five-seater touring models, powered by 4.6-litre 4-cylinder engines. A 3-speed selective transmission was used. The 1913 Vaughan Model 5 cost $2,500.　　　GMN

GWALIA (GB) 1922

Stanfield Ltd, Cardiff

One of the very few cars to have been built in Wales, the Gwalia used a 9hp Alpha engine, a 3-speed gearbox and a worm-driven rear axle. Its only unconventional feature was the suspension which was by a system of coil springs and bell cranks in the manner of the Citroën 2CV. Apart from the engine it was said that the whole car was built in Wales. With a three-seater clover-leaf body, the price was £250. GNG

G.W.K. (GB) 1911–1931

(1) G.W.K. Ltd, Datchet, Bucks. 1911–1914
(2) G.W.K. Ltd, Maidenhead, Berks. 1914–1931

The G.W.K. cyclecar was notable in that it was a successful instance of the application of friction drive. At first, weight was low, and the vertical twin-cylinder side-valve Coventry-Simplex engine, which lived at the rear, could push it along at about 35mph. Up to 1914, the G.W.K. was popular because of its economy. Its friction discs were of compressed paper at first, and then after 1919, of cork. By 1921 a four-cylinder 1,368cc Coventry-Simplex engine had replaced the twin, and a self-starter had been added increasing the weight. This went up again in 1924, when front-wheel brakes and a 1½-litre engine were fitted. These modern conveniences were offered in order to compete with quantity-produced light cars, but the little Austin Seven was faster, more economical, and already cheaper. The G.W.K. went out of production in 1926. Grice had already departed, in 1920, to make the very similar Unit, and in 1930 he tried to revive the G.W.K., showing another rear-engined car with friction drive bearing the original name, but it never appeared on the market. TRN

1913 G.W.K. 8hp two-seater. *T.H. Tarling*

GWYNNE (GB) 1922–1929

(1) Gwynne's Engineering Co Ltd, Chiswick, London W.4 1922–1925
(2) Gwynne Cars Ltd, Chiswick, London W.4 1925–1929

The name of Gwynne was known on centrifugal pumps before (and after) it appeared on cars, and the company also made aero and car engines before turning to road vehicles. Their first venture into the latter field, in 1920, took the form of acquiring the Albert, whose engines they had made. From the 1923 model year, they were known as Gwynne-Alberts. In 1922, Gwynne offered a light car under their own name. The engine of the Gwynne Eight was of Spanish origin, based on one of Arturo Elizalde's designs used in the Victoria (iv). It had four cylinders. Bore and stroke were 55 × 100mm, providing a capacity of 950cc. The push-rod overhead valves were neatly enclosed, the whole unit presenting a very clean outward appearance. High power – 24bhp – and light weight afforded a desirable combination of good performance and fuel economy, which was allied to low price. The Gwynne was noisy and uncomfortable in the extreme, but sold well at first on account of its other virtues. The two-and-two-halves 'chummy' style of body popular at the time was supplemented by more practical, if ugly, full four-seater and saloon bodies on longer chassis, while to pull the extra weight of these, a bigger and more flexible engine of 1,247cc, the Ten, was substituted. At the other extreme, a sports model was offered, but by this time, the middle 1920s, the family motorist who was the most important customer could find greater comfort and quietness more cheaply and the Gwynne passed from the motoring scene, after involving its creators in heavy loss. TRN

1921 G.W.K. 10.8hp two-seater. *National Motor Museum*

GYROSCOPE (US) 1908–1909

(1) Blomstrom Manufacturing Co, Detroit, Mich. 1908
(2) Lion Motor Car Co, Adrian, Mich. 1909

The Gyroscope was so named because of the horizontal, opposed 2-cylinder engine, which, with its horizontal flywheel, was claimed to increase stability and prevent skidding. Many other cars of this period had similar engines, but made no such claims. The 16hp engine connected with a friction transmission and shaft drive. Three body styles were marketed. GMN

1923 GWYNNE Eight tourer. *Autocar*

1917 HACKETT 22.5hp roadster. *McKean Collection, Free Library of Philadelphia*

1926 H.A.G. 5/25PS two-seater. *Neubauer Collection*

1917 HAL Twelve 6.4-litre roadster. *McKean Collection, Free Library of Philadelphia*

HAASE (US) 1904

Northwestern Automobile Co, Milwaukee, Wisc.

The two models of the Haase were tiller-steered, with 2-cylinder engines of 6 or 8hp. An optimistic 40mph was claimed for the more powerful model, which weighed 1,400lb. Speed control was accomplished by the lifting of the inlet valves. GMN

HACKETT (US) 1916–1919

Hackett Motor Car Co, Jackson, Mich.

The Hackett was an assembled car using a 4-cylinder G.B. & S. engine and was the successor to the earlier Argo. The catalogue for 1916 to 1918 listed both a touring car and a closed model; 1919 Hacketts were available only as tourers and roadsters. Following a reorganization, operations were transferred to Grand Rapids, Mich., where the car was continued as the Lorraine. KM

HADFIELD-BEAN see BEAN

H.A.G.; H.A.G.-GASTELL (D) 1922–1927

(1) Hessische Automobil-AG, Darmstadt 1922–1925
(2) Waggonfabrik Gebr. Gastell, Mainz-Mombach 1925–1927

H.A.G. produced only one type of car, a 5/25PS model which was of good technical design. The 4-cylinder 1,305cc engine had an overhead camshaft with vertical shaft drive by spiral bevel gear. In 1925 production was taken over by Gastell, a manufacturer of railway carriages and wagons, and the cars were subsequently known as H.A.G.-Gastell. A 1.5-litre sports version was quite successful in various German racing events. HON

HAGEA-MOTO (D) 1922–1924

Dipl. Ing. O. Bischoff & M. Althoven GmbH, Berlin-Wilmersdorf

A small car with a 4-cylinder 1,017cc 4/12PS proprietary engine by Steudel and friction drive. HON

HAGEN (D) 1903–1908

Kölner Accumulatorenwerke Gottfried Hagen, Cologne-Kalk

This firm, which is still in existence and produces batteries, branched out into car manufacture in 1903, building both private and commercial electric cars. Hagen cars, which were also marketed under the brand-names K.A.W. and Urbanus, were extensively used all over Germany, especially as taxicabs. HON

HAINES & GRUT (AUS) 1904

Haines & Grut, Melbourne, Victoria

The Haines & Grut was a high-wheel motor buggy similar to many made in America, although it seems to have been the only Australian vehicle of this kind. It had a 10/12hp opposed-twin engine, and belt drive. There were two forward speeds, and reverse was obtained by sliding the countershaft rearward to drive directly on the tyre. Of the five Haines & Gruts made, one survives today. GNG

HAL (US) 1916–1918

(1) H.A.Lozier Co, Cleveland, Ohio 1916
(2) Hal Motor Car Co, Cleveland, Ohio 1916–1918

These were the initials of H.A.Lozier who had previously built the Lozier car. The Hal was one of several makes which introduced the 12-cylinder, valve-in-head Weidely engine in 1916. This 6.4-litre power unit developed 87hp. Two-, four- and seven-seater models were built, as well as a limousine. The seven-seater weighed 3,550lb and was priced at $2,600, while the limousine cost $4,500. GMN

HALL (i) (US) 1904

Hall Motor Vehicle Co, Dover, N.J.

This was a four-seater rear-entrance tonneau with a 2-cylinder, 20hp engine in the rear of the chassis. The weight was 2,400lb and the price $3,000. GMN

HALL (ii) (US) 1914–1915

(1) Hall Cyclecar Manufacturing Co, Waco, Tex. 1914
(2) Hall Motor Car Co, Waco, Tex. 1915

This two-seater tandem cyclecar had a rear section which could be removed to make a light delivery van. Its underslung frame allowed a very low centre of gravity.

A 1½-litre 4-cylinder engine furnished 18hp. It had a 2-speed Fuller transmission with shaft drive, and with wire wheels it cost $395. GMN

HALL (iii) (GB) *1918–1919*
H.E. Hall & Co, Tonbridge, Kent

The Hall Flat-8 was an attempt to produce a smooth-running town car for private use, or as a taxicab. The prototype had a 20.6hp horizontal 8-cylinder engine specially made in the company's workshops, but used a number of components from other cars, such as a Talbot radiator and a Studebaker rear axle. With a very short bonnet, and long wheelbase, the car looked similar to a pre-war Lanchester or N.E.C. Probably only one was made, and this survives today. GNG

HALL & MARTIN see MARTIN (i)

HALLADAY (US) *1905–1922*
(1) Streator Motor Car Co, Streator, Ill. *1905–1913*
(2) Barley Mfg Co, Streator, Ill. *1913–1917*
(3) Halladay Motor Car Co, Lexington, Ohio *1917–1919*
(4) Halladay Motor Car Co, Attica, Ohio *1919–1920*
(5) Halladay Motor Car Co, Newark, Ohio *1920–1922*

Designed by L.P. Halladay, the first 20 Halladay cars were powered by 30hp 4-cylinder Oswald engines, replaced in 1907 by units of Rutenber manufacture: in various sizes the latter powered nearly all subsequent Halladay cars. A 6-cylinder 50hp engine was introduced for 1912, alongside 30 and 40hp fours, but from 1914 onwards all Halladays were sixes. In 1913 control of the company passed to Albert C. Barley, secretary and director of the Rutenber Motor Co, who made Halladays for four years. In 1916 he introduced a new and more glamorous car, the Roamer, and a year later he sold his interest in the Halladay company to a group of Ohio businessmen, and transferred Roamer production to Kalamazoo, Michigan.

The later Halladays were conventional touring cars, although a few sedans were also made. For 1922 a new 4-cylinder light car, the Falcon (iv), was introduced alongside the Halladay Light Six, but all production ceased in March 1922. GNG

HALLAMSHIRE (GB) *1900–1905*
Durham, Churchill & Co Ltd, Sheffield, Yorks.

The Hallamshire light car originally used a 7hp Simms engine, and most models had the Champion friction clutch which was a speciality of the firm. Later cars used the 10/12hp 2-cylinder Aster engine, or 4-cylinder engines of 12hp and 14/18hp, made by Forman and Aster respectively. They were well thought of locally, and achieved many successes in Yorkshire hill climbs and reliability trials. The company also made commercial vehicles under the name Churchill which remained in production until after World War 1. GNG

HALVERSON (US) *1908*
A. Halverson, New York, N.Y.

This juvenile car used a 4-cylinder F.N. air-cooled engine. Wheelbase was a diminutive 3ft 10in with track of only 2ft 2in. Total weight was given as 223lb. GMN

HAMILTON (i) (US) *1909*
Hamilton Carriage Co, Hamilton, Ohio

The Hamilton was a high-wheeler with a 16hp air-cooled opposed 2-cylinder engine. A planetary transmission was used and the 34 in wheels were fitted with solid rubber tyres. GMN

HAMILTON (ii) (GB) *1921–1925*
D.J. Smith & Co Ltd, Wickford, Essex

The Hamilton light car was offered in only one model, a two-seater with a 9hp 2-cylinder Precision engine and friction drive. Prices dropped steadily from £230 in 1921 to £150 when production ceased in 1925. Like several more illustrious makes the Hamilton used a circular radiator, but this feature did not save it from extinction. GNG

HAMLEN see LENHAM

HAMLIN-HOLMES; HAMLIN (US) *1919–1930*
(1) Hamlin-Holmes Motor Co, Chicago, Ill.
(2) Hamlin Motor Co, Harvey, Ill.

The Hamlin-Holmes prototype, which initiated a grandiose scheme to manufacture front-wheel-drive cars, was produced in 1919 in a touring model which was powered by a Lycoming 4-cylinder engine. It looked rather like a Model T Ford. Thereafter, pilot models appeared annually in various styles and using various engines, all of them for test purposes. In 1923, Hamlin-Holmes advertised a tourer as a production car, but production failed to materialize. A racing car was entered in the 1926 Indianapolis event, and 1930 a Hamlin (the Holmes name had been dropped) was advertised. The car had two axle systems allowing all weight to be carried on a dead axle. An exceptionally low centre of gravity was the selling-point of the Hamlin; it was achieved by placing the axles very low. The prototype

1918 HALL(iii) 20.6hp landaulette (unrestored) *Gordon Brooks*

1908 HALLADAY 35/40hp roadster. *The Veteran Car Club of Great Britain*

1904 HALLAMSHIRE 10hp two-seater. *Autocar*

343

1923 HAMPTON 11.9hp tourer. *Max Williamson*

1927 HAMPTON 11.9hp coupé. *G.N. Georgano*

1922 HANDS 9.8hp two-seater. *G.N. Georgano*

of the Hamlin Front-Drive car was a 4-door club sedan. The radiator was slanted and bonnet louvres were horizontal; in appearance, it closely resembled the Gardner Front-Drive prototype of the same year. The concern failed before subsequent models could be manufactured.   KM

HAMMER (US) *1905–1906*
Hammer Motor Co, Detroit, Mich.

This was a light car which in 1905 used a 2-cylinder engine of 12hp. In 1906, a 24hp 4-cylinder engine was used to power an 1,800lb five-seater tonneau. There was a choice of planetary or sliding-gear transmission and final drive was by shaft. The Hammer Motor Co was formed from part of the Hammer-Sommer Auto Carriage Co, which became defunct in 1905.   GMN

HAMMER-SOMMER (US) *1902–1904*
Hammer-Sommer Auto Carriage Co, Ltd, Detroit, Mich.

This car was made only in a five-seater, detachable tonneau model. The opposed 2-cylinder engine, mounted beneath the body, developed 12hp and a planetary transmission was used. The car was claimed to reach 35mph. This company split up and manufactured Hammer and Sommer cars separately.   GMN

HAMMOND (GB) *1919–1920*
Whitworth Engineering Co Ltd, Finchley, London N.

The Hammond was described as a light car from its 11.9hp rating, but a very long stroke (69 × 150mm) gave it a capacity of 2¼ litres. The chassis was conventional and it was one of the early post-war cars which were going to be built in vast numbers, in this case in a former aircraft factory on a 50 acre site. The price was to be about £400, but very few cars were made.   GNG

HAMPTON (GB) *1911–1933*
(1) Hampton Engineering Co, Hampton-in-Arden, Warwickshire *1911*
(2) Hampton Engineering Co Ltd, King's Norton, Birmingham *1912–1919*
(3) Hampton Engineering Co Ltd, Dudbridge, Stroud, Glos. *1919–1920*
(4) Hampton Engineering Co (1920) Ltd, Dudbridge, Stroud, Glos. *1920–1925*
(5) Stroud Motor Manufacturing Co Ltd, Dudbridge, Stroud, Glos. *1926*
(6) Hampton Cars (London) Ltd, Dudbridge, Stroud, Glos. *1927–1930*
(7) Safety Suspension Car Co Ltd, Cainscross, Stroud, Glos. *1931–1933*

W. Paddon sold other people's cars before deciding that he could build equally well himself. From 1912, he followed a one-model policy: the 12/16, a conventional 4-cylinder of 1,726cc, based on imported proprietary parts. A heavier Colonial version was also listed. In 1914, with light cars fashionable, a 2-cylinder 2-stroke of Hampton's own manufacture was announced, with pressed-steel frame and bevel drive. This model was soon withdrawn, and buyers were offered instead, a choice of a true cyclecar with an 8hp air-cooled Precision twin, 3-speed countershaft gears and belt final drive, or a conventional light car, with a 1,244cc Chapuis-Dornier engine. For the post-war expansion, part of a large ironworks was taken over in Gloucestershire. The first model made here was the 10/16 of 1919, with a 1,496cc ohv Dorman 4KNO engine. Pre-war type light car chassis were used, with variations in the wheelbase and with vacillation between half and three-quarter elliptic rear suspension. The following year a 1,795cc version was marketed, also powered by Dorman. The firm made their own gearboxes, and Lucas or Brolt electrical equipment was available.

Near the beginning of 1920 output was running at six cars per week; by the end of the year the company had suffered the first of its reformations. Designs were altered in detail only for 1921 and 1922. This period was marked by various sporting successes, in addition to the climbs of the notorious 1 in 2½ acclivity of Nailsworth Ladder both before and after the war. J.W. Leno managed a 'gold' in the 1924 Scottish 1,000 miles trial; Brian Marshall lapped Brooklands at over 89mph in 1922. For 1923, the 1,795cc was known as the 11/35, and the 9/21 Junior of 1,247cc was introduced, Meadows engines now being used. In 1924 a 14hp of 2,121cc was added to the range, whilst the 12hp (formerly 11/35) shrank to 1,496cc and acquired early front wheel brakes. Then the firm failed again. They were resuscitated by W.F. Milward, the works manager, aided by Leno and G. Dixon. Marginal improvements to the Hampton 12 were announced in late 1925, including a 3-bearing crank and more wheelbase variations. Similarities between Hamptons of this date and Charron-Laycocks may not have been entirely co-incidental, since both Milward and Dixon had been with that firm. More capital appeared in 1927, when Hampton Cars (London) Ltd was formed. This year's reorganization retained the 12hp as the 12/40, and added the 15/45, a 6-cylinder of 1,683cc. By 1928, 300 cars a year were being turned out, including the year's new model, the 9hp; mechanically similar to the old Junior, this was usually clad in clumsy fabric or metal saloon bodywork. For 1929 the 9hp and 12/40hp were continued, and a 6-cylinder 20hp was added, with the 2,931cc ohv Meadows engine.

With the trade recession menacing, the firm started to offer, as variants on the trusty 12/40, a supercharged sports model and adjustable rear suspension borrowed from the Hodgson. By 1930 they were involved with the Cowburn gearbox, incorporating coned rollers in place of gears, dependent on degrees of friction regulated by little coil springs. When Meadows credit ran out, the 12/40 was

eplaced by another 12hp of only 1,196cc, possibly of their own manufacture, whilst
00 ohv straight-8 engines of 2,262cc, with 50 matching chassis, were optimistically
rdered from Röhr in Germany. This chassis was based on a sheet-steel tray, with
ndependent suspension by double transverse half-elliptics at the front and long
antilevers at the rear. Models originally listed for 1931 were a revived 12/40, the
ontinued 9hp and 20hp, and the Röhr-engined 18hp, in Röhr or Hampton chassis
o choice. All these were later withdrawn, the short-stroke 12hp (80mm) became
vailable again, and an sv 4-bearing 6-cylinder of 2,414cc was obtainable in
ither type chassis, at £150 difference in price. The firm inevitably expired once
nore, but the 8-cylinder re-appeared ephemerally in Röhr's 1931 size of 2½ litres.
The receiver, Thomas Godman, formed a new company to offer the Röhr chassis
with a choice of the sv 6-cylinder or the 1932 Röhr engine, now of 2,736cc. It is
nlikely that any of these were sold, and the last Hampton made was probably
Milward's personal special, a Röhr-type car constructed from parts acquired at
he Dudbridge works sale, and used by him up to World War 2.　　　　DF

HANDLEY-KNIGHT; HANDLEY (US) 1921–1923
Handley Motors Inc, Kalamazoo, Mich.

This make was first known as the Handley-Knight and it used the sleeve-valve
4-cylinder Knight engine from its inception until early 1923. Thereafter, the
Models 6/60 and 6/40 used Midwest and Falls 6-cylinder engines exclusively. The
6/60 used a conventional radiator whereas its smaller counterpart, the 6/40, was
built with a V-type. On both models, small handle attachments, or loops encircled
he upper sections of the headlamps and helped enthusiasts to recognize the make –
If it carries handles, it's a Handley' (although the Reo of this period had the same
novel loops). Checker Cab bought up the Handley interests in May 1923.　　KM

HANDS (GB) 1921–1924
G.W. Hands Motor Co, Birmingham

When G.W. Hands, originator of the Calthorpe car, left that company he made
a light car bearing his own name for a short while. It was conventional in every
way, an assembled machine with a water-cooled, 4-cylinder, side-valve engine of
1,100cc by Dorman, and a Wrigley 3-speed gearbox and rear axle. It was, however,
oo expensive to succeed, and a new 15hp six with an overhead camshaft, introduced
n 1924, did not help. Hands returned to his old firm, taking this 15hp car with him
or production as a new Calthorpe.　　　　TRN

HANOMAG (D) 1924–1939
Hannoversche Maschinenbau AG vorm. Georg Egestorff, Hanover-Linden

Hanomag was founded before the turn of the century and was a well-known
producer of locomotives when they made their first acquaintance with road vehicles
in 1905, producing steam lorries under Stolz patents. The first private car appeared
in 1924 and was the 2/10PS two-seater, commonly known in Germany as the
Kommisbrot (army loaf). It was quite an unconventional design. The narrow wheel-
track eliminated the need for a differential, while the unique all-enveloping body
nevertheless enabled two passengers to sit side by side. The single-cylinder ohv
499cc engine was mounted in the rear, the axle being driven by chain. This model
was in production until 1928, by which time 15,775 had been built. It was followed
by a conventional 3/16PS sv 4-cylinder car and a number of other models. Of these
the Garant and Kurier (both of 1,089cc), Rekord (1,494cc) and the Sturm (6-
cylinder, 2,250cc) were very popular. The latter two models were also available
in very attractive open two-seater versions. Hanomags were successful in rallies
and trials. The company pioneered the use of diesel engines in private cars and
presented the Rekord Diesel with a 1,910cc engine developing 35bhp in 1936. A
world record for diesel-engined cars was gained in 1939 by an aerodynamic version
of the Rekord Diesel, which achieved a top speed of 95mph from a flying start. A
6-cylinder diesel engine was designed but was never used in a car because of the
outbreak of World War 2. An aerodynamic 1.3-litre saloon introduced in 1939 was
credited with over 70mph for only 32bhp.

After the war Hanomag presented a new private car, the Partner, at the
Frankfurt Motor Show of 1951. It was a front-driven three-seater with a 3-cylinder
2-stroke 697 engine. Although it was a very promising design it did not go into
production. Hanomag today is an important producer of lorries and vans of up to
3½ tons payload.　　　　HON

HANOVER (US) 1921–1924
Hanover Motor Car Co, Hanover, Pa.

The Hanover cyclecar was unusual in that its promoters intended it primarily
for export, which was a sensible idea in view of the unpopularity of the type on
its home ground. This helped it to be more successful than other American cyclecars:
800 were made, of which many were exported to Japan. The engine was a 2-cylinder,
air-cooled unit.　　　　TRN

HANSA (D) 1906–1939
(1) Hansa Automobil-Gesellschaft mbH, Varel 1906–1914; Bielefeld 1913–1914
(2) Hansa-Lloyd-Werke AG, Varel 1914–1929; Bremen 1929–1931
(3) Hansa-Lloyd und Goliath-Werke Borgward & Tecklenborg, Bremen 1931–1937

1924 HANOMAG Kommissbrot 499cc coupé.
G.N. Georgano

1934 HANOMAG Rekord 1½-litre drophead
coupé. *Neubauer Collection*

1938 HANOMAG Sturm 2.2-litre saloon.
Rheinstahl Hanomag AG

1912 HANSA Type E 3.8-litre tourer. *Autocar*

1934 HANSA 500cc coupé. *Borgward-Werke AG*

1902 HANZER 5hp two-seater. *C.E. Baker*

(4) Hansa Lloyd-Goliath-Werke Carl F.W. Borgward, Bremen *1937–1939*

The Hansa works were founded with the intention of producing small cars. The first was a 7/9PS car with a single-cylinder 720cc De Dion engine based on the French Alcyon. It appeared in 1906, and was sold under the name HAG. After a few more models with proprietary engines such as Fafnir the Hansa 6/14PS appeared in 1907 with a 4-cylinder engine of the company's own design. A wide range of models was offered during the following years. Among them were the Types D (10/30PS 2,612cc) and E (15/50PS, 3,815cc) of 1911 with overhead valves, a feature which was rare at that time. Hansa cars were produced in considerable numbers and they were renowned for their high technical standard and their good workmanship.

In 1913 Hansa took over the Westfalia works at Bielefeld and Hansa cars were built there in 1913 and 1914. The Type F (2,515cc) took part successfully in the 1914 Austrian Alpine Trial. In 1914 Hansa merged with Lloyd, the firm adopting the name Hansa-Lloyd. The production of Hansa cars was carried on until World War 1. After the war Hansa concentrated on light and medium-sized cars which were marketed as Hansas. The Lloyd factory specialized in the heavier cars and commercials, which were sold as Hansa-Lloyds. Post-war models were the P 8/36PS with a 4-cylinder 2,063cc engine, also available in a short-wheelbase sports version, and two cars, a 13/60PS (6-cylinder, 3,262cc) and a 16/70PS (8-cylinder, 3,996cc) which were equipped with American Continental engines.

In 1929 Hansa was taken over by Borgward-Goliath. Production in the Varel works ceased and Hansa private cars were subsequently built only in Bremen. The Konsul, Senator, Matador and Imperator were family and prestige cars with 4-, 6- and 8-cylinder engines with capacities up to 5.8-litres and outputs to 100bhp. The 3.2-litre Senator was an unusually large four for the period, and the Matador had a 2.6-litre Continental engine, and the combination of independent rear suspension and a backbone frame. In 1933 the small Hansa 400 was introduced. It had a 2-cylinder 2-stroke rear engine of 400cc and was later available with a 500cc engine. A new model, the Hansa 1100, with all independent suspension appeared in 1934. It was in production until 1939 and became very popular. Other models were the 6-cylinder '1,700' (also available in a twin-carburettor sports version), the '2,000' and the '3,500' Privat.

After 1938 Hansa cars were marketed as Borgwards. In 1958 the Hansa name was revived for the flat-four Goliath; it had previously been used as a type name for some Borgwards.   HON

HANSA-LLOYD (D) *1921–1929*
Hansa-Lloyd-Werke AG, Bremen

This make succeeded the Lloyd after the amalgamation with Hansa in 1914. Hansa continued to build private cars under its own name, while Hansa-Lloyd specialized in commercial vehicles – but also produced two luxury cars. These were the Treff As, with a 4-cylinder 4,056cc engine producing 60bhp, and the Trumpf As with 8-cylinder, 100bhp power units of 4,640cc or 5,220cc capacity. Hansa-Lloyd was taken over by Borgward-Goliath in 1929 and production of private cars ceased altogether, although commercials were continued.   HON

HANSEN (US) *1902*
Hansen Automobile Co, Cleveland, Ohio

The Hansen was a light runabout with a mudguard-less two-seater body, and a single-cylinder engine mounted under the seat. In September 1902 the company was succeeded by the General Automobile & Manufacturing Co who made an enlarged car called the General (ii).   GNG

HANSEN-WHITMAN (US) *1907*
Hansen Auto & Machine Works, Pasadena, Calif.

It is claimed that ten of these were built as five-seater touring cars. They used a 2-cylinder 2-stroke water-cooled engine. The drive was through a friction transmission and chains to the rear wheels. An unusual feature was the wicker seat backs.   GMN

HANSON (US) *1917–1923*
Hanson Motor Co, Atlanta, Ga.

One of the few cars built in Georgia, the Hanson was an assembled vehicle which used Continental 6-cylinder engines in both its Model 50 and larger Model 66 forms. Several hundred Hansons were produced in both open and closed models and sales, unlike many other cars built in the Southern United States, were not confined to the immediate area of manufacture.   KM

HANZER (F) *1900–1903*
Hanzer Frères, Petit-Ivry, Seine

Hanzer Frères began by making tricycles in 1899, and in 1900 introduced a voiturette powered by a front-mounted 3hp De Dion engine, and having 3 speeds. 1901 cars had 6hp Aster engines and 2 speeds, and were available with two- and four-seater bodies. They took part in several races including the Paris-Berlin. The 1902–03 range consisted of two single-cylinder models, of 5 and 6½hp, and a 9hp twin, and at this time they were taken over by Durey-Sohy who marketed the range under their own name for at least one year.   GNG

HARDING (i) (CDN) *1911*

Harding Machine Co, London, Ont.

This two-seater runabout used a 20hp 4-cylinder G.B. and S. engine. It was offered only as a runabout equipped with a torpedo body based on the American Hupmobile.   GB

HARDING (ii) (US) *1916–1917*

Harding Motor Car Co, Cleveland, Ohio

The Harding Twelve was made only as a seven-seater touring car. It was one of the earliest 12-cylinder cars on the American market. The engine, of 5.8-litres' capacity, was constructed from two 6-cylinder engine blocks which were mounted on a common crankshaft.   GMN

HARDINGE see PULLMAN (i)

HARISCOTT (GB) *1920–1921*

Harrison, Scott & Co, Bradford, Yorks.

The Hariscott was a little-known, assembled sports car using the 1½-litre sv Coventry-Simplex engine. A 4-speed gearbox was used, and maximum speed was said to be 60mph.   GNG

HARLÉ see SAUTTER-HARLÉ

HARPER (i) (GB) *1905–1906*

Harper Motor Co, Aberdeen

Although they had experimented with cars as early as 1898, the Harper brothers did not make a vehicle for sale until 1905. This was an all-weather landaulet based on the single-cylinder Cadillac, with the engine under the footboard, driving the rear axle via an epicyclic gearbox and single chain. The 2 forward speeds and the reverse were operated by pedals only.   GNG

HARPER (ii) (US) *1907–1908*

Harper Buggy Co, Columbus City, Ind.

This car was a small two-seater runabout, but not a high-wheeler. It was driven by a water-cooled, 2-cylinder opposed engine of 14hp. A planetary transmission was used.   GMN

HARPER (iii) (GB) *1921–1926*

A.V. Roe & Co Ltd, Stretford, Manchester

One of the oddest yet most practical of the 3-wheeled cyclecars that appeared in Britain in the 1920s was the Harper Runabout. It was designed by R.O. Harper and made in the aircraft factory of A.V. Roe & Co Ltd. Although it had two wheels at the rear, the Harper superficially resembled a motor scooter of the time more than any kind of car, with its tandem seats, handlebar steering, small wheels and centrally-mounted, 2-stroke, single-cylinder Villiers engine of only 269cc. However, this unit had a hand starter, there was 3-speed chain transmission, quarter-elliptic leaf springs were provided to all wheels and there was a true chassis-body unit of integral construction. The wheels were detachable and also had detachable rims. The two rear wheels had disc-type brakes. This interesting and comparatively complicated design was also efficient, providing 100 miles to the gallon of fuel and over 40mph for £100 (later reduced to £81). It deserved to survive, but the greater comfort and space, and conventional design, of normal light cars was bound to prevail.   TRN

HARRIS (US) *1923*

Wisconsin Automotive Corp, Menasha, Wisc.

A 6-cylinder assembled car, of which very few were produced.   KM

HARRIS-LÉON LAISNE see LÉON LAISNE

HARRISON (i) (US) *1905–1907*

(1) Harrison Wagon Co, Grand Rapids, Mich. *1905–1906*
(2) Harrison Motor Car Co, Grand Rapids, Mich. *1907*

The Harrison became a large car through several model changes and ended with a wheelbase of over 10ft. The 1906 and 1907 models featured a self-starting system which introduced acetylene into the proper cylinder for starting 'on the spark'. These cars used a 4-cylinder engine of 6.3-litres with overhead valves. Push-rods for the exhaust valves had a ring-shaped section so that they straddled the exhaust piping.   GMN

HARRISON (ii) (GB) *1971 to date*

Ken Harrison, Dartford, Kent

This interesting monocoque design revived interest in Formula 4, which had been dominated almost from its inception by Vixen cars. Front suspension consisted of parts from various Triumph models, but incorporating anti-dive features, and exceptional handling was achieved through remarkably low roll centres. A Formula 3 version was planned for 1972.   DF

1905 HARPER(i) 10hp landaulette.
Autocar

1921 HARPER(iii) 2½hp runabout. *Autocar*

1906 HARRISON(i) 4-cylinder tourer.
Automotive History Collection, Detroit Public Library

1951 HARTNETT 594cc tourer.

1915 HARVARD 14.4hp two-seater. *Keith Marvin Collection*

1917 HATFIELD(ii) Suburban five-seater. *Keith Marvin Collection*

HARROUN (US) 1917–1922
Harroun Motor Sales Corp, Wayne, Mich.

Named after the racing driver Ray Harroun who distinguished himself in 191
by winning the first Indianapolis 500 Sweepstakes, the Haroun was a low-price
car using its own make of 4-cylinder engine. The only body styles available wer
open models.   KM

HART (GB) 1900–1901
E.W. Hart & Co, Luton, Beds.

E.W. Hart was mainly an agent for electric and petrol-electric cars by suc
manufacturers as Lohner-Porsche and, later, Austro-Daimler, but he did show
under his own name a light electric two-seater called the Lutonia. This had a 2h
Bergmann electric motor geared directly to the rear axle.   GN

HARTMAN (US) 1914
George V. Hartman, Red Bluff, Iowa

George Hartman built a small number of two or four-seater cars powered b
4-cylinder Model engines. Most were $3\frac{5}{8} \times 4\frac{3}{4}$in units, but one or two cars ha
$3\frac{1}{2} \times 5$in engines.   GN

HARTNETT (AUS) 1951–1957
Hartnett Motor Co, Melbourne, Victoria

The Hartnett story is one of ambitious plans, frustrations, and lawsuits. Laurenc
Hartnett, one of the men behind the original Holden scheme, felt that there wa
a demand in Australia for a smaller car than that planned by General Motors
After negotiations in 1946 with Fiat and Renault, he acquired the rights of th
original 2-cylinder Grégoire (ii), shortly after the failure of the Kendall (ii) concer
in England. Backing from the State of Victoria was not followed by the expecte
support from the Commonwealth Government in Canberra. In spite of this Hartnet
was able to float his company and the car was announced as a 594cc ohv air
cooled flat-twin with fwd, rack and pinion steering and hydro-mechanical brakes
to sell for £549. Though the mechanical components were supplied to schedule
the contractor responsible for the supply of body panels failed to deliver them
and in the end only 120 Hartnetts were turned out, these having hand-made coach
work in saloon, tourer and station wagon forms. Plans had also been made fo
the manufacture of the 2-litre Hotchkiss-Grégoire in Australia, but these, under
standably, never materialized.

After the collapse of the Hartnett scheme, Hartnett took up the sponsorship o
Nissan products in the Commonwealth.   MCS

HARVARD (US) 1915–1920
(1) Pioneer Motor Car Co, Troy, N.Y.
(2) Adirondack Motor Car Co, Hudson Falls, N.Y.
(3) Harvard Motor Car Co, Hyattsville, Md.

The Harvard car, powered by a 4-cylinder Model engine, appeared only as an
open two-seater. From 1917 to 1920, Sterling engines were used. All Harvards
were made with right-hand drive, built for export to New Zealand. They featured
a hidden compartment for the spare wheel at the bottom of the rear deck.   KM

HASBROUCK (US) 1899–1901
Hasbrouck Motor Co, Newark, N.J.

The Hasbrouck was a light car with a large single-cylinder engine mounted in
the centre of the chassis, driving through a 2-speed epicyclic gearbox and chain
final drive. The engine had two 18in flywheels.   GNC

HASSLER (US) 1917
Hassler Motor Co, Indianapolis, Ind.

A small car of short life and limited production, the Hassler was available only
as a two-seater roadster at a price of $1,650. It was powered by a 4-cylinder Buda
engine of 3.7 litres capacity. Houk wire wheels were standard equipment. Front
suspension was by two semi-elliptic springs clipped at mid-point. Rear suspension
was by two semi-elliptic transverse springs with radius rods extending from the
axle housing to the gearbox.   KM

HATAZ (D) 1921–1925
Hataz Kleinautofabrik Hans Tautenhahn, Zwickau

This firm produced small cars with Steudel proprietary engines. The first model
was the 4/12PS with a 972cc 4-cylinder engine. A sports version developed 16bhp
and cars of this type took part in various racing events. At the Leipzig Fair of 1925
a line of cars with an increased engine output of 18bhp was shown, but production
had to cease soon afterwards as a result of financial difficulties.   HON

HATFIELD (i) (US) 1906–1908
Hatfield Motor Vehicle Co, Miamisburg, Ohio

This car was a high-wheeler also called the Buggyabout. It was designed for two
passengers and had an air-cooled 4-stroke, 2-cylinder opposed engine, friction
transmission, and double chain drive; steering was by wheel.   GMN

HATFIELD (ii) (US) *1917–1924*

Portland Car & Carriage Co, Sydney, N.Y.

The Hatfield was a conventional car powered originally by a 4-cylinder G.B. and S. engine. An early example of station wagon body was offered on this chassis. Later Hatfields had 4- or 6-cylinder Herschell-Spillman engines. For the last year or two of production, the open two-seater and tourer were available with sports style bodies, the most noticeable features of which were wire wheels and individual door steps. GNG

HAUTIER (F) *1899–1905*

té Hautier, Paris 16e

The Hautier company began by making an electric hansom cab, but added a petrol car to their range in 1900. This was a voiturette using a single-cylinder Soncin engine. By 1902 they had a range of three models with 1-, 2-, and 4-cylinder engines. These all had the same dimensions of 100 × 115mm, and the horsepower ratings were 7, 13 and 18hp respectively. Chain or shaft drive was available. GNG

1905 HAUTIER 16/20hp tonneau. *Lucien Loreille Collection*

HAVERS (US) *1908–1914*

Havers Motor Car Co, Port Huron, Mich.

Most Havers cars were powered by 6-cylinder engines. They were conventional in design, except for their long chassis. During the last year of manufacture a 55hp engine was used, of 6.2-litres capacity. In 1914 the Model 6-55 Speed Car for two passengers was priced at $2,250. GMN

HAWA (D) *1923–1925*

Hannoversche Waggonfabrik AG, Hanover

This firm, which manufactured railway carriages and wagons, started an automobile division in 1923 for the production of small electric cars. A two-seater (with tandem seats) and a van were available. Hawa also produced bodies for various other makes, such as Hanomag, Apollo and Mauser. HON

HAWK (US) *1914*

Hawk Cyclecar Co, Detroit, Mich.

The Hawk was a belt-driven cyclecar with a 9/13hp V-twin engine. It was advertised at $390 and could seat two passengers side by side. Its only distinctive feature was a sloping bonnet line. GMN

HAWKE (GB) *1969 to date*

1) D.R.L. Engineering Ltd, Waltham Cross, Herts. *1969–1970*
2) David Lazenby & Co Ltd, Hoddesdon, Herts. *1970–1972*
3) Hawke Engineering Ltd, Ware, Herts. *1972 to date*

Hawke's earliest successes, both on the tracks and in sales, were with spaceframe Formula Ford single-seaters, and the DL2A and DL2B cars of 1970 and 1971 maintained this precedent and gained several championships. The DL5 and the full-width 'Tyrrell'-nosed DL8 were Formula Super Vee machines, DL6A/B the 1971 Formula Atlantic/B model and DL7 a Formula 5000 car derived from the Leda LT20. During 1972 Sid Fox scored several victories with the side-radiatored DL9 Formula Ford car, and the DL10 was brought out for Formulas 3/B/Atlantic, based on a monocoque produced for the firm by Grand Prix Metalcraft. The firm then decided to retrench and concentrate on production only for Formula Ford. DF

1973 HAWKE DL10 Formula Ford racing car. *DRL Engineering Ltd*

HAWKINS *see* XENIA

HAWLEY (US) *1907*

Hawley Automobile Co Ltd, Constantine, Mich.

The Hawley was made in two models: a two-seater runabout on a 7ft wheelbase, and a four-seater tonneau on an 8ft wheelbase. The same 2-stroke, 2-cylinder engine was used for both. A friction transmission and final chain drive was common to both models. GMN

HAY BERG (US) *1907–1908*

Hay Berg Motor Car Co, Milwaukee, Wisc.

The only model of the Hay Berg was a three-seater roadster. It was powered by a 4-stroke, 4-cylinder water-cooled engine of 4.4 litres' capacity. This had a 3-speed transmission with shaft drive. The weight of this vehicle was 2,000lb. GMN

HAYNES (US) (1894) *1904–1925*

1) The Haynes-Apperson Co, Kokomo, Ind. *1904–1905*
2) Haynes Automobile Co, Kokomo, Ind. *1905–1925*

Elwood Haynes built his original single-cylinder car of buggy type in 1894. In 1898, with the Apperson brothers, he formed the Haynes-Apperson Automobile Co. In 1902, the Appersons and Haynes separated, although both companies remained in Kokomo. From June 1904 the cars were called either Haynes-Apperson or Haynes, while the company name was still Haynes-Apperson. This was officially changed to Haynes Automobile Company in September 1905.

The first production models of the Haynes (in 1904) were powered by 2- and 4-

1912 HAYNES 25hp tourer. *Kenneth Stauffer*

1923 HAYNES 31hp roadster. *National Motor Museum*

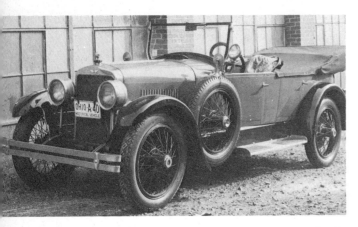

1923 H.C.S. 3½-litre tourer. *Kenneth Stauffer*

1929 H.E. 16/55 sports tourer. *National Motor Museum*

cylinder engines, sliding-gear transmissions and shaft drive. Only 4-cylinder engine were used in the years 1905–13. In 1912, three chassis were built, with a total of eight body types. In 1914, Model 26 was fitted with a 6-cylinder engine, and in 191 an electric gear change was standard on the larger chassis. For 1916, Haynes advanced to a 12-cylinder engine of 5.8-litres. This large engine was made by Haynes an continued to be manufactured through 1922, with no changes in bore or stroke. Th chassis varied in wheelbase during the post-World War 1 period from 10 to 11f The prices for the various models dropped from $4,200 for a seven-seater limousin in 1920, to $2,300 in 1925 for a five-seater sedan. Body styles in the Haynes rang were conservative, although one close-coupled four-seater coupé with distinctiv lines was made in 1923, and a Special Speedster, a two-seater roadster with wir wheels and attractive styling was introduced in 1921.　　　　　　　　GM

HAYNES-APPERSON (US) 1898–1904
The Haynes-Apperson Co, Kokomo, Ind.

Although Elwood Haynes had built his first car in 1894, none was made for sal until he joined forces with the Apperson brothers. By the end of 1898 Haynes Apperson cars were being made in two-, four- and six-seater models, all powered b a rear-mounted horizontally-opposed 2-cylinder engine of 3,120cc. The cars ha three forward speeds, spur gear transmission, and tiller steering. For three year this design was made without great change, although the straight dash gave way t a sloping version. In November 1901 the Appersons left the firm to make cars unde their own name, but the Haynes-Apperson name continued on the cars for nearl three years longer. By 1903 the left-hand tiller steering had been replaced by wheel, but this was still mounted on the left side, an unusual feature at the time o American cars. On 1904 models the engine was moved to the front under a conven tional bonnet, although it was still a horizontally-opposed twin. Prices ranged fron $1,450 for a two-seater runabout to $2,550 for a five-seater tonneau. From Jun 1904 the cars began to be referred to as Haynes, and the 1905 cars with vertica 4-cylinder engines were always known under this name. The company name wa not changed until September 1905.　　　　　　　　GN

HAZARD (US) 1914–1915
Hazard Motor Manufacturing Co, Rochester, N.Y.

This company largely concentrated on the production of engines for use b other manufacturers. For two years they ventured into the production of cars an two 4-cylinder models were offered, powered by Hazard engines of 24 and 30hp.　　MJW

H-B (H. BROTHERS) (US) 1908
H. Brothers, Chicago, Ill.

This high-wheeler for two passengers was priced at $500, or at $400 with 'com plete instructions for assembly'. It was of typical high-wheeler design with a 2-cylin der air-cooled engine, 36in diameter wheels with solid rubber tyres, planetary trans mission and single chain drive.　　　　　　　　GM

H-C (US) 1916
H-C Motor Car Co, Detroit, Mich.

This obscure make was marketed in roadster and touring versions at prices c $600 and $650 respectively. Both had a 4-cylinder, 28hp engine. Production wa limited to a very few units.　　　　　　　　GM

H.C.E. (GB) 1912–1913
(1) H.C.E. Cars, London, S.W. *1912*
(2) H.C.E. Cars, Harold Wood, Essex *1913*

The H.C.E. cyclecar used a 6/8hp Buckingham single-cylinder engine, and th choice of conventional gearbox or friction transmission. Final drive was by belt. Fo 1913 the same model was offered, but with the surprising refinement of front-whee brakes.　　　　　　　　GN

H.C.S. (US) 1920–1925
H.C.S. Motor Co, Indianapolis, Ind.

Harry C. Stutz sold his interest in the Stutz Motor Car Company of Indianapoli in 1919 and went on to make cars on his own account, in the same city. The H.C. was an expensive assembled machine (1921 price was $2,975), like its predecesso but its engines were by Weidely – a 4-cylinder, 3½-litre, overhead-valve unit – else sixes by Midwest. For a while, the H.C.S. sold reasonably well on the strengt of its promoter's name, but the firm died making taxicabs. The H.C.S. cars race at Indianapolis in 1923 were thinly disguised Millers.　　　　　　　　TR

H.E. (GB) 1920–1931
Herbert Engineering Co Ltd, Caversham, Reading, Berks.

The H.E. was one of the select company of British fast tourers of the 1920s. Lik so many of them, its characteristics included a generally straightforward desig good workmanship, sporting lines – and high price. The H.E.'s oval radiator wa particularly handsome and so was its aluminium, wire-braced coachwork b Morgan. Designed by R. J. Sully, it was a car of very modern design when it fir appeared in 1919. The proprietary engine, of 1,795cc, was a side-valve monobl

our with a detachable cylinder head. There was a separate 4-speed gearbox and
overhead worm drive – unusual in a car of this type. The only other unusual feature
of the H.E. was its rear suspension, which for many years was by underslung three-
quarter elliptic springs. The original H.E. gave way to the 14/20hp tourer of 1920,
with an engine of just over 2 litres' capacity, providing 40bhp at 3,000rpm, and a
stiffer frame. In 1922 a sports model called the '14/40' was added. It had dual coil
ignition, a tuned engine, a close-ratio gearbox and a shorter chassis. However, even
the tourer could achieve 67mph. For 1927, H.E. followed fashion by introducing a
six alongside the old four. This was a 2.3-litre unit rated at 15.7hp, still with side
valves. Performance was about the same as for the earlier tourer. It, too, had a sports
alternative, which in 1929 could reach 80mph. By this time the four had been
dropped and for 1930 was replaced, predictably, by a small 1½-litre six which could
be had in supercharged form. Presumably in the interests of cost-cutting, it used
quarter-elliptic springs at both ends.   TRN

HEADLAND (GB) 1897–c.1900
Headlands Patent Electric Storage Battery Co Ltd, Leyton, London E.
　Headlands mainly supplied their patent batteries to other firms, but they did exhibit
at the various shows a number of electric vehicles under their own name. These
included a two-seater phaeton with front-mounted motor which drove the front
wheels, the whole unit turning with the steering.   GNG

HEALEY (GB) 1946–1954
Donald Healey Motor Co Ltd, Warwick
　Donald Healey's first production used a welded-up chassis and trailing-arm type
independent front suspension, power being provided by the well-tried 2.4-litre 4-
cylinder ohv Riley engine. At the time of its introduction it was the world's fastest
series-production saloon (104.7mph for the flying-start mile) and cost £1,598.
Early competition successes included class victories in the 1947 and 1948 Alpine
Rallies, a second place overall in the 1949 event, and a win in the touring-car class
of the 1949 Mille Miglia. This model was made in small numbers until 1954, later
versions including the lightweight Silverstone two-seater of 1950, and some roomier
saloons and convertibles by Tickford. A 1950 export-only version for sale by Nash
had that firm's 3.8-litre ohv 6-cylinder engine, and took 4th place at Le Mans in
the same year. Only 506 were sold. A home-market version used the 3-litre Alvis
power unit. In 1952 Healey sought to reach a wider market with a 2.7-litre Austin-
engined sports two-seater, manufacture of which was taken over by Austin. With
the delivery of the last Nash-Healeys in August 1954, production at Warwick came
to an end.   MCS

HEALY (US) c.1912–c.1916
Healy & Co, New York, N.Y.
　The Healy was an electrically powered car, but detailed information on this
make has eluded considerable investigation. At least twenty of these cars were
registered in New York City in 1914 alone, and John D. Rockefeller Sr owned
1912, 1914 and 1916 models. Healy & Co were well-known coachbuilders, and
it is possible that they built the bodies, with chassis and running gear coming from
another factory.   GMN

HEBE (E) 1920–1921
Fabrica Española de Automóviles Hebe, Barcelona
　The Hebe was a light car powered by a 6/8hp 4-cylinder engine, made in touring
and sports form and, more unusually, as a miniature 2-door saloon.   GNG

HEDEA (F) 1913–1914
L. Accary, Paris 7e
　Also known as the Accary, this was a light car powered by a 10hp 4-cylinder
engine of 2,120cc.   GNG

HEIM (D) 1921–1926
Heim & Co, Badische Automobilfabrik, Mannheim
　Franz Heim, formerly a racing driver and an engineer with the Benz concern,
founded his own factory after World War 1 and presented his first car in 1921. It was
a 4-cylinder 2,086cc model. A 6-cylinder sports and a touring car both powered by
a twin-carburettor 2,385cc engine with overhead camshaft and detachable cylinder-
head came out in 1924. This was also available in a sports version with a 2-litre
engine. Production ceased in 1926.   HON

HEINE-VELOX (US) 1906–1909; 1921
(1) Heine-Velox Motor Co, San Francisco, Calif. 1906–1909
(2) Heine-Velox Engineering Co, San Francisco, Calif. 1921
　The first Heine-Velox was a high-priced 45hp, 4-cylinder machine that was made
for three years. After World War 1, Heine-Velox went into the ultra-luxury market,
seeking absolute quality in all respects. Their 1921 offering had a V-12 engine, its
chassis was furnished with hydraulically-operated four-wheel brakes and the complete car was the most expensive in America at the time, costing $17,000. Very few
were made.   TRN

1897 HEADLAND electric dogcart. *National Motor Museum*

1951 HEALEY 2.4-litre sports saloon.
British Motor Corporation

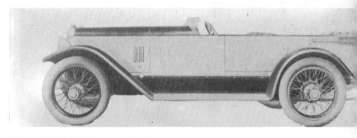
1921 HEIM 8/40PS tourer. *G.L. Hartner*

1921 HEINE-VELOX V-12 tourer. *Harrah's
Automobile Collection*

1959 HEINKEL (Trojan-built) 198cc 3-wheeler. *Trojan Ltd*

1901 HELIOS(i) *vis-à-vis. Oluf Berrum*

1899 HENRIOD(ii) 4hp duc. *National Motor Museum*

HEINIS (F) c.1925–c.1930
Etablissements Charles Heinis, Neuilly, Seine

Heinis made a small number of cars using a wide variety of engines. Apart from his own ohc designs, he used 4-cylinder S.C.A.P. engines of 1,100, 1,170 and 1,690cc and the straight-8 Lycoming of 5-litres. All these cars were produced in limited numbers, and were not listed in many of the better-known magazines.   GN

HEINKEL (D) 1955–1958
Ernst Heinkel AG, Stuttgart-Zuffenhausen

This former aircraft firm started production of engines and scooters after World War 2. In 1955 they presented a rear-engined bubble-car, with two front and one rear wheel. The engine was a single-cylinder 4-stroke air-cooled unit of 175cc. A later version of 198cc was also available with twin rear wheels. In 1958 the design was sold to Dundalk Engineering of the Irish Republic. Later this vehicle was built in England by Trojan.   HON

HEJKENSKIÖLD (S) 1918
G. Hejkenskiöld

This was a large four-seater cyclecar with 4-cylinder water-cooled engine and very spidery appearance. The climate in Sweden prevented the cyclecar from becoming popular there and the Hejkenskiöld never went into production.   C

HELBÉ (F) 1905–1907
Levêque et Bodenréder, Boulogne-sur-Seine

The Helbé derived its name from its makers (L et B), and was a light assembled car using $4\frac{1}{2}$, 6 and 9hp De Dion single-cylinder engines. The first Puch cars were based on this marque. Some components were made for them by Delage. For 1907 a 12hp 4-cylinder engine was added to the range.   GN

HELIOS (i) (S) 1901–1902
AB Södertälje Verkstäder, Södertälje

This company's first venture into car manufacture was a single-cylinder rear-engined *vis-à-vis* type based on a German design. Chain drive was employed. In 1902 the company shelved the Helios and began to make the American Northern buggy under licence.   C

HELIOS (ii) (CH) 1906–1907
Automobiles Helios, Zürich

The Swiss Helios was an 18/24hp 4-cylinder car designed by J.J. Muggli and built by Brunau, Weidmann & Co. It was exhibited at the 1906 Paris Salon and 1907 Zurich Show, but very few were made.   GN

HELIOS (iii) (D) 1924–1926
Helios Automobil-Bau AG, Cologne-Ehrenfeld

Only one model was produced by this firm, a 2/8PS car with a horizontally opposed 2-cylinder 972cc engine.   HON

HELO (D) 1923
Helo-Kraftfahrzeugbau Herrmann & Lommatzsch, Berlin SO 23

This was a 3-wheeled cyclecar that used a 3PS D.K.W. engine to drive the single front wheel.   HON

HELVÉTIA (F) 1899–1900
Compagnie des Voitures Electriques Helvétia, Combs-la-Ville, Seine-et-Marne

Although built in France, these cars were called Helvétia as they were designed by a Swiss, Jacques Fischer-Hinnen. A small number of electric victorias and cabs were made, and it was planned to built the cars in Switzerland, although this never materialized. In 1900 Jacques Fischer-Hinnen went to Prague to design electric cars which were built by Frantisek Krizik.   GN

HENDERSON (US) 1912–1915
Henderson Motor Car Co, Indianapolis, Ind.

This car was built in open two-seater and five-seater forms, powered by an L-head, 4-cylinder engine of 4.6-litres. Standard equipment included a Stutz transmission and McCue wire wheels. The roadster was priced at $1,300 and the five-seater at $1,400. The sons of the founder of this company were responsible for the famous Henderson motorcycle.   GMN

HENNEGIN (US) 1908
Commercial Automobile Co, Chicago, Ill.

This was a high-wheeler with solid rubber tyres and wheel steering, powered by a 4-stroke, air-cooled 2-cylinder engine. Two models were produced, one on a wheelbase of 6ft 3in, the other on one of 7ft 3in.   GMN

HENNEY (US) 1921–1931
Henney Motor Car Co, Freeport, Ill.

An estimated 50 custom-built sports tourers were made by this well-known mancturer of funeral cars. A small number of closed sedans and limousines were also roduced during the remainder of the decade, powered by Continental 6 or Lycoming engines. In 1960 the Henney Company produced an electric conversion of the enault Dauphine, known as the Henney Kilowatt. It had 36 2-volt batteries, a 7.2hp iotor, and a range of 50 to 60 miles. Only experimental models were made.   KM

IENOU *see S.U.P.*

IENRIOD (i) (CH) *1896–1898*
Ienriod frères, Bienne
   Fritz Henriod built an experimental steam car in 1886, and a petrol car in 1893. n 1896 he exhibited a car with a 4hp rear-mounted horizontal engine, and hot tube gnition. Later that year he was joined by his younger brother Charles-Edouard and small series of cars with single or horizontally-opposed twin engines was made. .ll used chain final drive. In 1898 the engine was moved to the front, but in the same ear Charles-Edouard left in order to make cars at Neuilly in France, and Fritz eased to make cars under his own name. A few years later he made cars called .N.A. at Boudry, near Neuchatel.   GNG

IENRIOD (ii) (F) *1898–1908*
Ienriod et Cie, Neuilly, Seine
   C.E. Henriod was a prolific inventor who claimed to have made the first car to un on alcohol fuel. This was in 1898, and he entered cars in alcohol tests for some ears after this. In 1902 he was offering two models, a 6hp single-cylinder voiturette alled the Simplon, which looked very like the contemporary De Dion, and a 12hp -cylinder car. Three Henriod cars were entered for the 1903 Paris-Madrid race, wo 12hp and a new 24hp 4-cylinder model. The latter was shown at the 1903 ialon together with the 6 and the 12hp. A feature of these cars which was to last intil the end of production was the gearbox combined with the rear axle. A 32hp -cylinder, air-cooled car was available in 1906, as well as smaller models. This ised the same system of cooling by laterally-mounted fans as the Swiss-built S.N.A. lesigned by C.E. Henriod's elder brother Fritz. His design of rotary valve engine was used by Darracq for a few years until the Clegg-Darracqs appeared.   GNG

HENRY (US) *1910–1912*
Henry Motor Car Co, Muskegon, Mich.
   The first model of this car was a 35hp, five-seater tonneau which sold for $1,750. For 1911, both 40 and 20hp engines were available, with a choice of five body styles. The 1911 two-seater roadster had running-board mounted toolboxes.   GMN

HENRY J (US) *1950–1954*
Kaiser-Frazer Corp, Willow Run, Mich.
   The Henry J, named after Mr Kaiser, was an early but ill-timed attempt at a 'compact', on an 8ft 4in wheelbase, introduced in October 1950. It was very cheaply finished and mechanically conventional. On early models no boot access was provided, though a lid later became optional and, finally, standard. Power was by sv Willys engines, the 68bhp 2.2-litre 4-cylinder from the Jeep, or the 2.6-litre 6-cylinder developing 80bhp. The light Henry Js were good performers, and their chassis were used for Brooks Stevens' experimental Excalibur J sports car of 1952 and the Darrin roadster of 1953–54. But the cheapest Henry J sold for $1,363 in 1951, despite a targeted price of less than $1,000, and with Chevrolets starting as low as $1,460, price was an ineffective sales weapon. Darrin had suggested a short-wheelbase Kaiser utilizing stock Kaiser sheet metal instead of the spartan Henry J body, and using the money saved for a V-8 engine, but his advice was ignored. About 126,000 Henry Js were produced, with 1,123 '1954' models making up the last of the run after the Kaiser-Willys merger. The cars were also made in assembly plants in Japan, the Netherlands and Israel, but were equally unsuccessful abroad: only 15,000 were built overseas.   RML

HENSCHEL (D) *1899–1906*
Berliner Maschinenfabrik Henschel & Co, Berlin-Charlottenburg
   This firm produced mainly electric cars and supplied Berlin's first electric taxicab in 1899. A two-seater petrol car was also offered, but very few were built. There is no connection with Henschel's of Kassel. the well-known locomotive builders who started to manufacture lorries in 1925.   HON

HE-PING (p); HO-P'ING (wg) (PEACE) (CHI) *1958 to date*
Automobile Repair Works, Tientsin, Hopei
   Announced in 1958, the first models of the He-Ping resembled American cars of the period, especially the Plymouth, but in 1965 a greatly revised version appeared, with styling very similar to that of the 1957 Chevrolet Bel Air. Specifications of the 1969 model included a 55bhp ohv 4-cylinder engine of 1,453cc, and coil ifs.   BE

HÉRALD (F) *1901–1906*
Sté Hérald, Levallois-Perret, Seine

1951 HENRY J 2.6-litre sedan. *Kaiser-Jeep Corporation*

1900 HENSCHEL electric coupé. *Neubauer Collection*

1958 HE-PING saloon. *David Scott*

353

1904 HERALD 10hp motor-cab. *The Veteran Car Club of Great Britain*

1916 HERBERT 11.9hp two-seater. *Autocar*

1933 HERCULES(v) 200cc coupé. *Neubauer Collection*

1905 HERMES-SIMPLEX 50hp roadster. *Neubauer Collection*

The first Hérald was a single-cylinder voiturette made in conjunction with Pierre Onfray. The same year, 1901, the Hérald company made a 14hp 2-cylinder car, and followed this in 1902 with two 2-cylinder models, a 9hp and a 12hp. These were continued in 1903 and two 4-cylinder cars were added, a 16 and 20hp. They had rather old-fashioned looking gilled-tube radiators and chain drive. The 1905/06 range consisted of a 10hp twin and two 4-cylinder cars, a 16 and 28hp. A number of Héralds were used as taxicabs in London.   GNG

HERBERT (GB) 1916–1917
Herbert Light Car Co, London N.W.

The Herbert was an assembled car powered by a 4-cylinder Sterling engine (S.U.P. in the prototype), Salisbury axles and Smith electrical equipment. It was named after Herbert Smith who obtained his engines through S. Smith & Sons of Cricklewood (no family connection), and assembled the cars in a mews garage off Albany St. They were distinguished by a sharply pointed radiator top.   GNG

HERCULES (i) (CH) 1902–1903
Hercules AG, Menziken

Mainly makers of commercial vehicles, Hercules built a few chain-driven cars with front-mounted engines of 1-cylinder 6hp, or 2-cylinder 12hp. They had tonneau bodies which could be converted to light trucks.   GNG

HERCULES (ii) (US) c.1907
James Macnaughton Co, Buffalo, N.Y.

The Hercules was an electric-powered car made in two- and four-seater models. The enclosed Model 141 landaulet had a wheelbase of 6ft 3in. Drive to the rear wheels was by a single chain.   GMN

HERCULES (iii) (US) 1914
Hercules Motor Car Co, New Albany, Ind.

This make succeeded the Crown (iv). The car was a four-seater costing $495, or $550 with electric starting. It had a 4-cylinder L-head engine of 2.2-litres, and a 2-speed selective transmission. The car was designed by R.W. Fishback who, it was claimed, had been the designer of at least one European make.   GMN

HÉRCULES (iv) (E) 1922
The Hercules cyclecar was built by a former racing motorcyclist, Juan Antonio Orus. It never passed beyond the prototype stage.   GNG

HERCULES (v) (D) 1932–1933
Nürnberger Hercules-Werke AG, Nuremberg

This firm has produced motor cycles from 1904 up to the present day and also built commercial vehicles between 1906 and 1926. In 1932 Hercules offered a 3-wheeled two-seater private car. The single rear wheel was driven by chain from the rear-mounted 200cc Ilo proprietary engine.   HON

HERFF-BROOKS (US) 1914–1916
Herff-Brooks Corp, Indianapolis, Ind.

The Herff-Brooks was a light car, with 4- or 6-cylinder L-head engines of 40 and 50hp respectively. The Six-50 roadster with 3-speed transmission cost $1,375.   GMN

HERMES (i) see ACCLES-TURRELL

HERMÈS (ii) H.I.S.A. (B/I) 1906–1909
(1) SA Hermès, Bressoux, Liège
(2) Hermes Italiana SA, Naples

This Italo-Belgian venture had the backing of racing driver Baron Pierre de Crawhez and used Italian labour and Belgian materials, though cars actually issued from both factories. Only one basic model appeared during the company's short life: a 4.2-litre 4-cylinder T-head machine with shaft drive, high-tension magneto ignition and a 4-speed gearbox with quadrant change. There was no foot accelerator, and ouput was quoted at 38bhp. A 40bhp version, built for the Coupe de la Commission Sportive in 1907, differed from production Hermès in having a Renault-style bonnet with sloping, flush-mounted frontal radiator. This was listed as a sporting variant in 1908, but a year later the prevailing industrial depression in Western Europe had swept the Hermès/H.I.S.A. away.   MCS

HERMES (iii) (US) 1920
Tsacomas Desmos, New York City, N.Y.

This was a light 4-cylinder four-seater car built by a Greek in New York and intended for export to Greece only. The radiator bore the name ΕΡΜΗΣ. At least two cars were made, but it is not certain whether either of them ever reached Greece.   GNG

HERMES-SIMPLEX (D) 1904–1906
E.E.C. Mathis, Sté Alsacienne de Construction Mécanique, Graffenstaden

In 1904 Ettore Bugatti parted company from De Dietrich for whom he had been

esigning, and joined forces with Mathis, the French agent for De Dietrich cars.
he result was the Hermes-Simplex car first displayed at the Paris Salon in 1904.
his had a 50hp 4-cylinder engine, with cylinders cast in pairs, 130 × 140mm, multi-
late clutch, 4-speed gearbox and transmission, chain drive and conventional semi-
lliptic springs. Overhead inlet valves were operated by rockers and pull-rods in turn
perated by a camshaft in the crankcase driven from the crankshaft by fibre gears.
xhaust valves were on the side. Cooling was by honeycomb radiator and water
ump. The brakes were unusual in that the hand lever operated the rear drum shoes,
ere being two pedals, one operating a band on the transmission, the other a second
and on the gearbox layshaft.

Later the range was extended to include three models: a 50hp (130 × 140mm),
60hp (140 × 140mm) and a 90hp (160 × 150mm). Some contemporary references
lso quote a small 28hp Model.

Mathis and Bugatti quarrelled in 1906 or 1907 and parted, Mathis continuing on
is own and Bugatti joining the Deutz company at Cologne.

A 40hp Hermes-Simplex chassis is known to exist today in France.　　HGC

1925 HERON(ii) 10.8hp tourer. *Autocar*

HERMON (GB) *1936*
Hermon Car Co Ltd, Orpington, Kent

The Hermon was a light car closely based on the 1½-litre British Salmson, but with
André-Girling coil independent front suspension and semi-elliptic rear suspension
n place of the Salmson's quarter elliptics. Probably not more than one car was made,
lthough it is possible that there was another using the 20/90 British Salmson
ngine.　　GNG

HERO (D) *1934*
The Hero was a 3-wheeled coupé powered by a 580cc D.K.W. 2-stroke engine
riving the rear wheels. Two bodies were available, 'a two-and-a-half-seater' and
four-seater.　　GNG

HERON (i) (GB) *1904–c.1905*
Heron Motor Co, Birmingham

The name of this first Heron car was an anagram of that of its promoter, J.J.
Horne. It was an extremely conventional machine, available in 1904 with 10, 12 and
4hp water-cooled 2-cylinder engines made by Aster, or with a 16hp 4-cylinder unit,
nd described as 'strong, simple and honestly built'. The chassis were supplied by
.J. West.　　TRN

HERON (ii) (GB) *1924–1926*
Strode Engineering Works, Herne, Kent

Made in the same works as the conventional Westcar, the Heron was a most un-
sual light car using a body of stitched plywood construction following Marks-Moirs
atents. The bodies were built by Samuel E. Saunders Ltd, of East Cowes, Isle of
Wight. The prototype was powered by a 997cc Ruby engine driving by belt (later
hains) to the rear axle. The first production Heron had an 11.9hp Dorman engine
nounted amidships, in a transverse position, driving the rear axle by chains. The
inal Heron was more sophisticated, and resembled a scaled-down Lancia Lambda
n appearance. It had a front-mounted 10.8hp Coventry-Climax engine and shaft
rive. In this model there was no chassis, and the engine and transmission were
nounted on a sub-frame.　　MJWW

1961 HERON(iii) Europa GT coupé. *Heron
Plastics Ltd*

HERON (iii) (GB) *1961-1965*
Heron Plastics Ltd, Greenwich, London S.E.10

The Heron Europa was available in kit form, based on a backbone chassis,
with most suspension parts by Triumph. An attractive fibreglass body was bonded
on, and a Ford engine fitted – usually the 105E. About three dozen were sold.　　DF

HERRESCHOFF (US) *1909–1914*
(1) Herreschoff Motor Co. Detroit, Mich. *1909–1914*
(2) Herreschoff Light Car Co, Troy, N.Y. *1914*

The Herreschoff began as a small car with a 24hp 4-cylinder engine, produced
in three models. Later models used 4- and 6-cylinder engines up to 3.8 litres. A
16hp light car was introduced in 1914.　　GMN

HERSCHELL-SPILLMAN (US) *1904–1907*
Herschell-Spillman Co, North Tonawanda, N.Y.

An early model (1904) was a five-seater tonneau. This was driven by a 4-cylinder
engine of 16/18hp and final drive was by chain. The main activity of the manufacturer was engine building.　　GMN

HERTEL (US) *1895–1900*
(1) Max Hertel, Chicago, Ill.
(2) Oakman Motor Vehicle Co, Philadelphia, Pa.; Greenfield, Mass.

The first Hertel was a very light car with bicycle-type frame, and the front wheels
carried in bicycle forks. It was powered by two 3½hp engines. The designer, Max
Hertel, afterwards made the Impetus cars at Pornichet in France. The Greenfield
factory of Oakman made engines for some early Locomobile petrol cars.　　GNG

1914 HERRESCHOFF 16hp two-seater. *The
Veteran Car Club of Great Britain*

1921 H.F.G. 9hp two-seater. *The Veteran Car Club of Great Britain*

1913 HILLMAN 9hp drophead coupé. *Rootes Motors Ltd*

1929 HILLMAN Fourteen drophead coupé. *J. Price*

HERTZ (US) 1925–1928
Yellow Cab Manufacturing Co, Chicago, Ill.

The Hertz car was the result of John Hertz' plan to rent out cars for self-drive. Hertz took over the old Shaw Livery Company of Chicago and marketed the remaining stock of large Shaw cars as Ambassadors. He redesigned the latter make in mid-1924 as the Ambassador Model D-1, a $1,695 sedan intended for car-hire operations. Late in 1925, the D-1 was renamed the Hertz and a touring model was added to the sedan to complete the line. The cars closely resembled contemporary Buicks. The car was withdrawn early in 1928 and since then standard makes have been used by the Hertz Drive Yourself concern.   KM

HESELTINE (US) 1916–1917
Heseltine Motor Corp, New York, N.Y.

This light car, with a choice of 8ft or 8ft 10in wheelbase, had a 2.3-litre 4-cylinder engine by Lycoming. Both two-seaters and four-seaters were priced at $695, including wire wheels.   GMN

HEWITT (US) 1906–1907
Hewitt Motor Co, New York, N.Y.

The Hewitt can claim to be the first V-8-powered American car, although the 7.9-litre engine was probably a French-built Antoinette. The Hewitt had selective transmission and shaft drive. The price of the chassis was $4,000. Also offered in 1907 was a model with a 10hp single-cylinder engine, on which the British Adams was based. After 1907, the Hewitt Motor Co concentrated on manufacturing heavy trucks.   GMN

HEWITT-LINDSTROM (US) 1900–1901
Hewitt-Lindstrom Electric Co, Chicago, Ill.

This company built mainly heavy electric trucks and buses, but they also made a few electric cars for town use, and a light two-seater runabout.   GNG

HEYBOURN (GB) 1914
A.W. Heybourn & Co, Maidenhead, Berks.

The Heybourn was a very light cyclecar using a 5hp single-cylinder Stag engine.   GNG

HEYMANN (US) 1898; 1904
(1) Heymann Motor Vehicle & Manufacturing Co, Melrose, Mass. 1898
(2) Heymann Motor Vehicle & Manufacturing Co, Boston, Mass. 1904

The first Heymann car was a two-seater carriage with tiller steering. The second, Boston-built, car was an unconventional machine with a 5-cylinder rotary engine mounted under a bonnet. Rated at 40hp, it had a capacity of 5 litres. Final drive was by shaft, and the price was $4,000.   GNG

HEXE (D) 1905–1907
Achenbach & Co, Hamburg

Achenbach started car manufacture by building Locomobiles under licence. In 1905 the first Hexe (german for 'witch') cars appeared, based on Nagant designs; the range comprised a 2-cylinder 9/10PS model and 4-cylinder cars of 14/16PS and 20/24PS. Three 4-cylinder models producing 18/20PS, 24/30PS and 40/45PS followed in 1906. The range was completed the next year with a 6-cylinder 30/35PS car. Production ceased in 1907 and Achenbach concentrated on importing Nagant cars. HON

H.F.G. (GB) 1920–1921
C. Portass & Son Ltd, Sheffield, Yorks.

The H.F.G. light car used a 9hp air-cooled flat-twin engine, placed transversely on the near side. The flywheel acted directly on a friction disc on the off side, whence the drive was taken by an offset propeller shaft to the rear axle. Engine and transmission were all under the bonnet, and a two-seater body was used.   GNG

H.H.; HÜTTIS & HARDEBECK (D) 1906–1907
Hüttis & Hardebeck Motorwagenfabrik, Aachen

This firm produced private cars, with 10, 24 and 28hp engines, for which the brand-name Ferna was also used. In 1907 the firm was affiliated to Brunau of Switzerland and production at Aachen ceased.   HON

HIDIEN (F) 1898–1902
E. Hidien, Châtillon-sur-Indre, Indre

Some 20 voiturettes were constructed at the tiny Forge des Lampes, with very little besides rough castings (obtained locally to Hidien's designs) being bought outside. The first model had a horizontal twin engine of square bore/stroke ratio, situated under the rear seat, and driving by chain. Two further types were essayed before production settled on a Renault-like design, using a vertical twin T-head motor placed in front of the radiator, and driving through a leather cone clutch and 3-speed gearbox to a transmission shaft. The bodies were light and scanty, but meticulously finished. Hidien eventually removed to Châteauroux and turned to manufacturing farm machinery.   DF

HIDLEY (US) *1901*

Hidley Automobile Co, Troy, N.Y.

The Hidley steamer was rated at 8hp. This was a two-seater runabout weighing 350lb. A multi-passenger trap was also built. GMN

HIGHGATE (GB) *1903–1904*

Highgate Motor Co, London N.

The 1903 Highgate (sometimes sold as the HMC) was a two-seater light car of the Lacoste et Battmann variety with a 6½hp single-cylinder engine by Aster or De Dion, and a gilled-tube radiator. In 1904 the car had a more refined appearance with a neat honey-comb radiator. Prices were reduced from 170gns in 1903 to 125gns in 1904. GNG

HIGHLANDER (US) *1921*

Midwest Motor Co, Kansas City, Mo.

The Highlander, the name of which frequently appears in trade journals as 'Hylander', was a typical assembled car powered by a Continental 6-cylinder engine. A conventional tourer and a sports version were available during the short life of the make. KM

HILDEBRAND (D) *1922–1924*

Martin Hildebrand Automobilwerke AG, Singen (Hohentwiel)

This firm produced a small three-seater with a 5/15PS engine which was also sold as the Hisiho. HON

HILL & STANIER (GB) *1914*

R. Hill, Stanier & Co, Newcastle-upon-Tyne

This was a cyclecar with a 6/7hp air-cooled 2-cylinder engine, and chain final drive. The price was to be £85 to £90, and delivery was planned for the summer of 1914, but very few were made. GNG

HILLMAN (GB) *1907 to date*

(1) Hillman-Coatalen Motor Car Co Ltd, Coventry *1907–1909*

(2) Hillman Motor Car Co Ltd, Coventry (*1910–1946*); Ryton-on-Dunsmore, Warwickshire (*1946–1970*); Linwood, Glasgow (*1963–1970*)

(3) Chrysler United Kingdom Ltd, Ryton-on-Dunsmore, Warwickshire; Linwood, Glasgow *1970 to date*

This car was originally known as the Hillman-Coatalen, the first cars being the work of Louis Coatalen, who designed a 25hp 4-cylinder for the 1907 Tourist Trophy. Pre-1914 production was on a small scale, and consisted initially of big sv machines with separately cast cylinders (a 6.4-litre four and a 9.7-litre six) and shaft drive. The traditional shape of Hillman radiator emerged in 1908, and continued on all models up to 1930. Neither a little-known 1.8-litre 2-cylinder of 1913 nor a very small six of 2 litres' capacity in 1914 made much impression, but much more successful was the 9hp Hillman, a monobloc 1,357cc sv four, selling at £200. This was brought up to date with electrics after World War 1, and progressively developed until 1925, by which time it had grown to 1.6 litres. A sports version with a V-radiator, outside exhaust, and polished aluminium bodywork was raced quite extensively in the early 1920s and Raymond Mays served his apprenticeship on one of these. All 1923–5 Hillmans came with drophead bodywork and winding windows. A conventional sv Fourteen with a 4-speed gearbox and magneto ignition was the only model offered from 1926 to 1928, and production of this was stepped up after Rootes took over in the latter year. In 1929 prices started at £295, and 'Safety' versions were fitted with safety glass and servo brakes. Less happy was a companion to the Fourteen, a 2.6-litre ohv straight-8 with coil ignition. However, Hillman moved into the mass-production class in 1932 with their excellent 1,185cc sv Minx at £159. This was progressively developed up to the outbreak of World War 2, with 4-speed gearbox and the options of free-wheel and radio in 1934, all-synchromesh boxes in 1935 (these were dropped again in 1939), integral luggage boot in 1936, and unitary construction in 1940. The underslung Aero-Minx sports model of 1933 formed the basis for the Talbot and Sunbeam-Talbot Tens which resulted from Rootes' acquisition of the S.T.D. group, and there was even a luxury Minx-based Humber Ten, though this was marketed only in New Zealand. Alongside these there were also some sv 6-cylinder cars, 1936 and later versions having transverse independent front suspension, but they gave way to another sv 1.9-litre Fourteen, sold with hydraulic brakes by 1940; these were not added to the Minx until the Phase II models of late 1947, which also featured steering-column change.

Post-war Minxes continued the model's reputation as a style leader of conventional mechanical specification. 1949 cars had full-width five/six-seater bodywork, there was a more powerful 1¼-litre engine in 1950, and a hardtop coupé version, the Californian, in 1953. In 1955 the range was extended to include the Husky short-wheelbase station wagon, while de luxe Minxes acquired 1,395cc short-stroke ohv power units, and licence-production was taken up in Japan by Isuzu. The model continued to keep abreast of the times with its cylinder capacity increased to 1½ litres in 1959, to 1.6 litres in 1962, and to 1.7 litres with a 5-bearing crankshaft in 1966. Automatic transmission became optional in 1960,

1939 HILLMAN Minx 10hp saloon. *Rootes Motors Ltd*

1954 HILLMAN Minx Californian 1¼-litre coupé. *Rootes Motors Ltd*

1965 HILLMAN Imp 875cc saloon. *Rootes Motors Ltd*

1973 HILLMAN Avenger GLS 1½-litre saloon.
Chrysler UK Ltd

1966 HINDUSTHAN Ambassador Mark 2
1½-litre saloon. *Hindusthan Motors Ltd*

1962 HINO Contessa 893cc saloon. *Hino Motors Ltd*

hypoid final drive replaced the spiral bevel type in 1961, and later cars had front disc brakes. From 1957 onwards the Rootes-owned Singer company's Gazelle had a Minx-type hull, and the Minx engine was used after 1959. A bigger Super Minx joined the range in 1962, and 1963 produced a challenger in the baby-car class, the Imp. Made in the Rootes' Group's Scottish factory at Linwood, it had an inclined, rear-mounted ohc 875cc, 4-cylinder engine, 4-speed all-synchromesh gearbox, and all-round independent suspension. In 1966 Imps did well in saloon-car racing, and Singer and Sunbeam versions followed, as well as a new Husky station wagon: the engine was used by a number of specialist manufacturers, notably Bond (iii), Ginetta, T.V.R. and Clan. It was also fitted to one version of the Greek Farmobil cross-country vehicle.

Chrysler acquired a majority interest in Rootes in 1964, the first consequences of the new management being the 1967 Minx and Hunter that replaced the existing Minx and Super Minx types. Design was entirely new, though the 1,496cc and 1,725cc engines (now inclined in the 'chassis') were retained. These were assembled in Iran under the name of Peykan. Vehicles assembled in South Africa used Peugeot engines. A Hunter won the 1968 London–Sydney Marathon. An entirely new shape from Hillman, the Avenger, appeared in 1970. Its suspension, by McPherson struts at the front and by rigid axle and coils at the rear, was similar to that of French Chryslers, there was a choice of 1,248cc or 1,496cc ohv 4-cylinder engines, disc brakes were fitted at the front, and automatic transmission was optional. Prices started at £765.

At the end of the 1970 season the Minx was dropped after an unbroken run of 38 years. Its replacement was a 54bhp Hunter De Luxe with the 1½-litre engine. Avengers went on sale in the U.S.A. as Plymouth Crickets. Two new Avengers were added during 1972: a station wagon and the twin-carburettor high-performance Tiger, a limited-production saloon with magnesium alloy wheels, capable of 105mph and retailing at £1,328. A 78bhp GLS version with power brakes, radial-ply tyres and wide-rim wheels appeared in 1973, when the Imp was continued, and the Hunter line-up ranged from the basic De Luxe up to the 93bhp 1.7-litre GLS with twin Weber carburettors and close-ratio gearbox. MCS

HILTON (US) *1921*
Motor Sales & Service Corp, Philadelphia, Pa.

The Hilton was a 4-cylinder car which was offered only in coupé form. Designed by Hilton W. Sofield, president of the Motor Sales & Service Corporation, the car was powered by a Herschell-Spillman engine and wire wheels were standard equipment. The factory itself was at Riverton, N.J. KM

HINDE see VAN GINK

HINDUSTHAN (IND) *1946 to date*
Hindusthan Motors Ltd, Uttarpara, West Bengal

This firm has devoted most of its energies to the production of Morris-based vehicles for the Indian market, though in the 1950s Studebakers, mainly the 6-cylinder sv Champion, were also built under licence. The first car produced was the Hindusthan Ten (alias the Series M Morris), but Hindusthan have also built the MO series Oxford (the Hindusthan 14), the Minor in 803cc and 948cc forms (the Baby Hindusthan), and the Series II Oxford, initially with sv engine, but from 1959 as the ohv Ambassador. This is still in production: it differs only in minor points of styling from its British-made prototype and engine capacity is still 1½ litres, though B.M.C. have now changed the styling of their corresponding model and enlarged their engines to 1,622cc. The 1971/2 price was Rs 15,091 and demand consistently outstrips supply. MCS

HINES (US) *1908–1910*
National Screw & Tack Co, Cleveland, Ohio

This car was designed by and named after William R. Hines, chief plant engineer of the manufacturer. The only model which was marketed was a five-seater touring car on an 8ft 10in wheelbase. It had a 4-cylinder engine of 4.2 litres. GMN

HINO (J) *1953–1967*
Hino Motors, Ltd, Tokyo

Although Hino was formed in 1942 by people who broke away from the Tokyo Jidosha Kogyo Co, it was concerned only with diesel trucks and buses until 1953. In March of that year, Hino obtained a licence to build the small 4-door Renault 4CV sedan. This model was assembled until 1961, when the firm began to market its own Contessa 900 sedan, with an 893cc rear-mounted engine.

The Italian stylist Michelotti redesigned the Contessa line in 1964. The 1300 line featured a 1.3-litre 60bhp rear-mounted 4-cylinder engine with 5-bearing crankshaft, independent suspension, rack-and-pinion steering and an all-synchromesh gearbox. A 70bhp coupé version was also available. In 1967 Hino joined the Toyota group and as a result private-car production ceased. BE

HINSTIN (F) *1920–1926*
SA des Etablissements Jacques Hinstin, Maubeuge, Nord

The Hinstin name was seldom seen on cars as their speciality was the assembly of components into vehicles which were sold by other firms under various names. Among the engines used were the 1,095cc Ruby, and the 1,100cc C.I.M.E. The latter engine was used in the car sold in England under the name Little Greg; this was described as the smallest model in the Grégoire range, being sold by the Grégoire agent, but it was, in fact, a Hinstin. Larger cars from the Maubeuge factory using Altos engines were known as Guilicks. GNG

H.I.S.A. see HERMES (ii)

HISPAKART (E) 1966 to date
Ramon Lopez Villalba, Madrid

The Hispakart is a light racing car built for Formula 4 events. It uses a very light polyester body and disc brakes on all wheels. Engines, rear-mounted and all of 250cc, can be Bultaco, Ducati or Montesa, with outputs varying from 29 to 40bhp. Maximum speeds are from 87 to 106mph. JRV

HISPANO-ARGENTINA (RA) 1940–1941
Hispano-Argentina Fabrica de Automoviles S.A., Buenos Aires

This company was founded by Carlos Ballesta Molina, who planned to make a large American-styled sedan powered by a 6-cylinder diesel engine. Few were made, and Molina then turned to a small car with a 1-litre 2-cylinder petrol engine. Shortages caused by World War 2 put an end to this model too. GNG

HISPANO-SUIZA (i) (E) 1904–1944
SA Hispano-Suiza, Barcelona

Although the Hispano-Suiza became most famous as a French make, its origins were Spanish, it was always made in Spain as well as in France (indeed, in greater numbers) and in the country of its birth it outlived its French offshoot as far as serious production was concerned. The Swiss engineer Marc Birkigt, who had designed the Barcelona-built La Cuadra car in 1900, was responsible for the design of a car made in the same city from 1901 to 1904 and called the Castro. The first Hispano-Suiza, of 1904, was in fact the 20hp Castro renamed. A range of large, beautifully-built, T-head pair-cast fours with live-axle drive and the luxury of water-cooled brakes was established and by 1907 they had found their way into the stables of King Alfonso XIII. Two similar sixes with 6.2- and 10.4-litre engines (30/40 and 60/65hp) joined them in the following year. All were expensive machines of conventional design, intended mainly for the carriage trade – although not the Alfonso XIII model of 1912. In 1910 an Hispano-Suiza racing voiturette won the Coupe de l'Auto race in France. It had a T-head engine with a very long stroke. The Alfonso was based on it. Various versions were made, but the best-known, a 3.6-litre car, had cylinder dimensions of 80 × 180mm. The range of cars of tourer type was retained. While the design of the Alfonso did not change, thanks to its extreme popularity abroad, the rest of the models, by 1913, were much more modern, consisting of monobloc 4-cylinder cars, still with long strokes, but with overhead valves operated by an overhead camshaft, all neatly enclosed. V-radiators replaced the former flat pattern in 1914. Two ohc fours, a 16hp and a 30hp, were listed until 1924. They were solid, reliable machines without front-wheel brakes, seen usually as taxis. By then, they had been overshadowed completely in the international field by the radically new H6B of 1919, which was made at the Paris factory and is dealt with under Hispano-Suiza (F). The next model to originate in Spain, and the first six since before 1914, was a cheaper version of the H6B intended for the less opulent Spanish market, consisting of a basically similar but smaller engine of 3.7 litres, with a detachable cylinder head, installed in an H6B chassis. This power unit needed the assistance of a lower set of gear ratios than those of the H6B, as it was expected to pull the same weight. This car was replaced by another 'utility' Hispano in 1930, a 3-litre model with pushrod-operated overhead valves like the contemporary small Hispano model in France. It had an interesting history; the design was to have been taken up by Hudson in America, but because of the Depression, American motorists were denied a Birkigt car. By 1935 it had been enlarged to 3,404cc, and there were three other sixes in the range: the 3,750cc Type 49, the 4,580cc Type 64, and the 8-litre Type 56bis, which had the same engine dimensions as the French-built H6C. The smaller sixes were made until 1944. In all, some 6,000 cars were produced by the Barcelona works, against about 2,600 from the Paris factory. One or two prototypes of the French V-12 were built at Barcelona but there was no series production TRN

HISPANO-SUIZA (ii) (F) 1911–1938
(1) Sté Française Hispano-Suiza, Levallois-Perret, Seine 1911–1914
(2) Sté Française Hispano-Suiza, Bois-Colombes, Seine 1914–1938

In 1911, a French company with a Paris factory was founded to assemble the Hispano-Suiza from Spain, a hitherto obscure make that had recently won sporting renown in France and was already an established manufacturer of luxury vehicles in its home country, enjoying royal patronage. The Spanish market was poor compared with the rich potential of France and other motoring countries and so it was that when a superb new model of Hispano of the most modern and advanced design was introduced, it came from the French factory. This was the

1921 HINSTIN 10hp two-seater. Porporato at the wheel. *Autocar*

1910 HISPANO-SUIZA(i) 40hp sedanca de ville. *Studios Miarnau, Barcelona*

1935 HISPANO-SUIZA(i) Tipo 60 RL 3.4-litre saloon. *Studios Miarnau, Barcelona*

1912 HISPANO-SUIZA(ii) Alfonso 3.6-litre two-seater. Coachwork by Grosvenor. *National Motor Museum*

1925 HISPANO-SUIZA(ii) 37.2hp coupé. Coachwork by Hooper. *National Motor Museum*

1935 HISPANO-SUIZA(ii) V-12 9.4-litre drophead coupé. Coachwork by Saoutchik *J. Rodriguez-Viña*

H6B of 1919, the first French-developed Hispano. It gained such immediate and lasting fame that henceforth, Hispano-Suiza was regarded as a primarily French make, and the products of the Spanish factory (though made in great numbers) fell into obscurity. The H6B was designed as the last word in advanced transport for the rich. The engine was the outcome of the company's experience of aircraft engine manufacture during World War 1 – a field in which it was already famous. Its six cylinders, totalling 6.6 litres, were of aluminium, with light steel liners. The cylinder head was fixed. A single overhead camshaft operated two valves per cylinder. This engine gave 135bhp at 3,000rpm. A 7-bearing, pressure-fed crankshaft coped with the power. Thus a good power-to-weight ratio was combined with reliability, according to the best aviation practice. The chassis was light, yet rigid, and extremely efficient servo-assisted four-wheel brakes were provided to check the 85mph which was available on top gear. In spite of a high final drive ratio of 3.4 to 1, the engine developed such excellent low-speed torque that 6 to 50mph in top gear occupied only 21 seconds.

The new Hispano was not quiet compared with the cars of competitors who counted silence above mechanical efficiency, but in its combination of most of the desirable qualities of a true luxury car – comfort, flexibility – and of the sporting machine – first rate reliability, performance, brakes and handling – it was unique in 1919. Not surprisingly, what amounted to a single-model policy was pursued for many years. Alongside the H6B, the H6C Sport or Boulogne model appeared in 1924. Bore and stroke were 110 × 140mm against the H6B's 100 × 140mm, giving eight litres. This fabulous machine was capable of up to 110mph and could be had in short-chassis form. Modified H6B's had won the Coupe Boillot at Boulogne in 1921, 1922 and 1923, in the last instance with the 8-litre engine, which accounted for the new car's name. The H6B and H6C were both still available in 1929, and, as the Tipo 56bis, the latter was made in Spain well into the 1930s. From 1924 to 1927, the former was made by Skoda of Czechoslovakia under licence. In 1930 Hispano-Suiza took over Ballot and fitted a smaller, 4.6-litre, 6-cylinder engine into a Ballot chassis. This Junior model, which had central gearchange, was not a car in the same class as its predecessors. In spite of the coming of the Depression, however, in 1931 Hispano-Suiza produced their biggest, most complex and most expensive design. This was the V-12 which abandoned, for the first time since 1919, the six-in-line, overhead-camshaft layout. Cylinder dimensions were 'square', at 100 × 100mm, providing 9½ litres and even greater low-speed torque than that of the old H6B. The overhead valves were operated by push-rods and rockers. Top gear ratio was now 2.75:1 and bottom 5.4:1, or about the same ratio as the top gear of many family saloons of the period. All V-12s could exceed 100mph and in its fastest, short-chassis open form, the model was said to attain 115mph. The V-12 was made until 1938. Meanwhile, the Junior had been superseded in 1935 by the 4.9-litre, 6-cylinder K6, which used push-rod overhead valves like its big brother. It too was current until 1938. Hispano-Suiza of Paris then abandoned car production, never to resume it. A prototype was built after World War 2, with front-wheel drive and a Ford V-8 engine, but it never achieved catalogue status. TRN

HISPARCO (E) *1925–1928*
P. del Arco y Compañia, Madrid

The Hisparco was a small sports car using a 750cc 4-cylinder engine and 4-wheel brakes. In 1926 a Hisparco won the 12-hour Mountain Circuit of Guadarrama, covering 449 miles at an average speed of 38mph. More than 150 were sold, of which some were Marguerites, Models BO, BO2 and BO5. JRV

HITCHCOCK (US) *1909*
Hitchcock Motor Car Co, Warren, Mich.

This was a small car with power supplied by a 2-cylinder, 2-stroke Speedwell engine of 20hp. Apparently very few cars of this name were manufactured GMN

HITCHON-WELLER *see* GLOBE

H.K. (F) *1907*
AS de Kostka, Paris

The H.K. light car was made in two models, a 10hp single-cylinder and a 12/16hp 2-cylinder. The smaller model was entered for the 1907 Coupe des Voiturettes, but did not start. GNG

H.L. (F) *1912–1914*
Hainsselin et Langlois, St Cloud, Seine-et-Oise

The H.L. used a fairly large 4-cylinder engine in a light chassis, and was described in British advertisements as 'Europe's reply to America'. The monobloc engines came in two sizes, a 10/15hp of 2.1 litres and a 12/18hp of 2.6 litres. In 1913 the latter was increased to 3 litres. The cars had 2-speed gearboxes in the rear axle, and independent front suspension by coil. A rounded radiator was used; body styles were two- and four-seater open tourers, and a landaulet. GNG

H.L.B. (GB) *1914*
H.L.B. Motors, Islington, London N.

The H.L.B. was a steam-driven cyclecar, probably the only one of its kind. It had a Stanley type boiler and a 2-cylinder double-acting engine, chain final drive and an armoured wood frame. The price was £125 which was not too expensive, but it appeared at an unpropitious time – June 1914. GNG

H.M.C. (GB) *1913*
Hendon Motor Cycle Co, London N.W.
This was a cyclecar which used an 8hp Chater-Lea engine, a 2-speed gearbox and belt final drive. The name H.M.C. was also used for the Highgate car. GNG

HOBBIE (US) *1908–1909*
Hobbie Automobile Co, Hampton, Iowa
This make was also known as Hobbie Accessible. It was a high-wheeler with solid rubber tyres, powered by a typical 2-cylinder, air-cooled engine mounted under the body. The car was tiller-steered and had double chain drive. GMN

HODGSON (GB) *1924–1925*
Hodgson Motors, Leeds, Yorks.
The Hodgson sports car used a 1½-litre Anzani engine, and was made in very small numbers only. A 4-speed gearbox and 4-wheel brakes were standardized, and a supercharger was an optional extra. Prices ranged from £295 for the standard 12/25 model to £585 for the 12/50 supercharged racing car. In 1929 Hodgson made a few more of the cars under the name British Eagle. GNG

HOFFMAN (i) (US) *1903*
Hoffman Automobile Mfg Co, Cleveland, Ohio
The Hoffman was a light steam car using a 6hp 2-cylinder engine and single chain drive. The firm also made a single-cylinder petrol car of similar external appearance, and from 1904 onwards concentrated on petrol cars which they sold under the name Royal Tourist. GNG

HOFFMAN (ii) (US) *1931*
R.C.Hoffman, Detroit, Mich.
Two prototypes of the Hoffman Front Drive car were built. The cars were powered by a Lycoming straight-8 engine and the wheels were carried on a solid load-bearing axle. Semi-elliptic springs were used and torque arms aided the front axle in taking the power. KM

HOFLACK (B) *1901*
Several voiturettes powered by Aster engines were made by this Ypres firm. GNG

HOFMANN & CZERNY (A) *1907–1910*
Hofmann & Czerny, Vienna XIII
In addition to motor cycles this firm produced one type of voiturette with a single-cylinder 8hp engine. HON

HOLBORN *see* McLACHLAN

HOLCAR (GB) *1897–1905*
M. Holroyd-Smith, London S.W.
Michael Holroyd-Smith was an inventor rather than a manufacturer, and although a price was given for his later cars, it is unlikely that more than one or two of each model were made. His first car had a rear-mounted 2-cylinder engine, and an unusual frame which passed outside the rear wheels. His second design of 1901 had a centrally-mounted V-twin engine of 6/8hp, while the third, known as the Holcar, had a front-mounted 20hp V-4 engine, shaft drive, and a five-seater tourer body. It was exhibited at shows (as were the earlier cars), and priced at £850. GNG

HOLDEN (AUS) *1948 to date*
General Motors-Holden's Pty Ltd., Melbourne, Vic.; Woodville, S.A.
The Holden company started life making bodies, their work appearing on imported Morris cars in the 1920s. Under General Motors ownership in the 1930s they assembled American and British G.M. products for the Australian market, offering fastback coupés in 1938, or three years before Detroit. The Holden, conceived after World War 2 as 'Australia's own car', was in fact a development of a 'compact' Buick dating back to 1938, which never saw production in its native land. In layout the FX-type Holden of 1948 was a straightforward General Motors design with a 4-bearing, 6-cylinder, ohv 2.2-litre engine, 3-speed synchromesh gearbox, column change, hydraulic brakes, coil-and-wishbone independent front suspension, hypoid final drive, and unitary construction. The wheelbase was 8ft 7in, and the standard sedan weighed 2,212lb. The initial Australian content was 92%, and it was promoted through a 600-dealer network. At a price of £A675 (about £540), its 80mph performance and toughness sold 7,725 cars in 1949, rising to 50,000 by 1952, when assembly was being undertaken in three States. The first Holdens were exported (to New Zealand) in 1954; by 1958 annual production had topped the 100,000 mark, and a year later the make accounted for 46% of all Australian private-car sales. Exports – now including the Near East and parts of

1913 H.L. 15hp two-seater. *H.N. Charles*

1903 HOFFMAN (i) 8hp tonneau. *Kenneth Stauffer*

1948 HOLDEN Model FX 2.1-litre sedan. *General Motors Holden's Pty Ltd*

1966 HOLDEN Premier 3-litre sedan.
General Motors Holden's Pty Ltd

1972 HOLDEN Statesman De Ville sedan.
General Motors Holden's Pty Ltd

1918 HOLMES(ii) 29hp tourer. *Keith Marvin*
Collection

Africa – exceeded 10,000 cars in 1963, and a year later the factory delivered 190,375 vehicles. A minor facelift had come with the FJ series of 1954, but the basic 1942 look remained for another two seasons until the introduction of the 70bhp FE type, a full six-seater with 13in wheels and recirculating ball steering. 1960 Holdens had 2.3 litres and 75bhp, plus the unsightly 'dog's leg' windscreen also found on Vauxhalls of the period, but two years later the range was again restyled, automatic transmission being introduced on the Premier series. 1964 Premiers had 2.9-litre engines, the cheaper Standard and Special using 2.4-litre 100bhp units. The 1965 HD type closely resembled contemporary 6-cylinder Vauxhalls and was available with front disc brakes. The 1967 line came with 2.4-litre (114bhp) and 3-litre (126 and 145bhp) engines and the same styling as before.

In 1969 came the Torana based on the Vauxhall Viva, but with a 6-cylinder engine and extended wheelbase. The HK line of Holdens came in two models, the standard Belmont and the de luxe Kingswood, with option of 5-litre Chevrolet V-8 engine. There was also a new coupé, the Monaro with 5.4-litre Chevrolet V-8 engine, and a long-wheelbase prestige model with air-conditioning called the Brougham. Holden produced their first Australian-built V-8s in 1970, in 4.1 and 5-litre versions. In 1971 the Brougham was dropped in favour of a new luxury line called the Statesman, in direct opposition to Ford's successful Fairlane. MCS

HOLDSWORTH (GB) 1903–1904
Light Car & Motor Engineering Co Ltd, Birmingham

This was a typical light two-seater using a 4½ or 6½hp Aster engine, wire wheels and drive by single chain or shaft. GNG

HOLLAND (i) (US) 1898–1908
Sam Holland, Park River, N. Dak.

Sam Holland was a blacksmith who built four cars, all of which were sold to local customers. The first two, built during the period 1898 to 1903, were single-cylinder cars with front-mounted engines and longitudinal springs forming the side members of the frame, as on the Curved Dash Oldsmobile. Two 4-cylinder cars were also made, and it was stated in 1908 that production was to begin soon but apparently it never did. GNG

HOLLAND (ii) (US) 1902–c.1905
Holland Automobile Co, Jersey City, N.J.

This company made engines of 6 and 12hp, and chassis with epicyclic gearing and single chain drive, ready to receive bodies. A steam car was attributed to this firm in 1905, but no details are known. GNG

HOLLEY (US) 1903–1904
Holley Motor Co, Bradford, Pa.

This small car had an attractive appearance with more than the normal amount of brass work. It was a two-seater car with a single-cylinder water-cooled engine with a coil radiator. It was steered by wheel and was priced at $650. GMN

HOLLIER (US) 1915–1921
Lewis Spring & Axle Co, Chelsea; Jackson, Mich.

Also known as Vincent-Hollier, this car was available originally with a V-8 engine of its own design, although a companion model powered by a 6-cylinder Falls engine was introduced for 1917. Only open models were built. KM

HOLLY (US) 1914–1916
Holly Motor Co, Mount Holly, N.J.

The Holly was made in a single chassis using a 60hp 6-cylinder engine. The two models, a roadster and a touring car, were listed at $1,000 for 1916. GMN

HOLMES (i) (US) 1906–1907
(1) Charles Holmes Machine Co, East Boston, Mass. *1906*
(2) Holmes Motor Vehicle Co, East Boston, Mass. *1906–1907*

This car was made in two five-seater touring models. The smaller car used a 2-cylinder opposed engine. The larger model had a 4-cylinder 3.3-litre engine. Both models had a Reeves friction transmission. GMN

HOLMES (ii) (US) 1918–1923
The Holmes Automobile Co, Canton, Ohio

Second in sales only to Franklin among air-cooled cars of the period, the Holmes Six was a highly regarded, if unbelievably ugly car. The louvred front with its series of horizontal slits in a herringbone pattern was generally described as looking like a caterpillar head. Holmes cars cost slightly more than Franklins. Approximately 500 units per year were sold in a full range of open and closed models. Holmes planned to launch a 4-cylinder car to augment their line of sixes, but by 1922 they were in financial difficulties and the company was declared bankrupt in May 1923. KM

HOLSMAN (US) 1903–1911
(1) Holsman Automobile Co, Chicago, Ill. *1903–1909*
(2) Holsman Equipment Co, Plano, Ill. *1910–1911*

The Holsman was a high-wheeler which was sold in considerable numbers in the Mid-West, and also in India and Australia. Engines were 10 and 12hp 2-cylinder, and 26hp 4-cylinder, both opposed air-cooled units. Rope drive was used up to 1905, steel cable from 1905 to 1909, and chains thereafter. GMN

HOL-TAN (US) 1908
Hol-Tan Co, New York, N.Y.
While the Hol-Tan Co was the sales agent for this make, these cars were built in St. Louis Missouri, by the Moon Motor Car Co. Prior to 1906, Hol-Tan had imported European cars including Fiats for the New York market. The larger model of the Hol-Tan had a long wheelbase (10ft 1in) for these years, with a 4-cylinder engine. Its selective, four-speed transmission was an early overdrive type, with a direct drive in third gear. GMN

HOLYOKE (US) 1901–1903
Holyoke Automobile Co, Holyoke, Mass.
The Holyoke was designed by the Swiss-born engineer, Charles R. Greuter, whose name is sometimes given to the make of car. It was made in single- and twin-cylinder form, and was notable for having overhead valves. In fact it is said to have inspired the 1903 ohv Welsh design. The first Holyoke was a large touring surrey with the 2-cylinder engine under the rear seats, but later a single-cylinder runabout was made. In 1903 the Holyoke assets were acquired by the Matheson Motor Car Co who used the Holyoke factory until 1906. GNG

HOMER LAUGHLIN (US) 1916
Homer Laughlin Engineers' Corp, Los Angeles, Calif.
This car was a combination of innovations and obsolete ideas. It had front-wheel drive by chains, with a friction transmission, and was powered by a 1.9-litre V-8 engine. The wheelbase was 9ft 4in with a turning circle of 22ft. The rear springs were a patented combination of two cantilever springs. Only one roadster was made. GMN

HONDA (J) 1962 to date
Honda Motor Co Ltd, Tokyo
The world's biggest and most successful motorcycle manufacturer turned to light vans and cars in 1962, exhibiting a small sports model at that year's Tokyo Show. This open two-seater had a dohc 4-cylinder 4-carburettor engine with hemispherical combustion chambers that could run up to 8,000rpm. Other features were a ladder-type frame, 5-speed gearbox, and separate chain final drive to each rear wheel. Initially 360cc and 500cc power units were used, the latter developing 40bhp, but the production version, the S800, had a 791cc engine and four forward speeds. It managed 100mph on 70bhp, but never became a best-seller and was discontinued in 1969. In 1964 Honda became the first Japanese contender for Formula 1 honours, trying a 1,500cc V-12 capable of 12,000rpm that eventually won the 1965 Mexican G.P. after lengthy teething troubles. Their 3-litre 12-cylinder car, however, never won a major race, its best showing being a 2nd for John Surtees in the 1968 French G.P. The 430bhp air-cooled RA 302 V-8 was a disaster, and was responsible for the company's withdrawal from Formula 1 at the end of that year.
More successful was Honda's second touring-car design, announced at the end of 1966 and still in production in 1972. This was a Mini-like baby saloon with transversely-mounted air-cooled ohc vertical-twin engine driving the front wheels. It also featured electric pump feed, a synchromesh bottom gear, and semi-elliptic rear suspension. A Honda-designed automatic gearbox was an option, and there were two choices of engine, with capacities of 356cc and 598cc. There was a move to bigger things in 1969 with the 4-cylinder 77, on similar basic lines and still air-cooled, but with a 5-bearing 1,298cc unit developing 96bhp, a sump-mounted gearbox, front disc brakes, and swing-axle rear suspension. Coupé versions had four carburettors and 110bhp. In 1971 the minicar theme was developed further with the Vamos, a rear-engined jeep-type vehicle using a platform frame, and the egg-shaped Z coupé, available on the home market with the 356cc engine in various stages of tune, options including a twin-carburettor 36bhp variant, the TS, and a 5-speed gearbox. For export the bigger engine was used, and standard colour was a vivid orange. However, though Honda sold over 315,000 cars in 1970 their impact on world markets never matched that of the motorcycles. For 1973 the company reverted to water cooling on the Civic, a challenger to models such as the Renault 5 and Fiat 127. Only 11ft 2in long, it used an ohc 1,169cc transverse engine in an all-independently sprung structure. GT versions had 69bhp and front disc brakes. MCS

HONG-QI (p); HUNG-CH'I (wg) (RED FLAG) (CHI) 1958 to date
No.1 Automobile Plant, Changchun, Kirin, Manchuria
A medium-sized car manufactured in sedan and convertible forms, the Hong-Qi is used mainly by government officials. It is powered by a 5.3-litre V-8 unit of 220hp at 4,400rpm through an automatic transmission. Various extras are available, including power steering, vacuum-assisted brakes, air conditioning, power windows and auto-tuning radio. Maximum speed is reported as 100mph. The original body design was abandoned as unattractive, after a limited production run, and considerable

1964 HONDA S.600 606cc sports car.
Shotaro Kobayashi Collection

1968 HONDA N.360 354cc saloon. *Honda Motor Co Ltd*

1973 HONDA Civic 1200 saloon. *Honda Motor Co Ltd*

1973 HONG-QI 6-cylinder limousine.
Andrew Wilson

1906 HORBICK 15/20 tourer. *Horsfall & Bickham Ltd*

1920 HORCH 15PS saloon. *Autocar*

modifications were made before manufacture was resumed. Fifteen specially built and numbered Red Flags were turned out for a Party anniversary some year ago, it was reported. The large factory complex was constructed with Soviet ai and concentrates primarily on the fabrication of Liberation trucks. Red Flags ar hand-assembled in very small quantities, only to the order of the First Ministr of Machine Building. In 1973 a 6-cylinder engine was also used.   B

HOOD (US) 1900–1901
Simplex Motor Vehicle Co, Danvers, Mass.

Also known as the Electronomic, the Hood steam car looked little different from its many contemporaries, but embodied one or two unusual ideas. The engine had single-acting cylinders and magnetically operated inlet valves, 3 small batteries being provided for the purpose. A flash boiler supplied superheated steam at a pressure o 200psi. A simple two-seater body was standard; the price was $1,000.   GNG

HOOSIER SCOUT (US) 1914
Hoosier Cyclecar Co, Indianapolis, Ind.

The Hoosier (the nickname for Indiana) was a tandem cyclecar, with a typica 2-cylinder, air-cooled engine. The drive was by a friction transmission and belts to th rear wheels. The only distinguishing feature of the body was its boat-tail.   GMN

HO-P'ING see HE-PING

HOPPENSTAND (US) 1948–1949
Hoppenstand Motors Inc, Greenville, Pa.

The Hoppenstand was a short-lived American minicar using a 350cc flat-twin air-cooled engine just in front of the rear axle, hydraulic transmission, an independent suspension all round by coil. Coupé and convertible models were avail able, and the Hoppenstand's appearance rather resembled that of the Frenc Rovin minicar.   GNG

HORBICK (GB) 1902–1909
Horsfall & Bickham Ltd, Pendleton, Manchester

The Horbick was the product of a well-known textile machinery firm. The 190 prototype had a 6hp M.M.C. engine, but the first production car of 1902 had 12hp 2-cylinder Forman engine, shaft drive and a four-seater tonneau body. 190 and 1904 cars used power units by Johnson, Hurley & Martin, but from 190 Horbick turned to White & Poppe for their engines which powered some of thei best-known models. These included the Minor with a 10/12hp 3-cylinder engine and the 4-cylinder 15/20hp Major. Their first 6-cylinder car, the 18/24hp of 1907 also was White & Poppe powered, but their largest model, the 45/60hp six, had a engine of Horbick's own manufacture. A number of these large cars were supplie to Indian potentates including the Niźam of Hyderabad. Horbicks were als catering for the taxicab market, when it was decided to concentrate on textil machinery as to continue the cars would involve too much expansion. In 190 they declined 'with thanks' an order for 2,000 London taxicabs, and gave up th manufacture of cars.   GNG

HORCH (D) 1900–1939
(1) A. Horch & Co, Cologne-Ehrenfeld 1900–1902
(2) A. Horch & Co, Reichenbach/Vogtland 1902–1904
(3) A. Horch & Co, Motorwagenwerke AG, Zwickau 1904–1939

August Horch was among the pioneers of car manufacture in Germany. He wa employed as an engineer with Benz from 1896 to 1899 when he started his ow factory at Cologne. The first motor car appeared in 1900. It had a 2-cylinder 5h front-mounted engine and shaft drive. The next models were a 2-cylinder 10/12h and a 4-cylinder 16/20hp. After the Zwickau works had been set up in 1904 Horc was able to increase production. The 18/22hp ohv 4-cylinder model of 1904 becam very popular and was the basis for several subsequent cars. A victory in th Herkomer Trial of 1906 was gained with this model, the first such success for Horch. Horch also pioneered with his *Torpedoform* aero-dynamic bodies for th Prince Henry Trials, which were built by Kathe of Halle. In 1906 a 6-cylinde 8-litre power unit was designed, developing 60bhp, but it was not a success and thi was one cause of differences between Horch and his partners. Horch himself lef the firm and started the Audi factory.

Various models with different engine sizes were included in the Horch range, from the small 6/18PS 1,588cc to the 25/60PS 6,395cc. All had 4-cylinder engines. Afte World War 1 the 33/80PS 8,440cc model appeared, which had actually been designe in 1914. It started a series of prestige cars for which the make became famous i the following years. Paul Daimler (son of Gottlieb) was engaged as chief enginee in 1923. Ohc 4- and 6-cylinder models with fwb appeared in 1923/4, but the first ne car under his management was the Horch 300 with a straight-8 3,230cc engine wit twin overhead camshafts. In 1927 the '305' and '306' appeared, which also feature straight-8 engines, with twin overhead camshafts and a capacity of 3,375cc developing 75bhp. These models differed only in wheelbase. They were followed by the '375' i 1928 with an 8-cylinder 3,974cc engine capable of 80bhp. After Daimler left Horc two more models (the Horch '400' and '405') were produced showing Daimle influence. The Horch 450 of 1930 was entirely new. It was a straight-8 with only one overhead camshaft. Two different wheelbases and engines of 4, 4½ and 5 litres were available. The last of these stayed in the range until 1939, later cars having 10-bearing crankshafts and all round independent suspension. Type numbers became a little confusing in the next few years, when some models were available with different wheelbases and engine capacities. A V-12 with 5,990cc (models '600' and '670') appeared in 1931, followed by the V-8 3,517cc '830B' in 1933, available in two wheelbase and engine sizes. By 1939 the range consisted of the '930V' and '830BL' (3,823cc, 92bhp) and the '951A', '853A' and '855' (4,944cc, 120bhp). These models were available with different wheelbases and a variety of body styles from a two-seater roadster to a large Pullman saloon. The Horch company was celebrated for luxurious 'prestige' cars which were sold at lower prices than other top makes; a V-8 cost £615 in England, and straight-8s from £985.

From 1932 Horch was a member of the Auto Union, and the racing cars bearing this name were built in the Horch works. In 1945 the factory was nationalized and in 1956 it brought out a new Horch. This had to be sold as the Sachsenring, as Auto Union, now based on Düsseldorf, hold the sole rights to the brand-names Horch, Audi and Wanderer. HON

HORLEY (GB) *1904–1907*

Horley Motor & Engineering Co, Horley, Surrey

Horley was one of the earliest companies to achieve the magic figure of 100gns for a complete car. This was a light shaft-drive two-seater powered by an 8hp single-cylinder M.M.C. engine, which was introduced in 1904 and made for three years. In 1906 the engine became a 9hp, and in 1907 it was replaced by an 8½hp 2-cylinder White & Poppe unit, and the price increased. The Horley company also made vans with Aster engines. The original 100gns model was sometimes called the No-Name. GNG

HORMIGER (E) *1909–1912*

Alvar Gonzalez, Gijon, Asturias

This was a firm of ship-builders who made marine engines and fitted a few of them into car chassis. Production was very limited. JR-V

HORNET (i) (GB) *1905–1907*

Horner & Sons, London E.C.

The Hornet was a light car powered by a 9hp 2-cylinder engine under the seat driving through an epicyclic gear and single chain to the rear axle. It had a dummy bonnet, and a two-seater body. Horner & Sons were only the selling agents; the car was said to have been made for them by the Lenox Autocar Company. An 18hp 4-cylinder model was also listed. GNG

HORNET (ii) *see* AMERICAN MOTORS

HORNSTED *see* MOLL

HORSE SHOE (F) *c.1908*

Horse Shoe was the name given in England to an imported French car. Two shaft-driven models were made, an 8hp single-cylinder two-seater and a 12hp 2-cylinder four-seater. Both were distinguished by the shape of a horse shoe, complete with 'nails', which surrounded the radiator. GNG

HORSTMANN (GB) *1914–1929*

Horstmann Cars Ltd, Bath, Somerset

The Horstmann started life as one of the more interesting and enterprising light cars. Its original engine was a 1-litre, 4-cylinder unit (enlarged in 1919 to 1½ litres), with a detachable head and horizontal overhead valves. The vertical rockers were operated positively by the camshaft. The valve gear was totally enclosed in a very tidy fashion. Forward of the flywheel, there were no chassis side members as such; the crank-case was extended to form the front of the frame and an undershield. The three forward speeds were housed in the back axle. The suspension too was unusual, consisting of cantilever springs and anti-roll bars at each corner. At the Junior Car Club's Burford Bridge rally in 1914, a Horstmann won the prize for the car with the most novel features: quite an achievement in an age when small-car design was extremely varied. By 1919 a full set of side curtains came with every car, a rare luxury in a light car of the time. A side-valve Coventry-Simplex engine of 1,368cc or 1,498cc was by this date available as an option, and by 1921 had supplanted the Horstmann engine altogether. Dashing sports and super sports models were offered, as well as the normal touring car, and all were now called Horstmanns, with English rather than German spelling. By 1923, the basic model was the 12/30hp with a 1½-litre side-valve Anzani engine. In 1924 it was joined for a year by the 9/20hp, with a 1,100cc Coventry-Simplex unit. Meanwhile, the company had been pursuing an ambitious racing programme. Racing Horstmanns had front wheel brakes as early as 1921 and pioneered supercharging in Britain two years later. These advances were reflected in the 1925 production cars, which were the first British light cars to have Lockheed hydraulic four-wheel brakes. They also had 4-speed gearboxes. However, they were very expensive, and could not compete with the big manufacturers. Horstmann tried, and failed, by cost-cutting: the 1928 range

1932 HORCH Type 670 6-litre V-12 drophead coupé. *Neubauer Collection*

1939 HORCH 3.8-litre V-8 drophead coupé. *Lucien Loreille Collection*

1923 HORSTMAN 10.5hp super sports car. *National Motor Museum*

*c.*1908 HOTCHKISS(i) 20/30hp landaulette. Coachwork by Barker. *National Motor Museum*

1931 HOTCHKISS(i) AM-80 3-litre tourer. Coachwork by Gurney Nutting. *Autocar*

1949 HOTCHKISS(i) Model 686 3½-litre saloon. *Autocar*

1951 HOTCHKISS-GRÉGOIRE 2-litre saloon. *Automobielmuseum, Driebergen*

consisted of the Anzani-engined car with normal, mechanical brakes, and a 9/25hp with 1¼-litre engine and three forward speeds. They were now much cheaper. The company's interest in unusual systems of suspension persisted to the end. In 1929 they were experimenting with a system of independent suspension by coil springs, but this did not find its way on to production cars and in any case no more of these were seen after that year. TRN

HOTCHKISS (i) (F) *1903–1955*

(1) Hotchkiss et Cie, St Denis, Seine *1903–1936*
(2) Automobiles Hotchkiss, St Denis, Seine *1936–1955*

The American Benjamin Berkeley Hotchkiss set up his ordnance factory at St Denis in 1867; the cars were the result of an arms slump. The work of Terrasse, these first Hotchkisses were T-headed fours with pair-cast cylinders, 5-ball-bearing crankshafts, lt magneto ignition, round honeycomb radiators, 4-speed gearboxes, and the famous Hotchkiss drive by live axle and open propeller shaft. Initially cylinder capacities were 4.6 litres and 7.4 litres, but the company's first racers of 1904 were 17.8-litre monsters notable for their aiv and chain drive. Though their 1905 successors conformed once more to touring-car practice, they were even bigger, with 18,815cc and an alleged 130bhp. Hotchkiss's last racing season was 1906 when their Grand Prix cars had 16.3-litre L-head units and quick-detachable wire wheels. Though these were unsuccessful, Hotchkiss sold 167 cars that year, with gate change standardized, and a choice of five models: a short-lived 4.2-litre petrol brougham, fours of 18, 30 and 42hp, and their first six. The last-mentioned was the large V type that evolved into a 9½-litre machine and was still being offered in 1912. Chassis price was £1,000 and it was capable of 60mph.

The slump following the Agadir crisis led to the abandonment of ball-bearing crankshafts; at the same time there was a move towards smaller cars with the 3.1-litre T type, with side valves in an L-head and ht magneto ignition. Two years later came something even smaller and more modern, the 12/16hp X type with 2-bearing crankshaft and three forward speeds at £390. Soon monobloc engines spread up the range to the 3.7-litre AB of 1912. From 1911 there were some smaller L-head sixes, the 4,678cc X6 and the 5½-litre AC6; 1912 sales were a record 598 units. Electric lighting was available from 1913, and all the 1914 models – the 2.6-litre AG, the 4-litre AF, the 5.7-litre AC, and the 6-cylinder AC6 – had semi-elliptic suspension all round.

The wartime demand for Hotchkiss machine guns led to the establishment of a branch factory under the Englishman Harry Ainsworth, this subsequently making engines for W.R. Morris until it was absorbed by him in 1923. At home Hotchkiss sold off their surplus works capacity at Lyons and concentrated on a revised AF with full electrics and a horseshoe-shaped radiator in place of the traditional round one. Its successor, the AH of 1921, had cantilever rear springs and torque tube drive, and a year later came the AL with ohv, and a detachable head; front-wheel brakes were added for 1923. There was also a prototype luxury car at the 1921 Paris Salon; this AK had a 6.6-litre 6-cylinder ohc engine, dual ignition, 4-speed unit gearbox, servo-assisted 4-wheel brakes, and a cruciform-braced frame, but it never went into production.

The return of Ainsworth to St Denis in 1923 coincided with the construction of a new factory and a more realistic type of car, the 2.4-litre 12CV AM, with 4-cylinder sv engine, 4-speed unit box, four-wheel brakes, wire wheels, and Hotchkiss drive once more. Between 1924 and 1928 it was the company's staple product, selling at the rate of over a thousand a year and offering a 70mph performance at a modest outlay. It persisted until 1932, acquiring ohv in 1926 and rod-operated brakes in 1928, and its engine was used in some Morris-Léon Bollées. Even better was the AM80 of 1929, largely the work of Bertarione. This was a short-stroke (80 × 100mm), 7-bearing ohv 3-litre six that owed a good deal to the AM2, though early cars featured torque tube drive; it was to be the basis from which all subsequent Hotchkisses were evolved. A silent 3rd gearbox featured on 1931 models, Hotchkiss drive reappeared in 1932, and 1933 improvements included Bendix brakes, cruciform-braced frames, down-draught carburettors and mechanical fuel pumps. AM80 engines were also fitted to Sizaire Frères and Tracta cars.

The 1933 range was expanded both up and down, with new 12CV (2-litre) and 13CV (2.3-litre) fours for the economy market, and an 85mph fast tourer, the 100bhp 3½-litre AM80S, for the enthusiast. This was based on the car with which Vasselle won the 1932 Monte Carlo Rally. Hotchkiss repeated this success in 1933 and 1934: in the latter year they collected two Glacier Cups in the Alpine Trial. There were further wins in the Monte Carlo in 1938 and 1939; on the latter occasion a Grand Sport Hotchkiss tied with a 3½-litre Delahaye. Radiators were moved forward on the 1934 Hotchkisses, and the 3-litre gave way to a 2,650cc 15CV that was not a success and lasted only one season. The 1935 cars had synchromesh and integral boots, and at the top of the 3½-litre 20CV range was the twin-carburettor Paris-Nice, a 115bhp sports car capable of 95mph. Hydraulic brakes appeared in 1936 (to be quietly dropped halfway through 1937). The sports 20CV engine was now giving 125–130bhp and when allied to a short 9ft 2in wheelbase resulted in the Grand Sport, a true 100mph saloon.

By 1938 the horseshoe radiator was now a wire-mesh grille, but despite the exigencies of French rearmament programmes the company managed to deliver 2,751 cars that year, made up of the two fours, the reinstated 3-litre 680, and the 3½-litre 686 in various forms, including seven-seater limousines with the single-carburettor 100bhp engine. Hotchkiss also came to the rescue of the ailing Amilcar concern, helping to make the Grégoire-inspired 1,185cc Compound, a small fwd saloon with unitary construction in Alpax; this was sold in England, though not in France, as a Hotchkiss. A 1.3-litre ohv development, the B67, was ready for production when France collapsed in the summer of 1940.

Hotchkiss never really recovered from World War 2, though Peugeot were briefly interested in the company and 686s won the first two post-war Monte Carlo Rallies of 1949 and 1950. The 13CV and 20CV were back in production, unchanged, by 1946, but the first year's output was a miserable 117 units. Hydraulic brakes and ifs did not appear until 1949 (though Hotchkiss had experimented with the latter in 1937), and a Cotal electric gearbox became a factory option. The 1951 models were 'facelifted' with V-screens, recessed headlamps and auxiliary coil rear suspension, but in the meantime there had been an expensive mistake: the acquisition of the rights to the Grégoire (ii) flat-4. This ingenious device was a development of the 1938 Amilcar theme featuring all-round independent suspension and a 4-speed overdrive gearbox, as well as fwd. Production models with 2.2-litre engines were said to achieve 95mph and 30mpg, but the teething troubles were endless, and Hotchkiss only managed to make 250 in the end. There was a shutdown in 1952 and the price of recovery was a merger with Delahaye that led inevitably to concentration on commercial vehicles. The old 13CV and 20CV received another facelift in time for the 1954 Paris Salon, but this was their swansong, though medium-powered trucks continued to be made until 1970, along with a version of the American Jeep built under licence.   MCS

HOTCHKISS (ii) (GB) 1920
Hotchkiss et Cie, Coventry, Warwickshire

Hotchkiss of Coventry, a British offshoot of the famous French firm, was set up during World War 1 to make engines in Britain. Their units became best known as the motive power for Morris and B.S.A. light cars, but before they were taken over by William Morris, they experimented with a small car of their own. It consisted of their 1,080cc air-cooled V-twin ohv engine installed with a 3-speed gearbox in a pre-war Morris Oxford chassis. It never went into production.   TRN

HOULBERG (DK) c.1913–1921
C. Houlberg, Odense

A small and handsome light car with a Bugatti-shaped radiator which was produced in Hans Christian Andersen's native town. Houlberg used 5/12hp 4-cylinder Ballot engines, and possibly Eysinks from Holland for a smaller model. Bosch magnetos and Zenith carburettors were used. Driving a car of his own, Houlberg competed keenly with his contemporary Thrige in the Copenhagen to The Skaw Tourist Trials of 1913 and 1914. Both roadsters and touring cars were offered, but the total output was little more than 30 cars.   TRA

HOUPT; HOUPT-ROCKWELL (US) 1909–1910; 1910–1912
(1) Harry S. Houpt Manufacturing Co, New Britain, Conn. *1909–1910*
(2) New Departure Manufacturing Co, New Britain, Conn. *1910–1912*

The Houpt was a large car powered by a 4-cylinder engine rated at 60hp, or a 6-cylinder unit of 90hp. Later models included a limousine and landaulet and prices ranged up to $7,500.   GMN

HOWARD (i) (US) 1900–1901
Howard Automobile Co, Trenton, N.J.

One of 19 new makes of steam buggy in 1900, the Howard was typical of its kind. A 2-cylinder vertical engine, single chain drive, tubular frame, tiller steering, wire wheels — all these features were found on other designs, including the most successful of the breed, the Locomobile.   GNG

HOWARD (ii) (US) 1903–1905
(1) W.S. Howard, Troy, N.Y. *1903*
(2) Howard Automobile Co, Yonkers, N.Y. *1903–1905*

This car was of modest size, but expensive. With a four-seater *Roi des Belges* body and a 25/30hp, 4-cylinder engine it cost $5,000. A smaller model with a 3-cylinder engine was also produced. This company was succeeded by Gas Engine & Power Co, in 1905, but apparently the Howard was not continued.   GMN

HOWARD (iii) (US) 1913–1918
A. Howard Co, Galion, Ohio

This car used a 5-litre, 6-cylinder engine. It had a 3-speed transmission and shaft drive. Apparently the only body style offered was an open five-seater.   GMN

HOWARD (iv) (US) 1913–1914
(1) Howard Motor Car Co, Connersville, Ind. *1913*
(2) Lexington-Howard Co, Connersville, Ind. *1913–1914*

This manufacturer also built the Lexington. The Howard was a large car with a wheelbase of 10ft 10in. Its L-head 6-cylinder Continental of 6.9 litres was rated at 60hp and used an early example of dual exhaust system.   GMN

c.1914 HOULBERG 5/12hp two-seater.
Thorkil Ry Andersen

1910 HOUPT-ROCKWELL 90hp tourer.
Automobile Manufacturers' Association

1904 HOWARD(ii) 24hp six-seater tourer.
Keith Marvin Collection

1948 H.R.G. 1½-litre sports car. *Bernard Alfieri Ltd*

1955 H.R.G. 1½-litre sports car. *H.R.G. Engineering Co Ltd*

1925 H.T. 2.8PS cyclecar. *Neubauer Collection*

HOWARD (v) (GB) *1913*

Howard Motor Works, Sutton, Surrey

This was a small-production cyclecar using an 8hp J.A.P. V-twin water-cooled engine, friction transmission and final drive by roller chain.　　GNG

HOWARD (vi) (US) *1929–1930*

Howard Motor International Corp, New York, N.Y.

The Howard 'Silver Morn' was announced as a revolutionary development in low-cost motors, but was, in fact, a conventional assembled car which was probably never made in any numbers at all. It was powered by a Continental Red Seal 6-cylinder engine, although advertisements spoke of an 8-cylinder chassis as well. Lockheed hydraulic brakes were featured, and the car had wire wheels and a ribbon-type radiator. With a complete range of smart body styles, prices ran from $695 to $2,395.　　GNG

HOWETT (GB) *1913*

Fowler's Garage, Hockley Brook, Birmingham

The Howett was a cyclecar which used a 10hp V-twin Blumfield engine, and friction transmission. The price was £100.　　GNG

H.P. (i) (F) *1913*

This was a little-known cyclecar with a 6hp single-cylinder engine. There were plans to sell it in England at £125 but nothing came of them.　　GNG

H.P. (ii) (GB) *1926–1928*

Hilton-Peacey Motors, Woking, Surrey

The H.P. was one of the last of the cyclecars, being a very simple 3-wheeler with a 500cc single-cylinder J.A.P. engine, chain drive to a 3-speed Sturmey-Archer gearbox, and final drive also by chain to the rear wheel. Other engines fitted to a few cars were 500cc Dunelts or British Vulpines, while a 344cc J.A.P.-engined model took 18 Class H records at Brooklands. The price was only £65, or less than half that of the contemporary Austin Seven, but most buyers wanted more comfort, and only about 40 H.P.'s were made.　　GNG

H.R.G. (GB) *1936–1956*

H.R.G. Engineering Co Ltd, Tolworth, Surrey

These initials stand for E.A. Halford, G.H. Robins, and H.R. Godfrey (the 'G' of G.N. (i)). Their car was intended to carry on the Frazer Nash tradition of a vintage-style sporting machine without frills, though the H.R.G. used bevel drive and not chains. The engine was the well-tried 1,496cc ohv 4-cylinder Meadows 4ED, ignition was by magneto, suspension was quarter-elliptic at the front and semi-elliptic at the rear, and the body a straightforward slab-tank two-seater. The result sold for £395 and with a weight of about 1,570lb it was capable of some 90mph. In 1938 an H.R.G. was the highest-placed British car at Le Mans, and the following year the marque won the 1½-litre class there. For 1939 pump-cooled ohc Singer engines were adopted, an '1100' using that firm's 9hp unit joining the 1½-litre. Synchromesh gearboxes and coil ignition were introduced, but magnetos were still optional until the demise of the traditional H.R.G. cars at the end of 1955. A solitary coupé used a Triumph engine.

There were few changes when the cars reappeared on the market in 1946, though there was a short-lived Aerodynamic 1500 with full-width bodywork. A distinguished competition record included Coupes des Alpes in 1948 and 1951 Alpine Rallies (a little-known H.R.G. innovation was the provision of a works van to support drivers of their cars in the 1949 event, forerunners of today's rally 'circuses'), class wins in the 1949 and 1950 Production Car Races at Silverstone, and a clean sweep of the 1½-litre class in the 1949 Belgian 24-Hour Race. Curiously enough, the zenith of the H.R.G.'s competition career coincided with a drop in sales: approximately 40 cars were delivered in 1948, 25 in 1949 and only 11 in 1950. The traditional H.R.G., however, survived until 1955; a twin-cam head announced in 1953 was never actually offered on this model, but the last 12 WS-types (all of which were exported) had the short-stroke Singer engine and hydraulic brakes in place of the cable-operated type used since 1936. An altogether more modern 1½-litre prototype (the '1100' had been dropped around 1950) with all-round independent suspension, disc brakes, twin ohc engine and aerodynamic body work, made its appearance in 1955, but this was not produced in series and H.R.G. concentrated on general engineering until the company closed down in 1966. A few months before the end a last prototype had appeared, using the Vauxhall VX 4/90 engine. Not more than 240 H.R.G.'s of all types were made.　　MCS

HSIEN-CHIN see XIAN-JIN

H.S.M. (GB) *1913–1915*

H.S.M. Motors, New Cross, London S.E.

The H.S.M. was an unusual cyclecar which, like the Seal, consisted of a two-seater sidecar permanently attached to a motor cycle, but steered by wheel from the sidecar. The engine was an 8hp J.A.P. The name H.S.M. was later applied to the batch of Triumph Dolomite 8-cylinder cars sold by High Speed Motors Ltd in 1938.　　GNG

H.T. (D) *1925*

Hans Thiele, Kraftfahrzeugbau, Berlin-Friedenau

A small car with a two-seater tandem body and a side-mounted 2.8PS 2-cylinder B.M.W. engine.　　　　　　　　　　　　HON

HUASCAR *see* GALBA

HUB (i) (US) *1899–1900*

Hub Motor Co, Chicago, Ill.

The Hub Electric was so called because of the four electric motors mounted in the wheel hubs. The cars were marketed by the Hub Company, and built by the Westinghouse Company of Pittsburg, Pa. Maximum speed was 15mph.　　GNG

HUB (ii) (US) *1907*

Hub Automobile Co, Boston, Mass.

The Hub was a very light two-seater with a tubular steel frame. Its engine was a single-cylinder, air-cooled unit of 10hp. It had steering by wheel and used a planetary transmission.　　　　　　　　　GMN

HUDLASS (GB) *1897–1902*

Phoenix Motor Works, Southport, Lancs.

Felix Hudlass had never seen a motor car when he began to make his first prototype in 1896. It used a front-mounted vertical twin engine of his own design and belt drive, and was capable of 15mph in top gear. Later models followed Benz principles with a large horizontal single-cylinder engine at the rear; one body style was a very early example of the enclosed 'doctor's coupé'. By 1902 the Hudlass was available with 6 and 10hp single-cylinder engines, and 12 and 20hp twins, now mounted in front under a conventional bonnet. Felix Hudlass left the firm in 1902 and later became chief engineer of the R.A.C., a post he held until 1947.　　　　　　　　　　GNG

HUDSON (i) (US) *1901–1902*

Beau-Chamberlain Manufacturing Co, Hudson, Mich.

The first car to bear the name Hudson was a light steamer with a vertical 2-cylinder engine, single chain drive and tiller steering. It bore no relationship to the later Hudson car.　　　　　　　GNG

HUDSON (ii) (US) *1909–1957*

(1) Hudson Motor Car Co, Detroit, Mich. *1909–1954*
(2) American Motors Corp, Kenosha, Wisc. *1954–1957*

The Hudson was created by Roy D. Chapin, and financed by J.L. Hudson, head of Detroit's famous department store of that name. The first product was a 20hp 4-cylinder car of conventional design, capable of 50mph, of which 4,000 were sold in its first season. These fours, one of which was entered in the 1914 Tourist Trophy were first supplemented and then supplanted by a 6-cylinder line. The first of these was the heavy (3,696lb) and fairly expensive ($2,350) Model 54 with a 4-speed overdrive gearbox, but the 4½-litre Super Six of 1916, with its high-compression sv engine, really made the company's name, and marked the first of a line of engines of this type which lasted almost to the end of production, giving generous outputs while still burning commercial-grade petrol. A Super Six made the first two-way transcontinental trip – New York to San Francisco and back – in 1916; Ira Vail took 9th place in the Indianapolis 500 Mile Race in 1919, and this model formed the backbone of New Zealand's 'service car' network in the 1920s.

Though Hudson's booming sales in the 1920s were largely due to the inexpensive companion make the Essex, the company also pioneered modestly-priced closed cars, and in 1922 their 'coach' (a 2-door saloon) sold for only $100 more than a tourer. Until 1929, the Super Six remained the staple Hudson model, and during its last three years of production it was powered by a 4.7-litre ioe unit derived from the original Essex Four of 1918. In 1930 it was replaced by a 3½-litre straight-8, later increased to 4,168cc in 1932 – this tough and well-liked unit remained in production until 1952, and powered such Anglo-Americans as the Railton and Brough Superior. These firms also used Hudson's 3½-litre six.

The 1930s were less favourable to Hudson, except in Britain, where the breed's popularity warranted the manufacture of a small-bore 2.7-litre 'export' six rated at only 16.9hp, which was still being made in 1940. The regular Hudson Six was a bigger machine of 3,455cc and was offered with independent front suspension in 1934 and 1935; in the latter year Electric Hand gear change became available. Fencer's mask radiator grilles followed in 1936, and steering-column change in 1939. The first post-war Hudsons were a continuation of the 1942 models, but 1948 brought the revolutionary Step-Down series with the company's high-compression sv in-line engines. These low-built cars had unitary construction of chassis and body, rear wheels mounted *inside* the chassis frame, and coil-spring independent front suspension. The 5-litre 145bhp 6-cylinder Hornet engine introduced for 1951, proved a great success in stock-car events, but before this the company had reached its post-war sales peak, with nearly 145,000 units delivered in 1950. Competition in the medium-price bracket was too strong, and

1900 HUDLASS dogcart. *The Veteran Car Club of Great Britain*

1914 HUDSON(ii) Model 54 40hp saloon. *American Motors Corporation*

1939 HUDSON(ii) Six 3.4-litre coupé. *American Motors Corporation*

1950 HUDSON(ii) Commodore Eight 4.2-litre sedan. *American Motors Corporation*

1904 BEESTON HUMBER 10/12hp tourer. *Rootes Motors Ltd*

1923 HUMBER 8/18hp chummy four-seater. *National Motor Museum*

1929 HUMBER 16/50hp coupé. Coachwork by Weymann. *National Motor Museum*

Hudson's venture in the compact car market in 1953, with the 3.3-litre 6-cylinder Jet at $1,833 (this was also the first Hudson to abandon the wet-plate clutch) was not successful.

In 1954 Hudson amalgamated with Nash to form the American Motors Corporation. Though all production was transferred from Detroit to Kenosha, and the Hudson range now shared its utinized hulls with the bigger Nash models, sales did not prosper. These last Hudsons had initially the old sv 6-cylinder units or Packard-built V-8s, while both Nash's Rambler and the Austin-built Metropolitan were sold by Hudson agents. The name was dropped at the end of the 1957 season.

MCS

HUFFIT (F) *1914*

Huffit Cyclecars Co, Paris

The Huffit cyclecar was powered by a 9/11hp Clément-Bayard engine, and weighed only 672lb.

MJWW

HUFFMAN (US) *1920–1925*

Huffman Bros Motor Co, Elkhart, Ind.

The Huffman was a typical assembled car of its time. A possible 3,000 units left the factory in six years of manufacture. A Continental 6-cylinder engine provided power and the cars were available in open and closed models. Sales were mainly confined to the Middle Western area of the United States. During the last few months of Huffman production, cars were equipped with Lockheed 4-wheel brakes and these later models frequently appeared with disc wheels in contrast to the standard artilleries used earlier.

KM

HUGHES (US) *1899–1900*

Hughes & Atkin, Providence, R.I.

The Hughes was a light two-seater buggy with wire wheels and tiller steering. Only 18 were built.

GNG

HUGOT (F) *1897–1899; 1905*

The first Hugot cars were very light voiturettes with a rear-mounted 2¼hp De Dion engine and a 2-speed gearbox. At least one model had the bodywork and mudguards made entirely of cane. These cars were to be sold in England in 1899 under the name of Paris. In 1905 a small number of two-seaters with single-cylinder 697cc engines at the front were made under the name Hugot et Pecto. They had belt drive, and one was entered in the 1905 6-day Reliability Trial for voiturettes, but it fell out on the first day.

GNG

HUMBEE SURREY (J) *1950–1962*

Mitsui Seiki Kogyo Co Ltd, Tokyo

Mitsui built machinery, gauges and tools before World War 2 and added a range of 3-wheeled vehicles after post-war reorganization. The Surrey was produced in light van versions and also as a three-seater private car with a single-cylinder, air-cooled 11½hp engine mounted in the rear of a plastic body. The layout was typically Japanese with a single wheel in front.

BE

HUMBER (GB) *1898 to date*

(1) Humber Ltd, Beeston, Notts. *1898–1908*

(2) Humber Ltd, Coventry *1898–1946*

(3) Humber Ltd, Ryton-on-Dunsmore, Warwickshire *1946–1970*

(4) Chrysler United Kingdom Ltd, Ryton-on-Dunsmore, Warwickshire *1970 to date*

Thomas Humber's bicycle firm, established in 1868, became a part of H.J. Lawson's intended automobile empire and as such was responsible for production of the abortive Pennington tricars. Car manufacture started with an experimental front wheel drive design, while motor tricycles and quadricycles were also produced. These led to a line of 3-wheeled forecars which persisted up to 1905. Little came of Humber's M.D. voiturette with 2-speed gear, but their more conventional 1901 offering had a 4½hp De Dion engine, De Dion-type transmission and shaft drive, as well as a single-spoke steering wheel which remained one of the company's trademarks in the early years and anticipated Citroën practice by more than half a century. A 12hp 2½-litre 4-cylinder car followed in 1902, but in 1903 two more ambitious vehicles appeared, a big 20hp four and a 3-cylinder version with mechanically-operated inlet valves, as well as Britain's first successful effort at a popular light car. This was the 5hp Humberette with a De Dion-type engine of 613cc and a 2-speed gearbox with two steering-column levers. All these cars had shaft drive – Humbers eschewed the chain. In 1904 the Humberette was made in a more powerful form and up to 1908 two separate lines of car were produced in the factories at Beeston and Coventry, the Beeston cars being the more expensive. 1905 saw a miniature four rated at 8/10hp, but with a capacity of 2 litres, which was developed the following year into a 10/12hp Coventry-Humber selling at £315; Beeston's offering that season was a 3½-litre T-head four selling for £472 10s. The 1907 versions of the Beeston-Humber had a capacity of 6.3 litres and pressure lubrication.

The 1908 range was quite extensive, ranging from a bid for the lightcar market with a 1½-litre 8hp vertical twin, pressure-lubricated and with Humber's own design f detachable wheels, at £195, up to a big 5½-litre six, also Coventry-made, at modest £450.

Financial difficulties led to the closure of the Beeston factory in 1908, but Coventry went on making the T-headed cars, all of which had 4-speed gearboxes by 1911. In 1912 new L-head models came out, the 11hp having a 1.7-litre monobloc engine, three forward speeds and splash lubrication; there was also a new cyclecar, the Humberette, with a 998cc air-cooled engine but otherwise on full-scale car lines, which was made up to the outbreak of World War 1. 1913/14 models cost £120, with £15 extra if water cooling was specified. Though Humbers had supported the first Tourist Trophies, an unusual departure for 1914 was the preparation of a team of 3.3-litre twin ohc 4-cylinder machines inspired by the Henry-designed Peugeots for that year's event.

After the war the company concentrated on solid family cars, noted for their excellent workmanship and all-weather equipment, as well as their conservatism. Side-valve engines were used up to 1922, but inlet over exhaust layouts appeared in 1923, in which year there was also a new small model, the '8/18' with 12 volt coil ignition at £275. Front wheel brakes had arrived by 1925, although Humbers adhered to the foot-operated transmission brake for several more seasons. The company sold over 4,000 cars in 1927, thanks to the 1,056cc '9/20', an excellent 2-litre 4-cylinder '14/40' and a new 20/55hp machine, Humber's first six for many years.

The cars were restyled in 1929, and the following year the effect of the Rootes takeover was seen in the new line of sixes, the 2.1-litre '16/50' and the 3½-litre Snipe and its long-chassis stablemate, the Pullman. 1930 was also the last year for the 9hp Humbers and thereafter the company's staple products were upper-middle-class family cars of over two litres' capacity, although a 1.7-litre '12' appeared in 1933 and formed the basis for the long-stroke 4-cylinder Rootes engines still being manufactured in 1966. Also at the end of 1932 overhead inlet valves were dropped. In 1936 the 6-cylinder cars acquired transverse ifs, while the biggest sixes were now of 4.1 litres' capacity. Only 6-cylinder cars were offered in 1938, and hydraulic brakes appeared on 16hp and 21hp models in 1939, and were also found on the first Super Snipe – a 'compact' evolved by mounting the 4.1-litre engine in the smaller chassis, which was excellent value at £398.

Snipe-based vehicles served the Allied Forces with distinction in World War 2 and the new models introduced in 1945 were really hold-overs from 1940, with hydraulics now standardized, together with a new four in the shape of a 1.9-litre side-valve Hawk based on Hillman's Fourteen of 1938/40. In 1950 a Super Snipe took second place in the Monte Carlo Rally. The Super Snipe and Pullman acquired overhead valves in 1953, and the Hawk a year later, while 1956 Super Snipes could be had with automatic transmission. Unitary construction was used on a redesigned Hawk in 1957, and two years later the Super Snipe (after a short period in abeyance) re-emerged as an altogether smaller 2,650cc car, also with unitary construction. This was soon replaced by a 3-litre development with disc front brakes. 1962 models had the four-headlamp pioneered in America in 1957. A small luxury Humber came out in 1964 in the shape of the Sceptre, based on Hillman's Super Minx, but with overdrive standard equipment. During 1967 all the big Humbers were dropped, to be replaced on the British market by the Australian-built Plymouth Valiant. Since 1968 the only Humber offering has been the 1.7-litre Sceptre, a prestige version of the Hillman Hunter. The 1973 models had twin-carburettor 79bhp engines, and there was a choice of a 4-speed all-synchromesh gearbox with overdrive on the two upper ratios or automatic transmission.   MCS

HUMBLE (AUS) 1903
Humble & Sons, Geelong, Victoria

This company made refrigerators and dairy equipment, wool presses and grain hoppers, and built at least one four-seater tonneau using some De Dion components.   GNG

HUMMINGBIRD (US) c.1946
Talmadge Judd, Kingsport, Tenn.

A small convertible coupé built for possible marketing, the Hummingbird was a one-off with a 20bhp 4-cylinder engine providing 50mpg.

This name was also used for a series of rebuilt pre-war Austin Sevens, sold by the Pippbrook Garage, Dorking, Surrey in 1949.   BE

HUMPHRIS (GB) 1908–1909
Humphris Gear & Engineering Co Ltd, Eastleigh, Hampshire

The Humphris was notable for its patent gearbox in the rear axle. This consisted of a disc with four circles of holes; pinions from the propeller shaft engaged with different sets of holes for each speed. Various engines were listed, including a 10/12, 12/14, 15/17 and 25/30hp.   GNG

HUPMOBILE (US) 1908–1940
Hupp Motor Car Corp, Detroit, Mich.; Cleveland, Ohio

Robert and Louis Hupp, the founders of this company, started with a 2.8-litre 4-cylinder light runabout, with two bucket seats and a bolster tank, distinguished by a 2-speed sliding-type gearbox. It sold for $750 and was joined in 1911 by a touring

1937 HUMBER Twelve drophead coupé.
G.N. Georgano

1952 HUMBER Super Snipe 4-litre saloon.
Rootes Motors Ltd

1965 HUMBER Super Snipe 3-litre saloon.
Rootes Motors Ltd

1973 HUMBER Sceptre 1.7-litre saloon.
Chrysler UK Ltd

1914 HUPMOBILE 15/18hp limousine.
Coachwork by Zimmermann of Berlin.
National Motor Museum

1932 HUPMOBILE New Century Six 3.7-litre
coupé. *Musée de l'Automobile, Le Mans*

1939 HUPMOBILE Junior Six 4-litre sedan.
Autocar

car with 3 forward speeds and a longer wheelbase of 9ft 2in, listed at only $900. Hupmobile, like Dodge and Chevrolet, adhered to the 4-cylinder sv unit for many years and made nothing else until 1924, though their cars acquired electric lighting and starting in 1914. A version with a 10ft 6in wheelbase was made available for seven-seater bodywork in 1916. Sales were good: 12,000 in 1913, and climbing up to 38,000 by 1923. By 1918 a rounded cowl and bonnet line had replaced the original angular configuration and fuel feed was by vacuum from a tank at the rear. Open models were listed at $1,250. Aluminium pistons were featured in 1924 and balloon tyres in 1925, the last year of the four. Interestingly enough, Hupmobile's 4-litre straight-8 appeared in 1925, a year before the first six. It was a conventional machine with contracting Lockheed hydraulic brakes, mechanical actuation being used on the 6-cylinder cars. The company stayed in the medium-price field, sixes selling at $1,295 in 1929, while prices of the M series sv eight started at $1,825. In 1929 Chandler's plant in Cleveland was acquired and was used for the manufacture of the less expensive Hupps. Like most of America's independent makes, the Hupmobile was hit hard by the Depression, sales dropping from 50,374 in 1929 to 17,450 in 1931, although in the next two years, in 1932 and 1933 some very handsome cars were made.

In 1934 the Aerodynamic range with three-piece wrap-around windscreens and headlamps faired into the bonnet sides appeared. An experimental fwd version was not proceeded with. The aerodynamic cars were made in 4-litre, 6-cylinder and 5-litre straight-8 forms, but sales were poor and the factory closed down halfway through the 1936 season. It was reopened, but the 1937 and 1938 models were of little interest apart from the standardization of automatic overdrive on the eights. Like Graham, Hupmobile tried to stay in business by adapting the body dies of the discontinued 810/812 Cord series to their conventional running gear. These Skylarks were built in the Graham factory; the last cars were completed in July 1940 but were sold as 1941 models.   MC

HUPP-YEATS (US) *1911–1919*
(1) R.C.H. Corp, Detroit, Mich. *1911–1912*
(2) Hupp-Yeats Electric Car Co, Detroit, Mich. *1912–1919*

These electric cars were four-seaters, in both open and closed versions. The motors were built by Westinghouse and had five selective speeds.   GMN

HURLINCAR (GB) *1913–1916*
Hurlin & Co Ltd, Hackney, London E.

The original Hurlincar used an 8/10hp V-twin J.A.P. engine and chain drive but from 1914 a more substantial light car was offered, with a 10hp 4-cylinder Ballot unit, and shaft drive. The company also sold the Aviette, an ultra-light cyclecar.   GNG

HURON (GB) *1970–1972*
(1) Huron Auto Race Developments Ltd, Enfield, Middlesex *1970–1971*
(2) Huron Auto Race Developments Ltd, Cobham, Surrey *1971–1972*

Designer Jo Marquart, Roy Ireland and Canadian Jack Smith advertised a range of racing models covering 2-litre Group 6 sports cars and single-seaters for Formulae 2, 3 and Atlantic with monocoque construction, and a space-framed Formula Ford machine. Sponsorship for the sports model was obtained from Holland; one was raced with BDA engine and D.A.F. Variomatic transmission. Further support was not encouraging and the name did not long survive, despite a reorganized company that assembled a few more cars at Cobham under Geoff Daly and Mike Chambers.   DF

HURST; HURMID (GB) *1900–1907*
(1) G. Hurst, Holloway, London N. *1900–1906*
(2) Hurst & Middleton Ltd, Holloway, London N. *1906–1907*

George Hurst's first cars were made in conjunction with Lewis A. Lloyd (Hurst & Lloyd), but in 1900 he set up on his own and made a small number of cars with 12hp 2-cylinder or 24hp 4-cylinder engines, shaft drive and a Panhard appearance. Production was spasmodic although one was sold to the Member of Parliament for Aberdeen in 1902. For 1906 Hurst brought out a 6-cylinder 30/40hp car as well as a 10hp twin and a 15/18hp four. The same year he was joined by R.E. Middleton, and for the last year of production, the cars were known as Hurmids.   GNG

HURST & LLOYD (GB) *1897–1900*
(1) Hurst & Lloyd, Holborn, London W.C. *1897–1898*
(2) Hurst & Lloyd, Wood Green, London N. *1898–1900*

George Hurst was a model maker of 293 High Holborn who made a number of engines with Lewis A. Lloyd. In 1897 they made a car with a 2-cylinder horizontal engine under the floorboards and flat belt drive. The following year they acquired a small works at Wood Green where a few of these cars were made. In 1900 Hurst left, and Lloyd was joined by W.E. Plaister. The remaining Hurst & Lloyd cars and all subsequent vehicles were sold as Lloyd & Plaisters.   GNG

HURTU (F) *1896–1930*
Compagnie des Autos et Cycles Hurtu, Albert, Somme; Neuilly, Seine; Rueil, Seine-et-Oise

Like Opel in Germany, Hurtu progressed from sewing-machines through bicycles to cars. They made a few hundred Bollée voiturettes for that concern, then went into car manufacture on their own account. Like most other pioneer motor manufacturers, they began by copying an established machine, in this case the belt-driven single-cylinder Benz, and incorporating improvements. Equally predictably, when this model was superseded in 1900 by a more modern car, the latter was a voiturette with a single-cylinder 3½hp De Dion engine and shaft drive. Single-, 2- and 4-cylinder Aster engines were also fitted. Indeed, the firm never departed very far from standard practice, for even the dashboard radiator used on smaller models from 1907 to 1920 was a common sight. They continued to specialize in light cars until 1914, their most popular offering being a 10hp machine of modern design with a monobloc 4-cylinder engine and unit construction of engine and gearbox, though an 8hp single was made as late as 1912. In 1922, however, a touring car with a 2-litre push-rod overhead valve engine and front-wheel brakes was introduced, and a good-looking sports alternative appeared two years later. However, the market for the classic French fast tourer declined towards the end of the 1920s, and Hurtu had no popular, cheap small car now to cater for the biggest market. Car production ceased in 1930.   TRN

HUSQVARNA (S) *1943*
Husqvarna Vapenfabriks AB, Huskvarna

The most famous Swedish motor cycle makers, Husqvarna built a prototype 3-wheeler planned for production after World War 2. It had a 500cc air-cooled 2-stroke engine with chain transmission to the single rear wheel. Lack of production facilities prevented the car from being made in numbers.   OB

HUTTON (GB) *1900–1905; 1908*
(1) J.E. Hutton Ltd, Northallerton, Yorks. *1900–1902*
(2) J.E. Hutton Ltd, Thames Ditton, Surrey *1903–1905*
(3) D. Napier & Son Ltd, Acton, London W. *1908*

Also known as the Simplex, the first Hutton was a voiturette powered by rear-mounted M.M.C., De Dion or Aster engines of 5 or 6hp, with a 2-speed belt transmission, and *vis-à-vis* body. These cars were made at Northallerton, but the next Hutton cars of 1903 to 1905 were made at Thames Ditton. They were conventional machines with 4-cylinder pair-cast engines of 12 or 20hp, and shaft drive. An experimental car was fitted with the Barber automatic transmission, but no cars so equipped were sold to the public.

The final phase of the Hutton came in 1908 when three 4-cylinder cars were made in the Napier factory for the 1908 Tourist Trophy. They were in fact of Napier design, but were named Hutton because S.F. Edge had decried the 4-cylinder engine so much in advertising and in correspondence that he was not anxious for such cars to run under the Napier name. However, the Hutton driven by W. Watson won the T.T., and is still in existence today. Another Hutton with an extra-long stroke (203.2mm compared with 178mm for the T.T. Winner) took 26hp class records at Brooklands in 1908.   GNG

H.W.M. (GB) *1950–1956*
H.W. Motors Ltd, Walton-on-Thames, Surrey

John Heath and George Abecassis supported Formula 2 racing energetically in the 1950–53 period with Alta-powered 2-litre and 2½-litre cars, and did much for Britain's prestige at a time when the national livery was seldom seen on the circuits. These cars had twin ohc 4-cylinder engines, all-round independent suspension and preselector (later, Jaguar synchromesh) gearboxes. In 1952 a 1-2-3 victory was achieved in the International Trophy at Silverstone, but in spite of frequent H.W.M. successes and Paul Frère's win in the Grand Prix des Frontieres at Chimay, the company lacked the finance to compete on even terms with the Italians. Very few cars were sold, though the company later made and raced larger sports cars with such engines as the 3.4-litre 240bhp Jaguar D engine, tubular ladder-type frame and a De Dion rear axle. The manufacture of cars ceased with John Heath's death in 1956.   MCS

HYDROMETER (US) *1917*
Automobile Boat Manufacturing Co, Seattle, Wash.

This was an early attempt at building an amphibian car and was the invention of William Mazzei. Built along the lines of a boat, and rather resembling the German Rumpler car of the 1920s, the Hydrometer was said to be able to reach 60mph in speed on land and 25mph in water. A Continental engine was used and propeller and rudder were mounted at the rear of the car. A two-seater roadster constituted the only model shown. The steering wheel operated both the front wheels and the rudder.   KM

HYDROMOBIL (D) *1903–1907*
Pittler Motorwagen-Gesellschaft, Berlin-Reinickendorf

W. von Pittler was one of the great inventors of his time. The main feature of his Hydromobil was its hydraulic transmission, the first one which worked satisfactorily.

Only prototypes of the Hydromobil were built and hydraulic transmission,

1914 HURLINCAR 10hp two-seater. *David Burgess Wise*

1900 HURST & LLOYD 2-cylinder tonneau. *Miss Doris Rowe*

1900 HURTU 8hp tonneau. *G.N. Georgano*

1920 HURTU 14hp tourer. *Autocar*

1908 HUTTON 26hp T.T. racing car. *Guy Griffiths*

1951 H.W.M. 2-litre Formula 2 racing car. Stirling Moss at the wheel. *Klemantaski Studio*

although used in certain commercial vehicles today, was not developed for private cars; Pittler was ahead of his time. He also built several prototypes with a friction drive of his own design. HON

HYLANDER *see* HIGHLANDER

HYSLOP (US) *1915*
Hyslop & Clark, Toledo, Ohio
By the time the Hyslop was marketed, the cyclecar had become rather more advanced in design. This make had semi-elliptical springs all round, with a 4-cylinder water-cooled engine and a V-shaped radiator shell. GMN

HYTHE *see* NEW CENTURY (i)

I

IBIS (F) *1907*

Automobiles Ibis, Levallois-Perret, Seine

The Ibis was produced in two models, an 8/10hp 2-cylinder and a 12/14hp 4-cylinder. Both cars used shaft drive.   GNG

IDEAL (i) (US) *1902–1903*

B. & P. Co, Milwaukee, Wisc.

This was a light two-seater car with a 5hp single-cylinder horizontal engine and 3-speed gearbox. Maximum speed was 25mph. The company also made steam engines for heavy lorries, but did not manufacture a steam vehicle themselves.   GNG

IDEAL (ii) (US) *1909–1914*

Ideal Electric Co, Chicago, Ill.

The Ideal electric car was built principally in closed models, most of them four-seaters. The controller allowed four forward speeds. This car weighed 2,500lb and was priced in the $1,800–1,900 range.   GMN

IDEAL (iii) (US) *1914*

The Ideal Shop, Buffalo, N.Y.

This cyclecar was built as either a single-seater or as a two-seater with tandem arrangement. The power was from a 2-cylinder Spacke engine which drove the vehicle through a planetary transmission and belts to the rear wheels.   GMN

IDEAL (iv) (E) *1915–1922*

Talleres Hereter SA, Barcelona

Shortage of imported cars during World War 1 led D. Laureano Hereter to start car manufacture in his engineering works. As there were few component suppliers the car was almost entirely made in the T.H. factory. The original series of 100 cars (Model D) used a 6/8hp 4-cylinder engine, but in 1918 the Type T.H. appeared with a 15hp 4-cylinder engine with inclined valves. Both these cars were successful in races, their successes including La Vuelta de Cataluña (1916), Carreras de Regularidad (1915 and 1916) and the Penya Rhin Races (1918). Nadal, one of the Ideal agents, tuned cars in his own workshop to such good effect that they began to defeat works-entered models. As a result, he was made manager of the firm and the former Chief Engineer, Custals, left to make his own car, the Nacional Custals.   JRV

IDEN (GB) *1904–1907*

Iden Motor Car Co Ltd, Coventry, Warwickshire

The Iden company was formed by George Iden, formerly works manager of M.M.C. Two 4-cylinder cars were made in 1904, a 12hp and an 18hp, with shaft drive and conventional appearance. For 1905 a 25hp car was introduced, but only made for one season. The smaller cars were continued for 1906 and 1907. At the end of 1907 a front-wheel drive car was made with a 12hp V-twin engine under the front seat, with drive via a 3-speed gearbox to the front wheels. It had a landaulet body, and was intended for taxicab work as much as for private use, but it was not made in quantity.   GNG

I.E.N.A. (I) *1922–1925*

Industria Economica Nazionale Automobili, Lodi

The I.E.N.A. was a conventional light car of the post-World War 1 period, powered by an 1,100cc 4-cylinder, water-cooled engine made by Chapuis-Dornier. Like most Italian cars of the age, it could also be had in sports form.   TRN

I.F.A. (D) *1948–1956*

Industrie-Vereinigung Volkseigener Fahrzeugwerke, Zwickau; Eisenach

This was not a brand-name but stood for a combine of several nationalized factories, including D.K.W., Audi, Framo, Phänomen, various tractor works and car-body manufacturers. But the I.F.A. emblem was used for some motor cycles and cars, especially for export. The cars were based on D.K.W. designs and built in the former Audi works at Zwickau. Two models were produced. Mechanically the first I.F.A. derived from the pre-1939 D.K.W. Meisterklasse with a 2-cylinder 2-stroke 684cc engine, front-wheel drive and pre-war body. It was produced from 1948 to 1955 and was succeeded by the A.W.Z. type P70. The I.F.A. F9 was based on a pre-war D.K.W. design which had not been put into production. It had a 3-cylinder 2-stroke 894cc engine, front-wheel drive and a new body. Production started in 1950 at Zwickau and was later transferred to Eisenach; it ceased in 1956 in favour

1918 IDEAL(iv) 15hp two-seater. *J. Rodriguez-Viña*

1905 IDEN 12hp tourer. *Autocar*

1954 I.F.A. Type F9 894cc convertible. *Neubauer Collection*

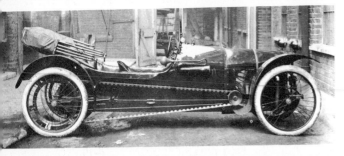

1913 IMP(i) 12hp cyclecar. *David Burgess Wise*

1961 I.M.P. 645cc GT coupé. *Intermeccanica Puch*

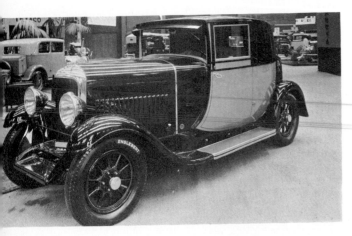

1909 IMPERIA(i) 28hp limousine. *The Veteran Car Club of Great Britain*

c.1929 IMPERIA(i) 1.8-litre coupé. Coachwork by Snutsel. *Geoffroy de Beauffort Collection*

of the new Wartburg. The Düsseldorf works of D.K.W. also used 3-cylinder 2-stroke engines in their post-war models and the body style used by the two makes was quite similar. HON

I.H.C. (US) *1911*
Independent Harvester Co, Plano, Ill.
The I.H.C. was a farmers' utility vehicle which could be used either for passengers or as a delivery car. It was powered by an air-cooled 24hp engine — mounted under the seat, despite the presence of a bonnet in front. It was a tiller-steered high-wheeler with drive by what was termed a 'V-chain belt'. The name I.H.C. was also applied to the earlier products of the International Harvester Corp (*see* International (iii)). GMN

ILFORD (GB) *1902–1903*
Ilford Motor Car & Cycle Co, Ilford, Essex
The Ilford light car had a 5hp front-mounted M.M.C. engine, 3-speed gearbox, and shaft drive. A four-seater *vis-à-vis* body was fitted. GNG

I.K.A. *see* KAISER CARABELA and TORINO

ILLINOIS (US) *1910–1914*
Overholt Co, Galesburg, Ill.
This car was produced as either a five-seater touring car, or as a baby tonneau. The 4-cylinder, 40hp engine was of 4.4 litres. The Model K of 1911 was quoted at $2,000. GMN

IMMERMOBIL (D) *1905–1907*
Max Eisenmann & Co, Hamburg
Two Immermobil models were produced on French lines. The 8hp model used a single-cylinder De Dion engine, while the 10/12hp was equipped with a 4-cylinder Reyrol unit. Bodies were of the two-seater voiturette type. HON

IMMISCH (GB) *1894–1897*
Acme & Immisch Electric Works Ltd, Chalk Farm, London N.W.
Acme & Immisch were large electrical engineers who made a few cars to order. In 1896 a 3-wheeler and a 4-wheeler *dos-à-dos* were built for the Sultan of Turkey. GNG

IMP (i) (US) *1913–1914*
W.H. McIntyre Co, Auburn, Ind.
The Imp was a cyclecar with a V-twin air-cooled engine, friction transmission and belt drive. Double cantilever springs were used in front and there was a single headlamp. With a 3ft track, 8ft 4in wheelbase and a weight of 600lb, this tandem two-seater was priced at $375. The company also built the McIntyre. GMN

IMP (ii) (US) *c.1955*
International Motor Products, Glendale, Calif.
Only 10ft long, the two-seater Imp was made of fibreglass and contained a 7½hp Gladden air-cooled rear engine. BE

I.M.P. (I) *1960–1961*
Intermeccanica Puch, Turin
The I.M.P. was an Austro-Italian hybrid using the engine of the Steyr-Puch and a two-seater GT coupé body made by Frank Reisner in Turin. The 645cc 2-cylinder engine developed 40bhp at 5,500rpm. Only 21 I.M.P.s were made. GNG

IMPERIA (i) (B) *1906–1949*
(1) Automobiles Imperia, Liège; Nessonvaux *1906–1929*
(2) SA des Automobiles Imperia-Excelsior, Nessonvaux *1929–1949*
The first Imperias were the work of the German Paul Henze, who himself handled an 8-litre car in the 1907 Kaiserpreis. At first only a 24/30hp four of 4.9 litres was marketed with lt magneto and coil ignition, 4-speed gearbox, and shaft or side-chain drive. The smaller 3-litre that followed was shaft-driven, and a 1,767cc monobloc four arrived during 1909. As late as 1911 an immense, Kaiser-preis-inspired chain-driven 9.9-litre 50/60 was still offered. In 1912 Imperia merged with Springuel, but though the latter name soon vanished, Jules Springuel took over the management, and some ioe Springuel designs were sold under the Imperia name. In 1914 a range of conventional, well-made sv fours, of 1.8 litres, 2.6 litres, 3.6 litres and 5 litres, was offered.
In 1919 Imperia took over the manufacture of the Spanish Abadal (this had always had a substantial Belgian content), offering both a 3-litre Type E, and the Hispano-Suiza-like 80 × 180mm 3.6-litre Type T, complete with handsome V-radiator as found on subsequent Imperias. These were made in small numbers until 1922, though a 6-litre twin-carburettor sohc Imperia-Abadal straight-8 with Perrot fwb on a 12ft wheelbase never progressed beyond the prototype stage. Equally short-lived was a promising sports car, the long-stroke 16-valve ohc 4-cylinder 3-litre with which de Tornaco won the 1922 Belgian GP. In 1923 M.A. van Roggen, now in charge at Nessonvaux, came up with his slide-valve 1,100cc 6CV, a small

urer of Panhard-like appearance, but with an unusual servo-assisted foot transmission brake – brakes on the front wheels were standardized in 1925. This one was quite successful, winning the small-car class of the 1926 Monte Carlo Rally and selling 504 units in 1927, but Van Roggen's 'empire-building' did not prosper: plans to produce 6CVs in France (at the Voisin works) and at the British G.W.K. factory proved abortive. The 1928 season brought a companion 1,642cc six, later enlarged to 1.8 litres and available in 3-carburettor sporting form, and in this period Imperia acquired Excelsior, Nagant (who were converted to making 6-cylinder engines), and the Matthys et Osy coachbuilding works. The slide-valve models survived until 1934, acquiring hydraulic brakes at the end, but in 1934 Imperia took out a licence to build fwd Adlers, and until 1940 these were their staple; the 995cc Trumpf-Junior, the 1,645cc Trumpf, and the later Zweiliter were all made. In 1935 the company fused with the only other surviving Belgian private-car maker, Minerva, and the big sleeve-valve models from Antwerp disappeared for good.

In 1947 there was a brief revival with the TA8, a synthesis of pre-World War fwd models by Adler and Amilcar, powered by the 1,340cc ohv 4-cylinder engine used in 1940 Amilcars. Features were gravity feed, hydraulic brakes, a 3-speed gearbox with dashboard change, and composite wood and metal coachwork. Three years later even this half-Belgian machine had given way to licence-production of a British car, the 2,088cc Standard Vanguard.   MCS

IMPERIA (ii) (D) 1935
Imperia-Werk AG, Bad Godesberg

This factory, well known for its motor cycles, had already experimented with cars in 1924/5, but production on a limited scale was not started until 1935. A 3-cylinder 2-stroke 750cc radial engine mounted in the rear was used for a streamlined two-seater coupé and for a small monoposto racing car, both with independent wheel suspension. Financial difficulties stopped production at an early stage.   HON

IMPERIAL (i) (GB) 1900–1905
Imperial Autocar Manufacturing Co Ltd, Manchester

The first cars of this make came in two models: a 3½hp single-cylinder *vis-à-vis* with the engine under the rear seat, and a 6hp 2-cylinder with a front-mounted engine, and four-seater tonneau body. Both cars had vertical water-cooled engines. Later the firm sold 6hp single-cylinder cars of the Lacoste et Battmann Type, of which only the bodies were built in England.   GNG

IMPERIAL (ii) (US) 1903–1904
Rodgers & Co, Columbus, Ohio

Four models of the Imperial were made, fitted with an opposed 2-cylinder, air-cooled engine. The drive system comprised a sliding-gear transmission and shaft to the rear axle. The steering column was hinged for ease of entrance to the driver's seat. The cars were also known as Columbus or Rodgers.   GMN

IMPERIAL (iii) (GB) 1904–1905
The Anti-Vibrator Co Ltd, Croydon, Surrey

This was an electric landaulet powered by two 3hp motors mounted in the rear wheels. It was unusual in having integral construction of body and chassis, and was lower in build than most electric town cars.   GNG

IMPERIAL (iv) (US) 1906–1907
Imperial Motor Car Co, Williamsport, Pa.

The Imperial Roadster, a four-seater, had a 4-cylinder Rutenber engine with dual ignition. This was water-cooled and had a capacity of 5.5 litres. A 3-speed transmission was used with shaft drive. The chassis had a wheelbase of 9ft and the complete car weighed 2,400lb.   GMN

IMPERIAL (v) (US) 1907–1916
Imperial Automobile Co, Jackson, Mich.

This Imperial company seems to have specialized in touring cars, having five models in one year (1910). In 1914, four chassis were offered with 4-cylinder engines of 4.9 and 5.2 litres, and 6-cylinder 5.7- and 7-litre units. The 44hp six cost $2,000 in its five-seater touring car form.   GMN

IMPERIAL (vi) (GB) 1914
Implitico Ltd, London E.C.

Made by a firm of lighting engineers responsible for the illumination of the Olympia Motor Shows, the Imperial was a simple cycle car powered by a Precision 8hp V-twin engine. Final drive was by belt, and with standard equipment, the car sold for £100.   GNG

IMPERIAL (vii) (US) 1954 to date
Chrysler Corporation, Detroit, Mich.

The name of Imperial, used by the Chrysler Corporation for their luxury-car line from 1926 onwards, became a make in its own right in 1954. The object of this move was to put the Imperial on a par with Cadillac and Lincoln in the public mind, but the cars remained large Chryslers, with overhead-valve V-8 oversquare

1948 IMPERIA(i) TA-8 1.3-litre sports car.
John Clothier

1934 IMPERIA(ii) 750cc coupé. *Jaeger Collection*

1901 IMPERIAL(i) 6hp tonneau. *G.N. Georgano Collection*

1955 IMPERIAL(vii) 5.3-litre sedan. *Chrysler Corporation*

1968 IMPERIAL(vii) 7.3-litre sedan. *Chrysler Corporation*

1966 INNOCENTI C 1098cc sports car. *Innocenti*

1972 INNOCENTI Mini Cooper 1300 saloon. *Innocenti*

engines and automatic transmission as standard equipment. Year-to-year improve ments followed those of Chrysler's other products, with 'flight-sweep' styling i 1955 and alternator ignition in 1960. 1955 Imperials had Chrysler's caliper dis brakes as standard. Since 1957 the name of Le Baron, a custom coachbuilder whos work often appeared on the Chrysler Imperials of the 1920s and 1930s, has bee associated with the costliest models. In 1966 the Imperial had an engine of ove 7 litres' capacity developing 350bhp; prices, at $5,733 upwards, were comparabl with Cadillac's De Ville series and the Lincoln Continental. Unitary constructic was adopted in 1967, and in 1971 Imperials were available with America's firs 4-wheel anti-skid brake system. That year's engines had a capacity of 7,211cc an an output of 335bhp, drastically reduced to 225bhp in 1972, when electronic ign tion was standardized. There were only detail changes for 1973.   MC

IMPETUS (F) *1899–1903*
Max Hertel, Automobiles Impetus, Pornichet, Loire-Inférieure

The Impetus cars were designed by the American, Max Hertel, who had previ ously been with the Oakman Motor Vehicle Company. They were elegant light car with 3 or 4hp De Dion engines, suspended at the rear on large C-springs. From 190 larger cars with 2-cylinder engines of up to 9hp were made. The small seaside resor of Pornichet was an unusual location for a car factory.   GN

INCAMP (E) *1952*
The Bilbao-built Incamp was a short-lived minicar of which only 12 were made
      GN

INDIAN (US) *1928–1929*
Indian Motorcycle Co, Springfield, Mass.

Only three Indian cars were built, these being experimental cars constructed unde the direction of Jack Bauer, son of the president of the concern. A roadster, a coup and one other type were constructed. One of these was powered with an Indian moto cycle engine; the other two with Continental fours. All used wire wheels and wer a little larger than the later American Bantam car.   KN

INDUCO (F) *1922–1925*
Automobiles Induco, Puteaux, Seine

Like the M.S., the Induco was in fact a Marguerite sold under another name The Marguerite Models B05 and B07 were bought by Induco who mounted tourin and Weymann saloon bodies. About 20 Inducos were sold.   GN

INDUHAG (D) *1922*
Industrie- und Handels- Gesellschaft mbH, Düsseldorf

A small 3-wheeled car with a single- or two-seater body. It was available as a electric car or with a 2/4PS 2-cylinder petrol engine. Transmission was to the two rear wheels in both versions.   HO

INGRAM-HATCH (US) *1917–1918*
Ingram-Hatch Motor Corp, Staten Island, N.Y.

This freakish car used a paraffin-burning, single overhead camshaft 4-cylinde engine. It was air-cooled and developed 40hp. Twin drive shafts transmitted th torque to a friction transmission, one for each axle half. Finally the wheels had combination of air and mechanical springs in place of spokes.   GM

INNES (US) *1921*
American Motor Export Co, Jacksonville, Fla.

The short-lived Innes was a small assembled car powered by an 18.2hp 4 cylinder Supreme engine and using Columbia axles and Grant-Lees transmission Body styles were a five-seater touring car, two-seater roadster, and light truck.   GM

INNOCENTI (I) *1961 to date*
Società Generale per l'Industria Metallurgica e Meccanica, Milan

The makers of the famous Lambretta scooter branched out into car manufactur in 1961 by undertaking licence-production of the Austin (i) 948cc A40 saloon All their subsequent cars have been variations on themes by the British Moto Corporation: in 1961 they also offered a Ghia-bodied Austin-Healey Sprite. Their 1963 IM3 was the fwd Morris 1100 with servo brakes, revised grille and 58bhp engine, selling for the equivalent of £472. 1963 Sprites had the 1,098cc engine and for 1965 there was the J4, an Italianized Austin 1100 in standard tune. Later in the year came a Mini, selling for LIT 860,000 or 110,000 lire more than the Fiat 850. In spite of the relatively high prices, Innocenti had sold 150,000 o their B.M.C.-based cars by November 1966. They added a version of the Mini Traveller for 1967 and also offered a 1¼-litre model of the Sprite, though no sport models were offered after 1971. Innocenti became part of the British Leyland Group in May 1972, when the range embraced the 998cc Mini saloon and Traveller the 1,275cc Cooper 1300, and the J5, an 1100 derivative.   MC

INSTITEC (RA) *1954–1955*
Industrias Aeronauticas y Mecánicas Estado (IAME), Córdoba

The Institec Justicialista was intended to be a mass-produced family car, made a saloon, station wagon and pick-up form, powered by a D.K.W.-inspired 2-cylinder 2-stroke engine driving the front wheels. The saloon's body was reminiscent of a scaled-down 1951 Chevrolet. There was also a Justicialista Sports powered by a Porsche engine, with fibreglass coupé body, and at least one of these was fitted with an air-cooled 3-litre V-8 engine. Several hundred cars were made by Institec, mainly 2-cylinder saloons, and the design was revived in the Graciela of 1960.   GNG

INTER (F) *1953–1956*

S.N.C.A.N., Lyons

Produced by an aircraft firm to the order of a Paris sales organization, the Inter was a tandem-seater cabin scooter of the Messerschmitt variety. A 175cc Ydral engine was used, and the front wheels were mounted on outriggers in the manner of the Reyonnah. Several hundred were sold.   GNG

INTERMECCANICA (I) *1967 to date*

Costruzione Automobili Intermeccanica, Turin

Intermeccanica was founded by Frank Reisner in 1959; their first production car was the I.M.P. Subsequently Reisner was concerned with the Apollo (iii), Griffith and Omega (vi) cars, all of which used Italian bodies and American engines, with assembly being done in America. Problems arising from this transatlantic enterprise led Reisner to manufacture in Italy and send complete cars to the United States. The first of such cars, the Intermeccanica Torino, was very similar to the Omega, with 4.7-litre Ford V-8 engine and two-seater convertible body. This was renamed the Italia in 1968 and subsequently fitted with a 5-litre and then 5.7-litre engine. Other Intermeccanica models have been the IMX fibreglass coupé and the Murena GT, a luxury station wagon powered by a 7-litre engine. For 1972 two Opel-powered models were introduced under the name Indra, using 2.8-litre Admiral or 5.4-litre Diplomat engines.   GNG

INTERNATIONAL (i) (GB) *1898–1904*

(1) International Motor Car Co, London *1898–1900*

(2) International Motor Car Co Ltd, London *1900–1904*

Oscar Seyd's firm never built a car, though some International offerings were assembled in their Great Portland Street Showrooms and a certain amount of work was also undertaken at the service depot in Kilburn, where International had been operating since 1896. The original International-Benz was in fact a French-built Roger, a car which had become hard to sell in France; International added their own improvements, among them a reverse, a British-built version of the 'Crypto' gear and bodywork made to their order. Single- and twin-cylinder variations on the Benz theme were offered until 1901, later cars being German-built after the demise of M. Roger's company. In 1899 International presented a 'light two-seater racing car' with wheel steering, a Benz-based 12hp with wheel steering, pneumatic tyres and double phaeton coachwork at £800, and a 9hp 'vibrationless' flat-twin (not on Benz lines) in addition to their regular range. They became a limited liability company in 1900, when two Coventry firms, Payne and Bates (Godiva) and Allard (i), were approached to make a new design for them. The Payne and Bates-built International (possibly the twin-cylinder Royal with steel frame and wheel steering, offered for £367 10s) proved unsatisfactory, but Allard's effort, the Charette, introduced in November 1900, sold in some numbers. This was a belt-driven light car with front vertical 823cc engine of De Dion type (designed to run at only 1,000rpm), a coal-shovel shaped bonnet and rack-and-pinion steering. It sold for £165. Early cars were rated at 5hp (later increased to 6hp) and there were 2-speed and 3-speed variants. All Charette chassis were delivered to London under their own power. This type was not offered after 1903 and apart from the Mountaineer motorcycle, the later cars of the International company were of French origin. The Armstrong (1902) was a single-cylinder 1,100cc machine with shaft drive on Renault lines and this gave way in 1903 to the Aster-engined Portlands, also shaft-driven and offered in a variety of sizes from a 6hp single at £205 up to a big 24hp 4-cylinder car with a 4-speed gearbox.

The smallest Portland was still available in 1904, but by this time the company was mainly concerned with importing the Diamant car. International were defunct by 1905.   MCS

INTERNATIONAL (ii) (US) *1900*

International Motor Carriage Co, Stamford, Conn.

This company showed a light car with a 2-stroke engine designed to run on paraffin at the Madison Square Garden show in 1900, but it did not go into production.   GNG

INTERNATIONAL (iii) (I.H.C.) (US) *1907–1911; 1961 to date*

(1) International Harvester Co, Chicago, Ill. *1907*

(2) International Harvester Co, Akron, Ohio *1907–1911*

(3) International Harvester Co, Chicago, Ill. *1961 to date*

The International was a popular high-wheeler built as a two-seater surrey or as a light delivery truck. It was powered by a horizontally-opposed 2-cylinder

1954 INSTITEC Justicialista Sports 1½-litre coupé.
Autosport

1901 INTERNATIONAL(i) Charette 6hp phaeton. *G.N. Georgano Collection*

1907 INTERNATIONAL(iii) motor buggy.
International Harvester Co

1967 INTERNATIONAL(iii) Travelall station wagon. *International Harvester Co*

1973 INTERNATIONAL(iii) Scout utility car. *International Harvester Co*

1928 INVICTA(iv) 3-litre drophead coupé. *National Motor Museum*

engine of 15hp. Friction transmission was used, with two forward speeds. Th[e] car was normally fitted with solid rubber tyres but a number of touring ca[rs] with standard wheels and pneumatic tyres were built in 1910 and 1911. Thes[e] models had 4-cylinder air-cooled engines made by International, with the excep[-] tion of the model J-30, which used a water-cooled 4-cylinder British-America[n] engine.

After 1911 the high-wheelers were made only in truck form, and although on[e] or two private car bodies were built on the small C-line chassis of the 1930[s] no more private vehicles were made by International until 1961. Then the fou[r-] wheel-drive 'Scout' cross-country vehicle was introduced, now available with [a] wide range of open or closed bodywork. This was supplemented by the Travelal[l], a 2- or 4-wheel-drive station wagon offered with 6-cylinder or V-8 ohv engin[e], though a 3,212cc four was standard on Scouts until 1972. For 1973 the bas[ic] engine was a 4.2-litre push-rod six; alternatives were V-8s of 5, 5.7 and 6.4 litre[s]. Other options include 3-, 4-, and 5-speed manual gearboxes, or automatic trans[-] mission. A new model was the Wagonmaster, a double cabin pick-up intended fo[r] fifth-wheel caravan towing.   GM[R]

INTERNATIONALE (NL) *1942*
Internationale Automobiel Mij, The Hague

This was a very light electric 3-wheeler built to combat the wartime absence o[f] petrol. Another similar Dutch vehicle was the Story.   GN[G]

INTER-STATE (US) *1909–1918*
(1) Inter-State Automobile Co, Muncie, Ind. *1909–1914*
(2) Inter-State Motor Co, Muncie, Ind. *1914–1918*

The first models of this make used 4-cylinder engines of 4.7 litres. In 191[1] specifications included electric lighting and starting, with an electric fuel pum[p]. In 1912, eight models were offered on three different chassis. The 4-cylinder Mod[el] 45 was introduced for 1913, but the company was reorganized in October 191[3] and a cheaper model introduced. This was the Model T with 4-cylinder Beave[r] engine that was built until 1918 when the plant was sold to General Motors fo[r] their production of the Sheridan.   GM[N]

INTERURBAN (US) *1905*
F.A. Woods Auto Co, Chicago, Ill.

This was a single-seat, front-wheel-drive electric vehicle. The body serve[d] as the frame. The electric motor could be exchanged for an 8hp 2-cylinde[r] internal-combustion engine. This could be done 'in ten minutes' for use on lon[g] trips. The car was steered by pivoting of the entire front axle.   GM[N]

INTREPID *see* ROTARY

INVICTA (i) (GB) *c.1900–1905*
H.E. Richardson, Finchley, London N.

The Invicta from Finchley was seen as a bicycle, a motor cycle and as [a] voiturette. Rather surprisingly for such a small concern, the latter two wer[e] powered by engines of the firm's own manufacture.   TR[

INVICTA (ii) (I) *1906*
Stabilimento Meccanico Carlo Mantovani & Cia, Turin

Carlo Mantovani had been technical director of Bender and Martiny (Perfect[a] and he built a few light cars with side-chain drive and 3-speed gearboxes in th[e] old factory. The 6/8hp Invicta was a twin and the 10/12hp a four with pair-ca[st] cylinders; neither lasted long.   MC[

INVICTA (iii) (GB) *1913–1914*
Clark's Engineering Works, Leamington, Warwickshire

The short-lived Invicta from Leamington was one of the cyclecar breed. It wa[s] powered by a watercooled V-twin J.A.P. engine of 8hp, driving through a 3-spee[d] gearbox and shaft primary drive to chain final drive.   TR[

INVICTA (iv) (GB) *1925–1938; 1946–1950*
(1) Invicta Cars, Cobham, Surrey *1925–1933*
(2) Invicta Cars, Chelsea, London S.W. 3 *1933–1938*
(3) Invicta Car Development Co Ltd, Virginia Water, Surrey *1946–1950*

In 1925 Noel Macklin and Oliver Lyle, both of them with experienc[e] of motor design and Macklin a former manufacturer as well (Eric Campbel[l], Silver Hawk) introduced a type of car that was quite new to the British marke[t]. The idea behind the Invicta was to combine in an assembled car the America[n] concept of flexibility and performance with British quality and road-holding[,] thus getting the best of both worlds. The Meadows 2½-litre, 6-cylinder engin[e] had push-rod overhead valves. Its low-speed torque permitted acceleration fro[m] a walking pace to 60mph in top gear, but a four-speed gearbox was provide[d] all the same, and the make's sustained high-speed cruising capabilities becam[e] legendary after winning the Dewar Trophy for long-distance reliability runs i[n] 1927 and 1929. In outward appearance the first Invicta was very staid, an[d] was marred by the fact that its brakes were poor. The rivets down the bonnet ere copied from the Rolls-Royce, the *ne plus ultra* of flexibility. During 1926, n engine with a bigger bore, providing 3 litres, was offered alongside the riginal unit, and by 1927 was the only one sold. In that year real speed arrived or the first time in the shape of the 4½-litre Invicta. This had a larger bore still, ith an 85mph maximum and really shattering acceleration in spite of pulling 3.9:1 axle ratio. By late 1929, the 3-litre had been dropped. The 1931 4½-litre ame in two types: the high-chassis, and the '100-mph' low-chassis model. The tter was lowered by underslinging the rear springs. It was capable of 95mph.

Unfortunately the splendid Invicta was always expensive, and its roadholding eputation was damaged among sportsmen, who were by now its most important ustomers, by a highly-publicized accident to S.C.H. Davis at Brooklands in 931. In spite of a win in the Monte Carlo Rally, a Coupe des Glaciers in the lpine Trial that year and almost equal success in the same events in 1932, nly about 1,000 Invictas were made before production ceased in 1935. Invicta ied to stave off the end by introducing a small car for a more popular market 1932. This 12/45 was not a success because the single overhead-camshaft -cylinder engine, made by Blackburne, was of only 1½ litres' capacity. However fficient it was, it could not cope with its heavy chassis without the aid of an xle ratio of 6:1. This gave the famed flexibility, but not the performance. The 2/45 was supplemented in 1933 by the supercharged 12/90, but only a handful ere made. Both cars were seen with Wilson self-changing gearbox, the weight f which cannot have helped. After Invicta ended, Macklin went on to make the ailton, a machine with the traditional Invicta performance characteristics lied to low price. For 1938, three new Invictas, in 2½-, 3- and 4-litre form, were lanned. They were all to have 6-cylinder, overhead-valve engines, all-synchromesh earboxes, and independent front suspension by a transverse spring. Nothing was een of these cars, the chassis of which seem to have been disguised Darracqs nd the bodies similar to those of the 3-litre D670 Delage.

The old name was revived briefly after World War 2, when it was attached to luxury car called the Black Prince, powered by a 6-cylinder Meadows engine of ree litres, with two overhead camshafts and two plugs per cylinder. This unit pro-uced 120bhp at 5,000rpm. Unlike earlier Invictas, the car's other characteristics ere highly unconventional. There was no gearbox; instead, a Brockhouse hydro-inetic turbo transmitter that provided automatic transmission on any ratio etween 15:1 and 4.27:1. Suspension was independent all round, by torsion bars. ut the new Invicta was another horribly expensive car, and although plans nvisaged an output of 250 a year, it met the same fate as its predecessors fter only a score or so had been made. A.F.N. Ltd., manufacturers of the Frazer ash, acquired the assets of the dead firm. TRN

OTA (GB) *1947–1952*
ota Racing Cars Ltd, Clifton, Bristol

The tubular ladder chassis developed by R.D. Caesar and R. Bickerton, ormed the basis of some of the first 500s (International Class I – hence the ame Iota). The marque's greatest achievement was perhaps at Silverstone in 950, when Frank Aitkens' Triumph-engined machine broke the Cooper monopoly, espite the presence of Stirling Moss. Probably the most famous Iota-based car was sprint Freikaiserwagen, with a supercharged Blackburne 1,096cc engine. An experi-ental sports car of 1951 had a 350cc Douglas flat twin engine, 4-speed gearbox nd chain drive; 70mph and 70mpg were claimed. DF

PE (D) *1919*
e Auto-Gesellschaft mbH, Berlin NW 7

A small car with a 4-cylinder 4/12PS engine which was not produced in umbers. HON

RADAM (PL) *1925–1939*
nz. Adam Gluck-Gluchowski, Krakow

Adam Gluck was an inventor who built a number of unconventional and dvanced light cars over a 15-year period, although probably none was produced or sale. His first car had a rear-mounted 600cc J.A.P. engine and a central riving position and later cars, with open and closed four-seater bodies, continued use rear engines. In 1935 he was working on a car with a 1,000cc flat-twin fuel jection engine of his own design, hydraulic torque converter, tubular backbone ame and swing axles.

The name Iradam was derived from Gluck's first name, combined with that of is wife, Irenny. The later cars also went under the name Adam Gluck. BE

RIS (GB) *1905–1915*
) Legros & Knowles Ltd, Willesden, London N.W. *1905–1907*
) Iris Cars Ltd, Willesden, London N.W. *1907–1909*
) Iris Cars Ltd, Aylesbury, Bucks. *1909–1915*

The first few Iris cars were cumbersome, crudely engineered machines with hain drive and it was not until the end of 1905 that the more familiar models ith shaft drive and the characteristic diamond-shaped radiator appeared. 15, 5 and 35hp 4-cylinder cars were made, supplemented by a 40hp six in 1907. In

1931 INVICTA(iv) 4½-litre sports saloon. Coachwork by Carbodies. *Carbodies Ltd*

1949 INVICTA(iv) Black Prince 3-litre drophead coupé. *Michael Sedgwick*

1912 IRIS 15.9hp tourer. *M.J. Worthington-Williams*

1954 ISETTA 236cc coupé. *Motor*

1965 ISO Grifo 5.4-litre GT coupé.
Iso SpA

1970 ISO Lele 5.7-litre saloon. *Iso SpA*

that year Iris Cars Ltd was formed as a selling company, but manufactu■
remained under the name Legros & Knowles. From then until the outbreak ■
World War 1, Iris produced a range of well-made if unexciting cars, rangin■
from a 15.8hp four to a 40hp six. From 1909 cars were assembled at Aylesbu■
from parts made at Willesden. The car's name was chosen from that of the Gree■
goddess Iris, 'The Speedy Messenger of the Gods', and the earliest cars carrie■
a mascot of the goddess. In 1907 appeared the advertisement entitled 'It Ru■
In Silence', which came to be thought of as the origin of the name.   GN

IROQUOIS (US) *1904–1908*
(1) J.S. Leggett Manufacturing Co, Syracuse, N.Y. *1904*
(2) Iroquois Motor Car Co, Seneca Falls, N.Y. *1905–1908*
In 1904, the Iroquois was a small car of advanced design, having slidin■
gear transmission and shaft drive, with a 20hp 4-cylinder engine. In later year■
model choices included 25/30hp and 35/40hp, 4-cylinder T-head engines.   GM

ISETTA (I) *1953–1955*
Iso SpA, Milan
For all its short span of three seasons, the Isetta was the car that started th■
'bubble' fashion and was made by a firm usually associated with motor cycle■
and scooters. Its proportions were exceptionally compact: the overall length wa■
only 7ft 4½in, and the narrow rear track of less than 2ft rendered a differenti■
unnecessary. The rear-mounted engine was an air-cooled 236cc twin 2-strok■
with common combustion chamber, rather on Trojan lines, but the specificatio■
included Dubonnet-type ifs, hydraulic brakes and a 4-speed-and-reverse al■
synchromesh gearbox. The large swing-up door was a characteristic of the egg■
shaped body. The steering wheel and column swung with it to give easy acces■
Cars were built under licence by V.E.L.A.M. in France, but the firm who real■
put the Isetta on the map were B.M.W. of Germany, who marketed a version wi■
their own single-cylinder 4-stroke engine in 1954 and continued to make it u■
to 1963. Isetta of Great Britain Ltd built 3- and 4-wheel models under B.M.W■
licence from 1957 to 1964. Iso did not resume car production until 1962, when th■
Iso Rivolta emerged as an entirely different type of vehicle.   MC

ISHIKAWAJIMA (J) *1916–1927*
Ishikawajima Dockyard & Engineering Co Ltd, Tokyo
From 1916 to 1918 various experimental cars were tested by this compan■
including a large semi-enclosed sedan. In 1918 a licence was obtained from th■
British Wolseley company to build and distribute their models throughout Asi■
and this agreement lasted until 1927. Shortly afterwards Ishikawajima set abou■
developing their own range of Sumida vehicles.   B

ISIS (CS) *1923–1925*
Beutelschmidt & Ruzichou, Prague
The Isis was a low-built cyclecar powered by a flat-twin engine. Only prototype■
were built.   GN

ISO (I) *1962 to date*
Iso SpA, Bresso, Milan
Iso's second effort at a 4-wheeler might be described as the antithesis of th■
Isetta of 1953 and was one of the new race of Euro-American GT saloon■
typified by the Facel Vega in France and the Gordon-Keeble in England. Is■
used the ohv V-8 Chevrolet Corvette engine in 5.4-litre, 260bhp form an■
mounted this on a platform chassis designed by Bizzarrini with 4-wheel dis■
brakes (inboard at the rear) coil and wishbone ifs, De Dion rear axle, limitec■
slip differential and centre-lock wire wheels. There was a 4-speed all-synchromes■
gearbox (automatic transmission was optional in 1966) and when the car came o■
the British marked it sold at £3,999. Its top speed was 142mph. From 1963 ther■
was an alternative model to the original Iso Rivolta in the shape of the Iso Grif■
a two-seater GT coupé available with 365bhp or 410bhp Chevrolet engine■
and a top speed of 162mph, mounted on a shorter wheelbase. This car ha■
considerable affinities with the GT Strada 5300 produced by Bizzarrini's own fac■
tory. A 4-door saloon, the Fidia, was introduced for 1968; coachwork was b■
Ghia. By 1969 the Grifo was available with a 7-litre 390bhp engine and ther■
was a Rivolta replacement, the Lele four-seater saloon. The 1972 versions of thi■
car had 5,735cc power units and retailed at 7,000,000 lire, or a million less tha■
the least expensive Lamborghini. Ford V-8 engines were used in 1973 Leles. MC

ISOTTA-FRASCHINI (I) *1900–1949*
(1) Società Milanese d'Automobili Isotta, Fraschini & Cia, Milan *1900–1904*
(2) Fabbrica Automobili Isotta-Fraschini, Milan *1904–1949*
Cesare Isotta and Vincenzo Fraschini went into partnership in 1899, importin■
French cars (Mors, Renault) and proprietary engines (Aster); when their compan■
was floated a year later the first cars to bear their names were thinly disguise■
Renaults with shaft drive and 5hp single-cylinder Aster power units. A 12hp twi■
appeared in 1902, but the first wholly Italian designs were not seen until 190■
These new Isottas followed the fashionable Mercédès idiom with pair-cast 4-cylinde■

gines, side valves in a T-head, lt magneto ignition, 4-speed gearboxes and side-
ain drive. Initially three models were listed — a 4,180cc 12, a 5,426cc 16 and
7,433cc 24 — and there were few major changes until 1908, though foot accelera-
rs and ht ignition came in 1906, and compressed-air starters were offered briefly
1907, when the largest car in the catalogue was the 11.3-litre Tipo C.

Like F.I.A.T. and Itala, the firm was quick to recognize the prestige value of
cing: in 1905 they built an unsuccessful 17.2-litre machine with gear-driven ohc;
1907 Minoia won the Coppa Florio; and in 1908 Trucco won the Targa Florio.
e last year brought numerous successes in the U.S.A., where 40 Isottas were
ld. By 1906 Isotta Fraschini were Italy's second-ranking manufacturers, after
I.A.T., but they were hard hit by the Agadir Crisis, and in 1907 there was a
ccessful takeover bid by Lorraine-Dietrich of France, whose intention it was to
egrate the Milan factory into their organization. By 1909, however, Isotta were
dependent again and had sold a manufacturing licence to Praga in Prague.

A novelty in 1908 was a 1,327cc racing voiturette with ohc 4-cylinder monobloc
gine said to run up to 3,500rpm; this went into limited production as the FENC
pe. More important, a successful uncoupled 4-wheel braking system was evolved
Oreste Fraschini and Giustino Cattaneo (who had joined the firm in 1905 and
as to be responsible for all Isottas up to 1935). This was available on production
odels by 1911, and three years later was standardized on the larger cars. The
09 range included a modern sv monobloc four, the ENC, available in 2.1-litre
d 2.2-litre forms, though the old combination of T-head engine and chain drive
rsisted until 1913. The smaller Isottas of 1914 closely paralleled the offerings
FIAT and Itala, coming in 2.3-litre, 3-litre and 4.4-litre sizes, with monobloc
gines, 4-speed gearboxes, and optional electrics. However, for the enthusiast the
mpany offered some 16-valve ohc sports cars with 4-wheel brakes and chain
ive — the 6.2-litre TM and the 10.6-litre KM. The latter boasted dual magneto
ition, could be had with pear-shaped or V-radiator, and was capable of 85—
mph on 140bhp. A development with 130bhp 7.2-litre engine was raced unsuc-
ssfully at Indianapolis in 1913, and there was also a shaft-driven variant of the
M, designated the TC.

After World War 1 Cattaneo switched to a one-model programme with the Tipo
a 5,880cc 9-bearing pushrod ohv straight-8 with alloy block, magneto ignition,
speed unit gearbox, central ball change, multi-plate clutch, semi-elliptic springing,
d coupled 4-wheel brakes. Output was 80bhp at a low 2,200 rpm, and the car
as conceived from the start as a chauffeur-driven carriage — hence the ponderous
ndling that attracted unfavourable comparisons with the contemporary 32CV
spano-Suiza. Most straight-8s were exported: of 1,370 delivered between 1919
d 1935 about 450 went to the United States and there were agencies in eight
reign capitals. In 1925 the Tipo 8 gave way to the 7.4-litre 8A with servo brakes,
gher gear ratios, and an output of 110—120bhp; the 135 bhp 8ASS sports version
as said to do 104mph. By 1929 a limousine cost £2,900 in London or $22,750
New York. Two years later came the last of Isotta's straight-8s the 8B. This
d a redesigned engine capable of 3,000rpm, coil ignition, and a stiffer and deeper
me; from 1932 it was available with a 4-speed preselective gearbox, a conversion
tiated by Antoine Lago, then the company London agent. In 1934 a 4-speed
nchromesh box was offered, but by now sales were down to a trickle (only 25—30
s were made all told, as against 950 8As) and the company, after unsuccessful
gotiations for a merger with Henry Ford, elected to concentrate on aero engines.
1936 they joined the Caproni organization, and their only roadgoing products
re diesel trucks made under M.A.N. licence.

There was a final comeback in 1947 with the Rapi-designed 8C Monterosa —
otta never marketed a six. This had a 90°ohc V-8 engine mounted at the rear
a platform chassis, with ifs by rubber in compression and swing-axle rear suspen-
on. The 5-speed all-synchromesh gearbox incorporated an overdrive top, brakes
re hydraulic, and a curious feature was an ignition warning light that went *out*
the event of trouble. Various cylinder capacities were tried: the 1947 Paris Salon
r had a 3.4-litre unit, but production models were to have had 2,544cc engines.
ototypes wore aerodynamic convertible and closed coachwork by Touring of
ilan, but less than 20 8Cs had been built when the factory was shut down by
der of the Italian government. The name was acquired by the Breda armaments
m, who attempted a revival of the diesel commercial vehicle range as late as 1958.

MCS

PANO-FRANCIA (F) *1913–c.1920*
P. Pelladeux, Biarritz

The Ispano-Francia cars were made, appropriately, only a few miles from
e Franco-Spanish frontier. In 1913 there was one model of 8hp single-cylinder
iturette, while the post-war range consisted of two models, an 8/10hp, possibly
e pre-war car revived, and a 16/20hp 4-cylinder car. In addition, the company
ade motor cycles and marine motors.

GNG

S.S.I. (I) *1953–1954*
tituto Scientifico Sperimentale Industriale, SpA, Milan

The I.S.S.I., or Microbo, was a very light (350lb) 3-wheeler powered by a single-
linder 125cc 2-stroke engine. It had a two-seater coupé body with a transparent
exiglass roof.

GNG

1914 ISOTTA-FRASCHINI 100hp tourer.
Autocar

c.1922 ISOTTA-FRASCHINI Tipo 8 6-litre
sporting tourer. *Autocar*

1930 ISOTTA-FRASCHINI Tipo 8A 7.3-litre
coupé. *Neubauer Collection*

1947 ISOTTA-FRASCHINI Tipo 8C Monterosa
3.4-litre saloon. *Autocar*

1966 ISUZU BELLETT 1600 GT saloon. *Isuzu Motors Ltd*

1972 ISUZU 117 1.8-litre coupé. *Isuzu Motors Ltd*

1909 ITALA 35hp limousine. *Museo dell' Automobile, Turin*

ISUZU (J) 1953 to date
Isuzu Motors Ltd, Tokyo

The present Isuzu company is an ultimate result of the merging of Jidos Kogyo (Ishikawajima-DAT) with Tokyo Gas and Electric (T.G.E.) to form Tok Jidosha Kogyo in 1937. Hino Motors split away in 1942 as an independent fir T.J.K. continued and was revamped as Isuzu Motors in 1949.

The merging companies had concentrated primarily on trucks and buses wi the Isuzu name used since 1934 on special designs, built to government standar by both Jidosha Kogyo and T.G.E. After merging, the name was retained a used in place of the other trade names, Sumida and Chiyoda, on all equipme constructed by the new firm.

Production of commercial vehicles has been an important factor with Isu ever since, and in 1953 they branched into new territory by acquiring a licen to build the Hillman Minx. In 1961 Isuzu replaced the Minx with motor cars its own design.

First of these was the Bellel, a conventional saloon with unitary constructi and coil-and wishbone ifs. Three types of 2-litre ohv 4-cylinder engine were ava able, the petrol models developing 88bhp and 98bhp, and the diesel 58bhp. Th was followed in 1966 by the 1½-litre 5-bearing Bellett series, available in vario forms up to a 90bhp twin-carburettor GT capable of 100mph. At the 1967 Tok Show came a replacement for the Bellel, the Florian with 1.6-litre ohc engine a servo-assisted drum brakes; an automatic option was offered as well as 3- a 4-speed all-synchromesh gearboxes. Also displayed was the 1,584cc dohc 117 spo coupé with front disc brakes, but this took more than two years to reach t production stage. At the same time Isuzu cashed in on the fashion for small Jee type vehicles with their 1,325cc Unicab; this had rear-wheel drive only and torsic bar front suspension. Florians for 1971 had 1.8-litre engines, and at the top the 1972 range were two new versions of the 117, one with Bosch fuel injecti and the other with capacity increased to 1,800cc. Isuzu are one of the smal Japanese manufacturers (22,027 cars only in 1970), and by 1972 General Mot had a one-third stake in the company. As a consequence the small car-based Isu pick-up truck went on sale on the West Coast of America as the Chevrolet L during the year. It had the 1,800cc Florian engine and retailed at $2,184.

I.T. (ITALMECCANICA) (I) 1950–1951
Italmeccanica, Turin

This was a sports car with Stabilimenti Farina body and torsion bar suspensic available with various versions of Ford or Mercury V-8 engines. It was introduc at the 1950 Turin Show and intended mainly for the American market, b production never started.

GN

ITALA (I) 1904–1934
(1) Fabbrica Automobili Itala S.A., Turin 1904–1929
(2) Itala S.A., Turin 1929–1931
(3) S.A. Costruzioni Automobilistiche, Turin 1931–1934

After leaving the Ceirano (i) concern Matteo Ceirano joined Guido Bigio form Itala, though he left in 1906 to start S.P.A., and Bigio remained in effecti charge until his death in a road accident seven years later. Early Italas follow the Mercédès idiom with 4-cylinder engines, side valves in a T-head, and lt magne ignition; they were, however, invariably shaft-driven. The first model was a 4.6-lit 24, but bigger types soon followed, some of them with twin water-cooled transm sion brakes. The company soon established a reputation on the circuits, Raggic 15.3-litre ioe Itala being the first large shaft-driven car to win a major race, t 1905 Coppa Florio. Cagno's stripped touring model was first in the 1906 Tar Florio, and a similar car won the Pekin–Paris marathon of 1907, in which ye Itala entered both a 14,432cc *grande voiture* (victor of the Coppa della Veloc at Brescia) and an oversquare 8-litre for the Kaiserpreis. A 12-litre 120bhp fo unsuccessfully contested the 1908 French GP, and was subsequently catalogu until 1912. These successes won Itala royal patronage (Queen Mother Margher of Italy had five), and induced the British B.S.A. and Weigel companies to produ some blatant copies of the successful 7.4-litre 35/40.

By 1908 the range was extensive: at the bottom end was a modest 2.6-lit 14/20 with ht magneto ignition and 4-speed gearbox, but for the wealthy there we two enormous sixes with capacities of 11.1 and 12.9 litres; the latter cost £1,6 as a chassis in England and was still catalogued as late as 1915 with the ol fashioned make-and-break ignition. More modern cars followed, L-head monobl units making their appearance in 1910 on the 1.9-litre 12/16, a small vehicle Italian standards that helped the company to sell 720 cars in 1911. That year al brought a new 2,235cc 14/18 on similar lines. In 1912 Alberto Balloco expe mented with an abortive variable-stroke engine; by contrast, his rotary-valve u was marketed, and quite a few were sold in various sizes ranging up to monste of over 8 litres' capacity, later ones having pear-shaped radiators in the now pi vailing Italian idiom. Some *avalve* Italas were actually raced in the 1913 Fren GP, though without success. By 1914 home-market buyers had the choice of models, three of them with rotary valves. Electric lighting was standard, a 14/20s came with electric starters as well.

Bigio's untimely death and an unsuccessful wartime attempt to build Hispan iza V-8 aero engines had a catastrophic effect on Itala, and their post-World War 1 range (based on the 2.6-litre Tipo 39 prototype of 1916) was merely the 14 idiom updated with spiral bevel back axles and full electrics. Tipo 50 was 2.8-litre sv four with fixed head and foot transmission brake, and the 54 and of 1922/3 were scaled-down 2-litre versions. Rather better was the 51S, a 55bhp velopment of the 50 with aluminium pistons that could achieve 80mph and won class in the Targa Florio races of 1921 and 1922. A new rotary-valve model 1922, the 4.4-litre 6-cylinder 55 with unit gearbox, twin carburettors and 4-wheel akes, was stillborn, but 4-wheel brakes were available on the fours by late 23, and these persisted until 1926.

Meanwhile G.C. Cappa had joined Itala from FIAT, and his 61 appeared in 24; this was an attractive 7-bearing pushrod light six of 1,991cc with alloy block d pistons, 3-speed unit gearbox, and 4-wheel brakes; it had received servo assis- nce by 1926 when an extra forward ratio was also provided. With its Rolls- oyce type radiator it was a handsome car that should have rivalled the O.M. po 665 (it cost £850 in England), but never did.

Despite assistance from the IRI, the government-run Reconstruction Finance orporation, Itala's finances went from bad to worse, and they lost 21 million e in 1929. An attempt to re-enter Grand Prix racing with a lilliputian V-12 in 100cc and 1,500cc forms failed utterly; a wooden-framed prototype was made 1926 and still exists, but it never ran under its own power. Nor did they succeed ith the 65, a redesigned dohc 2-litre based on the 61, but with coil ignition, twin ectric fuel pumps, and a rear axle passing through the chassis frame. Two re- ganizations followed, in 1929 and 1931, and in 1932 there was actually a new ala, a rehashed 2.3-litre development of the 61 designated Tipo 75.   MCS

VANHOE (CDN) *1903–1905*
anada Cycle and Motor Co, Toronto, Ont.

This was an electric car designed by Hiram Percy Maxim. Batteries were carried ver the front and rear wheels to balance weight: this was claimed to be a anadian invention widely copied in the U.S. A Westinghouse motor was suspended om the sprung body, propelling the 30in wheels by chain drive.   HD

VEL (GB) *1899–1906*
an Albone, Biggleswade, Bedfordshire

After producing bicycles for a number of years, Dan Albone turned first to otor cycles and then to motor cars. His study of early vehicles resulted in a ar of his own design. Coil-spring suspension was used to isolate the chassis from ad shocks and further passenger comfort was achieved by supporting the body n C-springs. The first Ivel used a Benz-type 3hp water-cooled engine, but in verse position to the Benz, i.e. with its combustion chamber at the rear. It ad 2 speeds, chain final drive and a four-seater *vis-à-vis* body. At the 1900 Stanley how, Ivel exhibited a landaulet with an 8hp 2-cylinder engine, but the firm was lways best-known for its agricultural tractors.   GB

VERNIA (GB) *1920*

There are very few references to the Ivernia, and it is not certain that it was ver built. The specifications published show it to have been a large car with 12ft heelbase and semi-elliptic 'underhung suspension'. The engine was a ponderous -cylinder unit of 4.8 litres (89 × 184mm).   GNG

VOR (GB) *1912–1916*
or Motors Ltd, London W.1

The factory address of the Ivor is uncertain, and little is known about the ake at all. Named after one of the directors, Ivor Henry Miller, the car had a 2/14hp Ballot engine, a patent 'shell-shaped' body and sliding doors. The dates epresent the period of the company's life, but it is unlikely that cars were made hroughout this period.   GNG

VRY (F) *1906; 1912–1914*
utomobiles Ivry, Ivry, Seine

There were two periods in which this firm made cars; in 1906 they made a tri- ar with a cone-shaped bonnet, and later two models of conventional 4-cylinder car, f 12 and 16hp.   GNG

ZARO (E) *1920*
onstrucciones de Automóviles Izaro Srl., Madrid

This car was made by D.J. Azqueta who named it after an island at the mouth f the river Mundaca, near his birthplace. The Izaros used 3-cylinder, 2-stroke and -cylinder, 4-stroke engines of 600cc and 750cc.   JRV

ZZER (US) *1911*
Model Gas Engine Co, Peru, Ind.

Only three Izzers were built and only as three-seater roadsters. This whimsical ame was dreamed up by a Dr Bissell who wanted an up-to-date car, not a has- een or 'was-er'. Wheelbase of this 4-cylinder car was 8ft 2¾in. One of the three s extant in Illinois.   GMN

*c.*1921 ITALA Model 50 2.8-litre sedanca de ville. *Museo dell'Automobile, Turin*

1925 ITALA Model 61 2-litre saloon. *Museo dell'Automobile, Turin*

1900 IVEL 8hp *vis-à-vis. Autocar*

1911 JACKSON(i) 9hp sports car. *Autocar*

1909 JACKSON(ii) 30/35hp tourer. *Kenneth Stauffer*

1950 J.A.G. 3.6-litre V-8 sports car. *Autocar*

JACK ENDERS (F) *1914–1920*
Enders Jack et Cie, Asnières, Seine

The Jack Enders was a light car made in touring or sports versions, using 2- 4-cylinder engines of 900 and 1,100cc respectively.　　　　　G

JACKSON (i) (GB) *1899–1915*
(1) Yorkshire Motorcar Manufacturing Co Ltd, Bradford, Yorks. *1899–1900*
(2) Reynold-Jackson & Co Ltd, London W. *1903–1915*

The original Jackson car used an imported single-cylinder engine, probably De Dion, but the few production cars made in Yorkshire used a 4hp horizon 2-cylinder Mytholm engine. (Later cars were called Mytholms.) In 1900 R. Reynol Jackson went to London where he sold the American Century, Buckmobile an Covert cars. In 1903 he began to sell cars under his own name, using Lacoste Battmann chassis and 6 or 9hp De Dion engines. The cars were original *dos-à-dos* dogcarts, but soon conventional seating was adopted.

Later Jacksons included a wide variety of vehicles such as early exampl of estate wagon and some astonishing sports cars using very long stroke I Dion single-cylinder engines. The 1909 Black Demon racer had a 9/11hp engi whose dimensions were 104 × 213mm, and a sloping slipper-shaped bonnet comin to a sharp point. Other cars in the 1909 range included a 6hp two-seater 100gns, a 9hp 2-cylinder and a 12/15hp 4-cylinder car. The 1913 light car used 4-cylinder Chapuis-Dornier engine and a pointed radiator à la Métallurgique, whi the company also made a 3-wheel cyclecar that year; this had a 1,350cc V-tw J.A.P. engine.　　　　　GN

JACKSON (ii) (US) *1903–1923*
Jackson Automobile Co, Jackson, Mich.

For their first year of production this company made both steam and petr cars, both called Jaxon. The steamer used a 3-cylinder vertical engine of 6h chain drive and a folding seat. It was out of production by 1904. The petrol c had a single-cylinder engine, and generally resembled the Curved Dash Oldsmobil A 2-cylinder car was introduced in 1904, and a 4-cylinder in 1906, in which ye there were three models, an old type 20hp 2-cylinder with engine under the sea and chain drive, and two front-engined, shaft-driven cars, a 20hp 2-cylind and a 30/35hp 4-cylinder. From then on, the Jackson followed convention lines, a Northway-engined six being introduced in 1913, and V-8 with ohv Ferr engine from 1916 to 1918.

Later cars had a Rolls-Royce type radiator, but the last model, made in 192 was a very ordinary looking car made by the Associated Motors combine wh had also acquired Dixie Flyer and National. The 1923 Jackson Six was sold in i final models as the National Model 6-51.　　　　　GN

JACQUEMONT (F) *c.1922–1925*
Automobiles Jacquemont, Paris 14e

The Jacquemont cyclecar used a large single-cylinder engine of 1,097cc an twin belt drive.　　　　　GN

JACQUES MULLER (F) *1920–1922*
Jacques Muller, La Garenne-Colombes, Seine

This was a shaft-driven cyclecar with 2-speed and reverse gearbox, quarter-elli tic springing and differential-less back axle, offered with a choice of air- and wate cooled 995cc V-twin Train engines, or a water-cooled sv four of 894cc by S.C.A. M. Muller sold out to B.N.C. in 1922.　　　　　MC

JACQUET FLYER (US) *1921*
Jacquet Motor Corp of America, Belding, Mich.

The Jacquet Flyer was a relatively high-priced sports car built in limite numbers for a few months. The car had a 4-cylinder engine with a capacity c 6.2 litres. Wire wheels were standard.　　　　　KN

JAEGER (US) *1932–1933*
Jaeger Motor Car Co, Belleville, Mich.

The Jaeger car was characterized by the elimination of spring shackles by sub stituting coil for semi-elliptic springs. In appearance, however, the car resemble most other low-priced cars of the period. It was powered by a 6-cylinder Con tinental engine, credited with 70bhp. The Jaeger sold at $700. Wire wheels wer standard and a V-radiator grille and three diagonal groups of four louvres on eac side of the bonnet identified it. Only a few coupés and convertible coupés were actually produced. KM

J.A.G. (GB) *1950–1952; 1954–1956*

1) J.A.G. Cars, Thames Ditton, Surrey

2) R.G.S. Automotive Components Ltd, Winkfield, Windsor, Berks.

The early J.A.G. featured a Ford V-8 3,622cc engine, and a stark 2-seater body. Such machinery falling from public favour, John A. Griffiths later introduced a Ford 1,172cc version. A model with an M.G. engine was also made, which achieved some competition success. The straightforward tubular ladder frame was also available separately, to form the base of a 'kit-built' car. Some fifty J.A.G.s in all were sold. DF

JAGUAR (GB) *1945 to date*

Jaguar Cars Ltd, Coventry, Warwickshire

Though the name Jaguar was applied to certain models of S.S. (ii) as early as 1936, it only became a make-name from 1945. From 1945 to 1948 the cars were really the 1940 S.S. models with hypoid back axles. They were made in 1.8-litre, 4-cylinder and 2.7-litre and 3½-litre, 6-cylinder forms with beam axles, push-rod-operated overhead valves, 4-speed synchromesh gearboxes and mechanical brakes. Like their predecessors they combined a high standard of elegance and performance at a modest price. The 4-cylinder engines were still made by Standard (i), but all post-war sixes were of Jaguar manufacture. Only sixes were made from 1949 onward and the new push-rod Mk Vs acquired independent front suspension and hydraulic brakes. In addition there was the XK 120, a revolutionary new sports two-seater with a 3.4-litre twin ohc 6-cylinder engine developing 160bhp, and modern aerodynamic styling. A production prototype was timed at 132.6mph and standard versions could reach 120mph, all for £1,263 – though very few were sold in England, only about 8 per cent of more than 12,000 of the model made up to 1954. The push-rod engines were dropped in 1951, in which year the big Mk VII saloon with the twin-cam engine made its appearance, combining American standards of roominess with British appointments and handling. A Mk VII won the 1956 Monte Carlo Rally; this model inaugurated a Jaguar dominance in big saloon-car racing that lasted until 1963, and more than 30,000 were made before it was replaced by the improved Mk VIII in 1957. It was available with automatic transmission in 1953 and with overdrive a year later, these two transmission options always being listed on subsequent touring Jaguars.

The company's official entry into racing was in 1950 – the idea behind this had been described as 'the fastest scheduled service over the Sarthe Circuit'. Consequently Jaguar never won the Sports Car Constructors' Championship, though they won at Le Mans five times – in 1951, 1953 (the year of the disc-braked C-types), 1955, 1956 and 1957, in which last event five of the unitary-construction D-types started and five finished, in 1st, 2nd, 3rd, 4th and 6th places. The cars were also a force to be reckoned with in almost every branch of motoring competition, among their greater achievements being two T.T. wins (1950 and 1951), victory in the Sebring 12-Hour Race (1955) and Ian Appleyard's Alpine Gold Cup (1953) for three successive unpenalized runs in his XK 120 in the Alpine Rally.

Racing experience was also applied to the touring cars and full unitary construction appeared in 1956 on the 2.4-litre, first of the compact twin-ohc saloons powered by a 112bhp short-stroke edition of the basic unit. In 1957, the 3.4-litre unit, now giving over 200bhp, was installed in the same hull, furnishing the company with yet another best-seller which helped them recover from a disastrous fire at the factory early that year. Disc brakes were standard on the sports-racing 'D' in 1954, but were also made available on sports and touring cars in 1958. The 1959 line offered three engine sizes: 2.4-litre, 3.4-litre and 3.8-litre, with outputs up to 250bhp in the XK 150 sports model, while the big Mk IX had power-assisted steering and the 3.8-litre unit as standard. In 1961 the E-type appeared with a 265bhp 3.8-litre engine, all-round independent suspension, and disc brakes all round (Jaguar have never fitted them on the front wheels only), offering a reliable 150mph for less than £2,100. Independent rear suspension and unitary construction found their way onto the big cars with the advent of Mk X in 1962. In 1964 there was the S-type (in 3.4-litre and 3.8-litre versions), also with independent rear suspension, bridging the gap between the compact Mk II and the Mk X.

In the meantime the Jaguar concern had expanded. Daimler (ii) was acquired in 1960, followed by Guy, since 1925 a truck manufacturer only, and the proprietary-engine firms of Coventry-Climax and Meadows. A redesigned version of the engine with a capacity of 4.2 litres was fitted to 1965 versions of the E-type and Mk X and at the same time all models save the Mk II received a 4-speed all-synchromesh gearbox; this was extended to the 1966 Mk II range. Another improvement was the Marles Varamatic variable-rate power-assisted steering on the new Mk X. During the year a 2 + 2 version of the E-type became available, this marking the reintroduction of an automatic gearbox option on a sports Jaguar, discontinued with the last XK 150s in 1960. The 420 saloon of 1967 filled a gap in the range. It was an improved S-type with Mk X appointments

1947 JAGUAR 3½-litre saloon. *Jaguar Cars Ltd*

1954 JAGUAR XK120 3.4-litre drophead coupé. *Autosport*

1967 JAGUAR E-type 4.2-litre sports car. *Jaguar Cars Ltd*

1968 JAGUAR Type 420 4.2-litre saloon. *Jaguar Cars Ltd*

1973 JAGUAR XJ 12 5.3-litre saloon. *Jaguar Cars Ltd*

1906 JAMES & BROWNE Vertex 45hp limousine. Coachwork by Lacre. *Autocar*

1964 JAMOS 650 GT coupé. *Bill Emery Collection*

and a 245bhp 4.2-litre engine. In the meantime the company merged with the British Motor Corporation to form British Motor Holdings, and in 1968 Jaguar became part of the British Leyland Group. A simplified version of the 2.4-litre saloon, the 240, was available at a low £1,390, and the E-type was altered to conform to the new U.S. Federal regulations, at the cost of a drop in output to 245bhp. New for 1969 was the XJ6, a new saloon with three-box unitary construction, servo-assisted disc brakes, rack-and-pinion steering, and the usual Jaguar options; it was offered with a choice of two 6-cylinder engines, the 4.2-litre and a new 2.8-litre, and helped the company to set a new production record of 32,000 cars in 1970.

Meanwhile experiments with a rear-engined prototype 502bhp four ohc V-12 sports racer in 1965 bore fruit on 1971's new Jaguar, the Series 3 E-type; this could be had with a 272bhp dohc 12-cylinder engine and transistorized ignition as an alternative to the well-tried six. Power-assisted steering was a factory option, and it sold for £3,123. This and the XJ were now the sole Jaguar models, but during 1972 the V-12 became available in a new version of the latter; this was sold only with automatic transmission.   MCS

JAMES (US) 1909
J. & M. Motor Car Co, Laurenceburg, Ind.

The James was an obscure two-seater high-wheeled buggy. It had an air-cooled engine with 2 opposed cylinders.   GMN

JAMES & BROWNE (GB) 1901–1910
(1) Martineau & Browne, Hammersmith, London W. *1901–1902*
(2) James & Browne Ltd, Hammersmith, London W. *1902–1910*

The James & Browne was designed by F. Leigh Martineau, and was chiefly known as a car with horizontal engine. The first models were a 9hp 2-cylinder, and 18hp 4-cylinder, both with a transverse crankshaft and the flywheel between the cylinders, or pair of cylinders. A 4-speed gearbox was used, and final drive was by chain. Although the earlier cars were bonnetted, the engines were mounted amidships, and most James & Brownes were equipped with town-carriage bodywork and engines under the chauffeur's seat. Even the little 9hp 2-cylinder model was made with a landaulet body of this design. In 1905 Martineau left the firm to go to the Pilgrim's Way Motor Company, for whom he designed more horizontal-engined cars, and the following year James & Browne introduced their first vertical engines. Known as the Vertex, two models were made, a 20hp four and a 30/40hp six, available with either chain or shaft drive. As with other firms such as Ader and Gillet-Forest, this switch to convention did not pay dividends, for there were too many good conventional cars already. Few of the Vertex models were sold, and the make disappeared by 1910.   GNG

JAMIESON (US) 1902
M.W. Jamieson & Co, Warren, Pa.

This was a light two-seater with a 7hp 2-cylinder engine, single chain drive and tiller steering. Few were made, but one survives today.   GNG

JAMOS (A) 1964
Built on the Steyr-Puch 650 TR chassis, the Jamos was a two-seater sports coupé powered by a 643cc 2-cylinder engine driving it at up to 90mph.   BE

JAMUN (GB) 1970–1971
Jamun Racing, Rochester, Kent

Constructed by Mike Sirett and Tony Munday, the sleek Jamun Formula Ford cars promised well but had an unlucky accident record.   DF

JAN (DK) 1915–1918
Jan Hagemeister, Copenhagen

Jan Hagemeister was financed by Mammen & Drescher, later by Landmands-banken. Jan cars were entirely Danish, with a 4-cylinder engine, Zenith carburettor and 3 forward speeds. The pointed radiator for the private cars was made of hammered metal. Both two- and four-seater cars and even trucks were offered. Chassis weight including a touring body was 900kg. A Jan limousine was bought by the Danish Royal Family. About fifty cars were produced before the firm went bankrupt. Jan later merged with Thrige and Anglo-Dane in 1918 to form De Forenede Automobilfabriker AS, makers of lorries.   TRA

JANÉMIAN (F) 1920–1923
M. Janémian, Bièvres, Seine-et-Oise

The Janémian cyclecar had a rear-mounted flat-twin engine of 1,100 or 1,400cc later replaced by a V-twin. Single chain drive was used, and the radiator faced sideways. Front suspension was by a single transverse spring.   GNG

JANNEY (US) 1906
Janney Motor Co, Flint, Mich.

The Janney was a light 4-cylinder experimental car which never got beyond the prototype stage. This company was formed by Wm.C. Durant, and occupied he old Buick plant at Flint. A total of four cars were built before the company was absorbed by Buick. The Janney became the 1908 Buick Model E-10, after being redesigned. GMN

JANSEN (NL) 1900–1901
B.A. Jansen, 's-Hertogenbosch

As well as manufacturing bicycles, Jansen imported Cambier and De Dion-Bouton cars into Holland, and the voiturette he built in small numbers used a front-mounted 3½hp De Dion engine. When the front-engined 6 and 8hp De Dion cars became available, he discontinued manufacture of De Tourists, as he called his own cars. GNG

JANSSENS (B) c.1902–c.1910
Ateliers A. Janssens, St Nicholas

The Janssens was a town car with front-mounted 2- or 4-cylinder engine driving the front wheels. It was originally made in the form of an *avant-train* unit to be attached to a horse-drawn vehicle, but later the company supplied a complete chassis. GNG

JANVIER (i) (F) 1903–1904
V. Janvier, Paris 14e

Also known as the Robin-Janvier or Flexbi, this was a 6-wheel car with three equally spaced axles. The front two axles steered, and the wheels were slightly smaller than the rear driving wheels. A 4-cylinder engine was used, and the car had a wide four-seater open body. GNG

JANVIER (ii) (F) 1926–1928
Janvier, Sabin et Cie, Châtillon-sur-Bagneux, Seine

Janvier were mainly makers of proprietary engines with long strokes, but they listed two chassis fitted with their 2-litre and 3-litre engines from 1926 to 1928. Earlier, they had entered a Picker-Janvier 3-litre (78 × 156mm) racing car in the 1912 Grand Prix de France at Le Mans (not to be confused with the proper French Grand Prix, which was held at Dieppe). Driven by Albert Guyot, it had a 5-speed gearbox; unfortunately clutch trouble delayed its start by two hours. GNG

JAPPIC (GB) 1925
Jarvis and Sons, Wimbledon, London S.W.19

The Jappic was a chain-driven single-seater cyclecar, suspended at front and rear on quarter-elliptics, which was offered with 500cc or 350cc J.A.P. motorcycle engines suitable for Class I or J record attempts. DF

JARVIS-HUNTINGTON (US) 1912
Jarvis Machinery & Supply Co, Huntington, West Virginia

This was a very large car with seven- and eight-seater bodies. The larger model had a wheelbase of 11ft 10in. Its engine was a 6-cylinder monster of 9.4 litres. The drive to the rear wheels was by double chains and the price was $5,000. GMN

JAVELIN see AMERICAN MOTORS

JAWA (CS) 1934–1939
Zbrojovka Ing. Janeček, Prague

The name Jawa originates from a combination of Janeček and Wanderer, adopted after the Czech firm had acquired a licence to produce German Wanderer motorcycles. In 1934 Jawa started to build D.K.W. cars under licence. The Jawa 700 had the D.K.W. 2-cylinder 2-stroke 684cc engine, front drive and chassisless wood-frame body, but used a longer wheelbase. It was available with various bodies, later versions having steel ones. Streamlined specimens of this make in open and closed form were quite successful in numerous sports events. A new model, the Minor, built to Tatra designs but based on D.K.W. principles, was introduced in 1937. It had a 2-cylinder 2-stroke 615cc engine and front drive. At first it was available as a very attractive two-seater roadster; later a saloon version was also offered. The Jawa Minor was the basis for the post-war Aero Minor. Motorcycle production continued after the war, and a number of prototype minicars were built between 1953 and 1956. HON

JAXON see JACKSON (ii)

J.B. (GB) 1926
Jones, Burton & Co Ltd, Liverpool

The J.B. was a medium-sized car using a 13.9hp 4-cylinder ohv engine made by Meadows. It never passed the prototype stage. GNG

J.B.M. (GB) 1947–1950
(1) James Boothby Motors Ltd, Horley, Surrey
(2) James Boothby Motors Ltd, Crawley, Sussex

The J.B.M. was a very light two-seater, with an excessively long wheelbase,

1915 JAN saloon. *Thorkil Ry Andersen*

1903 JANVIER(i) 6-wheel tonneau. *Autocar*

1938 JAWA Minor 1 616cc roadster.
Václav Petřík Collection

1923 J.B.R. 750cc two-seater.
Joaquín Ciuró Gabarró Collection

1914 J.B.S.(i) 10hp two-seater. *Autocar*

1951 J.B.S.(ii) 500cc racing car. A.J. Bottoms
at the wheel. *C.A. Bottoms*

1907 JEAN BART 16/20hp tourer and landaulette.
National Motor Museum

powered by a modified Ford V-8 engine giving 120bhp. The cars were assembled from re-conditioned components, and so no purchase tax was payable. The price was £750. DF

J.B.R. (E) 1921–1923
José Boniquet Riera, Barcelona

Boniquet was a dentist and former enthusiast of the engineless 'downcars' who built a number of cyclecars powered by 904cc Ruby engines. A 750cc racing model achieved considerable success, often against larger cars, in the Trofeo Armangué and Spanish Cyclecar Grand Prix. The prototype had an air-cooled engine and belt drive, but production J.B.R.s used water cooling and shaft drive. Boniquet later built the Storm cyclecar, and in 1947 built a prototype 3-wheeler under his own name. GNG

J.B.S. (i) (GB) 1913–1915
J. Bagshaw & Sons Ltd, Batley, Yorks.

The J.B.S. first appeared as a cyclecar with 8hp V-twin J.A.P. engine, although it did use shaft drive. For 1915 the makers went over to 4-cylinder models, using an 8hp Blumfield or 10hp Dorman engine. GNG

J.B.S. (ii) (GB) 1950–1952
J.B.S. Cars Ltd, Feltham, Middlesex

The first J.B.S. was evolved from the Cowlan special, lightened and with independent coil/damper units fitted to the tubular frame. J.A.P. or Norton 500cc engines were used, complying with Formula 3. The car was a success from the first, and severely shook Cooper supremacy in early 1951. After first designer/driver A.J. Bottoms and then R.M. Dryden had been killed, the heart went out of the firm, although C.A. Bottoms and Bottoms senior carried on for a year. The last few of over 120 cars made incorporated a De Dion-type rear axle. DF

JEAN BART (F) 1907
Automobiles Jean Bart, Nanterre, Seine

This was the Prosper-Lambert renamed. Three models were made, a 9hp single-cylinder, a 16/20hp 4-cylinder and a 40hp 4-cylinder. Production lasted less than a year. GNG

JEAN GRAS (F) 1924–1930
SA des Automobiles Jean Gras, Lyons

The Jean Gras began as a small 4-cylinder car with engines of 1200, 1500 and 1600cc, the 1500 being an ohc sports version. In 1926 the firm introduced a small six of 1½-litres, advertised as 'A Six in the price range of a Four'; some attractive low-slung saloon coachwork was fitted to this model. Jean Gras cars competed with some success in sporting events, including the 1926 Milan Grand Prix in which a specially reduced version of the 1200 achieved second place in the 1100cc class, driven by its builder, Jean Gras. GNG

JEANNIN (US) 1908–1909
Jeannin Automobile Mfg Co, St Louis, Mo.

The Jeannin was a high-wheeler with solid rubber tyres and a 10/12hp air-cooled engine. Steering was by wheel and the car had shaft drive. This was produced only as a two-seater runabout with a surrey top. GMN

JEANPERRIN (F) c.1900
Jeanperrin Frères, Gray, Haute-Saône

The only known model made by Jeanperrin Frères was a light four-seater *vis-à-vis* generally similar in appearance to the contemporary De Dion Bouton, powered by a single-cylinder 3hp engine. One survives in Switzerland. GNG

JEANTAUD (F) 1881; 1893–1906
C. Jeantaud, Paris

Charles Jeantaud built an experimental electric car in 1881, but serious production did not start until 1893. A large carriage with double transverse front springs, 2 speeds and chain drive ran in the 1895 Paris-Bordeaux Race. Production models favoured wheel steering, motors mounted under the driving-seat, side-chain drive and pneumatic tyres; there was even a hansom-cab version with a frontal bonnet. M. Jeantaud was the instigator of the Paris Motor-Cab Trials held in June 1898, which his designs won, and from his determination to promote the sales of his cabs sprang what has since become the World's Land Speed Record. A Jeantaud driven by the Chasseloup-Laubat attained 39.24mph over the kilometre at Achères in December 1898; the rival electric-cab maker Camille Jenatzy countered with 41mph, and a month later de Chasseloup-Laubat had achieved 43.69mph. The adoption of a primitive, V-nosed wind-cheating body enabled him to go on to 57.6mph, but he had no answer to Jenatzy's 100kph (66mph) with *La Jamais Contente*, and thereafter Jeantauds took no part in competition. The 1901 cars had front-mounted batteries. Postel-Vinay bi-polar motors and channel steel frames. There were 5 speeds, forward and reverse, and an electric brake. Speed and duration were given as 12½mph and 37½ miles respectively. By 1903 duration had been doubled. In 1903 and 1904 a range of petrol cars with 2-, 3- and 4-cylinder engines were offered, though these did not last long. In 1905 Jeantaud followed Krieger's lead in going over to fwd, and prices ranged from 7,000fr for a Petit Duc up to 15,000fr for formal-bodied vehicles. Charles Jeantaud committed suicide in 1906, and his company ended with him.   MCS

JEECY-VEA (B) 1925–1926
Motos Jeecy-Vea, Brussels

The Jeecy-Vea was a light car made by a firm whose main product was motor cycles. It was powered by a 750cc flat-twin Coventry-Victor engine, and was available with tourer or cabriolet bodies. However, competition from imported cars like Salmson and Amilcar was too great, and very few Jeecy-Vea cars were made.   GNG

JEEP (US) 1963 to date
Kaiser-Jeep Corp, Toledo, Ohio

Although the Jeep first appeared during World War 2, and was the sole product of Willys-Overland after 1956, it has been regarded as a make only since the formation of Kaiser-Jeep in 1963. At that time, the range consisted of 2- and 4-wheel-drive station wagons with 4- and 6-cylinder engines as well as updated versions of the original wartime Jeep. For 1965 these engines were supplemented by a 5.4-litre Rambler V-8 unit, used in the Wagoneer station wagon. The Jeep Universal utility vehicle was available with 3.2-litre 4-cylinder Perkins Diesel or 3.7-litre V-6 Buick engines, as well as the 2.2-litre 4-cylinder Jeep engine. Kaiser-Jeep merged with American Motors early in 1970, but the range continued unchanged. For 1971 there were utility and sporting versions of the Universal, with 4-cylinder or V-6 engines (the latter now manufactured by Kaiser-Jeep at Toledo), the more luxurious Jeepster series in station wagon, roadster and convertible forms, and the Wagoneer station wagon with options of 145bhp V-6 or 230bhp, 5.7-litre V-8 engines. The range for 1973 was similar, except that a 5-litre V-8 engine was available in the Universal, and the largest engine in the Wagoneer series was now a 5.9-litre V-8.   GNG

JEFFERY (US) 1914–1917
Thos. B. Jeffery Co, Kenosha, Wisc.

The Jeffery was the Rambler (ii) renamed after the founder of the company. It was made for four seasons in conventional 4- and 6-cylinder guises, with sv monobloc engines, the sixes giving about 60bhp. 1916 prices were $1,000 and $1,350 respectively. After the purchase of the company by Charles W. Nash, the cars were again renamed and went over to push-rod-operated overhead valves.   MCS

JEFFREY (GB) 1968 to date
Jeffrey Racing Cars, Minster Lovell, Oxon 1968–1971
Jeffrey Racing Cars, Shilton, Oxon. 1971 to date

The Marks 1, 2 and 3 Jeffreys were 750 Formula sports-racing cars, offered at first as a set of plans only, and later as a kit. The J4 road car and its 1972 successor the J5 utilized a tubular space-frame chassis, with Triumph front suspension and other running parts by Ford. A complete car less engine could be obtained from about £450, and performance was as could be expected from a weight of only 1,120lb. Up to August 1972 over 150 kits or chassis had been sold.   DF

JENARD (GB) 1956
G.A. Elsmore, Yeovil, Somerset

The Jenard Jabeka was a 2-seater sports car based on a tubular chassis, intended for Austin A40 or Coventry-Climax 1100cc engines. It utilized Austin front suspension, gearbox, and rear axle, which was linked to Woodhead-Monroe suspension units. Production never got under way.   DF

JENATZY (B) 1898–1903
Camille Jenatzy, Brussels

The famous racing driver Camille Jenatzy designed a number of electric or petrol-electric cars, mostly built by other firms. His first vehicle was a four-seater *dos-à-dos* electric car with chain drive built in 1898, while the following year he built 'La Jamais Contente', an electric car with a cigar-shaped streamlined body with which he took what was later called the World Land Speed Record at 66mph. From 1899 to about 1901 heavy electric cars and vans to Jenatzy designs were made by the Compagnie Internationale des Transports Automobile, in Paris. He began experiments with Petrol-electric drive in 1901 with a converted Mors, and in 1903 a number of petrol-electric cars of 12/15 and 20/28hp were made under the name Jenatzy-Martini at Martini's Belgian armaments factory at Liège. After this Jenatzy's name was not directly connected with any make of car, although his magnetic clutch was used in the 1904 Gordon Bennett Pipe racing cars.   GNG

JENKINS (US) 1907–1912
1) J.W. Jenkins, Rochester, N.Y. 1907

1903 JEANTAUD electric coupé. *The Veteran Car Club of Great Britain*

1966 JEEP Wagoneer 5.4-litre station wagon. *Kaiser-Jeep Corporation*

1916 JEFFERY 20/30hp sedan. *American Motors Corporation*

1938 JENSEN 3.6-litre sports tourer.
Jensen Motors Ltd

1966 JENSEN FF 6.3-litre coupé.
Jensen Motors Ltd

1972 JENSEN-HEALEY 2-litre sports car.
Jensen Motors Ltd

1907 JEWELL 8hp two-seater. *Keith Marvin*
Collection

(2) Jenkins Motor Car Co, Rochester, N.Y. *1908–1912*

The model changes in the Jenkins were very few. These cars all had 4-cylinder engines, with 140mm stroke and cylinder diameter gradually increased from 122mm to 124mm. The cars had a peculiarly peaked bonnet.　　　GM

JENNINGS (GB) *1913–1915*
Jennings Chalmers Light Car Co, Birmingham

The Jennings appeared in the middle of the cyclecar boom, but was more of true light car than most. Two models were made, both with Dorman engines, one being a flat-twin and the other a vertical twin. The engines were of 10hp rating, and both cars had shaft drive.　　　GN

JENSEN (GB) *1936 to date*
Jensen Motors Ltd, West Bromwich, Staffs.

The brothers Richard and Allan Jensen made their names as body stylists in the early 1930s, being responsible for the Avon Standards, well as coachwork for such chassis as the Wolseley Hornet and the Ford V8. Their 1937 3½-litre car was luxurious and elegant Anglo-American powered by the 3.6-litre Ford V8 engine and noted for its Columbia two-speed back axle, giving six forward speeds. Later additional models were marketed with the small 2.2-litre Ford V8 and 4.2-litre straight-8 ohv Nash engines, while individual cars had Steyr and Lincoln Zephyr units. A post-war Meadows-engined 3.9-litre ohv straight-8 with overdrive gearbox and coil-and-wishbone ifs never reached production, but the design led to series of hand-built vehicles in the 1939 tradition, with high gearing and big lazy engines. The saloon and Interceptor cabriolet of 1950 used an Austin 4-litre 6-cylinder A. 135 engine, and its styling anticipated the sports model of the Austin A40 (for which Jensen built the bodies). This was supplemented in 1954 by the very successful fibreglass-bodied '541' saloon, a big G.T. capable of 115mph with a modest fuel consumption. In 1957 Jensen became one of the first producers to fit disc brakes all round as standard equipment. The '541S' series of 1961 used the Rolls-Royce Hydramatic gearbox. Jensen were also responsible for the bodies on the bigger Austin-Healeys and (initially) for those of Volvo's P.1800 coupé. There was a reversion to American power units in 1963 with a 5.9-litre 305bhp V8 Chrysler engine in the Jensen CV8, which offered a choice of manual or automatic transmission. By 1966 330bhp was available from a 6.3-litre engine and the company broke new ground with the 'FF' with Ferguson-type hypoid final drive to all four wheels and disc brakes incorporating the Dunlop 'Maxaret' anti-skid device. When this model and the standard Jensens appeared in 1967, they had been completely redesigned with steel bodywork to Vignale specifications. Automatic transmission only was available on the 4-wheel drive cars and prices were high: £3,743 in basic form, and £5,340 for the 'FF' model. New in 1969 was the Jensen Director intended as a mobile office for executives and equipped with such luxuries as portable television set, a typewriter and a radio telephone. Air conditioning was optional on 1970 models. A high-performance 385bhp SP series appeared in 1972 when the FF was discontinued and the company announced their Lotus-powered Jensen-Healey two-seater. Interceptor production continued at the rate of 25 a week.　　　MC

JENSEN-HEALEY (GB) *1972 to date*
Jensen Motors Ltd, West Bromwich, Staffs.

Conceived by Kjell Qvale and Donald Healey to fill the gap left by the demise of the Austin-Healey 3000, the Jensen-Healey is a sports two-seater powered by a 1,970cc Lotus 4-cylinder engine with twin belt-driven ohc. Chrysler UK make the 4-speed all-synchromesh gearbox, the suspension (by independent coils and wishbones at the front and by coils and a live axle at the rear) and steering are by Vauxhall, and there are front disc brakes.　　　MC

JET (E) *1955*

This was a short-lived minicar made in Madrid, using a 197cc single-cylinder Villiers engine.　　　JRW

JEWEL (i) (US) *1906–1909*
(1) Forest City Motor Co, Cleveland, Ohio *1906*
(2) Forest City Motor Co, Massillon, Ohio *1906–1909*
(3) Jewel Motor Car Co, Massillon, Ohio *1909*

For 1906 and 1907 this make offered only a two-seater with a 2-stroke, single-cylinder engine of 8hp. During these years, the make was spelled 'Jewell'. In 1908, the Jewel 40 was introduced, powered by a Rutenber engine of 4 cylinders and 5.8 litres. Roadster and seven-seater touring models were mounted on a chassis of 10ft wheelbase. The Jewel was replaced by the Croxton-Keeton.　　　GMN

JEWEL (ii) (GB) *1921–1939*
John E. Wood, Bradford, Yorks.

The first Jewels were cyclecars powered by either Precision or Coventry-Simplex 2-cylinder engines, with friction transmission and chain final drive. Like most of their kind they were only made for about two years, but unlike most

...yclecar builders, John E. Wood then turned to the manufacture of small 4-cylinder cars, which he continued to turn out in very small numbers for a further 7 years. For 1923 he used an 8.9hp Coventry-Simplex unit, replaced in 1924 by 9.8hp Meadows. This was continued until 1939, although an 11.9hp engine was also listed. The cars were built to special order and there was considerable variation in minor details. Disc wheels were normally used, at least up to 1934, but wire wheels were available if desired. Most Jewels were tourers, but a 4-door saloon was also made during the 1930s. GNG

1935 JEWEL(ii) 10hp saloon. *Autocar*

JEWETT (US) *1923–1926*

Paige-Detroit Motor Car Co, Detroit, Mich.

The Jewett, named after H.M. Jewett, president of the Paige-Detroit Motor Car Co., was in reality a smaller Paige, but was sold as a make of its own, much as the Cleveland was sold as a smaller Chandler. It was a well-liked car and many of its models, particularly the open phaetons, appeared with exceptionally fine and sporty lines. Nevertheless, Jewett sales diminished and after more than 40,000 had been sold, the car was marketed as a Paige. Early cars had 4.1-litre engines but there was a small 2½-litre version, with fwb in 1925, and the last cars had hydraulic brakes. KM

JIDÉ (F) *1969 to date*

Jacques Durand, Châtillon-sur-Thouet, Deux Sèvres

This was a two-seater sports coupé powered by a Renault Gordini 1300 engine, sold in kit form or complete. GNG

JIN-BU (p) **CHIN-PU** (wg) **(PROGRESS)** (CHI) *1958 to date*

Tsin-Chien Mechanical Works, Chungking, Szechuan

The first models of this 2-door sedan had bodies of flat-sided design with split windscreens, four headlights and 95bhp water-cooled engine. Further models of this marque have probably been constructed since 1958. BE

JINGGANGSHAN (p): **CHINGKANGSHAN** (wg) (CHI) *1958 to date*

Peking No 1 Automobile Plant, Peking

This was a small rear-engined 2-door saloon of which a number of hand-built examples were displayed in 1958. It does not seem to have been in general production, but a recent model was said to have an air-cooled 4-cylinder radial engine developing 36bhp. The car was named after the Chingkang Mountains, where Mao Tse-Tung built his first revolutionary base in 1927. BE

1958 JINGGANSHAN saloon. *David Scott*

J.L. (GB) *1920*

A.E. Creese, East Dulwich, London S.E.

The J.L. was a sporting light car powered by a 1½-litre 4-cylinder Decolonge engine. It had a plywood body with pointed tail. GNG

J.M.B. (GB) *1933–1935*

J.M.B. Motors Ltd, Ringwood, Hampshire

The J.M.B. two- or four-seater 3-wheeler was not unlike the contemporary B.S.A. in general appearance, but less powerful. It used a 497cc single-cylinder J.A.P. engine mounted behind the seats, driving the rear wheel by chain. Total weight was 504lb; a speed of 55mph was claimed. The standard model cost £75 10s. A prototype 4-wheeler was built in 1935, but did not go into production. GNG

JOEL (GB) *1899–c.1902*

National Motor Carriage Syndicate Ltd, London E.C.

Named after Henry M. Joel, the designer, the Joel electric cars used two motors of 2hp each driving by chains to each rear wheel. Closed and open models were made, including the 1901 Brighton open two-seater, so called because it made the journey from London to Brighton on a single charge. GNG

1934 J.M.B. 5hp 3-wheeler. *M.J. Worthington-Williams*

JOHN O'GAUNT (GB) *1902–1904*

William Atkinson & Sons, Lancaster

Named after the famous 14th-century Duke of Lancaster, the John o'Gaunt was a light four-seater tonneau with a 4hp single-cylinder engine. Not more than 12 cars were made. GNG

JOHNSON (US) *1905–1912*

Johnson Service Co, Milwaukee, Wisc.

The original Johnson was a 4-cylinder steamer with an enormous bonnet and ornate enclosed body. The steam engine was a single-acting type of 30hp. After 1907, Johnson adopted internal combustion engines of three sixes, up to 50hp. This company also produced a large variety of commercial vehicles. GMN

JOHNSONMOBILE (US) *1959*

Horton Johnson, Inc, Highland Park, Ill.

Only one of this prototype 1904 Antique Runabout was produced. A 3hp Clinton air-cooled engine powered it, and the two-seater body was of waterproof plywood. BE

1903 JONES-CORBIN 8hp two-seater. *Kenneth Stauffer*

1921 JONSSON 15hp tourer. *Roland Swälas*

1930 JORDAN Speedway Eight 5.3-litre sports sedan. *Autocar*

JOMAR (US) *c.1954–1955*
Ray Saidel, Manchester, N.H.

The first Jomar was a small sports car powered by the British Ford Anglia engine of 1,172cc capacity. It had a full-width aluminium two-seater body. Later the name was applied to the British T.V.R. sports car when sold in the United States. GNG

JOMO (GB) *1967–1969*
K. Vickery, Redditch, Worcs.

The Jomo was produced at first in conjunction with Bill Longley, later to start the Dulon company. Little success attended this venture to market a competitive Formula Ford machine, and only a few were made. DF

JONES (US) *1915–1920*
Jones Motor Car Co, Wichita, Kans.

The Jones was a thoroughly conventional 6-cylinder car made mainly in open touring models. At first a 21.6hp engine was used, but this was replaced by a 29.4hp Continental for 1917 to 1920 models. The company also made trucks of up to 2½ tons capacity. GNG

JONES-CORBIN (US) *1902–1907*
(1) Jones-Corbin Co, Philadelphia, Pa. *1902–1904*
(2) Jones-Corbin Automobile Co, Philadelphia, Pa. *1904–1907*

The early model of this make offered single-, 2- and 4-cylinder 'genuine De Dion' engines of 8 to 30hp. This make used double-chain drive and its appearance revealed considerable European influence. A 45hp 4-cylinder car was listed at $4,500 in 1906. GMN

JONSSON (S) *1921*
Alfred Jonssons Motorfabrik, Lidköping

The Jonsson factory made marine engines, and a prototype car with a 2-cylinder paraffin engine in 1902. The second Jonsson car had a 4-cylinder 2212cc sv engine, a 3-speed gearbox, and a four-seater aluminium-panelled body. All parts except the Bosch magneto were made in the Jonsson works, and at least ten cars were ordered. However, only the one car was built; it still survives in private ownership in Lidköping. OB

JONZ (US) *1908–1911*
(1) Jonz Auto Co, Beatrice, Neb. *1909–1910*
(2) American Automobile Manufacturing Co, Beatrice, Neb. *1910*
(3) American Automobile Manufacturing, Ohio Falls, Ind. *1911*

The Jonz used a poorly-explained air/vapour cooling system for its 2-stroke engines. These were of 2, 3 and 4 cylinders, with rating of 20, 30 and 40hp respectively. Two- to five-seater open cars were offered, as well as a three-seater coupé and a taxicab. There is no evidence that this company was ever located in Kansas City, Mo., as is sometimes stated. GMN

JORDAN (US) *1916–1931*
Jordan Motor Car Co Inc, Cleveland, Ohio

Edward S. Jordan will be remembered as the man who broke away from nuts and bolts' advertising and introduced the element of emotional appeal into the sale of the automobile. (Indeed his advertising copy has become more famous than his cars.) These were among the best of the assembled creations, handsomely proportioned, and always powered by Continental engines. Wire wheels were standard on the first models, which had 5-litre 6-cylinder power units: 1918 prices started at $1,995. A year later coil ignition was standardized, and hydraulic fwb were introduced during 1924. 1925 was the first year of straight-eights, a 4.4-litre version being joined a year later by a small model with a 9ft 8in wheelbase. 1926 was Jordan's best year, with 11,000 cars sold, but they were unlucky in 1927 with their 'Little Custom', a luxury compact six with worm drive and a wheelbase of 8ft 11in, which failed to catch on. A handsome new radiator characterized the 1929 line, priced from $1,295 up. Like many American firms, Jordan's last effort was their greatest. This was the 1930 'Speedway' model, a 5.3-litre, 114bhp eight with a 4-speed gearbox, aircraft-type instrument panel, oddly shaped Woodlite headlamps, and European styling. Unfortunately at over $5,000 there were very few takers, and at the depth of the Depression there was little market for the cheaper Jordans, either. The company closed down in 1931. TRN

JOSWIN (D) *1920–1926*
Josef Winsch, Abt. Joswin Motorenfabrik, Berlin-Halensee

Motor cars from this firm were equipped with Mercedes engines. Two models were offered, the 25/75PS 6470cc and the 28/95PS 7290cc. Bodies were available from various firms, including Szawe. Joswin cars were of excellent quality and performance. HON

JOU (F) *1913–1926*
Automobiles A. Jou, Suresnes, Seine

The Jou was a conventional 4-cylinder car powered by a 1½-litre engine, which
s made without great change for over ten years.   GNG

UFFRET (F) *1920–1928*
Demeester, Colombes, Seine

Made by H. Demeester who had made voiturettes under his own name before
orld War 1, the first Jouffret was a solid-looking tourer using an 11hp Ballot
gine. Later cars used a variety of engines in the 1100 to 1500cc range by
.M.E. and S.C.A.P. Semi-elliptic springs were used, those at the front tapering
their front ends.   GNG

OURDAIN (F) *1920*
tomobiles Jourdain, Tours

The Jourdain was a 2-cylinder cyclecar. One was entered in the 1920 Coupe des
iturettes, but did not distinguish itself.   GNG

OUSSET (F) *c.1924–1926*
uis Jousset, Bellac, Hte-Vienne

The Jousset was a sporting light car using a variety of engines by C.I.M.E.,
by and S.C.A.P. The firm entered a streamlined saloon with a 1½-litre C.I.M.E.
gine for Le Mans in 1926, which failed to qualify.   GNG

OUVE (F) *1913*
uve et Cie, Paris

The Jouve was a cyclecar using an 8hp air-cooled J.A.P. engine, and belt drive.
e company also sold the Carden Monocar in France under the name Le Sylphe.
                                                                   GNG

OWETT (GB) *1906–1954*
Jowett Motor Manufacturing Co Ltd, Bradford, Yorks. *1906–1919*
Jowett Cars Ltd, Bradford, Yorks. *1919–1954*

The most famous motor car to come out of Yorkshire was the little flat-twin
ilt by Benjamin and William Jowett, who had earlier made V-twin engines
r cars and stationary work, and also the first Scott 2-stroke motor cycles. The
wett was one of the most practical light cars of its period, the 1920s and 1930s.
ter experiments lasting from 1906 to 1913, a machine with an 816cc water-
oled side-valve engine, a 3-speed unit-construction gearbox, worm final drive and
e-lever steering was put into production. A two-seater was the standard style
til 1923.

However, production was not seriously under way until after World War 1, when
e make first gained recognition outside its home shire. The engine was enlarged
907cc, bevel drive was substituted during the war and there was wheel steering
1914. The Jowett Seven had its drawbacks, such as a fixed-head engine which
ade owner-maintenance difficult, and it needed careful handling because of hard
ringing, high-geared steering and bad brakes, but its advantages far outweighed
em. Because the famous engine exerted its power output at very low engine speeds,
xibility and acceleration were excellent. The power unit was rugged, reliable and
ry economical. Fuel consumption could be as good as 55mpg. The whole car
eighed very little. Coil ignition and electric starting were standard fittings from
923, but the most important new convenience of that year was the introduction
the Long Four, a capacious four-seater, selling for £245, or £20 more than the
ll-current two-seater. The Long Four and the equally roomy saloon of 1926
ere bestsellers. In 1929, the engine was given a detachable cylinder head, and, at
st, internal expanding 4-wheel brakes were supplied with all cars except the
ort-lived 100 guinea 'chummy' model of that year. At the same time, the Black
rince saloon was introduced to give the make a more modern look; it had a fabric
dy with a high waistline and shallow windows, dummy hood irons and wire wheels,
in the most fashionable style.

In the 1930s weight went up and axle ratios went down, but economy and
lling power were still combined, thanks to the virtues of the original engine. A
andful of sports models had been made in the 1920s and now, in 1934, the
estrel sports saloon was offered, followed a year later by the twin carburettor
easel sports tourer. In the former year, a four-speed gearbox arrived and in 1935
centrifugal clutch and freewheel device could be had, to help gear-changing.
owever, the true revolution came in 1936, for this year was the last of the 907cc
win and the first of the Ten, with a flat-4 engine of 1166cc. A saloon only was
fered. For 1937, the twin was enlarged to 946cc and renamed the Eight, while all
ars were given Bendix brakes. Very late in the day, a synchromesh gearbox arrived
r the 1940 season.

After World War 2, the twin was finally dropped from Jowett passenger cars, but
machine that was to be almost as famous took the place of both the Eight and the
en, once again as the sole model. The Javelin, however, was an utterly different
onception. It was a small family car, but of the most advanced character. Indeed
was not 'British' at all, in the context of 1947, when traditional designs dominated
e home market. With its independent torsion-bar suspension front and rear, rigid
nitary body-chassis construction, good aerodynamic shape, light weight and high
earing, its fine handling, 80mph maximum speed and combination of excellent
cceleration and high cruising speed, it was more reminiscent of the pre-war

1920 JOSWIN 25/75PS sedanca de ville.
Henry Ford Museum, Dearborn, Michigan

1916 JOWETT 8hp two-seater. *G.N.*
Georgano

1926 JOWETT Long Four 7hp tourer. *M.A.*
Harrison Collection

1937 JOWETT 10hp saloon. *Autocar*

1952 JOWETT Javelin $1\frac{1}{2}$-litre saloon. *Jowett Cars Ltd*

1905 J.P. 24/30hp tourer. *G.N. Georgano Collection*

Lancia Aprilia, the Fiat 1100 or the B.M.W. The engine alone was a reminder Jowett practice, being a $1\frac{1}{2}$-litre flat-4. For 1950, the Javelin was joined by even more advanced car, the two-seater sports Jupiter. This had a space-fra designed by Eberan von Eberhorst, formerly of Auto-Union, and a 90mph perfor ance. The Jupiter, in turn, was developed in 1954 into the R4 Jupiter, a spor racing car of which only a handful were made. It was considerably shorter a lighter, with a fibreglass body, and was a 100mph machine. The competition rec of the Javelin and its developments was impressive. It included class wins in 1949 and 1951 Monte Carlo Rallies, and in the 1950, 1951 and 1952 Le Mans Hours race. Sadly, however, the old name died in 1954 after some 30,000 Javel and 1,200 Jupiters had been made. At the time of closure a revised twin, the CD-type, was under development. T

JOYMOBILE (NL) *1953–1954*
Washmobile Holland Co, Amsterdam
The Joymobile Turbomatic used a 45bhp 4-cylinder Delettrez diesel engine, a transmitted power to the rear wheels by means of a turbine. The liquid used this was stored in reservoirs in the tubular frame. It was intended to sell the at the equivalent of £750, but it never went into production. GI

J.P. (i) (F) *1905*
J. Prunello, Dumas et Cie, Puteaux, Seine
The J.P. was made in three models: a 10/12hp 2-cylinder and two 4-cylind models, a 16/20hp and a 24/30hp. Gnome engines were used, and the largest c employed double chain drive. GN

J.P. (ii) (GB) *1950–1954*
Joseph Potts Ltd, Bellshill, Lanarks.
A modified Cooper formed the basis of the first J.P. '500' racing car. Producti specification embraced a frame with two tubes on each side, and transverse le suspension. The last few of the 33 cars made used large-diameter oval secti side-members and a De Dion type rear axle. Successes were mostly local, thou Ron Flockhart largely made his name in a 998cc Vincent-H.R.D.-engined versic Production ceased when the firm's racing interests became diverted to motorcyc preparation.

JPL; LA VIGNE (US) *1913–1914*
J.P.L. Cyclecar Co, Detroit, Mich; Lavigne Motor Co, Detroit, Mich.
The JPL cyclecar was designed by J.P. La Vigne who was an early and ubiq tous engineer in the industry. The car used a 4-cylinder air-cooled engine w sliding-gear transmission, and had a completely underslung chassis. It was claim that petrol consumption was 30–40mpg, and that the top speed was 50mph. GN

J.P. WIMILLE (F) *1946–1950*
(1) S.E.T.A.M., Courbevoie, Seine *1946–1947*
(2) Ford S.A.F., Poissy, Seine-et-Oise *1947–1949*
(3) Compagnie Parisienne d'Automobile, Paris *1949–1950*
Designed by the racing driver Jean-Pierre Wimille, this car was an advanc rear-engined closed sports two-seater. The original design included a 2-lit V-6 ohv engine developing 80bhp, and a model was planned with torsion bar val springs developing 110bhp unblown or 200bhp blown. However, the prototype us a humble 11CV Citroën engine, and a later 1948 car had a 2.3-litre Ford V engine. The cars had Cotal electric gearboxes. The bodies were aerodynamic wi very short bonnets, and the early models had extremely poor rear vision, althou this was improved on later cars. Not more than seven were made in all, and t death of Wimille in the Buenos Aires Grand Prix in 1949 put an end to the projec GN

JUHÖ (D) *1922*
Julius Höflich AG, Fürth
A two-seater cyclecar with a single-cylinder 2/4PS 2-stroke engine which wa produced in limited numbers. HO

JULES (CDN) *1911–1912*
Jules Motor Car Co Ltd, Guelph, Ont.
This small torpedo touring car used a 30hp engine and carried four passenger Only two complete cars were built. A unique feature was the placing of the hor button in the middle of the brake pedal. C

JULIAN (US) *1922*
Julian Brown, Syracuse, N.Y.
Although its designer intended to produce this unusual coupé, only one car wa made. Radical in design, it featured a tubular frame, and a 60hp aircraft typ radial engine mounted at the rear. All moving parts were combined in a sing unit and these were automatically lubricated. K

JULIEN (i) (F) *1925–1926*
G. Julien, Blois, Loire-et-Cher

The Julien was a minute single-seater cyclecar using a single-cylinder 2CV engine under 200cc, and a two-speed gearbox.　　　　GNG

JLIEN (ii) (F) 1946–1949

des Etudes Automobile M.A. Julien, Paris 16e

The post-war Julien was also a minicar, appearing at the same time as the Rovin, which it was a rival. It used a 325cc single-cylinder engine which drove the rear eels by a single chain. An open two-seater was the only body style. In 1949 a new del with wider body was announced, but it did not go into production.　　GNG

JNIOR (i); F.J.T.A. (I) 1905–1910

bbrica Junior Torinese d'Automobili, Turin

The Junior, otherwise known as the F.J.T.A., was made by Giovanni Ceirano. was sold as a 9½hp single-cylinder voiturette, as a 12/14hp twin and as a 16/20hp r. The last was a completely conventional machine on Mercedes lines, with linders cast in pairs, side valves in a T-head and chain drive.　　TRN

JNIOR (ii) (E) 1955

stribuidora Marcom, Barcelona

The Junior was a 3-wheeler with a 197cc Villiers engine driving the single rear eel. The tubular chassis carried a two-seater body of reinforced plastic and suspen- n was by coil springs on all three wheels.　　JRV

JNIOR SPORTS (GB) 1920–1921

uminium & General Foundry Co, London E.C.1

The Junior Sports was a low-built two- or three-seater, powered by a 4-cylinder ters engine. It used a Moss gearbox and shaft drive.　　GNG

USSY (F) 1898–1900

A des Ets Jussy, Saint-Etienne, Loire

The Jussy works were among the first car builders in Saint-Etienne and made small number of light cars with single-cylinder engines and hot-tube ignition. roduction ceased in 1900, and in 1906 the company became the Société Anonyme s Ateliers du Furan, makers of the S.A.F. 3-wheelers.　　LL

USTICIALISTA *see* INSTITEC

UWEL (B) 1923–1927

The Juwel was a 9CV 1100cc 4-cylinder tourer for which the sponsors had mbitious plans for large-scale production. They acquired a large factory but soon n into difficulties, and replaced the rather pedestrian tourer by a low-slung ont-wheel-drive sports car with independent front suspension. This was in 1926, ut very few of the new model were made.　　GNG

W. *see* MIRAGE and WALKER (ii)

1949 J.P. WIMILLE 2.3-litre saloon. *Musée de l'Automobile, Rochetaillée-sur-Saone*

1947 JULIEN(ii) 325cc two-seater. *Lucien Loreille Collection*

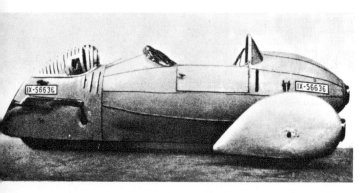

1935 KAISER(ii) 3-wheeler. *Neubauer Collection*

1947 KAISER(iii) Custom 3.7-litre sedan. *Kaiser-Jeep Corporation*

K.A.C. (DK) *1914*

A. Jacobsen, Københavns Automobil Central, Copenhagen

The 6/16 K.A.C. was a 4-cylinder car, but the engine make is not known. Bo roadsters and touring cars were offered and the price was 3,300kr and 3,500 kron respectively. In the Copenhagen to The Skaw run in 1915 a K.A.C. driven b A. Jacobsen himself won the prize for the best Danish car.   TR

KAHA (D) *1921–1922*

Elektromobilwerk Kaha GmbH, Wasseralfingen

This was a small electric single-seater.   HO

KAINZ (A) *1900–1901*

Josef Kainz, Vienna

The Kainz voiturette was powered by a 3½hp single-cylinder vertical engine und a bonnet. It had 3 speeds, and drive by spur gear to the rear axle.   GN

KAISER (i) (D) *1911–1913*

Justus Christian Braun-Premier Werke AG, Nuremberg

This company was formed in 1911 when the fire engine specialists Nürnberg Feuerlöschgeräte- und Maschinenfabrik vorm. Justus Christian Braun A combined with the Premier Cycle Company Ltd, which had factories i Nuremberg and Eger (Austria). A range of electric and petrol-driven vehicles wa sold under the name of Kaiser. These included a 6/18PS private car, but the mak was best known for its commercials. A later model was marketed as the Premie HO

KAISER (ii) (D) *1935*

Kaiser Fahrzeugbau, Aschersleben

A three-wheeled car with an aerodynamic single-seater body, rear-mounted engir and transmission to the single rear wheel by chain. Single-cylinder motor-cycle engin from 200cc to 600cc capacity by N.S.U. and Columbus-Horex were installed. Max mum speeds of 60–75mph were attained.   HO

KAISER (iii) (US) *1946–1954*

(1) Kaiser-Frazer Corporation, Willow Run, Mich. *1946–1953*
(2) Kaiser-Willys Sales Corp, Toledo, Ohio *1954*

The Kaiser was the most successful post-war 'invasion' of the American automo bile industry, the creation of a combine headed by shipbuilder Henry J. Kaise and Joseph W. Frazer of Graham-Paige. Howard Darrin styled the original proto type, but it was much revised by KF Styling under Robert Cadwallader. Fraze had rented, and KF later bought, the huge Willow Run plant built by Henry For for wartime manufacture of the B-24 Liberator bomber. Early plans called for low-medium-priced Kaiser and a more expensive 'custom' Frazer. The Kaiser prot type shown to the public in 1946 displayed unit construction, torsion-bar suspensic and front-wheel drive, and its (and Frazer's) new straight-through side styling s a trend that all the industry would follow. Complications and costs precluded the mechanical ideas from the production Kaiser Special, however, which had conver tional box-section frame, hypoid rear drive and coil-spring irs. The engine was a improvement on the pre-World War 2 Continental design, a sv 6-cylinder 3.7-litr unit developing 100bhp. This was gradually stepped up to 112, 118 and final 140bhp in the supercharged Kaiser Manhattan for 1954–5. But try as they migh the company could not permanently maintain their position, though they ranke eighth and built about 140,000 cars during both 1947 and 1948, to lead all th other American independents including Studebaker, Hudson and Nash.

The Kaiser car is remembered for its novel ideas and innovations. Among thes along with the first through-fenderline for 1947, were the Traveler and Vagabon utility models that looked like sedans but opened up at the rear like station wagon and had large flat beds created by drop-down seats; one of the first hardtops i the 1949 4-door Virginian; the first (with Frazer) post-war 4-door convertible; th Dragon line of luxuriously trimmed, padded-top sedans of 1951–3; and of cours the brilliant 1954–5 line of Manhattans and Specials with concave grille designe by A.B. Grisinger and 'safety-glo' tail lights, styled by Herbert Weissinger, extenc ing up along the rear fenders, along with Darrin's novel sliding-door Kaiser Darri roadster. The 1951–5 'anatomic design' Kaiser was among the most inspired U. sedan designs of the period.

Altogether Kaiser-Frazer produced over 747,000 cars and Kaiser-Willys com bined for 25,000 more in 1954–5. Of these, about 500,000 or more were Kaisers The make was phased out in 1955, when only 260 left-overs were sold as 195 odels and 1,006 Manhattans were exported to Argentina, where they were soon to be manufactured as the 'Kaiser Carabela' from 1958 to 1962.   RML

KAISER CARABELA (RA) *1958–1962*
Industrias Kaiser Argentina (IKA), Buenos Aires

When Kaiser ceased manufacture of the Manhattan sedan in America, the dies were shipped to Argentina, where it continued in production as the Carabela. Kaiser formed IKA in conjunction with the Argentine government, which owns 7.8% of the shares and was able to market the car at a price considerably lower than imported competitors. Carabelas were basically the same design as the former Willow Run machine but used a 6-cylinder Willys engine and heavier suspension for Argentine road conditions. Some exterior and interior trim modifications were introduced, including the use of leather upholstery. Both 2-door and 4-door sedans were sold along with a companion line of Jeep vehicles. In 1962 the Carabela was replaced on assembly lines by licence-built Ramblers, current models being called Torinos. IKA is the largest private employer in Argentina and its car products include Kaiser Jeeps, Renaults, and British Motor Corporation vehicles through its subsidiary, SIAM di Tella. In 1967 Renault purchased a controlling interest in IKA;   BE

KAISER JEEP *see* JEEP

KÄMPER (D) *1905–1906*
Heinrich Kämper Motorenfabrik, Mariendorf, Berlin

The Kämper concern was already well known as an engine manufacturer when car production was taken up. This was for a short period only, during which the vehicles were frequently used as taxicabs.   HON

K.A.N. (A) *1912–1915*
Königsgrätzer Automobilfabrik Alois Nejedly, Kukleny

Two types of small cars were produced with single-cylinder 7hp and 2-cylinder 1hp engines. About 400 cars were made.   HON

K & M (US) *1908*
Kreider Machine Co, Lancaster, Pa.

This was a high-wheeler with an air-cooled engine beneath the seat. A 2-speed selective transmission was used with chain drive. This vehicle could be converted into a 1½-ton truck, and also had a power take-off for driving other equipment.   GMN

KANE-PENNINGTON *see* PENNINGTON

KANSAS CITY (US) *1905–1909*
(1) Kansas City Motor Car Co, Kansas City, Mo. *1905–1909*
(2) Wonder Motor Car Co, Kansas City, Mo. *1909*

The Kansas City succeeded the Caps. As many as six models were introduced in one season, ranging from a two-seater roadster with a 2-cylinder, 24hp engine to a seven-seater touring car which used a 6-cylinder, 10-litre engine and cost $4,500.   GMN

KAPI (E) *1950–1958*
Automóviles Kapi, Barcelona, Valencia

The Kapi was a 3-wheeler powered originally by a Montesa motorcycle engine, later by a Hispano-Villiers. The first model, known as the Chi-Qui, had a single rear wheel, but on later models the single wheel was in front and the engine was mounted just in front of the offside rear wheel, in the fashion of the Gordon (iii). The Kapi company also offered a diminutive Jeep-type vehicle with 200cc engine.   JRV

KATO (US) *1907–1908*
Four-Traction Auto Co, Mankato, Minn.

The first Kato had 4-wheel drive via shafts fore and aft from the 2-cylinder, 24hp engine. The five/seven-seater car was on a wheelbase of 8ft 8in and was priced at $1,800. A later model used a 40hp engine.   GMN

KAUFFMAN (US) *1909–1912*
Advance Motor Vehicle Co, Miamisburg, Ohio

The Kauffman four-seater roadster was powered by an air-cooled 4-cylinder, 3.7-litre engine with overhead valves.   GMN

KAUZ *see* ANSBACH

KAVAN (US) *1905*
Kavan Mfg Co, Chicago, Ill.

The Kavan was a light runabout with a single-cylinder engine under the seat, and chain drive. The most remarkable point about the Kavan was its price — $200, or £40 at the current rate of exchange.   GNG

K.A.W. *see* HAGEN

KAYSER *see* PRIMUS

1954 KAISER(iii) Manhattan 3.7-litre sedan.
Motor

1912 K.A.N. 7hp two-seater. *Ing Adolf Babuška*

1952 KAPI Chi-Qui 125cc 3-wheeler.
G.N. Georgano

1912 K-D 4.9-litre tourer. *G. Marshall Naul Collection*

1915 KEARNS Model L 12hp two-seater. *Keith Marvin Collection*

1913 KEETON Six-48 6-litre tourer. *Floyd Clymer Publications*

1950 KELLER 2.6-litre sedan. *Autocar*

K-D (US) *1912*

K-D Motor Co, Brookline, Mass.

The K stood for Margaret E. Knight and the D for Mrs Anna F. Davidson, th founders of the company. Miss Knight designed the sleeve valve engine used in thi car. Its valving differed from Charles Knight's version in the use of a single split sleeve working outside the cylinder wall, instead of the better-known type witl double concentric sleeves. The engine was a 4-cylinder, 4.9-litre unit. The five-seate K-D was on a wheelbase of 11ft 5in and had wire wheels. Production of this car which cost $6,000, was very limited.   GMN

KEARNS (US) *1909–1915*

(1) Kearns Motor Buggy Co, Beavertown, Pa.
(2) Kearns Motor Truck Co, Beavertown, Pa.

Known as the Eureka buggy from 1908 to January 1909, this high-wheeler used 2-stroke Speedwell engines of 10/12hp (2-cylinder) or 15/18hp (3-cylinder) They had double friction drive and solid tyres, but unlike many of the high wheelers, had conventional bonnets. From the end of 1910 the company concentrat ed on trucks, but in 1915 they introduced a light car with 18hp 4-cylinder engine 3-speed gearbox, and shaft drive. They also made the Lu-Lu cyclecar in 1914 This had a 13.7hp 4-cylinder engine and shaft drive.   GNC

KEENELET (GB) *1904*

Keene's Automobile Works Ltd, London W.

The Keenelet steam car used a 14hp single-cylinder vertical engine, a semi-flasl boiler and friction cone transmission, the latter a rare feature in a steamer.   GNC

KEETON (US) *1908; 1910–1914*

(1) Keeton Taxicab and Town Car Works, Detroit, Mich. *1908*
(2) Keeton Motor Co, Detroit, Mich. *1910–1913*
(3) American Voiturette Co, Detroit, Mich.; Washington, Pa. *1914*

The Keeton had a complex history, intertwined with that of the Croxton-Keeton. The original car had a Renault-like radiator behind the 3.7-litre 4-cylinder engine. Its principal body-type was a landaulet on a wheelbase of 8ft 11in. The last model (after the separation from Croxton) used a 6-litre 6-cylinder engine and had a wheelbase of 11ft. The transmission had 4 forward speeds. Three body styles were offered at prices from $2,500 to $2,850. This firm built the Car Nation Cyclecar in 1914 and 1915.   GMN

KELLER (US) *1948–1950*

George D. Keller Motors, Huntsville, Ala.

An offshoot of the ill-fated Bobbi Kar, the Keller Chief and Super Chief were similarly short-lived but offered the buyer the unique choice of front engine on the sedan or rear engine on the convertible. 4-cylinder Continental or Hercules units were available and models shown were a three-seater convertible and a five-seater sedan and station wagon with independent suspension using rubber torsion bars. By the summer of 1949 only 18 pilot models had been built, and few cars, if any, were made after that. The original plans had envisaged an eventual production of 6,000 cars per month. Some Keller-designed station wagons were assembled in Antwerp in 1954–55, and sold under the name P.L.M. (Poelmans, Merksen-Antwerp).   BE

KELLER KAR (US) *1914–1915*

Keller Cyclecar Corp, Chicago, Ill.

The Keller Kar was a tandem, two-seater cyclecar. It used a conventional 2-cylinder air-cooled engine with belt drive. It was supplied in standard colours of black and red and sold for $375.   GMN

KELSEY (i) (US) *1913–1914*

Kelsey Car Corp, Connersville, Ind.

This Kelsey was an ephemeral, completely conventional 6-cylinder car of moderate price. It had no connection with other Kelsey cars.   TRN

KELSEY (ii) (US) *1921–1924*

Kelsey Motor Co, Newark, N.J.; Belleville, N.J.

C.W. Kelsey built the first Kelsey car, called the Auto-Tri in 1898 and subse-quently constructed several other one-of-a-type models. Between 1910 and 1912 he built the 3-wheeled Motorette. In 1921, he began manufacture of a friction-driven assembled car, augmenting this with a standard version in 1922. Gray and Lycoming engines were used in these 4-cylinder cars, though a 6-cylinder Falls-engined car was offered in 1921.   KM

KELSEY MOTORETTE *see* MOTORETTE

KELVIN (GB) *1904–1906*

Bergius Car & Engine Co, Glasgow

The Kelvin had a 14hp 4-cylinder engine, shaft drive, and a rear-entrance tonneau body. An unusual feature was the use of solid tyres. The engine, transmission and bodywork were all made on the premises formerly occupied by Albion, but after 14 cars had been produced the company turned to the manufacture of marine engines, in which field they are still active today.　　　　GNG

KEMPTEN (D) *1900–1901*

Süddeutsche Fahrzeugfabrik, Kempten

A voiturette with a 3hp proprietary engine was the only product of this South German firm.　　　　HON

KENDALL (i) (GB) *1912–1913*

Kendall Motors Ltd, Sparkhill, Birmingham

The Kendall cyclecar used an 8hp air-cooled V-twin J.A.P. engine, and a belt or worm drive.　　　　GNG

KENDALL (ii) (GB) *1945–1946*

Grantham Productions Ltd, Grantham, Lincs.

The first of the post-war 'people's car' projects, the Kendall appeared in two models. The first used a radial 3-cylinder engine mounted in the rear, and an angular 2-door saloon body, while the second had a front engine and front-wheel drive. This was the same design as the Aluminium-Français-Gregoire which was also the origin of the Dyna-Panhard, and used an integral body-cum-chassis frame of light alloy castings. A 594cc flat-twin engine was used, and the car was intended to sell for £200. The project was sponsored by Denis Kendall, M.P. and the factory was also to have made tractors. However, it closed in November 1946, after very few cars had been made.　　　　GNG

KENMORE (US) *1909–1912*

Kenmore Mfg Co, Chicago, Ill.

This was an unattractive car with large-diameter wheels and pneumatic tyres. Early models used 2-cylinder 2.1-litre engines and planetary transmissions. Later versions, with either air- or water-cooled engines, were said to be capable of 30mpg.　　　　GMN

KENNEDY (i) (GB) *1907–1910*

Hugh Kennedy & Co, Glasgow

Also known as the Ailsa (no connection with Ailsa Craig, which was another name for the Craig-Dörwald of Putney), the Kennedy used a 15/20hp 4-cylinder engine, and cost £395. Very few were made, but Hugh Kennedy later made the Rob Roy light car.　　　　GNG

KENNEDY (ii) (CDN) *1909–1910*

Kennedy Mfg Co, Preston, Ont.

The 1909 models were high-wheelers with De Tamble engines and shaft drive. A runabout and a surrey were offered. In 1910 the wheels were changed to 30in though everything else remained unaltered. About 50 of these cars were produced each year.　　　　HD

KENNEDY (iii) (GB) *1914–1916*

Kennedy-Skipton & Co Ltd, Leicester

This was a two-seater light car using an 11.9hp Salmon 4-cylinder engine, 3-speed gearbox and overhead worm rear axle.　　　　GNG

KENNEDY (iv) (US) *1915–1918*

W.J. Kennedy, Los Angeles, Calif.

This Kennedy was a four-seater coupé with a dashboard radiator and Renault-type bonnet, also known as the Petite. It used a 4-cylinder petrol engine, but had very much the appearance of an electric car.　　　　GNG

KENSINGTON (US) *1899–1904*

Kensington Automobile Co, Buffalo, N.Y.

The Kensington company made cars powered by petrol, steam and electricity. The steam and electric cars had a similar appearance, both being very simple two-seater runabouts, the steamer using a 2-cylinder 4hp engine and single chain drive. In 1902 a petrol car with an 11hp 2-cylinder Kelecom engine was introduced, and for one season all three motive powers were used. Steamers were dropped in 1903, and all manufacture ceased the following year.　　　　GNG

KENT (US) *1916–1917*

Kent Motors Corp, Belleville, N.J.

This was an assembled car using a 4-cylinder Continental engine of 3.6 litres. Four- and five-seater models were sold, complete with dash clock, for $985.　　　　GMN

KENTER (D) *1924–1925*

C. Kenter Automobilbau AG, Berlin-Charlottenburg; Leisnig

Kenter continued the manufacture of cars formerly sold as Komets. A 4/14PS two-seater with a Steudel engine and a 5/18PS four-seater with an Atos engine were produced.　　　　HON

1905 KELVIN 14hp tourer. *Museum of Transport, Glasgow*

1912 KENDALL(i) 8hp cyclecar. *G.N. Georgano Collection*

1946 KENDALL(ii) 6hp saloon. *Autocar*

1921 KENWORTHY Line-o-Eight tourer.
Floyd Clymer Publications

1914 KESTREL 10hp two-seater. *David Filsell Collection*

1952 KIEFT Formula 3 racing car. *I.C.B. Pearce*

1955 KIEFT 1,100cc sports car. *Autosport*

KENWORTHY (US) *1920–1922*

Kenworthy Motor Co, Mishawaka, Ind.

The Kenworthy shared with the Duesenberg the honour of being America's first production car to have an 8-cylinder in-line engine and 4-wheel braking. The 'Line-o-Eight' engine, as it was called, used overhead inlet and side exhaust valves. Unlike Duesenberg, the company also offered a more normal six and a 4-cylinder sports model. TRN

KERMATH (US) *1907–1908*

Kermath Motor Car Co, Detroit, Mich.

This was a small four-seater runabout with a tear-drop shaped radiator and bonnet. It used a 26hp 4-cylinder engine with 3-speed transmission and shaft drive. Because of lack of capital, only one Kermath was made. GMN

KESSLER (US) *1921–1922*

Kessler Motor Car Co, Detroit, Mich.

The Kessler was an assembled car using a 4-cylinder 2-litre engine of the firm's own design. A five-seater touring car with artillery wheels was the only model. At least one example was made of the Kess-Line-Eight, with straight-8 engine designed by William H. Radford. KM

KESTREL (GB) *1914*

Bristol Road Motor Garage Co, Gloucester

Wellings, the sponsor of this short-lived make, owned a leather-working company and a garage, the latter run by a mechanic called Clifford. They produced fewer than 15 of their cars, which had imported 4-cylinder, 1131cc engines and used leather for facing the friction discs on clutch, the countershaft and the slipping clutch differential. There was chain final drive, a 'gear' lever giving four positions only for the discs, and a complex system of pedals, ratchets and buttons to regulate the pressure on them. DF

KÉVAH (F) *1920–1924*

Etablissements Kévah, Paris 8e

The Kévah was made in two models, an 1100cc 2-cylinder and a 1057cc Ruby-engined 4-cylinder. The chassis was quite conventional and shaft drive was used. GNG

KEYSTONE (i) (US) *1899–1900*

Keystone Motor & Manufacturing Co, Philadelphia, Pa.

This was an unconventional steamer which had a 3-cylinder engine in each rear wheel hub, fed by steam from a tubular boiler mounted in the body. The company planned to make light cars and heavy trucks using this system. GNG

KEYSTONE (ii) (US) *1909–1910*

(1) Munch-Allen Motor Car Co, Dubois, Pa. *1909*
(2) Munch Motor Car Co, Yonkers, N.Y. *1910*

The Keystone Six-Sixty model was driven by a 6-cylinder, 7.8-litre engine. A two-seater roadster and two touring cars were made, all priced at $2,250. GMN

KEYSTONE (iii) (US) *1915*

H.C. Cook & Bros, Pittsburgh, Pa.

This Keystone used a 55hp Rutenber 6-cylinder engine and a 4-speed gearbox. Electric lighting and starting was advertised for all models. GNG

KIBLINGER (US) *1907–1909*

W.H. Kiblinger Co, Auburn, Ind.

The Kiblinger was a high-wheeled buggy with a 2-cylinder, air-cooled engine of 12hp under the seat. Nine different models were offered, the cheapest of which was a two-seater roadster for $450. This car was succeeded by the McIntyre. GMN

KICO (D) *1924*

Kieling & Co, Frankfurt am Main

This firm offered a light car with their own 4-cylinder engines of 4/12, 5/15, 6/18 or 7/21PS. HON

KIDDER (US) *1900–1901*

Kidder Motor Vehicle Co, New Haven, Conn.

The Kidder steam carriage used two separate cylinders of 3hp each, mounted horizontally on each side of the boiler. Drive to the rear axle was direct. A two-seater was the only body style (apart from a delivery van), and the car used tiller steering. The price was $1,000. GNG

KIDDY (F) *1921–1922*

Ateliers Lecourbe, Paris 15e

The Kiddy used a very small flat-twin engine of only 397cc, a 2-speed gearbox in unit with the engine, and a worm-driven rear axle. The maximum speed was little over 30mph. GNG

KIEFT (GB) *1950–1961*
(1) Kieft Car Construction Co Ltd, Bridgend, Glam. *1950–1952*
(2) Kieft Cars Ltd, Wolverhampton, Staffs. *1953–1956*
(3) Kieft Cars Ltd, Birmingham *1956–1961*

Cyril Kieft had considerable success in the halcyon days of Formula 3 with his all-independently-sprung 500cc Norton-engined racing cars designed by Ray Martin and driven by Stirling Moss, among others. Sports car production was limited; it included a centre-steered machine with a 1½-litre M.G. engine and an experimental sporting runabout with chain drive and a 650cc B.S.A. motor-cycle unit. Other engines used included the Bristol (ii), De Soto (ii), and Wooler flat-four. A 1100cc sports two-seater with all-round independent suspension and a 4-cylinder ohc Coventry-Climax engine ran at Le Mans in 1954 and was later catalogued at £1,560. In later days at Birmingham tuning and experimental work were the order of the day, although rear-engined Formula Junior racing cars with Triumph Herald and Ford 105E engines were made in 1960 and 1961.   MCS

KIM-10 (SU) *1940–1941*
Moskovskii Zavod Malolitrajnikh Avtomobilei (MZMA), Moscow

This four-seater sedan was the first to be built by the Moscow Light Automobile Works and had a 4-cylinder 30bhp engine. Transmission was 3-speed and suspension was by transverse springs. Maximum speed was reported as 56mph. Russian photos show that at least two different Kims were constructed. A picture from the Nami Institute shows a 4-door sedan with a strong Opel Kadett influence and rather like the post-war Moskvitch. A 2-door sedan had a different grille and shorter wheelbase.   BE

KIMBALL (US) *1910–1912*
C.P. Kimball & Co, Chicago, Ill.

This small electric car was made in both two-seater and four-seater models. Two motors operating at 80 volts drove the rear wheels by double chain drive. Steering was by wheel, and solid rubber tyres were standard.   GMN

KING (i) (GB) *1904–1905*
King & Co, Leicester

This was a short-lived make which used a 12hp vertical twin engine and single chain drive. The radiator bore some resemblance to that of the Daimler.   GNG

KING (ii) (US) *1910–1924*
(1) King Motor Car Co, Detroit, Mich. *1910–1923*
(2) King Motor Car Co, Buffalo, N.Y. *1923–1924*

Charles B. King built the first car in Detroit in 1896, with a 4-cylinder horizontal engine, and later designed 2- and 4-cylinder cars for Northern. He formed his own company in 1909 and its first product was a 4-cylinder 35hp car with central gear change. This and a companion 30hp model were made up to 1915 when a small V-8 of under 4 litres was introduced. From 1916 onwards only 8-cylinder cars were made, there being two models, of 26 and 29hp. Prices ranged from $1,400 for a 1917 tourer to $4,235 for a 1921 sedan. This inflation, although general in the industry, hit King sales, which slumped from a maximum of 3,000 per year in 1916 to only 240 in 1923, the year that King moved to a smaller plant at Buffalo. A number of Kings were sold in England before and after the war. They were handled by Salmons of Newport Pagnell who fitted some of them with their own coupé bodies.   GNG

KING (iii) (GB) *1967–1970*
Mike King Racing, Liss, Hampshire

A small number of racing cars were built under this name. The wedge-shaped Mark 5 Formula Ford machine retailed at £850 for a rolling chassis.   DF

KING & BIRD (GB) *1903*
King & Bird, Mansfield, Notts.

The King & Bird was a dog cart powered by a 4½hp De Dion engine. It is not known how many were built, but a number were registered in the Nottingham area in 1903.   MJWW

KING MIDGET (US) *1946–1969*
Midget Motors Corp, Athens, Ohio

The sole survivor of the post-World War 2 minicar boom in the United States, the Midget was a small two-seater of steel and aluminium construction. Early models contained a single-cylinder 8½hp Wisconsin air-cooled engine with manual transmission. Late cars used a 9¼hp Kohler engine with a unique automatic 2-speed-and-reverse transmission that was simple and dependable. Independent suspension was used and the chassis was made of perforated girders and tubing. Optional extras include doors, top, side curtains, speedometer, golf bag, racks, heater and hand controls for the handicapped. About 5,000 cars were made.   BE

KING-REMICK (US) *1910*
Autoparts Mfg Co, Detroit, Mich.

1940 KIM-10 1.1-litre saloon. *NAMI, Moscow*

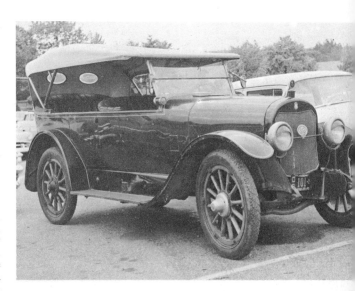

1918 KING (ii) 29hp V-8 tourer. *Kenneth Stauffer*

1965 KING MIDGET 9¼hp two-seater. *Midget Motors Corporation*

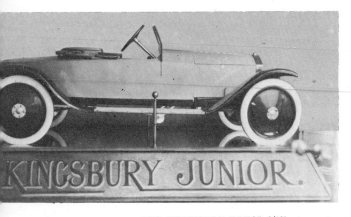

1920 KINGSBURY JUNIOR 8/10hp two-seater.
Autocar

1914 KISSEL 6-cylinder tourer. *National Motor Museum*

1925 KISSEL Gold Bug 8-75 speedster.
E.E. Husting

The King-Remick was a two-seater roadster, with racy lines. Its power was furnished by a 6.6-litre, 6-cylinder engine. **GMN**

KINGSBURGH (GB) 1901–1902

Kingsburgh Motor Construction Co, Granton, Edinburgh

The Kingsburgh company was formed in 1900, and the former works of Madelvic were acquired. A very small number of 12hp cars as well as a motor bus were made before the works were sold to Stirling's Motor Carriages Ltd. **GNG**

KINGSBURY JUNIOR (GB) 1919–1922

Kingsbury Engineering Co Ltd, Kingsbury, London N.W.9

The Kingsbury, named after the London suburb in which it was made, was a short-lived light car aimed at exploiting the post-World War 1 boom in popular motoring. It was powered by a 1,021cc, 2-cylinder, horizontally-opposed engine made in unit with a 3-speed gearbox, and had shaft drive. The Koh-i-Noor engine was made in Scotland by the company responsible for the Rob Roy car which also used the engine. The company had grandiose plans involving mass production of cars, motor cycles and the Kingsbury scooter, but they came to very little. **TRN**

KIRKSELL (US) 1907

Dr James Selkirk, Aurora, Ill.

Doctor Selkirk built a 50hp 4-cylinder car which he planned to sell at $3,000. It is unlikely that more than one was made. **GNG**

KISSEL (US) 1906–1931

Kissel Motor Co, Hartford, Wisc.

At first the name of Kissel was associated with agricultural equipment, then with stationary gas engines. A conventional shaft-driven 35hp 4-cylinder automobile called, rather unfortunately, the Kissel Kar (originally the Badger), was offered from 1906. It was made almost entirely by the company; few parts were bought out. A six with 'square' dimensions (121 × 121mm) appeared in 1909, electric starting came in 1913, and there was a short-lived V-12 powered by Weidely, built from 1917 to 1918. None of these had any sporting pretensions. From 1918, however, the policy of the company changed rapidly. The metamorphosis had begun in the previous year, when the Kissel Kar Silver Special Speedster was unveiled. It was named after its designer, C.T. Silver. At the New York Show of January 1918 the firm's new speedster policy was taken a step further with the Gold Bug, a development of the Silver Special Speedster. It earned its name because from 1919 chrome yellow was the make's standard colour. It had a Kissel-made 6-cylinder sv engine at first, of 4.3 litres, later 4.7 litres. More touring Kissels were offered as well, such as the Coach-Sedan and Tourster, which used the same engines as the Gold Bug. In 1924 external contracting Lockheed hydraulic brakes were a listed option. In that year, too, the alternative of a straight-8 with a modified Lycoming engine could be had. 1928 was the last year of Kissel-built engines. The handsome 1929 White Eagle with 3-litre 6-cylinder and 4- and 4.9-litre straight-8 engines, as well as internally expanding hydraulic brakes, could not compete at prices ranging from $1,595 to $3,885, and only 1,531 were sold. In 1930 Kissel assembled a few Ruxton cars on contract to New Era Motors, and in 1933 a reorganized company was hired to build Lever engines in order to demonstrate them to a large manufacturer for possible mass production. **TRN**

KITCHINER (GB) 1969 to date

Tony Kitchiner, London W.6

The first two Kitchiners were Formula 3 single-seaters, these being followed in 1970 by the K3A Formula 5000 monocoque. The smaller model was developed for a production Formula Ford machine. An interim special for Formula 5000 was the promising Kitchmac of 1972, using the suspension designed for the 1973 K8 Formula 5000 car grafted on to a McLaren monocoque. **DF**

KLAUS (F) 1894–1899

Th. Klaus, Boulogne-sur-Seine; Lyons

The first Klaus car was a 3-wheeler with a single-cylinder 2hp engine, and tiller steering to the single front wheel. This was followed by a 4-wheeler in 1897 with the same engine. The 1898 car had two 2½hp horizontal engines, one at each side of the car just inside the frame. These cars were mainly experimental, but they were exhibited at shows, and Klaus sold a few to acquaintances. **GNG**

KLEIBER (US) 1924–1929

Kleiber Motor Truck Co, Los Angeles, Calif.; San Francisco, Calif.

The Kleiber company was well known on the American west coast for its commercial vehicles. For six years it produced a small number of private cars which were marketed on the Pacific Coast only. These used a Continental 6-cylinder engine and other standard components. **KM**

KLEINE WOLF (D) 1950–1951

Georg Wolf, Niebüll

The Little Wolf was a minicar powered by a 200cc single-cylinder engine. It had independent suspension all round, and a one-piece body. Production was intended, at a price the equivalent of £150.　　　　　　　　　　　　　GNG

KLEINSCHNITTGER (D) *1950–1957*
Kleinschnittger Werk, Arnsberg

This firm produced a small open two-seater with a single-cylinder 2-stroke 125cc Ilo engine for several years. A two-seater coupé with a 250cc engine was announced in 1954 but was not put into production. The earlier cars were sold in Belgium under the name Kleinstwagen.　　　　　　　　　　　　HON

KLIEMT (D) *1899–1900*
C. Kliemt Wagenfabrik, Berlin

This firm produced electric cars in limited numbers.　　　　　HON

KLINE KAR (US) *1910–1923*
(1) B.C.K. Motor Co, York, Pa. *1910–1911*
(2) Kline Motor Car Corp, York, Pa. *1911–1912*
(3) Kline Motor Car Corp, Richmond, Va. *1912–1923*

James A. Kline was designer and general manager of the Pullman Motor Car Company up to 1909, when he founded the B.C.K. Company, with S.E. Bailey and Joseph C. Carrell. The first Kline Kars used 6-cylinder engines designed and built in the works, but following the formation of a new company, and the move from York to Richmond, the engines were bought out from the Kirkham Machine Company of Bath, N.Y., who built them to Kline's design. 4- and 6-cylinder units of 30 to 60hp were made, and the general design of the car was thoroughly conventional. The post-war 6-55 model used a Continental engine. By 1922 sales had slumped badly from the 800 to 1,000 per annum of the company's best years, and the following year they closed down.　　　　　　　GNG

KLINK (US) *1907–1909*
Klink Motor Car Mfg Co, Dansville, N.Y.

The 30hp Klink was available as a five-seater touring model or as a two-seater roadster at a standard price of $2,000. The 4-cylinder 4.4-litre engine had a 3-speed selective transmission. A 40hp four was introduced for 1908, and a 35hp six for 1909, but all production ended in September of that year, after about 20 cars had been made in all.　　　　　　　　　　　　　　　　GMN

KNAP (B; F) *1898–c.1909*
(1) Sté de Construction Liègeoise d'Automobile, Liège, Belgium *1898–1900*
(2) SA des Moteurs Knap, Troyes, Aube, France *1904–c.1909*

Georgia Knap built his first voiturette in France, at Troyes, but they were put into production at Liège. They were 3-wheelers, not unlike the Léon Bollée, although they had electric ignition even in the 1896 prototype. They had 2 speeds, and belt final drive. A series of 50 was planned, but it is not certain how many were actually made. However, the Sté Liègeoise d'Automobiles went so far as to organize races especially for Knap cars. After his contract at Liège had expired, Knap returned to Troyes where he began to experiment with engines of various sizes from single- to 6-cylinder, and to make motor cycles. In 1904 he introduced a light 4-wheel car with a single-cylinder engine and shaft drive. This was made in some numbers for about five years.　　　　　　　　　　　　　GNG

KNICKERBOCKER (US) *1901–1903*
Ward Leonard Electrical Co, Bronxville, N.Y.

This was a small 2-cylinder petrol car made by a well-known electrical equipment company. They also made an electric car under their own name.　　　GNG

KNIGHT *see* SILENT KNIGHT

KNIGHT OF THE ROAD (i) (GB) *c.1902*

This was the name given to a light car sold by the Motor Carriage & Chassis Company. It had a 5hp Aster engine, and was designed for commercial travellers. Another car sold by the same company was called the Esculapius, and was intended, appropriately, for doctors. This had a 5hp Ader engine.　　　　　GNG

KNIGHT OF THE ROAD (ii) (GB) *1913–1914*
Knight Brothers, Chelmsford, Essex

Knight of the Road and Knight Junior were two cars made especially for sale by Friswell & Company. They both had 4-cylinder engines, the former of 15.9hp and the latter of 11.5hp. The Knight of the Road had a full five-seater tourer body, while the Knight Junior was a two-seater.　　　　　GNG

KNIGHT SPECIAL (US) *1917*
Watson & Stoeckle, New York, N.Y.

This car used a Moline-Knight 4-cylinder engine and Entz magnetic transmission. The chassis cost $4,000, and custom bodies were available to purchaser's choice. One car was made, and plans were going ahead for modest production, but America's entry into World War 1 put an end to the project.　　　　　GNG

1925 KLEIBER 6-cylinder sedan. *Lucien Loreille Collection*

1950 KLEINE WOLF 200cc two-seater. *Autosport*

1920 KLINE KAR 6-55 tourer. *Automotive History Collection, Detroit Public Library*

1912 KNOX 40hp tourer. *Kenneth Stauffer*

1900 KOCH 6hp phaeton. *Geoffroy de Beauffort Collection*

1911 KOECHLIN 3-litre racing car. *Autocar*

KNÖLLNER (D) *1924*

Karl Knöllner Automobilfabrik, Ravensbrück bei Fürstenberg

The Knöllner factory produced the Carolette, a 3-wheeled two-seater with 2PS Helios engine, and the Carolus, a small 4-wheeler with 5/12PS engine.　　HON

KNOX (US) *1900–1915*

Knox Automobile Co, Springfield, Mass.

These cars were known as the Knox Waterless, or more familiarly as the Old Porcupine, from the fact that air-cooling was by means of 2in pins screwed into the cylinder jackets instead of the more common fins. The first car was a 3-wheeler with a rear-mounted 4hp single-cylinder engine, and epicyclic transmission. This was made until 1903, but the first 4-wheeler appeared in 1901, and had long springs extending from front to rear axle. Single chain drive was used until 1905, when double chains were introduced for the larger cars, these being replaced by shaft drive in 1907. In 1906 a Knox came through the Glidden Tour without losing a single point.

Water-cooling was optional from 1908, and the later Knoxes though luxurious and expensive, had lost the individuality of Old Porcupine. Large 4- and 6-cylinder cars were made, with prices ranging up to $6,400 for the 1915 66hp 6-cylinder limousine. Harry A. Knox, the founder, had left the company in 1904 to make Atlas and Atlas-Knight cars, also in Springfield.　　GNG

KOBOLD (D) *1920*

Kobold Kleinauto GmbH, Berlin-Charlottenburg

A small car which was in production only for a short time.　　HON

KOCH (F) *1898–1901*

Koch Frères, Paris

The Koch car was based on the first designs of Saurer, and used a 6hp horizontal single-cylinder opposed-piston engine mounted in the rear of the car and driving the rear axle through spur gearing. Quite a number were made, but more for military or colonial use than as ordinary private cars. Heavy oil fuel was used.　　GNG

KOCO (D) *1921–1926*

(1) Kleinauto- und Motorenwerke Koch & Co, Erfurt *1921–1922*

(2) Koco-Werke GmbH, Erfurter Kleinauto- und Motorenbau, Erfurt *1922–1926*

A small three-seater car which was available with 4/16PS and 5/25PS opposed twin-cylinder air- or water-cooled engines. In 1925 a 6/30PS model appeared with a 4-cylinder 1540cc engine.　　HON

KOEB-THOMPSON (US) *1910–1911*

Koeb-Thompson Motors Co, Leipsig, Ohio

This car was based on engine patents obtained by the founders, R.P. Thompson and Emil Koeb. Apparently the only model produced was a large five-seater with a 4-cylinder, 2-stroke engine. The car had rear platform springing.　　GMN

KOECHLIN (F) *1910–1913*

S. Gerster et Cie, Courbevoie, Seine

The Koechlin made its first appearance as an entrant in the 1911 Coupe des Voitures Legères, but unfortunately did not run. It used a 4-cylinder 2-stroke engine of 3 litres, and a 5-speed gearbox in which direct drive was on fourth. Koechlins were entered again in the Coupe de l'Auto of 1912 and 1913, but did not distinguish themselves. Two production cars were listed for 1912 and 1913, a 2.9-litre 4-cylinder and a 3-litre 6-cylinder, both with monobloc engines and 4-speed gearboxes.　　GNG

KOEHLER (US) *1910–1914*

H.J. Koehler Co, Newark, N.J.

This make was built by a sporting goods company which ventured into car and truck manufacture. The Montclair model was a five-seater with a 4-cylinder, 4.6-litre 40hp engine.　　GMN

KOLLER (RA) *1960*

The Koller was an international cocktail of a car. Assembled in the Argentine, it used a 3-cylinder 2-stroke Wartburg engine from East Germany and a fibreglass saloon body whose material was made under licence from Scott Bader & Company of Wellingborough, England. It had 4-headlamp styling, a wrap-around windscreen, and a hard-top type of body.　　GNG

KOLOWRAT (CS) *c.1920*

Count Alexander Kolowrat was already famous for his association with the firm of Laurin-Klement when, in 1920, he offered a light car bearing his own name. It was powered by a flat-twin 1100cc engine, and, like most of its kind on the Continent, boasted a plate clutch, 3 forward speeds and shaft drive. It was characteristic, too, in lacking a differential.　　TRN

KOMET (i) *see* STERLING (i)

KOMET (ii) (D) *1922–1924*
Komet Autofabrik Buchmann & Co, Leisnig
A small car with a 4/14PS Steudel proprietary engine. Production of this vehicle was continued by Kenter. HON

KOMNICK (D) *1907–1927*
1) F. Komnick Autofabrik, Elbing *1907–1922*
2) Automobilfabrik Komnick AG, Elbing *1922–1927*
Franz Komnick added an automobile department to his well-established engineering works in 1907. From the beginning Komnicks were distinguished by having their radiators placed behind the engine, as in many French cars of the period. The first models, the T-headed K10, K20, and K30, were famous for their durability. The later Komnick models were very popular, especially in their native East Germany and the East European states. Komnick cars participated in several long distance trials, including the Prince Henry Trials and several Russian events.
Until World War 1 Komnick offered a range of ioe 4-cylinder models from 1540 and 18bhp to 5536cc and 70bhp as well as an ohv 5½-litre. After the war only one model was produced, the C2 with an 8/40PS 2064cc engine with shaft-driven overhead camshaft and frontal V-radiator. A sports version was available with an engine output of 55bhp. Production of private cars ceased in 1927, but lorries and tractors stayed on the programme a few years longer. HON

KONDOR (D) *1900–1902*
Kondor Fahrradwerke AG vorm. Liepe & Breest, Brandenburg
This firm built various versions of a single-cylinder 5hp car. HON

KOPPEL (B) *1901–c.1903*
Compagnie Belge de Vélocipèdes, Liège
The Koppel had a vertical single-cylinder engine mounted at the rear of the car, and geared to the rear axle. The engine could be started by a lever from the seat. The front part of the frame containing the steering could be detached from the rear part containing the engine. It had a four-seater tonneau body. GNG

KOPPIN (US) *1915*
Koppin Motor Co, Fenton, Mich.
This two-seater cyclecar used a 2-cylinder air-cooled De Luxe engine of 1.2 litres. It had friction transmission and its price was $375. It is sometimes claimed that this make succeeded the Signet cyclecar. GMN

KORN ET LATIL (F) *1901–1902*
A. Korn et Latil, Paris 11e
This was a very light front-wheel-drive voiturette designed by Latil. Originally it used a 3¼hp Aster engine, later one of 6hp. Very few were made, but Latil soon became celebrated as a manufacturer of commercial vehicles. GNG

KORTE (GB) *1903–c.1905*
Rice & Co (Leeds) Ltd, Leeds, Yorks.
Korte, Atkinson & Co Ltd had made motor tricycles and De Dion type quadricycles since 1900, and in 1903 a new company introduced the Korte car. This had a 12/14hp 2-cylinder engine mounted transversely at the front of the car, driving through a 4-speed gearbox, and double chain drive. It could be fitted with four- or six-seater tonneau bodies. GNG

KÖRTING (D) *1922–1924*
Wilhelm Körting Automobilwerk, Wülfrath
Production started with a 4-cylinder 6/24PS model and this was followed by an 8/32PS. Both models were equipped with Selve proprietary engines. HON

KOVER (F) *1951–1952*
Sté Industrielle de Livry, Paris 15e
The Kover was a very small two-seater with a 125cc single-cylinder engine. Maximum speed was said to be 40mph. GNG

KRASTIN (US) *1902–1903*
Krastin Automobile Co, Cleveland, Ohio
This company made a 'tonneau touring wagon' with a 2-cylinder engine. The body could be converted from passenger to goods carrying. GNG

K.R.C. (GB) *1922–1924*
White, Holmes & Co Ltd, Hammersmith, London W.6
The K.R.C. light car originally used a 10hp V-twin Blackburne engine, replaced for 1923 by 4-cylinder engines, by Coventry-Climax or Janvier, of 7.5 or 8.9hp. Shaft drive was used, and models included a staggered seat sports car with cowled radiator and an ohv engine. A K.R.C. was entered in the 1922 200 Mile Race at Brooklands but retired with a cracked cylinder, although it was described as 'remarkably fast' before its retirement. GNG

1913 KOMNICK 17/50PS tourer. *Jaeger Collection*

1925 KOMNICK Type C 8/40PS saloon. *Neubauer Collection*

1901 KORN ET LATIL 3¼hp voiturette. *G.N. Georgano Collection*

1904 KRIÉGER electric brougham. *The Veteran Car Club of Great Britain*

1912 KRIT 16/20hp tourer. *Kenneth Stauffer*

1899 KÜHLSTEIN-VOLLMER *avant train* cab. *Neubauer Collection*

KREIBICH (CS) *1949*

The Kreibich was an experimental 3-wheeler with a 2-cylinder air-cooled engine and single rear wheel and an all-enveloping two-seater body. GNG

KREUGER (US) *1904–1905*

Kreuger Mfg Co, Milwaukee, Wisc.

This was a light touring car with a 2-cylinder air-cooled engine and shaft drive. The price was $1,000. GNG

KRIÉGER (F) *1897–1909*

(1) Compagnie Parisienne des Voitures Electriques (Système Kriéger), Paris *1897–1907*

(2) Compagnie Parisienne des Voitures Electriques, Colombes *1907–1909*

Like Jeantaud, Kriéger sprang to prominence in the 1897 Paris Motor Cab Trials, where the make won a prize for four-seaters. The first Kriéger was a fwd conversion of a horse-cab, with a separate electric motor in each front wheel. This gave not only power steering, but also 4-wheel braking, since there were separate brakes on the rear wheels. Their Milord carriage weighed 2,530lb and was credited with 15mph and a duration of 50 miles per charge. By 1898 the firm was in full production, rights being sold to the British Electromobile Co in Britain, whose 2½ ton Powerful of 1900 was in fact a Kriéger, to NAMAG (Lloyd) in Germany, and to S.T.A.E. in Italy, who made some Kriéger-type electrics around 1905. Design changed little through the years, though some voiturettes were marketed under the name of Electrolette in 1902 (60 percent of their weight was accounted for by the batteries!) and in the same year some bonneted cars, still with front-wheel drive, were built.

A so-called alcohol-electric ran in the 1902 Concours du Ministre, though its 4hp De Dion engine was strictly an auxiliary. More serious was a true petrol-electric with a 24hp Richard-Brasier engine and separate spur gear drive to each rear wheel, which was shown in 1903 and placed on the market a year later. The English price in 1905 was £800, but it cannot have been a great success as reports published in 1906 indicated that the factory was concentrating on regular battery-electrics. The works were moved to Colombes in 1907. A year later M. Kriéger patented a gas turbine-electric with rear-wheel drive, but shortly afterwards the company was reported to be in liquidation.

The last Kriégers of 1909 were taxicab chassis in which a 15hp Brasier engine drove the front wheels. The name reappeared during World War 2, in association with another famous French battery-electric name, Mildé, but the end-products were in fact electric conversions of La Licorne cars and Chenard-Walcker light vans. MCS

KRIM-GHIA (US) *1966–c.1969*

Krim-Ghia Import Co, Detroit, Mich.

These cars were Ghia-bodied versions of the Fiat 1500 and Plymouth Barracuda, build to Krim specifications. The Fiat sports model used a 4-cylinder 86hp engine, while the Barracuda roadster contained a 245hp Plymouth power plant. BE

KRIT (K.R.I.T.) (US) *1909–1916*

Krit Motor Co, Detroit, Mich.

Early models of the Krit were small three- and four-seaters with 4-cylinder engines. For 1911, a two-seater with an underslung chassis was built. The last models of this make were classed as light cars, with a 3.6-litre 4-cylinder engine. The price was $850 for either the roadster or touring version, and the cars used a swastika badge. GMN

KROBOTH (CS) *1930–1931*

The Kroboth was an advanced design of light car using a 500cc single-cylinder engine, tubular backbone frame and transverse semi-elliptic suspension at front and rear. Financial support was withdrawn from the project before production started. GNG

KRÜGER *see* ELEKTRA

KRUPKAR *see* MORRISON (ii)

KRUSE (D) *1899–1901*

Gebr. Kruse, Hamburg

This firm's production, which included electric and steam cars, was only on a small scale. HON

KÜHLSTEIN (D) *1898–1902*

Kühlstein Wagenbau, Berlin-Charlottenburg

Kühlstein took up production of electric cars in 1898. Most types were of their own design, but Jeantaud cabs were built under licence. After 1899 petrol-driven cars were also produced. *Avant trains* for the conversion of horse-drawn vehicles into motor cars were a speciality. After Ing. Josef Vollmer had been engaged by Kühlstein, the make was also known as the Kühlstein-Vollmer.

In 1902 Kühlstein car production was taken over by the electric concern A.E.G., who were extending their automobile department. Kühlstein continued to manufacture car bodies.

HON

KÜHN (D) 1927–1929
Otto Kühn, Halle (Saale)

Kühn built bodies, particularly for Opel, and introduced his own model in 1927. It was derived from the 4/16PS Opel and had a lengthened wheelbase. A subsequent model used the 6-cylinder 8/40PS Opel engine, Opel gearbox and rear axle, while the chassis and body were of Kühn's own design.

HON

KUNMING (CHI) c.1960 to date
Kunming Motor Vehicle Plant, Kunming, Yunnan

Some small 2-cylinder sedans selling for 4,000 yuan have been built in this plant, along with a jeep-like vehicle and buses. It is not certain if these were called Kunmings or given another brand name.

BE

KUNZ (US) 1902–1906
F.L. Kunz Machinery Co, Milwaukee, Wisc.

This was a small, rather attractive two-seater runabout with a single-cylinder engine. Although this car had a bonnet, the engine was in fact mounted under the seat. A 3-speed transmission was used, described as operating by 'a sliding wedge'. The price was given as $675.

GMN

KUROGANE (J) 1935–1962
(1) Nippon Nainenki Seiko Co, Ltd, Tokyo 1935–1959
(2) Tokyu Kurogane Kogyo Co, Ltd, Tokyo 1959–1962

The Kurogane company, called New Era until 1937, specialized in 3-wheelers, mostly built as commercial vehicles. A small car with V-twin air-cooled engine and 4-wheel drive was built from 1935 to 1940, but was probably mainly for military use; about 4,800 were made. After the purchase of Ohta Motors in 1957 a camping car was among the range of 4-wheel vehicles which Kurogane introduced. This Kurogane Baby camper was a four-seater with a canvas top and sides that let down for loading. It was powered by a rear-mounted 2-cylinder, 4-stroke, air-cooled engine developing 18hp.

BE

KURTIS (US) 1948–1955
(1) Kurtis-Kraft Inc, Glendale, Calif. 1948–1950
(2) Kurtis Sports Car Corp, Glendale, Calif. 1953–1955

Frank Kurtis, prominent sports and racing car designer, tried his hand at marketing his own cars on several occasions. A Kurtis-Kar, planned in 1948 with an 80hp engine, never materialized, but in 1949 the Kurtis Sports appeared with a distinctive two-seater body and Ford running gear. Bodies were built partially of fibreglass and 36 of this custom-made car were produced before Muntz Motors took over the design in 1949 to continue it as the Muntz Jet. 1954 brought the Kurtis 500-S competition car which was similar to the Indianapolis 500 racing model, except for some additions including wings and lights. 30 of this model were assembled, the engines available including the Mercury. A prototype of this machine delivered to a Hudson dealer in 1953 contained a 6-cylinder Hornet engine, transmission and axle. A 500-KK tubular chassis, adaptable to metal or fibreglass bodies, was also available during 1954–1955.

With the completion of 18 500-M sports cars in 1955, Kurtis turned to other fields of activity, including building airport servicing vehicles for jets and rocket sleds for Cook Electric Research Labs. The 500-M had a fibreglass body with scooped side panels, torsion-bar suspension and a 4-cylinder ohv supercharged engine. The capabilities of Kurtis-built racing cars were shown when they won 1st, 3rd, 4th, 5th, 6th, 8th, 9th and 10th places during the 1954 Indianapolis 500 Mile Race.

BE

KURTZ AUTOMATIC (US) 1921–1923
Kurtz Motor car Co, Cleveland, Ohio

The Kurtz, with its 6-cylinder Herschell-Spillman engine, was one of many assembled cars of its time, distinguished only by its preselector gear-change on the steering column.

KM

KYMA (GB) 1903–1905
New Kyma Motor Car Co Ltd, Nunhead, London S.E.

The Kyma first appeared as a very light 3-wheeler with a $2\frac{3}{4}$ or 4hp single-cylinder engine, belt drive and basket-work two-seater body. The single wheel was at the front in this model, but by 1905 the wheel was at the rear and the Kyma had a 6hp 2-cylinder engine and chain drive. The basket-work body remained, and a 4-wheeler was also available this year.

GNG

1900 KÜHLSTEIN 6hp two-seater. *Neubauer Collection*

1937 KUROGANE 1,300cc two-seater. *H. Igarashi*

1953 KURTIS racing and sports cars, with Frank Kurtis. *Associated Press Ltd*

1907 LABOR 20/30hp landaulette. *Lucien Loreille Collection*

1907 LA BUIRE 24hp landaulette. Coachwork by Beadle. *Autocar*

1913 LA BUIRE 12hp two-seater. *National Motor Museum*

LABOR (F) *1907–1912*

Weyher et Richemond, Pantin, Seine

The Labor was built by Weyher et Richemond to the designs of de Clèves-Chevalier who were the selling agents. It was a conventional shaft-driven 4-cylinder car made in two models, a 15/20hp and 20/30hp, the same basic models being made throughout the make's lifetime.　　　　　　GNG

LA BUIRE (F) *1904–1930*

(1) Chantiers de la Buire, Lyons *1904–1905*
(2) Société des Automobiles de la Buire, Lyons *1905–1909*
(3) Société Nouvelle de la Buire-Automobiles, Lyons *1910–1930*

Though the Chantiers de la Buire were engaged on automobile work under contract to Serpollet as early as 1900, their own designs did not appear on the market until 1904 – these were sometimes erroneously referred to in England as 'de la Buire' cars. They were conventional T-headed 4-cylinder machines with metal-to-metal clutches, 4-speed gearboxes, chain drive and pressed-steel frames, made in 16hp and 30hp sizes. A separate car division was formed in 1905 and a year later three fours were on the market; the smaller ones had capacities of 4.9 and 7.5 litres respectively, but the '80' was a herculean 13.6-litre affair. All had high-tension magnetos, Rover-type compression brakes and twin transmission footbrakes. The big La Buire had a long and distinguished career in British sprints and hill-climbs in the hands of J. Higginson, inventor of the Autovac. He started with ftd at Sunrising in 1907 and ended by being the entrant of the biggest car ever to record ftd at Shelsley Walsh in 1912. Otherwise La Buire were not interested in racing, apart from a 2nd place in the Coupe de la Commission Sportive of 1907, which resulted in a catalogued *type de course* model offered from 1908 to 1910. Bevel drive with twin crown wheels – a system favoured up to 1914 – made its appearance on a 2.7-litre 4-cylinder car in 1907. 1908 saw a '10/14' of 2.1-litre capacity and a 4.8-litre 6-cylinder, also shaft-driven. No fewer than nine models were on sale in 1909, and these included four sixes, their capacities ranging from a modest 3.6 litres up to an above average 9.5 litres. The company followed the majority of French makers in 1910 by offering L-head monobloc engines, initially in 3.2-litre form; these cars had multi-plate clutches and chain-driven camshafts, the latter being a La Buire innovation which was extended over the range. For the 1910 season the cars were known as Berthiers, after the technical director, M. Berthier who took over the company. In late 1910 the Société Nouvelle was formed, and the cars reverted to the La Buire name. Long strokes were a characteristic of late pre-war models: the '15' measured 80×160mm and the '20' 90×160mm. By 1912 unit gearboxes and differential-mounted transmission brakes had made their appearance, as had a round-nosed radiator, which was used throughout the range in 1914. A mechanical starter was fitted on the 1913 15hp model. Rather small fours of 1.7 and 2.3 litres were available in 1913, as well as the bigger '15' and '20', and 6-cylinder cars of 4.8 and 5.3 litres. The big La Buires still had two brake pedals, but the second one was now linked to the drums on the rear wheels.

The story after World War 1 is typical of so many distinguished French marques. A handsome V-radiator had little behind it save tradition; the 1919 '14/20' was a stolid 2,650cc affair with fixed head, side valves, pump and fan cooling, 4-speed unit gearbox, magneto ignition and spiral bevel final drive, selling for £1,075 in England. It was available with front-wheel brakes in 1922 and a year later came the optimistically-styled 14/46hp Speed Model with ohv and fwb and the same cylinder dimensions (75 × 150mm). An ohv 1.8-litre '12/38' with thermo-syphon cooling and central change offered 53mph for £525, but front-wheel brakes were extra until 1925. Thereafter La Buire had little new to offer and 1.8-litre and 2-litre 4-cylinder cars on similar lines persisted until 1930.　　　　　　MCS

LACONIA (US) *1914*

H.H. Buffum, Laconia, N.H.

The Laconia, a cyclecar, had double, parallel cantilever springs front and rear, an aluminium body and a V-twin air-cooled engine. The manufacturer is better remembered for his earlier effort, the Buffum.　　　　　　GMN

LACOSTE ET BATTMANN (F) *1897–1913*

(1) Lacoste et Battmann, Paris *1897–1905*
(2) Lacoste et Battmann Ltd, Paris *1905–1913*

This firm seldom sold cars under their own name, preferring to supply complete vehicles (and components) to other 'manufacturers', including several in England. Thus their products were marketed under such aliases as Napoleon (1903), Régal (i)

903), Gamage (1903), Speedwell (i) (1904), Cupelle (1905), Lacoba (1906) and implicia (1910). Some, but not all models of Jackson (i) in the 1905–6 period are so clearly of Lacoste origin. The diversity of types offered indicates that specification was tailored to the trade client's requirements.

The first Lacoste et Battmann was a 4hp motor quadricycle with electric ignition offered in 1897, and by 1902 the company had progressed to conventional voiturettes with Aster or Mutel engines, marketed as the 'L and B' by H. Cintrat, a dealer with premises both in Paris and in London. A good selection of models was available in 1903, smallest of which was a 6hp single-cylinder runabout styled in the manner of a De Dion, with underslung radiator, 3-speed gearbox and shaft drive, which cost £195. Bigger 12hp cars resembled the smaller Panhards and had 2-cylinder De Dion engines, while later in 1903 a 24hp 4-cylinder model with a Mutel engine was available. In 1904 a tubular-framed 700cc single could be bought for about £125, and a year later Régal, Speedwell and Jackson cars were being advertised as 'built on the Lacoste principles!' Like Darracq, the company was now British-registered and though cars were still made with armoured wood as well as steel frames, all the Lacoste vehicles sold in Britain had mechanically-operated inlet valves and rounded radiators; this helps to furnish clues to the identity of some more nebulous breeds. Over the next two seasons the choice was wide, including the singles, a 10hp 2-litre twin, a fairly small L-head 2½-litre four and two bigger fours of 3.3 litres and 4.9 litres. Though pair-cast engines were found on some of the 4-cylinder machines, a 12/16hp Lacoba exhibited at Manchester in 1906 had separate cylinders. Single-cylinder Lacostes ran (under their own name) in voiturette races sponsored by *L'Auto* in 1905 and 1907, René Thomas being one of the drivers on the former occasion. During the 1905–7 period the firm was said to be making a wide range with De Dion or Aster engines: in 1907, there were three singles, a twin and two fours, with ratings from 4½ to 24hp, and prices between 2350fr and 10,000fr. Light electric cars were also said to be available. The company was reported defunct in 1909, but a year later had staged a comeback with the Simplicia, which used a 1.8-litre 4-cylinder Aster engine in a tubular backbone chassis with transverse front suspension and central gearchange. It was on the British market at £320 and was still being made two years later, but by 1913 Lacoste et Battmann were out of business. MCS

LACOUR (F) 1912–1914
Lacour et Cie, Paris

The Lacour cyclecar used a 9hp V-twin engine, and a variable belt drive giving 3 speeds. GNG

LACRE (GB) 1904–1905
Lacre Motor Car Co, London W.

The Lacre company were well-known builders of car and commercial vehicle bodies, and also of complete commercials, but they only made one model of private car which could be called their own make. This was an electric brougham with two 2hp motors mounted on the rear axle. GNG

LA CUADRA (E) 1900–1901
, de la Cuadra y Cía, Barcelona

La Cuadra began by making electric buses, but his first car was powered by a 4½hp 2-cylinder petrol engine. It had a four-seater body, steering-column gear change and double chain drive. Only six were made before La Cuadra's money ran out, but a creditor, J. Castro, took over the works and began production of cars under his own name. The designer of both the La Cuadra and Castro cars was Marc Birkigt, later famous for Hispano-Suizas. GNG

L.A.D. (GB) 1913–1926
1) Oakleigh Motor Co, West Dulwich, London S.E. *1913–1914*
2) L.A.D. Productions Ltd, Farnham, Surrey *1923–1926*

The L.A.D. was one of the lightest and simplest of the cyclecars. Mainly sold in monocar form – although a two-seater was available to special order – the body resembled that of the Carden monocar, having a pointed nose and a completely exposed engine mounted at the rear. This was a 5½hp single-cylinder Stag unit which drove the rear axle via a short chain. Only one speed was provided and steering was by wire and bobbin. The price was £60. In 1923 two cyclecars, a 350cc single, and a 500cc twin were listed, the 350cc model continuing to 1926. GNG

LADA see VAZ

LADAS see BOWEN (i)

LA DIVA (F) 1902
Jules Zimmerman et Cie, Paris

This was a 2-seater voiturette with a Renault-style bonnet and a 3½ or 4½hp De Dion engine. GNG

LAD'S CAR (US) 1912–1914
Niagara Motor Corp, Niagara Falls, N.Y.

1920 LA BUIRE 14/22hp saloon. *Autocar*

1928 LA BUIRE 10 AA Long 10CV saloon.
Lucien Loreille Collection

1905 LACOSTE ET BATTMANN (CUPELLE)
8hp two-seater. *Arthur Ingram*

411

1923 LAFAYETTE Model 134 5.6-litre tourer.
Jacques Kupélian Collection

1926 LAFITTE 7hp two-seater. *Autocar*

1913 LAGONDA 11.1hp two-seater. G.F. Oates
at the wheel. *Old Motor*

This was a juvenile car for two small passengers. It was sold in kit-form, wi
blueprints, for home assembly. Its power came from a single-cylinder 3hp engi
with double chain or belt drive to the rear axle.   GM

LA DURANCE (F) 1908–c.1910
L. Conchy, Sisteron, Basses-Alpes
This was a light 3-wheeler powered by a single-cylinder 8hp engine. It had sid
by-side seating, and a single rear wheel.   GN

LADY (GB) 1899
Henry Cave, Coventry, Warwickshire
The Lady voiturette was powered by a 2½hp De Dion engine with drive b
flexible propeller shaft to the rear axle. It had a two-seater body.   GN

LA FAUVETTE (F) 1904
La Locomotion Moderne, Paris
This was a light car very similar to the contemporary De Dion in appearanc
It was powered by a 6½hp De Dion engine, and had shaft drive. Two- or four-seat
bodies were available.   GN

LAFAYETTE (US) 1920–1924
(1) Lafayette Motors Co, Mars Hill, Ind. 1920–1923
(2) Lafayette Motors Co, Milwaukee, Wisc. 1923–1924
The Lafayette was a luxurious, lavishly equipped V-8 designed by D. McCa
White, who had been responsible for the V-8 Cadillac of 1915. Its sv engir
developed 100bhp at 2,750rpm. Its thermostatically controlled radiator shutters wer
a pioneering feature. The price ran as high as $7,500 for the limousine. In 192
Nash Motors acquired control of Lafayette Motors and continued to make the bi
eight for a short while, as a luxury line, but soon dropped it. The Lafayette nam
was revived by Nash in 1934 for their cheapest line.   TR

LAFITTE (F) 1923–1928
SA de Construction de Voiturettes Th. Lafitte, Paris
The Lafitte was an unconventional light car powered by a 3-cylinder radial engin
of 736cc capacity, enlarged in its last year to 895cc. It had a system of friction driv
in which the whole engine swivelled to give variable ratio. When the friction disc
met face to face, a clutch was formed which gave a direct drive 'top' gear. With
two-seater fabric body, the English price was only £100 in 1926.   GN

LA FLÈCHE (F) 1912–1913
Guders Jack, Asnières, Seine
This was a tandem-seated cyclecar powered by an 8hp single-cylinder Buch
engine. Transmission was by friction discs, and final drive by single chain. Th
radiator was similar to that of the Adams, and the body was a tandem tw
seater in which the rear seats could be converted into a compartment fo
luggage or samples.   GN

LA FLEURANTINE (F) 1906
J. Lagarde et Cie, Fleurance, Gers
This attractively-named car was a 3-wheeled two-seater voiturette using a 2
cylinder engine and chain drive.   GN

LA FRANÇAISE *see* DIAMANT

LA GAULOISE (F) 1907
Sté des voiturettes la Gauloise, Issy-les-Moulineaux, Seine
This make was available in two models, one with a 6.2hp single-cylinder engine
and the other with a larger 4-cylinder engine.   GN

LA GAZELLE (F) 1913–1920
M. Tzaut, Neuilly, Seine
Tzaut had formerly been with the Clément-Bayard concern, and introduced hi
own light car at the Paris Salon of 1913. It was a conventional light car wit
a 4-cylinder 8hp Chapuis-Dornier engine, and shaft drive.   GN

LAGONDA (GB) 1906–1963
(1) Lagonda Motor Co Ltd, Staines, Middlesex
(2) Lagonda Ltd, Staines, Middlesex
(3) Lagonda Ltd, Feltham, Middlesex
(4) Aston-Martin-Lagonda Ltd, Newport Pagnell, Bucks.
Wilbur Gunn, the founder of the Lagonda Company, hailed from Springfield
Ohio. He came to England in about 1897. In 1898 he built an air-cooled cycle in
greenhouse at Staines. On this site the first vehicle to bear the Lagonda name wa
assembled in 1900, an improved version of the air-cooled cycle; and it was here tha
Lagondas were to be built until 1947.
To his new product Gunn gave the French form of the American Indian name fo
Buck Creek, the stream near his home town. In 1905 the company's first racing

ccess came when a V-twin cycle won the London–Edinburgh trial. This victory
couraged Gunn to enter the motor car field with a 20hp 4-cylinder machine.
veloped in 1906, it was brought out the following year as the Torpedo. A 6-
linder version followed; this car carried Wilbur Gunn and Bert Hammond to win
e Moscow–St Petersburg Reliability Trial in 1910. The big tourer was as a result
reatly favoured' by Tsar Nicholas II, and the Lagonda Car Company's early
rtune was made from exporting these cars to Russia until war broke out in 1914.
At home a dapper 14/4 replaced the earlier 12/4 in 1909. This gave way in 1913
an 11.1hp light car of radically advanced design. Among its more striking
novations were a rivetted monocoque body of unit construction; an anti-roll bar
assist the suspension; and the earliest known fly-off hand brake. It enjoyed a wide
arket, being subsequently enlarged into a 11.9 in 1920 and a 12/24 in 1924, though
er cars no longer had monocoque construction.
In 1925 Arthur Davidson designed the 1954cc ohv-engined model which marks
e beginning of the Lagonda as a sports car. The 14/60 engine featured 4 fully-
achined hemispherical combustion chambers, the first to be marketed, aspirated
interchangeable valves opposed at 90°. Twin camshafts were carried high in
e block. A Rubury braking system of prodigious efficiency was fitted. Grouped
assis lubrication nipples were featured, as was a clutch stop. The whole car was
perbly finished.
The 2-litre Speed Model, a modified version of the 14/60, was developed late
1927 for the 1928 season. The chief difference between it and the earlier car lay
the valve-timing overlap, twin carburettors on a direct manifold, and a raised
mpression ratio of 6.8:1. These alterations combined to give the Speed Model
urer an acceleration from rest to 80mph in 50 seconds, and the new model did well
competition. A 2½-litre 6-cylinder with push-rod operated ohv was introduced
1926, and this was subsequently enlarged to 3 litres in 1928. For 1930 the
assis of the 2-litre was lowered and during that year a supercharged version
came available. In 1932 came the last of the 4-cylinder 2-litres, the Continental,
nich had smaller wheels and a sloping radiator, and this finally gave way to
e 16/80, a 2-litre six with a push-rod operated ohv engine of Crossley manufac-
re. It was later fitted with an E.N.V. preselector gearbox. This was an attractive
r but, like all the 2-litres, it suffered from excessive weight.
In the meantime a version of the 3-litre known as the Selector Special appeared.
is was fitted with a Maybach gearbox that gave eight forward speeds, four high
d four low, by means of an internal reduction gear with semi-automatic control.
e model was something of a failure, however, and was quietly dropped.
At the 1933 Motor Show two outstanding cars were introduced: the 1,104cc
apier, with twin overhead camshafts (see under RAPIER) and the 4½-litre M45,
ving a similar Meadows 6-cylinder ohv engine to that in the now defunct Invicta.
last a Lagonda had real performance and it is noteworthy that the firm made
eir own very attractive coachwork.
For 1935 two additional models made their appearance, the 4½ Rapide and the
-litre, both using the same shortened chassis. It was no doubt this complexity
models which caused the company to get into financial difficulties, and a victory
Le Mans by a Rapide came too late to save the day.
When in the summer of 1935 Alan Good saved the Lagonda Company from
sorption by Rolls-Royce, he appointed W.O. Bentley as chief designer. The LG45
odel with which Bentley attacked the luxury market in 1936 had longer road
rings and Luvax dampers, but retained the M45R engine and chassis. Not until
e 1936 Motor Show could Bentley's influence on the Meadows engine be seen in
definitive form. The Sanction III unit featured an improved cross-flow inlet
anifold cast integrally into the head, onto which the carburettors were now
lted directly. Various other improvements including a lightened flywheel allowed
e line on the revolution counter to be moved up to 4,000rpm.
The last of the 4½-litre Lagondas was the LG6 of 1938. It had ifs, hydraulic brakes
d outboard rear springs, but still used the Meadows engine. The V-12 engine,
ought out for the 1937 season, is considered the finest of W.O. Bentley's designs.
is 180bhp unit could raise the car's speed from 7 to 103.45mph on top gear
thout snatching; and this flexibility could be supplemented by revving freely to
000rpm on the indirects. Regrettably the design was never developed fully, for
oduction was stopped in 1940, a few months after Rapide versions had been
aced third and fourth at Le Mans.
In 1947 the Lagonda firm was taken over by the David Brown complex. Contrary
spelling the end of the traditional Lagonda, the new merger enabled Bentley's
st motor-car design to be realized. This was the 2.6-litre model which appeared
1948. Its brilliant but unorthodox layout embraced a true cruciform chassis,
dependent rear suspension unique amongst British cars, and a twin ohc 6-cylinder
gine. A bored-out edition of the 2.6 was offered as the 3-litre in 1951, featuring
xurious styling, rich appointments and a top speed of 110mph. HRH the Duke of
dinburgh had two for his personal use, and for many years was an honorary
ember of the Lagonda Club.
The Lagonda Rapide was announced in 1961. Using a DB4 engine of 3,996cc
pacity, the car was set up on a platform chassis with independent springing all
und, servo-assisted disc brakes and a De Dion rear axle. An elegant, aluminium
perleggera body by Touring of Milan contributed greatly to the car's massive
celeration. The Rapide's top speed was a genuine 125mph with comfortable

1926 LAGONDA 14/60hp semi-sports tourer.
Harley J. Usill

1929 LAGONDA 2-litre high-chassis saloon.
Lagonda Club

1930 LAGONDA 3-litre sports tourer. *H.A.
Fitzpatrick*

1936 LAGONDA LG 45 4½-litre drophead
coupé. *G.N. Georgano*

1939 LAGONDA 4½-litre V-12 sedanca de ville.
Coachwork by H.J. Mulliner. *Lagonda Club*

1953 LAGONDA 3-litre saloon. *Lagonda Club*

1962 LAGONDA Rapide 4½-litre saloon.
Aston Martin-Lagonda Ltd

1909 LAMBERT(i) 15hp tourer.
Kenneth Stauffer

cruising at 120; its sumptuous finish and appointments were in keeping with [its]
price of £5,000. Production ceased in 1963, though a 4-door saloon version [of]
the V-8 Aston Martin DBS built for Sir David Brown in 1970 bore the Lagonda
emblem.   HA

LAGO-TALBOT *see* DARRACQ

LA GRACIEUSE (B) *1899*
La Société Electricité Mécanique Automobile, Brussels
   This was a light car powered by a 6hp engine with air-cooling by hollow radi[al]
discs of aluminium. It had coil ignition with auxiliary tube ignition, in case th[e]
accumulator gave out.   GN

LAIGLE (F) *1902–1903*
Laigle Paquet et Cie, Amiens
   The Laigle was a conventional four-seater car powered by 2- or 4-cylinder engin[es]
of 10/12 or 14/16hp.   GN

LA JOYEUSE (F) *1907–1908*
Voitures Légères Taine, Paris
   La Joyeuse was a 4-cylinder light car with shaft drive. One ran in the 1908 Cou[pe]
des Voiturettes.   GN

LA LICORNE *see* CORRE (i)

LA LORRAINE (F) *1899–1902*
Charles Schmid, Bar-le-Duc, Meuse
   This was a small *vis-à-vis* four-seater with a single-cylinder rear engine and th[e]
general appearance of a De Dion. Transmission was by a system of friction cone[s.]
                                                                         GN

LA MARNE (i) (US; CDN) *1920*
(1) La Marne Motor Co, Cleveland, Ohio
(2) Anglo-American Motors Ltd, Trenton, Ont.
   The La Marne was a low-slung, low-priced 8-cylinder car of which few wer[e]
built. The sole model, a hard-top tourer, was listed at $1,485, the concern advert[is-]
ing it as 'real value, $3,000'. Its 5.9-litre straight-8 engine developed 85bhp, an[d]
was of an ohc variety similar to the Hispano-Suiza. At least one was built [in]
Canada, by Anglo-American Motors who also planned to sell a 4-cylinder car a[t]
$975. The Canadian car has been erroneously listed as Le Marne.   K[M]

LA MARNE (ii) (F) *1920*
Brun et Forest, Chalons, Marne
   This was a short-lived touring car using a 12/15hp 4-cylinder engine.   GN

LAMBERT (i) (US) *1891; 1904–1917*
The Buckeye Mfg Co, Anderson, Ind.
   John W. Lambert's 3-wheeler of 1891 is considered the first petrol-engined vehic[le]
built in the United States. The Lambert (i) succeeded the Union (ii) in 1904. All th[e]
production Lamberts used a friction drive. Up to 1910, a chassis with a small 2-
cylinder engine was built with either four-seater or five-seater bodies; double and subsequently single chain drive was used. Shaft drive appeared on the big Lambert[s]
in 1907. Later models used 4- and 6-cylinder engines by Continental, Buda an[d]
Rutenber. After 1917 the marque continued for two years as a commercial vehicle[.]
                                                                         GM[R]

LAMBERT (ii) (F) *1902–c.1906*
A. Lambert et Cie, Paris
   Lambert used various proprietary engines including Aster or De Dion for thei[r]
smaller cars and Aster or Abeille for the larger ones. The 1902 range consisted o[f]
a 6hp single-cylinder two-seater, 9hp and 12hp 2-cylinder tonneaux. All used sha[ft]
drive and artillery wheels. By 1905 they were offering six models, from the 6h[p]
single-cylinder up to a 24hp 4-cylinder side-entrance tourer.   GN[C]

LAMBERT (iii) (F) *1926–1953*
(1) Automobiles Lambert, Macon *1926–1931*
(2) Automobiles Lambert, Reims *1931–1936; 1940–1945*
(3) Automobiles Lambert, Giromagny, Belfort *1948–1953*
   Germain Lambert was one of the most persistent producers of unusual small car[s,]
although his production was never large. He began at Macon with a Ruby-engine[d]
sports car with independent suspension all round, known as the Sans Choc. This wa[s]
followed by a front-wheel drive sports car, also Ruby-engined, made at Reims[.]
From 1933 to 1936 he made a very small fwd cyclecar with a single-cylinder 2h[p]
or 4½hp engine, which he named the Baby Sans Choc. The 2hp model was said t[o]
be suitable for children.
   The war years saw simple battery electric two-seaters emerging from the smal[l]
works at Reims, and after the war a new line of sports cars was announced fro[m]
Giromagny. These had 1,100cc engines described as Lambert-Rubys, for the Rub[y]
company was no longer in business. Forsaking his pre-war originality, Lambert use[d]

rear-wheel drive and a beam front axle with semi-elliptic springs. The car retained its pre-war appearance, and had something of the position of the Morgan on the French market. Performance, however, was good, the race engine giving 50bhp at 4,000rpm, and a Lambert won its class in the 1951 Bol d'Or. The last model used a streamlined Gran Turismo coupé body by Schmitt, but the market for such cars was too small for Lambert to stay in business.   GNG

LAMBERT-HERBERT (GB) 1913
Lambert-Herbert Light Car Co
    The Lambert-Herbert used an 8.9hp 4-cylinder engine, and was sponsored by Percy Lambert the racing driver. His death at Brooklands in October 1913 caused the winding-up of the company soon afterwards.   GNG

LAMBERT & WEST see WARREN-LAMBERT

LAMBORGHINI (I) 1963 to date
Automobili Ferruccio Lamborghini SpA, S. Agata Bolognese
    In 1946 Ferruccio Lamborghini was an amateur tuning Fiat 500s, but by 1949 he had started a tractor-building venture. His first vehicles were built up from Allied war surplus, but by 1966 the company had boomed into a big factory turning out twenty vehicles a day, with a profitable side-line in oil burners. The Lamborghini car appeared in 1963 as a hobby for its sponsor and was a 3½-litre 4-ohc V-12 with six Weber carburettors, developing 360bhp. The specification included a 5-speed ZF gearbox, self-locking differential, multi-tubular frame, all-round independent suspension by coils and wishbones and servo-assisted Girling disc brakes. Lamborghini's own GT coupé bodies had huge single windscreen wipers and retractable headlamps. Gian Paolo Dallara was responsible for design. Some 200 were delivered in 1965, by which time the new make was providing Ferrari with serious competition, though Lamborghini did not race his products.
    For 1966 GT models had 4-litre engines and henceforward the company made their own gearboxes and final drive units. Even more exciting was the P.400 Miura, introduced at Turin in November 1965, with its 4-litre unit mounted transversely at the rear, spur gear final drive and a top speed of 180mph. This was in production by the end of 1966. In 1967 there was a bizarre prototype on Miura lines, the Marzal with 175bhp 2-litre 6-cylinder engine, and 6-headlamp layout. It did not go into production, and a year later came a revised conventional V-12, the front-engined Espada. A 2 + 2 edition, the Jarama, followed in 1970. New in 1971 was a small V-8, the 2½-litre 220bhp Urraco, a development of the Miura with McPherson strut suspension replacing the coils and wishbones. This, the Espada and the Jarama were offered in 1973, when the Miura gave way to a new coupé, the Countach, powered by a 5-litre 440bhp version of the V-12 unit mounted longitudinally at the rear, behind its gearbox. With a claimed maximum speed of over 200mph, the Countach cost £15,200 on the British market. Lamborghini's cars wear the emblem of a bull, and have the unusual feature of synchromesh on reverse gear. MCS

LAMBRO (I) 1952
    The Lambro was a 3-wheeler of the Isetta variety, but had conventional doors in the side of the body. It had a 125cc rear-mounted engine which gave it a maximum speed of 40mph.   GNG

LA MINERVE (F) 1901–1906
Sté La Minerve, Billancourt, Seine
    The products of this company had no connection with the better-known Minerva cars. The first Minerve was a voiturette powered by a 3½hp single-cylinder engine, with chain drive to the rear axle. In 1902 the range had expanded to a 6hp single, 8 and 10hp twins, and a 16hp four, all with shaft drive. The 6hp was sold in England under the name Vesta.
    A 3-cylinder car was made in 1903, and sizes crept up in later years, the largest 1905 models being an 18 and a 24hp four. Design was conventional. The company also made stationary engines for industrial or agricultural use.   GNG

LAMMAS-GRAHAM (GB) 1936–1938
Lammas Ltd, Sunbury-on-Thames, Middlesex
    Instead of the Ford V-8 or Hudson units employed by most of the Anglo-Americans of the 1930s, the Lammas used the supercharged 6-cylinder Graham engine, although with 114mm stroke as against the 111mm of the standard engine. This gave a capacity of 3.7 litres, and 128bhp. Lammas-Graham bodies were very English in appearance, a drophead coupé, a 4-door saloon and a sports tourer. They were made by Abbot, Carlton and Bertelli respectively. Total production of Lammas-Grahams was less than 50.   GNG

LA MOUCHE see TESTE ET MORET

LA MOUETTE (F) 1909
Joanny Faure, Lyons
    This was a very rakish looking two-seater raceabout with a 4-cylinder engine driving the front wheels, and a dashboard radiator. Very few were made.   GNG

1952 LAMBERT(iii) Simplicia 1,100cc sports car. *Lucien Loreille Collection*

1966 LAMBORGHINI 400 GT coupé. *Automobili F. Lamborghini sas*

1966 LAMBORGHINI Miura P.400 coupé. *Automobili F. Lamborghini sas*

1938 LAMMAS-GRAHAM 3.7-litre drophead coupé. *G.N. Georgano*

1909 LANCHESTER 28hp tourer. *Francis Hutton-Stott*

1913 LANCHESTER 38hp limousine. *Keith Marvin Collection*

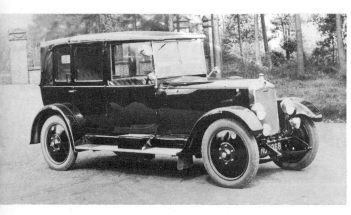

1923 LANCHESTER 21hp landaulette. *The Daimler Co Ltd*

1929 LANCHESTER 30hp straight-8 saloon. *Francis Hutton-Stott*

LA NATIONALE (F) *1899*
Sté La Nationale, Paris

This car was powered by a front-mounted 4hp V-twin engine geared to a counter shaft, with belt drive to the rear axle. The engine was designed to run on petrol or paraffin.
GN

LANCAMOBILE (US) *1899–1901*
James H. Lancaster Co, New York City, N.Y.

The Lancamobile was a light tiller-steered car with engine under the seat, and chain drive. It had a *vis-à-vis* body.
GN

LANCASTER (GB) *1902–1903*
E.H. Lancaster & Co Ltd, Sunderland, Co Durham

The Lancaster was one of many imported cars with a Lacoste et Battmann chassis and 6 or 8hp De Dion engine. Most cars used shaft drive, but a few were sold with chain drive.
GN

LANCHESTER (GB) *1895–1956*
(1) Lanchester Engine Co Ltd, Birmingham *1895–1904*
(2) Lanchester Motor Co, Birmingham *1904–1931;* Coventry *1931–1956*

The first Lanchester was remarkable in that, like the first Benz, it was designed from the ground up as a motor car, not as an adaptation of the horse carriage and in that it was a homogenous mechanical entity, owing nothing to the practice of the stationary engine and its power transmission. In the latter respect, the Lanchester was unique: the power unit and belt transmission of the Benz were derived from stationary practice. Frederick Lanchester's prototype was built in 1895 and improved upon two years later. Production models followed in 1900. The engine, centrally mounted, was horizontally-opposed, air-cooled, 10hp twin; each piston and cylinder had its own crankshaft and flywheel assembly, which rotated in opposite directions. Smoothness unparalleled in other contemporary cars resulted. By the standards of the day the engine was quiet. Epicyclic gears provided three forward speeds, with preselector control of the first and second. Engine and gearbox had automatic lubrication. There was worm final drive. In accordance with the best modern practice, the suspension, by cantilever springs at front and rear, was soft while the unit construction of the chassis and body provided great stiffness. The steering was by a side lever which, like the wick carburettor, was apparently old-fashioned but was in practice extremely efficient. Water-cooled engines were offered as an option from 1902, and bigger, faster models were made in 1904. However, in that year the first model with a vertical 4-cylinder engine was introduced, the 20hp, and the twins tailed off. The engine was moved forward to a position between the front-seat passengers, and it was given horizontal ohv's and pressure lubrication. A 28hp six arrived in 1906. This and the 20hp four were replaced respectively by the 38hp for 1911 and the 25hp for 1912. On the original Lanchesters, gearchanging and braking were effected by two levers, the only pedal being for the accelerator. By now, however, convention had demanded the substitution not only of a steering wheel, but also of the usual three pedals and gear lever, except that, of course, the epicyclic gears still enabled changes to be made without trouble or fuss. By 1912, Frederick's brother George was in charge. Although Frederick's design had gained a large and devoted following for the make, the public trend was increasingly towards convention, and George Lanchester's cars were to follow it.

George Lanchester was responsible for the Sporting Forty of 1914. Although only a handful were made, this car was a landmark because it was the first Lanchester to have its engine in the conventional position, covered by a bonnet. (It was also the only Lanchester to be called a sports car, and to have an sv engine.) From it was developed the Forty, which was at first the sole model offered. Its six cylinder, 6.2-litre engine was made in unit with its 3-speed epicyclic gearbox and had an ohc. The springs, half-elliptic at the front and cantilever at the rear, were underslung. Worm final drive was retained. This was a very fast, very expensive car in the Rolls-Royce class, and its makers felt bound to widen their net. Late in 1923 there appeared the Twenty-One, which was a scaled-down, simplified, modernized Forty. Its 6-cylinder engine was of 3.1 litres, it had a 4-speed sliding-pinion gearbox, and front wheel brakes were standard. In 1926 the bore was enlarged to provide 3.3-litres. In this form the car was sometimes known as the Twenty-Three. Alongside it, the Forty (with front wheel brakes from 1925) continued until 1929. It was replaced in that year by the Thirty, which was an up-to-date design with a straight-8 engine of 4½ litres, still with ohc, and a normal 4-speed gearbox. Like the Forty, it was a massive and magnificent car ideal for high-speed cruising. The Twenty-Three was dropped in 1931, when the B.S.A. group of companies, in which Daimler already provided a line of luxury cars, took over, although the Thirty was still catalogued in 1932. From now on, the name of Lanchester was applied to a line of much cheaper, smaller cars, beginning with the 15/18hp. This had a 2½-litre, push-rod ohv, 6-cylinder engine designed by George Lanchester, hydraulic brakes, and the Daimler fluid flywheel. It was a good car in its class, but like most Lanchesters to come, lost its character as the Eighteen, with fixed cylinder head and mechanical brakes, and became a cut-price Daimler. The group complicated matters further by introducing a 4-cylinder 10hp Lanchester as a more expensive version of e contemporary sv B.S.A.s. It had a 1.2-litre and then a 1.4-litre ohv engine. robably the best of the Lanchesters at this period was the Roadrider de Luxe 14hp f 1938, a small six with a detachable cylinder head and ifs. A few straight-8 Lanhesters were made from 1936 to 1939, but these were in fact 4½-litre Daimlers ith Lanchester radiators. Four were supplied to King George VI.

The first postwar Lanchester was a 4-cylinder ten of 1.3 litres on pre-1939 lines, ut with ifs, like all Lanchesters to come. It was replaced for 1952 by a new Fourteen, ith 2-litre, 4-cylinder engine and fluid flywheel. This car was basically a Daimler Conquest with two fewer cylinders and was the last Lanchester to qualify as a serious roduction car. In 1953–4, a handful of Dauphins were made. This was a true luxury ar, consisting of a 6-cylinder Daimler engine in a Fourteen chassis, surmounted y a luxurious coachbuilt body by Hooper; price was an unrealistic £4,010. Finally, ate 1954, Lanchester produced a completely new and original design, which was lso their last – the Sprite. The engine was an ohv, 4-cylinder unit of 1.6 litres; here was ifs, the brakes were hydraulic, but the Sprite incorporated unitary onstruction of body and chassis, and fully automatic Hobbs transmission instead f the fluid flywheel. The Sprite was never put into production, and the once-great nd always respected name of Lanchester died. TRN

ANCIA (I) *1906 to date*
abbrica Automobili Lancia e Cia, Turin 1906 to date

Vincenzo Lancia, the son of a wealthy soup manufacturer, was apprenticed to Ceirano in 1898 and went on to F.I.A.T. as chief inspector when that company ook over the Ceirano factory in 1899. In July 1900 he drove in his first race t Padua. Thereafter he was a member of the F.I.A.T. team until 1908, making he running in the 1905 Gordon Bennett Cup and taking 2nd place in the 1906 Vanderbilt Cup and the 1907 Targa Florio; but in 1906 he formed his own company. Production of the first Lancias was halted by fire at the factory in February 907, but during the year the Alfa (Greek letters were to be used as type designations ntil 1929) appeared as a 2½-litre 4-cylinder shaft-driven car with side valves in n L-head, a 4-speed gearbox and three-quarter elliptic rear suspension. A chassis ost £400 in England. In 1908 there was a companion 3.8-litre 6-cylinder, the Di-Alfa, of which only 23 were made: Lancia was not to produce another six or 42 years. Surprisingly enough, he did not race his cars, though Hilliard's Lancia von the 1908 Savannah race in America and two years later Billy Knipper won he Tiedeman Trophy on the same circuit. These circumstances led to the introduction of a near-Lancia, the S.G.V., to the American market in 1911: it was sponored by C.V. Tangeman, the former F.I.A.T. concessionaire in New York. Monobloc-engined Lancias made their début in 1909 with the 3.1-litre Beta, while capacity ncreased to 3.5 litres with the Gamma of 1910 and to 4.1 litres with the Delta of 1911, which had its water pump mounted in one of the engine brackets. There vas also a 2.6-litre 15hp model with a 4-speed rear-axle-mounted gearbox. Electric ighting was available on the 4.1-litre Eta at £757 in 1913. A year later full electrics claimed to be the first standardized installation by a European manufacturer) came on the 4.9-litre Theta: the use of foot operation for the starter together with a cut-out gave it five pedals, but in other respects it followed regular Lancia practice with its 4 forward speeds and a dry multi-disc clutch. From 1911 the cars had 4-spoke steering wheels, and also the symbolic emblem of a lance, designed by Count Carlo Biscaretti di Ruffia. During the World War 1 years, Theta derivatives served the Allied armed forces.

After the war came the Kappa, an improved 90bhp development of the Theta with detachable head, but the shape of things to come was visible in an abortive 12-cylinder ohc 6-litre car which appeared at the 1919 Shows, though it proved uneconomic to produce. The use of a very narrow-angle V of 22° made a monobloc casting possible. Though the Kappa gave place to the ohv Dikappa and to a 4.6-litre ohc V-8, the Trikappa with conventional chassis, Vincenzo Lancia's revolutionary Lambda was running in 1921, on show in 1922 and in full production by 1923. This used once again a very narrow-angle V-type engine and overhead camshaft (though this time with only 4 cylinders) which gave plenty of room for bodywork. Unitary construction was used for the standard torpedo body style, this being available with a detachable hard top. The cars had independent front suspension of vertical-coil type, found on all Lancias until 1956 and persisting in the range until 1963. Alloy blocks, pump cooling, fullpressure lubrication, vacuum feed and 4-wheel brakes were also featured. 13,000 of these, in nine series, were sold up to 1931. Capacity went up to 2.4 litres in 1926 with the Seventh Series and again to 2.6 litres and 69bhp with the Eighth in 1928/29. 4-speed gearboxes were standardized on the 5th Series (1925). Separate chassis became an option on the 7th Series, being standardized on the 8th and 9th: this last series had coil ignition. Separate chassis have always been available as an option on subsequent chassisless Lancias. Though looked upon as a sports car in export markets by virtue of its superior handling, the Lambda was never intended as such, and the later 'long' cars (11ft 2⅞in wheelbase) made excellent taxicabs.

From 1929 Lancia marketed a series of ohc cars with separate chassis and hypoid final drive, of which the first was the Dilambda with a narrow-angle ohc V-8 engine, electrically-welded frame, centralized chassis lubrication, fuel feed by twin electric pumps and (on later models) servo brakes. Nearly 1,700 were made up to 1932. An 11ft 5in wheelbase was available for formal coachwork and a saloon cost £1,295 in England.

1938 LANCHESTER 14hp Roadrider de Luxe Wentworth drophead coupé. *Francis Hutton-Stott*

1954 LANCHESTER Dauphin 2½-litre saloon. *Francis Hutton-Stott*

1911 LANCIA Eta 4.1-litre limousine. *Lancia & Cia*

1924 LANCIA Lambda 2nd Series 2.1-litre sedanca de ville. *Lancia & Cia*

417

1930 LANCIA Dilambda 4-litre tourer.
Lancia & Cia

1935 LANCIA Astura 3rd Series 3-litre saloon.
Lancia & Cia

1948 LANCIA Aprilia 1½-litre saloon. *Museo
dell'Automobile, Turin*

1951 LANCIA Aurelia B.20 2½-litre coupé.
Lancia & Cia

To replace the Lambda in 1931 came two variations on this theme, the model 1.9-litre 54bhp Artena, and the Astura, a small, 2.6-litre 73bhp V-8 with silent 3rd gearbox, which had grown up by 1934 to 3 litres with servo brakes. By 1939 it had acquired hydraulic actuation for these, had attracted some very elegant bodies from specialist coachbuilders and was the recognized transport for dignitaries of Mussolini's Italy. A return to unit construction came with the little 1.2-litre Augusta late in 1932: this was the usual ohc V-4 with hypoid rear axle, but hydraulic brakes were standard and its roadholding abilities compensated for a 65mph top speed and uninspired looks. From 1933 to 1937 the Augusta was made in a French factory at Bonneuil, under the name Belna. Bodies were by French coach builders including Paul Née and Pourtout. In 1937 came Vincenzo Lancia's last creation (he died that year), the 1,352cc Aprilia, which carried the Augusta formula one step further, with independent torsion-bar rear suspension, a well-streamlined saloon body, low weight (1,804lb) and engine output increased from 35 to 47bhp. No synchromesh was provided, but with a top speed of over 80mph and a fuel consumption of 30mpg it became the exemplar of European light-car design. Capacity went up to 1½ litres in 1939. The last Aprilia was made ten years later. Just before World War 2 came the 903cc Ardea, a miniature 29bhp version of the Aprilia with semi-elliptic rear suspension. Ten years later it was given a 5-speed gearbox.

The first entirely new Lancia since the founder's death appeared in 1950. The Aurelia, the work of Vittorio Jano (late of Alfa-Romeo) and Gianni Lancia, retained the hull, suspension and basic styling of earlier Lancias, but overhead camshafts had given way to a 1754cc, 56bhp push-rod V-6, and the top 3 ratios of the back-axle gearbox were synchronized. 1951 cars were available with an optional 70bhp 2-litre engine and that year the first of the classic short-chassis GT coupé versions also appeared, with 2 litres and 80bhp. This car collected both 2nd place in the Mille Miglia and a class win at Le Mans. A 3rd in the Mille Miglia and a 1-2-3 victory in the Targa Florio followed in 1953. Rally wins recorded by later GT Aurelias included the Liège-Rome-Liège (1953), the Monte Carlo (1954) and the Acropolis as late as 1958. In 1953 touring versions were available with 90bhp engines and there was also a seven-seater saloon, the B15, on a 10ft 8in wheelbase, not to mention a 2½-litre 118bhp GT, which had acquired a De Dion rear axle by the end of the year. Steering-column change was standard on all coupés to the end of production in 1959, only the open Spyders coming with factory-fitted floor change. Meanwhile in 1953 the Ardea had given place to the 1100cc Appia, a scaled-down Aurelia with a 38bhp engine. Its cylinder block was only 9½in long, a 2-bearing crankshaft being unusual with a 4-cylinder unit by this time. Though the Appia could exceed 75mph, it was hardly competitive (at the equivalent of £780) with F.I.A.T.'s equally new 1100-103 at £572. Encouraged by the success of the GT Aurelias, Lancia built some ohc sports-racing versions which evolved into the 3.3-litre D24. Results were encouraging, a failure at Le Mans being balanced by a 3rd in the Targa Florio and a 1-2-3 victory in the Carrera Panamericana (1953), and wins in both the Targa Florio and the Mille Miglia in 1954. Less successful were the Jano-designed 2.5-litre D50s for Formula 1. These had 4-ohc oversquare V-8 engines, space frames, double wishbone independent front suspension and 5-speed gearboxes mounted at the side of the differentials; their best performance was a 2nd place at Pau in 1955 and after Alberto Ascari was killed the whole operation was disposed of to Ferrari. At the same time the Lancia family lost control of the company.

Good seller though the Aurelia was, Lancia were no longer competitive with Fiat or the state-subsidized Alfa-Romeo factory, and their 1958 sales were 8,794 to Fiat's 169,532. 1956 had brought a revolution in the form of the Flaminia, still a 2.5-litre V-6 with rear-axle gearbox and hypoid final drive, but incorporating not only a revised form of unitary construction but also coil-and-wishbone independent front suspension. The 6-light saloon bodywork derived from the Aurelia-based Florida exhibited by Pininfarina at Turin in 1955. Standard engines gave 98bhp, but by 1958 there were short-chassis GT versions with 125bhp and disc brakes were fitted on all Flaminias. Capacity again went up to 2.8 litres in 1964, when the 3C sports coupé had 152bhp. Even more revolutionary was the Flavia of 1961, which was the work of Dr Fessia, designer both of the pre-war Fiat Topolino and of the C.E.M.S.A.-Caproni, from which both its fwd layout and ohv flat-4 engine were derived. Disc brakes, a 4-speed all-synchromesh gearbox and semi-elliptic rear suspension also featured in the specification, and a 92bhp GT coupé model was available in 1962. 1700cc bored-out versions were already being offered by Nardi and in 1963 Lancia themselves offered an alternative 1.8-litre unit. In 1964 the long-established Appia gave way to the Fulvia, which had much in common with the Flavia, though there was a reversion to an 1100cc V-4 engine. Sports versions developed 71bhp and 106mph was claimed from the Fulvia GT. The 1967 Lancia Programme included standard and sporting models of the Fulvia, Flavia and Flaminia, with Kügelfischer fuel injection available on the Flavia. There was continuing support for GT racing and rallies, the works team's record in the latter field including two successive wins for Källström and Häggbom (1969 and 1970) in the R.A.C. Rally, and victories in the 1972 Monte Carlo and Moroccan events. A car specially designed for rallies was the Stratos HF coupé, powered by a mid-mounted Fiat 132 or Dino engine. A small production run of these was built in 1973. The Flaminia was not offered after 1970, but 1969 brought a 1,991cc version of the Flavia coupé with 131bhp and dual-circuit servo-assisted disc brakes. This was followed in 1971 by a 5-speed saloon model using a miniature replica of the old Lancia grille. The 2-litre engine was standardized in all 1972 Flavias. Fulvias were available with 1.3-litre and 1.6-litre units, outputs ranging from 85 to 114bhp.

Lancia – a firm which has the reputation of never having made a bad car – made a remarkable recovery in the early 1960s, and built 40,000 cars in 1966, but mounting debts forced them to sell out to Fiat in November 1969.

The first signs of integration appeared in the new Beta model at the end of 1972. This fwd saloon was available with dohc 4-cylinder Fiat engines of 1.4, 1.6 or 1.8 litres, and LX versions had automatic headlamp beam levellings. MCS

LANDA (E) *1916–1927*
(1) Talleres Landaluce, Estrecho, Madrid *1916–1922*
(2) Sociedad Española de Automobiles Landa, Madrid *1923–1927*

The founder of the company, Juan Landaluce, was a very talented engineer who designed an unconventional 2-stroke engine which ran, not on a mixture of petrol and oil, but on petrol alone. The first Landa cars used a 2-cylinder engine of this design, giving 17bhp, but in 1919 a larger 2-cylinder 90 × 90mm 20bhp engine was introduced, followed in 1920 by a 4-cylinder unit, also 90 × 90mm, giving 34bhp. With these cars Landa won a number of races, including the Subida Cuesta Leones (class victory).

In 1922 company policy changed and large American-type 6-cylinder cars of entirely conventional design were introduced. Far more of these, some 400, were made than of the 2-stroke cars, and some survived as hearses in Madrid until the mid-1960s. JRV

LANDAR (GB) *1965 to date*
Landar Components Ltd, Birmingham 7

Designed and built by the Radnall brothers, a multi-tubular space frame, with stressed side panels, formed the basis of this sleek sports-racing car. Front suspension was by coil/damper units; at the rear were suspension rubbers and a tuned engine of B.M.C. Mini origin. Its overall height was 2ft 6in. A few space-framed Formula Vee machines, the R3 and R4, were built from 1967 onwards for Smithfield Garages Ltd. By September 1972, 35 of the transverse-engined Mini-based cars had been sold, 26 of them exported. Most were the R6 and R7 models, successful in their classes in hill-climbs as well as circuit racing to International Group 6 and S.C.C.A. formulas. The R5 and R8 were one-offs with rear-mounted Ford engines, built in 1967 and 1972 respectively. DF

L. & E. (US) *1922–1931*
Lundelius & Eccleston, Los Angeles, Calif.

Although the L. & E. was announced as early as 1922, the first car may not have appeared before 1924 when a 'car without axles' was built. The prototype (or prototypes) was a touring car, weighing 2,750lb. Power was supplied by a 6-cylinder air-cooled engine. A large factory was planned in Long Beach but this never materialized. Several subsequent experimental L. & E. cars were built after 1924. The 1932 model was announced in October 1931 and proved to be a handsome wire-wheeled sedan, somewhat resembling a Franklin of the period. The car had four transverse springs at both front and rear to support the wheels, each rear wheel being driven by a short shaft with two universal joints, the shaft connecting with a bevel gear and the differential unit hung from cross members on the frame. KM

LANDGREBE (D) *1921–1924*
C.O. Landgrebe, Dresden

The Landgrebe was a 3-wheeler looking like a Phänomobil. The engine was mounted above the front wheel and transmission was by cardan shaft. Two- and four-seater versions were available. HON

LANDINI (I) *1919*
Signor Landini was a flying instructor at Cameri, near Novara, who built a cyclecar steered by the feet, with a rudder bar replacing the steering wheel. Gear change and accelerator were controlled by moving the knees sideways, and power came from an 8hp Stucchi V-twin engine mounted on the offside running board, and driving the rear wheels by 2-speed gear and chain. The first Landinis had tandem seating for two, but later models had four seats and conventional wheel steering. It was intended to mass produce these cars at Cameri, but nothing came of the project. GNG

LANDRY ET BEYROUX *see M.L.B.*

LANE (US) *1899–1910*
Lane Motor Vehicle Co, Poughkeepsie, N.Y.

The first Lane, Model No. 1, was a four-seater with a 2-cylinder steam engine under the body. These cars grew larger, with boilers under front bonnets, although all used 2-cylinder engines, later of compound type, up to 30hp and operating at 350psi. The last and largest model was on a 10ft 5in wheelbase. A total of 22 different models were built during the company's manufacturing life. GMN

1963 LANCIA Flavia 1.8-litre coupé. Coachwork by Zagato. *Lancia & Cia*

1967 LANCIA Fulvia 1.1-litre saloon. *Lancia & Cia*

1973 LANCIA Beta saloon. *Lancia & Cia*

1909 LANE 30hp steam tourer. *Keith Marvin Collection*

1901 LA NEF 8hp 3-wheel tonneau. *Musée de l'Automobile, Rochetaillée-sur-Saone*

1926 LA PERLE 1½-litre 6-cylinder racing car, as raced in 1930. *Autosport*

1911 LA PONETTE 7hp two-seater. *Autocar*

LA NEF (F) 1901–1903
Lacroix et de Laville, Agen, Lot-et-Garonne

Sometimes known as the Lacroix-de Laville, this was a curious front-engined 3-wheeler with tiller steering and final drive by side belts of immense length. Single-cylinder De Dion engines were used. Although the dates of manufacture are believed to be correct, one of the surviving Nefs is fitted with a 1908 engine! Production figures are not known, but at least three other La Nefs survive today.　　　MCS

LANPHER (US) 1909–1912
Lanpher Motor Buggy Co, Carthage, Mo.

The Lanpher two-seater was a high-wheeler with an air-cooled 2-cylinder engine, solid rubber tyres, planetary transmission and double chain drive. It sold for $550.　　　GMN

LANSDEN (US) 1906–1908
Lansden Co, Newark, N.J.

This electric car, which was also known as the Electrette, had a peculiar elongated bonnet which housed the batteries. The two-seater roadster was powered by a 3½hp motor and weighed 1,950lb. Instruments were limited to a clock and odometer. It had an early example of left-hand steering by wheel.　　　GMN

LANZA (I) 1895–1903
(1) Sta Automobili Michele Lanza, Turin 1895–1898
(2) Fabb. Automobili Lanza, Turin 1898–1903

Michele Lanza owned a candle factory, but his interest in mechanics led him to build a car which was the first petrol-engined 4-wheeler to be made entirely in Italy. It had a rear-mounted 2-cylinder horizontal engine with hot-tube ignition, 3 forward speeds (no reverse) and chain drive. It had a vertical steering column with two handles, iron tyres on which the brakes operated, and a wagonette body. From 1895 to 1903 Lanza built a dozen cars, each varying from the other in some detail.　　　AZ

LA PERLE (F) 1913–1927
Louis Lefevre, Boulogne-sur-Seine

The pre-war La Perle was a belt-driven 2-cylinder cyclecar, but the marque did not become established until the early 1920s, when a light car with a 4-cylinder 1.4-litre Bignan engine was made. This car was entered in a number of races, including the 1921 Coupe des Voiturettes where a team of three competed, and the Boulogne Races where a La Perle won its class. For 1922 a Causan-designed ohv engine with capacity increased to 1½ litres was introduced, and in 1924 Causan produced a 1½-litre 6-cylinder engine with shaft-driven single overhead camshaft which developed over 60bhp. A road-going two-seater was capable of 85mph with this engine, and a supercharged racing car reached 105mph. About 300 of the 4-cylinder La Perles were made, and 75 sixes.　　　GNG

LA PETITE (US) 1905
Detroit Automobile Mfg Co, Detroit, Ill.

This two-seater car, designed by J.P. La Vigne (also known for the J.P.L.) had a single-cylinder air-cooled engine in front of the dash. The transmission had 2 forward speeds, and final drive was by shaft.　　　GMN

LA PONETTE (F) 1909–1925
Sté des Automobiles La Ponette, Chevreuse, Seine-et-Oise

The original La Ponette was a light two-seater using a 7hp single-cylinder engine of 827cc, a 2-speed epicyclic gear, and shaft drive. It had a dashboard radiator, and a very light doorless two-seater body. Single cylinder cars were made up to 1912, when a 4-cylinder Ballot 1460cc engine was introduced, and the following year the singles were discontinued. The singles were said to have been designed by an Englishman, John Averies, who afterwards made the Averies cyclecar. Post-war La Ponettes were thoroughly conventional, and used 4-cylinder engines by Ballot and S.C.A.P., as well as their own make, from 1.7 to 2.8 litres' capacity.　　　GNG

LA RAPIDE (GB) 1920
La Rapide Cyclecar Co, London S.W.

Despite its name, there is nothing to suggest that the La Rapide was anything but British. The engine, an 8hp air-cooled J.A.P., was unusually disposed, being bolted outside the body on the offside on two extended cross-members. Transmission was by primary chain to a Sturmey Archer 3-speed gearbox and thence by belt to the offside wheel only.　　　MJWW

L'ARDENNAISE (F) 1901
H. Lessieux et Cie, Rethel, Ardennes

This was a light car using a 5hp single-cylinder engine and shaft drive. The engine could be adapted to run on alcohol as well as petrol (a feature of a number of cars made in North Eastern France), and two- or four-seater bodies were available.　　　GNG

LARMAR (GB) *1946–1951*

Larmar Engineering Co Ltd, Ingatestone, Essex

The Larmar was designed for use by invalids, but took the conception of such vehicles far beyond the crude motorized bath-chairs which invalids had previously had to put up with. It was a proper 4-wheeled car with a collapsible hood, and used a 250cc single-cylinder engine mounted at the rear, driving by single chain to the nearside wheel. Cruising speed was 30 to 35mph, and the price (free of purchase tax) was £198. GNG

LAROS (I) *1932*

S.A. Fratelli Pellegatti, Milan

This was a small 4-cylinder car similar to the Fiat Balilla which a firm of outboard motor manufacturers planned to make. Prototypes were built, and production was planned to start in the spring of 1932, but Fiat bought up the designs to prevent competition. GNG

LA ROULETTE (F) *1912–1913*

Cyclecars La Roulette, Courbevoie, Seine

This cyclecar had an 8/10hp V-twin water-cooled engine, a tandem two-seater body, and final drive by double belts. One competed in the 1913 Cyclecar Grand Prix. GNG

LA SALLE (US) *1927–1940*

Cadillac Motor Car Co, Detroit, Mich.

Launched as a smaller and less expensive running-mate for the Cadillac, the La Salle was conceived in its entirety by General Motors' stylist Harley J. Earl – a very unusual practice for the period. Unlike other makers' 'cheap lines', it was manufactured to Cadillac standards throughout, though its wheelbase was 7in shorter and at $2,495 a sedan was about $700 cheaper. The engine was an sv V-8 of 5 litres' capacity. Synchromesh, safety glass and chromium plating were innovations shared with Cadillac in 1929 and the car grew steadily in size: first to 5.4 litres, then to 5.6 litres, with a further increase to 5.8 litres in 1930. The whole concept was changed in 1934 – though the La Salle was the guinea-pig for the turret-top steel bodies to be used in 1935 by all G.M. divisions save Buick, the car was cheapened in other respects, having a 4.2-litre straight-8 engine as used in the bigger Oldsmobiles. Its price was $1,595 (£725 in England). A reversion was made to the traditional V-8 in 1937, the cars sharing body shells with Oldsmobile and the more expensive Buicks, and the price was cut again to $1,205. The La Salle was squeezed out of the market by the lower list prices of the simpler Cadillac models. The 1940 cars were as good as their predecessors but at $1,446 as against $1,752 for a Cadillac, there was no longer room for the marque. MCS

LA SIRÈNE (F) *1900–1902*

(1) Fernandez et Cie, Paris 2e

(2) Cie 'La Sirène', Paris 2e

Known in 1900 as the Fernandez, La Sirène was a light car powered by a 5hp V-twin engine, with shaft drive. Two Sirène ran in the 1901 Paris-Berlin race, in which they were listed at 24hp. They were apparently not very different from the production cars, and *The Autocar* said 'how the 24hp is calculated is not known'. GNG

LA TORPILLE (i) (F) *1907–1923*

Léonce et Camille Bobrie, Saumur, Maine-et-Loire

The Bobrie brothers built a small number of tandem two-seater cyclecars powered by 6 or 8hp 4-cylinder Ballot engines. A few post-war cars had side-by-side seating, and the last two Torpilles used the 6/8hp Fivet engine. About 25 cars were made in all. GNG

LA TORPILLE (ii) (F) *1912–1913*

Perrin et Cie, Annonay, Ardèche

This was a tandem-seated 3-wheeler with a remarkably long body. The engine could be a single or a 4-cylinder unit. A conventional sliding gearbox was used, and chain final drive. The car had a sloping bonnet and dashboard radiator. GNG

LA TROTTEUSE (F) *1913–1914*

St Rémy, Seine-et-Oise

This was a light car made in two models, a single-cylinder 640cc, and a 4-cylinder 1327cc. Both cars had shaft drive, and were sold in two-seater form. GNG

LAUER (D) *1922*

Automobilwerk Lauer GmbH, Merseburg

A small 4-cylinder 5/15PS car which was built only in limited numbers. HON

LAUNCESTON (GB) *1920*

Launceston Engineering Co Ltd, Willesden Junction, London N.W.

The Launceston was a typical assembled car of the period, and very few were built. The four-seater touring 12/20hp model sold for £330 and displayed clean lines enhanced by Michelin disc wheels. MJWW

1930 LA SALLE 5-litre all-weather tourer. *General Motors Corporation*

1937 LA SALLE Model 37-50 5.3-litre sedan. *G.N. Georgano*

1940 LA SALLE Model 52 5.3-litre sedan. *Arthur Rippey*

1906 LAURIN-KLEMENT 1-litre two-seater.
Národni Technické Museum, Prague

1924 LAURIN-KLEMENT Type 450 4.9-litre
saloon. *Ing Adolf Babuška*

1903 L'AUTOMOTRICE 12hp spyder. *The
Veteran Car Club of Great Britain*

LAUREL (US) 1916–1920
Laurel Motors Corp, Anderson, Ind.

The Laurel was an assembled car with a G.B. & S. 4-cylinder engine, sold in two models, a four-seater roadster and five-seater touring car, both priced at $895. A distinguishing mark was the small script carrying the car's name on the sides of the bonnet above the louvres. KM

LAURENCE-JACKSON (GB) 1920
Laurence-Jackson Ltd, Wolverhampton, Staffs.

The Laurence-Jackson light car used an 8/10hp V-twin J.A.P. engine, friction transmission and final drive by single chain. The two-seater with disc wheels cost £295. GNG

LAURENT (i) (F) 1901
Laurent et Cie, Vierzon, Cher

The Laurent was a light voiturette powered by a 5hp 2-cylinder engine. A 4-speed constant-mesh gearbox was used, and final drive was by propeller shaft. GNG

LAURENT (ii) (F) 1907–1908
Laurent et Cie, St Etienne, Loire

This firm made a number of steam lorries, and were reported to have produced a few 4-cylinder petrol-engined cars of medium size. GNG

LAURIN-KLEMENT (A; CS) 1906–1928
Laurin und Klement AG, Prague; Mlada Boleslav; Pilsen (Plzen)

Laurin-Klement of Bohemia had an established reputation as makers of fine motor cycles before they went over to cars in 1906. They concentrated on fast voiturettes, as might be expected with such a background, and achieved at least equal fame in this field. The first Laurin-Klement car was a 6/7hp V-twin with overhead inlet valves and shaft drive. This was supplemented by the 14/16hp small four in 1908 and the more modern, monobloc 10/12hp a year later. There was even a straight-8, type FF, in 1907. These little cars gained a first-class sporting reputation in central and eastern Europe, thanks to the competitive instincts of Count Alexander Kolowrat, their backer. From 1912, however, the twin was dropped, and a range of heavier touring cars with 2.6-litre, 2.9-litre, and 3.8-litre engines superseded the light, lively Laurin-Klements of earlier days. Amalgamation with R.A.F. in 1913 resulted in a pair of Knight-engined models, the 3.3-litre 'MK', and the 4.7-litre 'RK', and a sv light car with 1.2-litre engine reappeared in the range. In the period after World War 1, when Bohemia had become part of the independent state of Czechoslovakia, big fours were made, two of them with Knight engines. There was also a 5-litre sleeve-valve six with fwb by 1924. Karl Loevenstein's armaments firm, Skodovy Zavody, took over in 1925, and although Laurin-Klements continued to be made, the new owners concentrated on cars under the name of Skoda. TRN

LAUTH-JUERGENS (US) 1907–1910
(1) Lauth-Juergens Co, Chicago, Ill. 1907–1910
(2) Lauth-Juergens Motor Car Co, Fremont, Ohio 1910

This car started a demonstration model by J. Lauth & Co, Chicago, in 1905. Limited production of a five-seater 'tourist' model began in 1907. It had a 4-cylinder, 40hp engine. After 1910, the make continued as a commercial vehicle. GMN

L'AUTOMOTRICE (F) 1901–1907
(1) Sté l'Automobile, Bergerac, Dordogne 1901–1903
(2) Sté l'Automotrice, Bergerac, Dordogne 1904–1907

The first car produced by the Societé l'Automobile was a voiturette powered by a 5hp Aster engine, with single chain drive. By 1904 the name was changed to the Societé l'Automotrice, and the cars were large 4-cylinder vehicles with honeycomb radiators and double chain drive. Engine sizes varied from 18/22 to 40/45hp. These cars were alternatively known as Radia from 1904 to 1905, and Baudouin-Radia from 1905 to 1907. GNG

L'AUTOVAPEUR (F) 1905–1906
Sté l'Autovapeur, Paris

The Autovapeur was a steam car using a Serpollet-type horizontal 4-cylinder engine, and a vertical multi-tubular boiler under the bonnet. The general appearance was that of a petrol-engined car. GNG

LA VA BON TRAIN (F) c.1900
Larroumet et Lagarde, Agen, Lot-et-Garonn

This was a two-seater, 3-wheeler voiturette powered by a single-cylinder De Dion engine. In its general layout it was not unlike the La Nef made in the same town, but it used wheel steering whereas the La Nef used a long tiller. One example of the La Va Bon Train survives today. GNG

LA VALKYRIE (F) 1905–1907
Sté Parisienne de Construction Automobile La Valkyrie, Montrouge, Seine

This was a conventional car made in two models, a 10hp 2-cylinder of 1728cc, and a 14/16hp four of 2270cc. Both models used shaft drive. GNG

LA VIGNE see JPL

LA VIOLETTE (F) 1910–1914
Franc et Cie, Levallois-Perret, Seine
Like many light cars of the time, the La Violette used a large single-cylinder engine of 700cc, friction transmission and final drive by a long chain to the nearside rear wheel. Later models (1913) included a 2-cylinder with similar layout, and a conventional 10hp shaft-drive 4-cylinder four-seater. GNG

LAVOIE (CDN) 1923
Lavoie Automobile Devices Ltd, Montreal, Que.
The Lavoie had a 4-cylinder engine of the firm's own design, unitary construction of chassis and body and 4-wheel brakes. Only a pilot model was built, in sedan form, and the public rejected this very advanced vehicle. KM

LAW (US) 1905
Law Automobile Corp, Hartford, Conn.
This car is described as having a 20hp engine and was sold for $2,500. This was a strictly local product and further information is lacking. GMN

LAWIL (I) 1969 to date
Lawil SpA Costruzioni Meccaniche e Automobilistiche, Milan
A Franco-Italian minicar designed for congested streets, the Lawil is powered by a front-mounted 246cc air-cooled 2-stroke vertical twin engine driving the rear wheels via a 4-speed gearbox. Length is 81.5in and the car is made in open and closed two-seater forms. It is sold in Britain under the name William. MCS

LAWSON MOTOR WHEEL see DOUGILL

LAWTER (US) 1909
Lawter Shredder Co, Newcastle, Ind.
One model of the Lawter had solid rubber tyres. Its engine was a horizontal, water-cooled 2-cylinder unit developing 20hp. Final drive was by planetary transmission and shaft. The other model was powered by a 16hp engine. GMN

L.B. (F) 1925
Lucien Borel, Villefranche de Lauraguais, Hte-Garonne
Borel assembled a small number of 2-cylinder cyclecars with front-wheel drive. GNG

LEACH (i) (US) 1899–1901
Leach Motor Vehicle Co, Everett, Mass.
The Leach steam car used a 6hp 2-cylinder vertical engine, single chain drive and tiller steering. With a two-seater body it looked little different from its contemporaries, but the makers did have the honesty to say that it was 'intended only for good roads'. The price was $600. GNG

LEACH (ii) (US) 1920–1923
Leach Motor Car Co, Los Angeles, Calif.
The first Leach used an L-head Continental engine, but the firm was best-known for the Power Plus Six made from 1922 to 1923. This was a 5.7-litre unit with single overhead camshaft that developed 107bhp. These cars were popular with movie stars of the day, although the make sold only in small numbers. Roadsters, touring cars and sedans were manufactured, and the make was among the first to offer the California Top: a fixed top and sliding windows which could be attached to an open touring car. A golf bag was standard equipment on the chummy roadster, and all 1922 models cost $6,500. GNG

LEADER (i) (NL) 1904–1905
Bosch, Zijlstra & Rupp, Arnhem
A small number of these cars were assembled from imported parts, using Aster or De Dion engines. GNG

LEADER (ii) (GB) 1905–1909
(1) Charles Binks Ltd, Apsley, Nottingham 1905–1906
(2) New Leader Cars Ltd, Apsley, Nottingham 1906–1909
Charles Binks had been a bicycle maker since 1901, and ultimately gained far more fame from the Binks carburettor than he did from his cars. The first of these was a conventional 10/12hp two-seater with 4 separately cast cylinders and shaft drive. A 14hp tourer and motor hansom were also made. The New Leader models for 1906 were a 10/20 and a 20/30hp 4-cylinder, and there was also listed a 60hp V-8, but little was heard of it. For 1908 and 1909 a 12/16hp 4-cylinder car was made. GNG

LEADER (iii) (US) 1905–1912
(1) Columbia Electric Co, McCordsville, Ind. 1905–1906

1900 LA VA BON TRAIN 8hp voiturette.
Musée du Château de Grandson

1923 LEACH (ii) Six California Top tourer.
National Motor Museum

1905 LEADER(ii) 10hp two-seater. *G.N.*
Georgano Collection

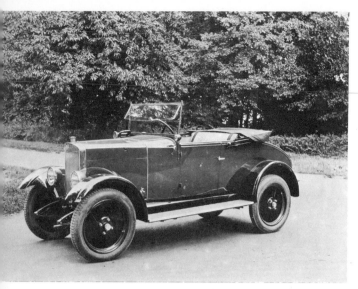

1925 LEA-FRANCIS G-type 10hp two-seater.
National Motor Museum

1929 LEA-FRANCIS V-type 12/40hp coupé.
National Motor Museum

1939 LEA-FRANCIS 12hp sports car.
G.N. Georgano

(2) Leader Mfg Co, Knightstown, Ind. *1906–1912*

Despite the original manufacturer's name, the Leader had an internal-combustion engine. Early models had 2-cylinder units with planetary transmissions and single chain drive. Later models used an F-head, 4-cylinder engine and sliding-gear transmission.   GMN

LEA-FRANCIS (GB) *1904–1906; 1920–1935; 1937–1953; 1960*
(1) Lea & Francis Ltd, Coventry, Warwickshire *1904–1935*
(2) Lea-Francis Cars Ltd, Coventry, Warwickshire *1937–1960*

Lea & Francis started as bicycle manufacturers, like so many car makers, but unlike most of the rest, never went over permanently and consistently to cars. These appeared in fits and starts. The first appeared in 1904, in the shape of a 15hp machine with a 3-cylinder horizontal engine, the oddest feature of which was its connecting rods over 3ft long. In the same year, however, Lea-Francis stopped making their cars, and Singer the Cycle Company began building them under licence and under the Singer name. R.H. Lea had in fact worked for Singer before branching out on his own. Thus began another famous car name. Lea-Francis made motor cycles from 1911, and they concentrated on these until 1920. In that year two cars reappeared beside the motor cycles; assembled 4-cylinder touring machines of 11.9 and 13.9hp. Few of either were made. Then, late in 1922, the company found its feet at last, with an equally conventional assembled light car. It had a 1,074cc 4-cylinder sv engine of 8.9hp by Coventry-Simplex, replaced in the following year by a 10hp Meadows unit of 1¼ litres with overhead valves. A car with 7hp Bradshaw flat-twin engine came to nothing. There were 3 forward speeds and quarter-elliptic springs at both ends. The 10hp was very popular, and was made until 1928. Like other Lea-Francises to come, it was well made, dependable, and lively. Its great moment came in the very important R.A.C. Small Car Trials of 1924, in which it made the best all-round performance. During 1925 a wider family market was sought with the 12/22hp J-type. This model had a longer wheelbase, allowing more spacious bodies, front-wheel brakes, a 1½-litre 4EC Meadows engine to cope with the weight and a 4-speed gearbox. For the sake of comfort, semi-elliptic springs were substituted at the rear on the P-type introduced for 1928, which also had a plate clutch and 4ED meadows engine.

The firm's first serious sports car was the L-type with 4ED engine, announced for 1925. The 12/40hp was one of the best assembled cars in Britain, and appealed more widely than the light cars. It was, indeed, current until the second cessation of car production in 1935. However, Lea-Francis also made some more ponderous, less lively cars, without the same degree of success. From 1925 until 1929, the Lea-Francis range duplicated some of the heavy 6-cylinder machines offered by Vulcan of Southport, with whom Lea-Francis had been associated since 1922. The 18hp was a 2½-litre car with cantilever rear springs and overhead worm drive. It was succeeded by A.O. Lord's Type T, with its advanced but unreliable LFS-type, double ohc engine of 1.7 litres. There was also, in 1928, a 2-litre six. These Vulcan/Lea-Francis cars ended with the demise of the Vulcan. However, an excellent Lea-Francis six was at last introduced for 1931: the Ace of Spades model, with their own 2-litre, single ohc engine. It continued alongside the old 12/40hp until 1935, together with a new 18hp car, which was a 2¼-litre enlargement of the Ace of Spades. However, a really powerful machine was also listed from 1928. This Hyper Sports was a quite different car, with its heavily-modified, Cozette-supercharged Meadows 1½-litre engine, low build and raked radiator. The sports-racing two-seater could attain 90mph, though a coupé and a short open tourer could also be had by those who did not intend to enter competitions. The Hyper Sports won the 1928 Ulster Trophy race.

A new company introduced two entirely new cars for 1938. They were designed by Hugh Rose, who had been responsible for the Riley Nine engine and, like the Riley, had 4-cylinder power units with push-rod overhead valves operated by two high camshafts. The Lea-Francis had ceased to be an entirely assembled car. A 12hp and a 14hp were available, with cubic capacities of 1½ and 1.6 litres. Both had a 4-speed synchromesh gearbox. A sports version of the 1½-litre was also sold, thus maintaining the old tradition. These two 'Leafs' were good cars, and as they were new, up-to-date models, they could be continued after World War 2. Most of those built in this period were Fourteens, which were heavier but had a bigger bore and a capacity of 1.8 litres. A tuned sports model of the 14hp arrived for 1948. At the end of that year, an export version of the 14hp, with torsion-bar independent front suspension, was shown and this suspension was adopted for both the 14hp and for the new 18hp, with a 2½-litre engine, in 1950. The sports model of the 18hp was a fine car, with 100bhp available. The models for 1953 had hydraulic brakes, but that was the last year in which the Lea Francis appeared as a competitive production car. By mid-1952, output had fallen to six cars a week. An expensive car of specialist appeal, the post-war years were too hard for it. In 1960 a few prototypes of a new sports car, the Leaf-Lynx, were made, but it never reached production. The power unit was a 2½-litre Ford Zephyr, there was independent front suspension and disc brakes were supplied, but the car was ill-favoured and ill received. No better luck attended the firm's attempt to make the Noble bubble-car.   TRN

LE BLON (F) *1898–c.1900*
Le Blon Frères, Paris

This was a light car with 4hp V-twin engine and belt drive. Chassis could be supplied 'suitable for any type of body'. Le Blon cars were sold in England under the name Le Lynx. GNG

LE BRUN (F) *1898–c.1900*
Automobiles Le Brun, Montrouge, Seine

The Le Brun was powered by a rear-mounted V-twin engine of Daimler type, of 6, 8, or 10hp. It had 3 speeds, and final drive was by double chain. Steering was by tiller, and the car was available with various bodies typical of the period, including a two-seater Duc and four-seater *vis-à-vis*. GNG

L.E.C. (GB) *1912–1913*
London Engine Co, Phonophore Works, Southall, Middlesex

The L.E.C. was a cyclecar using a 10hp 2-cylinder water-cooled engine and belt drive, and an imitation-Daimler radiator. The Phonophore company who made it were telephone manufacturers. GNG

LE CABRI (F) *1924–1925*
Automobiles Le Cabri, Asnières, Seine

This company made two small 4-cylinder cars, of 5hp and 7hp. The name was also applied to models of Gauthier and Salomon. GNG

LECOY (GB) *1921–1922*
Lambert Engineering Co Ltd, Harrow, Middlesex

The Lecoy light car used an 8hp V-twin J.A.P. engine and friction transmission. Suspension was by coil springs at the front, and cantilever at the rear. It was of very low and light appearance, more like a pre-war cyclecar, and cost £185. GNG

LÉDA (i) (F) *1908*
Thorand, Theim et Cie, Paris

This short-lived company made cars in four models: a single-cylinder 8/9hp, a 2-cylinder 6/9hp, and two 4-cylinder cars, an 8/10hp and a 10/12hp. GNG

LEDA (ii) (GB) *1969–1972*
Malaya Garages Ltd, Billingshurst, Sussex

The LT20 designed by Len Terry was a Formula 5000 monocoque that proved promising in the hands of Trevor Taylor, and also formed the basis for a Hawke model for the same formula. The successful LT27 was developed in 1972 by Tasman champion Graham McRae, who eventually renamed it the McRae GM1 and took over the manufacturing rights.

Malcom Bridgland's Malaya Garages also marketed Allan McCall's Formulas 3 and B design as the Leda-Tui, with plans for Formula Super Vee as well. This design featured a full monocoque up to the seat bulkhead, the engine then forming a fully stressed member. Works driver Bert Hawthorne was killed in the first Formula 2 car, but a second, the BH2 model developed independently by McCall, was raced later by John Watson. DF

LE DAUPHIN (F) *1941–1942*
André L. Dauphin, Paris 3e

The Dauphin was originally made as a pedal-driven tandem two-seater cyclecar, with provision for a 100 or 175cc Zurcher 2-stroke engine for those lucky enough to be able to obtain fuel in occupied France. Later it was supplied with a small electric motor. Steering was from the front seat in the original model, but from the rear in the electric car, in which form it looked remarkably like the Bedelia or Automobilette cyclecars of 30 years earlier. The bodies were made by the distinguished firm of Carosserie Kellner who, in happier times, had clothed such chassis as Delage and Hispano-Suiza. GNG

LEDOUX (CDN) *1914*
Ledoux Carriage Company Ltd, Montreal, Que.

Two conventional touring cars with aluminium bodies, a four and a six, were built to the designs of H.E. Bourassa. They ran well but World War 1 ended production plans. HD

LEEDS (RA) *1960–1964*
Leeds, Industrias Platenses Automotrices, La Plata

This short-lived firm marketed a couple of minicar designs both powered by the 324cc 2-stroke, 2-cylinder Villiers engine. The L4 Microcoupé was a conventional front-engined four-seater with bevel-driven rear wheels, all-round independent suspension, and a concave rear window in the Ford manner, but the Autoneta was an odd device. It was rear-engined, amphibious (a screw supplemented the chain drive), and independently sprung only at the front. The coupé body had gull-wing doors. MCS

LEESDORFER (A) *1898–1900*
Leesdorfer Automobilwerke, Leesdorf nr Baden

These cars were made under Amedée Bollée licence. The chassis were generally imported and completed in Austria. Two models, the Petit Duc and the Grand Duc, using 2-cylinder engines of 6hp and 9hp, were marketed. HON

1947 LEA-FRANCIS 14hp coupé. *National Motor Museum*

1898 LE BRUN phaeton. *Geoffroy de Beauffort Collection*

1941 LE DAUPHIN two-seater electric car. *Lucien Loreille Collection*

1902 LEGROS 12hp tonneau. *The Veteran Car Club of Great Britain*

1936 LEIDART 3.6-litre V-8 sports car. *National Motor Museum*

1903 L'ÉLÉGANTE 6hp voiturette. *G.N. Georgano*

LEFERT (B) *c.1902*
J. Lefert, Ghent

Lefert made a small number of electric cars, three of which were exhibited at the 1902 Brussels Salon. GNG

LEGNANO *see* F.I.A.L.

LEGRAND (i) (F) *1901*

The Legrand was a light car powered by two 3hp De Dion engines mounted under the seat. The two units were geared together, and final drive was by single chain. GNG

LEGRAND (ii) (F) *1913*
Albert Legrand, Paris

This Legrand had a conventional 4-cylinder monobloc engine and 3-speed gearbox, but dispensed with universal joints as the propeller shaft was flexible, being made of coiled wire. The car had a huge undertray which surrounded the whole chassis, and while it kept the transmission clean it must have added considerably to the weight. The Legrand was exhibited at the 1913 Paris Salon, but it is unlikely that it went into production. GNG

LEGROS (F) *1900–1913*
René Legros, Fécamp, Seine-Inférieure

The first legros car had a 4hp single-cylinder air-cooled engine mounted at the front and driving the rear wheels via a propeller shaft. The company also made an electric car, the Meynier-Legros, a heavy-looking vehicle with unequally-sized artillery wheels, and a Panhard-like bonnet under which the batteries were kept. By 1902 there were two petrol cars, with 8hp De Dion or 12hp Aster engines; these cars were known as La Plus Simple, a name which was used for Legros cars up to the end of production.

After 1903 production seems to have lapsed until 1906, when a range of 2-stroke cars was introduced. There were three 2-cylinder and two 4-cylinder models, from a 10/12 twin to a 24/30 four, and the same range was being made when production ceased in 1913. GNG

LE GUI *see* GUY (i)

LEICHTAUTO (D) *1924*
Leichtauto Gesellschaft mbH, Berlin

This was a light car of chassis-less tubular steel construction covered with canvas, powered by D.K.W. or Columbus rear-mounted engines. HON

LEIDART (GB) *1936–1938*
Leidart Cars Ltd, Pontefract, Yorks.

The Leidart was one of the lesser-known Anglo-Americans, and used a Ford V-8 engine and transmission in an English chassis. Bodies were simple open two- and four-seaters, and the car looked like a scaled-up Morgan 4-4. 1938 prices ranged from £400 for the two-seater to £575 for a saloon, although it is not certain that any of the latter were made. This also applies to a small model with a blown Ford 10 engine which was listed at £250. GNG

LEITNER (SU) *c.1911*
Leitner and Co, Riga

The Leitner private car was contemporary with the Russo-Baltique, also produced in Riga. BE

L'ÉLÉGANTE (F) *1903–c.1907*
J. B. Mercier, Paris

L'Elégante cars were very similar to De Dions in general layout and appearance, and most, if not all, used De Dion engines. 1903 models had 4 or 6hp single-cylinder engines, while later cars had engines of 9, 12, and 16hp. GNG

LE MARNE *see* LA MARNE

LE MEHARI (F) *1927*
F. Reynaud, Nouzonville, Ardennes

This was a cyclecar powered by two single-cylinder Train engines with a total capacity of 688cc. Drive was by long rubber belts. A sports model with front-wheel brakes was said to be capable of 60mph. GNG

LE MÉTAIS (F) *1904–1910*
Voiturettes Le Métais, Levallois-Perret, Seine

The Le Métais used mostly single-cylinder engines, of which De Dions were the most popular, although the firm claimed that one 9hp engine was of their own manufacture. The voiturettes also used friction drive, and competed regularly in light car races from 1906 to 1908. From 1907 a number of cars were made with 2- or 4-cylinder Gnome engines. GNG

LEMS (GB) *1903*

London Electromobile Syndicate, London N.W.

This was a very light electric two-seater runabout with tiller steering. Maximum speed was only 12mph, and the range per charge was 40 miles. The company were still advertising in 1905, but probably were only servicing cars by then.   GNG

LENAWEE (US) *1903–1904*

Church Mfg Co, Adrian, Mich.

This small, rear-entrance tonneau had left-hand drive. Its single-cylinder water-cooled engine was mounted under the front seat. Final drive was by shaft, and full-elliptic springs were used. The name Murray was used for earlier cars by this company.   GMN

LENDE (US) *1908–1909*

Lende Automobile Mfg Co, Minneapolis, Minn.

A five-seater car was the single model of the Lende. It was powered by a 4-cylinder, 5.2-litre engine and had a planetary transmission and shaft drive.   GMN

LENHAM (GB) *1968 to date*

Lenham Motor Co, Harrietsham, Kent

The tubular space-framed Lenham P70 GT cars became quite well known on the tracks, and were offered in closed or open form. For 1970, besides a Formula Ford model, three versions of the P80 spyder Group 6 car were offered, the Club model, the 2-litre European Championship version with Ford or B.M.W. engine and the over 2-litre type. Sponsor Roger Hurst developed one of these with a 3-litre Repco engine, and it was entered as the Darnval for the 1972 Le Mans. Later in 1970 a Formula F100 car was made. A separate company was formed which briefly marketed a Mark 2 Formula Ford machine, designed by Peter Coleman, under the name Hamlen before the Lenham-Hurst Racing Organisation took back the project and produced the type T80. This was continued in 1973 in addition to the Group 6 P90 with aluminium monocoque in place of fibreglass construction, and Ford or Tecno engines. One P90 was to be powered by a large Chevrolet engine for Interserie and Can-Am racing.   DF

LENOX (i) (US) *1908–1909*

Maxim & Goodridge, Hartford, Conn.

Also known as the Maxim-Goodridge, this was an electrically-powered car with solid rubber tyres. The batteries, weighing 800lb, were connected with a 3hp motor through a five-speed controller. These cars, mostly open victorias, were graceful in an archaic fashion, and sold for less than $2,000.   GMN

LENOX (ii) (US) *1911–1918*

1) Lenox Motor Car Co, Jamaica Plain, Mass. *1911–1914*

2) Lenox Motor Car Co, Boston, Mass. *1914–1918*

The Lenox was a well-designed car of pleasing appearance which used both 4- and 6-cylinder engines. The largest model was the 1913 six with a 6.2-litre engine. With electric starting, this five-seater cost $2,750. Buda engines were used latterly.   GMN

LENTZ (I) *1906–1908*

Società Italiana Automobili Lentz, Milan

Also sold under the name of Oria, the Lentz was a conventional shaft-driven 4-cylinder car made in 14/16hp and 20/24hp sizes.   MCS

LÉO (i) (F) *1897–1898*

The Léo cars were designed by Léon Lefébvre who later built the Bolide. Like the early Bolides, the Léo had a Pygmée horizontal 2-cylinder engine of 3 or 6hp, and final drive by belts. Two cars were entered in the 1896 Paris-Marseilles-Paris, but did not run.   GNG

LEO (ii) (GB) *1913*

The Leo was a cyclecar with an 8hp J.A.P. V-twin engine. The price was £105. It was sold by Derry & Toms, the London department store.   GNG

LEONARD (GB) *1904–c.1906*

J.J. Leonard & Co, Crofton Park, London S.E.

The Leonard was a light car with a 6hp De Dion engine, and armoured wood frame. In 1904 the company introduced the Medici which used a 10/12hp Tony Huber engine, and was said to be specially built for the medical profession.   GNG

LÉON BOLLÉE; MORRIS-LÉON BOLLÉE (F) *1895–1933*

1) Automobiles Léon Bollée, Le Mans *1895–1924*

2) Morris Motors Ltd, Usines Léon Bollée, Le Mans *1925–1931*

3) Sté Nouvelle Léon Bollée, Le Mans *1931–1933*

Léon Bollée was a son of Amédée Bollée *père*, the most important pioneer of steam road vehicles in France. Léon, however, turned to really small petrol cars. He was the first to do so, and therefore had to invent a new name for his Léon Bollée

1906 LE MÉTAIS 8/9hp tonneau. *Lucien Loreille Collection*

1972 LENHAM-REPCO P.80 3-litre sports car. *Lenham-Hurst Racing Organisation Ltd*

1916 LENOX(ii) tourer. *Keith Marvin Collection*

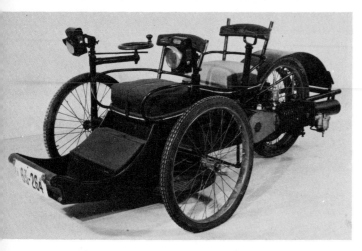

1896 LÉON BOLLÉE 3hp voiturette.
Museo dell'Automobile, Turin

1904 LÉON BOLLÉE 24hp tonneau. *R.J.
Stephens*

1932 LÉON BOLLÉE 12CV saloon. *Photo
Omnia. Lucien Loreille Collection*

car of 1895 – he called it a voiturette. It was a tandem two-seater 3-wheeler th[at]
was faster than any other petrol-engined vehicle on the road when it was working,
thanks to a powerful 3hp engine and light weight, but the power unit was unreliabl[e.]
It had a single air-cooled cylinder of 650cc and used hot-tube ignition. The[re]
were 3 forward speeds, with belt final drive. The frame was tubular. Four yea[rs]
after the voiturette appeared, Bollée superseded it with a 4-wheeler with independe[nt]
front suspension by double transverse leaf springs. It had a single-cylinder, wate[r]
cooled engine. Unlike the voiturette, it made no mark. The design rights were so[ld]
to Darracq, and around 1901 the name of Léon Bollée vanished. Meanwhile, th[e]
term voiturette had been taken up by the trade and public in general as the nam[e]
for a small light car.

The Léon Bollée reappeared in 1903 as an entirely normal, full-sized car i[n]
the more expensive class, backed by Vanderbilt money and designed for th[e]
American market. It was made in 28hp (4.6-litres) and 45hp (8-litres) versions, wit[h]
four cylinders and chain drive, and led on to a 11.9-litre six in 1907, in which yea[r]
the first shaft driven car appeared. From 1909 there was also a small modern fou[r]
the 10/14hp. The 1910 range embraced 9 models, including 2 of over 10 litr[e]
capacity. Electric lighting became available in 1913, but the Léon Bollée gre[w]
increasingly old-fashioned after World War 1 despite the introduction of ohv i[n]
1922 and fwb in 1923. Late in 1924 Sir William Morris bought the Le Man[s]
factory. From making a wide range of conservative French fours, it turned to thinly
disguised products of Cowley, Oxford, the idea being to breach the French tari[ff]
walls from the inside. The first Morris-Léon Bollée had a 12CV 2½-litre, 4-cylinde[r]
unit-construction engine made by Hotchkiss, the engine manufacturers controlled b[y]
Morris, but it had push-rod overhead valves and bore little evidence of its parentag[e.]
Not so the 18CV of 1928. This was a 3-litre straight-8 with single overhead cam
shaft that reflected Morris' takeover of Wolseley two years earlier. Morris' own ne[w]
six of 1928 was mirrored in the 15CV 2.6-litre Le Mans product of 1929. The bodie[s]
for the Morris-Léon Bollée were all made in France and were usually considerabl[y]
more dashing and attractive than their British counterparts. Chassis were made i[n]
France, and all cars had a 4-speed gearbox. At one time, 50 12CVs were being turn[ed]
out each week. However, Morris' enterprise was not a success, and he di[s]
continued it in the hard times of the Depression. A new syndicate was formed i[n]
September 1931 to sell the same range of cars under the name of Léon Bollée. Thi[s]
lasted for less than two years and few cars were made.   TR[

LÉON DUSSEK (F) *1906–c.1907*

The Léon Dussek was made in three models, all with 4-cylinder engines. The[y]
were the 16/20, 24/30 and 35/45hp. Cylinders were cast separately, and the car
had 4-speed gearboxes and double chain drive. The British agents, Motoria Ltd
said that shaft drive was also available.   GN[

LEONE (I) *1949–1950*
Officine Elettromeccaniche Vincenzo Leone, Turin

The Leone was a small sports car with tubular frame and ifs, based on Fia[t]
mechanical elements. A tuned 1100 engine was standard, but a 1,200cc versio[n]
was also available.   MC[

LÉON LAISNE; HARRIS–LÉON LAISNE; HARRIS (F) *c.1920–1937*
(1) L. Laisne et Cie, Lille *c.1920–1927*
(2) Automobiles Harris-Léon Laisne, Nantes *1927–1931*
(3) Automobiles Harris, Nantes *1931–1937*

The Léon Laisne or Harris-Léon Laisne was one of the experimental machine[s]
virtually test-beds for new systems of suspension or transmission, that abounded i[n]
France in the 1920s. The engines were relatively unimportant; they were motiv[e]
power only, bought from various proprietary engine makers. The uniqueness o[f]
the Harris-Léon Laisne lay in its suspension. There were no normal road spring[s]
or axles. The frame side members were tubular and contained coil springs an[d]
hydraulic stabilizers, operating through a system of levers to provide independen[t]
suspension for each wheel. This chassis was propelled originally by a 4-cylinde[r]
12CV C.I.M.E. unit, then by S.C.A.P. straight-8 and Hotchkiss 6-cylinder engine[s]
of different sizes. In 1933 the Harris Six used an English Standard 12hp, 6-cylinde[r]
engine.   TR[

LÉON RAMBERT (F) *1934*

Made in Clermont-Ferrand, the Léon Rambert was an ultra-light car made i[n]
single- or two-seater form, powered by 175cc or 250cc 2-stroke engines. Abou[t]
60 were made.   GN[

LEON RUBAY *see* RUBAY

LEPAPE (F) *c.1896–1901*
Hippolyte Lepape, Paris

Lepape was a prolific inventor who probably never made cars for sale. An early
design featured six wheels, a 6hp 3-cylinder radial engine and drive to the fron[t]
pair of wheels. In later cars he experimented with friction drive, and cooling o[f]
cylinders by radiation from a mass of metal surrounding the cylinder. This engine
was of 5hp, and was mounted in front, with final drive by belt.   GN[

E PIAF (F) *1951*

té Industrielle de Livry, Livry-Gargan, Seine

Le Piaf (slang for sparrow) was a minicar even simpler than most of the breed, ith a 175cc single-cylinder engine, a doorless body and two canvas seats. Maximum eed was said to be 40mph and it was remarkably cheap at 200,000 francs (about 200). GNG

EPRECHAN see AUTOGEAR (ii)

E ROITELET (F) *1921–1923*

The Parish-built Le Roitelet was a cyclecar with a 749cc 2-cylinder engine driving he front wheels. Front suspension was by centrally-pivoted transverse springs which turned with the steering. GNG

E ROLL (F) *1922*

Delauné, Bergé et Boudéne, Paris

This was a light car using a 900cc Chapuis-Dornier 4-cylinder engine and shaft rive. GNG

EROY (CDN) *1899–1907*

eRoy Mfg Co, Berlin (now Kitchener), Ont.

The Good brothers made early developments with single-cylinder petrol engines, roducing their first experimental car mounted on a buggy chassis in 1899. Other xperiments followed, and in late 1901 production began on a completely Canadian-uilt vehicle based on the curved-dash Olds. The manufacture of components to onstruct 32 cars places the LeRoy in the position of being Canada's first volume roduction automobile. The company later attempted manufacture of a 3-cylinder ar before their car production ceased in 1907. GB

ESCINA (US) *1916*

escina Automobile Co, Newark, N.J.

The Lescina, introduced in January 1916 at New York City's Grand Central alace, failed to last out the year, although its pians were grandiose. A total of ten ody styles were offered, from closed models to open cars and a panel delivery truck, n three different chassis of 10ft 5in, 9ft 4in and 8ft 10in wheelbase. The largest of hese, the Model V, was presumably not produced. Prices on the other two chassis anged from $555 to $1,288. The cars were assembled from standard proprietary omponents and initial plans included an auxiliary manufacturing plant in Chicago. KM

ESPINASSE (F) *1909*

Automobiles et Moteurs L. Lespinasse, Cauderan, Gironde

This company made a range of five models from a small 7hp 4-cylinder to a 20hp -cylinder car. In all models, the cylinders were cast separately. GNG

ESSHAFT (D) *1925–1926*

esshaft & Co, Berlin N 65

This was a small open three-wheeled vehicle with a single front seat and double ear seat. The engine was a 2-stroke 3.5hp by Rinne. HON

LESTER (i) (GB) *1913*

Lester Engineering Co, Shepherds Bush, London W.

The Lester cyclecar was powered by an 8hp J.A.P. or Precision engine, and had a very narrow single-seater body. Transmission was by friction discs, and final drive by chain or belts. A two-seater with staggered seating was also available. The price of the single seater was £80. GNG

LESTER (ii) (GB) *1949–1955*

1) H. Lester, Knebworth, Herts. *1949*
2) H. Lester, Thatcham, Berks. *1949–1951*
3) H. Lester Cars (1951) Ltd, Thatcham, Berks. *1951–1954*
4) The Monkey Stable, London N. *1954–1955*

Considerable experience in preparing competition vehicles showed Harry Lester hat the chassis rather than the engine was the limiting factor on the performance of the TC M.G. Hence the introduction of the tubular ladder frame, with coil ndependent front suspension. The engine was available linered to 1087cc or bored to 1467cc, with alternative ratios for the M.G. gearbox. Light two-seater bodies with cycle-type wings were fitted. J.C.C. Mayers, P.A.C. Griffiths, G. Ruddock and others achieved numerous successes; several of the cars were exported, and some 20 were built in all. For 1955 production of a new model was planned on a larger scale. A transverse leaf spring was fitted at the rear, and the 1467cc engine was now tuned for 100bhp. Fibreglass coupé bodywork was mounted on a light tubular frame, and an open two-seater was offered on the 1098cc Coventry-Climax engined version. However, motor racing's most tragic year claimed the lives of two of the leading members of the team who had sponsored the design – Jim Mayers and Mike Keen. Only seven cars had been laid down when the decision was taken to stop production. DF

1927 HARRIS-LÉON LAISNE 1.6-litre tourer.
Autocar

1951 LE PIAF 175cc minicar. *Autocar*

1913 LESTER(i) 8hp monocar. *G.N. Georgano Collection*

1951 LESTER-M.G. 1½-litre sports car.
Autosport.

1923 LEWIS(iv) 10hp two-seater. *Autocar*

1937 LEWIS AIROMOBILE 3-wheel coupé.
Special-Interest Autos

1921 LEYAT airscrew car. *Autocar*

LETHIMONNIER *see* SULTANE

LE TIGRE (F) *1920–1923*
R. Merville, Asnières, Seine
  This was a light car powered by a 4-cylinder sv Fivet engine of 1323cc. had a central steering position, and a three-seater torpedo body convertible to saloon. GN

LEVENN (F) *1900*
Ernst et Cie, Paris
  The Levenn voiturette used a 2-cylinder vertical air-cooled engine, and a early example of friction-disc transmission. A two-seater was the only bod style. GN

LEVER *see* ELCAR *and* KISSEL

LEWIS (i) (US) *1898–1902*
Lewis Cycle Co, Philadelphia, Pa.
  The Lewis was a spidery-looking vehicle with large wheels, powered by horizontal single-cylinder engine. It had friction transmission, the driven dis being made of compressed paper! GN

LEWIS (ii) (AUS) *1900–1902*
Lewis Cycle Works, Adelaide, South Australia
  The Lewis was the first car made in South Australia, and used a 4½hp single cylinder air-cooled engine, belt drive and wheel or tiller steering. GN

LEWIS (iii) (US) *1913–1916*
(1) Lewis Motor Co, Racine, Wisc. *1913*
(2) L.P.C. Motor Car Co, Racine, Wisc. *1914–1916*
  The Lewis was one of the first American cars with a long-stroke engine and wa sponsored by William Mitchell Lewis, formerly of the Mitchell Company; designe was René Petard, who was also responsible for contemporary Mitchells. In thi case the stroke was 152mm, compared with a bore of 89mm. The 6-cylinder engin was used to power a five-seater touring car. The weight of this vehicle was give as 3,250lb and the price in 1915 was $1,600. GM

LEWIS (iv) (GB) *1923–1924*
Abbey Industries Ltd, Abbey Wood, London S.E.
  The Lewis used a 10hp V-twin air-cooled M.A.G. engine, a 3-speed gearbox an shaft drive. A 4-cylinder water-cooled model was announced at the same time, bu never went into production. GN

LEWIS AIROMOBILE (US) *1937*
Lewis American Airways, Inc, Rochester, N.Y.
  This was a streamlined 3-wheeled five-seater saloon powered by a 2-litre flat-air-cooled engine designed by the former Franklin engineers, Doman and Marks Drive was to the front wheels. Only one prototype was built, although four othe cars were under construction when the company ran out of capital. The prototyp survives today in Harrah's Automobile Collection at Reno, Nevada. GN

LEXINGTON (US) *1909–1928*
(1) Lexington Motor Co, Lexington, Ky. *1909–1910*; Connersville, Ind. *1911–1913*
(2) Lexington-Howard Co, Connersville, Ind. *1914–1918*
(3) Lexington Motor Co, Connersville, Ind. *1918–1928*
  An assembled car from the beginning, the first Lexington was produced ir Kentucky in 1909 but operations were moved to Indiana less than a year later. At first 4-cylinder cars were built, with sixes introduced in 1915 and remaining in production for the duration of Lexington's existence. The Lexington appeared in various models and body styles offering a wide variety of types to the potential purchaser The peak production year was 1920 when some 6,000 were built. A year later the Ansted motor was adopted and prices ranged as high as $4,500. The concern went into receivership early in 1923, but production continued. The cars were highly regarded and had advanced lines for their day, the most famous models being the Lexington and Concord touring car and sedan of the early and mid-1920s. Also popular was the Minute Man Six, although the allusion to the Battle of Lexington-Concord in the American Revolution was odd as the Lexington was actually named after the Kentucky city of its origin. It was eventually absorbed by the Auburn Automobile Company; extremely limited production marked the Lexington's final years and the last of them were produced in 1928. KM

LEY *see* LORELEY

LEYAT (F) *1913–c.1921*
Marcel Leyat, Meursault, Côte d'Or
  Marcel Leyat was one of the small band of experimenters who, before and just after World War 1, tried to adapt aircraft propulsion to road vehicles. The *auto-*

mobile à hélice as conceived by Leyat was propelled by a 4-bladed tractor airscrew driven at first by an A.B.C. flat-twin air-cooled motor cycle engine. Later, a 3-cylinder Anzani unit was used. The airscrew was enclosed in a hoop and wire mesh grille to avoid nasty accidents. The Leyat was unconventional in every other way as well. The body-chassis unit offered two-seater accommodation in tandem, there was 4-wheel independent suspension, the only brakes were on the front wheels, and the rear wheels steered. Also known as the Hélica, the Leyat was made as an open two-seater, saloon, and delivery van. Production ceased in about 1921, but a final, ultra-streamlined 3-wheeler was tested at Montlhéry in 1927.   TRN

1920 LEYLAND Eight Speed Model four-seater.
Leyland Motors Ltd

LEYLAND (GB) *1920–1923*
Leyland Motors Ltd, Leyland, Lancs.

The Leyland was one of several instances in Britain of a manufacturer of commercial vehicles venturing into the luxury-car market just after World War 1. The 40hp Leyland Eight of 1920 was designed by J.G. Parry Thomas. Its engine had 8 cylinders in line, totalling 7.3 litres, and there was a single overhead camshaft. When it appeared at the Olympia Show in 1920, it caused a sensation on several grounds. It was the most expensive British car on the market, costing £3,050 complete, and it was also the most powerful, with 115bhp at 2,500rpm available with a single carburettor and 145bhp with two. Only 18 of these great cars were made. After he left Leyland, Parry Thomas developed the Eight for racing purposes. Two Leyland-Thomases, their engines now delivering 200bhp, were built. In 1929 another car was assembled from parts, and still exists today.   TRN

LE ZÈBRE (F) *1909–1932*
SA Le Zèbre, Suresnes; Puteaux, Seine

Towards the end of the first decade of the 20th century, most French light car makers were adding cylinders rather than deducting them, but the little 600cc 5hp Le Zèbre was popular in spite of having only one to start with. It had two forward speeds and shaft drive. Not until late 1912 did a 4-cylinder Le Zèbre appear. The bore was tiny, 50mm, but the stroke was long, at 120mm. Cubic capacity was 950cc, later reduced to 785cc. This car (and, by now, the single) had a 3-speed gearbox. It was continued for a short time after the war. The engineers who were responsible for the Le Zèbre achieved greater fame than their car. Salomon went on to help design the 5CV Citroën, while Lamy performed the same service for Amilcar.

In 1925 a completely new design of Le Zèbre appeared. It had a 2-litre sv engine with Ricardo head, 4-speed gearbox and fwb, and was still offered in 1930. The make's last appearance was at the 1931 Paris Salon when they exhibited an otherwise conventional light car, but with single-cylinder opposed-piston Lilloise diesel engine.   TRN

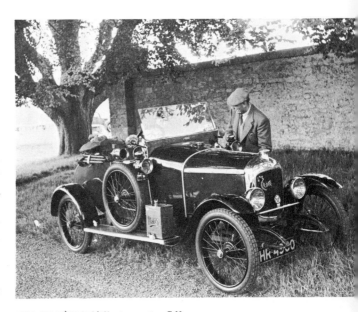

1921 LE ZÈBRE 8/10hp two-seater. *G.N.*
Georgano

LIBELLE (D) *1920–1922*
Kleinautofabrik GmbH, Sindelfingen
A cyclecar driven by a V-twin 4/10PS engine.   HON

LIBÉRIA (F) *1900–1902*
G. Dupont, Plessis-Trévise, Seine-et-Oise

The Libéria was a conventional light car made in two models, a 6⅓hp and a 12hp, both with Aster engines. The manufacturer competed regularly in the races of the time, including the 1901 Paris-Bordeaux, in which a Libéria was the only car to finish in the voiturette class apart from Renaults, the 1901 Paris-Berlin and the Paris-Vienna in 1902.   GNG

LIBERTY (i) (US) *1914*
Belmont Auto Mfg Co, New Haven, Conn.

This make succeeded the Liberty-Brush. It was a typical cyclecar with a V-twin air-cooled engine developing 15hp. Designer Joseph A. Anglada was also responsible for the Anderson (ii).   GMN

LIBERTY (ii) (US) *1916–1924*
Liberty Motor Car Co, Detroit, Mich.

This was a popular make for a short period. The Liberty discarded in 1920 the Continental 6-cylinder engine used at the beginning of its production and the company's own six was fitted until manufacture ceased. Production reached its highest point in 1919 when 6,000 cars were sold. The Liberty was purchased late in 1923 by the Columbia Motor Car Co which planned to market the car but did not succeed. The last units sold as 1924 models were actually 1923 cars. The Liberty and the Columbia were very similar in appearance.   KM

LIDKÖPING (S) *1923*
Lidköping Mek. Verkstad, Lidköping

Three prototypes were made of this light 4-cylinder four-seater car whose water-cooled engine gave 20bhp at 3,000rpm.   OB

LIFU (GB) *1899–1902*
The Steam Car Co (House's System) Ltd, London W.C.

1920 LIBERTY(ii) 23hp tourer. *Autocar*

1924 LILA Type J-C 10hp saloon. *Shotaro Kobayashi Collection*

1920 LINCOLN(iv) Six tourer. *Keith Marvin Collection*

1922 LINCOLN(vi) 5.8-litre sedanca de ville. *Ford Motor Co*

1932 LINCOLN(vi) Model KB 7.2-litre cabriolet. *Ford Motor Co*

Lifu steam cars were made under the patents of Henry Alonzo House by a number of subcontracting firms, for sale by the Steam Car Company. They used 2-cylinder compound engines driving the rear wheels by spur gear. Some models were bonnetted with a front-mounted condenser, while others employed forward control. The only known surviving Lifu is a 1901 10hp car built by Thomas Noakes & Sons of London, but it seems that other firms were also engaged in constructing the cars. It is, however, unlikely that they were ever built by the parent company, the Liquid Fuel Engineering Company of Cowes, Isle of Wight, whose factory was sold early in 1900, and who only made steam lorries and buses there. GNG

LIGHT (US) 1914
Light Motor Car Co, Detroit, Mich.

The name Light must have come from the manufacturer rather than the size of the car, for it was a conventional 30hp 6-cylinder vehicle, made only in touring form, and selling for $1,250. GNG

LIGIER (F) 1969 to date
Automobiles Ligier, Vichy, Allier

Guy Ligier, head of a large construction company, Rugby Football international and F1 racing privateer, laid down his original series of lightweight competition coupés in 1969. The prototype raced during 1970, using a 1.8-litre Cosworth FVC engine and a Y-shaped backbone chassis, and it was intended to market similar road cars. This original design was dubbed the JS1, in memory of Ligier's great friend and team-mate Jo Schlesser, killed during the 1968 French GP. In 1971 the JS2 appeared, designed by Michel Tetu, and its shapely fibreglass GT body style housed a 2.6-litre German Ford V-6, fuel-injected to 165bhp and in unit with a 5-speed Citroën SM transmission. It was intended to produce about 100 JS2s annually, at about £3,800 (or $9,300). Top speed was 150mph. In 1972 the JS3 sports-prototype also appeared, using a mid-mounted Cosworth-Ford DFV Grand Prix engine of 3-litres, and it raced successfully at Le Mans. DCN

LILA (J) 1923–1925
Jitsuyo Jidosha Seizo Co, Osaka

Upon completion of Gorham car manufacture, J.J.S. turned to a more advanced design. The Lila light car seated four in a fully enclosed cab and was powered by a 10hp engine giving a top speed of 30mph. Both car and truck models were sold and continued to be built until the company combined with the DAT works, after which only DAT trucks were manufactured. BE

LILIPUT (D) 1904–1907
(1) Bergmann's Industriewerke, Gaggenau 1904–1905
(2) Süddeutsche Automobilfabrik GmbH, Gaggenau 1905–1907

After the Orient Express cars, built from 1895 until 1903, Bergmann turned in 1904 to the manufacture of the friction-driven Liliput, designed by Willy Seck. Its single-cylinder 567cc engine developed 4bhp and at 2,500 marks it was the cheapest car then on the German market.

In 1905 the motor-car division of Bergmann's Industriewerke became independent as the Süddeutsche Automobilfabrik, but production of Liliput cars was continued. In 1906/07 the Liliput was available in a single-cylinder 6bhp and a 2-cylinder 9bhp version. Both were two-seaters. A four-seater model on the same lines was called the Libelle and had a 4-cylinder 12/16bhp engine. Both models were also advertised and marketed as Bergmanns, despite the reorganization of 1905. Liliput cars were built under licence by Schilling. HON

LINCOLN (i) (US) 1909
Lincoln Motor Vehicle Co, Lincoln, Ill.

This car was a high-wheeler with solid rubber tyres, using a 4-stroke, 2-cylinder air-cooled engine of 1.7 litres. Three models were made, two with shaft drive and one with a single chain. GMN

LINCOLN (ii) (US) 1911–c.1914
Lincoln Motor Car Works, Chicago, Ill.

After the closure of the Sears venture, the Lincoln Motor Car Works made a high wheeler of similar design to the Sears for a few years. Most were commercial vehicles. GNG

LINCOLN (iii) (US) 1914
Lincoln Motor Car Co, Detroit, Mich.

This Lincoln was an unsuccessful light two-seater. Its weight was 1,050lb and it cost $595. GMN

LINCOLN (iv) (AUS) 1919–1924
Lincoln Motor Car Co, Sydney, N.S.W.

The Lincoln was an attempt to place on the roads of Australia a car embodying the best of standard components and Australian workmanship, the latter including the radiator design and body. A Continental 6-cylinder engine was used for power and the touring car sold in 1923 for £A590 with wire wheels extra. The

Lincoln Motor Co of Detroit, Mich., requested the company to drop the Lincoln name in 1923, but it is not recorded that the Australians did so.   KM

LINCOLN (v) (GB) 1920

The Lincoln was a typical 3-wheeled cyclecar powered by an 8hp Blackburne engine and fitted with chain drive.   MJWW

LINCOLN (vi) (US) 1920 to date
Lincoln Motor Co, Detroit, Mich.

After Henry M. Leland's resignation from Cadillac in 1917, he evolved another big sv V-8 which came on the market under the name of Lincoln in 1921. It had a capacity of 5.8 litres and developed 81bhp. Cylinder heads were detachable and full-pressure lubrication was adopted at a time when many American makers pinned their faith to splash systems. Over 70mph was possible and it was not excessively expensive at $4,300, but the style of the bodies did not match the quality of the mechanical components, and Henry Ford acquired the company after it had encountered financial difficulties in 1922. Both Leland and his son Wilfred resigned a few months later, but Ford retained the traditions of quality, adding aluminium pistons from the time of his takeover. Lincolns were much used by both gangsters and police, the latter driving tuned versions capable of over 80mph and equipped with front wheel brakes, a luxury not available to the general public until 1927. President Coolidge bought a Lincoln in 1924, establishing a link between the marque and the White House which has lasted till this day: Franklin D. Roosevelt's Sunshine Special was one of the last 12-cylinder Ks, Harry S. Truman ordered an open Cosmopolitan in 1950 and John F. Kennedy bought a Continental in 1961.

Lincolns sold steadily in limited numbers – nearly 9,000 in 1926. Engine capacity went up to 6.3 litres in 1928. 1931 cars had a 12ft 1in wheelbase, downdraught carburation and 120bhp engines, but in 1932 there came a new 7.2-litre KB-type V-12 with vacuum booster brakes. This was joined the following year by a smaller 6.2-litre KA-type 12 at $2,700, and all subsequent Lincolns made up to 1948 were to have 12-cylinder power units. In 1934 both models gave way to a 6.8-litre K with aluminium cylinder heads, and a top speed of nearly 100mph. The Division could not, however, support itself on the dwindling prestige-car market, and for 1936 they offered a popular V-12, the 4.4-litre, 110bhp Zephyr. Unitary construction was adopted; other characteristics were a synchromesh gearbox, headlamps faired into the front wings, a fastback style and an alligator-type bonnet. The brakes, however, were mechanical, and Ford's traditional transverse suspension was used. It cost $1,320 and its engine was used in Anglo-American hybrids of the period: the Allard, Atalanta and Brough Superior. 1938 Zephyrs had a dashboard gear change. Hydraulic brakes followed in 1939, and column change in 1940. Meanwhile the Model K had at last been dropped; sales for the combined 1939 and 1940 seasons had been 120 of these cars and the black-bordered emblems on the last models were symbolic! To balance this, a new product had been launched in 1939, the Mercury. There were also some relatively inexpensive prestige cars – Edsel Ford's Zephyr-based Continental coupés and cabriolets, with 4.8-litre engines. Options in the last pre-war seasons included overdrive, a fluid coupling, and power-operated hoods and windows. No entirely new Lincolns appeared until 1949, when a change was made to Ford's new styling and coil-spring independent front suspension, while at the same time the 12-cylinder engine was replaced by an sv under-square 5½-litre V-8. Manual transmission was dropped finally from Lincolns in 1951, and 1952 models swept the board in the touring-car class of that year's Carrera Panamericana, the winner averaging 90mph. 205bhp ohv engines were introduced for 1953, and the 1956 line consisted of the 6-litre 285bhp Premiere and Capri, as well as a revived Continental at $10,000 made in very limited numbers. Dual headlamps were adopted for the 1957 cars, and 1958 Lincolns had unitary construction – this was the year of Lincoln-Mercury Division's disastrous Edsel. After 1961 the Continental became the staple Lincoln, an unusual body style being a 4-door convertible of a type not offered by the American motor industry for some years; this was discontinued in 1968, when Lincolns had 7,571cc 340bhp engines and front disc brakes (standardized in 1966). The short-wheelbase Continental III luxury 2-door hardtop introduced during the year reverted to the separate chassis and the traditional radiator grille. List price was $6,585. The company also built a $500,000 car, a bullet-proof Presidential limousine on a special 13ft 4in chassis.

All 1970 models had concealed headlamps and perimeter frames; that year's production of 58,771 units was well below Cadillac's level, but appreciably ahead of Chrysler's prestige Imperial. By 1973 cylinder capacity was 7,359cc, and improvements for the year were mainly concerned with safety. Most expensive Lincoln was the Continental IV, basically the 1972 revision of the Continental III with a Rolls-Royce style grille. Prices ranged from $7,322 for the Continental 4-door sedan to $8,774 for the Continental Mark IV coupé.   MCS

LINDCAR (D) 1922–1925
Lindcar Auto AG, Berlin-Lichtenrade

The Lindcar was a small car using proprietary components, such as Steudel or Atos engines. It was available with Z.F.-Soden preselector gear on request.   HON

1936 LINCOLN(vi) Zephyr 4.4-litre sedan. *Ford Motor Co*

1937 LINCOLN(vi) Zephyr 4.4-litre four-door convertible. Coachwork by Le Baron. *Keith Marvin Collection*

1941 LINCOLN(vi) Continental 4.8-litre convertible. *Henry Ford Museum, Dearborn, Michigan*

1967 LINCOLN(vi) Continental 7.6-litre coupé. *Ford Motor Co*

1906 LINON 14/20hp limousine. *Geoffroy de Beauffort Collection*

1910 LION-PEUGEOT 10hp tourer. *G.N. Georgano*

1954 LISTER-BRISTOL 2-litre sports car. Archie Scott-Brown at the wheel. *Autosport*

LINDSAY (GB) *1906–1908*
Lindsay Motor Car Co, Ltd Woodbridge, Suffolk

The Lindsay company had been makers of tri-cars for several years before they took up car production in 1906. Their first four wheeler was a 6hp tubular-framed voiturette with J.A.P. engine and Lowes variable gear selling for £140. They later made two models, one with a 12hp 4-cylinder Fafnir engine, and the other with a 28hp 4-cylinder Antoine engine. Both cars used shaft drive. In 1908 they introduced a 15.9hp car with short stroke (80 × 90mm) 1.8-litre engine. GNG

LINDSLEY (US) *1907–1908*
(1) J.V. Lindsley, Indianapolis, Ind. *1907–1908*
(2) J.V. Lindsley, Dowagiac Motor Car Co, Dowagiac, Mich. *1908*

This was a two-seater with large-diameter wheels and solid rubber tyres. It was powered by a 2-cylinder air-cooled engine of 10hp under the seat, with a planetary transmission. The manufacturer moved in 1908 to Dowagiac, Mich., and commenced to build 15 cars but the company failed before these were finished. These cars were completed by the Dowagiac Motor Car Co, and for this reason the name Dowagiac is regarded as a make by some historians. GMN

LINGTON (GB) *1920*
Lington Engineering Co Ltd, Bedford

The Lington's used a 10hp V-twin engine and shaft drive. It could be started from the driver's seat by a pedal. GNG

LINON (B) *1900–1914*
Ateliers Linon, Ensival-Verviers

The Linon company was established in 1897, and made a few cars of Gauthier-Wehrlé design before launching their own car in 1900. This was a voiturette with 3hp De Dion engine and belt drive. By 1902 Linon were making voiturettes powered by 3½, 4½ and 6hp De Dion engines, and larger cars powered by Linon engines of 8/10 and 16hp. They had steady, if unspectacular sales during the years up to 1914 during which time a wide range of models was made from 9 to 40hp, using not only their own engines but also units by Fafnir, Fondu, Ballot and Vautour. An 8hp single was made up to 1912 and the 1913 range consisted of three models, all with 4-cylinder monobloc engines: a 12, 16 and 22hp. GNG

LION (US) *1909–1912*
Lion Motor Car Co, Adrian, Mich.

The Lion was produced in at least three different body types, all powered by a 4-cylinder 40hp engine. The 1912 model, which cost $1,600 boasted of internal-expanding brakes with drums of 14in diameter. A fire in 1912 destroyed 150 cars in the factory and the company was unable to continue. GMN

LION-PEUGEOT (F) *1906–1913*
(1) Les Fils de Peugeot Frères, Beaulieu-Valentigney *1906–1910*
(2) SA des Automobiles et Cycles Peugeot, Audincourt *1910–1913*

The Lion-Peugeot started as an independent venture by Robert Peugeot in the motor cycle factory at Beaulieu-Valentigney, which had been used for car manufacture until the establishment of the SA des Automobiles Peugeot in 1897. These Michaux-designed voiturettes were produced in direct competition with the cars from Audincourt, and the original chain-driven single at £125 filled a gap left by the discontinuation of the original Baby. Already the company were trying their hand in the Coupe des Voiturettes, but made no impression in 1906 or 1907 against Sizaire-Naudin and Delage. The first of the classic racing V-twins made its appearance in 1908, and from 1909 to 1911 the marque was renowned for some very odd machines, which took advantage of regulations more concerned with bores than with strokes. The 1909 cars, victorious in both the Catalan Cup and the Coupe itself, were made with 1.9-litre engines, a single of 100 × 250mm and a twin of 80mm × 192mm, the former having three valves per cylinder, but the peak was reached in 1910 with the fantastic VX5, an 80 × 280mm V-twin with twin carburettors, developing 95bhp. The driver had to look round, rather than over the engine! There was a companion 65 × 260mm V-4, really two twins in series. In spite (or perhaps because) of this, Lion-Peugeot had to be content with 2nd place in that year's Coupe des Voiturettes. They tried once again in 1911 with a V-4, this time using the relatively modest stroke/bore ratio of 2:1.

By 1910 the production Lion-Peugeots had grown up into 1.7-litre transverse V-twins with 3-speed gearboxes and shaft drive, though chain-driven versions were still available as late as 1911. The reunion of the two rival Peugeot companies, however, signalled the end of these eccentricities: though a touring V-4 was announced in 1911 and was made with a 4-speed gearbox, pressure lubrication, and pedal-operated rear-wheel brakes, the Lion designation was dropped at the end of 1913. The 1.9-litre VD peugeot of 1914 marked the end of this line of development and none of the Lion derivatives survived World War 1. MCS

LIPSCOMB (GB) *1903–1905*
English Motor Car Co. Ltd. London N.W.

The Lipscomb was one of many assembled cars using 6hp De Dion-Bouton or Aster engines, sold from a depot in Euston Road. A larger car sold by the same firm was the 20hp Bayley, both cars obtaining their names from the company's director, Arthur Lipscomb Bayley. The Bayley was built for the English Motor Company by Craig-Dörwald.   GNG

LIPSIA (D) 1922–1924
Lipsia Automobilfabrik GmbH, Schleussig nr Leipzig

Two models were produced by this firm, powered by 6/20PS and 6/30PS engines.
HON

LIQUID AIR (US) 1901–1902
Liquid Air Power & Automobile Co, Boston, Mass.

The Liquid Air car resembled any light steam buggy of the period, but carried a tank of liquid air under high pressure whose expansion was supposed to drive an ordinary single-cylinder steam-type engine. The efficiency of such a system has been estimated at only 4%, and it is improbable that the car could have run any distance, if at all. The scheme was probably a stock promotion project.   GNG

LISTER (GB) 1954–1959
(1) Brian H. Lister, Cambridge 1954–1956
(2) B.H. Lister Ltd, Cambridge 1956–1959

A simple tubular frame, with coil independent suspension and a De Dion rear end, formed the basis of Lister production. At first, M.G. or Bristol engines were used, and it was with the latter type that the one-armed Archie Scott-Brown achieved a remarkable racing record. By 1956, other engines had been tried, including the A6GCS Maserati, and finally the Jaguar. A Formula 2 variant was produced in 1957. The Jaguar-engined cars continued to be successful, driven by Stirling Moss, Ivor Bueb, Walt Hansgen, and many others. In 1958 3-litre versions were produced for Le Mans, and a single-seater for the Ecurie Ecosse to run at Monza. For 1959, Frank Costin designed the bodies, and a space-frame car which was not produced. The general engineering side of the business was expanding, and finally squeezed out car production when this had reached a total of around 50.   DF

LITTLE (US) 1912–1915
Little Motor Car Co, Flint, Mich.

William H. Little was a former Buick manager whom William C. Durant employed to build cars in the Flint Wagon Works which had formerly made the Whiting. The first Little car was a 4-cylinder 20hp two-seater roadster priced at $650. It was joined by a 6-cylinder touring car, the 3.6-litre Little Six, in 1914. This was phased out the following year as it was too close in size and price to the Chevrolet Six, another Durant product. The Little roadster's styling influenced that of the Chevrolet Royal Mail roadster.   GNG

LITTLE DETROIT see DETROIT (ir)

LITTLEMAC (US) 1930–1931
Thompson Motor Corp, Muscatine, Iowa

Only a few Littlemac cars were built. They had short wheel-bases and were equipped with the former Star Four engine. Artillery wheels were standard and 2-wheel mechanical brakes were fitted. The price was $438.   KM

LITTLE PRINCESS (US) 1913–1914
Princess Cyclecar Co, Detroit, Mich.

This cyclecar was made in two- and four-seater versions, powered by 4-cylinder, 1½-litre air-cooled engines. Planetary transmission was used with shaft drive. The design later became the Princess (iii).   GMN

LITTLE SCOTSMAN see SCOTSMAN (ii)

LIVER (GB) 1900–1901
William Lea Motor Co Ltd, Liverpool

The Liver was closely based on the Benz, using genuine Benz engines, and body and chassis of English make but derived from Benz designs. 3½hp and 6hp models were made.   GNG

LLOYD (i) (D) 1906–1914; 1950–1963
(1) Norddeutsche Automobil- und Motoren AG, Bremen 1906–1914
(2) Lloyd Motoren-Werke GmbH, Bremen 1950–1963

The Norddeutsche Automobil- und Motoren AG (Namag), a subsidiary of the Norddeutsche Lloyd shipping line, was founded in 1906 for the production under licence of Kriéger electric cars, for which the brand-name Lloyd was used. The first petrol-driven car, designed by Joseph Vollmer, appeared in 1908 and was a 4-cylinder 15/35PS 3685cc model. A few more 4-cylinder models followed. Petrol-electric cars were produced from 1908. The make was not widely sold and in 1914 Lloyd amalgamated with Hansa, subsequent models being marketed as Hansa-Lloyds.

1959 LISTER-JAGUAR 3.8-litre sports car. *G. Marshall Naul*

1912 LLOYD(i) 22/50PS tourer. *Jaeger Collection*

1960 LLOYD(i) Arabella 897cc saloon. *Neubauer Collection*

1949 LLOYD(ii) 650 6hp two/four-seater. *Motor*

1960 L.M.B. Debonair GT coupé. *British Resin Products Ltd*

1900 LOCOMOBILE 5½hp steam buggy. *The Veteran Car Club of Great Britain*

Hansa-Lloyd was taken over in 1929 by Borgward who revived the name of Lloyd in 1950 when a small car with a 2-cylinder 293cc engine appeared. The body was of wood construction covered with leatherette. All-steel bodywork was standardized in 1954, and over 45,000 cars were sold in 1955. Engine capacity of this small Lloyd model increased to 596cc with the Alexander of 1957, which had an all-steel body. There was also an austerity two-stroke '250' at DM 2,980 which did not succeed. The last Lloyd was the 4-cylinder 897cc Arabella, introduced in 1957. The failure of the Borgward group also finished Lloyd in 1961, although the Arabella was continued in limited numbers until 1963 from stock parts. The Arabella de luxe model was marketed as a Borgward.   HON

LLOYD (ii) (GB) *1936–1951*
Lloyd Cars Ltd, Grimsby, Lincs.

The pre-1939 Lloyd was an ultra light open two-seater, powered by a rear-mounted 350cc single-cylinder engine. In 1946 the company announced the '650' model which was in production from 1948 to 1951. It used a 650cc vertical twin 2-stroke engine developing only 17½bhp. With a surprisingly large four-seater roadster body, the overall weight was 1,344lb, so performance was hardly spectacular (maximum speed was 46mph). The car had a tubular backbone chassis and the independent front suspension was by oil-damped horizontal coil springs. Rear suspension, also independent, was by vertical coil springs.

The price of the only model offered was £480 in 1948, when the Ford Anglia saloon cost only £293.   GNG

LLOYD & PLAISTER (GB) *1900–1911*
(1) Lloyd & Plaister, Wood Green, London N. *1900–1909*
(2) Lloyd & Plaister Ltd, Wood Green, London N. *1909–1911*

The original Lloyd & Plaister cars were Hurst & Lloyds remaining after George Hurst left to make his own car. Later Lloyd & Plaister made a number of 4-cylinder cars of 10, 16, 20 and 40hp, all with vertical engines, and with shaft drive for the three smaller models. The 40hp used double chain drive, but only six of these were made. About 50 L & P cars were made in all, as well as fire engines and railway inspection cars.

Lloyd & Plaister also manufactured the Allen-Liversidge 4-wheel brake system which was fitted to many makes of car including a 1908 16hp Lloyd & Plaister. (*See also* Vox.)   GNG

L.M. (GB) *1905–1922*
(1) William Cunningham, Clitheroe, Lanc. *1905–1919*
(2) Little Midland Light Car Co Ltd, Blackburn, Lancs. *1919–1920*
(3) Little Midland Light Car Co (1920) Ltd, Preston, Lancs. *1920–1922*

The original L.M. or Little Midland was a light two-seater powered by a 7½hp single-cylinder De Dion-type engine. It was made for a year or two around 1905, and then dropped, there being no further L.M.s until the cyclecar boom of the immediate pre-war period. In fact the L.M. appeared before almost any other British cyclecar, in 1911. It had a 7hp air-cooled V-twin J.A.P. engine, 2 speeds, and single chain drive. In its original form, the overall weight was only 448lb. In 1914 the buyer could have a water-cooled engine as an alternative, but it was still a J.A.P. When the post-war cars appeared, made in Blackburn and then in Preston, they were not greatly changed from their predecessors, except for disc wheels in place of wire, and a dickey seat.   GNG

L.M.B. (GB) *1960–1962*
L.M.B. Components Ltd, Guildford, Surrey

Leslie Ballamy had been renowned since the 1930s for his improvements to production chassis, particularly in respect of his conversions of transverse leaf-spring Fords to ifs. He was also concerned with the original Allard (ii). In 1960 100 tubular ladder chassis were laid down, the 'A' model being suitable for Ford sv engines, and the 'B' model for ohv Ford or B.M.C. 'B' series motors. A semi-swing axle front suspension was employed, with a transverse double canti-lever layout at the rear. Various proprietary fibreglass bodies were fitted, although following an agreement in 1961 with Edwards Bros of Tunstall, Staffs, many cars were assembled with their two/four-seater GT body and marketed as the E.B. Debonair.   DF

LMX (I) *1969 to date*
LMX Automobile s.r.l, Turin

The LMX was made in sports coupé or convertible forms with fibreglass coach-work on a forked backbone frame with McPherson strut-type suspension all round and disc brakes. The engine was a 2.3-litre German Ford V-6 developing 126bhp, though supercharged versions rated at 180bhp and 210bhp were also available.   MCS

LO CASCIO (I) *1905–1913*
Imprese Elettriche e di Automobili Giuseppe Lo Cascio & Cia, Naples

Lo Cascio announced their intention of manufacturing both petrol and electric cars, but no information is available on their products, and they may well have been dealers rather than makers.   MCS

LOCKWOOD (GB) *1921–1922*

Lockwood's Garage, Eastbourne, Sussex

The Lockwood was a miniature car advertised by its makers as 'the smallest car in the world'. It was primarily intended for use by children.　　MJWW

LOCOMOBILE (US) *1899–1929*

(1) Locomobile Company of America, Westboro, Mass. *1899–1900*

(2) Locomobile Company of America, Bridgeport, Conn. *1900–1929*

Locomobile was one of the two companies which resulted from the purchase of the Stanley brothers' steam-car design rights in 1899 by A.L. Barber and J.B. Walker. Walker separated from Barber and formed the Mobile concern, while his former partner did good business with the little Locomobile steam runabout. This consisted of a welded 'bicycle' framework, a carriage body, a twin-cylinder simple engine and a 14in boiler under the driver's seat. It was tiller-steered and chain driven and at $600 it looked a better bargain than it was, suffering from the crudest of lubrication arrangements and an astronomical water consumption: the boiler had to be refilled every 20 miles! In spite of this W.M. Letts managed to sell 400 in England in 1900 and 1901, at which time the four-storey Locomobile until 1903, with bigger boilers, culminating in a 10hp wheel-steered *dos-à-dos* which sold for $1,600.

Locomobile eventually sold their steam-car rights back to the Stanleys, but in the meantime A.L. Riker had designed a petrol car on Panhard lines, with a 4-cylinder engine, automatic inlet valves and pressed-steel frame. Radiators were of the Mercédès honeycomb type in 1905, in which year Joe Tracy competed in the last Gordon Bennett Cup Race with a very Mercédès-like T-headed chain-driven racer. More successful was Locomobile's ioe 'Old 16', built in 1906. George Robertson drove it to victory in the 1908 Vanderbilt Cup, while another Locomobile victory was first place in the touring-car category of the 1913 Glidden Tour, this achieved with a 1909 car that had already covered 100,000 miles. In the meantime the company had settled down to a long line of expensive and beautifully-made T-headed touring cars, the early ones being chain-driven fours. In 1907 $3,800 was asked for the $3\frac{3}{4}$-litre Model E and $4,500 for the $5\frac{3}{4}$-litre Model H. By 1909, the bigger four had grown up to 7.7 litres, and 1911 brought the debut of the famous T-headed 48, originally with 'square' engine dimensions of 114×114mm, but later growing up to $8\frac{1}{2}$ litres. It developed 90bhp, had dual magneto ignition (later coil) and was still being listed in 1929; its price was $4,800 in 1912, increased to $9,600 towards the end of its production run. Body styles were attractive, especially the open Sportifs and Gunboat Roadsters introduced during World War 1. There was also a smaller 38 to the same specifications.

Locomobile encountered financial difficulties in 1920, and after a short spell with Crane-Simplex and Mercer in the Hare's Motors group, was acquired by W.C. Durant's last empire in 1922. Durant continued the 48 and added another luxury car, the 90 with L-head monobloc engine, but the Locomobile factories were utilized for the production of the inexpensive Flint. In 1925 came the Junior 8, a competitor for the Chrysler with a $3\frac{1}{4}$-litre ohv engine, selling at $1,785. In 1929, the last year of production, the 48 and 90 were still available, but the staple car was a 4.9-litre Lycoming-engined straight-8 at $2,850, a sad end for a firm which had been advertising eleven years before that 'no stock parts or ready-made units are permitted'.　　MCS

LOEB *see* LUC

LOGAN (i) (US) *1903–1908*

Logan Construction Co, Chillicothe, Ohio

The Logan was a light car using the air-cooled Carrico engine, available in either two- or five-seater models. Model O for 1907 was a 'semi-racer' with a 4-cylinder engine, A Hassler transmission and shaft drive. The company subsequently limited itself to commercial vehicles.　　GMN

LOGAN (ii) (US) *1914*

Northwestern Motorcycle Works, Chicago, Ill.

This was a minor make of cyclecar with a 2-cylinder Spacke engine, a friction transmission and V-belt drive. The side-by-side two-seater was priced at $375.　　GMN

LOHNER (A) *1896–1906*

Jacob Lohner & Co, Vienna

The firm of Lohner, well-established as coachbuilders, was the first to start industrial production of motor cars in Austria in 1896. French Pygmée engines were used for the first Lohner cars. However, Lohner soon began to concentrate on electric cars, producing his first in 1898. Also in 1898 Lohner engaged a young engineer, Ferdinand Porsche, who for more than 50 years was to be one of the greatest names in the automobile world. His first car design was adopted by Lohner. This was built on the Radnabenmotor principle, in which an electric motor was fitted to each of the front wheels, dispensing with transmission systems. These cars were known as Lohner-Porsches. Lohner also developed cars using the *mixte* system, whereby energy for the electric motors was produced by a generator driven

1909 LOCOMOBILE Model 30 tourer. *Antique Automobile*

1926 LOCOMOBILE Junior Eight sedan. *Michael Sedgwick*

1908 LOGAN(i) Blue Streak 20/24hp roadster. *The Veteran Car Club of Great Britain*

1903 LOHNER-PORSCHE petrol-electric tonneau. *Neubauer Collection*

1962 LOLA Formula 1 racing car. John Surtees at the wheel. *Autosport*

1971 LOLA T212 2-litre sports car. *Geoffrey Goddard*

1972 Lola T300 Formula 5000 racing car. *Lola Cars Ltd*

by a petrol engine. A racing car on this principle participated in several races, driven by Porsche himself. Both systems worked quite satisfactorily, but proved too expensive in comparison with petrol cars. The patents were sold to Emil Jellinek in 1906. Electric as well as petrol electric cars were built to his order in the Austro-Daimler works. After 1906 Lohner built trolley-buses (Lohner-Stoll) for a few years, but did not take up production of private cars again. After World War 2 the company produced scooters. HON

LOIDIS (GB) *1900–1904*

A. Dougill & Co Ltd, Leeds, Yorks.

The name Loidis seems to have been given to a number of vehicles imported or made by Dougills. The German Lux (i) friction-drive car was imported under this name for a while, and a few cars were assembled using 6hp De Dion or 9hp Aster engines, Fafnir gearboxes and shaft drive. The name comes from Caer Loidis, the Celtic name for Leeds. GNG

LOLA (GB) *1958 to date*

(1) E. Broadley, Bromley, Kent *1958*
(2) Lola Cars Ltd, Bromley, Kent; Byfleet, Surrey *1958–1961*
(3) Lola Cars Ltd, Bromley, Kent *1961–1965*
(4) Lola Cars Ltd, Slough, Bucks. *1965–1970*
(5) Lola Cars Ltd, Huntingdon *1971 to date*

In 1956 Eric Broadley built a sports-racing car for the 100E Ford-engined class, which won every race he drove it in. This design was subsequently developed into the production model. Particularly in the hands of P. Ashdown, P. Gammon, M. Ross and M. Taylor, Coventry-Climax-engined versions swept all before them in 1959, the first full competition season as a marque. Noteworthy design features included a full space-frame of both round and square-section tubes, stressed floor, canted engine, coil ifs and rear drive shafts which doubled duty as upper suspension links.

Formula Junior was essayed in 1960, with a similar design incorporating an offset driver. Besides the works cars, D. Taylor and members of the Fitzwilliam Racing Team achieved some good placings. Hustled by Lotus successes, the rear-engined Mark 3 version appeared for 1961, and by 1962 a Mark 5 version was racing. That year the finance firm of Bowmakers sponsored a Formula 1 Lola team, based on the Junior designs, John Surtees, newly weaned from two wheels, put in some very commendable drives. At the 1963 Racing Car Show the sensational GT coupé appeared, with Ford V-8 engine behind the driver. Amongst the many who went wild over it were some senior Ford executives, and thus it formed the genesis of the great line of Ford GT sports-racers. Meanwhile, Lola themselves continued development of the single-seaters, achieving various successes in the new Formulae 2 and 3 in the hands of C. Amon, R. Attwood, M. Beckwith, D. Hobbs, J. Surtees and others. Monocoque structure was introduced in 1965, and the culmination of this line was perhaps the Type 90 with which Gragam Hill won the 1966 Indianapolis '500' race. Also in 1965, the Type 70 made its debut, and John Surtees ensured that it quickly made its mark.

Built to comply with Appendix C, Group 7 of the International regulations, these cars achieved an enviable reputation in their class, and as in the case of the early 1100cc sports cars, racing successes were reflected in the sales figures. Early cars had a punt chassis; the Mark 3 edition used a monocoque construction, with reinforcement from boxed side members containing fuel bags. 4.7-litre Ford or Chevrolet 5½-litre engines were offered as standard, and the body was of fibreglass, partly stressed. In 1967 a GT version also became available, the wheel thus turning full circle to the original progenitor of 1963. A single-seater, the Type 100, was still listed for the monoposto classes. With the announcement of an agreement between Lola and Aston-Martin, who unveiled a double ohc V-8 engine at the beginning of the year, came the hope that there might be an all-British competitor in the large sports-racing class, but after an unsuccessful Le Mans foray, development was shelved.

The first one or two numbers in Lola types denote the basic model, the last digit being used for any subsequent developments. The T110 was an abandoned Formula 1 project, T120 a one-off hill-climb car, T130 the chassis designed by Lola for the 1968 Honda Formula 1 car and T140 the Formula A/5000 model. The T142 version, priced at £5,500 for 1969, was particularly successful. T160 was the 1968 'Can-Am' car for Group 7 racing, but neither this car nor its successors, the T220 of 1970, T260 of 1971 and the T310 of 1972, ever quite managed to fulfil their obvious promise, despite on occasion drivers of the calibre of Jackie Stewart.

In sports-car racing the 2-litre FVC-engined cars were consistently in the money, winning the European Championship in 1971, mainly with the current T212 in the hands of Jo Bonnier, Guy Edwards, John Love, Ronnie Peterson and others. The T290 of 1972 was a worthy successor. Both the T200 Formula Ford and the T250 Formula Super Vee series, developed over several years, achieved some good performances in their respective classes. Another unraced Formula 1 car took the designation T230. In Formula 5000 Frank Gardner took the 1971 Rothmans Championship, partly with the T192, which he had been instrumental in developing in 1970, and partly with the new T300 based on a side-radiatored Formula 2 design.

A South American derivative was the project of Carlos Avallone of Sao Paolo, who laid down twelve sports cars based on T163 framework with T142 suspension.

The T280 sports-racing car, with 3-litre engine derived from the Cosworth DFV Formula 1 unit, was the only vehicle to challenge Ferrari consistently in speed during the 1972 Championship events, even after the death of the main sponsor, Jo Bonnier, at Le Mans. Unfortunately the cars were not as reliable as the Ferraris and no outstanding results were achieved. Excellent results, however, were achieved in 1972 Formula 5000 racing by Alan Rollinson and David Hobbs with the T300. Lola interest continued at Indianapolis also: the 1972 T270 wide-bodied aluminium monocoque was sponsored by the firm's U.S. distributor Carl Hass.

During 1970 Lola had sold over 200 cars and in 1971 they maintained their position as the world's leading racing-car maker with sales of 135 in a falling market.

DF

LOMAS (GB) 1966 to date
Lomas Racing, Knutsford, Cheshire

Early Lomas productions were Club sports racing cars, but the single-seater market was entered with an exceptionally light and simple Formula Vee kit, originally priced at only £147. By 1970 a more sophisticated kit was offered at £292, but unexpected difficulty was encountered with eligibility of the design for the class. There was a project for the model to be converted and sold as a production road sports car.

DF

LOMBARD (F) 1927–1929
Bollack, Netter et Cie, Argenteuil, Seine-et-Oise; Puteaux, Seine

André Lombard, who had driven Salmsons successfully in competitions, set up on his own to produce a sporting voiturette of advanced design bearing his own name, and manufactured for him by E. Brault. The driver sat far forward, beside the engine. The wheels were enclosed and the car was slung very low, the whole effect being far in advance of its time. Production cars, all with 4-cylinder, 1,083cc engines, and conventional seating but offered in several models, had twin ohc engines, with or without Cozette superchargers, and a 4-speed gearbox. The last new Lombard offered was a twin-cam 3-litre straight-8. Dhome's Lombard won the 1929 Bol d'Or 24 hour race. In 1929 Lombard ceased to sell cars under his own name; B.N.C. took over the stock of parts and assembled a few cars which they sold, and raced, under the name B.N.C.

TRN

LOMBARDA see ESPERIA

LONDONIA see OWEN (i)

LONDON SIX (CDN) 1921–1924
London Motors Ltd, London, Ont.

Approximately 100 London cars were produced in a four-year period. The cars were large and well built and powered by a Herschell-Spillman 6-cylinder engine which was tilted down at the rear. Other features of this massive quality car were aluminium bodies and laminated wood disc wheels.

KM

LONE STAR (US) 1920–1922
Lone Star Motor Truck and Tractor Corp, San Antonio, Texas

An assembled car, the Lone Star was available as a 4-30 or a 6-40 both using Lycoming power units. Open and closed models were listed. The cars were in fact made for the Lone Star Corporation by Piedmont Motor Car Co of Lynchburg, Va, who also made the Alsace, Bush and other cars.

KM

LONGTIN (B) 1902–c.1904
Longtin et le Hardy de Beaulieu, Jette St Pierre

This company made a small number of cars with 6hp single-cylinder engines, 10 and 14hp twins, or a 20hp four. The last-mentioned was chain-driven; the smaller cars used shaft drive.

GNG

LONSDALE (GB) 1900
Monk & Lonsdale, Brighton, Sussex

Designed by Albert Lambourne, who later built the Old Mill car, the Lonsdale was powered by a 2½hp air-cooled engine of the makers' own construction, and had belt drive.

GNG

LOOMIS (US) 1896–1904
(1) Gilbert J. Loomis, Westfield, Mass. 1896–1897
(2) Loomis Automobile Co, Westfield, Mass. 1901–1903
(3) Loomis Auto Car Co, Westfield, Mass. 1903–1904

Gilbert Loomis built a pioneer steam car in 1896, but did not put it into production. His first cars built for sale used 5hp Crest air-cooled engines. About 50 of these cars were made from 1901 onwards, and Loomis also made carburettors and silencers for other firms. In 1904 a 3-cylinder 18hp car appeared with single chain drive and rear-entrance tonneau body. Loomis afterwards worked as a designer for Pope-Tribune, Payne Modern and Speedwell.

GNG

1927 LOMBARD Type AL-3 racing car. *T.A.S.O. Mathieson*

1924 LONDON SIX sedan. *Keith Marvin Collection*

1903 LONGTIN 20hp tonneau. *Geoffroy de Beauffort Collection*

1912 LORELEY 8/24PS tourer. *Neubauer Collection*

1922 LORYC 904cc racing car. *Foto Claret*

1909 LOTIS 12/18hp tourer. *Autocar*

1954 LOTUS-M.G. 1¼-litre sports car. *N.W. Norman*

LORD BALTIMORE (US) 1913

Lord Baltimore Motor Car Co, Baltimore, Md.

The Lord Baltimore had a 4-cylinder L-head engine of 5.1 litres with a 4-speed selective transmission. It offered electric lights and starting by a compressed-air system. A five-seater tourer and a two-seater raceabout were produced. **GMN**

LORELEY (D) 1906–1927

Rudolf Ley AG, Arnstadt

Ley was a well-established engineering firm which introduced its first motor car, a 4-cylinder 6/10PS model with a 1.5-litre engine, in 1906. Loreley was the model brand-name adopted for Ley cars. The next car was a 6-cylinder 10/25PS 2.6-litre model, one of Germany's early sixes. It was followed by several 4- and 6-cylinder models during the next few years which were of a good technical standard. The 1912 6-cylinder had a capacity of little over 1½ litres. Small cars were a speciality which increased the availability and popularity of the make. Production of 1½, 2- and 3.1-litre 4-cylinder sv models continued after World War 1, and there was an ohc sports 1½-litre in 1924. Manufacture of private cars ceased in 1927 (light commercials were produced until 1929). Ley was one of the few firms which experimented with aerodynamic bodies to Jaray designs. **HON**

LORENC (B) 1903–1904

Transmission Lorenc, Brussels

The Lorenc was powered by two single-cylinder De Dion engines, one driving each front wheel independently by chain. It had a substantial four-seater tonneau body. There is possibly some connection between this car and the Hungarian firm of Lorenc & Lorenc of Budapest who were in the motor and cycle business, although it has not been established that they made complete cars. **GNG**

LORRAINE (i) (US) 1907–1908

Lorraine Automobile Mfg Co, Chicago, Ill.

The Lorraine was a large car with a 5.1-litre 4-cylinder engine. It had selective transmission and shaft drive. The range consisted of a seven-seater limousine and a two- or four-seater roadster. **GMN**

LORRAINE (ii) (US) 1920–1922

Lorraine Motors Corp, Grand Rapids, Mich.; Detroit, Mich.

The Lorraine was an assembled car which succeeded the Hackett and which was powered by a 4-cylinder Herschell-Spillman engine. Both open and closed models were sold but total production only reached a few hundred cars. **KM**

LORRAINE; LORRAINE-DIETRICH see DE DIETRICH

LORYC (E) 1920–1924

Talleres Lacy y Ribas SRL, Palma de Mallorca

The only car to be made in the Balearic Islands, the Loryc was a small sports car using a Ruby 4-cylinder 904cc engine, which usually carried two-seater sports or faux cabriolet bodies. It was based on the original model of the E.H.P. **JR-V**

LOS ANGELES (US) 1913–1915

Los Angeles Cycle Car Co, Buffalo, N.Y.

Chassis for this cyclecar were shipped to Los Angeles to be fitted with bodies, which explains the Buffalo address. The Los Angeles had an underslung steel frame, friction transmission and double chain drive and was powered by a 4-cylinder, water-cooled engine, or an air-cooled V-twin, both of 10hp. **GMN**

LOST CAUSE (US) 1963–1964

Lost Cause Motors, Louisville, Ky.

The Lost Cause concern was the idea of Charles Peaslee Farnsley, who founded it to offer buyers the kind of extras the motor industry did not normally provide. He began to supply Corvairs with 'custom' work by Enos Derham of the Derham Custom Body Works. This included such extras as racing rally timers and aircraft equipment such as altimeters and compasses. Among other items were picnic hampers, mint julep cups of vermeil, matching luggage and car rugs. The starting price of the lengthened-wheelbase Lost Cause cars was quoted at $19,600 but prices were expected to reach as high as $23,000. **KM**

LOTHIAN (GB) 1920

W.J.M. Auto Engineers Ltd, London S.W.9

The Lothian was a mystery car of which only brief specifications were published, and apparently no press descriptions or road tests. Two models were listed, a 10hp and an 11.9hp, both with 4-cylinder engines. **GNG**

LOTIS (GB) 1908–1912

Sturmey Motors Ltd, Coventry, Warwickshire

The Lotis was made by Sturmey Motors, who had previously made the British Duryea car and the Parsons light delivery van. The original Lotis models had 10/12 or 12/18hp 2-cylinder Riley engines mounted under the seat, but for 1909 e engines were moved forward under a coal-scuttle bonnet. From 1910 a range ~sing 4-cylinder White & Poppe engines of 18/21, 20/24 and 25/32hp was made. A light 'Colonial pleasure car' using paraffin fuel, and known as the Lotis-Parsons, ~as also planned. GNG

LOTUS (GB) *1952 to date*
1) Lotus Engineering Co, Hornsey, London N. *1952–1959*
2) Lotus Cars Ltd, Lotus Components Ltd, Cheshunt, Herts. *1959–1966*
3) Lotus Cars Ltd, Hethel, Norwich *1966 to date*

Possibly no man since World War 2 has done more towards launching ~opeless manufacturing projects than Colin Chapman. Stirred by his 'fairy-tale' ~uccess story, countless imitators essayed production of racing or kit-built sports ~ars on limited capital, and fell by the wayside, lacking Chapman's inimitable ~ombination of determination, engineering knowledge, business acumen and luck.

The first Lotus was a tuned Austin Seven, re-bodied on functional rather than ~esthetic principles. The Mark 2 of 1949, when fitted with a Ford 10 engine, was ~uccessful in hill and speed trials. Public notice came in 1951, when the Austin ~even engine of the Mark 3 was fitted with steel strips to 'de-siamese' the inlet ~orts. With ifs and a very light aluminium body, this car ran faster even on three ~ylinders than its adversaries could manage on the full complement.

For 1952, Chapman formed a company with Michael Allen, moved to premises ~nore commodious than the workshops at Allen's Wood Green home, and produced ~he Mark 3B and the successful Mark 4 trials car, which Mike Lawson used as a ~uccessor to his Mark 2. Mark 5 was a stillborn 750 formula car, and Mark 6 the ~rst model in regular production. Offered in kit form, this was based on a multi-~ubular frame with stressed aluminium panels, coil suspension and Ford running ~ear. A Consul engine was first fitted, de-stroked to bring it within the 1500cc ~lass. Later successful cars were also fitted with Ford 10 engines and various M.G. ~nits, including a 746cc J4, and these vehicles achieved numerous sports-racing ~uccesses in their classes over the next few years. A Mark 7 was started and aban-~loned (becoming the Clairmonte Special); the number was later used for an up-~lated version of the Mark 6. In 1953 a colleague of Chapman's at De Havilland's ~oined the merry part-time band. This was Frank Costin, who designed the efficient ~erodynamic body of the 1954 Mark 8. A complex full-width space frame accom-~nodated either a 1497cc M.G. engine or a 1098cc FWA Coventry-Climax, and ~ De Dion type rear axle with inboard brakes. Maintenance, via the small gaps in ~he frame tubing, was diabolical. By 1955 Chapman had gained sufficient confidence ~o work full-time in his company, producing the Mark 9, an improved version of ~he Mark 8. The De Dion-axled model was the Le Mans, a cheaper Club version ~eing available with Ford gearbox, and sometimes with Ford 10 engine. The Mark ~0 was a larger edition, accommodating the 2-litre Bristol engine. The promising ~erodynamic cars won a lot of races, but also suffered a lot of breakdowns – the ~Mark 6 providing the bread and butter. Notable Lotus exponents of the period ~ncluded Anthony, Ashdown, Allison, Davis, Coombs, Flockhart, Jopp, Lumsden, ~MacDowel, Naylor, Scott-Russell, Steed and Chapman himself.

For 1956 the Mark 9 was superseded by the Mark 11, and further names in ~he roll of honour included Bicknell, Bueb, Hawthorn, Hill, Schell, Scott-Brown, ~Sopwith, and Stacey. By now all versions except the 'Club' model had disc brakes. ~Club Lotus developed a fanatical camaraderie, assisting the designer to learn faults ~and improve detail. The reputation of unreliability was not, however, entirely justi-~ied – many of the faults could be laid at the door of the assemblers of 'kit-built' ~ars, and 156 racing wins were recorded in 1956. Mackay Fraser also took 1100cc ~lass records at Monza. In this year the first single-seater appeared – the Mark ~2 Formula 2 with FPF Coventry-Climax engine. The multi-tubular frame was ~tted with a ZF gearbox/axle unit, and the 'Chapman strut' suspension was intro-~luced. With cast magnesium alloy disc wheels and body similar to the one that ~Costin had designed for the Vanwall, its appearance belied is comparative lack ~of success.

In 1957 the 11 adopted the 'wishbone' front suspension of the Formula 2 car, ~and having achieved homologation under Appendix 'C' of the international ~egulations, Ian Walker's car won the British 'Autosport' series-production sports-~ar championship. Total production passed 300, whilst later in the year two ~ignificant new cars were shown. The Mark 7 followed the chunky functionality ~of line of the Mark 6, but employed a similar frame to the Mark 11. A 100E Ford ~ngine was standard, though a 'Super Seven' was available with Coventry-Climax ~ower and disc brakes. The Ford-engined car proved the more successful in its ~lass. The other surprise was the Mark 14, the prototype Elite fibreglass monocoque ~coupé, using a 1216cc engine designed by Coventry-Climax for the U.S.A. 1300cc ~GT class, mated to a B.M.C. 'B' gearbox.

1958 saw the introduction of the successful sports-racing Mark 15, with strut ~suspension at the rear, canted engine, very low lines, and a 5-speed gearbox ~ncorporated with the rear axle. The Coventry-Climax 1475cc unit was standard, ~hough 2-litre or 2.2-litre versions were also offered. An improved single-seater ~the Mark 16) appeared, at first with a horizontal engine layout. The outmoded ~small sports Mark 11 was replaced by the Mark 17, a light car using the new-~ype suspension, but this model was still no real match for the contemporary Lola ~n the class.

1957 LOTUS Mark 11 1.2-litre sports car. *Motor Sport*

1959 LOTUS Mark 14 Elite 1.2-litre special coupé. *Lotus Cars Ltd*

1961 LOTUS Super Seven 1½-litre sports car. *Autosport*

1962 LOTUS Mark 25 Formula 1 racing car. Jim Clark at the wheel. *Motor Sport*

1965 LOTUS Mark 26 Elan 1.6-litre convertible.
Lotus Cars Ltd

1966 LOTUS Mark 46 Europa 1.5-litre coupé.
Lotus Cars Ltd

1967 LOTUS Mark 49 Formula 1 racing car.
Peter A.C. Darley

In 1959 the Mark 16 was given a new frame and nearly upright engine, but the tortuous transmission and other design features gave works drivers Hill and Ireland continual disappointments. However, production of the Elite was at last commenced, with a new company in a new factory. At the end of the year the Mark 18 was announced, as a rear-engined Formula Junior. This model, Cosworth-Ford powered, swept all before it in 1960 in the hands of Arundell, Clark, Henry Taylor and Trevor Taylor. These successes were overshadowed by the marque's first Formula 1, by Stirling Moss at Monaco in Rob Walker's Mark 18 strengthened for the 2495cc Coventry-Climax engine.

Some 125 Mark 18s were sold that year, while even at this early juncture some 400 Sevens had been made. The Elite continued to achieve GT class wins, remaining a strong contender even after it had been superseded. As a road car however, this machine was noisy, lacking in creature comforts and not always reliable – nevertheless final production reached 988 in 1963.

1961 was a Ferrari year in Formula 1, but Moss's skill earned two major victories for the rather fragile Lotus 18. Meanwhile the Mark 20 had appeared becoming the leading Formula Junior car. In sports-car racing the Mark 19 ousted the Cooper Monaco from its supremacy. Innes Ireland and others also winning most major 1962 races with this model. A typical Lotus specification of this period would be a small-diameter tubular space frame, Chapman strut rear suspension with Armstrong coil/damper units, rear-mounted Cosworth-Ford engine driving though an inverted Renault or Volkswagen gearbox, and fibreglass body panels by Williams and Pritchard.

Early in 1962 a surprise replacement Formula Junior car was announced, with canted engine. Arundell, backed by Spence, continued the winning vein. The Formula 1 car was the Mark 24, and very promising too. Then came the bombshell – the stressed-skin monocoque Mark 25, which first appeared at Zandvoort in May. This was truly an epoch-making design, being eventually copied (as were many of Chapman's innovations) by nearly all serious racing-car constructors. In its first year, Clark and Lotus finished runners-up in the Championships.

Shortly afterwards a European journalist published doubts about the engine capacity of the omnipotent Formula Junior cars, which gave Chapman an opportunity to show his habitual aptitude for making the very best of a situation. He gained the maximum publicity and acclaim by laying a wager to repeat the questioned performance, hiring the Monza circuit to do so. Peter Arundell bettered his race speeds in the same car, which was subsequently checked as complying precisely with the Formula. In September a sports model put up a remarkable showing at the Nürburgring, powered by a twin ohc conversion designed by H. Mundy and R. Ansdale of the 5-bearing 1499cc 116E Ford Classic engine. This unit was fitted to the front-engined road car known as the Mark 26 or Elan. A sheet-steel box-sectioned backbone chassis was employed, branching at the front to hold the engine, and slightly at the rear for the Chapman strut suspension. Disc brakes were fitted. The body, styled by J. Frayling, featured retractable headlights operated by a vacuum unit. This model set standards of roadworthiness which enraptured motoring journalists, racing drivers and road enthusiasts alike – a well-known editor called it 'one of the finest "road-clingers" of all time'. With 1558cc engine and dual twin-choke Weber carburettors, 105bhp was developed in standard trim. Successive developments included the 1965 fixed-head coupé version (Mark 36), the very successful 1966 Series Two model (Mark 45), and the longer Plus 2, with extra seating and 118bhp. Sales were such that a move to more extensive premises was justified by 1966 – even by 1965 production was averaging 10 weekly, and in 1967 they passed 5,000.

Clark won seven of the ten *grandes épreuves* of 1963, annexing the Formula 1 championship for the Coventry-Climax powered 25, and Arundell continued his winning ways with a monocoque Mark 27 in Formula Junior. This was the first year of the Lotus-Cortina – the Elan engine and other major modifications transformed the staid Ford saloon into a 100mph sports car. The positive 'A' bracket location put too much torque on the rear axle casing, however, and for this reason the earlier models were not always very reliable. Later developments remedied this defect, and the model began to underline its racing successes (in the hands of Clark, Sir John Whitmore and many others) with wins in tough long-distance rallies (handled by Roger Clark, Elford, Söderström, etc.). The 1967 edition was slightly 'softer' and less Chapman-like in character: this was reflected in a reversal of the name to Cortina-Lotus. Mark 25 was superseded by Mark 33 in 1964, with modified rear suspension. Minor troubles robbed Clark of a second Championship victory, and the Mark 32 was trounced by the Brabhams and Coopers in the subordinate classes. Two noteworthy developments, however, were the Indianapolis cars and the Ford V-8-engined Mark 30 sports-racing model.

1965 was a better season; a Mark 35 in Jim Clark's hands redeeming the Formula 2 reputation, and Piers Courage securing a 'first time out' win in Formula 3 for the Mark 41 at the end of the year. This model surprisingly reverted to the tubular space-frame, in the interests of cheapness and ease of maintenance. Clark won races in every possible category, and besides repeating his 1963 Formula 1 triumphs, radically upset the American *status quo* by securing the Indianapolis laurels with the 4.2-litre Ford-engined Mark 38. A new Mark number, 37, was allotted to the perennial Seven in recognition of major chassis and body improvements.

The monocoque Mark 43 Formula 1 was designed for the disappointing H16

R.M. engine of 1966, and Courage and Pike showed potential customers that the Formula 3 cars could win races. Chapman, of course, generally picked the crest of a wave on which to launch a revolutionary new model, and this duly appeared at the end of the year. Two versions were available: the Europa for export, with reversed Renault R16 engine, and a Cosworth-Ford-powered model for racing. Common to both were a back-to-front Elan-type chassis, mid-engine location, and very low drag fibreglass GT body styled by Frayling. Another first-time win was achieved, by J. Miles at Brands Hatch.

Noteworthy single-seaters introduced during 1967 included the Mark 51, the first production Formula Ford car, and the Formula 1 Mark 49, with Ford-sponsored engine, which was the fastest car in Grand Prix racing. A fruitful association with the tobacco firm of John Player began in 1968, and though Lotus suffered a sad blow with the loss of Clark in a Mark 48 at Hockenheim, Jo Siffert and Graham Hill ensured that the 49B carried off the Formula 1 World Championship again.

In 1969 the consistently successful Mark 59 was introduced for Formulas 2, 3, and B, and a 4-wheel-drive turbine model, the Mark 56, led at Indianapolis. Developments during 1970 included a Series 4 version of the evergreen Seven, sold through Caterham Car Sales, with a new platform chassis and fibreglass body; the Mark 69 for the smaller racing classes; an unsuccessful wedge-shaped Formula 5000 (the Mark 70); and the 72 for Formula 1. This model regained the World Championship for Lotus, despite the loss of Jochen Rindt at Monza. The following year Emerson Fittipaldi gained more experience with this car before winning the World Championship in 1972 with the 72D, amazingly the third year of top-level racing for a basically unaltered design. The Brazilian driver made a good start to the 1973 Formula 1 season, winning the Argentine and Brazilian Grands Prix, still using the 72D. Manufacture of racing cars for sale had by now ceased, the works John Player Specials (as they were now known) alone maintaining the Lotus tradition. Infrequently new racing models still appeared: the Mark 73 of 1972 was a Formula 2 or 3 model with variable rate inboard front suspension and side radiators. Private owners continued to do well in many classes – during 1972 Keith Jarratt's 69F Formula Ford and Jon Fletcher's Modsports Elan were particularly hard to beat.

Steady development and increasing production were seen with the road cars. Sales figures in the United States alone exceeded 700 in 1971, when the Elan Plus 2S 130 received a more powerful 'big-valve' engine and the Europa earned a rear body line that improved visibility. An interesting 1972 model, possibly inspired by sales of a comparable rival marque, was the Elan sprint Estate marketed by Hexagon of Highgate and costing some £500 more than the standard product.   DF

1969 LOTUS Elan Plus 2 1.6-litre coupé. *Lotus Cars Ltd*

1973 LOTUS Elan Sprint 1.6-litre coupé. *Lotus Cars Ltd*

LOUBIÈRES (F) 1951–1953
Compagnie Normande d'Etudes

Also known as the Symétric, this was a petrol-electric car designed by Casimir Loubières. It used a transversely mounted 1100cc 4-cylinder engine driving a generator which fed four electric motors, one in each wheel. The system was not new, having been tried with a front-wheel-drive car as early as 1903 by Lohner-Porsche. An all-plastic body was used, the panels for the bonnet and front wings being used in reverse for the luggage boot and rear wings, hence the name Symétric. It never went into production.   GNG

LOUET (F) 1902–1908
(1) Sté des Automobiles Louet, Paris 15e *1902–1904*
(2) E. Louet et Badin, Auxerre, Yonne *1904–1908*

The first Louet was powered by an 18hp 3-cylinder vertical engine, and used double chain drive. In 1904 a full range of cars was offered including a 6hp single, 9hp twin and 12hp 3-cylinder. They also made 40 and 70hp 6-cylinder engines for marine use, and at the 1904 Paris Salon one of these with twin carburettors, was shown in a worm drive chassis with a wheelbase of 13ft 1½in. In 1905 a new 24/30hp 4-cylinder shaft-drive car was introduced, although the chain-driven 2-and 3-cylinder cars were still made.   GNG

1904 LOUET 9hp tonneau. *Geoffroy de Beauffort Collection*

LOUIS CHENARD (F) 1920–1932
Automobiles Louis Chenard, Colombes, Seine

Louis Chenard was one of the host of Parisian entrepreneurs who made small family cars in small numbers during the 1920s. His first machine was the 7/9CV of 1920, with a 4-cylinder, 1¼-litre engine and 3 forward speeds. A 4-speed gearbox and a greater variety of engines were soon available. In 1925, he was offering the 8CV and a 10CV, the latter a 1½-litre model.   TRN

LOUTZKY (D) 1899–1900
Gesellschaft für Automobilwagenbau, Berlin

Boris Loutzky was a very capable engineer who was better known for his designs for other factories. For a short time he produced small cars with 3½hp 2-cylinder vertical engines, bicycle-type front forks and bar steering.   HON

LOWELL (US) 1908
Lowell-American Automobile Co, Lowell, Mass.

This company was incorporated and announced the intention of manufacturing

1910 LOZIER 50hp Lakewood tourer. *Autocar*

1920 L.S.D. 8hp 3-wheeler. *Autocar*

1913 LUC 8/22PS tourer. *Neubauer Collection*

a car to be named the Lowell, with 4-, 6-, or 8-cylinder engines, at prices rangin from $1,250 to $2,500. Proof of actual production, however, is lacking. GM

LOYD-LORD (GB) *1923–1924*
Loyd-Lord Ltd, Chiswick, London W.4

The cars designed by A.O. Lord tended to be dogged by misfortune. Those offered under his own name were no exception. The Loyd-Lord was unusual, how ever, in that it started life as a conventional assembled car with a 4-cylinde 1795cc engine, but then developed eccentricities — evolution normally went t other way. The 11hp and 18hp Loyd-Lords of 1924 were both powered by 2-stro air-cooled supercharged engines, the smaller with 2 cylinders and the larger wi 4. A rotary supercharger was used. To aid cooling, the cylinders were separate cast and the aluminium cylinder heads were finned. TR

LOZIER (US) *1905–1917*
(1) Lozier Motor Co, Plattsburg, N.Y. *1905–1910*
(2) Lozier Motor Co, Detroit, Mich. *1910–1917*

The Lozier was one of the highest quality American cars of its era, and w highly favoured by the wealthy, conservative buyer. After three years of exper mental work, which included the building of a steam car, the Lozier compan launched their production car at the Madison Square Show in 1905. It had a 30/35 4-cylinder T-head engine, 4-speed gearbox and double chain drive, and cost $5,0C for the chassis alone. After 1907 shaft drive was adopted, and two models we available, a 40hp four and a 50hp six, the latter with a capacity of 9.3 litres. T cylinders were cast in pairs, and the T-head layout was still used. On this mod third gear was direct, fourth being an overdrive. Although closed models we available, the most popular bodies were the Briarcliff sports tourer, the Lakewoc torpedo and the Meadowbrook two-seater roadster. For a short period Lozier ha considerable success in racing. They won the 1910 National Stock Car Champio ship at Elgin, and in 1911 won the Vanderbilt Cup and came second at Indianapoli These successes were achieved with largely stock 6-cylinder cars.

In 1911 a smaller 6-cylinder, the 6-77, was introduced with an L-head engir which cost only $3,250 for the chassis. This car was designed by Frederic C. Chandler who left Lozier the same year with two other engineers, and forme the Chandler Company. This was the beginning of the end for Lozier, who broug out a 4-cylinder car in 1914 but found their sales hit by the Cadillac V-8 at t same price. They tried to interest Henry Ford in a take-over, but without succes From 1915 to 1917 prices were drastically cut, the 1916 Model 6-82 chassis costin only $2,775 as against $5,000 for the comparable 1913 6-72. The Model 84 4-cylind cost only $1,575, but production ended the following year. H.A. Lozier, son the founder, and brother of co-chairman E.R. Lozier, had left the company 1913, and afterwards manufactured the 12-cylinder Hal car at Cleveland. GN

L.P.C. *see* LEWIS (iii)

L-S (PL) *1936*
Wystawie Przemysw Mechanicznego i Elektrycznego, Warsaw

Alleged to have inspired the German Hanomag Type 1.3 of 1939, the Lux Spo contained an 8-cylinder 95hp engine and was built experimentally. F

L.S.D. (GB) *1920–1924*
(1) Sykes & Sugden Ltd, Huddersfield, Yorks. *1920–1923*
(2) L.S.D. Motor Co, Ltd, Mirfield, Yorks. *1923–1924*

Many jokes could be, and no doubt were, made at the expense of the little L.S.I 3-wheeler, generally to the effect that nobody was likely to part with pound shillings, or even pence to obtain one. Certainly few did. It was remarkabl ugly, though its outward imperfection concealed a normal V-twin J.A.P. air-coole engine and 3-speed transmission by shaft and final chains. The suspension was ver unusual: independent by coil springs at the front and with radius rods ar quarter-elliptic springs at the back. TR

L-T (S) *1923*
A.R. Lindström, Torsby

This was a neat-looking little car with a 20bhp air-cooled engine driving t front wheels via a 3-speed gearbox. An initial batch of 50 was planned, but on two were made. C

LUC (D) *1909–1914*
Loeb & Co GmbH, Berlin

The Loeb concern started to manufacture cars in 1909, after acting as agen for various well-known makes. Their first car was a 12/36PS, 3-litre model. Aft 1911 Loeb imported English Daimler chassis with Knight engines which were fitte with German bodies and sold as Luc-Knights. Two models were offered, one o 8/22PS, the other of 16/40PS. During 1913/14 a 10/30PS car with a 2,612cc s engine and a very advanced design of axle and rear suspension were produced. Loe went over to lorry manufacture during World War 1 and never returned to makir private cars. In 1920 the factory was taken over by Dinos. HO

JCANIA *see* OPPERMANN

JCAR (GB) *1914*

icar Ltd, Brixton, London S.W.

The Lucar was a light car using a 9hp 4-cylinder Aster engine and shaft drive.
ith electric lighting and starting, the two-seater cost 190gns.   GNG

JCCIOLA (I) *1947–1948*

, Penacchio, Milan

The Lucciola was a minicar with rear-mounted 250cc single-cylinder ohv engine,
speed-and-reverse gearbox, and chain primary drive. The frame was tubular and
e body was a two-seater rolltop convertible in the fashionable slab-sided idiom.
nly a few were made.   MCS

UC COURT (F) *1899–1936*

é des Ans. Etablissements Luc Court et Cie, Lyons

The Luc Court company was founded to make electrical machinery in 1892,
d their first car appeared seven years later. It had an 8hp 2-cylinder engine, double
ain drive and the unusual feature of a 5-speed gearbox. Later cars had a 20/24hp
cylinder engine, and in 1904 the speciality of the firm was a chassis which was
tachable from just behind the engine. It was said that the change to a new chassis
d body could be made in three minutes, and an advantage was that you could
oose a different countershaft ratio to suit the type of body being used. The 1906
nge consisted of a 10hp twin, and three fours from 10 to 40hp. In 1910 a new range
as introduced with inlet over exhaust valves: a 14hp four and an 18hp six, both
th long-stroke engines of 70 × 140mm. The four was continued with little change
til the end of private car production, and was used in a commercial chassis until
36. At the outbreak of World War 1, there were three basic models in the range:
e 14 and 18hp, and a large 20hp four of 3,600cc. An unusual feature was that all
odels still used chain drive, the chains running in oil-tight cases.

After the war the 14 was continued, joined for a short time by a 4,700cc four
hich was dropped in 1925. Luc Court output was never large, and private-car
oduction gradually dwindled during the later 1920s. For those who might want
e, the 14 was available to special order until 1936, after which date the engine
as no longer made, even for commercial vehicles. However, commercial chassis
ere made by Luc Court up to the early 1950s. One of the first Luc Courts, an 8hp
1901, survives in the Musée de l'Automobile at Rochetaillée-sur-Saône.   GNG

JCERNA (CH) *1907–c.1909*

-H Grivel, Lucerne

The Lucerna, or Aster-Lucerne, was an assembled car using Aster engines,
alicet et Blin frames and bodies made locally in Lucerne. 10/12, and 20/24hp
urs and a 20/24hp six were listed, all using shaft drive.   GNG

UCIA (CH) *1904–1908*

, Picker, Moccand et Cie, Chêne-Bougeries

Lucien Picker designed a 4-cylinder shaft-drive car in 1903 which so pleased its
rchaser, Charles Moccand, that he and Picker formed a company to make cars
Picker's design. They had 12/16hp or 24/30hp 4-cylinder engines, 3-speed
arboxes and double chain drive. Later models had inclined valves and hemi-
herical combustion chambers. About 100 cars were made before Picker became
chnical director of Megevet, engine builders, and the Lucia factory was acquired
Sigma (i).   GNG

UCIEN BOLLACK (F) *1929–1930*

ucien Bollack, Paris 16e

Lucien Bollack left the firm of B.N.C. in 1928 and, among other activities, took
e French agency for Lycoming engines. The following year he announced a car of
s own, assembled from American components. Naturally he used Lycoming
gines, straight-8s of either 4.3 or 5 litres' capacity, together with a Warner gear-
x and Columbia rear axle. A handsome 2-door saloon body was fitted and the car
oked not unlike a D.8 Delage. However, the Depression hit the Bollack project
fore the car could go into production, and despite the choice of engines offered,
is probable that only one car was made.   TRN

UCK UTILITY (US) *1913*

eburn Motor Car Mfrs Co, Cleburn, Texas

This short-lived car was a five-seater with a 4-cylinder 2.7-litre engine and a
speed transmission. It cost $2,000.   GMN

UFBERY (F) *1898–1902*

.E. Lufbery, Chaunay, Aisne

The first Lufbery cars used Daimler-type 2-cylinder engines and a combination
belt and epicyclic gearing which gave 5 forward speeds and 3 reverse. Final drive
as by double chains, and tiller steering was employed. Later cars used a 6hp 2-
linder engine of Lufbery's own design, but retained the unconventional gearing.
he cars were made in the works of the engineers Broquelin et Dupré.   GNG

1908 LUC COURT V4 9hp two-seater. *Lucien
Loreille Collection*

1926 LUC COURT H4 14hp saloon. *Lucien
Loreille Collection*

1936 LUC COURT H4-S2 14hp saloon. *Lucien
Loreille Collection*

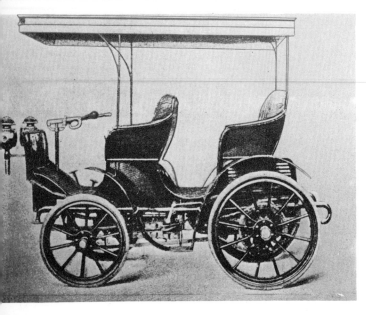

1901 LUFBERY 6hp phaeton. *Neubauer Collection*

c.1910 LUNANT 40hp tourer. *Lucien Loreille Collection*

1896 LUTZMANN 4PS *vis-à-vis. Neubauer Collection*

LUGLY (F) *1921*
SA des Automobiles Lugly, Courbevoie, Seine
   The Lugly was a conventional touring car using a 1.6-litre sv Balle engine.
GN

LU-LU (US) *1914*
Kearns Motor Truck Co, Beavertown, Pa.
   This oddly-named cyclecar was a side-by-side two-seater. It used a water-coole 14hp 4-cylinder engine, with a 3-speed transmission and shaft drive. The weigh was given as 930lb and it cost $398.
GM

LUNANT (F) *1900–1914*
Sté des Constructions de Cycles et Automobiles Lunant, Lyons
   J. Lunant was a bicycle maker who made a number of experimental cars an achieved small-scale production for a few years. He made an electric car in 190 and advertised two single-cylinder petrol cars in 1906, of 8 and 10hp. He als listed 4-cylinder cars of 16, 24 and 40hp 'built to order'. In 1913 one 4-cylind 10/12hp car with a monobloc engine and shaft drive was listed.
GN

LUNKENHEIMER (US) *1902*
Lunkenheimer Motor Vehicle Co, Cincinnati, Ohio
   Originally a carriage-building firm, the Lunkenheimer Company broadened i scope in 1902, building two cars, each of which had a 2-cylinder opposed engir housed under the front seat. Because of difficulties encountered in productio the car range was not continued, although the company survives as manufacture of industrial valves.
K

LURQUIN-COUDERT (F) *1906–1914*
Lurquin et Coudert, Paris
   This company built tri-cars from 1906, and their first 4-wheeler of 1911 (calle simply Coudert) was also one of the earliest of the cyclecars. It had a V-twi Train engine; final drive was by belts up to the beginning of 1912, and by frictio disc and chain thereafter.
GN

LUTÈCE (F) *1906*
G. Cochot, Colombes, Seine
   Cochot had made voiturettes as early as 1900, and his 1906 offering was a co ventional 4-cylinder car of 12/14hp with shaft drive. There were plans that it shou be sold in England by Teste & Lassen.
GN

LUTONIA *see* HART

LUTZ (US) *1917*
Lutz Motor Co, Buffalo, N.Y.
   This company was formed to manufacture steam cars, and was reported to b looking for a factory site in Buffalo, but there is no evidence that cars were eve made.
GN

LUTZMANN (D) *1893–1898*
F. Lutzmann, Dessau
   Lutzmann, whose designs were based on Benz principles, was one of the ear pioneers of motor-car manufacture in Germany. Output of Lutzmann cars wa not high although one model introduced in 1896, with a rear-mounted, 2-litr 4bhp horizontal engine, went into limited series production. Lutzmann was th only maker besides Daimler and Benz to exhibit at the first German motor sho held in Berlin in 1897 on the occasion of the founding of the Mitteleuropäische Motorwagen-Verein (Central European Car Club). In 1898 the production righ were bought by Opel, whose first cars were sold as Opels, 'System Lutzmann'.
HO

LUVERNE (US) *1903–1918*
Luverne Automobile Co, Luverne, Minn.
   This range of cars consisted of high-wheelers at first, but by 1909 more advance vehicles of 40hp were being built. Rutenber 6-cylinder engines of 38/40hp were use as well as some built by Beaver. Because of their uniformity of colour, inside a well as outside, later cars were known as 'Big Brown Luvernes'.
GM

LUWO (D) *1922–1923*
Kleinautobau Ludwig v. Wolzogen & Co KG, Munich
   A light car which used a 4/12PS Steudel proprietary engine.
HO

LUX (i) (D) *1897–1902*
(1) Lux-Werke, Ludwigshafen *1897–1898*
(2) Lux'sche Industriewerke AG, Ludwigshafen *1898–1902*
   The Lux company built special equipment for gas lighting before founding a automobile department. The first model was a four-seater with a horizontal opposed 2-cylinder engine, placed under the rear seat from which the car wa steered. It was very old-fashioned in comparison to the new Lux model whic

ppeared in 1901. This had a 2-cylinder front-mounted engine of 10/12hp. Produc-
on of this model lasted for only about one year. An electric car was also made
y this company, in addition to petrol and electric light commercials.   HON

UX (ii) (I) *1905–1907*
abbrica di Automobili e Cicli Lux, Turin
Lux cars were made by Eugenio Paschetta who had manufactured bicycles for
everal years. The cars had 2-cylinder 10hp engines at first, and after an agreement
ith Decauville, 16hp 4-cylinder engines.   GNG

UXIOR (F) *1912–1914*
erthaud et Moreau, Vincennes, Seine
The Luxior was a conventional 4-cylinder car powered by monobloc engines of
779 or 2257cc. It had a 3-speed gearbox and shaft drive.   GNG

.W.C. (US) *1916*
olumbia Taxicab Co, St Louis, Mo.
This manufacturer was primarily interested in cabs, but many taxis of the period
oubled as town cars. The limousine model was powered by a 4-cylinder, 27hp
ngine and cost $3,500.   GMN

YMAN (US) *1903–1904*
.F. Lyman, Boston, Mass.
Although it shared the same address as the Lyman & Burnham, this make was
issimilar in lay-out as well as in appearance. It was an expensive car ($6,250)
ith a 30/35hp 4-cylinder engine, sliding-gear transmission and shaft drive. The one
odel, a rear entrance, five-seater tonneau, was furnished with a removable
mousine top.   GMN

YMAN & BURNHAM (US) *1903–1904*
yman & Burnham, Boston, Mass.
This was powered by a 12hp, 2-cylinder engine, and had sliding-gear trans-
ission and shaft drive. The only body type was a five-seater rear-entrance
onneau. These cars were actually manufactured in Quincy, Mass. by the Fore River
hip & Engine Co.   GMN

YNCAR (GB) *1971 to date*
yncar Engineering, Taplow, Bucks.
A well-made monocoque single-seater designed by Martin Slater with partially
tressed engine, the Lyncar created much interest at the 1972 London Racing Car
how. John Nicholson's Formula Atlantic model was quite successful during 1972.
Cosworth DFV-engined version was planned for the 1973 hill-climb season.   DF

YNX (AUS) *1960–c.1962*
ynx Engineering, Sydney, N.S.W.
This was a conventional, but very neat, rear-engined single-seater. Cars were
ffered for Formula Junior with Ford 105E or Hansa flat-four engines, whilst a
ery successful hill-climb car used a 998cc Vincent twin.   DF

YONS-ATLAS; LYONS-KNIGHT (US) *1912–1915*
yons-Atlas Co, Indianapolis, Ind.
This make was an outgrowth of the Atlas Engine Co, an old builder of 2-stroke
ngines. The Lyons-Knight used sleeve valve Knight engines, of either 4 or 6
ylinders. The various models had generous dimensions, with wheelbases up to
0ft 10in. Five- and seven-seater touring models were offered, as well as a closed
mousine, the latter at a cost of $4,300.   GMN

1901 LUX(i) 10/12PS tonneau. *Allgemeiner
Schnauferl Club*

1913 LUXIOR 8CV coupé. *P. Kaefer*

1904 LYMAN & BURNHAM 12hp tonneau.
Keith Marvin Collection

1952 MACKSON Formula 3 racing car. Gordon Shillito at the wheel. *Autosport*

1899 MADELVIC electric brougham. *Museum of Transport, Glasgow*

1909 M.A.F. 8/10PS two-seater. *Neubauer Collection*

MACDONALD (US) *1923–1924*

MacDonald Steam Automotive Corp, Garfield, Ohio

This company attempted unsuccessfully to market a steam roadster called th[e] MacDonald Bobcat but the car failed to catch on. Closed models were also offere[d] but most MacDonald engines were ultimately used for those who wished to conve[rt] their petrol cars to steam.　　　　　K[

MACKLE-THOMPSON (US) *1903*

Mackle-Thompson Automobile Co, Elizabeth, N.J.

This two-seater runabout was driven by a single-cylinder, air-cooled engine [of] 5hp. It had three forward speeds and shaft drive. Its light weight (650lb) enable[d] it to reach 35mph.　　　　　GM[

MACKSON (GB) *1952–1954*

Guildford, Surrey

The Mackson 500 Formula 3 car was built under the aegis of the McGee refr[i]geration firm. Designed by Gordon Bedson, the car had a tubular frame with swing[-] axle rear suspension. Although various drivers, including Ken Wharton, raced th[is] model, successes were rare. Of the few buyers, probably M.G. Thomas was th[e] marque's most consistent and persevering protagonist.　　　　　D[

MACON (i) (US) *1915–1917*

All Steel Car Co, Macon, Mo.

This light car used a 4-cylinder, 2-litre Sterling engine. Wire wheels wer[e] standard equipment on this four-seater which was similar in general appearanc[e] to the Scripps-Booth.　　　　　GM[

MACON (ii) (GB) *1967–1971*

Macon Race Cars, Harrow, Middlesex

Tony Macon offered a conventional space-framed Formula Ford single-seate[r.] With Hillman Imp transmission, the price was a very competitive £850. The 196[ ] MR7 was priced at £1,345 complete in Formula Ford guise, and cars were mad[e] also for Formulas B, Super Vee (MR9) and Atlantic (MR10). Most were sol[d] in North America.　　　　　D[

MACQUE (AUS) *1913*

Allan Macqueen, South Melbourne, South Victoria

One of the very few cyclecars made in Australia, the Macque had a 2-cylind[er] horizontally-opposed 10hp engine, friction transmission and final drive by belt[s.] The price was £A170 for the air-cooled model, and £A185 for the water-coole[d] model.　　　　　GN[

MADELVIC (GB) *1898–1900*

Madelvic Motor Carriage Co Ltd, Granton, Edinburgh

The Madelvic company was formed by William Peck, the Astronomer Royal fo[r] Scotland. The car was an electric brougham in which power was transmitted t[o] the road through a small fifth wheel mounted in the centre of the vehicle, just behin[d] the two front wheels. The 3-wheeled *avant-train* could be attached to existin[g] horsedrawn vehicles. In 1900 the company was acquired by the Kingsburg[h] Motor Company. Some two-seater cars were also made with drive direct to th[e] front wheels.　　　　　GN[

MADISON (US) *1915–1918*

Madison Motors Co, Anderson, Ind.

The Madison was an assembled car built in small numbers and shown, first, a[s] a two-seater roadster and later as a four-seater roadster, and also a de luxe two[-] seater called the Dolly Madison model. A touring car was also made. A Rutenbe[r] 6-40 engine supplied the power with a Herschell-Spillman V-8 listed in 1916 only.　　　　　K[

MADOU (F) *1922–1925*

Automobiles Madou, Paris

Like many other small French manufacturers, Automobiles Madou used a variet[y] of proprietary engines according to the supply position at the time. The smalles[t] was a 900cc Chapuis-Dornier, while others were 985cc and 1,094cc Ruby, 1,170c[c] S.C.A.P., and 1,494cc C.I.M.E. units. Five Madous were Marguerite Model BO[ ] with Madou nameplates. At least one came to England and competed at the 192[ ] Autumn Meeting at Brooklands.　　　　　GN[

M.A.F. (D) 1908–1921
1) Markranstädter Automobil-Fabrik Hugo Ruppe, Markranstädt 1908–1911
2) Markranstädter Automobil-Fabrik vorm. Hugo Ruppe, GmbH, Markranstädt 1911–1921

This firm was founded by Hugo Ruppe, a son of Arthur Ruppe, after leaving his father's factory, known for Piccolo cars. M.A.F. cars, like the Piccolos, were air-cooled, 4-cylinder engines were used for various small cars in the 1200 to 1800cc range. Production was quite successful up to the outbreak of World War 1. After 1918, the pre-war model 8/18PS was continued and an 8/24PS model was added. A 14/38PS 6-cylinder model was turned out in small numbers. Production ceased in 1921 and the works were taken over by Apollo. HON

M.A.G. (H) 1912–1935
Magyar Altalanos Gepgyar, Budapest

The first M.A.G. cars used 4-cylinder engines of 25 and 35hp. In 1920 a reorganized company introduced a range of smaller cars known as Magomobil and Magosix. The former used a 1.8-litre 4-cylinder engine, and the latter a 1.6-, 2.1- or 2.4-litre six. They were the first cars to be made in Hungary on an assembly line, and a large number of both models were used as taxis, some surviving in use up to the 1950s. The Magosix had hydraulic 4-wheel brakes. GNG

MAGALI (F) 1905–1906
Gayon et Cie, Levallois-Perret, Seine

This company made two models, a 10hp and a 30hp, both using Lacoste et Battmann components. They also made motor cycles. GNG

MAGGIORA (I) 1905
Automobili Maggiora, Padua

These were 4hp and 8hp light cars powered by Austrian Laurin-Klement engines, but the company went into liquidation after less than a year. MCS

MAGNET (D) 1907–1926
Motorenfabrik Magnet GmbH, Berlin-Weissensee

This firm was well known for motor cycles and offered a 3-wheeled vehicle – a combination of motor cycle and sidecar – in 1907. By 1913 it was marketed as a three-seater with 830cc V-twin engine. A 4-wheeled car with a 4/14PS 800cc engine was introduced which was made with some minor alterations until 1926. HON

MAGNETIC (GB) 1921–1926
Magnetic Car Co, Ltd, Chelsea, London S.W.3

The British-built Magnetic car used the Entz magnetic transmission which had previously been tried out on the much larger Owen Magnetic and Crown Magnetic from America. For 1922 two Magnetics were listed, both with Burt-McCollum sleeve-valve engines. The smaller was a four of 2,614cc, while the larger was an eight of 5,228cc. The latter was not shown at Olympia, and may never have been built; it was not even listed after 1922. Magnetics appeared regularly at Olympia until 1925, but little was heard of them elsewhere, although at least one reached the second-hand market. In 1924 a new 2,888cc 6-cylinder ohv engine was used, and the cars had front-wheel brakes for the first time. In 1925 the six was continued, but with capacity enlarged to 3,297cc. GNG

MAGNOLIA (US) 1902
Magnolia Automobile Co, Riverside, Calif.

This company announced that a factory was being built and that 15hp touring cars would be made there, but it is not recorded that production ever started. GNG

MAHONING (US) 1904–1905
Mahoning Motor Car Co, Youngstown, Ohio

This car was available in single- or 4-cylinder air-cooled models. The 4-cylinder, 28hp model had three forward speeds, with final drive by single chain. GMN

MAIBOHM (US) 1916–1922
(1) Maibohm Motors Co, Racine, Wisc. 1916–1919
(2) Maibohm Motors Co, Sandusky, Ohio 1919–1922

The Maibohm was an assembled car using 4-cylinder engines during the first two years of manufacture and augmenting this with a Falls six in 1918. The smaller power unit was discontinued for the 1919 season. Open and closed models were available. The Maibohm name was changed to Courier in 1922. KM

MAICO (D) 1955–1958
Maico-Werke GmbH, Pfäffingen; Herrenberg

Maico had been well known for motor cycles from the early 1930s. In 1955 they started to make cars after acquiring the Champion (iv) designs. Initially a two-seater coupé was built, similar to the Champion, but in 1956 a four-seater saloon was added to the range, powered by a 398cc, and later 452cc, 2-cylinder Heinkel engine mounted at the rear. An open two-seater sports car was also made. Production of all cars ceased in 1958, although motorcycles continued to be built. HON

1930 MAGOSIX 2.4-litre saloon. *Neubauer Collection*

1920 MAIBOHM 20hp all-weather tourer. *Autocar*

1958 MAICO-CHAMPION 452cc saloon. *G.N. Georgano*

1920 MAIFLOWER 22.4hp two-seater. Prototype with Ford radiator. *Autocar*

1921 MAJOLA 12/20hp tourer. *Autocar*

1920 MAJOR 10hp two-seater. *Autocar*

MAIFLOWER (GB) *1919–1921*

Maiflower Motor Co, Ltd, Gloucester

Two young Army captains, M. Price and A.I. Flower, took advantage of the post-World War 1 car shortage, and used their gratuities to set up business as improvers of the Model T Ford. A replacement rear section was obtained for the lowered frame from Rubery Owen, and new front spring mountings were forged locally. Most mechanical parts remained standard, hidden behind a distinctive radiator and below a typically British body – tourer, two-seater or coupé. A number of cars were produced before the combination of the first post-war slump, the introduction of the horsepower tax and an element of internal discord brought manufacture to a halt.   DF

MAILLARD (F) *1900–c.1903*

M. Maillard, Incheville, Seine-Inférieure

The Maillard was first shown at the 1900 Paris Salon. It was made in two models, a 6 and a 10hp, enlarged the following year to 8 and 12hp respectively. The Maillard was made under licence in Belgium by the Société Générale de Constructions Aquila (no connection with the Aquila Italiana).   GNG

M.A.J. *see* JULIEN (ii)

MAJA (i) (A) *1907–1908*

Österreichische Daimler Motoren AG, Wiener-Neustadt

The Maja was a product of Austro-Daimler made briefly during a period when Emil Jellinek was interested in the company. Named after his younger daughter, as the Mercédès had been named after the elder, the Maja was a conventional 4-cylinder 24/28PS chain-driven car. Few were made.   HON

MAJA (ii) (D) *1923–1924*

Maja-Werk für Motor-Vierrad-Bau AG, Munich

This was a small car with an opposed twin-cylinder 500cc B.M.W. engine.   HON

MAJESTIC (i) (US) *1917*

Majestic Motor Co, New York, N.Y.

The only model of this make was an open five-seater costing $1,650. It used a V-8 engine of 4.6 litres, with Hotchkiss drive.   GMN

MAJESTIC (ii) *see* WHITEHEAD-THANET

MAJESTIC (iii) (F) *1926–1930*

Automobiles Majestic, Paris 16e

The Majestic was a conventional car using a 3-litre sv 6-cylinder engine, although an 8-cylinder model was announced for 1930.   GNG

MAJOLA (F) *1911–1928*

(1) J. Majola, St Denis, Seine *1911–c.1920*

(2) J. Majola, Chatou, Seine-et-Oise *c.1920–1928*

J. Majola was a maker of small high-efficiency engines before he turned to complete cars. His first was the Type A of 1911, a 1,300cc machine, designed by Doutre. This and the Type B, a 1000cc car that was also made after World War 1, both had single chain-driven overhead camshafts driving inclined valves, and hemispherical combustion chambers. They were beautifully made, very fast little cars. The 1,390cc Type DT of 1921 had four forward speeds, and was current until 1927. So was the smaller car, enlarged to 1,100cc, and renamed the Type F in 1923. The last new Majola was a cyclecar with an air-cooled flat-twin engine, introduced in 1927. The Majola had been made by Georges Irat since at least 1920, and in 1928 was absorbed by them completely.   TRN

MAJOR (F) *1920–1921; 1932*

Cyclecars Major, Paris

The short-lived Major cyclecar, built under Violet licence, made its mark in racing by winning the 1920 Cyclecar Grand Prix at Le Mans. Like most of Violet's creations, it had a 2-stroke engine. The two cylinders had a common combustion chamber, the inlet port being in one cylinder and the exhaust port in the other. As is obvious, the pistons moved together. Transmission was by friction disc.

In 1932 another Major, also a creation of Marcel Violet, was announced. It had a 3CV single-cylinder engine of 540cc, 3 speeds and shaft drive.   TRN

MALCOLM (US) *1914–1915*

Malcolm Jones Cyclecar Co, Detroit, Mich.

The Malcolm had a single headlight inset in the bonnet above the radiator. It was in the cyclecar class but had a 4-cylinder *en bloc* engine of 18hp, and room for three passengers. A V-twin with friction transmission and belt drive was also made. Some lists call this the Malcolm, and the larger car the Malcolm Jones.   GMN

MALDEN (US) *1898*

Malden Automobile Co, Malden, Mass.

The Malden was a light steam car with a two-seater body to which two extra front seats could be fitted. It had a vertical 2-cylinder engine, and wire wheels.

GNG

MALEVEZ (B) 1902–c.1904
Malevez et Michotte, Namur
The Malevez company were chiefly known for their steam buses and lorries, but they made a few light cars with 9hp 2-cylinder engines.

GNG

MALLIARY (F) 1901
G. Malliary, Puteaux, Seine
The Malliary voiturette used shaft drive from the vertical single-cylinder 5½hp engine to the rear axle. It had a tubular frame and wire wheels.

GNG

MALLOCK *see* U.2

MALTBY (US) 1900–1902
Maltby Automobile Co, Brooklyn, N.Y.
The Maltby runabout was a very light two-seater with tiller steering and bicycle-type wheels. The engine was mounted under the driver's seat, and suspension was full elliptic all round, the front spring being transversely mounted.

MJWW

MALVERNIA *see* SANTLER

MANCHESTER (GB) 1904–1905
Bennett & Carlisle Ltd, Manchester
Bennett & Carlisle were well-known retailers who assembled a few cars with Aster engines and chain drive. They advertised cars of 8, 10, 14, 20 and 30hp, but manufacture was always a sideline to retailing. The cars were sometimes known as Manch-Aster, a reference to their power units. The company later changed its name to Newton & Bennett, and sold the Italian-built N.B. cars.

GNG

MANEXALL (US) 1921
Manufacturer's & Exporters Alliance, New York, N.Y.
A small car, the Manexall had a 2-cylinder De Luxe air-cooled engine with a capacity of 1150cc, developing 13bhp at 2500rpm.

KM

MANIC (CDN) 1969–1971
Les Automobiles Manic (1970) Ltée, Granby, Que.
The first Manic, a rear-engined GT coupé with Renault mechanical components and its own fibreglass body, was introduced early in 1969 in Montreal, where production began. The company moved to a new factory in Granby in early 1971 but demand never matched expectations for this $3,000-up sportster.

HD

MANLIUS (US) 1910
Manlius Motor Co, Manlius, N.Y.
The Manlius was available as a small runabout or larger roadster. The roadster was powered by a 28hp air-cooled, 4-cylinder engine and was priced at $1,250.

GMN

MANNESMANN (D) 1923–1929
(1) Mannesmann Motoren-Werke & Co, Remscheid *1923–1926*
(2) Mannesmann Automobil-Werke AG, Remscheid *1927–1929*
Mannesmann were already manufacturers of commercial vehicles (Mannesmann-Mulag) when they took up production of private cars in 1923. The first models were light cars of 4/15 and 5/20PS, built until 1926. In 1927 a range of ohv 8-cylinder cars was introduced which were available with 3.4-litre, 55bhp, and 5.2-litre, 100bhp engines. The smaller car was available with Zoller supercharger.

HON

MANON (F) 1903–c.1905
H. Chaigneau, Paris 17e
The Manon light car used Aster or De Dion engines of 6 or 9hp, and was sold in England as the Mohawk-Manon by the Mohawk Motor & Cycle Company of Chalk Farm.

GNG

MAPLEBAY (US) 1908
Maplebay Mfg Co, Crookston, Minn.
This was a clumsy-looking two-seater runabout. It used a 22hp 4-cylinder, air-cooled Reeves engine with friction transmission; it cost $1,400.

GMN

MARATHON (i) (US) 1908–1915
(1) Southern Motor Works, Jackson, Tenn. *1908–1910*
(2) Marathon Motor Works, Nashville, Tenn. *1910–1915*
The Marathon was marketed in as many as four different chassis with ten different body types. These were powered by 30/35hp 4-cylinder engines, and sixes of 50hp. These units used the flywheel as an oil pump.

GMN

MARATHON (ii) (F) 1954–1955
Automobiles Marathon, Paris 17e

1970 MANIC GT 1300 coupé. *Hugh Durnford Collection*

1928 MANNESMANN 3.4-litre 8-cylinder saloon. *Neubauer Collection*

1950 MARAUDER 2.1-litre sports car. *Autocar*

1908 MARCA-TRE-SPADE 18/24hp chassis.
Autocar

1972 MARCH 722 Formula 2 racing car.
March Engineering Ltd

The Marathon used the body of the German Trippel with a rear-mounted Dyna-Panhard engine. Two models were made, the Corsaire GT coupé and the Pirate two-seater open sports car. GNG

MARAUDER (GB) 1950–1952
(1) Wilks, Mackie and Co Ltd, Dorridge, Warwickshire *1950–1951*
(2) Marauder Car Co Ltd, Kenilworth, Warwickshire *1951–1952*
The Marauder sports car used a Rover 75 engine and chassis, with a two-seater all-enveloping body built by Richard Mead of Dorridge. A 7.6:1 compression ratio and stiffer valve springs gave an extra 5bhp compared with the standard engine, and the chassis had stiffer suspension and a shorter wheelbase. Maximum speed was 90mph, although a 105bhp model capable of over 100mph was available to special order in 1951. Only 15 cars were made before production ceased. GNG

MARBAIS ET LASNIER (F) 1906
This company assembled a small number of cars, ranging in size from a 5hp single-cylinder voiturette to a 30hp 4-cylinder chain-driven tourer. GNG

MARBLE-SWIFT (US) 1903–1905
Marble-Swift Automobile Co, Chicago, Ill.
This was a two-seater car with a 2-cylinder, 10hp engine. It had friction transmission, double-chain drive and tubular axles. The coil radiator in front was surmounted by a magnificently large brass shell. GMN

MARCA TRE SPADE (I) 1908
Fratelli Bertoldo, Turin
Made by a well-known bicycle firm, the Marca was a conventional car with a 16/24hp 4-cylinder engine, 4-speed gearbox and double chain drive. GNG

MARCH (GB) 1969 to date
March Engineering Ltd, Bicester, Oxon
Beginning activities on a scale unusual for a new racing-car manufacturer, March caused considerable speculation when they announced their 1970 Formula 1 car, the 701. Only the moderately successful 693 Formula 3 pilot model had been produced previously. Design – by Robin Herd, the 'H' of March – was based on a conventional monocoque with no remarkable features, but despite an early Grand Prix victory by Jackie Stewart a somewhat disappointing season ensued. Victories were achieved also in Formulas 2, 3, Ford and Group 7 sports-car racing with the 702, 703, 708 and 707 models respectively, but in none of these classes did they find consistent success.
Better results came in 1971 when Roger Williamson won the Lombank Formula 3 Championship (713), but the outstanding ambassador for March was Ronnie Peterson, who earned second place in the Formula 1 Championship and took the Formula 2 Championship with the works 712. There was therefore keen anticipation when the 721 Formula 1 car was announced, with distinctive tray-shaped front wing, but 1972 proved to be a most disappointing year in this formula. Nor did the 721X, markedly lighter than the 1971 car (especially Peterson's special 'titanium' model), have the improved handling expected from putting the gearbox within the wheelbase. Eventually despair set in and a modified Formula 2 car was adopted, the 721G pioneered by privateer Mike Beuttler. However, in Formula Atlantic, Vern Schuppan, Bill Gubelmann, Chris Meek and Cyd Williams were conspicuously successful with the 722, which also managed some good results in Formula 2, and won the European hill-climb championship for Xavier Perrot. Sir Nicholas Williamson's handily-sized 712S BDA 2-litre took the British hill-climb championship. Other 1972 models included the 723 Formula 3, the 725 Formula 5000 with V-8 Rover-based engine, and a B.M.W.-powered Group 6 sports car. For 1973 there was a lighter and lower F2 car, the B.M.W.-powered 732, the F3 733, F5000 73A, and the 73S sports car using the same 2-litre B.M.W. engine as the 732. DF

MARCHAND (I) 1898–1909
(1) Orio & Marchand, Piacenza *1898–1900*
(2) Fratelli Marchand, Piacenza *1900–1906*
(3) Marchand & Dufaux, Piacenza *1906–1909*
Orio & Marchand was a sewing machine and bicycle firm which made a few small rear-engined cars of Decauville type. Later Marchands (1902) had front-mounted engines of 8, 10, 12, 16 and 20hp, and chain drive. By 1906 the range consisted of three 4-cylinder models, a 10/14, 18/22 and 28/35hp, and a 50/60hp six. They all had T-head engines with separately-cast cylinders, and double chain drive. Bodywork was very large and high, in some cases so high that passengers could stand up inside the closed models. AZ

MARCOS (GB) 1959 to date
(1) Speedex Castings and Accessories Ltd, Luton, Beds. *1959–1961*
(2) Monocoque Chassis & Body Co Ltd, Luton, Beds. *1961*
(3) Marcos Cars Ltd, Luton, Beds. *1962–1963*
(4) Marcos Cars Ltd, Bradford-on-Avon, Wilts. *1963–1970*

(5) Marcos Cars Ltd, Westbury, Wilts. *1970 to date*

Inspired by aircraft practice, Jem Marsh and Frank Costin developed a GT car with a composite chassis and lower body made of marine plywood. In the hands of Marsh and W.F. Moss, sufficient racing successes were achieved to overcome prejudice and scepticism. The first production model used a Ford 105E engine and gearbox, Nash Metropolitan or Standard 10 rear axle, and Triumph Herald steering and front suspension parts. Fibreglass body panels were fitted. This model was very successful, and J. Sutton gained the Autosport Trophy in 1961 and 1962 for victories in GT races. In 1964 a Volvo 1800-engined model was introduced, still with wooden chassis, but with all-independent suspension and one-piece body shell. Even with later simplifications, this sleek and distinctive motor car, styled by Denis Adams, was too much of a luxury product to sell in large numbers. It was supplemented by a 1½-litre Ford-engined version, and in 1966 a tuned 1,650cc alternative replaced the Volvo.

The Mini-Marcos arrived in 1965. This had a fibreglass body/chassis unit, accepted B.M.C. Mini components, but was still a true GT car in the Marcos manner. One of these was the only British car to finish the 1966 Le Mans Race. Including this model, nearly 1,000 cars had been sold (mostly in kit form) from the commencement of serious production in 1962 up to the end of 1966. Progress continued with the larger cars, including new models with 3-litre Volvo, V4 2-litre and V6 3-litre Ford engines, still available in component form as well as fully built. Top of the range was the futuristic V6 Mantis four-seater GT, with square-tube chassis frame, priced at £3,185 in 1970. Production was running at 4 cars per week and a move was made to larger premises, but a recession in the market led to a severe reduction in the firm's activities in 1972. The company was reorganized and the only model to continue in production was the Mini-Marcos. Incorporating a succession of minor improvements over the original cars, the Mark 4 edition sold at £295 as a kit without engine or suspension parts.   DF

MARCUS (GB) *1920*

Built in north-west London, the Marcus followed the 'carpet slipper' pattern of cyclecar design and was fitted with an air-cooled engine and belt drive. It was previously known as the Challenge and sold for £100.   MJWW

MARENDAZ (GB) *1926–1936*

(1) D.M.K. Marendaz Ltd, London S.W.9 *1926–1932*
(2) Marendaz Special Cars Ltd, Maidenhead, Berks. *1932–1936*

After production of the Marseal light car ceased, D.M.K. Marendaz went on to assemble some much more sporting machines that he called Marendaz Specials. They were low-hung, attractive cars, with very Bentley-like radiators. In the same chassis could be had a 1½-litre side-valve engine by Anzani (the 11/55hp model), the same unit supercharged and called somewhat optimistically the 11/120hp, and an 1100cc engine rated at 9/20hp. Record-breaking at Montlhéry in France and other energetic publicity gained the make a limited amount of popularity. For 1932, a small 1900cc six, known as the 13/70hp was offered. The side-valve engine was partly American and partly British in manufacture. It could be had with a supercharger. Hydraulic brakes with a reduction gear for the pedal were fitted, and the body, as always, was very good-looking. A bigger 2½-litre car, the 17/97, appeared for 1933. A new 2-litre 15/90hp six, powered by a Coventry-Climax engine with overhead inlet valves, was introduced in 1935. This car was successful in competitions, making a good name for itself. Its protagonists included Mr and Mrs A.E. Moss, the parents of Stirling Moss.   TRN

MARENGO (I) *1907–1909*

S.A. Automobili Marengo, Genoa

The first Marengos were small single- and twin-cylinder cars with shaft drive, but in 1909 the firm marketed a 1,326cc four rated at 10/12hp.   MCS

MARGUERITE (F) *1922–1928*

A. Marguerite, Courbevoie, Seine

Marguerite was an unusual manufacturer in that he not only marketed cars under his own name but sold them to a number of other firms including Induco, Madou and M.S. in France, and Hisparco in Spain. The Type A Marguerite, of which 12 were made, was powered by a 995cc 2-cylinder Train engine, but all subsequent cars used 4-cylinder engines, mostly made by Chapuis-Dornier. The Type B had a 900cc sv engine, and the Types BO5 and BO7 touring cars had 1,095cc and 1,494cc ohv engines. The Types BO and BO2 sports models had the 1,095cc engines, the latter in a lower chassis. Two BO2s used 1,100cc S.C.A.P. engines. The last five BO2s, made in 1928, were called Morano-Marguerites, because at that time the company was financed by Zamorano de Biedema. The same year he lost all his fortune at the Deauville Casino, and all production came to an end. About 450 cars were made by Marguerite in all, of which 200 were sold to other firms.   GNG

MARIE (F) *1907*

Built at Bayeux, the Marie was a single-seater car powered by a 1¾hp De Dion engine. Final drive was by belts.   GNG

1904 MARCHAND 12/16hp landaulette.
Museo dell'Automobile, Turin

1966 MARCOS 1600 GT coupé. *Marcos Cars Ltd*

1934 MARENDAZ 13/70hp coupé. *Arthur W. Ewing*

1910 MARION 30hp roadster. *National Motor Museum*

1923 MARKS-MOIR prototype two-seater. *Autocar*

1913 MARLBOROUGH(i) 8/10hp two-seater. *National Motor Museum*

1921 MARLBOROUGH(i) 10/20hp de luxe two-seater. *National Motor Museum*

MARIENFELDE *see M.M.B.*

MARINO (I) *1923–1927*
Società Automobili Marino, Padua

Initially Luigi Marino made a 1½-litre ohc 4-cylinder model with 4-speed gearbox, but in 1924 he adopted the 1,100cc C.I.M.E. engine and offered a range parallel with those of his French contemporaries. There was a 21bhp Normale, a 32bhp Tipo Sport, and a supercharged Gran Sport model capable of 77mph, all with three forward speeds. Two Marinos ran in the 1926 Gran Premio Vetturette at Monza, but both retired. The company survived until 1930, though latterly car manufacture was dropped. Luigi Marino made an experimental dohc 750cc sports car with rubber suspension in 1952.   MCS

MARION (US) *1904–1915*
Marion Motor Car Co, Indianapolis, Ind.

Early versions of the Marion had transversely-mounted 16hp Reeves air-cooled engines, and double chain drive. Their appearance was very similar to the contemporary Premier (also an Indianapolis car). 1906 Marions had conventionally-placed 16 and 28hp 4-cylinder Reeves engines, while later models used water-cooled engines by Continental and other firms of up to 48hp. A prototype roadster with 9,455cc V-12 engine was designed by George Schebler of carburettor fame, and built in 1908. Some quite big fours and sixes were made in the 1912–1914 period. Sales for a time were under the control of John N. Willys.   GMN

MARION-HANDLEY (US) *1916–1919*
Mutual Motors Co, Jackson, Mich.

The Marion-Handley was a continuation of the earlier Marion and was a fairly popular car for the few years it was produced. In appearance, the Marion-Handley resembled the typical assembled car of its time. Two models were available, a touring car and a four-seater roadster and these were available on two wheelbases: the 6-40 on 10ft and 6-60 on 10ft 5in. A Continental 6-cylinder engine was used for both. Artillery wooden wheels were standard equipment on the touring car, but wire wheels were offered as an option on the roadster.   KM

MARITIME SIX (CDN) *1913–1914*
Maritime Motors Ltd, Saint John, N.B.

This was based on the American Palmer-Singer and was widely advertised, although the extent of production is unknown. Expensive at $3,500, it was decidedly sporty with a Benz-style pointed radiator. Most of the models built were tourers.   RJ

MARKETOUR (US) *1964 to date*
Marketour Electric Cars, Long Beach, Calif.

This is a small electric car for shopping and running errands.   BE

MARKS-MOIR (AUS) *1923–1924*
Marks Motor Construction Co, Sydney, N.S.W.

The Marks-Moir frameless car used integral construction of Consuta multiply wood glued and sewn together by a special machine. The engine (Model T Ford on the prototype) was mounted amidships behind the two seats, and drove through a 2-speed epicyclic gearbox and an intermediate 2-speed sliding gear, giving 4 speeds in fact. The hull was of polished wood, the top of the bonnet and body were aluminium. Alford & Alder front-wheel brakes were fitted, and the 1924 model had a 10hp front-mounted Wolseley engine. Very few Marks-Moirs were made, but the design was used later by Heron (England) and Southern Cross (Australia).   GNG

MARLAND (F) *1970 to date*
Marland S.a.r.l., Issy-les-Moulineaux, Hauts-de-Seine

The first product of this company was a fibreglass coupé with Renault R8-Gordini engine, of which about 200 were made. In October 1971 the firm launched the Jorgia, a two-seater sports car with pre-war styling, powered by Citroën 2CV or Ami-6 engines.   LL

MARLBORO (US) *1899–1902*
Marlboro Motor & Carriage Co, Marlboro, Mass.

The Marlboro was a typical New England steam car in appearance, although it used a 5hp horizontal engine in place of the more usual vertical one. Final drive was by single chain, and four-seater bodies were available, in addition to the standard two-seater buggy.   GNG

MARLBOROUGH (i) (F/GB) *1906–1926*
(1) Malicet et Blin, Aubervilliers, Seine *1906–1924*
(2) T.B. André and Co Ltd, London *1909–1926*

This Anglo-French product started life as an entirely French car, but the British content increased until with the final 2-litre type the make was 100 per cent British. Malicet et Blin were well-known suppliers of components to the French industry, and the first car to bear the name of Marlborough was a conventional 7hp single-cylinder runabout exhibited at the 1906 Show in London by C.C.C. of

Taunton. The make's next appearance was in 1909, when T.B. André of shock absorber fame took over the agency. These Marlboroughs were conventional medium-sized machines with pair-cast cylinders, magneto ignition, 3-speed gear boxes, cone clutches and shaft drive, selling at a modest £270 for a 12hp of 2.8-litres capacity. There was also a bigger 3.1-litre four, and a short-stroke (85 × 90mm) six selling at £350. These cars had round radiators and were marketed until 1911, though by this time the six had acquired more conventional cylinder dimensions and a capacity of 3.6 litres. 1912, however, brought a change of direction and the Marlborough emerged as one of the first 4-cylinder cyclecars, with a 1130cc sv water-cooled power unit, a sharp V-radiator and shaft-and-bevel drive, selling for £185. Sir Francis Samuelson (with his wife as mechanic) drove one in the Year's Cyclecar Grand Prix, and by the outbreak of World War 1 it was an altogether more substantial affair with artillery wheels and a capacity of 1.2 litres. An electrically-equipped coupé could be bought for £275.

Post-war Marlboroughs were still largely French and had acquired round radiators, an extra 100cc, and four forward speeds. Subsequent improvements included 1½-litre British Anzani engines, rod-operated brakes and (in 1921) flat radiators. A rotary-valve machine was entered for the 1921 200 Miles Race at Brooklands, but did not start. The Anzani-engined 1922 Roadspeed model was guaranteed to reach 60mph, but a year later a differential-less light car used the familiar 1100cc ohv French C.I.M.E. power unit, these models being still listed in 1924 at £175. In 1923 T.B. André ventured into serious racing with the 1½-litre Marlborough-Thomas. Last of the Marlboroughs was a British-made 2-litre sporting six with an ohv Coventry-Climax engine, forced lubrication, 4-wheel brakes and 75mph top speed, but this never went into production. André made a brief comeback in 1933 with a small 2-cylinder sports car under his own name. MCS

MARLBOROUGH (ii) (NZ) 1919–1926

Designed by John North Birch, the Marlborough cars were large, beautifully-built machines powered by 5.8-litre 4-cylinder engines with five main bearings and full force-feed lubrication. Three cars were laid down, but only two completed, the first in 1919 at Blenheim, South Island, and the second in 1926 at Gisborne, North Island. The second car was renamed Carlton, a name also used by Birch for the small car he built two years later. GNG

MARLBOROUGH-THOMAS (GB) 1923–1924

T.B. André & Co, Weybridge, Surrey

The Marlborough-Thomas appeared as a separate venture from Marlborough in 1923. T.B. André and J.G. Parry Thomas, operating from a shed at Brooklands Motor Course, produced a handful of very exciting sports-racing cars powered by a 4-cylinder twin ohc engine of 1½ litres. The valves were closed by leaf springs, in a manner reminiscent of those of the Leyland Eight, also designed by Thomas. The low-built bodies were aerodynamically very efficient and aesthetically pleasing with their flared wings. TRN

MARMON (US) 1902–1933

(1) Nordyke and Marmon Co, Indianapolis, Ind. 1902–1925
(2) Marmon Motor Car Co, Indianapolis, Ind. 1926–1933

Howard Marmon's first cars were advanced machines, featuring air-cooled V-4 engines of oversquare dimensions, with mechanically-operated overhead valves and pressure lubrication. Something approaching independent front suspension was achieved by the use of double-three-point suspension, with a separate sub-frame for engine and transmission. Only the 2-speed gearbox of planetary type conformed to American practice of the period. These cars persisted until 1908, though 1907 brought the introduction of selective sliding-type gearboxes and a short-lived 60hp V-8. In 1908 buyers had the choice of air or water cooling and cylinder heads were detachable. The following year Marmon went over to conventional T-head in-line fours rated at 40/45hp and 50/60hp, and two years later only the 5.2-litre Model 32 with rear-axle gearbox was listed. Marmons did well in contemporary competition, with 54 1st places logged between 1909 and 1912; Ray Harroun won the first Indianapolis 500 in 1911 with a specially-built 6-cylinder car, the Wasp. An enormous 9.3-litre six rated at 48hp was available in 1914.

In 1916 the advanced ohv 6-cylinder 34 with aluminium cylinder block, body, bonnet and radiator shell, and double transverse rear suspension was introduced. Its engine capacity was 5½ litres, and its output 74bhp; developments of this model were still listed as late as 1927, acquiring Delco coil ignition in 1920, and the option of front wheel brakes in 1923. They were expensive: $5,000 was asked for a touring car in 1921. A not very successful 3.1-litre ohv straight-8 appeared in 1927, but the following season only eights were made, the cheapest sv 68 selling for $1,395. In 1928 Marmon also entered some front-wheel-drive cars at Indianapolis, but they were in fact only revamped Millers. The company sold 22,300 cars in 1929, thanks to a cheap new straight-8 at under $1,000, the Roosevelt. This brand-name, however, did not last, for the car appeared in the 1930 programme as the Marmon R, along with three other eights, the sv 69, and two big ohv cars with 4-speed gearboxes and capacities of 4.9 litres and 5.2 litres respectively.

Marmon's swansong was the magnificent 9.1-litre 200bhp 16-cylinder model of 1931. It was beautifully proportioned, and had an alloy engine. The list price

1911 MARMON Model 32 5.2-litre roadster.
Kenneth Stauffer

1917 MARMON Model 34 5½-litre cloverleaf roadster. *Don McCray*

1926 MARMON 74 5½-litre coupé. *National Motor Museum*

1931 MARMON V-16 9.1-litre convertible sedan. *Lucien Loreille Collection*

1930 MARQUETTE(ii) Six sedan. *National Motor Museum*

1906 MARS 6/7PS two-seater. *Dieter Schlaukötter*

was $4,925; there was a companion 8-125 in 1932, but only the Sixteen was listed for 1933. At the very end Marmon was testing a 150bhp V-12 with independent front suspension, De Dion rear axle, and tubular backbone frame, but this never saw production. MCS

MAROCCHI (I) *1900–1901*
Fratelli Marocchi, Milan

The Marocchi was a very small 3-wheeled two-seater, not much more than a motorized bath-chair in appearance. It had two 1½hp single-cylinder engines, one on each side of the front wheel, through which the car was driven. Steering was by tiller. GNG

MAROT-GARDON (F) *1899–c.1902*
Ph. Marot, Gardon et Cie, Corbie, Somme

This company were mainly known for motor tricycles and quads which they made from 1898, but in 1899 they announced a voiturette with 3hp engine and 3-speed gearbox. The following year the engine was increased to a 4½hp. For 1901 two models were made: a two-seater with a front-mounted horizontal 6hp engine driving the rear axle by chain, and a racing voiturette with a rear-mounted 7hp Soncin vertical engine, geared directly to the rear axle. GNG

MAROT-GINTRAC (F) *1905*
This Bordeaux company were mainly makers of stationary engines and motorboats, but they built a few cars with 4-cylinder 35/40hp engines. GNG

MARQUETTE (i) (US) *1912*
(1) Marquette Motor Co, Saginaw, Mich. *1912*
(2) Peninsular Motor Co, Saginaw, Mich. *1912*

The Marquette succeeded both the Rainier and the Welch. It was built in four body types, using 40 and 45hp engines. These were 4-cylinder T-head units, the larger engine being used only for the seven-seater touring model. The Marquette Motor Co was controlled by General Motors. GMN

MARQUETTE (ii) (US) *1929–1931*
Buick Motor Co, Flint, Mich.

This Marquette, introduced for the 1929 model year, was a small Buick with prices ranging from $990 for the business coupé to $1,060 for the sedan. A total of 13,850 of these 6-cylinder cars were marketed during 1929, but by 1930, presumably because of the Depression, it was decided to withdraw the make and the name disappeared from the list of American cars early in 1931. The only Buick product to use an sv engine, it had much in common with the contemporary Pontiac. KM

MARQUEZ (F) *1930*
Automobiles L.F. Marquez, Paris 5e

The Marquez was an expensive streamlined sports car with a straight-8 ohv S.C.A.P. engine of 2.3 litres. Very few were made. GNG

MARR (US) *1903–1904*
Marr Auto Car Co, Detroit, Mich.

The Marr was a two-seater runabout powered by a single-cylinder engine of 1700cc capacity. This was mounted under the seat. Steering was by wheel, and the vehicle weighed 1,000lb. GMN

MARS (D) *1906–1908*
Mars-Werke AG, Nuremberg-Doos

After manufacturing bicycles and motor cycles Mars started car production in 1906. A single-cylinder 6/7bhp and a 2-cylinder 8/10bhp model were listed, with friction drive on Maurer principles. HON

MARSEEL; MARSEAL (GB) *1919–1925*
Marseal Motors Ltd, Coventry, Warwickshire

In 1919, D.M.K. Marendaz, in conjunction with Seelhaft, began to make an orthodox light car from assembled components. It had a 1½-litre, 4-cylinder, sv engine by Coventry-Simplex, a 3-speed gearbox, a worm-driven rear axle and quarter-elliptic suspension. Seelhaft withdrew in 1923, upon which the car was renamed the Marseal, in order to appear less foreign. A 1¼-litre 11/27hp model was also made; this, and the 12/40hp 1½-litre were the best-known Marseals. They were solid, rugged cars, with a good performance, and did well in trials. Sports versions of both were made and so was an obscure six of 1750cc, with overhead valves. The sports 12/40 was said to be capable of 75mph. TRN

MARSH (i) (US) *1899; 1905–1906*
(1) Marsh Motor Carriage Co, Brockton, Mass. *1899*
(2) American Motor Co, Brockton, Mass. *1905–1906*

The 1899 Marsh was a steam car which was probably never produced in any numbers. From 1900 to 1905, Marsh built motor cycles which were known as Marsh-Metz from 1905 onwards, and from 1905 to 1906 a small car with a 10hp 2-cylinder air-cooled engine under the bonnet. In 1909 C.H. Metz bought the Waltham company and began to make the Metz car.   GNG

MARSH (ii) (US) 1919–1921
Marsh Motors Co, Cleveland, Ohio

The Marsh was a car of which only a few were actually built. It had a 3.3-litre 6-cylinder engine of L-head design.   KM

MARSHALL (i) see BELSIZE

MARSHALL (ii) (US) 1919–1921
Marshall Mfg Co, Chicago, Ill.

The Marshall was a typical assembled car of its time with a 4-cylinder Lycoming engine as its power unit. A touring car was the only body style offered.   KM

MARSHALL (iii) (GB) 1919–1920
P.F.E. Marshall, Gainsborough, Lincs.

Almost unknown, the Marshall was manufactured in very small numbers and is believed to have been fitted with the Coventry-Climax 'F' type 4-cylinder sv engine. This venture was in no way connected with Marshall Son & Co Ltd, also of Gainsborough, who made traction engines and steam rollers.   GB

MARSHALL-ARTER (GB) 1912–1915
Marshall-Arter Ltd, Hammersmith, London W.

The Marshall-Arter was a light car using originally a V-twin 10hp J.A.P. engine and drive by a flat spring in series with a propeller shaft. For 1914/15 the company turned to 4-cylinder engines by Chapius-Dornier, of 1,096 and 1,244cc. For a short time after its introduction the car was known as the Q.E.D.   GNG

MARSONETTO (F) 1965 to date
Ateliers Marsonetto, Lyons, Rhône

In 1958 Mario Marsonetto built a fibreglass coupé around Dyna Panhard components, and in 1965 a fwd four-seater sports car with fibreglass body, four-wheel independent suspension and disc brakes all round, powered by a Renault R8 engine. Named the Mars-1, this was made in small numbers until 1967 when it was replaced by the Marsonetto 1600, a luxurious GT coupé powered by a Renault R16-TS engine and capable of 140mph.   LL

MARTA (H) 1910–1914
(1) Hungarian Automobile Co Ltd (System Westinghouse), Arad 1910–1912
(2) Hungarian Automobile Works Ltd, Arad 1913–1914

The factory in which Marta cars were made was built in 1908 as a branch of the French Westinghouse company of Le Havre. Engines for railway use were made, followed by double-decker buses, and in 1910 the first cars appeared, with 16/20hp, 20/30hp and 30/40hp 4-cylinder engines. Shaft drive was employed on the smaller models, and chain drive on the larger. In 1912 the French company went bankrupt and control of the Marta concern passed to Austro-Daimler. A series of 18/22hp cars with 2½-litre 4-cylinder engines was made up to 1914. About 650 cars were made altogether, of which only 150 were under the Westinghouse regime. Lorries were made in the factory until 1926, as well as a few cars (see Astra ii).   GLH

MARTIN (i) (GB) 1905–1906
Hall & Martin, East Croydon, Surrey

Hall & Martin were car and motor cycle dealers who assembled a small number of cars using 10/12hp 2-cylinder Aster engines. Drive was by shaft and a four-seater tonneau body was fitted.   GNG

MARTIN (ii) (US) 1920–1922
Martin Motor Co, Springfield, Mass.

Also known as the Scootmobile, the Martin was a 3-wheeler on the same lines as the Scott Sociable, except that it used a pressed steel frame instead of the Scott's tubular one. Power came from a 616cc air-cooled V-twin engine, and the makers claimed a speed of 40mph and fuel consumption of 75mpg.   GNG

MARTIN (iii) (US) 1928–1932
Martin Aeroplane Co, Garden City, Long Island, N.Y.

The experimental Martin Aerodynamic car never got into production although it was widely acclaimed in car and scientific journals. It was designed by James V. Martin and General Billy Mitchell and carried a rear-mounted engine and independent suspension on all four wheels. Its radiator was mounted at the front.   KM

MARTIN (iv) (US) 1929–1932
(1) Martin Motors Inc, Washington, D.C.
(2) Martin Aeroplane Factory, Hagerstown, Md.; Garden City, Long Island, N.Y.

The Martin was an unsuccessful venture into the production of a midget car. The pilot models had been built as early as 1927 but despite considerable publicity to

1923 MARSEAL 11hp two-seater. *National Motor Museum*

1912 MARTA 18/22hp limousine. *G.L. Hartner Collection*

1922 MARTIN(ii) Scootmobile 616cc 3-wheeler. *Autocar*

1913 MARTINI 2.9-litre tourer. *Swiss Museum of Transport and Communications, Lucerne.*

1922 MARTINI Type TF 3.8-litre tourer. *Automobielmuseum, Driebergen*

sell the $200 mail-order midget, the car failed. It used a 4-cylinder Cleveland motorcycle engine of under 750cc, while the 5ft wheelbase chassis carried a two-seater coupé body. The price included the delivery crate, which could afterwards be used as a garage. Its 1931 catalogue referred to the car as the Dart, not the Martin. Often attributed to J.V. Martin, it was, in fact, designed by Miles H. Carpenter, creator of the Phianna.

KM

MARTIN (v) (GB) *1954–1956*
Ray Martin Racing Motors, Merton Abbey, London S.W.19

After Kieft turned from Formula 3 to sports cars, there was still a demand for the rubber-suspended swing-axle model to which Stirling Moss and Don Parker had drawn public attention. Ray Martin therefore continued independently producing an improved design, and a certain amount of success was achieved by C.D. Headland, Ninian Sanderson and others.

DF

MARTIN (vi) (GB) *1969 to date*
Martin Racing Developments, Dagenham, Essex

Brian Martin's first real successes were with the BM6 GT model, based on the Lotus 23 and fitted with a B.M.W. engine. The open BM7 and BM8 machines were available for Club or International Group 6 racing in 1970 and 1971. Class records in hill-climbs also fell to the FVC-powered BM8 of David Good. The 1972 Group 6 model was the BM9, which was built with FVC or B.M.W. engine, and a road car was also built. The BM10 for 1973 was designed for 2- or 3-litre engines, and cost £3,800 complete with gearbox.

DF

MARTIN ET LETHIMMONIER *see* SULTANE

MARTINI (CH) *1897–1934*
(1) Martini et Cie, Frauenfeld *1897–1903*
(2) Martini et Cie, St Blaise-Neuchâtel *1903–1906*
(3) Sté Nouvelle des Automobiles Martini, St Blaise-Neuchâtel *1906–1934*

Best known of the Swiss manufacturers was the Martini small arms factory, which built a petrol engine in 1889 and a prototype car in 1897. This was a chain-driven flat-twin with rear engine and 3-speed constant-mesh gearbox, though a second prototype of 1899 followed conventional Panhard lines. In 1901 the company experimented with more chain-driven vehicles using narrow-angle V-4 engines. A year later came some more serious production, the new Martinis being made under Rochet-Schneider licence, and to Mercédès ideas, which meant pair-cast 4-cylinder engines with side valves in a T-head, lt magneto ignition and 4-speed gearboxes, though pressed-steel frames did not replace the flitchplate type until 1904.

Early publicity stemmed, not from racing, but from a successful ascent of the Rochers de Naye rack railway. The firm came under the control of a British company run by H.H.P.Deasy and, though Deasy started to make cars under his own name in England in 1906, it did not revert to Swiss ownership until 1908. Sales in 1904 were 130 cars, some of which had engines with counter-clockwise rotation. The biggest 1905 Martini was a 6.9-litre 30/40. In 1906 one of these took part in an inconclusive long-distance road match against a 30hp 6-cylinder Rolls-Royce. Then in 1907 a new smaller model was introduced, the 3-litre 14/20 with shaft drive, as well as some unsuccessful contenders for the Kaiserpreis race. Alongside the traditional T-headers in the 1908 range was a 2.2-litre four with overhead inlet valves, but the company also built some advanced racers for voiturette events. These Charles Baehni designs had 1,086cc 4-cylinder ohc monobloc engines, semi-pressure lubrication, and ht magneto ignition; despite serious financial troubles between 1908 and 1910 these went into limited production with 1,290cc engines before giving way to an L-head light car, still with monobloc cylinders, in the latter year. At the same time L-head engines became general practice and sales picked up, some Martinis being exported to South America. By 1913 detachable steel wheels and full electrics were available, and a wide range embraced sv fours with capacities of 2.6, 2.9 and 3.6 litres, as well as a short-lived 3.6 litre with Knight double sleeve valves, and a 15CV sports model with 3-litre 16-valve ohc unit and hemispherical combustion chambers that gave 40bhp and did well in hillclimbs.

With Switzerland cut off from foreign imports by World War 1, Martini enjoyed a brief and final period of prosperity, sales climbing to 325 units in 1917. They also launched a cheap runabout, the long-stroke (60×120mm) sv 4-cylinder Martinelli with disc wheels and leather-covered cloverleaf coachwork. It could not, of course, compete against cheap post-war Citroëns and Renaults, but had a long career in the Swiss army, who were still using it in 1939. By contrast 1919's staple Martini was a restatement of the old 1914 formula, the 3.8-litre 4-cylinder TF, with the V-radiator of 1914 sports models, trough-and-dipper lubrication, a 4-speed gearbox and a foot transmission brake. It was well made, but far from competitive (the British price was £1,450), and inevitably there was another financial collapse in 1920, followed by a revival in 1924 after the share capital was acquired by Walter Steiger and his brother.

The Steigers had made sports cars in Germany, but their Swiss offering was a straightforward sv six, the 12/50PS FU, with 3.1 litres, 70bhp, 3-speed unit gearbox, central change, left-hand drive as standard, and 4-wheel brakes. For the luxury market there was a companion 4.4-litre 17/90PS that had acquired a Maybach overdrive gearbox and servo brakes by 1929. Sales were still poor, so Martini undertook licence-production of the 2½-litre 6-cylinder ohv W11 Wanderer (Type KM) which the Swiss dubbed the 'German Helvetia'. The Martini-Wanderer survived until 1932, but a year earlier the FUS had been replaced by the NF, a large and heavy car with the same type of engine, a 4-speed silent-3rd gearbox and hydraulic brakes on an 11ft 6in wheelbase. By 1933 both clutch and brakes had been given servo assistance and there was synchromesh, but though the power unit was also fitted to Martini's trucks, sales had dropped to a miserable 60 units a year and the St Blaise factory closed down for good in 1934.   MCS

MARTINOT ET GALLAND (D) 1898–1899
Ateliers de Construction de Bitschweiler, Thonn, Alsace

Like the pre-1918 Bugatti, Chatel-Jeannin and other Alsatian makes, the Martinot et Galland, although French-sounding, was a German car. It had a 5hp single-cylinder horizontal engine, wire wheels and solid tyres. Various kinds of two- or four-seater bodywork were fitted.   GNG

MARTIN STATIONETTE (US) 1954
Commonwealth Research Corporation, New York City, N.Y.

This was a 3-wheeled 'commuters' car designed by James V. Martin who had been responsible for the Martin (iii) cars. The Stationette had a bonnetless three-seater body and a rear-mounted 776cc 4-cylinder Hercules engine. Transmission was by Martin Magnetic fluid drive, and a maximum speed of 80mph was claimed. The price was fixed at $1,000, but production never started.   GNG

MARTIN-T (US) 1956–1964
Tanner Motor Co, Saginaw, Mich.

This was a small sports/racing car built by Martin W. Tanner that achieved considerable success in SCCA Class H events. In 1958 Tanner won the National Class H Modified championship. The first Martin-T was powered by a tuned Crosley engine, but subsequent cars used a more reliable Saab unit, also highly tuned. Seven cars were made in all, the last model having a rear-mounted engine.   GNG

MARVEL (i) (F) 1905–1908
Automobiles Marvel, Paris

The conventional Marvel was made in various 4-cylinder models. These included 15, 20/24, 25/30 and 30/40hp cars, with shaft drive on all but the largest model.   GNG

MARVEL (ii) (US) 1907
Marvel Motor Car Co, Detroit, Mich.

The single model of this make was a two-seater runabout, with a horizontal 2-cylinder engine. It used a planetary transmission and single chain drive.   GMN

MARWYN (GB) 1947–1951
(1) Marwyn Car Co, Bournemouth, Hampshire 1947
(2) Marwyn Car Construction Co, Ltd, Wareham, Dorset 1948–1951

One of the first 500cc racing cars to be marketed, B.E. Martin's design was based on a box-section frame with leaf suspension. Lord Strathcarron's J.A.P.-engined model, in particular, achieved some success in sprints and hill-climbs, but the marque's standing was never high. Even the much improved 1949 version, with independent front suspension, failed to establish itself. Quite a number of Marwyns ended up as the basis for one-off specials.   DF

MARYLAND (i) (US) 1900–1901
Maryland Automobile Mfg Co, Luke, Md.

The Maryland company made a wide range of steam vehicles, all with vertical 2-cylinder engines and single chain drive. Body styles included a runabout, surrey and phaeton, and prices ranged from $900 to $2,500.   GNG

MARYLAND (US) (ii) 1907–1910
Sinclair-Scott Co, Baltimore, Md.

This was a continuation of the Ariel of Bridgeport, Conn., with no technical changes for the first models. Later the wheelbase was expanded from 8ft 4in to 9ft 8in. A four-seater roadster and a five-seater touring car were complemented in 1908 and 1909 by a limousine and a town car.   GMN

MASCOT (S) 1920
Råverken, Hälsingborg

This was a curious cyclecar to which any motor cycle could be fitted, the cycle's rear wheel acting as the offside rear wheel of the car. Steering was by wheel, and the driver and passenger sat in tandem. Thus for S Kr 1,700 the buyer could have a car, providing he already had a sufficiently powerful motor cycle.   OB

MASCOTTE (GB) 1919–1921
Mascotte Engineering Co, Ltd, London W.10

The Mascotte was a very conventional light car using an 11.9hp Peters engine

1935 MARTINI NF 4.4-litre cabriolet. Coachwork by Höhner. *F. Hediger Collection*

1958 MARTIN-T sports car. *Glenn M. Beach*

1921 M.A.S.E. 6/8hp coupé. *Autocar*

1928 MASERATI 2-litre racing car. *Museo dell'Automobile, Turin*

1934 MASERATI 2.9-litre racing car. *Autosport*

1950 MASERATI A6 1½-litre coupé. Coachwork by Pininfarina. *Autosport*

of 1645cc. A 3-speed gearbox was fitted, and the price for a two-seater in 1919 was £475. In 1921 the stroke was increased from 110 to 120mm, giving a capacity of 1795cc.　　　　　GNG

M.A.S.E. (F) *1921–1924*

Manufacture d'Autos, Outillage et Cycles, St Etienne, Loire

The M.A.S.E. was a light car of more technical interest than many of its kind. It used a 995cc 4-cylinder ohv engine of its own make, although an 1100cc Ruby was also available. The body was a low coupé and front suspension was independent by two transverse semi-elliptic springs which took the place of a front axle. Rear suspension was by cantilever springs.　　　　　GNG

MASERATI (I) *1926 to date*

(1) Officine Alfieri Maserati SpA, Bologna *1926–1938*
(2) Officine Alfieri Maserati SpA, Modena *1938 to date*

This famous Italian marque gained its international reputation largely through the successes of its racing cars, rather than its sports models. The famous brothers from Bologna – Carlo, Bindo, Alfieri, Ettore and Ernesto – had links with motoring going back to pioneer days when Carlo, the eldest, raced motor cycles and cars and worked successively for Fiat, Bianchi and Junior, while Bindo and Alfieri joined Isotta-Fraschini. Carlo died in 1911 and Alfieri opened a tiny garage near the Ponte Vecchio, Bologna, in 1919.

During World War 1 the brothers began to manufacture Maserati sparking plugs, and in the early 1920s Alfieri successfully raced a fast 'special' he built, using one bank of an Isotta-Fraschini V-8 aero engine. Next he began racing Diatto cars which he modified extensively, and in 1925 the Maseratis undertook production of two 2-litre supercharged twin-ohc straight-8 Diatto GP cars. A year later Diatto withdrew from racing so the *Fratelli* took over the cars, reduced their capacity to 1½ litres to comply with the current Formula, and the Officine Alfieri Maserati was founded, using Neptune's trident, the traditional symbol of Bologna, as their trademark. Driven by Alfieri himself, the new Maserati won the 1½-litre class in its first race, the 1926 Targa Florio. More cars were built for private customers, and in 1929 they combined two 2-litre units in one chassis to produce the legendary 16-cylinder Maserati – the *sedici cilindri* – which exceeded 152mph at Cremona in 1929 and, with a sister 5-litre car, did well in racing. 1930 brought the famous 2½-litre GP car which won five major races that year; while more powerful derivatives added further laurels, including the 1933 French and Belgian Grands Prix.

When Alfieri Maserati died in 1932 Ernesto took over the reins, and with German domination of GP racing obvious after 1934, turned to the 1½-litre voiturette class, producing neat 4- and 6-cylinder twin-ohc single-seaters which gained numerous successes. In 1938 the big Orsi industrial group acquired the Officine Maserati, and the three remaining brothers became privileged employees, producing a new 16-valve 4-cylinder voiturette and the 3-litre straight-8 8CTF which won the Indianapolis 500 Miles in 1939 and 1940. The *Fratelli's* last effort was the A6G sports car, with new 6-cylinder single-ohc engine in 1½- and 2-litre forms which made its debut at the 1947 Geneva Show.

The Maseratis left to form the OSCA concern in Bologna late that year, but the Orsis developed their 4CL voiturette design into the 4CLT/48 with 2-stage supercharging and tubular frame; it won races when stronger opposition was absent but was far from fault-free. In 1952 they laid down a new Formula 2 car, based on the A6G; in 1953 they improved it so that Fangio won the Italian and Modena Grands Prix with it, and in 1954 came the highly successful GP 6-cylinder 250F Maserati built to the 2½-litre Formula. This car gained more honours for the Trident between 1954 and 1957, and gained for Fangio his fifth World Championship in 1957. By then, however, Maserati were expensively involved in Championship sports car racing as well, and the destruction of four highly costly 4½-litre V-8 Maseratis by crashes during the 1957 Venezuela Grand Prix, combined with default on cash payments by Argentina for goods supplied by the Orsi combine, caused the withdrawal of Maserati from racing. Thereafter they built expensive sports cars, but by 1960 were indirectly back in racing with the famous 'Birdcage' Types 60 and 61 with multi-tube space frames, and 2- and 2.8-litre 4-cylinder engines respectively, raced by private owners. The 61 won the Nurburgring 1,000km race in 1960 and 1961, and was succeeded by a rear-engined version with a 3-litre V-12 engine. This unit was the forerunner of the current racing Maserati engine as used in the 1966/67 Cooper Formula 1 chassis.

Since then the company has concentrated on high-performance luxury and sporting cars, developed from the dohc 6-cylinder 3500 series made until 1966, with servo-assisted 4-wheel disc brakes and semi-elliptic rear suspension. Latterly buyers had a choice of two power units, a 3,485cc version with 260bhp and a bigger one with 3,692cc and 270bhp; both had Lucas fuel injection as standard and could be had with 5-speed all-synchromesh gearbox or Borg-Warner automatic transmission. Since 1964 there had also been a 4-door saloon, the Quattroporte, powered by a dohc 4,136cc V-8 engine with four dual-choke Weber carburettors, retailing at 7,500,000 lire. The 1967 6-cylinder Sebring and Mistrale models had 4-litre engines, and a new 4.7-litre V-8 was introduced on the Mexico 2-door saloon and the Ghibli coupé; this latter had four retractable headlamps and did 174mph on 340bhp. A spyder version was listed in 1970, when both the sixes and the Quattroporte were dropped. In 1968 Maserati had become associated with Citroën of France, subsequently making a V-6 engine for the latter's high-performance SM model. The 1972 Maserati range included the Mexico, Ghibli and Indy, and their V-8 engines extended from a 260bhp 4.1-litre up to a 4.9-litre 335bhp unit used in the Ghibli SS. All these had four Weber carburetters, as did the firm's first road-going mid-engined car, the Bora two-seater coupé. This featured unitary construction, all-independent suspension, and a 5-speed transaxle. Its 4.7-litre engine was cooled by twin electric fans and developed 310bhp. A smaller version of the Bora was the Merak, powered by a carburettor edition of the 3-litre 190bhp V-6 engine as used in the Citroën SM.   CP

MASON (i) (US) 1898–1899
William B. Mason, Milton, Mass.

This steam car was similar to the first Stanleys, and used a Stanley boiler and burner together with the Mason patent regulator in which the fire was controlled by boiler pressure. This was used in a number of other steam cars, but it is unlikely that the Mason car itself was built in any numbers.   GNG

MASON (ii) (US) 1906–1910
(1) Mason Motor Car Co, DesMoines, Iowa 1906–1908
(2) Mason Automobile Co, DesMoines, Iowa 1908–1910

The Mason was launched as a five-seater powered by a 2-cylinder opposed engine of 24hp. It had planetary transmission and single chain drive. Very few changes were made in the design during the life of this make, although two- and four-seater versions were added in 1909. The Mason was succeeded by the Maytag, these two makes being Fred S. Duesenber's first essay in car design.   GMN

MASS (F) 1903–1923
PIERRON (F) 1912–1923
Automobiles Mass (L. Pierron), Courbevoie, Seine

This make is a curiosity in that throughout most of its effective life it was built in France for an English importer: in 1907 the works were under the direction of an Englishman, J.R. Richardson, and the Pierron, the Mass's *alter ego* for French consumption, was not offered until 1912. Even the name under which the car is best known is an abbreviation of the concessionaire's name, the guiding spirit being a Mr Masser-Horniman.

The Mass started life as the sort of straightforward single-cylinder voiturette associated with Lacoste et Battmann: frames were tubular, and buyers had the choice of either a 4½hp Aster engine (at £130) or a 6hp De Dion (at £183). A 1.7-litre De Dion-engined twin offered in 1904 had two carburettors. In 1905 there was not only a T-headed twin with auxiliary transverse rear suspension, but a big 3.9-litre 18/24hp chain-driven 4-cylinder in the Mercedes idiom. Single-cylinder cars with De Dion power units were still listed in 1906, but Gnome, and later Ballot engines were coming in, and the range also included a small L-headed 10/12hp four of 2.3 litres' capacity, a bigger 14hp with Hele-Shaw clutch and two large chain-driven machines with lt magneto ignition and 4.1-litre and 5.6-litre engines. In 1907 an 8-litre 40/50 (sometimes offered with chain drive and sometimes with shaft) was the biggest Mass so far, but of greater interest to the ordinary purchaser was a 2.4-litre 15 with a T-head Ballot engine at £315. The following year a 3.4-litre Special 15 with pump cooling offered more acre for £390.

Such 'period' improvements as L-head monobloc engines, unit gearboxes and pressure lubrication arrived with the 2-litre 10/12 (price £259) in 1910. It reverted to a separate gearbox in 1913, but meanwhile in 1911 the range had been tidied up, and the biggest type now offered was a 4.9-litre shaft-driven 20 at £470. Two years later big cars were back with an immensely long-stroke (80 × 180mm) 6-cylinder type, but the Mass was already sinking into obscurity, as is indicated by the fact that Mass Cars of London took on two American agencies, R.C.H. and Paige (the latter they sold in 4-cylinder form as 'Mass-Paige').

Interestingly enough the Pierrons sold in France at this time, while conforming in general specification, did not always have identical cylinder dimensions: in 1913 the smallest Mass is quoted as having 75 × 100mm, and the corresponding Pierron 68 × 130mm – both equivalent to 1.9 litres! All 1914 Masses featured Ballot engines, cone clutches, straight bevel final drive and detachable wheels of the company's own make. Only 4-cylinder models were offered, and all were 3-speed with the exception of the 2.8-litre 15.9, which also came with electric lighting. Biggest of all was a 5.3-litre model with cylinder dimensions of 100 × 170mm. The 15.9 was revived after World War 1 but its specification was virtually unchanged and even at £475 for a chassis in England it made no further impression.   MCS

MASSILLON (US) 1909
W.S. Reed Co, Massillon, Ohio

The Massillon had a 6-cylinder T-head engine of 7.8 litres, with two sparking plugs to each cylinder. The same chassis was used for both the roadster and the five/seven-seater touring car. A 3-speed transmission and shaft drive were employed.   GMN

MASTER (US) 1917–1918
Master Motor Car Co, Cleveland, Ohio

1950 MASERATI 4CLT 1½-litre racing car. *Motor Sport*

1963 MASERATI 3500GT Sebring coupé. Coachwork by Vignale. *G.N. Georgano*

1965 MASERATI Quattroporte 4.2-litre saloon. *Officine Alfieri Maserati SpA*

1905 MASS 8hp two-seater. *Lytton Jarman*

1923 MATCHLESS 10hp tourer. *Autocar*

1937 MATFORD V-8-72 2.2-litre saloon.
Lucien Loreille Collection

1907 MATHESON 40/45hp tourer. *General
Motors Corporation*

Better-known for their trucks, the Master company offered briefly a 6-cylinder car with 100bhp engine in roadster, phaeton and limousine form. Prices were $5,000 and up.　　　　GNC

MATADOR (i) (GB) *1966–1967*

Speedcraft, Tring, Herts.

The manufacture of the well-known Matador 'go-karts' also marketed a Formula 4 car of orthodox construction, with a tubular space-frame chassis wearing a lightweight fibreglass body. Only a handful were made before builder Roger Keele abandoned the project, though Dave Forrester's example was still competitive during the 1972 season.　　　　DF

MATADOR (ii) *see* AMERICAN MOTORS

MATAS (E) *1919–1922*

Matas y Cía, Barcelona

The Matas was a light car powered by 4-cylinder Dorman or Continental engines. Front suspension was by a single transverse leaf spring in the manner of the pre-World War 1 Sizaire-Naudin. In 1922 patents were sold to Stevenson, Ramagosa y Cía, who continued to make the car under the name S.R.C.　　　　GNG

MATCHLESS (GB) *1913–1914*

H. Collier & Sons Ltd, London S.E.

In 1913, the famous makers of motor cycles were responsible for a 3-wheeled car powered by an 8/10hp air-cooled V-twin engine. It had three forward speeds and shaft drive, usually the prerogative of 4-wheelers. They also built a small number of extremely advanced cyclecars in the post-World War 1 years; machines very different from the customary crudities that infested European roads at the time. The body and chassis were of rigid unitary construction, there was independent front suspension by double transverse springs, and front wheel brakes were supplied; a rare feature indeed in this class of car. The power unit was an air-cooled flat-twin of 1250cc. The body was both good-looking and roomy, with space for four passengers. However, all this could only be had at a price; and this was too high, for by 1923, a Morris Cowley four-seater could be bought for the £225 asked for the Matchless. About 50 Matchless 4-wheelers were made.　　　　TRN

MATFORD (F) *1934–1946*

SA Française Matford, Strasbourg; Asnières, Seine

Before 1934 the only Ford peculiar to France was a fwd conversion of the European 8hp Model-Y, the Tracford, but in 1934 an agreement was signed with the ailing Mathis concern whereby their factories were at first partially, and then entirely turned over to the manufacture of Ford vehicles. The cars were closely related to their American prototypes, the small 2.2-litre V8-60 being added to the range for 1936. A Matford won the Coupe des Dames in the 1936 and 1938 Monte Carlo Rallies. 1937 versions, the 72 and 76, resembled the Dagenham-built 22hp cars in styling, the same chassis being used for both models, while 1938 and 1939 models were much the same, but with V-windscreens. In 1947 the company was reorganized as Ford S.A.F. and cars were marketed under the Ford name.　　　　MCS

MATHESON (US) *1903–1912*

(1) Matheson Motor Car Co, Grand Rapids, Mich. *1903*
(2) Matheson Motor Car Co, Holyoke, Mass. *1903–1905*
(3) Matheson Motor Car Co, Wilkes-Barre, Pa. *1906–1910*
(4) Matheson Automobile Co, Wilkes-Barre, Pa. *1910–1912*

The first Matheson was a large chain-drive tourer powered by a 24hp 4-cylinder ohv engine. It was designed by Charles Greuter who had previously made the Holyoke car in the factory taken over by Matheson. Not more than 100 cars were made in the first three years of production, before the firm moved to Wilkes-Barre. Here larger cars of 40/45 and 60/65hp were made, the latter costing up to $7,500. 1908 saw the first six, a 48hp car still with overhead valves. It had shaft drive, although chains were still used on some fours until 1910. The improved 'Silent Six' was made until the end of production in 1912. Approximately 800 fours and 1,000 sixes were made in all.　　　　GMN

MATHIEU (B) *1902–1904*

Usines Eugène Mathieu, Louvain

Mathieu cars were made to the design of Eugène Mathieu in the factory formerly occupied by the makers of the Delin. The first car had an 8hp single-cylinder vertical engine, with shaft drive and a four-seater tonneau body. Later Mathieu cars had engines of 9 or 16hp. In 1904 Mathieu left Delin and became director of a factory at Saventhem which made a few cars under the name U.S. Brevets Mathieu up to 1906.　　　　GNG

MATHIS (D) *1898–1903; 1910–1914* (F) *1919–1935; 1945–1950*

(1) E.E.C. Mathis, Strasbourg *1898–1914*
(2) SA Mathis, Strasbourg *1919–1950*

The Mathis company, like Bugatti, changed its nationality with the return of

Alsace-Lorraine to France in 1918. The early cars made in Strasbourg up to 1903 were experimental prototypes only, though they included a really big 150 × 160mm 4-cylinder rated at 100hp and the first Mathis product sold to the public were the Hermes machines designed by Ettore Bugatti in 1904 to 1905. Bugatti set up as an independent consulting engineer, and Mathis supplemented his business by selling De Dietrich, Panhard, and Rochet-Schneider, as well as acting as Central European representative for Fiat and Minerva.

It was not until 1910 that the true Mathis went on sale, in the form of the 8/20PS, a straightforward 2-litre L-head monobloc 4-cylinder car with 3-bearing crankshaft, 4-speed separate gearbox, and shaft drive! the larger 2.8-litre model of this period was made for Mathis by Stoewer of Stettin. The firm's pre-war reputation was founded largely on well made miniature 4-cylinder machines, notably the 1,100cc Babylette and the 1.3-litre Baby. The former had a vertical-gate gear change, all its brakes on the rear wheels, and, surprisingly, a differential. A bolster-tank sports two-seater could be bought in England in 1914 for £195. Bigger cars had full-pressure lubrication, and came in 1½-litre, 1.8-litre (rated rather high in Britain at 16/20hp), and 2.6-litre sizes. There were also some 4.4-litre models with Knight double-sleeve-valve engines.

Mathis's interest in racing expressed itself in rather a peculiar way, since he tended to enter cars of unsuitable capacity for major races. Thus his 1.8-litre Coupe de l'Auto model of 1912 was set to run with the big cars in the concurrent Grand Prix, and in 1921 he ran a 1½-litre ohv 4-cylinder in the French GP, in a year when a 3-litre formula was in force!

After World War 1 the Mathis emerged as a neat little sv monobloc 8/15hp 4-cylinder with aluminium pistons, fixed head, trough-and-dipper lubrication, thermo-syphon cooling, full electrics, magneto ignition, and 4-speed gearbox. Capacity was 1131cc, and in 1921 an anglicized version was sold in London as the B.A.C., though later cars of this make had no French associations. The Mathises of the early 1920s, often with tiny engines (the T-type of 1923 had only 628cc), differential-less back axles, splash lubrication (and abysmal axle ratios of the order of 6:1, but always with 4 forward speeds) soon brought the company into fourth position behind France's big three – Citroën, Renault, and Peugeot – and production was running at 75 cars a day in 1927. The miniature 4-cylinder machines were credited with 63mpg, but in 1923 there was a new departure in the shape of a tiny 6-cylinder version. The 1.2-litre L-type with overhead camshafts and detachable head had some sporting pretensions, but more typical was the 1,140cc P-type tourer with a fixed-head sv power unit, 6:1 top gear, brakeless front axle, and differential-less back end. The wheelbase was 9ft, and the 4-speed box had central change: both sizes had V-radiators.

Interestingly enough Mathis favoured 4 cylinders, overhead camshafts, and 8-plug heads for their entries in the Touring Car GP, and were rewarded with class wins in 1923 and 1924, though their advanced 1925 machines with crab tracks, under-slung frames, and aerodynamic bodywork were less successful. The 6-cylinder touring cars had front-wheel brakes by 1924, and were continued until 1926, but 1925 brought a bigger family saloon to compete with Citroën, the 1.6-litre GM-type 4-cylinder with pressure lubrication, front-wheel brakes, and differential, sold at £295 in England. There was also a short-lived 1.7-litre ohc straight-8 with coil ignition: the output of 35bhp perhaps explains why nothing more was heard of this.

By 1927 Mathis were back to one-model policy with their 1.2-litre 4-cylinder MY at £255 for a fabric saloon. Its specification was entirely conventional with side valves, detachable head, 2-bearing crankshaft, magneto ignition, 6-volt electrics, and 4-speed gearbox. A 1.8-litre Emysix followed in 1928 with coil ignition, hypoid final drive, and two separate detachable heads for its monobloc engine: sold under the slogan 'Ware The Enemy – Weight', it justified this by turning the scales at only 2,184lb, and formed the basis for all Strasbourg's subsequent series-production sixes and eights.

Up to 1935 dull, solid sv family saloons were the staple of the SA Mathis. 4-speed Warner silent-3rd gearboxes appeared on the Emysix in 1929, and in 1930 there were bigger sixes of 2.4 litres and 4.1 litres, also with hypoid axles. William C. Durant laid plans to build 4-cylinder cars in his factories in 1930 under the name Matam (Mathis-America), but the Depression frustrated these. A very short-stroke (70 × 80mm) 1.2-litre, the PY type with spiral bevel final drive, appeared in 1931, when a 3-litre could be bought with hydraulic brakes in England for £476. Two bigger eights of 4.6 and 5.4 litres were made in very small numbers. Mathis engines were used in one model of the all-independently-sprung Harris-Léon Laisne, and both hydraulics and free wheels were standard on the big cars in 1932. This year a wide range embraced everything from the 904cc TY 4-cylinder up to the 3-litre FOH type straight-8.

Mathis, however, were slipping and an attempt was made to restore sales with the 1.4-litre Emyquatre of 1933, which had a box-section frame, independent front suspension, synchromesh and free wheel, and a modern-style 4-door saloon body with no running-boards. 6-cylinder cars acquired transverse independent front suspension at the same time. In 1934 a further attempt was made to bolster up the company by an agreement with Ford (i) whereby the Mathis factories would be used to manufacture Ford V-8s for the French market. Unfortunately Henry Ford and Emile Mathis saw this differently, and what in fact happened was that Matfords rapidly ousted Mathis cars from the production lines, thus fathering a line which survived until 1961, first under Ford and latterly under Simca control. Mathis

1913 MATHIS Babylette 1,132cc two-seater. *Neubauer Collection*

1920 MATHIS 10hp sports car. *Autocar*

1933 MATHIS EMY-4 8CV saloon. *Autocar*

1946 MATHIS 333 707cc 3-wheel coupé. *Autocar*

1966 MATRA Djet Six 1,250cc coupé. *Matra Sports*

1970 MATRA M660 3-litre sports car. *Matra Sports*

1972 MATRA M530 1.7-litre coupé. *Matra Sports*

cars for 1935 had all-round independent suspension, but they were the last of their line to be sold to the public.

Emile Mathis once again took possession of his factory in 1945, and essayed a comeback with a weird little front-wheel-drive 3-wheeler cloaked in egg-shaped coupé bodywork to the designs of Jean Andreau. The front wheels were independently sprung, and the 700cc flat-twin power unit was water-cooled with one radiator to each cylinder: all-up weight was a modest 840lb. It soon became apparent that the Government was not going to authorize production of this vehicle, but Mathis tried again in 1948 with an advanced 2.8-litre front-wheel-drive flat-6. Its output was 80bhp, the gearbox had overdrive on all three ratios, there was independent suspension all round, and the futuristic saloon body featured a panoramic windscreen. The Mathis reappeared at the 1949 Salon, but like La Licorne, Delaunay-Belleville and Bugatti, the firm never managed to get any post-war design into series production. In 1954 the Strasbourg plant was sold to Citroën, and another major, if uninspired, French marque vanished into limbo. MCS

MATICH (AUS) 1965 to date
Matich Cars, Castlecove, N.S.W.

After a successful career in sports-car racing, Formula Junior and the Tasman Series, Frank Matich turned to the construction of large sports cars for Group 7 events. His first Matich SR was based on a Lotus 19 and was powered by a Traco-tuned 4,990cc Oldsmobile V-8 driving through a 5-speed ZF gearbox. Since 1967 Matich has used the Australian-built Repco V-8 engine in his cars, all of which have been Group 7 machines. GNG

MATRA (F) 1965 to date
(1) Matra-Sports srl, Romorantin, Loir-et-Cher 1965 to date
(2) Matra-Simca, Division Automobile, Vélizy-Villacoublay, Seine-et-Oise 1969 to date

Engins Matra's primary interests are in aerospace and armaments, but in late 1964 they took over the assets of the defunct René Bonnet concern, and established Matra-Sports to run the existing Renault-engined sports cars and updated Formula 3 monocoque racing cars, using Cosworth-Ford engines. Production cars pursued the René Bonnet theme with Gordini-tuned 1,108cc Renault engines available in 70 and 94bhp forms, disc brakes on all four wheels and fibreglass bodywork. The 1966 Djet with hemispherical head was capable of 109mph, and in 1967 the company offered a 1250cc, 105bhp version as well as a new '2+2' with 1.7-litre German Ford V-4 engine.

In 1968 the Djet was dropped from the range, leaving the angular 530 coupé with mid-mounted 85bhp V-4 engine giving a top speed of 107mph. During 1969 Ford Cologne replaced their V-4 with a new twin-carburettor unit which Matra immediately adopted, while discussions were in hand for a Simca take-over of Matra-Sports. This was indeed concluded, so Matra-Simca came into existence as part of the American-based Chrysler empire. It was intended to continue the 530 Ford into 1973 when a new Chrysler-engined car appeared, the 1,294cc transverse mid-engined Bagheena three-seater coupé.

Matra cars quickly dominated the single-seater classes, and after winning in Formula 2 in 1967 they entered Formula 1 in 1968, the V-12 Matra-engined MS11 running under works colours, and a Cosworth-Ford-engined MS10 appearing under Ken Tyrrell's aegis for Jackie Stewart. The Ford car won three GPs that season, and a revised version won six GPs in 1969 to give Stewart and Matra the World Championship titles. Jacky Ickx and Johnny Servoz-Gavin won the European F2 Championship for Matra in these seasons, and then from 1970 to 1972 Matra ran their own V-12-engined F1 cars with little success. In sports-car racing the V-12 engine had replaced earlier BRM V-8 and Ford V-8-engined machines but likewise had little success until 1972, when Graham Hill and Henri Pescarolo won the Le Mans 24-hours for the marque. This V-12 engine was intended to form the basis of a high-performance prestige road car for the mid-1970s. MCS/DCN

MATTHEWS see SOVEREIGN

MATTHEY ET MARTIN (F) 1924–1925
Matthey et Martin, Paris 13e

This was a light car powered by an sv S.C.A.P. engine of 894cc, and using shaft drive. GNG

MAUDSLAY (GB) 1902–1923
Maudslay Motor Co Ltd, Parkside, Coventry, Warwickshire

The Maudslay Motor Company was a branch of a well-known engineering firm who had made marine engines for many years, and had built a steam carriage in 1835. Their first car had a 20hp 3-cylinder engine with single overhead camshaft, 4-speed gearbox and double chain drive. Many of the early Maudslays had bodies which were convertible from an open brake for summer use to a closed station omnibus. In 1904 a larger 3-cylinder car of 25hp was introduced, together with sixes of 40 and 60hp which were exactly double the size of the 20 and 25hp 3-cylinder models. Very few sixes were made, and the following year Maudslay introduced a range of fours on which they standardized until 1914, although a 16/20hp 3-cylinder was made until 1906. The round radiator which was to be a feature of Maudslays also appeared in 1905. Up to 1910 large fours of 20/30 and 35/45hp were made, shaft drive being introduced on the 1908 models. In 1910 a new 17hp four was announced, which had a silent chain gearbox for 1911. The larger models were gradually dropped, and by 1914 only the 17hp, called by the factory the 'Sweet Seventeen', was being made. All these cars retained the single ohc layout.

No post-war cars were made until 1923, when a very advanced car was shown at Olympia. Known as the 15/80, it had a 6-cylinder twin-ohc engine of 1991cc, and Perrot 4-wheel brakes. It never went into production, and from then on, Maudslay concentrated on the manufacture of heavy commercial vehicles.　GNG

MAURER (D) *1908–1909; 1923–1924*
(1) Johanna Maurer, Nuremberg *1908–1909*
(2) Automobilfabrik Ludwig Maurer, Nuremberg *1923–1924*

After Ludwig Maurer left Maurer-Union he founded a factory of his own, but in his wife's name, as he himself was barred from car manufacture for a period. 2-cylinder cars were built incorporating his friction-drive designs but production was on a small scale. Maurer later concentrated on the building of engines. After World War 1 he started manufacturing motor cycles, but he introduced another small car in 1923. This had a 2.6PS flat twin 2-stroke engine and a chain-driven rear axle.　HON

MAURER-UNION (D) *1900–1910*
(1) Nürnberger Motorfahrzeuge-Fabric 'Union', Nuremberg *1900–1908*
(2) Automobilwerke Union AG, Nuremberg *1908–1910*

Production of small friction-driven cars to Ludwig Maurer's designs started in 1900. The first models had single-cylinder engines and were very popular. With technical improvements and a slight increase in engine output they were produced until about 1908. In 1902 a 2-cylinder model appeared. After 1905 different versions of a 4-cylinder model were offered, but they were not manufactured in great numbers. These featured twin-disc drive and transmission by one or two chains, or by cardan shaft to the rear axle. Ludwig Maurer left the factory in 1908, but car production was carried on until 1910, Maurer designs were built in England by Dougill of Leeds.　HON

MAUSER (D) *1923–1927*
Mauser-Werke AG, Oberndorf

In 1922 the Mauser armaments factory started to produce the *Einspurauto,* a single-track 'car' with an auxiliary wheel on either side of the vehicle for moving off and stopping. In 1923 a 1½-litre, 6/24PS 4-wheeled car with overhead valves and front-wheel brakes was introduced.　HON

MAUVE (F) *1923–1924*
Cyclecars Mauve, Levallois-Perret, Seine

After building and racing the unconventional Elfe cyclecar for several years, Mauve turned to the manufacture of a car bearing his own name. This was quite conventional, and used a front-mounted 1,100cc single-ohc Anzani engine and shaft drive. He entered and drove one in 1923 Cyclecar Grand Prix.　GNG

MAVAG (H) *1938–1942*
Allami Gepgyar Mavag, Budapest-Köbánya

An old-established builder of railway carriages and railcars, Mavag began vehicle construction in 1923 with the assembly of trucks and buses. In 1938 they started production of licence-built German Fords, making body parts, tyres, etc. themselves and importing the engines. Models made included the 4-cylinder Eifel and two sizes of V-8, 2.2-litre and 3.6-litre. Native to Hungary was a seven-seater limousine, but other body styles followed German patterns. More than 600 Mavags were made, either as private cars or taxicabs.　GLH

MAVERICK (US) *1952–1955*
Maverick Motors, Mountain View, Calif.

Designed and built by H. Sterling Gladwin Jr, the Maverick was a fibreglass sports car powered by a 5.4-litre Cadillac V-8 engine. Only seven were made before Gladwin turned to other fibreglass products.　GNG

MAX (F) *1927–c.1929*
Mourlot et Cie, Billancourt, Seine

The Max was a diminutive cyclecar available with a single-cylinder 350cc engine or twins of 514 or 616cc. Friction transmission was used on the single-cylinder car, and a conventional 3-speed gearbox on the larger models.　GNG

MAXIM (GB) *1902–1905*
London General Automobile Co Ltd, London

This was the work of Hiram Stevens Maxim of Maxim gun fame, the father of Hiram Percy Maxim who was associated with Pope in the Columbia (i) venture in America. It was a conventional 16hp twin-cylinder car with mechanically-operated side valves in a T-head, cone clutch, 3-speed gearbox, and side-chain drive, selling

1909 MAUDSLAY 40hp tourer. Coachwork by Heley of Sevenoaks. *Autocar*

1904 MAURER-UNION 6PS voiturette. *Neubauer Collection*

1925 MAUSER 6/24PS saloon. *Neubauer Collection*

1924 MAXIMAG 10hp sports car. Coachwork by
Brichet of Geneva. *Autocar*

1923 MAXWELL Model 25 tourer. *Harrah's
Automobile Collection*

c.1924 MAYBACH W3 5.7-litre tourer.
Maybach Motorenbau GmbH

c.1934 MAYBACH Zeppelin 8-litre saloon.
Victor Rolff

for 450gns. Early examples had tubular radiators, but a honeycomb type had been adopted by 1903. Though cars were still being sold in 1905, the firm's principal business by this time was the supply of automobile lighting equipment.   MCS

MAXIMAG (CH) 1923–1928
SA Motosacoche, Geneva

Mountainous Switzerland has produced few small cars, but it was natural enough that Motosacoche of Geneva, famous for motor cycles and M.A.G. engines should be interested in this category. The Type A Maximag was powered by an 1100cc 4-cylinder engine. It had 3 forward speeds and, rare in a light car at so early a date, front-wheel brakes. A sports version was sold in addition to ordinary touring models, and this survived until the end of car production in 1928, when about 200 units had been made.   TRN

MAXIM-GOODRIDGE see LENOX (i)

MAXWELL-BRISCOE; MAXWELL (US) 1904–1925
(1) Maxwell-Briscoe Motor Co, Newcastle, Ind. Tarrytown, N.J. 1904–1913
(2) Maxwell Motor Corporation, Detroit, Mich. 1913–1925

This make, the work of Jonathan Maxwell and Benjamin Briscoe, appeared in 1904 as a flat-twin runabout with square (4 × 4in) cylinder dimensions, a conventionally bonneted style, mechanically-operated inlet valves, thermo-syphon cooling, and shaft drive. It sold for $750, and the make's early years were marked by distinguished performances in the Glidden Tours, with outright victories in 1911 and 1912. Inevitably, 4-cylinder versions followed, the D type being a big car rated at 30/40hp, though twins were still made as late as 1912, when the Messenger runabout was listed at $625 (£150 in England). 9,000 Maxwells had been sold by the summer of 1909, by which time the company had become part of the short-lived United States Motor Co – other members of this group included Stoddard-Dayton and Brush (ii).

With the collapse of the combine in 1912, Briscoe departed to form his own company, but Maxwell salvaged what was left, and continued to evolve inexpensive 4-cylinder cars from the Mascotte and Mercury which had sold for $950 and $1,150 respectively. Though a few sixes were made, Maxwell's staple during the rest of the make's career was a cheap sv monobloc four with 3-speed gearbox which sold for $750 in 1914, and $655 in 1916, the latter price including full electrical equipment. Total production of cars and trucks in 1917 topped the 100,000 mark, and post-war Maxwells had coil ignition.

Output went up to 32hp in 1921 with the coming of the new Good Maxwell. Walter P. Chrysler took over Maxwell and its associated company Chalmers in 1923, and the Chrysler Six, introduced for 1924, outsold Maxwell's 4-cylinder cars. The 1925 Maxwells were the last; they were replaced by a 4-cylinder Chrysler which ultimately gave way to the Plymouth (ii) in 1928.   MCS

MAXWERKE (D) 1899–1903
Elektrizitäts- und Automobil-Gesellschaft Harff & Schwarz AG, Cologne

This firm specialized in various types of electric cars, private as well as commercial vehicles. Petrol-driven and petrol-electric cars were listed but were of secondary importance.   HON

MAYA see CAMBER

MAYBACH (D) 1921–1941
Maybach Motoren-Werke GmbH, Friedrichshafen

Wilhelm Maybach left the Daimler company in 1907. Together with Count Zeppelin he founded a factory primarily for the production of aero engines, especially for the Zeppelin air-ships. These engines were designed by Karl Maybach, Wilhelm's son. After World War 1, Karl Maybach started to build a 22/70PS 5.7-litre 6-cylinder engine intended for motor cars. This engine was used by Spyker, but no other factories were interested, so Maybach decided to take up car production on his own. From the beginning Maybach aimed at a high quality car with outstanding driving comfort. The first Model W3 appeared at the 1921 Berlin Motor Show, and featured a very advanced 2-speed pedal-controlled transmission. This model was produced until 1926. It was followed by the ohv Model W5 (1926–1930) using a 27/120PS 7-litre engine in the same chassis, this being available with Maybach's *Schnellgang* 2-speed auxiliary box, giving 4 forward speeds. The Maybach 12 of 1929 had a V-12 7-litre engine, which was superseded one year later by the Zeppelin, also with a V-12 7-litre engine of 150bhp; after 1931 it was also available with an 8-litre 200bhp engine. The Zeppelin range was listed until 1939. Zeppelin chassis were also fitted with 6-cylinder engines of 7 litres capacity (already used in Model W5) and a new 5.2-litre engine developing 130bhp (the W6 and DSH models respectively). These cars retained beam axles to the end and were characterized by 7-speed boxes of great complexity. A Zeppelin chassis cost the equivalent of £1,300 in Germany.

In 1935 a new 6-cylinder model was presented, starting the SW range. This was the SW35 with a 3.5-litre 140bhp engine. Engine capacity was raised to 3.8 litres in the SW38 in 1936 and to 4.2 litres in the SW42 of 1940. Production ceased in 1941.

The Maybach Zeppelin shared with the Mercedes 770 the claim to be the most exclusive German car of the 1930s. This reputation was enhanced by Maybach's high standards of material and finish, of comfort and quietness in running. No less well-made were the 6-cylinder models which were in the first rank of German cars of this class. Maybach only built complete chassis, bodies being made by various firms to customers' special requirements. Best known of these firms was Spohn of Ravensburg. Spohn also built aerodynamic bodies to Jaray designs for the Zeppelin in 1932 and 1934, and for the SW35 in 1935. These versions were produced only in very limited numbers. Car production was not taken up again after World War 2. Altogether, some 2,000 cars are believed to have been made. In 1960 Maybach pooled their interests with Daimler-Benz in the manufacture of diesel engines for locomotives and ships. HON

MAYER (D) 1899–1900
Hugo Mayer, Berlin

A voiturette with the French Belvalette engine was produced by this firm. A small *avant train* with the engine mounted above the single wheel was built and also complete 3-wheeled vehicles using this component. HON

MAYFAIR (GB) 1900–1907
(1) Sports Motor Car Co Ltd, Kilburn, London N.W.; Kensington, London W. 1900–1901
(2) G.L.M. Dörwald & Co, Putney, London S.W. 1906–1907

The Sports Motor Car Company imported various cars which they sold under the name Sports or Mayfair. The latter was a single-cylinder two-seater voiturette, probably the Belgian Vivinus, although a shaft-drive 2-cylinder car was also advertised in 1900. The 1906–1907 Mayfair, sold by the makers of the Craig-Dörwald car, was available in four models, a 6hp (De Dion) single, a 10hp twin, and two fours, of 15 and 28hp. GNG

MAYRETTE (D) 1921–1924
Karl Mayr Kraftfahrzeugbau, Munich

This was a small car with a single- or two-seater body using the opposed twin-cylinder 500cc B.M.W. engine and chain transmission. A later version was a 3-wheeler with a single driven rear wheel and a 200cc J.A.P. engine. HON

MAYTAG (US) 1910–1911
Maytag-Mason Motor Co, Waterloo, Iowa

Maytag succeeded Mason in 1910, with no change in the car itself. These were medium-sized cars with 2- or 4-cylinder engines of 16hp or 30hp. The Model H roadster of 1911 had an early boat-tailed body. The company was out of the car business by the end of 1911, but is still famous for its washing machines. GMN

MAZDA (J) 1960 to date
Toyo Kogyo Co, Ltd, Hiroshima

Originally concerned with cork products, this company expanded into machine building and started manufacturing a range of 3-wheel trucks in 1931. A prototype saloon car was built in 1940, but it was not until 1960 that Mazda went into production with the R-360 coupé, available with manual or automatic gearbox. The Carol series of sedans and station wagons was added in 1962 and in 1964 the first of the Familia line was announced. The 360 coupé was powered by a V-twin engine of 356cc, had independent suspension and a 4-speed transmission. Maximum speed was 65mph. The Carol 360 was a 2-door saloon with a 20hp, 4-cylinder, air-cooled engine mounted transversely at the rear, and a fuel consumption of 53mpg. The Carol 600 sedan was a 4-door car with 28hp and a 65mph top speed.

The Familia series had front-mounted, water-cooled, 4-cylinder 42hp engines and was built in a variety of body styles. A unitized chassis was featured on the 800 De Luxe sedan. Transmission was 4-speed synchromesh and the car seated five passengers. The largest model in the Mazda range was the Luce 1500 1½-litre 4-door saloon. During 1967 the firm put into production their twin Wankel rotary engined sports coupé; capable of 120mph, it sold in England for £2,607. Four hundred of these cars had been built by the end of 1968, when two new rotary coupés were announced, the RX85 and the RX87. The former evolved into a 100bhp derivative of the Familia; the latter, which was styled by Bertone, featured fwd and front suspension by rubber in torsion, and had reached the market by 1971 as the R130. Conventional 1968 Mazdas had 987cc push-rod or 1,490cc ohc 4-cylinder engines, coil-and-wishbone ifs, and semi-elliptic rear springs. The last of the Minicars, the 360cc Carol 4-door saloon, survived into 1971, later ones with water cooling.

By 1969 the two regular models had grown up into the 73bhp Familia 1200 and the 1,796cc 1800 with front disc brakes. The 1971 Familias acquired ohc and capacity options were 985cc and 1,272cc, both with five main bearings. New to the range was an intermediate saloon, the Capella, available as the 92bhp 1500 or the 100bhp 1600. Familia, Capella and 1800 models were continued into 1972, along with the R100, R130 and Cosmo Wankel-powered coupés, this last with five forward speeds. In addition both Familia and Capella saloons were available

1936 MAYBACH Zeppelin 8-litre tourer. *Maybach Motorenbau GmbH*

1910 MAYTAG 30hp tourer. *Kenneth Stauffer*

1966 MAZDA Luce 1500 saloon. *Toyo Kogyo Co Ltd*

1973 MAZDA 818 1.3-litre coupé. *Toyo Kogyo Co Ltd*

1919 M.B.(i) 8/10hp two-seater. *Autocar*

1962 M.B.M. Formula Junior racing car.
National Motor Museum

1922 McFARLAN Series TV 9.3-litre sedan.
McFarlan Collection of Alvin J. Arnheim

1925 McFARLAN Series SV 4.3-litre coach-
brougham. *McFarlan Collection of Alvin J. Arnheim*

with twin-rotor Wankel units; the latter used a 1,146cc version developing 120bhp and 7,000rpm, as well as coil-spring rear suspension. New for 1973 were an improved 1300, the 81bhp 818 with redesigned styling, and the high-performance RX3 powered by a 982cc 2-rotor Wankel unit rated at 110bhp. Saloon, coupé and station-wagon versions of this latter were listed.   BE

M.B. (i) (GB) *1919–1921*
Merrall-Brown Motors Ltd, Bolton, Lancs.
    The original Merrall-Brown used a 10hp V-twin Precision engine, a 2-speed gearbox, acetylene lighting and chain drive. The rear wheels were set very close together giving the car the appearance of a 3-wheeler. By 1920 this model had been replaced by a conventional 4-wheeler powered by a 10/12hp Coventry-Simplex 4-cylinder engine. Chain drive was still used, but the new car had a modern low-built four-seater body. It gained a Bronze Medal in the 1920 Scottish Six Days Trial, and was the only four-seater light car to complete the course.   GNG

M.B. (ii) (I) *1924*
Motta & Baudo, Turin
    This interesting light car had patented all-round independent suspension and a chassis sharply inswept at front and rear. The engine was a 4-cylinder Chapuis-Dornier, but there was no series production.   MCS

M.B.M. (CH) *1959–1962*
Garage Monteverdi, Binningen, Basle
    The first M.B.M.'s were Formula Junior racing cars with rear-mounted D.K.W. engines, giving 85bhp and a speed of 140mph; later, Ford Anglia engines were used, giving 90bhp and 150mph. In 1961 a Formula 1 car with a Porsche engine was built, and also a sports car with a 1100cc Osca engine, disc brakes and De Dion-type rear axle. The last M.B.M. model was a GT coupé powered by a Ford Anglia engine. In 1967 Peter Monteverdi launched the Chrysler-engined Monteverdi GT coupé.   GNG

M.C.A. (D) *1962–1964*
M.C.A. Automobile Ulrich Otten, Bremen
    This firm built Volkswagen-based cars with fibreglass bodies in limited numbers. These were the Jetstar roadster with a 1198cc Volkswagen engine tuned to 45bhp, and the Jetkomet coupé with a 65bhp 1,493cc Volkswagen engine.   HON

M.C.C. *see* VAPOMOBILE

McCANDLESS (GB) *1954–1957*
R. and W.A.C. McCandless (Engineers) Ltd, Belfast
    Rex McCandless was best known for his design of a Norton racing motor cycle frame, which rider Harold Daniell said was like riding on a feather bed. Much later, he made some 4-wheel drive front-engined Formula 3 cars, the first of which betrayed their designer's past in having handlebar steering. Subsequently, production centred on a sports two-seater, developed in association with Cromie McCandless and L. McGladery. This car featured (as had the Formula 3) a backbone chassis, transmission brake and independent suspension on all wheels. Full-width or trials bodywork was available, and Ford 10 mechanical components were used.   DF

McCUE (US) *1909–1911*
The McCue Co, Hartford, Conn.
    The McCue had 4-cylinder L-head engines of 30 or 40hp. A runabout and a touring car were produced, with 3-speed selective transmissions, shaft drive and right-hand steering.   GMN

McCULLOUGH (US) *1899–1900*
Backbay Cycle & Motor Co, Boston, Mass.
    This was a light car using a 4½hp 2-cylinder horizontal engine and chain drive. It had a two-seater body.   GNG

McCURD (GB) *1923–1927*
McCurd Lorry Mfg Co Ltd, Hayes, Middlesex
    The McCurd was a light car made by a firm who were better known for their commercial vehicles. It had a 12/20hp 4-cylinder sv engine, a 4-speed gearbox and the two-seater cost £485. An unusual refinement was a watch in the centre of the steering wheel which, when pressed, sounded the horn.   GNG

McFARLAN (US) *1910–1928*
McFarlan Motor Car Co, Connersville, Ind.
    A small-production prestige car, the McFarlan was made by an offshoot of the earlier McFarlan Carriage Co. The company specialized in 6-cylinder motor cars from its inception until the last vehicles were produced, except for eights which were built as a sideline in the mid- and late-1920s. Several different engines were used between 1910 and 1916, when the concern adopted a larger Teetor-Hartley type and although various components were used, because of the infinite care given by the company to each of its cars the McFarlan was not considered an assembled

car in the same manner as many others of the time. By 1917, an elaborate range of both open and closed body types were available to the purchaser andMcFarlans became progressively larger and more expensive.

In the autumn of 1920, the enormous TV or Twin-Valve series was introduced, the engines being of McFarlan's own make and embodying triple ignition which necessitated 18 sparking plugs on each car. Noteworthy among models was the ornate and over-elaborate Knickerbocker Cabriolet, a town car selling for $9,000. The McFarlan was highly regarded among American makes although no more than 235 cars were produced in any given year.

In the autumn of 1923, the company introduced a smaller version of the huge TV McFarlan, the Single Valve or SV Six. Advertised as a 'companion car' to the larger car, it used a Wisconsin engine and was a quality product. Unfortunately, it was not a success and relatively few were sold. The SV was withdrawn from production by 1926. Another attempt to attract a lower-priced clientele was in the introduction of the Eight-in-Line series, these cars being priced similarly to the SV and available on the same chassis. Although their production did not approach that of the TV, this line, equipped with a Lycoming engine, was retained until McFarlan production ceased. Although the larger McFarlan did not change much in appearance between 1920 and 1927, the 1928 models were sleeker and lower. Only a few were built, however, and that year, the McFarlan assets were purchased by E.L. Cord.   KM

McGILL (US) 1922
McGill Motor Car Co, Fort Worth, Texas

The McGill was an assembled car, mainly produced as a tourer. A 6-cylinder engine with a capacity of 3450cc was standard. The touring models sold at $2,385.   KM

McINTYRE (US) 1909–1915
W.H. McIntyre Co, Auburn, Ind.

The McIntyre was a continuation of the Kiblinger. It appears that the principal of the original company changed his name, as the initials W.H. are identical. As many as four models of the McIntyre were available, with 4- and 6-cylinder engines and wheelbases up to 10ft. Later cars were of conventional design in contrast to the Kiblinger high-wheelers. From 1913 to 1914 this company built the Imp cyclecar.   GMN

McKAY (i) (US) 1900–1902
Stanley Mfg Co, Lawrence, Mass.

The McKay steam car was, in fact, a Stanley carefully redesigned so as not to infringe any of the patents which the Stanley twins had granted to Locomobile and Mobile. Locomobile nevertheless threatened to sue the Stanley company so they completely redesigned the car, replacing the vertical engine and chain drive by a horizontal engine and direct drive on the rear axle. This became the 1902 model of the new Stanley Motor Carriage Company.   GNG

McKAY (ii) (CDN) 1911–1914
(1) Nova Scotia Carriage Co, Kentville, N.S.
(2) Nova Scotia Carriage and Motor Car Co, Amherst, N.S.

Four-cylinder Buda engines were used in the 30hp torpedo (roadster) at $1,450 and the 40hp McKay tourer at $2,050. Production was rather haphazard – about 25 at Kentville and another 100 at Amherst after a major re-organization and the erection of a large factory. Based on the U.S. Penn, the McKay achieved some local racing success but lack of capital forced the firm out of business.   HD

McKENZIE (GB) 1913–1926
(1) Thomas McKenzie, Birmingham 1913–1920
(2) McKenzie Motors Ltd, Birmingham 1920–1926

The McKenzie was a light car whose design did not vary greatly throughout its lifetime. It appeared during the cyclecar boom, but always used a 4-cylinder engine and shaft drive. During the 1920s engines by Alpha or Coventry-Simplex were used, the former having a capacity of 1330cc, and the latter 1½ litres. A sports model was made, but the McKenzie never became well known in competitions.   GNG

McLACHLAN (GB) 1899–1900
(1) E.A. McLachlan, Stoke Newington, London N. 1899
(2) McLachlan Engine Co, Hackney, London E. 1900

McLachlan was a maker of heavy oil engines who fitted a few of his engines to light cars. The 1899 car was a 3-wheeler with a single-cylinder horizontal engine at the rear. It was priced at the low figure of £75. In 1900 he made a 4-wheeler called the Holborn, with a 3½hp single-cylinder engine.   GNG

McLAREN; McLAREN-ELVA (GB) 1964 to date
(1) Bruce McLaren Motor Racing Ltd, Slough, Bucks. 1964 to date
(2) Elva Cars (1961) Ltd, Rye, Sussex 1965–1966
(3) Elva Cars (1961) Ltd, Croydon, Surrey 1966–1968
(4) Trojan Ltd, Croydon, Surrey 1969 to date

Bruce McLaren followed Brabham's example in leaving the Cooper team to construct and drive his own cars. The prototype sports-racing machine was derived

1909 McINTYRE high-wheel surrey. *Antique Automobile*

1911 McKAY(ii) 30hp two-seater. *Hugh Durnford*

1920 McKENZIE 11.9hp two-seater. *Autocar*

from a Cooper-based special, the 'Zerex', converted for the American Roger Penske from an old single-seater machine. For 1965 a new 'Group 7' sports car was made, with large-diameter tubular chassis, and rear-mounted Traco-modified Oldsmobile engine driving through a Hewland gearbox. This model was also constructed at the rate of some two dozen annually by Elvas, who had greater production and marketing facilities. Driven by C. Amon and McLaren himself, *inter alia*, some major wins were earned. The Monopostos were less fortunate – mechanical troubles beset the Formula 1 cars of 1966 and 1967, although various power units by Ford, Serenissima and B.R.M. were tried. The monocoque construction, based on a 'Mallite' wood and alloy sandwich, was later used on some other single-seater models, succeeding the space-frame layout seen in 1966. The Elva-built 'production' Formula 2 and 3 monocoques, however, were based on an aluminium through centre section, with steel bulkheads, tubular sub-frames, and fibreglass covering, and this design was later converted for Formula 1 use. In 1967 the monocoque M6A works cars of Bruce McLaren and Hulme dominated the Can-Am series of races, and this pattern was repeated in 1968 with the M8A and the M8B in 1969. Production models built at Croydon (the M3, M6B and M12 for the respective years) sold well in the United States. Progress continued also with the Robin Herd-designed single-seaters, including the M4A Formula 2, and the M5A, M7 series and M9A 4-wheel-drive Formula 1 models.

In 1970 the M14A Formula 1 car and the M15A Indianapolis machine, designed by Roy Coppuck, were introduced. The very successful M10B model developed by Jo Marquart took the Formula 5000 Championship in Britain two years running, the 1971 Tasman Championship, and was also the car to beat in the hill-climbs. Tragedy came when Bruce McLaren was killed while testing an M8D Group 7 model. Nevertheless, the team succeeded once more in practically monopolizing the Can-Am series.

During 1971 the M8E team cars of Revson and Hulme once again looked after Group 7 racing, though the M8F and M20 cars of 1972 faced stiffer opposition. The M19 series of Formula 1 cars of 1971 and 1972, based on a Ralph Bellamy design initially featuring variable-rate suspension, were often front runners without being winners. The M16 did the job for which it was made in winning the 1972 Indianapolis in Mark Donohue's hands after coming second in 1971. M17 was allocated to an uncompleted sports-car project. For 1971 the M18 succeeded the M10B in Formula 5000. During 1972 customer cars, built as always at Croydon, included the M21 Formula 2 and the M22 Formula 5000 cars, the former proving most promising in the hands of Jody Scheckter. DF

1966 McLAREN-ELVA-Oldsmobile Group 7 sports car. Bruce McLaren at the wheel. *Motor Sport*

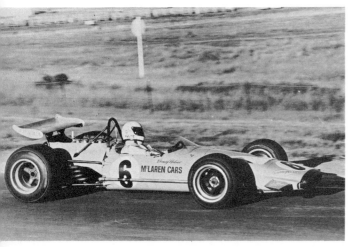

1970 McLAREN-Ford M14A Formula 1 racing car. Denny Hulme at the wheel. *McLaren Motor Racing Ltd*

1972 McLAREN-Chevrolet M20 Can-Am sports car. Denny Hulme at the wheel. *McLaren Motor Racing Ltd*

McLAUGHLIN (CDN) 1908–1922; McLAUGHLIN-BUICK 1923–1942
McLaughlin Motor Car Co Ltd, Oshawa, Ont.

The McLaughlin slogan was 'Canada's Standard Car'. In addition to being a slogan it became a statement of fact. Canada was founded in 1867, and so was the McLaughlin Carriage Company, which began by producing two hand-made sleighs. By the turn of the century McLaughlin carriages and sleighs were among the best known and most highly regarded in the country. An attempt to build cars from the ground up failed when the chief-engineer fell sick just as assembly was to start, whereupon McLaughlin agreed with W.C. Durant to put Buick engines and some other parts into their cars. The agreement was for 15 years, under terms very favourable to McLaughlin.

The first McLaughlin car was produced in 1908. Mechanically, it was like the contemporary Buick 4, but the body was all-Canadian. Production the first year was between 150 and 200 units. Output climbed to 423 the next year and to 1,098 by 1914. It rose slowly to around 6,000 yearly, spurting ahead to 15,000 in the final year of 1922. McLaughlin bodies continued to be different from Buick bodies, and considerably more elaborate for as long as they were made of wood. After that they became generally similar, though hoods, dashboards and other fittings and trim continued to be more luxurious on McLaughlins. A.P. Sloan, president of General Motors, once spotted a McLaughlin outside the New York City Buick showroom and flew into a rage lest Buick buyers should see it and demand similar quality. McLaughlin cars were sold on the reputation of McLaughlin carriages. Very early in their car-building enterprise the name was changed to Buick, but sales fell so drastically that it was changed back to McLaughlin. From about 1910 until the early 1920s, McLaughlin produced a very full range of cars including a four, a light six and the standard six. These were each available in all the usual body styles, often offering a choice in trim. The light six was basically the American Oakland with A McLaughlin nameplate.

In 1915 McLaughlin also began producing Chevrolets under licence, but again featuring a somewhat better-finished product than the American company. In 1918 the entire McLaughlin business was sold to General Motors and became General Motors of Canada. When the original 1907 agreement ran out in 1923 the name of the car was changed to McLaughlin-Buick. Differences in the Canadian car became minute and the McLaughlin prefix was dropped entirely early in World War 2.

In 1927 the company produced a custom touring car for a visit by the Prince of Wales, and in 1939 two huge convertible limousines for the visit of the King and Queen. HD

McNALLY (GB) 1969
McNally Engineering Ltd, Gateshead-on-Tyne, Co Durham

Gordon McNally marketed briefly in interesting Formula 4 single-seater based on a honeycomb monocoque, but only some half-dozen were sold.   DF

McNAMARA (D) 1965–1971
McNamara Racing KG, Lenggries

Francis McNamara began racing Formula Vee cars while serving in the U.S. Army in Germany. He established his FVee factory and the McNamara Sebring cars quickly proved successful and popular. In 1969 ex-Lola designer Jo Karasek developed an original Dan Hawkes F3 space-frame concept. The result was the Sebring Mark 3 that was driven internationally by Helmut Marko and Werner Riedl, but without success. In 1970 STP of America approached McNamara for an Indianapolis car and they built their first monocoque, which was unsuccessful. Litigation over this contract eventually led to the company's collapse in mysterious circumstances in 1971.   DCN

McRAE see LEDA (ii)

MÉAN (B) 1966 to date
(1) Méan Motor Engineering S.A., Liège-Guillemins 1966–1971
(2) Liberta Engineering S.A., Liège 1972 to date

Initially this firm made centrally-engined sports coupés and roadsters with tubular frames, all-independent suspension and (on some versions) all-disc brakes of Renault manufacture. Volkswagen, Porsche or Renault gearboxes were used, and a wide selection of power units included 1,108cc or 1,255cc Renault, the British Ford Cortina, the German Ford V-4 and V-6, N.S.U. and Peugeot 404. Méans were sold in kit form and in 1970 a racing car, the Liberta, was exhibited at the Brussels Show. The sole 1973 product is the Liberta fun car, rather more than a beach buggy. It uses a rigid box-section chassis and comes with a hardtop and integral roll bar. Power is provided by a rear-mounted Renault 8 or 10 engine.   MCS

MECCA (US) 1914–1916
(1) Mecca Motor Car Co, Teaneck, N.J. 1914–1915
(2) Times Square Automobile Co, Detroit, Mich. 1915–1916

The early Mecca was a cyclecar with a 1½-litre, 4-cylinder, water-cooled engine. In 1916 it became a light car of 1,800lb with a 3.2-litre 4-cylinder engine, and standard track. Both five-seaters and two-seaters were built.   GMN

MED-BOW, MEDCRAFT see SPRINGFIELD (ii)

MEDIA (GB) 1912–1916
Mead & Deakin, Tyseley, Birmingham

Although experimental cars had been made as early as 1907, the first Media which could be called a production car was a cyclecar of 1912. This was powered by a 5hp single-cylinder Fafnir engine, and had friction cone transmission. Later Medias had conventional gearboxes, and 4-cylinder engines, either a 750cc Salmon or a 1,243cc Chapuis-Dornier. Serious production never started, but after the war the promoters launched the Rhode light car.   GNG

MEDICI see LEONARD

MÉDINGER (GB) 1913
Médinger Car & Engine Co, Southall, Middlesex

The Médinger was a sporting cyclecar with a 1-litre 2-cylinder, 2-stroke engine, the whole machine being designed by the Sunbeam racing driver, Emile Médinger. The prototype was built at Wolverhampton, possibly in the Sunbeam works, and used chain drive, but the production cars were to have shaft drive. They were to have been made in the Phonophore Works where the L.E.C. cyclecar had been produced, but few, if any, were made there.   GNG

MEDUZA (PL) 1958
Wytwornia Sprzetu Komunikacyjnego, Mielec

The Meduza was a small prototype 2-door sedan similar in plan to the Mikrus. Only one was built and tested, according to Warsaw sources, and rejected in favour of Mikrus production.   BE

MEGY (F) 1901–1903
L. Megy, Paris

The Megy was an early attempt to make a fool-proof car. As well as an automatic transmission in which 'the gear ratio changed according to the conditions of the road surface', the clutch and brake were operated by moving the steering wheel up or down. At the 1903 Paris Salon Megy exhibited a tonneau, a limousine and a racing car.   GNG

MELDI (I) 1927–1933
Giuseppe Meldi, Turin

Formerly a tester for Moto Borgo motorcycles, and a manufacturer of side-cars in the early 1920s, Giuseppe Meldi built a series of cyclecars powered either by

1911 McLAUGHLIN 4-cylinder tourer. *Hugh Durnford*

1913 MÉDINGER 1-litre cyclecar. *G.N. Georgano Collection*

1914 MENDIP 11hp two-seater.
George R. Thatcher.

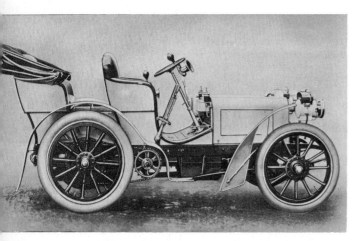

1901 MERCEDES 35PS tourer. *Daimler-Benz AG*

1904 MERCEDES 40/60PS tonneau. Charles
Cordingley at the wheel. *The Veteran Car Club
of Great Britain*

a Della Ferrera air-cooled 1-litre V-twin, Chapuis-Dornier 750cc four, or Citroën 5CV engine. Four-wheel independent suspension was featured, Lancia Lambda type at the front and swing axles at the rear. Two- or four-seater bodies were available, but only twelve Meldis were made in a six-year period. GNG

MELEN (GB) *1913–1914*
F. & H. Melen Ltd, Birmingham

After experimenting with air-cooling, the Melen company chose a water-cooled Alpha 2-cylinder engine of 1100cc for their shaft-driven light car. The price was 138 to 148gns according to equipment. GNG

MELKUS (D) *1959 to date*
H. Melkus, Leipzig

The most consistently successful of the 'Iron Curtain' racing-car constructors, Heinz Melkus has always raced his products himself with outstanding results — usually against cars which, if not also constructed by him, were mostly inspired by his designs. Production commenced with the Formula Junior class, and when this was superseded by Formula 3, the cars were mostly to this specification. Various suspension layouts have been tried, but the general configuration usually embraces a 3-cylinder Wartburg engine mounted behind the driver. Disc brakes were adopted in 1970. Melkus has built a few sports cars from time to time, including the RS 1000 of 1969, a mid-engined coupé with Wartburg engine and fibreglass body. DF

MENARD (CDN) *1908–1910*
(1) Windsor Carriage & Delivery Wagon Works, Windsor, Ont. *1908–1909*
(2) Menard Auto Buggy Co, Windsor, Ont. *1909–1910*

This 16hp 2-cylinder highwheeler sold for $625. It featured friction drive by chains and a steel-reinforced wooden front axle. It was designed by M.B. Covert of Detroit, who had previously designed the Covert steam and petrol cars. For 1910 the company turned exclusively to the production of trucks and fire engines. HD

MENDELSSOHN *see* PASSY-THELLIER

MENDIP (GB) *1914–1922*
(1) Mendip Engineering Co, Chewton Mendip, Somerset *1914*
(2) Mendip Motor and Engineering Co Ltd, Southmead, Bristol *1914–1921*
(3) New Mendip Engineering Co Ltd, Atworth, Melksham, Wilts. *1922*

The facilities at C. Harris's tiny Cutler's Green Iron Works in the early 1900s were such that when steam road vehicles were built, very few parts needed to be bought out. By 1911, the commercials had switched to petrol engines, and in 1913 a neat T-head motor of 1,092cc was made, with a most comprehensive basic casting embracing the manifolds and most of the auxiliaries mountings. Then they made a car to put it in, using a conventional channel frame, insulated from Sankey steel wheels by half-elliptics at the corners. Drive was by enclosed shaft to an overhead worm. A bull-nose radiator was fitted, and standard bodywork was a smart two-seater.

In 1914 the concern was taken over by W.H. Bateman Hope, and he subsequently moved the firm to larger premises in Bristol. Harris assembled a few cars at Weston-super-Mare. The engine grew up fast to 1,269cc and then 1,311cc, shrinking after World War 1 to 1,255cc. In 1919 and 1920 the fashionable disc wheels were worn, the engine size in the latter year finally stabilizing at 1,330cc developing 16bhp. A trade recession, coupled with Hope's death, led to the company's demise in 1921. The former works manager, G.R. Thatcher, created another company and assembled a few more cars from parts in stock, bringing the final total to around the 400 mark. DF

MENGES (US) *1908*
Menges Motor Carriage Co, Grand Rapids, Mich.

This was a large eight-seater touring car powered by a 4-cylinder engine. It was designed by A.L. Menges who was responsible for the Harrison, also built in Grand Rapids. MJWW

MENLEY (GB) *1920*
Menley Motor Co, Stoke-on-Trent, Staffs.

The Menley cyclecar was fitted with an 8hp air-cooled Blackburne engine driving through a 3-speed gearbox to a chain-cum-belt transmission. MJWW

MENOMINEE (US) *1915*
Menominee Electric Mfg Co, Menominee, Mich.

This company was mainly known for electric commercial vehicles, but they made an electric cabriolet to sell at $1,250. Planned production was 150 cars per year, but far fewer than that were actually made. GNG

MENON (I) *1897–1902*
Carlo Menon, Roncade di Treviso

The Menon voiturette used a 3½hp single-cylinder engine of which the cylinder block was air-cooled and the head water-cooled, although the first models were entirely air-cooled. The chassis was unsprung, and the light *vis-à-vis* body was suspended on four full-elliptic springs. About 20 of these cars were made before De Dion competition drove them from the market. The company continued to make motor cycles until 1929.   GNG

MENTASCHI (I) *1924*

Ditta Mentaschi & Cia, Milan-Lambrate

This concern exhibited a tandem-seater light electric car at the 1924 Milan Show, but it did not progress beyond the prototype stage.   MCS

MERAY (H) *1928–1932*

Meray Motorkerekpargyar Rt, Budapest

This motor-cycle firm made a number of 3-wheeled cars powered by rear-mounted single-cylinder J.A.P. engines of 500cc, driving the rear wheel by chain. The bodies were mostly closed coupés, and delivery vans were also made.   GNG

MERCEDES (D) *1901–1926*

1) Daimler Motoren Gesellschaft, Bad Cannstatt *1901–1903*
2) Daimler Motoren Gesellschaft, Stuttgart-Unterturkheim *1903–1926*

Emil Jellinek, wealthy admirer of Daimler cars, had persuaded the Daimler company and its chief designer Wilhelm Maybach to build a high performance car. This new car was the 35bhp 5.9-litre model which today is known as the forefather of modern motor cars and which owed nothing in appearance to horse-drawn carriages; features included honeycomb radiators, gate change, mechanically-operated inlet valves, and pressed-steel frame. The Mercedes design was copied by many manufacturers in Europe and America during the following years. This car was entered by Jellinek for the Nice Week of 1901 under his pseudonym Mercédès, his daughter's name. Driven by Wilhelm Werner it gained victory in the Nice Speed Trials and the La Turbie Hill Climb, these being the first successes connected with the name of Mercedes. Jellinek was already acting as unofficial agent for Daimler cars and had had a seat on the board of directors of the Daimler works since 1900. He sold the cars as Mercedes because of legal proceedings by Panhard-Levassor, who owned the Daimler licences for France. Sales and racing successes of cars bearing this name led the Daimler works in 1902 to adopt 'Mercedes' as a new brand name for private cars. Commercial vehicles were still marketed as Daimlers.

A range of tourers and racing cars followed, based on the 35PS model. Most prominent of this range were the Mercedes Simplex 18/22, 18/32, 40/45 and 60PS models which had a much lower weight than the 35PS; the '60' had inlet over exhaust and was capable of 70mph for a chassis price of £2,200. The very successful 60 and 90hp racing cars were based on the Simplex designs. Among their sporting successes were the Semmering Hill Climb in the years 1901 to 1909, the Gordon Bennett Race in 1903, the Ostend Speed Trials in 1904, and the World Record at Daytona in 1905. In 1902 Daimler took over the Motorfahrzeug- und Motorenfabrik Berlin AG in Marienfelde, which had been founded by a Daimler director and here Daimler concentrated production of their Daimler Marienfelde commercial vehicles. During a short period in 1906/7 Mercedes Electrique cars were built in Marienfelde under licence from Austro Daimler. One example of this species was added to the Kaiser's stable.

In 1907 Maybach left the company to found a firm of his own, specializing in aero engines. His last designs for Daimler were the 6-cylinder 37/70PS (9.5 litres) and 39/80PS (10.2 litres) models, with chain drive and T-head engines, derived from the 120hp racing car. Jellinek returned his rights for sole distribution of Mercedes cars in various countries to the Daimler company in 1905 and after selling his shares left the board of directors in 1908.

Paul Daimler followed Maybach as chief engineer and designer after spending a few years with Austro-Daimler. After 1908 most Mercedes models were equipped with shaft instead of chain drive, which was continued for the heavier 22/50, 28/60, 23/80 and 37/90PS types. Among numerous racing successes, the victory in the 1908 French Grand Prix was a highlight. Lautenschlager drove a 135PS racer especially built for this event. In 1909 Daimler acquired a licence for Knight engines and a range of models was produced, including the 4.1-litre 16/45 which was made until 1923. In 1909 Mercedes applied for registration of the now famous three-pointed star as a trade mark. It was registered and used from 1911 onwards.

From the start Mercedes cars were elegantly designed for high performance and favoured by royalty and the big financiers of the Old and the New World. The Kaiser owned several Mercedes. Among the most impressive successes were the 1st, 2nd and 3rd places in the 1914 French Grand Prix by Lautenschlager, Wagner and Salzer driving the 4.5-litre, 115bhp shaft-driven racing car which was developed for this event. One of these cars was brought to the United States and won the 1915 Indianapolis Race driven by Ralph de Palma. This model was successful after World War 1, when Count Masetti won the 1921 Italian Grand Prix and the 1922 Targa Florio. A few more first places were gained in hill climbs until 1927. The powerful ohc '28/95' 6-cylinder was just going into production when war broke out.

After the war Mercedes also started to experiment with supercharged engines for cars, after building blown aero engines during the war. The first production cars fitted with a Roots supercharger appeared at the Berlin Motor Show of 1921: the 4-cylinder 6/25/40PS, 1.5-litre and the 10/40/65PS 2.6-litre models. Paul Daimler

1928 MERCEDES-BENZ SS 38/250 tourer.
Daimler-Benz AG

1931 MERCEDES-BENZ Type 170 1.7-litre
saloon. *Daimler-Benz AG*

1935 MERCEDES-BENZ Type 130H 1.3-litre
saloon. *Daimler-Benz AG*

1938 MERCEDES-BENZ Type 540K 5.4-litre
coupé. *Daimler-Benz AG*

1954 MERCEDES-BENZ Type 300SL 3-litre
sports coupé. *Daimler-Benz AG*

1964 MERCEDES-BENZ Type 600 6.3-litre
pullman-limousine. *Daimler-Benz AG*

1972 MERCEDES-BENZ Type 350SLC 3½-litre coupé.
Daimler-Benz AG

retired from the company in 1922 and was succeeded by Ferdinand Porsche, who came to Mercedes from Austro-Daimler. Two more models with blown engines were produced, the 6-cylinder 15/70/100PS (4-litre) and the 24/100/140PS 6-litre. In 1923 the name of Rudolf Caracciola first appeared in association with Mercedes when he won the ADAC-Reichsfahrt; for the next 16 years his name was identified with the company's racing successes. In 1924 Mercedes began to merge their interests with Benz, and amalgamation followed in 1926. Subsequent models were sold under the name of Mercedes-Benz.   HON

MERCEDES-BENZ (D) *1926 to date*
Daimler Benz AG, Stuttgart-Untertürkheim; Mannheim

After amalgamation of Mercedes and Benz in 1926 the Benz 16/50PS model and the Mercedes models with supercharged engines were continued for some time. New 1926 models were the 6-cylinder 8/38PS 2-litre Stuttgart and the 12/55PS 3.1-litre Mannheim, both conventional and heavy sv machines with coil ignition, 3-speed gearboxes and wood wheels. These were developed into the 2.6-litre Stuttgart 260 and the 3½-litre Mannheim 350. A new model the Nürburg 460 with an 8-cylinder 4.6-litre engine was added in 1928 and this later grew into the Nürburg 500. These were the last models – except the 'Grosser Mercedes' – built to the classic chassis design with U-sectioned frame, rigid axles and semi-elliptic springs. The earlier Mercedes model 24/100/140PS became the sports model K with shortened wheelbase and a supercharged 6.25-litre 24/110/160PS engine. It was the fastest touring car on its time on the world market. From this model a range of very successful types was derived: the S (6.8-litre 26/120/180PS), the SS (7.1-litre 27/140/200PS), SSK (7.1-litre 27/170/225PS), and the SSKL (7.1-litre 27/170/300PS). They gained numerous victories and places in hill-climbs, and sports car races. Although they were not racing cars they nevertheless competed successfully in several events, winning, for example, the Ulster TT in 1929, the Irish Grand Prix in 1930, the Mille Miglia and Eifel Race in 1931, and the Avus Race in 1931 and 1932. In 1930 came the first 8-cylinder Grosser Mercedes with a 7.7-litre engine developing 150bhp, or 200bhp with supercharger. This first version was built until 1937 and had the old Mercedes chassis design, but the succeeding model 770 of 1938 had a modern lay-out with oval tubular frame and swing axles. The engine output was increased to 155/230bhp. A maximum speed of over 100mph was possible.

The 'economy class' was entered again in 1931 with the 6-cylinder, 1,692cc model 170, the first Mercedes car to use independent wheel suspension. The designs which followed included the rear-engined models 130H, 150H and 170H, with backbone frames, the 260D, the first diesel-engined private car to be series produced, and the supercharged 540K sports tourer.

In 1934 Mercedes-Benz took up racing again. For the 750kg Formula an 8-cylinder 3.36-litre supercharged model was designed, developing 354bhp. During the next three years engine capacities were raised to 5.66-litres giving an output of 646bhp. For 1938 and 1939 a V-12 supercharged model was built to the new 3-litre Formula specification, developing 476 and 483bhp. A 1½-litre, 254bhp racer had to be designed especially for the 1939 Tripoli Grand Prix and 1st and 2nd places in this race were the result. This was one of the last successes before the outbreak of World War 2, after a long and distinguished record which had begun in 1934 and only been interrupted by Auto Union, the two firms sharing nearly all major race successes between them. Several world records were also gained by Mercedes-Benz. In 1934 the standing-start mile was covered at 117.2mph at Gyor (Hungary), and the flying mile at 193.8mph on the Avus course. In 1936 a world record for the flying 10 miles was set with a V-12 aerodynamic-bodied car on the Frankfurt-Darmstadt autobahn with 207.2mph. The Frankfurt autobahn again saw a Mercedes record early in 1938 when the flying kilometre was covered at 268.9mph, the highest speed ever achieved on a public highway. Caracciola was the driver who gained these world records, and also a number of class records, for Mercedes. An aero-engined car was being prepared for an attack on the World Land Speed Record in 1939.

The former Benz works at Mannheim were used for the production of private cars until 1939. Since then commercial vehicles have been built in Mannheim and private cars in the Stuttgart-Untertürkheim works. At the outbreak of World War 2 the firm were testing a 6-litre V-12 intended as a replacement for the Grosser.

World War 2 halted development. The pre-war 1.697cc 170V was taken up again in 1947 and was available as the 170D with a diesel engine. These fours had back-bone-type frames; unitary construction made its appearance in the 1954 '180' series. The first ohc four was the sporting 190SL of 1955. The 6-cylinder models 220 and 300 followed in 1951. The 4-cylinder 170 was progressively increased in size and output from 1,697cc and 38bhp to the 1,988cc and 95bhp of the 200 introduced in 1965. Sports car manufacture recommenced in 1952 with the 6-cylinder, 3-litre, 215bhp 300SL with fuel injection, originally a fixed head coupé with gull-wing doors, but later sold as a roadster; over 3,250 were made. The 300SL was victorious at Le Mans in 1952. The 300SLR was a sports racing car with an 8-cylinder 3-litre engine of 300bhp and was very successful in competitions. In 1954 Mercedes-Benz again took part in formula racing with an 8-cylinder 2.5-litre version. Juan Manuel Fangio was World Champion in 1954 and 1955 on this model. Participation in racing was discontinued after 1955.

The top model of the Mercedes-Benz range of production cars was added in

1964. It was the 600, a luxury car with an 8-cylinder 6.3-litre 250bhp engine, continuing the tradition of the pre-war Grosser Mercedes. It is available in two wheelbase lengths, 10ft 6in and 12ft 10in. The latter has an overall length of 20ft 6in and is also available with a 6-door body. Early in 1968 the range was revised with a restyled body and new independent rear suspension for the 200, 230 and 250 models. A new 280 engine was introduced, used in the bodies of the former 300 saloons and 250SL sports car. Bridging the gap between the 300 and the 600 was the 300SEL, a 300 saloon using the big 6.3-litre V-8 engine. Power-assisted steering, automatic transmission and air conditioning were standard, and it was capable of 137mph, though attempts to race it at Spa in 1969 proved abortive. In May 1968 the company delivered its two millionth private car since the end of the war, and in 1969 came a tantalizing prototype sports coupé, the C-111 with rear-mounted fuel-injection 3-rotor Wankel engine developing 280bhp, a 5-speed ZF transaxle, limited-slip differential, and all-disc brakes. Weight was under 2,640lb. By 1970 it had been redesigned to take a 4-rotor unit with an equivalent capacity of 4.8 litres and an output of 350bhp; top speed was around 190mph. New production models were the 300SEL 3.5 saloon and 280SE 3.5 coupé, powered by 230bhp 3½-litre dohc V-8 units with fuel injection; by 1971 this engine had also been applied to the 350SL sports coupé, features of which were trailing-arm rear suspension and a foot-operated parking brake.

Smallest of the 1972–3 range was the 2-litre 200, available with 4-cylinder petrol or diesel engine, and during 1972 the medium-sized 280SE gave way to a new 2.8-litre dohc model. Output was 160bhp with carburettors or 185bhp with fuel injection.   HON

1911 MERCER Model 35-R roadster.
William S. Jackson

MERCER (US) *1910–1925; 1931*

(1) Mercer Autocar Co, Trenton, N.J. *1910*
(2) Mercer Automobile Co, Trenton, N.J. *1910–1925*
(3) Elcar Motor Car Co, Elkhart, Ind. *1931*

The Mercer was named after Mercer County, New Jersey, where it was made. The most famous Mercer of all was the Type 35 Raceabout of 1911, designed by Finlay R. Porter. The specification was ordinary enough, embracing at first a 5-litre, 4-cylinder, Continental-built T-head engine that produced a little over 10bhp per litre at a leisurely 1,700rpm. There were 3 forward speeds. The classic 'body work' consisted of a bolster tank, two bucket seats, and a monocle windscreen. However, in common with other speedsters, the mercer weighed very little and could pull a high axle ratio, which helped it to attain a guaranteed 70mph. In 1912, by contrast, a few cars were made with the Owen Magnetic's Entz transmission. A more efficient, L-head engine giving up to 89bhp at 3,000rpm according to tune was substituted in 1915. Also, it had a 4-speed gearbox. This 22 Series was designed by E.H. Delling. However, some of the old Raceabout's character was lost, in that the body of the new version had sides and a bench-type front seat, instead of the two stark bucket seats of the first type. Indeed, full touring models were offered as well. The Series 4 and 5, beginning in 1919, had yet another designer in A.C. Schultz, and even had an electric starter. Nevertheless, these cars were still European in concept in that the engines had a fixed head and a magneto, and drove through a plate clutch and, however much they had compromised with popular taste, they could still attain 75mph. A six with an ohv engine made by Rochester was introduced at the same time, and sixes alone were made from 1923. The old line of Mercers finally died two years later. However magnificent they may have been, they bore too little relation to what the public wanted to survive. Production never exceeded 500 units a year. An attempt was made to revive the name in 1931, but only two cars were built. The chassis was made by the Elcar Motor Co and the engine by Continental. The latter was a straight-8 providing 140bhp and 100mph.   TRN

1920 MERCER Series 6 tourer. *Don McCray*

MERCILESS (US) *1907*

Huntington Automobile Co, Huntington, (Ill?)

The 70hp Merciless had a wheelbase of 10ft 7in. The engine was a T-head 6-cylinder unit of 10 litres capacity. Drive was through a 4-speed transmission and drive shaft. The state in which this car was made is still in question.   GMN

MERCUR *see* EGO

MERCURY (i) (US) *1904*

Mercury Machine Co, Pittsburgh, Pa.

This was a two-seater with a 2-cylinder water-cooled engine of 7hp. A sliding-gear transmission was used and the weight of the vehicle was 1,250lb. Its price was $295 and a top cost $100 extra.   GMN

MERCURY (ii) (GB) *1905*

Ivanhoe Motor Co, Cricklewood, London N.W.

This company made a small number of 24hp 4-cylinder cars which they also called Ivanhoes. In 1906 they became agents for Weigel and planned to show these cars on their stand at Olympia, but permission was refused because they had said in their application that they would show Ivanhoes. In fact, only second-hand cars were shown on the stand, but they stressed that the Weigel could be seen at the works.   GNG

1918 MERCURY(v) sporting tourer. *Keith Marvin Collection*

1939 MERCURY(vi) 3.9-litre sedan. *Ford Motor Co*

1950 MERCURY(vi) 4.2-litre sedan. *Ford Motor Co*

1967 MERCURY(vi) Cougar 4.7-litre coupé. *Ford Motor Co*

MERCURY (iii) (GB) *1914–1923*
(1) Medina Engineering Co Ltd, Twickenham, Middlesex *1914–1920*
(2) Mercury Cars (Production) Ltd, Twickenham, Middlesex *1920–1923*

The Mercury was a conventional light car with a 10hp 4-cylinder monobloc engine and shaft drive. One model only was made before the war, but in 1920 there were three, a 9.5, 10.2 and 11.9hp. Bodies were the usual two- and four-seaters.
GNG

MERCURY (iv) (US) *1914*
Mercury Cyclecar Co, Detroit, Mich.

The Mercury cyclecar differed little from others of that breed, except that it had a self-supporting body which eliminated the chassis frame; in other words integral construction. The engine was a 9hp 2-cylinder air-cooled unit, and the car used friction transmission and belt final drive. Body styles were a monocar, a tandem two-seater and a light van.
GNG

MERCURY (v) (US) *1918–1920*
Mercury Cars Inc, Hollis, N.Y.

A small, assembled car of limited production, the Mercury used a Duesenberg or Weidely 4-cylinder engine and was equipped with a door in the floor to give the driver ready access to the service brake mechanism.
KM

MERCURY (vi) (US) *1938 to date*
Ford Motor Co, Detroit, Mich.

The Mercury, a product of Ford's Lincoln Division, was intended to rival G.M.'s Oldsmobile and Buick, and widen Ford penetration of the American market. The car was in effect an enlarged Model 91 Ford V-8 with a 3.9-litre 95bhp engine. At $957 it cost $230 more than its smaller sister, but $40 less than Buick's cheapest 4-door sedan. Hydraulic brakes were standard from the start and evolution followed established Ford lines, with no drastic changes until 1949, when the new low silhouette, hypoid rear axle, and coil-spring independent front suspension were incorporated. Capacity went up to 4.2 litres and its front-end styling emphasized the association with Lincoln. Mercury, like Ford, progressed to overhead valves and oversquare cylinder dimensions and in 1955 buyers had a choice of two V-8 engines of 188 and 198bhp. An inexpensive Medalist series was added in 1956 and in 1957 the standard power unit was a 255bhp 5.1-litre engine, with the option of a detuned Lincoln engine giving 290bhp. Mercury became bigger and more expensive in 1958 and 1959 to avoid clashing with the Edsel range from the same stable, and a 6.3-litre, 360bhp engine was available.

In 1961 Mercury broke with tradition, and offered for the first time something other than a V-8; not only was there the option of a 3.6-litre six in the regular range, but there was also a semi-compact, the 2.4-litre Comet, a model with a 9ft 6in wheelbase parallel with Ford's Falcon. The Comet sold for $2,084 in 1962, when the largest of the standard V-8s was a rather modest 4.8-litre. 1963 saw a return to bigger things, with 6.4-litre and 6.8-litre engines available in the top-price Monterey models, which also included a Breezeway sedan with forward-sloped rear window as already used on Ford of Britain's 1960 Anglia. Though the Comet was retained for 1966 with a 3.3-litre engine, the biggest Mercurys looked like Lincoln's Continental on a reduced scale; the wheelbase is 10ft 3in, with 6.4-litre, 6.7-litre and 7-litre engines available. For the more sporting motorist there was the Comet Cyclone with compact dimensions and a 6.4-litre V-8 unit. A 1967 sports coupé version, the Cougar, heralded a return to the waterfall-type radiator grille so generally popular in the early 1950s.

Subsequent Mercury developments were aimed at keeping station in the tricky medium-priced market, with the sporting element represented by the Cyclone and Cougar coupés (with V-8 engines of up to 390bhp) and the luxury sector covered by the Marquis Brougham, which in 1969 form aped the Lincoln with its concealed headlamps, and came with 7-litre V-8 unit and automatic as standard. Regular family cars were the Montego on a 9ft 9in wheelbase, and the stock Mercury of 10ft 4in. In 1971 there was a Mercury edition of Ford's Maverick compact, the Comet. Wheelbase was 8ft 7in, and engine options were sixes of 2.8 litres, 3.3 litres or 4.1 litres, or a small 4.9-litre 210bhp V-8. Basic price was a low $2,217, and it was continued into 1972 along with the Cougar, Montego, Monterey, Colony Park and Marquis lines, though new Federal regulations took their toll, and the most powerful engine option gave only 266bhp, as against 375 in 1970. Montegos had front disc brakes as standard, as had 1973 Cougars, which came with a traditional radiator grille in Humber-Sunbeam style. Most of the 1973 improvements concerned safety (e.g. reinforced bumpers and radial-ply tyres as standard on the big sedans). Ford's Lincoln-Mercury Division also distributed the German Ford Capri with 2-litre or 2.6-litre engine.
MCS

MERCURY SPECIAL (US) *1946*
Paul Omohundro, Los Angeles, Calif.

The aluminium-bodied Mercury Special sports never got beyond the prototype stage because of material shortage. A Mercury chassis and engine were used but it was intended to supply production models with Cadillac engines and transmissions, plus bodies of fibreglass.
BE

MERIT (US) *1920–1923*

Merit Motor Co, Cleveland, Ohio

The Merit, an assembled car, used a Continental 6-cylinder engine. Production was small.   KM

MERKEL (i) (US) *1905–1906*

Merkel Mfg Co, Milwaukee, Wisc.

This car, which was built in very small numbers, was a two-seater roadster, with left-hand steering by wheel. The final drive was by shaft.   GMN

MERKEL (ii) (US) *1914*

M.F. Merkel, Middletown, Ohio

This was a relatively heavy (1,060lb) two-seater cyclecar, with a 4-cylinder, water-cooled, 1½-litre engine. The drive was through a 3-speed transmission and drive shaft.   GMN

MERLIN (GB) *1913–1914*

New Merlin Cycle Co, Birmingham

The Merlin light car used a 9hp 2-cylinder Blumfield engine and shaft drive. The makers specialized in supplying components to other cyclecar manufacturers.   GNG

MERLYN (GB) *1961 to date*

Colchester Racing Developments Ltd, Little Bentley, Colchester, Essex

After starting with Formula Junior machines, Merlyn soon changed to rear engines, and thereafter progressed to Formulas 2 and 3. Both sales and racing successes were achieved with the tubular space-framed single-seaters, clad in attractive fibreglass bodies. Chris Irwin, in particular, scored several notable wins in Formula 3. From 1962 onwards a sports model was also available. Production centred on Formula 3 cars for a season or two. Then for 1968 the Mark 11 Formula Ford appeared, and was immediately successful. Tim Schenken took the major British championships in this and the following year. The Mark 12 was a Formula 2 car, Mark 14 another Formula 3 design, Mark 15 the Formula B counterpart, and Mark 16 was allocated to the Formula F100 model produced for 1970. The 1970 Formula Ford car was the Mark 17, which assumed the Mark 11's mantle by taking the British titles in the hands of Colin Vandervell.

Less was heard of the Formula 3, Group 6 sports-car racing and Formula B machines that took the next three Mark numbers. For 1971 the Mark 20 was revised and continued as the new Formula Ford car and continued as the car to beat in the class; Bernard Vermilio took the B.O.C. Championship. Leading drivers during 1972 included Tim and Tony Brise, Roger Arnott, Rob Cooper and Dave Ferris. Mark 21 was the Formula 3 car raced for the works by Ian Scheckter, Mark 22 an oval-track midget racer, and Mark 23 a revised Formula B or 3 machine. The continuing success of the Formula Ford cars enabled a steady production level to be maintained, and an improved model was planned for 1973. This was the Mark 24, with entirely new body and chassis.   DF

MERRY '01 (US) *1958–1962*

American Air Products Corp, Fort Lauderdale, Fla.

Sometimes referred to as the Merry Olds, this was a modern plywood and steel reproduction of the curved dash Oldsmobile. It used a 4hp single-cylinder Clinton air-cooled engine providing 35mph and 60mpg.   BE

MERZ (US) *1914–1915*

Merz Cyclecar Co, Indianapolis, Ind.

The body and bonnet of this cyclecar was of one-piece construction. A single headlight was inset above the false radiator. Its engine was a 1.1-litre, 2-cylinder De Luxe.   GMN

MESERVE (US) *1904*

W.F. Meserve, West Derry, N.H.

These were custom-built cars, using 4-cylinder 2-stroke 5.2-litre engines built by the Lowell Motor Co of Lowell, Mass. Final drive was by chain. A speed of over 40mph was claimed.   GMN

MESSERSCHMITT (D) *1953–1962*

(1) Regensburger Stahl- und Metallbau GmbH, Regensburg *1953–1956*
(2) Fahrzeug- und Maschinenbau GmbH, Regensburg *1956–1962*

The Fend design of 3-wheeled bubble car was taken over by Messerschmitt, the former aircraft company in 1953 and built in one of their works. The first model was the KR175 with a 175cc single-cylinder 2-stroke Sachs engine, which was replaced by a 200cc engine in 1955. This version was built until 1962, when production was discontinued. A very interesting vehicle was the 4-wheeled FMR Tg500 (Tiger) with a twin-cylinder 500cc Sachs engine, which was built from 1958 until 1960.   HON

MESSIER (F) *1926–1931*

Georges Messier, Montrouge, Seine

The 'Sans Ressorts' Messier was one of the many mobile testbeds for novel

1973 MERCURY(vi) Comet coupé. *Ford Motor Co.*

1961 MERLYN Formula Junior racing car.
Colchester Racing Developments Ltd

1972 MERLYN Mark 24 Formula Ford racing car.
Colchester Racing Developments Ltd

1959 MESSERSCHMITT Tg500 Tiger 500cc tandem two-seater. *G.N. Georgano*

1914 MÉTALLURGIQUE 38/80hp saloon.
Col. C.B. Krabbé.

1924 MÉTALLURGIQUE 12/40hp saloon.
Coachwork by Vanden Plas. *Raymond K. Wright*

1920 METEOR(vii) 27hp seven-seater sedan.
Keith Marvin Collection

systems of suspension current in France in the 1920s that got little farther than the experimental stage. As early as 1920, Georges Messier had been fitting his compressed-air pneumatic suspension to cars, including a model of Pilain in 1924, and in 1926 started building complete vehicles himself. They were powered by proprietary engines, starting with a 4-cylinder C.I.M.E. and going on to sixes and eights, the latter by Lycoming, but the means of propulsion was not what made the cars important. No more Messiers were made after 1931, but their designer went on to pioneer hydraulic landing gear for aircraft, and the Messier car suspension was the basis of that used today in the Citroën. TRN

MÉTALLURGIQUE (B) *1898–1928*
SA L'Auto Métallurgique, Marchienne-au-Pont

What was to become the most renowned sporting make of Belgium started life with a 4½hp, 2-cylinder car on Daimler lines. 2- and 4-cylinder chain-driven vehicles on a similar pattern followed. From 1905, however, a major change began. A range of lively, beautifully-made, modern cars, from an 8hp twin to two big fours, all featuring variable valve lift, steel frames and live axles, was offered. They were designed by Ernst Lehmann, formerly of Daimler. In case the owner wished to fit electric lighting, a dynamo for battery-charging was provided. In 1906, there appeared the superb 60/80hp fast tourer. Its 4-cylinder ioe engine gave 100bhp at 1,400rpm. A year later this and all other models acquired the sharp V-radiator that was to become the make's trademark. The 1908 range included the 40hp, a smaller version of the great 60/80, while a year later came the 26hp, which was to be the most famous model of all. These three types all had 4-speed gearboxes, a refinement comparatively rare in Belgium, that was extended to all models in 1911.

Most Métallurgiques made in Belgium were exported to Britain, and a German factory (Bergmann) was set up. All bodies were by Vanden Plas and were beautiful creations. A sports version of the 26hp providing 75bhp with the aid of light pistons and large valves, was listed in 1912. The other big Métallurgiques acquired sporting variants, too, but a small four also arrived, the 10/12hp of 1.7 litres. Sv engines were to be had in the more 'touring' models of 1913. The 5-litre 26hp was continued after World War 1, with the addition of Adex-type diagonally-compensated 4-wheel brakes. New in 1921 was a 3-litre sports car, one of which made the fastest lap in the 1922 Spa Grand Prix. However, a truly modern Métallurgique arrived in that year; a 2-litre, 4-cylinder fast tourer, in the postwar French tradition designed by Paul Bastien (who was later responsible for the Stutz Vertical Eight). The engine used a chain-driven overhead camshaft, there were front-wheel brakes, and the steering was notably light. This fine machine was the company's mainstay until the acquisition of its factory by Minerva and its machinery by Imperia in 1927. So ended a name with a remarkably consistent record of good cars. TRN

METEOR (i) (US) *1900*
Springfield Cornice Works, Springfield, Mass.

The first of many cars to bear the name Meteor, this was a light runabout powered by a 2¾ or 3½hp De Dion engine mounted in front, and driving by a long single chain to the rear axle. GNG

METEOR (ii) (US) *1902–1903*
Meteor Engineering Co, Reading, Pa.

The Meteor company was the successor to the Steam Vehicle Company of America, maker of the Reading steamer, and Meteor continued the Reading design for one year. The Meteor car itself was larger than the Reading, being a four-seater tonneau powered by a 4-cylinder horizontal engine of 10hp. It had wheel steering, a De Dion-type bonnet, and the appearance of a petrol-engined car. The price was $2,000, compared with $800 for the smaller Reading. GNG

METEOR (iii) (GB) *1903–1905*
Pritchett & Gold Ltd, Feltham, Middlesex

This company made both petrol and electric cars, although the latter were generally known as P & Gs. Two models of the Meteor were made, using a 12hp Blake engine or a 24hp Mutel engine, both 4-cylinder units, and both cars having shaft drive. GNG

METEOR (iv) (B) *1905–1906*
Felix Hecq, Brussels

The Belgian Meteor was made in two forms, a De Dion-engined voiturette and a 4-cylinder 16/20hp touring car. GNG

METEOR (v) (US) *1905–1906*
(1) Berg Automobile Co, New York, N.Y. *1905*
(2) Worthington Automobile Co, New York, N.Y. *1905–1906*

The Meteor had some advanced features such as aluminium engine parts, and shaft drive. The 18hp, 3-litre engine weighed 314lb, and had a speed range of 200 to 1,000rpm. The car was offered as a five-seater tonneau model. GMN

METEOR (vi) (US) *1907–1910*
(1) Meteor Motor Car Co, Bettendorf, Iowa *1907–1909*

Meteor Motor Car Co, Davenport, Iowa *1909–1910*

The Meteor differed from most Mid-Western cars, being powered by a 50hp 4-cylinder T-head engine. Circassian Walnut was used in the bodywork and prices ranged up to $4,000 for the seven-seater touring car or limousine.　GMN

METEOR (vii) **(US)** *1914–1930*

Meteor Motor Car Co, Shelbyville, Ind.; Piqua, Ohio

Meteor cars were produced until about 1916 as touring cars and roadsters, with Continental and Model 6-cylinder engines. A short-lived V-12 with Weidely engine was listed in 1916. The company then turned its efforts to ambulances and hearses and Meteor's private-car output was restricted to large sedans for funeral use and invalid cars until about 1923. Until 1930, however, private cars were built to special order. The company still survives.　KM

METEOR (viii) **(US)** *1919–1922*

Meteor Motors Inc, Philadelphia, Pa.

One of America's higher-priced luxury cars of the time, the Meteor, powered by a Rochester-Duesenberg 4-cylinder engine, was distinguished by careful workmanship, a variety of open and closed bodies and a radiator similar to the Austro-Daimler of the period.　KM

METEOR (ix) **(CDN)** *1949–1961; 1969 to date*

Ford Motor Company of Canada Ltd, Windsor, Ont.

This was identical to a Ford except for its special grille and trim and was retailed only in Canada by Mercury-Lincoln dealers in order to extend their market. This car replaced the Mercury 114, sold exclusively in Canada in 1947 and 1948, which was a standard Ford but with Mercury grille and trim. Standard 1946/8 Mercurys were also sold in Canada. From 1963 to 1970 the name Meteor was applied to Mercurys sold in Canada, but with Ford interiors and engines. The name was revived in 1969 for a full-size car on a 10ft 4in wheelbase, available in three series with 3.9-litre 6-cylinder engine, or V-8s of 4.9, 6.4 and 7 litres. Only V-8s were offered in 1972. The restyled 1973 Silver Anniversary models featured impact-absorbing bumpers.　HD

METEORITE **(GB)** *1912–1924*

(1) Meteorite Motors Ltd, London W.12 *1912–1921*
(2) Meteorite Cars Ltd, London W.12 *1921–1924*

This company began by making a cyclecar with an 8hp V-twin J.A.P. engine, but by 1915 had added a 10hp 4-cylinder and a 20.9hp 6-cylinder car with Aster engine to their range. The V-twin made a brief re-appearance in 1919, but the staple offering in the 1920s used a 10.8hp Coventry-Simplex engine. Saloon and Coupé bodies, as well as open tourers, were made by Strachan & Brown. The 10.8hp was made until 1924, and was joined in that year by a 13.8hp 6-cylinder car. Production ended in October 1924, and spares were transferred to C.E. Humphreys of Bedford. Humphreys are sometimes mistakenly listed as makers of the Meteorite.　GNG

METROPOL **(US)** *1913–1914*

Metropol Motors Corp, Port Jefferson, Long Island, N.Y.

This sporty car, without doors, was equipped with a 7.3-litre, 4-cylinder engine which had a cylinder bore of 108mm with an incredible stroke of 200mm. The resulting unit required a very high bonnet. Two- and four-seaters were produced. In 1914 the price of either body style was $1,475.　GMN

METROPOLITAN (i) **(GB)** *1901*

Metropolitan Motor Mfg Co, Fulham, London S.W.

The Metropolitan had a 7/8hp engine of the company's own design mounted in front under a short bonnet. The 2 vertical cylinders were widely spaced, with the flywheel in the middle, so that it was almost as if there were two separate engines. Transmission was by belts from the transverse crankshaft to a countershaft, and hence by single or double chain to the rear axle.　GNG

METROPOLITAN (ii) **(US)** *1922–1923*

Metropolitan Motors Inc, Kansas City, Mo.

This assembled car first appeared equipped with a Continental engine but this was replaced in the later months of 1922 by a 4-cylinder unit of the firm's own make, apparently because they wanted to market a smaller car.　KM

METROPOLITAN (iii) **(US)** *1954–1961*

American Motors Corp, Kenosha, Wisc.

The 1950 prototype of this car was called the Nash NXI, but it went into production in 1954 at the Austin Motor Company's plant in England, for sale by American Motors. The engine was a 1.2-litre Austin unit, the wheelbase was 7ft 1in, and the body a three-seater coupé or convertible. Only minor changes were made during the Metropolitan's seven-year life span.　GNG

METRO-TYLER **(GB)** *1922–1923*

Metro-Tyler Ltd, London W.10

1919 METEOR(viii) 30hp tourer. *Keith Marvin Collection*

1913 METEORITE 10hp two-seater. *David Burgess Wise*

1922 METEORITE 10.8hp saloon. *The Veteran Car Club of Great Britain*

The Metro-Tyler was one of the smallest of the post-war cyclecars, and used a 5/6hp air-cooled 2-cylinder 2-stroke engine of 550cc, built up from two of their motor cycle units. A 3-speed gearbox was used and final drive was by belt originally, with the option of chain for 1923. The price was very low at £125. GN

METZ (i) (US) 1909–1922

(1) Waltham Mfg Co, Waltham, Mass. 1909
(2) The Metz Co, Waltham, Mass. 1909–1922
(3) Motor Manufacturers of Waltham Inc, Waltham, Mass. 1922

C.H. Metz took over the Waltham company, which was making Waltham and Orient Buckboard cars. The first car to bear his own name was a light 12hp air cooled 2-cylinder roadster with friction transmission and double chain drive. It was sold on the Metz Plan, by which purchasers bought fourteen separate packages of parts, for home assembly. This design and 'plan' was continued through 1911 but in April of that year a new car with a 22hp water-cooled 4-cylinder engine was introduced, which was sold complete in the normal manner. It retained friction drive, as did all Metzes until 1917, and the two-seater roadster body of the earlier car. In 1916 the engine was enlarged to 25hp, and in 1919 a completely new car, the Master Six, was introduced, with a 45hp 6-cylinder engine, conventional gearbox and shaft drive. In 1922 this car was renamed the Waltham, thus reviving the name used by the old Waltham Manufacturing Company. GM

METZ (ii) (NL) 1909

The Amsterdam-built Metz was a 3-wheeler on the lines of the German Phänomobil, with 2-cylinder 3½hp Minerva engine and friction transmission. The body was a two-seater, but an extra rear seat could be mounted if necessary. GN

MEYER (US) 1919

A.J. Meyer Corp, Chicago, Ill.

The Meyer car was a curiosity as it was available in any model, for any number of passengers and with engines ranging from 2 to 12 cylinders. The Meyer patented wheels were made of pressed steel welded to the hub shell with rubber wedge between the shell and bearing collar. The special tyres were of hollow rubber construction of two hollow sections and centre wall and casing for flexibility. A specially-designed automatic gearshift was also standard. KM

MEYRA (D) 1952–1956

Wilhelm Meyer, Vlotho

This was a small 3-wheeler with front entrance on the Isetta pattern which was mainly intended for invalids. The single rear wheel was driven by chain from the 197cc single-cylinder Ilo engine. HON

M.G. (GB) 1924 to date

(1) Morris Garages Ltd, Oxford 1924–1928
(2) M.G. Car Co Ltd, Abingdon, Berks. 1929–1970
(3) Austin-Morris Division, British Leyland Motor Corp Ltd, Abingdon, Berks. 1970 to date

The name M.G. is synonymous with sports cars, but it has always been borne by more sedate vehicles as well; at first it had no true sporting connotation at all. In the early 1920s Cecil Kimber was in charge of the Morris Garages, the firm from which William Morris's new empire had sprung and which was the Morris agent in Oxford. It was an extremely common practice for manufacturers of staid, solid touring cars to offer mildly tuned alternatives with more dashing bodywork for the benefit of the man in the street who would pay a little extra for a more sporting vehicle. In 1920 Morris had discontinued his own sporting version of his Cowley and other Morris dealers had offered their own alternatives independently.

From 1922, Kimber began experimenting with special bodies, and two years later took the new 1.8-litre Oxford and modified it slightly into the M.G. Super Sports. A lightly-tuned engine, improved handling and handsome aluminium bodies effected the transformation. Backed by Morris reliability and service, the M.G. was a great success. When Morris went over to a flat radiator in place of the old 'bull-nose' for 1927, Kimber followed. By this time, he was calling his car the 14/40hp, because of its increased power compared with the 14/28hp of the standard Oxford. A year later there arrived the 2½-litre Morris Six with overhead camshaft for which Cecil Kimber designed a completely new cylinder block and head, a light body and a high axle ratio. The resulting 18/80hp M.G. was improved in 1930 with a 4-speed gearbox and stiffer chassis. This Mark II 18/80 was major modification of the Morris recipe. Earlier, when Morris had introduced his new ohc 847cc Morris Minor in 1928, Kimber adopted and adapted it to the M.G. style. The Minor chassis and engine were retained, with little alteration other than lowering the suspension and steering. The little fabric-bodied, pointed-tail two-seater M-type M.G. Midget of 1929, with its engine tuned to provide 20bhp, 65mph and excellent acceleration, was Britain's first really cheap and at the same time practical sports car. The sporting cyclecars of former times were too stark and noisy, and the imported French sports cars such as the Amilcar and Salmson were far dearer and in any case were going out of production. It was true that the M-type retained the Morris Minor's somewhat uncertain brakes and its wide-ratio 3-speed gearbox

1913 METZ Model 22 two-seater. *Harrah's Automobile Collection*

1926 M.G. 14/28hp two-seater. *Lytton Jarman*

1930 M.G. M-type Midget 8hp sports car. *British Motor Corporation*

…ut the performance wanted by a new, wide and undiscriminating market for sports cars was there.

M.G. went in for racing in 1930. The competition cars used superchargers, and special wheels, valves and springs, but shared many components with the touring models. This development began with the Double Twelve M-type, so named after works M-types won the team prize in the Brooklands Double Twelve Hour race of 1930, and with the formidable, if short-lived 18/100 Tigresse, which was derived from the 18/80 but was a true road-racing car, very highly tuned. Much fiercer than the Double Twelve replica was the much better known 746cc C-type, which weighed only 1,120lb, but in supercharged form was capable of 90mph. It won the 1931 Double Twelve, and the Irish Grand Prix and Ulster Tourist Trophy races of the same year. The M-type was developed into the J. Like most normal M.G. types, from the earliest one onwards, a variety of body styles could be had, but the best known was the J2 open two-seater sports of 1932, with its low lines, cutaway doors and slab-tank-mounted spare wheel at the rear. This style set the fashion for the sports cars of the 1930s. The J carried over developments from the racing C-type, demonstrating that racing improved the breed – the cylinder head was of more efficient design, the chassis was stiffer, the brakes were better and there was a 4-speed gearbox. The J3 was a supercharged version, while the J4 was a fine little blown sports-racing edition. The J was developed into the slightly more powerful P-type, which had a 3-bearing crankshaft – not before time.

As far as the general public was concerned, the ultimate development of the little 4-cylinder ohc engine was seen in the PB sports of 1935, with 939cc, but for out-and-out racing there was the supercharged Q-type, followed by the very modern 1935 R-type, with its wishbone and torsion-bar independent suspension of all four wheels. Apart from being 750cc supercharged instead of 847cc unsupercharged, the basic engine of the R-type was almost identical to that of the production P-type, and in fact the R-type engines carried P-type engine serial numbers.

Meanwhile, Kimber had taken the 1930 Wolseley Hornet, a small six (basically a lengthening of the Morris Minor) and turned it into the F-type M.G. Magna. Again, touring and sports versions were offered, with open and closed bodywork. It had a 1,271cc engine. The Magna was developed into the supercharged sports-racing K3 Magnette, which won its class in the 1933 Mille Miglia race, and triumphed outright in the same year's Ulster Tourist Trophy race, driven by Tazio Nuvolari. The unsupercharged 1287cc NE Magnette won the next year's Tourist Trophy. The more 'touring' Magnettes of the K and N series were designed to take four-seater bodies, though two-seaters were made. Larger and heavier, they were altogether more substantial machines than the Magnas they supplemented. In six competition seasons, the make also won the French d'Or race twice, the Brooklands 500 Miles race twice, the 1100cc class of the Grand Prix de France twice, and more than two dozen other important first places. Between 1930 and 1959, with and without works support, M.G. also captured many class speed records. In 1931, a special M.G. became the first 750cc car to exceed 100mph, and to cover more than 100 miles in the hour. M.G. became Britain's premier sporting marque.

After 1935, the company officially raced no longer, and no more competition cars were made for public sale. M.G. models tended to become bigger, and more comfortable. The 1936 Midget's 4-cylinder, ohc unit gave way to a 1,290cc long-stroke, push-rod ohv engine in the TA, which also had hydraulic brakes. This was succeeded by the shorter-stroke, 1¼-litre TB in 1939. The 1½-litre VA carried roomier bodies. The 6-cylinder cars became rather more staid, but the big 2-litre SA and 2.6-litre WA of the 1936–40 period were handsome, excellent and popular machines, catering for those who wanted an Alvis or a Lagonda but could not afford one. They were dropped after World War 2 in favour of the TC Midget, which was virtually the TB with a synchromesh gearbox, and its saloon and touring version, the Y-type. The latter was the first touring M.G. to have independent front suspension.

The TC Midget did more than any other machine to foster and spread the cult of the European sports car in America. The first real modernization in the design of the Midget came in 1949, with the introduction of the TD. This had wishbone and coil-spring independent front suspension, a box-section frame and rack-and-pinion steering, but though a little more power had been extracted from the engine, the handling was not noticeably improved. The TF of 1953 incorporated the firm's first concessions to aerodynamic principles in a production car, but was otherwise a transitional model. A 1½-litre engine became optional in the TF, and gave way to an Austin-designed unit of the same capacity in the completely new MGA that succeeded it for 1956. A very rigid chassis greatly improved handling, while an efficient aerodynamic shape provided a much higher maximum speed (nearly 100mph) and allowed a higher axle ratio. Both features made for fuel economy. A few MGAs were made with twin ohc engines, but in the hands of the average driver, these were temperamental, and the 1.6-litre, 78bhp push-rod ohv engine that was eventually fitted to all MGAs provided just as much performance with traditional M.G. dependability. The MGA 1600, like the Twin Cam, had disc brakes on the front wheels. Meanwhile, the boxy Y-type touring car contemporary with the TC had given way for 1954 to the attractive little 1½-litre ZA Magnette; a revival of an old name. It was, however, a 4-cylinder car. Basically, it was a livelier edition of the Wolseley in the B.M.C. range, and the practice of putting an M.G. radiator on the Corporation's smaller family saloons was continued, until now this is done on both the front-wheel-drive 1100 and the 1.6-litre Magnette IV.

1931 M.G. 18/80hp Mark II coupé. Coachwork by Weymann. *National Motor Museum*

1936 M.G. PB Midget 9hp sports car. *British Motor Corporation*

1936 M.G. TA Midget 10hp sports car. *British Motor Corporation*

1938 M.G. SA 2-litre saloon. *G.N. Georgano*

1965 M.G. MGB 1.8-litre GT coupé. *British
Motor Corporation*

1896 MIARI e GIUSTI (Bernardi) 3½hp
3-wheeler. *Museo dell'Automobile, Turin*

1912 MICHIGAN(ii) 40hp tourer. *Automotive
History Collection, Detroit Public Library*

The company's basic sports car having developed beyond its Midget heredity, a new, true Midget was introduced in 1961 as a cheaper alternative. This was basically the simple little Austin-Healey Sprite. The latest model has unit construction of body and chassis, a 1,275cc, push-rod ohv engine developing 65bhp at 6,000rpm, independent front suspension, and disc front brakes. In 1962 the MGA became the entirely new, unit-construction MGB with 95bhp 1,795cc engine, available as an open two-seater or GT coupé. For 1968 a new 7-main-bearing version of the 6-cylinder Austin-Healey engine was available with the MGB's bodies, the new car being called the MGC. An MGC was the first car to be owned by Prince Charles, but the model was not a great success, being withdrawn late in 1969 after 9,000 had been made. Also in 1968 the 1100 gave way to the 1,275cc 1300. However, one of the effects of the British Leyland merger was the elimination of the badge-engineered M.G.s. The Magnette IV disappeared during 1968, and the last 1300s were built during 1971. The 1970 MGBs had new grilles retaining only a vestige of the traditional shape, but this was the marque's first 50,000 year, and the quarter millionth MGB left Abingdon in May 1971. This model and the 1,275cc Midget III were the only M.G.s offered in 1972. TRN

M.G.P. (F) *1912*
Automobiles Jean Margaria, St Cyr, Seine

One model of the M.G.P. was listed, with a 12hp 4-cylinder monobloc engine of 2.3 litres' capacity. GNG

MIARI E GIUSTI (I) *1896–1899*
Miari, Giusti & Cia, Padua

This company manufactured the 3-wheeler designed by Professor Enrico Bernardi, which was probably the first Italian petrol-engined car. It had a horizontal single-cylinder engine of 624cc, a detachable cylinder head, and hot tube ignition. Drive to the single rear wheel was by chain. GNG

MICHEL IRAT (F) *1929–1930*
Automobiles Michel Irat, SA, Paris 17e

In 1929 Georges Irat reorganized the Chaigneau-Brasier company under his son's name. The sole model of Michel Irat, the Type CB2, was very similar to the small Chaigneau-Brasier. It had a 1086cc sv 4-cylinder engine. GNG

MICHIGAN (i) (US) *1903–1908*
Michigan Automobile Co, Kalamazoo, Mich.

Formerly called the Blood, the first Michigan was a very light two-seater powered by a 3½hp air-cooled engine. Priced at $450, it was one of the cheapest cars in America at the time. Later models were larger, using two-cylinder engines with two or four seater bodies. Prices of these ranged up to $1,250. GMN

MICHIGAN (ii) (US) *1908–1914*
Michigan Buggy Co, Kalamazoo, Mich.

This company began by making high-wheel buggies, but by 1911 was producing low-built tourers and roadsters powered by 33 or 40hp 4-cylinder engines. These were referred to in advertisements as the Mighty Michigan. GNG

MICRON (F) *1925–1930*
Automobiles Micron, Castanet-Tolosane, Toulouse

Designed by Henri Jany, the Micron was a very small cyclecar made mostly in single-seater form. It was powered by a single-cylinder engine of either 350cc or 500cc, and had front-wheel drive. Microns competed in the Bol d'Or races, and two are known to survive today, both in Spain. JRV

MIDDLEBY (US) *1908–1913*
Middleby Auto Co, Reading, Pa.

This make used only 4-cylinder air-cooled engines until 1911, when a 4-cylinder water-cooled engine was introduced, but without much success. Few model changes seem to have been made; for the first three seasons a standard chassis was used and all the engines were of 3.3 litres' capacity. Runabouts and five-seater tourers were produced, all with attractive peaked bonnets. GMN

MIDDLETOWN (US) *1909–1911*
Middletown Buggy Co, Middletown, Ohio

This was a high-wheel buggy with 2-cylinder engine, wheel steering and double chain drive. A light delivery truck was also built. In 1912 the firm became the Crescent Motor Company, which concentrated on cab-over-engine trucks. GNG

MIDLAND (US) *1908–1913*
Midland Motor Co, Moline, Ill.

The Midland used 4-cylinder Milwaukee engines in all models, until 1913 when one model had a 6-cylinder unit. The 4-cylinder engines, of two sizes (25/30 and 30/35hp), powered touring cars and roadsters. Six body types were made for 1913, the T-6 roadster having the 6.2-litre 6-cylinder engine. The roadsters were typical of the best style of the era. GMN

MIELE (D) *1911–1913*

Miele & Cie, Maschinenfabrik, Gütersloh

This firm is well known today for its washing machines. For a short period before World War 1 cars were also built, designed by Dipl. Ing. Klemm, who later made a name as an aircraft manufacturer. 6/17PS and 9/22PS types were made.　HON

MIER (US) *1908–1909*

Mier Carriage & Buggy Co, Ligonier, Ind.

This buggy-type car had wheel steering, mudguards, and a 12hp, 2-cylinder engine. It had solid tyres and double chain drive.　GMN

MIESSE (B) *1896–1926*

J. Miesse et Cie, Brussels

Though Jules Miesse built his first steam car in 1896, no vehicles were sold to the public until two years later. The production steamers used 3-cylinder single-acting engines and their flash boilers were housed under a conventional frontal bonnet. Frames were of armoured wood, and final drive was by side chains; the 10hp model was said to give 17bhp, and running costs of ½d per mile were claimed. Licence-production of the Miesse steamer was undertaken in England by Turner (ii), who continued to list vehicles of this type up to 1913, long after the Brussels factory had gone over to the internal-combustion engine.

Petrol-car experiments started in 1900, and by 1904 Miesse taxis were in service in the Belgian capital. By 1907 steam cars were no longer sold; the staple model was a 3.7-litre T-head 4-cylinder with shaft drive and gate change, priced at £475. This was joined a year later by a monobloc 60hp 6-cylinder for which 60mph was claimed. The monobloc layout had spread to the 4-cylinder cars by 1909, in which year the 24/30hp had a 5-bearing crankshaft. A 3.6-litre 'valveless' 20hp (in fact it had a curious combination of piston and slide valves) was offered in 1912 and 1913, along with a more conventional worm-driven 2.8-litre 15/18, and in the immediate pre-World War 1 period all Miesses had L-head monobloc engines, dry-sump lubrication, all brakes on the rear wheels, 4-speed gearboxes, rounded radiators, and electric lighting. Wire detachable wheels were also standard on cars sold in England, and both the 2.8-litre and the 4.4-litre were listed in standard bevel-drive and 'colonial' worm-drive forms. Rounded radiators were found on the post-war cars, which had overhead camshafts, 3-speed unit gearboxes, and wood wheels. The standard model was a long-stroke (69 × 130mm) 2-litre, but a straight-8 with the same cylinder dimensions and basic specification was also offered. The 2-litre sold for £500 in England in 1923.

In 1924 Miesse were reported to be making the Dunamis car, also a straight-8, but with an sv engine. After 1926 only trucks were made, though after World War 2 the company undertook the assembly of Nash cars for European markets. Miesse commercial vehicles are still made.　MCS

MIEUSSET (F) *1903–1914*

Ateliers de Construction Mécanique et d'Automobiles Mieusset, Lyons

The Mieusset company had made fire extinguishing equipment since 1867, and continued to do so long after car production had ceased. Their first cars were made in five models: a 6hp single-cylinder with chain or shaft drive, an 8/12hp twin, and three 4-cylinder models, of 12/16, 16/20, and 20/25hp. All these had double chain drive. By 1906 large fours of 40 and 60hp were available, and were continued without major change until 1914. In the last year of car production there were eight Mieusset models listed, from a 12/16 four to a 60/80 four which still used chain drive.

All were made in small numbers, as cars were never more than a sideline for the Mieusset firm. After the war lorries were made until 1925.　GNG

MIGNON (F) *1908*

C.E. Chepke, Paris

Mignon cars were either 8hp 2-cylinder voiturettes or 12/14hp 4-cylinder touring cars.　GNG

MIGNONETTE (F) *1900*

Wehrlé et Godard-Desmarest, Neuilly, Seine

The Mignonette voiturette was powered by either De Dion or Aster engines of 3hp. This was rear-mounted and geared to the rear axle. The car had a two-seater body and wheel steering.　GNG

MIGNONETTE-LUAP (F) *1899–1900*

Jiel-Laval et Cie, Bordeaux

This voiturette was powered by a rear-mounted 2¼hp De Dion engine. If this failed there were pedals connected by chain to the rear axle; it was said that the car was sufficiently light to be pedalled with ease to the nearest garage. Steering was by tiller.　GNG

MIKASA (J) *1957–1961*

Okamura Mfg Co, Ltd, Tokyo

The Mikasa touring car was front-wheel driven with a fluid torque converter and

1910 MIDDLEBY 25hp roadster. *Automotive History Collection, Detroit Public Library*

1911 MIDLAND 40hp roadster. *Kenneth Stauffer*

1921 MIESSE 20/30hp 8-cylinder saloon. *Autocar*

1904 MIEUSSET 16/20hp tonneau. *G.N. Georgano Collection*

1919 MILBURN Model 36L electric limousine.
Autocar

1900 MILDÉ ET MONDOS electric 3-wheeler.
Musée de l'Automobile, Rochetaillée-sur-Saone

1907 MILDÉ-GAILLARDET 30hp tourer.
Lucien Loreille Collection

a handsome four-seater body. The engine was an air-cooled 2-cylinder unit of 20hp and the vehicle weighed 1,350lb.   BE

MIKROMOBIL (D) *1922–1924*
(1) Automobil-Gesellschaft Thomsen KG, Hamburg-Wandsbek *1922–1924*
(2) Mikromobil AG, Hamburg-Wandsbek *1924*
    This was a small car with 6/18PS 4-cylinder 2-stroke engine.   HON

MIKRUS (PL) *1958–1960*
Wytwornia Sprzetu Komunikacyjnego, Mielec
    The Mielec Communications Plant produced this well-designed, 990lb, two-door sedan with a rear-mounted 2-cylinder air-cooled engine developing 14hp at 5,000rpm.
                                                                           BE

MILANO (I) *1906–1907*
Sta Milanese dell'Industria Meccanica, Milan
    The Milano used a 22/28hp 4-cylinder engine and shaft drive. It had a turbine fan cast on the periphery of the flywheel, and water-cooled brakes. The radiator was circular in shape.   GNG

MILBURN (US) *1914–1922*
Milburn Wagon Co, Toledo, Ohio
    The Milburn Wagon Company was established in 1848 as makers of horse-drawn vehicles. In 1909 the Ohio Electric was built in part of the Milburn factory, and this presumably paved the way for the production of Milburn's own electric cars, which were first made in December 1914. They were attractive to look at, having a lighter and more delicate appearance than most electrics. They were largely closed cars, although a few roadsters were made as well. In 1919 two models were made imitating the appearance of petrol cars; they were much less successful aesthetically than the undisguised electrics. Milburns were used by President Wilson's secret service men, and were among the most popular American electric cars. Over 7,000 were made. Some lists quote Milburn as late as 1927.   GNG

MILDÉ (F) *1898–1909*
Mildé et Cie, Levallois-Perret, Seine
    Charles Mildé made some of the best-known electric cars in France. His first vehicle used an underframe powered by a 3hp electric motor which, with the drive system, could be fitted to any carriage. By 1900 he was making light carriages with detachable *avant train* power units and also commercial vehicles with motors on the rear axle. A light 3-wheeler called the Mildé et Mondos used two motors on the rear axle, but by 1903 the range had settled down to a series of typical town cars in open and closed form. They had single compound-wound motors on the rear axle, 7 to 9 forward speeds (up to 22mph) and 2 to 3 reverse speeds.
    For 1904 a petrol-electric car was added to the range, powered by a 6hp single-cylinder De Dion engine. Petrol-electrics were a regular part of the range from then onwards and Frédéric Gaillardet, formerly chief engineer of Doctoresse and La Française (Diamant), was engaged to look after this side of the business. From 1907 or so, these cars were called Mildé-Gaillardets. 1905 electric cars had small bonnets and front-mounted engines which drove the rear axle via a propeller shaft. Commercial vehicles were made at least until 1914 and the name reappeared during World War 2, when electric conversions of La Licorne cars and Chenard-Walcker vans were sold under the name of Mildé-Kriéger.   GNG

MILES (GB) *1910–1912*
Joubert Miles, Sharpness, Gloucestershire
    Taking time off from a career spanning eighty years of cycle building, Miles constructed a few light tricars with tubular framework and many cycle parts. The prototype used an air-cooled motor, but the production version standardized an 8hp J.A.P., water-cooled by radiators mounted on each side.   DF

MILLER (i) (US) *1912–1913*
Miller Car Co, Detroit, Mich.
    The Miller was built on conventional lines with 30 and 40hp 4-cylinder engines. Roadsters and five-seater touring cars were sold at prices ranging from $1,250 to $1,450.   GMN

MILLER (ii) (US) *1915–1932*
(1) Harry A. Miller Inc, Los Angeles, Calif. *1915–1929*
(2) Rellimah Inc, Los Angeles, Calif. *1930–1932*
    Harry A. Miller, a recognized specialist in carburettors, first attracted notice in the world of motor cars when he built a replacement engine for Bob Burman's GP Peugeot in 1915, following this up by a 4-cylinder ohc light aero engine which was installed in several cars, including Barney Oldfield's Golden Submarine. During World War 1 Miller was associated with the Bugatti-Duesenberg aero-engine project, and his subsequent work reflects both this influence and that of Henry of Peugeot.
    By 1920 he had disposed of his wartime interests to Leach-Biltwell and in conjunction with Fred Offenhauser and Leo Goossen was working on the first of his advanced racing power units, a 3-litre double ohc hemispherical-head straight-8

commissioned by Tommy Milton. This was not ready in time for the 1921 Indianapolis 500 Mile Race and though a complete Miller did compete in 1922, ironically enough victory went to Milton's great rival, Jimmy Murphy, at the wheel of a GP-type Duesenberg with Miller engine.

With the coming of the 2-litre Formula, Miller cars began to make themselves felt. Throughout its career the company concentrated on track-racing machines which dominated late-Vintage 500 Mile Races (apart from 1924, 1925, and 1927, when Duesenberg won), but lacked the handling and brakes to complete on equal terms with European Grand Prix cars on their home ground. In spite of this, a Miller finished 3rd in the 1923 European G.P., but subsequent attempts by Leon Duray and Peter de Paolo to race them in Europe proved abortive. The basic Miller was still a straight-8 on the established lines, with dry-sump lubrication, eight carburettors, and Delco coil ignition: output was 120bhp. In 1924 appeared the first of the fwd cars with engine reversed in the frame and De Dion *front* axle. Jimmy Murphy, who had commissioned it, was killed before he could take delivery, but the car finished 2nd at Indianapolis in 1925. Millers were doing well in 1926, when America followed Europe in adopting the 91ci (1,500cc) capacity limit, and the new Miller 91 sold at $15,000 with front-wheel drive or $10,000 with conventional transmission. The engine was the old 2-litre unit with short-stroke crankshaft and magneto ignition: a centrifugal blower (as pioneered by Duesenberg) running at five times engine speed boosted power to 154bhp at 7,000rpm, and the 3-speed gearbox had ball change. All but one of the first ten finishers in that year's Indianapolis were Millers, while in 1927 Frank Lockhart took the International Class Flying-Mile record at 164mph on an unstreamlined single-seater Miller 91 tuned to give 252bhp. Lou Meyer (later of Meyer-Drake, the firm that took over the development of the Miller racing engine from Fred Offenhauser) won the 1928 '500', and Ray Keech won in 1929. Experiments were also made with Miller engines and cars in Europe. A Miller-powered Lea-Francis was prepared for record work in 1927. Ettore Bugatti purchased the two fwd racers that Leon Duray brought to Europe in 1928 (it may be significant that *Le Patron* produced a 4 × 4 sprint car, the Type 53, in 1932). Douglas Hawkes of Derby used a similar fwd machine as the basis for the successful Derby-Miller sprint and record cars of the early 1930s.

Though Millers won again at Indianapolis in 1930 and 1931, the advent of the 'junk formula' caused Harry Miller to sell out; but he was soon in partnership again with Goossen and Offenhauser as Rellimah, Inc. ('H.A. Miller' spelt backwards.) New designs included as abortive plan for a World Land Speed Record machine for Barney Oldfield, and a fearsome 5.1-litre 4-wheel-drive 4-ohc V-16. More significant historically, however, was the 3-litre 4-cylinder double ohc Miller with integral head which Shorty Cantlon drove into 2nd place at Indianapolis in 1930. This power unit was developed from a 1926 marine engine and formed the basis for the legendary Offenhauser (later Meyer-Drake) units which in 4½-litre unblown form with fuel injection dominated the Indianapolis scene until the 1960s.

Miller built only two road-going sports cars, a 325bhp V-8 in 1928, and a 4-wheel-drive V-16 in 1932. The latter cost $35,000, and the client had to have it finished elsewhere after bankruptcy forced Miller to close down in 1932.

Miller went on designing until his death in 1943. He ran three reworked 3.6-litre Ford V-8s in the 1935 Indianapolis Race: they had all-round independent suspension and front-wheel drive, but suffered from sheer lack of horse-power. Complexity killed the last of the Millers, the 1938 'Gulf Special' which resembled the Auto Unions and had rear-mounted 300bhp double ohc 3-litre 6-cylinder engines, and all four wheels independently sprung and driven. In 1938 there was also a more conventional car with exposed lateral oil and water radiators and disc brakes.   MCS

1932 MILLER-HARTZ fwd racing car.
Indianapolis Speedway Museum

1938 MILLER Gulf Oil Special 4-wheel drive
racing car. *Indianapolis Speedway Museum*

MILLOT (i) (F) *1901–1902*
Millot Frères, Gray, Hte-Saone

The Millot car used a 6 or 8hp vertical 2-cylinder engine with a chain-driven gearbox and twin chain final drive. A 12hp 4-cylinder tonneau was also made and, in 1902, an 8hp 4-cylinder car. Millot also made a number of mobile saw benches with rear-mounted single-cylinder engines of 9hp. These were made for a number of years from about 1900, and their crude appearance makes them seem older than the Millot cars proper.

There are at least three of the saw benches in existence, but so far as is known, none of the cars survives.   GNG

MILLOT (ii) (CH) *1906–1907*
Sté des Automobiles Millot, Zürich

The Swiss Millot cars were designed by Eugène Kauffmann who had built buses since 1904. An ambitious range of two fours (25/30 and 40/50hp), and two sixes (35/50 and 70/80hp) was announced. They had separately-cast cylinders, with shaft drive on the two smaller models, chain drive on the larger. They were high-quality machines with such refinements as water-cooled transmission brakes, but very few were made.   GNG

MILMOR (GB) *1959–1968*
H. Milborrow, London

A variety of sports-racing cars was built under this name, for the 1172, 750, 1200 and other formulas, and raced successfully for many years.   DF

1901 MILLOT(i) 6/8hp tonneau. *Geoffroy de
Beaufort Collection*

1904 MINERVA 10hp two-seater. *G.N. Georgano*

1913 MINERVA 26hp tourer. Coachwork by Snutsel. *Geoffroy de Beauffort Collection*

1930 MINERVA AK 5.9-litre cabriolet. Coachwork by Gaston Grummer. *Keith Marvin Collection*

1931 MINERVA AL 6.6-litre coupé de ville. Coachwork by Neuss. *Václav Petřík Collection*

MILNES (GB) 1901–1902

G.F. Milnes & Co Ltd, Wellington, Shropshire

Although sold under the name Milnes, these cars were really German, as the chassis were made by the Daimler company of Marienfelde. 12, 16 and 24hp models were available, with bodies by Milnes who were well-known tram manufacturers. Commercial Milnes-Daimlers were sold in far greater numbers than cars.   GNG

MILTON (GB) 1920–1921

Belford Motor Co, Edinburgh

The Milton was a light car with friction transmission. Engines were either 9hp Alpha or 10hp Decolange, although it is reported that a Dorman unit was tried as well. Front suspension was by a transverse semi-elliptic spring, and the whole body was hinged at the rear so that it could be lifted for servicing of the engine and friction discs. Not more than 20 Miltons were made.   GNG

MILWAUKEE (i) (US) 1900–1902

Milwaukee Automobile Co, Milwaukee, Wisc.

The Milwaukee steam car used a 5hp vertical 2-cylinder engine, and single chain drive. Various body styles were available, including a four-seater surrey steered from the rear seat.   GNG

MILWAUKEE (ii) (US) 1906

Eagle Automobile Co, Milwaukee, Wisc.

This was made only as a small two-seater on a wheelbase of 8ft 2in and powered by a 2-cylinder engine of 13–15hp. The transmission was the friction type. This may have been no more than a prototype model.   GMN

MINERVA (B) 1899–1939

(1) S. de Jong et Cie, Antwerp 1899–1902
(2) Minerva Motors SA, Antwerp 1903–1934
(3) Société Nouvelle Minerva, Antwerp 1934–1935
(4) SA des Automobiles Imperia-Excelsior, Antwerp; Nessonvaux 1935–1939

Belgium's greatest marque arose from humble beginnings – a bicycle factory opened in 1897 by Sylvain de Jong. He soon progressed to proprietary motorcycle engines (of which he became Europe's leading supplier), and to complete motorcycles in 1900, though a year earlier he had built a prototype voiturette and a primitive motor lorry. A 6hp 4-cylinder car on Panhard lines appeared in 1902, but serious car manufacture did not get under way until 1904. These early Minervas retained side-chain drive and armoured wood frames, but used mechanically-operated side valves in a T-head. They came in 1.6-litre 2-cylinder, 2.4-litre 3-cylinder and 3.2-litre 4-cylinder forms, and alongside them was an ingenious and successful cyclecar, the Minervette. Its 636cc single-cylinder engine was transversely mounted at the front, driving the offside rear wheel by chain via a 2-speed constant-mesh gearbox. It cost only £106. A year later the company had settled down to bevel-driven twins and fours, the latter being a 2.9-litre 14 with steel frame that was sold in London by the Hon C.S. Rolls.

The almost mandatory petrol brougham came in 1906, but more successful were a 3.6-litre 22 and a rapid 6.2-litre six introduced in 1907. This had gate change, and its engine developed 60bhp. Even faster were the firm's 8-litre Kaiserpreis cars with 5-bearing ioe engine and chain drive; they failed in the German race but won the Belgian Circuit des Ardennes. In 1909 there was an L-head monobloc four of 2½ litres' capacity, but at the same time the company adopted the Knight double-sleeve-valve engine, and thereafter all catalogued Minervas used Knights.

Though inevitably emphasis now shifted to chauffeur-driven carriages and silence, Minerva's Knights were by no means lethargic, as witness outright victories in the Swedish Winter Trials of 1911, 1913 and 1914, and distinguished performances in the Austrian Alpine Trials. The 3.3-litre cars that ran in the 1914 TT were good for 85mph and the team finished intact, in 2nd, 3rd and 5th places. Their success is reflected in the phasing-out of the motorcycles after 1910, and in a clientele that included Henry Ford as well as the Kings of Belgium, Sweden and Norway.

The 1910 models were all fours: a 2,234cc monobloc 16hp, a 4¼-litre 26hp, and a large 38 of 6.3-litre capacity. Electric lighting was available in 1912, when Citroën-type helical bevel gears made their appearance; two years later starters were an option and wire wheels were standardized, and the range extended from a modest 2.1-litre worm-drive monobloc 14 (which was popular as a taxi in Sweden) up to an enlarged 7.4-litre 38.

De Jong was quick to set Minerva on their feet after the German occupation of 1914–18, and by 1920 they were back in production with two models, a 3.6-litre 4-cylinder 20 and a 6-cylinder 30CV of 5,344cc, both with monobloc engines, vacuum feed, cone clutches, 4-speed gearboxes, cantilever rear springing and rear-wheel and transmission brakes, though plate clutches were standardized after 1921. Minerva, like Daimler, made their own bodies, a new coachworks being opened at Mortsel, an Antwerp suburb, in 1922; they also supplied engines to other firms, among them Mors and the curious Anglo-American Crown Magnetic. (Émile Mathis's 1913 sleeve-valve cars had been Minervas with Mathis radiators!) Smaller models followed: a 15CV 2-litre four in 1922, and a 20CV six of 3.4-litre capacity in 1923, this having 4-wheel brakes as standard, and a wheelbase of nearly 12 feet. In 1925, 2,500 cars found buyers, and a year later all Minervas had 4-wheel brakes, with some necessary Dewandre servo assistance on the big ones. The 1927 range included a replacement for the 30CV, the magnificent 5,954cc AK six with alloy pistons, light steel sleeves, and a 12ft 5½in wheelbase. There was, however, a new small 6-cylinder Minerva, the 2-litre 12-14CV; this came with a 3-speed unit gearbox, central ball change, and lhd, and sold for under £500 in England. It was made until 1933.

The carriage trade was not forgotten, for there were three new big cars in 1930: a 150bhp sports edition of the AK with full-pressure lubrication, and two straight-8s. Of these the 6.6-litre AL was a vast 9-bearing affair with dual ignition and right-hand change, whereas its 4-litre companion, the 22CV AP, had coil ignition and central change, and could be bought for less than £900. In 1932 there was a 20CV six with the same specification and cylinder dimensions of 75 × 112mm. However, none of these cars was suitable for the prevailing economic climate, and 1934 brought what was effectively the company's last model, the 2-litre M4, Minerva's first four since 1927. The sleeve-valve engine was retained, but in other respects it was typical of the prevailing idiom, with 3-speed synchromesh gearbox, mechanical brakes and pillarless saloon bodywork.

The M4 was not a success and in October 1935 Minerva merged with the only other Belgian factory still making private cars, Imperia of Nessonvaux. The traditional Minervas were continued for another season, and the AP survived until 1938, but thereafter the only cars sold to the public under the Minerva name were some fwd Imperias exported to France. Purely experimental was an astonishing vehicle exhibited at the 1937 Brussels Salon. This featured all-independent springing by torsion bars, and a transversely-mounted 3.6-litre Ford V-8 engine drove the front wheels via a torque converter. Only three prototypes were made.

In 1952 a comeback was planned with two Minerva models, both of foreign design. The smaller car was based on the 1947 Cemsa-Caproni, and the new luxury Minerva was to use the mechanical elements of the Armstrong Siddeley Sapphire, but neither materialized. The last Minerva was a jeep-type 4 × 4, the C20 of 1956. It was powered by a 4-cylinder sv Continental engine.　　　MCS

MINI (GB) *1970 to date*

Austin-Morris Division, British Leyland Motor Corporation Ltd, Longbridge, Birmingham; Cowley, Oxford

Previously marketed under the Austin (ii) and Morris (i) names, the various models of the fwd Mini, pioneer of the transverse engine configuration, were given the status of an individual make in 1970. The range extended from the basic 848cc type up to the 1,275cc GT and Mini Cooper S, though this was discontinued after 1971. The 998cc Clubman variant was also available as a station wagon. The millionth export Mini was delivered during April 1970.　　　MCS

MINIJEM (GB) *1966 to date*

(1) Jem Developments Ltd, London W.8 *1966–1968*
(2) Fellpoint Ltd, Penn, Bucks. *1968–1971*
(3) High Performance Mouldings, Cricklade, Wilts. *1971 to date*

This firm produced a two-plus-two-seater fibreglass body/chassis unit as part of a kit, to take B.M.C. Mini mechanical parts in their standard dispositions. Placed on the market in mid-1966, competition successes and an attractive appearance assisted in selling two dozen vehicles before the end of the year. A Mark II version was introduced in 1968 and by mid-1970 total production had exceeded 350. For 1971 it was intended to market also the Jem Futura, a strange device to fit onto a Volkswagen floorpan, designed by Robin Statham with a very steeply raked tinted windscreen covering most of the car, including the headlamps. Access was gained by tilting this screen, to which side windows and a short roof were attached.

When the firm was reconstituted late in the year, production recommenced with the Mark II only. For 1972 the complete body with average trimmings cost around £450 as a monocoque – the tubular steel backbone chassis previously employed was dispensed with.　　　DF

MINIMA (i) (F) *1911*

Éts Leroy, Levallois-Perret, Seine

This company made a voiturette powered by a single-cylinder 6/8hp Zédel engine.　　　GNG

MINIMA (ii) (I) *1935*

Antonio Passarin, Milan

The work of a boatbuilder, the Minima was a 3-wheeled monocar powered by a 120cc 2-stroke motorcycle engine. Final drive was by chain. Passarin also built a 250cc tandem 2-seater. Despite the prevailing motor-fuel shortage, there was no production.　　　MCS

MINIMUS (D) *1921–1924*

Minimus Fahrzeug GmbH, Pasing

The Minimus was a cyclecar with air-cooled V-twin 4/12PS engine and a two-seater tandem body. A later version had a 4-cylinder engine.　　　HON

1931 MINERVA AP 4-litre saloon.
Václav Petřík Collection

1938 MINERVA-IMPERIA TA-9B 1.6-litre saloon. *Lucien Loreille Collection*

1972 MINI 1275 GT saloon. *British Leyland Motor Corporation*

1910 MITCHELL 35hp tourer. *Kenneth Stauffer*

1923 MITCHELL Model F50 29hp sedan.
Automotive History Collection, Detroit
Public Library

1967 MITSUBISHI Debonair 2-litre saloon.
Mitsubishi Heavy Industries Ltd

MINNOW (GB) 1951–1952
Bonallack & Sons Ltd, Forest Gate, London E.7

The Minnow was a light 3-wheeler made by a firm of commercial vehicle body builders. A 250cc Excelsior Talisman 2-cylinder, 2-stroke engine drove the single rear wheel, and the car had a two-seater body and single headlamp. 45mph and 70mpg were claimed.   GNG

MINO (US) 1914
Mino Cyclecar Co, New Orleans, La.

The Mino was a single-seater cyclecar, using a 4-cylinder, water-cooled engine of 1.3 litres. Connected with this was a 2-speed transmission, with shaft drive. The car sold for $350.   GMN

MINUTOLI-MILLO (I) 1902–1903
Società Minutoli Millo & Cia, Lucca

Vittorio Millo built an experimental 3-wheeler in 1896, and in 1902 he designed an 8hp tonneau with 2.4-litre aiv 4-cylinder engine, lt magneto ignition, and shaft drive. A company was formed to manufacture this car, but Millo's death caused the collapse of the venture before any more could be produced. The prototype survives in the Museo dell' Automobile, Turin.   MC

MIOLANS (F) 1910
Valade et Guillemand, Neuilly, Seine

The Miolans was a light car shown at the 1910 Paris Salon. Its only unusual feature was the gearbox mounted on the rear axle.   GNG

MIRA (F) 1906
The Neuilly-built Mira was a light car made in single- and 4-cylinder forms with De Dion engines.   GNG

MIRABILIS (I) 1906–1907
Giuseppe de Maria, Turin

The Mirabilis was an ultra-light voiturette powered by a 3½hp engine of Giuseppe de Maria's own design and construction. The 1907 crisis in the Italian motor industry killed it before many were made.   GNG

MIRAGE (GB) 1970–1971
J.W. Automotive Engineering Ltd, Slough, Bucks.

J.W. (the initials stood for both John Wyer and John Willment) produced several special sports-racing cars with varying success for their own use and ran semi-works Porsche teams before embarking on the manufacture of cars for sale. These were the M5/160 Formula Ford single-seaters based on the Pringett Mistrale, priced complete at £1,450. One or two victories were recorded, but not many were made. The next Mirage, the M6, was once again a sports-racing special, in this case a Group 5 machine designed by Len Bailey for the Weslake V-12 engine, raced initially with a Cosworth DFV unit and some success.   DF

MISTRALE see PRINGETT

MITCHELL (US) 1903–1923
(1) Mitchell Motor Car Co, Racine, Wisc. 1903–1910
(2) Mitchell-Lewis Motor Co, Racine, Wisc. 1910–1916
(3) Mitchell Motors Co Inc, Racine, Wisc. 1916–1923

Mitchell and Lewis had been wagon builders since 1834, and their first car was a light two-seater powered by a 7hp air-cooled 2-cylinder engine, using single chain drive, and priced at $1,200. In 1905 a 9hp engine was used, and air or water cooling was available. 4-cylinder engines of 18 and 30hp appeared in the 1906 range, and in 1907 shaft drive was employed on all models. Until 1910, 20 and 35hp fours were made, having pair-cast cylinders in 1910 when they were joined by a 50hp 6-cylinder car. In 1913 a new range of T-head engines was introduced in a car designed by René Petard and known as the 'American-built French car'. A 40hp four and 50 and 60hp sixes were made in this range, which had high-cowled torpedo-style bodies and electric starters. Piston strokes were very long at 7 inches. At this time it was said that the Mitchell company made 96% of all components. In 1916 a short-lived 48hp V-8 was made, and the following year the company settled down to making a range of conventional sixes of no great distinction. In 1920 a sloping radiator gave rise to the epithet, 'the drunken Mitchell' and this was hastily replaced by a vertical radiator for 1921. However, the company had lost a lot of money on their 1920 models, and few of the redesigned cars were sold, as they lacked any distinctive qualities.

Their 6-cylinder engines had a capacity of 4.7 litres. After production ceased in 1923, the factory was bought by Nash.   GNG

MITSUBISHI (J) 1917–1921; 1959 to date
(1) Mitsubishi Kobe Dockyard Works, Kobe 1917–1921
(2) Mitsubishi Heavy Industries (Reorganized) Ltd, Tokyo 1959–1970
(3) Mitsubishi Motors Corp, Tokyo 1970 to date

The Mitsubishi Model A of 1917 was one of the first commercially manufactured

Japanese cars and was modelled on the Fiat. About twenty of these were built and sold and experimenting continued with other machines until 1921. Trucks and buses occupied most of the production of the Kobe works after this time and the factories were converted to tank manufacture during World War 2.

In 1959 the reorganized company turned out its first private car, the 500. This was a small four-seater propelled by a 2-cylinder, 4-stroke ohv air-cooled engine of 20hp. Second and third gears were synchromesh and the clutch was a single dry-plate type. By 1966 the Mitsubishi range included the 356cc Minica 360 saloon with air-cooled 2-stroke 2-cylinder engine, backed by the Colt saloons, of which the smallest had fastback styling and was powered by a 3-cylinder 2-stroke engine of D.K.W. type developing 41bhp. The larger 1000 and 1500 Colts used oversquare pushrod 4-cylinder units, and front suspension was by coils and wishbones in place of the transverse-leaf ifs of the smaller types. Biggest model was the Debonair, a 105bhp pushrod six with six-seater coachwork, four headlamps, and the choice of all-synchromesh or automatic gearboxes.

By 1970, when the car division became a separate entity, the faster Minicas had 38bhp engines. The pushrod Colts were also more powerful, with capacities of 1,088cc or 1,189cc, and there was a new range of Colt Galants with overhead-camshaft engines. These last reached the American market in 1971 and were sold through the Dodge dealer network after Chrysler had acquired a 35 per cent interest in Mitsubishi; at the same time the Debonair received a new ohc power unit. In 1972 the Minica was still offered, a new variant being the Skipper GT coupé with four headlamps. Pushrod Colts had bigger 1.4-litre engines, and the ohc 4-cylinder Mitsubishis embraced everything from simple 1.4-litre saloons up to the GTO-MR series, with twin-cam, twin-carburettor 1,597cc engine developing 125bhp, a 5-speed all-synchromesh gearbox, and servo-assisted front disc brakes. Mitsubishi have manufactured Jeep vehicles under licence since 1953. BE

1972 MITSUBISHI Colt 1.6-litre coupé.
Dodge Public Relations

M.J. (F) *1920*
Conventional cars with 1½-litre 4-cylinder engines were made under this name. GNG

M.L.B. (F) *1894–1902*
(1) Cie des Moteurs et Autos M.L.B., Hondouville, Eure
(2) Cie des Moteurs et Autos M.L.B., Passy, Seine
Also known as the Landry et Beyroux after its makers, this car had a single-cylinder 4hp vertical engine at the rear. It had a 3-speed sliding gear transmission and double chain drive. The makers entered a four-seater in the 1894 Paris-Rouen race, and cars of 5 or 6hp ran regularly in the town-to-town races of 1896 to 1898. Various bodies were fitted, including an enclosed cab. In 1901 a lighter car with wire wheels was built. GNG

M.L.T. (F) *1900*
Molas, Lamielle et Tessier, Paris 11e
The M.L.T. had a 20hp 4-cylinder single-acting engine actuated by compressed air stored in reservoirs at a pressure of 290 atmospheres. It had double chain drive and a six-seater brake body. A few lorries were also made. GNG

1896 M.M.C. phaeton (George Iden's prototype).
The Veteran Car Club of Great Britain

M.M.B. (D) *1899–1902*
Motorfahrzeug- und Motorenfabrik Berlin AG, Marienfelde, Berlin
This firm was founded by directors of the Daimler company. In spite of the protests of Daimler and Maybach they started to produce cars to Daimler patents, marketing them under the Daimler name. They were not the equals of the Cannstatt Daimlers in finish. Columbia electric cars were also manufactured under licence. An original M.M.B. 12PS petrol-driven car was offered in 1901. Apart from these ventures the factory specialized in commercial vehicles. After the death of Gottlieb Daimler the firm was taken over by the Daimler company in 1902. Production of commercials continued, these being sold under the name of Daimler-Marienfelde, or Milnes-Daimler in England. HON

M.M.C. (GB) *1897–1908*
(1) The Great Horseless Carriage Co Ltd, Coventry, Warwickshire *1897–1898*
(2) The Motor Manufacturing Co Ltd, Coventry, Warwickshire *1898–1907*
(3) The Motor Manufacturing Co (1907) Ltd, Clapham, London S.W. *1907–1908*
The Great Horseless Carriage Company was formed by H.J. Lawson with grandiose plans to make cars and commercial vehicles in large numbers. Premises were secured in the Motor Mills at Coventry, adjoining the works of the Daimler Company. A very small number of cars was turned out in 1897, with engines, gearboxes and frames by Daimler, bodies and wheels by the Great Horseless Carriage Co. They had 4hp engines with tube ignition, chain drive and tiller steering. In 1898 the company was reorganized as the Motor Manufacturing Company, with George Iden, previously an engineer with the London, Brighton & South Coast Railway, as works manager. Two lines of development were followed: the Daimler-based cars, and motor cycles and quads with M.M.C.-built De Dion engines. In 1899 a new range of cars designed by Iden appeared; they had rear-mounted horizontal 2-cylinder engines, and were made in various sizes such as the 4½hp Princess two-seater, the 6hp Sandringham Phaeton, or the 11hp Balmoral charabanc.

During its lifetime the M.M.C. firm went through several reorganizations and

1903 M.M.C. 25hp touring saloon. *G.N.*
Georgano Collection

1904 MOBILE(ii) 9hp tonneau. *G.N. Georgano Collection*

1957 MOCHET 175cc saloon. *Autosport*

changes of programme, and by 1901 the rear-engined cars had been dropped, and replaced by a range of cars with front-mounted vertical engines. These were a 5hp with an M.M.C.-De Dion engine, and 7, 10 and 12hp cars on Panhard lines. In 1902 the range was reduced to three, and an attempt was made to use interchangeable parts. The models were the 5½hp single, an 8hp twin, and a 12hp four. They were lower in appearance, but still looked rather ungainly, with large gilled-tube radiators. For 1903 the same range was made, although the four was now a 20hp, sometimes called a 25hp. They now had lower bonnets, some with honeycomb radiators, and used the Iden constant-mesh gearbox. A very luxurious long wheelbase touring saloon on the 25hp chassis was shown at the 1903 Paris Salon.

In December 1903 Iden resigned, and later made cars under his own name, and there was little change in the 1904 models. On the 8hp single-cylinder model, the buyer could have mechanical inlet valves as an alternative to automatic, but all models still used chain drive. In August 1905 the Motor Mills were sold to Daimler, and M.M.C. moved to new premises at Parkside. An ambitious range of six models from a 9hp single to a 30/35hp four were listed, but few were made. Two years later the company was revived and moved to London, where they planned to make a new 6-cylinder 35/45hp car, but only experimental models appeared. Alfred Burgess, the manager, then formed yet another company, still called M.M.C., with premises at Finchley, but this was only concerned with selling cars.　　GNG

M.M.F. (F) *1912*
Muller, Mignot et Cie, Levallois, Seine

This company made several cars with 4-cylinder 2,120cc engines.　　GNG

M.M.W. (D) *1901–1903*
(1) Magdeburger Motor & Motorfahrzeugfabrik GmbH, Magdeburg *1901*
(2) Magdeburger Motor-Werke Max Stang & Co, Magdeburg *1901–1903*

This firm produced one basic type which was available with various bodies for use as a private or commercial vehicle.　　HON

MOBBEL *see* PICCOLO

MOBILE (i) (US) *1899–1903*
Mobile Company of America, Tarrytown, N.Y.

The Mobile Company was founded by J.B. Walker who, together with A. Lorenzo Barber, had acquired the Stanley patents. After a disagreement Barber left to make the Locomobile at Bridgeport, Conn., while Walker retained the former Stanley works at Tarrytown where he made the Mobile. At first this was almost identical with the Locomobile, and differences were restricted to body styles. Mobile offered as many as 20 different models in 1902, and 15 in 1903, by which time about 6,000 vehicles had been made. They ranged from a $550 Runabout, which was one of the cheapest American steamers, to a $3,000 enclosed limousine, which was the most expensive.　　GNG

MOBILE (ii) (GB) *1903–1907*
Mobile Motor & Engineering Co Ltd, Birmingham

This company began by selling the Waddington light car which used De Dion or Aster engines, and the first Mobiles were similar. They used the 6hp single-cylinder De Dion or Aster in a two-seater, the 8hp De Dion single, also in a two-seater, and the 10hp Aster twin in a four-seater tonneau. All cars had shaft drive, and were typical of the assembled light vehicles of the time. In 1907 the Calthorpe Motor Company acquired the assets of Mobile.　　GNG

MOBILETTE (US) *1965 to date*
Mobilette Electric Cars, Long Beach, Calif.

This is an electric runabout of a type quite popular in southern California for shopping.　　BE

MOCHET (F) *1951–1958*
Charles Mochet, Puteaux, Seine

Charles Mochet, who had built the C.M. cyclecar from 1924 to 1930, introduced another minicar in 1951. His CM125 represented true minimal motoring and could be conducted without a driving licence. The simple tubular frame was crab-tracked, the front wheels were independently sprung, and it rode on bicycle-type wheels, of which only the rear ones were braked. Bodywork was austere with a front end reminiscent of the early flat-twin Tatras. Power came from a 3½bhp 2-stroke single-cylinder 125cc Ydral engine mounted at the rear. Mochet was able to sell 40 of these little cars a month, and there was a more ambitious development in 1953, in the shape of a 4-speed version with hydraulic brakes and a 750cc C.E.M.E.C. flat-twin engine. By 1957 the company was making a 175cc 4-seater roll-top convertible with full electrics (including wiper and trafficators), which offered 37mph and 65mpg for the equivalent of £315, but rising prosperity in Europe sounded the death-knell of the cyclecar and the Mochet disappeared from the market.　　MCS

MÖCK (D) *1924*
Gebr. Möck, Tübingen

This light car was produced only in limited numbers. It used a 4-cylinder 5/20PS engine of 1.33-litre capacity. HON

MODEL (US) 1903–1909
(1) Model Gas Engine Co, Auburn, Ind. *1903–1904*
(2) Model Gas Engine Works, Auburn, Ind. *1904–1906*
(3) Model Automobile Co, Peru, Ind. *1906–1909*

Early versions of the Model used long-stroke 2-cylinder opposed engines. Engines of 12 and 16hp were available. An unusual transmission gave three forward and two reverse gears. Final drive was by single chain. Later models had engines of 20 and 24hp. This manufacturer also built the Star (iv). The Model Gas Engine Works were building engines as late as 1912, which would indicate that the Model Automobile Co was an offshoot of this company. GMN

MODERN see PAYNE-MODERN

MODOC (US) 1913
Chicago Motor Co, Chicago Heights, Ill.

The Modoc was a conventional 30/40hp 4-cylinder car sold by the mail order firm of Montgomery-Ward. The price was $1,250. GNG

MOHAWK (i) (US) 1903–1904
Mohawk Auto & Cycle Co, Indianapolis, Ind.

This was a small car, made as a two- or five-seater, with single- and 2-cylinder engines, giving 7hp and 18hp respectively. The smaller car was steered by tiller, while the larger used a steering wheel. Both had wire wheels and pneumatic tyres. GMN

MOHAWK (ii) (US) 1914–1915
Mohawk Motor Co, Boston, Mass.

The Mohawk was available in either two- or five-seater models. It was powered by a 4-cylinder Farmer engine with overhead valves. GMN

MOHAWK-MANON see MANON

MOHLER (US) 1901
Mohler & Degress, Astoria, Long Island, N.Y.

This was a light two-seater powered by a single-cylinder vertical engine mounted at the front. It had shaft drive. GNG

MOHS (US) 1968 to date
Mohs Seaplane Corp, Madison, Wisc.

Bruce Baldwin Mohs' Ostentatienne Opera Sedan was one of the most unusual and expensive cars made in America. Powered by either a 5-litre or 9-litre V-8 engine, it was a four-seater sedan with rear entry for safety. Other safety features included cantilever seats that swung laterally on turns and pivoted to horizontal in the event of a head-on collision, and an extra wide track of 6ft 2in. All cars were equipped with refrigerator and two-way all-transistor radio with two base stations for home and office. Prices were from $19,600 for the 5-litre model, and $25,600 for the larger car. Four were built. For 1971 Mohs introduced a new series, the Model C and D KamperKars; these were metal-top convertibles to sleep three people, with hingeless doors that moved out from the side on linear bushings. Model C had a 6.4-litre International engine, Model D an 8.7-litre V-12 F.W.D. unit normally used in Seagrave fire apparatus. For 1973 they were renamed SafariKars, and the V-12 engine was dropped. GNG

MOLINE; MOLINE-KNIGHT (US) 1904–1913; 1914–1919
Moline Automobile Co, E. Moline, Ill.

The Moline was launched as a modest five-seater car with flat-twin or 4-cylinder engines. The twin was chain-driven, with a 2-speed planetary transmission. In 1912, Moline was among the first manufacturers to make a feature of a long-stroke engine (6in), of 35hp. In 1914 the sleeve-valve Knight engine was used; it was standardized a year later, when a 4-speed gearbox was adopted. Body types included a limousine and a closed sedan. In 1916, the wheelbase was shortened and smaller engines were used. The last models offered 4-cylinder power units of 3.6 and 5 litres. In 1919, the Moline-Knight became the R. & V. Knight. GMN

MÖLKAMP (D) 1923–1926
Möllenkampwerke AG für Fahrzeugbau, Düsseldorf; Cologne

The production plants of Priamus at Cologne were taken over by the Möllenkamp-werke in 1923. Production of motor cars under the name of Mölkamp started with a 6-cylinder 10/50PS 2590cc model. After 1924 a 6/30PS model with a 4-cylinder 1460cc engine was built under Ceirano licence. Production ceased in 1926. HON

MOLL (D) 1922–1925
Moll-Werke AG, Chemnitz

The Moll was a light car powered by a 6/30PS Siemens & Halske 4-cylinder engine of 1595cc. This was sold in England in 1922 and in 1923 by L.G. Hornsted under the

1968 MOHS Ostentatienne Opera Sedan. *Bruce Baldwin Mohs*

1906 MOLINE Model C tourer. *Automotive History Collection, Detroit Public Library*

1924 MOLL 6/30PS tourer. *G.L. Hartner*

1922 MONET-GOYON 500cc cyclecar. *Autocar*

names Hornsted or Summers. After this another cyclecar, the Mollmobil, designed by Fritz Görkeb was built from 1924. It was a small two-seater with tandem seating. D.K.W. engines were used, at first of 164cc, later of 198cc.   HON

MOLLA (F) *1922*
Molla et Cie, Paris
The Molla was a cyclecar using a 2-cylinder engine and belt drive.   GNG

MOLLE (F) *1907–1910*
Emile Molle, Riom, Puy-de-Dôme
Molle was a pioneer of the 2-stroke engine who built 9 cars with engines of his own construction and shaft drive. Seven had 2-cylinder engines of 1,525cc, and two single-cylinder engines of 1,330cc.   LL

MOLLER (US) *1920–1921*
Moller Motor Car Co, Lewistown, Pa.
The Moller was an 850lb car, constructed on European lines and designed with right-hand drive, intended primarily for export. It was powered by a 4-cylinder 1½-litre engine. Few were manufactured.   KM

MOM (F) *1906–1907*
Ateliers de Construction Mécanique, Paris
Two cars were listed by this firm, a 6hp single-cylinder voiturette and a 10/12hp 4-cylinder car. The makers also said that they could make cars from 20 to 120hp; as they also manufactured engines for motor boats, presumably they visualized using their marine engines in these made-to-order cars.   GNG

MOMO (US) *1971 to date*
Momo Corp, Forest Hills, N.Y.
A typical Italo-American GT coupé, the Momo Mirage used a 5.7-litre 350bhp Chevrolet V-8 engine in a Stanguellini-built chassis, with four-seater 2-door coachwork by Frua. A choice of 5-speed ZF manual gearbox or GM Turbo Hydramatic transmission was offered.   GNG

MONARCH (i) (US) *1903*
This was a very light two-seater runabout with a 5hp single-cylinder engine and tiller steering. It was sold by the P.J. Dasey Company of Chicago, who also sold the Buffalo-built Morlock, but it is not certain if the Monarch was also built by Morlock.   GNG

MONARCH (ii) (US) *1905–1909*
Monarch Motor Car Co, Chicago Heights, Ill.
The Monarch was a motor buggy with large diameter wheels. 2- or 4-cylinder air-cooled engines were mounted beneath the seat. A planetary transmission with shaft drive was used. Both two- and four-seater bodies were made.   GMN

MONARCH (iii) (US) *1906*
Joseph S. Heller, New York, N.Y.
This Monarch was a two-seater runabout powered by a 7½hp single-cylinder horizontal air-cooled engine. It weighed 900lb, drove through a 3-speed epicyclic transmission, and was priced at $500.   MJWW

MONARCH (iv) (US) *1908*
Monarch Machine Co, DesMoines, Iowa
This high-wheeled motor buggy was a four-seater with a 4-cylinder, 3.2-litre, water-cooled engine. The drive was by planetary transmission and double chains. The weight was 1,500lb and the price was $750.   GMN

MONARCH (v) (GB) *1912–1914*
R. Walker & Sons, Tyseley, Birmingham
The Monarch light car was powered by an 8hp 2-cylinder Precision engine. A 2-speed epicyclic gear and shaft drive were employed, and the car sold at 110gns for the air-cooled model, 120gns for the water-cooled one.   GNG

MONARCH (vi) (US) *1914–1917*
Monarch Motor Car Co, Detroit, Mich.
This Monarch was advertised as 'The Car with the Silver Wheels'. Originally it had a Continental Six engine, but at least as early as 1916, the makers used a V-8 engine of 4.6 litres. The five-passenger open model weighed 3,000lb and was priced at $1,500.   GMN

MONARCH (vii) (GB) *1925–1928*
Monarch Motor Co Ltd, Castle Bromwich, Birmingham
This was an assembled car with a 13.9hp ohv Meadows 4-cylinder engine and a 4-speed gearbox. Only a saloon model was listed, made by Mulliners and costing £525. Very little was heard of the car, and although it was listed up to 1928, probably only prototypes were made.   GNG

MONARCH (viii) (CDN) *1946–1961*
Ford Motor Co of Canada Ltd, Windsor, Ont.

Identical to the American Mercury except for special grille and trim, the Monarch was sold only in Canada by Ford dealers to widen their market coverage. For the 1958 model year there was no Monarch as the marque was replaced by the Edsel.   HD

MONCRIEFF (US) *1901–1902*
The J.A. Moncrieff Company, Pawtucket, R.I.

Although it was called a Steam Wagon, the Moncrieff was a two-seater car of slightly more solid appearance than many of its contemporaries. It used a 7hp 2-cylinder engine, tiller steering and solid tyres on its wooden wheels.   GNG

MONDEX-MAGIC (US) *1914*
Aristos Co, New York, N.Y.

This rare car had a Fischer slide-valve engine, in which the sleeves oscillated as well as having a reciprocating motion. Two sizes of 6-cylinder engines were used, of 4.2 litres and 7 litres. The prices of these large cars ranged from $4,500 for a four-seater to $6,500 for a closed limousine.   GMN

MONET-GOYON (F) *1921–1926*
Etablissements Monet et Goyon, Macon, Saone-et-Loire

This well-known motor-cycle firm made a number of small cars in three basic models. The first was a 3-wheeler known as the Auto Mouche with a single-cylinder engine mounted over the front wheel. This was replaced in 1923 by a rear-engined 4-wheeler powered by 269 or 500cc single-cylinder engines, with chain final drive. This, in turn, was replaced by a front-engined car with a 350cc engine, and chain drive to the rear axle. All these cars used Villiers engines, which were also used exclusively in Monet-Goyon motor cycles until the late 1920s.   GNG

MONICA (F) *1971 to date*
Compagnie Française de Produits Métallurgiques, Balbigny, Loire

This new French car results from collaboration between the British Deep Sanderson company, who built the prototype, and a French railway-wagon manufacturer. The prototype had a 2.6-litre Martin V-8 engine; production models had a 3½-litre unit, also a Martin V-8, composite space-frame, and sheet aluminium chassis, ZF 5-speed transmission and 4-door saloon body. For 1973, a 6-litre Chrysler V-8 engine was adopted. Maximum speed is 150mph. The car is named after Monique, wife of Jean Tastevin who is head of C.F.P.M.   LL

MONITOR (i) (US) *1909*
Monitor Automobile Works, Janesville, Wisc.

This was a solid-tyred vehicle with a 2-cylinder engine. Mainly commercial models were made, but a few two-seater runabouts and four-seater surreys also appeared.   GNG

MONITOR (ii) (US) *1915–1922*
(1) Cummins Monitor Co, Columbus, Ohio
(2) Monitor Motor Car Co, Columbus, Ohio

An assembled car which offered the buyer 4-, 6- or 8-cylinder cars between 1915 and 1917 and fours and sixes only from 1918 on. The bulk of production came in the years after 1918 when the 4-cylinder G.B. & S. or 6-cylinder Continental engine was used to power the cars. Closed and open models were offered.   KM

MONITOR (iii) (F) *1920–1921*
Charles Rouquet et Cie, Suresnes, Seine

The Monitor cyclecar was built in two versions, both using the same 747cc V-twin Train engine. One model was front-engined and drove via long belts, the other had the engine behind the seats and drove through a chain running in an oil-bath case. A single-seater model was also made.   GNG

MONK & LONSDALE *see* LONSDALE

MONNIER (F) *1908*
Monnier et Cie, Juvisy-sur-Orge

This company listed two models, a 6/7hp single-cylinder, and a 10/12hp four. They probably used proprietary engines such as De Dions, but the 4-cylinder model was said to have the maker's own carburettor.   GNG

MONO (D) *1909–1912*
Mono-Werke Roger & Niebuhr, Automobil- und Maschinenfabrik, Hamburg 15

One type, the 6/16PS, was the only model produced by this firm.   HON

MONOS (D) *1928–1930*
Monos Fahrzeug-Gesellschaft mbH, Berlin-Lichtenberg

This was a 3-wheeled cyclecar design by Fritz Görke. The technical layout followed his earlier designs, characterized by the side-mounted engine and chain drive to one of the two rear wheels. A two-seater tandem body was used.   HON

1972 MONICA 3½-litre saloon.
Compagnie Française de Produits Métallurgiques

1926 MONOTRACE 510cc tandem two-seater.
Musée de l'Automobile, Rochetaillée-sur-Saone

1915 MONROE 15hp two-seater. *Kenneth Stauffer*

1967 MONTEVERDI 7.2-litre GT coupé. *Autocar*

1972 MONTEVERDI 375L 7-litre coupé. *Automobiles Monteverdi*

1910 MOON 35hp tourer. *Automotive History Collection. Detroit Public Library*

MONOTRACE (F) *1924–1930*
Ateliers du Rond Point, Sainte Etienne, Loire

Based on the Mauser Einspurato, the Monotrace was a 2-wheeled car with 2 small auxiliary wheels to balance the car when it was stationary. The body seated two in tandem, and the car was powered by a 510cc single-cylinder engine. A motor-cycle gearbox and chain drive were used. GNG

MONROE (US) *1914–1924*
(1) Monroe Motor Co, Flint, Mich. *1914–1916*
(2) Monroe Motor Co, Pontiac, Mich. *1916–1918*
(3) William Small Co, Flint, Mich. *1918–1922*
(4) Premier Motor Corp, Indianapolis, Ind. *1923–1924*

The Monroe was a fairly popular low-priced car which was powered by 4-cylinder engines by Mason or Sterling, and from 1918 of the company's own make. Open models constituted the factory's output for the first three years of manufacture, but a sedan was added in 1917 and closed cars were subsequently listed as well as open models. In 1923, it was rumoured that Monroe would be taken over by Premier (i) and appear as a smaller model of that make, but instead Stratton Motors obtained Monroe and continued production. Shortly thereafter, Premier obtained control of both Monroe and Stratton and marketed Monroe briefly in a redesigned model which included a flat, squared radiator in place of the earlier rounded type. Few were built and the final cars were marketed as the Model B Premier. KM

MONTEVERDI (CH) *1967 to date*
Automobile Monteverdi Ltd, Basle-Binningen

Peter Monteverdi, B.M.W. agent and creator of the M.B.M. competition cars, exhibited his first luxury GT at the 1967 Frankfurt Show. Styled with some assistance from Frua, it was a 2+2 coupé with 7.2-litre 375bhp Chrysler V-8 installed in a box-section space-frame with De Dion rear axle, power-assisted steering, and dual-circuit disc brakes. Bodies were made by Fissore in Italy, and automatic transmission was standard. New in 1970 was the Hai, a mid-engined two-seater coupé using a 6.9-litre, 450bhp Chrysler Hemi V-8 in unit with a 5-speed ZF transaxle. It cost £9,000 on the home market and was capable of 180mph. In 1971 the range was rounded out with two further types, both front-engined: the 375C, a short-wheelbase coupé or convertible on which a manual gearbox was optional; and the 375L, a 4-door saloon on a 10ft 5in wheelbase. Production runs at 75–80 cars a year. MCS

MONTIER (F) *1923–1932*
Garage Montier, Paris 14e

Charles Montier was a Ford agent who built various sporting versions of the Model T. Modifications included a lowered chassis, ohv engine with lightened pistons and a conventional 4-speed gearbox. A Montier finished 14th in the 1923 Le Mans 24-Hour Race, and various single-seater specials competed in French races throughout the 1920s. By 1926 Montiers had front-wheel brakes, and after the demise of the Model T in 1927 Charles Montier and his son Guy turned to modifying the Model A. GNG

MONTU (I) *1900*
Officino Meccanica Montu, Alessandria

This cycle-maker announced that he would add cars to his repertoire in 1900, but no further details were forthcoming. MCS

MOON (US) *1905–1930*
Moon Motor Car Co, St Louis, Mo.

Like so many American car manufacturers, Moon started life making buggies; buggies were to the American industry what bicycles were to Europe. The first Moon cars were designed by Louis P. Mooers, who had been responsible for the Peerless. The Model A of 1906 was a conventional, expensive 30/35hp 4-cylinder with a Rutenber engine and shaft drive. In 1912, 5.2- and 5.8-litre fours with dual ignition were sold. A six was introduced in 1913, and three years later the four had vanished, in favour of 3.6- and 5-litre Continental-powered cars. The 1919 Moon was a good-looking, well-made, though assembled, machine powered by a 3.6-litre engine by Continental. The radiator was by now a copy of that of the Rolls-Royce, showing the class of market at which the Moon was aimed. There was an ohv engine in 1921, and a smaller, side-valve unit, also by Continental, was listed as well. Moon refinements included four main bearings (a rarity in American 6-cylinder engines of the time), demountable rims on detachable wheels and, from 1924, Lockheed hydraulic 4-wheel brakes. Two years later there arrived the Diana (named after the moon goddess) which had an sv straight-8 engine of 4 litres, and imitated the radiator shape of the luxurious Minerva from Belgium; the 1927 2.8-litre Moon Six also appeared with this radiator. The first Moon to use an 8-cylinder engine was the Aerotype of 1928, a 4.4-litre side-valve machine. A new six, the 6-72, accompanied it and was continued into 1929. That year brought one of the best-looking of the company's products, the Prince of Windsor, named after the Prince of Wales. The specification was a 4.4-litre straight-8 engine and a 4-speed gearbox – an unusual refinement, this – in a dropped frame with hydraulic brakes and automatic chassis lubrication. Unfortunately, this attempt to produce a European-type high-quality car ended after Moon acquired control of New Era Motors Inc., the firm which brought out the front-wheel-drive Ruxton. The new venture promptly collapsed, killing two famous names, Moon and Kissel. TRN

MOORE (i) (US) *1906*
Moore Automobile Co, Walla Walla, Wash.

This was an assembled car with 4-cylinder engine and 5ft track. Most roads in the U.S. were built for wagons with a 4ft 8in track, but the State of Washington's roads were built for 5ft tracks. The Moore Automobile Co was organized in order to compel Eastern manufacturers to supply Washington State with 5ft-track cars. When Franklin and several other companies began to do this, Moore promptly ceased manufacture. GNG

MOORE (ii) (AUBURN-MOORE) (US) *1906*
H.S. Moore, Cleveland, Ohio

This five-seater had a 2-cylinder water-cooled engine which was mounted amid-ships. It used a planetary transmission and single-chain drive. GMN

MOORE (iii) (US) *1906–1908*
Moore Automobile Co, New York, N.Y.

One chassis was offered by this manufacturer, at a price of $5,000. It was equipped with a 4-cylinder water-cooled engine, a 4-speed selective transmission and shaft drive. Continental racing tyres were standard equipment on this car. GMN

MOORE (iv) (US) *1916–1921*
(1) Moore Motor Vehicle Co, Minneapolis, Minn. *1916–1917*
(2) Moore Motor Vehicle Co, Danville, Ill. *1917–1921*

The Moore was a very conventional 4-cylinder tourer with a 22hp Golden, Belknap & Schwartz engine. Originally priced at a modest $550, it had risen to $895 by 1919 as a result of war-time inflation, but the design changed little. A total of 612 Moores was made. GNG

MOORE (v) (US) *1917*
Indianapolis, Ind.

This 2-wheeled two-seater was a curious hybrid which combined the features of a car and a motor cycle. It was powered by a 22hp air-cooled engine and was complete with 3-speed transmission and shaft drive, but it had handlebar steering and was without bodywork. The name of its manufacturer is not known. GMN

MOOSE JAW STANDARD (CDN) *1917*
Canadian Standard Auto Tractor Co, Moose Jaw, Sask.

Five local residents tried to produce a luxury car with wire wheels, 12ft wheelbase and Continental 6-cylinder engines. Only five cars were built, each backer getting one, and the company was wound up. The car was sometimes also known as the Continental. GB

MOPS (D) *1925*
Schmidt & Bensdort GmbH, Mannheim

This was a small 3-wheeled car with one driven rear wheel and a 350cc engine. HON

MORA (US) *1906–1911*
Mora Motor Car Co., Newark, N.Y.

The Mora was a relatively small car which used both 4- and 6-cylinder engines of 3.7 and 4.6 litres capacity respectively. The most common Mora seems to have been the tiny Model 20 of 1910 and 1911. This company also made the Browniekar through a subsidiary organization. In 1911 the Frank Toomey Co of Philadelphia took over the concern but it is not known whether the new company produced any 1912 Mora models. Total production of Moras was less than 1,500 cars. GMN

MORAVAN *see* AVIA (i)

MORETTI (I) *1945 to date*
(1) Fabbrica Automobili Moretti SpA, Turin *1945–1961*
(2) Moretti Fabbrica Automobili e Stabilimenti Carozzeria SAS, Turin *1962 to date*

Unlike many of Italy's small specialist firms, Moretti started by making almost everything themselves. Their first model to be shown in public was La Cita, a 350cc minicar with a front-mounted 14bhp vertical-twin ohv engine, welded, straight-tube frame, hydraulic brakes and transverse independent front suspension. Coupé and station wagon versions were available, and 60mph and 80mpg were claimed. Alongside this a very small double ohc 4-cylinder engine was developed, and by 1950 the twin had been supplanted by versions of this with 600cc and 750cc single-cam units mounted in backbone frames. The twin-cam unit was retained for a rear-engined Formula 3 500cc racer with De Dion back axle and there was also a twin-cam sports coupé with all-round independent suspension.

By 1954 quite a wide range of Morettis was available, the small cars being offered in 27bhp 2-bearing single-cam, and 51bhp 3-bearing twin-cam forms, while in

1924 MOON 20hp tourer. *Autocar*

1929 MOON 8-80 White Prince of Windsor roadster. *Autocar*

1910 MORA Light Four 24/28hp tourer. *Automotive History Collection, Detroit Public Library*

1952 MORETTI 600cc saloon. *Autosport*

1962 MORETTI 500D two-seater coupé.
Moretti SpA

1928 MORGAN(ii) Aero 9hp 3-wheeler.
National Motor Museum

1949 MORGAN(ii) 4/4 10hp sports car.
Autosport

1972 MORGAN(ii) Plus 8 3½-litre sports car.
Morgan Motor Co Ltd

addition there was a Michelotti-styled sports saloon using a 1.2-litre twin-cam engine which sold in America for $2,850. Clients were required to deposit 50 per cent of the purchase price before an order was accepted. The range continued to expand, with 4-door saloon and 'cab-over-engine' station wagon variants of the 750. In 1957 a special-bodied version of Fiat's Nuova 500 was offered, but as late as 1958/9 an immensely complicated variety of Morettis could still be bought, with three models of 750: the 27bhp Touring, the 43bhp Super Touring, and the 55bhp double ohc GT, a single-cam 820cc variant, a 50bhp 1-litre engine on similar lines, and a rear-engined Formula Junior racer. All had coil-and-wishbone suspension front and rear, and the Golden Arrow coupé had Dunlop disc brakes.

This elaborate programme was not justified by modest sales (116 in 1958), and from 1960 onward Moretti turned to versions of regular Fiat models, the change of direction being reflected by the change of the company's title in 1962. Up to 1963 there was a very expensive 163bhp spyder based on the 6-cylinder Fiat 2300, with capacity enlarged to 2.5 litres, but subsequently Moretti have concentrated on the smaller models. The 1967 range included an 850 4-door saloon and an electric conversion of the 500 which did not go into production. Since 1970 they have classed themselves as coachbuilders rather than car manufacturers, and in Italy Morettis are sold through the Fiat dealer network. Among the types offered in 1972 were a 128 coupé and a Jeep-type open car based on the 500.   MCS

MORGAN (i) (GB) 1905–1906
Morgan and Co Ltd, Leighton Buzzard, Beds.

Made by a well-known firm of coachbuilders, this was a conventional shaft-driven car with 5.8-litre T-head 4-cylinder Mutel engine, distinguished only by its Sparks-Boothby hydraulic clutch, soon abandoned in favour of an ordinary leather cone. Only about five were made and their lack of success resulted in Morgans' becoming Adler concessionaires in 1907, and abandoning motor manufacture.
MCS

MORGAN (ii) (GB) 1910 to date
Morgan Motor Co Ltd, Malvern Link, Worcs.

The Morgan was the best-known, and best, of the British 3-wheelers that were popular while the horsepower tax gave them an advantage. H.F.S. Morgan's tricycle was also the first of its type, going into production in 1910. At the front of a tubular chassis frame was an sv, air-cooled V-twin motor-cycle engine of 1,100cc by J.A.P., transversely mounted. Transmission was by dog clutches and chains, providing two forward speeds. The steering was direct. The front wheels had independent front suspension, by sliding pillars and coil springs. There were two seats. A reasonable amount of power plus light weight meant an excellent performance. The vehicle was safer than most 3-wheelers because its road-holding was above average. This recipe made the Morgan popular with sportsmen, for whom the Grand Prix model was produced in 1914: the first catalogued competition Morgan. Soon afterwards, an exiguous four-seater, the forerunner of the Family model of the 1920s, was listed.

After World War 1, Morgan continued to cater for all markets. Names changed, but the Sports or Standard model was the normal two-seater, also available in De Luxe form; the Family model was the more capacious type, and the long-tailed Aero, later the Super Sports, was the Morgan intended for serious speed work. Engines were water- or air-cooled to choice, most being supplied by J.A.P., or by Blackburne in the case of the competition models. From 1925 all the latter's power units had overhead valves. By 1927 the Super Sports could attain 80mph in standard trim, while the less sporting types now had internal expanding front wheel brakes and electric starting. Geared-down steering and (if required) three forward speeds followed in 1929. Even so, Morgan were losing customers to new, cheap sports cars such as the M-type M.G. Three speeds and reverse in a normal gearbox (though still with chain final drive) were available from 1931 and standard after 1932, and a modified 8hp Ford 4-cylinder engine could later be had instead of the twin. Four years later the first 4-wheeled Morgan was introduced, the excellent little 4/4. It used an 1,122cc 4-cylinder Coventry-Climax engine with overhead inlet valves, developing 34bhp. It was still light in weight, and retained the Morgan independent front suspension, so its performance and handling qualities were well up to form. It could attain 75mph. The twins were last catalogued in 1939.

Just before World War 2, a 1267cc Standard 10hp engine with ohv head was substituted in the 4/4. When this was no longer available, from 1950, Morgan fitted a tuned Standard Vanguard unit giving 70bhp. In this Morgan Plus Four, as the car was renamed, performance became still more lively, and when the 90bhp Triumph TR2 engine became available in 1954, maximum speed rose to 100mph for the first time. With the advent of the Plus Four, there was no longer a small Morgan, but this gap was made good in 1955, when the Series 2 4/4 arrived. This used the very hard-wearing, 1172cc sv Ford Ten engine which had powered F4 Morgan. (The latter was the last 3-wheeler, which had been made until 1950.) The result was a cheap, pleasant and reliable sports car of the old school. Later, the ohv Ford 105E engine was substituted. The latest version has a 1,599cc 98bhp engine, a 4-speed all-synchromesh gearbox, front disc brakes, and the traditional Morgan suspension. The Plus Four kept pace with Triumph's TR engine development, also acquiring disc brakes and, eventually, the 2,138cc 105bhp TR4 unit. A streamlined coupé, the Plus Four Plus of 1964, was a brief deviation from the classical Morgan line which met with little approval and was discontinued after only 50 had been sold. When

Triumph changed to a six during 1968, Morgan adopted a new engine for their bigger cars, and the Plus Four became the Plus Eight, powered by Rover's 3½-litre 160bhp V-8 and capable of 125mph. The 1973 versions of the model use the 4-speed all-synchromesh Rover gearbox in place of the Moss box previously fitted.

TRN

MORGAN (iii) (D) *1924–1925*
Morgan Auto-AG, Berlin

This car followed the unusual layout of the Sunbeam-Mabley. It was a 3-track vehicle with one rear wheel driven by shaft and spiral bevel gear. The two side wheels were of the same size as the two others and were not retractable as auxiliary wheels. An opposed twin-cylinder 500cc 2/12PS engine was placed in the rear.   HON

1913 MORRIS(i) Oxford 10hp two-seater. *British Motor Corporation*

MORISSE (F) *1899–1914*
P. Morisse et Cie, Etampes, Seine-et-Oise

The first Morisse was a voiturette powered by a 3hp single-cylinder engine under the seat, but driving by belt to the front wheels. The engine could be started from the driver's seat. In 1901 rear-driven cars with horizontal or vertical engines of 5½hp were made, and by 1904 a variety of proprietary engines were being used. These included a 6 or 9hp De Dion single, 10hp De Dion or Tony Huber twins and 24hp Tony Huber or Fossier fours. The latter cars had double chain drive, the others shaft. Development followed conventional lines, and by 1912 there were four 4-cylinder monobloc-engined cars, of 9/11, 10/12, 14/16 and 16/20hp. These later cars were often called S.E.M.s.   GNG

MORLOCK (US) *1903*
Morlock Automobile Co, Buffalo, N.Y.

This vehicle was a somewhat crude four-seater with *dos-à-dos* seating. Its single-cylinder 5hp engine was mounted beneath the seat, with a single chain driving the rear axle.   GMN

MORRIS (i) (GB) *1913 to date*
(1) W.R.M. Motors Ltd, Cowley, Oxford *1913–1919*
(2) Morris Motors Ltd, Cowley, Oxford *1919–1970*
(3) Austin-Morris Division, British Leyland Motor Corp Ltd, Cowley, Oxford *1970 to date*

W.R. Morris (later Lord Nuffield), an Oxford cycle and motor agent, launched his Morris-Oxford light car in 1913. This was made from proprietary parts, the engine being a 1-litre T-head four by White and Poppe. At £175 it was one of the best of the true light cars (as opposed to cyclecars) and over 1,000 had been sold by the end of 1914. A larger model, the famous Cowley, arrived on the scene in 1915; this was assembled from American components, the engine being by Continental. After World War 1 Morris marketed two 1½-litre L-head sv fours, with power units by Hotchkiss of Coventry; the Cowley differed from the Oxford mainly in its more austere equipment and the absence of a starter. In an inflationary climate, Morris was brave enough to reduce his prices (a Cowley two-seater cost £465 in October 1920, £299.10s. a year later, and £225 in October 1922) and ensured a steady flow of production by acquiring his suppliers, such as Hotchkiss, Wrigley (transmissions) and Hollick and Pratt (bodies).

The 'bullnoses' were soon best-sellers backed by a nation-wide service organization, and in 1925 Morris outsold all his competitors with 54,000 cars. From 1924 to 1926 the staple Morrises were the 1½-litre Cowley and the 1.8-litre Oxford, both with 3-speed gearboxes and the wet-plate clutches which persisted on some models right up to 1939. The Oxford acquired front wheel brakes in 1925, and they were available as an option on Cowleys a year later. 1927 produced the flat radiator and also a venture into the export market with the unsuccessful Empire Oxford of 2½ litres, which had a 4-speed box and worm drive. Equally unsuccessful was a plan to market Gallicized Morrises built in the Léon Bollée plant at Le Mans.

Meanwhile Cecil Kimber had produced the first of the Morris-Oxford-based M.G. sports cars, and a new name had been born. Morris had made a few sixes in the early 1920s, but his first serious attempt in this direction was a 2½-litre ohc model for 1928, its engine inspired by the Wolseley 16/45, a make which had come under Morris control the previous year. 1929 saw another ohc Morris, the 847cc Minor at £125. Never a best-seller, it none the less served as the basis for M.G.'s Midget. The 1930 6-cylinder Morrises had hydraulic brakes, extended down the range until they were universal by 1934, and in 1931 Morris managed to offer a simplified sv two-seater version of the Minor for £100. The early 1930s proved very difficult for the company, which had no obvious best-seller and too many different models. Sliding roofs and electric fuel pumps by the Morris-owned S.U. concern were innovations for 1932 and 1933 cars pioneered the semaphore-type traffic indicator in Britain. That year Morris's sv 1.3-litre Ten-Four came out as an answer to Austin's Ten and Hillman's Minx. All 1934 models had synchromesh and the bigger sixes the added refinement of a free wheel.

The best-seller came at last in 1935 with the 918cc sv Series I Eight, which retailed at £132.10s. for a fully-equipped saloon and helped Morris reach their first million cars by the summer of 1939. In a bigger category were the Series II models with modern styling, 3-speed gearboxes, and built-in jacking systems, ranging from a revised Ten-Four up to a 3½-litre 6-cylinder Twenty-Five at £280. These were

*c.*1924 MORRIS(i) Oxford 1.8-litre limousine. Coachwork by Sanders of Hitchin. *Bernard Sanders*

1930 MORRIS(i) Minor 847cc two-seater. *British Motor Corporation*

497

1938 MORRIS(i) Twenty-five Series III 3½-litre saloon. *British Motor Corporation*

1950 MORRIS(i) Minor 918cc saloon. *British Motor Corporation*

1966 MORRIS(i) 1800 1.8-litre saloon. *British Motor Corporation*

contemporary with the Series I, though introduced some months after it. All 1938 Morrises except for the Eight had push-rod ohv engines (already applied to Wolseley and M.G.). Later that year Riley was absorbed into the Nuffield empire. Two 1939 winners were a revised Series E 8hp with a 4-speed gearbox and headlamps faired into the wings, and the 1,140cc ohv Series M Ten, which introduced integral construction to Cowley and was made after World War 2 by Hindusthan in India.

Only the 8 and 10 were made in the first post-war years, the first really new Morrises for ten years being the 1949 cars designed by Alec Issigonis. Of these the MM series Minor used the old 8hp sv engine, but boasted integral construction, rack-and-pinion steering and torsion-bar independent front suspension and set a new standard in popular car handling. A million of the basic design had been sold by January 1961. Its companion models, also chassisless and with independent front suspension were a new sv 1½-litre Oxford and the 2.2-litre ohc MS type Six.

The amalgamation of Nuffield and Austin (ii) to form the British Motor Corporation in 1952 resulted in a gradual process of rationalization. First the Minor went over to Austin's 803cc ohv A30 engine in 1953. The Series II Oxford and its less powerful companion, the Cowley, of 1954 had Morris hulls, but their engines were also ohv Austins. In 1955 the range was completed by a new Isis using the 2.6-litre B.M.C. 6-cylinder unit – this was discontinued in 1958. In the late 1950s some cars were made and sold in Australia under the Morris name which were in fact more closely akin to other makes in the B.M.C. group. The 6-cylinder Marshall was really an Austin A105, while both the Major and its Austin counterpart, the Lancer, were based on the Wolseley 1500.

With the arrival of the Farina-styled 1½-litre saloons in 1959, differences between Austin and Morris had been reduced to house colours and radiator emblems. The front-wheel-drive Mini (1960) was shared between the two makes and though its bigger stablemate, the 1100 of 1963 with Hydrolastic suspension, was initially a Nuffield monopoly, the inevitable Austin variant followed a year later. In the case of the third front-wheel-drive model, the 1800, Austin were ahead of Morris in introducing it by nearly eighteen months. The 1968 range comprised the fwd Mini, 1100/1300, and 1800 as well as the conventional 1,600cc Oxford and the indestructible Minor 1000, now with 1,098cc engine and still selling close on 60,000 a year. This sole survivor of independent Morris design did not disappear until the end of 1970. Minis became a separate make that year. From 1971 Morris versions of the 1100 and 1300 disappeared; the name was reserved for the Marina, an orthodox rear-wheel-driven family saloon with Minor 1000 front suspension, semi-elliptics at the rear, and drum brakes on the simpler variants. Push-rod 1,300cc and 1,800cc B.L.M.C. 4-cylinder engines were used, and the original 2-door coupé and 4-door saloon were joined by a station wagon in 1973. The largest fwd cars were still available with Morris badges – there was a version of the 6-cylinder 2200 in 1972.

MCS

MORRIS (ii) *see* AUSTIN (iii)

MORRIS & SALOM (US) *1895–1897*
Morris & Salom, Philadelphia, Pa.

The first car by this firm was known as the Electrobat. It had front-wheel-drive by two Lundell electric motors, with larger wheels at front than at the rear. One was entered in the 1895 Chicago Times-Herald Race but did not finish. Later, some cars with equal wheels were also made.

GNG

MORRIS-COMMERCIAL (GB) *1930–1931*
Morris-Commercial Cars Ltd, Birmingham

Only one private-car type was made by Morris's truck division, and this was a development of their 6 × 4 army command car designed for comfortable on- and off-road motoring. The 6D had a 4,256cc 6-cylinder engine in place of the 2½-litre sv four used in the lorries, features of the design including limousine body-work, hydraulic brakes and wire wheels. Top speed was over 70mph, but a chassis price of £866 explains why probably fewer than 20 found buyers.

MCS

MORRISON (i) (US) *1890–c.1896*
William Morrison, Des Moines, Iowa

This was the second electric car to be built in America, and the first to be sold commercially. Sturges cars were Morrisons used by Harold Sturges for publicity purposes in 1895–96.

GNG

MORRISON (ii) (GB?) *1904–c.1905*
Krupkar Ltd, London S.W.

This was a 3-wheeler with a 6hp 2-cylinder engine driving the front wheels. It was shown at the 1904 Crystal Palace Show by Krupkar Ltd, Who imported cars of German origin, including the Cudell, Horch and Opel, and sold them as Krupkars, or Cudell-Krupkars, Opel-Krupkars etc. They obtained their name from the use of metal from Krupps of Essen in the cars.

The origin of the Morrison is uncertain.

GNG

MORRISS (GB) *1908–c.1911*
H.E. & F. Morriss, London N.

The Morriss steam car was made by Frank Morriss and his brother. Only four cars were built, using a 2-cylinder slide-valve engine of Morriss design, and four-seater tourer bodies.   GNG

MORRISS-LONDON (US) *1919–1925*

(1) Crow-Elkhart Motor Car Co, Elkhart, Ind.
(2) Century Motor Co, Elkhart, Ind.

The Morriss-London was an assembled car built for export to England only under an agreement with the manufacturer and F.E. Morriss of 64 Piccadilly, London. The cars were nearly identical with the Crow-Elkharts which were built until 1924 by the parent company, and were distinguished by a slightly pointed radiator. They were available as touring cars or landaulets, the latter designed for use as taxicabs. Artillery, wire or disc wheels were optional and although some Morriss-Londons were completely built in the United States, most of the coachwork was added in England, a number of bodies being made by Morgan. From 1922 to 1925 sales were taken over by Saunders Motors Ltd of London N.W.11.   KM

MORS (F) *1895–1925; 1941–1943*

(1) Société d'Electricité et d'Automobiles Mors, Paris *1895–1907*
(2) Société Nouvelle des Automobiles Mors, Paris *1908–1943*

Emile Mors was an electrical engineer, which may account for the ingenious ignition system (by low-tension coil and dynamo) found on his first cars with aiv V-4 engines, dry-sump lubrication, water-cooled heads and air-cooled barrels. These power units were rear-mounted, and the belt-and-pulley change-speed gear was in the Benz idiom. Production in 1898 was running at 200 cars a year and front-mounted engines made their appearance on the Petit Duc, an 850cc flat-twin with partial water cooling, cone clutch and final drive by side chains. Steering was by handlebar and the car cost £294 in England in 1900. It was still listed in 1901, though later examples were wheel-steered.

The Mors racing cars designed by Brasier at first rivalled and then surpassed the hitherto invincible Panhards, winning the Paris-St Malo and Paris-Bordeaux in 1899, following this with victories in the Paris-Toulouse-Paris and Bordeaux-Périgeux-Bordeaux in 1900, and the Paris-Berlin and Paris-Bordeaux in 1901. in 1902 the 60hp 9.2-litre competition machines had shock absorbers and in 1903 capacity had gone up to 11.6 litres, with mechanically-operated overhead inlet valves and streamlined bodywork of the upturned-boat type. Gabriel won the Paris-Madrid race on one of these, while the Hon. C.S. Rolls recorded 84.68mph over the kilometre at Welbeck on a similar machine. The 1904 racers saw a reversion to T-head power units, but this was the last year in which Mors made any impression on the circuits. Though Jenatzy drove for the team in the 1908 Grand Prix, he took 9th place, and the 2½-litre cars prepared for the cancelled 1914 Coupe de l'Auto never reappeared.

Though full water cooling was not adopted till 1902, vertical 4-cylinder engines made their appearance late in 1899, followed in 1900 by lt magneto ignition. 1901 cars had what amounted to one carburetter per cylinder, with a huge central float chamber. From 1902 onwards the cars followed conventional lines; 1903 models retained the chain drive, but had mechanically-operated sv in a T-head, pressed-steel frames, Dubrulle lubricators and Mercedes-style honey-comb radiators. Brasier had already departed to work for Georges Richard. In 1904 Charles Schmidt, also of Mors, went to design European-style cars for Packard in America – this had no connection with the American Mors cars made from 1906 to 1909. Also new in 1904 was the 'shouldered' radiator shell which persisted on the marque almost to the end. 4-cylinder cars only were made in 1905; they came in 2.3-litre, 3.2-litre, 4.3-litre, 5.7-litre and 8.1-litre sizes, and the largest model, rated at 40/52hp, had an auxiliary transverse spring at the rear and cost £1,224. In 1906 the aluminium water jacketing introduced in 1903 was abandoned, while cone clutches gave way to the contracting-band type which Mors never departed from. Ignition was now by ht magneto and options included the Huillier windscreen (patented by a Mors director) and compressed-air starting. A cab-over-engine petrol brougham was listed on the 17hp chassis. In 1907 L-head monobloc engines arrived with the small 10hp and 15hp models, which also had shaft drive and pressure lubrication: at the top of the range was a 50hp 6-cylinder with gate change and lt magneto ignition which sold at £1,375 in England.

The 1908 depression was a blow from which Mors never really recovered, though the company was reconstructed under André Citroën's management and in 1909 they made 2,000 cars, sales being aided by bigger shaft-driven 2.5-litre and 3.7-litre models. Chain drive and make-and-break ignition were to persist on the biggest Mors until 1912, though there was a shaft-driven 3.6-litre 6-cylinder in 1911 and the L-head monobloc 12/15hp with 4-speed gearbox was quite popular in 1913/14. Poppet and Knight sleeve-valve models in great diversity were offered during the last two pre-World War 1 seasons, the latter coming in 2.1-litre, 3.7-litre, 4.4-litre and 7.2-litre sizes with engines by Minerva. By 1914 only the small cars retained sv power units; Citroën double helical bevels were standard, and an sv sports 17/20hp was offered with electric lighting. Only Minerva-built Knight engines were used after 1918, the radiators wearing a triple-S monogram as a riposte to Panhard's double-S (for *sans soupapes*). Mors, however, had fewer resources than their former rivals, and not even good looks and a 70mph performance (plus front wheel brakes in 1921) could save the 3.6-litre Sporting 20. A 2-litre car, also Minerva-engined, appeared in 1922, but

1973 MORRIS(i) Marina 1800 TC coupé.
British Leyland Motor Corporation

1930 MORRIS-COMMERCIAL 6D 4.2-litre limousines.
Norman Painting Collection

1903 MORS 70hp Gordon Bennett racing car. Salleron at the wheel. *The Veteran Car Club of Great Britain*

1923 MORS 14/20hp tourer. *G.N. Georgano*

1966 MOSKVITCH 408 1.4-litre saloon. *Thomson & Taylor (Brooklands) Ltd*

1902 MOTOBLOC 8hp tonneau. *Musée de l'Automobile, Rochetaillée-sur-Saone*

by 1925 most, if not all the company's facilities had been absorbed by Citroën. There was a brief renaissance with electric cars during World War 2, but the last vehicles to bear the name of Mors were the Speed motor scooters made from 1952 to 1956.

MCS

MORSE (i) (US) *1904–1909*
Morse Motor Vehicle Co, Springfield, Mass.

Launched at the end of 1904, the Morse steamer had a 3-cylinder horizontal single-acting 20hp engine, with direct drive to the rear axle. It had a five-seater tonneau body, and a bonnet like that of a petrol car. Made from 1904 to 1906, it was joined by a conventional 4-cylinder petrol car, which lasted until 1909. The company was then re-organized as the Easton Machine Company, and made the Morse (ii).   GNG

MORSE (ii) (US) *1909–1916*
Euston Machine Co, South Easton, Mass

The Morse used 4-cylinder, ohv engines of 24 and 34hp and 4-speed transmissions with direct drive in third. Prices for four open models ranged from $3,900 to $4,200 over the years 1911 to 1914.   GMN

MORSE (iii) (US) *1914–1917*
Morse Cyclecar Co, East Pittsburgh, Pa.

This cyclecar had an unusual drive system to the front wheels by chain. It was powered by a 1.1-litre V-twin engine. The body was steel, but an aluminium body, lighter by 50lb, could also be had.   GMN

MORVI (IND) *1911–1912*
Morvi Motor Works, Morvi State

The Morvi was designed by Ralph Ricardo who had previously been responsible for the Dolphin (i), and was built under his supervision in India in the workshops of his employers, the Morvi State Railway. It had a single-cylinder T-head engine and shaft drive. Ricardo left the company before series production could begin, and probably only one Morvi was made.   MJWW

MOSER (CH) *1914–1924*
Moteurs Moser, St Aubin, Neuchâtel

Fritz Moser's first vehicle was a cyclecar with air-cooled V-twin engine and chain drive. He also made engines for other firms; like Zedel he opened a branch at Pontar-liter in France to make engines for the French market, but did not, apparently, manufacture complete cars there. In 1920 he made several prototypes of a 3-wheeler with a V-twin engine, but his production car had 4 wheels. A 4-cylinder light car was also made from 1920 to 1924.

From 1914 to 1918 a number of 4-cylinder light two- and four-seaters designed by Rudolf Egg were made in the Moser factory. The 1918 model had a Zürcher engine and electric lighting, whereas the Moser 2-cylinder had acetylene lighting.   GNG

MOSKVITCH (SU) *1947 to date*
Moskovskii Zavod Malolitrajnikh Automobilei, Moscow

Born of war reparations, the first Moskvitch 400 was in reality the pre-war German Opel Kadett sedan, whose dies the Russians removed from Germany to build this 'Son of Moscow'. It was of unit construction with a 4-cylinder engine of 23hp which was later increased to 26 in the Model 401 of 1954. Some tourers and station wagons were built on this chassis in addition to the sedans.

In 1956 a newly designed Model 402 replaced the former Opel style. Engine power was increased to 35hp at 4,200rpm and a 4-wheel-drive 410 was introduced.

A somewhat modified 407 series was announced in 1958 with 45hp and available in sedan, taxi, ambulance, station wagon, delivery, and 4-wheel-drive forms. A 403 sedan was constructed in 1963, overlapping 407 production; it was similar to the other series but had different trim and could likewise be obtained as a station wagon or delivery.

The greatly changed 408 series was displayed in 1966 and showed the Russians' determination to expand their car export business. This five-seater sedan compared favourably with other makes of similar size and was equipped with a 4-cylinder, 1.4-litre ohv engine of 60hp. The transmission was a 4-speed synchromesh; it had independent front suspension with leaf springs at the rear. Station wagon and delivery models were produced and options included four headlamps, electric windscreen wipers and sun visors.

An unusual variation of the Moskvitch was the Scaldia sedan, assembled in Belgium by Sobimpex with the Russian chassis and a British Perkins Diesel engine. Early in 1968 came the 412 series with 80bhp ohc hemi-head engine of 1,480cc, and by 1972 this was the staple Moskvitch.   BE

MOT ET SARALEGUI (F) *1902*
This was a light two-seater voiturette with tandem seating, the driver being in the front seat.   GNG

MOTOBLOC (F) *1902–1930*
(1) G. Carde, fils et Cie, Bordeaux
(2) SA Motobloc, Bordeaux

The Schaudel of 1898, which became the Motobloc, featured unit construction of engine and gearbox, the earliest known instance of this form of design and the reason for the name Motobloc. Furthermore, the change-speed gears were actually in the crankcase. The power unit was a transversely-mounted, inclined twin with chain drive. This odd little voiturette survived until 1904, after which it was perpetuated only as a van chassis, and a conventional vertical 4-cylinder engine – still made in unit with the gearbox - was substituted. This was a highly efficient unit that soon acquired overhead inlet valves, and it was also very smooth, thanks to the positioning of the flywheel between the two pairs of cylinders. A mid-mounted flywheel was also used in the 6-cylinder engine of 1909 and on all models throughout the 1920s. Only fours were made up to 1927, ranging from 1,327cc to 3 litres in capacity. Independent front suspension was introduced in 1928, and the 1929/30 range consisted of a 9CV, 1,453cc four, and two sixes, a 10CV (1,683cc) and a 15CV (3,013cc).　　　TRN

MOTOCOR (I) *1921–1924*
Motovetturetta Carrozata Originale Resistentissima, Turin

The Motocor was a 3-wheeler powered by a variety of motorcycle engines, according to customers' choice. The driver sat alone in front, with two passengers behind him. Commercial versions and motor cycles were also made by this company.　　　GNG

MOTORETTE (US) *1910–1912*
C.W. Kelsey Mfg Co, Hartford, Conn.

The famous 3-wheeled Kelsey Motorette was produced in limited numbers for little over two years. Designed and manufactured by the automobile pioneer C.W. Kelsey, the car had a single wheel at the rear. The first models were air-cooled and power was supplied by a 2-stroke 2-cylinder engine. Steering was by tiller. As the first cars showed a tendency to roll on turns, Kelsey developed the stabilizer or anti-sway bar which counteracted this. By 1911, Motorettes were water-cooled and to promote advertising the manufacturer sent two men from Hartford across the continent to California. The factory price of the Motorette was $385. A delivery van was priced somewhat higher. A third model, a rickshaw, was added and exported to Japan. Several hundred units were built before the company failed and these were marketed throughout the United States as well as Japan, Denmark, Mexico and Canada.　　KM

MOTORMOBILE *see* VILAIN

MOUETTE (F) *1923–1925*
Automobiles Mouette, Paris 16e

The Mouette car was sponsored by L. van der Eyken who also made the Fox (i). It was a conventional car using S.C.A.P. or Ruby engines, mainly in the 1,100 to 1,500cc range.　　　GNG

MOURRE (F) *1921–1923*
Antoine Mourre, Paris 14e

The Mourre cyclecar used the same design as the 2-stroke Major, and was said by some to be the 1920 Major renamed. Two Mourres were entered in the 1921 Grand Prix des Cyclecars, and the car driven by its designer, Violet, finished second. (He had won this race in 1920, driving a Major). Despite these successes, neither Mourres nor Majors were entered in later cyclecar races. The 1923 Mourre used a conventional 4-cylinder 4-stroke engine of 950cc made by Fivet.　　　GNG

MOVEO (GB) *1931–1932*
Moveo Car & Engineering Co, Preston, Lancs.

The Moveo was an attempt to make what today would be called a Gran Turismo coupé, using proprietary parts, notably a 2,973cc Meadows ohv 6-cylinder engine. It had dual ignition, 4-speeds and was available with a supercharger. A close-coupled four-seater coupé was built for demonstration purposes, but coachwork was supposed to be to individual choice. Other Meadows engines of 3,280 and 4,430cc were also available, but it is likely that the 3-litre prototype coupé was the only Moveo made.　　　GNG

MOYEA (US) *1902–1904*
(1) Moyea Automobile Co, New York, N.Y. *1902–1904*
(2) Consolidated Motor Co, New York, N.Y. *1904*

This car was built under Rochet-Schneider licence, was powered by a 4-cylinder, 25hp engine and had a 4-speed transmission and shaft drive. The bodies were built by Springfield Metal Body Co, Springfield, Mass. The 1903 chassis were built by the Alden Sampson Manufacturing Co, Pittsfield Mass., who subsequently purchased Consolidated Motor Co in order to obtain the licence from the French manufacturer.　　　GMN

MOYER (US) *1909–1915*
H.A. Moyer, Syracuse, N.Y.

The early offerings by this manufacturer were two models with 4-cylinder engines and a 6-cylinder car was added in 1913. This line was later reduced to a single chassis in which was fitted a 5.2-litre 4-cylinder engine. Both two-seater and five-seater models were made at prices ranging from $2,200 to $3,000.　　GMN

*c.*1923 MOTOBLOC 12CV tourer. Coachwork by Louis Maffre. *National Motor Museum*

1910 MOTORETTE 7hp 3-wheeler. *Henry Ford Museum, Dearborn, Michigan*

1913 MOYER 30hp two-seater. *National Motor Museum*

1923 M.S. 1,095cc two-seater. *Autocar*

1955 M.T. 125cc 3-wheeler. *G.N. Georgano*

1912 MULTIPLEX(i) tourer. *P.J. Amabile Jr Collection*

MOZOTA (F) *1906*

B. de Mozota, Paris

Three models of this car were listed, a 10/12, 24/30 and 40/60hp, all with 4-cylinder engines.　　　　GNG

M.P.M. (US) *1914–1915*

Mount Pleasant Motor Co, Mount Pleasant, Mich.

The M.P.M. was a conventional medium-sized car made in 4- and 8-cylinder versions. The company planned to move to Alma or Saginaw at the end of 1915, but apparently never did so.　　　　GNG

M.R.E. (GB) *1972 to date*

M.R.E. Racing Services Ltd, Bourne End, Bucks.

After building components such as magnesium racing wheels, oil tanks, exhaust systems and suspension units, M.R.E. introduced a simple space-frame racing car for Formula 3 or Formula Ford, known as the 3s3 and Fs3 respectively.　　　　GNG

M.S. (F) *1923–1925*

(1) Automobiles M.S., Sèvres, Seine-et-Oise *1923–1924*
(2) Sté Nouvelle des Automobiles M.S., Suresnes, Seine *1924–1925*

Morin Sylvestre bought engines and chassis from Marguerite and mounted his own bodies, of which the canework cabriolets were the most striking. Models included one with a 995cc 2-cylinder Train engine, and others with 961 and 1,095cc 4-cylinder Chapuis-Dornier engines. About 60 M.S. cars were sold.　　　　GNG

M.S.L. (GB) *1911–1912*

Motor Showrooms Ltd, London W.C.

The M.S.L. was assembled at premises in Long Acre from parts imported from France. Two models were offered, a 10/14 and a 12/16hp, both with monobloc 4-cylinder engines. Body styles were open two or four-seaters. In September 1911 it was announced that there were plans to manufacture the entire car in England. Nothing came of this and M.S.L. advertising ceased during 1912.　　　　GNG

M.T. (E) *1955*

Built in Nervion, the M.T. was a 3-wheeled minicar powered by a 125cc engine driving the single rear wheel.　　　　GNG

MUELLER (US) *1895–1900*

Mueller & Co, Decatur, Ill.

Hieronymous A. Mueller imported a Benz in 1892 or 1893, to which he made various modifications such as replacing the 2 forward speeds by 3 and adding a reverse, making a new cooling system, and using his own sparking plug and car-burettor. This car was driven in the 1895 Chicago Times-Herald Race by his son Oscar B. Mueller, and finished 2nd. Mueller senior built five more cars and planned to become a manufacturer, but was killed in a workshop explosion in 1900. The parent company concentrated on the making of brass forgings.　　　　GNG

MUELLER-NEIDHART (S) *1952*

The Mueller-Neidhart was a light car intended for mass-production in Sweden and Holland. It had a tubular backbone frame and a Swiss-designed Neighart compressed rubber suspension. Only prototypes were made.　　　　GNG

MULLNER (A) *1913–1914*

The Mullner was one of the few pre-war Central European cyclecars. It was powered by a 6/7hp 2-cylinder Zédel engine, with chain drive to one rear wheel.　　　　GNG

MULTIPLEX (i) (US) *1912–1913*

Multiplex Mfg Co, Berwick, Pa.

The Multiplex was built in three versions on a standard wheel-base: a two-seater roadster, a two-seater raceabout and a five-seater touring car, powered by Waukesha 4-cylinder engines. A four-speed transmission was used with direct drive in third gear. Less than 20 of these cars were manufactured.　　　　GMN

MULTIPLEX (ii) (US) *1954*

Multiplex Mfg Corp, Berwick, Pa.

The Multiplex 186 was a short-lived sports car powered by a 2-litre 4-cylinder or 2.7-litre Willys F-head 6-cylinder engine. The chassis had independent front suspension.　　　　MCS

MUNSON (US) *1899–1902*

Munson Electric Motor Co, La Porte, Ind.

The Munson was probably the first petrol-electric car to be made and sold in America. 2- and 4-cylinder engines were used, and only chassis were provided. They could be fitted with any kind of body, either private or commercial.　　　　GNG

MUNTZ (US) *1949–1954*

(1) Muntz Car Co, Inc, Glendale, Calif. *1949–1950*

(2) Muntz Car Co, Inc, Evanston, Ill. *1950–1954*

Derived from the Kurtis Sports, the Muntz four-seater convertible was built by Earl Muntz, a prominent radio and television manufacturer. The Glendale works turned out 28 cars powered by the 5.4-litre Cadillac V-8 engine, but when production moved to Evanston the wheelbase was lengthened by 3in to 9ft 7in, and a Lincoln V-8 engine was adopted. Most of these were sv units, but the last few were the 1953 205bhp ohv engines. Early Muntz bodies were of aluminium, but later most were steel. A total of 394 Muntz cars was made.   BE

MURAD (GB) *1948–1949*
(1) Murad Machine Tool Co Ltd, Aylesbury, Bucks
(2) Murad Developments Ltd, Aylesbury, Bucks

For a small firm to market a competitive saloon in the 1½-litre class was a remarkable achievement; at the same time to introduce several advanced features and also 'buy out' no major components was a shear impossibility. Yet the Murad reached well beyond the prototype stage, and nearly succeeded. The ohv engine had hydraulic tappets, and a form of semi-Heron combustion chamber. Independent front suspension was by coil, with enormous lower wishbones, and the use of rubber bushes restricted the number of lubrication points.   DF

MURDAUGH (US) *1901*
Murdaugh Automobile Co, Oxford, Pa.

This two-seater small car had a 'reach' frame and was driven by a 3¼hp engine. It was steered by a tiller. Drive was by a single chain from a friction transmission.   GMN

MURENA *see* INTERMECCANICA

MURRAY (i) (US) *1902–1903*
Church Mfg Co, Adrian, Mich.

The Murray was a light runabout on similar lines to the Curved Dash Oldsmobile, built by a former Olds engineer. It had a 6hp single-cylinder water-cooled engine, epicyclic gearbox and single chain drive. About 1,000 Murrays were produced before the makers turned to a larger car, the Lenawee.   GNG

MURRAY (ii) (US) *1916–1918*
Murray Motor Car Co, Pittsburgh, Pa.

The Murray Eight with its V-8 motor and Rolls-Royce style of radiator, was a prestige car of the World War 1 period which sold at a reasonable price and had an enviable clientele of owners and enthusiasts. The cars featured both an electric clock and a slanted windshield as early as 1917.   KM

MURRAY-MAC (US) *1921–1928*
Murray Motor Car Co, Atlantic, Mass.

The Murray-Mac was the earlier Murray Eight after it had been taken over by John J. McCarthy. Few Murray-Macs were produced and these appeared throughout the 1920s, one or two at a time. The Murray Eight designs were retained and standard engines of 6-cylinder type as well as other standard components were used.   KM

MUSTANG (US) *1948–1949*
Mustang Engineering Corp, Seattle, Wash.

This was a prototype six-seater sedan with a door in the centre of each side, built in Seattle, Wash. The rear-mounted 59hp, 4-cylinder Hercules engine was in unit with the transmission and axle for ease of removal and repair. The car was designed by a former Lincoln service manager, Roy C. McCarty.   BE

MUSURUS (F) *c.1921–1922*
Janvier, Sabin et Cie, Châtillon-sur-Bagneux, Seine

Musurus Bey was a wealthy Turkish enthusiast who commissioned the Janvier engine firm to build a few cars bearing his name. They had rounded-V radiators in the Delaunay-Belleville or N.A.G. idiom and were powered by large T-head Picker Janvier 4-cylinder engines.   MCS

MUTEL (F) *c.1902–c.1906*
Mutel et Cie, Paris 15e

Mutel were well-known makers of proprietary engines which were fitted to a wide variety of French makes, as well as a few in England. They made very few cars, although some cars with Mutel engines in M.A.B. chassis were sold under the name Mutel; these seem to have been special orders rather than production cars.   GNG

M.V.M. (GBG) *1956*
Manor View Motors, Catel, Guernsey, C.I.

The only car ever to have been built for sale in the Channel Islands, the M.V.M. was a light sports two-seater powered by a rear-mounted 325cc Anzani 2-cylinder 2-stroke engine. It had a ladder-type tubular frame, independent suspension all round, and a fibreglass open body. The price was intended to be between £356 and £375, and the car might have given some competition to the Berkeley had it been produced, but only prototypes were made.   GNG

1951 MUNTZ 5.3-litre convertible. *Autosport*

1948 MURAD 1½-litre saloon. *Motor*

1918 MURRAY(ii) Model 70-T town car. *Keith Marvin Collection*

1926 MURRAY-MAC sedan. *Keith Marvin Collection*

M.W. *see* WEGMANN

M.W.D. (D) *1911–1912*
Motor-Werke mbH, Dessau
    Two models of touring cars were produced which sold reasonably well. The 8/22PS model was continued by the Anhaltische Automobil- und Motorenfabrik AG (Der Dessauer).   HON

M.W.F. (A) *1905–1907*
Maschinen- und Waggonbaufabrik (AG), Simmering
    This firm — specialists in railway carriages — continued the production of Wyner cars in their own works. Like Wyner they build mainly cars with 8/10hp single-cylinder De Dion engines.   HON

MYRON (CS) *1934*
Automobil- und Flugmotorenfabrik Myron, Zlin
    A prototype of this make was exhibited at the Prague Salon of 1934. It had a 2-cylinder 2-stroke engine of 800cc and a two-seater chassisless body. Another version had a 2-cylinder 2-stroke rear engine with a capacity of 1 litre, a central tubular frame and a four-seater body. Neither version went into series production.   HON

MYTHOLM (GB) *1899–1902*
(1) Brown & Buckton, Hipperholme, Yorks *1899–1900*
(2) Yorkshire Motor Car Mfg Co, Ltd, Hipperholme, Yorks *1900–1902*
    Brown and Buckton were engine builders who made a few experimental cars. They were acquired by the Yorkshire Motor Car Manufacturing Co who used Mytholm engines in the cars designed by R. Reynold Jackson. They were 4hp horizontal 2-cylinder units, and the cars had single chain drive. A few were made after Jackson left the firm, and these were called Mytholms.   GNG

N

NACIONAL (i); NACIONAL PESCARA (E) *1929–1932*
Fabrica Nacional de Automóviles, Barcelona

Sponsored by the Marquis Raoul de Pescara and designed by his brother Enrique and the Italian Edmond Moglia, the Nacional Pescara was a curious mixture of European and American ideas. The engine was a 9-bearing ohc straight-8 of 2.8 litres' capacity. It had an aluminium block and head and nitralloy liners and developed 80bhp. Detroit influence was reflected in the Delco coil ignition, 3-speed unit gearbox, hydraulic brakes, hypoid rear axle and disc wheels. Few were made: a proposed 3.9-litre sports car with 10 cylinders in line, understandably, never got off the drawing board. The Revolution of 1931 removed one of the firm's staunchest supporters, King Edmond Alfonso XIII, and plans to build Nacional Pescaras under licence in the Voisin works in France came to nothing. Competition models, however, had a distinguished record; these had dohc engines that gave 180bhp in blown form as well as electron wheels and fuel tanks. A stripped two-seater weighed only 1,344lb. The Nacional Pescaras of Zanelli and Tort won the 1931 European Mountain Championship. The cars were still taking part in hill climbs as late as 1935, when Zanelli won the 3-litre class at Kesselberg and Val de Cuech.   MCS

1930 NACIONAL(i) 2.8-litre roadster. *Autocar*

NACIONAL (ii) (MEX) *1949–1952*
Fabrique DM-Nacional, Mexico City

The Nacional was built in part of the factory of Distribuidora Mexicana, a big furniture-making concern. It was designed by Antonio Ruiz Galindo, son of the owner of DM. Striking convertible bodies to owners' orders were built on any stock American chassis, mainly Mercury. About 15 were made before Galindo turned to the retailing of Fiats.   GNG

NACIONAL CUSTALS (E) *1919*
Sr Custals, Barcelona

After he left Ideal (iv), Custals produced a very small number of cars of his own, based on Ideal designs.   JRV

NACIONAL-G (E) *1939–1940*
Natalio Horcajo (Tecnico Industrial), Zaragoza

Built by Natalio Horcajo and Martin Gomez, this was a light car powered by a 700cc 2-cylinder 2-stroke engine, with a 3-speed gearbox, tubular backbone frame, and independent suspension all round. A 2-door saloon body was fitted, and a military version was also made. There were plans to make 5,000 per year, but these were stopped at the instigation of the German government, whose overall plan for Europe did not envisage an industrialized Spain. Only four prototypes were made of this interesting car, which might have become the first mass-produced people's car of Spain.   JRV

1940 NACIONAL-G 700cc saloon. *Natalio Horcajo*

NACIONAL SITGES (E) *1933–1937*
This was a small factory in the famous summer resort of Sitges which produced cars based on Peugeot designs. During the Spanish Civil War the factory produced light tanks, but none reached the front as the engine proved too feeble to propel them.   JRV

NACKE (D) *1901–1913*
Automobilfabrik E. Nacke, Coswig

Nacke started production of cars in 1901, using the name Coswiga for his cars at first, but production was on a small scale. By 1906 he was making large 4-cylinder chain-driven cars of 5.2 and 6.8 litres, but later he concentrated on smaller shaft-driven cars. Nacke enlarged his programme after 1909, offering a range of 4-cylinder models with overhead inlet valves in the following years but these never became well-known. He began to specialize in commercial vehicles and gave up production of private cars in 1913. Commercials were continued until the late 1920s.   HON

N.A.G. (D) *1902–1934*
(1) Allgemeine Elektrizitäts-Gesellschaft, Berlin *1902–1908*
(2) Neue Automobil-Gesellschaft, Berlin *1908–1915*
(3) Nationale Automobile-Gesellschaft, Berlin *1915–1934*

The electrical concern A.E.G. became interested in the production of motor cars and bought the Allgemeine Automobil-Gesellschaft (A.A.G.). They set up the Neue Automobil-Gesellschaft (N.A.G.) organization to sell the cars produced in the A.E.G. factory. The A.A.G. Klingenberg was continued until 1902 when A.E.G. acquired the firm of Kühlstein and its chief designer Joseph Vollmer. He designed the first N.A.G. cars, the 2-cylinder Model A and the 4-cylinder Model B. Several

1906 NACKE 45/50PS tourer. *Neubauer Collection*

1920 N.A.G. Model C.4 2½-litre tourer.
Autocar

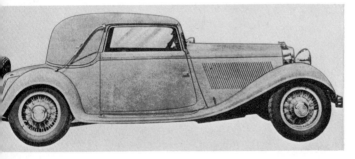

1931 N.A.G. 4½-litre V-8 drophead coupé.
Neubauer Collection

1912 NAGANT 30hp saloon. Coachwork by
d'Ieteren. *Autocar*

1927 NAMI-1 2-cylinder tourer. *NAMI, Moscow*

improved models followed. N.A.G. also produced commercials, especially buses, which appeared on the roads in large numbers. In 1908 A.E.G. withdrew from car production, which was taken over by N.A.G. A light car with a 6/12PS 1,570cc engine was marketed as the Puck after 1908; later it was renamed the Darling and re-engined with a 6/18PS unit. At least one N.A.G. was used by the Kaiser. The firm also produced electric and petrol-electric cars. A great variety of models was offered until 1914, headed by the K 8 with a 33/75PS 9-litre engine.

After World War 1 N.A.G. concentrated on their C 4 with a 4-cylinder 33PS 2,536cc engine. This model was the basis of the C 4b or Monza sports version, which was quite successful in several events. In 1926 they took over the Protos factory and the Presto works were acquired one year later. Ohv sixes were sold under the name N.A.G.-Protos. A V-8 100bhp 4.5-litre model appeared in 1931 and then N.A.G. started experimenting with front-wheel drive. The V-8 engine was also used in a front-drive model, but this never reached the public. The small front-drive N.A.G. Voran of 1933 had an opposed 4-cylinder 1,468cc engine and was based on Voran designs. This model was not a success and led to the end of car production in 1934. Commercials were continued in conjunction with Büssing for some years.   HON

NAGANT (B) *1900–1928*
(1) Nagant Frères, Liège
(2) SA des Automobiles Imperia-Excelsior, Liège

The first Nagant, made by an armaments manufacturer, was the opposed-piston Gobron-Brillié from France, built under licence as the Gobron-Nagant. 2- or 4-cylinder models were available, with four and eight pistons respectively. After 1905 these unconventional machines were dropped in favour of some typical Belgian cars – orthodox, well-made, very strong. They had chain drive until the 1909 season, and ht magneto ignition had replaced the lt type a year earlier. L-head engines made their appearance on a 2.6-litre car in 1909. The make was sold in England under the name of Nagant-Hobson. Until 1911 there was nothing about the Nagant to attract attention to it, but then came the 4-cylinder 14/16hp, which had an efficient engine capable of 3,000rpm with side valves. A light car of 1913 could turn at 4,000rpm, an extremely high speed for the time. Needless to say, these Nagants, with their very good power outputs, were much in evidence in competitions: 4½-litre twin-ohc cars ran in the 1914 Grand Pix. During this period, Nagant had an outside interest in the shape of an arrangement to build the French Rochet-Schneider for the Belgian firm of Locomotrice.

The company's interest in competitions persisted after World War 1; the model used was a long-stroke 3-litre which at first had side valves, and then overhead inlets. The 15 CV was a 4-cylinder, 2-litre machine with all-overhead valves and Adex-type 4-wheel brakes. It was enlarged to just over 2-litres in 1925. A Nagant won the 3-litre class in the Spa 24 Hours Race of that year. In 1927, a supercharged engine was exhibited at the Brussels Show, but that was the end of Nagant's interest in high performance. The last new model was an sv 2-litre six with Ricardo head, a common recipe that promised flexibility, not speed. Then came absorption by Imperia, and the end of a line of fast yet immensely durable cars.   TRN

NAIG (D) *1909–1911*
Neue Automobil-Industrie GmbH, Berlin-Charlottenburg

A voiturette was produced by this company but only in very small numbers.   HON

NAMELESS (GB) *1908–1909*
Nameless Motor Car Co, Hendon, London N.W.

A small number of cars were made by this firm, powered by the 15.9hp 4-cylinder White & Poppe engine. The chassis price was £290.   GNG

NAMI-1 (SU) *1927–1930*
Spartak Works (assisted by Nauchnii Avto-Motornii Institut), Moscow

300 units of this four-seater tourer were produced at the start of the first Soviet plan for quantity car manufacture. Its engine was a 2-cylinder air-cooled unit developing 20hp at 2,600rpm, permitting a top speed of about 50mph. Emphasis was on stamina rather than appearance, since Russian driving conditions were far from ideal at the time.

The NAMI (Scientific Auto-Motor Institute) design bureau has since deveoted its time to assembling prototypes of vehicles to be considered for production, including bicycles, motor cycles, racing cars, trucks, electric vans and the Bielka small car.   BE

NANCE *see* TOURAINE

NANCÉIENNE (F) *1900–c.1903*
Sté Nancéienne d'Automobiles, Nancy

This company built cars and commercial vehicles, mainly the latter, under Gobron-Brillié patents. A number of them were designed to run on alcohol fuel, and a Nancéienne won the 1901 Paris-Roubaix race for alcohol-fuelled cars. A 10hp car averaged 27mph with four passengers in the Paris-Berlin race.   GNG

NAPIER (GB) *1900–1924*
(1) D. Napier and Son Ltd, Lambeth, London S.E. *1900–1903*

2) D. Napier and Son Ltd, Acton, London W. *1903–1924*

This precision-engineering firm was founded in 1808 and among its products were printing presses. In 1899 Montague Napier sought to revive its declining fortunes by experimenting with cars, his first product being a vertical-twin engine with coil ignition built as a replacement unit for an 1896 Panhard owned by his fellow-cyclist S.F. Edge. In 1900 Edge formed the Motor Power Company to distribute cars, and for the next twelve years he was to act as Napier's sole distributor, racing captain, and super-publicist, bludgeoning the make into the headlines. In the same year the first complete Napier car successfully competed in the British 1,000-Mile Trial. This was a 2.4-litre front-engined aiv twin on Panhard lines (its rear-mounted radiator apart) with 4-speed gearbox, side-chain drive and armoured wood frame, soon followed by the company's first four, the 4.9-litre 16hp, noted for its triple automatic inlet valves and substantial aluminium content (this model, however, retired in the Paris–Toulouse–Paris race).

In 1901 Napier and Edge produced a more serious racing contender, the 17,157cc 50 (its engine developed 103bhp at 800rpm). This two-tonner was disqualified from the Gordon Bennett Cup because no British-made tyres could stand up to its weight, but it was actually catalogued (at £1,500) though not more than two were made. In the same year the American Charles J. Glidden set off on the first of his globe-circling tours that were to last until 1908: he used Napiers throughout, starting with a 16hp. In 1902 there was a small 2½-litre four rated at 12hp, as well as a new light 6½-litre shaft-driven racer, still with aiv and flitchplate frame, with which Edge scored a lucky win in the Gordon Bennett Cup, and put Napier (and Britain's motor industry) on the map. Within a year production had soared to 250 units per annum, and Napier were established in a new and bigger factory at Acton.

In 1904, however, came the introduction of the world's first commercially successful six, the 18hp with 5-litre engine and mechanically-operated overhead inlet valves, and before the year was out a 15.1-litre racing version was on the road. This, the famous L48, was an excellent sprint machine (Arthur Macdonald took the World Mile Record at 104.65mph in January 1905) but its 2-speed gearbox restricted its usefulness in circuit racing. Overhead inlet valves also featured in Napier's new 1904 4-cylinder racer, and a year later automatic inlets had been discarded, apart from an abortive 18hp four built for the first Tourist Trophy.

With a new trademark in the shape of the 'water tower' radiator filler cap, the company was moving towards the luxury 6-cylinder market, with chassis prices approaching the £1,500 mark, and reaching £2,500 with the vast oversquare 90hp by 1907. If Edge's American venture in Boston never produced a car, San Giorgio of Italy offered a variety of Napier types between 1906 and 1909. Side valves in L-heads and pressed-steel frames were now standard practice, with a 6-cylinder 60hp of 7.7-litre capacity as the best-known model, though a chain-driven four of 40hp was still offered in 1909. In July 1907 Edge celebrated the opening of Brooklands Track by covering 1,582 miles in 24 hours on a stripped Sixty, and his Napiers had two very successful seasons there. In 1908 Edge withdrew his team of 11½-litre 6-cylinder cars from that year's Grand Prix when the ACF refused to countenance his Rudge-Whitworth quick-detachable wire wheels. This marked Napier's official retirement from racing.

New for 1908 was an improved L-head 5-litre six with square cylinder dimensions, dual ignition, a 3-speed gearbox, and shaft drive, as well as the first Colonial models with raised ground clearances and hoods convertible into tents. The smaller fours sold steadily, but so committed was Edge to the 6-cylinder concept that he contested (and won) the 1908 T.T. with a team of fours running under the *nom de guerre* of Hutton. Some even more modest Napiers appeared in 1909: a 1.3-litre 10hp twin-cylinder taxicab chassis with 3-speed unit gearbox; and the 15hp, a straightforward 2.7-litre four with pair-cast cylinders, offered with bevel or worm drive. Sales boomed, reaching their peak in 1911 with 801 units delivered, though an 11-model range could no longer compete against Rolls-Royce's solitary Silver Ghost in the luxury market, in spite of Napier's award of the R.A.C. Dewar Trophy in 1910 for a run from London to Edinburgh in top gear. The big 65 and 90 were still offered in 1912, and the 6,840cc 6-cylinder 45 lasted until World War 1, but more typical of latter-day Napier thinking was the 4.7-litre 30/35, a six with 3-speed gearbox and wire wheels. It had acquired electric lighting by 1914, when its companion models were a pair of fours, the faithful 15 and a bigger, 4-speed 3.2-litre 16/22.

The company's post-war showing was half-hearted; Edge's departure in 1912 was an event from which they never recovered. The new 40/50hp T75 six of 1919 had a 6.2-litre ohc monobloc engine with aluminium cylinders and steel liners and dual ignition, other features being a 4-speed separate gearbox with central change, cantilever suspension, and a foot transmission brake. Though 4-wheel brakes and balloon tyres made their appearance in 1924, production ceased in the latter part of that year after only 187 had been delivered. Of the 4,258 Napiers built since 1900, no fewer than 1,800 dated from their peak period of 1909–11.

More than one attempt was made to revive the make. In 1931 Napier were the underbidders (to Rolls-Royce) for the Bentley assets, and even after World War 2 there were rumours of a super-car to bear the name. The last motor vehicle sponsored by the company was, however, a 3-wheeler tractive unit of 1931 that was subsequently marketed by Scammell as the Mechanical Horse.　　MCS

1900 NAPIER 8hp double phaeton. *D.R. Grossmark*

1914 NAPIER 30/35hp limousine. *National Motor Museum*

1922 NAPIER 40/50hp limousine. Coachwork by Cunard. *D.R. Grossmark*

1956 NARDI 750cc coupé. *G.N. Georgano*

1914 NARDINI 12/15hp two-seater. *D.C. Field Collection*

1918 NASH Model 681 tourer. *American Motors Corporation*

1926 NASH Model 21 Light Six 3-litre sedan. *American Motors Corporation*

NAPOLEON (US) *1916–1917*

(1) Napoleon Auto Mfg Co, Napoleon, Ohio
(2) Napoleon Auto Mfg Co, Traverse City, Mich.

This was a light, assembled car with five-seater or seven-seater touring bodies on a standard chassis. It was powered by a 4-cylinder engine of 2.7 litres.　GMN

NARDI (I) *1947–1956*

(1) Nardi-Danese, Turin *1947–1950*
(2) Officine Enrico Nardi, Turin *1951–1956*

Enrico Nardi, a former racing driver and engineer, helped to build an interesting racing special designed by the Italian A. Monaco in 1934–35, assisted Enzo Ferrari in building his first car, the 1½-litre 8-cylinder 815 sports car of 1940, then went into partnership with Renato Danese between 1947 and 1950. They built fast sports 750s, using either BMW-based flat-twin air-cooled engines, or Fiat-based 4-cylinder units in multi-tubular frames. Nardi also produced Lancia-engined specials and, in 1955, built a remarkable twin-hulled sports car for Le Mans, the Bisiluro with the under-750cc Giannini twin-ohc engine installed, together with the transmission, in one hull. More recently, Nardi have been well known in Italy as manufacturers of special manifolds, crankshafts, camshafts, and other speed accessories.　CP

NARDINI (F) *1914*

The Nardini was a light car built in France to the order of Monsieur Nardini who sold it in England from premises in Shaftesbury Avenue, London. Altos engines were used, and it has been suggested that the chassis was made at the Altos works, but there is no proof of this. The engines were both 4-cylinder units, of 1,094 and 1,779cc, and the cars were of conventional layout.　GNG

NASH (US) *1917–1957*

(1) Nash Motor Co, Kenosha, Wisc. *1917–1954*
(2) American Motors Corp, Kenosha, Wisc. *1954–1957*

Charles W. Nash, the former President of General Motors, acquired the Thos. B. Jeffery Co in July 1916, and from the 1918 season onwards the cars were marketed under his name. The first Nash was a 4-litre six with push-rod-operated overhead valves, followed in 1922 by a 4-cylinder car which also had overhead valves at a time when most American manufacturers adhered to the L-head. Rubber-mounted engines appeared in the same year, when Nash sold 41,000 medium-priced cars (the four cost $985, the six about $500 more). in 1924 Nash acquired the defunct Mitchell concern at Racine and the ailing Lafayette Co of Milwaukee, producers of a luxury V-8 (when the latter name was revived in 1934 it was used for an uninspired sv 6-cylinder machine selling for under $600). They also produced, in 1925–26, the 6-cylinder Ajax, an sv machine that they developed into a cheap line. During the latter part of the Vintage era the company concentrated on 6-cylinder cars, with side valves in the cheaper models and overhead valves in the higher-priced range, though 1930 saw a 4.9-litre straight-8 with dual coil ignition and overhead valves, a type that was progressively developed until 1942. Engines of this type were used in the British Jensen of 1939.

The company successfully rode out the Depression though sales dropped to below 15,000 cars in 1933, when Nash were building a really big eight with an 11ft 10in wheelbase and a capacity of 5.3 litres as well as two sixes and a smaller straight-8. Synchromesh had been adopted in 1932, and overdrive became an option in 1935, when the bigger Nashes had the fashionable fastbacks and spatted rear wheels. Other options widely publicized in the later 1930s were seats convertible into a bed and the firm's 'Weather Eye' system of air conditioning. Coil-spring independent front suspension and steering-column gear-change followed in 1939, in which year a version of the Ambassador Six was available in England with the option of a Perkins 4.7-litre diesel engine in place of the usual push-rod ohv petrol unit. Unitary construction appeared for the first time on the inexpensive sv 6-cylinder 600 sedan, introduced for 1941 at $785. This was the ancestor of the famous Rambler series and reappeared in 1945. Only 6-cylinder cars were made from 1945 until 1954, and with the advent of the Airflyte range in 1949 unitary construction was standardized. These cars had all four wheels enclosed, and a one-piece wrap-around windscreen.

In 1950 there came the experimental NXI convertible with an Austin A40 engine, later made for Nash by Austin of Birmingham as the Metropolitan, while in 1951 there appeared the 3.8-litre Nash-Healey roadster, a British Healey with an ohv 6-cylinder Nash engine. From 1950 onwards the Rambler accounted for most of Nash's production, but the original name survived the amalgamation with Hudson and the creation of American Motors in 1954. In 1955 the big Nashes were fitted with an ohv 5,244cc V-8 engine, this and its Ultramatic transmission being made by Packard. A 5.8-litre A.M.C.-built eight was adopted in 1957, but sales were negligible and the 1958 models were known as Rambler Ambassadors.　MCS

NATHAN (GB) *1965–1970*

Roger Nathan Racing Ltd, Fortis Green, London, N.2

As Frank Costin was the 'Cos' of Marcos, it is not startling to note that the centre monocoque section of the Costin-Nathan sports-racing car was wooden. Space sub-frames, and fibreglass bodywork were attached thereto. A highly tuned

Hillman Imp engine was fitted, in either 849cc or 998cc guise. The all-up weight of the GT version was only 8½cwt, and the open variety recorded some notable lap times in its first competition season.

Costin left the firm to work elsewhere while Nathan continued development of the model successfully until 1968. For 1969 the Astra RNR1 was introduced, with tubular sub-frames attached to the partially wood monocoque, and with this and its successor the RNR2 a long run of racing victories was recorded. The open version, ready to race with Coventry-Climax 2-litre engine, was priced at £4,150. Many victories were in the hands of Nathan himself. Jeremy Lord, whose RNR1 had taken 40 out of 44 races in 1970, had further successes in 1972 after an unhappy season in 1971 with a rival marque. About 45 cars were made.   DF

NATIONAL (i) (US) 1900–1924
(1) National Automobile & Electric Vehicle Co, Indianapolis, Ind. 1900
(2) National Motor Vehicle Co, Indianapolis, Ind. 1900–1916
(3) National Motor Car & Vehicle Corp, Indianapolis, Ind. 1916–1924

The first National vehicles were light electric runabouts, which were supplemented in 1903 by a petrol-engined car with a 4-cylinder Rutenber engine, 3-speed gearbox and shaft drive. In 1905 electric cars were dropped and the round radiator which was to characterize Nationals for several years was introduced. 1906 saw the 6-cylinder model, one of the first sixes in America; as on the four, cylinders were separately cast, but in 1908 there appeared a range of cars with pair-cast cylinders, and in the same year the round radiator was replaced by a shield-shaped design. From 1909 to 1915, 4- and 6-cylinder cars up to 60hp and $5,000 were made, and in the years 1909 to 1912 many competition successes were achieved, including victory in the Elgin National Trophy and Illinois Trophy in 1911, and the Indianapolis 500 Mile Race in 1912. The driver was Joe Dawson, who won at an average speed of 78.7mph.

In 1915 a new range of models was announced with 6- or 12-cylinder engines in the same chassis. The six was a Continental Red Seal, and the twelve was National's own make, but curiously the most expensive of the range was the old six, known as the Newport Six. The twelve was dropped in 1920 and for the last four years Nationals were undistinguished cars, although of good quality. A merger in 1922 between National, Dixie Flyer and Jackson led to a range of three cars for 1923/24, of which only the largest, the '6-71' was a genuine National. Although bearing the National name, the '6-31' was a Dixie Flyer and the '6-51' a Jackson.   GNG

NATIONAL (ii) (GB) 1904–1912
Rose Bros, Gainsborough, Lincs.

Originally in the tobacco wrapping machinery business, Rose Bros, in association with Lamb Bros and Baines Bros, designed and built a 10/12hp 2-cylinder and an 18/22hp 3-cylinder car. These were later followed by a 4-cylinder version, but the 6-cylinder announced in 1906 does not appear to have been a practical proposition as no available records show this model. The National appeared at various hill climbs and speed trials throughout the country.   GB

NAVAJO (US) 1953–1955
Navajo Motor Car Co, New York, N.Y.

This was a two-seater sports car powered by a 130bhp Mercury V-8 engine. The fibreglass body had an appearance similar to that of the Jaguar XK-120, and maximum speed was 125mph.   GNG

NAVARRE (US) 1921
A.C. Schulz, Springfield, Mass.

Designed by the engineer A.C. Schulz, for many years assistant chief with both Locomobile and Marmon, the 6-cylinder Navarre was to have been priced at $5,000 and $6,000 for open and closed models respectively. Although production was planned, only one closed model was shown and the Navarre name never appeared on the price lists.   KM

NAZZARO (I) 1911–1923
(1) Fabbrica Automobili Nazzaro, Turin 1911–1916
(2) Automobili Nazzaro, Florence 1919–1923

Like Vincenzo Lancia, Felice Nazzaro was a celebrated Fiat racing driver who turned to car manufacture. More successful than Lancia at the wheel, Nazzaro made relatively few cars, and his firm did not prosper to become a household word like Lancia's. The first Nazzaro car used a 4-cylinder monobloc engine of 4,398cc, and a 4-speed gearbox. Imported to Great Britain by Newton & Bennett, it usually carried less sporting coachwork than one might have expected from a racing driver's car. However, Nazzaro won the 1913 Targa Florio on one of his cars, and the following year entered a team of three specially-built 4½-litre cars for the Grand Prix. They had 4-cylinder 16-valve engines with single overhead camshafts. None of them finished the race. In 1916 Nazzaro left his firm, and the post-war cars were made by a new company at Florence. Before they appeared, the name was in the news when Meregalli won the 1920 Targa Florio on a pre-war Nazzaro. The new cars had 4-cylinder ohc engines of 3½-litres capacity and V-radiators. The last models, made in 1922, had two exhaust valves per cylinder.   GNG

1936 NASH Lafayette 3½-litre coupé. *American Motors Corporation*

1951 NASH Ambassador Six 3.8-litre sedan. *American Motors Corporation*

1913 NATIONAL(i) Model 40 roadster. *Kenneth Stauffer*

c.1906 NATIONAL(ii) 24hp tourer *Rose Fosgrove*

1912 N.B. 12hp saloon. *Autocar*

1939 NEANDER 1-litre tandem two-seater.
Neubauer Collection

1910 N.E.C. 30hp tourer. *Autocar*

N.B. (I/GB) *1913–1915*

John Newton Fabbrica Automobili, Turin

The N.B. was an English-designed car made in Italy in the former Valt factory, which was entirely owned by John Newton. Two 2-cylinder cars were made, but all production N.B.s were 12hp 4-cylinder cars with a long stroke (dimensions were 70 × 140mm) giving a capacity of 2,155cc. They were conventional, well-made cars, and about 1,000 were made, being sold on the English market by Newton & Bennett of Manchester. In 1914 the name was changed to Newton by order of the Italian Government, and in 1915 the works were sold to Diatto.   GNG

NEALE (GB) *1897*

Douglas Neale, Edinburgh

Douglas Neale built a very high electric dogcart with a four-seater *dos-à-dos* body which, with the wheels, was built by Drew of Edinburgh. Drive was to one rear wheel only. Four were sold, at a price of £150 each.   GNG

NEANDER (D) *1934–1939*

Neander Motorfahrzeug GmbH, Düren-Rölsdorf

Ernst Neumann-Neander – originally an artist – started his work in the car industry as a body designer in the years before World War 1. After the war bodies of his design were used for various makes; the best known of these were the Szawe cars. He designed and manufactured an interesting motor cycle before turning to cyclecars in 1928. The first model was a single-seater with a side-mounted 350cc engine, of which only a few prototypes were built. The next appeared in 1934 and became known as the Pionier. The engine was placed in front of the front axle. Front drive without differential, independent suspension and a two-seater tandem aluminium body were some of its features in addition to many unorthodox technical details. The Pionier was produced only in limited numbers. It was followed by Neumann-Neander's two 'Kurvenleger' experimental 3-wheelers. In one of these models, this special design enabled the wheels alone to be tilted inwards when cornering, in the other, bodywork and wheels were tilted inwards simultaneously. In 1937 a monoposto racing car appeared – based on the Pionier – which was also available as a tandem two-seater and used a 1,000cc J.A.P. engine. A small series was produced and during 1938 and 1939 these cars, which were capable of about 90mph, took part in several competitions.   HON

N.E.C. (GB) *1905–1920*

New Engine Co Ltd, Willesden, London N.W.

The N.E.C. was a town car with a horizontal underfloor engine, and either a negligible bonnet or none at all. They were designed by G.F. Mort who also designed 2-stroke aero engines, some of which were bought by A.V. Roe. The first N.E.C. of 1905 used a 4-cylinder engine of 24hp, and this was followed by a 15hp 2-cylinder in 1906, a 20hp twin and a 30hp 4-cylinder in 1908, and a 40hp four in 1910. All seats were within the wheelbase and they were very roomy cars, the larger models having, instead of occasionals, proper rear-facing seats as in the Mercedes-Benz 600 Pullman Limousine. They were mainly made with limousine or landaulet coachwork, although a few two-seaters were sold, and a 30hp open tourer competed in the 1907 Scottish Reliability Trial. The 30 and 40hp models were listed after World War 1, but those sold were probably pre-war stock. By 1921 the company was engaged in general engineering and the manufacture of car components.   GNG

NECKAR (D) *1959–1967*

Neckar Automobilwerk AG, Heilbronn

In 1959 N.S.U.-Fiat changed their name to Neckar, but cars were marketed under both names until 1966. In that year all claims to the name N.S.U. were relinquished. After 1967 the production of special German models ceased, and standard Turin types were assembled under the Fiat name.   HON

NÈGRE (F) *1897*

H. Nègre, Amiens, Somme

The Nègre steam car had a 4-cylinder horizontally-opposed engine, Serpollet-type boiler and chain drive. It had a two-seater body with an extra forward-facing seat at the front, in front of the engine and the boiler.   GNG

NEIMANN (D) *1931*

The Neimann 3-wheeler had a neat, sporty appearance with a tail like a GP Morgan. It was powered by a 600cc air-cooled V-twin engine.   GNG

NELSON (US) *1917–1921*

E.A. Nelson Motor Car Co, Detroit, Mich.

Emil A. Nelson, who had formerly served with Oldsmobile, Packard and Hupmobile, designed the Nelson car along European lines and powered it with a 2.4-litre 4-cylinder aero-type engine with overhead camshaft. A few roadsters were built in 1917 and 1918 as well as a handful of closed models, but the bulk of production was of touring cars. Approximately 350 cars were built up to the end of 1920 and although the cars may have been sold as late as 1921, production had probably ceased by then.   KM

NEMALETTE (D) *1923–1925*
Netzschkauer Maschinenfabrik Franz Stark & Söhne, Netzschkau

This was a 3-wheeled two-seater with a single front wheel. Transmission was to the rear wheels. HON

NEMO (GB) *1970–1971*
Race Cars International, Hornsey, London N.19.

This was an attractive monocoque design by Max Boxstrom for Formulas 2, and Atlantic, but the venture did not prosper and the car was raced only in the Formula 3 class. DF

NERUS (GB) *1969–1971*
Checkpoint Engineering Ltd, Hastings, Sussex

Two versions of the Nerus were made, the successful 'Silhouette' Formula F100 car, and the Group 6 sports-racing two-seater. Cedric Selzer designed the space-frame tubular chassis and Marchant & Rose built the fibreglass bodies. Only a handful of cars were sold. DF

NESSELSDORF (A; CS) *1897–1920*
1) Nesselsdorfer Wagenbau-Fabriks-Gesellschaft vorm. k.k. priv. Wagenfabrik Schustala & Co, Nesselsdorf; Vienna *1897–1920*
2) Koprivnická vozovka as, Koprivnice *1920–1923*

This company already had a name for horse-drawn vehicles and railway carriages when they built their first motor car in 1897. This was equipped with a 5hp Benz flat-twin engine and was given the name Präsident. It was driven to Vienna to appear at an exhibition. One of the engineers concerned with the Präsident was Edmund Rumpler, who was later to be associated with Adler, and after World War 1 built cars under his own name. Hans Ledwinka had just started work with the Nesselsdorf company and was also involved in this first car. Ten more of these cars, powered by Benz-type flat-twin engines and with chain drive to the countershaft, pneumatic tyres and four speeds, were built in 1899. Because the Nesselsdorf factory did not have suitable production facilities the engines were contracted out to the firm of William Hardy of Vienna. Nesselsdorf began making their own engines in late 1900. During 1900 the first racing successes were achieved by Baron von Liebig. He persuaded the company to build a pure racing car which was designed by Ledwinka, and again equipped with a Benz engine. The 1900 touring Nesselsdorf was similar to the earlier ones, but a change was made in 1901, when the engine was placed under the chassis and the carriage style of bodywork was given up. Three different models – Type A with an 8hp, Type B with a 12hp and Type C with a 4-cylinder 24hp engine – were available. However, these models did not prove very successful and when Ledwinka returned to Nesselsdorf after a few years with Friedmann in Vienna, building steam cars, he was given the task of reorganizing the automobile division and of designing new types.

The first was the Type S of 1906. This was a very successful model and can be regarded as the beginning of the make's worldwide reputation. A 3.3-litre, 4-cylinder engine with the cylinders cast in pairs was used, developing 30hp. Very advanced was the overhead camshaft, driven by vertical shaft, the so-called *Glockengetriebe*. The succeeding Type T differed from its predecessor in using a monobloc engine. The 6-cylinder U 40/50PS and U 20/65PS, which were built until the outbreak of World War 1, were based on the same principles. During the war, Ledwinka had moved to Steyr. The end of the war saw the town of Nesselsdorf within the frontiers of the new state of Czechoslovakia and renamed Koprivnice. Types T and U were continued after the war. Ledwinka returned to the company for a second time, but his subsequent designs were known by the make's new name of Tatra. HON

NEUSTADT-PERRY (US) *1902–1907*
Neustadt Motor Car Co, St Louis, Mo.

This company made a variety of cars with petrol and steam engines. The steamers were made from 1902 to 1903 only, and were powered by 10hp 2-cylinder vertical engines mounted under the rear seat and driven by single chain. Petrol cars used single and 2-cylinder engines in the light runabouts, and 4-cylinder engines in the larger touring cars. High-wheel buggies were made from 1904 to 1907, using air or water cooling, epicyclic or friction disc transmission, and final drive by single or double chains. GNG

NEW BRITISH (GB) *1921–1923*
Charles Willetts Junr Ltd, Cradley Heath, Staffs.

The New British was a light car using a 10hp V-twin Blackburne engine which was available in air- or water-cooled forms. Transmission was by friction discs, and final drive by chain. The only body style was a two seater. GNG

NEW CENTURY (i) (GB) *1902–1903*
Suffield & Brown, Willesden, London N.W.; Poplar, London E.

Suffield & Brown showed two cars at the Agricultural Hall in 1903, a steam car called the Hythe with a 3-cylinder compound engine, tubular boiler under a bonnet, and chain drive, and a petrol car with a very large 2-cylinder horizontal engine. They also announced that they made electric cars with Joel motors. GNG

1917 NELSON 4-cylinder tourer. *Automotive History Collection, Detroit Public Library*

1897 NESSELSDORF Präsident 5hp four-seater. *Neubauer Collection*

1921 NEW BRITISH 10hp two-seater. *Autocar*

1913 NEW HUDSON 4½hp cyclecar. *M.A.*
Harrison Collection

1900 NEW ORLEANS 7hp voiturette. *G.N.*
Georgano

*c.*1909 ORLEANS 30/40hp landaulette. *National*
Motor Museum

NEW CENTURY (ii) (GB) *1902–1904*

Hoyle Brothers & Co Ltd, Brighouse, Yorks.

Announced in the same year as the previous New Century, the Yorkshire car was a light two-seater with a single-cylinder engine mounted at 25° from the horizontal at the front of the car. Final drive was by chain.   GNG

NEW ENGLAND (i) (US) *1898–1900*

New England Motor Carriage Co, Waltham, Mass.

This was a typical light steam buggy with a vertical 2-cylinder engine, chain drive and tiller steering. It had little to distinguish it from its contemporaries, including two other makes (Waltham and American Waltham) made in the same town at the same time.   GNG

NEW ENGLAND (ii) (US) *1899–1901*

New England Electric Vehicle Co, Boston, Mass.

This company was formed to manufacture electric cars under the patents of the Barrows Vehicle Company of Willimantic, Conn. The design was a 3-wheeler with the single front wheel driving.   GNG

NEW ERA (i) (US) *1902*

The Automobile and Marine Power Co, Camden, N.J.

This was a tiller-steered two-seater buggy, with a 7hp single-cylinder engine under the seat. Drive was by double chain. Its weight was 950lb and its price $850.   GMN

NEW ERA (ii) (US) *1916–1917*

(1) New Era Engineering Co, Joliet, Ill. *1916*
(2) New Era Motors, Inc, Joliet, Ill. *1917*

This light car was made only as a five-seater tourer. It had a 4-cylinder, L-head engine, and was priced at $660.   GMN

NEWEY (GB) *1913–1921*

Gordon Newey Ltd, Birmingham

The Newey company had sold an assembled car, the Newey-Aster in 1907, and in 1913 began to make a small car with a 10hp Aster 4-cylinder engine and conventional design. After the war they re-introduced this model, and added a 12/15hp car with a Chapuis-Dornier engine of 1,750cc. Very few of the post-war cars were made, owing to Mr Newey's failing health. In 1916 Newey announced the G.N.L. car. This had a 4-cylinder 2.4-litre American engine and chassis, and open two- and four-seater bodies made in England.   GNG

NEW HUDSON (GB) *1912–1924*

New Hudson Cycle Co Ltd, Birmingham

Well-known makers of cycles and motorcycles, New Hudson introduced a very small two-seater car with wheels and mudguards which betrayed their bicycle origin very clearly. A 4½hp single-cylinder engine was used, and transmission was by an epicyclic gear.

The post-war New Hudson was a 3-wheeler with an M.A.G. 2-cylinder 8.96hp engine and chain drive.   GNG

NEW IMPERIAL (GB) *1914*

New Imperial Cycles Ltd, Birmingham

The New Imperial was the product of a cycle firm. It used a small 4-cylinder engine of 10hp, a 3-speed gearbox and shaft drive.   GNG

NEWMOBILE (GB) *1906–1907*

Newmobile Ltd, Acton, London W.

This company listed a 24hp 6-cylinder car, but nothing is known of its origin. Small commercial vehicles were also advertised.   GNG

NEW ORLEANS (GB) *1900–1910*

(1) Burford, Van Toll & Co, Twickenham, Middlesex *1900–1901*
(2) New Orleans Motor Co Ltd, Twickenham, Middlesex *1901–1905*
(3) Orleans Motor Co Ltd, Twickenham, Middlesex *1905–1910*

The New Orleans began life as the Belgian Vivinus voiturette built under licence in England. It had a single-cylinder air-cooled engine of 3½hp mounted at the front. Transmission was by belt to fast and loose pulleys on a countershaft, and thence by spur gears to the rear axle. Two forward speeds were provided. This car was first on sale at the beginning of 1900, and before the end of the year it had been supplemented by a 2-cylinder model of 7hp, and otherwise similar layout. In 1901 a completely new 7hp car appeared, with water-cooled engine, conventional clutch and 3-speed gearbox, and shaft drive. The small belt-drive car was still available in 1904, together with a 9hp twin, and 12 and 15hp 4-cylinder cars.

In 1905 the company name was changed to Orleans, and the cars followed suit, although they were occasionally called New Orleans for some time. A 22hp 4-cylinder car was made in 1906, and the first 6-cylinder model, a 35hp, appeared in 1907. In 1909 they were making a 30/40hp 4-cylinder and a 35/45hp 6-cylinder car but very few were sold. As the Orleans became larger it lost its individuality, and one of the 4-cylinder models was anything like as popular as the little belt-drive voiturette had been. GNG

NEW YORK SIX (US) *1928–1929*
1) Automotive Corporation of America, Moline, Ill.
2) New York Motors Corp, Moline, Ill.

The New York Six was a subsidiary car to the Davis (i). Both makes were taken over by the Automotive Corporation of America in order to extend the Davis range. Few of these cars were built. They had a radiator and bonnet louvres similar to the Reo Wolverine car of the same era. KM

NIAGARA (i) (US) *1903–1907*
Wilson Auto Mfg Co, Wilson N.Y.

The two-seater Niagara could be converted into a four-seater car by opening the front to provide an extra seat. It was a tiller-steered car with a single-cylinder, 5hp engine under the seat. With wooden wheels and pneumatic tyres, its appearance was rather primitive. GMN

NIAGARA (ii) (US) *1915–1916*
Mutual Motor Car Co, Buffalo, N.Y.

This was a lightweight five-seater tourer powered by a 36hp 4-cylinder engine. It was of thoroughly conventional design, and cost $740. GNG

NICLAUSSE (F) *1906–1914*
J. et A. Niclausse, Paris 19e

The firm of Niclausse were well-known boiler makers, and cars were never more than a sideline for them. Their first model had a 30/40hp 4-cylinder T-head engine with separately-cast cylinders and shaft drive. This model was continued throughout the maker's lifetime, although the designation changed to 35/50hp later on. Smaller cars of 12/16 and 20/30hp were introduced in 1909, the former a monobloc four, the latter with pair-cast cylinders. These models, too, were continued without major change until 1914. GNG

NIELSON (US) *1907*
Nielson Motor Car Co, Detroit, Mich.

The only model of the Nielson was a two-seater runabout with a single-cylinder 12hp air-cooled engine located behind the seat. With friction transmission and double chain drive, it was priced at $800. GMN

NIKE (i) (E) *1917–1919*
J. Alejandro Riera S. en C., Barcelona

The Nike was designed by Antonia Riera Cordoba, a member of the family of J. Alejandro Riera who were well-known manufacturers of perfume. It was powered by a J.A.R. 12–15hp 4-cylinder engine designed and built by Riera, and had as a mascot a replica of the Winged Victory of Samothrace. A Nike was exhibited at the 1919 Barcelona Show, but not more than five were made in all. GNG

NIKE (ii) (GB) *1968 to date*
Nicholls Engineering & Development Ltd, Bideford, Devon

The name Nike was encountered less frequently than this firm's products, for besides building the Elden chassis, their own later cars were often sold as Bakers, the name of the U.S. importer. A Formula Vee single-seater was the first production Nike, designated Mark 3 in recognition of earlier specials. This was followed by a conventional Formula Ford car, of which some dozen were made. The next five models were a Formula 5000 single-seater, another Formula Ford, a two-seater model, a hill-climb car with N.S.U. Wankel engine, and a Formula F100 machine. Introduced in 1971, a number of the Mark 10 Formula Fords were made in succeeding years. Mark 11 was a monocoque model for Formulae B and 3. DF

NIKKEI–TARO *see* N.J.

NINON (F) *c.1930*
G. Vincent, Nantes

Better-known for their motorcycles, this firm for a brief period marketed a light 3-wheeler, using many cycle parts, which they called the Mototri. In 1946 a more conventional minicar was built, with two-seater body of well-rounded lines, but this model never reached beyond the prototype stage. DF

NISSAN (J) *1937–1943; 1960 to date*
Nissan Motor Co, Ltd, Yokohama

The Nissan Motor Co. was formed in 1934 and continued production of the Datsun, taking over from a previous firm. It was then decided to expand into the field of larger private cars. Assisted by American Graham-Paige technology, the company brought out the Nissan Model 70 five-seater sedan and phaeton in 1937. Machine tools, dies, gauges and related equipment were purchased from G-P, who also supplied Nissan with engine blocks and gave further aid where required. Similar in appearance to the Graham Six sedan of the period, the Nissan was

1907 NICLAUSSE 12/16hp landaulette. *Juan Coma-Cros*

1937 NISSAN Model 70 sedan. *Nissan Motor Co Ltd*

1967 NISSAN Silvia 1.6-litre coupé. *Nissan Motor Co Ltd*

1921 NOMA Six 27hp speedster. *National Motor Museum*

1949 NORDEC 10hp sports car. *Autocar*

1908 NORDENFELT 16hp two-seater. Coachwork by Hewers. *Autocar*

powered by a 6-cylinder, 85hp engine which permitted a speed of 75mph. From 1940 to 1941 a Model 50 series was also built which was more like a German Opel in styling.

Nissan continued to manufacture during World War 2, supplying military equipment to the Japanese armed forces. The marque was temporarily abandoned after the war in favour of manufacture of Datsun vehicles and Austin A40 and A50 cars, built under licence from 1953 to 1960. However, the Patrol, a Jeep-type vehicle, was always sold as a Nissan.

On 1 April 1960 the Nissan name reappeared when the Cedric sedan was announced to replace the Austin. A large car by Japanese standards, the Cedric Special was powered by a 118hp, 2,825cc engine; the Custom and 1900 series contain a 95hp, 4-cylinder ohv engine with a cast-iron block and a 3-bearing crankshaft. At the top of the 1967 range was the 4-litre President V-8.

Nissan took over Prince Motors in 1966, and the two ranges were rationalized. Yue Loong have made Nissan products under licence in Taiwan since 1958. The Nissan group's heavier commercial vehicles invariably carry the Nissan name, but since the spread of Japan's export drive in the middle 1960s the tendency has been to sell private cars as Datsuns, and in some markets (notably Britain) even the larger 6-cylinder machines are Datsuns rather than Nissans. The later models are described under Datsun. BE

N.J. (J) 1954–1956
Nippon Keijidosha Co, Kawaguchi, Saitama

Also known as the Nikkei-Taro, the N.J. was a small roadster with a two-cylinder 12hp air-cooled engine. The company also built small commercial vehicles for a few years. BE

NOBEL *see* FULDAMOBIL

NOBLE (US) 1902
Noble Automobile Mfg Co, Cleveland, Ohio

Two models of the Noble were made, a 6hp single-cylinder runabout, and a 10hp 2-cylinder touring car. Both had 2 forward speeds and chain drive. GNG

NOËL (F) 1913–c.1921
Lucien Noël, Courbevoie, Seine

The pre-war Noël was a tandem-seated cyclecar steered from the rear seat. It had an 8.9hp 2-cylinder engine, and an underslung chassis. One was driven by its designer in the 1913 Cyclecar Grand Prix at Le Mans. It did not distinguish itself, but in the 1920 Cyclecar Grand Prix a Noël came third. The production car of the 1920s had side-by-side seating with a 4-cylinder 904cc Ruby engine. GNG

NOËL BENET (F) 1900
Noël Benet, Offranville, Seine-Maritime

The Noël Benet was a two-seater voiturette powered by a single-cylinder De Dion engine driving the front wheels. One survives, in the Musée de l'Automobile at Rochetaillée-sur-Saône. GNG

NOMA (US) 1919–1923
Noma Motors Corp, New York, N.Y.

Although the Noma was an assembled car, with a choice of Continental or Beaver 6-cylinder engines available, it was attactively low-slung and sporty with a distinctive oval radiator and wire wheels. Open and closed models were produced, all of them equipped with individual step plates in place of running boards. Several hundred cars were built by Noma during five years of production. KM

NOMAD (GB) 1967 to date
Nomad Cars, Hastings, Sussex

Mark Konig's 1966 Nomad Group 6 sports-racing prototype used a 2-litre B.R.M. V-8 engine and had a long and distinguished career in international events. Replicas of the Mark 2 of 1969, similarly clothed with Williams and Pritchard fibreglass body, were also advertised for public sale. Designer Bob Curl achieved more success producing the Gropa in conjunction with Andrew Mylius, this being a conversion of the old B8 Chevron to Group 6 specification. The Nomad was revived by Mike Adda with a smaller car for 1972, the Mark 3B with BDA 1300 engine, and there was also a side-radiatored Formula Ford project. DF

NO NAME *see* HORLEY

NORCROSS (US) c.1907
United Electrical Mfg Co, Norcross, Ga.

This car is something of a mystery as it was offered for sale only through local advertisements. The 1907 versions were four- and five-seater touring cars, and a roadster with a price range of $800 to $850. GMN

NORDEC (GB) 1949
North Downs Engineering Co, Whyteleafe, Surrey

The Nordec company were sole manufacturers of the Ballamy patented suspension and Marshall-Nordec (Roots-type) superchargers. Both of these were incorporated in the Nordec car, which had a Ford 10 engine in a modified Ford 8 chassis with independent front suspension. The two-seater body was slightly like a scaled-down Allard, but rather high in appearance. A lower model was scheduled for production and sale at an intended price of £650 including purchase tax.   GNG

NORDEN (S) *1902–1906*
AB Södertälje Verkstäder, Södertälje
This was the name given to the Northern of Detroit assembled in Sweden. It was a two-seater buggy with a 5hp single-cylinder engine and two forward and reverse speeds.   OB

NORDENFELT (B) *1906–1909*
The Nordenfelt used engines by Barriquand et Marre, and was reported to have all other components made by John Cockerill of Liège, although the latter firm have always denied their connection with this, or any other, car. It first appeared at Olympia in 1906 with a 24/30hp 4-cylinder engine and conventional chassis with shaft drive. Bodies were by Hewers, Withers and other coachbuilders. Later models included a 30/35 and 40/45.   GNG

NORFOLK (GB) *1904–1905*
A. Blackburn & Co, Cleckheaton, Yorks.
The Norfolk was made in two models, a 10hp and a 12hp, differing only in the cylinder bore (88mm and 95mm respectively, the stroke of both models being 120mm). They had 2-cylinder engines, 3-speed gearboxes and chain drive. Only about 12 were made, of which one survives.   GNG

NORIS (D) *1902–1904*
Süddeutsche Motorwagen-Industrie Noris Gebr. Bauer, Nuremberg
Three different models were available with proprietary engines of French origin. A single-cylinder 6PS, a 2-cylinder 12PS and a 4-cylinder 24PS car were listed.   HON

NORMA (GB) *1912–1914*
Norma Motor & Engineering Co Ltd, Hammersmith, London W.
The Norma was a conventional shaft-driven light car powered by a 4-cylinder 10½hp engine. The makers had previously announced the Pinnace, a most unusual cyclecar with a stream-lined boat-shaped body, and rear-mounted J.A.P. V-twin engine. One of these ran in the 1912 London-Exeter trial, but not many of them were sold.   GNG

NORRIS (GB) *1914*
Stockport Garage Co, Stockport, Cheshire
The Norris light car was powered by a 4-cylinder engine of 966cc. It had 3 speeds and shaft drive, and sold for 165 guineas. This price included genuine leather upholstery.   GNG

NORSK (N) *1908–1911*
Norsk Automobil & Vognfabrik AS, Oslo
This company made a small number of single-cylinder 8hp cars with friction drive, and one 4-cylinder tourer.   OB

NORSK GEIJER (N) *1926–1930*
AS C. Geijer & Co, Oslo
The Geijer company was a well-known coachbuilding firm which built the first Norwegian bus bodies in 1921. In the late 1920s they assembled a small number of cars (less than 20) using Lycoming engines and hydraulic 4-wheel brakes. The largest model had a straight-8 65bhp engine and a wheelbase of 10ft 7in, but a 4-cylinder car was also made.   OB

NORTH BRITISH *see* DRUMMOND (i)

NORTHERN (US) *1902–1909*
(1) Northern Mfg Co, Detroit, Mich. *1902–1905*
(2) Northern Motor Car Co, Detroit, Mich. *1906–1909*
The Northern company was founded by two ex-Oldsmobile engineers, J.D. Maxwell and C.B. King. Their first and most popular car was the Silent Northern, a single-cylinder two-seater runabout not unlike the Oldsmobile, but with a straight dash. These cars were made under licence in Sweden as the Norden. Bonnetted, flat-twins were sold from 1904 and in 1906 King designed a 4-cylinder 18hp car with air-operated brakes and clutch. In 1908 he left the company – later to make the King (ii) car – and in 1909 Northern merged with E.M.F.   GMN

NORTH-LUCAS (GB) *1923*
Robin Hood Engineering Works, Putney, London S.W.15
The North-Lucas Radial was an experimental vehicle made by R. Lucas, who

1908 NORSK 4-cylinder tourer. *Oluf Berrum*

1928 NORSK GEIJER straight-8 saloon. *Oluf Berrum*

515

1920 NORTH STAR 4hp cyclecar. *Autocar*

1914 N.S.U. 8/14PS tourer. *Neubauer Collection*

1958 N.S.U. Prinz 598cc saloon. *N.S.U. Werke AG*

had designed the Lucas Valveless car, and O.D. North. The design was based on that of Edmund Rumpler's Tropfenwagen. The unit-construction body and chassis was clad in a streamlined envelope of aluminium and fabric. At the rear was a 5-cylinder air-cooled radial engine of 1½ litres, while the suspension at each end was independent, by coil springs around hydraulic shock absorbers. TRN

NORTH STAR (GB) *1920–1921*
North Star Works, Lee Green, London S.E.

The North Star was a very small cyclecar using a 4hp single-cylinder Blackburne engine, a gradua gear and single belt drive. The price was £159, low for the inflationary post-war period, and the car was sold by Sir J.F. Payne-Gallwey, Brown & Co Ltd, who also handled the Edmond and Swallow light cars. GNG

NORTHWAY (US) *1921*
Northway Motor Sales Co, Natick, Mass.

The Northway was built for a few months only by the parent truck concern of the same name. Resembling the Roamer or Kenworthy, the car carried a Rolls-Royce-type radiator and used a Northway 6-cylinder engine. A roadster, a touring car and sedan priced from $4,200 to $5,200 constituted the range. Individual mudguards with step plates were substituted for running boards. Several were made and marketed before production was discontinued. KM

NORTHWESTERN *see* HAASE

NORTON (GB) *1913*
Tom Norton Ltd, Llandrindod Wells, Radnorshire

No connection with Norton motorcycles, this was an unconventional cyclecar which had two separate sidecar bodies. A front-mounted V-twin air-cooled engine drove through epicyclic gears and shaft to the rear axle. Very few were made as the firm encountered manufacturing difficulties. GNG

NORWALK (US) *1910–1922*
(1) Norwalk Motor Car Co, Norwalk, Ohio *1910–1911*
(2) Norwalk Motor Car Co, Martinsburg, W. Va. *1911–1922*

The Norwalk's most distinguishing feature (up to 1916) was its underslung frame. The first model used a 4-cylinder, 4.1-litre engine. This grew to a long, low and formidable car with a 4-speed transmission and direct drive in third gear, powered by a 6-cylinder engine of 8.6 litres. With a six-seater touring body its cost was $3,750. Smaller models with 35hp to 45hp engines were also built up to 1916. The Norwalk cars manufactured after 1918 were of standard size with 3.1-litre, 6-cylinder engines. A five-seater touring car was priced at $975. See also Stork Kar. GMN

NOTA (AUS) *1971 to date*
Nota Engineering Pty Ltd, Parramatta, N.S.W.

The Type IV, sold in Britain as the Nota Fang, sported a transverse rear-mounted B.L.M.C. engine in a tubular steel chassis, with low-drag fibreglass body. Weight was a mere 1,064lb and overall height exactly 3ft. DF

NOVARA (US) *1917*
Herreshoff Mfg Co, Bristol, R.I.

The Novara was a magnificent two-seater runabout with a body of mahogany. The influence of yacht design, the main business of Herreshoff Manufacturing Co, is evident in the appearance of the Novara. Its 4-cylinder engine with overhead valves was rated at 37hp and was built by the American & British Manufacturing Co, Bridgeport, Conn., which later made the Porter (ii). There was no connection with the Herreshoff car. GMN

NOWA (D) *1924–1926*
Nowa-Werk, Nowawes, Potsdam

This small firm produced two models of light cars, a 5/18PS 1.3-litre and a 6/28PS 1.58-litre, but both of them in small numbers only. HON

N.P. (GB) *1923–1925*
S.L.C. Co Ltd, Newport Pagnell, Bucks.

The N.P. was made by a subsidiary of Salmons & Sons Ltd, the coachbuilders. 11.9hp and 13.9hp Meadows ohv engines were used in a thoroughly conventional chassis. Bodies were open two- and four-seaters, and were, naturally, made by Salmons. A total of 395 cars were made in three years, but costs were too high to show a profit, and the Salmons Light Car Company was wound up. GNG

N.S.U. (D) *1905 to date*
(1) Neckarsulmer Fahrradwerke AG, Neckarsulm *1905–1910*
(2) Neckarsulmer Fahrzeugwerke AG, Neckarsulm; Heilbronn *1910–1931*
(3) NSU-Werke AG, Neckarsulm *1958–1969*
(4) Audi N.S.U. Auto Union AG, Neckarsulm *1969 to date*

N.S.U. were already important producers of bicycles and motorcycles when they started car manufacture in 1905 by building Pipes under licence. Cars of their own design appeared in 1906. These were 4-cylinder models of 6/10PS and 15/24PS and in the following years N.S.U. concentrated very successfully on small cars. A very popular car was the 5/12PS 1,132cc model which was produced until 1914 and in improved 5/15PS and 5/20PS forms until after World War 1. There was also a 1,100cc verticle twin in 1909, and some bigger N.S.U.'s with 2.6-litre and 3.3-litre engines. During the post-war years N.S.U. were quite successful in sporting events with their 5/20PS 1.3-litre and 6-cylinder 6/30PS 1.6-litre sv sports models; the latter was also available with Roots blower. The newly built factory at Heilbronn was sold to Fiat in 1930 and production of cars was given up a year later. Production of motor cycles was carried on in the Neckarsulm factory.

In 1958 N.S.U. decided to take up car production again and presented the Prinz, a small rear-engined car with a 20bhp (later 30 bhp) ohc air-cooled vertical twin engine of 598cc, and all wheels were independently sprung. It was also available as the Sport Prinz with a 30bhp engine and G.T. coupé body. Larger cars on similar lines were produced during the following years: the 4-cylinder models 1000 (990cc) and 110 (1,085cc). By 1967 the 1-litre TTS version offered 70bhp and 95mph.

An important N.S.U. development was the first Wankel-engined car. The first model with this rotary engine was the Spider, a roadster version of the Sport Prinz. The Wankel engine developed 50bhp from what was assessed as the equivalent of 500cc capacity. A legal dispute arose between N.S.U. and N.S.U.-Fiat after the former's resumption of car production over the use of the name N.S.U. on cars. A final agreement was reached in 1966 when N.S.U.-Fiat gave up all claims to the designation N.S.U. and adopted the name Neckar instead. New for 1968 was the fwd twin-Wankel Ro 80 saloon with a capacity equivalent to 2 litres. This advanced car featured alternator ignition, a 3-speed semi-automatic gearbox with central change, power-assisted steering, all-independent coil springing, and disc brakes at front and rear. It was expensive (DM17,300 in 1972), but top speed was 108 mph, and over 12,000 found buyers in the first 18 months. The K70, a projected development with manual gearbox and orthodox ohc 4-cylinder engine, was shelved, and did not reappear until 1971, when it emerged under the Volkswagen emblem. This was the result of the 1969 merger with Audi, which brought N.S.U. under VW control. Development of the older rear-engined types continued; most potent of the 1972 range was the 1,177cc TT, capable of 96mph, but all these models were phased out in the latter part of 1972, leaving the Ro 80 to carry on a famous name.   HON

N.S.U.-FIAT (D) 1930–1966
(1) NSU-Automobil AG, Heilbronn 1929–1959
(2) Neckar Automobilwerk AG, Heilbronn 1959–1966
In 1930 Fiat acquired the newly erected N.S.U. plant at Heilbronn and started to assemble cars there for the German market. First model to be produced was the 2½-litre 521 (1930–3), but other pre-war types turned out were the 508, 1500, 508C and 500; this last was offered as a fabric coupé and a sports two-seater as well as with standard Italian bodywork.

After World War 2 the German Fiat Company (Deutsche Fiat AG) started to sell original imported Fiat cars on the German market, while the Heilbronn works assembled various models not only for Germany, but also special versions for export, which were not officially in the Fiat programme. These were the N.S.U.-Fiat Weinsberg 500 two-seater Limousette and Coupé, the N.S.U.-Fiat Jagst 770 Riviera Spyder and Riviera Coupé with bodies by Vignale, and the Neckar 850 Adria saloon. Fiat-based cars sold on the German market by the organization included the Bianchina 500, Bianchina Panoramica and Autobianchi Primula. After the resumption of car production by N.S.U. a dispute arose over the use of N.S.U. as a brand-name for cars. As a result N.S.U.-Fiat changed their name to Neckar in 1959, but were allowed to continue marketing their cars under both names. Then in 1966 N.S.U.-Fiat relinquished all claims to the name of N.S.U. and all their cars have subsequently been sold as Neckars.   HON

NUG (D) 1921–1925
Nug-Kraftfahrzeugwerke Niebaum, van Horn & Co, Herford
This small make was not widely known, although it took part in some race meetings. The engine was 4-cylinder 960cc ioe engine, developing 18bhp at 2,100rpm. Maximum speed was 50mph. Saloon and open models were made, and the cars had V-radiators and wire wheels.   HON

NU-KLEA STARLITE (US) 1959–1960
Nu-Klea Automobile Corp, Lansing, Mich.
A 2,100lb electrically powered two-seater car with a plastic body and two motors driving the rear wheels.   BE

NYBERG (US) 1912–1914
(1) Nyberg Automobile Works, Anderson, Ind. 1912
(2) Nyberg Automobile Works, Indianapolis, Ind. 1913–1914
The Nyberg was made in as many as four different models, ranging up to the Model 6-45. This was a seven-seater which used a 6-cylinder 5.4-litre engine and cost $2,100.   GMN

1968 N.S.U. Ro.80 saloon. *N.S.U. Werke AG*

1939 N.S.U.-FIAT 500 sports car. *Autocar*

1960 N.S.U.-FIAT Weinsberg 500 coupé. *Neckar Automobilwerk AG*

1911 OAKLAND 25hp tourer. *Don McCray*

1924 OAKLAND 6-54 sedan. *General Motors Corporation*

1962 OGLE SX-1000 998cc coupé. *David Ogle Ltd*

OAKLAND (US) *1907–1931*

Oakland Motor Car Co, Pontiac, Mich.

The original Oakland was the work of A.P. Brush, designer both of the original single-cylinder Cadillac and of the Brush Runabout. It was a 2½-litre vertical-twin with planetary transmission, selling for $1,300. The power unit rotated anti-clockwise. In 1909, when General Motors took over, the company was also marketing a conventional 4-cylinder car with sliding-type gearbox at $1,600. For the next few years fours were the staple product, 3.3- and 4.4-litre engines being used in 1912. 1913 Oaklands had rounded-V radiators reminiscent of the Belgian Métallurgique, and were made in 4- and 6-cylinder forms with electric lighting and starting. Left-hand drive was adopted in 1915, when the bigger '6-49' model used a Northway engine. Four models – a 5½-litre V-8, two sixes, and a four – were offered in 1916, in which year the firm's own small ohv 6-cylinder unit appeared. This was in a car modestly priced at $795, of which Oakland sold over 35,000 in 1917. From 1919 to 1923, this ohv car was the only model listed, but in 1924 the firm brought out a new and inexpensive sv six which offered both front wheel brakes and Duco cellulose finish for $995. 1926 saw the introduction of the companion make, Pontiac, but unlike other makers' cheap lines this rapidly overshadowed the Oakland, sales of which dropped from some 58,000 in 1926 to 30,826 in 1929.

An inexpensive sv V-8 on the lines of Oldsmobile's Viking was introduced as a replacement for the six in 1930, but demand continued to fall and after 1931 only Pontiacs were made.   MCS

O'CONNOR (US) *1916*

O'Connor Corp, Chicago, Ill.

The O'Connor was offered in six different models. The larger models used 25hp 6-cylinder engines. The prices ranged from $755 to $985.   GMN

OCTO (F) *1921–1928*

L. Vienne, Courbevoie, Seine

The original Octo light car used a 1.6-litre Ballot 4-cylinder engine, and friction transmission. It was replaced in 1922 by a car with a conventional gearbox and 972cc Ruby sv engine. An ohv version of this was used to power a sports model with flared wings, and in 1926 front-wheel brakes were added. For the last two years of its life the Octo used a slightly larger Ruby engine of 1,097cc   GNG

O.D. (D) *1933*

O.D. Werke, Dresden

This company was mainly known for their 3-wheeled delivery vans and trucks, but they made a few 'combination cars' for four passengers or goods, powered by D.K.W. or Ilo engines. These were mounted directly above the single front wheel.   GNG

ODELOT (US) *1915*

Lawrence Stamping Co, Toledo, Ohio

The Odelot (Toledo in reverse) was a two-seater runabout, with a 4-cylinder 20hp engine. It was equipped with bucket seats and wire wheels. This car sold for $450 with a black bonnet and mudguards, and a choice of green, red or yellow cowl and seats.   GMN

ODETTI (I) *1922–1923*

SA Automobile Odetti, Milan

The Odetti was a light car powered by a 10hp 2-cylinder 2-stroke engine of the company's own design. It had integral construction of body and chassis, and shaft drive. Very few were made, as it hardly passed the prototype stage.   GNG

OFELDT (US) *1899–c.1902*

F.W. Ofeldt & Sons, Nyack-on-the-Hudson, N.Y.

Made by a company well-known for their steam launches, the Ofeldt steamer had a V-twin engine and tiller steering. Later the company built a 4-cylinder steam engine and fitted it to a delivery wagon, but it is not certain how many private cars were actually built.   GNG

OGLE (GB) *1961–1964*

David Ogle Ltd, Letchworth, Herts.

This firm at first consisted mainly of an industrial design team, undertaking

pecial one-piece fibreglass bodies as a sideline. The 'production' $1\frac{1}{2}$-litre used
mechanical parts from an integral-construction Riley, with the basic platform
reinforced by a tubular structure developed by Tojeiro, carrying coil rear suspension
and a 4-seater GT saloon body. In 1962 this was replaced by the SX1000 B.M.C.
Mini-based car. Production of this luxurious little two/four-seater rose to six
weekly in 1963, and continued for a while after David Ogle's death in a road
accident. The design was later revived as the Fletcher G.T. Ogle also built two
examples of the SX250, a GT coupé powered by the $2\frac{1}{2}$-litre Daimler V-8 engine.
The body design of this car was later used for the Reliant Scimitar. DF

OGREN (US) 1915–1923
1) Ogren Motor Car Co, Chicago, Ill. 1915
2) Ogren Motor Works, Chicago, Ill; Waukegan, Ill. 1916
3) Ogren Motor Car Co, Milwaukee, Wisc. 1916–1923
Designed by Hugo W. Ogren, this was a high-quality car powered by a 6-cylinder
Continental engine of over 5 litres' capacity. Priced at $4,375 for the tourer,
it had attractive lines with individual door steps. In 1922 a new company,
Commander Motors Corp., was formed to build a new car called the Commander,
also designed by Hugo Ogren, but none appeared. GNG

OHIO (i) (US) 1909–1913
1) Jewel Carriage Co, Cincinnati, Ohio 1909–1912
2) Ohio Motor Car Co, Cincinnati, Ohio 1912
3) Crescent Motor Co, Cincinnati, Ohio 1913
The Ohio used a 40hp 4-cylinder engine for most of its models. Seven body
styles were offered in one year on a chassis using shaft drive and with a wheelbase of 9ft 7in. GMN

OHIO (ii) (US) 1910–1918
Ohio Electric Car Co, Toledo, Ohio
The Ohio electric car used Crocker-Wheeler motors, with 4-speed controllers.
Steering in all models was by tiller and pneumatic tyres were fitted. As many as
four closed models were offered in a year. GMN

OHTA (J) 1922; 1934–1957
1) Ohta Jidosha Seizosho Co, Ltd, Tokyo 1922; 1934–1935
2) Kosoku Kikan Kogyo Co, Ltd, Tokyo 1935–1945
3) Ohta Jidosha Kogyo Co, Ltd, Tokyo 1947–1957
Ohta was once one of the largest car firms in Japan. A two-door, four-seater
tourer, Model OS, was built as a prototype in 1922 but it was not until 1934 that
the first production Ohta was marketed. The 1934 Ohta was powered by a 4-cylinder
side-valve engine of 736cc and this remained the basic power unit through the
pre-war years. With financial aid from Mitsui, the company was able to produce a
number of body styles including sedans, tourers, roadsters and trucks. Model OC
was built in 1936 and an improved Model OD was made from 1937–39.
After the war Model PA was introduced and many were used as taxis. This
car was a four-seater with independent suspension and a 4-cylinder L-head engine
of 23hp providing 47mph. Model OE was another four-door, 4-cylinder machine
with a body reminiscent of the British Sunbeam-Talbot.
A rather unusual model was the VK-2 that combined a pickup body with a
five passenger club coupé. It contained a 4-cylinder unit giving 45hp. One of
the last Ohtas was Model PK-1. This was a small four-door sedan with a pressed
rail chassis and a wheelbase of 84.5in. A 4-cylinder sv engine of 25hp at 4,000rpm
drove it at 60mph.
Kurogane absorbed Ohta in 1957 and discontinued car production although
Ohta trucks continued for a few more years. BE

OKEY (US) 1907–1908
Okey Motor Car Co, Columbus, Ohio
The Okey runabout was powered by a 2-stroke, 3-cylinder engine of 2.6 litres.
This was claimed to produce 22hp at 1,300rpm. The car used a planetary trans-
mission and shaft drive. GMN

OLD MILL (GB) 1914
Albert Lambourne Ltd, Brighton, Sussex
The Old Mill was named after Old Mill Works, built on the site of Black Mill
which was demolished in 1906. It was a quality light car powered by a 10hp Dorman
engine. The car had exceptionally long $\frac{1}{4}$-elliptic springs at the front, and a
mechanical starter operated from the dashboard. It was expensive at £220 for an
open two-seater, and only 13 cars were made. GNG

OLDSMOBILE (US) 1896 to date
(1) Olds Motor Works, Lansing, Mich. 1896–1943
(2) Oldsmobile Division of General Motors Corp, Lansing, Mich. 1943 to date
Ransom Eli Olds built an experimental three-wheeled steam car in 1891, following
this six years later with a single-cylinder petrol-engined vehicle of dogcart type.
He then made a small number of electric cars, before producing his famous Curved

1912 OHIO(ii) electric brougham. *William S. Jackson*

1936 OHTA Model OS 736cc tourer. *Shotaro Kobayashi Collection*

1914 OLD MILL 10hp coupé. *National Motor Museum*

1903 OLDSMOBILE 5hp curved-dash runabout. *The Veteran Car Club of Great Britain*

1916 OLDSMOBILE 6-cylinder sedan. (This was the one millionth General Motors car). *General Motors Corporation*

1937 OLDSMOBILE L-37 4.2-litre sedan. *Harley J. Usill*

1946 OLDSMOBILE 76 3.9-litre sedan. *G.N. Georgano*

1966 OLDSMOBILE Tornado 7-litre coupé. *General Motors Corporation*

Dash Runabout, the world's first mass-production automobile. This consisted of a very short and simple buggy-type chassis with two long springs serving as auxiliary side-members, on which was mounted a single-cylinder moiv engine of 1.6 litres' capacity, with trembler coil ignition, a 2-speed epicyclic transmission, and central chain drive. The engine possessed an immense silencer and turned at 500rpm – 'one chug per telegraph pole'. Despite a fire at the factory in March 1901, which destroyed everything except a single prototype, the little Olds was an instant success, 2,100 being sold in 1902 and 5,000 in 1904. Though at its best as a town runabout, it made a number of epic runs, notably Whitman's and Hammond's drive from San Francisco to New York in 1903. This type of car was made under licence in Germany as the Polymobil, and Ultramobil.

By 1904 Ransom Olds had left to found the Reo company and the Oldsmobile started to grow up. Dummy-bonnetted versions were available in 1905. These were followed by a twin-cylinder 2-stroke car with frontal engine and a conventional gearbox selling for $1,250, and by the Palace touring car, a four of square cylinder dimensions which combined pressure lubrication and automatic inlet valves. Oldsmobiles grew bigger and bigger; by 1908 the smallest was a 3½-litre four and the largest a six of over 8 litres' capacity, and this trend was not reversed when General Motors took over in 1909. Compressed-air starters were available in 1911 and the 1912 line was obviously designed for the carriage trade, being headed by the immense Limited, with a 6-cylinder 11½-litre engine, a wheelbase of 11ft 6in, wooden wheels of 43in diameter and a top speed of over 70mph, all for $5,000. Even the baby of the family, the 4-cylinder Defender had a capacity of 5 litres and cost $3,000, while all the range boasted 4-speed gearboxes. Oldsmobiles were a little smaller at 7 litres in 1914 and had acquired Delco electric lighting and starting, though right hand drive was retained.

The company did not return to prosperity until the following year, when a modestly-priced sv 4-cylinder 42 with streamlined dash was marketed and over 7,500 were sold. This was followed in 1916 by an sv V-8 with a Fiat-like radiator selling at about $1,500, which Oldsmobile continued to offer until 1923. They also listed both a 2.8-litre six and an ohv Northway-engined four in the early 1920s. In 1924 only the six was available, and a wide range of 'sport equipment' (such as trunk bars and step plates) was advertised. Over 44,000 were sold, and tourers were listed at $785. Mechanical pump feed and front-wheel brakes followed in 1927 and bodies were restyled in 1928.

Sales climbed to over 100,000 in 1929, in which year Oldsmobile launched the abortive 8-cylinder Viking. Synchromesh was available in 1931, and a 3.9-litre straight-8 closely resembling the Buick in outward appearance joined the range in 1932. 1934 cars had independent front suspension, and turret top styling characterized the 1935 models. In 1938, when a 6-cylinder sedan could be bought for $967, Oldsmobile became the first of the G.M. group to offer the option of an automatic gearbox, evolved by 1914 into the famous Hydramatic. 273,000 cars were sold in 1941.

Oldsmobile became G.M.'s technical leader after World War 2; Hydramatic was optional on all models in 1946 and in 1948 the company's official half-centenary was made the occasion to give the cars 'Futuramic' styling, a preview of what G.M.'s other cars were to look like in 1949. Oldsmobile's 1949 4.9-litre ohv oversquare Rocket V-8 was the first of its kind to appear, and by 1951 the old sixes had been dropped altogether. The Rocket was giving 202bhp in 1955 and 305bhp from 6.1 litres in 1958. In this year G.M.'s X-frame was standardized, air suspension was optional, the cars came in two wheelbase lengths and manual transmission was available only on the cheaper models.

Oldsmobile's compact, the F-85 of 1961, was an interesting car with unitary construction, coil springing all round, a 9ft 4in wheelbase and an aluminium V-8 of only 3½ litres' capacity, developing 155bhp. Fastest of the full-size V-8s was the Starfire convertible with 330bhp, while a sporting version of the F-85 came out the following year in the shape of the Cutlass. In 1963 there was a companion Jetfire model, capable of 110mph, and listed at $3,633 with a turbo-supercharger. The aluminium V-8 was replaced on 1964 model F-85s by Buick's V-6, and a Jetstar line of economy cars was evolved by fitting a modestly-rated 8-cylinder engine in the regular chassis. 1966 Oldsmobiles covered a wide range from the small six up to V-8s of 383bhp, but the Division achieved a real technical breakthrough once more with the big Toronado coupé. This had front wheel drive and Hydramatic transmission, and was powered by the most potent version of Oldsmobile's 7-litre engine. The 1968 models were made in various capacities up to 7½ litres. The largest ones had automatic transmission and power steering as standard, and the 442 with 360bhp 6,555cc V-8 engine and 4-speed manual gearbox represented the fashionable sporting image. By 1971 the Cutlass Supreme, 88, 98 and Cruiser station wagons had acquired front disc brakes, but a year later even the Toronado boasted no more than 265bhp. The same basic range was still available in 1973, with single headlamps and front disc brakes standardized on the Cutlass along with the new GM energy-absorbing front bumper. New to Oldsmobile was a compact, the Omega with 3-speed manual box and drum brakes. Engine options were a 4,097cc six or a 5,735cc V-8.   MCS

OLIVER (US) *1905*

Oliver Trackless Car Co, South Bend, Ind.

The car was a five-seater, with side-entrance. The power came from a 700cc 2-cylinder engine under the bonnet, driving the rear axle by chain. Its cost was $1,500, with a weight given as 1,750lb.   GMN

OLYMPIAN (US) *1917–1921*
Olympian Motors Co, Pontiac, Mich.

The Olympian was an assembled car with a 4-cylinder engine. Two models were available, a touring car and a four-seater roadster, designated as the Tourist and the Gypsy respectively, both of which sold at $695.   KM

O.M. (I) *1918–1934*
(1) SA Officine Meccaniche, Brescia *1918–1928*
(2) O.M. Fabbrica Bresciana di Automobili, Brescia *1928–1934*

The Officine Meccaniche was a locomotive-building firm that absorbed Züst in 1918, and continued the production of that firm's 4.7-litre sv 4-cylinder 25/35hp until 1923. Alongside this, however, they introduced their own designs, with conventional sv monobloc engines, detachable heads, 12-volt coil ignition, thermo-syphon cooling, and single-plate clutches. They were the work of an Austrian named Barratouché and changed little with the years, so much so that it is true that only one O.M. theme reached the public – first as a four, and then as the famous 2-litre 6-cylinder Superba. The company showed, but did not market, a 3-litre straight-8 development in 1928. First of the series was the 465, a 1,327cc four rated at 12/15hp in Italy. Output was 18bhp and there were three forward speeds. In 1921 came the 1,410cc 467, and a year later this gave way to the 1½-litre 469, available from the start with 4-wheel brakes and very successful in Italian sporting events. It survived until the end in 1934, some models having magneto ignition; in its final form, the 469S4 of 1930, it had a 1.7-litre engine, though by this time it was usually seen in light commercial guise. The 2-litre six was first marketed in 1923, always with 4-wheel brakes and (until 1925) with straight bevel back axle. Initially developing a modest 40bhp, it was giving 60bhp in single-carburettor touring form by 1926, and sports models were capable of 75mph. Competition successes included the 1925 Tripoli GP; 4th at Le Mans in 1925 and 1926; and a victory for Minoia and Morandi in the first Mille Miglia of 1927.

In 1926 O.M. built a dohc straight-8 for the 1,500cc Grand Prix Formula, but its 3-speed gearbox was against it, and its best showing was a 2nd place in the 1927 European GP. The 665 was extensively modified for the British market by Rawlences, the concessionaires in London, and cars appeared with dual ignition, 12-plug heads of Ricardo type, 4-speed gearboxes of E.N.V. make with right-hand change, and Dewandre servo brakes. In 1929 Rawlence produced an ohv conversion with three carburettors and dual ignition that ran in the T.T. and the Double-Twelve. It was catalogued in England, though never in Italy, where in the same year some works-built supercharged 80bhp sv machines appeared with raked radiators and underslung frames, followed by improved 1930 versions on which capacity was increased to 2,350cc. This model was not offered to the public, though standard 1930 O.M.s had 2.2-litre engines; this size persisted until 1934 and supercharged sports editions were also listed.

Though O.M.s could still race to some purpose (there was a 2nd in the 1931 Mille Miglia), the emphasis was shifting towards commercial vehicles powered by Saurer diesel engines made under licence, and in 1930 the stock of private cars on hand was sold to the Esperia concern, run by two former O.M. executives, Coletta and Mangano. It seems unlikely that they built any vehicles, and when Fiat acquired O.M. in 1933 the private cars were doomed.

Curiously, a new design was announced in 1934; this one, the OMV or Alcyone, had synchromesh, hydraulic brakes, and overhead exhaust valves, but though it did the round of the shows, it was not made in series. A 1½-litre ohc four designed by Olivo Pellegatti did not even get off the drawing-board. O.M. still exist as makers of trucks, tractors and railway rolling-stock, but since 1968 they have been a *sezione* of Fiat.   MCS

OMAHA (US) *1912–1913*
Omaha Motor Car Co, Omaha, Nebr.

The only unusual feature of this make was its underslung frame. It used an L-head 4-cylinder engine of 3.8 litres, with shaft drive. Both roadster and seven-seater bodies were mounted on a chassis with a wheelbase of 9ft 10in. Another Omaha was listed as having been made in 1899, but details are not known.   GMN

OMÉGA (i) (F) *1900*
Kreutzberger Frères, Paris

The Oméga voiturette was made in two models, with 3½hp or 5hp engines. They were both single-cylinder horizontal units, with opposed pistons in the style of the Gobron-Brillié. The two crankshafts were geared to a common shaft from which final drive was by chain.   GNG

OMEGA (ii) (d) *1921–1922*
Omega Kleinautobau GmbH, Berlin-Charlottenburg

A small 3/10PS 4-cylinder model was produced by this firm. In 1922 it was renamed the Omikron.   HON

1973 OLDSMOBILE Omega 4.1-litre coupé.
General Motors Corporation

1930 O.M. 2.2-litre sports car. Coachwork by Zagato. *G.N. Georgano*

1931 O.M. Superba Tipo 665 2.2-litre saloon.
Museo dell'Automobile, Turin

1928 OMÉGA(iii) Six 3-litre sports car. *Musée de l'Automobile, Le Mans*

1909 OMNIA 15/20hp landaulette. *C. Poel Jr*

1903 ONFRAY 10hp tonneau. *The Veteran Car Club of Great Britain*

OMÉGA (iii) (F) *1922–1930*
Automobiles Oméga-Six, Boulogne-sur-Seine

The Oméga-Six, designed by Gadoux, was a beautifully-made, advanced car that made its bow at the 1922 Paris Salon. The maker's object was to provide a miniature modern luxury car on the lines of the Hispano-Suiza, an intention reflected in the design. The 11 CV, 6-cylinder, 2-litre engine had a single overhead camshaft, there was a 3-speed gearbox, and front-wheel brakes were fitted. Later models had a 3-litre engine, a 4-speed gearbox and a 2-speed axle for fast cruising. Not many of the Oméga-Six were made: presumably those who could afford Hispano-Suiza prices preferred to buy the famous name itself. TRN

OMEGA (iv) *see* PREMIER (iii)

OMEGA (v) (GB) *1925–1927*
W.J. Green Ltd, Coventry, Warwickshire

Made by the firm who produced the Omega motorcycle, this £90 3-wheeler had a 980cc J.A.P. engine, driving the rear wheel by chain. GNG

OMEGA (vi) (US) *1966–1967*
Suspensions International Corp, Charlotte, N.C.

Steve Wilder took over the former Griffith project and renamed the cars Omega. With 5-litre Ford V-8 engine and all-steel body by Intermeccanica of Turin, they were assembled first in the tuning shops of Holman & Moody, and later in a hangar at Charlotte Municipal Airport. In 1967 Frank Reisner of Intermeccanica concentrated all production in Italy, and renamed the cars Intermeccanica Torino. GNG

OMIKRON (D) *1922–1925*
(1) Omikron Kleinautobau GmbH, Berlin-Charlottenburg *1922–1924*
(2) Berlin-Forster Automobilfabrik GmbH, Berlin-Charlottenburg *1924–1925*

The Omikron succeeded the Omega (ii). 4/16 and 5/20PS Steudel-engined models were produced. Omikron cars participated in several national races. HON

OMNIA (NL) *1907–1911*
(1) Houwing & Co, Stompwijk *1907–1908*
(2) NV Omnia Motoren, Voorburg *1908–1911*

The Omnia was a conventional car made in 2-, 3- and 4-cylinder models of 10/12, 18/24 and 55hp. All models had water-cooled in-line engines and shaft drive. In 1909 a 9hp single-cylinder voiturette was added to the range, and the 2-cylinder model was widely used as a taxi. After 1909 only one model was made, a 15/20hp 4-cylinder car which was similar to the 18hp Spyker except for the radiator, and was probably made under Spyker licence. GNG

OMNIMOBIL (D) *1904–1910*
Aachener Stahlwarenfabrik AG, Aachen

This was not a car make, but a construction kit marketed as the Omnimobil. It was used by numerous German manufacturers to produce cars under their own name. The Omnimobil set consisted of all necessary components, including a complete engine with gearbox, chain or shaft transmission, axles, steering assembly etc. From 1904 a 2-cylinder 6PS engine was supplied, while later a 4-cylinder 16PS engine was also available. The Aachener Stahlwarenfabrik started to produce their own complete Fafnir cars in 1908 and the production of Omnimobil sets was given up in 1910. HON

OMNOBIL (D) *1922*
Deutsche Elektromobil- und Motorenwerke AG, Wasseralfingen

This firm made electric cars with single- and tandem two-seater bodies. HON

ONE OF THE BEST *see* ADAMS (i)

ONFRAY (F) *1901–c.1905*
Cie Française de Cycles et Automobiles, Paris

The first Onfray was powered by a 6hp single-cylinder horizontal engine of the company's own make. It had chain drive, and body styles were a two-seater tonneau or three-seater spyder. In 1903 the firm was making a range of light cars, mostly with shaft drive. The 6 and 8hp cars had radiators mounted at the side of the bonnet like those of the contemporary Renault, while the 9 and 10hp cars had frontal radiators. All had vertical engines, and the 10hp had chain drive. GNG

ONLY (US) *1909–1915*
Only Motor Car Co, Port Jefferson, N.Y.

The name for this make came from the original single-cylinder engine of massive capacity. This 2.1-litre cylinder had a ball-bearing mounted crankshaft, with a flywheel at each end. The car was built as a two-seater 'racytype', and was claimed to achieve 60mph. A four-seater version was made for 1911. After 1912 a 4-cylinder engine with $7\frac{7}{8}$in stroke was used, and only a five-seater model was offered. GMN

ONNASCH (D) *1924*

Traugott Onnasch, Köslin

Onnasch produced two models of 3-wheelers with one driven rear wheel: a 3½hp single-cylinder and an 8hp 2-cylinder using Bekamo engines. A small 4-wheeled model was also produced.   HON.

O.P. (F) *1921–1924*

Automobiles O.P., Levallois-Perret, Seine

Alternatively known as the Phrixus, the O.P. was a light car with sv Chapuis-Dornier engines of 898 or 1,095cc, although one model was listed with an ohv engine of 1,093cc, apparently of O.P.'s own make. The smaller car had a conventional 3-speed gearbox, but the larger used friction transmission. As late as 1922 the O.P. had the anachronism of acetylene lighting.   GNG

OPEL (D) *1898 to date*

(1) Adam Opel, Rüsselsheim *1898–1928*

(2) Adam Opel AG, Rüsselsheim *1928 to date*

The Opel concern was well-established in bicycle and sewing machine manufacture when the five Opel brothers decided to start car production. They bought the production rights of the Lutzmann and the first Opel-Lutzmann car appeared in 1898 with a rear-mounted single-cylinder engine. This was soon replaced by a 2-cylinder engine. The model was not very successful and the Opel brothers looked for another design. They reached an agreement with the French firm of Darracq and started to produce cars under licence in 1902, Opel importing Darracq's chassis and mounting their own bodies. These cars were advertised as Opel-Darracqs. Import of Darracq cars continued after Opel introduced the first of their own designs in 1902. This was a 10/12hp car with a 2-cylinder 1,884cc engine. In 1903 they produced their first 4-cylinder car, a 20/24hp model. The range was completed with a 2-cylinder 8/14hp and a 4-cylinder 35/40hp car in 1905 and in the following year co-operation with Darracq was discontinued.

The firm was very active in sports and racing events; in 1905 Opel gained more than 100 victories. The Herkomer and Prince Henry Trials saw Opel entries and in the 1907 Kaiserpreis Race a third place was gained. Until 1911 Opel was one of the leading German car producers, offering a wide range of models from the very popular 2-cylinder 8/14PS 'Doctor's Car' to a 33/60PS 9,240cc luxury model. In 1911 the factory was destroyed by fire, but after complete rebuilding which allowed the application of the most modern production techniques, Opel regained their position. The 10,000th car was delivered in 1912, and the production of lorries was taken up in 1913. The biggest of the 1914 range, the 10.2-litre 40/100PS, had overhead valves and was credited with 75mph. The small 5/14PS and 6/16PS cars became very popular in the years up to World War 1, and the heavier types were built in greater quantities. During the first years after the war political reasons prevented the resumption of large-scale production.

In 1923 the Opel range covered seven models from 9/32PS to 30/80PS; five of them were cancelled when Opel installed an assembly line in 1923/24 and started mass production of cars on American principles, being the first German company to do so. The new 4/12PS model – presented in 1924 – was almost a copy of the Citroën 5CV. It had a 4-cylinder 951cc engine and a two-seater body. It was commonly known as the Laubfrosch (tree frog) because of its green paint. Sales of this model amounted to 39,000 by 1927. Opel started to build up a widespread service organization covering all German districts; they were the first German producers to guarantee repairs at fixed prices. After 1926 a four-seater body was used on a lengthened Laubfrosch chassis and engine capacity was raised to 1,016cc. This model was made until 1929. Heavier models followed, such as the 4-cylinder, 2,612cc 10/45PS and various 6-cylinder cars, still with side valves. In 1928 Opel were Germany's largest car manufacturers, producing 37.5% of all cars in that country. It is interesting to note that Opel were then the biggest bicycle producers in the world.

Interesting experiments were carried out by Opel with rocket-driven cars in 1927 and 1928 in co-operation with the rocket specialists Valier and Sander. Fritz von Opel drove the rocket-car on the Avus track at over 125mph.

The approach of economic crisis in the late 1920s made the Opel family decide to change their firm into a joint-stock company. The majority of the shares were acquired by General Motors. In 1929 Opel's first 8-cylinder car was introduced, the 24/110PS, 5,970cc Regent. In the same year a 4/20PS 1,016cc car appeared as the successor to the range of small models which had started with the Laubfrosch.

The 1930s were characterized by three model ranges. The small 4/20PS was developed into the 1-litre (1931/33), 1.2-litre (1933/35), P 4 (1936/38) and the Kadett (1937/39), the latter having an engine capacity of 1,074cc. It sold in England for a mere £135. The Regent 1.2-litre (1932/33) grew into the 1.3-litre (1934/35) and the Olympia (1935/37), both having a 1,279cc engine. The 1938 Olympia had an increased engine capacity of 1,488cc and an output of 37bhp. The 6-cylinder models of the 1920s were developed into the 1.8-litre (1931/33) and 2-litre (1934/37), the 2,473cc Super (1937/38) and the Kapitän (1938/39) with the same engine. The 6-cylinder 3,620cc Admiral rounded off the pre-war range of models. Dubonnet-type independent suspension was introduced in the 1934 2-litre, and was standard in all models by 1939.

1910 ONLY 12hp single-cylinder roadster. *Automotive History Collection, Detroit Public Library*

1913 OPEL 4/8PS tourer. *Adam Opel AG*

1924 OPEL Laubfrosch 4/12PS two-seater. *Adam Opel AG*

1936 OPEL Olympia 1.3-litre saloon. *Adam Opel AG*

1938 OPEL Admiral 3.6-litre drophead coupé. Coachwork by Hebmüller. *Jockisch Collection*

1965 OPEL Diplomat 5.4-litre V-8 coupé. *Adam Opel AG*

1972 OPEL Manta S 1.9-litre coupé. *General Motors Corporation*

1958 OPPERMAN Stirling 400cc coupé. *Autosport*

During the 1930s Opel ranked first in European car production. The 1935 Olympia was the first mass-produced car with a chassis-less all-steel body. The P 4 at 1,450 marks was the cheapest car on the German market, a true four-seater of 32bhp capable of 55mph. The end of World War 2 brought the enforced dismantling of the Kadett production lines. They were transferred to Russia and the Kadett, identical to the pre-war model, re-appeared as the Moskvitch. At the Opel works production started again in 1947 with the Olympia, followed in 1948 by the Kapitän. Bodies and engines were similar to the pre-war designs. While bodies changed frequently during the following years the engines were built according to the old proved design. In 1962 a new Kadett appeared, built in a new factory at Bochum. It had a 993cc, 40bhp engine, increased in 1965 to 1,078cc. The Olympia became the Rekord in 1953 and its 1,488cc engine was supplemented by 1,680cc and 1,897cc units in 1959 and 1965 respectively. Overhead camshafts were adopted for this series in 1965. As the Rekord L 6 it was also available with the 2,605cc Kapitän engine. The Kapitän's 2,473cc power unit was increased to 2,605cc in 1959 and to 2,784cc in 1965. The name Admiral was also revived in 1964 for a car with Kapitän engines. In the same year the Diplomat was introduced to top the Opel range. V-8 Chevrolet engines of 4,638cc (190bhp) and 5,354cc (230bhp) were used for this model. Kapitäns and Admirals were also available with Diplomat engines on request. Car production rose from 6,028 in 1948 to 623,989 in 1965. The 1968 range was widened still further by the addition of fast-back 2- and 4-door Kadetts, and a new Olympia based on the Kadett, but available with 1.1-litre, 1.7-litre or 1.9-litre engines.

A sporting image began to emerge in 1969, with active support for rallies and the introduction of a GT coupé combining Kadett mechanical elements with retractable headlamps and front disc brakes; with the optional 1.9-litre ohc engine it was capable of 115mph. Opel components were also used in Belgian versions of General Motors' new make, the Ranger. A new high-performance six appeared in 1970, the Commodore GS, its 2.8-litre engine offered with the option of fuel injection. A year later came Opel's answer to the Anglo-German Ford Capri, the Manta coupé. This had double-wishbone ifs and a choice of 4-cylinder ohc power units with outputs of up to 90bhp. The same theme was perpetuated in a saloon, the Ascona, which had front disc brakes as standard and was available with 1,584cc or 1,897cc engine. In May 1971 the factory converted an Opel GT to electric propulsion, and this car covered a flying kilometre at 117.2mph, breaking the official electric car record held since 1899 by Camille Jenatzy's *La Jamais Contente*.

Redesigned versions of the intermediate Rekord series appeared in 1972; in addition to new 1.7-litre and 1.9-litre ohc engines, there was a 2.1-litre diesel option. During the year Opel replaced Volkswagen as the home market's best-selling make. They offered a formidable diversity of models: the Kadett with 1,078cc or 1,196cc engines; the Rallye Kadett with the option of a 1.9-litre 90bhp unit; the ohc 4-cylinder Asconas and Rekords; the GT and Manta coupés; the 6-cylinder Commodore and Admiral series; and the 5.3-litre Chevrolet-engined Diplomat V-8. Front disc brakes were standard on all but the basic Kadetts, and only these and the V-8 retained push-rod-operated ohv. The Admiral and Diplomat apart, Opel had fallen into line with Vauxhall, using rigid axles and coils at the rear, though various forms of ifs were found. New for 1973 were a high-performance Ascona, the 1900SR, and its Manta equivalent, the Berlinetta. Both had 90bhp 1,897cc engines.

HON

OPES (I) *1946–1948*
Officine Precisione e Stampaggio, Turin

The Opes light car was powered by a 3-cylinder air-cooled radial engine of 702cc (later 784cc), which drove the front wheels. Light alloys were widely used in the chassis. The body was a 2-door saloon.

GNG

OPESSI (I) *1935–1936*

Pierino Opessi was an agent for Lynx motorcycles who built a prototype Lynx-engined 3-wheeler and displayed it at the 1936 Milan Motorcycle Show. Both sv and ohv versions were planned.

MCS

OPHIR (US) *1901*

The Ophir was in most respects a typical light steam runabout of the period, with a 2-cylinder engine and tiller steering. However, in place of the usual single chain drive, it had shaft drive in which the propeller shaft was an extension of the crankshaft running at quite a sharp angle from just below the floor to the rear axle.

GNG

OPPERMAN (GB) *1956–1959*
S.E. Opperman Ltd, Elstree; Borehamwood, Herts.

The Unicar was a boxy fibreglass 2/4-seater saloon with independent suspension and rear-mounted 2-stroke 2-cylinder engine. 85mpg was claimed when using the Excelsior 225cc unit; with the 328cc version 75mph was advertised. As the cost was still under £400 some ephemeral sales success was achieved. The car was also sold in kit form. The London Motor Show of 1958 saw this model supported by the distinctive Stirling, a miniature GT coupé albeit with the same layout. This model cost nearly £100 more than the cheapest of the full-sized saloons, and very few were sold.

DF

OPPERMANN (GB) 1898–1907

1) Carl Oppermann, London N. *1898–1902*
2) Carl Oppermann Electric Carriage Co Ltd, London N. *1902–1907*

Carl Oppermann's first electric was an Arthur Mulliner-bodied victoria which was a true horseless carriage with centre-pivot steering. Both the batteries and the 3½hp motor were tucked away under the body, and it could do a modest 8mph. By 1899 car influence became apparent and Oppermanns had tubular frames, wheel steering and worm drive, while fwd versions were available. The firm made their own batteries. The 1901–02 range included a neat Electromobile victoriette – a designation which led to some confusion with the better-known Electromobile(i) – with a 'motor mounted to swing about the lower rear axle', leather wings, electric sidelamps and even an odometer, all for £352, while there was a light-weight 1hp runabout at only £160. By 1905 Oppermann had progressed to a styling resembling that of contemporary petrol cars, with the motor under a frontal bonnet, shaft-and-worm drive and 4 forward speeds; one of these was sold to the King of Siam. Subsequently the firm was largely concerned with taxicabs, and the 1906 6hp was available with central chain drive as an alternative to the well-tried worm gear. The make was not listed after 1907 and in 1912 Carl Oppermann was running a garage in Kensington.   MCS

OPUS-H.R.F. (GB) 1966 to date

(1) Rob Walker Corsley Garage Ltd, Warminster, Wilts. *1966–1970*
(2) H.S.P. Motor Co, Bristol 4 *1970–1972*
(3) H.S.P. Motor Co, Bristol 2 *1972 to date*

Reminiscent of a transatlantic Model T-based dragster, the Hot-Rod-Ford from Rob Walker's Corsley Garage was envisaged as a cheap 'fun car', suitable for sporting use on or off the road. The chassis was designed to accept standard Ford Anglia components, with Ford Popular front suspension. A simple bath-tub type open fibreglass body was offered. It was claimed that by using second-hand mechanical parts and home assembly, a car could be completed for less than £200. With a 1,300cc Ford engine, total weight remained below 672lb in road trim. Sales began towards the end of 1966. The car was consistently developed by Roy Dickenson of Bristol, who sold about a dozen annually and undertook some redesign to counter a scarcity of various mechanical parts.   DF

OREL (F) 1905–1914

Automobiles Orel, Argenteuil, Seine-et-Oise

The Orel began life as a voiturette with an 8hp V-twin engine, and in 1907 a 7hp single-cylinder and a 12hp 4 were listed. Two of the singles ran in the Coupe des Voiturettes of that year, but did not distinguish themselves. In the following years Orels gradually increased in size, and by 1912 the single had been dropped, the range consisting of an 8/10hp twin, and 14 and 18hp fours, all using Buchet engines. The following year a Knight-engined model was added, with a 20/24hp sleeve-valve engine of 2½-litres' capacity.   GNG

ORIA see LENTZ

ORIAL (F) 1923–1924

This was a small cyclecar using a 904cc 4-cylinder Ruby engine, made under Sénéchal licence.   GNG

ORIENT see WALTHAM (ii)

ORIENT EXPRESS (D) 1895–1903

Bergmann's Industriewerke, Gaggenau

The motor-car division of this firm started production in 1895. The first models, a 3-wheeler and a 4-wheeler with single-cylinder engines, were designed by Joseph Vollmer and based on Benz principles. Voiturettes with single- and 2-cylinder engines followed and a 4-cylinder model appeared in 1903. Orient Express cars were also marketed under the Bergmann name.   HON

ORION (i) (CH) 1900

Zürcher & Huber, Automobilfabrik Orion, Zürich

The Orion was a light car with a single-cylinder front-mounted engine, shaft drive and a three-seater *vis-à-vis* body. Only six were made, after which the company went over to the manufacture of commercial vehicles which they produced successfully until 1910.   GNG

ORION (ii) (GB) 1914

The Orion was a belt-driven cyclecar with a 4-cylinder 8.9hp engine, sold from a showroom in Gloucester Road, London. The factory location is uncertain.   GNG

ORIX (E) 1952

Designed by Juan Ramirez, the Orix bore a remarkable similarity to the Volkswagen, but was powered by a 610cc flat-twin engine. About twelve were made.   GNG

ORLEANS see NEW ORLEANS and OWEN (i)

1905 OPPERMANN electric tonneau built for the King of Siam. *Autocar*

1966 OPUS-H.R.F. 1,300cc two-seater. Stirling Moss at the wheel. *Rob Walker Corsley Garage Ltd*

1899 ORIENT EXPRESS 6hp phaeton. *M.W. Wood*

1920 ORPINGTON 11hp two-seater. *Autocar*

1913 ORYX 10/30PS tourer.
G.L. Hartner Collection

1953 OSCA 1.3-litre Le Mans coupé. *Autosport*

1967 OSCA PR.2 1.6-litre coupé. *Automobili
Osca*

ORLO (US) *1904*
Jackson Automobile Co, Jackson, Mich.

The Orlo was a side-entrance five-seater costing $1,125. Its 16/17hp 2-cylinder engine was mounted under the front seat and drive was through a single chain. The radiator for the water-cooled engine was finned coil mounted beneath the front of the bonnet. The firm was also responsible for the better-known Jackson (ii).   GMN

ORMOND (US) *1904–1905*
United Motor & Vehicle Co, Boston, Mass.

The Ormond was an expensive steam car made in very limited numbers. It had a 4-cylinder opposed engine of 15hp, and carried elaborate seven-seater bodywork. The price was $3,000.   GNG

ORPINGTON (GB) *1920–1924*
Smith & Milroy Ltd, Orpington, Kent

The Orpington was one of several cars assembled in Britain that utilized Ford Model T components, in this case axles, brakes and steering. The 1½-litre, 4-cylinder engine was a Coventry-Simplex and the gearbox was by Moss. The result was an economical, roomy machine, but still far too expensive to compete with much better cars – £52 more than the comparable Morris in 1924.   TRN

ORSON (US) *1908–1909*
Brightwood Manufacturing Co, Springfield, Mass.

The Orson was probably the only example of a car built by a co-operative of wealthy businessmen for their own use. Named after Orson Kilbourn, son of the designer, it was a large conventional 4-cylinder car whose chassis was made by the Brightwood Manufacturing Co, and bodies by the Springfield Metal Body Co. There were a hundred subscribers whose combined wealth was said to total $250m, and each paid what the car cost (average $4,000), no profit being made. The 100 cars were completed in about a year, after which the sponsors decided that the American market was almost saturated, and so did not put the car on general sale. It was called by the press 'the bankers' car', and the showrooms were appropriately at 52 Wall Street.   GNG

ORYX (D) *1907–1922*
(1) Berliner Motorwagen-Fabrik GmbH, Berlin-Reinickendorf *1907–1909*
(2) Oryx-Motorenwerke, Zweigniederlassung der Dürkoppwerke AG, Berlin-Reinickendorf *1909–1922*

Oryx followed the make of B.M.F., producing private cars; commercials were sold under the name of Eryx. The first Oryx car was the 6/10PS with 1,555cc engine. In 1909 the factory was taken over by Dürkopp, but Oryx continued to build their own models, all with small monobloc engines. Various versions were produced until the outbreak of World War 1. After the war Oryx ceased to exist as an independent company as it was integrated into the Dürkopp works. Production of private cars was discontinued in 1922.   HON

OSCA (I) *1947–1967*
Officina Specializzata Costruzione Automobili, Bologna

Nine years after the three surviving Maserati brothers – Ernesto, Ettore and Bindo – had sold out to the Orsi interests in 1938, they returned from Modena to their native Bologna and founded the Oscar concern on 1 December 1947. In a small factory, initially with minimal equipment, their first product was a single-ohc 1,100cc sports car which, in Luigi Villoresi's expert hands, won its second motor race, the Naples Grand Prix of 1948. Thereafter Osca turned out very successful twin-ohc 750, 1,100, 1,500 and 1,600cc sports cars which did well in races, particularly in the Mille Miglia. As late as 1954 a 1,500cc Osca, brilliantly driven by Stirling Moss, won the Sebring 12 Hours Race in Florida from many larger-engined cars.

In 1951, Osca built a 4½-litre unsupercharged V-12 Formula 1 car which won at Goodwood; they next produced a 2-litre 6-cylinder Formula 2 car with De Dion rear axle, and in 1959 they built several Fiat-engined Formula Junior cars which went well but were rather heavy – an Osca tendency. That same year Fiat built a 1.6-litre version of the twin-cam Osca engine, putting it in a high performance GT car, and subsequently Osca used the same unit in a GT range of their own, bodied by Vignale, Zagato or Fissore. Growing old, and lacking suitable successors, the brothers sold their Osca business to Meccanica Verghera, makers of the MV Agusta motorcycle, in 1963. The last Osca model was the 1,600 PR2 of 1966, for MV decided to close down Osca completely.   CP

OSCAR (GB) *1969–1970*
Oscar Car Co, Lambourn, Berks.; Aldershot, Hampshire

This company, an offshoot of Oselli Engineering, manufactured a Formula Ford designed by Frank Boyle, who later produced the Fireball cars. It had unusually large brakes and a low frontal area. The kit was priced at £550 and the prototype gave promising results, but persistent engine troubles deterred buyers.   DF

OSTERFIELD (GB) *1907–c.1909*
Douglas S. Cox, West Norwood, London S.E.

Two models of the Osterfield were made, a 19.6hp four, and a 40hp 8-cylinder car.   GNG

OTAS (I) *1969–1971*
Otas Costruzioni Automobilistiche, Turin

This was an Aldo Sessano-styled sports coupé based on the 903cc 4-cylinder fwd Autobianchi A112. Output was raised from 44 to 59bhp, but it cost one-and-a-half times as much as a standard saloon.   MCS

O.T.A.V. (I) *1905–1908*
Officine Turkheimer Automobili e Velocipedi, Milan

The O.T.A.V. voiturette, or Turkheimer as it was known in its early years, was powered by an air-cooled, single-cylinder engine of 5½hp. There were two cooling fans, one in the normal position forward of the engine, and another, crankshaft-driven, in a housing in the crankcase. Epicyclic gears provided 2 forward speeds, driving through 2 belts. The O.T.A.V. single was current until 1908, but there was also a 10hp twin with 3 forward speeds, and in 1907 a full-sized 4-cylinder, 2.8-litre machine that may have also counted as a Junior, for in that year the firm became associated with the Fabbrica Junior Torinese Automobili, who were known for conventional vehicles.   TRN

1908 O.T.A.V. 5½hp two-seater. *Autocar*

OTOMO (J) *1924–1927*
Hakuyosha Ironworks, Ltd, Tokyo

After experimenting with several Ales prototype touring cars in 1920–21, engineer Junya Toyokawa introduced a production model in 1924 under the name Otomo. This light car was powered by an air-cooled, 4-cylinder ohv 943.8cc engine driving a three-speed gearbox. The bodies were built at the factory and were available as two-seaters, four-seaters, tourers, sedans, and vans.

In 1926 a larger model was sold using a water-cooled four cylinder ohv engine of 24hp. A total of 270 cars were produced before the company was liquidated due to foreign competition in the export trade. This was the first Japanese car to be driven on a foreign road as it was sold in Shanghai, China.

The Hayukosha Works was virtually self-supporting as all machining and casting was done within the plant and many of the machines used, including shapers, grinders, milling and gear-hobbing machines, were of their own manufacture.   BE

OTTO (i) (F) *1901–1914*
Sté Générale des Voitures Automobiles Otto, Paris 15e

The original Otto was made in two models, a 10hp with 2-cylinder horizontal engine, and a 20hp with a 4-cylinder vertical engine. Both had chain drive. The following year 2- and 4-cylinder models were both of 10hp; they had De Dion type bonnets with gilled tube radiators mounted low between the front dumb irons. There is little trace of cars from 1903 until the appearance of the F.L. models in 1909. Said to have been named after the Eiffel Tower (pronounced Eff Ell), they were conventional 4-cylinder cars with 12/16hp monobloc engines. In 1912 a 6-cylinder 18/24hp model was introduced.   GNG

OTTO (ii); OTTOMOBILE (US) *1909–1912*
(1) Otto Gas Engine Works, Philadelphia, Pa. *1909–1911*
(2) Ottomobile Co, Mt Holly, N.J. *1912*
(3) Ottomobile Co, Philadelphia, Pa. *1912*

The initial models of the Otto were roadsters; later touring and limousine models were added. These cars looked long and low, this effect being enhanced by a wheelbase of 10ft 3in. The later models used a 4.2-litre 4-cylinder engine. The bodies had no overhang, being bracketed front and rear by the wheels. The last models were known as Ottomobiles and used engines of 4.6 or 5.1 litres' capacity.   GMN

1924 OTOMO 943cc saloon (*left*); *c.*1926
AUBURN (*right*). *Shotaro Kobayashi Collection*

OTTO (iii) (D) *1923–1924*
Otto-Werke GmbH, Munich

This aircraft company built light motorcycles (Flottweg) after World War 1 and introduced a 27/85PS car in 1923. It was built in limited numbers only, but was a successful competition car – especially in the hands of its designer Gustav Otto, son of Nicolaus August Otto, the inventor of the 4-stroke gas engine, which laid the foundation for the development of the motor car.   HON

OTTOCAR (OTTOKAR) (US) *1903–1904*
Otto Konigslow, Cleveland, Ohio

The single model of the Ottocar was a light two-seater roadster. It was driven by a single-cylinder water-cooled engine of 6hp. Also used were a planetary transmission and single-chain drive. Painted Brewster green, it was priced at $750.   GMN

OTTOLINI (I) *1900–1901*
Fabbrica Automobili Ottolini, Milan

This small firm made a few 5hp single-cylinder cars with four forward speeds and belt drive.   MCS

1903 OTTO(i) 10hp tonneau. *The Veteran Car Club of Great Britain*

1909 OTTO(i) 9CV coupé. *Musée de l'Automobile Le Mans*

1910 OTTO(ii) 35hp roadster. *Kenneth Stauffer*

1907 OURS 14/16hp tourer. *Lucien Loreille Collection*

OTTOMOBILE see OTTO (ii)

OURS (F) *1906–1909*
SA des Automobiles Ours, Paris
   This company made conventional touring cars with 3- or 4-cylinder in-line engines of 10/12 and 14/16hp, and round radiators in the style of Delaunay-Belleville. Their main business was in the manufacture of taxicabs, of which 150 were running in Paris in 1908.   GNG

OUZOU (F) *1900–1901*
Emile Ouzou et Cie, Levallois-Perret and Poissy, Seine
   The Ouzou voiturette was powered by a 6hp single-cylinder Soncin engine and had single chain drive.   GNG

OVENDEN (US) *1899*
W.C. Ovenden, West Boylston, Mass.
   Ovenden made a light steam buggy with which he intended to go into production, but he only sold one car.   GNG

OVERHOLT (US) *1909; 1912*
The Overholt Co, Galesburg, Ill.
   The four-seater Overholt used solid rubber tyres and a 2-cylinder, air-cooled engine of 12/14hp. It had friction transmission and chain drive.   GMN

OVERLAND see WILLYS

OVERMAN (US) *1899–1904*
(1) Overman Wheel Co, Chicopee Falls, Mass. *1899–1900*
(2) Overman Automobile Co, Chicopee, Mass. *1901–1904*
   The Overman Wheel Co were manufacturers of Victor bicycles and began development work on cars in 1896 when H.A. Knox was hired to design a petrol engine. This was never put on the market and Knox left, later to manufacture Knox, and Atlas cars. A steam car, the Victor, appeared in 1899. It was typical of the many New England steamers of the period, with 4hp vertical 2-cylinder engine and single chain drive. In 1900 the Victor bicycle business was sold to the Stevens Arms & Tool Co, and for a few months Overman leased the top floor of the building to assemble Victor cars. In January 1901 a new company was formed, and they took over space in a factory at Chicopee, where Victor steamers continued to be built. In 1902 A.L. Riker joined the firm, and they became associated with Locomobile. The first Locomobile petrol cars were developed at Chicopee as well as new Overman petrol cars and the steamer. By 1904 the firm was wholly absorbed by Locomobile. Meanwhile the Chicopee Falls plant was used for the manufacture of Stevens-Duryea cars.   GNG

OWATONNA (US) *1903*
Virtue & Pound Mfg Co, Owatonna, Minn.
   Virtually nothing is known about this vehicle other than that it was powered by a 9hp petrol engine and was placed on the market early in 1903.   GMN

O-WE-GO (US) *1914–1915*
O-We-Go Car Co, Owego, N.Y.
   This was a tandem two-seater cyclecar with a V-twin air-cooled Ives engine rated at 10/12hp. It had a friction transmission and belt drive. The only distinguishing feature was that the headlights were mounted on the front wings, later a feature of the Pierce-Arrow.   GMN

OWEN (i) (GB) *1899–1935*
(1) Automobile Transport Co, London W.
(2) Orleans Car Co, London W.
   There have been a number of mystery makes of car of which it is hard to establish that any vehicles were made. Most were listed for a year or two only, but Owen's shadowy marque persisted for 36 years, with no satisfactory proof that a single vehicle left the factory, if indeed there ever was a factory. The first mention of an Owen is of a 10hp 2-cylinder car with shaft drive in 1899. This appears as the first Owen in lists of the 1920s but there is no contemporary reference. However, in 1901 E.H. Owen of 72 Comeragh Road, West Kensington, announced the Twentieth Century Voiturette with a 3½hp vertical single-cylinder engine mounted in front, and belt drive to a countershaft, which was geared to the rear axle. In December 1901 he was prepared to book orders for Twentieth Century cars of 9, 12, 16 and 24hp, for delivery in the new year. There follows a short gap, but in the 1905 Buyers' Guides the Automobile Transport Company listed cars under four different names: the 10hp Parisia, the 20hp Londonia, the 30hp Twentieth Century, and the 40hp Owen's Gearless. From this point the picture becomes increasingly complex, with cars of various sizes appearing under the names given above as well as the Owen Petelectra (a petrol-electric design), and Atalanta. These continue with models of up to 60hp until 1911, when there is an abrupt break until after World War 1.

In 1920 there appeared a new marque, the Orleans, listed in 10, 15 and 20hp form, until 1935, as a companion to the Owen. This re-appeared in 1920 with two models, the 20hp with a long-stroke 4-cylinder engine (76×165mm) and only 1 forward speed. In contrast the 40hp Owen-Dynamic had an infinite variety of speeds from a petrol-electric drive. These cars were priced (provisionally) at £550 and £1,100 respectively. They were dropped in 1921 in favour of a 28hp V-8 of 5,302cc with Owen starter and carburettor, dual ignition and 2-speed gearbox. This model was priced at £2,250 for the chassis, at a time when a Silver Ghost or 40/50 Napier chassis only cost £2,100. The V-8 became a 7,634cc straight-8 in 1925; with a wheelbase of 12ft 6in, this model was listed in *The Autocar* to 1928, and in some other tables until 1935. Few illustrations of any of these cars appeared apart from a line drawing of the 1901 voiturette and some doubtful photos in a 1908 Buyers' Guide in which the 10hp 2-cylinder and 35hp 4-cylinder Londonia are illustrated by the same car, a typically American-looking tourer. The post-war V-8 appeared in a small illustration in the 1921 *Autocar* Buyers' Guide, but it bears an uncanny resemblance to the Kenworthy, apart from a few minor variations which could easily have been altered by retouching. The premises at Comeragh Road (renumbered No. 6 after World War 1) are quite unsuitable for any kind of factory. Rumours that the works were in Birmingham are unproven, as is the suggestion that the Owen was an Irish car. It is a mystery which for the moment can only be explained by the persistent optimism and fertile imagination of E.H. Owen.   GNG

OWEN (ii) (US) *1910–1914*
Owen Motor Car Co, Detroit, Mich.

The Owen used a 50hp, 6.9-litre 4-cylinder engine. It had a central gear change and was one of the first cars with this improvement. The single model was a seven-seater touring car for $4,000. Its 42in tyres gave a ground clearance of 12in.   GMN

OWEN MAGNETIC: CROWN MAGNETIC (US) *1914–1922*
(1) Baker, Rauch & Lang Co, Cleveland, Ohio; Wilkes-Barre, Pa. *1914–1919*
(2) Owen Magnetic Motor Car Corp, Wilkes-Barre, Pa. *1919–1922*

The American battleship *New Mexico* was provided with gearless Entz magnetic transmission across an air gap. Ray M. Owen, of Baker, Rauch & Lang, the manufacturers of electric cars (Baker, Raulang), adapted it for automotive use in the Owen Magnetic, a luxury car introduced in 1914. A normal 6-cylinder petrol engine generated the electric power which operated the transmission. The Owen Magnetic disappeared in 1921, but J.L. Owen took over the system and offered it in a car called the Crown Magnetic: a push-rod ohv six of nearly 7 litres' capacity. With British engines, he also sold it in the United Kingdom (British Ensign). Electrical transmission, with its smoothness and flexibility, obviated the need for gear-changing, but was expensive and unconventional.   TRN

OWEN-SCHOENECK (US) *1915–1916.*
The Owen-Schoeneck Co, Chicago, Ill.

The Owen-Schoeneck was a conventional touring car powered by a 5.2-litre 4-cylinder Herschell-Spillman engine.   GNG

OWEN-THOMAS (US) *1909*
Owen-Thomas Motor Car Co, Janesville, Wisc.

This unusual vehicle was powered by a 6-cylinder engine of 4.1 litres, with a crankshaft which ran in four ball-bearings 9in in diameter, and rotary valves in the cylinder heads. Ball-bearings were also used in the valve-train, in the transmission and in the fan-shaft. The steering was on the left-hand side with centre controls. The five-seater, with a wheelbase of 11ft, was priced at $3,000. A two-seater version had a wheelbase of 9ft. In November 1909 the Wisconsin Engine Company purchased the rights of Owen-Thomas and planned to make the car at Corliss, Wisconsin.   GMN

OXFORD (i) *see* DETROIT-OXFORD

OXFORD (ii) (CDN) *1913–1915*
Oxford Motor Cars & Foundries Ltd, Montreal, Que.

The Oxford was the handsome, well-made product of a family of French Canadian industrialists. 4- and 6-cylinder models were offered but production was limited to a handful of sixes: touring cars and one roadster. Almost all components were imported from America. When these became hard to get during World War 1 and sales failed to match expectations, the car-manufacturing section of the family business was liquidated.   HD

1910 OWEN(ii) 50hp tourer. *Automobile Manufacturers' Association*

1918 OWEN MAGNETIC 33hp roadster. *Kenneth Stauffer*

1914 OXFORD(ii) 6-cylinder tourer. *Hugh Durnford*

1915 PACKARD Twin Six 6.9-litre tourer. *Henry Ford Museum, Dearborn, Mich.*

1925 PACKARD 5.9-litre saloon. Coachwork by Freestone & Webb. *Monty Bowers*

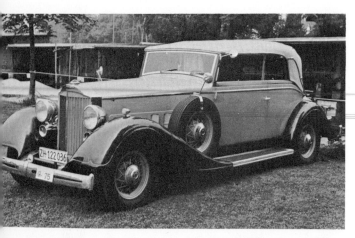

1934 PACKARD Eight 5.3-litre cabriolet. Coachwork by Graber. *G.N. Georganc*

PACIFIC (US) *1914*

Portland Cyclecar Co, Portland, Ore.

The Pacific was a two-seater cyclecar with tandem seating, which used an air-cooled, 2-cylinder engine of 1.1 litres. It is, claimed that this model was succeeded by a full-sized car named the Portland.   GMN

PACIFIC SPECIAL (US) *1914*

Cole California Car Co, Oakland, Calif.

This company listed a 33hp 4-cylinder roadster and tourer for one year only, at a price of $1,950. There was apparently no connection with the better-known Cole Motor Car Company of Indianapolis.   GNG

PACKARD (US) *1899–1958*

(1) New York & Ohio Automobile Co, Warren, Ohio *1899–1901*
(2) Ohio Automobile Co, Warren, Ohio *1901–1902*
(3) Packard Motor Car Co, Warren, Ohio *1902–1903*
(4) Packard Motor Car Co, Detroit, Mich. *1903–1955*
(5) Studebaker-Packard Corp, Detroit, Mich. *1955–1958*

The brothers J.W. and W.D. Packard bought a Winton in 1898 and determined to improve upon it. The result was the first 12hp Packard of 1899. This followed traditional early-American lines with a single horizontal cylinder, central chain drive, buggy styling and wire wheels, but was more advanced than its competitors in having a 3-speed and reverse gearbox and automatic spark advance. This gave way to the wheel-steered Model C, which proved capable of 40mph. An even more powerful single sold for $3,000 in 1903 and on one of these Fetch and Krarup successfully drove from San Francisco to New York in 61 days. In the same year a very big four of over 12 litres' capacity was designed on European lines by Charles Schmidt, late of Mors. This sold for $7,500 and led to the famous Model L, the first car to bear the classic Packard radiator. It had side valves in an L-head and the gearbox was mounted in unit with the back axle; a similar engine was used in the racing car Gray Wolf, a streamlined lightweight capable of 75mph. 1906 Packards had T-head engines and magneto ignition in place of coil; engine capacity was $5\frac{3}{4}$ litres, increasing to 7 litres in 1907 with the introduction of the famous '30', from which 60bhp was claimed. For the next few years these high-quality fours engaged all Packard's attentions, the '30' at $4,200 being joined by a short-wheelbase 18 intended for use as a town carriage. Dry-plate clutches were adopted in 1910 and in 1911 a third model joined the range: Packard's first six, the $7\frac{1}{4}$ litre '48'.

Sixes only were offered in 1913, when electric lighting and starting were standardized. Spiral bevel final drive followed in 1914. Revolutionary was the world's first series-production 12-cylinder, the Twin-Six, which was announced in 1915 for 1916: it was also the first American touring car to use aluminium pistons and was quite modestly priced at $2,600. First series cars had the unusual combination of left-hand drive and left-hand gear-change, abandoned on later series which also had detachable cylinder heads. A special racing car version, the 905 with a much bigger engine, recorded 149.9mph in the hands of Ralph de Palma at Daytona in 1919. From 1916 to 1920 only the Twin Six was made, but it was then joined by a straightforward sv Single-Six selling from $2,350 up. This car was given front-wheel brakes in 1924 and remained in production until 1928, accounting for most of Packard's sales while it was current. A 5.9-litre 84bhp straight-8 with front-wheel brakes as standard replaced the Twin-six during 1923; it came in two wheelbase lengths. A tourer cost $3,750 and it was the ancestor of the whole line of 'Senior' Packards up to 1939. 1925 cars had centralized chassis lubrication and over 40,000 sixes were sold, as against less than 5,700 eights. Innovations for 1927 were a hypoid back axle, and a bigger 8-cylinder engine of 6.3 litres' capacity, developing 106bhp. Only eights were made in 1929, in which year a 5.3-litre Standard model was catalogued at $2,435, while in 1930 a limited series of '734' sports models with high axle ratio, 145 bhp engines and 4-speed gearboxes was introduced. 1932 Packards had V-radiators. An inexpensive Light 8 at $1,750, using the 5.3-litre engine, proved uneconomic to make, but there was also an excellent 7-litre V-12 and all cars had synchromesh gearboxes and vacuum-servo brakes. The company's styling with its traditional radiator shape continued up to 1939.

In 1935 Packard made a bid for the low-priced market with the 3.7-litre straight-8 '120' with hydraulic brakes and independent front suspension, priced from $980, as against $2,475 for the Standard-eight, $2,990 for the Super-eight and $3,820 for the Twelve. The new model accounted for 24,995 of the 31,889 cars sold by Packard that year and was joined two seasons later by a very similar 3.6-litre six, the '115' at $860; this and the '120', now enlarged to 4.6-litres, were made in a separate factory. In 1938, 50 per cent of the company's labour force was engaged in making the senior Packards which accounted for no more than 8 per cent of total production!

In 1937 hydraulic brakes and independent front suspension were standardized throughout the range. 1939 was the last year of the true senior Packards; column change was introduced and overdrive was available on all models except the Twelve. Air conditioning was a 1940 option and 1941 brought the first of the handsome Clipper line, made in 4-litre 6-cylinder and 4.6-litre straight-8 versions. Expensive cars were still made, with custom bodywork by Rollson, Le Baron and Darrin available on the 5.8-litre chassis. During World War 2, body dies for the bigger, conventionally-bodied Packards were sold to the Soviet Government, the result being the 1945 Z.I.S.

Production was resumed with the Clipper 6 and 8 in 1946, but Packard never regained their former pre-eminence. Styling was unfortunate and the company retained the old straight-8 until 1954, though they evolved their own 'Ultramatic' automatic transmission in 1949 and had power brakes, steering and window lifts in 1954. Super-luxury cars included the eight-seater Executive limousine at $6,900 in 1953 and the big Caribbean convertible.

The 1954 merger with Studebaker brought about a new 260bhp, ohv V-8 with an ingenious inter-linked torsion-level suspension, while engines were sold to American Motors for their Nash and Hudson lines. Sales fell to a depressing 13,000 in 1956 and though the Packard lingered on until 1958, the last two seasons' cars were nothing more than disguised Studebakers.   MCS

1937 PACKARD 120 4.6-litre convertible coupé
G.N. Georgano

PACKET (US) *1916–1917*
Packet Motor Car Manufacturing Co, Minneapolis, Minn.

Formerly known as the Brasie, the Packet was a two-seater cyclecar, selling for $325. It has a 1.6-litre 4-cylinder engine.   GMN

PACO (US) *1908*
Pietsch Auto & Marine Co, Chicago, Ill.

This make was a two-seater high-wheeler, which used a 10/12hp engine, a 4-stroke, 2-cylinder unit mounted under the seat. With a false bonnet and wheel steering the price was $400.   GMN

PADUS (I) *1906–1908*
Fabbrica Automobili Padus, Turin

The Padus was a voiturette sold in 6hp single-cylinder and 10hp 2-cylinder models. Three Padus cars were entered in the 1908 Turin voiturette race, but they all failed to finish.   GNG

1939 PACKARD Eight 6.3-litre tourer.
Coachwork by Derham. *Keith Marvin Collection*

PAGE (US) *1906–1907*
Page Motor Vehicle Co, Providence, R.I.

This car was a two-seater runabout with a 2-cylinder, air-cooled engine of 10hp. It had a 2-speed transmission and shaft drive. It sold for $750.   GMN

PAGÉ (US) *1921–1924*
Victor W. Pagé Motors Corp, East Stamford, Conn.

The Aero-Type Four designed by Victor W. Pagé, an inventor, designer and engineer, had an aircraft-type 4-cylinder engine. This rare make was available as a four-seater roadster with disc wheels as standard equipment at $1,250, and as a coupé at a slightly higher price.   KM

PAIGE-DETROIT; PAIGE (US) *1908–1927*
Paige-Detroit Motor Car Co, Detroit, Mich.

The first model of the Paige-Detroit was a two-seater roadster powered by a 2-stroke, 3-cylinder engine of 2.2 litres. In 1910, the power unit was changed to a 4-stroke, 4-cylinder engine, and the following year the car's name was changed to Paige. For 1914, a 6-cylinder model with a rating of 36hp was added. In 1916 two sixes were built with capacities of 3.7 and 4.9 litres (1915 was the last year in which 4-cylinder engines were used). The larger model, the Six-46 was made as a seven-seater touring car and in three closed types. The smaller six was offered only as a five-seater tourer.

The 1919 models were known as Paige-Linwood (Duesenberg engine) and Paige-Larchmont (Continental engine).

The most notable Paige model was the Daytona roadster, first produced in 1922. This was a sporty three-seater with a 6-cylinder, 6-litre engine. The third seat was a drawer-like affair on the right side which pulled out over the running-board. This car had wire wheels and was named to commemorate the 1921 record of 102mph by a stripped version of this model. The Daytona was continued until 1926.

From 1921 on, the radiator shell was remarkably similar to that of the more familiar and later Bentleys. For the last model year of 1927, the Paige was offered with three chassis using 6-cylinder engines, and one with a straight-8 engine.

A cheaper car built by Paige from 1923 to 1926 was the Jewett. In 1928, the Paige became the Graham-Paige.   GMN

1955 PACKARD Clipper 5.8-litre sedan.
Autosport

PALLADIUM (GB) *1912–1925*
(1) Palladium Autocars Ltd, Kensington, London W. *1912–1919*

1921 PAIGE Daytona 6-litre roadster. *Kenneth Stauffer*

1914 PALLADIUM 18/30hp tourer. *Autocar*

1924 PALLADIUM Victory 11.9hp tourer. A.E.R Gilligan, the well-known cricketer, at the wheel. *Autocar*

1911 PALMER-SINGER 50hp tourer. *Kenneth Stauffer*

(2) Palladium Autocars Ltd, Putney, London S.W.15 *1919–1925*

The first Palladiums were assembled from French components. Three models were listed in 1912, of 10, 12 and 15hp, all with four cylinders and overhead inlet valves. Sv engines were substituted in 1913. These orthodox cars were joined by a six for 1915 and Palladium experimented with a very interesting cyclecar in 1919. It was powered by a flat-twin 1.3-litre air-cooled engine, the cooling being effected by means of a fan blowing into cowlings on the cylinders. The transmission was in the back axle, and was by friction disc. No more passenger cars came from Palladium until 1922, when a conventional 12hp 4-cylinder, with an sv Dorman engine, was introduced. It had a 4-speed gearbox, which was an unusual refinement in a light car at the time. In the following year appeared a more sporting edition, with a tuned engine that furnished a 60mph maximum speed. This performance was the more usable because in the same year front wheel brakes became standard fittings. The Palladium was now a well-liked and formidable proposition among trial drivers, but it was an expensive little car of a specialist appeal and never won general popularity.   TRN

PALLISER (GB) *1968–1972*
Palliser Racing Design Ltd, London S.W.4

The brainchildren of Hugh Palliser Dibley, an ex-racing driver, Palliser cars were made for most racing classes. In the United States they were sold through Bob Winkelmann, who himself raced the first Formula B model. In 1969 the Palliser-Winkelmann WDF1 was the best-selling Formula Ford car in the States, and the WDF2 of 1970 also did well, earning the I.M.S.A. Championship series for Jim Jenkins. Thus encouraged, the firm took over larger premises for 1971, marketing new space-frame cars for Formulas 3, B, Atlantic, Ford, Super Vee, 5000 and sports cars (Group 6). Unfortunately, although most of these models were of sound design and satisfactory performance – in Britain Vern Schuppan gained the Yellow Pages Formula Atlantic Championship – this expansion coincided with a contraction in the market and increasing demands in Dibley's other job as an airline pilot. The firm retreated first to their original small workshops, then ceased completely. Designer Len Wimhurst here carried on with servicing existing models and also built further similar cars for the subordinate formulas under his own name.   DF

PALM (US) *1918–1919*
Distributed by E.W. Brown Motors Pty, Ltd, Melbourne, Victoria

The Palm car was nothing more than a pirated Model T Ford. It was basically a Canadian Ford with the steering wheel changed to the right-hand position and a Palm emblem replacing the obliterated Ford insignia. In 1920, the Renown emblem replaced the Palm and the cars were known by the former name. Although the car was simply a rechristened Ford, it is important to list it under the Palm and Renown names to avoid possible confusion.   KM

PALMER (US) *1906*
Palmer Automobile Manufacturing Co, Ashtabula, Ohio

This was a two-seater car of the buggy type with a single-cylinder engine rated at 8hp. The drive was through a planetary transmission and cables, rather than chains. The car weighed 800lb.   GMN

PALMER-SINGER (US) *1907–1914*
Palmer & Singer Manufacturing Co, Long Island City, N.Y.

The Palmer & Singer company had been agents for Matheson and Simplex cars, and the first P & S cars were built in the Matheson factory. 4- and 6-cylinder models were made, the largest six being a 10-litre 60hp and, unusually for such a large car at that time, it had shaft drive. A 28/30hp 4-cylinder roadster was called the Skimabout; other 4-cylinder models were town cars with dashboard radiators and Renault-style bonnets. Victory in the Long Island Derby at Brighton Beach led to the 1913 models being called Brightons; these were very handsome cars with pointed radiators and streamlined torpedo bodies. In an effort to avert bankruptcy the company announced their 1915 range in late 1913. This included one car with a 6.2-litre 6-cylinder sv Magic engine, made under Fischer patents. However, the company failed, and was replaced by the Singer Motor Co Inc, makers of the Singer (ii) car from 1915 to 1920.   GMN

PALMERSTON; PALM (GB) *1920–1923*
Palmerston Motor Co Ltd, Boscombe, Bournemouth, Hampshire

This company made two models of light car, both using flat-twin Coventry-Victor engines and shaft drive. The Palmerston appeared first and used a 5/7hp engine, while the larger Palm was only available from 1922 to 1923, and used a 9hp engine.   GNG

PAN (US) *1918–1922*
Pan Motor Co, St Cloud, Minn.

The Pan was the tangible result of what became one of the biggest stock swindles in the history of the American car industry. Samuel Conner Pandolfo conceived the idea of a practical car built in a single plant by workers who lived in company housing. He built his own village around a large factory, and started production of touring cars and roadsters with a Pan 4-cylinder engine. An adjustable lever allowed the seats of Pan cars to be made into a double bed. Pandolfo also planned to build a tractor but was arrested, convicted of using the mails to defraud, and imprisoned. The company went out of business in 1922 after building 737 cars.

KM

PAN AMERICAN (i) (US) *1902*
The Pan American Motor Co, Mamaroneck, N.Y.

This company announced a 16hp 4-cylinder car with tonneau body, designed by W.M. Power.

GNG

PAN-AMERICAN (ii) (US) *1917–1922*
Pan-American Motor Corp, Chicago, Ill.; Decatur, Ill.

Formerly the Chicago (vi) the Pan-American was a 6-cylinder assembled car which used a Continental engine, one of many of its kind. Approximately 4,000 cars were turned out in Pan-American's six years of production, including the American Beauty model, built in 1920 and 1921, which is sometimes misrepresented as a make in its own right.

KM

PANDA (US) *1955–1956*
Small Cars Inc, Kansas City, Mo.

The Panda was a light two-seater with alternative power units of a flat-twin 1,100cc Kohler, or a minute 4-cylinder 582cc Aerojet. The wheelbase was only 5ft 10in, and the price was $1,000.

GNG

PÁNEK (CS) *1921–1922*
B. Pánek, Rakovnice

This firm built a few 2-cylinder 12hp cyclecars in 1921.

HON

PANHARD (F) *1889–1967*
(1) Panhard et Levassor, Paris *1889–1898*
(2) Société des Anciens Etablissements Panhard et Levassor, Paris *1899–1965*
(3) SA André Citroën, Paris *1965–1967*

One of the greatest names in the history of motoring, Panhard and Levassor sprang from a woodworking-machinery firm founded by Périn and Pauwels in 1845, which passed into the hands of René Panhard and Emile Levassor on Périn's death in 1886. In the same year Levassor's friend Edouard Sarazin acquired the Daimler patent rights for France; he died in 1887 and his widow subsequently married Levassor.

A car with a centrally-mounted V-twin Daimler engine was running successfully in 1891, and after experiments with rear engines the partnership settled for what was to become the classic automobile layout – engine at the front, gearbox amidships, and driven rear wheels, though as yet the gears were exposed, and final drive was by central chain. These early Panhards had 4 speeds forward and reverse, and sold for 3,500fr. Solid rubber tyres were adopted in 1892, and in 1894 a car was fitted with a Maybach float-feed carburettor in place of the surface type, an improvement standardized in 1895. A Panhard was awarded joint 1st place (with Peugeot) in the 1894 Paris-Rouen Trial, and the following year enclosed gearboxes were used for the first time. Emile Levassor was the moral (if not the technical) victor of the Paris-Bordeaux-Paris Race that year, when wheel steering and the 2.4-litre vertical-twin Phénix engine also made their appearance. On all Panhards up to 1900 the side-brake was inter-connected with the clutch. 4-cylinder engines were used in 1896 racers, and made available to the public in 1898; the marque's win in the Paris-Marseilles-Paris Race was, however, clouded by Emile Levassor's death as the result of a spill during the race.

Gradually the classic Panhard configuration took shape; aluminium gearbox casings were first seen in 1897, as was the rear-mounted G and A radiator. Wheel steering and pneumatic tyres came into general use in 1898, and frontal tubular radiators in 1899. By 1900 the touring Panhard had crystallized into the archetype of the medium-sized car: armoured-wood frame, quadrant change, automatic inlet valves, drip-feed lubrication, final drive by side chains, plus such features as piano-type pedals (dropped in 1907), and cylindrical controls on the steering-wheel (still found in 1911). Makers like M.M.C. and Star (i) in Britain, and Dürkopp in Germany produced near-Panhards, and Montague Napier installed his first car engine of 1899 in a Panhard chassis. In 1899 Commandant Krebs of the Panhard board produced a rear-engined single-cylinder voiturette of retrogressive design, with centre-pivot steering, but the licence was quietly sold to Clément.

So far only Mors had challenged Panhard's racing supremacy. 1898 victories included the Marseilles-Nice Race, Paris-Amsterdam-Paris and the Paris-Bordeaux Race, in which last Charron averaged 26.9mph. A year later Girardot (later to partner Charron in the C.G.V. venture) was averaging 32.5mph to win the Paris-Ostend Race. Though 1900 was a Mors year apart from Charron's victory in the first Gordon Bennett Cup, and 1901 was little better, apart from the exploits of the *voitures légères* with 3.1-litre 4-cylinder engines, Panhard did well under the 1,000-kilogram formula of 1902 with their 13.7-litre 70: this retained automatic inlet valves and the flitch-plate frame, but recorded wins in the Circuit des Ardennes and the Circuit du Nord. Mechanically-operated inlet valves were seen on the 1903 racers, while in 1904 the firm was using 15.4-litre engines, vast V-radiators,

1890 PANHARD 4-seater *dos-à-dos. SA André Citroën*

1912 PANHARD 15.9hp tourer. *G.N. Georgano*

1921 PANHARD 16CV saloon. *SA André Citroën*

1926 PANHARD 35CV straight-8 saloon. *SA André Citroën*

1933 PANHARD 6CS.2 2½-litre saloon. *SA André Citroën*

1937 PANHARD Dynamic 2½-litre coupé. *SA André Citroën*

1946 PANHARD Dyna 610cc saloon. *SA André Citroën*

and shaft drive on their competition cars, being rewarded with victories in the Circuit des Ardennes and the Vanderbilt Cup, the driver in both races being the American, George Heath. Mercedes, Brasier, and F.I.A.T. were, however, in the ascendant, and though Panhard continued to race up to 1908 (trying dashboard radiators in 1907) they never regained their former position.

The same conservatism permeated their touring cars. In 1900 the Hon. C.S. Rolls's Panhard was by far the fastest machine in the 1,000-Miles Trial, and the 1.7-litre 7hp twin of 1901 (still with tube as well as lt electric ignition) was a good seller at £340. That year brought the Krebs automatic carburettor and the Centaure engined governed on the inlet, while the company briefly took up the manufacture of the De Boisse 3-wheeler. Tube ignition was still available as a standby in 1902, in which year Dr Lehwess tried to drive round the world in a 25hp Panhard omnibus weighing 3 tons – he got no further than Nizhni Novgorod. Sales were still a respectable 1,200 in 1904, but the cars were hard to sell, and the Hon. C.S. Rolls gave up his London agency for this reason. A chain-driven 3-cylinder 8/11hp with a 1.8-litre engine at £425 was hardly the answer (though it was still catalogued in 1908), but in 1904 the bigger cars went over to shells for their tubular radiators, mechanically operated inlet valves, and ht magneto ignition.

At the top end of the range in 1905/06 were the Model Q, a 50hp 4-cylinder of 10.5 litres with 5-bearing crankshaft at £1,580, and an even bigger 11-litre 6-cylinder with a bonnet 5ft long which sold for £1,400 in 1906. Multiplate clutches arrived in 1907, and shaft drive (on the smaller cars) in 1908, in which year compressed-air starters were also available, and the range included a 1.2-litre twin and a 5-litre chain-drive six. Pressed-steel frames at last ousted armoured wood, and though a monstrous chain-driven 4-cylinder could still be bought in 1909, a truer sign of the times was a monobloc 2.4-litre 12/16 with ht magneto ignition. Gate change was standard in 1910, and the biggest model was now a chain-driven 6-cylinder 6-litre. 1911 was the last year of the twins, and also the first production year for the Knight sleeve-valve engine introduced on a 4.4-litre 25hp with separate cylinders, a choice of chain or shaft drive, and a chassis price of £580. 42bhp and 59mph were claimed for this, and a smaller Knight-engined 2.6-litre 15hp was available in 1912, when Panhards had all their brakes on the rear wheels, the classic V-radiator (used until 1936) made its appearance on de luxe versions, and wire wheels were available. V-radiators and 4-cylinder engines were universal in 1914; only the small cars had poppet valves, and the big sleeve-valve 4.8-litre and 7.4-litre versions were seen with skiff-type bodywork of great elegance.

Though 2.2-litre poppet-valve cars were made from 1919 to 1922, Panhard settled down to a long association with the Knight engine, and managed to extract some performance from it by the use of light steel sleeves from the middle 1920s. Other oddities were expanding-band brakes, a push-on handbrake, and a peculiar X-gate gear change which took some learning. In 1922 the sleeve-valve range was extended at both ends by a rather ponderous 1.2-litre ten with central change, left-hand drive, thermo-syphon cooling and a cone clutch instead of the usual wet-plate, and by a big 6.3-litre straight-8 with front-wheel brakes, twin magnetos, and twin carburettors, which was made until 1930.

All 1924 models had front-wheel brakes, dynamotors, and 4-speed gearboxes and the smaller ones had splash lubrication. The 4.8-litre 4-cylinder was quite a fast car which took the World Hour Record at 115.3mph in 1925, and in its 5.3-litre 1929 form it could exceed 90mph. The straight-8s with bored-out 7.9-litre engines also had a long career in record work which did not end until 1934, but another aspiring record-breaker – an ultra-narrow 1½-litre single-seater steered by a hoop around the cockpit – came to nothing.

The first 6-cylinder sleeve-valve car was the 3.4-litre 20/60 of 1927, soon followed by the 1.8-litre 16/45 and the 2.3-litre twin-carburettor 18/50. Silent-3rd gearboxes were adopted in 1929, and a year later an all-silent type had been evolved – in 1931 this was fitted to 3.5-litre 6-cylinder and 5-litre 8-cylinder cars with centralized chassis lubrication, coil ignition, a sheet steel platform between the rear cross-members of the frame, but still having wood wheels and the X-gate. This range continued until 1936, though later ones had free wheels, automatic clutches and wrap-round windscreens reminiscent of the Arrol-Johnstons of the early 1920s; they were expensive, the big 8-cylinder 8DSR costing 95,000fr or 15,000fr more than the most luxurious Renault.

For 1937 there was the startling Dynamic, still a sleeve-valve six (it came in 2.5-litre, 2.7-litre and 3.8-litre sizes) but with backbone chassis, hydraulic brakes, worm drive, and all-round torsion bar independent suspension. Faired-in headlamps, wheel spats front and rear, and a central driving position completed a bizarre ensemble, though a reversion to left-hand drive was made with the 1939 models.

There was a complete *volte face* after 1945, and the Panhard became a utility car of considerable performance with the advent of the Dyna series. These were air-cooled fwd flat-twins of 610cc based on a Grégoire (ii) design, in which torsion bars served as valve springs for the ohv gear; the light alloy bodywork was by Facel-Métallon, front suspension was independent, rear suspension by a live axle and torsion bars, and the 4-speed gearbox had an overdrive top and dashboard change. The original version was followed by a 32bhp 750cc version in 1950, and two years later there was an 850cc 5CV as well. Specialist cars using Panhard mechanical elements were D.B. (from 1948), Veritas (1950), Marathon (ii) (1954), and Arista (ii) (1957). Even faster Dynas were evolved and the special Monopole of

Hémard and de Montrémy won the Index of Performance at Le Mans three years in succession (1950–1952); further wins in this category were scored in 1953 (with a works-sponsored streamliner designed by Riffard) and again in 1963. Rally successes included a Coupe des Alpes in the 1952 Alpine Rally, a class win in the 1954 Monte Carlo Rally, and an outright win in 1961. Panhard's offered their own sports variant, the Junior, in 1953; this 38bhp roadster was followed a year later by a supercharged, 62bhp version.

Far more ambitious was the 1954 Dyna saloon, a bulbous and ugly machine in alloy (no castings were used). Both the engine-transmission group and the dead rear axle were removable as units, a petrol heater was standard, and it could carry six people at 80mph with a 40mpg petrol consumption. It was expensive in England at £1,055, but it pushed sales up from around 14,000 in 1951 to 30,000 in 1957, and it survived in the range for ten years. All-steel bodywork was standardized in 1958, and from 1961 there was a high-performance (over 90mph) version, the 60bhp Tigre at £1,127. Over 100mph was claimed from the hotter 24CT and CD sports coupés introduced for 1964. In 1955 Citroën took an interest in the company, and ten years later the old-established Panhard concern was fully integrated into the SA André Citroën, thus giving its new owners greater factory space. In 1967, Panhard's last year, only the coupé versions of the Dyna were being manufactured, in 50bhp and 60bhp 850cc forms, the 24CT with all-round disc brakes.   MCS

1964 PANHARD 24CT 848cc coupé. *Autosport*

PANTHER (i) (D) *1902–1904*
Panther Fahrradwerke Oskar Vormbaum, Magdeburg

This manufacturer of bicycles and motorcycles introduced a small 3-wheeled two-seater with two driven rear wheels in 1902. A De Dion-Bouton engine was used. In 1903 a 4-wheeled car appeared with a 20hp engine. The car division of this firm was taken over by Dürkopp in 1904 and transferred to Bielefeld.   HON

PANTHER (ii) (GB) *1906–1908*
F.M. Russell & Co Ltd, Willesden, London N.W.

The Panther was an imported car sold by F.M. Russell who also handled the Westminster. It had a 14hp 4-cylinder engine, and sold at £350 for the chassis.   GNG

PANTHER (iii) (I) *1954–1955*
(1) Panther Diesel SpA, Milan
(2) Industria Sammarinese Costruzione Automobili, Milan

The Italian Panther was the only Diesel-engined minicar, and one of the few cars designed exclusively for use with this type of power unit. The engine was a 520cc twin driving the front wheels, and a two-seater coupé body was fitted. A 480cc petrol-engined version was made in 1955 by I.S.C.A.   GNG

PANTHER (iv) (US) *1962–1963*
Panther Automobile Co, Bedford Hills, N.Y.

This was a fibreglass sports car powered by a 2.6-litre V-8 engine developing 190bhp. Claimed maximum speed was 150mph, and the price $4,995.   GNG

1954 PANTHER(iii) 480cc coupé. *Associated Press Ltd*

PANTHER (v) (GB) *1972 to date*
Panther West Winds Ltd, Walton-on-Thames, Surrey

The Panther J72 is a fairly close replica of the pre-World War 2 S.S.100 two-seater sports car, powered by a 3.8-litre Jaguar 6-cylinder engine basically similar to that used in the Mark 2 saloons. The Panther has a Jaguar XJ6 gearbox, tubular chassis, beam axles and disc brakes. Maximum speed is 114mph.   GNG

PANTHÈRE (F) *1922–1923*
Automobiles Panthère, Paris 15c

The Panthère was a light car powered by a 904cc 4-cylinder Ruby engine. A conventional 3-speed gearbox and shaft drive were used.   GNG

PANTZ (F) *1900–1901*
Charles Pantz, Pont-à-Mousson, Meurthe-et-Moselle

Pantz cars used 2-cylinder horizontal engines of 6 or 9hp. Steering was by tiller, and transmission by fast-and-loose pulleys giving 4 forward and 2 reverse speeds. M. Pantz made lorries for several years after he abandoned the production of private cars.   GNG

PARAGON (i) (US) *1905–1907*
Detroit Automobile Manufacturing Co, Detroit, Mich.

This car with its distinctive 700cc, 2-cylinder 5hp engine was not aptly named. The total weight of this very small two-seater was 650lb.   GMN

PARAGON (ii) (GB) *1913–1914*
K. Portway & Co, Manningtree, Essex

The Paragon was a belt-driven cyclecar with air- or water-cooled engines by J.A.P. or Fafnir. The price was £115.   GNG

PARAGON (iii) (US) *1921–1922*
Paragon Motor Car Co, Connellsville, Pa.

1972 PANTHER(v) J72 3.4-litre sports car. *Panther West Winds Ltd*

1956 PARAMOUNT 1½-litre tourer. *Paramount Cars Ltd*

1921 PARENTI 35hp V-8 tourer. *Automobile Manufacturers' Association*

1899 PARISIENNE Victoria Combination 2¾hp voiturette. Dan Albone, maker of the Ivel car, at the tiller. *Gordon Brooks*

This 6-cylinder phaeton was to have been made at Cumberland, Md., but the few cars produced were built elsewhere. The Paragon had an engine of the company's own design and disc wheels were standard equipment. KM

PARAMOUNT (GB) *1950–1956*

(1) Paramount Cars (Derbyshire) Ltd, Swadlincote, Melbourne, Derbyshire *1950–1952*

(2) Meynell Motor Co Ltd, Swadlincote, Melbourne, Derbyshire *1952–1953*

(3) Paramount Cars (Leighton Buzzard) Ltd, Linsdale, Bucks, *1953–1956*

The Paramount used a Ford Ten engine in a ladder-type under-slung chassis, with a hand-built aluminium body on a wooden frame. On the early models a Wade or Shorrocks supercharger was an optional extra. The Leighton Buzzard firm (associated with Camden Motors) was the first to get the car into production, as only six were made in Derbyshire. With the Ford Ten engine maximum speed was 70mph, but this was increased late in 1955 with the adoption of the 1508cc Ford Consul engine. In 1956 the remaining stock of cars was acquired by Welbeck Motors Ltd of London, and sold at £795 each (£214 less than the list price). The cars were mostly four-seater tourers, a rare body style in England at this time, but a few saloons were also made. GNG

PARANT (F) *1906–1907*

Parant frères, Neuilly, Seine

The Parant was a conventional touring car powered by a 24/30hp 4-cylinder Ballot engine. Transmission was by a 3-speed gearbox, and final drive by side chains. GNG

PARENT (F) *1913–1914*

Paul Faitot (Automobiles Parent), Maisons-Alfort, Seine

Two models of the Parent were made, one with a large single-cylinder engine of 704cc, and the other with a 4-cylinder engine of 905cc. Both cars used shaft drive, and had sharply-pointed radiators. GNG

PARENTI (US) *1920–1922*

Parenti Motors Corp, Buffalo, N.Y.

This car was designed without axles, transverse springing being used as a substitute: two springs were located in the front and one in the rear. Plywood was extensively used in the construction of both frame and body. The Parenti was powered by a V-8 air-cooled engine of the firm's own design but for 1922 a water-cooled Falls six was substituted. To attract the public, Parenti salesmen exhibited some of the first models in bright orange, yellow and purple.

Whether it was the design of the Parenti or its price ($5,000 for the town car and formal limousine) which defeated the car is not now known. Relatively few cars were sold, however, before the company failed. KM

PARENT-LACROIX (F) *c.1900–c.1903*

Parent et Lacroix, Villefranche, Rhône

Designed by Petrus Lacroix, this car was a voiturette made in very small numbers. Details of specification are not known. GNG

PARISIA *see* OWEN (i)

PARISIENNE (F) *1899–1903*

Sté Parisienne E. Couturier et Cie, Paris

This company made bicycles and tricycles but were mainly known for the ultra-light voiturette called the Victoria Combination. This had a 2¾hp De Dion or 3½hp Aster engine mounted over the front axle, and driving the front wheels. Both front axle and engine turned with the steering, which was by tiller. They were generally thought to be very flimsy, but in a 1900 trial, one averaged 18mph over a route of 150 miles without an involuntary stop. Over 400 were made in two years; it was also known as the Eureka. The company also made more conventional cars known as the Duc-Spider two-seater and Duc-Tonneau four-seater. These had 5 or 6½ Aster engines under a bonnet, driving the rear axle by shaft. GNG

PARIS-RHÔNE (F) *1947–c.1950*

The Lyons-built Paris-Rhône was an electric 3-wheeler with a two-seater coupé body by Faurax et Chassende. GNG

PARIS SINGER (GB) *1900*

Paris Singer Ltd, Clapham, London S.W.

This car has no connection with either of the other Singers, being made by a son of Isaac M. Singer, founder of the sewing machine company. The Paris Singer had a 4½hp 2-cylinder horizontal engine mounted under the seat and driving by chains. Although it was described as being 'as noiseless as many electric vehicles', it never went into production. GNG

PARKER (i) (GB) *1901–1902*

Thomas H. Parker; Wearwell Motor Co, Wolverhampton, Staffs.

Designed by Thomas Parker, this car was built in the works of the Wearwell company, makers of the Wearwell cars and Wolf motorcycles. It was a steamer with a 10hp compound 2-cylinder engine, a flash boiler under the bonnet, and shaft drive. It had the general appearance of a Daimler. Parker also designed some electric cars, including the Bushbury Electric Cart of 1897. This was a 3-wheeler steered by reins.   GNG

PARKER (ii) (CDN) *1921–1923*
Park Motor Car Co Ltd, Montreal, Que.

The Parker looked identical to the American Birmingham, but while it used the same Haskelite bodies it had a traditional suspension system instead of the Birmingham's Wright-Fisher independent front suspension. Parkers were built in the former Forster plant, but only a handful of them. A Continental 6-cylinder engine was used, and the biggest model was called the Royal Six.   HD

PARKIN (US) *1908*
Parkin & Son, Philadelphia, Pa.

The Parkin was a 6-cylinder, 60hp car that cost more than $3,000. Its manufacturer tried unsuccessfully to make a name in local races in 1908. Once source claims that the Parkin was produced as early as 1903.   GMN

PARNACOTT (GB) *1913–1920*
A.E. Parnacott, Penge, Kent

At least two distinct prototypes of the Parnacott were made, but production never started. The pre-war car used a 3½hp air-cooled F.N. engine, and the 1920 model a 1,478cc flat-twin water-cooled unit, all-independent suspension and shaft drive. A price of £300 was fixed for the latter car.   GNG

PARR (GB) *1901–1902*
J. Parr & Co Ltd, Leicester

The Parr light car used a 5hp single-cylinder engine of the company's own manufacture, and double chain drive. One was entered in the 1901 Glasgow Reliability Trials, but retired on the first day. In 1902 an 8hp car was made.   GNG

PARRY; NEW PARRY (US) *1910–1912*
(1) Parry Auto Co, Indianapolis, Ind. *1910–1911*
(2) Motor Car Manufacturing Co, Indianapolis, Ind. *1912*

The Parry was built as a two- or five-seater open car with 20 or 30hp 4-cylinder ohv engines. After reorganization in 1911, the name was changed to New Parry. The last models, with 4-cylinder engines developing 35hp, were priced at $1,750.   GMN

PARSONS (US) *1905–1906*
Parsons Electric Motor Carriage Co, Cleveland, Ohio

The Parsons was a diminutive two-seater electric car with a 5ft 6in wheelbase and 3ft 10in track. Its 8hp motor was connected to the drive axle by double chains. It weighed 900lb and cost $1,600.   GMN

PARTIN; PARTIN-PALMER (US) *1913–1917*
(1) Partin Manufacturing Co, Chicago, Ill. *1913–1915*
(2) Commonwealth Motors Co, Chicago, Ill; Rochelle, Ill. *1915–1917*

The Partin was a six-seater, powered by a 6-cylinder Rutenber engine. After combining with Palmer Motor Car Co, late in 1913 (with no change in the company name), this became the Partin-Palmer. The latter was made in two versions. The smaller model, with a 22hp 4-cylinder engine, with full electrical equipment, was a two-seater selling for $495. The larger model, designated the 38, was a five-seater with a 6-cylinder Mason engine, on a longer wheelbase. It was replaced by the 32, a Lycoming-powered four which, with minor alterations, became the Commonwealth.   GMN

PARVILLÉ (F) *1927-c.1929*
Edouard Parvillé Paris 8e

The Parvillé was an electric car powered by a 5hp motor driving the front wheels.   GNG

PASCAL (F) *1902–1903*
Automobiles Pascal, Paris 18e

The Pascal cars were made in the Bardon factory, and were said to have been designed by Baron Henri de Rothschild who gave his services free to Paris hospitals under the pseudonym of Dr Pascal. The car was a large chain-drive tonneau powered by a 24hp 4-cylinder engine, and cost £860 in England. In September 1902 there were plans to change the car's name to Le Roi Soleil, after the famous racehorse owned by the Baron, but at the Paris Salon that year it was still known as the Pascal.   GNG

PASHLEY (GN) *1953*
W.R. Pashley Ltd, Birmingham

The Pashley 3-wheeler used a 197cc Villiers 2-stroke engine, and was very much like the Bond Minicar in layout. The price was fixed at £265 (the Bond was £269), but production never started. The firm also made motor rickshaws.   GNG

1910 PARRY 30hp tourer. *Automotive History Collection, Detroit Public Library*

1903 PASCAL 24hp tonneau. *The Veteran Car Club of Great Britain*

1906 PASSY-THELLIER 16/20hp landaulette.
Lucien Loreille Collection

1915 PATHFINDER 40hp tourer. *Don McCray*

1916 PATERSON 25hp tourer. *Kenneth Stauffer*

PASING (D) *1902–1904*

Automobilwerk Pasing Albert Regensteiner, Pasing

This firm produced a voiturette reminiscence of Klingenberg designs with a single-cylinder rear-mounted engine.　　　　HON

PASSE PARTOUT *see* REYROL

PASSONI (I) *1905*

Cycle-type wire wheels and a tubular frame characterized Maurizio Passoni's voiturette exhibited at the 1905 Turin Show.　　　　MCS

PASSY-THELLIER (F) *1903–1907*

Sté Passy-Thellier, Levallois-Perret, Seine

The first Passy-Thellier cars used 8 and 10hp 2-cylinder Aster engines and 12 and 16hp 4-cylinder engines by Abeille and Aster respectively. They used shaft drive, and various models competed in Paris-Vienna and Paris-Madrid races. For 1903 a 24hp 4-cylinder Buchet-engined car was added. Later cars were sometimes known as Mendelssohns, one of the directors being E.G. Mendelssohn-Bartholdy, of the same family as the famous composer. In 1906 a company was formed to sell the cars in England, by which time a 6/8hp single-cylinder car had been added to the range, although other models were similar to those of the 1903 range.　　　　GNG

PATERSON (US) *1908–1923*

W.A. Paterson Co, Flint, Mich.

The Paterson started as a typical Mid-Western motor buggy. The Model 14 had solid rubber tyres and an air-cooled 2-cylinder engine, with planetary transmission and double chain-drive. By 1910 this had evolved into a car with a 30hp 4-cylinder engine, sliding-gear transmission and shaft drive, in three body styles. The use of 4-cylinder engines was continued into 1915 when the line was complemented by a car with a 6-cylinder, 4.7-litre engine and a longer wheelbase. After 1915, only sixes were made. It is likely that all the sixes were built by Continental; at all events from 1919 until 1923 this was the engine make. The body styles were conservative and there were no outstanding types. The distinguishing feature of the later models was a radiator and bonnet cross-section with sharp shoulders, probably in imitation of the Packard.　　　　GMN

PATHFINDER (US) *1911–1918*

(1) Motor Car Manufacturing Co, Indianapolis, Ind. *1911–1915*
(2) The Pathfinder Co, Indianapolis, Ind. *1916–1918*

The Pathfinder succeeded the New Parry and was noted for several advanced body innovations, such as the disappearing top, the boat-tailed roadster and spare wheels under cover. The various models were large with 10 to 11ft wheelbases. Early Pathfinders had 4-cylinder engines; V-radiatored sixes followed, and in 1916 a model with a 6.4-litre 12-cylinder Weidely power unit was launched.　　　　GMN

PATIN (F) *1898–1900*

Cie Electrique O. Patin, Paris

Patin electric cars were made in various models from a light tandem two-seater to a heavy-looking five-seater victoria with unequal artillery wheels. In 1899 a 3-wheeled voiturette with its motor driving the front wheel was made, known as the Patin et Requillard.　　　　GNG

PATRI (F) *1923–1925*

Etablissements Patri, Paris 17e

Two models were made by this company, a 5hp 2-cylinder cyclecar known as La Forinette, and a 6hp 4-cylinder car with an ohv Chapuis-Dornier engine.　　　　GNG

PATRIA (D) *1899–1901*

Weyersberg, Kirschbaum & Co AG, Solingen

After manufacturing tricycles and quadricycles, this firm went on to offer a voiturette with a single-cylinder proprietary engine in 1899.　　　　HON

PATTERSON-GREENFIELD (US) *1916–1918*

C.R. Patterson & Sons, Greenfield, Ohio

This was the product of a well-known Negro family of carriage builders who had been in business since the 19th century. The car was a conventional machine, made mostly in tourer form and powered by a 30hp 4-cylinder engine. About 30 were made.　　　　GNG

PAULET (F) *1922–1925*

Sté Mécanique du Rhône, Marseilles

The Paulet was a high quality car with a single ohc 3.9-litre 6-cylinder engine of the company's own design and manufacture. About 200 cars were made.　　　　GNG

PAWI (D) *1921*

Paul Victor Willke, Berlin-Reinickendorf

The Pawi was a conventional light car powered by a 4-cylinder 1,598cc 6/18PS engine. It had a 4-speed gearbox and torpedo tourer or delivery van bodies. Probably only prototypes were made, although the firm also made motorcycles. GNG

PAWTUCKET (US) *1900–1901*

Pawtucket Steam Boat Co, Providence, R.I.

This company made a small number of an unusual vehicle, a single-seater steam car. It had a 7hp 2-cylinder engine, and solid tyres on its 32in wheels. GNG

PAYDELL (GB) *1924–1925*

Paydell Engineering Co, Hendon, Middlesex

The Paydell was a medium-sized car powered by a 13.9hp 4-cylinder ohv Meadows engine. The specification was conventional, and at £575 it cannot have attracted many buyers. GNG

PAYNE-MODERN (MODERN) (US) *1907–1909*

Modern Tool Co, Erie, Pa.

The Payne-Modern used ohv air-cooled 4- or 6-cylinder engines of V configuration, with 60° between the cylinder banks. The gearshift lever was mounted on the steering column, and the final drive was by shaft. The semi-elliptic springs were inclined so that the outboard ends were above the frame, while the inside ends were beneath the level of the frame. Both touring and roadster models were made, with 4-speed gearboxes. GMN

PAYZE (GB) *1920–1921*

Payze Light Car Co Ltd, Cookham, Berks.

The Payze light car used a 10hp Coventry-Simplex engine. With a three-seater cloverleaf body, the price was £450. GNG

P.D.A (GB) *1912–1913*

Pickering, Darby & Allday Ltd, Birmingham

The P.D.A. cyclecar used V-twin engines by Precision, Blumfield or J.A.P. in conjunction with shaft drive and a 2-speed gearbox on the rear axle. No more than 15 were made. GNG

PEACE *see* HE-PING

PEARSALL-WARNE *see* WARNE

PEARSON-COX (GB) *1909–1916*

Pearson & Cox Ltd, Shortlands, Kent

The Pearson-Cox was the last new make of steam car to appear in Great Britain, and this was probably the last company to make steamers in Britain. The design incorporated a 3-cylinder compound engine, semi-flash boiler and shaft drive. The original engine was a 12hp unit, and the cars were generally two-seaters, but in 1913 a larger 15hp model was made with full five-seater bodywork. Few of these cars were made, mostly to special order. In 1913 a petrol-engined cyclecar was made, powered by an 8hp J.A.P. V-twin, with belt drive to a gearbox on the rear axle, again to special order only. GNG

PECK (CDN) *1913*

Peck Electric Limited, Toronto, Ont.

The very elegant Peck coupé cost $4,000 but offered a choice of chain or shaft drive and wheel or tiller steering. The factory serviced Toronto buyers' cars, though its slogan insisted that the car 'Keeps Pecking'. It was also available as a roadster, with chain drive and wheel steering standard. HD

PECO (ZA) *1965 to date*

The Formula V (Volkswagen-based) champions of 1965 and 1966 offered this smart single-seater based on a square-tube chassis frame, with a fibreglass body. In 1967 a British version, known as the C.G.V., was developed. DF

PEDERSEN (US) *1922*

The Pedersen was a shaft-drive light car with a 9hp 2-cylinder air-cooled engine. It was intended for mail-order distribution. GNG

PEEL (GBM) *1962–1966*

Peel Engineering Co Ltd, Peel, Isle of Man

The only car ever to have been produced for sale in the Isle of Man, the Peel is a very light 3-wheeler. The original model, the P.50, was one of the smallest cars ever made, with a single-seater coupé body only 4ft 5in long, and a 49cc D.K.W. engine. The later Trident had two seats in tandem, and an electric model was tried in 1965. About 100 Peels of all types were made. Subsequently fibreglass coupé bodies were made for B.M.C. Minis. GNG

PEER GYNT (D) *1925*

Dickmann AG, Berlin W.57

This was a very light cyclecar powered by a singe-cylinder 2-stroke engine. GNG

1920 PAYZE 10hp two-seater. *M.A. Harrison Collection*

1909 PEARSON-COX Model F 12hp steam car. *Autocar*

1963 PEEL P.50 49cc single-seater coupé. *G.N. Georgano*

1904 PEERLESS(i) 24hp tourer. *Burton H. Upjohn*

1923 PEERLESS(i) 5.4-litre coupé. *Keith Marvin Collection*

1925 PEERLESS(i) 5.4-litre tourer. *National Motor Museum*

1929 PEERLESS(i) Six-81 3.7-litre sedan. *Keith Marvin Collection*

PEERLESS (i) (US) *1900–1931*

(1) Peerless Mfg Co, Cleveland, Ohio *1900–1905*
(2) Peerless Motor Car Co, Cleveland, Ohio *1905–1931*

The Peerless was known in its heyday as 'One of the three P's' (Packard, Peerless and Pierce-Arrow), the great trio of American motoring. It first appeared in 1900, the product of a concern which had built clothes wringers and bicycles since 1869. Its début was not auspicious, the 1900 prototype being a typical horse-less carriage with bicycle wheels and a single-cylinder De Dion-Bouton engine. This was followed in 1901 by the Type C Motorette, with a 3½hp single-cylinder water-cooled engine, priced at $1,300. This was augmented later in the year by the Type B, similar but smaller and cheaper.

Louis P. Mooers came to Peerless as chief engineer in 1901 and it was he who shaped the policy of the company during its first formative years. He designed the 1902 range of cars. These were shaft-driven and the engine was mounted vertically at the front of the car in what was to be the conventional arrangement in most cars, but was an innovation at the time. Selective sliding-gear transmission was used and side-entrance tonneaus were included in the range, possibly the first cars of this type. The prototypes of the 1902 line were equipped with a single-cylinder Mooers-designed engine, although the production cars had 2-cylinder power plants. The 1903 series were based on 1902 Peerless racing cars (also designed by Mooers). Two models were available, a 24 and a 35hp, both with 4-cylinder T-head engines of Mooers design. The year 1903 was notable for the appearance of the Peerless limousine, probably America's first closed car that was not custom-built.

In 1904, Mooers designed the famous Peerless Green Dragon racing car, a behemoth with a 6in × 6in bore and stroke. Driven from track to track by Barney Oldfield, 'The Boy in Green' test driver for the company's racing cars, the Green Dragon brought Peerless an enviable reputation as Oldfield continued to break records – frequently his own! He crashed the Green Dragon in 1905, but a new car was built and continued the record set by its earlier namesake.

By this time, the company was rapidly expanding and production was increased. The Peerless was regarded as one of the prestige cars of America and was priced accordingly. In 1907, the first 6-cylinder model was introduced although the fours continued for many years. Changes were largely limited to perfection of details. In 1912, prices ranged from $4,200 to $7,200. By 1913, Peerless cars were equipped with self-starters of the firm's own design.

An important development in Peerless design was the introduction of a V-8, a year after the rival Cadillac concern. This Peerless V-8 appeared late in 1915 and was reasonably priced in comparison with the expensive sixes which were discontinued at this time. With 80bhp at 2,700rpm, low speeds as well as high were possible in top gear. In appearance the V-8 closely resembled the Cadillac. The 1915 model continued without basic change until 1922, by which time its appearance had become outmoded. For 1923, bodies were lowered and rounded and the rear platform spring given up. Strangely enough, the newer design also closely resembled the contemporary Cadillac.

By 1923, business was good with some 5,000 cars being sold. A year later, a six was introduced as a companion car to the larger eight, now termed the 'Equipoised Eight'. In 1925, for the first time, an outside engine was utilized in a six by Peerless. This was a Continental and was used on the 6–80 chassis. Prices ranged from $1,400 for the cheapest six to more than $4,100 for the most expensive eight. Between 1926 and 1929, Peerless continued to market two lines of sixes and one of eights at prices from $1,895 to $3,795. But despite a wide price range, sales were falling steadily, possibly because of generally uninspired and rather unattractive bodies. In 1929, the Peerless range was redesigned, the new models resembling the Marmon or Stutz to a considerable degree. A Continental straight-8 replaced the old V-8 engine. The two sizes were continued and towards the end of 1929, with sales increasing, the outlook seemed brighter. Count Alexis de Sakhnoffsky was hired to design the 1930 line. These cars were the sleekest and best-looking Peerless had ever produced. Three sixes and one eight were offered with prices ranging from $995 to $2,195. The eight was dropped shortly after its introduction.

Then came the Depression and this finished the Peerless. The make had slipped from 25th to 28th place among American car manufacturers from 1928 to 1929 and to 30th place in 1930.

It was early in 1931 that the company decided to attempt to recapture its former position by introducing a new prestige car which would compare with the Cadillac V-16 and the Marmon Sixteen. This was the Peerless V-16; only one prototype was built and this still survives today. Built in 1931, it was to have been produced as a 1933 or possibly even a 1932 model. This car was almost entirely built of aluminium. With a 42lb frame, an aluminium engine of 7.6 litres and 173bhp at 3,300rpm it was one of the handsomest cars ever made in the United States then or at any other time. Its custom sedan body was built by Murphy.

Actual production of Peerless cars ended on 30th June 1931. The plant remained idle for more than two years then, prohibition having been repealed, the Peerless Motor Car Company became the Peerless Corporation, brewers of Carling's Ale and as such, it survives to this day.   KM

PEERLESS (ii) (GB) *1957–1960*
Peerless Cars Ltd, Slough, Bucks.

A square-section tubular frame, clad with a 2-door fibreglass saloon body, formed the basis of the four-seater Peerless GT. Engine, transmission, front suspension and controls were Triumph TR3, whilst rear suspension was by leaf springs with a De Dion axle. In the twelve months following a successful Le Mans run in 1958 approximately 250 cars were sold, but a degree of roughness both in performance and in detail finish thwarted the development of any lasting popularity. The sponsors had originally sold reconditioned American Peerless lorries after World War 1.   DF

1958 PEERLESS(ii) 2-litre coupé. *British Resin Products Ltd*

PEGASO (E) 1951–1958
Empresa Nacional de Autocamiones SA, Barcelona

The only post-war Spanish car to have achieved international fame, the Pegaso was a complex and expensive sports car built in the training works of the old Hispano-Suiza factory. It was first shown to the public at the 1951 Paris Salon as a 2½-litre V-8 with four overhead camshafts, dry sump lubrication and a 5-speed gearbox incorporated in the rear axle. Suspension was by torsion bars all round, and the rear axle was of the De Dion type. This car was the Tipo Z.102 developing 180/230bhp, and it was followed by the Z.102 B (2.8-litre, 210bhp), Z.102 SS (3.2-litre, 210/280 bhp) and Z.103 (4.0-, 4.5- and 4.7-litre); the Z.103 had push-rod overhead valves. Performance varied considerably according to compression ratio and axle ratio. Carburation was by 2, 4 or 8 Webers, and the cars could be supplied with Roots-type superchargers. Only three of four Z.103s were made.

Pegasos never made a significant mark in international competition, although they did well in some Spanish races, and one took records for the flying kilometre and flying mile in Belgium in 1953. A curious asymmetrical car with the driver's seat on the offside was entered for Le Mans in 1953.

In 1958 the designer, Wilfredo Ricart, retired, and company policy changed in favour of concentrating on heavy lorries and buses, which had always been their main production. Only 125 Pegasos were built, mostly to special order.   JRV

1951 PEGASO Z.102 2½-litre drophead coupé. *Autosport*

PEGASSE (F) 1924–1925
M. Arboval, Boisguilbert

The Pegasse was a cyclecar powered by a 2-cylinder engine, and with final drive by chains.   GNG

PEILLON (F) 1899–1900
Made at Boulogne-sur-Seine, the Peillon 2½hp voiturette was exhibited at the 1899 Paris Salon.   GNG

PEKA (D) 1924
Pe-Ka Fahrzeugwerk, Dresden A.16

This light 3-wheeler followed the same general arrangement as numerous other makes in Germany in that period. It had a single front wheel and the rear axle was driven by a rear-mounted 1.5PS D.K.W. engine. A single-seater body was fitted.   HON

PELHAM see BAILEY & LAMBERT

PENDLETON (US) 1905
Trumbull Manufacturing Co, Warren, Ohio

The Pendleton was a five-seater tonneau. Its 4.6-litre 4-cylinder engine was rated at 28/30hp.   GMN

PENELLE (F) 1900–1901
C. Penelle, Melun, Seine-et-Marne

The Penelle was a car of Benz-like appearance powered by a 6hp 2-cylinder Buchet horizontal engine. This drove by belt to a countershaft on which a train of spur wheels meshed with pinions on a differential shaft, from which final drive was by chain.   GNG

PENN (US) 1911–1913
Penn Motor Car Co, Pittsburgh, Pa.

The Penn Thirty had a 4-cylinder engine of 3.7 litres. It was built in two-seater and five-seater versions, both with 8ft 9in wheelbases. A 45hp model was also listed.   GMN

1955 PEGASO Z.103 4.7-litre sports car. *E.N.A.S.A.*

PENNINE (GB) 1914
The Pennine cyclecar was built near Halifax, and used an 8hp V-twin J.A.P. engine. The price was £110.   GNG

PENNINGTON (US; GB; US) 1894–1895; 1896–1899; 1899–1902
(1) E.J. Pennington, Cleveland, Ohio 1894–1895
(2) Great Horseless Carriage Co Ltd, Coventry, Warwickshire 1896–1897
(3) Pennington and Baines, London 1898–1899
(4) Pennington Motor Co Ltd, London 1899
(5) Anglo-American Rapid Vehicle Co, New York, N.Y. Philadelphia, Pa. 1899–1902

1896 PENNINGTON Autocar 2hp 3-wheeler.
National Motor Museum

1909 PENNSYLVANIA Type D 29hp tourer. *The Veteran Car Club of Great Britain*

This complicated list of companies must be regarded as principal *claimants* to manufacture, since Edward Joel Pennington was the company promoter and charlatan *par excellence* of the horseless-carriage era; total production during his heyday probably amounted to no more than 15 vehicles, of which not one went to a private buyer. Pennington himself claimed to have built an electric 3-wheeler in 1887, an airship in 1890, and the first of his internal-combustion devices in 1893, but it was not until 1894 that he devoted himself seriously to the motor car. His ideas included a fuel-metering device in place of a carburettor, the much-discussed 'long-mingling spark', (which was not found on any Penningtons made after 1896), steel-tube cylinders without water-jacketing, large section 'unpuncturable' pneumatic tyres, and the ability to run on ordinary lamp-oil – a claim which does not seem to have been put to practical test. The first Pennington was a motorcycle, which was said to have sailed through the air for 65 feet, and to have attained 57mph. From this evolved the first 'Victoria', a primitive quadricycle made up of two ladies' bicycles joined together by a central platform which housed the working parts. Before he left America he had persuaded the Hitchcock cycle firm in Cortland, N.Y., and Thomas Kane and Co of Racine, Wisconsin, to finance his astonishing projects – hence the name Kane-Pennington applied to the engines in his earlier English press releases. It was announced that six Kane-Pennington 'motocycles' were to be entered for the Chicago *Times-Herald* race of 1895, but none materialized. By the end of the year Pennington and his prototypes were in London.

Thereafter, a stream of wild claims, challenges and projects poured from Pennington's fertile brain: fire-engines, 'war-motors', and even an airscrew-driven motor cycle which was actually exhibited at the Cycle Show in December 1896. The presence of water jacketing on the Victoria's cylinders was an initial disappointment; none the less, Pennington was able to sell his patent rights to H.J. Lawson's British Motor Syndicate for a reported £100,000 and by the summer of 1896 it was announced that Coulthard's of Preston were going into production with a commercial vehicle powered by a 16hp V-4 Kane-Pennington engine. Pennington himself was assigned a storey of the Lawson-owned Motor Mills at Coventry, whence emerged the best-known of his cars, the 3-wheeled Torpedo. This had a parallel-twin engine of immensely long stroke (62.5mm × 305mm, or 1.9 litres); though the long-mingling spark was not used in practice, the fuel-metering nozzle was, and the only other engine control was an ignition switch. The tubular frame was made by Humber, the vehicle was intended to be steerable either by driver (at the rear on a saddle) or front passenger, and four transverse saddles were mounted on top of the frame for additional passengers. Pennington asserted that it could carry nine people, it certainly managed 40mph on occasion and defeated a Bollée in a much-publicized tug of war, but its retirement from the London-Brighton Emancipation Run was occasioned by the bursting of one of the 'unpuncturable' tyres. Five were probably made at Coventry, and in March 1897 the Irish Motor and Cycle Co was floated in Dublin. This concern collapsed five months later without doing anything, and even the Great Horseless Carriage Co gave up advertising early delivery of Penningtons.

In 1898 the inventor was back, publicizing (from a new London address) the Raft-Victoria, a 3½hp device with front-wheel drive, rear-wheel steering, trembler-coil ignition and a horizontal under-floor engine with horizontal rope (later belt) drive, all for less than £100 – later increased to £115 10s on the strength of over 400 orders booked! Hubert Egerton attempted to drive one of these from Manchester to London, but gave up at Nuneaton after 72 sparking plugs had been consumed. An illusion of series-production (which deceived S.F. Edge, among others) was created by commissioning two Lancashire firms (later to make the Rothwell and Bijou cars respectively) to build components for the Raft-Victoria, but not more than three were completed, one of these having bodywork by Stirling of Granton (the Stirling-Pennington of 1899). When frustrated customers pressed for the return of their deposits, a new company was hurriedly formed, but this was short-lived, and in October 1899, Pennington returned to his native land, where he managed to sell his rights for $750,000 to the Anglo-American Rapid Vehicle Co; this concern offered either to refund the outstanding deposits or supply would-be clients with American made 'Pennington or Daimler' cars.

The self-styled 'largest motor vehicle company in the world', however, made nothing more than a handful of 4-wheeler, wheel-steered derivatives of the old Torpedo, said to do 72mph and to be the subject of an order of 1,000 vehicles for use by the British Government in the South African War. Pennington was back in England in the winter of 1900/01 with his latest 'war motor', a reworked tricar with cylinders of 12 in stroke and a light shield over the forecarriage, which careered around Richmond Park for a while. Nothing was heard of Anglo-American after 1902, but Pennington was involved in the Tractobile steam-driven fwd attachment for buggies (1901), the Continental sparking plug with self-contained combustion chamber (1905), a scheme to market a 16hp car for only £60 (1907) and with yet another supposititious airship (1910). He died in 1911.   MCS

PENNSY (US) *1916–1919*

Pennsy Motor Co of Pittsburgh, Pittsburgh, Pa.

This medium-sized car sold for $855 in 1917, as either a two-seater or as a five-seater. It used a 4-cylinder engine of 3.1 litres, rated at 30/35hp. A six was added in 1918.   GMN

PENNSYLVANIA (US) *1907–1911*
Pennsylvania Auto-Motor Co, Bryn Mawr, Pa.

The earliest Pennsylvania was a four-seater with a 32hp 4-cylinder engine, on a 9ft 4 in wheelbase. The models grew rapidly larger, culminating in the Model H for 1910–11 which had a 9.1-litre 6-cylinder engine. The large seven-seater version was on an 11ft 5in wheelbase.　　　　GMN

PEOPLE'S (US) *1900–1902*
People's Automobile Co, Cleveland, Ohio

As a result of a prolonged strike by employees of the Cleveland tramways company, a concern was formed to build and operate motorbuses in opposition to the tramways. This People's Automobile Company also built a few cars with single-cylinder engines. One of the founders of the company was Paul Gaeth who later built the Gaeth car.　　　　GNG

PEREGRINE (GB) *1961*
Peregrine Cars Ltd, Waltham Abbey, Essex

The Peregrine was, needless to say, a species of Falcon, but produced by an independent company, although in the old Falcon premises. It followed a typical British kit-car formula of coil-suspended space-frame chassis, two-seater fibreglass body in sports or touring form, and Ford 105E engine and transmission.　　　DF

PERFECTA (I) *1899–1903*
Bender e Martiny, Turin

This company marketed a wide range of vehicles: Gaillardet-engined electrics, petrol cars with De Dion engines, motor tricycles and quads. A belt-driven single-cylinder machine based on the German Orient Express was offered in 1900 and it seems probable that most Perfectas were foreign imports. The name was also used by Darracq for motor quads made for the trade in 1899–1900: a further indication of the possible source of some of Bender e Martiny's wares.　　　MCS

PERFECTION (US) *1906–1908*
Perfection Automobile Works, South Bend, Ind.

The Perfection was made in both 4- and 6-cylinder versions. The latter was rated at 70hp, with a 7.8-litre capacity. This five-seater sold for $2,500.　　GMN

PERFETTI (I) *1922–1923*
Perfetti Automobili, Milan

Although a small proprietary 4-cylinder engine was used, the Perfetti was otherwise a highly original car. The driver sat in the centre of the body, with a passenger on each side of him, and one behind. The steering column was nearly horizontal. It is unlikely that the car passed the prototype stage.　　　GNG

PERFEX (i) (US) *1912–1914*
Perfex Co, Los Angeles, Calif.

The Perfex was a sturdy-looking two-seater roadster with a 22.5hp G.B. and S. 4-cylinder engine of 3 litres' capacity and 3-speed transmission. It cost $1,050.　GMN

PERFEX (ii) (GB) *1920–1921*
Perfex Manufacturing Co Ltd, Bournemouth, Hampshire

The English Perfex was a medium-sized assembled car using the same engine as the American Perfex, a 22.5hp 4-cylinder G.B. and S. Open two- and four-seaters and a saloon were available, but very few of them were sold.　　　GNG

PERL (A) *1921–1927*
Automobilfabrik Perl AG, Liesing

Perl started to manufacture commercial vehicles in 1907 and this production was supplemented by electric lorries and tractors. In 1921 a small private car was introduced. This 3/14PS type had a 898cc engine and a two- or three-seater body. It was followed by the Norma and the Suprema with the same engine capacity but slightly increased output, and also available with four-seater bodies. Later this firm merged with Gräf & Stift.　　　HON

PERREAU (F) *1923–1925*
Automobiles Perreau, Epinay, Seine

This was a short-lived light car using a 7hp 4-cylinder Ruby engine of 1,088cc, and shaft drive.　　　GNG

PERRY (GB) *1913–1916*
Perry Motor Co Ltd, Tyseley, Birmingham

Made by a firm of cycle-fitting manufacturers who had built motor-tricycles in 1899, and forecarriages in 1903, the original Perry light car used a 6.4hp vertical twin engine of 875cc, a 3-speed gearbox and shaft drive. A sporting model was available with raked steering column and shortened gear lever but apparently no modifications to the engine. This was said to be capable of 'close on 40mph'. For 1915 a 4-cylinder car with 11.9hp 1,795cc engine was introduced, and about 700 of these were made until production ceased in 1916. The Perry company was absorbed

1920 PERFEX(ii) 22.5hp tourer. *Autocar*

1921 PERL 3/14PS coupé. *Technisches Museum.*
Vienna

1914 PERRY 11.9hp two-seater. *National Motor*
Museum

1909 PETREL 30hp roadster. *National Motor Museum*

1896 PETTER 3hp dog-cart. *Petters Ltd*

1899 PEUGEOT four-seater phaeton. *SA Peugeot*

by A. Harper Sons & Bean Ltd in 1919, and the 4-cylinder car was launched with some modifications as the 11.9hp Bean. GNG

PESTOURIE ET PLANCHON (F) 1922

This was a small car with body and chassis constructed entirely of wood. The engine was a water-cooled 4-cylinder unit of 904cc, and the rear wheels were mounted close together, giving the appearance of a 3-wheeler. GNG

P.E.T. (US) 1914

P.E. Teats, Detroit, Mich.

The P.E.T. was a cyclecar with a 4-cylinder engine on a chassis of 3ft 6in track and 8ft 8in wheelbase. Price was given as $350. GMN

PETER-MORITZ (D) 1921–1925

Automobilwerke Peter & Moritz, Zeitz; Naumburg

The Peter-Moritz was a 2-seater cyclecar on Rover Eight lines with a 2-cylinder opposed engine of 1,315cc capacity. The first versions were air-cooled, later versions water-cooled. HON

PETER PAN (US) 1914–1915

Randall Co, Quincy, Mass.

This cyclecar had a 4-cylinder water-cooled engine with overhead valves which produced 24hp at 3,200rpm. Both two- and four-seater models were made. They had a V-shaped radiator, 3-speed transmission and shaft drive, and were priced at $400 to $450. GMN

PETERS (US) 1921–1922

Peters Autocar Co, Trenton, N.J.

The Peters was a short-lived air-cooled car powered by a 2-cylinder engine of 1,144cc capacity, developing 14bhp. The types offered were a roadster, a two-seater speedster and a light station wagon, all priced at $345 and all with wire wheels. KM

PETERS-WALTON-LUDLOW (US) 1915

Peters-Walton-Ludlow Auto Engineering Co, Philadelphia, Pa.

This was a cyclecar with a 9hp 2-cylinder engine, but, unusually for such vehicles, a five-seater tourer body was offered. The price of this car was $390. GNG

PETIT (F) 1909

Built at Tarare, Rhône, this was a voiturette powered by a single-cylinder Aster engine. Transmission was by friction discs. GNG

PETREL (US) 1908–1912

(1) Petrel Motor Car Co, Kenosha, Wisc. 1908–1909
(2) Petrel Motor Car Co, Milwaukee, Wisc. 1910–1912

This make is said to have succeeded the Earl (i). The Petrel was made in two-seater roadster and in five-seater touring versions, with L-head 4.9-litre engines. The early models used friction transmissions and double chain drive. By 1910 this self-proclaimed 'Aristocrat of Medium Priced Cars' had reduced its wheelbase to 9ft and had adopted shaft drive. The 30hp 4-cylinder two-seater model cost $1,350. For 1912, the name of the make was changed to F-S, after the parent company Filer and Stowell. GMN

PETTER (GB) 1895–1898

(1) Jas. B. Petter and Sons, Yeovil, Somerset 1895–1896
(2) Hill and Boll, Yeovil, Somerset 1897–1898

Percival W. Petter designed the prototype single-cylinder dog-cart, which developed 3bhp from the rear-mounted engine. Hot-tube ignition and automatic inlet valve were featured, and drive was by chain to either rear wheel, thus ingeniously permitting 2 gear ratios. Subsequent models employed a more powerful horizontal 2-cylinder unit. Production was taken up by a prominent coachbuilding firm, Hill and Boll, who later formed the Yeovil Motor Car and Cycle Co. Some electric cars were also made, and it is likely that about a dozen complete vehicles were sold. DF

PEUGEOT (F) 1889 to date

(1) Les Fils de Peugeot Frères, Beaulieu-Valentigney 1889–1897
(2) SA des Automobiles Peugeot, Audincourt 1897–1910
(3) SA des Automobiles et Cycles Peugeot, Lille 1902–1928; Audincourt 1910–1926; Sochaux 1910–1926
(4) SA des Automobiles Peugeot, Sochaux 1928 to date

The Peugeot family, who are still in control of the concern that bears their name, had a long and successful career as manufacturing ironmongers – their products included tools, coffee mills, umbrella spikes and corsetry – before the first of the companies connected with the motor car was founded in 1876. Cycle manufacture was undertaken in 1885, and four years later a 3-wheeler steam car was built in association with Léon Serpollet. It had a tubular frame and a flash boiler, and in 1890 it was successfully driven from Paris to Lyons, the object of the journey being a visit to the Chantiers de la Buire, a firm later associated both with Serpollet steamers and with petrol cars of their own design. Steam was soon dropped, however, in favour of Daimler-engined cars introduced at Emile Levassor's instigation: these had rear-mounted V-twin power units, cycle-type wire wheels, and handlebar steering, and the cooling water circulated through the tubular frames.

In 1891 a Peugeot made the first long-distance cross-country journey undertaken by a petrol car from Beaulieu-Valentigney to Paris, then on to Brest in company with a cycle race, and back by the same route. The firm also claims to have delivered the first petrol-driven car to a private customer in France. Sales rose steadily: 5 in 1891, 29 in 1892, 72 in 1895 and 300 in 1899. Sir David Salomon imported a 4hp car into Britain in 1895, and another early customer was the Hon. C.S. Rolls of Rolls-Royce fame. In 1894, when a whip for chasing away dogs was a recognized extra, Lemaître finished 2nd in the Paris-Rouen and in the following year Peugeot was the technical, if not the moral, victor of the Paris-Bordeaux; more significant in this latter event was André Michelin's entry of a similar machine with pneumatic tyres. 2.7-litre vertical-twin engines were used in 1895, replaced in 1896 by a Rigoulot-designed unit of Peugeot manufacture. This had horizontal parallel cylinders with their heads pointing rearward and a transverse countershaft, and this basic type was still offered in commercial and town-brougham forms as late as 1905 – though in 1902 phaetons on this chassis were being sold off in England at £385.

A separate company took over car manufacture at Audincourt in 1897. The cars grew bigger: 3.3-litres in 1898, and a gigantic 5.8-litre credited with 30bhp in 1900. At the other end of the scale there was a 3hp light carriage weighing only 784lb in 1899. That year electric ignition was also available, though the older cars retained tube ignition up to 1902. Wheel steering made its appearance in 1900 and a 3.3-litre front vertical engine was used in the Paris-Berlin Race of 1900. Also in this year the original 'Baby' was introduced, with a 785cc front-mounted aiv single-cylinder engine, a tubular frame and a 3-speed gearbox. It also had rack-and-pinion steering at an early date, and sold in England (where it was marketed by Friswells) in 1903 for £195.

In 1902 the Lille factory was opened and a complicated range included everything from a motor-quad at £110 up to 2- and 4-cylinder cars on Mercedes lines with pressed-steel frames, moiv T-head engines, lt magneto ignition and honeycomb radiators with rectangular header tanks of distinctive appearance. These were built under licence in England by Siddeley. All Peugeots save the Baby had moiv in 1903, when a 9hp T-headed twin could be bought for £325. Also in 1903 Robert Peugeot started to build motorcycles in the old Beaulieu-Valentigney factory, branching out into cars in 1906 under the name of Lion-Peugeot. 1904 brought some experiments with naphtha as fuel in an old-type 2-cylinder car and a year later the singles acquired mechanically-operated valves. A wide range included 4-cylinder short-stroke cars with engines of 1.9 litres, 3.6 litres, 5 litres, 5.4 litres and 7.1 litres. Oversquare engines (which Peugeot had tried in the Paris-Vienna race of 1902) were seen in 1906, as was a footbrake working on the rear wheels – this was to become a regular feature of the marque.

All but the smallest models had gate change in 1907 and in 1908 came Liegard's experimental desert cars (which anticipated the Citroën-Kégresse of the 1920s) and also the first six, a 10.4-litre of 60hp. Pedal-operated rear wheel brakes and ht magneto ignition were regular practice in 1909 (though lt ignition was retained on a big sporting 50hp at £890) and the 10hp twin and a small 2.2-litre 4-cylinder car had shaft drive as standard; the 3-litre 16, the 4.6-litre 22, and a new small six rated at 20hp could be had with shaft or chains. L-head monobloc engines made a belated appearance on a 2-litre 4-speed model in 1910, when the unnecessary rivalry between the two Peugeot companies came to an end with the creation of the SA des Automobiles et Cycles Peugeot. At the same time the Sochaux works, where car production was later to be concentrated in 1928, were opened.

The trend was now towards single-camshaft engines and 4-speed gearboxes, but 1912 saw two new departures, the re-entry into racing with Henry-designed machines and the introduction of the new Bébé. The racing cars were 16-valve double ohc 4-cylinder shaft-driven affairs of advanced design, made in 7.6-litre Grand Prix and 3-litre Coupe de l'Auto forms. Sunbeam's sv cars vanquished the smaller Peugeot, but in the Grand Prix Boillot successfully defeated the giant FIATs and ushered in a new era of racing cars. In 1913 Goux won the Indianapolis 500 Mile Race on a 5.6-litre development with gear-driven camshafts and dry-sump lubrication, as well as taking the World Hour Record at 106.22mph, and the 3-litre model won the Coupe de l'Auto. 1914 brought less success, since Peugeot's 4½-litre cars with stream-lined tails and front wheel braking were defeated by Mercedes at Lyons, and the 2½-litre Coupe de l'Auto versions did not appear until André Boillot's Targa Florio victory in 1919.

During World War 1, Peugeot did magnificently in the U.S.A., winning the Grand Prize and the Vanderbilt Cup in 1915, as well as taking 2nd place at Indianapolis, where the marque was victorious in 1916. Howard Wilcox won for Peugeot again in 1920, and the significance of the Henri-designed cars is to be seen in the twin ohc engines produced by Harry Miller in the 1920s and 1930s. After an abortive attempt at Indianapolis in 1920 with a weird triple ohc 3-litre 4-cylinder car with *five* valves per cylinder, Peugeot abandoned the *grandes épreuves* for good.

In the touring-car field, the 856cc Bébé of 1912 was an Ettore Bugatti design

1908 PEUGEOT Type 116 16hp tourer. *SA Peugeot*

1913 PEUGEOT Bébé 6hp two-seater. *SA Peugeot*

1921 PEUGEOT Type 153 3-litre sporting tourer. Coachwork by Geissberger of Zürich. *G.N. Georgano*

1928 PEUGEOT Type 183 2-litre saloon. *SA Peugeot*

1929 PEUGEOT Type 201 1.1-litre coupé. *SA Peugeot*

1938 PEUGEOT Type 402B 2.1-litre saloon. *SA Peugeot*

1938 PEUGEOT Darl'mat 2.1-litre coupé. *Lucien Loreille Collection*

with a 10bhp T-head monobloc engine and a peculiar transmission consisting of twin concentric propeller shafts meshing with two rows of teeth on the crown wheel. 1914 cars had three forward speeds, and sold for £160. In 1913 there was a new 4-speed 14/18 with worm drive and full-pressure lubrication, as well as a big long-stroke 40/50hp with combined piston and slide valves, which had given way within twelve months to a more conventional poppet-valve 7.5-litre car, said to develop 92bhp. Bigger Peugeots had bevel drive, the smaller ones worm; just before the war came the 2.6-litre Type 153 with worm drive. The 12hp V-4 (a legacy of the old Lion-Peugeot company) was made up to the outbreak of war.

The Type 153 survived World War 1, leading to a series of 3-litre 4-cylinder cars with sv, and later ohv engines. One of these was tried in 1923 with the Peugeot-Tartrais 2-stroke diesel engine, but a 37mph top speed and no great improvement in fuel consumption put an end to this line of development. A 1.4-litre 10hp had side valves, worm drive, central change and left-hand drive, and was developed on the same lines until the later 1920s, while for the luxury market there was a twin-carburettor 6-litre cuff-valve 6-cylinder, selling for £1,200 as a chassis in 1922. This was still being made in 1924. Most important was a successor for the Bébé, the 668cc Quadrilette, an alleged ancestor of the Austin Seven, though all the two cars had in common were L-head engines and the same suspension arrangements: transverse at the front and quarter-elliptic at the rear. The Peugeot had a fixed cylinder head, a 3-speed gearbox mounted in unit with the differential-less worm-drive back axle, a punt-type frame, and hand and foot brakes working on separate rear wheels. A rear track of only 2ft 6in necessitated staggered or tandem seating, lighting was by acetylene, and in its original form at £298 it had no starter.

This model was continued until 1930, acquiring a conventional chassis in 1923, a 719cc engine in 1926 and front-wheel brakes in 1929, by which time the added weight of five-seater bodywork resulted in the adoption of a 7.25:1 top gear! A 950cc development, still with quadrant change and rear-axle gearbox, but with the refinements of front-wheel brakes and detachable head, was offered for £185 in 1927.

Peugeot also produced some fine sleeve-valve sports cars, starting with the Type 174 of 1922, which had a 5-bearing crankshaft, twin-pump lubrication and the bevel drive of Sochaux' bigger models. In later, dry-sump form it was capable of 140bhp and its victories included the 1924 and 1925 Touring-Car Grands Prix, as well as 2nd and 3rd places in the 1925 Targa Florio. The streamlined fabric saloons raced in 1925 had headlamps which retracted into the scuttle sides. Some smaller sleeve-valve touring cars were made for competition in 1923 and 1927, André Boillot winning the Touring G.P. in the latter year on one of these, while there was also a 3.8-litre 6-cylinder touring model of similar type in 1928. All Peugeots save the little 7/12hp had front wheel brakes by 1924.

In 1927 the company acquired the factories of Bellanger and De Dion Bouton. 1928 produced the first of a new line of models with the 2-litre 6-cylinder Type 183, which appeared with coil ignition at £380 in 1931. A year before the company had introduced Type 201, a straightforward worm-driven sv 1,100cc family saloon with transverse front suspension and coil ignition. There was also a limited-production sports type, the 201X, using the supercharged ohc Bugatti Type 48 engine (half a Type 35), while Audi in Germany offered the regular 201 engine in their short-lived 5/30PS model; some compensation, perhaps, for Peugeot's abortive attempt to build cars at Mannheim in 1927. The 201 was continued until 1937, acquiring transverse independent front suspension with the C series of 1932 and a synchromesh gearbox in 1934, while in that year the firm catalogued a coupé model with electrically lowered hardtop – an anticipation of Ford's Sunliner of at least twenty years later. The six-seater 1½-litre 301 with box-section frame and similar basic specification had come out during 1932 and in 1935 Peugeot introduced their last six, the short-lived 601 with a 2,150cc sv engine.

A complete facelift came with the 1936 402, which retained the worm-drive, synchromesh and independent front suspension, but had an ohv 2.1-litre, 4-cylinder engine developing 55bhp, dashboard change and a fully aerodynamic body on which not only the head-lamps but also the battery were housed between the grille and the radiator proper. The Fleischel automatic gearbox originally announced as an option on this model never saw production, but a 4-speed box of Cotal type was an optional extra. A sports two-seater version capable of 95mph ran at Le Mans in 1937, being offered in England for £495 in 1939. These sports models were known as Peugeot-Darl' Mats, being specially prepared by Emile Darl' Mat. They had modified 402 engines in the 302 chassis, and were made in open sports, cabriolet and coupé forms. About 200 were made between 1936 and 1939. The 402 saloon bodywork was used by Berliet on their Dauphine model of 1938/39. In 1938 Peugeot adapted the new formula to a cheap 1,100cc saloon, the 202 with a 30bhp short-stroke unit, which sold for the equivalent of £117 in France and helped Peugeot to take second place (behind Citroën) in home sales during the last complete season before World War 2. 52,796 cars were delivered in this period.

During World War 2 the company made a number of light electric cars. Known as the VLV, they had two-seater cabriolet bodies, and were capable of 30mph. Unlike some war-time electrics, they were not adaptations of existing cars, but were of completely fresh design.

After the war Peugeot were quick to reinstate the 202 in production, selling 14,000 of them in 1946, but a year later they had their first new model available, in the shape of the best-selling 203. The worm-drive and batteries mounted behind the grille reflected 1936 practice, but entirely novel were the 42bhp oversquare 1.3-litre engine with hemispherical head and wet liners, all-coil suspension (independent in front), a 4-speed gearbox with geared-up top and peculiar 'gate', unitary construction, hydraulic brakes and rack-and-pinion steering. A sliding roof (hitherto seldom found except on British cars) was an optional extra. This incredibly tough family car was sold until 1960, winning the 6,500 Mile Redex Trial in Australia in 1953 and taking 2nd place in the 1954 Monte Carlo Rally. From 1949 to 1954 it was the staple Peugeot model. Meanwhile, in 1950, the company had absorbed Chenard-Walcker, keeping that firm's forward-control light van in production under the Peugeot name: they also had a substantial holding in Hotchkiss.

In 1955 came the 1½-litre 403 with all-synchromesh gearbox, selling for £1,129 in England. This was another best-seller, being available with 2-pedal control in 1958, with the option of an Indénor diesel engine in 1959, and then with the 203's 1,290cc engine when that model was finally retired at the end of 1960. The millionth 403 left the works in April 1962. The 404 of 1960 saw the introduction of Pininfarina's angular styling (and a marked resemblance to both the B.M.C. A55 and the Fiat 1800/2100). Its 1.6-litre 72bhp engine was inclined, strut-type independent front suspension was now used, and there was a reversion to a direct top gear. The later coupé and convertible versions marked the introduction of Kügelfischer fuel injection as an optional extra, while a diesel version was also available.

During 1964 there was a partial pooling of resources with Citroën, this involving joint ownership of the Indénor diesel-engine plant and other facilities. The 404 was also proving itself as tough as previous Peugeots, a victory in the Australian Ampol Trial of 1956 being followed up with a class win in the 1964 East African Safari, and 2nd place in general classification in the 1965 events. In 1965 came the very advanced 204, a new 1,100cc saloon with a 58bhp transverse ohc engine driving the front wheels, independent rear suspension, and front disc brakes. The 403 was dropped at the end of 1966 after 1,200,000 had been sold, and in 1968 a new variant of the 204 appeared with 1,255cc ohc diesel engine. A new big Peugeot, the 504, appeared in 1969; this retained rear-wheel drive and push-rod-operated ohv, and its 1.8-litre 5-bearing unit developed 82bhp. The range included automatic-transmission, station-wagon, coupé and cabriolet versions; fuel injection was standard on the two latter. New in 1970 was the 304, a scaled-up 204 with 1.3-litre engine on which coupés and cabriolets were once again available. A year later fwd Peugeots were given alternator ignition, a 1.6-litre unit was standardized for the 404, and 504s came with 2-litre petrol or 2.2-litre diesel engines, though the older 1.8-litre type was still fitted to utility models. In the 1973 range were the 204, 304, 404 and 504, as well as a newcomer, the 104. This was a 4-door saloon powered by a 956cc ohc engine driving the front wheels.　　　　MCS

PEUGEOT-CROIZAT (I) *1905–1907*
(1) SA Brevetti Automobili Peugeot, Turin *1905–1906*
(2) Peugeot-Croizat SA, Turin *1906–1907*

This firm built cars under Peugeot licence, types marketed being the later single-cylinder Baby with honeycomb radiator and its capacity increased to 695cc, and the 2.2-litre Type 71 chain-driven T-head four. The venture was short-lived, and by 1908 the unsold stock of singles was being remaindered off in London.　　MCS

PEYKAN *see* HILLMAN

PFA (PL) *1923–1924*
Poznanska Fabryka Automobilowa, Liwoszna

Only a few prototypes are reported to have been built of the PFA coupé. Further information is scarce.　　　　BE

PFLÜGER (D) *1900*
Vereinigte Accumulatoren- und Electricitätswerke Dr Pflüger & Co, Berlin

This company produced electric cars on a small scale.　　　　HON

PHÄNOMEN (D) *1907–1927*
(1) Phänomen Fahrradwerke Gustav Hiller, Zittau *1907–1910*
(2) Phänomen-Werke Gustav Hiller AG, Zittau *1910–1927*

Phänomen built bicycles and motor cycles before turning to car production. The Phänomobil, a 3-wheeled vehicle with the engine mounted above the single front wheel which it drove by chain, appeared in 1907. This first model had a V-twin air-cooled engine of 880cc. After 1912 a 4-cylinder engine of 1,536cc was used. The Phänomobil was built until 1927 and was a very popular and economical vehicle. It was available as a two- or four-seater with various body styles. In 1911 Phänomen also offered a 4-wheeled 10/12PS, 2,580cc car and a 16/45PS 3,968cc model followed. They were manufactured to high standards of quality but were not built in large numbers. They were continued after World War 1 in improved form.

The Model 412 of 1924 was a new design with a 4-cylinder, 3,128cc 50bhp engine with shaft-driven overhead camshaft, which was also available in a short-wheelbase 65bhp sports version. Car production ceased in 1927 and Phänomen subsequently concentrated very successfully on their Granit vans and light lorries with compressed-air cooling. The factory was nationalized in 1945, and today produces light commercials under the name of Robur.　　　　HON

1950 PEUGEOT Type 203 1.3-litre saloon. *SA Peugeot*

1967 PEUGEOT Type 204 1.1-litre coupé. *SA Peugeot*

1973 PEUGEOT Type 504 2-litre saloon. *SA Peugeot*

1907 PHÄNOMOBIL 4/6PS 3-wheeler. *Neubauer Collection*

1900 PHEBUS-ASTER 3½hp voiturette. *E.R. Harrison*

1913 PHILOS 8CV two-seater. *Lucien Loreille Collection*

1912 PHOENIX(ii) 11.9hp two-seater. *Autocar*

PHÉBUS (i) (F) *1899–1903*
Noé Boyer et Cie, Suresnes, Seine

Noé Boyer was the commercial director of the Phébus branch of the Clément-Gladiator & Humber Ltd, makers of bicycles and tricycles. Phébus-Aster motor tricycles had been made for a few years when the first Phébus-Aster car appeared. It was a light two-seater voiturette powered by a 3½hp Aster engine, with 2 speeds and spur-gear drive. The first cars imported to England were called Automobilettes; they had 2¼hp engines and no bonnets.   GNG

PHÉBUS (ii) (F) *1921*
Cyclecars Phébus, Lyons

The Phébus cyclecar had a 2-cylinder engine, and was probably only built in prototype form.   GNG

PHELPS (US) *1903–1905*
Phelps Motor Co, Stoneham, Mass.

The Phelps, in its original version, was a five-seater with rear entrance and a 3-cylinder water-cooled engine. Its radiator was a finned coil mounted beneath the front of the car. The body was hinged at the rear and could be raised to expose the entire running gear. Later models used 3- and 4-cylinder engines and honeycomb radiators. It was succeeded by the Shawmut.   GMN

PHÉNIX (F) *c.1912–1914*
Automobiles Phénix, Puteaux, Seine

The Phénix was a product of Prunel frères, Dumas et Cie who had previously been responsible for the J.P. and Prunel cars. At the 1912 Paris Salon three Phénix models were shown; a 10, 12, and 15hp, all with 4-cylinder engines and shaft drive.   GNG

PHIANNA (US) *1916–1922*
(1) Phianna Motors Co, Newark, N.J. *1916–1918*
(2) M.H. Carpenter, Long Island City, N.Y. *1919–1922*

One of America's finest prestige motor cars, the Phianna, successor to the S.G.V., was built in limited numbers for its six years of existence. The earlier cars had oval radiators and laminated walnut and ash fans mounted co-axially with the flywheel. In 1919, the radiator was changed to a square type and bonnet louvres were eliminated. The 4-cylinder Phianna engine was continued. Although the Phianna wheelbase was not as large as many contemporary cars of similar price, comfort was achieved by the use of 5ft rear springs. The Phianna was a favourite with several heads of government as well as with a number of United States officials in Washington. Plans for a larger and longer 6-cylinder Phianna were outlined, and pilot cars were constructed, but the make failed in 1921. Cars were assembled from stock and marketed until 1922.   KM

PHILIPSON (S) *1946*
Gunnar Philipson, Augustendal

The Philipson was planned as a modernized D.K.W. to be built in a plant formerly used to assemble Chrysler and Dodge vehicles. The 2-cylinder 700cc 2-stroke engine and front-wheel drive was retained but hydraulic brakes were added and the bodywork was altered to improve appearance. Little or no production seems to have followed the introduction of the prototype.   BE

PHILOS (F) *1912–1923*
SA Nouvelle des Automobiles Philos, Lyons

The pre-war Philos was made in one model using a 1,131cc 4-cylinder Ballot engine, but post-war cars, while of the same general size and price range, used a variety of engines by Altos, Ballot, Ruby and S.C.A.P., ranging from 1,088cc to 1,775cc. All were 4-cylinder units and the cars were of conventional design, although a curved V-radiator gave them a distinctive appearance.   GNG

PHIPPS-GRINNELL (US) *1901–1912*
Phipps-Grinnell Automobile Co, Detroit, Mich.

The Phipps-Grinnell electric car was made in very small quantities of not more than 15 to 20 per year, at least until 1911, when the firm announced that expansion would take place. This make was succeeded by the Grinnell.   GNG

PHOENIX (i) (GB) *1902–1904*
Phoenix Motor Works, Southport, Lancs.

The Phoenix Motor Works had been the home of the Hudlass car before Felix Hudlass left the firm; the few Phoenix cars made were closely based on the 12hp 2-cylinder Hudlass. In 1904 a new 10hp 3-cylinder car was introduced, and the name changed to Barcar. As in the American Compound, and the first 3-cylinder Arrol-Johnston, the middle cylinder had a larger bore than the other two, and worked off the exhaust gases of its smaller neighbours.   GNG

PHOENIX (ii) (GB) *1903–1928*
(1) Phoenix Motor Co., London N. *1903–1911*
(2) Ascot Motor and Manufacturing Co, Letchworth, Herts. *1911–1928*

The Phoenix Motor Company's first vehicles were motorcycles, and the Trimo and Tricar three-wheelers, though as early as 1904 the firm marketed a short-lived conventional light car with 6hp De Dion engine. They were named after the Phoenix Cycling Club, of which J. van Hooydonk, their deviser, was a member. They were motor tricycles with two wheels and the passenger in front. Machines of this type were cheap, economical and had a good performance because they were light. In these respects, they were the forerunners of the cyclecar. The Phoenix tricycles had brakes on the front wheels. Transmission was by chain. The Quadcar of 1905 had four wheels and developed into a more car-like creation, with side-by-side seating and a dummy bonnet in front. The power unit was a horizontal water-cooled Minerva single or Fafnir twin transversly mounted. A true car appeared for the first time in 1908: a voiturette with a 10hp vertical 2-cylinder engine, still transversely-mounted, and retaining chain primary and final drive. In between was a 3-speed gearbox. The brakes were as excellent as ever. This type was made until World War 1, but in 1913 a more orthodox light car was added. It used an 11.9hp 4-cylinder in-line engine in front of a dashboard radiator, a metal-to-metal clutch, a 3-speed gearbox and worm drive. After the war, this car was continued, but it was a slow and old-fashioned vehicle. The 11.9 was given a flat radiator in 1921 and a stablemate, the 3-litre ohc 18hp in 1920. A more modern design was offered two years later: the 12/25hp, with an ohv Meadows engine and 4-speed gearbox. A Meadows-engined six was introduced in 1925.　　　　TRN

PHOENIX (iii) (ET) *1955–1956*

Cairo Motor Co Ltd, Cairo; Alexandria

The Egyptian Phoenix was the work of an Englishman, Raymond Flower, and was conceived as a super-sports car to contest Le Mans. Plans specified a 1,960cc dohc 4-cylinder Turner (iii) engine of 145bhp with fuel injection, mounted in a multitubular frame with a De Dion back axle, but the prototype had twin carburettors. Also planned was a minicar using 197cc or 250cc 2-stroke Villiers engine, but though this was undergoing trials late in 1956, the deterioration in Anglo-Egyptian relations that followed the Suez Crisis killed both projects. The only Phoenix model to reach the public was the Flamebird, a two-seater sports coupé built up round Fiat 1100 elements, of which 30 were manufactured. The Phoenix Minicar subsequently evolved into the Meadows-built Frisky.　　　　MCS

PHOENIX (iv) *see* FENG HUANG

PHÖNIX (H) *1905–1915*

(1) Phönix Automobile Works, Budapest *1905–1910*
(2) Machinery, Mill, and Automobile Works, Budapest *1911–1915*

The Hungarian Phönix cars and buses were based on the Cudell-Phönix, designed by Karl Slevogt for the German company, but not made in large numbers by them. Various sizes of cars were made, powered by 4-cylinder ohv engines, and using chain drive. These included a 16hp and a 35/40hp. The same factory was used later by M.A.G. for the production of Magomobil and Magosix cars.　　　　GNG

PHRIXUS *see* O.P.

PICCOLO (D) *1904–1912*

(1) A. Ruppe & Sohn, Apolda *1904–1908*
(2) A. Ruppe & Sohn AG, Apolda *1908–1910*
(3) Apollo-Werke AG, Apolda *1910–1912*

This firm made agricultural machinery before starting car production in 1904. With their Piccolo cars they were one of the pioneers of air-cooled engines in Germany. The first Piccolo of 1904 had an air-cooled V-twin 6PS 704cc power unit and was available with two- or four-seater bodies. It was a, cheap and very popular car and was produced in large numbers until 1907. During the first years of production the engine was placed unenclosed at the front of the car, but after 1906 it was covered by a bonnet. In the same year an air-cooled in-line 4-cylinder 12PS model appeared which was superseded in 1907 by a V-4 12PS car. A simplified Piccolo model with an air-cooled, single-cylinder, 624cc engine developing 5bhp was introduced in 1910 and marketed as the Mobbel. In the same year the firm became the Apollo-Werke and a new range was offered under the new name, but the air-cooled cars were sold until 1912 as Piccolos, thereafter as Apollo-Piccolos.　　　　HON

PICK; NEW PICK (GB) *1898–1925*

(1) J.H. Pick & Co, Stamford, Lincs. *1898–1908*
(2) New Pick Motor Co Ltd, Stamford, Lincs. *1908–1915*
(3) Pick Motor Co Ltd, Stamford, Lincs. *1915–1925*

Jack Pick built his first car, a simple dogcart, in 1898, and sold it to a local doctor for £85. The local gentry became interested in his activities, and Pick cars became well-known in the area. By 1900 a two-seater with a 2¾hp vertical air-cooled engine at the rear, tiller steering and a sprung frame was advertised. The springing was provided by laminating the chassis between steering head and the remainder of the frame. During 1901 the engine was moved to the front, and the car took on a more solid appearance. An example of the 5hp 1901 model still survives, and regularly appears on the Brighton run.

1905 PICCOLO 6PS voiturette. *Neubauer Collection*

1912 PICK 20hp coupé. *R.H. Long*

1923 PICK 22.5hp two-seater sports car. *Autocar*

1910 PICKARD Model H Tourer. *Harrah's Automobile Collection*

1913 PIC-PIC 30/40hp limousine. *Autocar*

1900 PIEPER 3½hp voiturette. *G.N. Georgano*

The range was increased in 1903, when a 6hp flat-twin was made, along with 10 and 12hp models. These had chain drive to the gearbox, and single chain final drive. By 1908 the cars were called New Pick, after the firm had moved to new premises on the Great North Road. One model was made, the 14/16hp, a conventional 4-cylinder (separately-cast) shaft-drive car with 2 forward speeds, top being direct drive. In 1910 the New Pick Racer was advertised, said to be 'well capable of 50mph'. In 1911 a new long stroke (90mm × 127mm) monobloc engine and 3-speed gearbox was introduced, and this model was continued without major change until the end of production. The bore was increased to 95mm for 1912 (giving a capacity of 3,601cc), and in 1915 the car's name reverted to Pick.

The company seemed to be dormant in early post-war years, but in 1923 a sporting two-seater was introduced with a top gear ratio of 2½ to 1. At 40mph the engine was only turning at 1,000rpm, and was said to be quiet and unhurried at 60mph. However, these attractions did not seem to sell many Picks, and in 1925 Jack Pick turned from car manufacture to the greengrocery business.   GB

PICKARD (US) *1908–1912*
Pickard Bros, Brockton, Mass.

The Pickard used 4-cylinder, air-cooled engines of 3.3 and 4.9 litres with sliding-gear transmissions and shaft drive. The brake-bands were lined with camel hair, and the bonnets were oval in cross-section.   GMN

PICKER-MOCCAND *see* LUCIA

PIC-PIC (CH) *1906–1924*
(1) Sté des Automobiles à Genève, Geneva *1906–1910*
(2) Piccard-Pictet et Cie, Geneva *1910–1924*

Piccard-Pictet began motor manufacture by making racing cars for the Dufaux brothers, but their own machine, the 'Rolls-Royce of Switzerland' was designed in 1906 by Marc Birkigt. Although built in the Piccard-Pictet factory, the cars were known as S.A.Gs until 1910. They were fours of 20/24 and 35/40hp, while a 28/32hp six followed in 1907. All were conventional, beautifully-made cars with an excellent performance. In 1910 a modern small monobloc four was added: the 14/16hp 2.4-litre. For 1912 one model, the 30hp, was given a single-sleeve-valve engine of Burt-McCollum type; poppet-valve Pic-Pics were a 16hp and two models of 20hp with different strokes (90mm and 150mm, and 90mm × 170mm). Two 4½-litre sleeve-valve Pic-Pics with front-wheel brakes ran in the 1914 Grand Prix, but both retired.

During World War 1 Pic-Pics were bought in large numbers by the Swiss Army; they were very durable, and 1918 models were still in use in the late 1930s. Both the basic post-war models used single-sleeve-valve engines; these were a 2.9-litre 4-cylinder, and a 5.9-litre V-8. However, the company's sales were badly hit by cheap imported cars and Piccard-Pictet were bankrupt by 1920. The new company concentrated on making turbines, but a few Pic-Pics were made by the Sté des Moteurs Gnome et Rhône. The last of these was shown at the Geneva Motor Show in 1924.   TRN

PIEDMONT (US) *1917–1922*
Piedmont Motor Co, Inc, Lynchburg, Va.

This assembled car was produced in a variety of open and closed body styles powered by 4- and 6-cylinder Lycoming and Continental engines. The concern also made cars from other firms, notably Alsace, Bush, and Lone Star.   KM

PIEPER (B) *1899–1903*
Sté des Etablissements Pieper, Nessonvaux, Liège

The original Pieper was a voiturette with a single-cylinder 3½hp, or a 6hp 2-cylinder engine, and belt drive. In 1900 these were joined by an electric two-seater with a range of 50 miles per charge, and also by a petrol-electric car. This had the same appearance as the pure electric, but had a 3½hp petrol engine coupled to an electric motor under the seat. In 1902 a 12hp 4-cylinder chain-drive tonneau was made. Later Auto-Mixte petrol-electric vehicles were made to Pieper designs.   GNG

PIERCE; PIERCE-ARROW (US) *1901–1938*
(1) The George N. Pierce Co, Buffalo, N.Y.
(2) Pierce-Arrow Motor Car Co, Buffalo, N.Y.

Of the many prestige cars built in the United States, probably none enjoyed more favour for a longer period than the Pierce-Arrow. This car began humbly enough. The first model, the Pierce Motorette, appeared in 1901. It was produced by George N. Pierce, a builder of bicycles and birdcages and was powered by a 2¾hp De Dion engine. This initial venture proved successful and was followed in 1902 by a similar car but with the output increased to 3½hp. For 1903, the Arrow name appeared and the company introduced a 15hp 2-cylinder car, with a 6½hp machine as a sideline.

In 1904 the name was changed to Great Arrow and the cars had power units capable of 28hp. It was such a car which won the Glidden Tour, a reliability test, and from this point onward, the name was one to be reckoned with. Power was gradually increased as was the size of the car through the immediate years and by 1908, the Pierce Great Arrow boasted 60bhp at 1,000rpm. Up to 1909, steering-column change was used. This was the last year in which the word Great appeared in the Pierce nomenclature.

The Pierce-Arrow was introduced in 1909 and such was the firm's reputation that production was limited and the supply seldom met the demand of the public. An interesting option on the enclosed-drive limousine for 1911 and later was a bulge in the roof to allow ladies to enter through the rear doors without crushing the elaborate hats then in fashion against the roof.

In 1913, the first Pierce-Arrows appeared with the headlamps attached to the tops of the front mudguards, although this innovation was optional. The greater percentage of Pierce Arrow motor cars were to appear with this type of headlamp fitting, but the earlier arrangement was available until the early 1930s.

By 1914, Pierce-Arrow cars were available in three sizes. The 66 (reputedly the largest stock car built in the United States) was powered by a 6-cylinder engine with a 5in × 7in bore and stroke, giving a capacity of 12.7 litres. The wheelbase was 12ft 3½in and the tyres were 37in. A complete line of bodies was offered with prices ranging from $5,850 to $7,300. The 8½-litre 48 was built on a wheelbase of either 11ft 2½in or 11ft 10in with a price range of $4,850 to $6,300 and the 38, with a wheelbase and prices of 10ft 7in or 11ft and $4,300 to $5,400, constituted the smallest line. Transmission was 4-speed with direct drive on top gear.

By 1915, with somewhere between 12,000 and 13,000 cars having been built and of these a good percentage still on the road, the Pierce-Arrow was considered as a top prestige car compared with anything in its price class or even about it. Except for 1928, the name never appeared on the radiator, as it was felt the cars were easily recognizable without it. In frequent cases, Pierce-Arrows of this period were sold with a single chassis and two bodies, one open and one closed, which could be alternated with the seasons. Tyres were reduced to 35in in size and the plant was expanded about 1916 to accommodate the increased orders, not only for private cars, but for the commercial vehicles which the company had been building since 1911. The enormous 66 was discontinued during 1917 and the 38 and 48 were continued at prices ranging from $4,800 for the cheapest 38 to $7,000 for the most expensive 48, exclusive of custom bodies. In 1920, the two cooling vents located above the bonnet were eliminated and the cowl parking lights were removed, all lighting being replaced in the headlamps. The last right-hand-drive Pierce-Arrows were built late this year, Pierce-Arrow being one of the very last American cars to change over to left-hand steering. A new series was introduced for 1921, the line being split in size between the 38 and 48 models. These retained the 6-cylinder engine. For the first time, bonnet louvres were used.

By 1923, sales were dropping and less than two years later, the company introduced a smaller companion car, the Model 80. This was the first Pierce-Arrow to be equipped with 4-wheel brakes. Its L-head 6-cylinder engine developed about 70bhp. Prices ranged from $2,895 to about $4,000. They sold reasonably well in comparison with the larger 36 but the company was showing an annual deficit and production was diminishing. In 1928, the stockholders voted to place the company under the control of the successful Studebaker Corporation because of prevailing business conditions.

A new model was introduced for 1929, the company adopting a straight-8 engine of over 6 litres in place of the old six. The car was offered on two wheelbases at prices beginning at $2,775, and this was Pierce's best year, with 9,700 cars delivered. For 1930, three different 8-cylinder engines were offered the prospective purchaser. Because of the relationship between Pierce-Arrow and Studebaker, a number of the Pierce-Arrow cars bore a striking resemblance to the Studebaker President Eight, largest of the Studebaker line. Demand continued to fall, and production with it, in 1931, and for 1932 the company introduced two 12-cylinder lines in addition to its eight, but even then, only 2,692 units were built during the year. These twelves came in 140bhp, 5½-litre, and 150bhp 7-litre forms, priced from $3,900 up.

For 1933, Pierce introduced a special show car, the Silver Arrow, of which only five were made but which served as an intimation of the shape of cars to come. Priced at $10,000, the Silver Arrow had a 12-cylinder 175bhp engine and no running boards. A tapered back, split rear window and spare wheels concealed in compartments behind the front wheels made this one of the most talked about cars of the year. It was displayed at the 1933 Chicago World's Fair.

In 1933, a group of Buffalo businessmen made the Pierce-Arrow an entity of its own once more. Ab Jenkins was breaking racing records with Pierce-Arrows and although the publicity was excellent, business was not. After 1934, the basic changes in design were slight. The company turned out both eights and twelves but by 1935, with less than 1,000 cars produced, it was apparent that the end of the make was in sight. Retaining its classic radiator, the Pierce-Arrow limped through 1936 and 1937, with a handful produced in 1938 when the company went out of business.   KM

PIERCE-RACINE (US) 1904–1909

Pierce Engine Co, Racine, Wisc.

This company made its first car in 1894, and the second in 1899, but public sale did not begin until 1904. The 1904 model was a two-seater with a water-cooled 8hp engine, selling for $750. Four models were made in 1906. The Model D lasted from 1907 to the end of production in 1909. This was a 40hp car with shaft drive, claimed to be capable of 60mph. The company was bought in 1910 by the J.I. Case Threshing Machine Co, makers of the Case.   GMN

1904 PIERCE Arrow 15hp roadster. *Henry Ford Museum, Dearborn, Mich.*

1911 PIERCE-ARROW 66 tourer. *Henry Austin Clark*

1933 PIERCE-ARROW 7-litre V-12 convertible sedan. Coachwork by Le Baron. *Kenneth Stauffer*

1938 PIERCE-ARROW 1801 6.3-litre convertible. *Bernard Weis*

1904 PIERRE ROY 6CV tonneau. *G.N. Georgano*

1912 PILAIN(i) 10/12hp two-seater. *Autocar*

1930 PILAIN(ii) 5CV coupé. *Lucien Loreille Collection*

PIERRE ROY (F) *1902–c.1908*
Pierre Roy, Grand Montrouge, Seine

The Pierre Roy was a conventional car made originally with a 10/12hp 2-cylinder engine and shaft drive. Later models had 4-cylinder engines of 14/20 and 24/30hp, still using shaft drive.   GNG

PIGGINS (US) *1909*
Piggins Brothers, Racine, Wisc.

The Piggins was a very large car with wheelbases up to 11ft 1in. T-head, 6-cylinder engines of 36hp and 50hp were used. The latter unit was of 7.8 litres' capacity and drove a seven-seater weighing 3,700lb which cost $4,500.   GMN

PILAIN (i) (F) *1902–1920*
SA des Automobiles Pilain, Lyons

François Pilain made his first cars, with 2- and 4-cylinder engines, in 1902, but had dropped the twin by 1904. The drive was independent of the rear axle, by two shafts to internally-toothed rings, with a dead axle beneath. The principle was the same as that used by De Dion, the aim being to allow the axle to move in relation to the frame without recourse to chain drive. The engines had side vales in a T head, and there were 4 forward speeds. Round radiators and lt magneto ignition were featured, and 1906 cars came in 4.1-litre and 8.6-litre sizes, both with 4-cylinder engines. Ht ignition and pressure lubrication followed in 1908. There was a 1.9-litre car with monobloc engine in 1909, and a small 2.4-litre six in 1912. A wide 1913 range covered everything from a 1-litre lightweight up to 6.3 litres, including an ultra-long-stroke 4.2-litre (85×185mm) four. The Pilain was an expensive if excellent machine that did not long outlive World War 1 in its original form. It was then developed into the extraordinary S.L.I.M.   TRN

PILAIN (ii) (F) *1930–1935*
E. Pilain, Levallois-Perret, Seine

Emile Pilain, who had been responsible for the original Rolland-Pilain, produced a light car on his own account in 1930 for the mass market. It was a 919cc, water-cooled sv four, with a 3-speed gearbox and Perrot brakes. It was rated at 5CV, and in 1932 there was also a 1.2-litre version with free wheel.   TRN

PILGRIM (i) (GB) *1906–1914*
Pilgrim's Way Motor Co Ltd, Farnham, Surrey

The first Pilgrims were large town cars with under-seat engines. the 5½-litre 4-cylinder unit was mounted horizontally across the frame with the cylinders pointing forwards, and drove a 2-speed epicyclic preselector gearbox. After 18 of these cars had been made the company turned its attention in 1911 to a 10/12hp two-seater with front-wheel drive and a Renault-like bonnet.   GNG

PILGRIM (ii) (US) *1914–1918*
Pilgrim Motor Car Co, Detroit, Mich.

This was termed a light car, weighing only 1,450lb. The five-seater model was powered by a 4-cylinder, water-cooled engine of 2.3 litres.   GMN

PILLIOD (US) *1915–1918*
Pilliod Motor Co, Toledo, Ohio

This car had an advanced single-sleeve-valve engine and was one of the earliest examples of the extensive use of aluminium. This allowed the 4.4-litre engine to produce 27hp with a weight of 390lb. The Pilliod was available in two, four- and five-seater forms.   GMN

PILOT (i) (US) *1909–1924*
Pilot Motor Car Co, Richmond, Ind.

Throughout its life, the Pilot was an assembled car, with little evidence of imagination in either engineering or style. It started as a two-seater roadster which was soon joined by five-seater touring versions. These early models used a 4-cylinder, 35hp engine. In 1913, a 6-cylinder model was added and this was also the last year of the 4-cylinder cars. The 6-cylinder engine of 4.9 litres was built by Teetor and developed 90hp. For 1916, a 4.7-litre V-8 was added to the range. In this year the purchaser had an odd choice of either right- or left-hand steering position, with centre controls. Model 6-45 originated in 1916, with a Teetor six of 3.8 litres. With variations only in the wheelbase, this model was built until the end in 1924. In 1922, a 6-cylinder Herschell-Spillman engine of 50hp was added as the Model 6-50 and was continued into 1924. In the last year of production, three chassis were offered. Two had H-S engines and the smallest, the 6-45, had a Teetor unit.   GMN

PILOT (ii) (GB) *1909–1914*
(1) Motor Schools Ltd, London, N.W. *1909–1911*
(2) Pilot Motors & Friction Cars Ltd, London, N.W. *1911–1914*

The Pilot was made by a firm who specialized in driving and maintenance instruction, but unlike the Academy it was not provided with dual control. Its main feature was friction drive by belt and cone pulley, and a variety of engines were used. The cars using 16hp White & Poppe or 19.6 Hillman engines were only experimental, but from 1911 onwards two models were catalogues, the smaller with a single-cylinder 7hp Coventry-Simplex, and the larger with a 10hp 4-cylinder Chapuis-Dornier engine. Mainly two-seater bodywork was provided.　　GNG

PILOT (iii) (D) *1923–1925*
Pilotwagen AG, Bannewitz; Werdau

A 4-cylinder 6/30PS car was produced by this firm. After the Sächsische Waggon-fabrik had acquired a controlling interest in the company in 1924 the bodies were built in Werdau.　　HON

PINART (B) *1901*
Ernest Pinart, Brussels

Pinart cars used 6 or 9hp 2-cylinder engines, or a 12hp 4-cylinder unit. They had 3-speed gearboxes and chain drive.　　GNG

PINGUIN (D) *1954*
Ruhr Fahrzeugbau, Herne, Westphalia

The Pinguin was a 3-wheeled coupé powered by a 200cc Ilo air-cooled engine driving the single rear wheel.　　GNG

PINNACE *see* NORMA

PIONEER (i) (AUS) *1897*
Australian Horseless Carriage Syndicate, Melbourne

The Pioneer was probably the first internal combustion-engine car to be built in Australia. It was made by William Grayson and had the general appearance of a Benz, although the horizontal 2-cylinder engine was said to be Grayson's design, and ran on paraffin.

Despite the gradiose name of the company, and the report that they had orders for six months' production, not more than six Pioneers were made.　　GNG

PIONEER (ii) (US) *1909–1911*
Pioneer Car Co, El Reno, Okla.

This was a light-weight car driven by a 4-cylinder, 30hp engine through a planetary transmission. The Model B Surrey cost $1,050.　　GMN

PIONEER (iii) (US) *1914*
American Mfg Co, Chicago, Ill.

The Pioneer Cyclecar used a 9hp 2-cylinder air-cooled engine and semi-tandem or staggered seating for two. Transmission was by friction discs, and final drive by belts.　　GNG

PIONEER (iv) (US) *1959*
Nic-L-Silver Battery Co, Santa Ana, Calif.

The Pioneer, or Lippencott Pioneer as this little electric was also known, had a fibreglass body and motors linked to the rear wheels. Suspension was by torsion bars and there was a toggle switch for forward or reverse.　　BE

PIONEER (v) *see* XIAN-JIN

PIPE (B) *1898–1922*
Compagnie Belge de Construction Automobile, Brussels

The Pipe, one of Belgium's best-built and most expensive cars, is said to have been so named because its manufacturers also made metal pipes. Their first car was made in 1898, but the earliest of which anything is known was the 2-cylinder 6hp of Panhard-Levassor type, with chain drive, offered in 1900. By 1902 there was a similar 4-cylinder car of 15hp, and in 1904 a range of four models all of the same basic design, of which 100 were made that year.

Petrol-electric transmission, in the form of the Jenatzy Magnetic Clutch, was tried in 1904–5, but it was only fitted to a few cars. At the Paris Salon in December 1904, however, a more lasting Pipe feature appeared: inclined push-rod-operated overhead valves. The 28/32hp and 50hp models of 1905 had these, and also Truffault shock absorbers. None of these features was entirely new, but all were symptoms of very advanced design. No fewer than 300 Pipes were made in 1907, and one of their racing cars took 2nd place in the Kaiserpreis race that year, but oddly enough, when they were at the height of their fame, production seems to have ceased for two years.

When it was resumed, little was left of former distinctiveness. A small side-valve car was offered in 1910 and 1911, to be succeeded in 1913 by a range of entirely conventional, if still beautifully-made machines with quiet, flexible, very long-stroke side-valve engines, all with four cylinders and live axles. Automatic ignition advance was the only novelty now offered. The sole survivor of former days was the 11-litre, chain-driven 80hp model.

After World War 1, car production was not resumed immediately as the factory had to be completely rebuilt. At the 1921 Brussels Show Pipe exhibited two 4-cylinder models, a medium-sized 3-litre car, and a 9-litre giant. Few were made of either car, but production of lorries continued until 1932.　　TRN

1908 PILGRIM(i) 30hp landaulette. *Autocar*

1913 PILOT(ii) 10/12hp two-seater. *National Motor Museum*

1904 PIPE 60hp Gordon Bennett racing car. *Geoffroy de Beauffort Collection*

1947 PLAYBOY 2.6-litre two-seater. *Autocar*

1931 PLYMOUTH(ii) Model PA 3.2-litre sedan.
National Motor Museum

1935 PLYMOUTH(ii) PJ 3.3-litre sedan.
G.N. Georgano

PIPER (GB) *1966 to date*
(1) Campbells Garages, Hayes, Kent *1966–1967*
(2) Piper Cars Ltd, Wokingham, Berks. *1967–1971*
(3) Emmbrook Engineering Ltd, Wokingham, Berks. *1971–1972*
(4) Piper F.M. Ltd, Ashford, Kent *1972 to date*

A range of sports-racing cars, GT coupé and Formula 3 single seaters, designed by Tony Hilder, was offered by George Henrotte, a former 500cc driver. Composite structures were adopted – a platform chassis with tubular appendages was used for the sports car, with an alloy and glassfibre body. Coil/damper unit suspension was adopted. Various Ford and B.M.C. engines were fitted. The GT coupé was developed by a separate company under Brian Sherwood as the GTT, and during 1969 a few of the GTR racing models were built, with 2-litre B.R.M. and B.M.W. engines as well as Ford. Plans were afoot for a new single-seater and road and racing V-8-engined vehicles. After Sherwood died at the end of the year the firm concentrated only on the GTT two-seater, with square-section chassis tubing and 1600 Ford GT engine, priced as a complete kit at £1,355. About 50 were sold before they were phased out in favour of the P2 in 1971. This was a basically similar but longer, wider car with better roadholding, pop-up headlamps and other detail changes. A 2-litre Ford engine was used in the 1973 model.   DF

PITT (GB) *1902–1903*
Pitt Yorkshire Machine Co, Liversedge, Yorks.

A 9hp four-seater tonneau with Renault-type bonnet was made by this firm, but there is no proof that it ever went into production.   GNG

PITTEVIL (B) *1900*
Built in Antwerp, the Pittevil was a 2-cylinder voiturette with belt drive.   GNG

PITTLER *see* HYDROMOBIL

PITTSBURGH (i) *see* AUTOCAR

PITTSBURGH (ii) (US) *1909–1911*
Fort Pitt Motor Manufacturing Co, New Kensington, Pa.

Pittsburgh cars were driven by T-head 6-cylinder 9.1-litre engines. Aluminium bodies were furnished for the runabout and two touring models. These cars had an advanced exhaust system for the period, and the manufacturer claimed an added 300rpm engine speed by proper exhaust design. The single 1911 model was a seven-seater touring car.   GMN

PIVOT (F) *1904–c.1907*
Automobiles Pivot, Puteaux, Seine

The Pivot was a conventional car made in 1-, 2- and 4-cylinder form. The twins were a 6/7hp and a 9/11hp, both with 4-speed gearboxes and shaft drive. In 1905 there was a range of three 4-cylinder shaft drive cars, of 16, 24, and 30hp, and in 1906 the range consisted of 6 and 8hp singles, and 8/10 and 10/12hp twins, the latter made in touring and town car form. Some advertisements listed models from 10 to 50hp, but this was probably wishful thinking.   GNG

PLANET (i) (GB) *1904–1905*
Automobile Engineering Co Ltd, Clapham, London S.W.

Four models of the Planet were made, a 6hp with single-cylinder De Dion engine, a 12hp 2-cylinder, and 24 and 30hp 4-cylinder cars. The 6hp had a two-seater body, and the larger cars, four-seater rear-entrance tonneaus. All had shaft drive except the 30hp, which was driven through double chains. Prices ranged from £152 for the 6hp to £499 for the 30hp.   GNG

PLANET (ii) (D) *1907*
Planetwerke Max Bohm, Berlin-Charlottenburg

A 2-cylinder 7PS and a 4-cylinder 10PS type were marketed by this firm. A characteristic was the planetary gear that gave the make its name.   HON

PLASTI-CAR (US) *1954*
Plasti-Car Inc, Doylestown, Pa.

Powered by a Renault 4CV engine, the Plasti-Car was available in two forms, the open Rouge and the hard-top Marquis, both two-seaters. Bodies were in fibreglass, but an aluminium version of the Marquis, built in Europe, was available.   GNG

PLAYBOY (US) *1946–1951*
Playboy Motor Car Corp, Buffalo, N.Y.

Playboy nearly outlasted the flood of short-lived post-war American makes. The company struggled valiantly and managed to manufacture 97 examples of this compact three-seater convertible before bankruptcy. It was driven by a 40bhp 4-cylinder Continental (originally Hercules) L-head engine, had an automatic transmission and a 7ft 6in wheelbase. Price was $985.   BE

P.L.M. *see* KELLER

PLUTO (D) *1924–1927*

(1) Automobilfabrik Zella-Mehlis GmbH, Zella-St Blasii *1924–1927*

(2) Pluto Automobilfabrik AG, Zella-St Blasii *1927*

After production had ended at the Ehrhardt factory a new car manufacturing company was established, again under Ehrhardt influence. They built the Amilcar under licence which appeared in 4/20PS, 1,004cc and 5/30PS 1,054cc two-seater sports forms. The latter model was also available with a Roots blower, and was then designated the 5/30/ 65PS.   HON

PLUTON (F) *1901*

Sté Industrielle d'Automobile Pluton, Levallois-Perret, Seine

The Pluton was powered by a 5hp De Dion engine mounted in front, with chain final drive. Three-seater spider or four-seater tonneau bodies were available.   GNG

PLYMOUTH (i) (US) *1910*

Plymouth Motor Truck Co, Plymouth, Ohio

Although this was offered to the public as a five-seater touring car with 40hp engine, only one was actually built.   GMN

PLYMOUTH (ii) (US) *1928 to date*

Chrysler Corporation, Detroit, Mich.

The 4-cylinder 21hp Plymouth appeared in 1928 at a list price of $725 for a sedan. It replaced the earlier 4-cylinder Chryslers and represented a serious challenge for Ford and Chevrolet in their lowest price class. Its side valves, internal-expanding hydraulic brakes and ribbon-type radiator gave it a close resemblance to the 1928 Chryslers and De Sotos, and it sold over 100,000 in its first year, even improving its sales position in the bleak economic climate of 1932. Plymouth adhered to four cylinders until 1933, when the PD-series 6-cylinder was listed at less than $600. 1934 de luxe models had independent front suspension, but this was dropped after a year and did not reappear for some time. The standard engine in the later 1930s had a capacity of 3.3 litres, rather smaller than that used in comparable Chevrolets and Fords: a small-bore 2.8-litre version was made for export up to 1939, but the name Plymouth was not usually found on cars sold in England, which were nominally Chrysler Kew and Wimbledon sixes. After World War 2 evolution followed that of other Chrysler Corporation cars closely, the old-fashioned styling losing the division its long-held third place in American sales to Buick. Further, Plymouth retained the L-head six as its staple power unit right up to 1955, when Flight Sweep versions were introduced with over-square ohv V-8 engines on accepted American lines in a variety of powers from 157 to 177bhp. The capacity of these was 4.3 litres, while the six, now of 3.8 litres, remained available. These 1955 cars were lower and longer than their predecessors and could be obtained with synchromesh, overdrive or automatic gearboxes.

The Fury models of the ensuing decade represented a breakaway from the traditional Plymouth stolid family car, while the Division was also responsible for Chrysler's contribution to the compacts, the Valiant launched for 1960. This had rather more European styling than its competitors, with a dummy spare-wheel moulding on the tail; interesting items of specification were its unitary construction, alternator ignition, and inclined in-line 2.8-litre ohv 6-cylinder engine. The influence of the GT car on America resulted in the Barracuda of 1965, a fastback coupé using the Valiant's 8ft 10in wheelbase and a 4½-litre V-8 power unit. Plymouth, like Ford and Chevrolet, was aiming at comprehensive coverage of the low and medium price market in 1966, with the compact Valiant, the sports-compact Barracuda, the medium-sized Belvedere, the full-size Fury, and the luxurious 'V.I.P.' 4-door hardtop, offered only with a 5.2-litre V-8 engine and selling for $2,930. An increasing emphasis on sporting models was detectable by 1968, when in addition to the established Barracuda there were two other sports coupés, the GTX and the Road Runner. All three were available with 4-speed manual gearboxes and the 6,981cc 425bhp hemi-head V-8 also used by Dodge. In 1970, when Valiant prices started at a low $2,172, there was also a Valiant sports coupé, the Duster.

In 1971 Plymouth added a sub-compact to their range when they offered the 1½-litre Hillman Avenger as the Plymouth Cricket. The 1972 range embraced the Valiant on a 9ft wheelbase, the Barracudas and Satellites, and the full-size Furys with V-8 engines and automatic transmission as standard. Engines ranged from the Valiant's 3.2-litre and 3.7-litre sixes up to the largest Chrysler unit, a V-8 of 7,210cc. Electronic ignition was offered on the costliest Barracuda model. Casualties of new Federal regulations were the hemi-head engine and convertibles, and the same range with minor improvements, among them manually-operated sun roofs, was offered in 1973.   MCS

P.M. (B) *1921–1926*

Sté Auto-Mécanique P.M., Sclessin, Liège

The P.M. was a conventional light car powered by a 4-cylinder Peters engine of 1,795cc. The name was taken from the initials of the founder, Pierre Malherbe, but also conveniently fitted those of another director, Pierre Mullejans. The company owned the majority of shares in the English Carrow Car Co, and the later Carrows used the same engine as the P.M. In 1924 a new model appeared with a 4-cylinder single-ohc engine.   GNG

1960 PLYMOUTH(ii) Valiant 2.8-litre sedan.
Chrysler Corporation

1968 PLYMOUTH(ii) Barracuda 6.3-litre coupé.
Chrysler Corporation

1973 PLYMOUTH(ii) Valiant sedan.
Chrysler Corporation

1952 POBIEDA 2.1-litre saloon. *Associated Press Ltd*

1914 PODEUS 10/30PS tourer. *Neubauer Collection*

1956 POIRIER Monoto XW5 125cc 3-wheeler. *David Filsell Collection*

1972 POLSKI-FIAT 125P 1½-litre station wagon. *FSO*

P.M.C. (i) (US) *1908*
C.S. Peets Manufacturing Co, New York, N.Y.
The P.M.C. was a two-seater runabout with solid rubber tyres. It was powered by a 2-cylinder opposed engine of 12hp. Its cost was $550, with a top for $30 extra
GMN

P.M.C. (ii) *see* PREMIER (ii)

PNEUMOBILE (US) *1915*
Cowles-McDowell Pneumobile Co, Chicago, Ill.
The Pneumobile appears to have been the first American car to use air-springs in place of mechanical springing. The cylindrical springs also acted as shock absorbers. It was built as a seven-seater on a wheelbase of 11ft. It had a 6-cylinder, 4.8-litre Buda engine. In appearance this was quite an advanced car, with a radiator of compound curvature.
GMN

POBIEDA (Victory) (GAZ M.20) (SU) *1946–1958*
Zavod Imieni Molotova, Gorky
This original design was conceived by a group headed by Andrei Lipgart and was the first post-war sedan from the giant Gorky auto plant. Built to help overcome the great shortage of cars and other transport, it was of unit construction and fitted with a 4-cylinder 2.1-litre, 50bhp engine driving through a 3-speed synchromesh transmission. Suspension was independent at the front and by semi-elliptic springs at the rear with a rigid axle. Fuel consumption was put at 21mpg with a top speed of 65mph.
Rugged construction characterized this car, for it was required to withstand the variety of road and weather conditions found in the Soviet Union. A medium-sized 4-door sedan was the primary version available and many were, and still are, in use as taxis. In addition a number of touring models were built, and in 1955 the model M-72, a 4-wheel-drive sedan, was added to the series, utilizing the basic Pobieda body shell.
Thirteen years saw little change in the M-20's appearance, although some modifications were made on the M-20B. The more modern Volga (M-21), eventually replaced the Pobieda on the assembly lines but the design lives on in the form of the Warszawa, built under licence by FSO in Poland, with an ohv engine.
Snowmobiles have been seen in Russia fitted with altered Pobieda bodies and propelled by an aircraft engine assembly mounted on the rear; the source of this combination is unknown.
BE

PODEUS (D) *1910–1914*
Paul Heinrich Podeus, Wismar
Podeus started by producing lorries, but built private cars from 1910. A 9/24PS, 2,248cc and a 10/30PS 2,536cc model were manufactured, but were not widely known. Lorries, and in later years crawler tractors, remained the Podeus speciality.
HON

POGGI (I) *1959*
This was a front-engined Formula Junior car with Fiat components, designed by Eugenio Poggi and sponsored by Massimino.
DF

POINARD (F) *1952*
This small motorcycle firm built a prototype 3-wheeler powered by a 125cc engine.
GNG

POIRIER (F) *1928–c.1958*
Etablissements G. Poirier, Fondettes, Indre-et-Loire
Although primarily makers of invalid carriages, this firm advertised various 3-wheelers for general sale. Early back-to-back versions and monocars were superseded in 1935 by the Monoto single- or tandem-seater voiturettes, with tubular frames. Before World War 2, 175cc Train or Sachs engines were favoured; Peugeot and Gnome-et-Rhône were also obtainable. After the war, shaft transmission was adopted, and alternative engines were the 98cc Sachs or 125cc Ydral.
DF

POKORNEY *see* TRICOLET

POLONIA (PL) *1924*
M. Karpowski, Warsaw
A six-seater tourer prototype with a 45hp 6-cylinder engine, the Polonia never reached production. The one existing car was used as a lottery prize.
BE

POLSKI-FIAT (PL) *1968 to date*
Fabryka Samochodow Osobowych, Warsaw
The first cars to bear this name were members of the Fiat 508 and 508C family made under licence by the Polish government between 1932 and 1939; latterly they were almost entirely Polish-made, only instruments being imported. The 125P made by FSO is, however, distinct from any native Fiat model, using the body styling of the 124 in conjunction with the floor pan, suspension and engines from the superseded 1300/1500 series first seen in 1961. Certain parts are made in the former Stoewer factory at Szczecin (Stettin).
MCS

POLYMOBIL (D) *1904–1909*

Polyphon Musikwerke AG, Wahren

This firm, known for precision machine tools, started car production by building the Oldsmobile under licence. It differed in several points from the original design. Most significant was the absence of the curved dash, which was replaced by an additional seat. From 1904 to 1905 this model was known as the Gazelle, later like all other Polyphon cars – as the Polymobil. It was produced until 1908, was quite popular and was available with wheel instead of tiller steering. A four-seater version was characterized by a bonnet, steering wheel and longer wheelbase. The engine was mounted under the front seat. In 1907 two cars of Polyphon's own design were introduced, the 2-cylinder 8/10PS and the 4-cylinder 16/20PS. After 1909 a new range of models appeared, offered under the name of Dux.   HON

POMEROY (i) (US) *1902*

Pomeroy Motor Vehicle Co, Brooklyn, N.Y.

Sometimes mistakenly listed as Pomroy, this was a small electric runabout made for less than one year.   GNG

POMEROY (ii) (US) *1920–1924*

(1) Aluminium Company of America, Cleveland, Ohio *1920–1922*
(2) Pierce-Arrow Motor Car Co, Buffalo, N.Y. *1923–1924*

The Pomeroy was not, as is sometimes claimed, an 'all-aluminium car', but it did contain about 85% of aluminium parts, notable exceptions being the semi-elliptic springs and the gears. It was designed by L.H. Pomeroy who was also responsible for the Prince Henry Vauxhall and Double-Six Daimler, and was made in two models. The first was made by Alcoa and used a 4-cylinder 4-litre engine (six of these were made), while the second was made in the Pierce-Arrow factory and used a 6-cylinder engine similar to the Pierce-Arrow 80, except for a smaller bore. These cars were never sold to the public, and large-scale manufacturers were unwilling to commit themselves to a material of which one company had a near monopoly of supplies.   GNG

PONDER (US) *1923*

Ponder Motor Manufacturing Co, Shreveport, La.

The Ponder was the continuation of the earlier Bour-Davis car after that make had been taken over by J.M. Ponder. A Continental 6-cylinder engine was used in this short-lived assembled car.   KM

PONTIAC (i) (US) *1907–1908*

Pontiac Spring and Wagon Works, Pontiac, Mich.

This was a two-seater high-wheeler with right-hand steering by wheel. It was powered by a 2-cylinder, water-cooled engine mounted under the body. The drive was through a friction transmission and double chains to the rear wheels. The cost was $600.   GMN

PONTIAC (ii) (US) *1915*

Pontiac Chassis Co, Pontiac, Mich.

A chassis without body was all that this company marketed. It was furnished with a 4-cylinder engine, by Perkins, rated at 25hp, driving through a 3-speed transmission.   GMN

PONTIAC (iii) (US) *1926 to date*

(1) Oakland Motor Car Co, Pontiac, Mich. *1926–1932*
(2) Pontiac Motor Co, Pontiac, Mich. *1933 to date*

Oakland's Pontiac Six was intended as a lower-priced running mate, and prices of this conventional 3-litre sv six started at $825. Only closed bodies were offered initially, but a sale of over 140,000 cars was an indication of acceptance, especially when followed by an increase to 210,890 in 1928. The 1930 Pontiacs closely resembled Buick's Marquette, and had 3.3-litre engines, the six being joined in 1932 by a V-8 which was really a revamped 1931 Oakland.

In 1933 Pontiac scored an important success with a 3.7-litre, 77bhp straight-8 selling for less than $600 with General Motors' new no-draught ventilation, the 6-cylinder models being dropped for the time being. The 1934 cars had Dubonnet-type independent front suspension, and 'turret-top' all-steel bodies. Fencer's mask radiator grilles were found on the 1935 Silver Streak line. Capacities of the six and the eight were 3.6 litres and 4.1 litres respectively in 1937. In 1939 Pontiac's cheaper cars had body shells very similar to those of the Chevrolet, as befitted a make which ranked next in the G.M. hierarchy – though in fact only $20 separated the cheapest Pontiac 4-door sedan from the corresponding Oldsmobile model.

Pontiac's Torpedo Streamliners brought back the fastback style in 1941, and the immediate pre-war models were continued with little alteration until 1949, when the whole group's products were restyled, and Pontiacs emerged with lower bodies, redesigned X-frames, and the option of Hydramatic transmission. Though maintaining high sales – they beat Plymouth into 4th place overall in 1954 – Pontiac remained conservative in engine design, and the well-tried 127bhp sv straight-8 was not supplanted until 1955, when all U.S.-produced Pontiacs

1923 POMEROY(ii) 4-litre sedan. *Aluminum Co of America*

1931 PONTIAC(iii) Model 401 3.3-litre coupé. *Arthur Ingram*

1939 PONTIAC(iii) Quality Six 3.6-litre sedan. *G. Marshall Naul*

1961 PONTIAC(iii) Tempest 3.2-litre coupé. *General Motors Corporation*

1968 PONTIAC(iii) Bonneville 6½-litre hardtop.
General Motors Corporation

1973 PONTIAC Grand Am coupé.
General Motors Corporation

1914 POPE-HARTFORD 35hp two-seater.
Western Reserve Museum, Cleveland, Ohio

1906 POPE-TOLEDO Type 12 35/40hp tourer.
Burton H. Upjohn

received a 4.7-litre ohv V-8. The L-head six was retained for some models made for the Canadian market.

Along with some of the other staider American makes, such as Plymouth and Mercury, Pontiac strove to build their reputation on performance in the later 1950s; the 1958 Super Tempest attained 330bhp, and in 1959 Pontiac came out with a wide-track chassis and concentrated on a 6.4-litre V-8 available in a variety of powers from 245 to 345bhp.

The Division's compact, the Tempest arrived in 1961, and was an unusual ohv oversquare four of 3.2 litres' capacity, mounted in a unitary-construction hull, with its 3-speed synchromesh gearbox in the rear axle. Floor change was standard: it was listed at $2.240. A small V-8 was available as an option in 1963. The big Pontiacs went over to G.M.'s perimeter-type frame in 1963, when the V-8 engine was available in a variety of guises from a 'cooking' 215bhp version burning regular-grade petrol at $2,725 up to the sporting Grand Prix coupé with 303bhp and a revolution counter as standard equipment, at $3,489. The Tempest's 4-cylinder engine was dropped in 1965 in favour of a 140bhp six or 5.4-litre eight. Sporting qualities were emphasized in 1966, by which time the Tempest had grown from a 9ft 4in wheelbase to 9ft 8in, and the range included the G.T.O. Grand Prix and 2 plus 2 models, all disposing of more than 330bhp from engines of 6.4 and 6.9 litres' capacity. In 1967, 3.8-litre ohc 6-cylinder engines were introduced: in the sporting Firebird Sprint this unit developed 215bhp.

By 1970 the more sporting Pontiacs (GTO, Firebird and Grand Prix) had front disc brakes, and all full-sized Pontiacs came with automatic transmission as regular equipment. New for 1971 was a compact, the Ventura II on a 9ft 3in wheelbase. The 1972 range covered most sectors of the market, from the Ventura at $2,394 up to the luxury Grand Ville with 220bhp 7,456cc V-8 engine at $4,368. For the sporting motorist there were the Le Mans Sport, the GTO, and a wide selection of Firebirds up to the Trans Am with 300bhp V-8 unit, giving it a top speed of about 120mph. Peculiar to Canada was the Laurentian, a hybrid Chevrolet-Pontiac on a 10ft 3½in wheelbase, available with 110bhp 6-cylinder or 165bhp V-8 unit. In the main 1973's improvements concerned styling, the cars being longer and wider, but new were the Grand Am 2- and 4-door hardtops, with 6½ or 7½-litre V-8 engines, power steering, power disc front brakes and 3-speed automatic gearbox.　　　　　　　　　　　　　　　　　　　　MCS

POPE (F) *1933–1934*
L.A. Pope, Paris

The Pope was designed by an American living in France. Its 900cc ohc V-4 engine drove the front wheels via a 4-speed unit gearbox, other features being a backbone frame, transverse ifs, and rear suspension by reversed quarter-elliptics. The power unit was quick-detachable for purposes of servicing. A coupé was demonstrated to the press but there was no series production.　　　MCS

POPE-HARTFORD (US) *1903–1914*
Pope Manufacturing Co, Hartford, Conn.

This is one of the best-remembered cars of the period; Pope-Hartfords were apparently reliable vehicles although the design was very conservative. A single-cylinder model was included in the 1905 range, and 2-cylinder models were made as late as 1906. Double chain drive was retained in some models for 1908.

In price and size the Pope-Hartford came between the larger Pope-Toledo and the inexpensive Pope-Tribune.

In 1912, 4- and 6-cylinder models, of 50hp (6.4 litres) and 60hp (7.7 litres) respectively, were part of a large range of 17 different models. This type of marketing led to the collapse of the Pope group of companies, which at one period encompassed five makes of cars as well as motorcycles and bicycles. Pope-Hartford also offered, in 1911, the FIAT-Portola, a chain-driven FIAT chassis fitted with their own engine.　　　　　　　　　　　　　GMN

POPE-ROBINSON *see* ROBINSON (i)

POPE-TOLEDO (US) *1903–1909*
Pope Motor Car Co, Toledo, Ohio

Of the several makes produced by the Pope companies, this was the elite car. It grew out of the Toledo steamer, although none of the Pope-Toledos had steam engines. All models were distinguished by peaked bonnets and were powered by 4-cylinder, water-cooled engines; 1904 models retained automatic inlet valves. Early Pope-Toledos were rear-entrance tonneaux, but by 1907 limousines and seven-seater touring cars were being built. The company was taken over in 1909 by the Apperson-Toledo Motor Co, who discontinued this make.　　GMN

POPE-TRIBUNE (US) *1904–1907*
Pope Manufacturing Co, Hagerstown, Md.

This was the smallest and least expensive of the several Pope-owned makes. Two- and four-seater models, using single- and 2-cylinder engines, were built, both with shaft-drive. In 1907, a 4-cylinder car was brought out. The prices of the several models ranged from $500 to $900. After financial difficulties in 1907, the Pope-Tribune was dropped.　　　　　　　　　GMN

POPE-WAVERLEY *see* WAVERLEY

POPP (CH) *1898*
Lorenz Popp, Basle

Lorenz Popp was financed by E. Burkhardt who was the Benz agent for Switzerland, and the two Popp cars made were on Benz lines, with a rear-mounted 2-cylinder 7hp engine, a 2-speed belt transmission and chain final drive. A two-seater and a four-seater were built; the former survives today in the Swiss Transport Museum at Lucerne.   GNG

POPPY CAR (US) *1917*
Eisenhuth Motor Co, Los Angeles, Calif.

This company announced a 5-cylinder car with 'self-starting motor, conventional transmission done away with, and a secret reverse system'. The car was to sell at the low price of $650, but there is no evidence that it was made.   GNG

PORSCHE (A; D) *1948 to date*
(1) Porsche Konstruktions-GmbH, Gmünd (Austria) *1948–1950*
(2) Dr Ing.h.c. F. Porsche KG, Stuttgart-Zuffenhausen *1950 to date*

Ferdinand Porsche, well-known designer of Lohner, Austro-Daimler, Steyr and Mercedes cars as well as Auto Union racers and the Volkswagen, started to produce cars on his own account in 1948.

Prototypes and a first series of 50 cars with light metal bodies were built in Austria, but real production started in 1950 at Stuttgart, where Porsche had owned a factory since before World War 2. This first model was the Type 356 which was built in various versions until 1964. Its rear-mounted engine was a Volkswagen-based air-cooled 4-cylinder unit of 1,086cc, developing 40bhp. Except for minor alterations its body style remained unchanged until the last model, the 2000GS of 1964, which developed 130bhp from its 1,966cc engine.

From the beginning Porsche was active in racing and gained innumerable wins in all continents in road and track racing and in hill climbs. The first works entry was for Le Mans in 1951, and it won the 1,100cc class. Several records at Montlhéry followed the same year. A 1,500cc class win in the Mille Miglia, another 1,100cc class win at Le Mans, and 1st, 3rd and 4th places in the Liège-Rome-Liège Rally were the outstanding successes of 1952. Le Mans, Mille Miglia, Nürburgring, Targa Florio, Carrera Panamericana are just some of the circuits which saw further Porsche triumphs. Formula 1 and 2 racing was also attempted, but this was only an interlude, as Porsche concentrated on sports car and GT events.

In 1964 Porsche introduced the Type 905 (Carrera GTS), built specially as a competition car, in which form the 1,966cc engine developed 180bhp. The 'civil' version was capable of 155bhp. The coupé body was made of fibreglass. Also in 1964 the Type 911 was introduced with a new body and a 1,991cc, flat-6 engine capable of 130bhp. The Type 912 replaced the 356C in 1965; it had the 911 body and the 4-cylinder 1,582cc engine of the 356C. A new competition model, the Carrera 6, based on the 911, was brought out in 1966 with a twin-ohc 1,991cc engine giving 210bhp. Again fibreglass was used for the body. A works-authorized four-seater saloon version of the 356 was made by the Swiss coachbuilder Beutler, who also built the bodies for the first 50 Austrian Porsche cars. The 907 2.2-litre prototypes were 1st and 2nd in the 1968 Sebring 12-hour race, other good performances of the season being a 2nd at Le Mans, and wins in the Monte Carlo and Swedish Rallies. The last year of the 4-cylinder 912 was 1969, but on the competition side the company evolved the 4,494cc 520bhp flat-12 917 sports car with 4ohc, fuel injection, dry-sump lubrication, multi-tubular space-frame and a 5-speed transaxle. Theoretical top speed was 240mph, and it was actually catalogued at DM140,000 (about £14,600). It was not immediately successful, either in sports car or Can-Am racing, but 1970 was a Porsche year, with victories in the Buenos Aires 1,000 Kilometres, the Daytona 24, the Sebring 12 Hours, the Nürburgring 1,000 Kilometres, Le Mans and the Österreichring 1,000 Kilometres.

The 6-cylinder 911 touring series was progressively developed: semi-automatic transmission was an option in 1968, and fuel injection in 1970, when capacity was increased to 2,195cc. Bigger 2,343cc units were standardized in 1972, when the 911S with fuel injection offered 190bhp and 143mph; this range was continued into 1973 with minor improvements. Competition successes continued: Porsche won the Sports Car and GT Championships in 1971, and 1972's score included the Arctic Rally and a 3rd at Le Mans. In America the marque returned to Can-Am events with the 917-10, a formidable spyder version of the basic 917 theme with a 5-litre turbocharged engine developing 950bhp. The company announced a return to the Grand Touring category of racing in 1973 with a lightweight 911-based coupé, the Carrera RS. It had a spoiler and a 2,687cc engine producing 210bhp. The Carrera won the 1973 Daytona 24-Hour and Targa Florio Races.   HON

PORTER (i) (US) *1900–1901*
Porter Automobile Co, Boston, Mass.

The Porter steam car used a 2-cylinder engine and had a maximum speed of about 25mph. Steering was by tiller which was usual on such cars, but the aluminium body had less angular lines than most of the Porter's contemporaries. The price was $750.   GNG

1904 POPE-TRIBUNE 7hp two-seater. *The Veteran Car Club of Great Britain*

1962 PORSCHE Flat-8 racing car. Dan Gurney at the wheel. *Motor Sport*

1963 PORSCHE Type 356C 1.6-litre coupé. *Dr Ing F. Porsche KG*

1973 PORSCHE Carrera RS 2.7-litre coupé. *Dr. Ing. F. Porsche KG*

1921 PORTER(ii) town car. *Keith Marvin Collection*

1956 POWERDRIVE 322cc 3-wheeler. *Motor*

1921 PRAGA Grand 3.8-litre saloon. *Autocar*

PORTER (ii) (US) *1919–1922*

American & British Manufacturing Corp., Bridgeport, Conn.

The Porter was a high-priced luxury car designed by Finlay Robertson Porter, formerly designer of the T-head Mercer and the F.R.P.; it was the logical successor to the F.R.P. from an engineering standpoint. Using a 4-cylinder engine of the firm's design, the Porter car, which somewhat resembled the Rolls-Royce, was equipped with a right-hand steering position, an anomaly on American roads. A variety of custom body builders, including Brewster, Holbrook and Demarest, supplied open and closed coachwork to the Porter chassis at prices from $10,000. A total of 34 cars constituted the complete Porter output.   KM

PORTHOS (F) *1906–1914*

Sté Générale des Automobiles Porthos, Billancourt, Seine

The first Porthos had a 24/30hp 4-cylinder T-head engine, and was joined in 1907 by a 50/60hp 6-cylinder car. Also in 1907 Porthos entered a straight-8 racing car of 10.857cc in the Grand Prix. Driven by ex-Rugby footballer Garcet, it finished 8th. In the 1908 Grand Prix Porthos entered a team of three 6-cylinder cars, but with less success. The original company was wound up in 1909, and no Porthos cars were made until the formation of a new company in 1912. Then quite a wide range was offered: 16/20 and 24/30hp fours, and 20/25 and 30/40hp sixes. For 1914 a small 10hp four was added to the range.   GNG

PORTLAND *see* INTERNATIONAL (i) *and* PACIFIC

POSTAL (US) *1907–1908*

Postal Auto & Engine Co, Bedford, Ind.

The Postal was an unsophisticated tiller-steered high-wheeler, with rear fenders only. Its 2-cylinder engine was placed under the seat for two passengers. Its weight was 900lb and its price was $475.   GMN

POWELL SPORT WAGON (US) *1954–1956*

Powell Sport Wagons, Compton, Calif.

The Powell utility had the rare distinction of being a 'used' new car as all were built of reclaimed Plymouth cars. A 1941 Plymouth chassis was the basis of this machine and added to it were rebuilt 90bhp Plymouth 6-cylinder engines, dating from 1940 to 1950. The metal and fibreglass pickup body was a boxy design with provision for a camping unit on the back and fishing rods in the rear bumpers.   BE

POWERCAR (US) *1909–1912*

Powercar Auto Co, Cincinnati, Ohio

Although this car had sliding-gear transmission and shaft drive, its 4-cylinder engine, rated at 30hp, hardly justified the make's name. In its final year of manufacture both a touring model and a torpedo roadster were offered.   GMN

POWERDRIVE (GB) *1956–1958*

Powerdrive Ltd, Wood Green, London N.22

The Powerdrive was one of a crop of economy cars which appeared in England in the mid-1950s. It was a low, wide 3-wheeler whose aluminium body could seat three abreast. The engine was a 322cc 2-cylinder, 2-stroke Anzani, and the price was £412. After production ceased, the design reappeared with modified body as the Coronet from Denham.   GNG

PRADO (US) *1920–1922*

Prado Motors Corp, New York, N.Y.

Built in extremely restricted numbers, the Prado was an 8-cylinder car using as its motive power a converted Curtiss OX-5 aircraft engine. Bore and stroke were 4in × 5in (101 × 127mm, giving a capacity of over 8 litres). Disc wheels and individual cycle-type mudguards were standard.   KM

PRAGA (A; CS) *1907–1947*

(1) Pražská Továrna na Automobily, Prague *1907–1929*

(2) Českomoravská-Kolben-Danek, Prague *1929–1947*

This firm of general engineers took out a manufacturing licence for Isotta Fraschinis, and also built some 2- and 4-cylinder cars on Renault and Charron lines. In 1911, however, Frantisek Kec joined the company as chief engineer, being responsible for all subsequent private-car types. His idiom was straightforward: sv monobloc engines, 4-speed gearboxes and semi-elliptic springing. He laid down three basic models: the 1,128cc Alfa; the 2.3-litre Mignon; and the 3.8-litre, 45bhp Grand. The change of national status after World War 1 brought no radical change of design, though in 1924 Praga introduced a baby four-seater, the 707cc Piccolo. This was enlarged to 824cc in 1925, and to 856cc in 1927, when Kec turned to multi-cylinderism with a new 1,496cc 6-cylinder Alfa (which had 4-wheel mechanical brakes and a hydraulic servo) and a straight-8 Grand of 3.4 litres.

In 1929 Praga merged with the Breitfeld and Danek aero-engine firm, and their products now embraced motorcycles, aero-engines and complete aircraft as well as cars and trucks. The 1930 Grands had hydraulic brakes and 4.4-litre, 90bhp engines, and the Alfa grew up to 1.8 litres and the Piccolo to 995cc. In 1934 deliveries of 2,250 units made the Praga a national best-seller, thanks to the Piccolo's successor, the Baby, which combined the existing engine with a forked backbone frame (as used on subsequent small cars), all-independent suspension, and a 3-speed synchromesh gearbox. It sold for the equivalent of £180. Less successful was the 1,660cc Super-Piccolo with coil ifs, and aerodynamic saloon bodywork with countersunk headlamps and spats to all four wheels, which grew up into the more conventionally styled Lady of like capacity.

In 1935 the Grand was replaced by a big six, the 3.9-litre Golden; this had a hypoid rear axle, a synchromesh gearbox, and transverse-leaf ifs, and could be had with an electrically-selected Cotal box. Also in the immediate pre-war range were a 2½-litre Alfa on similar lines, and a new 1,128cc Piccolo based on the 1934 Baby. Then in 1938 Keč at long last essayed ohv with a sports two-seater edition of the Lady for the Czechoslovak Thousand-Mile Race.

After World War 2 the company concentrated on trucks powered by the Golden's 6-cylinder engine, though a few private cars of this type were made for ministerial use in 1946 and 1947. The factory's current products are light commercial vehicles based on French Saviem-Renault designs.   MCS

PRATT (US) 1907
Pratt Chuck Works, Frankfort, N.Y.

The Pratt was one of the few 6-wheeled cars produced in the United States. Four wheels were mounted at the rear and two at the front. Both the front and the intermediate set were steerable, the intermediate pair turning in a lesser angle than the leading pair. Power was supplied by a 75hp engine to the rear pair of wheels only, through the medium of an ordinary transmission gear and a 2-part rear-axle shaft. The touring-car, the only model listed, was 14ft long.   KM

PRATT-ELKHART; PRATT (US) 1911–1917
(1) Elkhart Carriage & Harness Manufacturing Co, Elkhart, Ind. 1911–1915
(2) Pratt Motor Car Co, Elkhart, Ind. 1916–1917

This make started as a medium-sized car with a 4-cylinder engine of 4.4 litres. The last models had longer wheelbases (11ft) and were powered by a 6-cylinder, 5.7-litre engine rated at 50hp.   GMN

PREMIER (i) (US) 1903–1925
(1) Premier Motor Mfg Co, Indianapolis, Ind.
(2) Premier Motor Corp, Indianapolis, Ind.

The Premier started life as a conventional machine made on modern lines, with a pressed-steel frame, mechanically-operated inlet valves, and shaft drive. A four-cylinder air-cooled car was made in 1905. Its designer was G.A. Weidely, who made his name with proprietary engines. A line of conventional water-cooled big fours and sixes followed, starting with a 24/28hp model in 1907. From 1913, sixes alone were built, the '48' at $3,250 having a capacity of over 8 litres. The special racing Premiers of 1916 had a twin ohc, 4-cylinder, 16-valve engine reminiscent of the Peugeot. The touring Premier of 1919–20 was notable mainly for its use of the Cutler-Hammer Magnetic Gear Shift, an electric transmission system controlled by a lever mounted on the steering wheel. The ohv 4.8-litre engine was an unusually advanced six, with aluminium block, crankcase and pistons, and iron liners.   TRN

PREMIER (ii) (GB) 1906–1907; 1912–1913
Premier Motor Co Ltd, Birmingham

The Premier company were concessionaires for the Italian Marchand car, and the 1906 4-cylinder Premier was, in fact, a Marchand. Towards the end of 1906 they launched a short-lived two-seater of their own design powered by a 10/12hp Aster engine, but no further cars appeared until the cyclecar boom of 1912. This brought two distinct designs: the P.M.C. Motorette 3-wheeler with a rear-mounted 6hp single-cylinder engine driving the rear wheel by chains; and the more conventional Premier, a 4-wheeler using an 8hp 2-cylinder engine, and chain drive.   GNG

PREMIER (iii) (D) 1913–1914
Justus Christian Braun Premier-Werke AG, Nuremberg

After producing the Kaiser cars this firm offered a new model in 1913 under the name of Premier. It was a two-seater sports car with a 1,030cc 4/12PS engine. This car was also built in the company's Austrian factory at Eger and was marketed as the Omega.   HON

PREMOCAR (US) 1921–1923
Preston Motor Corp, Birmingham, Ala.

The first Premocars offered to the American public were available in two distinct types, a low-priced 6-cylinder model which had a Falls ohv engine, and a 4-cylinder model with a Rochester-Duesenberg unit which sold for a considerably higher figures. The four was almost immediately dropped, however, and most of the Premocars built were sixes.   KM

PRESCOTT (US) 1901–1905
Prescott Automobile Manufacturing Co, New York, N.Y.

1932 PRAGA Grand 4.4-litre cabriolet.
Václav Petřík Collection

1939 PRAGA Piccolo 1.1-litre saloon. *G.N. Georgano*

1907 PREMIER(i) 24hp roadster. *Automotive History Collection, Detroit Public Library*

1920 PRESCOTT 7½hp steam surrey. *National Motor Museum*

1905 PRIAMUS 15/20PS tonneau. *Neubauer Collection*

1966 PRINCE(ii) Gloria Super Six 2-litre saloon. *Nissan Motor Co Ltd*

This was a tiller-operated steamer with a 2-cylinder Mason engine rated at 7½hp. The body was an open four-seater, with a fold-down seat in front of the driver, or a standard four-seater surrey. Specifications for the Prescott included brass brake-shoes and a steam-operated air pump for inflating the tyres. GMN

PRESTO (D) *1901–1927*
(1) Presto-Werke Günther & Co, Chemnitz *1901–1907*
(2) Presto Werke AG, Chemnitz *1907–1927*

Presto were bicycle and motor cycle manufacturers who first exhibited cars at the Leipzig Motor Show in 1901. It is not known whether these were of their own design as they were building small numbers of Delahayes under licence in about 1907. A car of Presto design took part in the 1908 Prince Henry Trial, but there was no production worth mentioning until about 1910. From then on until 1914 various types were offered but not widely sold. Production of the 8/25PS, 2,078cc model, which appeared in 1913, was continued after World War 1 until 1919. After 1921 Presto concentrated on their 30bhp, 2,350cc Type D, which later became the Type E with its engine output increased to 40bhp.

In 1926 Presto acquired the Dux works. They produced two 6-cylinder models, the 2.6-litre Type F and the 3-litre Type G, which were continued as N.A.G.-Prestos after N.A.G.'s take-over in 1927. HON

PRIAMUS (D) *1901–1923*
(1) Kölner Motorwagenfabrik GmbH, vorm. Heinrich Brunthaler, Cologne *1901–1903*
(2) Motorfahrzeugfabrik 'Köln' Uren, Kotthaus & Co, Cologne *1904–1909*
(3) Priamus Automobil-Werk GmbH, Cologne-Sülz *1909–1921*
(4) Priamus-Werke AG für Fahrzeugbau, Cologne-Sülz *1921–1923*

The name Priamus was not used for this make until 1904. The first model of 1901 was a voiturette with a single-cylinder 6PS engine. In 1904 single-, 2-, 3- and 4-cylinder models were listed. These small and medium-sized cars were augmented by larger models in 1905 and 1906. Priamus cars participated in the Herkomer Trials, but without significant success. A pre-war design, the Priamus 8/24PS, only went into production after World War 1. The 9/30PS model of 1920 was only built for a short time before the firm was forced to abandon production because of financial difficulties. Möllenkamp took over and attempted unsuccessfully to continue production of the 9/30PS. This last model was also marketed as the P.A.G. HON

PRIDEMORE (US) *1914–1915*
Pridemore Machine Works, Northfield, Minn.

This was a tandem two-seater cyclecar with a 2-cylinder, air-cooled engine rated as 12/18hp. The transmission was of the friction type and final drive was by chains. The frame was underslung. GMN

PRIMA (F) *1906–1909*
Sté des Automobiles Prima, Levallois-Perret, Seine

The Prima was made by Léon Lefèbvre who had formerly been the maker of the Bolide. Three models of Prima were listed, a 9hp single-cylinder and two fours, a 10/12hp and a 15/20hp. Two single-cylinder voiturettes were entered in the 1907 Coupe des Voiturettes but were not successful, despite the fact that one was driven by René Thomas. GNG

PRIMO (US) *1910–1912*
Primo Motor Co, Atlanta, Ga.

The Primo company used small 25hp 4-cylinder engines, with Schebler carburettors, to power their various models. Prices ranged from $1,250 for a two-seater roadster to $1,750 for the five-seater touring car. GMN

PRIMUS (D) *1899–1903*
Pfälzische Nähmaschinen- und Fahrräderfabrik vorm. Gebr. Kayser, Kaiserslautern

After manufacturing sewing machines and bicycles this firm progressed to motor tricycles in 1899 and a single-cylinder 5PS voiturette in 1900; 2- and 4-cylinder models also appeared shortly afterwards. HON

PRINCE (i) (I) *1921–1923*
Automobili Costruzioni di V. Carena e Mazza, Turin

A conventional specification – 1,460 sv 4-cylinder engine, magneto ignition, and three forward speeds – characterized the Prince, which wore a radiator in the contemporary Fiat idiom. Prevailing industrial unrest killed the venture. MCS

PRINCE (ii) (J) *1952–1967*
(1) Tama Motors Co, Tachikawa *1952*
(2) Prince Motors Co, Tachikawa *1952–1954*
(3) Fuji Precision Machinery Co Ltd, Tokyo *1954–1961*
(4) Prince Motors Ltd, Tokyo *1961–1966*
(5) Prince Motors Ltd (Division of Nissan Motor Co), Tokyo *1966–1967*

The Prince originated in the former Tachikawa Aircraft Works, which started producing Tama electrics at the end of World War 2. As the supply of petrol became plentiful and the cost of lead for batteries increased, the Tama was abandoned in favour of a conventional ohv 4-cylinder 1½-litre saloon. This was placed on the market in 1952 and named the Prince in honour of Crown Prince Akihito. It has grown up three years later into the Skyline, with coil-spring independent front suspension, De Dion rear axle, 4-speed synchromesh gearbox, and 60bhp engine. It was exhibited at the 1957 Paris Salon, the first Japanese car to be promoted in Europe. A 1.9-litre Gloria was put on the market in 1961, and a 2-litre ohc 6-cylinder was put into production in 1964. Top of the 1966 line was the 2½-litre 134bhp Grand Gloria saloon, available with automatic transmission. In 1967 the 1,484cc Skyline saloon and the 2-litre Gloria were still offered, and the former received a new ohc engine in 1968, but these latter models went out under the Nissan/Datsun name. BE

PRINCEPS (i) (GB) 1902–1903
Princeps Autocar Co, Northampton

The Princeps was a light car with tubular frame and two-seater body. It was powered by a rear-mounted 4hp Aster engine, and had a 2-speed gearbox. GNG

PRINCEPS (ii) (GB) 1920

The Princeps light car was powered by a 10.5hp Coventry-Simplex engine and had friction transmission and chain drive. Two-seater, four-seater and delivery van models were offered. GNG

PRINCESS (i) (US) 1914–1918
Princess Motor Car Co, Detroit, Mich

The original Princess was a light two-seater, costing $475, powered by a 1.6-litre 4-cylinder Farmer engine. It had a Renault-style bonnet, although the radiator was mounted in front of the engine. For 1916 this model was supplemented by a conventional-looking five-seater tourer powered by a 3-litre G.B. & S. engine. GMN

PRINCESS (ii) (GB) 1923
Streatham Engineering Co Ltd, London S.W.2

This was a light car powered by an 8.9hp V-twin air-cooled engine. The company's main business was in the manufacture of shock-absorbers. GNG

PRINCESS (iii) see VANDEN PLAS

PRINCETON (US) 1923–1924
Durant Motors, Inc, Muncie, Ind.

The Princeton was William C. Durant's attempt to produce a prestige car for a market between that covered by the largest Flint and the smaller Locomobile, both Durant subsidiaries. Produced in the former Sheridan plant, the Princeton used an Ansted 6-cylinder ohv engine. Few were marketed. KM

PRINETTI & STUCCHI (I) 1898–1902
Prinetti & Stucchi, Milan

Prinetti & Stucchi were well-known makers of motor tricycles which did well in early races. Their voiturette had two front-mounted vertical single-cylinder engines, and final drive by belts. It had a tubular frame, and the body was suspended by C-springs at the rear. GNG

PRINGETT (GB) 1969–1971
Pringett Racing Ltd, Eastbourne, Sussex

Pat Rochfort designed the multi-tubular Pringett Mistrale Formula Ford single-seater primarily for driver training. Gerry Corbett, whose brother-in-law R.W. Pringle was a co-director, constructed the cars. Works driver Sid Fox and others achieved some victories during 1970, but only 14 chassis were made in all. DF

PRITCHETT & GOLD (GB) 1903–1904
Pritchett & Gold Ltd, Feltham, Middlesex

Well-known for the manufacture of accumulators, this company made a few electric cars which they sold under their own name, as well as petrol-engined cars called Meteor. The P. & G. Electric was a two-seater open car with a sloping bonnet in the style of the Renault. GNG

PROBE (GB) 1969–1971
(1) Adams Probe Motor Co, Bradford-on-Avon, Wilts. 1969–1971
(2) Caledonian Probe Motor Co, Irvine, Ayrshire 1971

The futuristic-looking Probe cars were styled by former Marcos designer Dennis Adams and built by himself and his brother Peter. Driving position in the very low coupé body was almost horizontal – the Probe was intended as a design exercise rather than a serious production machine. Nevertheless, about twelve were sold, the last two being assembled by a new company in Scotland. Power was provided by a rear-mounted British Leyland 1800 engine. GNG

PROD'HOMME (F) 1907–1908
Etablissements Prod'homme, Ivry-Port, Seine

1899 PRINETTI & STUCCHI 4hp voiturette.
Museo dell'Automobile, Turin

1970 PROBE 16 1.8-litre coupé.
G.N. Georgano

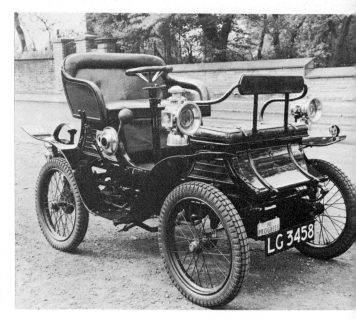

1901 PROGRESS(i) 4½hp voiturette. *D.C. Field Collection*

1914 PROJECTA 9hp cyclecar. *Autocar*

1905 PROTOS 17/35PS tourer. *Siemens Museum*

1926 PROTOS Type C1 10/45PS tourer. *Ruprecht von Siemens*

1903 PRUNEL 9hp tonneau. *The Veteran Car Club of Great Britain*

This company made 2- and 4-cylinder cars with opposed-piston engines, on the lines of the Gobron-Brillié.　　　　　GNG

PROGRESS (i) (GB) *1898–1903*
Progress Cycle Co Ltd, Coventry, Warwickshire

Progress cycles were made by E.J. West who later made the West-Aster cars as well as chassis for other firms. The Progress voiturette originally had a 3½hp or 4½hp De Dion or M.M.C. engine mounted at the rear of a tubular frame, and two-seater, or four-seater *vis-à-vis* bodies. In 1902 a new model appeared with pressed steel frame and front-mounted engines by Aster or De Dion. An 8hp Daimler 2-cylinder engine was also available, and bodies were by Mulliner. By the end of 1903 the Progress company was in liquidation, but the Aster-engined model re-appeared in 1904 basically unchanged as the West-Aster.　　　　　GNG

PROGRESS (ii) (GB) *1934*
Haynes Economy Motors Ltd, Manchester

The Progress 3-wheeler was powered by 980cc 2-cylinder engine, and had a single front wheel.　　　　　GNG

PROGRESS (iii) *see JIN-BU*

PROJECTA (GB) *1914*
Percival White Engineering Works, Highbury, London N.

The Projecta cyclecar was powered by a J.A.P. V-twin engine, and had a 2-speed transmission with belt final drive. Its most unusual feature was the very low, canoe-shaped body which acted as a frame.　　　　　GNG

PROSPER-LAMBERT (F) *1901–1906*
Sté Prosper-Lambert, Nanterre, Seine

Prosper-Lambert entered the market with a shaft-driven light car powered by a 7hp single-cycle De Dion engine. A 12hp 2-cylinder car was added to the range for 1902/03, in which year the catalogue stated that engines were of the company's own design. Four of these cars were driven in the 1903 Paris-Madrid race. By 1905 a 16hp 4-cylinder model was added to the range, and 1906 saw a range of five cars offered, the 9hp single, 10 and 12hp twins, and 16 and 30hp fours. All had shaft drive. For 1907 the cars were sold under the name Jean Bart, after which they disappeared from the market altogether.　　　　　GNG

PROTOS (D) *1900–1926*
(1) Motorenfabrik Protos Dr Alfred Sternberg, Berlin *1900–1904*
(2) Motorenfabrik Protos GmbH., Berlin *1904–1908*
(3) Siemens-Schuckert-Werke GmbH, Automobilwerk Nonnendamm, Berlin *1908–1926*

The first Protos car was a small single-cylinder model. As it was not very satisfactory a new 12/14 model was brought out. This was powered by the 'Kopensmotor', an engine which consisted of two 'working' cylinders and a third set at 180° to the others and containing a freely operating piston as a counterbalance to prevent uneven running. From the beginning Protos cars were built with shaft drive. In 1905 a 6-cylinder model with an engine output of 100bhp was introduced. It was not put into production but was the first in a range of very successful 6-cylinder cars. The make became widely known when a 4-cylinder 17/35PS Protos took part in the 1908 New York-Paris Race and finished second behind the American Thomas team. In 1908 Protos was taken over by the Siemens-Schuckert electrical concern, which had already taken up car manufacture.

The name Protos was used for all subsequent models and production of the 4-cylinder 17/35PS (4.6-litre) and 6-cylinder 26/50PS (6.8-litre) cars was continued for some time; these were quite popular during the years up to World War 1, and Protos was considered among Germany's best makes. Electric lighting and starting appeared in 1913.

After the war the factory concentrated on one model, the 4-cylinder Type C with a 30bhp 2,596cc engine which was later superseded by the Type C1 with an engine of the same capacity but developing 45bhp. In 1926 Siemens-Schuckert decided to give up car production, and sold their car division to N.A.G. Protos cars were built for a short time under N.A.G. management, but production ceased later in 1926. However, until 1932 certain N.A.G. products were sold under the N.A.G. Protos name.　　　　　HON

PROVINCIAL (GB) *1904–c.1905*
Provincial Electric Construction Co Ltd, Liverpool

This company exhibited two cars at the 1904 Liverpool Show. They were conventional assembled cars, a 6½hp single-cylinder two-seater, and a 12hp 2-cylinder four-seater tonneau.　　　　　GNG

PRUNEL (F) *1900–1907*
Société des Usines Prunel, Puteaux, Seine

The first Prunels were conventional voiturettes with 3hp De Dion engines, chain drive, and cycle-type wire wheels, and were marketed by E.J. Brierre under the name of Atlas. This name was also applied to a 4½hp De Dion-powered quadricycle, but by 1903 Prunel had blossomed out into a range of cars powered by Aster, Herald, Pieper, and De Dion engines: the company claimed to make everything else themselves. The big 4-cylinder 20hp had a capacity of 3.8 litres, a flitch-plate frame, automatic inlet valves and chain drive. The company went over to mechanically-operated inlet valves in 1904, when the 10hp model used a Gnome engine, and the 15 a Mutel unit. The 1905 range included twins of 1.8 litres and 2½ litres, as well as 3½-litre and 4.9-litre fours, the big 24/30 selling for only £460 in England. With the 1906 range, shaft drive was available to order, and there was an even bigger Prunel rated at 40/50hp.

In its later years the story of this company becomes very involved; not only was the Boyer car built in the same factory, but vehicles sponsored by the Prunel brothers (and probably built by them as well) were marketed in England under the names of Gnome (1905), Gracile (1906), and J.P. (1907). Prunel were still quoted as manufacturers in 1914, but there is no indication that any cars were made after 1907. However, the 1912–14 Phénix cars were apparently made in the Prunel factory. MCS

P.T.V. (E) 1956–1962
Sociedad de Automóviles Utilitarios, Manresa, Barcelona

The P.T.V. was one of the most successful post-war Spanish minicars, and its sales rivalled those of the Biscuter. It was certainly a more comfortable vehicle. It had a rear-mounted 2-cylinder 2-stroke Ausa engine of 250cc capacity, independent suspension all-round and hydraulic brakes. The body was a two-seater cabriolet and its maximum speed exceeded 60mph. About 1,250 were made. JRV

PUBLIX (US/CDN) 1947–1948
Publix Motor Car Co, Buffalo, N.Y.; Fort Erie, Ont.

This 3-wheeled convertible coupé was 6ft in length, with an aluminium body and chassis. It was powered by an air-cooled 1.75hp Caufflel engine mounted in a special shock-absorbing rig connected to the drive mechanism and the rear wheels. The steering wheel could be shifted from the left-hand side to the right at will. BE

PUCH (A) 1906–1925
(1) Johann Puch Erste Steiermärkische Fahrrad-Fabriks-Aktiengesellschaft, Graz 1906–1914
(2) Puchwerke, AG, Graz 1914–1925

Puch was already well-known for his bicycles when he built an experimental prototype motor car in 1901. A second prototype was ready in 1903 but, as with the first car, production was not started. Only in 1906 did car manufacture really begin with a V-Twin 8/9PS 904cc voiturette. Another 2-cylinder model was built in 1908, the 9/10PS which also was available in sports form. After 1908 Puch used 4-cylinder engines and in 1912/13 the 16/40PS and 27/60PS models were fitted with Daimler-Knight engines. Puch then concentrated on his Alpenwagen Type VIII with a 14/38PS 3,560cc engine. This car was produced until 1923. Another Alpenwagen, the Type VII, appeared in 1919 but was only built for about one year.

Car production was given up in 1925, Puch concentrating very successfully on motorcycles. In 1928 Puch emerged with Austro-Daimler and in 1934 Steyr was integrated (Steyr-Daimler-Puch AG).

Since 1957 the Fiat 500 has been built under licence by Steyr-Daimler-Puch in the former Puch factory at Graz. HON

PULCINO (I) 1948
Antonio Artesi, Palermo

This chain-driven minicar with 125cc 2-stroke engine, 4-speed gearbox, and neat two-seater bodywork was displayed at the 1948 Fiera del Mediterraneo. MCS

PULLCAR (GB) 1906–1908
Pullcar Motor Co Ltd, Preston, Lancs.

The Pullcar used a transversely-mounted 4-cylinder 15.9hp White & Poppe engine under the driver's seat. This drove the front wheels through a 3-speed epicyclic gearbox. The Pullcar was used mainly as a taxi (it was licensed by the Metropolitan Police), but several were used by private owners, including J.S. Critchley. GNG

PULLMAN (i) (US) 1903–1917
(1) Broomell, Schmidt & Steacy, York, Pa. 1903–1905
(2) York Motor Car Co, York, Pa. 1905–1909
(3) Pullman Motor Car Co, York, Pa. 1909–1917

A.P. Broomell's first Pullman car was a 6-wheeler named after the Pullman railroad cars. This model proved impractical, and in 1905 Broomell introduced a 4-wheeled car under the name York. By 1907 the cars were again known as Pullmans, and had 20 or 40hp engines and shaft drive, priced at $1,850 to $3,500. By 1912 the largest model was the 60hp 6-cylinder Model 6–60, a 8½-litre car with compressed-air starter, although smaller fours were also made. In 1915 the Cutler-Hammer push-button magnetic gear change was introduced, on the 6–46A with Continental engine. Later in 1915 a new management took over and introduced a much cheaper line of cars, powered by 3-litre 4-cylinder G.B. & S. engines and

1960 P.T.V. 250cc two-seater. *G.N. Georgano*

1913 PUCH Alpenwagen Type VIII 14/38 PS tourer. *Steyr-Daimler-Puch AG*

1907 PULLCAR 15.9hp landaulette. J.S. Critchley in passenger seat. *Autocar*

1903 PULLMAN(i) 6-wheel tourer.
Hardinge Co

1973 PUMA(i) Spyder 1600 sports car.
Puma Veiculos e Motores SA

1902 PURITAN(i) 6hp steam car. *Keith Marvin
Collection*

selling at prices from $740 to $990. As late as 1925 cars with similar specification to these were being advertised in Britain under the name London-Pullman, although American production ceased in 1917. The London-Pullmans were presumably old stock, possibly fitted with British bodies.   GMN

PULLMAN (ii) (US) *1907–1908*
Pullman Motor Vehicle Co, Chicago, Ill.
   This car had a 4-cylinder water-cooled engine of 7.0 litres. A 3-speed sliding-gear transmission and shaft drive were used. The only model, a seven-seater touring car, was priced at $3,600. There is no known connection with the better-known Pullman (i) of York, Pa.   GMN

PUMA (i) (BR) *1964 to date*
(1) Sociedade de Automoveis Luminari Ltda, São Paulo *1964–1966*
(2) Puma Veiculos e Motores Ltda, São Paulo *1966 to date*
   The Puma started life as the D.K.W.-Malzoni, a GT coupé conceived by Italian-born Genaro Malzoni round the mechanical elements of the 3-cylinder fwd D.K.W. made under licence in Brazil by Vemag. Serious production began with the formation of the Puma company in 1966. However, Volkswagen do Brasil acquired Vemag in 1967, after only 135 cars had been made, and Malzoni turned his attention to the 1,500cc rear-engined Volkswagen, on which he fashioned a Porsche-like coupé of fibreglass. By 1969 the cars had acquired disc front brakes and the option of a 68bhp, 1,600cc engine. Production in 1970 was 207 Pumas. During 1971 the 1600 went on sale in Switzerland. The 1972 GTE1600 weighed 1,499lb and had a top speed of 103mph. For 1973 a new range of front-engined Pumas were added, with 4-cylinder 2½-litre or 6-cylinder 4.1-litre Chevrolet engines.   MCS

PUMA (ii) (GB) *1969 to date*
Fairfield Engineering, Dymock, Gloucestershire
   Designed by Tony Hilder, earlier associated with the Piper, this was originally a full-length Mallite monocoque single-seater with torsion-bar suspension. Cars were built for Formula Atlantic and Formula 3 in association with Alan McKechnie Racing. The 1972 model, while retaining the Mallite inner skin, had an Arch Motors monocoque with rear sub-frame and revised suspension.   DF

PUNGS-FINCH (US) *1904–1910*
Pungs-Finch Auto & Gas Engine Co, Detroit, Mich.
   The Pungs-Finch started as an advanced vehicle, with shaft drive and a sliding-gear transmission but few improvements were made during its life. In 1905 there appeared the even more advanced Finch Limited, with inclined overhead valves operated by a gear-driven overhead camshaft, and capacity of over 10 litres. Only one was made. The last Pungs-Finch, for 1910, was the Model H which had a 4-cylinder, 40hp T-head engine of 5.8 litres. Both a two-seater and a five-seater model was available.   GMN

PUP (US) *1947*
Pup Motor Car Co, Spencer, Wisc.
   With an automatic clutch, the 600lb Pup was a small two-seater offering either a 7½hp single-cylinder or a 10hp 2-cylinder engine in the rear.   BE

PURITAN (i) (US) *1902–1903*
Locke Regulator Co, Salem, Mass.
   The Puritan steam car used a 6hp 2-cylinder vertical engine and single chain drive, but among its more modern features were wheel steering (the column folded for easy access to the seats), and a foot throttle.   GNG

PURITAN (ii) (US) *1913–1914*
Puritan Motor Co, Chicago, Ill.
   This cyclecar used a 10hp De Luxe engine and V-belt drive. The body was a side-by-side two-seater. Semi-elliptic springs were used in front, and three-quarter elliptics at the rear.   GMN

PUZYREV (SU) *c. 1899*
B.P. Puzyrev, St Petersburg
   Puzyrev was one of the earliest producers of Russian private cars. Details of specifications are lacking.   BE

P. VALLÉE (F) *1952–1957*
Société Colas, Blois, Loir-et-Cher
   These attractive little two-seaters were fitted with the 125cc Ydral engine, thus circumventing the need for a driving licence. Rubber suspension was featured. In 1957 a new model was announced, in 125 and 175cc forms, under the name Chantecler.   DF

PYGMÉE (F) *1965 to date*
Voitures de Course Pygmée, Annecy, Haute-Savoie
   Father Marius and son Patrick dal Bo built their first single-seaters under the

Pygmée name in the mid-1960s, when Patrick raced a spidery-looking F3 machine internationally. Formule France, improved Formula 3 and eventually solidly-engineered monocoque F2 cars stemmed from this beginning, and during 1971 an ambitious four-car F2 team included Jean-Pierre Beltoise, the French champion. Recurrent troubles gave the dal Bos little reward.   DCN

PYRAMID (GB) *1914*

Payne's Engineering Co, Chiswick, London W.

The Pyramid cyclecar used an 8hp V-twin J.A.P. engine, friction transmission, and final drive by belts. The price was £125.   GNG

QUADRANT (GB) *1906–1907*

Quadrant Cycle Co Ltd, Birmingham

Mainly known for their motorcycles and tricars, Quadrant made a few 4-wheeled cars powered by White & Poppe engines. These were of 14/16 and 20/22hp.   GNG

QUAGLIOTTI (I) *1904*

Auto Garage Quagliotti, Turin

The Quagliotti was one of many ephemeral makes put together from proprietary parts in small workshops for local sale. Light cars used De Dion or Aster engines, but a 16hp Aster-powered four was also planned.   MCS

QUASAR-UNIPOWER (GB) *1968*

Universal Power Drives Ltd, Perivale, Middlesex

Made by the producers of the Unipower GT, this is a city car of unconventional form, designed by Vietnamese-born Quasar Khanh. It consists of a metal-framed box of toughened safety glass on a 4-wheeled steel tube chassis, powered by a B.M.C. 1,100cc engine, with automatic transmission, mounted transversely at the rear. Maximum speed is around 50mph. It seats five people on a base 5ft 4 in long × 5ft 6in wide; it is 6ft 2in high and looks like a transparent cube. It has sliding doors at the sides and also a door at the front. The roof safety glass is green-tinted and heat-absorbing.   GNG

QUEEN (i) (CDN) *1901–1903*

Queen City Cycle & Motor Works, Toronto, Ont.

Not related to the later U.S. Queen, this single-cylinder runabout was steered by wheel and featured a forward-opening folding seat for two extra passengers. Its performance was considered poor even by the standards of the day and production ceased when the company president bought a Cadillac.   GB

QUEEN (ii) (US) *1904–1907*

C.H. Blomstrom Motor Co, Detroit, Mich.

The Queen started as a single-cylinder car with single chain drive. Later models used 2- and 4-cylinder engines, but all of them were relatively small. These cars had very graceful lines. The manufacturer also marketed Blomstrom and Gyroscope cars.   GMN

QUENTIN (F) *1908–1912*

Quentin et Cie, Levallois-Perret, Seine

The Quentin company made motorcycles, and a few very light cars with single-cylinder engines and differential-less shaft drive.   GNG

QUICK (US) *1899–1900*

(1) H.M. Quick, Paterson, N.J. *1899*
(2) Quick Manufacturing Co, Newark, N.J. *1900*

The Quick was a light two-seater buggy with a 2-cylinder 4hp horizontal engine, single chain drive and tiller steering.   GNG

QUINSLER (US) *1904*

Quinsler & Co, Boston, Mass.

This was an attractive two-seater car with a removable dickey seat for a third person. It used a front-mounted De Dion engine. Steering was by wheel and the price was $950.   GMN

QUO VADIS (i) (F) *1900–c.1902*

Laurent et Touzet, Lyons

These cars used a front-mounted 2-cylinder Aster engine driving the front wheels. They had a centrally pivoted front axle, a primitive and unsatisfactory system even in 1900.   GNG

QUO VADIS (ii) (F) *1921–1923*

Automobiles Quo Vadis, Courbevoie, Seine

The Quo Vadis was described as 'une voiture légère de grand luxe', but was probably no more than the usual cyclecar of the time.   GNG

1968 QUASAR-UNIPOWER 1,100cc city car
Universal Power Drives Ltd

1905 QUEEN(ii) 4-cylinder tourer. *Senator N. Larsen*

1924 RABAG-BUGATTI 6/25PS tourer.
Neubauer Collection

1909 R.A.F. 40/45PS tourer. *Jaeger Collection*

1937 RAILTON 4.2-litre drophead coupé.
Coachwork by Ranalah. *Railton Owner's Club*

RABA (H) *1912–1925*
Magyar Waggon es Gepgyar Reszenytarsasag, Györ

The Raba works was founded in 1896. They built chassis for Csonka in Budapest and Spitz in Vienna, and also trucks under their own name. An electric train was delivered to the London Underground in 1905. In 1912 they began production of Raba cars built under Praga licence. The 35/45hp shaft-driven Raba Grand was made until 1925, after which commercial vehicles were again the sole products. These were made until 1944, and in 1968 licence production of M.A.N. diesel trucks was started.   GLH

RABAG-BUGATTI (D) *1922–1926*
Rheinische Automobilbau AG, Düsseldorf; Mannheim

This firm produced Bugatti cars (Types 22 and 23) under licence. Engines and chassis were built in Mannheim by Union-Werke, known for the Bravo, while the bodies were built in Düsseldorf. Models of 6/25PS 1,453cc and 6/30PS 1,495cc were listed. Both open and closed bodies were listed, and sports models were very successful in German and international race events. Rabags were distinguished from their French cousins by a lipped top to the radiator. As Rabag was a part of the Stinnes concern (like Aga and Dinos) production ceased in 1926 after the failure of this combine.   HON

RABOEUF (F) *1914*
M. Raboeuf, Amiens

The Raboeuf was a light car powered by a 10hp Chapuis-Dornier engine. A 3-speed gearbox with direct drive on top was used in conjunction with shaft drive. A two-seater and dickey body was standardized, and the car might have met with more success had it not been launched so near the beginning of World War 1, and had the factory not been so close to the front line.   GNG

R.A.C. *see* DIAMOND (i)

RADIA *see* L'AUTOMOTRICE

RADIOR (F) *1921*
J. Chapolard, Automobiles Radior, Bourg, Ain

The Radior was an assembled car using a 10hp Ballot engine. Only prototypes were made.   GNG

RAE (GB) *1969 to date*
G. Rae, Malvern, Worcs.

Having constructed several specials for Club sports-car racing, Gordon Rae offered a space-framed model for Formula 1200 and the Clubman's racing classes.   DF

R.A.F. (A) *1907–1913*
Reichenberger Automobilfabrik, Reichenberg

This factory was founded by Baron von Liebig together with two partners. The baron achieved his place in automobile history through being the first man to undertaken a long distance journey by car. In 1894 he drove a Benz Victoria from the Bohemian town of Reichenberg to Mannheim and beyond, a total of 575 miles which he covered in 69 hours. R.A.F. specialized in the heavier type of touring cars, building them to a high standard. The first type was a 24/30PS and this was followed by the 30/35PS. The R.A.F. 40/45PS became known as the Alpentyp because of its participation in the Austrian Alpine Trial. A licence for Daimler-Knight engines was taken out in 1912 and 40PS and 70PS models — the latter with a 6-cylinder engine — were introduced. In 1913 R.A.F. merged with Laurin & Klement.   HON

RAGLAN (GB) *1899*
Raglan Cycle Co, Coventry, Warwickshire

This well-known cycle company made a car closely based on the Benz, but it was not put into production.   GNG

RAILSBACH (US) *1914*
L.M. Railsbach, Saginaw, Mich.

The manufacturer classed this make as a light car, although its 3ft track would place it in the cyclecar category. It had a water-cooled 4-cylinder, 1.2-litre engine. The two-seater with staggered seating sold for $350.   GMN

RAILTON (GB) *1933–1949*

(1) Railton Cars, Cobham, Surrey *1933–1940*
(2) Hudson Motors Ltd, London W.4 *1940–1949*

This was the work of Reid Railton, well-known as a designer of cars for the World Land Speed Record, and was assembled in the old Invicta (iii) works after that company's activities had been transferred to Chelsea. It set the formula for the Anglo-American sports hybrids of the 1930s, and the basis was a 4-litre Terraplane 8 chassis (from mid-1934, a 4.2-litre Hudson 8) lowered and given stiffer suspension. On this was mounted coachwork in the British style, and the rectangular bonnet (with rivets along it) and radiator closely resembled those of the Invicta. The result, which sold in tourer form for £535 in 1934, was capable of 90mph, could be driven almost anywhere in top gear, and possessed startling acceleration: the Light Sports of 1935 could reach 60mph in under ten seconds.

Mechanically, the cars followed Hudson evolution with hydraulic brakes added in 1936; they also grew heavier and more expensive, with saloons selling for £698 that year. Cheaper versions were available in 1938/39 with the 2.7-litre and 3½-litre 6-cylinder Hudson engines, and a 10hp baby Railton introduced in 1938 at £299 had Standard (i) mechanical components. Rather more than 1,400 were made; a handful were assembled after World War 2, but the ban on dollar imports and a list price of over £4,000 put a stop to the best of the Anglo-Americans.   MCS

RAIMONDI (I) *1898*

Fabbrica Biciclette e Automobili Ippolito Raimondi, Parma

The firm's title indicates a serious intention to market cars, but in fact only one Raimondi was built. It was a belt-driven light car with single-cylinder engine, probably of De Dion make.   MCS

RAINERI (I) *1958–1960*

The Raineri was a typical example of Italian front-engine Formula Junior cars. It was powered by a Fiat 1100 engine in a space-frame chassis with all-independent suspension from a Fiat 600. A later version used the Lancia Appia V-4 engine.   GNG

RAINER (US) *1905–1911*

(1) Rainier Co, Elyria, Ohio; Saginaw, Mich. *1905–1907*
(2) Rainier Motor Car Co, Saginaw, Mich. *1907–1911*

The first Rainier was a 22/28hp touring car. In 1906 it had progressed to a 30/35hp 4-cylinder engine. By 1908, the range had increased to three, with a landaulet priced at $5,800, and this 'Pullman of Motor Cars' was guaranteed to be free of repairs for one year. In 1911, four body types were built on a chassis with a 10ft wheelbase. The engine was a 45/50hp 4-cylinder unit with a 4-speed transmission. In 1912, the Rainier was succeeded by the Marquette (i).   GMN

RAK (PL) *1961 to date*

J. Jankowski, Warsaw

The leading Polish racing-car constructor Jankowski, like Melkus, generally employed Wartburg components, being the most 'tunable' of the few alternatives available for modification to the Formula 3 and the old Formula Junior classes.   DF

R.A.L. (B) *1908–1914*

Automobiles Raskin, Liège

The R.A.L. was a light car powered by 4-cylinder engines of either 1,593 or 1,743cc. It had a conventional chassis and open or closed two-seater bodies.   GNG

RALEIGH (i) (GB) *1905; 1916; 1933–1936*

Raleigh Cycle Co Ltd, Nottingham

Apart from their production vehicles, Raleigh made a number of experimental cars at different times. The first, in 1905, was designed by T.J. Biggs, formerly of Eastmead & Biggs, and used a 4-cylinder 16hp Fafnir engine. Only one car was made. Predictably, the company showed an interest in the cyclecar boom, but after experimenting with 2-cylinder engines they settled on a 4-cylinder Alpha unit of 11hp for their shaft-driven light car. Few of these were made.

In 1922 Raleigh built an experimental flat-twin to rival the Rover Eight, but it was never marketed, and it was not until 1933 that the first real production Raleigh appeared. This was a 3-wheeler using a 742cc V-twin engine, a 3-speed gearbox and shaft drive, known as the Safety Seven. It had a full four-seater body, and cost £110/5/-. The designer was T.L. Williams who subsequently bought the manufacturing rights from Raleigh, and founded the Reliant Motor Company at Tamworth.   GNG

RALEIGH (ii) (US) *1920–1922*

Raleigh Motors Inc, Reading, Pa.; Bridgeton, N.J.

Probably less than 25 Raleigh motor cars ever got into the hands of customers. These were assembled cars with 6-cylinder Herschell-Spillman engines.   KM

RALF STETYZ (PL) *1926–1928*

Tow. Akc. Konstrukcji Mostowych 'Rudski' (Rudski & Ska), Warsaw

Prototypes of the Ralf Stetyz were built at Boulogne-sur-Seine and appeared

1908 RAINIER 30/35hp tourer. *Automotive History Collection, Detroit Public Library*

1968 RAK Formula 3 racing car. *Jerzy Guzdek*

1936 RALEIGH(i) Safety Seven 742cc 3-wheeler. *National Motor Museum*

1929 RALLY 1,100cc sports car. *Autocar*

1911 RAMBLER(ii) Model 64 tourer. *American Motors Corporation*

1968 RAMBLER(iii) Javelin 5.6-litre coupé. *American Motors Corporation*

1963 RAMSES 600cc saloon. *Egyptian Light Transport Co*

at the 1923 Paris Salon, but the production cars were made at the Rudski Works in Warsaw. Designed by Stefan Tyszkiewicz, the car was made in two models, a 1½-litre four, and a 2.7-litre six which in fact had a Polish-built Continental engine. In 1928 a fire destroyed the factory, and no attempt was made to rebuilt it.   BE

RALLY (F) *1921–1933*
Automobiles Rally, Colombes, Seine

The Rally was a typical French sporting voiturette of its period, starting life as a 2-cylinder cyclecar put together largely out of Harley-Davidson motorcycle parts, and growing up in 1922 into a normal 4-cylinder, water-cooled machine. The engine was of proprietary manufacture, and could be had in two sizes. S.C.A.P., Ruby, C.I.M.E. and Chapuis-Dornier units were used. There were 4 forward speeds. By 1927 there were four models, the most powerful being a sports racing car with a Roots-supercharged twin overhead camshaft engine, and the most sophisticated an 1,100cc straight-8. Both these models were made only in prototype form. Later cars were basically customized Salmsons.   TRN

RAMAPAUGH *see* BALL

RAMBLER (i) (US) *1900–1903*
(1) Rockaway Bicycle Works, Rockaway, N.J.
(2) Rockaway Automobile Co, Rockaway, N.J.

This company made a light two-seater runabout powered by a water-cooled single-cylinder engine. Final drive was by single chain. The price was $650.   GNG

RAMBLER (ii); (iii) (US) *1902–1913; 1950–1970*
(1) Thos. B. Jeffery Co, Kenosha, Wisc. *1902–1913*
(2) Nash Motor Co, Kenosha, Wisc. *1950–1954*
(3) American Motors Corporation, Kenosha, Wisc. *1950–1970*

Despite the interval of 37 years, these two makes are directly connected. The original Rambler derived its name from the bicycles built by Gormully and Jeffery, who had a branch factory in Coventry in the 1890s. In 1902 form it was a light runabout in the American idiom with a single horizontal cylinder, chain drive, cycle-type wire wheels and tiller steering, selling for $750. In the first season 1,500 cars were sold, a figure which places the makers in the same category as Oldsmobile, among the world's first mass producers.

By 1905 the Rambler had grown into a sizable twin-cylinder machine with front bonnet, and with the introduction of a 4-cylinder model in 1907 the make had moved up into the semi-luxury class; another parallel with Oldsmobile, but one which had less unfortunate financial consequences, for Rambler sold over 3,000 cars in 1911 and 4,435 in 1913, the last year of production. The bigger of two fours offered in 1912 had a 7-litre engine with separate cylinders. 1914 models went under the name of Jeffery. Advanced features of these late Ramblers were sidelamps faired into the scuttle, and detachable wooden wheels.

Nash Motors, successors to the Jeffery company, revived the name in 1950 for the first of the modern generation of American 'compacts'. This was a 2.8-litre sv six with a wheelbase of 8ft 4in and an overall length of under 15ft, priced at $1,800. It featured unitary construction of chassis and body, and weighed only 2,576lb at a time when a regular Chevrolet sedan turned the scales at around 3,600lb. Nash sales went up by 50,000 as a result of the Rambler, which was offered as a Nash until 1957, acquiring styling by Pininfarina in 1952, the option of an automatic gearbox in 1953, and an alternative v-8 engine in 1957. Some cars were also sold under the Hudson name after the merger which brought American Motors into being in 1954.

From 1958 on, all A.M.C. cars were known as Ramblers, the former full-sized Nashes continuing as Rambler's Ambassador model. The Rambler was the first of the contemporary compacts, and set a fashion imitated later by the Big Three. In the recession year, 1958, George Romney's criticisms of large cars were widely quoted. In 1958 the low-priced American model reverted to the 8ft 4in wheelbase, and 1961 saw the introduction of a die-cast aluminium ohv push-rod six which eventually supplanted the old sv unit. The last vestiges of the 1949 Nash Airflyte styling vanished in 1963, and disc brakes were offered as an option in 1965, in which year a sporting fastback coupé, the Marlin, was introduced. 1967 models were made on three wheelbase lengths – 8ft 10in, 9ft 4in, and 9ft 8in – and with a choice of ohv 3.8-litre 6-cylinder or 4.8- and 5.6-litre V-8 engines. From 1968 the name Rambler became less prominent in the range, new models such as the Javelin being known under their own names. For the 1970 season the name Rambler was dropped altogether in the U.S.A. and Canada, although the Hornet was sold as a Rambler in export markets. For the 1971 season the name Rambler was no longer used at all.   MCS

RAMSES (ET) *1959 to date*
Egyptian Light Transport Co, Cairo

Ramses cars are based on the N.S.U. Prinz series, and the specification includes a rear-mounted 600cc ohc air-cooled 2-cylinder engine, 4-speed all-synchromesh gearbox, and all-round independent suspension. Four-seater saloon and convertible models are offered as well as light commercial vehicles. A 4-door saloon was added to the range in 1971.   MCS

RAMUS (F) *1900*

Ateliers de Constructions Mécaniques Ramus frères, Chambéry, Savoie

The Ramus voiturette used a front-mounted 4hp single-cylinder horizontal engine, and transmission by fast-and-loose pulleys. GNG

RANDALL (US) *1904*

J.V. & C. Randall, Newtown, Pa.

The Randall was a 3-wheeled vehicle, with a fringed top. It was steered by a tiller acting directly on the front wheel, and powered at the rear by an air-cooled 12hp 2-cylinder engine with chain drive. It was a four-seater, and 20mph was claimed for it. GMN

RAND & HARVEY (US) *1899–1900*

Rand & Harvey, Lewiston, Maine

This was a light steam buggy, powered by a 2-cylinder engine, which probably never passed the prototype stage. GNG

R. & V. KNIGHT (US) *1920–1924*

R. & V. Division of the Root & Vandervoort Engineering Co, East Moline, Ill.

Although the R. & V. Knight was never a popular car, with production never exceeding 760 per year, it was of outstanding quality. Known as the Moline-Knight between 1914 and 1919, it was sold with a complete line of body styles in the $2,500 to $4,000 price range. Its 4.2-litre sleeve-valve Knight engine developed 57bhp at 2,400rpm.

The radiator was distinctive and slightly pointed and all cars were sold with unusually full equipment including tyre chains, windscreen wipers, etc. The cars had a steel and pressed-lead seal around the entire engine and the two years' guarantee which came with the car depended on this remaining unbroken, although authorized service stations could reseal this if work on the car became necessary. KM

RANGER (i) (US) *1908–1910*

(1) Ranger Motor Works, Chicago, Ill.

(2) Ranger Automobile Co, Chicago, Ill.

The Ranger was a small two-seater runabout, of the buggy type, with a 2-cylinder, air-cooled engine, planetary transmission and tiller steering. It cost $395. GMN

RANGER (ii) (GB) *1913–1914*

Ranger Cyclecar Co Ltd, Coventry, Warwickshire

This Ranger was another product of E.J. West, and was, in fact, the 1912 West Cyclecar renamed. The original model used a 2-cylinder Precision engine, 2-speed gearbox and chain final drive, but 1914 models used a Blumfield twin or Alpha 4. GNG

RANGER (iii) (US) *1920–1922*

Southern Motor Manufacturing Association, Houston, Tex.

Ranger cars for 1920 and 1921 were powered by a 4-cylinder engine of the firm's own make, and a touring car, sport roadster and a conventional roadster were offered. The 4-cylinder car with artillery wheels was continued in 1922, the five-seater touring model selling at $1,485. A 6-cylinder line was introduced this year, the larger cars having wire wheels as standard equipment. Cycle mudguards and aluminium step plates were also featured on the Pal o'Mine, Blue Bonnet, Commodore and Newport sport types. The 6-cylinder touring car cost $3,550. Few of the sixes were built. KM

RANGER (iv) (ZA) *1968 to date*

General Motors South African (Pty) Ltd, Port Elizabeth

Promoted as 'South Africa's Own Car', the Ranger was a synthesis of General Motors' overseas design, the hull coming from Opel's Rekord, the front suspension from the Vauxhall Victor, and the optional Tri-Matic automatic gearbox from Holden. Front disc brakes were standard, and buyers had the choice of 2,120cc or 2,507cc 4-cylinder pushrod Chevrolet engines. At the top of the 1972 range was the SS2500 hardtop coupé with vinyl roof, dual-choke Weber carburettor and 4-speed manual gearbox. The 1973 models used the Mk II Opel body shell. Other models produced by GMSA included the Firenza, a Vauxhall Viva-based 4-door sedan with 2½-litre Chevrolet engine, and the De Ville Constantia and Kommando, variations on a Holden theme. Standard models had 6-cylinder units of 3,769cc and 4,093cc, but the most expensive De Ville used a 5.7-litre 205bhp V-8 engine, and came with Turbo-Hydramatic automatic gearbox and front disc brakes as standard. All these models were sold under the Chevrolet name. MCS

RANGER (v) (B) *1970 to date*

General Motors Continental SA, Antwerp

The Belgian Ranger derived from its South African prototype, but was intended for European markets, hence the use of Opel engines, either the 1,897cc 5-bearing ohc four or the 2½-litre pushrod six. Disc front brakes and 4-speed gearboxes were standard, with the usual automatic option, initially on saloons alone. The 1972 range also embraced the E-OES11 series with 1.7-litre engine. The most expensive type was the GTS coupé. This had a 130bhp 6-cylinder engine, came with a choice of manual or automatic gearbox, and had a maximum speed of 115mph. MCS

1924 R. & V. KNIGHT 4.2-litre sedan.
Automobile Manufacturers' Association

1913 RANGER(ii) 8hp cyclecar. *J.S. Spicer*

1971 RANGER(v) 1.9-litre saloon.
General Motors Corporation

1908 RAPID(ii) 20hp tourer. *Autocar*

1938 RAPID(iii) 350cc two-seater. *Autocar*

1934 LAGONDA RAPIER 10hp sports tourer.
G.N. Georgano

RAOUVAL (F) *1899–1902*
Sté Mécanique Industrielle d'Arzin, Arzin, Nord

The Raouval was powered by a 2-cylinder 8hp Pygmée engine. It was a solid-looking car with a four-seater tonneau body and chain drive.　　　GNG

RAPID (i) (CH) *1899–1900*
Zürcher Patent Motorwagen-Fabrik Rapid, Zürich

This company was formed to manufacture the 3-wheeler designed by Rudolf Egg, and formerly built by Egg & Egli. A number of changes were made in the design: the engine was no longer a De Dion, but a Swiss-built unit of De Dion pattern, and the Rapid was heavier and better equipped. A 2-wheeled trailer for luggage could be bought. However, fewer cars were built by Rapid than by the other licence holders, Weber of Uster.　　　GNG

RAPID (ii) (I) *1905–1921*
Società Torinese Automobili Rapid, Turin

This was another of Giovanni Battista Ceirano's companies, although ill-health forced his retirement soon after its foundation. Though a 9½hp single was shown at Paris in 1905, and 2.3-litre twins were catalogued as late as 1909, the basic Rapid was a T-head four with separately-cast cylinders, pump cooling, ht magneto ignition, 4-speed gearbox, gate change and shaft drive, with an ingenious arrangement of three torque and radius rods mounted above and below and parallel to the propeller shaft. Initially two types were offered, the 4.6-litre 16/24 and the 7.4-litre 24/40, the latter having a 5-bearing crankshaft. In 1906 came the huge 10.6-litre 50/70, still shaft-driven. Round radiators were used until 1908. Racing was never seriously supported, though a 16/24 ran in the 1906 T.T., and another Rapid finished last in the 1907 Coppa Florio. Ioe and pair-cast cylinders appeared on the 2.7-litre 12/16 of 1907, another bi-block design being the 3.1-litre T-head 16/20 of 1908; a wide range of T-head types continued to be available until 1912.

Modern designs were, however, on the way: along with the option of compressed-air starters in 1910, Rapid offered a pair of L-head monobloc fours with 1,570cc and 2,614cc engines, joined by a 2-litre in 1912; a curious digression was a 15hp racing model using the 80mm bore of the 2.6-litre car, and a piston stroke of 300mm. In 1915 a one-model programme was adopted with the 1.6-litre 10/12. Features were monobloc cylinders, a 3-speed gearbox, detachable steel wheels and no transmission brake. Full electrics were available in 1916. This model was revived after World War 1. Rapid were latterly more concerned with general repair work, however, and the company was liquidated in 1921, the remnants going to S.P.A. and C.I.P.　　　MCS

RAPID (iii) (CH) *1946*
Rapid Motormäher AG, Dietikon, Zürich

Based on a light car design of Josef Ganz (of Standard Superior), the first prototype appeared in 1938 under the name Erfiag. It had a 350cc rear-mounted single-cylinder M.A.G. engine, and an open two-seater body. It was put into production after the war by Rapid, but only a first batch of 36 cars was built. Rapid hastily returned to the manufacture of motor scythes and light, 2-wheeled tractors.　　　GNG

RAPIER (GB) *1933–1940*
(1) Lagonda Ltd, Staines, Middlesex *1933–1935*
(2) Rapier Cars Ltd, Hammersmith, London W.6 *1935–1940*

Late in 1932 the Lagonda Company decided to supplement their successful but conservative 2- and 3-litre cars with a small racing-type sports model of high quality. Timothy Ashcroft was retained as its designer; development got under way early in 1933. Production encountered difficulties, however, and the car was not officially released until July 1934. It was in full production by the time of the Motor Show, and was enthusiastically received.

It was powered by a robust engine of 1,104cc capacity with twin over-head camshafts driven by chains and a massive fully-balanced crankshaft running on 3 main bearings of 2in diameter – the same as those of the 4½-litre engine. The valves were opposed at 90° in the cross-flow head, serving four beautifully-machined hemispherical combustion chambers. Twin SU carburettors were fitted; the compression ratio was 7.5:1. This was an unburstable engine with a potential of 6,000rpm; 5,500 could be used safely on the gears.

The chassis was one of the first to be fitted with Girling brakes, whose 25ft stopping distance at 30mph was a remarkable figure for the time. A directly-mounted E.N.V. preselector gearbox took the drive to a 5.8:1 rear axle; ratios of 17.95, 10.56 and 7.18 were to be had on the intermediate gears. In full touring trim the car's top speed was 75mph.

In addition to a standard four-seater tourer body which was the most popular, Abbott offered a drophead and fixed-head coupé on the Rapier chassis. Eagle supplied a sporty two-seater; and bodies by Corinthian, Ranalah, Maltby and Silent Touring were available.

Lord de Clifford was the first to seize upon the Rapier's poential for development. Soon after driving one in the 1934 Le Mans race, Dobson and de Clifford Ltd of Stains offered a semi-racing version with a bored-out engine and a standard gearbox with a choice of ratios as an alternative to the E.N.V. unit. Above the Lagonda badge on the radiator was a supplementary badge bearing the words 'De Clifford Special'; a number survive today.

When the Lagonda Company was re-formed in the middle of 1935 it was found that the Rapier's sales had not kept pace with its acclaim. A small, high-quality sports car could not survive under the market conditions of the day, so the design was discontinued. The car was saved from oblivion by the formation of the Rapier Company, however, with Ashcroft, Major W.H. Oates and N. Brocklebank putting up the capital. All production machinery and spares passed to the new company, who continued to manufacture the car as the Rapier from August 1935. Save for the badge it was identical to the Lagonda Rapier, and all Lagonda guarantees were honoured. It was offered in supercharged form in 1936, continuing in sporadic production until 1940. From a total production of 300 cars, some 175 survive.   HAF

RASKIN *see* R.A.L.

RATIER (F) *c. 1926–1928*
Montrouge, Seine
    The Ratier was a neat-looking little sports car with a 750cc single ohc engine. A closed coupé body was available, and a sports two-seater was raced at Brooklands by Sir Francis Samuelson.   GNG

RATIONAL (i) (GB) *1901–1906*
Heatly-Gresham Engineering Co Ltd, Royston, Herts.
    The original Rational had a single-cylinder horizontal engine and a 2-speed epicyclic gearbox. The chassis was suspended in the normal way but an extra set of semi-elliptic springs was used between chassis and body, giving the car a very high and old-fashioned appearance, even for 1901. Production models used horizontal 2-cylinder 10hp engines and epicyclic gearboxes, but abandoned the unusual suspension. Not more than 17 cars were made in all, but the company also made a few taxicabs with under-floor engines and central driving position.   GNG

RATIONAL (ii) (GB) *1910–1911*
K.J. McMullen, Brimpton, Berks.
    Kenrie James McMullen undertook the manufacture of light cars in his stable. He was aided by his butler, and an odd-job man called Scroggins. Surplus Fafnir motorcycle engines were acquired, and mounted, four at a time, in a V on an alloy crankcase. Cooling was by fans and carburation by Longuemare. Either coil or magneto ignition was offered; neither proved satisfactory. Much was made of the overhead worm drive, but Scroggins did not make this: a local traction engine manufacturer was known to have a customer called McMullen who frequently purchased steering-gear units. Another unusual feature was the presence of a large 'torsion spring' between clutch and gearbox. It was intended to be a £100 car, but the price rose faster than the sales graph. A V6-cylinder Rational was listed; capacity was 3 litres, and price £255. In 1911 McMullen departed, leaving behind not only parts of incomplete Rationals, but also the remains of an unsuccessful aeroplane.   DF

RAUCH & LANG; RAULANG (US) *1905–1928*
(1) Rauch & Lang Carriage Co, Cleveland, Ohio *1905–1916*
(2) Baker, Rauch & Lang Co, Cleveland, Ohio *1916–1922*
(3) Rauch & Lang Electric Car Manufacturing Co, Chicopee Falls, Mass. *1922–1928*
    Rauch & Lang were an old-established carriage building firm (founded 1853) when they began to make electric cars in 1905. These followed the usual pattern of such vehicles, being mainly closed town cars, although a few open phaetons were also made. The biggest Rauch & Langs were heavier vehicles and included a six-seater limousine with separate outside seat for the chauffeur. Some cars had 4-doors, a very unusual feature in electric cars. In 1916 they became parts of the Baker, Rauch & Lane group and production declined. From 1919 onwards they were sometimes listed as Raulangs, and from 1922 this became the official name of the cars.
    By this time production had been transferred to the Stevens-Duryea factory at Chicopee Falls where the number of private cars made was very small. The factory, which was still turning out a few Stevens-Duryeas, also made petrol and electric taxi-cabs under the name R. & L., and bodies for Stanley Steamers.   GNG

RAVEL (i) (F) *1900–1902*
SA des Automobiles Louis Ravel, Neuilly, Seine
    The Ravel light car had a 5hp V-twin engine mounted under the seat, driving the rear axle through spur gearing. There was another Ravel car, also made at Neuilly, by Joseph and Edouard Ravel. This had a 15hp, 2-cylinder, 2-stroke engine, but it is not thought to have been a production car. Joseph Ravel had made a light liquid-fuelled steam car in 1868.   GNG

RAVEL (ii) (F) *1923–1928*
SA des Automobiles Ravel, Besançon, Doubs
    The Ravel was a medium-sized car with a 12CV 2.1-litre 4-cylinder ohv engine, a 4-speed gearbox and front-wheel brakes from the beginning of its life. A smaller car of 1,460cc was added in 1925, and a 2½-litre six was listed in addition to the fours, for 1928 only.   GNG

1905 RATIONAL(i) 10hp limousine. Coachwork by Sanders of Hitchin. *Bernard Sanders*

1910 RATIONAL(ii) 14hp two-seater. *David Filsell Collection*

1909 RAUCH & LANG electric stanhope. *The Veteran Car Club of Great Britain*

573

1925 RAVEL(ii) 12CV two-seater. *Autocar*

1914 R.C.H. 16hp tourer. *Automotive History Collection, Detroit Public Library*

1953 R.E.A.C. 750cc sports coupé. *Autosport*

RAWLSON (GB) *1971 to date*

Rawlson Ltd, Dover, Kent

The 1971 GT prototype was raced with some success with Cona coffee machine sponsorship. The CR8 coupé of 1972 was offered either as a Group 5 machine or as a road car, the latter in association with Liberta S.A. of Liège, and using either Renault or Simca running parts.   DF

RAYFIELD (US) *1911–1915*

Rayfield Motor Car Co, Springfield, Ill.

The Rayfield's distinguishing feature was its radiator mounted behind the engine in Renault style, with sloping bonnet. The 4- and 6-cylinder engines developed 18 and 22/25hp respectively. The 4-cylinder engine used for the first three years was a diminutive 1.4-litre unit.   GMN

RAYMOND (i) (US) *1912–1913*

Raymond Engineering Co, Hudson, Mass.

The Raymond was a 4-cylinder light roadster, which sold for $445.   GNG

RAYMOND (ii) (F) *c.1923–1925*

The French Raymond was an assembled car powered by a Model T Ford engine, and possibly using other Ford parts as well. It was sold from the Rue du Faubourg St Honoré, Paris, but the factory address is uncertain.   GNG

RAYMOND MAYS (GB) *1938–1939*

Shelsley Motors Ltd, Bourne, Lincs.

Named after the racing driver and sponsor of the E.R.A. racing cars, the Raymond Mays was a hand-built car powered by the 2.6-litre Standard V-8 engine. It had transverse leaf independent front suspension, and tourer or dh coupé bodies. Only 5 cars were built before World War 2 intervened.   GNG

R.C.H. (US) *1912–1916*

Hupp Corporation, Detroit, Mich.

This was a small car with a wheelbase of little more than 7ft. The first models had left-hand drive, and central change. Both two- and four-seater models were produced, powered by 4-cylinder engines with a 3-speed selective transmission. R.C. Hupp resigned from Hupmobile in 1911 to form this company.   GMN

R.E.A.C. (F) *1953–1954*

Built in Casablanca, the R.E.A.C. was one of a number of sports cars using the Dyna-Panhard engine and front-wheel drive. It had an unconventional fibreglass body and turret-like circular hard top coupé.   GNG

READ (US) *1913–1914*

Read Motor Co, Detroit, Mich.

The Read car was an undistinguished, inexpensive ($850) five-seater touring car with grey body and black striping, powered by a 4-cylinder 3.3-litre engine.   GMN

READING (i) (US) *1900–1903*

(1) Steam Vehicle Company of America, Reading, Pa. *1900–1902*

(2) Meteor Engineeing Co, Reading, Pa. *1902–1903*

The Reading was a typical light steam carriage, although 4-cylinder engines were available as well as the more usual twins. The company was absorbed by the Meteor Engineering Company in 1902, who introduced a larger car under their own name, although the light Reading design was continued to the end of 1903.   GNG

READING (ii) (US) *1910–1913*

Middleby Auto Co, Reading, Pa.

This car was a companion make to the Middleby but larger, on a 10ft wheelbase. A two-seater speedster, selling for $1,350, had a 4-cylinder, 4.1-litre engine.   GMN

REAL (US) *1914–1915*

H. Paul Prigg Co, Anderson, Ind.

The Real cyclecar had a spruce frame. The rear-mounted engine was an air-cooled 2-cylinder Wizard and drive to the rear wheels was by belts.   GMN

REBEL *see* AMERICAN MOTORS

REBER (US) *1902–1903*

(1) Reber Manufacturing Co, Reading, Pa. *1902–1903*

(2) Acme Motor Car Co, Reading, Pa. *1903*

The Reber was a five-seater, with rear entrance, driven by a vertical 2-cylinder engine. This unit was water-cooled, and the coil radiator was mounted beneath the frame in front of the sloping bonnet. Drive was by double chain. This make became the Acme (i).   GMN

REBOUR (F) *1905–1908*

Automobiles Rebour, Puteaux, Seine

The Rebour company was said to have supplied chassis to other firms before they started making their own cars. These were conventional machines with pair-cast 4-cylinder engines, 4-speed gearboxes and double chain drive. Models were of 10/12, 18/22, 20/25, and 40/50hp. A number were exported, especially to Germany and to Spain, where they were sold under the name Catalonia.   GNG

RED ARROW (US) 1915

Red Arrow Automobile Co, Orange, Mass.

The Red Arrow was made by the successors to the Grout Brothers Automobile Company. As a change from the steamers and large petrol cars made by Grout, the new company made a cyclecar with a 12hp 2-cylinder engine.   GNG

RED BUG (US) 1924–1928

1) Automotive Electrical Service Co, Newark, N.J.
2) Standard Automobile Corp, North Bergen, N.J.

Sometimes listed as the Auto Red Bug, this vehicle was the Briggs & Stratton Buckboard redesigned with an electric motor powered by a 12 volt battery driving the nearside rear wheel. A brake acted on the opposite rear wheel. Otherwise the Red Bug offered no more amenities than the Briggs & Stratton, but at least it was quieter. The name was also applied to the petrol-engined Buckboard.   GNG

RED JACKET (US) 1904

O.K. Machine Works, Buffalo, N.Y.

This five-seater, rear-entrance car used a water-cooled, 2-cylinder engine. Its transmission was a 3-speed selective type, and final drive was by double chain. Lighting was by a single headlamp. With much brass, including upholstery binding strips, it cost $1,500.   GMN

REDPATH (CDN) 1903

Berlin (later Kitchener), Ont.; Toronto, Ont.

A typical single-cylinder runabout known as the Redpath Messenger was the only model produced. It featured a $4\frac{1}{2} \times 4\frac{1}{2}$in engine mounted under a rounded, slightly streamlined bonnet, and shaft drive. Three of these cars were built.   GB

REEVES (US) 1896–1898; 1905–1912

1) The Reeves Pulley Co, Columbus, Ind. 1896–1898; 1905–1910
2) Milton O. Reeves, The Reeves Sexto-Octo Co, Columbus, Ind. 1911–1912

The first five Reeves vehicles were known as Motocycles. Designed by Milton O. Reeves, they had 6 or 12hp Sintz 2-cylinder 2-cycle marine engines, variable belt transmission, and double chain final drive. Size varied from a three-seater car to a twenty-seater bus.

In 1905 a new series of cars appeared powered by 12 or 18/20hp 4-cylinder air-cooled engines of Reeves design and manufacture, joined by water-cooled fours and sixes, and an air-cooled Big Six in 1906. Chain drive was used on the Big Six, the other cars having shaft drive. Smaller 2-cylinder cars with solid tyres and chain drive followed. The last production Reeves was a 2-cylinder high-wheeler known as the Buggymobile or Go-Buggy. Production ceased in 1910 and Milton Reeves began experimenting on his own account with multi-wheeled cars. The 1911 OctoAuto was based on an Overland, and had a 15ft wheelbase with overall length of 20ft 8in. The first SextoAuto was the OctoAuto with a normal front axle, the second SextoAuto was based on a Stutz. A price of $5,000 was quoted for this car, but only one was made.

Reeves engines were supplied to many firms, including Aerocar, Auburn, Auto-Bug, Chatham, Maplebay, Moon and Sears.   GNG

REFORM (A) 1906–1907

Chein & Goldberger, Vienna

Reform cars were available with single- and 2-cylinder engines of 8hp. Production was not on a large scale.   HON

REGAL (i) (F) 1903

D.C. Selbach, Paris

Régal was one of the names under which Lacoste et Battmann cars were sold. Originally a light two-seater with a 6hp De Dion engine, later Régals were powered by 2- and 4-cylinder engines by Aster and Mutel.   GNG

REGAL (ii) (US) 1907–1920

Regal Motor Car Co, Detroit, Mich.

In 1907 Regal made 50 of their 20hp 4-cylinder cars, but the following year they took them all back, and gave the owners a new 1908 model free. Apparently this generosity was not repeated in following years, and they settled down to making a range of conventional 4-cylinder cars. The best-known was the 3.2-litre 18/20hp 'underslung' model, which, like the American Underslung, had frame members which passed underneath the axles. It was made in open two-seater, and closed coupé form. Other models were the 20/30hp and 40hp which had normal chassis design. Regals were imported into England by Seabrook of Great Eastern Street, and from 1911 to 1915 the models sold in England were known as R.M.C.s or Seabrook-R.M.C.s. In

1907 REBOUR 20/25hp limousine. *Lucien Loreille Collection*

1904 RED JACKET 2-cylinder tonneau. *Keith Marvin Collection*

1911 REEVES OctoAuto 8-wheeled tourer. *Automotive History Collection, Detroit Public Library*

1911 REGAL(ii) 18/20hp two-seater. *Autocar*

1907 REGINA(i) GALLIA electric landaulette. *Lucien Loreille Collection*

1911 REINHARD 2-litre tourer. *Lucien Loreille Collection*

*c.*1962 REJO 1,172cc sports car. *E. Selwyn-Smith*

1915 a 10/15hp four of 2.1-litres with unit construction of engine and gearbox wa introduced, together with a short-lived V-8. At the 1919 Olympia Show Seabrook showed a large R.M.C. tourer powered by a 3.8-litre 6-cylinder engine, but shortl afterwards American production ceased, and Seabrooks began to make their ow light cars. GN

REGAL (iii) (CDN) *1910*
This was a 30hp car made as a touring car or runabout at Walkerville, Ont. it had no connection with the better-known Berlin-built Regal (iv). GN

REGAL (iv) (CDN) *1914–1917*
Canadian Regal Motor Car Co, Berlin (later Kitchener), Ont.
The Regal was a light-weight touring car which resembled the Detroit mode bearing the same name. Available with a Lycoming 4-cylinder engine at $875 o a V-8 at $1,350, it had a radiator filler concealed under the bonnet. The compan was under the direction of Henry Nyberg, who had built the U.S. Nyberg car befor going to Canada. In 1917 the company moved to a new plant and started producin Dominion trucks. About 200 Regal cars were built. G

REGAS (US) *1903–1905*
Regas Automobile Co, Rochester, N.Y.
The Regas was powered by 2- or 4-cylinder engines, both of V configuratio These were of 2.1 and 4.1 litres respectively. The cylinders were air-cooled, by a ingenious system which combined radiation and circulation of air. These cars use a Marble-Swift friction transmission. GM

REGENT (D) *1903–1904*
Maschinenfabrik W. Stutznäcker, Dortmund
This old-established ironworks started manufacture of cars in 1903, but produc tion was not on a great scale. HOM

REGINA (i) (F) *1903–1908*
Société l'Electrique, Paris 11e
Both petrol and electric cars were sold by this firm, the petrol cars being Dixi while the electrics were known as Gallias. They were made in the usual styles, bu had exceptionally light and elegant lines. They had compound motors actin directly on the rear axle, and 6 speeds. The Galliette was a light runabout wit motor under the chassis, driving by shaft. A number were sold in America, probabl the only European electric cars to be marketed there. GN

REGINA (ii) (F) *c.1922–1925*
Automobiles Regina, Paris 18e
This Regina was a 3-wheeler with single front wheel and a 4-cylinder engin mounted transversely at the rear. This could be started from the driver's seat. Th Regina was available as an open two-seater or, surprisingly, as a four-seate saloon. GN

REGINETTE (F) *c.1922*
The Paris-built Reginette was an ultra-light single- or two-seater cyclecar pow ered by a rear-mounted 2½hp 2-stroke engine of 247cc capacity. The chassis con sisted of ash-wood slats that were claimed to be 'D'une souplesse extraordinaire – necessary as there was no other springing. The 'Type Plage' was a bodiles two-seater resembling the Briggs & Stratton Buckboard, but for an extra 300 franc the buyer could have a light metal cowling over his feet and sides, which styl was termed the 'Type Sport'. GN

REGNER (F) *1905–1906*
Daniel Regner, Paris
The Regner was a very light two-seater voiturette with a single-cylinder 6h engine and belt final drive. GN

REID *see* WOLVERINE (i)

REINERTSEN *see* REX BUCKBOARD

REINHARD (F) *1911–1914*
Sté de Construction des Moteurs Reinhard, Lyons
The Reinhard cars used a sleeve-valve engine of Valentin Reinhard's own design The first cars had 4-cylinder engines of 2-litres capacity and chain drive, but th later model, known as 'Melanie' had a 3-litre engine and shaft drive. Only 2 Reinhards were made and M. Reinhard failed in his attempt to sell his engine desig to Delaugère-Clayette and Minerva. GN

REISACHER-JULIEN (F) *1900*
Éts Reisacher-Julien, Marseilles
This company built a small series of cars with Reisacher engines and Julie bodies. GN

REISSIG (D) *1912–1914*

Automobilwerk 'Siegfried' Arno Köhl-Krügel, Reissig nr. Plauen

This firm produced cars on a small scale. Only one type, of 9/26PS, is known. Usually the cars were marketed under the name of Reissig, but Siegfried was also used. HON

REJO (GB) *1958–1962*

Rejo Cars, Greenwich, London S.E.10

A very small number of sports/racing cars were produced under this name with Ford 100E and 105E engines. The 1172 Formula car used a Heron fibreglass body. A number of Rejo's own fibreglass body shells were also sold. Designer Rod Easterling, who had been in partnership first with Jim Osborn and later with Ron and David Inglis, also produced on his own a rear-engined monocoque sports car with Cosworth F.J. engine. One of these in the hands of John Anstice-Brown was still winning sufficient races in 1971 to take the Castrol/Motoring News Championship. DF

REKORD (D) *1905–1908*

Internationale Automobilcentrale Dr Mengers & Bellmann, Berlin

This firm produced cars with 6 to 80hp engines, and used French components almost entirely. The make participated in the Herkomer Trials in 1905 and 1906 but did not figure prominently in the results. HON

RELAY (US) *1904*

Relay Motor Car Co, Reading, Pa.

The Relay used a 24hp 3-cylinder engine with overhead valves. Final drive was by propeller shaft and a five-seater tonneau body was standard. GNG

RELIABLE DAYTON (US) *1906–1909*

Dayton & Mashey Automobile Works, Chicago, Ill.

The Reliable Dayton cars were two-and four-seater high-wheelers. Their 2-cylinder air-cooled engines were located under the body, with rope drive to the rear wheels, and solid rubber tyres. The dummy bonnet in front was complete with dummy radiator. GMN

RELIANCE (US) *1903–1907*

Reliance Automobile Manufacturing Co, Detroit, Mich.

This car was produced as a five-seater side-entrance tonneau, with a fixed top. It was powered by a 2-cylinder water-cooled engine of 3.2 litres, had shaft drive and cost $1,250. GMN

RELIANT (GB) *1952 to date*

(1) Reliant Engineering Co (Tamworth) Ltd, Tamworth, Staffs. *1952–1963*
(2) Reliant Motor Co Ltd, Tamworth, Staffs. *1963 to date*

This company was established in 1935 by T.L. Williams to take over the design of the Raleigh 3-wheeler van with single front wheel. From 1939 onwards this was powered by Reliant's own version of the Austin Seven engine, and in 1952 a private car version, the Regal, with a four-seater body, was introduced. The price was £352. Fibreglass bodywork was adopted in 1956. The first 4-wheeled model was announced for 1962, and was evolved in association with Sabra of Israel; this car, the Sabre, was a sports two-seater with a 1.7-litre Ford Consul engine (later replaced by the 6-cylinder 2.6-litre Zephyr), coil-spring independent front suspension, ladder-type frame, and front disc brakes. Its styling provoked mixed reactions, but by 1966 it had evolved into the handsome Scimitar fibreglass GT coupé with all-synchromesh gearbox, still Ford-powered.

Reliant was also responsible for the other Sabra designs, specializing in the evolution of inexpensive family cars for series production on a limited scale in emergent countries: in 1966 they produced the FW5 saloon for manufacture in Turkey as the Anadol. The Austin-based engines of the 3-wheelers were replaced in 1963 by a die-cast alloy 600cc ohv 4-cylinder unit of Reliant design and manufacture; two years later this engine was also applied to the Rebel, a small 4-wheeler saloon with fibreglass bodywork selling for £525. 1967 Scimitars had the 144-bhp Ford V-6 engine, a similar 2.5-litre unit being optional for 1968. In April of that year the 50,000th 3/25 3-wheeler was delivered, and with the acquisition of Bond (iii) in 1969 Reliant became the second largest all-British manufacturer on an annual production of 20,000 units. Also in 1969 they set a new styling fashion with the GT Estate Scimitar, which sold so well that the original coupé model was discontinued during 1970. Engines of 700cc were fitted to 1970 versions of the 3-wheeler and Rebel, and the introduction of Ford's Granada in 1972 led to the standardization of its 135bhp 3-litre engine in the Scimitar. Reliants for 1973 were the Scimitar GTE, the 3/30 3-wheeler, and a new 750cc version of the Rebel. MCS

RELYANTE (F) *1903*

Relyante Motor Works, Walthamstow, London E.

Although listed as British cars, Relyantes were imported French machines of different makes. The 6½hp single-cylinder was a Lacoste et Battmann, the 12hp twin a Delahaye, while the 10hp steamer was a Serpollet. GNG

1952 RELIANT Regal 747cc 3-wheeler. *Reliant Motor Co Ltd*

1965 RELIANT Scimitar GT 2.6-litre coupé. *Reliant Motor Co Ltd*

1972 RELIANT Rebel 700cc saloon. *Reliant Motor Co Ltd*

1938 REMI-DANVIGNES 1,100cc sports car.
Autocar

1907 RENAULT 20hp limousine. *Lucien Loreille Collection*

1914 RENAULT 35hp torpedo tourer. *Lucien Loreille Collection*

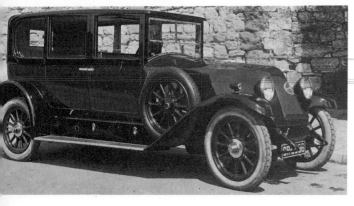

1924 RENAULT 26.9hp limousine. *The Veteran Car Club of Great Britain*

REMI-DANVIGNES (F) 1935–1939
Remi-Danvignes et Cie, Paris 11e

Although the small sports car had flourished in France in the 1920s, hardly any were made by the late 1930s, with the exception of the Remi-Danvignes. This was made in two models, a 750cc vertical twin with overhead camshaft, and an 1,100cc 4-cylinder Ruby-engined car. Both models had low two-seater bodies, and independent suspension all round.
GNG

REMINGTON (i) (US) 1900–1901
Remington Auto & Motor Co, Kingston, N.Y.

This car used a 4-cylinder engine of unusual design, burning a mixture of hydrogen and acetylene gas. The 1901 model was called the Remington Standard, the name of the famous typewriter made by the same firm.
GNG

REMINGTON (ii) (US) 1900–1904
Remington Motor Vehicle Co, Utica, N.Y.

This car was built as a five-seater tonneau at $1,350 and as a two-seater runabout at $850. Each was driven by a 2-cylinder 2-stroke engine of 10hp. This was water-cooled, and drive to the rear axle was by belt.
GMN

REMINGTON (iii) (US) 1914–1915
Remington Motor Co, Rahway, N.J.

The Remington began as a sophisticated cyclecar with a 1,750cc 4-cylinder engine and shaft drive. The Hollister automatic transmission was preselective and actuated by the clutch, a system employed successfully 20 years later by Hudson. In 1915, a V-8 engine was used in a car with standard track on a 9ft 8 in wheelbase. The cars were designed by Philo E. Remington, grandson of the founder of the famous arms company.
GMN

RENAULT (F) 1898 to date
(1) Renault Frères Billancourt 1898–1909
(2) SA des Usines Renault, Billancourt 1909–1945
(3) Régie Nationale des Usines Renault, Billancourt 1945 to date
(4) Régie Nationale des Usines Renault, Flins 1952 to date;
(5) Régie Nationale des Usines Renault, Havre-Sandouville 1963 to date

Louis Renault's first prototype of 1898 had a 1¾hp 273cc air-cooled De Dion engine mounted under a 'meat-safe' bonnet at the front of a tubular chassis with shaft drive and differential back axle. The 3-speed-and-reverse gearbox incorporated a direct top gear patented by its designer. This car was wheel-steered, but early production Renaults had tiller steering. The small company founded by Louis and his brothers Marcel and Fernand delivered 60 cars in the first six months. In 1899 Louis and Marcel took 1st and 2nd places in the Paris-Trouville Race, and Louis followed this up with a win in the voiturette class of the Paris-Ostend Race. 1900 models had water-cooled 500cc De Dion engines and lateral radiators, and were sold in England as M.C.C. Triumphs. That year 179 cars were sold, and both Corre (i) in France and Argyll in Scotland were close imitations of the Renault. Wheel-steered Renault racers won their classes in the Paris-Bordeaux and Paris-Toulouse-Paris (1900) and the Paris-Berlin (1901) Races.

In 1902 single and 2-cylinder De Dion and Aster engines were still being used in touring models, but the car with which Marcel Renault finished 2nd in the Paris-Vienna Race (as well as winning the light-car class) was a sample of things to come with its 3.8-litre Viet-designed and Renault-built 4-cylinder unit. Mechanically-operated side valves in an L-head made their appearance on the 6.3-litre light racers evolved for the 1903 Paris-Madrid Race (in which Marcel Renault met his death), and by 1904 the design of the cars had crystallized into a form that was to be followed until 1928, and to have many imitators. Engines were of L-head type, their cylinders initially cast in pairs. Ignition was by ht magneto, while cooling was by thermo-syphon, the hallmark of the Renault being the huge dashboard radiator. The sliding-type gearbox had quadrant change, and the bevel drive with its direct top gear was inherited from 1898.

There was a brief reversion to pump cooling in 1905 on some cars built for the Gordon Bennett Eliminating Trials, but this year also brought the first of the 1,100cc 2-cylinder models (Types AX and AG), the company's pre-1914 best-sellers and the ancestors of the celebrated '*Taxis de la Marne*'. A short-chassis AX two-seater could be bought for 5,000fr or £250 in 1908. Szisz's 13-litre Renault won the first French Grand Prix in 1906, but though the marque tried again the following year, they dropped out of racing thereafter. In the 1906 to 1908 period compressed-air starters were available on the bigger models. King Edward VII bought a 3-litre 4-cylinder 14/20 in 1906, in which year fours of 2.1 litres, 4.4 litres, and 7.4-litres were also listed. Over 3,000 Renaults were sold in 1907, but there were few major changes up to 1914. Direct copies were made in England by Dodson and in the U.S.A. by Croxton and (in the case of one town-car model) Palmer-Singer. After Fernand Renault's death in 1908, the company was renamed: 1908 also saw the first 6-cylinder, a 9.5-litre 50/60, followed two years later by a smaller 18/25hp car. Later improvements included pressure lubrication in 1911, and by 1913 the company were fitting detachable wood wheels of their own design and manufacture on all but the 2-cylinder models. A labour force of 5,200 made more than 10,000 Renaults – one-fifth of all French private-car production, and the first monobloc fours were appearing.

Renault, like Fiat, still declined to make bodywork, though they listed standardized open styles on the smaller and cheaper chassis. The 1914 range embraced the twin in two wheelbase lengths, 4-cylinder cars with capacities of 2.1 litres, 2.6 litres, 3.6 litres, 5.1 litres, and 8.5 litres, and two sixes with 5.1 litre and 7.5-litre engines. Bigger Renaults used a transverse helper spring in conjunction with semi-elliptics at the rear, all the big cars came with electric lighting as standard equipment, and the de luxe 15.8hp had an electric starter as well.

1919 Renaults were very similar to the pre-war article, but the quadrant change had gone, and the entire range (three fours and a six) had full electrical equipment. All the 4-cylinder cars had monobloc engines, but the FI-type 6 had its cylinders cast in threes. In 1921 this model grew up into the elephantine 9.1-litre 45, a 90mph Edwardian survival which was listed until 1928/29, and had fixed cylinder heads, wood wheels and a choice of two wheelbase lengths (12ft 6in and 13ft 1in). The radiator capacity was 12 gallons, and in 1926 a lightweight streamline saloon version became the first car to average more than 100mph over 24 hours. The bigger Renaults acquired front-wheel brakes in 1922: at the same time the dashboard radiator was merged with the bonnet line.

From 1923 came an economy car to challenge the rising star of Citroën and to fill the gap left by the twins, the 951cc KJ-type with 3-speed gearbox and the transverse rear suspension that was to be a feature of the make up to 1940. Also offered that year were two medium-sized fours, the '45', and the 4.8-litre Type-JY 6-cylinder, which was nearly as big as the 45, but not nearly as fast. Some 6-wheeler trans-Sahara vehicles were evolved in 1924 using the 13.9hp 4-cylinder engine. In 1925 Renault won the Monte Carlo Rally for the first time (other victories were in 1935 and 1959). All 1925 Renaults had front-wheel brakes, detachable heads followed in 1927 on the 14/45hp and on a new 3.2-litre light six which also had coil ignition, and for 1928 there was a 1½-litre six with coil ignition, and transverse rear springing: this was slow and undergeared, but persisted until 1931. Only the smaller fours now had cone clutches.

1929 brought real deviation – the 7.1-litre Reinastella, Renault's first straight-8, with frontal radiator, pump cooling, and servo brakes, listing at £1,550 for a chassis. By 1931 frontal radiators, coil ignition, disc wheels, unit gearboxes, and transverse rear suspension were universal. Smallest and cheapest model was the little Monasix at £199: there were also a 2.1-litre four, a 3.2-litre six, and two eights, the Reinastella and cheaper Nerva model at around the £400 mark. There was a reversion to thermosyphon cooling in 1932, and 1933 brought the introduction of synchromesh and downdraught carburettors on the sixes and eights; synchromesh had spread to 4-cylinder versions in 1934, and at the same time these smaller Renaults discarded gravity feed.

Renault design in the middle and later 1930s was stolid and uninspired, deriving largely from American practice: features were 3-speed gearboxes with dashboard change, umbrella-handle handbrakes, recessed rear number plates, mechanical brakes, and full-width bodywork justifying the slogan 'There's More Room in a Renault'. The 1936 range included what was a very big four by the standards of the day, an sv 2.4-litre which sold very well until 1940, and was used in some light-commercial and station-wagon models as late as 1951. A 1-litre 8.3hp selling for £140 from 1938 on had unitary construction. The rest of the pre-war range consisted of two medium-sized fours, a 4.1-litre six, and a 5.4-litre straight-8.

After Louis Renault's death in prison in 1944 (he had been accused of collaboration with the Nazis), Renault was nationalized, and under Government control two private-car models were made: a revised 4-door 1-litre Juvaquatre, now with hydraulic brakes, and the 760cc 4CV developed secretly during the war years. This very advanced little machine had a rear-mounted 4-cylinder ohv engine developing 19bhp, 3 forward speeds, all-round independent suspension, hydraulic brakes, and spider-type wheels with detachable rims. Top speed was 60mph, and assembly was undertaken in London for the British market (the Renault works at Acton assembled cars from the late 1920s until 1961), while Hino of Japan built the model under licence, and their subsequent designs showed traces of Renault ancestry. Production of the 4CV reached 100,000 in 1950, half a million had been made in 1954, and over a million found customers before the model was withdrawn in 1961. Sporting versions were made to give as much as 38bhp, and from 1951 onward capacity was reduced to 750cc.

The rear-engined theme was the backbone of Renault private-car development until the early 1960s, but in 1951 they came out with the Frégate, last of the conventionally-planned machines; this was a short-stroke 2-litre four with all-round independent suspension, hypoid final drive (never found on the rear-engined cars) and a 4-speed all-indirect gearbox. Though later versions had bigger 2.1-litre engines and the Transfluide semi-automatic transmission, it was never a best-seller. In 1955 the option of the Ferlec automatic clutch was introduced on the 4CV, and a year later came a new rear-engined light car, the 845cc Dauphine with a 30bhp long-stroke engine, selling for £796 in England. Despite controversial handling, it became the first French model to sell more than two million examples, and was made under licence in Italy by Alfa-Romeo, and in Brazil by Willys-Overland. Also in 1956 Renault took gas-turbine records with the experimental Etoile Filante.

1933 RENAULT Primastella 13.9hp saloon.
Geoffroy de Beauffort Collection

1939 RENAULT Viva Grand Sport 27hp sports saloon.
W.D. Beckingham

*c.*1955 RENAULT Frégate 2-litre convertible.
G.N. Georgano

1968 RENAULT 1100 saloon. *Renault Ltd*

1972 RENAULT 15TS 1.6-litre coupé. *Renault Ltd*

1904 REPTON 4hp 3-wheeler. *Autocar*

Further Dauphine developments resulted from Amédée Gordini's association with the company: the 1957 Dauphine Gordini had a 4-speed gearbox and 38bhp, and was followed in 1959 by the Floride sports coupé. This acquired a 956cc engine in 1962, in which year Renault challenged Citroën's 2CV with a fwd utility car, the 747cc R4 with all 4 wheels independently sprung, and hypoid final drive. Sales in 1963 amounted to 668,867 cars, the plant at Le Havre was opened to supplement the automated factory at Flins which had been operating since 1952, and once again there was a big Renault product – the American Rambler made under licence. Supplementing the Dauphine was a new and roomier rear-engined saloon, the 956cc R8 at £671, with its radiator mounted behind the engine, and all-round disc brakes (standardized on all rear-engined Renaults the following season). Gordini and automatic versions were also listed, followed by the 1,100cc R8 Major, and by 1966 it was possible to buy a Gordini-tuned R8 variant capable of over 100mph in England for £984. The 4 (now enlarged to 845cc), the Gordini-Dauphine, the 8 family, and the Caravelle (as the Floride had been renamed) made up the 1967 Renault line, along with the ingenious 16, introduced in 1965. This was a fwd 1½-litre 63bhp saloon with front disc brakes and station-wagon styling.

The Dauphine and the Rambler-Renault were dropped in 1968, and competition activities became increasingly the province of Renault's associate, Alpine: works-entered Renault cars were not seen in rallies after 1969. New for 1968 were 4s with 4-speed gearboxes, and a 1,565cc 16TS with crossflow head. This higher-capacity engine was standardized in the 16 range by 1971. The 1969 16s could be had with automatic gearboxes; a new fwd model was the 6, an enlarged 4 with the 845cc engine. The move towards front-wheel drive took a further step in 1970 with the 12, a 1,300cc saloon on which the 4-cylinder engine lay in front of the gearbox. Other features were front disc brakes and rear suspension by rigid axle and coils; a Gordini version used a 1,565cc engine. Price of the basic model on the home market was 9,980 francs. It gradually supplanted the rear-engined 8 and 10, which had virtually disappeared by the end of 1971.

By 1972 the 4, 6, 12 and 16 had been joined by the Rodeo, a jeep-type vehicle based on the 4, as well as the 15/17 range of sports coupés. The most potent of these was the 17TS with hemi-head fuel-injection engine developing 120bhp, all-disc brakes, and an electric sunroof. Early in the year came Renault's answer to the Fiat 127, the compact fwd 4-cylinder 5. This featured a 43bhp, 956cc 5-bearing engine (an economy 782cc version was available for the home market), all-independent suspension, a 4-speed all-synchromesh gearbox with dashboard change, alternator ignition, disc front brakes and a lift-up tailgate.

Since World War 2 Renault mechanical components have featured in several specialist makes of car, among them Alpine, Autobleu, Réné Bonnet, Brissonneau, Matra, Méan and (since the introduction of the Europa in 1967) Lotus. In 1972 Renaults were being assembled or manufactured in 27 foreign countries, including Bulgaria, Rumania and Yugoslavia.   MCS

RENAUX (F) 1901–1902
Sté l'Energie, Paris

Better known for their tricycles, the Société l'Energie made a light car powered by an 8hp Buchet engine, and using shaft drive.   GNG

RÉNÉ BONNET (F) 1962–1964
Réné Bonnet, Champigny-sur-Seine, Marne

The Réné Bonnet was a continuation of the D.B. line with one great difference. After Deutsch's departure, M. Bonnet transferred his allegiance to Renault, offering both the Djet with admidships engine and rear drive, and the Le Mans and Missile with front-mounted engines and front-wheel drive. Fwd versions had disc brakes on the front, the Djet having them all round, all wheels were independently sprung, and bodies were of fibreglass. 850cc and 1,100cc power units were used. The cars won the Index of Energy at Le Mans in 1962 and 1963, the most powerful road-going variants offered 81bhp. A Renault-engined Formula 3 car with a 5-speed gearbox made its appearance in 1964, but in 1965 both sponsorship and name changed, when Engins Matra took over. The name became Matra Djet, while the Formula 3 programme continued, with Cosworth-Ford powered-cars.   MCS

RENFERT (D) 1924–1925
Josef Renfert, Motorfahrzeugfabrik, Beckum

The Renfert was a small car with a 3/12PS 2-cylinder, 2-stroke engine of 780cc.   HON

RENFREW (GB) 1904
Scottish Motor Carriage Co Ltd, Glasgow

One model of the Renfrew was made, a 4-cylinder 16/20hp five-seater tourer priced at £400. Very few were sold, but they were entered in a number of hill-climbs and Scottish Automobile Club Reliability Trials of the period.   GNG

RENNIE (GB) 1907
Rennie Motor Manufacturing Co, Brighton, Sussex

The Rennie was an assembled car sold in three 4-cylinder models, a 10/12, 12/15 and 25/30hp. A 30hp 6-cylinder car was also listed.   GNG

RENOWN *see* PALM

REO (US) *1904–1936*

(1) R.E. Olds Co, Lansing, Mich. *1904*

(2) Reo Car Co, Lansing, Mich. *1904*

(3) Reo Motor Car Co, Lansing, Mich. *1904–1936*

The name derives from the initials of Ransom E. Olds, who left Oldsmobile to form a new company. The first Reos were single-cylinder 8hp runabouts with under-floor engines, dummy bonnets, planetary transmissions, and chain drive; they sold for $685, reduced to $500 by 1909. A companion 16hp twin at $1,250 had a capacity of 3.4 litres and a carburettor for each cylinder. These represented the company's main effort up to 1909, though a short-lived four had been marketed in 1906. 1911/12 brought the Reo The Fifth, another 4-cylinder car with 3.7-litre ioe engine, which offered central change and left-hand drive for $1,055.

Reo cars were steady sellers right up to the Depression of 1929–31, and the company did very well with their subsequent ioe fours and sixes, which were made with V-radiators during the World War 1 period. In 1918, 4-cylinder cars sold for $1,225, $1,550 being asked for the 5-litre 6-cylinder version. Only a four was made in 1919, but for 1920 Reo standardized a six, their famous ioe Model-T with 'back-to-front' gear change, and two foot-operated brakes with no hand lever; 2-wheel brakes were deemed sufficient right up to the end of production in 1926. 1927 saw a switch to side valves and hydraulic four-wheel brakes, and in 1928 the company offered the Wolverine, a cheaper car with a Continental engine which sold for $1,195, as against the $1,685 asked for the Flying Cloud with Reo's own engine. This was the company's best year, with 29,000 cars sold. The Wolverine was dropped in 1929, and production centred on two versions of the Flying Cloud with 3½-litre and 4.4-litre engines. An 8-cylinder Flying Cloud followed in 1931, along with a bid for the luxury market with the 5.9-litre straight-8 Custom Royale, styled by Alexis de Sakhnoffsky. It had automatic chassis lubrication, and could be obtained in three wheelbase lengths, the longest being 12ft 8in.

The Reo 4-speed automatic gearbox was available on all models from 1933 onwards, as an alternative to synchromesh, but though the 4.4-litre Flying Cloud with Graham-like sedan bodywork could still be bought for $845 in 1936, that was the end of Reo's private cars. Trucks and buses continued to be made, from 1957 as a division of White. In 1967 amalgamation of design with Diamond T led to a new brand name, Diamond-Reo, and in 1971 this was sold by White to become an independent make. MCS

REON (GB) *1967 to date*

Reon Engineering, Heath and Reach, Leighton Buzzard, Beds.

This small part-time firm started production by constructing 750 Formula specials. By 1971 the models available, either from plans, as kits or complete cars, ranged from the Reon 2, a wedge-shaped semi-monocoque 750, through the 2b Formula 1200 model, the 2c and 2d Clubman's machines, the 3 and 5 space-framed 750 and Formula Ford types to the Reon 6 Formula 4 monocoque. DF

REPTON (GB) *1904*

Repton Engineering Works, Repton, Derbyshire

The Repton was a very small 3-wheeler powered by a 4hp water-cooled engine. It had a single-seater body, 2-speed epicyclic gearbox in which top gear was direct, and a maximum speed of 25mph. Very unusual for the time was the use of front-wheel brakes. GNG

REPUBLIC (US) *1911–1916*

(1) Republic Motor Car Co, Hamilton, Ohio *1911–1912*

(2) Republic Motor Car Co, Tarrytown, N.Y. *1913–1916*

This car, called 'the classiest of all', used a T-head, 4-cylinder engine rated at 35/40hp. The crankshaft was off-set, and each cylinder had two sparking plugs. GMN

RESTELLI (I) *1920–1923*

SA Officine Meccaniche Isola Bella, Milan

The Restelli sports car used a 1,490cc single-ohc 4-cylinder engine of the company's own design. In 1922 there was also a 1,459cc twin-ohc unit. There was no chassis, the engine, gearbox and back axle being rigidly connected, and attached to trunnions on which the springs were mounted. Very few Restellis were made, but one of them was driven by Antony Lago in English trials in 1924. GNG

REVELLI (I) *1941*

Mario Revelli, Turin

During World War 2 Revelli built two 3-wheeled battery-electric city cars. One of these had chain drive to the offside rear wheel, but on the second Revelli the transaxle layout incorporated the motor as well. There was no series production. MCS

REVERE (US) *1917–1926*

(1) ReVere Motor Car Corp, Logansport, Ind. *1917–1922*

(2) ReVere Motor Co, Logansport, Ind. *1922–1926*

1909 REO 16hp tourer. *Kenneth Stauffer*

1931 REO Custom Royale Eight 5.9-litre sports saloon. *Autocar*

1928 REO 25/65hp 4.2-litre coupé. *Automobile Manufacturers' Association*

1920 REVERE Model C 5.9-litre roadster. *Keith Marvin Collection*

1914 REX SIMPLEX 17/38PS sporting tourer. *Jaeger Collection*

1903 REX(ii) 10hp tonneau. *G.N. Georgano Collection*

The ReVere was a short-lived luxury car that was best known in speedster form. In its fiercest guise, it was powered by a horizontal-valve 5.9-litre Rochester-Duesenberg racing engine providing 103bhp at 2,600rpm and 85mph. Alternatively, there was a smaller, 81bhp unit. A 4-speed gearbox was supplied. Formal bodies, such as that for King Alfonso XIII of Spain, were also worn. As happened so often with cars of this exotic type, the ReVere lost appeal in its later years. Continental 6-cylinder engines were fitted in 1924. When balloon tyres arrived the ReVere was furnished with two superimposed steering wheels, one with a lower ratio for parking.

TRN

REVOL (F) 1923–1925
J.F. Revol, Fontenay-aux-Roses, Seine

The Revol was a cyclecar powered by a 2-cylinder engine, either by Train or Anzani.

GNG

REX (i) (REX-SIMPLEX) (D) 1901–1923
(1) Deutsche Automobil-Industrie Friedrich Hering, Ronneburg *1901–1904*
(2) Deutsche Automobil-Industrie Hering & Richard, Ronneburg *1904–1908*
(3) Automobilwerk Richard & Hering AG, Ronneburg *1908–1921*
(4) Elitewagen AG, Ronneburg *1921–1923*

Before this firm started to build their own cars they offered various components for car construction, such as chassis, wheels, axles, etc. Their first cars appeared in 1901, using De Dion engines, and were marketed under the name of Rex, but the single-cylinder 6hp 698cc model was called the Rex Simplex. This name was later used for all other models. After 1907 the firm produced engines of their own design.

Rex-Simplex participated in the Prince Henry Trial, 1908, and until 1914 they had a reputation for high technical standards. Best known were their models 9/16PS (2,120cc), 10/28PS (2,680cc), and the very successful 17/38PS (4,500cc), which was produced from 1908 until 1914. After 1911 Dr Valentin was engaged as chief designer. When he went to Russo-Baltique some of his designs for this company were based on the Rex-Simplex. After World War 1 two improved pre-war types were continued, the 10/30PS and the 13/40PS. In 1921 the factory was taken over by Elite and only the 13/40PS was continued for a time as the Elite-Wagen.

HON

REX (ii) (GB) 1901–1914
(1) Birmingham Motor Manufacturing and Supply Co Ltd, Birmingham *1901–1902*
(2) Rex Motor Manufacturing Co Ltd, Coventry, Warwickshire *1902–1914*

Though always best known for their motor cycles, Rex made cars under a confusing variety of names, these including Ast-Rex, Airex, Rexette, Rex-Remo, and even Rex-Simplex which had no connection with the products of the German firm of Richard and Hering. The original Birmingham concern added cars to its repertoire in 1901, with a conventional 900cc single-cylinder voiturette. This cost £168 and had bevel drive, a 2-speed gearbox, and a curious cylindrical radiator, at first mounted low down at the front, and later moved to the rear.

The fusion with Allard (i) and the move to Coventry in June 1902 resulted in a wider range of cars, including some 3-speed singles, and a 'square' 2.4-litre vertical-twin. In 1903, when there were rumours – which came to nothing – of a racing car for the Gordon Bennett Eliminating Trials, the manufacture of pedal cycles was abandoned and a good variety of models with Panhard-style radiators was offered at prices from £198/10s to over £400. In addition a motor cycle-based tricar became available, and by 1904 this had evolved into the Rexette with car-type frame, a seat for the driver instead of a saddle, a water-cooled single-cylinder engine started by a handle and a 2-speed gearbox. It became even more car-like in 1905 with the adoption of wheel steering and 3-wheel brakes for a list price of £105, and the 1906 'Rexettes' had transverse V-twin engines and were available with 2-seater forecarriages.

Though the 12hp 2-cylinder Rex-Simplex car was sold in 1904 and 1905, the tricar was the principal product (the motor cycles apart) until the 1906 season, when the Ast-Rex appeared. This was a conventional shaft-driven vehicle with 3.7-litre 4-cylinder Aster engine and 3-speed gearbox, selling for £510. It did not last long, giving way to the Airex line, announced as V-4s with two forward speeds only in 1906. Production Airexes, however, were air-cooled 1.3-litre aiv V-twins rated at 9/11hp; they had shaft drive, 3-speed gearboxes, coil ignition and round 'radiators', all for £194/5s. 1907 also brought a reversion to the motor-cycle-type tricar with the handlebar-steered Litette at £78/15s, though this was still powered by a 726cc water-cooled engine and a wheel-steered version was made in 1908. Though the tricars survived for another season, these last Triettes were strictly on 2-wheeler lines.

Meanwhile Rex had returned to full-sized cars with the Rex-Remo models introduced for 1908; these were straightforward T-headed 4-cylinder affairs with shaft drive, magneto ignition, 3-speed gearboxes and quadrant change. An interesting feature was the use of a 'honeycomb' grille to conceal the gilled-tube radiator. They were made in 2.6-litre and 2.8-litre forms until 1911, the last examples having detachable wire wheels.

After this Rex concentrated on motor cycles, though there were two more abortive attempts to produce a car. The first of these was a water-cooled V-twin cyclecar of 1912, which had an underslung frame and friction drive; the second came after a reorganization of the firm in 1914, and was a conventional light car with a 1,100cc sv 4-cylinder Dorman engine, intended for production in private and commercial forms. World War 1 intervened, and in 1922 Rex merged with another Coventry motor cycle producer, Acme. This combined operation expired in 1928, and though there was a brief revival in 1932, it lasted only a year.   MCS

REX (iii) (US) *1914*
Rex Motor Co, Detroit, Mich.
    The two-seater Rex cyclecar had a 4-cylinder, water-cooled engine of 15/18hp. A friction transmission and shaft final drive were used.   GMN

REX BUCKBOARD (US) *1902*
Pennsylvania Electrical & Railway Supply Co, Pittsburgh, Pa.
    This was a very simple car on the lines of the Orient Buckboard, powered by a 4½hp engine. It was designed by Rex Reinertsen, an employee of the Pennsylvania Supply Company, and built in their workshops.   GNG

REXER *see* WEYHER ET RICHEMOND

REYMOND (F) *c.1901*
Automobiles Reymond et Cie, Chalons-sur-Saône, Saône-et-Loire
    This light car had a 12hp V-twin engine and single chain drive. The one surviving example has a two-seater body, but no details have been found in any motor journal of the period.   GNG

REYNARD (GB) *1931*
Reynard Car & Engineering Co Ltd, Highgate, London, N.6
    The Reynard was a low-built sports car powered by a twin-carburettor Meadows 1½-litre ohv engine. Only prototypes were made.   GNG

REYONNAH (F) *1951–1954*
Robert Hannoyer, Paris 4e
    The Reyonnah was one of the few examples of a folding car. The front wheels were on sponsons which projected from the sides of the very narrow tandem-seating body, and which could be folded under the car so that their track was no greater than that of the rear wheels, which were mounted very close together. Power came from a 175cc Ydral engine, and the perspex hood opened sideways in the style of the Messerschmitt.   GNG

REYROL (PASSE-PARTOUT) (F) *1901–1930*
(1) Société des Automobiles Reyrol, Neuilly, Seine *1901–1906*
(2) Société des Automobiles Reyrol, Levallois-Perret, Seine *1907–1930*
    Apart from the 1926 Passe-Partout, these two makes were identical; in 1905 the same model was marketed as a Reyrol in England and as a Passe-Partout in France. Initially, however, the cars were always Reyrols, and their first manifestation was a primitive single-cylinder voiturette with a 5hp Aster or De Dion engine, belt-and-spur gear transmission, and a small steering wheel perched atop a vertical column. The Yorkshire Motor Vehicle Co was formed in England in 1901 to produce this type, but was bankrupt before the year was out.
    By 1905 the company had progressed to a more conventional lightweight with armoured-wood frame, 3-speed gearbox, and shaft drive, which was said to be France's cheapest car at 2,700fr (£110 in England). Engines available were the 4½hp aiv De Dion and the 6hp moiv Buchet. 785cc and 942cc Buchet units were catalogued in 1906, and pressed-steel frames were available in 1907, in which year there was also a small monobloc 4-cylinder of less than 2 litres, selling for £225. Dashboard radiators were used on the cars which ran in the 1907 and 1908 Coupes des Voiturettes, but underslung coolers were found on the production versions, now with De Dion units: 40mph was claimed from these. Two 4-cylinder models were also available, the bigger of which was known as the 12/14 Passe-Partout or 12/16 Reyrol. From 1909 onward only 4-cylinder cars with 3-speed gearboxes were marketed, and in 1913 these came in 1½-litre, 1.7-litre, 2.1-litre, 2.3-litre, and 2.7-litre guises.
    After World War 1, the Chapuis-Dornier engine was standardized, and there were three sv Reyrols, the biggest of which had a capacity of 2.1 litres. A 2.3-litre ohv model, also Chapuis-Dornier-powered, appeared in 1924, and a small 1.2-litre ohv car in 1925. 1926 Reyrols cost 15,000fr, and had front wheel brakes and 1½-litre ohv Chapuis-Dornier engines. In this year the Passe-Partout name was applied specifically to a 1,100cc light car with worm-driven front wheels, 3-speed gearbox, and cone clutch. This was the last of the Passe-Partouts, but 1,100cc and 1,500cc Reyrols, generally with saloon bodywork, were available until 1930.   MCS

R.F. (GB) *1966-1971*
Racing Frames Ltd, Ware, Herts.
    This multi-tubular spaced-framed machine, with stressed body panels, and inboard independent suspension by rubber, was offered for Formula 4 racing. Subsequently chassis were constructed for other firms, this business being associated with Ehrlich Engineering Ltd of Bletchley, Bucks., makers of the E.M.C. racing cars.   DF

1951 REYONNAH 175cc two-seater. *Associated Press Ltd*

1907 REYROL Coupe des Voiturettes racing car. *Autocar*

1955 R.G.S.-ATALANTA 3.4-litre sports car. *R.G. Shattock*

1924 RHEMAG 4/24PS sports car. *Neubauer Collection*

1922 RHODE 9.5hp occasional four-seater. *Autocar*

R.G.S.-ATALANTA (GB) 1947–1958
R.G.S. Automobile Components Ltd, Winkfield, Windsor, Berks.

R.G.S. Automobile Components Ltd, Winkfield, Windsor, Berks.
Richard G. Shattock used the remnants from the Atalanta firm to assist in the production of his post-war all-independent suspension sports-racing cars. A Brooke marine engine was originally used, followed by a 1,496cc Lea-Francis, Ford and finally Jaguar units. With the 'C' type engine, the car proved very successful. However, those who bewailed the demise of the first Atalanta never flocked to purchase its successor. Only a dozen or so chassis were constructed, mostly multi-tubular types in kit form. In latter years, fibreglass bodies were also available.
DF

R.H. (F) 1927–1928
Etablissements Raymond Hebert, Levallois-Perret, Seine

The R.H. was a rakish-looking small sports car with a low, doorless two-seater body, the lower part of which was part of the frame. It was powered by an 1,100cc C.I.M.E. engine. Like some vintage Chenard-Walckers, brakes were on the front wheels and transmission only.
GNG

RHÉDA (F) 1898–1899
Sté des Automobiles Rhéda, Paris

The original Rhéda was a two-seater 3-wheeler powered by a 2½hp single-cylinder horizontal engine, but a 4-wheeler was introduced in 1899.
GNG

RHEMAG (D) 1924–1926
Rhenania Motorenfabrik AG, Berlin; Mannheim

Only one model was listed by this firm. It was a 1,065cc ohv 24bhp sports car with alloy engine available with two- and four-seater bodies.
HON

RHODE (GB) 1921–1931
Rhode Motor Co, Birmingham

A minority of British light cars of the 1920s catered more for the sporting customer than the family man. One of the best was the Rhose, made by F.W. Mead and T.W. Deakin, who had already gained a name for their motor-cycle sidecars, and who had also built the Media cyclecar. Their car was exceptional in that all its mechanical components except the gearbox were made by Rhode themselves. The engine, a 4-cylinder of 1,087cc and 9.5 rated hp, had an overhead camshaft and produced 19bhp. There was no differential, and the springing was by quarter-elliptics at each end. Fast, reliable, noisy and not very handsome, the 9.5 was full of character, but deficient in mass appeal. To overcome this, a full four-seater with the added luxury of a self-starter and differential was introduced for 1924, with a 1,232cc, 10.8hp engine and a lower axle ratio to cope with the extra weight. In the following season, the stark old 9.5 disappeared, and in 1926 the 10.8 itself was refined by means of a quieter, smoother engine with push-rod overhead valves. In this form, it was called the 11/30hp.

In fact, if not in theory, the last traces of sporting tradition vanished with the introduction in 1928 of a completely new car, the Hawk. It was a long and heavy fabric-bodied saloon; at first with an ohc version of the 11/30hp engine, and latterly with a 1½-litre push-rod ohv Meadows unit. Although styled in the 'sports saloon' fashion of the late 1920s, the Hawk was not a fast car. The company also made, from 1925 to 1927, the M. & D. light truck, which was powered by a 15.9hp ohc engine.
TRN

RIBBLE (GB) 1904–c.1908
Jackson & Kinnings, Southport, Lancs.

The first Ribbles were 3-wheelers made in single- or two-seater form. Curiously, the single-seater had an 8hp engine which drove it at 50mph, whereas the two-seater's engine was only of 4½hp. Later Ribble cars were 4-wheelers with 4-cylinder engines of 10/12 or 12/16hp.
GNG

RICART (E) 1922–1928
Ricart y Perez, Barcelona

The first Ricart was a 4-cylinder 16-valve competition car of about 1 litre capacity. An exciting 1½-litre twin-ohc six succeeded it in 1926. This machine had provision for a supercharger. Both these cars were designed by Wilfredo Ricart, later of Ricart-España, Nacional, Alfa-Romeo, and Pegaso. Neither went into production, it seems, though an sv, 6-cylinder, 12hp touring Ricart was built for official use.
TRN

RICART-ESPAÑA (E) 1928–1929
Industria National Metalurgica, Barcelona

After the collapse of the España company, the founder, D. Francisco Battlo, joined forces with Wilfredo Ricart to build a high quality car, the Ricart-España. The engine was a 6-cylinder ohv 2.4-litre with twin carburettors. It carried imposing open and saloon bodywork, and a number found favour with provincial governors and bishops, but lack of sufficient credit brought production to an end. A small number of the twin-ohc Ricart racing cars was also made under the Ricart-España name.
JRV

1928 RICART-ESPAÑA 2.4-litre tourer. *J. Rodriguez-Viña*

RiCHARD (US) *1914–1917*
RiChard Automobile Mfg Co, Cleveland, Ohio

This car had a 4-cylinder engine with a piston stroke of nearly 230mm, giving a capacity of 7.3 litres. The resulting bonnet was considerably higher than the rest of the body. Initially, a seven-seater touring body was made. Later, the wheelbase was extended to 11ft 5in to accommodate a nine-seater body with a boat-tail. This model was listed with a 9-litre V-8 engine.   GMN

RICHARDSON (i) (GB) *1903–1907*
J.R. Richardson & Co Ltd, Saxilby, Lincs.

Three models of Richardson were made, the 6½hp single, the 12/14hp twin, and the 24hp 4-cylinder car. The two smaller engines were made by Aster. All cars had tubular frames and shaft drive. In 1905 the 4-cylinder model was replaced by a slightly smaller one of 18/20hp.   GB

RICHARDSON (ii) (GB) *1919–1922*
C.E. Richardson & Co Ltd, Sheffield, Yorks.

The post-war Richardson was a cyclecar powered by either a 990cc J.A.P. or a 1,090cc Precision engine, both air-cooled. Transmission was by friction, and final drive by single chain. Early models had an ugly sloping grille, but this was replaced in 1921 by a better-looking vertical one. About 600 Richardsons were made in all.   GNG

RICHELIEU (US) *1922–1923*
Richelieu Motor Car Corp, Asbury Park, N.J.

The Richelieu was designed by Newton Van Zandt, formerly with ReVere: this accounts for the general similarity between the two makes. (It has been said that the Richelieu prototype was built in the ReVere factory.) It was a luxury car powered by a 4-cylinder Rochester-Duesenberg engine. The 4-door models cost $6,000, the open cars slightly less. These handsome cars with high, rounded radiators were discontinued in 1923 after fewer than 50 had been delivered.   KM

RICHMOND (i) (US) *1902–1903*
Richmond Automobile & Cycle Co, Richmond, Ind.

The Richmond Steam Runabout differed little from its contemporaries with its 6hp vertical engine and chain drive. The body style was a four-seater with *dos-à-dos* arrangement.   GNG

RICHMOND (ii) (US) *1908–1917*
Wayne Works, Richmond, Ind.

Until 1911, the Richmond used air-cooled engines, all 4-cylinder units of 22 to 30hp. By 1913, larger models, on wheelbases of up to 10ft 1in, were using water-cooled engines of 5.2 litres. Five-seater touring cars and two-seater runabouts were the only body types offered.   GMN

RICKENBACKER (US) *1922–1927*
Rickenbacker Motor Co, Detroit, Mich.

Captain Eddie Rickenbacker was already famous, as a racing driver and a World War 1 aviator, when he began to offer a remarkable car bearing his name. It bore his personal symbol of a hat in a ring, and was powered by a small sv 6-cylinder engine, which was very smooth thanks to its two flywheels. This unit developed 58bhp at 2,800rpm. The chassis frame was boxed and rigid, and there were internal expanding brakes on all four wheels. The 1923 Rickenbacker was the first cheap car to have front-wheel brakes. The last Rickenbackers were 4.4-litre straight-8s of the same design. This engine gave 107bhp at 3,000rpm in sports form, and was said to propel the Rickenbacker at 90mph.

The whole machine was exceedingly well made, as well as original, but high quality, low price and unconventionality killed it. The design was bought by J.S. Rasmussen in Germany and used in two models of the Audi.   TRN

RICKETTS (US) *1908–1909*
Ricketts Auto Works, South Bend, Ind.

The Ricketts used Brownell 4- and 6-cylinder engines of 35 and 50hp respectively. A baby tonneau and a five-seater touring car were available on a 9ft 8in wheelbase; the Model D was a seven-seater touring model on a longer wheelbase, priced at $2,250. These cars all had 3-speed selective transmissions and shaft drive.   GMN

RICORDI & MOLINARI (I) *1905–1906*
Società Italiana Costruzione Automobili Ricordi-Molinari, Milan

The company's staple product was an 8hp single-cylinder tonneau with 3-speed gearbox and shaft drive, distinguished by a round radiator. Max Ricordi's father, Giuseppe, is said to have imported Italy's first car in 1890, and marketed a Ricordi-Benz in 1900. This was almost certainly of German origin.   MCS

RIDDLE (US) *1916–1926*
Riddle Manufacturing Co, Ravenna, Ohio

The Riddle firm which existed from 1831 until 1926, was one of the earlier

1919 RICHARDSON(ii) 8hp cyclecar (with 1921 grille). *W.R. Alexander*

1922 RICHELIEU 5.5-litre tourer. *Automobile Manufacturers' Association*

1927 RICKENBACKER 4.4-litre coach sedan. *Automotive History Collection, Detroit Public Library*

1896 RIKER electric 3-wheeler. *Henry Ford Museum, Dearborn, Mich.*

1909 RILEY 12/18hp torpedo tourer. *Autocar*

1922 RILEY 10.8hp tourer. *Mrs Fellowes*

manufacturers of motor ambulances and hearses. In the 1920s and probably as far back as 1916, a handful of invalid sedans were built to special order. These cars had bodies without pillars on the right-hand side to facilitate entrance and egress for wheel chairs or beds. A few were bought as passenger cars for bearers' use at funerals. They closely resembled the contemporary Cadillacs and were powered by a Continental 6-cylinder engine developing 50bhp. KM

RIDER-LEWIS (US) 1908–1910
Rider-Lewis Motor Car Co, Muncie, Ind.

This make was advertised as 'The Excellent Six', which referred to its 40/50hp engine with overhead camshaft and valves. 4-cylinder cars of 26hp were also built. Body types available included a five-seater touring car, a two-seater roadster, a limousine, landaulet and 'tonneauette'. GMN

RIDLEY (i) (GB) 1901–1907
(1) John Ridley (afterwards Ridley Autocar Co Ltd), Coventry, Warwickshire *1901–1904*
(2) Ridley Motor Co Ltd, Paisley, Renfrewshire *1906–1907*

The Ridley was a very light two-seater using a 3½hp De Dion or 5hp Buchet engine, and an ingenious combined gearbox and back axle designed by John Ridley. After the failure of the Coventry company John Ridley ordered semi-finished chassis from Horsfall & Bickham, makers of the Horbick, to which he added his own design of single-cylinder water-cooled engine, and completed assembly at his private address in Paisley. A new company was formed in 1906, but few cars were sold. GNG

RIDLEY (ii) (GB) 1914
Thorofare Motors Ltd, Woodbridge, Suffolk

The Ridley light car was a neat-looking little vehicle with a Rolls-Royce-style radiator. It was powered by a 2-cylinder Blumfield engine, had friction transmission and belt final drive. GNG

RIEGEL (F) 1902
Transformations Automobiles Riegel, Paris

The Riegel was an *avant-train* unit for conversion of horse-drawn vehicles. Power came from a 10hp flat twin engine, which, with gearbox and wheels could be easily changed from one vehicle to another. GNG

RIEJU (E) 1954–1956
Rieju y Juanda SA, Figueras, Gerona

This motor-cycle factory produced a small number of minicars powered by 2-cylinder Hispano-Villiers engines. JRV

RIGAL (F) 1902–1903
English Motor Co, London W.

Originally shown by the British Germain company, the Rigal bore no resemblance to any Germain. Its single-cylinder De Dion engine and general appearance indicate that it was one of the many vehicles originating from Lacoste et Battmann. GNG

RIKAS (D) 1922–1923
Rikas Automobil-Werke, Berlin SW 68

The Rikas was a small car with a 4-cylinder 6/14PS engine which was built in limited numbers. HON

RIKER (US) 1896–1902
(1) Riker Electric Motor Co, Brooklyn, N.Y. *1896–1899*
(2) Riker Electric Vehicle Co, Elizabethport, N.J. *1899–1900*
(3) Riker Motor Vehicle Co, Elizabethport, N.J. *1901–1902*

One of A.L. Riker's first electric vehicles, a two-seater phaeton, won a race at Providence, R.I., running against several petrol-engined cars. This sporting tradition was continued in 1900 when a special low-slung torpedo racer established a number of records for electric cars, including the mile in 1 minute 46 seconds.

Production Rikers included two-seater runabouts, four-seater *dos-à-dos*, an enclosed coach driven from a hansom cab position, and heavy trucks. In December 1900 Riker merged with the Electric Vehicle Co, makers of the Columbia, and only the trucks were continued under the Riker name. After A.L. Riker sold his company to the Electric Vehicle Co, he offered them his designs for a petrol car. They were not interested, so he formed the Riker Motor Vehicle Co. The first car from this company was an 8hp 2-cylinder machine with chain drive, followed later in 1901 by a 16hp 4-cylinder car. This design was the basis of the first Locomobile petrol-engined car. Riker was also concerned with the Overman Automobile Co, which made a few cars before the works were taken over by Stevens-Duryea. GNG

RILEY (GB) 1898–1969
(1) Riley Cycle Co Ltd, Coventry, Warwickshire *1898–1912*
(2) Riley (Coventry) Ltd, Coventry, Warwickshire *1912–1948*
(3) Riley Motors Ltd, Abingdon, Berks. *1948–1969*

The first Riley car was a small single-cylinder belt-driven voiturette which did not go into production. Motor tricycles followed in 1900, and a handlebar-steered tricar with 2 forward speeds, and a 517cc engine with mechanically-operated inlet valves in 1903. Tricars were made until 1907, later examples being twins with driver's seats in place of saddles, water cooling and wheel steering. The 1,034cc V-twin engine was also fitted to the company's first 4-wheelers, which had amidships-mounted power units with their gearboxes alongside and chain drive, and sold for £168. Bigger V-twins of 2 litres' capacity, more conventional layout and round radiators were made from 1908 onwards. These incorporated pressure lubrication, shaft drive, constant-mesh 3-speed gearboxes, and Riley's own patent detachable wheels, the demand for which brought car production almost to a standstill and was responsible for the formation of the new company in 1912. In 1914 the 2-cylinder cars were still being made, but there was also a new 2.9-litre sv monobloc four with worm drive, which was offered again after World War 1 by the Riley Engine Co, though it soon disappeared from the market.

The first post-war Rileys were the Elevens with sv 1½-litre 35bhp engines, alloy pistons and full electrical equipment which were selling for £550 in 1920, acquiring spiral bevel final drive in 1921. The Redwinger sports version with wire wheels and polished-aluminium coachwork appeared in 1923, offering 70mph for £450, and the sv cars were continued until 1928, with a 1,645cc engine and the option of front-wheel brakes in 1925. One of these Twelves was used to prospect Kenya's road system in 1926, and in 1927 there was even a supercharged development of the Redwinger available, though this was overshadowed by Percy Riley's advanced new Nine, with a 1087cc 32bhp 4-cylinder engine, twin camshafts and high push-rods, a unit which was to form the basis of all Riley designs made up to 1957.

In 1928 came the handsome Monaco fabric sports saloon version at £298, a best-seller from the start, and the lowered and tuned Brooklands sports, inspired by the late J.G. Parry Thomas, which weighed 1,120lb, had a twin-carburettor 50bhp engine, and was capable of 80mph, all for £395. A twin carburettor variant of the touring Nine followed in 1929, along with a new 1.6-litre 6-cylinder Fourteen of similar styling at £495.

Rileys had a distinguished competition record in the following years: class wins in the 1929, 1930, and 1931 Tourist Trophies were followed by Whitcroft's outright victory in 1932, while two more wins were recorded by F.W. Dixon on the later 1½-litre 4-cylinder in 1935 and 1936. A 4th place at Le Mans in 1933 led to 2nd, 3rd 5th, 6th, 12th and 13th places in 1934, not to mention three successive wins – 1934, 1935, and 1936 – in the B.R.D.C. 500 Mile Race at Brooklands. Leverett won the light-car class of the 1931 Monte Carlo Rally on a Nine, while the 6-cylinder racing Rileys of 1933–34 formed the genesis of the E.R.A., and nearly twenty years later the late Mike Hawthorn was to make his name in Club Racing on sports Nines and 1½-litres. Both the Nine and the 14-6 were progressively developed, the former acquiring vacuum feed in 1931, a lowered chassis and semi-panelled bodywork in 1932, and an optional (later standard) preselector gearbox in 1934. A super-sports 6-cylinder 1½-litre with water-cooled centre main bearing appeared in 1932, being followed in 1933 by the touring Mentone version at £348. 1933 also brought two advanced body styles, the fastback Kestrel saloon (listed up to the end of the old Riley company in 1938) and the more-conservatively styled Falcon on which the doors opened into the roof. A Salerni automatic transmission was offered on the 14-6, but did not go into regular production.

Two handsome sports two-seater variants were listed in 1934/35, the 9hp Imp on a 7ft 6in wheelbase and the 1,654cc 6-cylinder M.P.H. which gave over 90mph for £550, while a newcomer in 1935 was the classic 1½-litre Four with Wilson gearbox, rod-operated Girling brakes and centralized chassis lubrication, a best-seller in its class at £335, and available in single- and twin-carburettor versions: subsequent developments were the 85mph Sprite two-seater and the Kestrel-Sprite and Lynx-Sprite saloon and tourer which offered more room but the same highly-tuned engine for £398. A cheaper Nine, the Merlin with pressed-steel bodywork, came on the market in 1936, along with the 1½-litre, a 6-cylinder 6-15, and a 2.2-litre V-8, of which very few were made, its engine made up of two 9hp blocks. 1937 Nines came with new 6-light Monaco bodies and twin-carburettor 42bhp engines as standard, while other new models were an abortive 3-litre luxury V-8 made by a subsidiary company, Autovia Cars, and a more successful long-stroke 2.4-litre Big Four on classic lines, with an 85bhp engine and Borg-Warner 3-speed synchromesh gearbox incorporating an overdrive at £385. Overdrive was optional on 1938 1½ litres.

Finances, however, were insecure and Riley were acquired by the Nuffield Organization later in that year. Under the new management only the 1½-litre and the Big Four were continued, with disc wheels, conventional synchromesh gear-boxes and Wolseley-like bodywork. Their post-World War 2 successors used the same engines, but were altogether more handsome cars with independent torsion-bar front suspension and fabric tops, the bigger engine's output being boosted first to 90bhp and then to 100bhp: this unit was also used by Healey in the 1946–54 period, while some open three-seater versions with column change were made by Riley for export. Hypoid back axles and full hydraulic brakes were incorporated in 1952.

After the Nuffield-Austin amalgamation the 1½-litre was continued into 1955 with relatively little change, but the 1954 2½-litre Pathfinder shared its bodywork with Wolseley's 6-90, the new chassis being a B.M.C. design with coil rear suspension

1931 RILEY Brooklands Nine sports car. *Gerald Hennings*

1936 RILEY Lynx 1½-litre sports tourer. *G.N. Georgano*

1952 RILEY 1½-litre saloon. *National Motor Museum*

1966 RILEY Elf Mark 3 998cc saloon. *British Motor Corporation*

1915 RITZ 10hp two-seater. *David Filsell Collection*

1921 ROAMER 5-litre tourer. *National Motor Museum*

and cam-type steering. Even this disappeared after 1957 in favour of a version with a 2.6-litre 6-cylinder ohv B.M.C. engine, and subsequent Rileys were merely luxury versions of B.M.C. themes, starting with the One-Point-Five (basically a Wolseley 1500), and working through variations of the Farina-styled 1½-litre and 1.6-litre saloons, the Mini, and, from 1966, the 1100/1300 family with Hydrolastic suspension, known in Riley guise as the Kestrel. Riley's Mini, the Elf, had a built-out boot and (from 1963) a 998cc engine in place of the standard 848cc Austin/Morris type. This meaningless badge-engineering was stopped by British Leyland in 1969. MCS

RIP (F) *1908–1912*
SA des Voitures Automobiles Rip, Rive-de-Gier, Loire

The most unusual feature of the Rip was its suspension by transverse coil springs at front and rear. The engine was either a 5/6hp single, or a 10/12hp monobloc four. The cars were fitted with dashboard radiators and the bonnets were of the Renault type. GNG

RIPERT (F) *1899–1902*
Automobiles Ripert, Marseilles

Ripert cars were made in very small numbers in a little workshop in Marseilles. Two models were made, of 6 and 12hp, both using front-mounted 2-cylinder horizontal engines; 4 speeds were provided, and final drive was by belt. GNG

RITTER (US) *1912*
Ritter Automobile Co, Madison, Wisc.

This was listed for the year 1912 only, as a torpedo roadster using a 4-cylinder engine of 1.8 litres. The wheelbase was 7ft 6in and the price $685. GMN

RITZ (US) *1914–1915*
(1) Ritz Cyclecar Co, New York, N.Y. *1914*
(2) Driggs-Seabury Ordnance Corp, Sharon, Pa. *1915*

This cyclecar was claimed to be 'The Miniature Car for Everyone' although it carried only two passengers side-by-side. It had a V-twin engine of 10/12hp, tubular front axle, and quarter elliptic springs. Drive was by shaft, with planetary transmission. By 1915 a 1.2-litre four with sv monobloc engine and detachable head was selling in England for £120. GMN

RIVAT ET BOUCHARD (F) *c.1900*
Rivat et Bouchard, Lyons

This company produced a small number of motor cycles, and at least one voiturette, but proper production never started. GNG

RIVIERA *see* SCHNADER

R.L.C. (GB) *1920–1921*
Argyll (London) Motor & Engineering Co Ltd, Hornsey, London N.

The R.L.C. was an unconventional light car, made in the London service depot (not the Scottish factory) of Argyll. It used a 1,212cc 3-cylinder radial engine and friction drive. It was also known as the Rubury-Lindsay, after its designer Capt. J.M. Rubury, and A.H. Lindsay, manager of the Hornsey service station. TRN

R.M.C. *see* REGAL (ii)

R.N.W. (GB) *1951*
R.N.W. Products Ltd, Farnham, Surrey

Named after its designer R.N. Wellington, this was a two-seater minicar powered by a 197cc Villiers engine at the rear. The car had independent suspension all round, but only 2-wheel brakes. GNG

ROACH (US) *1899*
W.E. Roach (formerly Roach & Barnes), Philadelphia, Pa.

The Roach light car used a 2-cylinder engine mounted under the seat, wire wheels and tiller steering. Probably only prototypes were made. GNG

ROADER (US) *1911–1913*
Roader Car Co, Brockton, Mass.

The Roader was a small two-seater roadster with a 4-cylinder, 2.1-litre engine. With its wheelbase of about 8ft, and a price of $650, this appears to have been a forerunner of the light car which appeared after the cyclecar craze. Roader was an American term for a spirited horse. GMN

ROAMER (US) *1916–1930*
(1) Barley Mfg Co, Streator, Ill. *1916–1917*
(2) Barley Motor Car Co, Kalamazoo, Mich. *1917–1930*

Albert C. Barley, who earlier made the Halladay from Streator, Illinois, sold his Roamer frankly as a cheap Rolls-Royce – which it was in radiator shape if not in any other significant respect. It was an assembled car. By 1920, it was produced with four sizes of proprietary engine. The best-known was a 5-litre, 6-cylinder unit by Continental. The powerful 4-cylinder, horizontal-valve Rochester-Duesenberg engine and a Rutenber unit were also used in the period up to 1920. The rear suspension was by double cantilever springs – an unconventional touch. Touring and sport models were offered. From 1922 to 1925 a rather small six was sold, on its own: by this time, production of the Rochester-Duesenberg engine had stopped. By 1927, all Roamers were 4.9-litre straight-8s, and remained so to the end.

TRN

ROBE (i) (US) *1914*

W.B. Robe Co, Portsmouth, Ohio

The Robe cyclecar used a 4-cylinder, water-cooled engine and shaft drive. Further details are unknown.

GMN

ROBE (ii) (US) *1921*

W.B. Robe and J.D. Strong, Nansemond, Va.

W.B. Robe's second venture into car building concerned a small 4-cylinder car with suspension that consisted of a full-length leaf spring on each side, in the manner of the Curved Dash Oldsmobile. The cylinder block was made of 'Robe metal' (really aluminium), and Ford Model T valves and rear axle were used. Not more than four were made.

GNG

ROBERTS (US) *1915*

Roberts Motor Co, Sandusky, Ohio

The Roberts company was primarily concerned with the manufacture of proprietary petrol engines for use by other manufacturers, and offered a range of engines from 3 to 60hp. They had already been in business at least five years when the Roberts car was announced. It was fitted with a 6-cylinder 60hp engine of their own manufacture, the cylinders cast in pairs.

MJWW

ROBERT SERF (F) *1926–1933*

Automobiles Robert Serf, Colombey-les Belles, Meurthe-et-Moselle

The Robert Serf light car was made in two models, the 7CV with 1,470cc 4-stroke 4-cylinder engine, introduced in 1926, and the 4CV, powered by a 597cc 2-cylinder 2-stroke engine, introduced in 1933. The latter was available as an open two-seater, saloon, or light van. About 100 Robert Serf vehicles were made.

GNG

ROBERTSON (i) (GB) *c.1900–1902*

William Robertson & Sons Ltd, Dundee

This company was registered in 1900 with a capital of £12,000, and listed as a maker of tricycles, voiturettes and cars, but no details can be traced of their production.

GNG

ROBERTSON (ii) (GB) *1915–1916*

James Robertson, Manchester

Launched on the market after World War 1 had broken out, the Robertson cyclecar used an 8hp J.A.P. or Precision engine, a 2-speed gearbox, and chain final drive.

GNG

ROBERTS SIX (CDN) *1921*

Canadian Automobile Corp, Lachine, Que.

Several body styles of the Roberts Six were announced, to sell between $4,500 and $5,800. Possibly only a prototype was built.

HD

ROBIE (US) *1914*

Robie Motor Car Co, Detroit, Mich.

The Robie cyclecar used a 4-cylinder Perkins engine of 1.6 litres and was produced as a side-by-side two-seater. The only distinguishing feature was a rounded radiator, similar to that of the contemporary Delage Grand Prix car.

GMN

ROBINET (F) *1906–1907*

F. Robinet et Cie, Nantes, Loire-Inférieure

The Robinet was an extraordinary vehicle which was a cross between the sketchier voiturettes of the Paris-Madrid era, and the later cyclecars. It had a very narrow wooden frame with two seats in tandem; between the two seats was the engine, a 10hp V-twin Deckert which drove through a 2-speed Bozier gear and single chain. As in the Bédélia, the driver sat in the rear seat.

GNG

ROBINSON (i); **POPE-ROBINSON** (US) *1900–1904*

(1) John T. Robinson & Co, Hyde Park, Mass. *1900–1902*

(2) Robinson Motor Vehicle Co, Hyde Park, Mass. *1902*

(3) Pope-Robinson Co, Hyde Park, Mass. *1902–1904*

The Robinson superseded the Bramwell-Robinson. The early models were two-seaters with water-cooled 2.2-litre 2-cylinder engines behind the seat. The 1900 model had left-hand steering with an aluminium steering wheel. Later models were five-seater rear-entrance tonneaus, powered by 4-cylinder T-head engines of up to 4.4 litres. The final drive was by double chain. They were expensive, high-quality cars, among the best made in New England at that time.

GMN

1904 POPE-ROBINSON 24hp tonneau. *Dr Alfred Lewerenz*

1907 ROBINSON(ii) 12hp two-seater. *T. H. Tarling*

1913 R. & P. 6/8hp cyclecar. *G.N. Georgano Collection*

1922 ROB ROY 8hp two-seater. *Glasgow Museum of Transport*

1963 ROCHDALE Olympic coupé. *Rochdale Motor Panels*

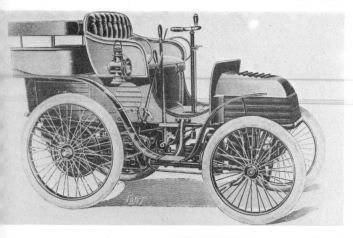

1900 ROCHET 9hp tonneau. *Geoffroy de Beaufort Collection*

ROBINSON (ii) (GB) 1907
Charles Robinson, Kettering, Northamptonshire

The Robinson was remarkable for the use of exhaust gases in the cooling system. The exhaust entered the 'radiator' at the bottom, and was cooled by a fan as it progressed to a header tank at the top. Here it mixed with cool air which was drawn into the tank by a circular orifice, and passed to the finned cylinder heads via a sheet-iron cowl. While it must have reduced the cooling effect of the fresh air, the exhaust accelerated the flow of air to the cylinders. Also this must be the only car in which the cooling system also acted as a silencer. Otherwise the Robinson was quite conventional with a 4-cylinder 12hp engine, shaft drive and a two-seater body. Of the three made, one survives today.　　　　GNG

ROBINSON & HOLE (GB) 1906–1907
Robinson & Hole Ltd, Thames Ditton, Surrey

Designed by Angus Maitland, who afterwards made the Beacon cyclecar, the Robinson & Hole used a 16/20hp, T-head 4-cylinder engine with a conventional chassis and shaft drive. Two- and five-seater touring cars were offered, but only six cars were made. A projected 24/30hp car was never completed.　　　　GNG

ROBINSON & PRICE (GB) 1905–1906; 1913
Robinson & Price Ltd, Liverpool

This company made two attempts at car manufacture, the first in 1905 with a 6½hp single-cylinder and a 10/12hp twin, both cars using Fafnir engines and shaft drive. Very few were made, and the company concentrated on general engineering and repair work until 1913. Then, with the coming of the cyclecar boom, they made a two-seater with a single-cylinder 6/8hp Coventry-Simplex engine and chain drive. This was generally known as the R. & P., a name sometimes given to the earlier cars.　　　　GNG

ROB ROY (GB) 1922–1926
Kennedy Motor Co, Ltd, Glasgow

The Rob Roy from Scotland, named after Sir Walter Scott's hero, started life as a cyclecar powered by the same 8hp water-cooled flat-twin engine that was installed in the Kingsbury Junior. In its later years, it grew up into a fully-fledged light car with 4-cylinder sv Coventry-Climax and Dorman engines of 10 and 12hp. In 1924, all three models were listed.　　　　TRN

ROBSON (US) 1908–1909
Robson Mfg Co, Galesburg, Ill.

The Robson was offered in four basic chassis with either single-, 2- or 4-cylinder engines. In the largest chassis was a 40/45hp, 4-cylinder engine, 3-speed selective transmission and shaft drive. Four body types were available in this chassis, including a two-seater 'beetle-backed' roadster.　　　　GMN

ROC *see* WALL

ROCH-BRAULT (F) 1898–1899
Sté Française d'Automobile Roch-Brault et Cie, Paris

Maurice Roch-Brault made a few examples of a petrol car which he built in collaboration with Gabriel Malliary, who later built a car under his own name at Puteaux. The Roch-Brault design was made in Belgium in 1899 by Vincke of Malines, under the name Vincke-Roch-Brault.　　　　LL

ROCHDALE (GB) 1957 to date
Rochdale Motor Panels and Engineering Ltd, Rochdale, Lancs.

The Rochdale started life as just another assembled or kit-built small car, with tubular frame and such body styles as the Riviera drophead coupé and the Olympic two/four-seater saloon. Then the firm distinguished itself by developing the Olympic into a true monocoque body-chassis unit, comprising a one-piece fibreglass moulding. At first, B.M.C. mechanical parts were fitted, the Riley 1.5-litre engine proving most popular. From 1963 the Mark 2 was available, with Triumph front suspension, and the Ford 116E engine was most in favour. Although no longer sold as a complete kit, this model was still available as a body-chassis unit in 1972, priced at £328, and altogether some 600 were sold.　　　　DF

ROCHESTER (US) 1901–1902
Rochester Cycle Manufacturing Co, Rochester, N.Y.

The Rochester was one of many light steam buggies of the period. It had a vertical 2-cylinder engine, single chain drive and tiller steering. Like most of its contemporaries, it had full elliptic springing at the rear, and a single transverse elliptic at the front, but an 'unusually flexible frame' was said to allow 15in of vertical movement by either front wheel without appreciable disturbance of body level.　　　　GNG

ROCHET; ROCHET-PETIT (F) 1899–c.1905
(1) Compagnie Generale des Cycles et Autos, Paris 11e
(2) Sté Rochet, Paris 11e

The first cars made by this firm were based on the designs of Edouard Rossel of Lille. They used front-mounted 2-cylinder engines 'of Daimler type' of 6/8hp, 4-speed gearboxes and double chain drive. In 1900 a 12hp was added, and a wide variety of body styles was available, including an enclosed limousine. Smaller cars with 4½hp single-cylinder Aster engines were made in 1902, and in 1904 Danneels of Ghent secured the licence to build Rochets for Belgium, Holland and Great Britain. GNG

ROCHET FRÈRES (F) 1898–1901
Rochet frères et Cie, Lyons

This company is sometimes confused with the Parisian Rochet, but their products were lighter, and fewer cars were made, although one survives in the collection of Henri Malartre. It is a light *vis-à-vis* with front-mounted single-cylinder De Dion engine, 3 speeds and belt final drive. GNG

ROCHET-SCHNEIDER (F) 1894–1932
SA des Etablissements Rochet-Schneider, Lyons

In its early years, the Rochet-Schneider copied successful designs as they came out. It started life as a derivation of the Benz, with a horizontal single-cylinder engine and belt drive, but its appearance was more like that of the contemporary Peugeot. At the 1901 Paris Salon, two cars of Panhard type were revealed: a 2-cylinder 8hp and a 12hp 4-cylinder. However, the most advanced type of car was now the Mercedes, so for 1903 the existing models were redesigned to follow Cannstatt practice, except for their armoured wood frames. What they lacked in originality, Rochet-Schneiders gained in power, good construction, and long life. From 1903, when the new 20/22hp was offered, they grew in reputation as strong, fast cars of conventional pattern.

A 4.4-litre live-axle 18hp joined the bigger chain-driven machines in 1906, and ht magneto ignition made its appearance in 1907, when the range was headed by a 10.9-litre chain-driven six with pair-cast cylinders. A year later the smaller cars had L-head monobloc power units. By 1911 this trend had spread to the bigger Rochet-Schneiders, among them a 4.8-litre 4-cylinder and a 5.5-litre six.

Six types were offered in 1914, with 4- and 6-cylinder monobloc engines of between 15 and 50hp. All had side valves. Commercial vehicles were also made. A range of equally stolid, but sturdy machines was offered after World War 1, in 12, 18 and 30hp forms. All were basically pre-war vehicles. From 1923, ohv engines were available on some models. By 1929, four 4-cylinder cars and a six were listed, the 14hp and 20hp with overhead valves.

The last new model was the 26 CV, a 4½-litre ohv six with dual ignition and servo brakes. With wire wheels and elegant coachwork, it was a very handsome vehicle, and with a smaller, 21CV six lasted until Rochet-Schneider abandoned private car production. Commercial vehicles were made until 1951, when the company was taken over by Berliet. The Rochet-Schneider was made under licence in its early days by four firms: Nagant and F.N. in Belgium, Florentia in Italy and Martini in Switzerland. TRN

RÖCK (H) 1905–1918
Stephen Röck Machinery Works, Budapest-Kelenföld

The Röck general machinery works built some models of Csonka cars, including the 16hp in which Stephen Röck did well in the 1909 Prince Henry Trial. From 1913 cars were built under German Lloyd licence, these being the 21/35 and 22/50hp models. GLH

ROCKAWAY see RAMBLER (i)

ROCKEFELLER YANKEE (US) 1949–1950
Rockefeller Sports Car Corp, Rockville Center, L.I.

This was a fibreglass four-seater sports car using the standard Ford V-8 engine together with many other Ford components such as axles, suspension and steering. The car could be supplied without engine and transmission for those buyers who wanted to fit a more powerful engine. Price of the car complete was $2,495. GNG

ROCKET (i) see SCRIPPS-BOOTH

ROCKET (ii) (US) 1948
Hewson Pacific Corp, Los Angeles, Calif.

The choice of a 4- or 6-cylinder rear engine was offered on this prototype, which was rather 'teardrop' in shape, and fitted with an early example of the padded instrument panel. BE

ROCK FALLS (US) 1919–1925
Rock Falls Mfg Co, Sterling, Ill.

Powered by a Continental 6-cylinder engine, these cars were mainly used as funeral cars. Less than 50 per year were manufactured. KM

ROCK HILL (US) 1910
Rock Hill Buggy Co, Rock Hill, S.C.

1903 ROCHET-SCHNEIDER 16hp tonneau.
The Veteran Car Club of Great Britain

1931 ROCHET-SCHNEIDER 4½-litre saloon.
Gili de Heredia

1913 RÖCK 21/25hp tourer.
G.L. Hartner Collection

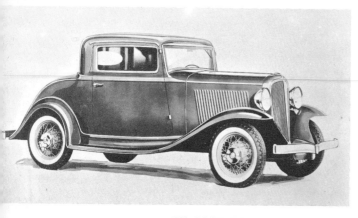

1932 ROCKNE 3.1-litre coupé. *Studebaker-Packard Corporation*

1932 RÖHR Type F 3.3-litre saloon. *Neubauer Collection*

This five-seater car, of toy tonneau design, was equipped with a 4.1-litre, 4-cylinder engine. It had 3-speed selective transmission and shaft drive. A peculiar option was the track: either the standard 4ft 8in, or 5ft. This car was an unsuccessful venture by this manufacturer who later, through a subsidiary, made the more successful Anderson (ii).

GMN

ROCKNE (US) 1931–1933
Rockne Motors Corp, Detroit, Mich.

The Rockne was in effect a small Studebaker. Apparently it was thought that a hero's name would sell the car: Knute Rockne, the great American football coach, held this position at Notre Dame University in South Bend, Ind., where the Studebaker Corporation was also based. In 1931 it was announced that Rockne had been appointed to the Studebaker staff as sales manager, but shortly afterwards he was killed in a plane crash and the Rockne Corporation was set up in Detroit. The cars had 3.1-litre 6-cylinder engines and a complete range of body styles at prices from $585 to $675. The 1933 models had wing mudflaps. The Rockne was withdrawn from the Studebaker list for 1934 after a total of 30,293 had been sold. KM

ROCOURT-MERLIN (F) 1900
Éts Rocourt et Merlin fils, Marseilles

Merlin was a coachbuilder who made a few cars powered by Abeille engines.

GNG

RODGERS see IMPERIAL (ii)

RODLEY (GB) 1954–1955
Rodley Automobile Co Ltd, Leeds, Yorks.

The Rodley light car was powered by a 750cc V-twin J.A.P. engine mounted at the rear, with final drive by chain. An angular coupé body was provided, which was claimed to be a four-seater, but the rear seats were very cramped. 50mpg and 50–60mph were advertised, and production was supposed to reach 50 per week, but in fact few were made.

GNG

ROEBLING-PLANCHE (US) 1906–1909
Walter Automobile Co, Trenton, N.J.

This car was an ancestor of the famous Mercer. The name Roebling came from the famous wire-rope family, and Planche from the French designer. Although this make used 4-cylinder engines exclusively, Roebling-Planche ranged from a 20hp, five-seater landaulet for $3,500 to a two-seater racing model with a massive engine rated at 120hp. This latter model cost $12,000.

GMN

ROGER (i) (F) 1888–1896
Emile Roger, Paris 17e

Emile Roger bought a Benz at the 1887 Paris Exposition, and the following year began to sell, and then to manufacture, them in France. Some of the parts may have been of French manufacture but design followed Mannheim exactly, early cars being 3-wheelers which gave way to 4-wheelers in 1894. By 1895 Roger was advertising cars of from two to ten passengers, so presumably the range extended up to the Benz 'omnibus'. The Macy-Roger, which competed unsuccessfully in the 1895 Chicago Times-Herald race, was in fact a French-built Roger, and so were the Anglo-French cars sold from premises in Birmingham, although the latter were sometimes claimed to be English cars. The early International (i) cars were also Rogers.

GNG

ROGER (ii) (GB) 1920–1924
Thomas Roger & Co Ltd, Wolverhampton, Staffs.

The Roger light car used a 10.8hp Coventry-Climax engine and friction drive. Front suspension was by a transverse semi-elliptic spring, and the two-seater cost £245 in 1922. Shaft drive was optional from 1923.

GNG

ROGERS (US) 1911–1912
Rogers Motor Car Co, Omaha, Nebr.

The Rogers was a two-seater, high-wheeler with an 18hp, air-cooled 2-cylinder engine. This was placed under the single seat and the drive was through friction transmission and double chains. With a surrey top, it cost $750.

GMN

RÖHR (D) 1928–1935
(1) Röhr Automobilwerke AG, Ober-Ramstadt 1928–1930
(2) Neue Röhrwerke AG, Ober-Ramstadt 1930–1935

This firm produced their cars in the former Falcon plants. The first model was the Type R of 1928 which was a sensation when it was introduced. A sheet-steel platform frame allowed a low centre of gravity and light weight. Suspension was by two transverse leaf springs for the front and semi-elliptic springs for the rear axle. The straight-8 engine of 2,262cc developed 50hp. H.G. Röhr was not able to make a success of this advanced car and had to resign from his firm in 1930. He was engaged by Adler and later went to Mercedes-Benz. The firm was re-established by a group of financiers. The 1931 Type RA had a 2.5-litre engine. A number of 2¼-litre engines and chassis were imported into the United Kingdom by Hampton who after assembling them and fitting their own bodies and radiators sold them as the Hampton R. It is said that 50 chassis and 100 engines were ordered, but it is unlikely that more than half a dozen were delivered. The Type F of 1932 had an 8-cylinder 3,287cc 75bhp engine. A small series of the Olympier version of this model, designed by Porsche, was also produced. The engine output was increased to 100bhp, or 140bhp with a Roots blower.

In 1932 Röhr acquired a Tatra licence and introduced the Junior with a 4-cylinder opposed engine of 1,486cc and 30bhp, centre tubular chassis and independent suspension. This model was produced from 1932 to 1935 but new financial troubles resulted in production of this promising car coming to an end. The Tatra licence was taken over by Stoewer who also bought up a number of half-finished Röhr Junior cars, which after completion were distributed by Stoewer as the Greif Junior.　　HON

ROLAND (D) 1907
Kraftwagen-Gesellschaft Roland, Berlin-Wilmersdort

A single-cylinder and a 2-cylinder model of voiturette type were offered by this company, but no further details are known.　　HON

ROLLAND-PILAIN (F) 1906–1931
SA des Etablissements Rolland-Pilain, Tours

1921 ROLLAND-PILAIN 18CV coupé de ville.
Autocar

Unusual among French marques of its period, Rolland-Pilain made their greatest impact after World War 1. Their first product was a 20hp 4-cylinder model with a monobloc engine, though smaller 2.2-litre shaft-driven cars were available in 1909 and a 3-speed 1½-litre 8/10CV in 1910, in which year the company was also experimenting with 'valveless' engines and 4-wheel brakes. Though racing was in the doldrums, they went to the trouble of building a big chain-driven car for the 1911 Grand Prix de France, and a complex 1912 range started with a 9CV of 1.7 litres and went up to a chain-driven 4-cylinder 60 of 130 × 270mm. The 6-cylinder 18CV had a 'valveless' engine, and even in 1913 chain drive was still optional on the biggest fours of 20CV and 24CV. Only 1.9-litre and 4-litre 4-cylinder cars with sv monobloc engines and unit gearboxes were listed in 1914.

These basic types, still with pedal-operated transmission brakes, were available again after World War 1, but far more advanced was the 2.2-litre 14/16 of 1921, which boasted not only overhead valves and a detachable head, but also front-wheel brakes (hydraulic at the front and mechanical at the rear). This car was still catalogued in 1926. Even more ambitious was the 2-litre twin ohc straight-8 GP car of 1922, with desmodromic valves, ball-bearing crankshafts and 4-wheel hydraulic brakes. A victory at San Sebastian in 1923 was the limit of their success on the circuits, but the type found its way into the catalogue as the Type A22 at 90,000fr, and one of the racers also ran with a 2-litre, 6-cylinder cuff-valve Schmid engine. In 1925 came a 2-litre ohv 4-cylinder with 4-wheel mechanical brakes, selling for £725 in England, while a 1½-litre development, the D26, was introduced for 1927. In 1929 Rolland-Pilain, along with several other French firms, tried a Franco-American theme by introducing a range of big luxury chassis with sv Continental engines. Both the 6-cylinder, 3-litre, and the 4-litre straight-8 had centralized chassis lubrication, though the elegant bodywork was marred by the use of artillery wheels. At the 1930 Paris Salon the Rolland-Pilain shared a stand with the B.N.C. (also going through a Franco-American phase), but this was the end, though the firm's Paris depot was still advertising spare parts for Bignan as well as Rolland-Pilain in 1934.　　MCS

1933 ROLLFIX 200cc coupé. *Neubauer Collection*

ROLLFIX (D) 1933–1936
(1) Rollfix-Eilwagen GmbH, Hamburg-Wandsbek *1933–1934*
(2) Rollfix-Werke Frederic Schröder KG, Hamburg-Wandsbek *1934–1936*

A two-seater 3-wheeler Rollfix appeared in 1933 with its single rear wheel driven by a 200cc Ilo engine. Another model was a 3-wheeled estate car with a rear-mounted engine and two driven rear wheels.　　HON

ROLLIN (US) 1923–1925
Rollin Motor Co, Cleveland, Ohio

Rollin White had been chief engineer of the White company before he made his own cars. These were of European rather than American type, with an efficient 4-cylinder, 4-bearing, 2.4-litre engine, low fuel consumption, 4-wheel brakes and low-pressure tyres. The engine was similar to that used in the Cletrac 'F' tractor: both companies operated under the same roof. The quality in general was extremely high, and the price low ($975 in 1923), but the Rollin's 'foreignness' told against it.　　TRN

1924 ROLLIN 16/45hp sedan. *Autocar*

ROLLING *see* DUPRESSOIR

ROLLO (GB) 1911–1913
Rollo Car Co Ltd, Birmingham

The Rollo cyclecar was made in two models, a monocar powered by a 4½hp Precision single-cylinder engine, and a tandem two-seater powered by an 8hp J.A.P. engine. Both models used tubular frames and belt final drive. In 1913 a side-by-side two-seater was also available; prices ranged from £73 for the monocar to £105 for the side-by-side two-seater.　　GNG

1913 ROLLO 8hp cyclecar. *The Veteran Car Club of Great Britain*

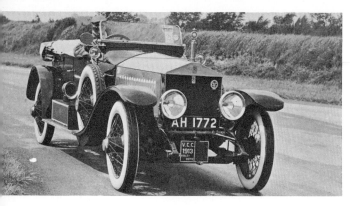

1913 ROLLS-ROYCE(i) Silver Ghost Continental tourer. *National Motor Museum*

1923 ROLLS-ROYCE(i) Twenty limousine. Coachwork by Barker. *National Motor Museum*

1929 ROLLS-ROYCE(i) 20/25hp coupé. Coachwork by Weymann. *National Motor Museum*

1931 ROLLS-ROYCE(i) Phantom II coupé. Coachwork by Weymann. *National Motor Museum*

ROLLSMOBILE (US) *1958 to date*

(1) Starts Mfg Co, Fort Lauderdale, Fla. *1958–c.1960*
(2) Horseless Carriage Corp, Fort Lauderdale, Fla. *c.1960 to date*

Using 3hp Continental air-cooled engines, Rollsmobiles are built as 3/4 scale replicas of the 1901 Oldsmobile and the 1901 Ford. Equipped with automatic transmissions and sealed-beam headlights, the cars may be licensed for highway travel. Bodies with mahogany overlay and 20in chrome-plated sulky wheels add a touch of authenticity to this modern 'antique'. Cruising speed is reported to be 30mph and fuel consumption 100mpg.

BE

ROLLS-ROYCE (i) (GB) *1904 to date*

(1) Royce Ltd, Manchester *1904–1906*
(2) Rolls-Royce Ltd, Manchester *1906–1908*
(3) Rolls-Royce Ltd, Derby *1908–1945*
(4) Rolls-Royce Ltd, Crewe, Cheshire *1946–1971*
(5) Rolls-Royce Motors (1971) Ltd, Crewe, Cheshire *1971 to date*

The Rolls-Royce was the result of a meeting between Henry Royce, a manufacturer of electric cranes in Manchester, and the Hon. C.S. Rolls, a pioneer motorist then selling Panhards in London, who wanted a quality car to boost falling sales. The first cars were based on the 1.8-litre (later enlarged to 2-litre) vertical-twin 10hp ioe Royce with shaft drive, but the range was expanded to embrace a 3-litre, 3-cylinder, 'light' and 'heavy' versions of a 4-cylinder Twenty, and a 6-litre pair-cast six retailing at £900. A Light Twenty with geared-up top, driven by Rolls, won the 1906 Tourist Trophy, and also broke the Monte Carlo-London record.

An abortive 3½-litre V-8 petrol brougham with square cylinder dimensions was shown in 1905, but 1906 was the start of a one-model policy based on the 40/50hp 6-cylinder, later to win immortality as the Silver Ghost, which made its début at Olympia that year. This had a conventional 7-litre sv engine with pressure lubrication and dual ignition, as well as the 4-speed overdrive gearbox. Output was a modest 48bhp, but the car's reputation was assured after a successful 15,000 mile R.A.C.-observed trial in 1907, from which the Ghost emerged with flying colours: the first ones at Manchester, and from 1908 on at Derby. At £985 for a chassis it was backed by a unique inspection scheme, and in mid-1909 it was revised with a longer-stroke 7.4-litre engine and conventional 3-speed box. The cars reverted to 4 speeds in 1913, when cantilever rear suspension was adopted; later modifications were full electrics (1919) and Hispano-Suiza-type mechanical servo 4-wheel brakes (1924). The 'Best Car In The World' – a reputation well established by 1914 – was not normally entered in competitions, but in 1911 a car was successfully driven from London to Edinburgh and back on top gear for a fuel consumption of 24.32mpg, and a works team swept the board in the 1913 Austrian Alpine Trials. Armoured-car versions of the Ghost gave yeoman service both during and after World War 1.

Production was resumed after the Armistice, the chassis price being inflated to £2,100. In 1920 an American factory was opened, this making the Rolls-Royce (ii) until 1931. Post-war inflation led Rolls-Royce to abandon their one-model policy in 1922 and to introduce a 3.1-litre ohv 6-cylinder Twenty with a 3-speed unit gearbox and central change at £1,100 for a chassis. This was regarded by Rolls-Royce enthusiasts as heresy, but the Twenty was an excellent if sluggish car which lost none of the traditional quality; nearly 3,000 were made up to 1929. In 1925 it acquired a 4-speed box, right-hand change, and the servo 4-wheel brakes of the Ghost, which was retired that year in favour of a 7.7-litre Phantom I with overhead valves and vertical radiator shutters. An improved Phantom II with hypoid back axle and redesigned combustion chambers was listed for 1930, while the Twenty emerged as the more powerful 20/25 with a 3.7-litre engine. A Continental version of the bigger car gave a genuine 90mph with closed coachwork. Refinements of the early 1930s included synchromesh (on the 20/25 in 1932, and on the Phantom a year later), and centralized chassis lubrication (1933).

In 1931 the company bought Bentley Motors, after Napier had made an unsuccessful bid. The Bentley emerged two years later as a Rolls-Royce-based 3½-litre: it was not to lose its identity until the 1950s. Sir Henry Royce died in 1933, and the entwined 'R's of the radiator emblem were changed from red to black, supposedly in mourning. The smaller Rolls-Royces acquired hypoid final drive in 1936, in which year an alternative power unit of 4¼-litres' capacity was offered, first as an option, and then as standard: thus the 20/25 grew up into the 25/30. In this year Rolls-Royce stopped making their own carburettors, though electrical equipment was not bought out until after World War 2. Aero-engine influence (the company had been making these units since 1914 and had been responsible both for the Schneider Trophy R engine of 1931 and the Merlin of 1935) was reflected in the 12-cylinder Phantom III first shown in 1935. Its capacity was 7.3 litres, and it was the first Rolls-Royce to have independent front suspension. Later examples had overdrive gearboxes. It offered 90–95mph for £2,600 and up. This model was still being made in 1939, along with a development of the 25/30, with independent front suspension, the Wraith, which could be bought for around £1,600 complete.

Post-war production was transferred from Derby to Crewe and the first new model was the Silver Wraith, with a 4¼-litre engine, overhead inlet valves and hydraulic actuation for the front brakes, costing around £4,300 in 1947. The

Phantom III was not revived, but sixteen ioe 5.7-litre straight-8 Phantom IVs were made for heads of state from 1949 onwards. Among the customers was H.R.H. Princess Elizabeth, who was to become the first reigning British monarch to use Rolls-Royces officially. The 6-cylinder cars continued up to 1959. 1949 brought the first factory-bodied model, the export-only Silver Dawn, using the standard Bentley saloon body, left-hand drive, and steering-column change. In 1952 capacity went up to 4.6 litres and a long-chassis version was listed with an 11ft 1in wheelbase. The General Motors Hydramatic transmission became an option in 1953, and the famous manual box with right-hand control was finally dropped two years later with the advent of a 4.9-litre Silver Cloud, a restyled saloon with 15in wheels, which could be bought with power-assisted steering and full air conditioning. 1960 cars were identical in outward appearance, but were powered by entirely new over-square alloy 6.2-litre V-8 engines. Power-assisted steering was now standard, though the hydro-mechanical servo brakes were retained. The standard saloon cost £6,093, and a limousine version on a 12ft wheelbase, the Phantom V, was some £3,000 dearer. A four-headlamp layout was introduced in 1963, and a year later Rolls-Royce started to supply a 4-litre version of their ioe 6-cylinder engine to B.M.C. for installation in the Vanden Plas Princess.

At the 1965 Shows Rolls-Royce introduced an entirely up-to-date design, the Silver Shadow. This boasted unitary construction, self-levelling, all-round independent suspension, and servo-assisted disc brakes with three separate circuits. It retained the 1960 V-8 engine, also the (now dummy) traditional radiator. The Phantom V with its separate chassis was kept on, a ceremonial limousine for heads of state being listed at £10,695. A Silver Shadow convertible was available in 1968 for £10,449; 1969 brought both a long-wheelbase version of the model and the enlargement of the engine to 6,745cc. In 1970 a new 3-speed automatic gearbox (already used on lhd export models since late 1965) replaced the earlier 4-speed type, and the Phantom VI replaced the Phantom V; production of these state carriages ran at about 50 units a year. Similar modifications were applied to the parallel Bentleys. The sensational bankruptcy of February 1971 found the Car Division still profitable; indeed, within a month the company had announced their high-performance Corniche 2-door saloon and convertible with coachwork by H.J. Mulliner-Park Ward, at prices from £12,829 upward, and that December the 10,000th Silver Shadow left Crewe. By late 1972 prices of the more expensive models had risen to £14,399 for the Corniche and £15,559 for the Phantom limousine.   MCS

ROLLS-ROYCE (ii) (US) 1921–1931
Rolls-Royce of America Inc, Springfield, Mass.

The American Rolls-Royce company was formed in November 1919 to build the famous British cars in an American factory and so avoid high import duties. The plant was bought from the American Wire Wheel Co, and the Silver Ghost went into production there in 1921. It had a 6-cylinder 7.4-litre sv engine developing 80bhp, and came in two wheelbases, 12ft and 12ft 6½in. Right-hand drive was used until 1923. Unlike the British company, Rolls-Royce of America always advertised coachwork and supplied complete cars if customers wished. Most bodies were by Brewster, and in 1926 this firm was taken over by Rolls-Royce. In 1926 came the New Phantom, or Phantom I as it was later called. This had a 6-cylinder 7.7-litre engine with overhead valves, and again came in two wheelbases, 11ft 11½in and 12ft 2½in. The Depression badly hit sales of the American Rolls-Royce, and production at Springfield came to an end in 1931, although a few British cars were assembled there later. A total of 2,944 American Rolls-Royces was made, of which 1,703 were Silver Ghosts and 1,241 were Phantom Is.   GNG

ROLUX (F) 1938–1952
P. Martin, Lyons

The Rolux was a very small minicar powered by a 125cc single-cylinder air-cooled engine mounted at the rear. It was probably unique at the time of its introduction in 1938, but found itself quite in the fashion during the minicar boom of the late 1940s. The private cars had very simple doorless two-seater bodies, and commercial versions were also made. About 1,000 Roluxes were made before the company returned to making the goods-carrying tricycles and New-Map motor cycles which had always been their main business.   GNG

ROMANELLI (CDN) 1970
Romanelli Motors Ltd, Montreal, Que.

Designed and built by Francesco Romanelli, an Italian immigrant to Montreal, this was an ambitious sports car using its own design of 6-litre V-12 engine of cast aluminium alloy which developed 520bhp. A 5-speed Romanelli-designed transaxle gave a maximum speed of 203mph on top gear. The car had a fibreglass two-seater coupé body, and sold for $9,000. Only the prototype was built.   GNG

ROMER (US) 1921
Romer Motors Corp, Danvers, Mass.

The Romer was an assembled car with a Continental 6-cylinder engine and other components, sold at prices ranging from $1,975 to $2,700. The car was discontinued late in 1921 although the company went on to make a few 1¼-ton trucks, production of these continuing until mid-1922.   KM

1938 ROLLS-ROYCE(i) Phantom III sedanca de ville. Coachwork by Barker. *National Motor Museum*

1950 ROLLS-ROYCE(i) Silver Wraith saloon. Coachwork by Park Ward. *Autosport*

1968 ROLLS-ROYCE(i) Phantom V limousine. Coachwork by H.J. Mulliner, Park Ward. *Rolls-Royce Ltd*

1928 ROLLS-ROYCE(ii) Phantom I speedster phaeton. Coachwork by Brewster. *National Motor Museum*

1912 RONTEIX 8hp chummy four-seater.
Autocar

1929 ROOSEVELT 3.3 litre sedan. *National Motor Museum*

1935 ROSENGART LR14S 1.6-litre saloon. *Jacques Kupélian Collection*

RONTEIX (F) *1906–1914*

J. Ronteix, Levallois-Perret, Seine

The Ronteix light car originally used a 905cc 4-cylinder engine, transverse leaf front suspension and an unusual change speed mechanism. The clutch shaft ended in a bevel which could be made to mesh with any of three rows of teeth on the crown wheel. This system, also used by Sizaire-Naudin, was employed on the Ronteix up to 1913 when it was replaced by a normal sliding gearbox. In the 1913 Cyclecar Grand Prix at Le Mans Ronteix cars finished first and fourth. Production cars for 1913 and 1914 had engines of 966, 1,130 and 1,460cc. They had shaft drive, but chain drive was said to be available at a reduced price. The smaller car was sold in England as the Cummikar.   GNG

ROO (AUS) *1917–1919*

Roo Motor Car Manufacturing Co, Sydney, N.S.W.

The Roo was a light car powered by a flat-twin engine and using an underslung chassis. A consumption of 50mpg was claimed, and large-scale production planned, but only two and a half cars were built.   GNG

ROOSEVELT (US) *1929–1931*

Marmon Motor Co, Indianapolis, Ind.

The Roosevelt, named after President Theodore Roosevelt, was in fact the smallest of the Marmon line, and was introduced on New Year's Day, 1929. With its trim lines and horizontal bonnet louvres, it closely resembled the smaller Peerless or Stutz of the time and was the only straight-8 priced at under $1,000. The 1930 Roosevelt was renamed the Marmon-Roosevelt and the radiator emblem embodying the late President's likeness was dropped. The line was discontinued early in 1931.   KM

ROOTS & VENABLES (GB) *1896–1904*

Roots Oil Motor & Motor Car Co, London S.E.

The first Roots car was on the road early in 1896. It was a tiller-steered 3-wheeler powered by a $2\frac{1}{4}$hp vertical single-cylinder oil engine. By April 1897 Roots & Venables were making a 4-wheeler two-seater or four-seater *dos-à-dos* with a 3hp oil engine, chain drive and tiller steering. At this time the only other British firms delivering cars for sale were Daimler, the Coventry Motor Company (Coventry Bollée), and Petter; of these, two were based on foreign designs. As production facilities were inadequate, many parts for Roots cars were made by the Birmingham Small Arms Company, while from 1902 the cars were, in fact, made by Armstrong-Whitworth. Rear-engined cars of 3 and 6hp were made in 1900, and by early 1902 there were two front-engined models. The range consisted of the old $3\frac{1}{2}$hp rear-engined model on solid tyres, a $4\frac{1}{2}$hp front-engined car, also on solids, and a 7hp front-engined car on pneumatics. They still used heavy oil exclusively, and a $4\frac{1}{2}$hp car was the only oil-engined vehicle to compete in the 1903 1,000 Miles Trial. For 1904, their last year of production, two models were made, with a 5hp single-cylinder engine, and a 12hp 2-cylinder vertical engine.   GNG

ROPER-CORBET (GB) *1911–1912*

The origin of this car is uncertain, but it was sold by the London & Parisian Motor Co Ltd, whose managing director was Capt. Bertram Corbet. It was a conventional machine with a 15.9hp 4-cylinder engine and a Rolls-Royce type radiator. One was shown at the 1911 Olympia Show on the stand of Melhuish & Company, the coachbuilders.   GNG

ROSE NATIONAL *see* NATIONAL (ii)

ROSENGART (F) *1928–1955*

(1) Automobiles L. Rosengart, Neuilly-sur-Seine *1928–1937*
(2) Société Industrielle de l'Ouest Parisienne, Paris *1937–1955*

The first Rosengarts were made in the old Bellanger factory under the direction of Lucien Rosengart and Jules Salomon (the designer of the original Citroëns). They were Austin Sevens built under licence, and differed from their British prototypes mainly in matters of styling: for example the ribbon radiator shells, not adopted by Birmingham until late 1930. Production had reached 28 cars a day by the summer of 1930, and the Austin theme was continued until the end of pre-World War 2 production, though 1932 and subsequent cars had a longer wheelbase and semi-elliptic rear suspension. By 1939, when a roadster could be bought for the equivalent of £78, the chassis had channel-section side members. In the 1932 range there was also a 1,100cc 20bhp 6-cylinder, which was virtually an elongated 5CV with 3-speed gearbox and vacuum-servo brakes. A line of fwd 4-cylinder sv cars began in 1933, with transverse independent front suspensions, built under Adler licence and based on the German company's 1.6-litre Trumpf. A more conventional rear-driven version was sold as the '8/40'.

Fwd cars were still marketed in 1939, but by this time they were based on the 11CV Citroën, from which they derived their 1.9-litre ohv engines, 3-speed synchromesh gearboxes, and hydraulic brakes. Sporting 2-door saloon and cabriolet bodies were mounted on a platform-type chassis. Similar bodies were used on the 1947

Super-Trahuit, but the Super-Traction fwd structure now housed a 95bhp 3.9-litre sv Mercury (vi) engine. Such a car was an unrealistic proposition in the prevailing economic climate, and 1952 brought a return to the Austin Seven theme – the sv 747cc engine now gave 21bhp, and the Ariette and Artisane saloons had modern styling, transverse independent front suspension and hydraulic brakes. Speeds of 60mph were claimed.

The last of the line, the Sagaie of 1954, abandoned the old sv four in favour of a 40bhp, 750cc, ohv air-cooled flat-twin engine. Saloon and convertible models were made, and it was said to do 75mph, but failed to compete with Renault and Panhard. MCS

ROSS (i) (US) 1905–1909
Louis S. Ross, Newtonville, Mass.

The Ross steamer used a single-acting 2-cylinder engine of 2.1-litres, rated at 25hp at an operating pressure of 375psi. The main model was a wooden-bodied five-seater touring car. It weighed 2,800lb and was priced at $2,800. In 1908 a two-seater runabout was also built, for $2,250. GMN

ROSS (ii) (US) 1915–1918
(1) Ross & Young Machine Co, Detroit, Mich. 1915
(2) Ross Automobile Co, Detroit, Mich. 1915–1918

The original Ross was a five-seater, with a Herschell-Spillman V-8 engine of 3.7 litres, rated at 45hp, which sold for $1,350. Later models used a Continental 6-cylinder, 5.2-litre engine. The Ross was an assembled car, although six body styles were offered, both open and closed. GMN

ROSSEL (i) (F) 1898–1899
Edouard Rossel, Lille

Rossel's first car had a Daimler vertical engine, but in 1899 he built one using a power unit of his own design. Rights to manufacture this were sold to Rochet of Paris, and as their first cars were said to have engines 'of Daimler type', Rossel had probably not changed radically the original Daimler design. After selling his petrol-car designs, he made steam tractors for pulling canal barges. GNG

ROSSEL (ii) (F) 1903–1926
(1) F. Rossel et Cie, Sochaux-Montbéliard, Doubs
(2) SA des Automobiles Rossel, Sochaux-Montbéliard, Doubs

The Rossel was designed by a Peugeot engineer who retained his links with that company, forming a joint company to make aero engines in 1910, and eventually selling his works to them. The first Rossel car had a 22hp 4-cylinder engine with square dimensions (108 × 108mm), and chain drive. By 1905 a slightly larger 22/26hp and a 28/35hp, the latter with over square dimensions of 120 × 110mm were listed, and 1906 brought yet larger cars of 40/50 and 50/65hp. The largest Rossel was the 6-cylinder 60/80hp (12 litres) of 1907.

This range was continued for several years, but by 1910 smaller shaft-drive cars of 10, 12 and 16hp were available. Cylinder dimensions of these cars were more conventionally long-stroke (75 × 150mm for the 12) although an oversquare six (120 × 110mm) of 40hp was continued at least until 1913. The larger cars still had chain drive at the outbreak of World War 1.

Post-war Rossels showed no modern ideas, and the range varied from the old 12hp to a 25hp 4 of 5½ litres' capacity. The final model was a 3½-litre six introduced in 1923, but the marque had no particular quality to attract buyers, and in 1926 the factory was sold to Peugeot. GNG

ROSSELLI (I) 1899–1904
Emmanuel A. Rosselli Fabbrica Italiana di Automobili, Turin

Rosselli made a few motorcycles and voiturettes powered by V-twin engines of 3 to 7hp. GNG

ROTARY (i) (US) 1904–1905
Rotary Motor Vehicle Co, Boston, Mass.

Despite its name, the Rotary did not use a revolving engine in the manner of the Adams-Farwell, but its design was unorthodox enough. It had an 8hp single-cylinder vertical engine with two connecting rods and two crankshafts. The latter were geared to a central shaft which drove a conventional gearbox and live axle. The design was supposed to eliminate vibration. An alternative, and perhaps appropriate, name for the car was Intrepid. GNG

ROTARY (ii) (US) 1922–1923
Bournonville Motors Co, Hoboken, N.J.

The Rotary touring car, powered by a 5-litre 6-cylinder, rotary-valve engine of the company's own manufacture, cost $6,000 when introduced, but was available at $3,800 in 1923. The rotary-valve principle as used in the car was invented by Eugene Bournonville, president of the company, as early as 1914. The solid sleeve which was the rule in the heads of most sleeve-valve engines was changed to an adjustable sleeve and shoe which acted as a seal. Few of these rakish looking cars, designed by Bournonville himself, were built. KM

1938 ROSENGART LR-4 7hp saloon. *G.N. Georgano*

1951 ROSENGART Ariette 7hp drophead coupé. *Autocar*

1914 ROSSEL(ii) 12/14hp two-seater. *Autocar*

1910 ROTHWELL 25hp tourer. *P.N. Stott*

1949 ROUSSEY 700cc saloon. *Autocar*

1908 ROVER 20hp landaulette. *The Rover Co Ltd (courtesy H.B. Light)*

1912 ROVER 12hp tourer. *G.N. Georgano*

ROTHWELL (GB) *1901–1916*

Eclipse Machine Co Ltd, Oldham, Lancs.

After some unsuccessful experiments with a Pennington-designed front-wheel-drive car, the Rothwell brothers produced a conventional 6hp single-cylinder light car at the end of 1901, followed by larger 12 and 15hp 4-cylinder vehicles. The most successful Rothwell was the 25hp produced from 1910 to 1916. This was a sturdily built car with a 4-cylinder engine of Rothwell's own design and manufacture, using dual ignition. Alternative axle ratios were available, and prices ranged from £335 for a two-seater to £575 for the long-wheelbase ¾ landaulette. About 600 Rothwells were made in all.　　　　GNG

ROUGH (GB) *1899–1900*

R. Rough & Co, Hereford

The Rough car used a 2hp engine and friction transmission. A few experimental cars were built, and Rough planned to enter one in the 1900 1,000 Miles Trial. Although production was planned, it never started.　　　　GNG

ROUSSEL (F) *c.1908–1914*

Etablissements Roussel, Charleville, Ardennes

This company made conventional light cars in 10 and 12hp sizes, both with 4-cylinder engines. Two- and four-seater bodies were available.　　　　GNG

ROUSSEY (F) *1949–1950*

Roussey frères, Meudon, Seine-et-Oise

The Roussey light car used a 700cc horizontally-opposed 4-cylinder 2-stroke engine, driving the front wheels. The only model was a 2-door saloon.　　　　GNG

ROUSSON (F) *c.1910–1914*

Rousson et Chamoix, Feurs, Loire

Rousson cars were conventional 4-cylinder machines. The 1913 range consisted of five models, ranging from a 8CV of 1,460cc to a 16CV of 3,632cc. All cars had monobloc engines, and were available with two- and four-seater open coachwork.　　　　GNG

ROUXEL (F) *1899*

Rouxel et Cie, Boulogne-sur-Seine

The Rouxel was a voiturette powered by a single-cylinder 2¼hp Aster engine. It had cycle-type wheels, and a very light appearance.　　　　GNG

ROVER (GB) *1904 to date*

(1) The Rover Co Ltd, Coventry, Warwickshire; Birmingham *1904–1945; 1919–1925*
(2) The Rover Co Ltd, Solihull, Warwickshire *1945 to date*

This famous cycle firm (which built J.K. Starley's electric car in 1888) was offering tricars of conventional design in 1903, progressing from machines with cycle-type frames and belt drive to water-cooled and wheel-steered twins at £85 in 1905. The firm's first production 4-wheeler was an interesting 8hp 'single', the work of E.W. Lewis, which appeared in 1904. It had a tubular backbone frame, column change, a camshaft brake, and wire-and-bobbin steering, soon replaced by rack-and-pinion type. A smaller and less powerful 6hp followed at £105; one of the 8hp cars was used by Dr Jefferson in 1906 to drive from London to Constantinople.

The first 4-cylinder Rover was a 16/20hp with shaft drive and 3.1-litre engine, followed by a small monobloc 10/12. In 1907 the shield-shaped radiator was introduced, vestiges of which survived until 1949. Courtis won that year's TT on a 20hp of conventional design which was listed at a modest £400. The 8hp had acquired right-hand change by 1908, though the camshaft brake persisted, while in addition to the singles and the 20hp there were conventional L-head models of 1.6 and 2.5 litres in 1909. Rover's own detachable wheels were optional in 1910, and in 1911 the 15hp 4-cylinder went over to pressure lubrication. Knight sleeve-valve engines were adopted, on an alternative version of the 8hp (it cost £30 more than its poppet-valve counterpart), and on a new vertical-twin 1.9-litre 12hp. 1912 was the last year of the singles and twins, a new era arriving with the Clegg-designed 2.3-litre 4-cylinder monobloc 12hp at £350. This had worm drive, inlet ports cast in the head, a water-jacketed carburettor, and electric lighting, and was the only model offered by 1914. It survived in the range until 1924, being known latterly as the Fourteen. Later cars had their headlamps attached to the radiator shell.

Rover built 12/16hp Sunbeams to War Department account between 1914 and 1918, but reverted to the small economy class in 1920 with a near-cyclecar, the Eight, powered by a 1-litre (later enlarged to 1,130cc) flat-twin air-cooled sv unit, and retaining the 12hp Rover's worm final drive. It was made under licence in Germany by Peter and Moritz. Some 17,000 were sold up to 1925, prices dropping steadily from £300 to £160. Electric starters were not optional until 1923, and were never standardized. Its successor was an ohv water-cooled in-line four, the 9/20, which cost £215, acquired front-wheel brakes in 1926, and was available with a detachable hardtop coupé body in 1927, after which it gave way to a 1.2-litre Ten, also with worm drive. 1929 Tens had chromium plating, and sunshine roofs were available on closed models. A big 3½-litre six of 1924 did not go into production, but from 1925 to 1928 the company made some advanced 4-cylinder ohc cars with

2.1- and 2.5-litre engines with hemispherical combustion chambers. Though the smaller 14/45 won the R.A.C.'s Dewar Trophy for 50 consecutive ascents of Bwlch-y-Groes these were expensive machines to make, and Rover's breakthrough into a bigger class came with a straightforward 2-litre ohv bevel-drive six which sold well at £410, and was developed into the stylish if not very practical Light Six of 1930, noted for its raked screen and close-fitting cycle-type mudguards. This was the model which beat the 'Blue Train' in a race across France. It gave 70mph for £325. At the other end of the scale the same engine was made to propel a limousine on a 10ft 10in wheelbase.

V-radiators, lowered frames, and conventionally-mounted headlamps distinguished the 1931 cars, which ranged from the worm-driven Ten at only £189 for a saloon up to the 2.6-litre, 60bhp Meteor 20 with prices from £398. This last was evolved into a pleasant 90mph sports model which won its class in the 1933 R.A.C. Rally. 1932 saw the addition of a small six, the 1.4-litre Pilot at £225, and an abortive experiment, the unconventional rear-engined 2-cylinder air-cooled Scarab light car with all-round independent suspension, intended to sell for £89. Though a cheap worm-driven Ten was still listed in 1933, this was the year Rover adopted the free wheel, and turned to making cars still in the medium-price class, but of generally superior quality – a position in the market they have held till the present day. 1934 cars had 4-speed gearboxes, ohv engines, and spiral bevel final drive. They consisted of a new 1.4-litre Ten at £238, a 4-cylinder 12 at £268, a 1.6-litre 6-cylinder 14 derived from the earlier Pilot at £288, and a 16hp Meteor saloon at £438, as well as 3-carburettor sporting sixes with 14 and 20hp engines. After a brief venture with hydraulic brakes, Rover reverted to mechanical actuation on all their cars in 1936. Extensive restyling took place for 1937 on all models save the Ten, which was brought into line two seasons later. Big cars were still offered: there was a 2.1-litre 16hp and a new 2½-litre Speed 20 – and automatic chassis lubrication.

The 1937 style lasted until the 1949 season. Changes included synchromesh in 1939, the replacement of wire wheels by disc types in 1940, a rationalization of the range after World War 2, and a switch to ioe engines in 1948, when only a 1.6-litre 4-cylinder 60bhp and a 2.1-litre 6-cylinder 75hp were offered, both with independently-sprung front wheels. Also new in 1948 was the 4 × 4 Land-Rover cross-country vehicle, initially using the 60hp engine; this vehicle has been progressively developed ever since and was available with a diesel engine from 1958 on. Only the '75' was made in 1950, but it was completely restyled, with slab-sided full-width bodywork, integral headlamps, steering-column change, and hydro-mechanical brakes, amended to full hydraulic two years later. The free-wheel was retained and the price was £1,106: this shape had a long production life which did not end till 1964. The range was widened once more in 1954 with a 2-litre four and a 2.6-litre 6-cylinder 90bhp version.

Meanwhile the company's wartime work on gas turbines had led to the world's first successful turbocar which appeared in 1950, using a 75 chassis and rear-mounted 200bhp engine. It recorded 151.965mph over the flying kilometre in 1952, and was followed by further experimental cars of which the first designed as an entity was the T3, a 110bhp 4-wheel-drive coupé with fibreglass bodywork which was shown at Earls Court in 1956.

Development of the 1950 P4 theme continued, with the introduction of overdrive (and the abandonment of the free-wheel) on the 90 in 1956, and the adoption of vacuum servo brakes. There was a 105bhp version of the Rover 90, the 105S, in 1957, and also an alternative model with Rover's own 2-speed automatic transmission, dropped in favour of the Borg-Warner system after two seasons. Integral construction was introduced on the new 3-litre of 1959; this was a big car with a 10ft 10½in wheelbase, and the option of overdrive or automatic, but retaining the overhead inlet valves of the smaller models. The price was £1,764. The 4-cylinder 60hp was dropped after 1962. From late 1959 all models had front disc brakes, and power-assisted steering appeared on the 3-litre in 1961.

In 1962 a new and more practical turbocar appeared, the 140bhp T4 saloon with front-wheel drive and disc brakes on all 4 wheels: it did not go into production, though its structure served as a prototype for the advanced 2000 of 1964, which first supplemented and then supplanted the last 2.6-litre developments of the old P4, withdrawn at the end of that year. The 2000's 4-cylinder ohc engine developed 90bhp, all four forward gears were synchronized, a De Dion rear axle was used, and all 4 wheels had servo-assisted disc brakes. Like the 3-litre it had unitary construction, with detachable body panels, and its 100mph performance helped it to do well in rallies, with works support which had been initiated in the days of the 3-litre. The Rover-Leyland merger of 1966 brought the last of the major British independents under the control of the 'big battalions', but car design was unaffected, and during the year there were two new versions of the 2000, one with automatic, and the other, the TC, with a 114bhp twin-carburettor engine. Engines provided the main news of 1967: the old ioe 2.6-litre six was adapted for use in the Land-Rover, and the company acquired a licence to build the discarded 3½-litre light-alloy ohv Buick V-8, which powered a new edition of the 3-litre. This 3.5 was available only with automatic transmission, but on 160bhp maximum speed was up to 108mph. A year later the V-8 was wedded to the 2000 structure to make the Three Thousand Five, a 114mph saloon, though this was not available with a manual gearbox until 1972.

The 8-cylinder Rover-Buick engine was to have further applications, among them Morgan's Plus-8, an experimental mid-engined Alvis coupé, and the GKN-

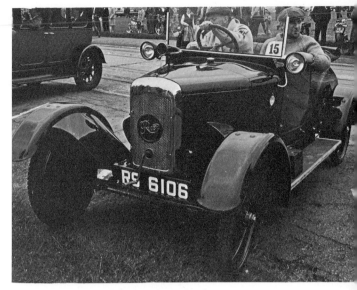
1924 ROVER Eight two-seater. *George A. Oliver*

1939 ROVER 16hp sports saloon. *The Rover Co Ltd (courtesy H.B. Light)*

1964 ROVER 2000 saloon. *The Rover Co Ltd (courtesy H.B. Light)*

1973 ROVER Range Rover 3½-litre estate car.
The Rover Co Ltd

1954 ROVIN 3CV two-seater. *Robert de Rovin*

1972 ROYALE RP12 Formula Atlantic racing car.
Royale Racing Ltd

1904 ROYAL ENFIELD 8hp two-seater. *G.N.
Georgano Collection*

Lotus 47, a Europa derivative. In 135bhp form the unit also powered the Range Rover announced in June 1970 as a more luxurious station wagon development of the Land-Rover. This used rigid axles and coils all round. Other features were an all-synchromesh gearbox, permanently engaged 4-wheel drive, and all-disc brakes. Top speed was over 95mph. Range Rovers were used for a successful British Army expedition across the Darien Gap in Central America in 1972. The 2000, Three Thousand Five, 3.5-litre, Land-Rover and Range Rover comprised Rover's 1972–3 offerings.

MCS

ROVIN (F) 1946–1959
Robert de Rovin, Saint-Denis, Seine; Colombes, Seine

The first cars to bear the Rovin name were cyclecars built by Raoul de Rovin in the late 1920s, but they were not sold to the public. In 1946 his brother Robert established himself in the Delaunay-Belleville factory at Saint-Denis.

The Rovin was a neat little rear-engined minicar with backbone chassis, chain primary and shaft final drive, 3-speed synchromesh gearbox, all-round independent suspension, and 12-volt electrics. The first cars had 260cc ohv air-cooled singles, but by the time the Rovin reached the public in any quantity it was fitted with an oversquare sv water-cooled flat-twin of 425cc developing 10bhp. By 1949/50 the original austere and doorless 2-seater bodywork had been replaced by a unitary-construction hull of slab-sided aspect, with winding windows, not unlike B.M.C.'s later Metropolitan in appearance.

By 1952 the cars had grown up into the 3CV model with 462cc and 13bhp, and over 50mph was claimed. Even at a price of about £350 this could not compete with Citroën's 2CV, and though the Rovin outlived such competitors as the Mochet, the Julien, and the Reyonnah, it was finished by 1959.

MCS

ROYAL and ROYAL PRINCESS (US) 1905
Royal Automobile Co, Chicago, Ill.

The Royal was a tiller-steered electric runabout with a piano-box body guaranteed to go 75 miles on one charge. Four models were available; another model named the Royal Princess was a 2-cylinder, petrol-engined five-seater with planetary transmission and single chain drive which sold for $1,500.

GMN

ROYALE (GB) 1969 to date
(1) Racing Preparations Ltd, Park Royal, London NW10 1969–1971
(2) Royale Racing Ltd, Huntingdon 1971 to date

The first Royales marketed were conventional Formula Ford machines, which were as successful as any in the class. The RP4 of 1970 took the Tarmac Formula F100 Championship in the hands of Ray Allen and RP5 was a successful Formula B design. In 1971 the RP6A Formula Ford, RP8 Formula B/Atlantic, RP9 Formula Super Vee and RP10 Group 6 sports-car models were advertised, RP7 being an abortive Formula 5000 project. Later came the impressive RP11 Formula 3 and RP12 Formula Atlantic pointed-nosed monocoques, and founder Bob King moved to premises nearer his main suppliers at Huntingdon. During 1972 Manfred Schurti took the European Formula Super Vee Championship, disputed in Britain by Mike Hayselden's RP9 and the newer RP14 of Tony Roberts, while the U.S.A. Championship was led by Bill Scott and in Formula 3 racing Tom Pryce's RP11 proved very fast. New models for 1973 included the RP16 Formula Ford and the RP17 for Group 6 sports-car racing.

DF

ROYAL ENFIELD (GB) 1901–1905
Enfield Cycle Co Ltd, Redditch, Worcs.

Produced by the famous armaments and cycle firm, these vehicles were initially motor quadricycles powered by 2¾hp and 3½hp single-cylinder De Dion engines. From these the company progressed to conventional light cars using De Dion singles, and twins made both by Ader and in their own works. In 1906 the car-manufacturing side was divorced from other activities, and more ambitious vehicles were made under the name of Enfield.

MCS

ROYAL RUBY (GB) 1913–1914; 1927
Royal Ruby Cycle Co, Manchester

The first 4-wheeler made by the Royal Ruby company was a cyclecar powered by a 10hp V-twin J.A.P. engine. It had 2 speeds and shaft drive, although a belt-drive model was to be added to the range later. After World War 1 they made no cars until 1927, when a very light 3-wheeler powered by a 5hp single-cylinder J.A.P. engine was announced. It did not last for more than one season.

GNG

ROYAL STAR (B) 1904–1910
(1) Sté de Construction Mécaniques, Antwerp
(2) SA Royal Star, Antwerp

The Royal Star was made in single-, 2-, and 4-cylinder models from 1904, joined by a 25hp six with dual ignition in 1906. In 1910 the name of car and company was changed to S.A.V.A.

GNG

ROYAL TOURIST (US) 1904–1911
(1) Royal Motor Car Co, Cleveland, Ohio 1904–1908

(2) Royal Tourist Car Co, Cleveland, Ohio *1908–1911*
(3) Consolidated Motor Car Co, Cleveland, Ohio *1911*

The Royal Tourist was the successor to the Hoffman (i). The first model was a rear-entrance tonneau with a 2-cylinder engine of 18/20hp. All subsequent models used 4-cylinder engines of up to 48hp. In 1908, this car was the first to have the horn bulb at the hub of the steering wheel, with the horn under the bonnet. During the last three seasons the same chassis was used. In 1911 the company combined with the Croxton-Keeton Motor Car Co to form the Consolidated Motor Car Co. GMN

ROYAL WINDSOR *see* DOMINION(i)

ROYCE (GB) *1904*
Royce Ltd, Manchester

Three prototype 1.8-litre twin-cylinder cars were made by F.H. Royce on Decauville lines in 1904. They had overhead inlet and side exhaust valves and shaft drive, but the design was not offered to the public until Royce joined forces with the Hon. C.S. Rolls to make the Rolls-Royce later in the year. MCS

ROYDALE (GB) *1907–1909*
Roydale Engineering Co Ltd, Huddersfield, Yorks.

The Roydale was made by a short-lived subsidiary of Learoyd Bros & Co Ltd, fancy worsted and woollen manufacturers. It was designed by Charles Binks, who had formerly made the Nottingham-built Leader, and used a Binks carburettor. Two 4-cylinder models were manufactured, an 18/22hp and a 25/30hp, both with monobloc engines, Mercedes-type radiators and shaft drive. GNG

R.P.S. (GB) *1972 to date*
Race Publicity Syndicates, Norwich

One of the myriad firms founded by ex-Lotus employees, the first designs offered by this company were single-seaters for F5000 and Formula Ford. DF

R.T.C. (GB) *1922–1923*
René Tondeur Co Ltd, Croydon, Surrey

This was a cyclecar powered by an 8.3hp air-cooled V-twin Blackburne engine. Transmission was by direct twin-belt drive to the rear-axle, and it was claimed that a centrifugal governor automatically varied the effective diameter of the belt pulleys, thus providing a variable gear. GNG

RUBAY (US) *1922–1924*
The Rubay Co, Cleveland, Ohio

Leon Rubay was a bodybuilder who, like Brewster, went over to car manufacture. His machine was of European type, an advanced and efficient light car featuring front-wheel brakes and a 1,600cc 4-cylinder ohc engine, producing 36bhp at 3,000rpm. Such a vehicle had no appeal in America, where bigger cars with more cylinders and costing less were the fashion. In 1924, the company was acquired by Baker, Rauch & Lang, formerly makers of electric cars. TRN

RUBINO (I) *1920–1923*
Officine di Netro SA, Turin

The Rubino was a conventional 2.3-litre 4-cylinder sv touring car designed by Lamberti, formerly of S.P.A. It was said to be an excellent hill-climber, but the economic situation prevented any quantity production. The design was taken over by Pietro Scaglioni's Tau concern. MCS

RUBURY-LINDSAY *see* R.L.C.

RUBY (F) *1910–c.1922*
Godefroy et Levêque, Levallois-Perret, Seine

This firm was always more celebrated for their engines than for their cars, although in pre-war days they offered quite a wide range of the latter. In 1912 there were six models, three singles and three 4-cylinder cars, from 6 to 12hp, all using friction transmission and chain final drive. They were sold in England as the Elburn-Ruby up to 1912, and as the Tweenie from 1912 to 1914. After the war Ruby concentrated more on engines, but made a few small 4-cylinder cars, still with friction drive. One of these, driven by Levêque, finished second in the 1920 Cyclecar Grand Prix at Le Mans. Levêque also made the Super cyclecar from 1912 to 1914. GNG

RUDGE (GB) *1912–1913*
Rudge-Whitworth Ltd, Coventry, Warwickshire

The Rudge cyclecar used a number of features familiar on the Rudge-Multi motorcycle, including a variable gear by expanding pulley. It was powered by a 750cc single-cylinder air-cooled engine, and final drive was by belts. The body was a staggered two-seater, and the whole car had a very low appearance. It never achieved the frame of the Rudge motorcycles, and was actually on the market for less than a year. GNG

1904 ROYAL TOURIST 18/20hp tonneau.
Antique Automobile

1907 ROYDALE 25/30hp landaulette. *The Veteran Car Club of Great Britain*

1922 R.T.C. 8.3hp cyclecar. *Autocar*

1921 RUMPLER 2.6-litre saloon. *Deutsches Museum, Munich*

1914 RUSSELL(ii) tourer. *Hugh Durnford*

c.1914 RUSSO-BALTIQUE tourer. *G.L. Hartner*

RUGBY *see* STAR (v)

RUGER (US) *1969 to date*
Sturm, Ruger & Co, Inc, Southport, Conn.

The Ruger is a replica vintage car with the lines of a 4½-litre Bentley, powered by a 7-litre Ford V-8 engine developing 425bhp. Suspension is non-independent, by semi-elliptic springs all round.   GNG

RUHL (B) *1901*
Built at Verviers, the Ruhl was a 4-cylinder car based on the contemporary Dasse. Very few were made.   GNG

RULER (US) *1917*
Ruler Motor Car Co, Aurora, Ill.

The Ruler was a 4-cylinder 2.7-litre car built on the 'frameless' principle, i.e. the chassis was entirely eliminated. Instead of the usual chassis or frame, the Ruler had a patented 3-point cradle with two wheels as two points and a ball and socket in the centre of the front transverse member as the third point. In the cradle were the clutch, transmission and differential. The body could be removed by unfastening the ball on the forward end of the cradle and disconnecting the brakes and rear springs. The engine had a roller-type camshaft with lubrication by means of the flywheel rim, and was equipped with overhead valves.   KM

RULEX (GB) *1904*
R.L. Motor Engineering Co Ltd, London W.C.

The Rulex was a very light voiturette powered by a single-cylinder engine. The 3½hp model cost 70gns, and the 4½hp model 80gns.   GNG

RUMPF (B) *1899*
Sté le Progrès Industriel, Brussels

This company was formed to manufacture machine tools and engines, as well as complete cars. The Rumpf car had a 6½hp 2-cylinder engine, a 4-speed gearbox, and double chain drive. A three-seater *vis-à-vis* body was provided.   GNG

RUMPLER (D) *1921–1926*
Rumpler Motoren-Gesellschaft mbH, Berlin

Dr Edmund Rumpler began his career in car design with Nesselsdorf and Adler at the turn of the century. He soon left cars for the aircraft industry. After World War 1 he again concentrated on cars, using aircraft design principles. At the Berlin Motor Show in 1921 he introduced his 'teardrop car', an extremely unconventional vehicle in technical details as well as in body style. A 6-cylinder 2.6-litre engine developing 36bhp was mounted in the rear, and transmission was to the rear swinging half axles. The engine was built by Siemens & Halske to a Rumpler design. It had an unusual 'star' layout with two pairs of 3 cylinders each in radial formation on a common crankshaft.

In 1924 another teardrop car appeared, based on the first model, but using a conventional 4-cylinder 2.6-litre 50bhp engine. Production of these cars was not on a large scale. A licence was taken by Benz, but the Rumpler principles were used only for a racing and a sports car. In 1926 Rumpler began to take an interest in front-wheel drive; he used his 4-cylinder 2.6-litre of the last teardrop model turned round for front drive. However, the product was not satisfactory and only limited numbers were built.   HON

RUPPE *see* PICCOLO

RUSSELL (i) (US) *1902–1904*
Russell Motor Vehicle Co, Cleveland, Ohio

This make of motor buggy, with small diameter wire wheels, used a diminutive 4-cylinder engine of 6hp, placed under the body. The engine was claimed to be self-starting and was available with either hot-tube or magneto ignition. The steering was by tiller.   GMN

RUSSELL (ii) (CDN) *1905–1916*
(1) Canada Cycle & Motor Co, Toronto, Ont. *1905–1910*
(2) Russell Motor Car Company Limited, Toronto, Ont. *1912–1916*

The Russell was Canada's foremost luxury car in the years before World War 1, and the only successful Canadian car to originate with a bicycle company. CCM was founded in 1899 and the following year was producing a few De Dion-engined tricycles and quadricycles as well as Locomobile steamers through its subsidiary, National Cycle. The Ivanhoe electric was also built briefly.

The first Russell was introduced in 1905. It was a 2-cylinder model with front-mounted engine, shaft drive and the gearchange on the steering column. It met instant success. A four was added in 1906 and year by year Russells got bigger and more luxurious. In 1910 the Russell was the first North American car with a Knight engine and prices reached $5,000. Success was steady until 1913 when production problems crippled the introduction of superb new Russell-Knight fours and sixes and sales plummeted.

For 1915 Russell moved back into the medium-price field with a poppet-valve light six for $1,750 and started to recoup with war contracts. Production ended with the purchase of CCM's automobile interests and Canadian rights to the Knight engine by Willys-Overland.　　　　　　　　　　　　　　　　　　　　HD

RUSSO-BALTIQUE (SU) *1909–1915*

Russko-Baltyskij Waggonyj Zawod, Riga

Before 1914, Russian passenger cars tended to be obscure foreign machines assembled in Russian factories under native names. The best-known, the Russo-Baltique, was made in a steelworks at Riga on the Baltic. It is uncertain just how many makes were reincarnated in the Tsar's dominions under that name. Some were derived from the Rex-Simplex from Germany; others were replicas of the Belgian Fondu. They were put together under the supervision of a Swiss engineer, H. Potterat.

The first Russo-Baltique, called the 24/30hp, appeared in 1909. It had a 4-cylinder engine of 4½ litres' capacity. Three years later, there were four models, including the 24/30hp, all with four cylinders, the biggest a monster of 7.2 litres. Fondu and Rex-Simplex were virtually unknown outside their countries of origin, and hardly famous inside them, but as the Russo-Baltique, they performed to some purpose in the earliest Monte Carlo and San Sebastian Rallies of 1911 and 1912, as well as in the Russian Reliability Trials of 1909 and 1910. Production ceased at the outbreak of war, in 1915, before a plan to make Hispano-Suizas under licence could get under way.　　　　　　　　　　　　　　　　　　　　TRN

1951 RUSSON 197cc three-seater. *Autocar*

RUSSON (GB) *1951–1952*

Russon Cars Ltd, Stanbridge, Beds.

The Russon differed from most of the post-war minicars in that the designers tried to make a reasonable-sized car, even though a very small engine was used. It had a wide, roomy three-seater aluminium body and tubular frame with independent suspension all round. The prototype used a 197cc J.A.P. engine, but this was replaced by a 2-cylinder Excelsior Talisman of 250cc for the production cars. However, only 15 of these were made.　　　　　　　　　　　　　　　　　　GNG

RUSTON-HORNSBY (GB) *1919–1924*

Ruston & Hornsby Ltd, Lincoln

Ruston & Hornsby were always better known for agricultural rather than passenger vehicles. They made a paraffin-engined tractor in 1897. World War 1, however, saw them building more sophisticated machinery, in the shape of Clerget and BR2 aero engines. Like so many other firms engaged in wartime mass production, they foresaw a vast new market for cheap cars with the coming of peace, for which they now had the tools and experience.

Their first offering was the A1 Ruston-Hornsby of 1919, a completely conventional machine, designed to compete with American imports, and built for quantity production. It was powered by a 4-cylinder engine of 2.6 litres, rated at 15.9hp. There were 3 forward speeds. The 20hp A3 joined the A1 in 1920; it had a bigger bore, providing three litres. They were solidly-made, comfortable cars, but slow, heavy to handle, and not cheap. A smaller 15hp was added in 1923, but manufacture of private cars was discontinued in the following year.　　　　TRN

1922 RUSTON-HORNSBY 15.9hp all-weather tourer. *Ruston & Hornsby Ltd*

RUTHERFORD (GB) *1907–1912*

Highclere Motor Car Syndicate Ltd, Highclere, Newbury, Berks.

The 30/40hp Rutherford steam car used a Serpollet-type flash generator and 3-cylinder vertical single-acting engine. It had shaft-drive, a five-seater touring body and the appearance of a conventional petrol-engined car. The original price of £575 was reduced by 1911 to £400 for a larger-engined car, but the popularity of steamers in England was fast waning, and few Rutherfords were sold. For the first two years of its life, the car was known as the E.J.Y.R., after its designer, E.J.Y. Rutherford.　　　　　　　　　　　　　　　　　　　　GNG

RÜTTGER (D) *1920–1921*

Carl Rüttger Motorpflug- und Automobilwerke, Berlin-Hohen-Schönhausen

This company specialized in the production of tractors, but introduced a 10/4PS private car in 1920. Only a few prototypes were built.　　　　　HON

RUXTON (US) *1929–1931*

New Era Motors Inc, New York, N.Y.; Moon Motor Corp., St Louis, Mo.; Kissel Motor Car Co, Hartford, Wisc.

The Ruxton was a front-drive car which, like its rival, the Cord L-29, was built in limited numbers during roughly the same period. The Ruxton was the idea of Archie M. Andrews, a promoter and financier who was also a director of the Hupp Motor Corporation. An experimental car embodying the front-drive principle was built late in 1928 and named after William V.C. Ruxton, one of Andrew's acquaintances who showed an interest in the production of this type of car. A long, low prototype was built in the spring of 1929. This car was powered by a 4.4-litre Continental Straight Eight engine which produced a maximum of about 100bhp at 3,400rpm. All Ruxton cars followed this initial pilot model both in engine and overall design.

1929 RUXTON 4.4-litre roadster. *Kenneth Stauffer*

Actual production began in June 1930 in both the Moon and Kissel factories; Ruxtons of either origin had to struggle in an increasingly competitive market. Sedan bodies were built by Budd on dies and tooling used by some models of the English Wolseley. Open models were built by Raulang. The cars were low, rakish, and carried no running boards. The price of the sedan, at $3,195, was approximately that of its rival, Cord. Because of the collapse of Moon and Kissel and a flagging Depression market, Ruxton failed late in 1930 or early 1931 after between 300 and 500 cars had been built, some of which were not actually sold until 1932. Of these, two were phaetons, one a town car and the remainder almost equally divided between roadsters and sedans.   KM

R.W.N. (D) *1928–1929*
Rudolf Weide, Motorfahrzeugbau, Nordhausen

This was a 3-wheeler with two-seater body. There was a single front wheel, the rear wheels being driven by the rear-mounted engine. There was a choice of 200cc, 350cc or 500cc engines.   HON

RYCSA *see* GILDA

RYDE (GB) *1904–1906*
Ryde Motors Ltd, West Ealing, Middlesex

The Ryde used a 3-cylinder in-line engine of 14/16hp, a conventional 3-speed gearbox and shaft drive. Two-seater and four-seater tonneau bodies were provided, as well as a delivery van. In 1904 there was also a short-lived 10hp flat-twin model.   GNG

1904 RYDE 14/16hp tonneau. *G.N. Georgano Collection*

RYJAN (F) *1920–1926*
(1) Grillet, Chatou, Seine-et-Oise *1920–1925*
(2) Grillet, Nanterre, Seine *1925–1926*

The Ryan was a conventional touring car powered originally by an ohc S.C.A.P. engine of 1,690cc, replaced in 1924 by an sv S.C.A.P. of approximately the same size. For the last two years a 2-litre Altos engine was used.   GNG

RYKNIELD (GB) *1903–1906*
(1) Ryknield Engine Co Ltd, Burton-on-Trent, Staffs. *1903–1905*
(2) Ryknield Motor Co Ltd, Burton-on-Trent, Staffs. *1906*

The Ryknield was a conventional small car using a 10/12hp vertical-twin engine and shaft drive. In 1905 a 15hp 3-cylinder model, with ht magneto ignition was added to the range, as well as a chain-driven 24hp 4-cylinder of over 6 litres capacity. In November of that year the works closed down. Buses were later made by a new company, which exhibited a 20hp 4-cylinder prototype in 1906. In the period 1911 to 1914 Baguley, Salmon and Ace cars were made in the same factory.   GNG

RYLEY (i) (GB) *1901–1902*
Ryley, Ward & Bradford, Coventry, Warwickshire

Messrs Ryley, Ward and Bradford had experimented for two years with a light voiturette which they put on the market in September 1901. It had a 2¾hp M.M.C. single-cylinder engine, 2 speeds, shaft drive and a tubular frame. In 1902 they made a larger car with a 5hp Aster engine and 3 speeds.   GNG

1904 RYKNIELD 10/12hp victoria. *G.N. Georgano Collection*

RYLEY (ii) (GB) *1913*
J.A. Ryley, Birmingham

This was a cyclecar powered by a 6hp J.A.P. V-twin engine, and using belt drive.   GNG

RYNER-WILSON (GB) *1920–1921*
Ryner-Wilson Motor Co Ltd, Wimbledon, London S.W.19

The Ryner-Wilson hardly progressed beyond the prototype stage, but it employed several unusual features. The engine was a 6-cylinder 15.7hp 2,290cc unit, which used push-rod operated overhead valves grouped in sets of four on the heads of each pair of cylinders. Two Vici carburettors were used, and lubrication was on the dry-sump principle.   GNG

RYTECRAFT SCOOTACAR (GB) *1934–1940*
(1) British Motor Boat Mfg Co Ltd, London W.C.1 *1934–1939*
(2) B.M.B. Engineering, London W.C.1 *1939–1940*

This curious little vehicle had its origin in a fairground 'dodgem' car, and to the end of its days never entirely lost the appearance of one. The first road-going cars were powered by a 98cc Villiers Midget engine giving a maximum speed of 15mph. They were single-seaters, with one speed, no springs and an automatic centrifugal clutch.

Design was gradually improved, and by 1940 a 250cc Villiers engine was being used, and amenities included a 3-speed and reverse gearbox, a two-seater body and full electric lighting. Some cars were built with the styling of Vauxhalls or Chrysler Airflows, for publicity purposes, and commercial versions (Scootatruck) were also made. The price was at first £70, increased to £80 for the later models; this was surely the best £10 worth ever known in car prices. Although production ceased in 1940, a few cars were assembled after World War 2.   GNG

1937 RYTECRAFT Scootacar 250cc minicar. *Autocar*

S

S.1 (DK) *1949–1950*

E. Sommer, Copenhagen

Built by the Jaguar distributor for Denmark, this was a light car powered by a 2-cylinder Jowett Bradford engine. The 2-door saloon body bore a remarkable similarity to the contemporary Armstrong Siddeley. GNG

SAAB (S) *1950 to date*

(1) Svenska Aeroplan AB, Linköping *1950–1965*

(2) SAAB Aktiebolag Ltd, Linköping *1965–1968*

(3) SAAB-Scania Aktiebolag Ltd, Lindköping *1968 to date*

Although the Svenska Aeroplan Aktiebolaget began testing their car during the war, and showed a prototype to the press in 1947, production did not start until 1950. This was the Model 92 which used a 764cc 2-cylinder 2-stroke engine of DKW type developing 25bhp, and driving the front wheels. Suspension was by torsion bars all round, and the aerodynamic 2-door saloon body was not very different from that used today. Excellent road-holding made it a popular car for rallies and in 1955 more power was provided with the Model 93. This used a 3-cylinder engine of 748cc capacity giving 38bhp. Suspension was now by coil springs and hydraulic shock-absorbers. The GT model of this car was tuned to do nearly 100mph.

The 1966 model was the 96 (841cc, 46bhp, or with tuned Monte Carlo 850 engine, 60bhp), equipped with triple carburettors and duo circuit brakes (discs on front wheels). Since the late 1950s the Saab has been increasingly successful at rallies, Erik Carlsson winning the 1960, 1961 and 1962 R.A.C. Rallies, and the 1962 and 1963 Monte Carlo Rallies. For several years the company had been experimenting with open sports and GT cars, and in 1966 a fibreglass GT coupé went into limited production.

In 1950 only 1,246 cars left the factory, but in 1965 the figure was 48,300, of which 17,000 were exported. In 1967 came the first 4-stroke SAABs with 1½-litre German Ford V-4 engines, and towards the end of the year details were released of the new 99 2- and 4-door saloons, though serious production did not begin until 1969. These used a 5-bearing 1,709cc 4-cylinder ohc in-line engine of Triumph manufacture, mounted above the 4-speed all-synchromesh gearbox; other features were all-disc brakes and rear suspension by rigid axle and coils. Fuel injection was available on 1970 versions, and there were two capacity increases, to 1,854cc in 1971 (when the free wheel was abandoned) and to 1,985cc during 1972. New in 1968 was a fibreglass sports coupé, the Sonett, based on the Ford-engined V-4 type; this was also the last season for the traditional 2-stroke power units and it marked a merger with the old-established Scania-Vabis truck firm, also the Swedish importers of the Volkswagen. The 4-cylinder engines brought rally successes again for SAAB, who won the R.A.C. British event in 1968, the Scottish in 1969, the R.A.C. and Swedish in 1971, and the Swedish and the Thousand Lakes in 1972. OB

S.A.B.A. (I) *1925–1928*

Sta Automobili Brevetti Angelino, Milan

The S.A.B.A. was a revolutionary car using a central backbone frame and 4-wheel drive and steering. Front and rear suspension were by transverse leaf springs, and the car had brakes on the front wheels and transmission. A conventional 1-litre 4-cylinder engine was used. It was announced in July 1927 that the S.A.B.A. was reaching the production stage, but it does not seem ever to have been sold. However, a conventional car, the S.A.B.A. Stelvio, was also made. GNG

SABELLA (GB) *1906–1914*

Sabella Motor Car Co Ltd, Camden Town, London N.

The first car built by Fritz Sabel was a hand-propelled vehicle, to which he fitted a 1hp engine. He exhibited small cars with single- and 2-cylinder engines, the latter with shaft drive, at the Stanley Shows of 1906 and 1907, but did not go into production until the time of the cyclecar boom of 1912/13. His cyclecars had 10hp J.A.P. engines, and belt final drive. GNG

SABLATNIG-BEUCHELT (D) *1925–1926*

Beuchelt & Co, Grünberg

One model was produced by this firm, which specialized in manufacturing railway carriages. The car was equipped with a 1,496cc 6/30PS engine. HON

SABRA (IL) *1960 to date*

Autocars Co Ltd, Haifa

1966 SAAB 96 sports saloon. *Svenska Aeroplan AB*

1973 SAAB 99 EMS 2-litre saloon. *Svenska Aeroplan AB*

1912 SABELLA 10hp cyclecar. *G.N. Georgano Collection*

605

1965 SABRA Carmel 1.2-litre saloon.
Reliant Motor Co Ltd

1968 SABRA Luxe 12/50 saloon. *Autocars Co Ltd*

1903 SAGE 12hp tourer. *The Veteran Car Club of Great Britain*

1906 ST LOUIS 32/36hp tourer. *Keith Marvin Collection*

Named after the succulent cactus that is Israel's national emblem, the country's first indigenous make of car was evolved in association with Reliant of Great Britain, and used Ford (ii) mechanical components. The first Sabra was a sports car identical with Reliant's Sabre, joined in 1962 by a small station wagon using the 997cc Anglia engine and gearbox in a box-section frame with coil-spring independent front suspension. Bodywork was of fibreglass, and this model was evolved into the similarly-bodied Sussita and its saloon counterpart the Carmel, both with the 1.2-litre Cortina unit. Saloons had swing-axle independent rear suspension. In 1967 the Cortina-powered Gilboa 12 4-door saloon was introduced, as well as a version with 1,147cc Triumph unit. Since 1969 1,296cc Triumph engines have been standardized. The Carmel is assembled in Greece where it is known as the Attica Carmel 12. MCS

SACHSENRING (D) *1956–1959*
VEB Sachsenring Automobilwerke, Zwickau

The nationalized Horch works introduced a new car in 1956 with a 6-cylinder ohv 2,407cc engine under the name of Horch, but this designation was changed to Sachsenring. It was produced until 1959. The Trabant has been built since 1956 in the same factory. HON

S.A.F. (i) (F) *1908–c.1912*
Sté Anon. des Ateliers du Furan, Sainte-Étienne, Loire

The company that had made the Jussy cars from 1898 to 1900 returned to the motor business in 1908 with a tandem tricar similar to the British Riley or Royal Enfield. The engine was a 500cc vertical single-cylinder developing 4½hp, mounted under the driver's seat. The two front wheels were independently suspended, and drive to the rear wheel was by chain. LL

S.A.F. (ii) (S) *1921–1922*
AB Svenska Automobilfabriken, Bollnäs

The S.A.F. was an assembled car using an American 4-cylinder engine made by G.B. & S. It had a light six-seater body and cantilever rear springs. Production was intended to reach 1,000 per year, but not many cars were in fact made.

The name S.A.F. was also used for cars made by the Süddeutsche Automobil Fabrik of Gaggenau. OB

SAFETY (US) *1901*
Safety Steam Automobile Co, Boston, Mass.

This simple two-seater steam buggy had a single-cylinder engine of 2.5in bore and 4in stroke. It had a 'reach' frame with elliptical springs and tiller steering. GMN

SAFIR (CH) *1907–1908*
Automobilfabrik Safir, Zürich

The Safir company built a large factory in order to produce cars and commercial vehicles under Saurer licence. Mainly lorries were made, but there were also two models of private cars, a 30hp and a 50hp. They had shaft drive and compressed-air starters. The works soon closed because of financial difficulties, but a claim to fame was that the first Saurer Diesel engine for road vehicles was made in the Safir factory in 1908. GNG

S.A.G. *see* PIC-PIC

SAGE (F) *1900–1906*
Ateliers P. Sage, Paris 15e

The Sage company made a large range of cars, all of solid construction and appearance, and powered by a variety of proprietary engines. The 1902 range consisted of four models, using 2- and 4-cylinder engines of 10 to 24hp, by Abeille, Mutel, Brouhot or Aster. They had gilled-tube radiators and double chain drive, and there was one town car with engine under the seat. In 1904 Filtz engines were used in some models and the cars had acquired honeycomb radiators of round section, not unlike those of Hotchkiss. 1906 cars, which came in a range of 10 to 50hp, were available with Gassner petrol-electric drive. GNG

SAGER (CDN) *1910*
United Motors Ltd, Welland, Ont.

This 4-cylinder touring car of 30hp was priced at $1,650. It was named after Frederick Sager, a company official who had worked with Oldsmobile. GB

SAGINAW (i) (US) *1914–1915*
Valley Boat & Engine Co, Saginaw, Mich.

The Saginaw was a two-seater cyclecar with belt drive. Its only distinguishing feature was that the headlamps were inset into the front mudguards in Pierce-Arrow fashion. It is said that this manufacturer built the Valley Dispatch truck at Elkhart, Indiana in 1927. GMN

SAGINAW (ii) (US) *1916*
Lehr Motor Co, Saginaw, Mich.

In the latter part of 1916 a few 1917-model Saginaws were built. They were equipped with Massnick-Phipps V-8 engines. Before the end of the year the name had been changed to Yale.   GNG

ST JOE *see* SHOEMAKER

St JOHN (US) *1903*
S.H. St John & Son, Canyon City, Colo.

The St John car had a single-cylinder engine mounted under the rear seat, and single chain drive. It was started by spinning the flywheel which was loose from the engine, so that there was no problem of overcoming compression. The makers wanted to sell the patent, so they probably did not make the car in any numbers.   GNG

ST LAURENCE (GB) *1899–1902*
John Tavendale, Laurencekirk, Kincardineshire

John Tavendale was a millwright and cycle maker who produced a small number of cars. His first, called a Mearns Motor, used engine castings from the Endurance Motor Co of Coventry, and had a high dogcart body. Later he built about six smaller cars with 6hp single-cylinder Accles & Turrell engines.   GNG

ST LOUIS (US) *1898–1907*
(1) St Louis Motor Carriage Co, St Louis, Mo. *1898–1906*
(2) St Louis Motor Car Co, Peoria, Ill. *1906–1907*

The early models of this manufacture were *dos-à-dos* four-seaters with single- and 2-cylinder engines. These were tiller-steered, and the engines were beneath the seat. 1902 cars were wheel steered, and that year came George P. Dorris' first four, a chain-driven experimental machine. Dorris was responsible for subsequent designs. In 1904 this make was still using a single wooden brake-shoe operating on the transmission. The last models, Types XV and XVI, used water-cooled 4-cylinder engines, sliding-gear transmissions, and shaft drive.   GMN

ST VINCENT (GB) *1903–1910*
William McLean (St Vincent Cycle & Motor Works), Glasgow

The Vincent works assembled a small number of cars and commercial vehicles using 2- and 4-cylinder Aster engines, and they were also known as Scottish Aster. A 12hp car was entered in the 1905 Scottish Reliability Trials, but withdrew on the third day. Production of cars was only spasmodic, and after 1910 ceased completely, although taxicabs were made for a few years longer.   GNG

S.A.L. *see* ESPERIA

SALMON (GB) *1914*
Baguley Cars Ltd, Burton-on-Trent, Staffs.

The Salmon was a four-seater light car powered by an 11.9hp 4-cylinder engine. It was introduced in July 1914, and only three were made. The earlier 8hp light car made by the same company was sometimes called the Salmon, but its correct name was Ace.   GNG

SALMSON (F) *1921–1957*
Société des Moteurs Salmson, Billancourt, Seine

Renowned for their water-cooled (and later air-cooled) radial aero engines, Salmson entered the car industry by taking out a manufacturing licence for the G.N. in 1919. 3,000 of these machines were turned out in two years. The first Salmsons proper appeared in 1921. These Emile Petit designs had flimsy cyclecar-type chassis with shaft drive and differential-less back axles, with a St Andrew's Cross motif on the radiator. The standard engine was an odd 1100cc monobloc four with a single push-rod per cylinder, which also operated the inlet valves as a *pull*-rod. Ignition was by Salmson's own type of magneto and cooling was by thermo-syphon. This ohv unit worked reasonably well at low speeds, gave 45mph and 45mpg, and a two-seater could be bought in England for £265, the price dropping steadily to £158 by 1926. At the same time Petit produced something far more advanced for the Cyclecar Grand Prix in the shape of a twin-ohc unit of similar capacity with dual magneto ignition and 2-bearing crankshaft: with one of these Lombard won the race, as well as taking 2nd place (behind a G.N.) in the 200 Mile Race at Brooklands. This was followed by 1st and 2nd places in both these events in 1922, class wins in both the Cyclecar Grand Prix and the first Le Mans 24 Hour Race in 1923, at San Sebastian in 1925, and in both Le Mans and the Targa Florio in 1926. 1927 marked the peak of Salmson's competition career, with 2nd and 3rd places in general classification at Le Mans (as well as Class and Biennial Cup wins), and a 2nd place in the Coupe de la Commission Sportive run under fuel consumption rules.

The firm also built a 750cc engine for the 1923 Cyclecar Grand Prix – it won its class but was never produced commercially. Nothing came, either, of Petit's ingenious 1927 1,100cc twin-blown twin-ohc straight-8 with desmodromic valves, said to give 140bhp at 8,000 rpm.

Touring Salmsons progressed to twin overhead camshafts with the advent of the 1.2-litre 10hp in 1922; there was still no differential or front wheel brakes (though the latter had appeared on the racers), but a starter was standard and quarter-

1921 SALMSON 1,100cc racing car. André Lombard at the wheel. *National Motor Museum*

1927 SALMSON Model G 1,100cc sports car. *National Motor Museum*

1934 SALMSON S4C 1½-litre coupé. *Neubauer Collection*

1939 SALMSON S4E 2.3-litre saloon. *Lucien Loreille Collection*

1953 SALMSON 2300 2.3-litre coupé.
Autosport

1904 SAMPSON 40hp Gordon Bennett racing
car. *G. Marshall Naul*

elliptic springs had given way to semi-elliptics. From 1925 onwards the twin-cam 1100cc sports cars came into their own, and by 1926 the adoption of a cowled radiator completed their classic outline. There were variations of specification, but all the sports models came with front wheel brakes, balloon tyres, and differential-less back axles, and ranged from the 3-speed Grand Prix with splash lubrication and 2-bearing crank at £265, giving over 70mph, to the G.P. Special, which had full-pressure lubrication and 4 forward speeds, available in Cozette-blown form at £475. Meanwhile the 10/15 had acquired front-wheel brakes, and at the end of 1926 the differential arrived on a bigger 12/24 with dynamotor, V-radiator, and a 9ft 4in wheelbase giving room for more commodious coachwork.

The vogue for small French sports cars vanished as quickly as it had come, though Salmson once more collected the Biennial Cup at Le Mans in 1928, and the twin-cam sports models were still listed in Britain as late as 1931. The arrival of the M.G. Midget killed what sales there were, and Salmson, like Amilcar, tried their hand at small luxury machines; a twin-cam 1.6-litre six for 1929 never went into production, but its successor, the S4, had a longer run. This retained the twin-cam engine and 3-bearing crank, magneto ignition, gravity feed, and 3-speed gearbox, but it usually wore saloon bodywork, and was not notably fast for a price of £325. It had grown up by 1933 into the 4-speed 1½-litre S4C with rear tank, which formed the basis for the 12hp British Salmsons made at Raynes Park from 1934 onward. The 1.6-litre S4D of 1935 still had a magneto, but featured transverse independent front suspension and a 4-speed Cotal electrically-selected gearbox, and twin-ohc saloon cars in two engine sizes were listed in 1939. The bigger of these boasted 2.3 litres and 70bhp, and had hydraulic brakes. Its English price was £495. The same models reappeared in 1946, when a few 90bhp competition versions were made with 2.3-litre engine. Over a thousand Salmsons found customers in 1950, but thereafter the decline was rapid.

A new 2.2-litre Randonnée model with a light alloy engine and Cotal gearbox came out in 1951, and 1953 produced the 2300 aerodynamic coupé with half-elliptic instead of cantilever rear springing, wire wheels, and a tuned version of the twin-cam engine giving 105bhp and over 100mph. This was made in small numbers until 1957, but a year previously the end had been heralded when Renault acquired the company. Last of the Salmsons was a long-wheelbase version of the 2300 with 4-door saloon bodywork.   MCS

SALOMON (F) *1931*

The famous engineer Jules Salomon who was responsible for the original Ciroëns and the Zèbre, designed an ultra-light car to be sold under his own name. Also known as Le Cabri, it was a two-seater with a single-cylinder water-cooled engine of 386cc, and was intended to cost the equivalent of £70 in France. M.Salomon hoped to find a motorcycle firm to manufacture it, but did not succeed.   GNG

SALTER (US) *1909–1912*

Salter Motor Co, Kansas City, Mo.

The Salter was built in five-seater touring models and two-seater roadsters, both types costing $1,750. Both used an F-head 4-cylinder, 6.3-litre engine and a planetary transmission.   GMN

SALVA (I) *1906–1907*

Società Anonima Lombarda Vetture Automobili, Milan

Unlike many of the ephemeral Italian concerns, Salva made big 4-cylinder cars with 4-speed gearboxes and (probably) chain drive. The smallest of the range was a 16/25hp, but there were also a 28/45 and a 60/70. The factory was a casualty of the Agadir Crisis of 1907.   MCS

SALVADOR (i) (US) *1914*

Salvador Motor Co, Boston, Mass.

The Salvador cyclecar was powered by a water-cooled 4-cylinder Farmer engine. It had a 3-speed selective transmission, shaft drive and what was termed a 'gearless differential'. It was a two-seater and sold for $485.   GMN

SALVADOR (ii) (E) *1916*

Industrias Salvador, Barcelona

The Spanish Salvador was a cyclecar powered by a 10hp V-twin M.A.G. engine. Final drive was by shaft, and front suspension was by transverse semi-elliptic springs.   GNG

SALVATOR *see* UNDERBERG

SALVO (GB) *1906*

Swan & Co, London N.

A 24/30hp 4-cylinder limousine with shaft drive was shown at the 1906 Stanley Show. Swan & Company were dealers, and the Salvo may have been bankrupt stock from another company.   GNG

SAM (PL) *1954–1956*

Designed by Antonin Weiner, the Sam was a small sports car powered by a variety of engines including Triumph, D.K.W. and B.M.W. motorcycle units, and car engines from I.F.A., Syrena, Fiat and Lancia. Twelve were made, mostly two-seaters, although at least one single-seater racing car was built. Driven by Weiner, Jerzy Szulczewski and Ludwig Bielak, they won several Polish championships. GNG

S.A.M. (I) *1924–1928*
Società Automobili e Motori, Legnano, Milan

The S.A.M. was a sporting voiturette, on the French model, but this type failed to catch on in Italy. The B23 and B24 had sv engines, but the C25 and V25 were more exciting, with their 1,100cc ohv engine producing 22bhp at 3,200rpm. TRN

SAMPSON (US) *1904; 1911*
(1) Alden Sampson Manufacturing Co, Pittsfield, Mass. *1904*
(2) United States Motor Corp, Alden Sampson Division, Detroit, Mich. *1911*

The 1904 Sampson was a copy of the Moyea, for which Sampson had built chassis in 1903. It had a 4-cylinder engine which produced 18hp at 810rpm, and a 4-speed sliding-gear transmission with final drive by double chains. The Sampson missed a minor opportunity of fame by failing to have a car ready for the Gordon Bennett Cup trial in 1904. The later model, called the Sampson 35, had a 4-cylinder, 35hp engine. The five-seater four-door model, with a claimed 17 coats of paint, sold for $1,250. GMN

SAMSON (US) *1922*
Samson Tractor Co, Janesville, Wisc.

Although only one Samson car was produced, the make is unique in being the only car ever advertised by General Motors which never went into production. Built by the Samson Division of General Motors, the Samson was a nine-seater touring car powered by a Chevrolet FB engine and had auxiliary seats which could readily be removed, with the rear seat, to convert the car into a truck. The Samson truck was built until 1923. KM

SANCHIS (F) *c.1906–1912*
Enrique Sanchis, Paris; Courbevoie, Seine

This company began by making tri-cars, and progressed to a series of what were described as 'voiturettes extra-légeres', of 4½ to 10hp, and 4 to 2 cylinders. A light two-seater car, with unit construction of body and chassis, was shown at the 1906 Paris Salon. Towards the end of their life they were sold by L. Pierron whose cars were called Mass in England. GNG

SANDFORD (F) *1922–1939*
S. Sandford, Paris 17e

The Sandford was a French version of the highly successful Morgan 3-wheeler from England, but was a considerably more sophisticated vehicle. It usually had 4-cylinder water-cooled engines, for the sake of smoothness and flexibility, and from 1924 boasted front-wheel brakes. The Sandford also had 3 forward speeds. In 1927, there were three models: the Tourisme, Sport and Super Sport. In the early 1930s, the range consisted of a 5CV family car with a 900cc Ruby engine, a sports model of around 1,100cc, and a supercharged version of the latter. A 4-wheeler was made from 1934, using a 1,100cc Ruby engine and independent suspension all round, while in 1933 the economy versions of the 3-wheeler used the 954cc Ruby flat-twin engine. From 1936 to 1939 Sandford imported the Morgan 4/4, to which he attached his own radiator grille, and in mid-1939 he planned an Anglo-French sports car using a Ruby engine in the Morgan chassis. World War 2 killed this project, and post-war plans to revive the 3-wheeler came to nothing. TRN

S & M (US) *1913–1914*
S & M Motors Co, Detroit, Mich.

The S & M (Strobel & Martin) Six-43 model was an assembled car using a 6-cylinder Continental engine. The only model was a distinguished looking five-seater tourer. This was on a wheelbase of 10ft 10in and had early side-mounted spare wheels. For $2,485, standard equipment included two dash compartments, electric cigar lighter, two vacuum bottles fitted into the rear compartment and Houk wire wheels. In 1914 this became the Benham. GMN

S & M SIMPLEX (US) *1904–1907*
Smith & Mabley Manufacturing Co, New York, N.Y.

The original version of the S & M Simplex, Model AA, was a two-seater with an 18hp 4-cylinder engine and double chain drive. For 1905 and 1906, the engine was increased to 30hp and had a capacity of 5.2 litres. This was on a chassis of 8ft 10in wheelbase, priced at $5,000. Bodies were to order only. There was a special two-seater racing version with a 70hp engine. In 1907, a longer chassis was made and in it there was an 8.5-litre, 4-cylinder T-head engine with a 4-speed transmission. Smith & Mabley became defunct in 1907 and were succeeded by the Simplex Auto Co. The S & M Simplex was, therefore, the ancestor of the great Simplex (ii). GMN

SANDRINGHAM (GB) *1902–1905*
Frank Morriss, King's Lynn, Norfolk

1906 SANCHIS tri-car. *Joaquín Ciuró Gabarró Collection*

1930 SANDFORD 1,100cc sporting 3-wheeler. *Musée de l'Automobile, Le Mans*

1904 S & M SIMPLEX 18hp tourer. Coachwork by Quimby. *Automotive History Collection, Detroit Public Library*

1924 S. & S. 27hp Brighton limousine.
Keith Marvin Collection

1923 SAN GIUSTO 748cc chassis. *Museo dell' Automobile, Turin*

1928 S.A.R.A. 1.8-litre drophead coupé. *Autocar*

Frank Morriss was official car repairer to King Edward VII, and as well as selling Benz and Daimler cars, he specialized in modifying old Daimlers. The main Morriss improvements were conversion from tiller to wheel steering, rebuilding the gearbox, and increasing the cylinder bore from 90 to 100mm. The cars sold under the name Sandringham were said to be of Morriss's own design, but probably owed a good deal to Daimler. They had 10hp 2-cylinder engines and chain drive, and more were sold as wagonettes and hotel buses than as private cars.　GNG

S. & S. (US) *1924–1930*
Sayers & Scovill Co, Cincinnati, Ohio
　The S. & S. cars were successors to the earlier Sayers and a sideline to the Sayers and Scovill hearses. They were large, expensive 6- and 8-cylinder cars produced as sedans and limousines for funeral use, invalid cars and, in a few instances, as cars for customers wanting something different from the standard cars of other makes. The S. & S. catalogue of 1929 listed an eight-seater Lakewood sedan with 5.3-litre straight-8 engine at $4,295 as its only private car. After 1929 or 1930, S. & S. passenger cars were only available to special order.　KM

SANDUSKY (US) *1902–1903*
Sandusky Automobile Co, Sandusky, Ohio
　The Sandusky was a typical light runabout with a single-cylinder engine under the seat, single chain drive and tiller steering.　GNG

SAN GIORGIO (I/GB) *1906–1909*
SA Industriale San Giorgio, Genoa
　This company produced Napier cars under licence, the works being under the supervision of Arthur Macdonald, the Napier racing driver. Three models of 6-cylinder car were made, the 25hp, 40hp and 60hp. Bodies came from a factory at Pistoia under the same management, which built them under licence from Kellner of Paris.　GNG

SAN GIUSTO (I) *1922–1924*
SA San Giusto, Milan; Trieste
　Of all the short-lived cyclecars produced in Italy just after World War 1, the San Giusto was the most unusual and interesting. With its central backbone chassis, transverse-spring independent suspension of all four wheels, front-wheel brakes (in 1924), rear-mounted, air-cooled, 748cc 6hp 4-cylinder engine and 4 forward speeds, its specification was very advanced.　TRN

SANTAX (F) *1922–1924*
　The Santax was a very small cyclecar powered by a single-cylinder 2-stroke engine. As it was under 125cc the owner paid no tax on it, nor did he have to pass a driving test.　GNG

SANTLER (GB) *1898–c.1924*
(1) C. Santler & Co, Malvern Link, Worcs. *1898–1914*
(2) Santler & Co Ltd, Malvern Link, Worcs. *1914–c.1924*
　Santler was a bicycle maker who made a few cars from time to time. He claimed to have helped Karl Benz to design his first car of 1885, and only to have left Benz because he would not give him credit for his help. Be that as it may, Santler's first car, known as the Malvernia, certainly bore a close resemblance to the Benz of the 1890s. He subsequently made a light, front-engined car in 1902 and a small series of 10hp two- and four-seaters in 1914. In the early 1920s Santler made a few very Morgan-like 3-wheelers under the name Santler Rushabout.　GNG

SANTOS DUMONT (US) *1902–1904*
Columbus Motor Vehicle Co, Columbus, Ohio
　Named after the famous balloonist, the Santos Dumont car was first made with a 2-cylinder engine mounted under the front seat, chain drive, and a four-seater tonneau body. The 1904 model had a 20hp 4-cylinder engine mounted vertically under a bonnet, and was priced at $2,000. From February 1904 the car was usually advertised under the name Dumont.　GMN

S.A.R.A. (F) *1923–1930*
Sté des Autos à Refroidissement par Air, Courbevoie, Seine; Puteaux, Seine
　The S.A.R.A. was the only French car of the 1920s to make a success of air cooling. It began life as a two-seater light car, low-built and weighing very little, powered by an 1,100cc ohv engine. A centrifugal turbine blower impelled air into a jacket around the cylinders, providing very effective cooling. The rest of the S.A.R.A. was typical of French voiturette practice of the time — three forward speeds, shaft drive, no differential, and front suspension by a transverse spring. Road-holding was good. The S.A.R.A. acquired four seats and front-wheel brakes in 1925 and four forward speeds in 1927, but the first really new model appeared in the following year, when the S.A.R.A. grew up into a full-sized car, with a 6-cylinder engine of 1,806cc, retaining the same design, and half-elliptic front springs. It was made in saloon and coupé form, and for two years was built under licence in Scotland under the name Scotsman(ii).　TRN

SARALEGUI *see* MOT ET SARALEGUI

S.A.S. (F) *1927–1928*
Automobiles S.A.S., Paris

The S.A.S. was a low-slung saloon available with a number of different C.I.M.E. engines of 4- and 6-cylinders. Smallest was the 1,215cc sv six, and largest the 1,598cc ohv four. GNG

S.A.T.A.M. (F) *1941*
Ets Satam, La Courneuce, Seine

This was a two-seater electric coupé with a maximum speed of 30mph. The batteries were mounted half under the bonnet, and half behind the seats. GNG

SAUBER (CH) *1969 to date*
P.P. Sauber AG, Hinwil/Zürich

Saubers are Group 6 competition cars made in very small numbers, with tubular frames, all-independent suspension, all-disc brakes, and mid-mounted engines. The C-1 uses a 997cc Ford engine developing 120bhp with a 4-speed gearbox, but the 5-speed C-2 is powered by the 1,790cc dohc Cosworth-Ford unit. MCS

SAURER (CH) *1897–1914*
Adolphe Saurer AG, Arbon

Adolphe Saurer's first car appeared in 1897, and had a 6hp single-cylinder opposed-piston engine mounted at the rear. It had a four-seater body and tiller steering which was replaced by a wheel in 1898. The design was acquired by Koch of Neuilly, France, who made it in some numbers, especially for colonial use. The next series of Saurer cars appeared in 1902; designed by Adolphe's son Hippolyte, they were conventional 24/30hp 4-cylinder cars with T-head engines, 4-speed gearboxes, and chain drive. This model was later enlarged to 30/35hp (5.3 litres) and was joined by a 50/60hp (9.2 litres). These cars were made in small numbers up to 1914. They were mostly tourers or limousines, many of the bodies being built by Switzerland's best-known early coachbuilder, Geissberger of Zürich. Commercial vehicle production began in 1903, and soon became so important a part of the Saurer programme that private cars were dropped.

Saurer were pioneers of the Diesel engine, and are today Switzerland's largest commercial vehicle manufacturers. GNG

SAUTEL ET SÉCHAUD (F) *1902–c.1904*
Sautel et Séchaud, Gentilly, Seine

This was a 3-wheeler not unlike the Léon Bollée in general layout, except that the engine was vertical instead of horizontal. It was a single-cylinder unit of 3½hp mounted behind the rear seat, and driving through a 2-speed gearbox. All controls were on the steering column, gear changing being effected by moving the column forward or backward. GNG

SAUTTER-HARLÉ (F) *1907–1912*
(1) Sté Sautter, Harlé et Cie, Paris *1907–1908*
(2) Harlé et Cie, Paris *1908–1912*

Although little known as car makers, the firm of Sautter Harlé had been established as an engineering concern since 1825, and had made the heavy oil engines used in Koch cars at the turn of the century. Their own cars were characterized by a Renault-style bonnet, but had the radiator slung low in front. A 2-cylinder 10/12hp and a 4-cylinder 16/20hp were the first models, both with shaft drive. They were supplemented in 1910 by a 12hp 4-cylinder of 1,944cc, and an 18hp 4 of 3,053cc. GNG

S.A.V.A. (B) *1910–1923*
Sté Anversoise pour Fabrication de Voitures Automobiles, Antwerp

This Belgian marque is significant as the first sporting machine sponsored by the David Brown organization (who were the United Kingdom concessionaires in 1912–14) and also for its unusual valve gear. The first S.A.V.A.s were, however, conventional 4-cylinder 2.5-litre cars with L-head monobloc engines, thermo-syphon cooling, and cone clutches, though the constant-mesh 4-speed gearbox was unusual, as was the fuel feed by gearbox-driven pump. Sv cars were still made in 1913 but there were also 3-litre and 5.1-litre models of sporting character with dual ignition and overhead exhaust valves, a layout more frequently found on motorcycles. Larger versions of these eoi cars were listed in 1914, but for the Tourist Trophy S.A.V.A. prepared some 70bhp 3.3-litre racers on which the inlet valves were now overhead. There were still two plugs per cylinder, and a 3.4-litre production version with camshaft-driven fuel pump was planned for 1915, only to be frustrated by World War 1 and the German invasion of Belgium. The devastation of Belgium prevented S.A.V.A. from making an effective comeback until 1923, when the 1915 type was revived, albeit with a reversion, once more, to the eoi layout. Front-wheel brakes were optional on the new 3.4-litre cars, which were offered along with a less interesting 2-litre model. Belgium's automobile industry, however, was already contracting, and S.A.V.A. were among the first casualties, selling out to Minerva late that year. MCS

1972 SAUBER C-2 1,790cc sports car.
P.P. Sauber AG

1903 SAUTEL ET SECHAUD 3½hp 3-wheeler.
The Veteran Car Club of Great Britain

1920 S.A.V.A. 24/30hp two-seater. *George A. Oliver*

1913 SAXON 1.4-litre two-seater. *Don McCray*

1919 SAYERS Model BP 27hp tourer. *Keith Marvin Collection*

1920 S.B. electric cyclecar. *Autocar*

SAVER (GB) 1912
Saver Clutch Co Ltd, Manchester

The Saver car was an unconventional machine powered by a 14hp Hewitt piston-valve engine, as used in the Davy and in some Crowdys. A 2-speed gear was incorporated in the clutch (on the strength of which it was called a gearbox-less car), and it had a worm-driven rear axle. A curious boat-shaped two-seater body was used, but no price was quoted, and the car was more of a test-bed for new ideas than a serious commercial proposition. GNG

SAVIANO SCAT (US) 1960
Saviano Vehicles, Inc, Warren, Mich.

The Scat (Saviano Cargo And Touring) was a utility vehicle powered by a 25hp Kohler air-cooled engine. It had a 2-door, four-seater, body. BE

SAXON (US) 1913–1923
Saxon Motor Car Co, Detroit, Mich.; Ypsilanti, Mich.

The Saxon appeared in the winter of 1913–14 as a small two-seater roadster with a 1.4-litre 4-cylinder engine, and 2-speed rear-axle gearbox, soon replaced by a 3-speed unit. Electric lights were available at extra cost. At $395 (£105 in England), these wire-wheeled cars caught the public fancy and although they looked more like cyclecars than conventional small automobiles, sales were high from the first. Peak year was 1916, with 27,800 delivered. Continental and Ferro engines were used and after several thousand Saxons had been sold, wooden artillery spoke wheels were available as an option. Various improvements were noted through 1915 and a small number of delivery vans were produced to augment the roadster in the Saxon range. By 1915, electric lighting was standard equipment. A 2.9-litre 6-cylinder touring car still with rear-axle gearbox appeared in 1915 as a companion to the 4-cylinder roadsters which were retained until 1917, when Saxon reached tenth place in sales among American manufacturers. In 1920, a 4-cylinder ohv car reappeared and by 1921, sixes were discontinued. In the years following this re-appearance the Saxon models were known as Saxon-Duplex. Production dropped rapidly, the last cars being sold early in 1923. KM

SAYERS (US) 1917–1924
Sayers & Scovill Co, Cincinnati, Ohio

The firm of Sayers & Scovill had been building chassis as well as bodies for hearses and ambulances since 1907 and entered the private-car market in 1917 with a touring car to sell for $1,295. A Continental 6-cylinder engine was used and artillery wheels were standard. The Sayers was an especially fine car from the standpoint of body workmanship. A roadster was added to the line for 1918 and a sedan, limousine and coupé shortly after. In 1923, the production of the Sayers was suspended in favour of a larger car to be called the S. & S. KM

S.B. (D) 1920–1924
S.B. Automobilgesellschaft mbH, Berlin

The letters S.B. stand for Slaby and Beringer, Dr Slaby being the designer of this unique electric vehicle. It was a small single-seater using a chassis-less, wooden body. By adding a 2-wheeled trailer the car could be converted into a 6-wheeled two-seater. A later version had a body with two seats side by side. After S.B. was taken over by D.K.W. the car was also available with a D.K.W. motorcycle engine instead of an electric motor, but this experiment was not satisfactory. The principle of constructing chassis-less bodies of wood was applied to D.E.W. and D.K.W. cars. The 1920 single-seater was sold in England by Gamages, the London store, for £150. HON

SBARRO (CH) 1971 to date
(1) Ateliers d'Études de Construction Automobiles sarl, Les Tuileries de Grandson 1971–1972
(2) Sté de Fabrications d'Automobiles Sbarro, Gressy 1973 to date

The first Sbarro was a Lola-based super-sports coupé with 5,358cc V-8 Chevrolet engine, but in 1973 the company introduced a rear-engined 3-seater built in their new works. Power came either from twin N.S.U. Ro80 Wankel units developing a total of 230bhp or from a single, blown Volkswagen K70 engine. MCS

S.B.K. (S) 1904–1906
Svenska Belysning-Kraft AB, Tidaholm

These cars, of which only five were made, were of the ordinary buggy type, using single- or 2-cylinder engines, chain drive and tiller steering. OB

SCACCHI (I) 1911–1915
Scacchi & Cia, Fabbrica Automobili, Chivasso, Turin

The Scacchi was a medium-sized car called a 20/30hp, with a 4-cylinder monobloc engine and 4-speed gearbox. It was launched on the English market at £485 complete, but few were sold under this name, as Luigi Storero contracted to sell all Scacchi's production, providing he could call the cars Storeros. Some Scacchis were sold under the name Caesar; this may represent Cesare Scacchi's outlet for the cars which did not pass through Storero's hands. There was also a 50hp model. GNG

SCALDIA see MOSKVITCH

SCAMPOLO (D) 1950–c.1961
Recklenhausen Technical Research Bureau, Recklenhausen

The original Scampolo 500, with a rear-mounted D.K.W. 2-stroke engine, was developed by engineering students. The well-known B.M.W. twin was also used, and a later Formula Junior version was Wartburg-powered.   DF

SCANIA (S) 1902–1912
Maskinfabriks AB Scania, Malmö

The Scania company of Malmö was a successor of a branch of the Humber Cycle Co. Their first car was designed by Reinhold Thorssin and used an under-seat engine and complex chain transmission. Thorssin soon left to join A.M.G. in Gothenburg, and the first production Scanias had 2-cylinder Kamper engines under a bonnet. One of these early cars was sold to Crown Prince Gustaf of Sweden who used it for many years. From 1908 to 1911 about 30 4-cylinder cars were made, with engine outputs varying from 12 to 36hp. In 1911 the firm merged with Vabis; the Malmö factory was devoted to lorries, and cars were made in the Vabis factory at Södertälje.   OB

SCANIA-VABIS (S) 1914–1929
AB Scania-Vabis, Södertälje

After the firms of Scania and Vabis joined forces they concentrated on two 4-cylinder models, of 20 and 60bhp. The smaller had a monobloc engine, the larger had cylinders cast in pairs. It was with the 60bhp model that Scania-Vabis introduced their sharply pointed V-radiator and V-windscreen.

Post-World War 1 models were similar in design, and few were made. In 1924 the company decided to concentrate on commercial vehicles, and only four cars were made from 1924 to 1929, all to special order. Not more than 500 cars were made by the three firms of Scania, Vabis and Scania-Vabis in the period 1897 to 1929.   OB

S.C.A.P. (F) 1912–1929
SA des Automobiles S.C.A.P., Billancourt, Seine; Boulogne-sur-Seine; Courbevoie, Seine

S.C.A.P. (Société de Construction Automobiles Parisiennes) were best known for the engines they supplied after World War 1 to the manufacturers of assembled cars, but they also made a few cars of their own. Initially, they offered five models, all sv monobloc fours between 8CV and 15CV, the smallest with 3 forward speeds. They had Ballot engines. These pre-1914 S.C.A.P.s were notably successful in hill-climbs and other competitions, and sports versions were sold. After making aero engines during the war, the firm introduced their Type L 10CV, which was still a conventional small four except for its rear suspension, which consisted of two linked half-elliptics, and a transverse cantilever spring pivoted at its centre to the chassis. The Type M of 1923 was a typical baby car of the time, with an 1,100cc engine. Around 1924, the 1½-litre Type O replaced the 10CV, but from then on until 1927, the firm devoted most of its efforts to making engines for other people's cars. The last new S.C.A.P. was the 2-litre, ohv straight-8 of 1929.   TRN

S.C.A.R. (F) 1906–1915
Sté de Construction Automobile de Reims (Rayet, Liénart et Cie), Witry-les-Reims, Marne

The S.C.A.R. was first seen outside France in the 1906 Tourist Trophy. The original 18/20hp was a straightforward 2½-litre T-headed four with separate cylinders, ht magneto ignition, 3-speed gearbox, and shaft drive. The only unusual feature was the 5-bearing crankshaft, and the radiator resembled that of a Mors. A year later there was a companion 4.1-litre model, as well as a pair-cast 6-cylinder 6-litre, both also shaft-driven. By 1910 S.C.A.R.'s, while still cooled by thermo-syphon, had detachable heads, a single camshaft, 4 forward speeds, and Renault-style dashboard radiators. Smallest of the range was a 1.3-litre twin at £215, for which 38mpg was claimed, but better-known was a 2.4-litre 4-cylinder car which was raced at Brooklands, and there was also a pair-cast 6-cylinder of 3.6 litres' capacity. The later S.C.A.R.s were made on similar lines, but were all fours with a 140mm stroke, which was used in conjunction with a small 69mm bore in the case of the 11.9hp type. In 1914 there were also 2.8-litre and 3.2-litre versions, with all brakes on the rear wheels. The factory was in the front line during World War 1, and was destroyed by enemy action.   MCS

SCARAB (US) 1934–1939
Stout Engineering Co, Detroit, Mich.

Developed from the experimental Sterkenberg car designed by John Tjaarda, the Scarab was designed by William B. Stout. It had a streamlined saloon body with no bonnet, a rear-mounted Ford V-8 engine and integral construction. Apart from the driver's, the seats could be moved to any position, and a card table set up if desired. A price of $5,000 was quoted, and a few cars were made to special order, several orders coming from Hollywood stars. In 1946 Stout built another version of his streamlined car, but this did not go into production.   GNG

1951 SCAMPOLO 500cc racing car. *Autosport*

1914 SCANIA-VABIS 22hp tourer. *Scania-Vabis AB*

1924 SCANIA-VABIS limousine.
Scania-Vabis AB

1913 S.C.A.P. 15CV sporting four-seater.
Coachwork by Carrosserie Générale Automobile.
Autocar

1911 S.C.A.R. 11.9hp two-seater. *Autocar*

1909 SCHACHT 12hp motor buggy. *Henry Ford Museum, Dearborn, Mich.*

S.C.A.T. (I) *1906–1923*
Società Ceirano Automobili Torino, Turin

Giovanni Ceirano the younger, previously with Ceirano (i) and Junior, formed a new company in 1906, marketing a range of T-headed fours with lt magneto ignition, 4-speed gearboxes and shaft drive. Unusually by Italian standards these were quite modest vehicles – the largest model was a 22/32hp of 3.8 litres, enlarged to 4.4 litres in 1910 – and this realistic policy enabled the young concern to ride out the Agadir Crisis of 1907–8. The first monobloc-engined S.C.A.T. came in 1910 and a year later L-head units with ht ignition were the order of the day. Compressed-air self-starters came in 1912. S.C.A.T.s won the 1911, 1912 and 1914 Targa Florio races, their drivers including Ernesto Ceirano, Giovanni's son, and Cyril Snipe, nephew of another Torinese manufacturer, John Newton. Inevitably Newton and Bennett handled both Newton and S.C.A.T. in Britain, but there was no other connection. At the top of the immediate pre-war range were a 4.7-litre 25/35 and a vast 100 × 200mm ohc 60/70, though this one, surprisingly, was sold only with shaft drive.

During World War 1 S.C.A.T. made Hispano-Suiza aero-engines under licence. In 1917 Giovanni Ceirano sold out to a Hispano-controlled French syndicate that continued the manufacture of the 2.1-litre and 4.7-litre types after the war. New fours of 1,551cc and 2,951cc were introduced in 1922, as well as a short-lived 2.2-litre six for which 40bhp was claimed, but a year later Giovanni Ceirano was in control again, liquidating Ceirano (ii), his latest venture, and continuing production of his own designs in the S.C.A.T. works. For a short while these were called S.C.A.T.-Ceiranos. MCS

S.C.H. (B) *1927*
The S.C.H. was a light sports car with an 8CV 4-cylinder engine and all-round independent suspension. GNG

SCHACHT (US) *1905–1913*
(1) Schacht Manufacturing Co, Cincinnati, Ohio *1905–1909*
(2) Schacht Motor Car Co, Cincinnati, Ohio *1909–1913*

Up to 1909 the Schacht models were high-wheelers with 12hp 2-cylinder engines under the seat and chain drive. Steering was by wheel. After 1909, the make became more conventional with 40hp 4-cylinder engines. Some of the later cars were sold with combination truck/tourer bodies. As Le Blond-Schacht, the company made trucks up to 1938. GMN

SCHARF GEARLESS (US) *1914*
Scharf Gearless Cycle Car Co, Westerville, Ohio

This cyclecar had a friction transmission, hence the name. Drive to the rear wheels was by chain. The car had a 4-cylinder, 1-litre engine. Wheelbase was 8ft 4in. GMN

SCHAUDEL *see* MOTOBLOC

SCHAUM (US) *1901*
Schaum Automobile Co, Baltimore, Md.

The Schaum had full elliptical springs, double chain drive and tiller steering. This two-seater car was driven by a petrol engine rated at 4hp. GMN

SCHEBERA *see* CYKLON

SCHEELE (D) *1899–1910*
(1) Heinrich Scheele, Cologne *1899–1906*
(2) Kölner Elektromobil-Gesellschaft Heinrich Scheele, Cologne *1906–1910*

This firm was among the German pioneers of electric cars. Various models for private use were offered until 1910, and commercials were listed until the mid-1920s. In 1901 Scheeles were sold in England under the name Imprimis. HON

SCHEIBLER (D) *1900–1907*
(1) Motorenfabrik Fritz Scheibler, Aachen *1900–1903*
(2) Scheibler Automobil-Industrie GmbH, Aachen *1903–1907*

The first Scheiber cars were characterized by flat-twin engines and friction drive. These were superseded by conventional chain driven cars with 4-cylinder engines of up to 6.9 litres in 1904/05, and smaller single- and 2-cylinder models in 1906/07. After 1907, commercial vehicles only were made. HON

SCHILLING (D) *1905*
V. Chr. Schilling, Suhl

Using Omnimobil components and the 6/12PS, 4-cylinder Fafnir engine this firm produced a voiturette which was also marketed under the name of V.C.S. They also made the Liliput under licence. HON

SCHLOSSER (US) *1912–1913*
W.H. Schlosser Mfg Co, New York, N.Y.

The Schlosser had a 4-cylinder, 7.7-litre engine. The five-seater was priced at $2,370. GMN

SCHMIDLIN (F) *c.1925–1926*
Constructions Jean Schmidlin, Paris
　The Schmidlin was a light car powered by a 985cc 4-cylinder Ruby engine. It had a 3-speed gearbox and shaft drive.　　　　GNG

SCHNADER (US) *1907*
Milton H. Schnader, Reading, Pa.
　This car was previously called the Riviera. It was made only as a five-seater open model, powered by a flat 2-cylinder engine of 3.2 litres. Its transmission was of a planetary type and final drive was by shaft.　　　　GMN

SCHNEIDER *see* BRILLIÉ and TH. SCHNEIDER

SCHRAM (US) *1913*
Schram Motor Car Co, Seattle, Wash.
　This was a large car with a 6-cylinder engine of 6.2 litres' capacity, developing 38hp. The five-seater was priced at $2,300.　　　　GMN

SCHUCKERT (D) *1899–1900*
Elektrizitäts-Aktiengesellschaft vorm. Schuckert & Co, Nuremberg
　Electric vehicles, private cars as well as commercials, were produced by this company. The firm was taken over by Siemens in 1903 and reappeared as a car manufacturer in 1906.　　　　HON

SCHULZ (D) *1904–1906*
Maschinenfabrik G. Schulz, Magdeburg
　This was a little-known make, although the firm exhibited at the Berlin Show and participated in the 1905 Herkomer Trial. 18hp and 28hp models were produced.　　　　HON

SCHURICHT (D) *1921–1925*
(1) Automobilwerk Walter Schuricht, Pasing *1921–1924*
(2) Bayerisches Automobilwerk AG, Pasing *1924–1925*
　Schuricht built a small car with 4-cylinder 4/12PS and 5/15PS, and later 5/18PS engines and two- or three-seater bodies.　　　　HON

SCHÜTTE-LANZ (D) *1922–1923*
Schütte-Lanz Kleinautomobil GmbH, Zeesen
　This firm manufactured bodies, but in 1922 they introduced a small car of their own design. Production was limited to a series of prototypes.　　　　HON

SCIOTO *see* ARBENZ

SCIREA (I) *1914–1927*
(1) Officine Scirea, Milan *1914–1915*
(2) Officine Scirea, Monza *1924–1927*
　Initially a maker of aero-engines, Antonio Scirea built an 8/10hp light car with 1.2-litre ioe engine and 3-speed gearbox in 1914, but production was interrupted by World War 1. There were no new Scireas until 1924, when the company introduced a 1,500cc machine, still with overhead inlet valves, but now with four forward speeds. A sports version of 1927 was the last of the line.　　　　MCS

SCOOTACAR (GB) *1957–1964*
Scootacars Ltd, Leeds, Yorks.
　The Scootacar was an extremely narrow 3-wheeler, with seating for two in tandem, although the rear seat was very cramped. Originally powered by a 197cc Villiers engine, it was later given a 324cc Villiers unit.　　　　GNG

SCOOTMOBILE *see* MARTIN (ii)

SCOOT-MOBILE (US) *c.1946*
Norman Anderson, Corunna, Mich.
　Built mostly from aircraft parts, the Scoot-Mobile was a prototype 3-wheeler with automatic gear change, 3-wheel brakes, and a speed of 40mph.　　　　BE

SCORPION (i) (GB) *1960*
Rytune Ltd, Hastings, Sussex
　This was an 'export-only' Formula Junior car, based on the original front-engined Elva, and usually fitted with a D.K.W. engine.　　　　DF

SCORPION (ii) (GB) *1969–1971*
W. Hayward, Christian Malford, Wilts.
　This successful space-framed Formula 1200 sports-racing car was available for sale in kit form. It had an unusual front suspension system with swing axles and horizontal coil springs.　　　　DF

SCOTIA (GB) *c.1907*
　Few details are known of the Glasgow-built Scotia, except that a car with a

1905 SCHEELE electric landaulette. *Neubauer Collection*

1961 SCOOTACAR 324cc 3-wheel coupé. *G.N. Georgano*

1924 SCOTT SOCIABLE 578cc 3-wheeler.
National Motor Museum

1905 SCOUT 14hp Tourist Trophy car.
Autocar

1920 SCOUT 15.9hp coupé. *Autocar*

16/20hp 4-cylinder engine was listed in 1907. It may have been built on a commercial vehicle chassis. GNG

SCOTSMAN (i) (GB) *1922–1923*
Scotsman-Motor Car Co, Glasgow

The Glasgow-made car of this name was a conventional 4-cylinder family machine, sold in several types; the 10hp with a 1,460cc engine, the 11hp of 1,492cc, and (on the same chassis) the 14/40hp Flying Scotsman, with a 2.3-litre, 45bhp ohc Sage unit. All models used British-built proprietary engines. The radiator was shaped like a Scottish thistle, and one of the backers was the singer Sir Harry Lauder. TRN

SCOTSMAN (ii) (GB) *1929–1930*
Scotsman Motors Ltd, Edinburgh

The second car to bear this name was a short-lived Scottish version of the 6-cylinder, air-cooled S.A.R.A. from France, its engine being made under licence, and other parts coming from components suppliers. Only a handful were built. Some of the 1930 cars used the 11.9hp Meadows 4ED engine, and were known as the Little Scotsman. TRN

SCOTT (i) (US) *1899–1901*
(1) St Louis Electric Automobile Co, St Louis, Mo. *1899–1900*
(2) Scott Automobile Co, St Louis, Mo. *1900–1901*

The Scott was a light electric two-seater of very simple appearance and limited range. The St Louis Electric Automobile Company was organized by A.L. Dyke, who later made cars under his own name. GNG

SCOTT (ii) (F) *1912*
Scott et Cie, Paris

Little is known about this company apart from the fact that two models of 4-cylinder cars were listed for 1912 only. One had a 15hp engine of 2,120cc and the other a 20hp of 3,770cc. GNG

SCOTT-NEWCOMB *see* STANDARD (x)

SCOTT SOCIABLE (GB) *1921–1925*
Scott Autocar Co Ltd, Bradford, Yorks.

Alfred Angas Scott's odd little offset 3-wheeler was a clever device, with its triangulated tubular frame, but it was probably too reminiscent of a motor cycle and sidecar to persuade people who wanted something better to buy it. Two of the Scott's wheels were in line, and the third was offset to one side, that is to say there was one wheel at each corner of the frame. All were enveloped by a wooden side-by-side two-seater body, and the whole ensemble was propelled, naturally enough, by Scott's famous water-cooled 2-stroke 2-cylinder engine, of 578cc, driving through a 3-speed gearbox to the offside rear wheel by shaft. Steering was by wheel. TRN

SCOTTISH ASTER *see* ST VINCENT

SCOUT (GB) *1904–1923*
(1) Dean and Burden Bros Ltd, Salisbury, Wilts. *1904–1908*
(2) Scout Motors Ltd, Salisbury, Wilts. *1908–1921*
(3) Whatley & Co, Pewsey, Wilts. *1921–1923*

The Burden brothers had been selling Scout engines for motorcycles, boats and agricultural machinery since 1902. In 1904 the business was expanded and registered, and 4-cylinder cars and commercial vehicles offered. Designs were conservative, and sales remained largely local. A 14/17 model was entered in the 1905 Tourist Trophy, and in 1906 J.P. Dean drove a standard 17/20 tourer of 2,926cc into 9th place. Surprisingly, a 6-cylinder 4,389cc car was introduced that year. In 1907 a move to larger premises was made, production now running at around 100 cars annually. Models ranged from a 12hp 2-cylinder to an enlarged 6-cylinder of 5,638cc. By 1911 various other 4-cylinder models had been introduced, but the six had been dropped. The first monobloc engine was the 10/12 1,870cc of 1912. Unusually, World War 1 brought no prosperity: prolonged bickerings over Admiralty contracts debilitated the firm. When released in 1920, only one private-car model was offered. This, the 2,613cc 12/14 of 15.9 rated hp, was sold to Wiltshiremen on the marque's pre-war prestige rather than on the associations of the khaki paintwork. The first post-war slump found the firm deficient in strength or flexibility. Whatley and Co, the firm that picked up the remnants, assembled a few more cars. DF

SCRIPPS-BOOTH (US) *1913–1922*
The Scripps-Booth Co, Detroit, Mich.

James Scripps-Booth planned to make a tandem two-seater cyclecar steered from the rear, but the production model had front-seat steering. It was powered by a Spacke air-cooled V-twin engine, had a 2-speed planetary transmission, and final drive by two leather V-belts. About 400 were sold at $385 each, up to the end of 1914. These cyclecars were sometimes known as Rockets. From 1914 to 1916 a staggered-seat roadster, the Model C, was made, powered by a 25hp Sterling 4-cylinder ohv engine, and using shaft drive. This was replaced in 1916 by the Model

D, with a Ferro V-8 engine, made in roadster, touring and town car models. Both Models C and D had pointed radiators, some of the Model D town cars being very similar to the Mercedes in this respect.

In July 1918 Scripps-Booth was acquired by General Motors, and the cars rapidly lost their individuality. The 1918 Model G had a Mason-built Chevrolet 490 engine, transmission and rear axle, and so was really a Chevrolet in Scripps-Booth clothing, but at a much higher price than the Chevrolet. 1919 to 1923 models had Oakland chassis and Northway engines, with Scripps-Booth bodies and radiators. In 1921 even the V-radiator was abandoned.   GNG

SEABROOK (GB) 1920–1928
(1) Seabrook Bros Ltd, London E.C. 1920–1926
(2) Seabrook Bros Ltd, London S.W.3 1926–1928

Seabrook Bros were a firm of factors who imported the Regal (later R.M.C.) before the war, and began to make their own car in 1920. This was an advanced machine with an 11.9hp 4-cylinder engine using aluminium pistons and cylinder heads. It proved too expensive to make, and was replaced in 1921 by a 9.8hp model with a Dorman engine. In 1923 an 11.9hp Meadows-engined model was added, which became the only model from 1925 onwards.   GNG

SEAGRAVE (US) 1960
Seagrave Fire Apparatus Co, Columbus, Ohio

After examining several independently designed prototype compact cars from a Detroit firm, the Seagrave Co, long known for its fire-fighting equipment, decided against producing them. One of the cars was 13ft long, stood 4ft high and used a 4-cylinder Continental engine of 65hp.   BE

SEAL (GB) 1912–1924
(1) Haynes & Bradshaw, Manchester 1912–1920
(2) Seal Motors Ltd, Manchester 1920–1924

The Seal was a most unusual 3-wheeler which resembled a motorcycle and side-car, but was steered from the side-car. The first model used a 770cc 6hp J.A.P. V-twin engine, a Sturmey-Archer hub gear box, and belt drive. Steering was by tiller. The 1914 model had a 980cc 8hp J.A.P. engine, used on all subsequent Seals, a 3-speed countershaft gear box, chain drive, and wheel steering. A 1920 model had Seal's own gear box and shaft drive, but the following year a return was made to chain drive and a Burman gearbox. Two-, three-, and four-seater models were made in the 1920s, the latter being called the Family model and having full weather protection.   GNG

SEARCHMONT (US) 1900–1903
(1) Searchmont Motor Co, Philadelphia, Pa. 1900–1902
(2) Fournier-Searchmont Co, Chester, Pa. 1902–1903

In November 1900 the Searchmont company acquired the rights to manufacture the light car developed by the Keystone Motor Company. Known as the Wagonette, this car had a 5 or 10hp rear-mounted engine, two-seater body and tiller steering. It was made until 1902 when, under the direction of the French racing driver Charles Fournier, a new range of front-engined cars with 8 or 10hp 2-cylinder engines and double chain drive was made. Very expensive at $2,500 for the 10hp, they were nevertheless the first American-built cars to have forced-feed lubrication. They were designed by L.S. Chadwick who later made the famous Chadwick car. In 1903 a 32hp 4-cylinder car was made.   GNG

SEARS (US) 1906–1911
Sears Motor Car Works, Chicago, Ill.

The Sears was a high-wheeler built in both passenger and utility versions, for marketing by the Sears, Roebuck mail-order Company. All models had solid-rubber tyres and 2-cylinder horizontally-opposed air-cooled engines, and were steered by tiller. The most advanced model was the 1911 closed coupé selling for $485. Some 3,500 Sears cars were sold. The firm made a brief return to the mail-order car business in 1952 (see Allstate).   GMN

S.E.A.T. (E) 1953 to date
Sociedad Española de Automóviles de Turismo, Barcelona

Spain's biggest private-car producers opened their factory in July 1953, and have concentrated on the manufacture of Fiat designs. Until 1956 their staple offering was the 1400 4-cylinder saloon, but this was joined in 1957 by the rear-engine 600. In 1959 S.E.A.T. followed Fiat in adopting the angular Pininfarina line, but combined the hull of the 6-cylinder 1800 model with the 1400 engine and transmission. In 1963 the parent company's 1500 engine first became an option in this car, and then supplanted the old type. Some Siata-modified cars were also made and sold, and in 1966 the 850 joined the range. A S.E.A.T. 4-door saloon version was catalogued in 1968, when production passed the six-figure mark for the first time, and another special Spanish model made its appearance. This 1430 was a de-luxe 4-headlamp 124 with 1,430cc pushrod engine. In 1970 283,678 cars were delivered, and S.E.A.T. assumed the role of supplier of obsolete Fiat models for which an export demand still existed – initially the 600D, but from late 1971 the

1916 SCRIPPS-BOOTH Model D town car. *Don McCray*

1924 SEAL 980cc family 3-wheeler. *M.J. Holben*

1902 SEARCHMONT 10hp tonneau. *Kenneth Stauffer*

1963 S.E.A.T. 600D 4-door saloon. *S.E.A.T.*

1920 SECQUEVILLE-HOYAU 10CV coupé de ville. *Autocar*

1928 SELVE Selecta 3.1-litre fwd saloon. *Autocar*

850 saloon and coupé as well. Alongside these production of the 124/125 family continued.　MCS

SEATON-PETTER (GB) 1926–1927
British Dominions Car Co Ltd, Yeovil, Somerset

The British Dominions Car Company was run by Douglas Seaton, and the cars were made in the works of Petters, the oil-engine makers who had built some early cars under their own name. The Seaton-Petter had a vertical twin 2-stroke engine of 1.3 litres, 3 forward speeds, and ¾-elliptic springs all round. The body was a high, roomy four-seater, the rear seats being detachable to allow the car's use as a light truck. The price was a remarkably low £100.　TRN

SEBRING (US) 1910–1911
(1) Sebring Motor Car Co, Sebring, Ohio *1910*
(2) Sebring Automobile Co, Sebring, Ohio *1911*

The Sebring used 6-cylinder engines exclusively. These were of 3.9 litres, and 35hp. Three body types were offered on a 10ft 2in wheelbase. Some models had monocle-type windscreens.　GMN

SECQUEVILLE-HOYAU (F) 1919–1924
SA des Anciens Ets Secqueville-Hoyau, Gennevilliers, Seine

The 10CV Secqueville-Hoyau was a short-lived light car of very high quality and correspondingly high cost; one of several similar attempts in different countries to provide a type of machine that nobody wanted. The 4-cylinder, 1¼-litre engine was an efficient unit, with its inclined side-valves, aluminium pistons and tubular connecting rods. Other luxury touches were a 3-bearing crankshaft, 4 speeds, and electric starting (unusual in a small car at the time), and a radiator of Rolls-Royce shape. It was a good-looking car, carrying well-proportioned bodywork with pleasingly low lines, helped by underslung springs. The company had started life making aircraft components, and had built Bugatti aero engines under licence during World War 1, which probably accounted for the *canard* that their new car was also designed by Bugatti.　TRN

SEETSTU (GB) 1906–1907
James McGeoch & Co, Paisley, Renfrewshire

The Seetstu was a light two-seater 3-wheeler powered by a 3hp 2-stroke engine. The name is said to be derived from Paisley dialect 'seestu', meaning 'see you'; another explanation is that it means 'seats two'. Only six or seven were built.　GNG

SEFTON (GB) 1903
Liverpool & Manchester Motor Manufacturing Co, Liverpool

This company were well-known dealers who sold De Dietrich, Régal, and other cars. It was announced that they were to manufacture the Sefton voiturette, delivery van and car, but no details are known. If there were any made, they were probably assembled vehicles; the fact that the company sold the Régal points to the use of Lacoste et Battmann components.　GNG

SEIDEL-AROP (D) 1925–1926
Arop Gesellschaft mbH, Automobilbau, Berlin

The Arop company produced one 8/25PS, 1,020cc model only, designed by Seidel.　HON

SEKINE (US) 1923
I. Sekine & Co, New York, N.Y.

I. Sekine was an importer who built, or had built, a car for sale in the Japanese market for a short time. The Sekine had no differential, the drive being taken from a 4-cylinder engine of just under 2-litres capacity, angled at 17° from the longitudinal axis of the car to the left rear wheel, thence through fabric universals to the right wheel by way of a shaft. There were no conventional axles, their place being taken by double transverse springs. The sole brake was connected to the right rear wheel. Only a touring car model was made.　KM

SELDEN (US) 1906–1914
Selden Motor Vehicle Co, Rochester, N.Y.

This manufacturing company was founded by George B. Selden of patents fame. The early models of the car used 4-cylinder Continental engines, under a peculiarly shaped bonnet. By 1912 the Selden had grown to a vehicle with a 10ft 5in wheelbase with a 4-cylinder 47hp engine. It is ironic that this make succumbed just as Selden's rival at law, Henry Ford, was booming with his Model T. Commercial vehicles were, however, manufactured until 1932.　GMN

SELF (S) 1916; 1919; 1922
Axel H. and Per Weiertz, Svedala

The two Weiertz brothers constructed three prototypes of cyclecars with pointed 'radiators' and long bonnets covering their air-cooled engines. The first car had a single-cylinder engine, the second a 4-cylinder, and the third a V-twin. The brothers later worked for Thulinverken and designed the Thulin Type B.　OB

SELLERS (US) *1909–1912*
(1) Sellers Automobile Co, Elkhart, Ind.
(2) Sellers Motor Car Co, Hutchinson, Kan.
This was a conventional 4-cylinder touring car built largely for local consumption. GNG

SELVE (D) *1923–1929*
Selve Automobilwerke AG, Hameln
After World War 1 the Norddeutsche Automobil-Werke, manufacturers of the Colibri and Sperber, were taken over by the Selve concern, who were already producing Basse & Selve engines for the car industry. Their first cars were the 6/24PS 1½-litre and the 8/32PS 2-litre models. The 8/40PS 2,090cc type (later increased to 9/40PS and 2,352cc) was also available in a sports version developing 65bhp. The 6-cylinder 2,850cc models of 1925 and the 3,075cc Selecta of 1927 completed the range. The latter was manufactured until 1929, when car production was discontinued. A front-driven 6-cylinder car — designed by Henze — was introduced at the Berlin Motor Show in 1928 but not put into production. HON

S.E.M. *see* MORISSE

SEMAG (CH) *1920*
Seebacher Maschinenbau AG, Zürich
This was a light car powered by an 11hp 4-cylinder engine. It was designed by Rudolf Egg, and bore a radiator similar in shape to that of the Moser, another Egg design. Financial troubles prevented the Semag from going into production. GNG

SENATOR (US) *1906–1910*
Victor Auto Co, Ridgeville, Ind.
The Senator used air-cooled engines of up to 4-cylinders and 3.3 litres with 3-speed selective transmission. Three body types were available at $2,000. GMN

SENECA (US) *1917–1924*
Seneca Motor Car Co, Fostoria, Ohio
The Seneca was a typical assembled car with tourers and roadsters the only body types available. All Senecas were 4-cylinder cars, a Le Roi engine being used before 1922 and a Lycoming being substituted afterwards. Only a few hundred Senecas were built during any year and about half of the output was exported, most of the other half being sold in and around Fostoria. KM

SÉNÉCHAL (F) *1921–1929*
(1) Sénéchal et Cie, Courbevoie, Seine *1921–1925*
(2) Sté Industrielle et Commerciale de Gennevilliers, Seine *1925–1929*
The Sénéchal, the product of a racing driver, Robert Sénéchal, was one of the more successful French sporting voiturettes. The first model, the B4, was powered by a 4-cylinder Ruby engine of 900cc, driving through a 2-speed gearbox and shaft transmission, and had front suspension by a single transverse spring. By 1922, the Sénéchal had become completely normal by acquiring 3 speeds, and two engine sizes were available, the bigger a 975cc, with overhead valves. This was called the Grand Sport, and the 900cc car the Sport. A year later, the Sport had gone, and an 1,100cc machine was added.
In 1925 the firm was taken over by Chenard-Walcker, and engines were henceforth made by the controlling company. The 1,100cc and the 975cc SZ had front-wheel brakes by 1926. In 1927 the range consisted of the SZ and the 1500 Special, a car with a bigger bore, providing 1½ litres. Both of these models had 4 speeds. The Sénéchal gained most of its renown by winning the Bol d'Or race three times running, in 1923–25. TRN

SENG ET HENRY (F) *1901–1902*
The Seng et Henry was a light car powered by a front-mounted 2-cylinder vertical engine, with a 4-speed gearbox and shaft drive. The clutch and brake were operated by movement of the steering wheel. GNG

SENSAUD DE LAVAUD *see* DE LAVAUD

SERA (F) *1960*
Sera SA, Paris 17e
The Sera was a two-seater sports car using Dyna-Panhard engine and chassis components. GNG

SERENISSIMA (I) *1965–1970*
Scuderia Serenissima, Bologna
This was a revival of the Chiti-designed A.T.S. sports coupé, now once again under Count Volpi's sponsorship. The V-8 engine had two overhead camshafts per block where the A.T.S. had had only one, but the unit's amidships mounting, the space-frame, and the all-round disc brakes were inherited from the earlier car. It was made in 300bhp, 3-litre and 340bhp, 3.5-litre versions, and one ran at Le Mans in 1966 without success. Serenissima engines were also tried in the 1966 Formula 1

1920 SEMAG 11hp tourer.
Ferdinand Hediger Collection

1925 SÉNÉCHAL 8hp sports car. *Autocar*

McLaren racing cars, but were dropped for the 1967 season, though Group 6 McLaren-Serenissimas were seen in 1968 and 1969. Attempts to revive the make included a Ghia-bodied 3½-litre coupé at the 1968 Turin Show, and in 1970 Moreno Baldi acquired some of the assets of the company – the last sign of activity from either Serenissima or A.T.S.   MCS

1965 SERENISSIMA 3-litre sports car.
Autosport

SERPENTINA (US) 1915
Claudius Mezzacasa, New York City, N.Y.

This was an experimental car using the diamond pattern wheel layout as on the Sunbeam-Mabley.   GNG

SERPOLLET (F) 1887–1907
(1) Léon Serpollet, Paris 1887–1900
(2) Gardner Serpollet, Paris 1900–1907

Léon Serpollet was one of the pioneers of the steam road vehicle, and contributed more to the development of the private passenger steam car than anyone else, with his multi-tube flash boiler of 1888. For the first time, steam could be raised quickly, by instantaneous evaporation of water in heated tubes. The unit was economical, for it only generated as much steam as was immediately required, and it was compact, allowing its use in passenger vehicles of reasonable size. Within eight years, Serpollet was using paraffin oil firing instead of coke, which again helped the steam passenger car. A dual pump fed oil to the burner and water to the boiler in constant proportions. By 1899 Serpollet had developed a 5hp engine with four vertical cylinders and poppet instead of slide valves, centrally-mounted. So far, very few Serpollet steam cars had been marketed, but in 1900, backed by finance from the American Frank Gardner, the latest model, now with horizontally-opposed cylinders, was put on sale in 5, 8 and 10hp form. Serpollet supported competitions, himself achieving 75mph over the flying kilometre with a racing car in 1902. Serpollets finished 3rd, 4th, 5th and 6th in the 1902 Circuit du Nord. The 6-cylinder cars prepared for the 1904 Gordon Bennett Eliminating Trials were less successful. The 1903 models had their water tank at the front instead of the rear, providing a 'bonnet' in the fashionable manner. A year later the dual pump, previously hand-operated, was driven by a donkey engine on two new models, the 15hp and 40hp, and the engine as well as the boiler moved up to the front. The condenser was the 'radiator'. A small 9hp utility model was also new; in this, oil was fed by pressure only. By 1906 engine and boiler had retired from their frontal position, which cannot have helped sales, and a year later Serpollet, and his car, died. TRN

1899 SERPOLLET 12hp landaulette. *National Motor Museum*

SERPOLLET-ITALIANA (I) 1906–1908
Serpollet Italiana SA, Milan

This ambitious venture took over the old Ricordi e Molinari works with the intention of building Serpollet steam cars and commercial vehicles; examples of these were exhibited at the 1907 Milan Show. The company also offered a light single-cylinder 8hp petrol runabout of unknown provenance.   MCS

SERVITOR (US) 1907
Barnes Manufacturing Co, Sandusky, Ohio

The 12/14hp Servitor had an air-cooled, 4-cylinder engine and a patented 2-speed transmission with final drive by shaft. The only model was a two-seater.   GMN

SEVERIN (US) 1920–1922
Severin Motor Car Co, Kansas City, Mo.

Using a Continental 6-cylinder engine, the Severin was a typical assembled car of the early 1920s.   KM

SEYMOUR-TURNER see TURNER (ii)

S.F.A.T. (F) 1903–1904
Sté Française des Autos Thermo-Pneumatiques, Paris

The S.F.A.T. design eliminated the gearbox by the use of compressed air drive. A conventional 4-cylinder engine drove an air compressor which drove the rear wheels through a turbine. It was shown at the 1903 Paris Salon, but there is no record of how it performed.   GNG

S.G.V. (US) 1911–1915
(1) Acme Motor Car Co, Reading, Pa. 1911
(2) S.G.V. Co, Reading, Pa. 1913–1915

The S.G.V. succeeded the Acme (ii), and was inspired by the Lancia. These were high quality cars with luxury features such as Circassian walnut dashes. All models had 4-cylinder engines, of up to 4.3 litres. As many as six body types were available, with limousines selling for $3,850. In 1913, the S.G.V. introduced the Vulcan electric shift with 4 forward speeds. This transmission was actuated by push-buttons mounted in a steering-wheel spoke.   GMN

SHAD-WYCK (US) 1917–1918
Shadburne Brothers, Frankfort, Ind.

The Shad-Wyck was in fact a Bour-Davis assembled by Shadburne Brothers

1904 SERPOLLET 18hp tulip phaeton. *The Veteran Car Club of Great Britain*

after the first failure of the Bour-Davis company in 1917. About 25 cars were sold under the name Shad-Wyck; a plan to assemble Dixie Flyers in the same factory was never realized. GNG

SHAMROCK (IRL) 1959–1960
Shamrock Motors Ltd, Tralee, Kerry

The Shamrock was a four-seater convertible with fibreglass body and detachable top, powered by a 1½-litre ohv B.M.C. engine. Only four were made. GNG

SHANGHAI (CHI) 1965 to date
Shanghai Motor Factory, Shanghai

This is a medium-sized saloon powered by a 90bhp 6-cylinder engine of about 2 litres capacity. A considerable number of Shanghais are in use in China, both for Government officials and as taxis. GNG

SHARON (US) 1915
Driggs-Seabury Ordnance Corp, Sharon, Pa.

The Sharon was a short-lived tandem cyclecar with an underslung chassis. Its 4-cylinder engine was rated at 12/15hp and power was transmitted through friction drive. This prolific manufacturer also produced the Twombly (iii), Driggs-Seabury and Ritz. GMN

SHARP (US) 1914–1915
Sharp Engineering & Manufacturing Co, Detroit, Mich.

At $295 the Sharp was one of the cheapest of the cyclecars. It was a two-seater with an 800cc, 2-cylinder, air-cooled engine. It had a 2-speed gearbox, and shaft drive. GMN

SHARP-ARROW (US) 1909–1910
(1) William H. Sharp, Trenton, N.J.
(2) Sharp-Arrow Automobile Co, Trenton, N.J.

William Sharp was a professional photographer who appears to have produced two small cars as early as 1905. The later and larger cars were actually manufactured at the plant of the Mercer Automobile Co, also in Trenton. The available models were a touring car, roadster and a 'speedabout'. These used a 6.4-litre 4-cylinder Beaver engine. The company faded away after Sharp was killed driving a Sharp-Arrow in practice for the 1910 Savannah Races. GMN

SHATSWELL (US) 1901–c.1903
H.K. Shatswell & Co, Dedham, Mass.

Shatswell sold accessories and components, especially for steam cars. They advertised a complete set of components, including a Mason engine, for home assembly of a light steam runabout. GNG

SHAW (i) (US) 1920–1921
Waldron W. Shaw Livery Co, Chicago, Ill.

For many years builders and operators of taxicabs, the Shaw Company introduced its private car line in 1920 with a phaeton powered by a 4-cylinder Rochester-Duesenberg engine and selling for $5,000. This was augmented by a roadster, sports-phaeton, coupé, sedan and limousine, and the cars were sold in limited numbers. For a brief time, the Shaw name was temporarily dropped in favour of Colonial. In 1921, the Duesenberg four was replaced by a Weidely 12-cylinder power unit, but few were marketed. The Shaw was taken over late in 1921 by the Yellow Cab Company which sold the remaining cars with a Continental engine under the Ambassador name. KM

SHAW (ii) (US) 1924–1930
Shaw Manufacturing Co, Galesburg, Kansas

The Shaw Sport Speedster was an ultra-light two-seater, designed mainly for children. It was powered by a 2½hp engine of either Shaw or Briggs & Stratton manufacture, and had only one speed. Early models had belt or chain drive, but shaft was available from 1926. Prices varied from $120 to $151. GNG

SHAWMUT (US) 1905–1909
Shawmut Motor Co, Stoneham, Mass.

The Shawmut – the name is of American Indian origin – succeeded the Phelps. Its 4-cylinder, 6.4-litre engine was rated at 35/40hp and powered touring cars and roadsters. A 4-speed transmission and shaft drive was used. GMN

SHEFFIELD-SIMPLEX (GB) 1907–1922
Sheffield-Simplex Motor Works Ltd, Tinsley, Sheffield, Yorks.

The Sheffield-Simplex started life in 1904 as the Brotherhood-Crocker, a conventional 20hp, 4-cylinder, chain-driven machine on Mercedes lines. It was renamed Sheffield-Simplex in 1907, but was dropped two years later in favour of three new machines. One was a car in the luxury class. This 45hp had only 2 forward speeds, of which the lower was an emergency gear in the back axle. The square (114mm × 114mm) 6-cylinder engine was so flexible that the universal bugbear of gearchanging

1912 S.G.V. roadster. *Antique Automobile*

1972 SHANGHAI 6-cylinder saloon. *Andrew Wilson*

1909 SHARP-ARROW 6.4-litre roadster. *Kenneth Stauffer*

1924 SHAW(ii) 2½hp speedster. *Dr Alfred Lewerenz Collection*

1914 SHEFFIELD-SIMPLEX 30hp tourer.
National Motor Museum

1968 SHELBY(ii) GT-500 7-litre coupé. *Shelby
Automotive*

1924 SHERET 7/8hp family tourer. *Autocar*

1921 SHORT-ASHBY 8hp two-seater. *Autocar*

could be abolished. All normal running was supposed to be done on the one, direct gear. However, gears improved any car, even if using them was not absolutely essential, so a 3-speed gearbox in the back axle was added in 1911. The clutch and footbrake were operated by the same pedal. The other new Sheffield-Simplexes for 1910, the 20/30hp and the 14/20hp, were anything but original in most respects, being frank copies of the Renault from France. The first was a six, and the second a four with Allen-Liversedge front-wheel brakes. All three cars were discontinued for 1913, being replaced by the 30hp, which had an engine of the same dimensions as the smaller six, but was notably smooth and quiet. The radiator was in the normal place, and there was a 4-speed gearbox behind the engine, driving to a Lanchester-type underslung worm back axle. Starting and lighting were electric. The Sheffield-Simplex was now, in fact, a modern, beautifully-built, but quite conventional car. It was continued after World War 1, acquiring front-wheel brakes as an option in 1921, but, presumably to facilitate casting, its 6 cylinders were now cast separately instead of in pairs; a retrograde step. It was extremely expensive, costing £2,700 complete at this time, and very few were built.   TRN

SHELBY (i) (US) *1902–1903*
Shelby Motor Car Co, Shelby, Ohio

The Shelby used a horizontal single-cylinder double piston engine on Gobron-Brillié lines. In other respects it was a conventional light car with a De Dion-type bonnet and low-mounted radiator, shaft drive and a four-seater tonneau body.   GNG

SHELBY (ii) (US) *1962–1970*
(1) Shelby-American Inc, Santa Fe Springs, Calif. *1962*
(2) Shelby-American Inc, Venice, Calif. *1962–1967*
(3) Shelby Automotive, Ionia, Mich. *1967–1968*
(4) Ford Motor Co, Detroit, Mich. *1968–1970*

The first of racing driver Carroll Shelby's Cobras used a 3.6-litre Ford V-8 engine in a modified British-built A.C. chassis. Early production versions used a 4.3-litre engine, but the majority of the 1,140 Shelby Cobras had 4.7 or 7-litre units. In 1965 Shelby began building the 4.7-litre GT-350 coupé, a tuned and lightened version of Ford's Mustang, and this was joined in 1967 by the GT-500 which used the 7-litre engine. The Cobra was discontinued in 1968, and the name applied to the Mustang-based cars. At about the same time, Ford took over manufacture of this car and continued until early 1970, when the Shelby line was dropped. Total production of Shelby GTs was 14,810.   GNG

SHEPHARD (F) *1900*
E.F. Shephard, Levallois-Perret, Seine

The Shephard was powered by a 5hp 2-cylinder Doré engine mounted transversely under a perforated bonnet. It had shaft drive to the gearbox, and chain final drive. A light two-seater body was provided.   GNG

SHEPPEE (GB) *1912*
Sheppee Motor Co, York.

Made by a firm of steam lorry manufacturers, the Sheppee was a heavy-looking steam car powered by a 25hp engine with 2 double-acting high pressure cylinders. The engine and many components came from the firm's lorries, and very few cars were made. They had tourer or cabriolet bodies.   GNG

SHERET (GB) *1924–1925*
Arnott & Harrison Ltd, Willesden, London N.W.10

The Sheret was a more expensive version of the New Carden, also made by Arnott & Harrison. It used the same engine, but had a three-seater body, chain drive in place of the Carden's spur gear, 3 speeds in place of 2, and quarter elliptic springs all round, instead of the Carden's transverse semi-elliptic at the front.   GNG

SHERIDAN (US) *1920–1921*
Sheridan Motor Car Co, Muncie, Ind.

The Sheridan was a short-lived General Motors product which was to have been produced both in 4- and 8-cylinder types, although the latter failed to appear on the market. The car was equipped with a Northway engine and sold for less than $2,000. Production was in the old Interstate car factory and the Sheridan was presumably made to fill the gap between the Chevrolet and Oakland cars in the G.M. empire. The 8-cylinder model was to have appeared just below the Cadillac size and price range. In 1922, the factory was acquired by William C. Durant and was henceforth used for the manufacture of Durant Six and Princeton cars.   KM

SHIBAURA (J) *1954*
Exhibited at the 1954 Tokyo Motor Show, this minicar was driven by an air-cooled motorcycle engine. No further information was reported.   BE

SHIELS (AUS) *1933*
Phoenix Motors Pty Ltd, St Kilda, Victoria

This was a light sports car powered by an 18hp 6-cylinder engine driving the front wheels. The prototype was built by Phoenix Motors to Shiels' design, but production never started.   GNG

SHOEMAKER (US) *1906–1908*
(1) Shoemaker Automobile Co, Freeport, Ill. *1906–1908*
(2) Shoemaker Automobile Co, Elkhart, Ind. *1908*

The Shoemaker was a five- or seven-seater car with a 35/40hp 4-cylinder engine. It had a 3-speed gearbox and shaft drive. Among the features of the car were a tubular front axle and camel-hair brake shoes. In June 1908 the Shoemaker company was bought by the St Joe Motor Car Company who became the Sellers Automobile Company the following year.   GMN

SHORT-ASHBY (GB) *1921–1923*
(1) Short Bros Ltd, Rochester, Kent *1921–1922*
(2) Ashby Motors Ltd, Manchester *1922–1923*

The Short-Ashby (or Short, or Ashby) was an attempt by an aircraft manufacturer to make a small car, in the lean times that faced the aero industry after World War 1. Although designed by Victor Ashby, it was a very 'French' machine, with a 4-cylinder, 970cc Ruby engine, front transverse spring and rear cantilevers. Transmission was by friction disc, giving 3 speeds. As with many other friction-drive makes, there was the option, latterly, of a conventional 3-speed gearbox. 1923 cars were called Ashbys, being no longer made by Short Brothers.   TRN

1951 SIATA 1400 Rallye tourer. *Siata Auto SpA*

S.H.W. (D) *1924–1925*
Schwäbische Hüttenwerke AG, Böblingen

Only three prototypes were built of this car, which had some advanced features for its time. It was the work of Professor Kamm, who later was closely connected with the foundation of the Research Institute for Automobile Engineering at Stuttgart and the designing there of the experimental K-Wagen. The S.H.W. was intended as a small, economical car for a wide public. Its main feature was the cup-shaped self-supporting body – built in aluminium alloy by the Zeppelin works – which was completely closed at the bottom. Front drive and a ZF-Soden preselector gearbox were used, the engine being an opposed twin 4/20PS of 1,000 cc. This car did not go into mass production – not because of technical but because of financial difficulties. The three prototypes were run for about 50,000 to 65,000 miles and proved successful in the A.D.A.C. 24 Hours Race on a Taunus circuit in 1925.   HON

S.I.A.M. (I) *1921–1923*
Società Italiana Automobili Milano, Milan

The S.I.A.M. had a 2-litre single-ohc 6-cylinder engine. It apparently never passed the prototype stage.   GNG

SIATA (I) *1949–1970*
(1) Società Italiana Applicazione Trasformazione Automobilistiche, Turin *1949–1959*
(2) Siata-Abarth, Turin *1959–1961*
(3) Siata Auto, Turin *1961–1970*

1952 SIATA 208 2-litre V-8 coupé. *Siata Auto SpA*

As its name implies, Ambrosini's company, founded in 1926, has always specialized in tuned and 'customized' versions of other makes, chiefly Fiat. By 1933 they were extracting 48bhp from the basic Balilla design, which developed only 22bhp in standard form, and their ohv head for the 1936 500 Topolino enjoyed a wide currency: they also marketed a handsome little cabriolet version of this model with a V-grille. A rear-engined 750cc machine, the Bersaglieri, was announced in 1948, but the first production Siata car was the Amica, which used ohv Fiat 500 B/C mechanical components in their own steel tube frame, clothed with full width cabriolet bodywork, and was available not only with a 22bhp tuned standard engine, but also with a Siata-modified 750cc 3-bearing version developing 25bhp. The next Fiat model to receive the Siata treatment was the oversquare 1400 of 1950, which emerged with output boosted from 44 to 65bhp, open or closed sporting bodywork, and a grille which had a hint of M.G. about it – the Rallye two-seater of 1951 had a 5-speed gearbox and was a close imitation of the M.G. TD-type. Special Fiat 1400s were still being offered in 1958. In 1952 American power units were adopted, a few cars being made both with the 722cc ohc Crosley and the big hemi-head V-8 Chrysler, the latter unit mounted in a chassis with separate gearbox, torsion-bar independent front suspension, and De Dion rear axle. From 1952 to 1955 some handsome *derivazioni* were evolved round FIAT's limited-production V-8 2-litre, these offering Vignale coachwork, a 5-speed gearbox, and 110mph for $6,000 in America. A brief essay into the popular market was made in 1953 with the Mitzi minicar: this had all-round torsion-bar suspension and a rear-mounted 400cc sv vertical-twin engine. Thereafter Siata concerned themselves with Fiat derivatives, using 600 and 1100 mechanical elements. In 1960 resources were pooled with Abarth, both companies retaining their separate existences, and two years later Siata transferred their attention to the 1300 and 1500 Fiat models. 1,400 cars were made in 1964, most of these being twin-carburettor 94bhp variants of the regular Fiat 1500 saloon, though a handsome GT coupé was offered as well. Last of the Siatas was the Spring, a sports two-seater based on the rear-engined Fiat 850; it marked a reversion to the mock-M.G. theme of 1951.   MCS

1964 SIATA TS 1500 1½-litre coupé. *Siata Auto SpA*

1904 SIDDELEY 6hp two-seater. *Bristol-Siddeley Ltd*

1913 SIDDELEY-DEASY 14/20hp two-seater. *Autocar*

c.1906 SIEMENS-SCHUCKERT electric landaulette. *Neubauer Collection*

SIBLEY (i) (GB) c.1902
John Sibley & Co, Maidstone, Kent

This company advertised that they were motor car, lurry (*sic*) and wagon builders, and would make motor vehicles to any design. It is not known if they were ever commissioned to build a vehicle, or if they had to be content with sales and repairs.   GNG

SIBLEY (ii) (US) 1910–1911
Sibley Motor Car Co, Detroit, Mich.

The Sibley was a two-seater roadster with a 4-cylinder 3.6-litre engine rated at 30hp, driving through a 3-speed selective transmission. Eugene Sibley, one of the founders of this company, was later to form the Sibley-Curtis Motor Co of Simsbury, Conn. This firm made only two cars, in 1912, and one of the partners was killed in a road accident in one of them.   GMN

SIBRAVA (CS) 1920–1923
J. Sibrava, Prague

Sibrava made Walter 3-wheelers under licence for a year or two from 1920, and a few 4-wheeled cars of his own design in 1923.   GNG

S.I.C. (I) 1924
Società Italiana Cyclecars, Chiavari

Italy, like other European countries, produced a crop of short-lived cyclecars just after World War 1. One of the smallest was the S.I.C., powered by a 2-cylinder, 500cc, 2-stroke engine. It had 2 forward speeds.   TRN

SICAM (F) 1919–c.1922
S.I.C.A.M., Pantin, Seine

The Sicam was a small cyclecar powered by a 496cc 2-cylinder 2-stroke Violet engine. Transmission was by chains and dog-clutches in the manner of G.N. and Frazer Nash, but only two speeds were provided. Front suspension was by helical springs, with a transverse leaf spring at the rear.   GNG

SIDDELEY (GB) 1902–1904
(1) Siddeley Autocar Co Ltd., Coventry, Warwickshire 1902–1903
(2) Vickers, Son, and Maxim Ltd, Crayford, Kent 1903–1904

J.D. Siddeley's first cars were merely thinly-disguised Peugeots on Mercédès lines, with vertical engines, mechanically-operated inlet valves, honeycomb radiators, and side chain drive, offered in 2.3-litre, twin-cylinder and 3.3-litre, 4-cylinder 18hp forms. The 6hp single-cylinder runabout was made for Siddeley by Wolseley and was merely that firm's light car fitted with a more conventional style of bonnet and radiator. It cost £175. In 1905 Siddeley replaced Herbert Austin as General Manager of Wolseley, and was responsible for the vertical-engined Wolseley-Siddeley cars.   MCS

SIDDELEY-DEASY (GB) 1912–1919
Siddeley-Deasy Motor Manufacturing Co Ltd, Coventry, Warwickshire

These cars were derived from the Deasys with dashboard radiators and pair-cast cylinders introduced for the 1910 season by the old company under J.D. Siddeley's management. Two of the four 1912 models — 4-cylinder machines of 1.9 and 2.6 litres' capacity — were identical to their 1911 counterparts, but the remaining two featured Knight sleeve-valve engines; these cars were the 3.3-litre 18–24 and a big 6-cylinder town carriage, the 24–30 costing £685 in chassis form. Poppet-valve units were dropped in 1913, when there was a smaller 2.6-litre 14–20 in the range, and the company also marketed the B.S.A.-based 13.9hp Stoneleigh with frontal radiator. Electric lighting was standardized on 1914 models, which could also be had with electric starters. The amalgamation with Armstrong-Whitworth after World War 1 resulted in the 30hp Armstrong Siddeley.   MCS

SIDÉA (F) 1912–1924
Sté Industrielle des Automobiles 'Sidéa', Mézières-Charleville, Ardennes

Pre-war cars of this make used Chapuis-Dornier engines and were available in five models, from 6 to 14hp, all with 4 cylinders. Post-war production did not start until 1922, and a number of different proprietary engines were used, including the sv 1½-litre Fivet and the single ohc 1,690cc S.C.A.P. Chassis design of all Sidéas was quite conventional. The last cars were called Sidéa-Jouffret.   GNG

SIEGEL (D) 1908–1910
Feodor Siegel, Schönebeck

Siegel built one type of car with a 2-cylinder 9hp engine. It was available with two- or four-seater bodies or as a delivery van.   HON

SIEGFRIED *see* REISSIG

SIEMENS-SCHUCKERT (D) 1906–1910
Siemens-Schuckert GmbH, Automobilwerk Nonnendamm, Berlin

This electric concern started production of cars in 1906. In the range were electric cars, petrol-electric cars on the Pieper system, and a petrol-driven car with a 6/10PS 1½-litre Körting engine. After the acquisition of Protos in 1908 Siemens-Schuckert gave up their own production of petrol-driven cars but continued a range of electric cars until 1910.   HON

SIGMA (i) (CH) *1909–1914*
Sté Industrielle Genevoise de Mécanique et Automobiles, Chêne-Bougeries

Made in the former Picker-Moccand factory, the Sigma took its name from the initials of the company. The cars carried the Greek letter *Σ* in the middle of their round radiators. They were medium-sized 4-cylinder vehicles, originally with 8/11hp sv engine. In 1911 the company acquired a licence to build the Knight sleeve-valve engine in 18 and 28hp sizes, and they also made 15 and 25hp poppet-valve engines. Sigmas achieved many successes in hill-climbs, and took second place in the 1910 Targa Florio, driven by de Prosperis, the Sigma agent for Sicily. He entered again in 1912 and 1913, but came no higher than 11th, and 15th respectively.   GNG

SIGMA (ii) (F) *1913–1928*
Sté des Automobiles Sigma, Levallois-Perret, Seine

Pre-war Sigmas used a variety of 4-cylinder Ballot engines, in sizes from 8 to 20hp, chassis being made by Malicet et Blin. Just after World War 1 a short-lived 2-cylinder car was made, but most of the vintage Sigmas used 4-cylinder proprietary engines and were of very conventional layout. The 1,494cc C.I.M.E. engine of 1925 had a single overhead camshaft, but other models had sv units, by S.C.A.P. or Ballot, from 894cc to 1,614cc.   GNG

SIGNET (US) *1913–1914*
Fenton Engineering Co, Fenton, Mich.

The Signet was sometimes called the Fenton. It was a two-seater, side-by-side cyclecar. The power was furnished by a 2-cylinder, air-cooled De Luxe engine of 9/13hp, with friction transmission and belt drive.   GMN

SILENT KNIGHT (US) *1906–1909*
Knight & Kilbourne Co, Chicago, Ill.

This car was built to advertise Charles Y. Knight's 4-cylinder, 40hp sleeve-valve engine. The drive was through a selective transmission and drive shaft. As a five-seater touring car, it was priced at $3,500. The Silent Knight was not a success, and the Knight engine did not gain popularity in America until after it had been adopted by Daimler and other European makes.   GMN

SILENT SIOUX *see* FAWICK

SILHOUETTE (GB) *1970–1972*
Silhouette Cars Ltd, London S.E.8

The Silhouette GS70 was a smart two-seater fibreglass GT car using a Volkswagen floorpan and running gear. The interior (and the exterior of a show car) was trimmed with a carpet-like material called Velvetex, and the basic body kit cost £450.   DF

SILVA-CORONEL (F) *1927–1928*
The Silva-Coronel was powered by a small straight-8 engine of 2½ litres' capacity. Five cars were built.   GNG

SILVER HAWK (GB) *1920–1921*
Silver Hawk Motors Ltd, Cobham, Surrey

After severing his connection with the Eric-Campbell, Noel Macklin went on to make an out-and-out sports car, the Silver Hawk. Not being backed by a touring car of any description, this was a highly unusual, and dangerous, project, which met with the expected fate. The new machine was basically similar to the Eric-Campbell, but used a tuned 1,373cc, sv engine rated at 10/35hp, and wore a dashing aluminium two-seater body with an outside exhaust pipe. Macklin was next associated with the name of Invicta.   TRN

SILVERTOWN (GB) *1905–c.1910*
The Silvertown Co, Silvertown, London E.

This was an electric car made by a subsidiary of the India Rubber, Gutta-Percha & Telegraph Works Ltd. Batteries and chassis were made by the parent firm, and bodies by W. & F. Thorn Ltd. The usual town cars were built, but in 1908 a car was made with optional 4-wheel drive, having two motors, one mounted on each axle casing.   GNG

SIMA-STANDARD (F) *1929–1932*
Automobiles Sima-Standard, Courbevoie, Seine

After the demise of the Sima-Violet, the name of S.I.M.A. (Société Industrielle de Matériel Automobile) became associated with another, equally unpromising small car. The 5CV Sima-Standard was designed to compete directly with the giants – Renault, Citroën, Peugeot, and the rest – by providing something of several of them in its make-up. Its 860cc sv engine was built up from Citroën parts, but almost everything else was Amilcar. It came in open two-seater and saloon versions, and lasted until 1932 when it was replaced by a short-lived 1.3-litre 7CV car.   TRN

1919 SIGMA(ii) 10hp tourer. *Autocar*

1921 SILVER HAWK 10/35hp sports car.
National Motor Museum

1905 SILVERTOWN electric landaulette.
Coachwork by W. & F. Thorn. *Autocar*

1925 SIMA-VIOLET 496cc sports car. *Lucien Loreille Collection*

1936 SIMCA-FIAT 6CV saloon. *Lucien Loreille Collection*

1950 SIMCA-GORDINI 1½-litre Le Mans coupé. *National Motor Museum*

1951 SIMCA Aronde 1.2-litre saloon. *Simca Industries*

SIMA-VIOLET (F) *1924–1929*

Sté Industrielle de Matériel Automobile, Paris; Courbevoie, Seine

Violet was the motor car industry's most persistent exponent of the 2-stroke air-cooled engine, producing a succession of designs for various concerns. It speaks well for them that one, the Sima-Violet, enjoyed some success, even though it was both unconventional and a late arrival on the cyclecar scene. It was powered by a very low-slung, air-cooled, horizontally-opposed 2-cylinder engine of less than a half a litre's capacity. The 2-speed gearbox was on the back axle, and front suspension was by a single transverse spring. Alcyon built an identical 2-cylinder car. A 4-cylinder, 1½-litre racing model, very low and modern in appearance, was offered in 1927. *TRN*

SIMCA (F) *1935 to date*

(1) Sté Industrielle de Mécanique et Carrosserie Automobile, Nanterre, Seine *1935–1961*; Poissy, Seine-et-Oise *1954–1970*
(2) Chrysler France SA, Poissy, Seine-et-Oise *1970 to date*

H.T. Pigozzi's company was formed in November 1934, to manufacture Fiat cars under licence for the French market in the former Donnet factory. Pre-1940 production models were virtually identical to their Italian counterparts, the types offered being the Tipo 508 Balilla, the 2-litre Tipo 518 Ardita, and the later 500 (Simca 5) and 1,100 (Simca 8). Outside France, however, the make's reputation stemmed from the competition successes of Amédée Gordini's specially tuned versions, mainly based on the 508 family, though he also extracted 28bhp from the Topolino engine. Most successful of these were the aerodynamic 508C two-seaters which won the Bol d'Or, the small sports-car race at Reims, and the Paris-Nice Rally, as well as the Index of Performance at Le Mans in 1939. A 1.2-litre version of the basic Fiat unit developed 65bhp. After World War 2, Gordini continued to develop competition cars under Simca sponsorship until 1951, and evolved an 1,100cc single-seater with twin-tube frame and all-round independent suspension, which furnished keen competition for the Cisitalia and did very well in 1947, with wins in the Bol d'Or and at Nîmes, not to mention a 1-2-3 victory in the Coupe des Petites Cylindrées at Reims. The cars acquired hemispherical heads and 5-bearing crankshafts in 1948, winning their class in the Belgian 24 Hour Race, as well as being victorious once again in the Bol d'Or. Later Simca-Gordinis used 1½-litre Wade-blown 1½-litre power units, and the breed's career culminated in Trintignant's win in the 1951 Albi Grand Prix. Thereafter the company withdrew its support from Gordini, who set up on his own as a manufacturer.

In 1942 Simca joined Baron Petiet's Groupe Française Automobile selling organization along with Delahaye/Delage, but withdrew from the G.F.A. after the war, when production of the Simca 5 and Simca 8 resumed in basically 1939 form. An ohv Simca 6 (the equivalent of Fiat's later 500C) was introduced for 1948, and in 1949 a 50bhp sports version of the 8CV with handsome coupé bodywork by Facel Metallon was marketed; a car of this type won its class in the 1949 Alpine Rally, while standard Simca 8s scored two class wins in the 1950 Monte Carlo event. This year the Simca 8 was restyled, and emerged with a 40bhp 1.2-litre engine and steering-column change. In the summer of 1951, however, an entirely new car, the Aronde, made its appearance; the engine was a 45bhp derivative of the old 8CV, but the rest of the car was entirely new, with unitary construction, coil-and-wishbone independent front suspension, and hypoid final drive. Production jumped to 50,000 cars in 1952 and the Aronde made numerous attacks on long-distance records held for many years by the Citroën 'Petite Rosalie', achieving 100,000 kilometres at 100km/h in 1953. The Aronde had a production run of over 12 years. The half-millionth car was delivered in January 1957, and the millionth in February 1960. Simca also participated in several takeover bids, buying Unic (now only making trucks) in 1951, Ford (v) in 1954, Saurer's French branch in 1956, and Talbot in 1959. A 50bhp sports version of the Aronde was announced in 1953, and Gemmer cam steering was adopted in 1954, in which year the model was introduced to the British market at a list price of £896. With the acquisition of the French Ford company, their 2.3-litre sv V-8 Vedette reappeared under the Simca name, the Ford factory at Poissy first supplementing and then supplanting the original Simca works at Nanterre, which was turned over to Citroën in 1961. The V-8 sold fairly well, and was given a more powerful 84bhp engine in 1958. Production ceased in France in 1961, though as late as 1967 the Chambord and Présidence versions, now with 112bhp and ohv, were still being made under licence in Brazil.

1956 Arondes had 48bhp 1.3-litre engines as standard, though 57bhp Special units were found in the sports coupés and convertibles and the Montlhéry saloon; station wagons had the 45bhp Service type. 1957 saw a family derivative, the Ariane, using the hull of the V-8 Vedette and the regular Aronde engine — it was made until 1963. In 1958 Chrysler acquired a minority interest in Simca, and it was announced that the American company's Adelaide factory would build Arondes for the Australian market; this small holding had become a controlling interest by 1963, and the Chrysler 'pentastar' emblem was to be seen on all Simcas in 1967. Aronde development continued: a cheap 6CV 1,100cc model was listed in 1960, and the 1961 range used 5-bearing engines in various ratings up to 62bhp, later increased to 70bhp. A new departure for 1962 was the 1000, a 944cc rear-engined 4-door saloon with radiator mounted alongside the power-unit, 5-bearing crankshaft, all-round independent suspension, and 4-speed all-synchromesh gearbox: at

6,490NFr it was cheaper than Citroën's Ami 6, and production rose to over a quarter of a million cars. Within a year this had evolved into a Bertone-bodied coupé with all-round disc brakes, while the first of the Simca-Abarths was available in the shape of a twin ohc 1,300cc model. In 1963 all-synchromesh boxes were also found on the conventional 4-cylinder 1300 and 1500; outputs were 61bhp and 83bhp, and the bigger car had front disc brakes, which were added to the 1300's specification in 1966. 1964 was the last year of the Aronde, which had been continued as a very inexpensive item at 6,950NFr for an 1,100cc saloon. In 1966 the 1000 became available with a 3-speed semi-automatic gearbox, full automatic (by Borg-Warner) being an option on the 1500 series; during the year the millionth Simca 1000 left the factory.

1968 brought two new versions of the 1000, the high-performance GLS and the austerity 777cc Sim'4 for the home market; at the same time Simca switched to fwd with their transverse-engined 53bhp 1100. On this the gearbox was mounted left of the engine, rear suspension was independent, by wishbones and torsion bars, and front disc brakes were fitted. An interesting hybrid evolved in England was the Radbourne-Abarth 1200, basically a 1200 coupé fitted with a Fiat 124 engine. In 1970, the company changed its name and the Chrysler (iii) was added as a prestige line. Also Simca took Matra, and their racing team, under their wing. A 76bhp 1.2-litre version of the 1100 appeared in 1971, helping the fwd Simca to become France's best-selling car early in 1972. The principal novelty for 1972 was yet another 1000 derivative, the 1,294cc Rallye saloon. The conventional rear-driven 1301 and 1501 were continued into 1973, along with the 1000 and 1100 families.

MCS

SIMMS (i) (GB) 1901–1908

(1) Simms Manufacturing Co Ltd, Bermondsey, London S.E. *1901–1903*
(2) Simms Manufacturing Co Ltd, Kilburn, London N.W. *1904–1908*

The first car built by Simms had a 3½hp engine of their own manufacture, single chain drive and an aluminium body. It was not made for sale, and the first production cars did not appear until 1903. These had 4-cylinder engines of 20/24 or 30/35hp, which were available either separately to other manufacturers or with chassis. These models were known as the Welbeck, and the later cars were often known as Simms-Welbecks. In 1904 there were 10 and 12hp 2-cylinder cars in addition to the fours, and a 30/35hp pair-cast six was introduced in 1907. Some 1905 models were fitted with pneumatic bumpers at the front. which were unsightly but were said to enable the cars to escape unscathed from quite serious crashes. 1907 was the last year that Simms showed cars at Olympia.

GNG

SIMMS (ii) (US) 1920–1921

Simms Motor Car Corp, Atlanta, Ga.

The Simms was only available as a five-seater tourer with its own design of 4-cylinder engine. Few were sold and no price was announced.

KM

SIMPLEX (i) (NL) 1899–1914

NV Maatschappij Simplex, Amsterdam

The first Simplex was a belt-driven *vis-à-vis* made on Benz lines, but by 1902 a new model was introduced with a vertical single-cylinder Fafnir engine mounted at the front, wheel steering and single chain drive. Shaft drive came in soon afterwards, and 1907 an 8hp 2-cylinder and 14/16hp 4-cylinder car were made. The largest model was the 35hp 4-cylinder model of 1911, still with Fafnir engine. A considerable number of the smaller cars were sent, partly knocked down, to the Netherlands East Indies, and assembled there. Production ceased with World War 1, and although a prototype 3-wheeler with 10hp V-twin engine was shown in 1919, it never went into production.

GNG

SIMPLEX (ii) (US) 1907–1917

Simplex Automobile Co Inc, New Brunswick, N.J.

After the 1907 bankruptcy of Smith & Mabley, the firm was taken over by Herman Broesel, who formed the Simplex Automobile Company. The best-known model of the new company was the 50hp, a massive chain-driven car of high quality whose 4-cylinder T-head engine had a capacity of 10 litres. The chassis price was $4,500 and bodies were made for Simplex under contract by such firms as Quimby, Demarest, Holbrook and Brewster. In 1908 a stripped version won the 24 hour race at Brighton Beach, and famous drivers who drove for Simplex included George Robertson, Al Poole and Joe Tracy. The cars were designed by Edward Franquist who introduced a 38hp 7.8-litre shaft-drive model in 1911, and a 75hp 10-litre chain-drive roadster in 1912. By 1914 this was the only chain-driven model in the range, and was said to be the last chain-driven American car. Some of these cars had a sharply-pointed V-radiator, although most Simplexes used a flat, Mercedes-type radiator.

The 1914 range consisted of the 38hp, 50hp and 75hp fours, and a 50hp six, but towards the end of that year a new model appeared which heralded a complete change in the Simplex company. This was the 46hp L-head Simplex Crane Model 5, designed by Henry M. Crane who had replaced Franquist as chief designer after a company reorganization. The new car was a very high quality machine and carried beautiful coachwork, mainly by Brewster, but it lacked the sporting qualities of

1968 SIMCA 1100 saloon. *Simca Industries*

1907 SIMMS-WELBECK 20/25hp landaulette. *The Veteran Car Club of Great Britain*

1899 SIMPLEX(i) *vis-à-vis. Automobielmuseum, Driebergen*

1913 SIMPLEX(ii) 75hp two-seater. *Don McCray*

*c.*1900 SIMPSON 10hp steam car. *Museum of Transport, Glasgow*

1927 SIMSON-SUPRA Type J 12/60PS tourer. *Neubauer Collection*

its predecessor. It was made until 1917, and bodies were still being fitted to Crane chassis in 1921. By this time the company had been bought by Hare's Motors, and a re-organized company, the Crane-Simplex Company of New York, made a few cars in 1923 and 1924. GNG

SIMPLEX (iii) (F) *1920*

The French Simplex was quite a large open tourer with a bullnose radiator, but underneath the bonnet there was a horizontal single-cylinder engine of 735cc. A special balance weight coupled to the connecting rod and to an eccentric was supposed to avoid vibration. Front wheel brakes were fitted. GNG

SIMPLEX PERFECTA (GB) *1900*
Randolph Works, Normanton, Derby

This was a 4hp four-seater voiturette for which only £100 was asked. The makers did, however, ask buyers to deposit the sum at their bank before work on the car commenced. GNG

SIMPLIC (GB) *1914*
(1) Wadden & West, Cobham, Surrey
(2) G.W. Wadden, Weybridge, Surrey

True to its name, this was a very simple cyclecar powered by an air-cooled 5/6hp J.A.P. engine. An epicyclic gear was used, and final drive was by belts. GNG

SIMPLICITIES (US) *1905*
Simplicities Automobile Co, Middletown, Conn.

The only model of this make was a five-seater with rear entrance which used a water-cooled 4-cylinder engine of 24hp with a 3-speed gearbox. The manufacturer claimed that a number of these cars were exported to Great Britain before 1905. GMN

SIMPLICITY (US) *1906–1911*
Evansville Automobile Co, Evansville, Ind.

This company offered touring cars, roadsters and limousines, with friction transmission. The latter feature presumably determined the name of this make. The engines used were all 4-stroke, 4-cylinder, water-cooled units. The Simplicity may have used double chain drive as late as 1911. GMN

SIMPLO (US) *1908–1909*
Cook Motor Vehicle Co, St Louis, Mo.

This small four-seater runabout had solid rubber tyres and a 4-stroke, 2-cylinder engine, with friction transmission and double chain drive. The car sold for $650, or for $700 with pneumatic tyres. GMN

SIMPSON (GB) *1897–1904*
John Simpson, Stirling

John Simpson was an inventive engineer who made about 20 steam cars of varying design, mainly for his own interest and use, although a number were sold. One of his early cars used a 6hp 4-cylinder single-acting engine, and had double suspension; the chassis was sprung on the axles, and the body was sprung on the chassis. Later cars had engines of 6, 10 and 12hp, always of Simpson's own design, flash boilers and automatic fuel and water regulators. GNG

SIMS (I) *1908–1909*
Società Italiana Merz e Stinchi, Turin

Only one model of the Sims car was offered, a 10/12hp four of 1,767cc. Cylinders were cast monobloc, but there were side valves in a T-head, low-tension magneto ignition and chain drive. MCS

SIMSON; SIMSON-SUPRA (D) *1911–1932*
Simson & Co, Suhl

The Simson armaments factory began car production in 1911, building 6/18 and 10/30PS models. After World War 1, the firm concentrated on cars. Cars of 1,559cc (22bhp), 2,595cc (40bhp) and 3,538cc (45bhp) were made until in 1924 a new model, the Simson Supra Type S, appeared, designed by Paul Henze. The name Simson Supra was used for all subsequent models. The engine was a 4-cylinder, 1,950cc unit with twin overhead camshafts driven by a vertical shaft. It had four valves per cylinder and developed 60bhp. The high quality finish and the technical features of the engine made it a sensation at the Berlin Motor Show, although the chassis was quite conventional. The Type SO was a simplified single ohc version developing only 40bhp. In 1926 the Type R was introduced with a 6-cylinder 3,108cc push-rod engine developing 70bhp. Type RJ was based on the R with a capacity of 3,358cc. The last Simson Supra was the Type A with a straight-8 sv 4,673cc engine. This was only made in limited numbers during 1931 and 1932, after which Simson discontinued car production. The name survives on motorcycles produced by East Germany's nationalized industry. HON

SINCLAIR (GB) *1899–1902*
E.H. Clift & Co, London W.

The first car made by this company was called the Clift electric victoria, but petrol-engined cars went under the name Sinclair, after the road in Kensington where they were built. Two types were made, with 5 or 7hp rear-mounted horizontal engines or a 10hp vertical engine at the front. Both used shaft drive. GNG

SINGER (i) (GB) *1905–1970*

(1) Singer & Co Ltd, Coventry, Warwickshire *1905–1936* Birmingham *1927–1936*
(2) Singer Motors Ltd, Coventry, Warwickshire *1936–1956* Birmingham *1936–1956*
(3) Singer Motors Ltd, Ryton-on-Dunsmore, Warwickshire *1956–1970*

The Singer cycle firm acquired the manufacturing rights of the Perks and Birch motor wheel in 1901, and made front-wheel drive tricycles as well as motor bicycles. These gave way to a line of conventional tricars, which were still available as late as 1907 with water cooling, wheel-steering and 6hp and 9hp engines. Car production started in 1905 with a 15hp 3-cylinder machine designed by Alex Craig, and made under licence from Lea-Francis. It had horizontal cylinders with overhead camshafts and 30in connecting-rods, and final drive was by chain. 2-cylinder versions were also made, but the beginning of a new line came with a conventional 2.4-litre 4-cylinder in 1906: an experimental 6-cylinder engine was exhibited, but not offered for sale. Only orthodox cars with front vertical engines were listed in 1907, the smaller ones (a short-stroke 900cc twin, a 1.4-litre 3-cylinder, and a 1.8-litre 4-cylinder) having T-head White and Poppe power units, the larger fours of 2.4 litres and 3.7 litres using Aster engines. Thereafter White and Poppe engines were standardized, and in 1909, when the company was reorganized, there was a 2.5-litre sixteen with 3-speed gearbox and all brakes on the rear wheels, selling for £380. L-head fours of 2.6 litres and 3.3 litres were introduced for 1911, in which year the biggest car had worm drive, Sankey steel detachable wheels were featured, and the circular *motif* in the radiator core was discarded. The White and Poppe-powered Singers had quite a brisk performance, G.O. Herbert's 'Bunny Junior' being capable of 3,000rpm, and wresting the Brooklands 16hp class records from Coatalen's Sunbeam, while a modified 15hp with lengthened stroke and overhead inlet valves ran in the 1912 Coupe de l'Auto. This year saw the introduction of Singer's first best-seller, the 1,100cc L-head Ten with pair-cast cylinders and 3 speed gearbox in unit with the back axle. Though qualifying as a cyclecar in terms of weight, it was in fact one of the first modern baby cars, and sold for £185: Haywood's tuned version put 72 miles into the hour at Brooklands, and the fortunes of the Rootes brothers' motor business were founded on the sale of this model. The following year Singer's own engines spread up the range with a new monobloc 2.4-litre fourteen, available with electric lighting, and fitted with Singer-made shock absorbers. By the outbreak of World War 1 only the big 20hp retained the White and Poppe unit, and very few of these were made. Motorcycle manufacture ceased in 1915, and the few Tens being made to civilian account had a new rounded radiator and electric lighting. Tens were also supplied to the Armed Forces during the war.

The first post-war years saw a concentration on the 10hp model, now with full electrics, but otherwise little changed. A 60mph sports version cost £500 in 1920, and 33bhp was claimed from a racing version which ran in the 1921 200 Mile Race. In 1922 the gearbox was placed amidships, and by 1923 the car had been completely redesigned with an ohv monobloc engine and unit box. For one season only (1923) a cheapened version was offered under the Coventry-Premier name, this being a motorcycle and cyclecar concern which Singer had acquired in 1921.

It was in 1921 that a trend towards a complicated range began which was to bring about the firm's subsequent financial difficulties, though in 1928 Singer ranked third behind Morris and Austin among all-British private-car manufacturers. Their first production six was available in 1922, this being a long-stroke 2-litre with side valves, thermo-syphon cooling, magneto ignition, 3 forward speeds, spiral bevel final drive, and disc wheels, selling for £675. 4-wheel brakes were optional on this model in 1924, and had spread to the Ten two years later, and a smaller 1.8-litre ohv power unit was introduced in 1927. Also in 1924 fabric bodies were listed, though curiously enough Singer avoided these during the late 1920s when fabric was fashionable. By 1927 also the Ten had grown up into a 1.3-litre Senior with plate clutch, and a new and very successful baby car had come on the scene in the shape of the 848cc ohc Junior, initially with 3-speed gearbox and brakes on the rear wheels only. It was a roomy four-seater with 4 doors, a 7ft 6in wheelbase, and a price of only £418.10s., and it was made until 1932, as well as being the ancestor of all Singer models up to the Rootes takeover in 1956. 1928 brought the abandonment of cone clutches, the provision of 4-wheel brakes on the Junior, and the introduction of an improved 42bhp 1.9-litre ohv six with a 7-bearing crankshaft. There was also a short vogue for fully convertible saloons with wind-down roofs. 1930 Singers had wire wheels and coil ignition, but things became impossibly complicated in the 1931–33 period, when the marque went in for ribbon radiator shells, not to mention the 'Kaye Don' six with waterfall-style radiator grille and twin carburettors, selling for £480. Eight models were listed in 1932: the Junior with 4 speeds and rear tank, a 972cc Junior Special version destined to grow up into the Nine, both with overhead camshafts, a sv 1.3-litre 4-cylinder Ten, and four 6-cylinder cars ranging from a short-lived 1½-litre sv 12/6 at £235 up to the big ohv push-rod Kaye Don. Hydraulic brakes were standardized on all but the biggest six

1908 SINGER(i) 12/14hp doctor's coupé. Coachwork by H.J. Mulliner. *Autocar*

1925 SINGER(i) Ten tourer. *Rootes Motors Ltd*

1935 SINGER(i) 11hp saloon. *G.N. Georgano*

1936 SINGER(i) 9hp Le Mans sports car. *National Motor Museum*

1950 SINGER(i) SM 1500 saloon. *National Motor Museum*

1957 SINGER(i) Gazelle 1½-litre saloon. *Rootes Motors Ltd*

1909 SIRRON 12/16hp two-seater. Mr Norris at the wheel. *Autocar*

in 1933, when the first 972cc sports Nine was introduced; these cars challenged M.G. and did very well in reliability trials, which suited their rather low gearing. In standard form they offered 70mph and 5,300rpm for £185, though even their 4th place (and best-placed British car) in the 1937 TT failed to make up for the catastrophe of the 1935 race, when the whole team was eliminated by spectacular steering failures. This unfortunate affair also sounded the death-knell of an excellent 4-bearing 1½-litre sporting six introduced during 1933.

The permutations went on. Singer's own 'perm-mesh' clutchless change came in 1934, in which year there was also a 1½-litre ohc Eleven with independent front suspension and fluidrive transmission at £245. This could be bought with a full-width aerodynamic saloon body known as the Airstream. All 1935 cars had ohc engines, fluidrive and independent front suspension being applied also to the de luxe 9hp saloon and the 2-litre 6-cylinder model at the top of the range. In 1936 there were six models, cheapest of which was the 9hp Bantam with 3-speed gearbox, electric pump feed and 12-volt electrics, looking very like the Morris 8, and competitively priced at £120 for open models. Inevitably another reorganization followed, and more models. A 42bhp Twelve with an engine of just over 1½ litres' capacity sold for £225, had an X-frame, and marked a reversion to the beam front axle, but a similarly-powered sports model was almost stillborn, and after 1937 there were no more true sports cars or 6-cylinder models. Instead, a 1.2-litre Ten with the option of 3 or 4 forward speeds was listed for 1938 at prices from £169.10s. up, and the company's confidence in its ohc power units was reflected in the issue of a bore guarantee with the 1939 models. The Nine (now of 1,074cc) reverted to mechanical brakes, and a semi-sports roadster style was offered as an alternative to the saloon on this chassis. 1,100cc and 1½-litre engines were supplied to H.R.G., who continued to use Singer power units for the rest of their series-production career.

After World War 2 car production was concentrated at the Birmingham works (opened in 1927), and Singer re-introduced their pre-war types. In 1948, however, the saloon models were replaced by a full-width, slab-sided 1½-litre model, the SM 1500. This retained a separate chassis, and featured column change, hypoid final drive, and coil-spring independent front suspension. At £799 it was more expensive than its rivals, and sales slumped once the era of the seller's market came to an end. Neither this nor the improved 1951 1½-litre roadster, also with independent front suspension, could compete against the big manufacturers. None of the company's subsequent innovations – the option of twin-carburettor power units in 1953, experiments with a fibreglass-bodied roadster in 1954, or the Hunter saloon of 1955 with conventional radiator grille, fibreglass bonnet top and (on paper, at any rate) a rather expensive twin-ohc engine as an alternative – could save the day. Early in 1956 Rootes Motors purchased Singer, and by the end of the year the Hunter had been replaced by a Hillman Minx-based Gazelle retaining Singer's 52bhp ohc engine. Even this last vestige of the old days had been phased out of production by the end of 1958, and since then the name of Singer has been carried by de luxe variants of the basic Hillman types, acquiring such Hillman improvements as optional automatic transmission in 1960 and hypoid final drive in 1961.

At the beginning of 1970 the range consisted of the rear-engined ohc Chamois (Imp), and the 1,496cc Gazelle and 1,725cc Vogue, both members of the Arrow family corresponding to Hillman's Minx and Hunter. All these disappeared soon afterwards as part of the rationalization the Chrysler Corporation imposed on the old Rootes Group. MCS

SINGER (ii) (US) 1915–1920
Singer Motor Co Inc, Mount Vernon, N.Y.

The Singer was the successor to the Palmer-Singer, which had been produced since 1906, and was one of the finest and most expensive luxury cars manufactured in America in its few years of existence. Distinguished by a sharply pointed radiator and a wide choice of custom bodies from leading coachbuilders, the cars produced between 1915 and 1919 were powered by a Herschell-Spillman 6-cylinder engine. In 1920, the series HEH20 line was introduced. This series, which proved to be the last, had a 12-cylinder Weidely engine. Prices on the last Singer cars were as high as $9,000. Wire wheels were standard. KM

SINGLE-CENTER (US) 1906–1908
Single-Center Buggy Co, Evansville, Ind.

This motor buggy had a 4-stroke 2-cylinder water-cooled engine of 2.6 litres. The drive was by double chains, and the wheelbase was only 7ft. It was available with either solid rubber or pneumatic tyres.

The significance of the name Single-Center is not clear, but it may have referred to a swivelling front axle. GMN

SINPAR (F) 1907–1914
Automobiles Sinpar, Courbevoie, Seine

The Sinpar began life as a voiturette powered by a single-cylinder De Dion engine of 4½hp or an Anzani of 7hp. Both models had dashboard radiators and shaft drive. In 1912–14 a 4-cylinder car with an 8hp monobloc engine was made. This was identical to the 8hp Demeester, but was sold under the Sinpar name. In recent years the name has been born by a light, Renault 4-based Jeep-type vehicle. GNG

SINTZ (US) *1903–1904*

Claude Sintz Inc, Grand Rapids, Mich.

Clark Sintz was one of America's pioneer builders of gasoline engines, which were used in such early cars as the 1894 Haynes and 1897 Reeves. The first car to bear the Sintz name was made by Reeves in 1897, but in 1903 Clark's sons Claude and Guy went into business to manufacture tonneau cars powered by 16hp 2-cylinder 2-stroke engines. Only six were built. GNG

SIRRON (GB) *1909–1916*

(1) Cresswell, Norris & Co Ltd, South Kensington, London S.W.
(2) Sirron Cars Ltd, Fulham, London W.
(3) Sirron Cars Ltd, Southall, Middlesex

The Sirron car derived its name from that of H.G. Norris, one of its promoters, spelt in reverse. It was a conventional shaft-driven car of medium size, using proprietary French engines, although a small 10/12hp of 1914 to 1916 used an Alpha engine. The larger cars were called the 12/16 (2,212cc) and the 16/20 (2,553cc), although both were rated at 15.9hp, having the same 80mm bore. It began life in the unlikely location of Cornwall Gardens Mews, in the heart of residential South Kensington, but soon moved to Fulham. GNG

SIVA (i) (I) *1967–1970*

S.I.V.A. srl, Lecce

The S.I.V.A. Sirio was a two-seater GT coupé powered by a German Ford 20M V-6 engine, mounted amidships. The engine, tuned by Conrero, had its power increased from the normal 90bhp to 130bhp. GNG

SIVA (ii) (GB) *1969 to date*

(1) Neville Trickett Design Ltd, Bryanston, Blandford, Dorset *1969 to date*
(2) Siva Motor Car Co Ltd, Aylesbury, Bucks. *1972 to date*

Nearly 200 Edwardian-style cars had been produced by this firm up to September 1972, their popularity possibly assisted by the regular appearance of one on a television programme. The original types, like Trickett's previous Opus-H.R.F. design, used Ford mechanical parts. Later versions were available also with Citroën 2cv or Volkswagen ingredients, known as the Parisienne, Raceabout (two-seater) and San Remo (four-seater) respectively. Other models available, usually as kits, were the Siva Buggy and Mule, both based on Mini parts, and the Llama with Imp constituents.

In 1971 the Volkswagen-based Siva Spyder was announced and developed during the year as the S160 GT, with stressed fibreglass gull-wing body and very full specification. A yet more ambitious design was the S530 GT of 1972, with triple pontoon monocoque chassis, racing type suspension and large V-8 Chevrolet engine. For 1973 Trickett introduced a new VW-based coupé, the Saluki. DF

SIZAIRE-BERWICK (F/GB) *1913–1927*

(1) Sté Nouvelle des Autos Sizaire, Courbevoie, Seine *1913–1927*
(2) F.W. Berwick & Co Ltd, Park Royal, London N.W. *1920–1925*

After leaving Sizaire-Naudin, Maurice Sizaire designed an almost completely conventional luxury car, the Sizaire-Berwick. It was made initially in France, with a 4-litre 20hp sv monobloc engine, and full electrical equipment, and from 1920, also in Britain by F.W. Berwick, the British agents for Sizaire-Naudin. Rated at 25/50hp, the post-war car had an sv 4½-litre engine with only 4 cylinders (unusual in a machine of this class), but it was a very smooth-running unit. It developed 60bhp at a modest 2,000rpm. The pre-war radiator was a copy of the Rolls-Royce, but after Derby instituted legal proceedings, its front was changed from a flat surface to a shallow V with a flat apex. From 1923, after Austin had gained a controlling interest, the British company also turned out two models with Austin Twenty and Twelve engines, as well as a 3.2-litre six. Production of British Sizaire-Berwicks ceased after 1925, though a French version powered by an American 6-cylinder Lycoming engine was shown at the 1927 Paris Salon. TRN

SIZAIRE FRÈRES (F/B) *1923–1931*

(1) Sté Nouvelle des Autos Sizaire, Courbevoie, Seine *1923–1929*
(2) Sté Belge des Automobiles Sizaire *1929–1931*

In 1923, there emerged from the Sizaire works in Courbevoie the world's first production car to have all-independent suspension; the Sizaire Frères Type 4RI. The system was basically similar to that of the old transverse-spring Sizaire-Naudin, considerably refined, and applied to all four wheels. As before, Maurice Sizaire was responsible for it, while his brother Georges looked after experimental work. The power unit was a 11CV of 2 litres, with a single overhead camshaft, and developed 50bhp. The 4RI was capable of almost 70mph. A 16-valve sports version of this advanced fast tourer was listed in 1926. The suspension system remained unchanged throughout the car's career, though Lockheed brakes arrived in 1928, and various proprietary engines were used. These included, in the same year, an ohv Hotchkiss and a Willys-Knight sleeve-valve six. In 1929 production ceased in France, but Georges Sizaire began small-scale manufacture in Belgium, where the car was known as the Belga Rise. This usually had Willys-Knight engines, but Hotchkiss or Minerva units could be ordered. TRN

1971 SIVA(ii) 530 5.3-litre coupé.
Aylesbury Automation Ltd

1920 SIZAIRE-BERWICK 25/50hp coupé.
National Motor Museum

1927 SIZAIRE FRÈRES 2-litre saloon. *B.K.*
Goodman Collection

1910 SIZAIRE-NAUDIN 12hp roadster. *The Veteran Car Club of Great Britain*

1920 SIZAIRE-NAUDIN 12/15hp tourer. *Autocar*

1921 SKEOCH 3½hp cyclecar. *Autocar*

1929 SKODA 645 2½-litre saloon. *Motokov*

SIZAIRE-NAUDIN (F) *1905–1921*

(1) Ets Sizaire et Naudin, Paris 15e
(2) Sté Nouvelle des Autos Sizaire, Paris 15e

The Sizaire-Naudin was one of the pioneers of that typical French breed, the small sporting voiturette. Designed by Maurice Sizaire and built by Louis Naudin, it first appeared at the end of 1905 as a 1906 model, and quickly won acclaim for cheapness, simplicity and strength. The 100mm × 120mm (918cc), single-cylinder engine of De Dion type, but with an overhead inlet valve, was normal enough, and the armoured-wood frame was old-fashioned. However, the independent front suspension, by transverse leaf spring and sliding pillars, had been seen only on the defunct Decauville 'voiturelle' and Ader, and the transmission, which provided direct drive on all 3 forward speeds by means of a propeller shaft that shifted to engage corresponding rings of teeth on the crown wheel, was entirely Sizaire-Naudin's own. Though unconventional, the suspension and drive worked well enough, as was proved by the car's wins in the Coupe de l'Auto race in 1906, 1907 and 1908, and in the Sicilian Cup race in 1907. Until 1910, the power output of the single-cylinder engine was increased by enlarging the bore, and then progressively lengthening the stroke (as was fashionable at a time when racing formulas had the effect of restricting bore). By that year, dimensions on the production car were 120mm × 140mm (over 1,500cc). The limit of this type of design had been reached, and 4-cylinder engines were replacing it. A small, long-stroke four, also with overhead inlet valves, was offered alongside a single. The latter survived until 1913, but by then the Sizaire-Naudin had grown up in every way. They were modern, conventional family cars, with sv, L-head monobloc 4-cylinder engines made by Ballot, and normal front suspension. These vehicles were continued for a short time after World War 1. TRN

S.J.R. (US) *1915–1916*

S.J.R. Motor Co, Boston, Mass.

The S.J.R. was a small car which offered only a single model, a four-seater roadster, at $945. The car was low hung an equipped with wire wheels. The windshield was slanted and the appearance was that of a foreign car. Powered by a 4-cylinder Wisconsin engine, few were marketed before the company failed. KM

SKELTON (US) *1920–1922*

Skelton Motor Car Co, St Louis, Mo.

The Skelton was an assembled car with a 4-cylinder Lycoming engine. Touring cars and roadsters were available at $1,295 each. KM

SKENE (US) *1900–1901*

J.W. Skene Cycle & Automobile Co, Lewiston, Maine

The Skene company boasted that every part of their light steam buggy was made at their works, which, if true, distinguished it from many assembled machines. In design, however, it was conventional, using a vertical 2-cylinder engine of 5hp, single chain drive and tiller steering. An unusual feature was that a single-seater body could be fitted, as well as the typical two-seater stanhope. GNG

SKEOCH (GB) *1921*

J.B. Skeoch, Dalbeattie, Kirkcudbright

This was a very light cyclecar powered by a 348cc single-cylinder Precision engine. It had a Burman 2-speed gearbox and single chain drive. Not more than 10 were made. GNG

SKIRROW (GB) *1936–1939*

H. Skirrow, Lea Bridge Stadium, London, E.10

Harry Skirrow's midget racing cars were the best-known machines built for dirt-track racing. The design featured a 1,000cc J.A.P. engine tuned to give 80bhp and driving all four wheels by chains. About 100 Skirrows were made, selling for £175 each. Several were exported to Australia, and in the late 1940s Jack Brabham drove one with considerable success. GNG

SKODA (CS) *1923 to date*

(1) Akc. spol. drive Skodovy zavody, Plzen (Pilsen); Mlada Boleslav *1923–1945*
(2) Skoda np, Mlada Boleslav *1945 to date*

Skoda was one of the most important industrial concerns of the Austro-Hungarian empire. After World War 1 it was included in the territory of the new Czechoslovak republic. The company branched out into car production, building Hispano-Suizas under licence. The first of these appeared in about 1923. The engine was the 37.2hp 6-cylinder 6.6-litre, while the bodies were of Skoda's own design. Production was in the Skoda works at Pilsen. In 1925 Skoda took over the Laurin & Klement works at Mlada Boleslav, and production of private cars under the Skoda name began in this factory. The first models were based on earlier Laurin-Klement designs. For the next few years the range included various 4-, 6- and 8-cylinder models of conventional design. More advanced ideas were introduced with the 420 model in 1933. The engine was a 995cc unit developing 20bhp, the chassis was on Tatra lines with a centre tubular layout and rear swing half-axles. The 420 ushered in the 1930s range of models with which Skoda became famous. The 420 developed into the

Popular and the same technical features were to be found in the 4-cylinder Rapid (1,380cc and 22bhp) and the 6-cylinder Superb (2,480cc and 50bhp). Model 932 was an experimental version with rear engine. The Popular also appeared with a streamlined coupé body and was quite successful in a number of sporting events, including the Monte Carlo Rally. All models gradually increased capacity and output, and changed from side to overhead valves. The range was supplemented by the 1.8-litre Favorit and the Monte Carlo with a Popular chasis and Rapid engine. In 1939 the range consisted of four types, the most important being the 1100 OHV (1,089cc and 32bhp) and the 6-cylinder, 3,140cc 85bhp model.

After World War 2, the Skoda 1100 OHV and 1200 OHV – based on pre-war designs – appeared, and were developed into the well-known 40 or 50bhp Octavia with a capacity of 1,089cc, the Octavia Super (1,221cc and 45bhp) and the Felicia, a two-seater Octavia version with a 50bhp engine. The Octavia/Felicia range was discontinued, with the exception of the station wagon models, after the introduction of the Skoda 1000 MB (MB for Mlada Boleslav) in 1964, a rear-engined 988cc 40bhp model. The Octavia wagons were discontinued in 1969, and a year later came a new version of the 1000MB, the S110 with 1,107cc engine and disc front brakes. Even faster was the S110R coupé of 1971. The 1972 range embraced variations on the basic rear-engined theme with 48bhp, 53bhp and 62bhp power units. Disc front brakes were standard.   HON

1929 SKODA 860 3.9-litre 8-cylinder cabriolet. *Motokov*

SKRIVA (F) *1922–1924*
Automobiles Skriva, Paris 7e
 The Skriva was a conventional car powered by the sv 2.4-litre Sergant engine.
                                                                GNG

S.K. SIMPLEX (GB) *1908–1910*
Smeddle & Kennedy Ltd, Newcastle-upon-Tyne
 The S.K. Simplex was a light two-seater, powered by a 10hp 2-cylinder engine with single overhead camshaft. It had a conventional gearbox and shaft drive.   GNG

SKYLINE (US) *1958*
Skyline Inc, Jamaica, N.Y.
 The Skyline X50 was a two-seater sports car based on the Henry J with a push-button-controlled retractable hard top.   GNG

1954 SKODA 440 1,100cc saloon. *Motokov*

S.L.I.M. (F) *1920–1929*
Sté Lyonnaise de l'Industrie Mécanique et Autos Pilain, Lyons
 The S.L.I.M., or S.L.I.M.-Pilain, was the successor to the Pilain, and while it retained that car's De Dion-type final drive it also utilized compressed air to actuate the starter, the horn, the automatic jacking system, and the 4-wheel brakes. The engine, too, was of unusually sophisticated design, progressing from a 3.8-litre four with a single overhead camshaft to a 16-ohv unit employing 2 low camshafts. By the time the latter engine was in use, the pneumatic system had been abandoned in favour of more conventional mechanism.   TRN

S.L.M. (CH) *1899; 1934–1935*
Schweizerische Lokomotiv- und Maschinenfabrik, Winterthur
 S.L.M. are a well-known locomotive-building firm who made a number of short-lived excursions into the field of road vehicles. Their first was a four-seater light car with a single-cylinder opposed-piston engine; only one prototype was built. Steam lorries were made around 1906, and front-wheel-drive petrol lorries from 1924 to 1932, and in 1934 came S.L.M.'s second, and more dramatic, venture into car building. This was the S.L.M.-Pescara, powered by a 3.6-litre V-16 aluminium engine with Roots supercharger, which developed 150bhp at 4,000rpm. It was designed by the Marquis de Pescara who had previously made the Nacional Pescara in Spain. Three engines were made, but only one complete car, a very handsome two-seater drop-head coupé.   GNG

1965 SKODA 1000 MB 988cc saloon. *Czechoslovak News Agency*

SLOANE (GB) *1907*
Sloane Motor Works, London S.W.
 This company advertised a range of four cars, a 6½hp single (De Dion engine), and a 8hp single, a 10hp twin and a 14hp 4-cylinder car. No trace can be found of actual manufacture or sale.   GNG

S.M. (GB) *1904–1905*
S.M. Car Syndicate Ltd, Willesden Junction, London N.W.
 The S.M., or Shave-Morse, was designed by George J. Shave, formerly works manager of the Locomobile Company of Great Britain, and Irving J. Morse. It had a 4-cylinder vertical single-acting steam engine under the bonnet, with a flash boiler at the rear. Final drive was by double chain. 8½hp and 20hp models were said to be available. The S.M. Car Syndicate made steam lorries until about 1912, and made an experimental front-wheel-drive car with a 2-cylinder Aster engine in 1909.   GNG

S.M.B. (I) *1907–1910*
Sta Meccanica Bresciana, Brescia
 This was a conventional medium-sized car powered by 4-cylinder 20hp T-head

1923 S.L.I.M. 15hp sports car. *Autocar*

1908 GREAT SMITH 50hp tourer. *Keith Marvin Collection*

c.1960 SMZ single-cylinder two-seater. *G.N. Georgano*

engines of 3.8 or 4.2 litres. It had a 4-speed gear box and shaft drive, and a circular radiator. GNG

SMITH; GREAT SMITH (US) *1898–1911*
Smith Automobile Co, Topeka, Kans.

From 1898 to 1905 the Smith company made a number of light buggy-type cars sometimes known under the name Veracity. They then turned to the manufacture of larger 4- and 6-cylinder shaft-drive cars called Great Smith. It was claimed that a Great Smith was the first car to climb Pike's Peak entirely under its own power, but they were too expensive, and did not sell well. In 1911 H. Anton Smith, the builder, decided to abandon car manufacture, and made a large bonfire in which he destroyed all the files and records of the Smith Automobile Company. GMN

SMITH FLYER (US) *1917–1919*
A.O. Smith, Milwaukee, Wisc.

The single model of the Smith Flyer was a 5-wheeled buckboard. In addition to the four main wheels of bicycle type there was a smaller wheel at the rear driven by the single-cylinder engine. This design was later made by Briggs and Stratton. KM

SMYK (PL) *1958*
Szczecinska Fabryka Motocykli, Szczecin (Stettin)

Of unorthodox design with a tilting front-of-the-car entrance, this small sedan was powered by a 15hp Junak 4-stroke motor-cycle engine. Only 20 were built. BE

SMZ (US) *1956–1969*
Serpukovskii Motocikletnii Zavod, Serpukov

A 4-wheeled, two-seater minicar that could be equipped with invalid controls. It was reported to be supplied to disabled Soviet veterans at no charge and sold to the general public at low cost. Mounted in the rear was a one-cylinder 2-stroke engine of an estimated 10hp providing a fuel economy of 60mpg and a maximum speed of 50mph.

The SMZ came with a canvas top but it is thought that some models were also built with solid tops. A 3-wheeled version of this car was produced at the factory and was known as the SZL. This had a rear-mounted 7.3hp engine, and four forward speeds. In 1969 a new minicar named Sputnik replaced the SMZ and SZL. BE

S.N.A. (CH) *1903–1913*
Sté Neuchâteloise d'Automobiles, Boudry, Neuchâtel

S.N.A. cars were designed by Fritz Henriod, who had previously made cars under his own name at Bienne. They were all air-cooled, being known as 'Autos-sans-eau'. In 1903 the range consisted of horizontally-opposed twins of 6/8, 10/12 and 18/20hp. They had shaft drive, and some models had electric lighting. In 1907 a new 4-cylinder car appeared, the 25/30hp; it had 4 separate cylinders. Two fans mounted laterally directed air on to the cooling fins. It was made steadily but in small numbers until 1913. GNG

SNOECK *see* BOLIDE

SNYDER (i) (US) *1906–1908*
D.D. Snyder & Co, Danville, Ill.

The Snyder was called a motor buggy by the manufacturer, and had large diameter wheels and solid rubber tyres. The original tiller steering was changed to a steering wheel in the 1908 models. The power unit was a 4-stroke, 2-cylinder opposed engine of 10/12hp. A planetary transmission and double chain drive were used. GMN

SNYDER (ii) (US) *1914*
Snyder Motor & Manufacturing Co, Cleveland, Ohio

This cyclecar was built in three models. The smallest had a 2-cylinder, air-cooled 9hp engine, the largest a water-cooled, 4-cylinder, 1.6-litre unit. GMN

SOAMES (GB) *1903–1904*
Langdon-Davies Motor Co Ltd, Southwark, London S.E.

The Soames car was full of original ideas, having a constant-mesh gearbox which, together with the engine, was mounted on a sub-frame separate from the chassis which supported the body. The engine was an 11hp 2-cylinder vertical unit, and final drive was by double chains, but mounted close to each other, instead of near the wheels as in most double chain drive cars. GNG

SOCIÉTÉ DES PONTS MOTEURS (F) *1913–1914*
Sté des Ponts Moteurs, Paris

This company made an *avant train* attachment which could be fitted to any vehicle. Power came from a V-twin engine of 1,100cc, and a 3-speed gearbox was used. The track of attachment was variable to suit that of the vehicle it powered. This type of machine was not uncommon at the turn of the century, when many people wanted to motorize their horse-drawn carriages, but was something of an anachronism by 1913. GNG

SÖDERBLOM (S) *1903*

Söderbloms Gjuteri & Mekaniska Verkstad, Eskilstuna

A well-known lorry maker, Söderblom built one car to special order, with a 10hp 2-cylinder engine, friction-disc transmission and chain final drive.　　OB

SOLETTA (CH) *1956*

Ingenieurbureau für Fahrzeugbau, Solothurn

Although only built in prototype form, the Soletta was the first post-war Swiss-designed and built car. It had a four-seater 2-door saloon body, and was powered by a rear-mounted flat-twin Condor motor cycle engine of 750cc.　　GNG

SOLIDOR (D) *1905–1907*

Bèaulieu & Krone, Berlin

French Mendelssohn (Passy-Thellier) cars were marketed in Germany under this name. Complete chassis or parts for assembling were imported, while bodies were of German manufacture. Single-, 2- and 4-cylinder models with engine outputs between 8 and 30bhp were made.　　HON

SOLIGNAC (F) *1900–c.1903*

Sté des Voitures Electriques, Paris

The Solignac was an *avant train* attachment for the conversion of horse-drawn carriages. It was powered by an electric motor.　　GNG

SOLOMOBIL (D) *1921–1922*

Kraftwagenfabrik Solomobil GmbH, Berlin

This firm made a 3-wheeler 4/10PS and a 4-wheeler 6/12PS cyclecar with air-cooled V-twin engines.　　HON

SOMÉA (B) *1921*

SA des Automobiles Leroux-Pisart, Brussels

Leroux-Pisart had been making the A.L.P. assembled light car for two years when they engaged Paul Bastien to design a new and more individual car. This was the Soméa which had a 2-litre single ohc engine, and a good performance. However, Leroux-Pisart had manufacturing difficulties, and only three Soméas were made. Bastien afterwards designed the 2-litre Métallurgique, and was one of the team responsible for the Stutz Vertical Eight.　　GNG

SOMMER (US) *1904–1907*

Sommer Motor Co, Detroit, Mich.

This company was an offshoot of the Hammer-Sommer Auto Carriage Company which was dissolved in 1904. The first Sommer car was similar to the Hammer-Sommer, with 12hp 2-cylinder engine mounted under the seat. It had a De Dion-type bonnet, but by 1906 this had been replaced by a conventional bonnet with front radiator. Mechanically the 1907 models were unchanged, as was the price of $1,250.　　GNG

SONCIN (F) *1900–1902*

Emile Ouzou et Cie, Paris 9e

The Soncin voiturette had a 4½hp engine of the company's own manufacture, which was also used to power racing tricycles. The body was a two-seater. In 1902 the company became Grégoire et Cie.　　GNG

SORIANO-PEDROSO (F) *1919–1924*

SA des Automobiles Soriano-Pedroso, Biarritz; Neuilly, Seine

Although built in France, the Soriano-Pedroso was made by two Spaniards, the Marquis Ivanrey de Soriano and the Marquis de San Carlos de Pedroso. Prototypes were built at Biarritz and production models at Neuilly. The car was a small sporting vehicle powered by sv Ballot engines of 1,131cc or 1,590cc, although the former could be underbored to 1,094cc for racing purposes. The most unusual feature of the cars was their final drive by side chains. They were entered in the 1920 Cyclecar Grand Prix but without success, and the 1921 Brooklands 200 Mile Race, where they did not start. Both of the partners subsequently built cars under their own names, though neither was a production model. The Soriano was a streamlined record-breaking car powered by a 904cc Ruby engine; the Pedroso was a sports car with a twin-ohc straight-8 3-litre engine of the Marquis' own design. Both of these cars still exist.　　GNG

SOURIAU (F) *1912–1914*

A. Souriau et Cie, Montoire, Loire-et-Cher

Also known as the Obus, the Souriau was a 3-wheeler whose single front wheel both drove and steered. An experimental model appeared in 1907. Engines were either a 5hp single-cylinder of 625cc, or an 8hp 4-cylinder of 1,460cc.　　GNG

SOUTH BEND (US) *1914*

South Bend Motor Car Works, South Bend, Ind.

This company made a two-seater roadster with a 4-cylinder 50hp engine, priced at $1,800.　　GNG

1921 SOMÉA 2-litre skiff-body sports car.
Autocar

1920 SORIANO-PEDROSO 1,131cc sports car.
Geoffroy de Beauffort Collection

1912 SOURIAU voiturette. *Jacques Kupélian Collection*

1966 SOVAM 1100 coupé. *Automobiles Sovam*

1972 SP2 3½-litre estate car. *Derek Skilton*

1909 S.P.A. 70/80hp 6-cylinder tourer.
Joaquín Ciuró Gabarró Collection

SOUTHERN (i) (US) *1906*
Southern Automobile Mfg Co, Jacksonville, Fla.

The Southern was a high-wheeler reported as being built in 1906. This was, undoubtedly, the first attempt at car production in the citrus belt.　GMN

SOUTHERN (ii) (US) *1909*
Southern Motor Works, Jackson, Tenn.

The Southern was more advanced than its manufacturer's address might suggest. It used a 4-stroke, water-cooled engine of 30hp, a 3-speed selective transmission and shaft drive. Either a five-seater touring body or two-seater roadster were available, both of these models being priced at $1,500.　GMN

SOUTHERN (iii) (US) *1921–1922*
Southern Automobile Manufacturing Co. Memphis, Tenn.

The Southern Six was a rarely-seen assembled car, produced in strictly limited numbers. With 6-cylinder Herschell-Spillman engines, the few Southern Six cars which did appear were well built and sold in the $3,000 price range.　KM

SOUTHERN CROSS (AUS) *1933–1935*
Marks Motor Construction Ltd, Sydney, N.S.W.

First Southern Cross cars had a laminated timber frame and spring anchorages were interleaved with the wood. They used a 65bhp horizontally-opposed 4-cylinder sv engine with aluminium cylinder heads, the design having been attributed to Sir Charles Kingsford-Smith. Conventional frames were used by 1934, when a sedan with McGill torque converter transmission was offered for £295. Subsequent cars may have been equipped with engines made in the United States.　KM

SOUTHERN SIX (AUS) *1921–1922*
Australian British Motors Ltd, Sydney, N.S.W.

This was an assembled car using a 6-cylinder 2.4-litre Sage engine and Wrigley gearbox. It was sold in tourer form only.　GNG

SOVAM (F) *1964–1969*
SA Morin Automobiles, Parthenay, Deux-Sèvres

The Sovam fibreglass sports coupé used Renault engines in 850cc, 1,100cc or 1,300cc sizes, front-mounted and driving the front wheels. The all-round independent suspension was by torsion bars. The last 1,300cc cars had 5-speed all-synchromesh gearboxes and a top speed of 121mph.　GNG

SOVEREIGN (US) *1906–1907*
Matthews Motor Co, Camden, N.J.

Sometimes known, after the makers, as the Matthews, this car had a large 4-cylinder engine of 48hp, dual ignition, and double chain-drive. It was claimed that the aluminium tourer body could seat eight, and the car was advertised as being 'especially adapted for protracted touring'. Maximum speed was 70mph.　GNG

SP (GB) *1972 to date*
Hooe Garage (East Sussex) Ltd, Battle, Sussex

The SP series of cars are intended as very limited production machines made to customers' orders, using Rover engines in tubular chassis. The prototype SP Highwayman was a 6-cylinder vintage-style sports tourer, and the SP2 was a sports estate car powered by a Rover V-8 engine. Production is not expected to exceed five cars per year, and prices will be in the region of £6,000.　GNG

S.P.A. (I) *1906–1926*
Società Ligure Piemontese Automobili, Turin

Matteo Ceirano's S.P.A. was a finely-built, modern, generally conventional vehicle in the Italian tradition. The first cars were big fours of 24 and 60hp, with side valves and live axles. There were two sixes by 1907, one of them with its flywheel attached to the forward end of the crankshaft. By 1910 L-head monobloc engines, unit gearboxes and ht magneto ignition had arrived, and like other manufacturers, S.P.A. offered a modern small four for 1912, the 14/16hp. In that year, 500 cars were sold. S.P.A. won the 1909 Targa Florio, gained successes in many other events, and offered sporting alternatives to their touring cars, but no true competition car was listed until after World War 1. This was some time coming; the immediately post-war S.P.A.s were a touring sv four of 2.7 litres and a six of 4.4 litres, together with a sporting variant of the four. Then in 1922 appeared the exciting and advanced 30/40hp Super Sports. It had the same cubic capacity as the touring six, but its 6 cylinders each had four valves, which were operated by two overhead camshafts. The cylinders were of alloy, with steel liners, and aluminium pistons were used. This was an engine of racing rather than touring type. Two carburettors, dual ignition and front-wheel brakes completed a most sophisticated specification. The general appearance of the S.P.A. 30/40hp was reminiscent of German sports cars of the time, for some wore a sharp V-radiator and high, straight-topped, rather square bodies.

The 30/40, and the other S.P.A.s, vanished when the firm was absorbed by FIAT in 1925.　TRN

SPACKE *see* BROOK-SPACKE

S.P.A.G. (F) *1927–1928*
Automobiles S.P.A.G., Asnières, Seine
The S.P.A.G. car was built by A. Simille and G. Péquinot, whose initials (transposed to make them easier to remember) formed the car's name. Engines of 1,100cc (touring) and 1,500cc (sport) were used, and four body styles were announced: saloon, sports saloon, tourer, and roadster. A competition model did well in the 1927 Bol d'Or, but only seven cars were made.   GNG

SPARTAN (i) (US) *1911*
C.W. Kelsey Manufacturing Co, Hartford, Conn.
Although the Spartan was introduced as a companion product to the Motorette 3-wheeled cars being built by the Kelsey Manufacturing Company at the time, it never went into production. The only model built was a conventional five-seater touring car.   KM

SPARTAN (ii) (GB) *1969–1971*
Bob Sparshott Fabrications Ltd, Wheathampstead, Herts.
This firm constructed a small and cheap Formula 4 monocoque, still includuding desirable sophistications such as fully Rose-jointed suspension. Production was planned of a Mark 2 version also suitable for Formula 3, but the project did not reach fruition.   DF

SPATZ (D) *1955–1957*
Bayerische Autowerke GmbH, Traunreut
This was a small car with a rear-mounted 250cc 14bhp engine and 3-seater body. The firm of Victoria, well-known for its motor cycles, was involved in its production. After 1957 the car was marketed under the name of Victoria.   HON

SPAULDING (i) (US) *1902–1903*
Spaulding Motor & Auto Co, Buffalo, N.Y.
This company made a number of light runabouts powered by single-cylinder engines. They were said to be preparing a touring car for 1903, but it is uncertain if it was made.   GNG

SPAULDING (ii) (US) *1910–1916*
Spaulding Manufacturing Co, Grinnell, Iowa
This Spaulding used 4-cylinder water-cooled engines with either planetary or sliding-gear transmissions. As many as thirteen models were offered in one year. Apparently all models were on a standard chassis of 9ft 4in wheelbase.   GMN

SPEEDEX (GB) *1960*
Speedex Castings and Accessories Ltd, Luton, Beds.
Principally manufacturers of accessories and tuning aids, Speedex supplied the Mercury space-frame chassis for the construction of two- or four-seater sports cars, using Ford mechanical parts.   DF

SPEEDSPORT (B) *1924–c.1927*
Assembled in Brussels, the Speedsport was one of a number of European modified versions of the Model T Ford. Early Speedsports were spidery two-seater sports cars with a shortened wheelbase, two bucket seats and a large trunk mounted incongruously behind them. Later cars carried some quite handsome two-door saloon bodywork.   GNG

SPEEDWAY (US) *1904–1905*
Gas Engine & Power Co, Morris Heights, N.Y.
This was a five-seater side-entrance tonneau with a 28hp, 4-cylinder engine. The car had a pleasant appearance, a 4-speed transmission and shaft-drive at prices ranging from $4,700 to $5,350. The Gas Engine & Power Co later combined with the manufacturer of the Howard (ii).   GMN

SPEEDWELL (i) (GB) *c.1900–1907*
(1) Speedwell Motor and Engineering Co Ltd, Reading, Berks.
(2) New Speedwell Motor Co Ltd, London
By 1904 this firm held at least eight foreign agencies, but they were still selling various lesser-known imported cars under their own name. Models ranged upwards from single-cylinders of 700cc, the buyer of a de luxe model enjoying a genuine De Dion engine, rather than merely one 'of De Dion type'. Some versions included Léon Bollée parts. In the 1905 Tourist Trophy 4-cylinder cars of 2,011 and 2,497cc were entered; the 1906 contender was of 3,922cc. A 3-cylinder was also available, and so were Gnome-engined models of 4,084cc (4-cylinder) and 6,126cc (6-cylinder). By this time the company was building its own designs, including a patented rear axle, split horizontally and with a torque rod below, with a system of mounting the wheels that was claimed to eliminate wheel-wobble and like vices. Another feature was a spring take-up in the clutch. For 1907, Aster engines were used.   DF

1923 S.P.A. 2.7-litre saloon. Coachwork by Reliance Motor Works Ltd. *Autocar*

1924 S.P.A. 4.4-litre tourer. *Lucien Loreille Collection*

1927 S.P.A.G. 1½-litre racing car. *Lucien Loreille Collection*

1904 SPEEDWELL(i) 6hp dogcart. *G.N. Georgano*

1907 SPEEDWELL(i) 25hp tourer. *A.J. Dew*

1909 SPEEDWELL(ii) 50hp tourer. *Automotive History Collection, Detroit Public Library*

1910 SPEEDWELL(ii) 50hp tourer. *Kenneth Stauffer*

SPEEDWELL (ii) (US) *1907–1914*

Speedwell Motor Car Co, Dayton, Ohio

Early models of the Speedwell used a 40hp, 4-cylinder engine with shaft drive. Six different body styles were offered in 1909. Later models were very large, with 6.9-litre, 6-cylinder engines. In 1913 the buyer had a choice of a Mead rotary valve engine, or one with standard poppet valves. GMN

SPEEDY (i) (GB) *1905*

Jackson Brothers & Lord, Salford, Lancs.

This was a light 3-wheeler with a tandem two-seater body, 4hp engine, and belt drive. GNG

SPEEDY (ii) (GB) *1920–1921*

Pullinger Engineering Co Ltd, Peckham, London S.E.

The Speedy was a cyclecar announced with a great flourish, and promises of mass-production (5,000 in the first year), but very few were made. It had an 8hp air-cooled V-twin engine, chain drive to the 2-speed gearbox, and belt final drive. With a two-seater streamlined body the overall weight was 672lb. The price was to be only £150. GNG

SPEIDEL (CH) *1915–1922*

Paul Speidel, Geneva

Paul Speidel built a small number of light cars as well as motorcycles. His first two cars, one a tandem two-seater, used Chapuis-Dornier engines, but after the war he used an 8hp 4-cylinder Swiss-built M.V. (Muller-Vogel) engine. This drove via a 4-speed gearbox and propeller shaft. The last Speidel was a racing car powered by a 620cc 2-cylinder M.V. engine, and capable of 70mph. GNG

SPENCER (US) *1921–1922*

Research Engineering Co, Dayton, Ohio

Few Spencers were ever produced. The car used a 4-cylinder engine of the company's own make and was equipped with artillery wheels. The price of the five-seater touring model wa $850. KM

SPENNY (US) *1914–1915*

Spenny Motor Car Co, Chicago, Ill.

This company made a 4-cylinder 30hp roadster and tourer to sell at $1,075, and a 6-cylinder tourer priced at $3,750. GNG

SPERBER (D) *1911–1919*

Norddeutsche Automobilwerke, Hameln

The Norddeutsche Automobilwerke (N.A.W.) started production of cars with the Colibri, which was developed into the Sperber with a 1,592cc 6/15PS engine. In 1913 two new and smaller 4-cylinder models of 5/15PS and 6/15PS appeared. These were carried on until 1919, when the N.A.W. factory was taken over by Selve. HON

SPERLING (US) *1921–1923*

Associated Motors Corp, Elkhart, Ind.

The Sperling was built with right-hand drive for the export market. The cars were distinguished by a slightly V-shaped radiator. Both open and closed models appeared in the company's catalogues. KM

SPERRY *see* CLEVELAND (i)

SPHINX (i) (F) *1912–1925*

(1) F. Terrier, Courbevoie, Seine *1912–1916*

(2) Sphinx Automobiles Etablissements Perfecto, Puteaux, Seine *1920–1925*

Sphinx light cars were designed by an Englishman, J.H. Forster, and some pre-war models were made in England under the name Globe (ii). Single-, 2- and 4-cylinder engines were used, one of the fours having the cylinders in V-formation. All cars had belt or chain final drive. Post-war cars had the alternative of a 1,400cc flat twin, or a 1,323cc 4-cylinder engine, the former, at least, still using belt drive. This car was sold in England as the Foster (ii) in 1922 and Anglo-Sphinx in 1923. GNG

SPHINX (ii) (US) *1914–1915*

Sphinx Motor Car Co, York, Pa.

This was a light, five-seater tourer with a 4-cylinder Lycoming engine of 2.7 litres. The only unusual feature of this car was the use of cantilever springs all round. The manufacturer was succeeded by the Du Pont Motor Car Co who made a similar car under the name Du Pont for 1915 only. GMN

SPHINX (iii) (D) *1920–1925*

(1) Sphinx Automobilwerke AG, Zwenkau *1920–1925*

(2) Georg Kralapp Automobilwerke, Zwenkau *1925*

One model was produced by this firm in limited numbers. A 4-cylinder 1,320cc engine of 22bhp was used. HON

SPIDOS (F) *c.1921–1925*
Cyclecars Spidos, Lyons

The Spidos was a cyclecar powered by an ohv Ruby engine of 1,100cc. Driven by their designer, de Vassiaux, they won several local races and hill-climbs.　GNG

SPINELL (D) *1924–1925*
Spinell Motorfahrzeuge GmbH Otto Krell Jr, Berlin

This was a sports two-seater with a light metal body and a 1.5/PS, 12bhp 500cc Kühne engine.　HON

SPITZ (A) *1902–1907*
Arnold Spitz, Vienna IX

Spitz originally was a dealer, handling the De Dion-Bouton, Benz and Mercedes in Austria. Otto Hieronimus, the well-known racing-driver, designed a car which was produced to Spitz's order by Gräf & Stift. Several types with single-, 2- and 4-cylinder engines were made. After 1907 Spitz cars were built by the Ungarische Maschinen- und Waggonfabrik, of Raab, Hungary.　HON

S.P.M.A. (F) *1908*
Sté Parisienne de Mécanique Appliquée, Courbevoie, Seine

The S.P.M.A. was a light car powered by a 10/12hp 4-cylinder engine. It had friction drive by a small pulley acting on two large discs.　GNG

SPOERER (US) *1907–1914*
Carl Spoerer's Sons Co, Baltimore, Md.

Original models of the Spoerer had 30hp and 50/60hp 4-cylinder engines. For 1910 this was reduced to one engine of 40hp in four different body types, including a seven-seater. Later, as many as eleven models were offered, with engines of 25 and 40hp. Prices for these cars ranged up to $4,150.　GMN

SPORTS (GB) *1900–1901*
Sports Motor Car Co, Kensington, London W.; Kilburn, London N.W.

The Sports was an imported or assembled car powered by an 8hp 2-cylinder engine. It had a 4-speed gearbox, and shaft drive. Two models were made, the Sports Car, a two-seater, and the four-seater Sports American Phaeton. The latter used a Gauthier-Wehrlé transmission, and may well have been a product of this firm. The Sports Motor Car Co also sold various imported cars under the brand-name of Mayfair.　GNG

SPRINGER (US) *1904–1906*
(1) John H. Springer, New York, N.Y. *1904*
(2) Springer Motor Vehicle Co, New York, N.Y. *1904–1906*

The original Springer was a two-seater with a 2-cylinder water-cooled engine of 12hp for which 12mph was claimed. A larger five-seater was soon offered, with an air-cooled 4-cylinder engine of 40hp.　GMN

SPRINGFIELD (i) (US) *1904*
Springfield Automobile Co, Springfield, Ohio

The Springfield had a single-cylinder, 2-stroke, water-cooled engine of 1.6-litres, rated at 8hp. The drive was through a planetary transmission and single chain. A two-seater was the only body style made.　GMN

SPRINGFIELD (ii) (US) *1907*
Med-Bow Automobile Co, Springfield, Mass.

This car was made only as a five-seater. It had a 4-cylinder, 5.2-litre Rutenber engine with special high-lift valve cams. The price was $2,500.　GMN

SPRINGFIELD (iii) (US) *1908–1911*
Springfield Motor Car Co, Springfield, Ill.

This car, it was announced, was made to order. Available were both a torpedo and a touring model for $2,500 on a wheelbase of 10ft 8in. These had F-head 4-cylinder, water-cooled engines of 6.1 litres. 3-speed selective transmissions were used.　GMN

SPRINGUEL (B) *1907–1910*
SA des Automobiles Springuel, Liège

The prototype Springuel appeared in 1903, but production did not start until 1907. The car had a 24hp 4-cylinder engine with pair-cast cylinders, 4-speed gearbox and double chain drive. It was made in small numbers, mostly in open tourer form, up to 1910, when the company was acquired by Imperia. The later cars manufactured in the Springuel factory were known as Springuel-Imperias, and were similar to Imperia models.　GNG

SPRITE (US) *1914*
W.S. Frasier & Co, Aurora, Ill.

This two-seater, side-by-side cyclecar was driven by a 2-cylinder air-cooled engine. Its weight was 700lb and its cost was $425.　GMN

1914 SPERBER Typ F40 6/20PS tourer.
Neubauer Collection

1923 SPERLING sedan. *Keith Marvin Collection*

1924 SPINELL 500cc cyclecar. *Neubauer Collection*

1902 SPYKER 12hp limousine. *C. Poel Jr*

1911 SPYKER 40hp landaulette. Queen Wilhelmina's first car. *C. Poel Jr*

1919 SPYKER 13/30hp two-seater.
C. Poel Jr

SPUTNIK *see* SMZ

SPYKER (SPIJKER) (NL) *1900–1925*

(1) De Industrieele Maatschappij Trompenburg, Amsterdam *1899–1916*
(2) Nederlandsche Automobiel- en Vliegtuigenfabriek Trompenburg, Amsterdam *1916–1925*

The Spijkers (the simpler spelling was used for the cars) set up in business as coachmakers at Hilversum in 1880, taking a Benz agency in 1895, and modifying the German cars to their own ideas. The first true Spyker appeared in 1900, a 5hp with front-mounted air-cooled flat-twin engine, 2-speed and reverse gear, and shaft drive (Spykers never used chains). This car was not a commercial success; more promising were a 1.9-litre twin and a companion four introduced in 1902, with separately cast cylinders, side valves in a T-head, coil ignition, and armoured frames. The bigger 20hp car had a 5-bearing crankshaft, full-elliptic front suspension was used; there was also a petrol brougham version. The close fit of the bonnet was the first step towards the dust sealing that became a strong Spyker selling point, accentuated by the full undershielding of later models.

In 1904 Jacobus Spijker tried a 'circular' 4-cylinder engine, its curious shape the result of comprehensive but ineffectual water-jacketing. This was available in 12/16hp, 20/24hp and 30/36hp sizes, along with a huge 8.7-litre 6-cylinder 4×4 racer, with brakes on all wheels. This never reached production though three or four 32/40hp fours were made with the 4×4 configuration, and sold at a price of £960. Conventional pair-cast engines and semi-elliptic front springs came in 1905, and during the same year round radiators were adopted. The 1906 Spykers had ball-bearing crankshafts; the biggest of a range of four 4-cylinder cars was the 7.9-litre 25/38. Pressed-steel frames arrived on the 1907 models, smallest of which was a short-stroke (80×90mm) four with ht magneto ignition intended for taxicab service. The next major departure came in 1909, when the company adopted Valentin Laviolette's ingenious T-head, transverse-camshaft layout, a feature of all Spykers up to 1917, and offered in a wide diversity of models. A 2-cylinder light car did not progress beyond the prototype stage, but the fours extended from a 1.7-litre 12hp up to a 7.2-litre 40, all with thermo-syphon cooling; at first only the larger ones had four forward speeds, and all but the smallest now wore three-quarter elliptic springs at the rear. The 12hp had a 3-speed transaxle, and some models were available with Allen-Liversidge 4-wheel brakes as an optional extra in 1911, though these (like a 4.2-litre monobloc 6-cylinder) were apparently not a success. Electric lighting was available in 1913 and standard by 1915. V-radiators appeared during 1914, when the company introduced a sports version of the 3.4-litre 20 with light steel pistons, capable of 68mph.

A shortage of raw materials reduced production to a trickle by 1916, and the first new post-World War 1 Spyker, the 3.3-litre 13/30, reverted to an L-head layout, as well as making liberal use of American components (Delco coil ignition, Stewart vacuum feed, Stromberg carburettor). It had a 3-speed unit box with central change, and was noteworthy only for the peculiar aerocoque sports coachwork with aerofoil wings and tail fin fitted to some examples. In 1920 the company tried importing Mathis light cars from France and selling them with Spyker badges, but the last real Spyker was the Frits Koolhoven-designed 6-cylinder 30/40. It featured a 5.6-litre sv Maybach engine, dual ignition and a 2-speed fan, and there were four forward speeds. Front-wheel brakes came in 1923, but though Queen Wilhelmina of the Netherlands purchased two landaulettes in 1921, and S.F. Edge used a two-seater for a successful attack on his Double-12-Hour record at Brooklands in 1922, there was little future for such a car at £1,950. The last of 150 examples left the Spyker works in 1925.   MCS

SQUIRE (GB) *1934–1936*

Squire Car Manufacturing Co Ltd, Henley-on-Thames, Oxfordshire

Adrian Squire's aim was to build a 1½-litre sports car of the highest possible standard, regardless of price. He used a specially-built twin-ohc Anzani engine developing 105bhp, a Roots supercharger, ENV preselector gearbox and hydraulic brakes. Bodies were by Ranalah, Vanden Plas and, for the short-chassis two-seater, Markham of Reading. Prices began at £1,195 for the two-seater, but by 1936 had dropped to £795. Twelve cars were laid down, seven of them having been completed when the company was liquidated in July 1936. The name, goodwill and spares were purchased by Val Zethrin who assembled three more cars.   GNG

SQUIRE SS 100 (US) *1971 to date*

Auto Sports Importers Inc, Philadelphia, Pa.

This is a replica of the pre-World War 2 British S.S. 100 sports car, using a 4-litre 6-cylinder Ford engine and a fibreglass body made in Milan.   GNG

S.R.C. (E) *1922–1925*

Stevenson, Ramagosa y Cía, Barcelona

Formerly the Matas, the S.R.C. was an assembled car using British 11.9hp engines by Dorman or Meadows.   GNG

S.S. (i) (GB) *1900*

S.S. Motor Car Co, London E.C.

This company's offices were in Holborn Viaduct, but the factory address is uncertain. The car had a 5hp horizontal single-cylinder engine, constant-mesh 3-speed gearbox and chain final drive.   GNG

S.S. (ii) (GB) 1931–1945

(1) Swallow Coachbuilding Co Ltd, Coventry, Warwickshire 1931–1934
(2) S.S. Cars Ltd, Coventry, Warwickshire 1934–1945

William Lyons and William Walmsley started the manufacture of sidecars in Blackpool in 1922, following this up in 1927 with a line of handsome open and closed sporting bodies on popular chassis such as Austin (i), Morris, Fiat, Swift and Standard (i). The company moved to Coventry in 1928, and from the Swallow saloon version of the 16hp Standard came the first S.S.I of 1931. This used Standard mechanical components throughout, but a special underslung frame was made for the Swallow though the 2,054cc 6-cylinder sv engine was left untuned. The long bonnet, diminutive coupé body and helmet-type front wings gave it a distinctive look, which suggested a price in the region of £1,000 – the S.S.I., in fact, cost £310. A 2½-litre 20hp engine was available, and there was a companion S.S.II based on the 1,052cc Standard Little Nine. A sale of 776 machines the first season was remarkable for a new make at the depths of the Depression. The 1933 6-cylinder models with full-flow wings were better proportioned, and a sports tourer was available for the first time. 1934 cars had X-braced frames, synchromesh gearboxes, and larger and more powerful engines – the 2.7-litre Twenty gave 68bhp. Twin carburettors and a higher-lift camshaft featured in 1935, in which year the company's first sports car made its appearance: this 90 was sold only with the 20hp engine, and had a short chassis and slab-tank two-seater bodywork.

The Jaguar name first appeared in 1936, on a handsome 4-door sports saloon, with a 2.7-litre ohv 104bhp engine, still made by Standard, but redesigned by Harry Weslake and W.M. Heynes. These cars were good for 85–90mph and sold for only £385. The sv S.S.I and S.S.II models were continued for one more season with Standard engines, a Standard unit also being used in the 1.6-litre version of the Jaguar, but much more exciting was the short-chassis ohv 100 two-seater. Its handling was tricky, but it proved hard to beat in British rallies of the later 1930s. In 1938 the 2½-litre was continued, but the small sv four had given way to a 1.8-litre unit, used after the war by Standard in their versions of the Triumph. A new 125bhp 3½-litre was listed not only in saloon and drophead coupé forms, but also as a 100 two-seater, offering a genuine 100mph for only £445. Over 5,000 cars were sold in a year interrupted by war. The 1940 models were available with heaters.

In 1945 the name of the company was changed to Jaguar Cars Ltd, and the sidecar interests were sold. Under different ownership the Swallow company was responsible for the Swallow Doretti in 1954.   MCS

S.S.E. (US) 1916–1917

S.S.E. Co, Philadelphia, Pa.

The S.S.E. was made in nine body styles, on a standard chassis in which was a 6-cylinder, 4.7-litre engine. This was an expensive car with prices from $5,000 for the five-seater tourer, to $8,000 for the closed berline.   GMN

STABILIA (F) 1908–1930

(1) Automobiles Stabilia, Neuilly, Seine 1908–1910
(2) Giraldy et Vrard, Neuilly, Seine; Asniéres, Seine 1911–1920
(3) Vrard et Cie, Asnières, Seine 1920–1930

This so-called auto inversable was made intermittently in limited numbers, the prototype appearing in 1905. The main feature was an underslung frame. The first cars had auxiliary transverse rear springing, 2.2-litre 4-cylinder engines with pair-cast cylinders and forced lubrication, and left-hand steering. By 1912, 1½-litre, 1.7-litre, and 2.7-litre versions were marketed, and the 1913 cars had very odd rear suspension, the coil springs being held in tension by wire cables. The company was reorganized in 1920, when a 2.8-litre 14CV, with pump-and-fan cooling, 4-speed gearbox, multi-disc clutch, and foot transmission brake was offered. Rear suspension was cantilever. Standard units in 1924–26 were the 1½-litre and 2-litre Altos, and manufacture virtually ceased in 1927, though the small Gobron of the period was marketed under the Stabilia name – with an equal lack of success. A final effort was made late in 1930 with a small ohc straight-8 of 1.4 litres' capacity, still with underslung frame, but now with reversed quarter-elliptics at the rear. Ignition was by twin magnetos, and 80bhp was claimed.   MCS

STACK (GB) 1921–1925

G.F. Stack & Co, East Croydon, Surrey

The Stack light car used a 766cc V-twin engine and friction transmission. This was of the usual type, but a refinement was a device to vary the pressure of the driving disc according to the ratio selected. Final drive was by single chain.   GNG

S.T.A.E. see KRIÉGER

STAFFORD (i) (US) 1910–1915

Stafford Motor Car Co, Topeka, Kans., Kansas City, Mo.

1920 SPYKER 13/30hp aerotype sports car.
Autocar

1935 SQUIRE 1½-litre sports car. *National Motor Museum*

1935 S.S.1 20hp Airline saloon. *Jaguar Cars Ltd.*

1938 S.S. Jaguar 100 3½-litre sports car. *Jaguar Cars Ltd*

1914 STABILIA 2.7-litre two-seater. *Autocar*

1921 STACK 6hp two-seater. *Autocar*

1920 STAFFORD(ii) 11.9hp tourer. *Autocar*

The Stafford used a 4-cylinder water-cooled engine of 4 litres which had an early example of overhead camshaft driven by a chain. The final drive was through selective transmission and drive shaft.
GMN

STAFFORD (ii) (GB) *1920–1921*
Stafford Associated Engineering Co Ltd, Battersea, London S.W.

Like many post-war firms the Stafford company hoped to make a large number of cars cheaply by buying out all their components. Engines were by Dorman, mainly the 11.9hp 1,794cc, although a car with a 16/20hp 2,650 engine was also listed. Few Staffords were made, although one survives today in Yorkshire.
GNG

STAG (GB) *1913–1914*
The Stag Co, Sherwood, Nottingham

Stag engines were used in a number of ultra-light cyclecars such as the Heybourn and the L.A.D., and they also made a few cars of their own. These had a 5/6hp single-cylinder engine, a Jardine 3-speed gearbox and belt final drive. A vaned flywheel acted as a fan.
GNG

STAIGER (D) *1923–1924*
Automobilfabrik Staiger, Stuttgart

This firm produced as their only model a small 4-cylinder 4/12PS cyclecar with a two- or four-seater body.
HON

STAINES-SIMPLEX (GB) *1906–c.1912*
Staines Motor Co Ltd, Staines, Middlesex

Also known as the S.S.S. (Staines Silent Simplex), this car was first exhibited at the 1908 Cordingley Show, although it was stated that the company had had nearly two years experience in building cars. It was an assembled car with a Coventry-Simplex 8/10hp 2-cylinder engine and shaft drive. The bonnet and radiator were on the Renault pattern. A 4-cylinder car with a 15/20hp Coventry-Simplex engine was also offered, but very few appear to have been sold. In fact *The Motor* said that the company's main business was in hiring out chauffeur-driven cars, and that the chauffeur/machinists, when unemployed in the hiring department, were assembling cars to order.
GNG

STANBURY (GB) *1903*
Stanbury & Co, Liverpool

Stanburys were well-known cycle and motor factors, and made at least one car. This, a 12hp model, was said to have passed its tests 'with flying colours', but no more was heard of it.
GNG

STANDARD (i) (GB) *1903–1963*
Standard Motor Co Ltd, Coventry, Warwickshire

R.W. Maudslay's company started modestly with a single-cylinder machine with an under-floor engine of markedly oversquare (5in × 3in) dimensions, which was the work of Alex Craig who also designed for Maudslay (made by the same family as the Standard's founder), Lea-Francis, and Singer. A 12/15hp bonneted twin was also available, while 4-cylinder engines were offered as proprietary units. In 1906 Standard offered Britain's first inexpensive sixes with side valves, 3-speed gearboxes, and shaft drive; a fairly large 24/30hp being followed by a really big 50hp at £850, and a 3.3-litre 20 at £450, these cars being energetically marketed in London by Charles Friswell. 6-cylinder cars dominated Standard design for several years, the 20 doing well in its subsequent 4-litre form; a fleet of 70 was shipped to India for the Delhi Durbar in 1911. The shouldered radiator first carried the Union Jack badge in 1908. In 1909 a 2.7-litre 4-cylinder 14 with cylinders cast in pairs was being offered for £350, other fours following until the sixes were finally dropped at the end of 1912. A big car in miniature, the 9.5hp Rhyl, was announced in 1913 with a 3-speed gearbox, worm drive, and all brakes on the rear wheels, at £185. Electric lighting was available on this model in 1915, and at the outbreak of World War 1 there were also two bigger Standards, both sv monobloc fours with capacities of 2.4 and 3.3 litres.

In 1919 an enlarged 1.3-litre version of the Rhyl, the SLS, was the staple product, but this had grown up by 1921 into the 11.6hp SLO with exposed overhead valves – these early Vintage Standards also had no sides to their radiator shells. There was a short-lived ohv 8hp in 1922, but the most successful mid-Vintage model was the 13.9hp SLO4, still with overhead valves and worm drive, which had rigid side-curtains and could be bought for £375 in 1924. From 1923 these cars carried the emblem of the 9th Roman Legion as their radiator mascot. 10,000 Standards were sold in 1924. Front-wheel brakes were standard on the 13.9hp cars in 1926. Some less successful 2.2-litre ohv 6-cylinder cars were marketed in 1927, in which year saloons could be bought with sliding roofs, while financial difficulties were circumvented by the hurried introduction of the very reliable 1,155cc worm-drive Nine with an sv engine and fabric bodywork for 1928. Within a year a roomier, longer-wheelbase version was listed, as well as supercharged and unsupercharged sports two-seaters, and the first of the Avon Standard Specials, a low-built two-seater styled by the Jensen brothers, had made its appearance. The Avon, both in its original form and in its later manifestations (the work of C.F. Beauvais) continued in a variety of semi-catalogue forms on many Standard chassis from the Nine to the 20hp up to 1937. 1929 was the year of chromium plating, of the first of a line of sv sixes with coil ignition and 7-bearing crankshafts that was to persist up to 1940, and of the appointment of Captain J.P. Black, from Hillman, as Managing Director. Under his control Standard rode out the Depression with steadily increasing sales, but at the cost of magneto ignition, worm-driven back axles and the traditional radiator, all of which had disappeared by 1931, when Standard were offering the Big Nine, a really roomy small saloon for less than £200, and low-priced 16 and 20hp sixes. This range was rounded out in 1932 by a 1-litre Little Nine at £155, and in this year William Lyons, whose 1930 Swallow-bodied Standards had anticipated the new 1931 radiator, launched his first S.S. cars. These used specially-built Standard chassis and his own style of bodywork, and were to evolve into the Jaguar. Standard-built engines were used in all Lyon's cars up to 1940 and survived on 4-cylinder Jaguars until 1948. Cruciform-braced frames and silent-third gearboxes were features of the 1933 Standards, while that year's complex range included a couple of short-lived sixes of under 1,500cc, the option of preselector gearboxes on some models, and a long-wheelbase 20hp landaulette. Synchromesh, free wheels and integral boots came in 1934, when a new best-seller was the well-equipped 1.3-litre Ten, and there were six models for 1935, including a sporting 10/12hp consisting of a Ten chassis and body, and a 1.6-litre twin-carburettor 12hp engine. Much the same cars were offered in 1936, but this year also brought the fastback Flying Standards with luggage accommodation and spare wheels streamlined into the tail, though retaining the Bendix brakes of earlier versions. Initially offered only in 12, 16, and 20hp sizes, the style was universal by 1937, when buyers had the choice of four 4-cylinder and two 6-cylinder types, from the Nine at £149 to the Twenty at £299, as well as a rapid compact V-8 with a 2.7-litre 80bhp sv engine in a Twelve chassis. It failed to catch on, though its fencer's mask grille was found on all Standards from 1938 to 1947, and the engine was used by Raymond Mays. Other makers buying components from Standard were Railton, whose Ten was based on a Standard chassis, and Morgan, for whom a special ohv 10hp engine was made from 1939–50.

A 1939 best seller was the 1-litre Eight at £129, the first British small saloon with independent front suspension: similar layouts were found on Super versions of the Ten and Twelve, but this year's Flying Standards no longer had fastbacks. Of the extensive pre-World War 2 range, only the Eight, Twelve, and Fourteen were continued after the war, the Fourteen using a 1.8-litre engine in the Twelve chassis, although Standard products now included Triumph (iii), acquired in 1945.

Late in 1947 came the company's first true post-war design, the unitary-construction Vanguard with a 2.1-litre ohv wet-liner 4-cylinder engine, full-width six-seater bodywork, hydraulic brakes, and a 3-speed gearbox with column change. It sold for £544, though for some time it was practically unobtainable on the home market, and was the only model catalogued between 1949 and 1953. Cars were made under licence in Belgium by Imperia, and the engine also went into the bigger Triumphs, the Ferguson tractor, the earlier Plus-Four Morgan, and, in 2-litre form, into Triumph's successful TR series. Overdrive became an option in 1950; the body was restyled in 1953, 1956, and 1959; a diesel version with separate chassis was marketed in 1954 and 1955; and a luxury Sportsman version with a 90bhp engine, a traditional grille, and overdrive as standard appeared in 1957, though this was too expensive at £1,231, and did not last long. Towards the end automatic Vanguards were available, but the tough old four was dropped in 1961.

There were other models. An 803cc ohv Eight with coil-spring independent front suspension and very basic appointments was announced late in 1953 at £481, followed shortly after by a more luxurious 948cc 10hp at £581. These were never quite best-sellers despite such later options as 2-pedal control, triple overdrive (on the Eight) and the addition of a luxury Pennant version of the Ten in 1957. Fairthorpe used this engine, which later served as the basis for the Triumph Herald, but production of the small Standards tailed off in 1959. There were other variations on the Vanguard theme: the Ensign with a 1.6-litre 62bhp engine was cooly received, though it was revived in 1962 with a 75bhp, 2,138cc unit and 4-speed gearbox. After the Leyland take-over in 1961, the company's efforts concentrated increasingly on the Triumph range, but Standard's final fling in 1962 was once again Vanguard-based, though it broke new ground with a 2-litre short-stroke ohv 6-cylinder engine later used in the Triumph 2000. The last Standards were delivered in the summer of 1963. The name died because the term, 'standard', when applied to cars, had been debased; it had come to mean the opposite of 'de luxe' – and this despite the comfortable appointments of the Luxury Six.   MCS

STANDARD (ii) (STANDARD TOURIST) (US) 1903–1907
Standard Motor Construction, Jersey City, N.J.

This make succeeded the U.S. Long Distance. The only model was a five-seater in wood at $3,250, or in aluminium for $3,500. The engine was a 4-stroke, 4-cylinder one of 25hp.   GMN

STANDARD (iii) (I) 1906–1912
Fabbrica Automobili Standard, Turin

Also known as the F.A.S., this car was a conventional machine with a 14/20hp 4-cylinder engine and 4-speed gearbox. The company had no known connection with any other firm bearing the name Standard.   GNG

1907 STANDARD(i) 30hp tourer. *J.R. Davy*

1925 STANDARD(i) 13.9hp Pall Mall saloon. *National Motor Museum*

1929 STANDARD(i) 9.9hp Teignmouth saloon. *J.R. Davy*

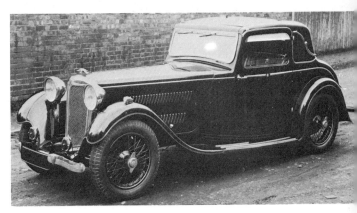

1933 STANDARD(i) 16hp coupé. Coachwork by Avon. *National Motor Museum*

1940 STANDARD(i) 8hp 4-door saloon.
National Motor Museum

1947 STANDARD(i) Vanguard 2.1-litre saloon.
Standard-Triumph Ltd

1953 STANDARD(i) Eight 803cc saloon.
Standard-Triumph Ltd

1917 STANDARD(viii) 34hp V-8 tourer.
Kenneth Stauffer

STANDARD (iv) (US) *1909–1910*
(1) St Louis Motor Car Co, St Louis, Mo. *1909*
(2) St Louis Car Co, St Louis, Mo. *1910*

From 1906 to 1909 this company made three models of the Mors under the name American Mors, but in 1909 they introduced a car of their own design. This had an ohv 50hp 6-cylinder engine of 7.8 litres capacity. Five body styles were listed, including a limousine at $4,000. The rear springs were of the platform type. GMN

STANDARD (v) (US) *1910*
Standard Gas Electric Power Co, Philadelphia, Pa.

This car had a 4-cylinder, 3.7-litre engine with a 3-speed sliding-gear transmission and shaft drive. The only feature of interest was electric starting. The single model for 1910 was a four-seater torpedo which weighed 2,000lb. GMN

STANDARD (vi) (D) *1911–1912*
Standard Automobilfabrik GmbH, Berlin-Charlottenburg

Cars of this make were characterized by the use of Henriod rotary-valve engines, but the system proved unsuccessful and production was not on a large scale. Two 4-cylinder models of 10/28PS and 13/35PS were listed. HON

STANDARD (vii) (US) *1912–1915*
Standard Electric Car Co, Jackson, Mich.

This electric car used Westinghouse motors and was claimed to have a range of 110 miles on a charge. It was operated from a tiller on the left-hand side. The controller gave six forward speeds, the maximum speed being 20mph. The Model M, a four-seater closed model, cost $1,885. GMN

STANDARD (viii) (US) *1912–1923*
(1) Standard Steel Car Co, Butler, Pa. *1912–1923*
(2) Standard Auto Vehicle Co, Butler, Pa. *1923*

For most of its life the Standard was built by a firm whose main product was steel and composite railway carriages and wagons. Up to 1916 it was a conventional 38hp 6-cylinder car built in touring and closed models, at prices up to $3,600. In 1916 an 8-cylinder model was introduced which was to become the staple product of the company. Smaller than the six, it was rated at 29hp (50bhp) and cost only $1,950 for the most expensive model. For 1917 it was increased to 34hp (80bhp) and by 1921 prices were up to $5,000. In 1923 a new company acquired the design from the Standard Steel Car Co. They assembled a few of the V-8s, but did not introduce any new models, and were out of business the same year. GNG

STANDARD (ix) (US) *1914*
Standard Engineering Co, Chicago, Ill.

This was a cyclecar powered by an air-cooled 2-cylinder Spacke engine. Transmission was by friction discs, and final drive by single chain. GNG

STANDARD (x) (US) *1920–1921*
Standard Engineering Co, St Louis, Mo.

The Standard Steam Car was equipped with a Scott-Newcomb 2-cylinder, horizontal paraffin-burning steam engine and was advertised as being able to raise a head of steam in less than 60 seconds. The car carried a Rolls-Royce-type condenser and closely resembled the then well-known Roamer. A touring model was the only body style available. It was sometimes known as the Scott-Newcomb. KM

STANDARD (xi) (D) *1933–1935*
Standard Fahrzeugfabrik GmbH, Ludwigsburg

This firm, owned by Wilhelm Gutbrod, obtained the licence for the production of a small car designed by Josef Ganz. The car appeared under the name of Standard Superior. It had a 2-cylinder, 2-stroke engine of 396cc developing 12bhp or of 494cc and 16bhp. Special features of this design were an aerodynamic body, rear engine, centre tubular chassis and independent suspension. Production was given up in 1935, but vans and estate cars were built until 1939. Another car built to Ganz designs was the Swiss Rapid (iii). HON

STANDISH (US) *1924–1925*
Luxor Cab Manufacturing Co, Framingham, Mass.

The Standish, of which only a few were ever completed, was produced by the Luxor taxicab company, itself a subsidiary of the Crawford/Dagmar empire. The Standish cars were designed with a pointed radiator and powered by a Continental six engine. The radiator was later used on the Elysée truck, also a subsidiary division of M.P. Moller's Dagmar and taxicab enterprise. Like the Dagmar, most Standish cars were seen with brass rather than nickel trim. They were made in the taxicab factory formerly occupied by the R.H. Long Co, makers of the Bay State car. KM

STANGUELLINI (I) *1946–c.1966*
Officine Stanguellini Trasformazione Auto Sport e Corsa, Modena

One of the best-known of the Italian *amelioriazioni* based on Fiat products is the Stanguellini. Its founder, Vittorio Stanguellini, used to modify Fiat Balillas before World War 2, and established his own marque in 1946, building fast sports specials out of the inevitable Fiat components. Of these, the Bialbero (twin-cam) in 750cc and 1,100cc two-seater spider forms was notably successful in competitions. In 1959 Stanguellini built a batch of 50 Formula Junior single-seaters, using Fiat-based 1,100cc engines mounted at the front of a tubular frame. These proved the most successful Junior cars of the year, winning numerous races, including the Prix Junior at Monaco. Subsequently Stanguellini followed the fashion set by the British and switched to rear-engined cars, always beautifully made but unsuccessful against their more powerful British rivals.   CP

STANHOPE (GB) *1915–1925*

(1) Stanhope Motors (Leeds) Ltd, Leeds, Yorks. *1915–1922*
(2) Bramham Motors Ltd, Leeds, Yorks. *1922–1924*
(3) Stanhope Bros Ltd, Leeds, Yorks. *1925*

The Stanhope was an unconventional 3-wheeler in which the single front wheel was driven by two belts. These ran on a fixed axle, which did not turn with the wheel, of course. An automatic variable gear was provided, and the engine was a J.A.P. V-twin of 8hp. From 1922 to 1924 the car was known as the Bramham, but in 1925 it reappeared as the Stanhope. There was also a fwd 4-wheeler powered by a 10hp ohv Blackburne engine, available as a two-seater, four-seater or saloon.   GNG

STANLEY (i) (US) *1897–1927*

(1) Stanley Dry Plate Co, Newton, Mass. *1897–1899*
(2) Stanley Manufacturing Co, Lawrence, Mass. *1899–1901*
(3) Stanley Motor Carriage Co, Newton, Mass. *1901–1924*
(4) Steam Vehicle Corporation of America, Newton, Mass. *1924–1927*

The Stanley twins, F.E. and F.O., were partners in a photographic dry plate business in Newton, where they produced their first light steam car in 1897. This proved a great success, over 200 being sold in the first year of production. In 1898 a Stanley was timed over a mile at Charles River Park at 27.40mph. Among the customers were A.L. Barber and J.B. Walker, who purchased the manufacturing rights of the vehicle, and produced it as the Locomobile and Mobile respectively. In 1899 some Stanleys were advertised by the Locomobile Co of America under the name Stanley-Locomobile. The Stanleys proceeded to evolve an entirely new design, which appeared in 1902 with a simple non-condensing engine, driving directly on the rear axle. The boiler was mounted at the front, frames were of wood, and steering was by tiller. Locomobile went over to petrol cars at the end of 1903, but the Stanleys prospered, listing an 8hp model at $750, and selling their cars to police and fire departments. More powerful versions rated at 10 and 20hp were available by 1904, and by 1906 the Stanley had assumed its characteristic appearance, with coffin-like bonnet concealing the boiler, and wheel steering. It could out-accelerate petrol cars, and that year Frank Marriott was timed at 127.66mph on Daytona Beach with the streamlined Woggle-Bug. Marriott tried again the following year, but a spectacular crash at about 150mph destroyed the car. Stanley's 1908 Gentleman's Speedy Roadster was capable of 60mph, and would run over 50 miles on a filling of water. 1913 cars were electrically-lighted, and 1915 brought the introduction of steel framed and V-shaped frontal condensers on a 10ft 10in wheelbase chassis which lent itself to seven-seater coachwork. However, the advent of Cadillac's electric self-starter in 1912 had signalled the end of the steamer, with its need for a long warm-up from dead cold. The 1920 Model 735 Stanley resembled a conventional petrol car in outward appearance with a flat radiator of typically American aspect, but the boiler was still under the bonnet, and the double-acting 2-cylinder engine still drove direct on the back axle. Acceleration was well above par for the standards of the day, and the car would cruise at 45mph, with more available. But at around the $2,600 mark sales were low (about 600 per annum), and the Stanleys had retired from the company during World War 1. The firm was reorganized in 1925, and the last Stanleys had hydraulic front-wheel brakes and balloon tyres.   MCS

STANLEY (ii) (US) *1907–1910*

(1) Stanley Automobile Manufacturing Co, Mooreland, Ind. *1907*
(2) Troy Automobile & Buggy Co, Troy, Ohio *1908–1910*

This Stanley was a five-seater touring car weighing 1,550lb. It was powered by a 2-cylinder, water-cooled engine of 3.6 litres. A friction transmission was used, with a single chain to drive the rear axle.   GMN

STANLEY-WHITNEY *see* WHITNEY (i)

STANWOOD (US) *1920–1922*

Stanwood Motor Car Co, St Louis, Mo.

The Stanwood was a typical assembled car of its day, offering both open and closed body styles. The engine was a Continental six and other standard components were employed.   KM

STAR (i) (STARLING, STUART) (GB) *1898–1932*

(1) Star Motor Co, Wolverhampton, Staffs. *1898–1902*

1934 STANDARD(xi) Superior saloon. *Neubauer Collection*

1953 STANGUELLINI 1,100cc sports car. Mike Hawthorn at the wheel. *Autosport*

1904 STANLEY(i) 8hp runabout. *Rea Publicity (Western) Ltd*

1910 STANLEY(i) Model 71 20hp tourer.
Keith Marvin Collection

c.1920 STANLEY(i) Model 735 sedan. *Keith Marvin Collection*

1899 STAR(i) 3½hp *vis-à-vis. The Veteran Car Club of Great Britain*

Star Engineering Co, Wolverhampton, Staffs. *1902–1909*
(3) Star Cycle Co, Wolverhampton, Staffs. *1905–1909*
(4) Star Engineering Co Ltd, Wolverhampton, Staffs. *1909–1928*
(5) Star Motor Co Ltd, Wolverhampton, Staffs. *1928–1932*

Edward Lisle Sr's Star Motor Co, an offshoot of the Star Cycle Co, produced its first car in 1898, and offered it for sale in the following year. This was a Benz-based machine, with a single-cylinder, water-cooled 3½hp engine, belt primary drive and chain final drive. It was an improvement in that water circulation was assisted by a pump. In 1900 there followed a 2-cylinder car with 3 forward speeds, still on Benz lines. 1901 brought De Dion-engined single-cylinder vehicles, and 1902 an 8hp twin of Panhard type in addition. Other, larger cars of Panhard ancestry joined the 8hp, up to a 20hp four. By 1904, although a De Dion-powered single and Panhard-type twin were still there, the bigger machines were of Mercédès pattern, with honeycomb radiators, mechanically-operated inlet valves, and pressed-steel frames. All Stars up to 1914 were extremely well-made, well-furnished, conventional, rather expensive cars lacking in technical originality, showing a line of development very similar to that followed by many other firms. 6-cylinder models made their first appearance in the 1907 range. The best-known Star of the period was the excellent 15hp of 1909, a shaft-driven 2.8-litre four which had become the 3-litre 15.9hp by 1914. A great variety of other, basically similar models were turned out, not only by Star but also by the Star Cycle Co. The latter, run by Edward Lisle Jr, had made motor tricycles and bicycles, and produced the Starling car in 1905. It had 2 forward speeds and a De Dion single-cylinder engine, but was otherwise of Panhard type, with armoured wood frame and chain drive. One year later the company supplemented it with the more modern Stuart, which had 2-cylinders, 3 speeds and shaft drive. This name was dropped in 1908, all models being called Starlings, but these, too, disappeared in 1909 when Star's cheaper line was entrusted to the new Briton Motor Co, a more independent concern that was still run by Edward Lisle Jr. So popular was the Star that its makers were among the six largest in the country before 1914.

The 15.9hp was continued after World War 1, together with another sv four of pre-war origin, the 20hp of 3.8 litres. A modern light car of fashionable type, the 11.9hp, arrived in 1921. It used a 1,795cc sv engine with a detachable head, made in unit with a 3-speed gearbox which had central change. By 1924, the 11.9 had grown up into the 2-litre 12/25hp. It shared cylinder dimensions with the 18hp, which was a new 3-litre six. The 12/25 could be had as a very fine fast touring car with overhead valves and 54bhp, in which form it was called 12/40hp. Thereafter, the range reverted to its pre-war complexity. By 1927, there were three sv models and two additional and more up-to-date cars with overhead valves. The 14/40hp, new in 1926, was a solid 2-litre, ohv machine which, in spite of having only 4 cylinders and 3 forward speeds, was a notably smooth and flexible car, thanks to a 5-bearing crankshaft. The ohv 20/60hp, a 2½-litre six with the same bore and stroke as the 14/40 and a 7-bearing crankshaft, was the most luxurious model. A light six, the popular ohv 18/50hp, joined the range in 1928, the year of the company's acquisition by Guy, and replaced the 14/40 for 1929. By this time, the sv cars had gone, leaving the two sixes. As the 18hp Comet and the 21hp Planet, they were revised with handsome bodies and very full, luxurious equipment, including one-shot chassis lubrication, thermostatically-controlled radiator shutters and a built-in jacking system. Two other engines, of 14hp (2 litres) and 24hp (3.6 litres) were also obtainable for 1932, as alternative Comet and Planet power units. These were the last new Stars, for they were too expensive to make, and the times favoured the mass-produced economy car. Production ended in March 1932, but the unsold stock was sold by McKenzie and Denley of Birmingham, and the Star was quoted in the *Buyer's Guide* lists until 1935. TRN

STAR (ii) (US) *1903–1904*
(1) Star Automobile Co, Cleveland, Ohio
(2) H.S. Moore, Cleveland, Ohio

This car was driven by a single-cylinder, water-cooled engine of 1.9 litres, mounted beneath the front seat, with false bonnet and coil radiator in front. A champion planetary transmission and double chain drive was used. Both two- and five-seater models were made, the latter with rear entrance. GMN

STAR (iii) (US) *1908*
Star Automobile Co, Chicago, Ill.

Star runabouts were offered in three models, selling for $500, $600 and $700 respectively. The smallest was an open two-seater, and shaft drive was employed on all models. MJWW

STAR (iv) (US) *1908*
Model Automobile Co, Peru, Ind.

The short-lived Star from Peru was offered in conventional 2- and 4-cylinder forms. The twin was chain-driven, while the big, expensive four ($4,000) had shaft drive. TRN

STAR (v) (US) *1922–1928*
Durant Motor Co of New Jersey, Elizabeth, N.J.; Lansing, Mich.; Oakland, Calif.

William Crapo Durant's Star Four was one of the more serious attempts to take away some of the Model T Ford's market, for the cheapest practical car. Unlike the Ford, the Star was an assembled machine. It had a 2.2-litre, 4-cylinder engine by Continental, and was conventional in design in every way except the gearbox, which was separate; a feature common to all the vehicles in Durant's empire, but very unusual in American mass-produced cars by the early 1920s. The touring car cost only $443 in 1923, which helped Star to be the seventh biggest seller in America that year. It was sold outside the United States as the Rugby. In 1926, a 2.8-litre six was introduced. Fwb appeared in 1927 but a year later the make disappeared in the collapse of the Durant interests. By this time, 250 cars a day were being turned out. Only the Four was still called the Star for the 1928 model year, as the Six was now known as the Durant Model 55.   TRN

STARIDE (GB) 1952–1954
Erskine Engineering, Southampton

Michael Erskine, maker of the Staride speedway motor cycles, collaborated with J.D. Habin (who had raced a Cooper) and Dean Delamont (from the Kieft design team) to produce a Formula 3 machine with the best features of both these marques. The result was twelve Erskine Starides, with tubular chassis and swing-axle rear suspension, and a fair measure of success in the hands of Habin, R. Anderson, R. Bicknell, J. Coombs, A. Loens, N. Sanderson and others.   DF

STARIN (US) 1903–1904
The Starin Co, North Tonawanda, N.Y.

The Starin was a typical light runabout powered by a 6hp horizontal single-cylinder engine, mounted under the seat. Drive was via a 2-speed epicyclic gear and single chain to the rear axle.   GNG

STARLING see STAR (i)

START (CS) 1921–1930
Královéhradecká tovarna automobilu Start, Hradec Králové

Two small cars were initially built by this firm, a 2-cylinder 1,100cc, and a 4-cylinder 1,450cc model. At the 1929 Prague Show a new light car with a 1-litre air-cooled 4-cylinder engine was shown.   HON

STATES (US) 1915–1919
(1) States Cyclecar Co, Detroit, Mich. 1915–1916
(2) States Motor Car Co, Kalamazoo, Mich. 1917–1919

The States succeeded the Greyhound cyclecar and initially used a 1.2-litre 4-cylinder engine. When the cyclecar went out of fashion the company turned to a larger car with 22hp G.B. & S. 4-cylinder engine, or their own 6-cylinder engine. These came with roadster, phaeton and sedan bodies, at prices from $895 for the four, and $995 for the six.   GNG

STATIC (US) 1923
Static Motor Co, Philadelphia, Pa.

This company was listed as the maker of the Static Super-Cooled Six, but no details are available.   GNG

STATUS (GB) 1972 to date
Status Co, New Buckenham, Norwich

The first production car offered under this name was the Minipower Mark 1, the brainchild of ex-Lotus employee Brian Luff. The Mini engine was rear-mounted in a welded tubular space-frame, with fibreglass body. Inboard rear coil/damper suspension units like a Formula 1 racing car were featured. The chassis and body could be bought for £450. A completed car could weigh as little as 1,008lb.   DF

STAUNAU (D) 1950–1951
Staunau Werk, Hamburg-Harburg

The Staunau was available with 400cc and 750cc 2-cylinder, 2-stroke Ilo engines and had front-wheel drive. It was produced in limited numbers for about one year.   HON

STAVER; STAVER-CHICAGO (US) 1907–1914
(1) Staver Carriage Co, Auburn Park, Ill. 1907–1910
(2) Staver Motor Co, Chicago, Ill. 1911–1914

For its first two seasons, the Staver was a typical high-wheeler with a 2-cylinder engine and double chain drive. Later models used 4-cylinder monobloc engines of 30, 35, and 45hp. Capacities ranged up to 5.2 litres in 1912. Body types were limited to four- and five-seaters, with wheelbases up to 10ft. In 1914 a 6-cylinder car was made.   GMN

STEAMOBILE (US) 1900–1902
(1) Keene Automobile Co, Keene, N.H. 1900–1902
(2) Steamobile Company of America, Keene, N.H. 1902

This was a typical tiller-steered steam buggy, powered by a 7/9hp 2-cylinder vertical engine, and having single chain drive. A *dos-à-dos* four-seater body was

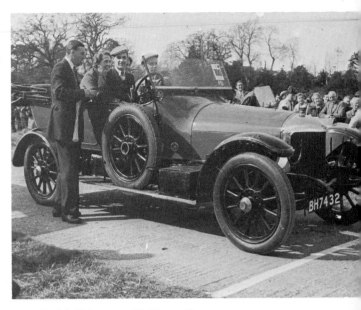

1914 STAR(i) 15.9hp tourer. *The Veteran Car Club of Great Britain*

1927 STAR(i) 20/60hp coupé. *Autocar*

1926 STAR(v) 2.2-litre tourer. *William S. Jackson*

1904 STEARNS(i) 24hp tonneau. *Keith Marvin Collection*

1907 STEARNS(i) 30/60hp tourer. *Burton H. Upjohn*

1929 STEARNS-KNIGHT 6.3-litre convertible. *Keith Marvin Collection*

1924 STEIGER 10/50PS tourer. *G.L. Hartner*

available in addition to the two-seater. The Steamobile had a curved dash like that of the Oldsmobile, although it was higher-built. GNG

STEARNS (i); STEARNS-KNIGHT (US) 1899–1930
F.B. Stearns Co, Cleveland, Ohio

This company's first product was a typical gas buggy in the American idiom with horizontal underfloor engine, planetary transmission, chain drive, and bicycle-type wheels. In its 1901 form it had one enormous cylinder ($6\frac{1}{4}$in bore and 7in stroke) and wheel steering. By 1902 the Stearns had grown into a bonneted $5\frac{1}{2}$-litre 25hp twin retailing for $3,000. 1905 cars were altogether more European, with their mechanically-operated side valves, paired cylinders, and Mercédès-style radiators. A 40hp four sold for $4,000, and led to even greater things, such as a chain-driven 45/90hp six, with the rear pair of cylinders vanishing into the scuttle. Capacity was 13 litres, and it could achieve close on 90mph. The smaller $8\frac{3}{4}$-litre 4-cylinder 30/60 was a 60mph car available with shaft or chain drive at $4,600. In 1909 there was a modest 15/30hp town carriage with a monobloc engine. The trademark of these cars was the white line running round the inside of the radiator shell. Sporting machines subsequently gave way to staidier cars with the Knight double-sleeve valve engine, 1914 versions being a 5.1-litre four and a 6.8-litre six, both with electric lighting and starting. By 1917 Stearns were cashing in on the V-8 fashion with a 5.4-litre car, but fours and sixes engaged the company's attention during the early and middle 1920s, the former disappearing in 1926, one year after the firm had been acquired by Willys-Overland. This change of ownership did not affect the quality of the Stearns, which was kept on as a prestige line. During the make's last two seasons – 1929 and 1930 – there was a 27.3hp six retailing at $2,095, and a big 6.3-litre straight-8 with a 9-bearing crankshaft and 12ft 1in wheelbase, for which prices started at $5,500. MCS

STEARNS (ii) (US) 1900–1904
Stearns Steam Carriage Co, Syracuse, N.Y.

Designed by E.C. Stearns, this car had no connection with the better-known Cleveland-built Stearns. It was a steam car of conventional design using a 2-cylinder slide-valve engine of 8hp, chain drive and steering by side tiller. A wide variety of body styles was offered, including a six-seater with three rows of seats and roll-down canvas sides. The latter model was introduced in 1902, and has been called, probably correctly, the world's first production station wagon. GNG

STECO (US) 1914
Stephens Co, Chicago, Ill.

This cyclecar had an ash frame and used a 2-cylinder, air-cooled engine of 10hp. Final drive was by belt. The body was designed for two passengers in tandem, and the price was $450. GMN

STEELE (US) 1915
The William Steele Co, Worcester, Mass.

This company made trucks but are reported to have built a small number of 2-cylinder cyclecars during the boom period for such vehicles. GNG

STEEL SWALLOW (US) 1907–1908
Steel Swallow Auto Co, Jackson, Mich.

This two-seater runabout was probably not as swift nor as silent as its name implied. It had an air-cooled 2-cylinder engine under the bonnet. With a friction transmission and a 7ft wheelbase, its cost was $700. GMN

STEIGER (D) 1920–1926
(1) Walter Steiger & Co, Burgrieden 1920–1925
(2) Steiger AG, Burgrieden 1925–1926

Steiger produced some prototypes during World War 1, but real production was started in 1920. The first model was the 10/50PS, 2.6-litre, an advanced design by Paul Henze, featuring an overhead camshaft driven by vertical shaft, and the use of light metal for the engine. Steiger was also active in racing and competed in the Avus, Solitude, Semmering, Monza, Targa Florio and other events. The racing engines had a capacity of 2,899cc and developed 100bhp giving a maximum speed of 106mph. Production of cars ceased in 1926, but single cars were built for a few more years by a former Steiger representative in Düsseldorf from spare parts. Walter Steiger himself went to Switzerland and designed a car for Martini, known as the Martini-Steiger. HON

STÉLA (F) 1941–1944
Véhicules Electriques Stéla, Villeurbanne, Lyons

This firm was probably the largest producer of electric vehicles in war-time France. The first cars had angular lines and carried their batteries on the running boards, but in 1942 came the Type RCA, a streamlined 4-door, five-seater saloon. A number were used as taxis in Lyons, and Admiral Darlan, head of the Vichy government, had two for his personal use. Production of Stéla passenger cars ceased with the liberation, but commercial vehicles continued to be made until 1948. GNG

STELKA (CS) *1920–1921*
Pribramska Strojirna a Slevarna Spol sro, Pribram

The Stelka was a 2-cylinder light car named after the owner of the company, Rudolf Stelsovsky. Very few were made before the company was reorganized. In 1925 a few more cars were made under the name A.S.P.A.   GNG

STELLA (i) (F) *1900–1901*
Sté de Constructions Mécaniques Stella, Levallois-Perret, Seine

This was a light voiturette with a tubular frame powered by Aster or De Dion engines of 2½hp. An epicyclic gear and belt drive were used, and the weight was only 336lb.   GNG

STELLA (ii) (CH) *1906–1913*
Compagnie d'Industrie Electrique et Mécanique, Geneva

After C.I.E.M. abandoned petrol-electric drive they made a range of conventional 4-cylinder cars under the name Stella. The first model was a 10hp, followed by 14/18, 18/20 and 24/30hp cars. The cylinders were pair-cast until 1910, when monobloc engines were introduced. 3- or 4-speed gearboxes were used, and the cars had round radiators similar to those of the Hotchkiss. About 200 cars were made under the names C.I.E.M. and Stella.   GNG

STELLITE (GB) *1913–1919*
Electric and Ordnance Accessories Co Ltd, Birmingham

This was an 1,100cc economy car made by a subsidiary of Wolseley. The 4-cylinder monobloc engine had overhead inlet valves and a detachable head, and steering was by rack and pinion, but the back-axle-mounted gearbox had only two forward speeds, and the frame was of armoured wood! Quite a few were sold at £157 10s for a two-seater, and 3-speed versions were available by 1915. The latter reappeared in 1919 at £285, but by 1920 the make had given way to Wolseley's own ohc Ten. The name was later revived for an austerity edition of the latter model.   MCS

STEPHENS (i) (GB) *1898–1900*
R. Stephens, Clevedon, Somerset

Stephens was a cycle and general engineer who made a small number of cars, including two nine-seater buses which plied between Clevedon and Portishead in 1900. The 1898 prototype still exists; it has an 8hp 2-cylinder horizontal engine built into the frame, and drive is taken by belts to a countershaft and thence by chains to the rear wheels. Front suspension is independent, and the car has wire wheels, although production cars had wooden wheels. About 12 Stephens vehicles were made altogether.   GNG

STEPHENS (ii) (US) *1916–1924*
(1) Moline Plow Co, Moline, Ill. *1916–1921*
(2) Stephens Motor Car Co, Freeport, Ill. *1922–1924*

The Stephens was a highly regarded car that used a 3.7-litre sv Continental engine up to 1918, and thereafter a similar-sized ohv unit of the company's own manufacture. Nearly 25,000 were sold during the years of production and a variety of open and closed models constituted its catalogue. Until 1922, Stephens were prosaic in appearance, if good dependable cars. That year, the Salient Six Model 10 appeared as the 1923 line and the moderately-rounded radiator was replaced by a high rounded type similar to that used by Kissel or ReVere. Among its more aesthetically appealing types, the new line featured a four-seater, close-coupled sports phaeton with cycle mudguards and side-mounted spare wheels. Wire wheels were used for this model which was sold in French grey with apple-green wheels and trim.   KM

STERLING (i) (US) *1909–1911*
Elkhart Carriage and Motor Car Co, Elkhart, Ind.

The Sterling succeeded the Elkhart and preceded the Elcar, and the company also made a 4-cylinder assembled car, the Komet, in 1911. The Sterling was built in five open body styles, ranging in price from $1,500 to $1,850. They used a T-head, 4-cylinder engine of approximately 4 litres' capacity. The rear springs were of the old-fashioned platform design.   GMN

STERLING (ii) (GB) *1913*
Sterling Engineering & Automobile Co Ltd, Leeds, Yorks.

This was a cyclecar powered by an 8hp V-twin J.A.P. engine. Final drive was by V-belts.   GNG

STERLING (iii) (US) *1914–1916*
Sterling Motor Car Co, Brockton, Mass.

The Sterling was a small five-seater touring car weighing 1,250lb. It had a 4-cylinder engine and was priced at $650, with electric lighting.   GMN

STERLING (iv); AMS-STERLING (US) *1915–1923*
(1) Sterling Automobile Mfg Co, Paterson, N.J.: Amston, Conn. *1915–1917*
(2) Amston Motor Car Co, Amston, Conn. *1917*
(3) Consolidated Car Co, Middlefield, Conn. *1917–1923*

1942 STÉLA Type RCA electric saloon. *Lucien Loreille Collection*

1910 STELLA(ii) 18/20hp saloon. *Swiss Museum of Transport & Communications. Lucerne*

1898 STEPHENS(i) 8hp dogcart. R. J. Stephens at the tiller. *D.R. Grossmark*

This was an assembled car powered by a 4-cylinder, 2.3-litre Le Roi engine with overhead valves. The two-seater roadster was listed at $590. One source gives the name of the second make as Royal Amston, but this cannot be confirmed. Later models, made by the Consolidated Car Company, used 4-cylinder Le Roi or 6-cylinder Herschell-Spillman engines. GNG

STERLING-KNIGHT (US) 1923–1925
Sterling-Knight Motors Co, Cleveland and Warren, Ohio

Introduced in October 1923, the Sterling-Knight was one of the lesser-known Knight-engined cars. The 6-cylinder car failed in early 1925 after a total production of about 425. KM

STESROC (GB) 1905–1906
Johnson Bros. Knaresborough, Yorks.

Little is known about these cars, except that the makers advertised 'steam motor carriages' of 8, 10 and 15hp, at prices from £200 to £400. They said that their cars were sold on the deferred payment system. No contemporary descriptions or tests have been traced. GNG

STEUDEL (D) 1904–1909
Horst Steudel Motorwagenfabrik, Kamenz

At first Steudel built cars with De Dion or Aster engines. Their two models with 2-cylinder 5/10PS and 4-cylinder 6/12PS Fafnir engines were better known. After Steudel discontinued car production they took up engine manufacture. HON

STEVENS-DURYEA (US) 1902–1927
(1) J. Stevens Arms & Tool Co, Chicopee Falls, Mass. 1902–1906
(2) The Stevens-Duryea Co, Chicopee Falls, Mass. 1906–1923
(3) Stevens-Duryea Motors Inc, Chicopee Falls, Mass. 1923–1927

In 1900 J. Frank Duryea, one of the famous Duryea brothers, organized the Hampden Automobile & Launch Co at Springfield, Mass., to build a car called the Hampden. It is unlikely that it was ever built under this name, but late in 1901 he joined the Stevens company, a well-known armaments firm, and the car was built by them in the former Overman plant at Chicopee Falls. It had a 6hp 2-cylinder horizontal engine, tubular frame and two-seater stanhope body. Starting was from the driver's seat, and the price was $1,200. A 4-cylinder car was introduced in 1905, and the company's first six in 1906. This was an enormous machine, with a capacity of 9.6 litres. It had shaft drive and 3-point engine support, and cost $5,000. From 1907 only 6-cylinder cars were made; large, high quality conservative machines whose design changed little over the years. They were mostly touring and town cars, although a few two-seater roadsters were made around 1914. The last basically new model was the Model D of 1915, a 47.2hp six of 7,740cc which developed 80bhp at 1,800rpm. This was continued as the Model E in 1920, by which time inflation had brought the price as high as $9,500 for a limousine. Production continued until 1924 at about 100 cars per year, and a few cars were still being sold off as late as 1926 or 1927. In its final years the company was also manufacturing Raulang electric cars and taxicabs. GNG

STEWART (US) 1915–1916
Stewart Motor Corp, Buffalo, N.Y.

This was a large car, with a 6-cylinder 4.7-litre Continental engine. The radiator was mounted to the rear of the engine, which allowed a sloping bonnet. Three- or seven-seater models were available at $1,950. The manufacturer was better-known for commercial vehicles. GMN

STEWART-COATS see COATS

STEYR (A) 1920–1940; 1953 to date
(1) Österreichische Waffenfabriks-Gesellschaft AG, Steyr 1920–1926
(2) Steyr-Werke AG, Steyr 1926–1935
(3) Steyr-Daimler-Puch AG, Steyr 1935–1940
(4) Steyr-Daimler-Puch AG, Graz 1953 to date

As an arms factory Steyr had to look for new employment after World War 1 and put into effect an earlier plan for starting car production. In 1920 their first model appeared under the name of Waffenauto, designed by the famous Hans Ledwinka. It had a 6-cylinder 12/40PS ohc engine of 3,325cc capacity. This first model laid the foundation for the excellent reputation of Steyr cars. Ledwinka left Steyr in 1921, but subsequent models were based on his designs. The Steyr Type IV was a 4-cylinder 7/23PS 1,814cc. The Type VI Sport was very successful both as a touring and as a sports car; it had a 6-cylinder 15/90PS 4,014cc engine, while the VI Klausen sports and racing version was powered by a 19/145PS 4,890cc unit. A third place in the 1923 Targa Florio was one of the successes of these cars. A range of other 6-cylinder models followed, of which the 6/30PS, 1,560cc Type XII was notable for its independent rear suspension, though it retained semi-elliptics at the front. In 1929 Ferdinand Porsche, who had returned to Austria after working with Mercedes, was engaged as chief engineer. His first design was the 6-cylinder, 8/40PS, 2,078cc Type XXX. However, Porsche stayed only for one year. His last design for Steyr

1922 STEPHENS(ii) Salient Six 25hp sedan.
Kenneth Stauffer

1908 STEVENS-DURYEA limousine. *Henry Ford Museum, Dearborn, Mich.*

1915 STEWART 29hp tourer. *Keith Marvin Collection*

was the Austria, a big 8-cylinder model of 100bhp and 5.3 litres, but this model only appeared in prototype form. The same bank was giving Steyr and Austro-Daimler financial backing and they did not want both companies to build large cars. A community of interests was formed between Steyr and Austro-Daimler in 1929, and this led to a merger in 1935. About 500 1.2-litre Opels were made under licence in 1932, followed by a range of popular models of Steyr design: the 100 (4-cylinder, 32bhp, 1,385cc), the 120 (6-cylinder, 50bhp, 1,990cc), the 200 (4-cylinder, 35bhp, 1,498cc) and the 220 (6-cylinder, 55bhp, 2,260cc), now with all wheels independently sprung. In 1936 the Type 50 appeared with a 4-cylinder, opposed engine of 22bhp and 984cc. This was developed into the 25bhp, 1,158cc Type 55 in 1938. These were very popular and economical cars with aerodynamic integral construction, but production had to cease in 1940 as a result of World War 2, after about 13,000 cars of the two types had been built.

Production of Steyr cars was not resumed after the war, but from 1949 Fiats were assembled for the Austrian market. In 1953 there was a special version of the 1900 powered by a Steyr-designed 1,997cc engine, available in 65bhp and 85bhp forms, and with a 4-speed gearbox as an alternative to the 5-speed Fiat type. In 1957 the company started to make Fiat's Nuova 500, with revised rear suspension and their own 493cc engine. This evolved into the hotter 650cc 650T and 650TR; the latter was good for 85mph and became a major force in rallies, gaining the Pole Sobieslaw Zasada the 1966 European Championship. This exciting little car was not, however, catalogued after 1968, and 1973's staple offering was the standard Steyr-Puch 500 in 20bhp form.　　　　　　　　HON

STICKNEY (US) 1914
Charles A. Stickney Co, St Paul, Minn.

This was a tandem two-seater cyclecar, with driver's controls in the rear seat. The engine was a 2-litre, T-head 4-cylinder unit, with water cooling. A friction transmission was used with double chain drive. The wheelbase of 10ft gave a low profile while the bonnet had a distinct slope, with a V-shaped radiator.　　　GMN

STIGLER (I) 1921–1925
Officine Meccaniche Stigler SA, Turin

Stigler were makers of battery-electric commercial vehicles who also produced a few private cars. These were small two- and four-seaters of conventional appearance with disc wheels and dummy bonnets and radiators. Endurance between charges was quoted as 62 miles at 22mph.　　　MCS

STILL (CDN) 1899–1900
Still Motor Co Ltd, Toronto, Ont.

This firm was formed to take advantage of a new type of double-acting electric motor designed by William Still. A variety of commercial and passenger vehicles were built and sold.　　　HD

STILSON (US) 1907–1910
(1) Pittsfield Motor Carriage Co, Pittsfield, Mass. 1907
(2) Stilson Motor Car Co, Pittsfield, Mass. 1907–1910

Five models of the Stilson were produced, all powered by 6-cylinder Herschell-Spillman engines. The transmission used was a patented unit with early hydraulically-controlled clutch. These were large cars with wheelbases from 10 to 11ft 9in, and weighing up to 3,300lb.　　　GMN

STIMULA (F) 1905–1914
De la Chapelle frères et Cie, St Chamond, Loire

This company made motor cycles and tri-cars for several years before commencing car manufacture. Like many French manufacturers, they made a single-cylinder 8hp model (probably with a De Dion engine), and a variety of fours from a 10/12hp of 1,726cc to a 16/20hp of 2,815cc. Two single-cylinder cars were entered in the 1907 Coupe des Voiturettes, but that seems to have been all Stimula did in the sporting line. The company was still listed in the early 1920s, but were probably no longer making cars then.　　　GNG

STIRLING (GB) 1897–1903
(1) J. & C. Stirling, Hamilton, Lanarkshire 1897–1898
(2) Stirling's Motor Carriages Ltd, Hamilton, Lanarkshire 1898–1902
(3) Stirling's Motor Carriages Ltd, Granton, Edinburgh 1902–1903

Stirlings had been coachbuilders for nearly 50 years when they made their first Stirling-Daimler stanhope in January 1897. It used a 4hp Daimler engine, and followed Daimler lines closely. Within a year they were ordering engines and chassis from Daimler in lots of 50, and building their own dogcart and wagonette bodies on them. They were the first motor company in Great Britain to pay dividends, shareholders receiving 5% each year from 1897 to at least 1900.

In 1900 they began to import the Clément-Panhard voiturette with a 5hp single-cylinder engine and centrally-pivoted front axle. This was sold as the Stirling-Panhard or Clément-Stirling, and carried very high doctors' coupé bodywork as well as the usual open two-seater. Stirling-Daimlers were still being made in small numbers in 1902, but by this time the firm was concentrating on commercial vehicles,

1920 STEYR Type II 3.2-litre limousine. *Steyr-Daimler-Puch AG*

1929 STEYR Type XX 2.1-litre drophead coupé. *Steyr-Daimler-Puch AG*

1937 STEYR Type 50 984cc saloon. *Steyr-Daimler-Puch AG*

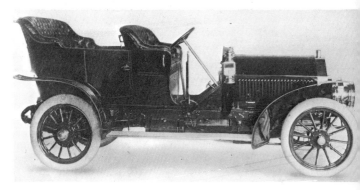

1907 STILSON 6-cylinder tourer. *G. Marshall Naul*

1902 STIRLING-DAIMLER 12hp tonneau. John Stirling at the wheel. *Museum of Transport, Glasgow*

1908 STODDARD-DAYTON 45hp tourer. *Kenneth Stauffer*

1931 STOEWER Repräsentant 4.9-litre drophead coupé. *Neubauer Collection*

and car production ceased very soon afterwards. Lorries and buses, mainly the latter, were made until 1907.　　　　GNG

STODDARD-DAYTON (US) 1904–1913
(1) Stoddard Mfg Co, Dayton, Ohio *1904–1905*
(2) Dayton Motor Car Co, Dayton, Ohio *1905–1912*
(3) U.S. Motor Co, Stoddard-Dayton Division, Dayton, Ohio *1912–1913*

This was one of the great American cars of the era. The first models used 4-cylinder Rutenber engines of 3.3 litres and were designed by a young English engineer, H.S. Edwards. These had the gear change on the steering column. Pearl grey was the standard colour. In 1907, both 4- and 6-cylinder engines were used, the fours having overhead valves. For 1910, a total of twelve models was offered, on three different chassis; these included a 50hp engine on a wheelbase of 10ft 8in. For 1911, a 6-cylinder, 8.6-litre Knight engine was introduced. This model was sometimes referred to as the Stoddard-Knight. Three other models, with 4-cylinder, poppet-valve engines, were continued through 1913. The Stoddard-Dayton had an illustrious racing career, including victory in the inaugural Indianapolis race meeting of 1909. The Stoddard-Dayton ceased to exist with the collapse of the U.S. Motor Co.　　　　GMN

STOEWER (D) 1899–1939
(1) Gebrüder Stoewer, Fabrik für Motorfahrzeuge, Stettin *1899–1916*
(2) Stoewer-Werke AG vorm. Gebr. Stoewer, Stettin *1916–1939*

This factory developed out of the Stoewer ironworks and was among the pioneers of the German car industry. After manufacturing motor cycles, tricycles and quadricycles for two years, Stoewer turned to cars in 1899. The first model had a rear-mounted 2-cylinder engine. 4-cylinder cars followed in 1901, and electric cars were also produced. Best known were the 2-cylinder Type T (2,280cc and 3/12PS), the 4-cylinder P4 (3,052cc and 11/22PS), the G4 (1,500cc and 6/12PS) and the 6-cylinder P6 (8,820cc and 34/60PS), evolved in the 1905–1907 period all with shaft-drive. The B1 of 6/16PS and the B6 of 9/22PS which appeared in 1910 were also built by Mathis under licence. The G4 model was the basis for the B5, which in 1912 became famous by setting up a record at Brooklands with 67.7mph. The new range of models which appeared in 1913 was also based on successful earlier cars. They were the C1 (6/18PS), C2 (10/28PS) and C3 (6-cylinder and 19/45PS). Shortly before the outbreak of World War 1 the Stoewer range was headed by the F4 with a 4-cylinder, 8.8-litre 33/100PS ohc engine. After the war an enormous Stoewer appeared, the type D7, using a 6-cylinder 11.2-litre 42/120PS aero engine, as well as some conservative sv 4- and 6-cylinder models with rear wheel and transmission brakes. Fwb appeared in 1925. Stoewer introduced 8-cylinder cars in 1928. These were the Superior, Marschall, Gigant and Repräsentant with engines ranging from 2 litres and 45bhp to 4.9 litres and 100bhp. The firm re-entered the economy class in 1931 with the V5, a front-driven model with a V-4 1,188cc engine, followed by the front-drive models R140 (1,369cc), R150 (1,488cc) and R180 (1,769cc). Another 8-cylinder was the fwd Greif V-8 with a 2,488cc engine, which was replaced by the conventional 6-cylinder 3,609cc Arcona in 1938. In 1934 the 1½-litre 4-cylinder and 2½-litre V-8 were shown at the Brussels Salon by Monsieur Dewaet under the name D.S. (Dewaet-Stoewer). The Greif Junior was built under Tatra licence with an opposed 4-cylinder 1,474cc engine. It succeeded the Röhr Junior. In the middle of the range was the Sedina with a 4-cylinder engine of 2.4 litres.

Production of private cars was given up at the outbreak of World War 2 in 1939. The factory was destroyed during the war and production was not resumed.　　HON

STOLLE (D) 1924–1927
Vorster & Stolle Motoren AG, Munich 23

Cars of this make were designed by the well-known engineer Martin Stolle. Although this design was very promising, only a few cars were produced as this firm was one of the manufacturers affected by the collapse of the Stinnes concern. The 6/40PS Stolle had a 4-cylinder 1.5-litre engine with shaft-driven overhead camshaft. It was also available with a sleeve-valve engine of the same capacity and output.

A two-seater sports car and a four-seater tourer were listed, and the cars were credited with 75mph.　　HON

STONEBOW (GB) 1901
Payne & Bates, Foleshill, Coventry, Warwickshire

This vehicle was marketed under the name of Stonebow by R.M. Wright & Co of Lincoln. Although 5 and 7hp models were advertised, only the smaller single cylinder car resembling the Benz appears to have been successful. Similar vehicles were sold by the makers under the name of Godiva.　　GB

STONELEIGH (GB) 1912–1924
Stoneleigh Motors Ltd, Coventry, Warwickshire

The first Stoneleighs were identical with the sleeve-valve B.S.A. as made by Daimler before World War 1, except for their radiators. Indeed, the make never seems to have been independent, because, when it cropped up again for 1922, it was attached to a short-lived light car made by Armstrong Siddeley. This was powered by a 1-litre, V-twin, air-cooled engine, with inclined overhead valves and aluminium pistons. The three-seater body was of unusual design, with a single seat and central steering wheel in front and two seats behind.   TRN

STORCK (US) 1901–1903
Frank C. Storck, Red Bank, N.J.

Frank Storck was a cycle repairer who assembled a small number of light steam cars of the Whitney type, and sold them for $750 each.   GNG

STORERO (I) 1912–1919
Storero Fabbrica Automobili, Turin

This short-lived Italian make of quality was founded by Luigi Storero, a pioneer of Italian motoring, who built and raced motor cycles and tricycles in the late 19th century, and was a colleague and close friend of Giovanni Agnelli, co-founder of F.I.A.T. Storero was the first driver to race a F.I.A.T. outside Italy, in the 1903 Paris-Madrid, and his interest in the marque led him to establish a wide sales and garage network in Italy. This organization was taken over by Fiat in 1908, and Storero took to marketing special de luxe versions of the larger Fiat models. Then, in 1912, he launched the Storero 20/30, made for him by Cesare Scacchi, a big 4.4-litre, 35bhp 4-cylinder car with sv monobloc engine in unit with a 4-speed gearbox. This gearbox was unusual at that time in having a direct third speed and overdrive top. The radiator of the Storero bore a badge consisting of a large S in a circle. Equipment of the car was to luxury standards, it ran with notable silence, and production for 'una clientela raffinata' was naturally to a limited scale. Between 1914 and 1916 some 6-cylinder Storeros, the Types C and C2, were produced. Capacities were 5.5 and 4.4 litres respectively.   CP

STOREY (GB) 1919–1930
(1) Storey Machine Tool Co Ltd, New Cross, London S.E.; Tonbridge, Kent 1919–1920
(2) Storey Motors, Clapham Park, London S.W. 1921–1925
(3) Storey Motors Ltd, Clapham Park, London S.W. 1925–1930

Announced in October 1919, the prototype Storey used a 14.3hp Coventry-Simplex engine, and had a 3-speed gearbox in unit with the overhead worm back axle. The first production cars used Chapuis-Dornier engines of 14.3 and 20hp, although these were replaced towards the end of 1920 by Storey engines of 10, 12, 15.9 and 20hp. The gearbox was brought forward to the usual position on the two larger models, and the overhead worm axle replaced by a spiral bevel gear. A little over 1,000 cars were made in the two factories at New Cross and Tonbridge, but by the end of 1920 Will Storey's company was declared bankrupt. His brother Jack restarted production on a much smaller scale at Clapham Park, using Storey engines until the supply ran out, followed by various proprietary makes, mainly Meadows.

A new limited company was formed in 1925, and three models were listed, a 10/25 and a 14/40 four, and a 17/70 six. These cars had open two-seater bodies, and either Rudge-Whitworth wire, or Sankey artillery wheels. However, during the nine years at Clapham Park, not more than 50 cars were made, less than 5% of the first year's production at New Cross and Tonbridge.   GNG

STORK KAR (US) 1919–1921
Stork Kar Sales Co, Martinsburg, W. Va.

The Stork Kar was a conventional tourer car powered by a 4-cylinder Lycoming engine. Specifications were identical to those of the later Norwalks, also made in Martinsburg, and to the Piedmont, from Lynchburg, W. Va. As Piedmont sold their cars under a number of different names, it is possible that both the Stork Kar and the Norwalk were in fact made by Piedmont.   GNG

STORM (i) (E) c.1924–1925
José Boniquet Riera, Barcelona

The Storm was a light car powered by a 6/8hp 4-cylinder Ruby engine, built in small numbers by the designer of the J.B.R. cyclecar. The name was derived from the words Siempre Triunfante Optimo Rendimiento Motor.   GNG

STORM (ii) (US) 1954
Sports Car Development Corp, Detroit, Mich.

The Storm Z-250 sports car had a 250bhp Dodge V-8 engine and a two-seater Bertone body.   BE

STORMS (US) 1915
William E. Storms, Detroit, Mich.

The Storms was apparently the only American-built electric cyclecar, produced with either three-seater or two-seater (side-by-side) bodies. Prices ranged from $750 to $950.   GMN

STORY (NL) 1941–1944
The Story was one of a number of small electric cars which appeared in Europe during the wartime absence of petrol. It was a two-seater 3-wheeler of neat appearance, with the single wheel in front.   GNG

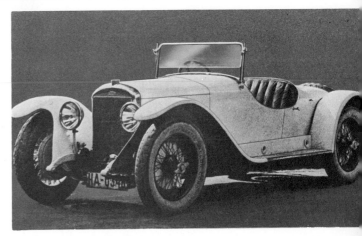

1926 STOLLE 6/40PS sports car. *Neubauer Collection*

1922 STONELEIGH 9hp three-seater. *Th. van Wyk*

1913 STORERO Model A 20/30hp landaulette. *Museo dell'Automobile, Turin*

1920 STOREY 20hp Kent two-seater. *The Veteran Car Club of Great Britain*

1912 STRAKER-SQUIRE 15hp coupé. *The Veteran Car Club of Great Britain*

1924 STRAKER-SQUIRE 24/90hp tourer. *National Motor Museum*

STRAKER-SQUIRE (GB) 1906–1926

(1) S. Straker & Squire Ltd, Fishponds, Bristol *1906–1918*
(2) Straker-Squire Ltd, Edmonton, London N. *1918–1926*

The first road vehicles of Sidney Straker and L.R.L. Squire were steam wagons, made from 1901, followed by petrol buses. During 1906 Straker acquired the licence to make the Cornilleau-Ste Beuve car from France as the 25hp Straker-Squire-C.S.B. By mid-1907 a straightforward four of 16/20hp was being offered under the name of Straker-Squire. Late that year, a smaller 12/14hp was added. It was the company's first wholly home-grown model, and was at first called a Shamrock, not a Straker-Squire. The best-known of the pre-World War 1 Straker-Squires was certainly the 15hp of 1910–14, a sporting 3-litre with a 4-cylinder, sv engine and an excellent performance, designed by A.H.R. Fedden. In 1919 a completely new and in some respects very modern car was announced. It was also a 6-cylinder machine with a capacity of 4 litres, still designated the 20/25hp, but had a single overhead camshaft and aluminium pistons, and to ease manufacturing problems, its cylinders were separately cast. Its valve gear was exposed. The whole unit resembled the Rolls-Royce Eagle aero engine the company had made during World War 1. In spite of an old-fashioned appearance, this was a powerful, if noisy engine that gave the Straker-Squire an 80mph performance. Brakes and steering were suitably good. Unfortunately, even when the car went into production in 1921, as the 24/90hp, very few were made. The pre-war 15hp was resurrected, and for 1923, a dull little light car with a 1½-litre ohv Dorman engine was added. By 1926 only the 24/90 and the light car remained, both with hydraulic 4-wheel brakes.　　TRN

STRALE (I) 1967

Strale, Turin

This was a typical hybrid GT coupé of the period with 6.3-litre ohv V-8 engine of American origin, fibreglass coachwork, 4-speed gearbox, and a De Dion rear axle. 180mph was claimed with the most powerful engine option giving 431bhp.　MCS

STRATHMORE (US) 1899–1902

Strathmore Automobile Co, Boston, Mass.

This company advertized two-seater cars and vans, but no details are available. Steam as well as petrol-driven vehicles were listed.　　GNG

STRATTON (i) (US) 1909

C.H. Stratton Carriage Co, Muncie, Ind.

This make was a high-wheeler with solid rubber tyres and right-hand steering by wheel. It was built in two- and five-seater versions. Its 2-cylinder horizontally opposed air-cooled engine was under the bonnet in front, and drive was by double chain.　　GMN

STRATTON (ii) (US) 1923

Stratton Motors Corp, Indianapolis, Ind.

This car with a 4-cylinder engine of Stratton design was an attempt by Frank S. Stratton, formerly sales manager of the Grant Company, to market his own car. For a short time, the concern obtained control of Monroe and built the latter, but shortly after both Monroe and Stratton were absorbed by Premier.　　KM

STREETER & SMITH (ZA) 1913

Streeter & Smith, Cape Town

The first, and almost the only, vehicle to be designed and built in South Africa, the Streeter & Smith was a cyclecar similar to many being made in Europe. It was powered by an 8hp air-cooled Precision engine, had a 3-speed Armstrong gearbox, and belt final drive. A price of £100 was fixed, but very few were actually sold.　　GNG

STRINGER (US) 1901

Stringer Automobile Co, Marion, Ohio

This company made a steam carriage with a 4-cylinder engine, and 'enclosed chainless drive'. It never went into production.　　GNG

STRINGER-WINCO (GB) 1921–1932

Stringer & Co, Sheffield, Yorkshire

The successor to the pre-war Winco, the Stringer-Winco was a light car powered by a 4-cylinder 1,088cc Alpha engine. In 1922 it was succeeded by the Stringer Type S, or Stringer-Smith. This had an 11.9hp 1,794cc Meadows engine. Smaller cars with 9 and 11hp Alpha engines were listed until 1932, but it is unlikely that any were sold as late as this, and throughout the 1920s production must have been very small.　　GNG

STRØMMEN; STRØMMEN-DODGE (N) 1933–1940

AS Strømmen Værksted, Strømmen

The famous bus manufacturing firm of Strømmen assembled American Dodge cars from 1933 to 1940, and built a number of long wheelbase seven-seater saloons from 1933 to 1936. These were known simply as Strømmen, whereas the normal assembled cars were called Strømmen-Dodge. Output of all models varied between 800 and 1,000 per year.　　OB

STRONG & ROGERS (US) *1900–1901*

Strong & Rogers, Cleveland, Ohio

This company made a light electric two-seater powered by a 2½hp motor. On one model the seat and tiller bar were covered with goatskin, the handle being of pearl with sterling silver ferrules. The wooden body had hand-carved decorations. For all this the price of $2,000 was perhaps not excessive, although cheaper models were also available.   GNG

STROUSE (US) *1915–1916*

Strouse, Ranney & Knight Co, Detroit, Mich.

The Strouse two-seater roadster was priced at $300 with 3ft 6in track or $325 with standard track. It was powered by a water-cooled, 4-cylinder engine, with friction transmission and single chain drive.   GMN

STRUSS (US) *1897*

Henry Struss, New York City, N.Y.

The Struss was a two-seater with a straight dash and rear-mounted 4hp 4-cylinder engine built by Richard Burr. Final drive was by side chains. Struss was specially commissioned to build this car, and apparently made no others.   GNG

STUART (i) *see* **STAR** (i)

STUART (ii) (US) *1961*

Stuart Motors, Kalamazoo, Mich.

This was a proposed electric car, seating two adults and several children, with a 4hp motor driven by eight 6-volt batteries. The enclosed body was of fibreglass and the range was about 40 miles per charge at 35mph.   BE

STUDEBAKER (US/CDN) *1902–1964; 1964–1966*

(1) Studebaker Corp, South Bend, Indiana *1902–1954*
(2) Studebaker-Packard Corp, South Bend, Indiana *1954–1964*
(3) Studebaker Corp of Canada Ltd, Hamilton, Ontario *1964–1966*

The brothers Henry and Clem Studebaker opened a blacksmith's and wagon-building shop in South Bend in 1852, horse-drawn vehicles of their construction serving in both the American Civil War and World War 1, and production continuing until 1919. Their first cars were electrics, made in modest numbers from 1902 to 1912: these were joined in 1904 by the Model-C petrol car, a typically American 16hp flat-twin with amidships engine, 2-speed gearbox, and chain drive. This was followed a year later by a vertical 4 on more European lines, selling for $3,000. For the next few seasons, however, Studebaker elected to act as selling agents for cars built to their order, and their more expensive offerings were built by Garford of Elyria. The cheaper machines were the E.M.F. and Flanders built by the Everitt-Metzger-Flanders Co, and these two makes accounted for 9,700 cars in 1910. 1913 saw a brace of Studebaker models made at South Bend, both with sv monobloc engines, dual ignition, and electric lighting and starting: the 3-speed gearboxes were mounted in unit with the back axles, and the 6-cylinder version was claimed to be the first such car to retail in the U.S.A. for less than $2,000. In 1914 there was a smaller, 15/20hp 3.2-litre 4 with coil ignition only. Studebaker sold over 45,000 cars in 1915, and their sixth position in 1916 U.S. sales was matched by a seventh place in 1920. 1919 was the last year for 4-cylinder cars, and the 1920 models, while retaining separate gearboxes, abandoned the transaxle layout. Models available were 6s of 4.7 litres and 5.8 litres, the latter establishing a line of really large 6-cylinder cars which survived until 1928. An inexpensive 3.3-litre Light 6 joined the range in 1921, and 1923 Studebaker models had all-metal bodies with welded steel pressings. Balloon tyres were standardized in 1925, in which year contracting-type hydraulic fwb were an option: open cars were made with permanent tops of the 'California' type and detachable side-curtains. Fwb were standard in 1926, but the company reverted to mechanical actuation in 1927, in which year a 'compact', the Erskine, was marketed. Studebaker went after stock-car records in a big way in the later 1920s, an outstanding performance being 25,000 miles in 25,000 minutes. The 1929 range consisted of two 6s, the 'Dictator' and 'Commander' (at $1,265 and $1,495 respectively), and a brace of straight-eights of 4-litres' and 5.5-litres' capacity. Pierce-Arrow was acquired in 1928, but regained its independence five years later. In 1930 Studebaker, with Plymouth, pioneered the free wheel, offered initially on 8-cylinder cars alone, but available throughout the range by the latter part of the year, when the cheapest model, the Light 6, could be bought in England for £295.

Another compact appeared under the Rockne nameplate in 1932. Special versions of the 'President 8' distinguished themselves in the Indianapolis 500-Mile Race, Cliff Bergere's Studebaker Special finishing 3rd, while in 1933 6th to 12th places were filled by similar cars. Studebaker went into receivership in 1933, but came back strongly in 1934 with an unattractively-styled three-model range – the 3.4-litre 'Dictator 6', the 3.6-litre 'Commander 8', and the 4.1-litre 'President 8', all with synchromesh, free wheel, and X-braced frames. Subsequent evolution followed accepted American lines: transverse ifs, automatic overdrive, and hydraulic brakes once more in 1935: a hill-holder (modernized version of the sprag) in 1936: headlamps half-faired into the wings in 1938: and column change in 1939, when

1913 STUDEBAKER Model AA 27.2hp tourer. *M.A. Harrison*

1923 STUDEBAKER Big Six 5.8-litre tourer. *Keith Marvin Collection*

1929 STUDEBAKER President 8 5.5-litre sedan. *Studebaker-Packard Corporation*

1939 STUDEBAKER Commander 3.6-litre sedan. *Autocar*

1956 STUDEBAKER Golden Hawk 5.8-litre coupé. *Studebaker-Packard Corporation*

1906 STURTEVANT Automatic 40/50hp tourer. *M.A. Harrison*

1914 STUTZ coupé. *John Newman Collection*

1929 STUTZ Black Hawk Six 4-litre sedan. *G.N. Georgano*

Raymond Loewy became responsible for the Corporation's styling. 1939 was also the first year for one of America's longest-lived modern economy cars, the 2.7-litre 6-cylinder sv 'Champion' selling at $765. Fluid couplings were available on the 1942 range, which included Studebaker's last straight-8s. The revolutionary post-war 'coming or going' style with wrap-around rear window was launched by Loewy on the 1946/47 models with 2.8-litre and 3.7-litre 6-cylinder engines. Sales climbed to 239,000 in 1949, and the inevitable ohv V-8 — a relatively small one of 3.8 litres — replaced the bigger 6 in 1951. Studebaker's answer to the big battalions was the low and elegant line of the 1953 cars, which unfortunately became more cluttered down the years, and finances were not improved by the merger with Packard in 1954. An interesting departure was the sporting 'Hawk' coupé powered by Packard's V-8 engine and Ultramatic transmission in 1956: 1957 versions had blown Studebaker engines, the only example of a factory-equipped super-charger (save the 1954 Kaiser) since the Graham. The company managed to get their 'Lark' compact sedan tooled and into production in ten months in 1959, and this descendant of the old sv 'Champion' was the only model now offered with the exception of the 'Hawk'. The small 6 achieved ohv at long last in 1961, and 1962 saw the exciting fibreglass-bodied 'Avanti' coupé with disc brakes on the front wheels, a 4-speed gearbox, and optional supercharger. It annexed 29 stock-car records, including a flying mile at 168.15mph, but neither this nor the continuing 'Lark' range could save Studebaker. A wide choice of models — two 6s and three 8s — was listed for 1964, but early in the season South Bend stopped making cars, and production was transferred to the Canadian plant which had been assembling Studebakers since 1912. Even as an 'import', the Studebaker did not sell well: the last examples of the *marque* had 3.2-litre 6-cylinder and 4.7-litre 8-cylinder Chevrolet engines, but even these were abandoned in the spring of 1966. Production of the 'Avanti' was continued on a small scale by an independent factory in South Bend.

MCS

STURDGESS *see* ELDEN

STURGES *see* MORRISON (i)

STURMEY *see* LOTIS

STURTEVANT (US) *1904–1908*
Sturtevant Mill Co, Boston, Mass.

Sturtevants were large cars with 10ft wheelbases and powered by 4- or 6-cylinder engines. The 4-cylinder engine was of 7.3 litres' capacity. An automatic transmission was standard on Sturtevants from 1905 on. The Flying Roadster, a three-seater weighing 2,200lb, was priced at $4,000.

GMN

STUTZ (i) (US) *1911–1935*
(1) Ideal Motor Car Co, Indianapolis, Ind. *1911–1913*
(2) The Stutz Motor car Co of America, Indianapolis, Ind. *1913–1935*

The Ideal Motor Car Company was the name of the firm which made the first Stutz racing cars, but it was changed to the Stutz Motor Car Company in 1913. Harry C. Stutz' most famous passenger car was the Bearcat speedster of 1914 — probably the best known of all American sports cars. It followed the usual recipe of a low-hung chassis, a big, slow-turning proprietary engine (in this case, a T-head, 4-cylinder Wisconsin unit, producing 60bhp at 1,500rpm), and very little else, just a bonnet, wings, raked steering column, two bucket seats, and a fuel tank behind them. A Stutz-made 3-speed gearbox was integral with the rear axle; an uncommon feature. This component had been sold by Stutz before he made complete cars. A 6.2-litre 6-cylinder engine was available, but seldom seen. The Stutz Bearcat was the most popular of its breed, in spite of its high price, and its appeal was boosted by Stutz successes with ohc, 16-valve racing cars. It was the Mercers' greatest rival. Touring Stutzes were made as well, but were comparatively little known. Total production grew from 759 cars in 1913 to 2207 in 1917. Two years later, Stutz left to make another car, the H.C.S., although the cheaper Stutzes of the 1915 period were also known as H.C.S. The gearbox was moved back to the normal position in 1921, and shortly after this Stutz began making their own engines: an sv four giving 88bhp and a 75bhp ohv six. The latter was developed to give 80bhp in the 4.7-litre Speedway Six of 1924, the last of the old line.

In 1926, there was a change of management, and Frederick E. Moskovics, the new president, initiated a radically new policy. Paul Bastien, who had designed the splendid 2-litre Métallurgique from Belgium, was responsible for the Stutz AA, or Vertical Eight. It was a beautifully-made fast tourer, more typical of Europe than America. Its specification embraced a straight-8 4.7-litre engine with a single overhead camshaft, and dual ignition, including two plugs per cylinder. Power output was 92bhp at 3,200rpm. This was a modern, reasonably efficient engine by any standards, and distinctly advanced in these respects by American standards. There were, however, only 3 forward speeds. The hydraulic brakes were very good indeed, and the underslung worm final drive allowed the fitting of low-built, good-looking bodies. Centralized chassis lubrication and safety glass were provided. Glamorous though the AA was, it was sold on the slogan of 'The Safety Stutz', and a year's free passenger insurance was given with each car. In 1927, the engine was enlarged to 4.9 litres, now giving 95bhp, and a speedster option, the Black Hawk, was added. In the following year, Weymann fabric body construction was adopted; another European touch. The engine was enlarged again in 1929 and this made 113bhp available. Better still, there were 4 forward speeds. Special Black Hawk speedsters were 2nd at Le Mans in 1928, but they came no higher than 5th in 1929. These cars had Roots superchargers and vacuum servo brakes. The type was put on sale as the Bearcat, reviving a famous name. Stutzes also competed at Le Mans in 1930, 1931 and 1932. Unfortunately, a Stutz lost a well-publicized challenge match at Indianapolis with a Hispano-Suiza, and Frank Lockhart was killed at Daytona Beach while trying to take the World Land Speed Record with a Miller-engined car built by the company, both setbacks taking place in 1928.

Sales fell, and a range of cheaper models with, it was hoped, wider appeal was introduced for the next year, alongside the existing models. These cars had little in common with the classic models, so were called Black Hawks, not Stutzes. One used a 6-cylinder, ohc engine of 4 litres' capacity made by Stutz, and the other a straight-8 sv unit by Continental. At the other end of the scale, there appeared in 1931 the superb DV (dual valve) 32, to compete with the new multi-cylinder cars being brought out by Lincoln, Cadillac, Marmon, and others. The design was basically similar to that of the SV16, still current, but there were two overhead camshafts and four valves per cylinder: 32 in all. The DV32 was listed in speedster form, as the Bearcat, and, on a shorter chassis, as the Super Bearcat. These stubby, formidable cars were guaranteed to exceed 100mph. The expensive, high-quality, specialist Stutz went the way of most of its kind in the Depression years. Instead, the company sold, and later made a light delivery van, called the Pak-Age Car. This had a rear engine and all-independent suspension, and was current from 1928 to 1938, after which manufacture was taken over by Diamond T. TRN

1933 STUTZ DV32 5.2-litre drophead coupé. Coachwork by Rollston. *Keith Marvin Collection*

STUTZ (ii) (US) *1970 to date*
Stutz Motor Car of America, New York, N.Y.

Unlike replica cars such as the Auburn and Cord, the makers of the Stutz Blackhawk coupé merely borrowed the name of the pre-war car for their machine. It was powered by a 6½-litre Pontiac V-8 engine stripped and modified so that the original output of 365bhp was raised to 425bhp. This was mounted in a modified Pontiac chassis, and the Virgil Exner-designed body was hand-built by Carrozzeria Padana of Modena, Italy, where the final assembly of the cars was done. The first model, the 2-door hardtop, was priced at $22,500; a new model for 1972 was a 4-door saloon using an lwb Cadillac chassis, and selling for $31,250. GNG

STUTZNACKER *see* REGENT

STUYVESANT (US) *1911–1912*
Stuyvesant Motor Car Co, Sandusky, Ohio

The 6-cylinder Stuyvesant was a large and expensive car for the period, with a 10ft 8in wheelbase. The four-door five-seater touring car was listed at $4,200. The engine was of 9.4 litres, and had a 4-speed transmission. GMN

SUBARU (J) *1958 to date*
Fuji Heavy Industries Ltd, Tokyo

One of the companies formed from the disbanded Nakajima Aircraft Co, Fuji Heavy Industries built the Rabbit motor scooter. They introduced their rear-engined unitary-construction 360 minicar in 1958. The transversely-mounted air-cooled 2-stroke twin engine developed 16bhp, suspension was all-independent by torsion bars, and initially a 3-speed synchromesh gearbox was used, though by 1969 there were four forward speeds; the basic model was still quoted as late as 1971. A light commercial version, the forward-control Sambar, was also made as a station wagon. A full-sized Subaru appeared in 1968, the front-engined 997cc fwd FE. All-independent springing was retained, but new features were pushrod ohv and water-cooling, as well as an electric fan and an electric fuel pump. The 4-speed gearbox had synchromesh on all its ratios, the 67bhp sports version had Ajebono front disc brakes. The FF was the first Japanese car fitted with radial-ply tyres as standard. A 1,088cc unit was standardized in 1970, and a 1,300cc 80bhp version became available in 1971.

In 1970 Subaru had updated their minicar, producing the roomier R2 on a lengthened wheelbase with a 30bhp engine and synchromesh on bottom gear. Nearly 160,000 cars were made that year. The 1972 range included saloon and station wagon models of the R2, and a wide range of FF derivatives extended from the basic 62bhp 1.1-litre 2-door saloon at 449,000 yen up to the Leone GSR, a semi-fastback 2+2 coupé that cost 719,000 yen. This one had a twin-carburettor 1,361cc engine giving 93bhp, and was credited with 106mph. Curiously, drum brakes were standard, though front discs were used on the intermediate 1.3-litre types. MCS

1971 STUTZ(ii) Blackhawk 6.6-litre coupé. *Stutz Motor Car Co of America*

SUBURBAN LIMITED (US) *1911–1912*
(1) Suburban Motor Co, Detroit, Mich.
(2) De Schaum Motor Car Co, Detroit, Mich.

This was built in runabout, torpedo and touring models. All were on a chassis with 9ft 2in wheelbase. The common engine was a six with 4.3-litre capacity. Like

1967 SUBARU 360 saloon. *Fuji Heavy Industries Ltd*

1968 SUBARU 1000 saloon. *Fuji Heavy Industries Ltd*

1927 SUÈRE 10CV saloon. *Autocar*

1906 SULTANE 16/20hp tonneau. *Oliver Herbosch*

other De Schaum promotions, this make may never have progressed beyond the prototype stage.   GMN

SUCCÈS (B) *1952*

The Succès was a 3-wheeler powered by a rear-mounted 2-cylinder 2-stroke engine.   GNG

SUCCESS (US) *1906–1909*
Success Auto-Buggy Manufacturing Co, St Louis, Mo.

This high-wheeled motor buggy started with an air-cooled, single-cylinder engine and ended as a line of four models with either 2- or 4-cylinder engines. The late versions came with a choice of water or air cooling. They all used a planetary transmission with chain drive.   GMN

SUÈRE (F) *1909–1930*
J. Suère, Paris

Suère were best known as manufacturers of small cars. In 1913, these were an 8CV single-cylinder, an 8CV four, and a 10CV four with a slightly larger bore. All had side valves, 3 forward speeds and shaft drive, and did well in competitions. Their designs were unremarkable, with the exception of the tiny 1½-litre sv V-8 of 1919 (prototype 1914). The conventional 1.8-litre four, and the modern 1,200cc 4-cylinder light car and 2-litre six which replaced it, both with 4-speed gearboxes, were more popular.   TRN

SUFFIELD & BROWN *see* NEW CENTURY (i)

SULMAN SIMPLEX (AUS) *1923*
Tom Sulman, Camperdown, N.S.W.

This was a cyclecar powered by a 2-cylinder Lake engine.   GNG

SULTAN (US) *1909–1912*
Sultan Motor Co, Springfield, Mass.

The Sultan company specialized in taxicabs, but also manufactured similar vehicles for private use. These had closed four-seater landaulet bodies. Power was supplied by 4-cylinder engines of 2.2 litres and 6-cylinder engines of 3.7 litres. A 3-speed transmission was used with shaft drive. A predecessor, the Elektron Manufacturing Co of Springfield, Mass., had obtained rights to manufacture the French Sultan.   GMN

SULTANE (F) *1903–c.1910*
Lethimonnier et Cie, Paris 16e

This company made solid, conventional touring cars, beginning with a 4-cylinder 10/14hp of 2.4 litres. Engine size and number of models were gradually increased, and in 1907 there were five 4-cylinder cars from a 9/12hp of 1.8 litres to a 45/60hp of 7.8 litres. In this year a 7/9hp 2-cylinder model was added for the first time. In 1906 a company was formed at Springfield, Mass., to make the car in America, where it was known as the Sultan. It was announced that models from 12 to 60hp would be made, and production lasted until 1910.   GNG

SUMIDA (J) *1933–1937*
Jidosha Kogyo Co, Ltd, Tokyo

Sumida, named after a river flowing through Tokyo, had a rather complex history but for the purposes of this book the years 1933 to 1937 are of primary interest. During its 1928–1937 span, the major amount of production was devoted to trucks and related equipment. Much of this seems to have been channelled to government use as great emphasis was placed on the need for military vehicles and car firms were subsidized for this purpose.

Ishikawajima combined with the DAT Automobile Manufacturing Co in 1933 to form Jidosha Kogyo and for some time thereafter Sumida built military staff cars on special order. The large Model H four door sedan showed similarity to the General Motors La Salle of the period. Model K-93 was a six wheel military touring car very much like the specially built and imported Hudsons used in the Manchurian War. Type JC was a four-wheel drive staff car issued in 1937. Tanks and armoured cars of Sumida design also served the Japanese forces in World War 2.

Jidosha Kogyo combined with Tokyo Gas and Electric in 1937 to form Tokyo Jidosha Kogyo and the Sumida name was dropped in favour of Isuzu, a name already in use by the firm. This marque manufactured commercial vehicles until after the war when cars were added. In 1942, Hino Motors was formed by splitting away from the company and has continued to function independently ever since.   BE

SUMINOE (J) *1954–1955*
Suminoe Engineering Works, Ltd, Tokyo

The Suminoe works built bodies for Datsun Motors and manufactured this feather-weight two-seater of their own design. It has a 2-cylinder 12.5hp air-cooled engine mounted at the rear of a transversely sprung chassis that stood on thin motorcycle type wheels.   BE

SUMMERS *see* MOLL

SUMMERS & HARDING (GB) *1913*

This was a cyclecar powered by an 8hp V-twin J.A.P. engine, and with belt final drive. Later in 1913 it was renamed the Flycar, but few seem to have been sold under either name.   GNG

SUMMIT (i) (US) *1907*

Summit Carriage-Mobile Co, Waterloo, Iowa

Also known as the Carriage-Mobile, this was a high-wheel motor buggy powered by a 10hp single-cylinder engine.   GNG

SUMMIT (ii) (AUS) *1922–1926*

Summit Motors, Sydney, N.S.W.

The Summit was an assembled car using a 4-cylinder Lycoming engine similar to that used in the Auburn and the Gardner. Artillery wheels were standard and a moderately rounded radiator gave the car a measure of distinction in appearance. The frame was imported from the United States and holes for left-hand-drive fittings appeared on all Summit cars.   KM

SUN (i) (D) *1906–1908*

Sun Motorwagen-Gesellschaft E. Jeannin & Co KG, Berlin

This company was founded by Emile Jeannin, brother of Henri Jeannin of A.A.G. and Argus. A range of shaft- and chain-driven models was offered: 4-cylinder cars of 18/22hp and 28/32hp and the 6-cylinder 40/50hp and 65/75hp. Sun cars took part in the Herkomer and Prinz Heinrich Trials of 1907 and the Kaiserpreis Race.   HON

SUN (ii) (US) *1915–1918*

(1) Sun Motor Car Co, Buffalo, N.Y. *1915*
(2) Sun Motor Car Co, Elkhart, Ind. *1916–1918*

The Sun from Elkhart was a small, low-priced, conventional six, rated at 22hp. The men behind it, R. Crawford and R.C. Hoff, were former Haynes personnel. Touring, roadster, and sedan models were listed.   TRN

SUN (iii) (D) *1920–1924*

(1) Sun Automobil-Kleinkraftwagen Ges., Berlin-Charlottenburg *1920–1923*
(2) Sun Motorfahrzeuge Henri Jeannin, Berlin-Schöneberg *1924*

Henri Jeannin was very well known in the motoring world before the turn of the century. After World War 1 he founded a new company and produced a small two-seater car with an air-cooled V-twin engine. There was no connection with the pre-war Sun company, which was founded by Emile Jeannin, Henri's brother.   HON

SUN (iv) (US) *1921–1924*

The Automotive Corp, Toledo, Ohio

The Sun Runabout from Toledo was an ephemeral light car, of the breed killed in America by the Ford and others. It was powered by a 4-cylinder, air-cooled, ohv engine of Cameron manufacture, and had 3 forward speeds. Suspension was by quarter-elliptic springs at both ends.   TRN

SUNBEAM (GB) *1899–1937; 1953 to date*

(1) John Marston Ltd, Wolverhampton, Staffs. *1899–1905*
(2) Sunbeam Motor Car Co Ltd, Wolverhampton, Staffs. *1905–1935*
(3) Sunbeam Motors Ltd, London W.11 *1936–1937*
(4) Sunbeam-Talbot Ltd, Ryton-on-Dunsmore, Warwickshire *1953–1970*
(5) Chrysler United Kingdom Ltd, Ryton-on-Dunsmore, Warwickshire *1970 to date*

John Marston's tinplate and japanware firm, which had been making bicycles since 1887, built its first 4hp belt-driven prototype car in 1899, followed by another machine with a twin-cylinder engine in 1901. The first model to see series production was, however, the diamond-formation and allegedly skidproof Sunbeam-Mabley voiturette with 2¾hp De Dion engine, a number of which were sold for £130 in the 1901–1904 period. More conventional was the 12hp marketed under T.C. Pullinger's direction in 1903, which was based on a Berliet design and had a flitch-plate frame, chain drive with Sunbeam's patent oil-bath chain cases, and a 2.4-litre 4-cylinder engine with automatic inlet valves. A 3.6-litre 6-cylinder car was on the market briefly in 1904, but Sunbeam soon progressed to Shaw-designed T-head fours, though another short-lived six appeared in 1907. Sunbeam's great years started in 1909 when Louis Coatalen joined the firm from Hillman. In that season the company was offering three L-head fours with chain drive, and capacities of 3.4, 4.5, and 6.3 litres, plus an odd 3.2-litre twin-cylinder Station Cart. Coatalen's first effort was a T-headed 14/18hp, available with either shaft or chain drive. This was followed a year later by a 2.4-litre 12/16 on similar lines, but with pressure lubrication and an overdrive gearbox, while overhead valves were tried out on a racing car, the Nautilus, at Brooklands in 1910. An improved 12/16 of 3 litres' capacity with monobloc engine ran in the 1911 Coupe de l'Auto race, foreshadowing an immensely successful touring development which sold initially for £375. It had an L-head engine and was made up to 1921. In 74bhp racing guise it scored a 1-2-3 victory in the 1912 Coupe de l'Auto, following

1954 SUMINOE Flying Feather 350cc two-seater.
Matsubayashi Photo; Lucien Loreille Collection

1903 SUNBEAM 12hp tonneau. *National Motor Museum*

1913 SUNBEAM 12/16hp drophead coupé. Coachwork by Grosvenor. *National Motor Museum*

1921 SUNBEAM 24hp limousine. *G.N. Georgano*

1930 SUNBEAM 23.8hp saloon. *National Motor Museum*

1935 SUNBEAM 21hp saloon. *G. N. Georgano*

this up with a 3rd place in 1913. In 1914 Sunbeam built Henri-inspired twin-ohc 4-cylinder racers both for the Tourist Trophy and for the French Grand Prix, and at the outbreak of World War 1 the range consisted of the 12/16 in standard and sporting forms, a 4-litre 16/20 of similar general design, and a 6.1-litre 6-cylinder car rated at 25/30hp, all offered with electric lighting. The company concentrated on aero engines during the war years, though a 4.9-litre twin-ohc 6-cylinder machine was sent to Indianapolis in 1916 and took 3rd place, while Rovers took over production of the 12/16 for the Fighting Services. Renamed the 16, it reappeared in civilian form with full electrical equipment at £790, along with a smaller version of the pre-war 25/30 powered by a 4½-litre engine.

Sunbeam amalgamated with Talbot and Darracq in 1920 to form the S.T.D. combine, and the next five years saw an energetic racing programme. Twin-ohc 108bhp straight-8s were made for the 3-litre formula of the immediate post-war years, followed by some unsuccessful 2-litre fours, and finally the twin-ohc 6-cylinder 'Fiats in green paint', designed by Bertarione, which won the French and Spanish G.P.s in 1923, and ran supercharged in 1924, as well as having a long and distinguished competition career in later years. Chassagne won the Tourist Trophy on a 3-litre straight-8 in 1922, while one of the regular 3-litre sports models finished 2nd at Le Mans in 1925. Sunbeams took the World's Land Speed Record five times in the 1922–27 period: Lee Guiness started with 133.75mph on the 350hp V-12 sprint car, a figure which Campbell subsequently raised, first to 146mph and then to 150.87mph on the same machine. In 1926 Segrave attained 152.3mph on the 4-litre V-12, a car which was also used for road racing, and the following year he became the first man to exceed 200mph on land with the twin-engined chain-drive 45-litre monster. Sunbeam's last record car, the Silver Bullet of 1930, was unsuccessful.

Touring Sunbeams of the 1920s were cars of great refinement if not outstanding performance. The basic 16 and 24hp types were redesigned with push-rod overhead valves in 1922, ohc sporting versions being also listed, while a more modest 2-litre 14hp with unit gearbox was available at £725. Front-wheel brakes arrived on the 6-cylinder 16/50 in 1924, and were optional also on the 14/40 which replaced the 14hp model. An impressive 3-litre 6-cylinder twin-ohc sports car with dry-sump engine was made in small numbers between 1925 and 1930, but it was 'too fast for its chassis' as well as being expensive to make and buy. A big straight-8 with a push-rod engine, available in 4.8-litre and 5.4-litre forms, was introduced in 1926 at prices from £1,295 up and front-wheel brakes became standard on all models. All cars had the V-radiator by 1927, when the fours were dropped, and the standard touring sixes were the 2-litre 16hp at £550, the 2.9-litre 20hp at £750, and the 3.6-litre 25hp at £950, all with plate clutches, spiral bevel final drive, and cantilever rear suspension. Thereafter Sunbeam design changed little, and sales declined though quality was maintained. Semi-elliptic springs were found at the rear of the smaller 1930 models, in 1931 the cars acquired hydraulic brakes and radiator shutters, and the 16's engine was enlarged to 2.2 litres. The 1932 cars' silent-third gearboxes gave way to synchromesh on 1933 16 and 20hp Sunbeams. That year there was also a 2.9-litre Speed Model with crash box at £745, though its main competitor was S.T.D.'s other fast tourer, the Talbot 105. The old firm's last new model was a ponderous 1.6-litre ohv four, the Dawn of 1934, with preselector gearbox and independent front suspension. This was offered again in 1935, along with the 20, the 25, and the Speed Model, but the collapse of the S.T.D. combine brought receivership and purchase by Rootes, and an ohv Roesch-designed 4½-litre straight-8 announced for 1937 never went into production. There were no Sunbeams in 1938, and when the Sunbeam-Talbot range was announced for 1939 it was based on the later Rootes Talbots.

The name of Sunbeam did not reappear until 1953, when it was given to a sports two-seater version of the 2.3-litre ohv 4-cylinder Sunbeam-Talbot 90, the Alpine, which sold for £1,269, and collected four Coupes des Alpes in that year's Alpine Rally, following this up with a Gold Cup (for Stirling Moss) and a Coupe des Dames (for Sheila Van Damm) in 1954. In 1955 the basic 90 saloon model was marketed as the Sunbeam MK III, and further laurels included the Malling/Fadum win in that year's Monte Carlo rally. The type was listed until 1957, being joined in 1956 by a Hillman Minx-based sports saloon, the Rapier, with a 1.4-litre square 4-cylinder 62bhp engine, unitary construction, and overdrive as standard equipment, at £986. This did well in subsequent Alpines and Monte Carlo Rallies, as well as winning its class in the 1956 Mille Miglia, and by 1958 had grown up to 1½ litres and 68bhp, acquiring a less Hillman-like grille in the process, though overdrive was now an extra. A sports two-seater version, another Alpine, with integral construction, was listed for 1960, and subsequent evolution was on regular Rootes lines: diaphragm clutches in 1964, with the option of automatic on the Alpine, all-synchromesh gearboxes in 1965, and 1.7-litre 5-bearing engines in 1966. 1964 brought two new developments of the basic theme, an Italian-bodied Venezia sports saloon based on the Humber Sceptre, and the Tiger, which was an Alpine with rack-and-pinion steering and a 4.3-litre, 164bhp Ford V-8 engine, this despite the Rootes-Chrysler connection. In 1966, the Rapier V, Alpine V, and Tiger comprised the Sunbeam range, though in the United States the Hillman Imp was also sold under the Sunbeam name. A 51bhp Sunbeam version of the Imp was available in the home market in 1967, and this was followed by the more sporting Stiletto coupé for 1968.

An entirely new Rapier on Hillman Hunter lines was announced for that year, its fastback styling inspired by Plymouth's Barracuda. It had an 88bhp engine, a close-ratio gearbox, and overdrive as standard.

During 1968 the old Alpine was discontinued (the Tiger had already gone), and the Rapier range was rounded out, first by the H120 of 1969 with twin-carburettor Holbay-tuned engine giving 105bhp and Rostyle wheels, and then by the Alpine, a simplified version of the basic theme introduced for 1970. These three fastbacks were still being made in 1973, along with the Sunbeam Sport based on the Imp saloon. The Stiletto was discontinued during 1972.   MCS

SUNBEAM-TALBOT (GB) *1938–1954*

(1) Sunbeam-Talbot Ltd, London W.11 *1938–1945*
(2) Sunbeam-Talbot Ltd, Ryton-on-Dunsmore, Warwickshire *1946–1954*

The Rootes-built Sunbeam-Talbots from the old Talbot factory were luxury fast-touring versions of basic Hillman and Humber models distinguished by their Talbot radiators, wheel discs and metallic colour schemes. The Ten at £265 was based on the Hillman Minx, the 3-litre on the Humber Snipe, and the 4-litre on the Super-Snipe, the 6-cylinder cars having hydraulic brakes. A hydraulic-braked 56bhp 2-litre car using the Hillman 14 engine was announced for 1940, but did not go into production until after World War 2, when the Ten was also reintroduced. These cars, manufactured at Ryton, sold for £684 and £799 respectively, but were replaced in 1948 by more modern ohv cars of similar capacity, with wrap-round windscreens, steering-column change and hypoid back axles but still with semi-elliptic springing. The smaller 80 was dropped at the end of 1950, and the staple Sunbeam-Talbot was now the revised 90 with independent front suspension and a 70bhp engine.

The first public appearance of the original 90 had been in the 1948 Alpine Rally, when Sunbeam-Talbot won the Manufacturers' Team Prize, and the new model repeated this success in 1952, in which year they also won second place in the Monte Carlo Rally. The post-war cars had been sold as Sunbeams in France (to avoid confusion with M. Lago's Talbots, *alias* Darracq), and when the Alpine roadster appeared in 1953 this too assumed the name of Sunbeam. For the 1955 season, the saloons were renamed Sunbeam MKIII, though the Talbot part of the car's ancestry is perpetuated in the manufacturer's title.   MCS

SUNSET (US) *1901–1904*
Sunset Automobile Co, San Francisco, Calif.

The Sunset steamer, although made on the West Coast, was very similar to its many contemporaries from New England. It had a vertical 2-cylinder engine, chain drive and tiller steering. The price was $900.   GNG

S.U.P. (F) *1919–1922*
Usines du Paquis, Cons-la Granville, Ardennes

The S.U.P. was an assembled car powered by a 1,843cc Sergant engine, or a 1,775cc unit of the maker's own construction. It had a 4-speed gearbox and conventional chassis.

The director of the Usines du Paquis was Albert Henon, and the cars were some-times known as Henons.   GNG

SUPER (F) *1912–1914*
Levêque frères, Asnières, Seine

The Super cyclecar was made by Levêque who was also responsible for the Ruby car and engine, although he was not apparently assisted by Godefroy with the making of the Super. It was a machine of lighter construction than the Ruby, using originally a single-cylinder Anzani engine, tandem seating and belt drive. In 1913 Levêque drove a Super into 4th place in the Cyclecar Grand Prix at Amiens. This car had a 2-cylinder engine of 964cc.   GNG

SUPER TWO (GB) *1960–1965*
Super Accessories (L.R. Montgomery & Co Ltd), Bromley, Kent

Super Accessories made a wide range of equipment for Austin Seven and Ford Ten enthusiasts, and the Super Two sports car cost only £99, without engine. The chassis, ifs, and many other items were specially made for Super Accessories by Bowden Engineering of Ottery St Mary, Devon, while the aluminium two seater bodies came from Hamblin Ltd. Just over 200 Super Two kits were delivered in all.   DF

SUPERIOR (i) (D) *1905–1906*
Superior Fahrrad- und Maschinen-Industrie Hans Hartmann, Eisenach

After manufacturing bicycles this firm began production of voiturettes with Omnimobil components and 2- and 4-cylinder Fafnir engines. Production was discontinued after a short period.   HON

SUPERIOR (ii) (CDN) *1910*

William English, a wagon maker of Petrolia, Ont., built about 60 light trucks with 4-cylinder Atlas engines and planetary transmissions. Extra seats could be added to convert the trucks to private cars.   GNG

1965 SUNBEAM Tiger 4.3-litre sports car.
Rootes Motors Ltd

1972 SUNBEAM Rapier H120 1.7-litre coupé.
Chrysler UK Ltd

1940 SUNBEAM-TALBOT 10hp tourer.
Sedgwick & Marshall Collection

1948 SUNBEAM-TALBOT 90 2-litre saloon.
Rootes Motors Ltd

1913 SUPER 8/10hp cyclecar. *National Motor Museum*

1960 SUPER TWO 1.2-litre sports car. *Super Accessories Ltd*

1921 SURREY 10hp two-seater. *Autocar*

SUPERIOR (iii) (US) *1914*
Crescent Motor Car Co, St Louis, Mo.

For a few months, this car was called Crescent. It was a five-seater with a 4-cylinder, 3.3-litre engine and right-hand drive. GMN

SUPER KAR (US) *1946*
Louis R. Elrad, Cleveland, Ohio

The Super Kar was a prototype 3-wheeled midget with a 15hp air-cooled engine in a streamlined body. BE

SURAHAMMAR *see* VABIS

SURREY (GB) *1921–1930*
(1) West London Scientific Apparatus Co Ltd, Putney, London S.W.15 *1921–1922*
(2) Surrey Service Ltd, Putney, London S.W.15 *1922–1927*
(3) Surrey Light Cars, Putney, London S.W.15 *1927–1930*

The Surrey was an assembled light car that utilized some Ford Model T parts, including the front axle and steering. It was powered originally by a 1½-litre 4-cylinder Coventry-Simplex engine. There was a choice of transmission, either by friction disc and chain to a solid rear axle, or else through a Meadows 3-speed gearbox to live axle. Electric starting and lighting were optional extras as late as 1923, by which time friction drive had been discarded. Later cars had V-radiators and Meadows engines of 9.8 and 11.8hp, and there was even a sv six, the 18.2hp New Victory Six. TRN

SURREY '03 (US) *1958–1959*
E.W. Bliss Co, Canton, Ohio

Looking like a 1903 Curved Dash Olds, the Surrey had an 8hp Cushman air-cooled engine with chain drive and modern refinements such as Sealbeam headlights and improved brakes. It could be purchased in kit form or fully assembled. BE

SURRIDGE (GB) *1912–1913*
Robert Surridge, Camberwell, London S.E.

The Surridge was a cyclecar powered by a Fafnir V-twin engine of 8hp, and using friction transmission and chain final drive. It had an ash frame, reinforced by steel plates. GNG

SURTEES (GB) *1969 to date*
(1) Team Surtees Ltd, Slough, Bucks. *1969–1970*
(2) T.S. Research and Development Ltd, Edenbridge, Kent *1970 to date*

The first Surtees model was the TS5 Formula 5000, immediately successful in the hands of Trevor Taylor and David Hobbs on both sides of the Atlantic. This was followed by the TS7 Formula 1 car, frequently raced by ex-World Champion John Surtees himself. The TS8 Formula 5000 car for 1971 gave major victories that year for Mike Hailwood and Allan Rollinson, and Hailwood's TS8A was second in the 1972 Tasman Championship. The TS11 of 1972 for the same Formula was also successful internationally.

The TS9 Formula 1 cars, like the earlier models with full-length monocoques, gave Surtees, Hailwood, Tim Schenken and Andrea de Adamich some promising performances in 1971 and 1972. During 1972 the Formula 2 works team of TS10s, driven by Surtees, Hailwood and Schenken, did very well, and there were plans to extend the workshops to build versions for Formulas B and Atlantic as well during 1973. The TS14 was the 1973 works Formula 1 model. Surtees cars follow accepted design principles, relying on meticulous attention to detail for their continuing success. DF

SUTTON (AUS) *1900–1901*
Austral Otis Co, Melbourne, Victoria

The Sutton car was a most original vehicle powered by a 6hp paraffin engine which drove the front wheels by chains. The tiller steering turned the rear wheels. It was designed by Henry Sutton, and it was announced that the Austral Otis Company were to manufacture it in quantity, but there is no evidence that they did. GNG

SUZUKI (J) *1961 to date*
Suzuki Motor Co, Ltd, Hamamatsu

In addition to their very successful motor cycle line, Suzuki builds 4-wheeled vehicles that began with the Suzulite utility car produced in 1961. This was a front-wheel-drive 2-door car capable of seating four or carrying merchandise in the rear compartment. The engine was a 2-cylinder, air-cooled, 20bhp unit. Ball-joint suspension was used.

By 1966 Suzuki, like other Japanese makers, were moving away from minicar themes with their 800 Fronte, a development of the original 360 using a 41bhp, 785cc 3-cylinder 2-stroke engine, a 4-speed all-synchromesh gearbox, and all-independent springing. Top speed was 72mph. The 1969 SS versions of the original 360 gave 36bhp and 77mph, but the 3-cylinder model was no longer quoted. However, 1971 brought an ingenious Fronte-based 359cc 4 × 4, the Jimny. Various minicar models with 2-stroke engines were offered in 1972. BE

S.V.A. (I) *1949*
Società Valdostana per la Costruzione di Motori, Aosta
This exciting prototype had an 813cc ohc blown flat-4 engine and 5-speed gearbox. Production was planned, but never materialized.　　　MCS

SVEBE (S) *1948–1952*
Five 500cc racing cars were built by Bengt Peterson, who later constructed Robardie go-karts. The final Svebe was a one-off Brabham copy of 1966 for the constructor's son Ronnie, soon to become a Grand Prix star.　　　DF

SVELTE (F) *1904–1907*
SA de Constructions Mécaniques de la Loire, St Etienne, Loire
This company were well-known manufacturers of fire-arms and bicycles, and made a small number of conventional 4-cylinder cars. There were five different engine sizes from 16 to 50hp.　　　GNG

S.V.P. (F) *1905–1906*
Sté de Voitures Populaires, Paris
The S.V.P. was a light two-seater powered by an 8hp engine driving by flat belt to a countershaft, and thence by reduction gears to the rear wheels.　　　GNG

SWALLOW (GB) *1922*
Sir J.F. Payne-Gallwey, Brown & Co Ltd, London S.W.1
The Swallow was marketed by the same firm who sold the Edmond and North Star cars. It was made in two models, one with a 2-cylinder Blackburne engine, and the other with a 4-cylinder Dorman. Both cars had 2-speed epicyclic gearboxes and worm driven rear axles.　　　GNG

SWALLOW DORETTI (GB) *1954–1955*
Swallow Coachbuilding Co (1935) Ltd, The Airport, Walsall, Staffs.
This car used the engine, gear-box and transmission of the Triumph TR-2, with a tubular steel frame and flush-sided body of Swallow's own design. It was a brisk comfortable tourer rather than a sports car, and for the extra comfort and equipment buyers paid £230 more than for a TR-2. Most Dorettis had Laycock overdrive, and were capable of just over 100mph. The body style was an open two-seater, although one G.T. coupé was made.　　　GNG

SWAN (F) *1923*
E. Bloch, Neuilly, Seine
The Swan was made in two models, the smaller with a 1,244cc engine, and the larger with a 2-litre, both 4-cylinder sv Altos units. They were conventional shaft-driven cars.　　　GNG

SWEANY (US) *1895*
The Charles S. Caffrey Co, Camden, N.J.
The Sweany was a most original steam car driven by four small 3hp single-cylinder engines acting directly on each wheel. Steam at 150psi was provided by a single water-tube magnesium-lined boiler mounted at the front of the car. Hardly surprisingly, it never went into production.　　　GNG

SWIFT (i) (GB) *1900–1931*
(1) Swift Motor Co Ltd, Coventry, Warwickshire *1900–1919*
(2) Swift of Coventry Ltd, Coventry, Warwickshire *1919–1931*
Swift progressed from sewing-machines through bicycles, motor tricycles and quadricycles to cars. Their first was a voiturette with a tubular chassis, powered by an M.M.C. single-cylinder engine of De Dion type, but with an original transmission system. There was direct drive on both the 2 forward speeds, provided by two rings of teeth on the crown wheel and two pinions. The design was unreliable, for the rear axle was unsprung and attached to a flexible chassis. It was soon dropped in favour of normal transmission, and the axle was sprung from 1903. These single-cylinder cars, with various makers' engines installed, were the only offerings until 1904, when an excellent Swift-made twin of 10hp was added. Bigger 3- and 4-cylinder machines were made at the time, and in 1909 a short-lived single-cylinder 7hp, also sold by Austin was added, but most sales came from the 2-cylinder light car. In 1912 this was replaced by a 7hp 2-cylinder cyclecar with shaft drive, made by the Swift Cycle Co Ltd. For 1914 the Swift Light Car, which was virtually the cyclecar with a pressed steel, in place of tubular, chassis, was offered by the Swift Motor Co Ltd. The Cycle Co made no further cars, and the formation of Swift of Coventry in 1919 merged the two companies. An 1,100cc 4-cylinder Ten replaced the 2-cylinder car in 1914. This Ten was continued after World War 1, with a new 2-litre Twelve beside it. The latter had 4 forward speeds but was otherwise similar. After this, only 4-cylinder cars were made, irrespective of current fashions. They were immensely strong and simple, inefficient in terms of power output but not utility. The Ten was redesigned on more modern lines in 1923. A slightly smaller engine with detachable head and coil ignition was made in unit with a 3-speed gearbox, though the model reverted to a magneto in 1925. As the 12/35hp, the Twelve was brought up-to-date with the same features, becoming the

1972 SURTEES TS10 Formula 2 racing car.
Team Surtees Ltd

1964 SUZUKI Fronte 800 saloon. *Shotaro Kobayashi Collection*

1955 SWALLOW DORETTI 2-litre coupé.
Autosport

1913 SWIFT(i) 7hp cyclecar. *D.C. Field*

1930 SWIFT(i) 10hp saloon. Coachwork by
Swallow. *Autocar*

1931 SWIFT(i) 10hp two-seater. *Michael Sedgwick*

c.1957 SYRENA 744cc saloon. *G.N. Georgano*

1923 SZAWE 10/50PS all-weather tourer.
Neubauer Collection

14/40hp in 1926. In the same year the Ten's engine was enlarged to 1,200cc. Wire wheels were optional from 1927, and 4-speed gearboxes came in 1929. The 1930 Ten had a narrow 'ribbon' radiator shell, and was available with Swallow 2-door saloon coachwork as well as fabric saloon and tourer styles. This was supplemented in 1931 by the 8hp Cadet 2-door saloon which in its cheapest form cost only £149. Swift could not compete with the mass-producers, however, and the make died shortly after.   TRN

SWIFT (ii) (CDN) *1911*
Swift Motor Car Company of Canada Limited, Chatham, Ont.
One prototype, possibly based on the U.S. Anhut, was produced by this firm of marine-engine builders.   HD

SWIFT (iii) (US) *1959*
(1) Swift Manufacturing Co, El Cajon, Calif.
(2) WM Manufacturing Co, San Diego, Calif.
Three models of this little car were built for the driver who wanted something unusual. The Swift-T, Swift-Cat, and Swifter were rather like 5/8 scale versions of the 1910 Ford, Stutz Bearcat and 1903 Cadillac, and were propelled by single-cylinder Clinton air-cooled engines with governors to limit engine strain. Drive was by belts and the two-seater bodies were the same basic unit, with different trim and accessories.   BE

SYCAR (GB) *1915*
This was a 'motorcycle and sidecar' type 3-wheeler on similar lines to the Seal; only the 'sidecar' and front wheels were coupled together. Chain-cum-belt drive was employed, and the standard engine was a 4¼hp air-cooled single of unspecified type. The Sycar was said to weigh only 280lb complete, and the price quoted was £58. Production does not seem to have been essayed.   MCS

SYLPHE (F) *1920*
Sté S.E.D.A.S., Bois-Colombes, Seine
This was an ephemeral light car powered by a 6hp 4-cylinder engine. It should not be confused with Le Sylphe, which was the name given to the Carden Monocar sold in France in 1914 by Jouve et Cie.   GNG

SYNNESTVEDT (US) *1904–1908*
Synnestvedt Machine Co, Pittsburgh, Pa.
So far as can be determined, this make consisted only of electric-powered cars, although some writers claim that petrol models were also built. The Synnestvedt two-seater had 40 battery cells connected with a 4-speed controller and an 8hp motor. The rear axle was chain-driven. The wheelbase was 6ft 3in. A steering wheel was used, not the more common tiller.   GMN

SYRACUSE (US) *1899–1903*
Syracuse Automobile Co, Syracuse, N.Y.
This was a light electric two-seater with tiller steering. Designed by William Van Wagoner, it was originally known as the Van Wagoner.   GNG

SYRENA (PL) *1955–1972*
Fabryka Samochodow Osobowych, Warsaw
An original design of the FSO works, the fwd Syrena sedan remained essentially unchanged throughout its career. Initially it was offered with a 744cc in-line water-cooled 2-stroke twin engine developing 30bhp, but a 992cc 3-cylinder unit was available in 1963-4, and from 1967 onwards Syrenas used rather smaller 842cc vertical-threes developing 40bhp. A few Syrena-Sport prototypes were made as well.   BE

SZAWE (D) *1920–1922*
Szabo & Wechselmann Automobilfabrik, Berlin W 8
Szabo & Wechselmann were originally coachbuilders and started car production in 1920. The cars – a 2.5-litre 38bhp and a 2.6-litre 50bhp – had no special mechanical features but were of luxurious finish. The radiator was of hammered German silver, pipes and linkages were nickel-plated, engine and chassis were polished. The bodies were designed by Ernst Neumann-Neander. In 1922 Szawe and Ehrhardt amalgamated and the cars were subsequently called Ehrhardt-Szawes until production ceased in 1924.   HON

SZL *see* SMZ

T

TADEC; TAYDEC (GB) *1969 to date*

T.R. Clapham (Engineers) Ltd, Keighley, Yorks.

Tom Clapham's Group 6 sports-racing cars were campaigned with some note in European championship races by Peter Hanson. With Cosworth FVC engine, the 1971 model with full-length composite aluminium and magnesium monocoque was offered at £5,250. For 1972 the sports cars were dropped and a single-seater developed for Formulas 2, 3 and Atlantic; it was in the last class (with the Mark 5) that the marque was most successful.   DF

TAKURI (J) *1907–1909.*

Tokyo Jidosha Seisakusho, Tokyo

The seventeen Takuris built were of conventional design with a 4-cylinder engine and chain-drive. The four-seater tourer was equipped with a luggage rack, and a single headlight.

The Takuri is believed to be the first commercially produced passenger car in Japan and was also known as Yoshida after the name of the company president.

Prior to this the company engineers, Uchiyama and Yoshida, had constructed the first motor car built in Japan, in 1902, and had also produced a twelve-passenger bus for a Hiroshima firm.   BE

TALBOT (GB) *1903–1938*

Clement-Talbot Ltd, North Kensington, London W.10

From 1903, Clement-Talbot Ltd, a company backed by the Earl of Shrewsbury and Talbot, began importing the French Clément car into Britain; in spite of its name and an interest held by Adolphe Clément, the concern was British, and by the end of the year its cars were called Talbots. The 1904 models were a 6hp single, and 11hp twin, and two big fours. All of them had shaft drive and side valves in T-heads, except for the biggest, the 27hp voiture de luxe, which used overhead inlet valves and a single camshaft. Trucks, buses and boats were also advertised. Promotion, which was at first in the hands of the managing director, D.M. Weigel, was energetic and successful.

By the end of 1904, an impressive factory had been built, complete with test track, and in the following year British-assembled, and partly British-made Talbots emerged from it. A wide variety of types was listed, from an 11hp twin to a great 50hp 4-cylinder model. One model that was to be famous, the 12/16hp, had already been designed. French cars were still being imported by the company. However, the 20hp of 1906 was the first British-made Talbot. It was designed by C.R. Garrard, and while still conventional, had an unusually efficient engine of 3.8 litres' capacity. Both this and the 2.7-litre '12/16' were fast cars that quickly made a name for themselves in competitions; their slogan became 'The Invincible Talbot'. For 1907 a 3-litre 15hp, a car in the same mould, superseded the '12/16'. By 1908 it was the only British chassis offered, into which could be installed 15hp, 25hp or 35hp engines. Their popularity was due to a combination of smoothness, reliability, speed and reasonable price. The French range was still listed. A six was introduced for 1910, and the 4½-litre 25hp was revised by G.W.A. Brown with an L-head valve arrangement. This model, highly tuned and lightened, and fitted with a racing body, became the first car to cover 100 miles in an hour, at Brooklands in 1913 in the hands of Percy Lambert. In the same year a new model, the 2.6-litre 15/20hp, was introduced. This and the 25hp, now called the '25/50', were the famous cars that kept the name before the public eye in competitions. A sports model of the latter was also listed. By this time, the French range had been dropped.

In 1919 Clement-Talbot was taken over by another French-sounding, but in fact British-owned firm, the Société Alexandre Darracq of Paris. Darracq proceeded to acquire Sunbeam as well, but Talbot private-car policy was at first unaffected. The 25/50hp and 15/20hp models were continued. For 1922, however, the new 1-litre Darracq light car was offered as the 8/18hp Talbot. In the Talbot tradition, it was a solid car with above-average performance and handling. The push-rod overhead valve engine had coil ignition, there were only two seats, there was no differential, and suspension was by quarter-elliptic springs all round. Both acceleration and brakes were excellent; in other words, this was a light car more typical of France than of England. Georges Roesch, who had been Chief Engineer since 1916 and had already devised the Talbot 12hp of 1919, a car which was never put on the market, quickly revised the '8/18' as the 10/23hp, which was more 'English' in that it had a long, wide, roomy body, and a differential, with an enlarged bore and 1,100cc to cope with the added weight.

From 1923 to 1926, the company tried to exist on the '10/23' and a series of obscure small sixes of which few were made. The pre-war big fours had been dropped,

1907 TAKURI 12hp tourer. *Shotaro Kobayashi Collection*

1905 TALBOT 12/16hp tourer. *National Motor Museum*

1919 TALBOT 25/50hp limousine. *The Veteran Car Club of Great Britain*

1924 TALBOT 12/30hp coupé. *Rootes Motors Ltd*

1929 TALBOT 14/45hp saloon. *Autocar*

1934 TALBOT 105 21hp sports tourer. *National Motor Museum*

1947 TAMA E4S-47 electric saloon. *Tokyo Electric Motorcar Co*

but nothing as popular had been found. Clement-Talbot were at a very low ebb when Georges Roesch saved them with a one-model policy, based on a small six of the type just becoming fashionable. However, the 14/45hp Talbot was better than the rest because it combined efficiency and high quality with comfort, roominess and smoothness. Considering all this, the price was not high. It was, in fact, Roesch's intention to provide the characteristics of the Rolls-Royce 20hp with half the engine size, weight and price. The cubic capacity was only 1,665cc (61 × 95mm). The reciprocating parts, including the overhead valves, were very light, and the compression ratio was notably high, enabling revolutions and power output to be high also. Even so, the engine was an unusual combination of silence and flexibility. The brakes were excellent, though it was surprising to find only quarter-elliptic springs at the rear. The car's main drawback was weight: bodies were very spacious, mounted on a deep, stiff but heavy frame with a long wheelbase. However, most customers did not want ultra-high performance; the 60–65mph of the '14/45' was very good for such a large car with so small an engine.

The company's crisis had allowed no time for development, so the new car came straight off the drawing board to the public; but it was so good a design that there were no major snags, and Talbot sold all they could make. The engine was very difficult to work on without garage equipment, but the '14/45' was designed for replacement rather than repair of parts: another very modern, if not entirely desirable, feature. The design was obviously capable of great development, and during 1930 the first stages were announced – the Talbots 75 and 90. Both had the same size of engine; the '14/45' with an enlarged bore, providing 2¼ litres. The '75' was a touring model available alongside the '14/45' to those who wanted a little more performance, while the '90' was a more highly-tuned sports car, giving over 80mph with the same refinement. It was sold in closed as well as open form, but the most handsome body was the standard sports tourer. Additionally, a cheaper Light Six 14/45 with a shorter chassis was added at the lower end of the range.

With the '90' began Talbot's second lease of life as a distinguished sporting make. Third and fourth places in the Le Mans 24 Hour Race were followed by class wins in the Irish Grand Prix, the Ulster Tourist Trophy Race and the Brooklands 500 Miles Race. In spring 1931 the Talbot 105 was introduced with a new, 75 × 112mm engine providing 3 litres. To improve the breathing, the valves were in a staggered arrangement instead of being in line as hitherto. All types of body, from saloon to four-seater sports, were offered on this chassis. The last was a 100mph machine. The bigger engine was difficult to start, in spite of assistance from two 12-volt batteries, for the starter was not geared down. It was no help when the optional Wilson self-changing gearbox was fitted from 1933. In competitions, the name went from strength to strength. The '105' came 3rd in the Irish Grand Prix and at Le Mans, 4th in the Tourist Trophy and 2nd in the 500 Miles Race. A 105 tourer took home a Coupe des Glaciers after a fault-free performance in the Alpine Trial. The Coupe des Alpes team prize was won in 1932 by Talbot 105s, and in that year came a 2nd place in the Brooklands 1,000 Miles Race (which replaced the Double Twelve), and 3rd place at Le Mans and in the 500 Miles Race.

These racing successes were won by cars prepared by Fox & Nicholl Ltd with works support; in spite of the fame and success of the Talbot, the Sunbeam-Talbot-Darracq group had been in financial trouble since 1930 and earlier, and racing was a luxury. At the end of 1932, however, Fox & Nicholl's participation was discontinued and the great run of triumphs ended. The normal production cars continued to do well. In 1932 the Talbot 65, a new model basically the same as the '14/45', was announced. The '95', consisting of the '105' engine in a longer wheelbase for more sedate use, was introduced for 1933. In the following year cars with the self-changing gearbox were given a centrifugal clutch to avoid drag, and for 1935 there appeared the last developments of the standard type, the '110'. This superb machine had a larger bore than the 105, giving 3½ litres. Early in 1935, however, Rootes gained control of Clement-Talbot. The '65' was dropped for 1936 in favour of the Rootes Talbot Ten, a Hillman Minx-based design, and by 1938 the last Roesch survivor, the '110' was gone.   TRN

TALBOT-DARRACQ *see* DARRACQ

T.A.M. (F) 1908–c.1925

(1) Sté de Travaux Mécaniques et Automobiles, Courbevoie, Seine
(2) H. Gendron, Boulogne-sur-Seine

The original T.A.M. was a light car powered by a 12hp 4-cylinder engine. By 1913 three models were listed: a 10/12hp with Chapuis-Dornier engine and V-radiator, a 12/14hp with Decolonge engine and flat radiator, and a 16/20hp. Post-war models consisted of the 10/12 and 12/14, the latter engine now called a Sergant instead of a Decolonge. Taxicabs and delivery vans were also made.   GNG

TAMA (J) 1947–1951

(1) Tokyo Electric Motorcar Co, Tachikawa 1947–1949
(2) Tama Electric Motorcar Co, Tachikawa 1949–1951

The Tama electric was a result of the conversion of the former Tachikawa Aircraft Co to vehicle manufacture after World War 2. The 4½hp Model E4S-47 was the first. It was a 2-door sedan seating four. This was followed in 1948 by two new sedans, the Junior and the Senior, with improved performance. The Senior seated five and had a 5½hp motor giving it a speed of 35mph with a range of 125 miles per charge. With the promise of increasing petrol supplies, Tama abandoned electrics at the end of 1951 and reformed as Prince Motors in 1952, introducing the new Prince car in that year.   BE

TAMAG (D) 1933
E.W. Taschner GmbH, Krefeld
The Tamag was a small aerodynamic 3-wheeled coupé with two driven front wheels, using a 200cc engine.   HON

TAMM (D) 1922
The Tamm was a cyclecar with an air-cooled 2-cylinder engine. Transmission was by friction disc to a shaft and by bevel to the right-hand rear wheel.   HON

TAMPLIN (GB) 1919–1927
(1) Tamplin Motors, Staines, Middlesex 1912–1923
(2) Tamplin Motors, Cheam, Surrey 1923–1927
The Tamplin cyclecar, like the A.V., was a lineal descendent of the pre-World War 1 Carden, and was in fact designed by Captain Carden. It was at first a tandem two-seater with a centrally-mounted 980cc V-twin J.A.P. engine, chain primary and belt final drive, and 3 forward speeds. The independent front suspension was by coil springs and sliding pillars. Bodies were of fibreboard. In 1922 the Tamplin became a more conventional side-by-side two-seater with all-chain drive, front-mounted engine, and quarter-elliptic front springs. Sports versions in 1923 had polished aluminium bodies and Blackburne engines. The impressive total of just under 2,000 was made, and the car was still said to be available to special order in 1927.   TRN

TANKETTE (GB) 1919–1920
(1) Ronald Trist & Co Ltd, Watford, Herts.
(2) Tankette Ltd, London N.4
The Tankette was a curious little 3-wheeler made to catch the tail-end of the cyclecar boom. Powered by a 2¾hp single-cylinder 2-stroke Union engine, drive was transmitted by a Burman two-speed gearbox and chain to the double rear wheel. The chassis, if such it could be called, consisted of a frame built up with flat steel strips on either side of ash members, bolted together and sprung on quarter elliptics fixed rigidly fore and aft.
The front axle consisted of concentric steel tubes which enabled the wheels to be pushed inward so that the car could pass through a 3ft doorway into the owner's home. It appears that potential buyers did not appreciate the advantages of garaging the car in the front room, and few were sold.   MJWW

TARKINGTON (US) 1922–1923
Tarkington Motor Car Co, Rockford, Ill.
The Tarkington was a short-lived car using a 6-cylinder engine of the company's own manufacture. Only one model was produced, a five-seater touring car. Wire wheels were standard on all cars built.   KM

TARRANT (AUS) 1901–1907
Tarrant Automobile & Engineering Co, Melbourne, Victoria
Although production was very small, the Tarrant was the best-known early Australian car. The first production car had a 6hp 2-cylinder M.M.C.-De Dion engine, belt transmission and chain final drive. Later cars used 10hp 2-cylinder, and 14 and 16hp 4-cylinder engines, all with shaft drive. The last three 2-cylinder chassis, made about 1905, were fitted with the 11.9hp 3-cylinder White & Poppe engine, but the 4-cylinder engines were made in Melbourne. A 1906 14hp car won the Six Days Victorian Reliability Trial of that year. Despite the variety of models, not more than 20 Tarrants were made altogether.   GNG

TASCO (US) 1948
American Sports Car Co, Hartford, Conn.
Designed by Gordon Buehrig, former Cord engineer, the Tasco sports had a Derham body on a Mercury chassis. The unorthodox machine featured a radiator-cowl bumper, mudguards that turned with the front wheels and a removable perspex roof. Only one of these cars was constructed.   BE

TATE (CDN) 1912–1913
Tate Electrics Ltd, Windsor, Ont.
This ambitious firm offered the usual coupé, as well as a roadster, delivery cars of 500 and 1,000lb capacity, and trucks of 2,000 and 4,000lb capacity. Seating arrangements in the coupé put the driver in front, facing forward, as in petrol cars. The coupé cost $3,600 and the roadster $2,700. All vehicles had wheel steering.   HD

TATIN (F) 1899
V.Tatin, Paris
The Tatin was a very simple 3-wheeler powered by a horizontal single-cylinder engine of 2¼hp.   GNG

1923 TAMPLIN 8hp two-seater. *Autocar*

1920 TANKETTE 2¾hp cyclecar chassis. *Autocar*

1907 TARRANT 14/16hp two-seater. *Autocar*

1927 TATRA Type 11 1,056cc tourer.
Czechoslovak News Agency

1934 TATRA Type 57 1,160cc sports car.
Václav Petřík Collection

1935 TATRA Type 80 6-litre V-12 saloon.
Keith Marvin Collection

TATRA (CS) *1923 to date*
(1) Tatra-Werke AG, Kopřivnice *1923–1935*
(2) Ringhoffer-Tatra-Werke AG, Kopřivnice *1935–1941*
(3) Tatra, np, Kopřivnice *1945 to date*

At first the Tatra was a continuation of the Nesselsdorf, producing the pre-war Types T and U, the latter a 6½-litre ohc 6-cylinder. The first real Tatra car of 1923 was completely different from the last Nesselsdorf models. After his return from Steyr, Hans Ledwinka produced a car which became one of the classics in the history of automobile design. It was characterized by an air-cooled opposed-twin engine of 1,056cc developing 12bhp, a central tubular frame, and special rear swing axles and differential. It was known as the Type 11, and was the basis of later Tatra models, commercial vehicles as well as private cars. Type 12 was identical with the Type 11, but had 4-wheel brakes. The Tatra design was not intended for sporting events, but nevertheless two of these cars participated in the 1925 Targa Florio and gained 1st and 2nd place in the 1,100cc class, driven by Fritz Hückel and Karl Sponer. These were standard production cars, except that two inlet valves instead of one were fitted, and the front transverse-leaf springing was replaced by swinging half axles. Josef Vermirovsky was another competition driver on the small Tatra model; his successes included winning a 5,000 kilometre (3,107 miles) trial from Leningrad via Tiflis to Moscow in 1925. About 25,000 cars of Types 11 and 12 were built up to 1930. Some 4-cylinder models followed, built on the same lines with air-cooled opposed engines, central tubular frames and swing axles: the 30 (1,680cc, 40bhp) and 52 (1,910cc, 40bhp). There were also the in-line 6-cylinder Type 70 of 3,400cc and 60bhp, and the 6-litre V-12 Type 80 with 100bhp, both featuring the same frame construction and swing axles. The Type 80 was built only in limited numbers, like the single-cylinder, 528cc Tatra 3-wheeler (Type 49).

The next important development was the Tatra 57 which appeared in 1932. It had the central tubular frame and swing-axles which were traditional by this time, and an air-cooled opposed 4-cylinder engine of 1,160cc developing 22bhp. Engine capacity was later increased to 1,690cc, and the car was built until 1938. The German Röhr Junior was the Tatra 57 design built under licence. Under the name of Austro-Tatra the light Tatra models were also manufactured in Vienna.

Ledwinka and Tatra were destined to make automobile history again with the Type 77 of 1934. Its all-enveloping body was built strictly to aerodynamic principles. A central box-type frame was used, and in its forked rear end – behind the rear axle – an air-cooled V-8 engine of 3,400cc was placed. It developed 70bhp and gave the car a maximum speed of 95mph. The 1937 Tatra 87 incorporated the same technical principles and used a basically similar body. Engine capacity was reduced to 2,960cc; output was 75bhp – a result of weight reduction. This car was capable of 100mph. In the same year the Tatra 97 was introduced with the same body, but an opposed 4-cylinder unit of 1,760cc and 40bhp was fitted. After the district of Kopřivnice had come under German occupation, and the restriction of numbers of types which had been introduced in Germany in the late 1930s was enforced in Czechoslovakia too, production of the Tatra 97 ceased and only the 87 was continued until about 1941. In 1945, after the war, the Tatra works were nationalized by the Czechoslovak government, and production was devoted to the front-engined Type 57B and the rear-engined Type 87. These were replaced in 1948 by a single model, the 2-litre rear-engined Tatraplan, derived from the pre-war Type 97. This was made until 1954, after which there was a three-year period when no private cars were made. In 1957 the Tatra 603 was introduced; this again had an air-cooled V-8 engine of 2,472cc mounted in the rear. It is still in production today as the T3-603, with twin-carburettor engine, servo-assisted disc brakes, and power assisted steering, although Tatra concentrate on commercial vehicles and railway carriages. In preparation for 1973 was the 3.4-litre T613, a development of the existing theme.   HON

TAU (I) *1924–1926*
Pietro Scaglione, Turin

Scaglione took over the design rights of the Rubino car, but though the Tau was still a 2,297cc 4-cylinder, the L-head configuration gave way to a T-head layout on the touring Tipo 95, and to pushrod-operated ohv on the 90 Sport, which disposed of 50bhp and was capable of 75mph. There were four forward speeds. Taus had Lancia Lambda-like tourer bodies, as well as the mock-Rolls-Royce radiator style then fashionable in Italy. About a hundred were made.   MCS

TAUNTON (i) (US) *1901–1904*
Taunton Motor Carriage Co, Taunton, Mass.

This was a small tiller-steered runabout with a single-cylinder engine under the seat. Normally a two-seater, two additional seats could be provided by dropping the front dash.   GMN

TAUNTON (ii) (GB/B) *1914–1920*
Taunton Cars Ltd, Liège

The taunton was of British design, but it was intended to produce it in Belgium. It had a 14.4hp 4-cylinder engine with overhead inlet valves, and a pressed steel frame which included the bottom half of the sump and gearbox. Six cars were hand-made in England in 1913, and a factory acquired at Liège in which it was planned to make 1,500 cars a year to sell at £175 for a two-seater. Only two cars were completed before World War 1 broke out. A revised model was announced in 1920, but the proposed revival did not materialize.　　　　　　　　　　GNG

TAUNUS (D) *1907–1909*
Taunus Automobilfabrik GmbH, Frankfurt-am-Main

This small company, manufacturers of lorries and buses, produced only one known private car, a 6/12hp model. From 1939 to 1967 the name Taunus was used for German Fords.　　　　　　　　　　HON

TAURINIA (I) *1902–1908*
(1) Società Taurinia, Turin *1902–1907*
(2) Taurinia Fabbrica Automobili, Turin *1907–1908*

The first Taurinias were straightforward 9½hp singles with De Dion engines and shaft drive, one of which won the voiturette class of the 1904 Susa-Moncenisio hill-climb. By 1905 the firm had progressed to a bigger car with a 10/12hp 4-cylinder Fafnir engine, and during the last two seasons this had grown up into a 14/18 of 3 litres' capacity with side valves in an L-head and lt magneto ignition.　　MCS

TAUZIN (F) *1899*
Tauzin et Cie, Levallois-Perret, Seine

The Tauzin voiturette was powered by a front-mounted 3½hp V-twin engine, and used a 3-speed gearbox and shaft drive. A light two-seater body was fitted.　　GNG

TAYDEC *see* TADEC

TAYLOR (GB) *1922–1924*
Taylor's Motors Ltd, Newcastle upon Tyne

The prototype Taylor had a 10hp Coventry-Simplex engine and Meadows 4-speed gearbox, but for production cars of 1923–24 a 14hp Meadows engine was used.　　　　　　　　　　GNG

TAYLOR-SWETNAM (GB) *1913*
Taylor, Swetnam & Co, Coventry, Warwickshire

This was a light car powered by a 2-cylinder engine of the company's own make, with a 3-speed gearbox and shaft drive. With a two-seater streamlined body, the price was £140. They were said to be bringing out a car with a 4-cylinder French engine for 1914.　　　　　　　　　　GNG

T.B. (GB) *1920–1924*
Thompson Bros (Bilston) Ltd, Bilston, Staffs.

Made by a well-known firm of boiler makers, the T.B. was a neat-looking little 3-wheeler powered by a 961cc 2-cylinder J.A.P. engine. It had a 2-speed gearbox and shaft drive to the single rear wheel. Some models had disc wheels, and the radiator was similar in shape to that of the Brescia Bugatti.　　GNG

T.D.C. *see* CROMPTON (ii)

TECNO (I) *1964 to date*
Tecno Automobili, Bologna

The Pederzani brothers' Tecno concern is the great success story of Italian racing-car mass production. They began building karts in 1962 and in 1964 produced 250cc Ducati-engined Formula 4 cars for sale. In 1965 an 850 Formula car appeared with Fiat 850 engine, and in 1966 the first F3 Tecno was built, Cosworth-Ford-engined and with fuel tank amidships giving a far-forward cockpit. This was unsuccessful and was quickly replaced by a more conventional car, but with a similarly short wheelbase. Many of these new cars were sold in 1967 when they dominated F3. In 1968 ten Formula 2 and 43 F3 cars were sold.

Tecno also developed their own Ford engines, and in 1970 Clay Regazzoni won the European F2 Championship for Tecno. In 1971 the Pederzanis concentrated on the Formula, and built their own engines yet again. Meanwhile F3 production had been reduced while Formula 1 engine and chassis developments took place. A space-frame prototype appeared initially, mounting the 3-litre flat-12 Tecno engine, and new monocoque chassis raced with the engine under Martini colours in 1972.　　　　　　　　　　DCN

TECO (i) (GB) *1905*
Thornton Engineering Co, Ltd, Bradford, Yorks.

The Teco was assembled from English and French components, including those of the Bailleul. Production was intended, but only one was made.　　GNG

TECO (ii) (D) *1924–1925*
Teco-Werke GmbH, Stettin

This firm produced only one model, which was powered by a 4-cylinder 5/30PS engine.　　　　　　　　　　HON

TEMPELHOF *see* B.M.F.

1937 TATRA Type 87 2.9-litre V-8 saloon.
Czechoslovak News Agency

1957 TATRA Type 603 2½-litre V-8 saloon.
Czechoslovak News Agency

1923 TEMPERINO 1,100cc racing car. *Museo dell'Automobile. Turin*

1922 TEMPLAR 3.2-litre tourer. *Kenneth Stauffer*

1935 TEMPO V-600 600cc convertible. *Tempo-Werk*

1934 TERRAPLANE 3½-litre roadster. *American Motors Corporation*

TEMPERINO (I) *1919–1925*
Vetturette Temperino SA, Turin

The Temperino brothers had grandiose ideas of marketing a mass-produced cycle-car with universal appeal, to be made by Farina, the coachbuilders, but production was held up during World War 1, and comparatively few reached the public. An air-cooled 1,100cc V-twin engine, with overhead inlet valves, drove by shaft to the offside rear wheel only, avoiding the need for a differential. The 3-speed gearbox was integral with the rear axle. Other features were rack-and-pinion steering, acetylene lighting (electric in 1922), and a front-mounted kick-starter. Racing versions had 4 speeds and a slightly larger engine.　　　TRN

TEMPLAR (US) *1917–1924*
Templar Motors Corp, Cleveland, Ohio

The Templar was the best-known of several American attempts to make a high-grade small car just after World War 1, but was just as surely doomed by the development of American tastes in automobiles. It was a well-proportioned machine, with radiator and body well within the wheelbase. Materials and finish were superb, the aluminium bodies being given 27 coats of paint. The 3-litre (later 3.2 litre) 'Top-Valve' (i.e. overhead-valve) engine was smooth in spite of having only 4 cylinders, and very clean in appearance. It was also more efficient than most American power units. Much aluminium was found beneath the bonnet, too. Standard equipment in the roadster included a compass and a Kodak camera. A 3½-litre six was also listed for 1917 only. A 4.3-litre 6-cylinder engine was listed at the end of the Templar's career.　　　TRN

TEMPLE-WESTCOTT (US) *1921–1922*

This was a 6-cylinder assembled car, whose chassis were made at Amesbury, Mass., and bodies by the Bela Body Co, Framingham, Mass. Only about 20 made.　　　GNG

TEMPO (D) *1933–1956*
Vidal & Sohn Tempo-Werk, Hamburg-Harburg

This firm specialized in small 3-wheeled vans and introduced a private car based on the same design in 1933. It had one driven front wheel and a 200cc Ilo 6hp – later 9hp – engine. This model was built until 1935. Several estate cars, based on the vans, were offered until 1940. In addition to the 3-wheeled models a front-driven 4-wheeled car was introduced in 1935 with a 600cc Ilo engine. Estate-car versions of the post-war 3-wheeled vans were also available until 1956.　　　HON

TENNANT (US) *1914–1915*
Tennant Motors Co, Chicago, Ill.

This firm made a conventional 30/35hp 4-cylinder roadster and also a five-seater tourer.　　　GNG

TENTING (F) *1891–1899*
Sté Nationale de Construction de Moteurs H. Tenting, Boulogne-sur-Seine

The Tenting Works were established in 1884 to make gas engines, and the first car appeared in 1891. It had a rear-mounted horizontal 2-cylinder engine of 4hp, a variable-speed friction transmission (surely the first example of this system) and steering by swivelling forecarriage. Final drive was by chain to the offside rear wheel. Later cars had V-twin engines and conventional steering, and competed in some of the early town-to-town races, such as the Paris-Marseilles-Paris 1896. In 1898 Tenting was said to be building a twenty-six-seater bus powered by a 16hp 4-cylinder engine. After February 1899 cars were no longer made under the name of Tenting, but the company continued to make engines.　　　GNG

TERRAPLANE (US) *1932–1937*
Hudson Motor Car Co, Detroit, Mich. .

The Terraplane replaced the original compact Essex Six late in 1932. It was a conventional 2.6-litre sv 6-cylinder car with a 3-speed gearbox selling for $475 in the U.S.A. and £295 in England; though it failed to make much impression at home, its 70mph top speed and low running costs brought it many admirers in Europe. A companion 4-litre straight-8 for 1933 had a 94bhp engine and offered 85mph for only £385; it formed the basis for the first Railtons. The 1934 line was restyled with a striking V-grille and independent front suspension, and used Hudson's 3½-litre 6-cylinder engine, though 2.6-litre versions were made for export. The cars were again restyled, along with the Hudsons in 1936, when hydraulic brakes were added. After 1937, the name was dropped and its place taken by Hudson's new small six, the 112.　　　MCS

TERRIER (GB) *1959–1961*
L. Terry, Winchmore Hill, London N.21; Thornwood, Essex

Aided by driver Brian Hart, Len Terry commenced his series of successful and painstaking designs with a winner in the form of his 1,172cc Ford-engined two-seater sports car. This was followed by a low-cost Formula Junior, with a front-mounted Ford 105E engine, multi-tubular chassis frame, and coil/damper unit suspension.　　　DF

TERROT (F) *1912–1914*
SA des Etablissements Terrot, Dijon, Côte d'Or

Terrot had made bicycles since the 1890s, and became one of France's best-known motor-cycle manufacturers. They made a few experimental voiturettes in 1900 and 1902, and a small series of conventional light cars from 1912 to 1914. These came in two models, the 8hp 1,244cc and the 10hp 1,460cc. Both used 4-cylinder monobloc engines with side valves, and shaft drive.   GNG

TESTE ET MORET (F) *1898–1903*
Teste et Moret, Lyon-Vaise, Rhône

Also known as La Mouche, the Teste et Moret was a light two- or four-seater car powered by a single-cylinder De Dion engine. It had friction transmission and a tubular frame. A 10hp 2-cylinder racing model was made in 1902. Teste et Moret's designer was T.C. Pullinger who went to Sunbeam after the Lyons firm ceased production.   GNG

TEXAN (US) *1918–1922*
Texas Motor Car Association, Fort Worth, Tex.

An assembled car, the Texan had a Lycoming 4-cylinder engine and other standard components together with outsize tires, presumably suited for service in the oil-fields of Texas. About 2,000 cars and 1,000 trucks were made.   KM

TEXAS (US) *1920*
Texas Truck & Tractor Co, Dallas, Tex.

This car is often confused with the Texan built at Fort Worth, but there is no connection between the two makes. Despite the company name, there is no record of any trucks or tractors being built, and the Texas, which was a conventional assembled car, was offered for one year only.   MJWW

TEXMOBILE (US) *1921–1922*
Little Motors Kar Co, Dallas, Tex.

This was a small car powered by a 22½hp 4-cylinder L-head engine of the company's own make.   GNG

T.G.E. *see* CHIYODA

T.H. *see* IDEAL (iv)

THAMES (GB) *1906–1911*
Thames Ironworks, Shipbuilding & Engineering Co, Ltd, London E.

Said to have been the origin of Millwall Football Club, the Thames Ironworks had been makers of steam and petrol-engined commercial vehicles since 1902. At the 1906 Olympia Show they exhibited a large 45hp 6-cylinder car with shaft drive. By 1908 a 15hp twin and a 24hp four had been added to the range, as well as a larger six of 60hp. One of the latter, driven by Clifford Earp, took a number of records at Brooklands in 1907 and 1909. These included all class records from 50 to 300 miles, and from one to three hours.

In 1910 the Thames range was at its largest, consisting of an 8hp single-cylinder car with worm drive, a 12hp twin which was often made in taxicab form, a 15.9hp monobloc four, and 24 and 60hp sixes. After 1911, only commercial vehicles were made.   GNG

THANET *see* WHITEHEAD-THANET

THEIS (D) *1933*
Dipl. Ing. K. Theis, Berlin-Charlottenburg

This was a small aerodynamic 3-wheeled coupé with two driven front wheels, using a 200cc engine.   HON

THIEULIN (F) *1907–1908*
Automobiles Thieulin, Besançon, Doubs

The Thieulin was a conventional 4-cylinder light car. A racing two-seater, driven by Thieulin himself, ran in the 1908 Grand Prix des Voiturettes.   GNG

THOLOMÉ (F) *c.1920–1922*
M. Tholomé, St Ouen, Seine

The Tholomé cyclecar was built in 2- and 4-cylinder versions, the latter having the 1,100cc Ruby engine. Transmission was by friction disc or 2-speed gearbox, and final drive by chain. A side-by-side two-seater body, known as 'une carrosserie bateau', was fitted.   GNG

THOMAS (i) (US) *1902–1919*
(1) E.R. Thomas Motor Co, Buffalo, N.Y. *1902–1911*
(2) E.R. Thomas Motor Car Co, Buffalo, N.Y. *1911–1919*

The first Thomas-built car was the Autotwo of 1899, but from 1900 to 1902 Thomas built engines only, having granted a licence to the Buffalo Automobile & Auto-Bi Company to build light cars and motorcycles (*see* Buffalo (i)). In 1902

1898 TESTE ET MORET voiturette. *Lucien Loreille Collection*

1907 THAMES 60hp two-seater. At Brooklands with Clifford Earp at the wheel. *Autocar*

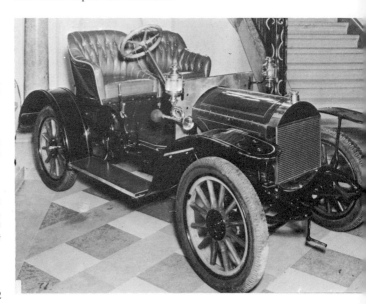

1908 THIEULIN 4-cylinder two-seater. *Musée de l'Automobile, Rochetaillée-sur-Saone*

1910 THOMAS(i) Flyer 72hp tourer. *Kenneth Stauffer*

1919 Thor(ii) 15hp coupé. *Autocar*

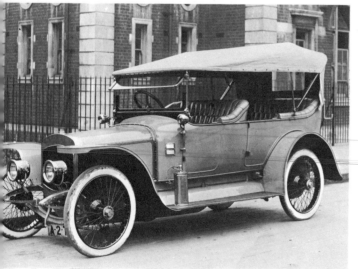

1912 THORNYCROFT 18hp tourer. *Transport Equipment (Thornycroft) Ltd*

Thomas took over Buffalo's operations and in July 1903 introduced a touring car powered by a 24hp 3-cylinder in-line engine. A De Dion-type bonnet was used with a gilled-tube radiator slung low in front, but by November 1903 this had been replaced by a conventional bonnet and honeycomb radiator. These cars used double chain drive. For 1905 the model was called a 24/30hp, and this year saw the introduction of larger 40 and 50hp 4-cylinder cars, together with a 60hp six. The name Thomas Flyer was applied to the cars from 1905 onwards, and a wide range of bodies was offered, from two-seater racer to limousine. The most famous model was the K-6-70, with a 72hp 6-cylinder engine; it was one of these which won the 1908 New York to Paris Race. This car, which was sold at auction in 1913 for $200, is now a priceless part of Harrah's Automobile Collection at Reno.

One chain-driven model was continued into 1909, but later Thomases tended to be more sedate, with emphasis on town cars and landaus. In 1911 and 1912 only 6-cylinder models were made. The Model 6-70 was continued to the end, its massive 12.8-litre engine being the largest in the range. Cars were listed up to 1919, available to special order only. GMN

THOMAS (ii) (GB) 1903
W.F. Thomas, Birmingham

The English Thomas used an 8hp 2-cylinder engine mounted at the front, driving via friction transmission and chain final drive. A 6hp single-cylinder, and a 10hp twin were planned, but not built. GNG

THOMAS-DETROIT (US) 1906–1908
E.R. Thomas-Detroit Co, Detroit, Mich.

This car differed very little from the parent Thomas (i). For 1908, it was powered by a 6.1-litre 4-cylinder engine with two sparking plugs per cylinder. A 3-speed transmission with shaft drive was used. This firm then became the Chalmers Motor Co. GMN

THOMOND (IRL) 1925–1929
J.A. Jones, Dublin

Said to have been the first car built in the Irish Free State, the original Thomond used a 1,750cc 4-cylinder ohv engine, a 4-speed gearbox, and five-seater saloon bodywork. Later models were more sporting and did well in Irish trials. The 12/48hp of 1929 had a fabric coupé body, and probably used the Meadows 4ED engine. GNG

THOMPSON (i) (US) 1901–1902
Andrew C. Thompson, Plainfield, N.J.

This was a light electric runabout powered by a $1\frac{1}{4}$hp motor geared directly to the rear axle. A speed of 12mph, and a range of 25–30 miles were modest even for 1901, but with a special battery, the range could be extended to 60 miles. GNG

THOMPSON (ii) (US) 1906
Thompson Automobile Co, Providence, R.I.

This was a heavy steam brake which could carry six passengers on bench seats facing each other, and two forward facing passengers at the front. GNG

THOMSON (i) (AUS) 1896–1901
Thomson & Co, Melbourne, Victoria

The prototype Thomson steamer was built in 1896, and had a 5hp vertical compound 2-cylinder engine mounted in front, and double chain drive. A six-seater body was fitted. It was driven over 2,000 miles in experimental trials, including a run of 493 miles from Bathurst, N.S.W. to Melbourne. From 1900 to 1901 about 10 production cars were made. Herbert Thomson planned to make a twin-engined steam car capable of 40mph, as well as a 3 ton lorry, but he turned to the importation of cars instead. GNG

THOMSON (ii) (US) 1900–1902
Thomson Automobile Co, Philadelphia, Pa.

This was a light two-seater powered by a 5hp single-cylinder engine, priced at $500. An unusual feature in so small a car was double chain drive. GNG

THOMSON (iii) (F) 1913–1928
Etablissements Industriels Raymond Thomas, Talence, Gironde

This firm supplied components to the motor industry, and made marine engines, but they preferred to buy from outside the engines used in their cars. These were mostly fairly small units such as the $1\frac{1}{2}$-litre Aster or Altos, or 2-litre Altos, but they did list a car powered by the enormous 6.6-litre 4-cylinder T-head Janvier engine. This model was introduced in 1914, and theoretically at any rate, could still be bought in 1926. Quite what sort of a market they were aiming at is not known, for although the 40CV Thomson was appreciably cheaper than an equivalent Renault or Hispano-Suiza, potential purchasers of the latter are unlikely to have pondered for very long over a Thomson catalogue. GNG

THOMSON (iv) see WILES-THOMSON

THOR (i) (GB) 1904–c.1906
Thor Motor Car Co, London S.W.

This firm exhibited at the 1904 Cordingley Show a two-seater car powered by a 6/8hp Simms engine, with a 3-speed gearbox and shaft drive. It had solid tyres and a somewhat rustic appearance, more that of a commercial vehicle, and indeed a number were made with van bodies. In 1905 the Thor has a 12/14hp 2-cylinder engine and chain drive, but retained the solid tyres. The 8hp model was still listed. GNG

THOR (ii) (GB) 1919–c.1921
Simpson, Taylor Ltd, London S.W.

There is no known connection between the two Thor cars except that they both hailed from the Westminster district of London. The post-war car was assembled from American components, and used a 4-cylinder engine of 2,255cc. GNG

THORN ET HOGAN (F) 1901–1902
Thorn, Hogan et Cie, Puteaux, Seine

This was an Anglo-American concern who made a light car 'especially for English and American roads'; i.e. with greater ground clearance than the average French light car. It was powered by a 10hp vertical-twin engine and had shaft drive. A four-seater tonneau body was fitted, and the car had the general appearance of a Panhard. GNG

THORNYCROFT (GB) 1903–1913
John I. Thornycroft & Co, Ltd, Basingstoke, Hampshire

Thornycrofts had been making steam lorries for about seven years when they put their first cars on the market. They were a 10hp twin and a 20hp 4-cylinder car, both with automatic inlet valves, gilled-tube radiators and shaft drive. By 1905 they were of much more modern appearance, with honeycomb radiators similar to the Mercedes, and mechanically-operated inlet valves. The 20hp had become a 24hp, and the following year a new 14hp 4-cylinder model was introduced with monobloc engine and overhead valves. From 1905 to 1908 the firm competed in the Tourist Trophy races, their best performance being Tom Thornycroft's 5th place in the 1908 race. In 1909 there were three models, an 18hp four, a 30hp four, and a 45hp six, all with monobloc engines and overhead valves. However, commercial vehicle production was becoming more important, and all models but the 18hp were dropped after 1912; car production ceased altogether at the end of 1913. GNG

THRIF-T (US) 1955
Tri-Wheel Motor Corp, Springfield, Mass.

A 3-wheeled utility car, the Thrif-T had a 7ft 1in wheelbase, weighed 900lb and possessed a flat-twin Onan engine of 10hp. Body combinations included a canvas-topped five-seater model, a pickup and a delivery. BE

THRIGE (DK) 1909–1918
Thomas B. Thrige AS, Odense

This company was founded in 1894. Today it is well known for its electric motors of all types. The first Thrige vehicle was a truck driven, of course, by electricity. In 1911 the petrol car they had developed was ready for production. Thrige offered a range of vehicles, using Ballot and Daimler-Knight engines for private cars and White & Poppe, Continental and Hercules for heavy trucks. In 1914, 50 light cars were produced, all with 4-cylinder 4/12hp Ballot engines. They had 3-speed gearboxes, leather cone clutch and lacked a differential, like Mathis. The price asked was 3,800 Danish kroner. A 4/12hp Thrige scored a 1st in the 1914 Copenhagen to The Skaw run, being the best Danish car entered. The normal Thrige passenger car was an 8/22hp with a Ballot engine cast en bloc. Thrige cars had a considerable sale before the firm's merger with Jan and Anglo-Dane in 1918 to form De Forenede Danske Automobilfabriker AS, after which only Triangel trucks and motor buses were offered. TRA

THRUPP & MABERLY (GB) 1896
Thrupp & Maberly, London W.

Thrupp & Maberly were well-known carriage builders who fitted a small number of their vehicles with electric motors at their premises at 425, Oxford Street. One of these was a victoria made for the Queen of Spain. GNG

TH. SCHNEIDER (F) 1910–1931
Automobiles Th. Schneider, Besançon, Doubs; Boulogne-sur-Seine

Théophile Schneider had been one of the founders of Rochet-Schneider before he started making cars on his own account. These were conventional enough, with their 4- or 6-cylinder sv engines and shaft drive. The only feature not shared by a majority of French cars was the dashboard radiators. In spite of this conservatism, Th. Schneider competed energetically in first-class racing, taking part in the Coupe de l'Auto race, the French Grand Prix, and the Belgian Grand Prix in 1912, and the French Grand Prix in the two succeeding years; but because of conservatism, perhaps, it was without success. In 1914, seven 4-cylinder models, from 1.8 to 6.1 litres, were offered, as well as a 3.2-litre six.

1914 THRIGE 8/22hp limousine. *Thorkil Ry Andersen*

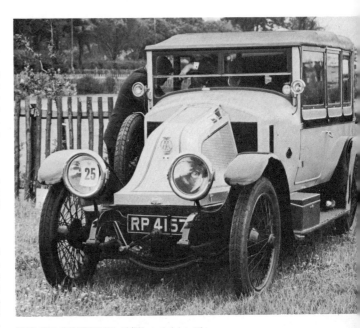

1912 TH. SCHNEIDER 18/22hp cabriolet. *The Veteran Car Club of Great Britain*

1923 TH. SCHNEIDER 15hp tourer. *Autocar*

1927 THULIN Type B 1.7-litre saloon.
Oluf Berrum

1920 THURLOW 10hp 3-wheeler. *Autocar*

1973 TICI 848cc two-seater. *TiCi Cars Ltd*

The same policy was followed after World War 1: the manufacture of conventional, strong motor cars with a high turn of speed, though now with frontal V-radiators. The basically pre-war 14CV was offered in 4- and 6-cylinder form from 1919 to 1923, and there was a light car, the 1,170cc VL *(voiture légère)* from 1926. The most exciting and best-known Th. Schneider was the 10CV, introduced in 1922, an sv 2-litre fast tourer in the best French tradition. By 1925 it had acquired ohv and front-wheel brakes, and survived until the end of car manufacture. The VL was also sold in ohv form by 1927. These were the longest-lived and most popular models in a complex range. Production ceased in 1929, but cars were still being sold off in 1931.

TRN

THULIN (S) *1920–1928*

AB Thulinverken, Landskrona

The Thulinverken aeronautical company entered car manufacture with a 4-cylinder vehicle based on the German Aga model, but entirely made in Sweden. It was typically German in appearance with a sharply pointed radiator and concave body sides. Only about 300 were made before the firm's bankruptcy in 1924. Three years later the Weiertz brother, who were connected with the Self, joined a newly reconstituted firm, and designed the Type B, an attractive low-built saloon with all seats between the axles, and powered by a 4-cylinder, 1.7-litre ohv engine giving 36 to 38bhp; 4-wheel brakes were used, the rear brakes being mounted inboard. Only 13 of these promising cars were made (one with a 6-cylinder Hupmobile engine), before competition from the newly established Volvo company forced Thulin out of business.

OB

THURLOW (GB) *1920–1921*

Thurlow & Co, Wimbledon, London S.W.19

Although a prototype Thurlow 3-wheeler had appeared in 1914, production did not start until after the war. The car was powered by a 10hp V-twin Precision engine which drove by chain to a 3-speed Sturmey-Archer gearbox. Final drive was by belts. The engine could be started from the driver's seat, the starter being connected to the exhaust valves which were automatically lifted during the first half of the lever's travel.

GNG

THURNER (D) *1970 to date*

Rudolf Thurner, Bernbeuren

N.S.U. TT 1200 components form the basis for this plastic-bodied sports coupé, marketed as the Thurner RS.

HON

TiCi (GB) *1966 to date*

TiCi Cars Ltd, Shepshed, Loughborough, Leics.; Sutton-in-Ashfield, Notts.

The original TiCi was a two-seater town car 6ft long and weighing only 560lb. Performance from the rear-mounted Triumph Daytona motor-cycle engine was quite impressive, but the support that the project received was not, a notable exception being the interest shown by ex-B.R.M. sponsor Raymond Mays. A slightly enlarged version with Mini engine became available in 1972, styled as a 'fun car', and available in kit form. Designer Anthony Hill retained the fibreglass monocoque-tub form of construction, with suitably strengthened pick-up points for the engine and suspension.

DF

TIC-TAC (F) *1920–1924*

F. Dumoulin, Puteaux, Seine

In its original form the Tic-Tac cyclecar was powered by a 4-cylinder 985cc Ruby engine, and used chain drive. This car was entered in the 1920 Cyclecar Grand Prix, where it distinguished itself mainly by getting in the way of the faster cars. Later Tic-Tacs used shaft drive and larger engines by Chapuis-Dornier and Janvier. One model had a 1½-litre engine with 3 valves per cylinder, but still no sporting successes came to the marque.

GNG

TIDAHOLM (S) *1906–1913*

Tidaholm Bruks AB, Tidaholm

The Tidaholm had probably the oldest ancestry of any car-making firm; the company traced their history back to the ownership of a mill in 1403. Lorries were made from 1903, and were always their main production. The first private vehicle was a 1-ton lorry chassis on which estate bus or shooting brake bodies could be mounted. These vehicles were capable of 20mph, and one was supplied to King Gustaf V. In 1909 a Tidaholm car was shown with a Bugatti-designed ohc 4-cylinder engine, but very few were made, and production was concentrated on commercial vehicles, which were made until 1933.

OB

TIFFANY (US) *1913–1914*

Tiffany Electric Car Co, Flint, Mich.

The Tiffany succeeded the Flanders electric cars. The sole model, an open two-seater, had very sweeping body lines fore and aft, with wire wheels and cycle mudguards. It was powered by a Wagner electric motor, was lever-steered, and cost $750. The name Tiffany only applied to the car from October 1913 to March 1914, after which the Flanders name was revived.

GMN

TIGER (US) *1914*

Automobile Cyclecar Co, Detroit, Mich.

This cyclecar was made in two-seater and four-seater models. These were powered by a 4-cylinder Farmer engine with overhead valves and shaft drive.   GMN

TILEY (US) *1904–1906; 1908–1913*

Tiley Pratt Co, Essex, Conn.

The Tiley used 4-cylinder Rutenber engines of 32/36hp. These were water-cooled, and had sliding-gear transmission and shaft drive. A very few cars with 6-cylinder engines were also built. Less than 25 Tileys were constructed.   GMN

TILICUM (US) *1914*

Yukon Auto Shop, Seattle, Wash.

The Tilicum cyclecar used a 2-cylinder 14hp engine. Its transmission was a crude system with V-belts and split pulleys on the rear axle. Torque variation was accomplished by moving the entire rear axle forward or backward, the maximum movement being 3in.   GMN

TINCHER (US) *1903–1908*

(1) Chicago Coach & Carriage Co, Chicago, Ill. *1903–1904*
(2) Tincher Motor Car Co, South Bend, Ind. *1904–1908*

This company made large, heavy cars powered originally by 4-cylinder engines of 20 or 45hp, with massive bonnets and gilled-tube radiators, and twin chain drive. Brakes on rear wheels were operated by compressed air. Later models were as large as 50 or 80hp. The 1906 '50' cost $5,000. In 1907 Studebaker acquired the company.   GNG

TINY (GB) *1913–1915*

Nanson, Barker & Co, Ltd, Esholt, Yorks.

The Tiny cyclecar was powered by an 8hp V-twin Precision engine, and used shaft drive. A 10hp Dorman 4-cylinder engine was used in 1915. After the war Nanson, Barker & Company made the larger Airedale car.   GNG

TISCHER (US) *1914*

Linton G. Tischer Tri-Car Co, Peoria, Ill.

The Tischer was a 3-wheeled car, with the single, powered wheel in the rear. This was driven by a belt from a 9hp, 2-cylinder, air-cooled engine, through a friction transmission.   GMN

TITAN (i) (GB) *1911*

Titan Motor Wheel Co, Coventry, Warwickshire

This was a 3-wheeler powered by a 5½hp single-cylinder water-cooled Fafnir engine. The frame was of ash, and there was a 2-speed epicyclic gear and final drive by chain to the back wheel. A price of £78 15s was quoted.   MCS

TITAN (ii) (GB) *1965 to date*

(1) C. Lucas (Engineering) Ltd, Highgate, London *1965–1967*
(2) C. Lucas (Engineering) Ltd, King's Lynn, Norfolk *1967–1968*
(3) C. Lucas (Engineering) Ltd, Huntingdon *1968–1971*
(4) Titan Cars Ltd, St Neot's, Hunts. *1971 to date*

The first two Titan models were a one-off sports car and a Formula 2 single-seater, but it was the Mark 3 Formula 3 car of 1967 that really brought the name to notice. This was followed up by the 1968 Mark 4 Formula Ford and succeeding designs concentrated on this formula. The cars used space-frames by Arch Motors and bodies by Specialised Mouldings, and generally followed conventional design principles. They were consistently successful. Most production went for export, but the Mark 6 models raced in Britain by Ken Bailey and Derek Lawrence during 1972 were almost unbeatable.   DF

TMF (US) *1909*

Termatt, Monahan & Farney, Oshkosh, Wisc.

This was a high-wheeler with a 2-stroke 4-cylinder engine. Not more than three were built.   GMN

TOBOGGAN (GB) *1905–1906*

Toboggan Tri-car Co, Ltd, London E.C.

Although it was called a tri-car, the Toboggan was more car-like than most of its kind, having wheel steering and proper seats for driver and passenger. It was powered by either a 4½hp Aster or 6hp Fafnir engine with the radiator immediately behind the passenger seat. Friction transmission and chain final drive were used.   GNG

TOJEIRO (GB) *1952–1962*

Tojeiro Automotive Developments Ltd, Barkway, Royston, Herts.

The first Tojeiro sports cars used a simple tubular frame, similar to the contemporary Lester. The most popular engine was the M.G., bored to 1,467cc, until Cliff Davis's Bristol-engined version achieved a fine run of successes in 1951 and 1954. The designs were then sold to A.C. for their Ace, and subsequent models were

1915 TINY 8hp two-seater. *M.J. Worthington-Williams*

1972 TITAN(ii) Mark 6 Formula Ford racing car. *Titan Cars Ltd*

1959 TOJEIRO-JAGUAR 3.8-litre sports car. *Autosport*

1920 TOM POUCE 730cc cyclecar. Designer Blanc at the wheel. *Autocar*

1966 TORINO 380 3.8-litre coupé. *American Motors Corporation*

1935 TORNAX Rex 700cc sports car. *M.H. Meier*

based on space frames. Jaguar engines were fitted from 1956 onwards, but perhaps the most interesting model was the 1,098cc Coventry-Climax-engined car of 1958, which included a single disc brake and an inverted Volkswagen gearbox in unit with the De Dion type rear axle. In 1959 a 1½-litre version was made, and in 1960 a Formula Junior was obtainable. The last of a line of some 50 vehicles were the rear-engined Coventry-Climax powered coupés built for the Ecurie Ecosse.　　DF

TOLEDO (i) (US) *1900–1903*
(1) American Bicycle Co, Toledo, Ohio *1900–1902*
(2) International Motor Car Co, Toledo, Ohio *1902–1903*
　　The first Toledo cars were steamers, powered by vertical 2-cylinder double-acting engines of 6¼hp. Steering was by tiller, and several different body styles were made, prices varying from $800 to $1,600. In 1902 a petrol-driven car with a 18hp vertical 3-cylinder engine was introduced. The steamers were dropped at the end of 1902, and the petrol cars were known as Pope-Toledo from 1903 onward.　　GNG

TOLEDO (ii) (US) *1913*
Toledo Autocycle Car Co, Toledo, Ohio
　　Also known as the Autocycle, this was a 2-cylinder cyclecar with shaft drive.　　GNG

TOM *see* FERBEDO

TOMOS *see* CITROËN

TOM POUCE (F) *1920–1924*
(1) Blanc et Guillon, Puteaux, Seine *1920–1923*
(2) Garage Ernault, Dommartin, Somme *1923–1924*
　　The original Tom Pouce (Tom Thumb) cars were powered by a 730cc 2-cylinder 2-stroke engine, which was replaced by a 1,100cc Ruby 4-cylinder unit in the later cars. A conventional 3-speed gearbox and shaft drive were used, and some models had staggered seating. One was driven by Blanc, the co-builder, into 4th place in the 1920 Cyclecar Grand Prix.　　GNG

TONELLO (I) *1921–1923*
Automobili Guido Meregalli, Milan
　　This was a sports car with 1.7-litre ohc 4-cylinder engine developing 50bhp, for which over 80mph was claimed. Dual-magneto ignition and an adjustable-rake steering column were interesting features.　　MCS

TONY HUBER (F) *1902–1906*
Automobiles Tony Huber, Billancourt, Seine
　　Tony Huber was mainly a maker of proprietary engines used in a wide variety of makes, but he did manufacture a number of cars under his own name. They included an 8 and an 11hp 2-cylinder, the latter with chain drive, although other models, larger as well as smaller, all used shaft drive. 4-cylinder cars included a 14hp, a 16/18hp and a 20/25hp. Although relatively few Tony Hubers were made, two examples of the 8hp 2-cylinder model survive in England.　　GNG

TOQUET (US) *1905*
Toquet Motor Car & Construction Co, New York, N.Y.
　　This rare car was furnished with a T-head, 4-cylinder 7½-litre engine rated at 45hp, fitted with a flyball governor, and connected so that the clutch and brake operated the throttle. The transmission was of 2 speeds, and progressive, while the final drive was by shaft. The weight of the five-seater was 3,200lb.　　GMN

TORINO (RA) *1966 to date*
(1) Industrias Kaiser Argentina SAIC, Córdoba *1966–1968*
(2) IKA-Renault SAIC y F, Córdoba *1968 to date*
　　This company has made a diversity of foreign designs, among them Jeeps, Ramblers and (until 1967) the B.M.C.-Farina family of 1½-litre sedans and station wagons inherited from Di Tella. Since the fusion with Renault interests in 1968 it has also made these cars in various sizes. Entirely Argentinian, however, was the Pininfarina-styled Torino, with 3-litre or 3.8-litre ohc 6-cylinder engine, coil-spring rear suspension, and ZF manual gearbox, at first with three forward speeds, though four speeds were standard from 1970. By 1972 the bigger engine was also standardized, disc brakes were used on the more potent S, TS, and GS versions, and this last, powered by a 185bhp engine, was credited with 124mph in coupé form. Two customized versions made by outside firms were the Comahue and the Tulia.　　MCS

TORNADO (GB) *1958–1964*
(1) Tornado Cars Ltd, Rickmansworth, Herts. *1958–1963*
(2) Tornado Cars (1963) Ltd, Rickmansworth, Herts. *1963–1964*
　　One of the leaders in the kit-built field, and one of the largest users of fibreglass bodies, Tornado achieved success with both two-seater open and two/four seater GT versions. A simple ladder frame, with coil suspension and Ford 8 or 10 components, was utilized for the Typhoon. Subsequent models, with similar chassis and

proprietary running gear, were the 1,000cc Tempest, the 2-litre Triumph-engined Thunderbolt, and the Talisman for Ford 109E engines. In 1960 there was even a 'sports brake' station wagon version.　　　　　DF

TORNAX (D) *1934–1937*
Tornax Fahrzeug- und Apparatebau GmbH, Wuppertal-Langerfeld
This motor-cycle firm introduced a two-seater sports car in 1934 under the name of Tornax Rex. The DKW front-drive unit with a 700cc engine was used in a central tubular chassis. The car had independent suspension all round.　　　HON

TORPEDO (GB) *1909*
F. Hopper & Co, Ltd, Barton-on-Humber, Lincs.
The old-established firm of Hopper marketed the Torpedo during 1909, but the car was, in fact, manufactured by the Star Cycle Company of Wolverhampton, only the finishing touches being added by the Barton firm. Originally a 6hp single-cylinder model was offered, replaced by a 2-cylinder car.　　　GB

TOURAINE (US) *1912–1915*
(1) Nance Motor Car Co, Philadelphia, Pa. *1912–1913*
(2) Touraine Co, Philadelphia, Pa. *1913–1915*
The Touraine was a larger car than average, with wheelbases up to 11ft 2in. It was driven by a 6-cylinder T-head engine of 6½-litres. Two-, five- and seven-seater open models were offered at prices from $2,200 to $3,200.
After 1915, this company became the Vim Motor Truck Co, building only commercial vehicles.　　　GMN

TOURAND (F) *1900–1907*
(1) Tourand et Cie, Le Havre, Seine-Inférieure
(2) Tourand et Cie, Suresnes, Seine
The first Tourand had a 6hp 2-cylinder Crozet engine, with double chain drive. Production lapsed for a few years, but in 1905 a range of 4-cylinder shaft-drive cars was introduced. These included a 16/20 and an 18/24hp car, although models of 40, 60 and 70hp were theoretically available. At least one 80hp racing car was made in 1906 or 1907.　　　GNG

TOURETTE (GB) *1956–1958*
(1) Carr Bros, Purley, Surrey *1956*
(2) Progress Supreme Co, Ltd, Purley, Surrey *1957–1958*
The Tourette was a very light 3-wheeler powered by a 197cc Villiers engine, with a 4-speed gearbox and optional reverse. Buyers had the alternative of a plastic body at £299 or an alloy on ash frame body at £325. The cheaper model was the least expensive car on the British market.　　　GNG

TOUREY (F) *1898*
Jules Tourey, Paris
The Tourey car had a 4hp single-cylinder horizontal engine mounted at the rear, with three-seater 'light carriage' or four-seater 'Petit Duc' bodywork.　　　GNG

TOURIST (i) (US) *1902–1909*
Auto Vehicle Co, Los Angeles, Calif.
The Tourist was the best-known West Coast make of the era. These cars used 2- and 4-cylinder water-cooled engines, and were mainly five-seater touring models. The smaller engines had a friction transmission while a sliding-gear type was employed with the 4-cylinder engine and was priced at $1,700.　　　GMN

TOURIST (ii) (D) *1907–1920*
(1) Tourist Automobil-Werk GmbH, Berlin-Tempelhof *1907–1911*
(2) Berliner Automobilfabrik 'Torpedo' Georg Beck & Co, Berlin *1911–1920*
This was a 3-wheeler with a V-twin air-cooled 7hp engine. The engine was in the front transmission to the rear wheels being by shaft and chains. Open two- or three-seater bodies were used during the first years, while later versions were also available with closed bodies.　　　HON

TOWANDA (US) *1904*
Towanda Motor Vehicle Co, Towanda, Pa.
This car was one of several of the period which were built without an engine, this being supplied by the customer. Steering was by wheel, and the rear axle was fitted for single chain drive.　　　GMN

TOWNE SHOPPER (US) *1948*
International Motor Car Co, San Diego, Calif.
The aluminium-bodied Towne Shopper was a prototype two-seater for running errands. It had a 2-cylinder, 10.6hp rear engine and weighed 600lb.　　　BE

TOYOTA (J) *1936 to date*
(1) Toyota Automatic Loom Works, Kariya City *1936*
(2) Toyota Motor Co, Ltd, Toyota City *1937 to date*

1910 TOURIST(ii) 7hp 3-wheeler. *Neubauer Collection*

1936 TOYOTA Model AA 6-cylinder saloon. *Toyota Motor Co Ltd*

1943 TOYOTA Model BA 4-cylinder saloon. *Toyota Motor Co Ltd*

1949 TOYOTA Model SA 4-cylinder saloon. *Autocar*

The Toyota Works, a flourishing textile concern, began experimenting with cars and in 1935 completed the A-1 prototype. In the first years of manufacture, Toyota concentrated on the AA and AB models, a 4-door sedan and a tourer respectively, based on the A-1. These machines were powered by 6-cylinder, in-line, ohv engines of 65hp at 3,000rpm, and had bodies reminiscent of the Chrysler Airflow.

In 1938 the design was revised as the model AC, and this was joined by the newly styled 2,258cc AE series in 1939.

During World War 2 a number of experimental types were constructed, including the BA sedan with a 4-cylinder 48bhp engine and the larger B with a 6-cylinder engine of 85bhp and a seven-seater body. When the war was over the SA model was marketed and was the first of the firm's products to use the Toyopet trade mark. In more recent years its use has been limited to machines for the home market, with the Toyota name replacing it on exports.

The Model SA was a neatly styled 2-door sedan with 27bhp, a backbone chassis and independent coil-spring front suspension; a total of 215 cars were built from October 1947 to May 1952. The Toyota firm expanded rapidly, adding many models of cars, trucks and buses to its range. Production boomed from 700 cars a month in 1955, and 11,750 in 1958, to 50,000 by 1964. By 1955 the 1,453cc ohv 4-cylinder Crown was available, with 3-speed synchromesh gearbox, column change, hydraulic brakes, and hypoid final drive. A 1-litre car, first of the Coronas, followed in 1958.

In 1961 the 700 series was introduced and in 1964 the Corona and Crown private cars were redesigned for an increased export trade. In 1967 the Publica 700 was the smallest of the Toyotas, using a 2-cylinder air-cooled engine. The conventional 1,100cc 60bhp Corolla sold in England for £700 and the handsome and well-equipped Corona line was powered by 1½-litre 74bhp and 1.6-litre 95bhp engines. The Crown models had 6- and 8-cylinder units. The Crown Eight was the largest Toyota built for 1967 and contained a 115bhp V-8 engine, and Toyoglide automatic transmission. There were also two sports models with twin-ohc engines, a four and a six, and the big Land Cruiser, a 4-wheel-drive vehicle using Toyota's 3.9-litre push-rod 6-cylinder truck engine.

Like Nissan, Toyota explored Group 7 racing, as well as building up an empire. Hino were absorbed in 1966, their private cars being discontinued shortly afterwards. Daihatsu followed in 1968, which was Toyota's first million year. Meanwhile the Crown series had been re-engineered with perimeter frames, and emerged with the formidable choice of two 2-litre engines (a pushrod four or an ohc six), and four transmissions, 3- or 4-speed manual and 2- or 3-speed automatic. The Crown 8, never a great success, gave way to the unitary-construction Century 8 with 3-litre all-aluminium engine developing 150bhp, and such options as power-assisted steering and air suspension. With an overall length of 16ft 2in, it was one of Japan's largest private cars. The Publica, Corolla and Corona series were continued into 1969. New during 1970 were the Carina and Celica. The former was a conventional pushrod four sold in 1.4-litre and 1.6-litre forms, with live axle and coil rear suspension, bridging the gap between the Corolla and the Corona. The later represented serious international competition for cars like the Fiat 124 Sport and the M.G.B.-GT. It had a 1,588cc dohc 4-cylinder engine developing 115bhp, front disc brakes and a 5-speed all-synchromesh gearbox.

Toyota's 1972 line-up was complex and comprehensive. Rear suspension alternated between orthodox semi-elliptics (Publica, Corona) and live axles with coils. Front disc brakes were standard on the Corona and the Celica, and offered on the more expensive variants of other series. The smallest Toyota was still the 790cc air-cooled flat-twin Publica on a 7ft 1in wheelbase; it was also available with 1-litre and 1.2-litre in-line water-cooled fours. Corollas had 7ft 10in wheelbases, and came with pushrod engines of 1.2, 1.4 or 1.6 litres: a 5-speed gearbox was used on the high-performance SR coupé. The Corolla's two larger engine options were common to the Carina, though the 1600GT ran to two carburettors and dohc. Most Coronas used 1,707cc or 1,858cc single-cam engines and 4-speed gearboxes, though extremes of the range were a 3-speed 1½-litre for the home market, and the 5-speed twin-cam 2-litre GSS with 140bhp. The Celica remained a dohc 1600, the Crown was now available only with 6-cylinder engines (in 2-litre, 2.3-litre or 2.6-litre sizes), and the Century's output was increased to 170bhp. The 4×4 Land Cruisers were continued, these being made under licence in Brazil with Mercedes-Benz diesel engines. Toyotas were also being manufactured or assembled in twelve other countries.　　　　　　　　　　　　　　BE

TRABANT (D) *1959 to date*
VEB Sachsenring Automobilwerk, Zwickau

In 1959 the first Trabant model (the 50) appeared, succeeding the Zwickau P70. The 500cc 2-cylinder 2-stroke engine was based on the P70 engine. In 1962 the engine capacity was increased to 594cc. Like the P70, the Trabant has a fibreglass body and front-wheel drive. Over 300,000 had been made by 1965.　　HON

TRACFORD (F) *1934–1935*
Automobiles Tracford, Gennevilliers, Seine

This was an ingenious conversion of the European 933cc Model Y Ford, on which the engine/gearbox unit was reversed, and the suspension, though still transverse, was independent at front and rear. A longer wheelbase (8ft 8in compared with 7ft 6in) left room for more elegant sporting bodywork to be fitted.　　MCS

1966 TOYOTA 2000GT 2-litre coupé. *Toyota Motor Co Ltd*

1968 TOYOTA Publica 800 saloon. *Toyota Motor Co Ltd*

1973 TOYOTA Crown 2600 Special saloon. *Toyota Motor Co Ltd*

TRACTA (F) *1926–1934*
SA des Automobiles Tracta, Asnières, Seine

Towards the end of the 1920s, several French manufacturers took up front-wheel drive, but only one made a success of it in this period. J.A. Grégoire's Tracta was unusual, too, in that racing cars preceded production cars. Indeed, the Tracta was always primarily a sporting make.

First made in 1926, and raced during 1927, the Tracta was offered to the public at the Paris Salon of the latter year. An ohv 4-cylinder engine of 1,100cc drove the front wheels, with the assistance, if required, of a Cozette supercharger. The 4-speed gearbox was in front of the engine. Sliding-pillar independent front suspension was used, with inverted quarter-elliptics at the rear. The front wheels were pronouncedly crab-tracked, and the front brakes were inboard.

These compact, low-built sports cars were entered consistently in the Le Mans 24 Hours Race, finishing in 1927, taking second place in their class in 1928 and winning it in the following two years. By 1929, there were two models: a two-seater that came just within the 1½-litre racing class, and a 1,600cc four-seater saloon. They were capable of 80mph and nearly 70mph respectively. The latter model was continued until 1934, accompanied by two 6-cylinder types, with 2.7-litre Continental sv and 3-litre Hotchkiss ohv engines.   TRN

TRACTION AÉRIENNE (F) *1921–c.1926*
Sté La Traction Aérienne, Neuilly, Seine

Like the Leyat, the Traction Aérienne was driven by a 4-bladed propeller, powered by a 1½-litre flat-twin engine. With a two-seater saloon body the overall weight was less than 670lb. It had 4-wheel brakes and was steered by the front wheels, unlike the Leyat which had rear wheel steering.

A road test reported that it was a noisy vehicle and had slow acceleration, but that the suspension on rough surfaces was remarkably good. Later models were sold under the names Eolia and Hélica.   GNG

TRACTOBILE (US) *1900–1902*
Pennsylvania Steam Vehicle Co, Inc, Carlisle, Pa.

The Tractobile was an *avant train* attachment for horse-drawn vehicles, but was unique in that it was steam powered. The boiler was made up of five separate units, each with 40 small tubes, and one or more units could be removed for cleaning. Two vertical cylinders acted on each front wheel direct, although it is difficult to see this in surviving photographs. As the Tractobile was an enterprise of E.J. Pennington, it may be wondered whether any ever ran at all, or if they were merely a stock-promotion scheme.   GNG

TRAEGER (D) *1923*
A. Traeger, Freiburg (Silesia)

A small car with a 4-cylinder 5/18PS engine appeared under this name and was produced in limited numbers.   HON

TRAIN (F) *1924–1925*
Motorcycles et Moteurs Train, Courbevoie, Seine

Train were well-known makers of small engines for motorcycles and cyclecars who made a few complete cars as well. They had single-cylinder engines of 344cc.   GNG

TRAK-KART (GB) *1965–1970*
Trak-Kart Co, Enfield, Middlesex

The Trak-Kart KE4, produced by a well-known manufacturer of go-karts, was the first Formula 4 car on public sale. The kit was priced at £274.   DF

TRASK-DETROIT *see* DETROIT STEAM CAR

TRAVELER (i) (US) *1906–1913*
(1) Traveler Motor Car Co, Evansville, Ind. *1906–1910*
(2) Traveler Auto Co, Evansville, Ind. *1911–1913*

Models of the Traveler were of moderate size, with 30 to 36hp 4-cylinder, L-head engines. Both two-seater runabouts and five-seater touring cars were made. All models had selective, 3-speed transmissions and shaft drive.   GMN

TRAVELER (ii) (US) *1914–1915*
Traveler Motor Car Co, Detroit, Mich.

Model 36 of the Traveler (1914) used a 4-cylinder L-head engine of 3.6 litres. It had a 3-speed transmission and a wheelbase of 10ft. A two-seater roadster was priced at $1,275, with a five-seater version at $20 more. Model 48 had a 6-cylinder engine of 5.6 litres, with a wheelbase of 10ft 10in. This model was also made in two- and five-seater versions, the latter selling for $2,000.   GMN

TREBERT (US) *1907*
Trebert Gas Engine Co, Rochester, N.Y.

The Trebert Gas Engine Co was fairly well known for building petrol engines and offered a seven-seater touring car for just one model year. This was on an 8ft 7in wheelbase with semi-elliptical springs in front and platform springs at the

1965 TRABANT 601 Universal 594cc estate car.
VEB Sachsenring Automobilwerke

1927 TRACTA 1,100cc coupé.
Automobielmuseum, Driebergen

1921 TRACTION AÉRIENNE 1,526cc saloon.
Autocar

rear. The 4-cylinder, T-head engine was rated at 30hp and used a 3-speed gearbox and shaft drive. This single model weighed 2,800lb and was priced at $1,850. GMN

TRESKOW (D) 1906–1908
Robert Treskow Motorwagenfabrik, Schönebeck

In addition to motor cycles this small firm produced a car with a 2-cylinder 10PS engine. Production was only on a limited scale. HON

TRIBELHORN (CH) 1902–c.1920
(1) A. Tribelhorn, Feldbach 1902–1918
(2) Electrische Fahrzeuge AG, Altstetten 1918–c.1920

Tribelhorn were mainly builders of electric commercial vehicles, but they made a number of private cars, mostly open two- or four-seater victorias. In 1918 they introduced a 3-wheeler chassis with single front wheel and two-seater body with batteries under the seat. This chassis was widely used by the Swiss Post Office, and demand by them and other commercial customers prevented many private 3-wheelers from being made. GNG

TRIBET (F) 1909–1914
Tribet et Cie, Villeneuve-la-Garenne, Seine

Tribet cars were conventional shaft-driven cars made originally in two models, a 4-cylinder 8/10hp and a 6-cylinder 12/16hp, both with circular radiators. Two 4-cylinder cars were entered for the 1910 Coupe des Voiturettes, but both broke down. By 1913 there were three models, of 8, 10 and 12hp, all with 4-cylinder engines. GNG

TRIBUNE (US) 1913–1914
Tribune Motor Co, Detroit, Mich.

This company was formed by L.G. Hupp who had been with Hupmobile. The Tribune was a light five-seater car with a 4-litre 4-cylinder Buda engine. GMN

TRI-CAR (US) 1955
The Tri-Car Co, Wheatland, Pa.

Known as the Suburbanette, the Tri-Car was a 3-wheeled coupé with a three-seater fibreglass body. A Lycoming vertical twin engine drove the single rear wheel through a Westinghouse-Schneider torque converter, and the car had Goodrich rubber suspension. A maximum speed of 65mph was claimed. GNG

TRICOLET (US) 1904–1906
(1) Richards Automobile & Gas Engine Co, Guthrie, Ind.
(2) H. Pokorney Automobile & Gas Engine Co, Indianapolis, Ind.

This 3-wheeler, originally known as the Pokorney, had an air-cooled, 2-cylinder engine in the rear. Its two-seater body was mounted on a 5ft 6in wheelbase. The planetary transmission had no reverse. A tiller steered the single front wheel. A 4-wheeled model was available for an extra $25. GMN

TRIDENT (i) (F/GB) 1919–1920
The Trident was a curious 3-wheeler powered by an 8hp 2-cylinder engine mounted on, and driving, the single front wheel. The engine was on the near side, while the 3-speed gearbox, clutch and magneto were on the off side. Suspension was by four laterally-mounted and interconnected cantilever springs. The Trident seated two in tandem, and alternative models planned included a one-passenger taxicab and a delivery van. The prototypes were made in France, but it was announced in August 1919 that the Trident was soon to be made in England by Vickers Ltd. Delivery was quoted as six to eight months, and the price £160, both figures quite encouraging for the period. However, it is unlikely that British production ever started. GNG

TRIDENT (ii) (GB) 1965 to date
(1) Trident Cars Ltd, Woodbridge, Suffolk 1965–1968
(2) Trident Cars Ltd, Ipswich, Suffolk 1968 to date

Much interest was shown in the Fiore-bodied T.V.R. Trident exhibited at Geneva in 1965. However, when the firm underwent its next metamorphosis, this design was sold to W.J. Last, of Woodbridge, one of their agents. Development work continued in 1966, aiming for 3-car-a-week production in 1967. A 4,727cc Ford V-8 engine was fitted in a cruciform-based boxed platform chassis. Front suspension was by coil, and rear conventional half-elliptics. Four-seater open or closed bodies were offered. During 1967 the Ford-engined car was replaced by the new Clipper with Chrysler V-8; it incorporated a much-revised chassis and some styling changes within the same overall concept. A smaller model, the Ford V-6-engined Venturer, was introduced at this time and the range was supplemented further in 1971 with the announcement of the Tycoon with 2.5-litre Triumph engine. DF

TRIMOBILE see AVON

TRI-MOTO (US) 1900–1901
Western Wheel Works, Chicago, Ill.

1919 TRIBELHORN electric two-seater. *PTT-Museum, Berne*

1919 TRIDENT(i) 8hp 3-wheeler. *Autocar*

1965 TRIDENT(ii) 4.7-litre coupé. *Trident Cars Ltd*

1941 TRIPPEL Type SG 6 2½-litre amphibious car. *Neubauer Collection*

Also known as the Crescent Tri-Moto, this was a very light front-wheel-drive 3-wheeler on the lines of the Lawson Motor Wheel made in England. Steering was by tiller. It was sold by the American Bicycle Company, which was an enterprise of Colonel Pope.   GNG

TRIOULEYRES (F) 1896
Compagnie Générale des Automobiles, Paris

This was one of the Benz derivatives which appeared during the 1890s. It had a 5hp horizontal engine at the rear, and used belt drive to the countershaft, and final drive by chain. Two- and four-seater cars ran in the 1896 Paris-Marseilles race.   GNG

TRIPPEL (D) 1934–1944; 1950–1952
(1) Trippelwerke, Homburg/Saar 1934–1940
(2) Trippelwerke GmbH, Molsheim 1940–1944
(3) Protek-Gesellschaft für Industrie-entwicklungen mbH, Tutlingen; Stuttgart 1950–1952

The name Trippel became associated with amphibious cars when Hans Trippel introduced his first vehicle of this type in 1932. Several versions were developed, production beginning with the SG 6, a 4-wheel-drive car with a 4-cylinder Adler engine; it later acquired a 6-cylinder $2\frac{1}{2}$-litre Opel unit. Another model, which appeared in 1937, was the SK 6, with a 2-litre Adler engine and front-wheel drive. Both types were developed further and after 1940 were produced in the Bugatti works at Molsheim, Bas-Rhin, which was under German occupation at that time. A new type, the SG 7, had a rear-mounted air-cooled Tatra V-8 engine and 4-wheel drive.

In 1950 Trippel introduced a new small car – not an amphibian. It had a rear-mounted opposed twin 498cc Zündapp engine and an all-enveloping body. It was manufactured in limited numbers. In 1953 it reappeared as the Marathon, but did not go into full-scale production. A few were built under licence by SIOP of France using a rear-mounted Dyna-Panhard engine. Production under licence was also planned in 1957 in Germany, but this project came to nothing. At the 1959 Geneva Show Trippel exhibited another amphibian, the Eurocar, which was later marketed as the Amphicar.   HON

TRIUMPH (i) (US) 1900–1901
Triumph Motor Vehicle Co, Chicago, Ill.

This company made an electric stanhope known as the Ellis, and announced that they would accept orders for petrol or steam cars, for delivery in 90 days.
                                                                    GNG

TRIUMPH (ii) (US) 1906–1909
Triumph Motor Car Co, Chicago, Ill.

These were open cars in four- and five-seater models. Their engines were 4-cylinder units of 30hp and 45hp. In 1907 this car used 'the *only* self-contained, automatic, self-starting motor in the world'. This starting method stored exhaust gases in a tank under the seat, at a pressure of 125psi. This gas could be bled back into the cylinders for starting.   GMN

TRIUMPH (iii) (GB) 1923 to date
(1) Triumph Cycle Co, Ltd, Coventry, Warwickshire 1923–1929
(2) Triumph Motor Co, Ltd, Coventry, Warwickshire 1930 to date

This famous motor-cycle factory made a tricar in 1903, but 4-wheelers were not offered until 1923, when a 1.4-litre sv 4-cylinder 10/20 with a Ricardo-designed engine and 4-speed gearbox was listed at £430; production was undertaken in the factory formerly occupied by Dawson (iii). This gave way in 1925 to a 1.9-litre 13/30 at £495, the first British car to have Lockheed contracting-type hydraulic brakes. Neither this nor its 15hp successor made much impression, but in 1928 Triumph introduced the 832cc sv Super 7, with unit gearbox, hydraulic brakes, and worm final drive, which sold well both at home and overseas. There was a supercharged sports version listed at £250 in 1929–30, and the manufacture of small family saloons of superior quality was pursued until 1933–34. Ribbon-type radiators were featured in 1930, and in 1931 came a 1.2-litre small six, the Scorpion, really a Super 7 with 2 extra cylinders, and endowed with very low gearing. Ioe Coventry-Climax power units made their appearance in the Super 9 of 1932, when Triumph saloons had pillarless doors, and 4-speed gearboxes were adopted. The bigger 1933 models had electric fuel pumps, and during the season a 1,122cc ioe Ten joined the range at £225.

Though these family models were still being made in 1934, there were also the more sporting Glorias with 1,100cc 4-cylinder and $1\frac{1}{2}$-litre 6-cylinder ioe power units, cruciform-braced frames, and free wheels, which in open form could exceed 70mph: one of these, driven by Donald Healey (responsible for the design of 1936–39 Triumphs) won the light-car class of the 1934 Monte Carlo Rally. An abortive and very Alfa-Romeo-like 2-litre twin-ohc supercharged straight-8 was listed at £1,225 in 1935, but that year's Gloria-Vitesse models were far more successful, especially in 2-litre, 6-cylinder form. Metallic finish was available, and the saloon models were sold with screenwashers as standard equipment.

In 1936 the car and motor-cycle businesses were divorced, and from 1937 onwards the cars became heavier; synchromesh was adopted, Triumph-built engines

1951 TRIPPEL 498cc coupé. *Autocar*

1927 TRIUMPH(iii) 15hp saloon. *Michael Sedgwick*

1929 TRIUMPH(iii) Super 7 supercharged sports car. *Autocar*

1939 TRIUMPH(iii) Dolomite 2-litre roadster. *Autocar*

1946 TRIUMPH(iii) 1800 saloon. *Standard-Triumph Ltd*

1965 TRIUMPH(iii) 1300 saloon. *Standard-Triumph Ltd*

1973 TRIUMPH(iii) Toledo 1½-litre saloon. *Standard-Triumph Ltd*

with full overhead valves supplanted the ioe Coventry-Climax units, and models ranged from a 1½-litre, 4-cylinder Gloria saloon at £288 up to the 1.8-litre, 4-cylinder and 2-litre 6-cylinder Dolomites, with ugly fencer's mask radiator grilles at £348 and £368 respectively.

The Dolomites were comprehensively equipped, with centralized chassis lubrication and radio as an factory extra, and the handsome if rather American looking roadster coupés of 1938–40 were regular *concours* winners.

From the summer of 1938 only Dolomites were catalogued, the smallest model being a compact 1½-litre (actually 1,767cc) on a 9ft wheelbase at £313, but during 1939 a conventionally-styled 12hp sports saloon appeared at £285. Only 50 were made since Triumph went into receivership just before World War 2, and when the cars reappeared after VJ Day they were products of Standard, their new 1800 having the 65bhp 1.8-litre ohv 4-cylinder unit made for the 1½-litre Jaguar. Other features were Girling brakes, and an unusual right-hand column change for the 4-speed gearbox. Both the roadster at £799 and the saloon at £831 were traditionally styled, the latter having a razor-edge body of the type favoured by British specialist coach-builders in the later 1930s.

By 1949, 2.1-litre Standard Vanguard engines and 3-speed gearboxes had been adopted, and 1950 brought a curious little razor-edged 2-door saloon, the Mayflower, with a 10hp sv engine, which persisted until 1953.

In that year the first of a successful line of sports cars appeared, descended from an abortive 1950 design with retractable headlamps, fully aerodynamic bodywork with power top, and overdrive gearbox, which had been a casualty of the Korean War. The new TR2 weighed only 1,888lb, had a 2-litre, 90bhp development of the Vanguard engine, independent coil-and-wishbone front suspension, 2LS Lockheed brakes, hypoid final drive, and the useful combination of over 100mph and 25mpg in regular service. It distinguished itself in competition, early successes including an outright win in the 1954 R.A.C. Rally and the team award in the 1956 Alpine Rally, as well as being an outstanding dollar-earner. The TR3, its successor, acquired front disc brakes in 1956, and was made until 1962. The power unit was adopted by Morgan (1954), Swallow Doretti (1954), Peerless (ii) (1958), and its successor Warwick (ii) (1960).

After the discontinuation of the razor-edged 2.1-litre Renown saloon early in 1955, the TR was the staple Triumph until mid-1959, when the Herald saloon appeared, using a development of the 948cc Standard 10 engine in a separate chassis. It has all-round independent suspension (the first small British family saloon to be so equipped), a collapsible steering wheel, and Michelotti styling. It could be bought in 38bhp single carburettor and 50bhp twin-carburettor versions for prices starting at £702. This model did not really prosper until Standard-Triumph was taken over by Leyland in 1961, when a more powerful 1,147cc development with the option of front disc brakes appeared, followed two years later by the 12/50 with disc brakes as standard, and a sunshine roof. A 1.6-litre 6-cylinder development with four head-lamps, the Vitesse came in 1962, and the Spitfire sports two-seater was a further Herald derivative announced for 1963. 4-cylinder Triumph engines are used by Amphicar, Bond (iii), and Fairthorpe.

In 1962 the TR4 with restyled bodywork, a 2.1-litre engine, rack-and-pinion steering, and all-synchromesh box, was introduced, acquiring independent rear suspension as the TR4A in 1965, while the Triumph features were also incorporated in a 90bhp 2-litre 6-cylinder saloon, the 2000, which was a successful introduction in 1964. Triumph's new car in 1966 was the 1300, still with all-synchromesh gearbox, all-round independent suspension, and front disc brakes, but also featuring front-wheel drive and a 61hp development of the basic Herald engine. 1967 Vitesses had the 2-litre engine, also used in the new GT6 hardtop coupé, a Spitfire derivative. A TR5 sports car, with a 2½-litre 6-cylinder fuel injection engine at last replacing the tough old Vanguard unit and a 75bhp TC version of the 1300 saloon, were introduced in 1968. It was also announced that sohc 4-cylinder engines were being manufactured for SAAB's new 99 model, though all the new 1969 Triumphs retained push-rod engines. These included revised versions of the GT6 and Vitesse with wishbone rear suspension, and a more expensive companion for the 2000, the 2.5 PI using a detuned TR6 fuel-injection unit; this one was rallied by the works, the Culcheth and Syer car coming 2nd in the 1970 World Cup event. In 1970 Triumph introduced the Stag, a luxury sporting 2+2 powered by a 3-litre dohc V-8 engine of their own design developing 145bhp. This featured alternator ignition, a choice of synchromesh and overdrive or automatic transmission, all-independent springing, power-assisted rack and pinion steering, and vacuum servo brakes with discs at the front. A big and heavy car weighing 3,020lb, it carried semi-convertible coachwork with built-in rollbar.

In the 1971 range was a Herald replacement, the Toledo 2-door saloon. This combined the 1300 structure with the 1,296cc Herald 13/60 engine driving the rear wheels. Rear suspension was by live axle and coils, and all-drum brakes were standard, though front disc brakes, four doors and a 1,500cc engine were used on an export-only model. The 1300 was replaced by a more powerful 1500, and in August 1971 4-door Toledos in basic form reached the home market. That summer the Herald/Vitesse range was finally phased out (apart from Indian production of 'Standard' Heralds) and after many delays Triumph's medium-sized luxury Dolomite was finally launched at the beginning of 1972. This followed Toledo lines with front disc brakes, but was powered by a 91bhp twin-carburettor edition of the 1,854cc ohc engine as supplied to SAAB. Principal 1973 improvements were the standardization of front disc brakes on the Toledo, and of overdrive on manual versions of the 2.5 PI and Stag.   MCS

TRIUMPH (iv) (D) *1933*
Triumph Werke AG, Nuremberg
   This well-known motor-cycle manufacturer built a few 3-wheeled coupés powered by 350cc engines driving the single rear wheels.   GNG

TRIVER (E) *1952*
   The Triver was a small rear-engined coupé with narrow-track rear wheels on the Isetta pattern. The engine was a 2-cylinder Hispano-Villiers.   JRV

TROJAN (GB) *1922–1936; 1961–1965*
(1) Leyland Motors Ltd, Kingston-on-Thames, Surrey *1922–1928*
(2) Trojan Ltd, Croydon, Surrey *1928–1965*
   The Trojan, designed by Leslie Hounsfield, was a comparatively rare case of an extremely unconventional design seizing and holding a good-sized, faithful market for a number of years. Perhaps the nearest analogy is the Hanomag Kommisbrot in Germany, at the same time. It was strange, in the first place, to find Leyland Motors, manufacturers not only of trucks but also of the ultra-luxurious Leyland Eight, venturing into the opposite extreme of truly elementary motoring. Like the Ford, the Trojan aimed at low price, at simplicity of driving and maintenance, and at being a universal tool. There analogies ended. A horizontal, 2-stroke, 4-cylinder engine lived under the floor. On pre-1914 prototypes it had been vertically mounted between the seats. It had a cubic capacity of 1½ litres, but developed only 10bhp. Transmission was by a 2-speed epicyclic gearbox (an important feature, because it provided an easy gearchange) and duplex chain to a solid axle. Although the engine was slow-revving, such power as was developed came in at very low engine speeds. The Trojan's low-speed pulling power in general and hill-climbing ability in particular, became a legend. Its oddities went much further. For the sake of cheapness and reliability, solid tyres were fitted on most of the early Trojans and were still available in 1929. Passenger comfort was looked after adequately by the very long and soft cantilever springs at each corner. Those who disagreed could have pneumatic tyres if they liked. The chassis consisted of a flat steel box, to which was attached a roomy, if hideous, open four-seater body. By 1925, the price was only £125, making the Trojan the cheapest British four-seater on the market. It was also the slowest, and never had front wheel brakes, but its advantages outweighed its drawbacks for many customers who cared nothing for appearances.
   From 1928, manufacture was taken over by Trojan Ltd. By this time, the market was hardening against even the most tenacious of unconventional vehicles, and also, a more modern and attractive design was called for. The outcome was the RE-type, which retained the old car's engine and transmission, cloaked in a good-looking fabric body with low lines and cycle-type wings. The engine was now at the rear, driving forward by chain. There were three forward speeds, and because pneumatic balloon tyres were universal, half-elliptic springs were used. However, the RE was little faster, still lacked front wheel brakes, and was more expensive. It was a doomed attempt to compromise, that retained the fundamentals of an obsolete design. Well into the 1930s, the primeval type was still made to special order, but that was now the limit of the design's popularity, except in the commercial vehicle field. A centrifugal clutch was incorporated in 1932 and a fluid flywheel two years later, but then the RE was gone. At the 1935 Show they exhibited the Mastra, a 2.2-litre 6-cylinder car, still a 2-stroke and still rear-engined, but with synchromesh, fwb, heater, and built-in jacks. It did not go into production and no more passenger cars were made until 1962, when the company began to make, under the name of Trojan 200, the Heinkel 'bubble-car', which had gone out of production in its native Germany. By way of contrast, Trojan also took over production of the Elva sports car.   TRN

TROLL (N) *1956*
Troll Plastik- og Bilindustri, Lunde i Telemark
   The only post-war Norwegian car, the Troll used a 700cc 2-cylinder 2-stroke engine of Gutbrod design (they purchased parts from the bankrupt Gutbrod company), a plastic two-seater coupé body and 4-wheel independent suspension. Of the planned first batch of 15 cars, only 5 were made before the company failed.   OB

TRUE (US) *1914*
Badger Brass Mfg Co, Kenosha, Wisc.
   The True cyclecar carried two persons in tandem with the driver in the rear. It had a 2-cylinder, 10hp engine; the wheelbase was 8ft 8in.   GMN

TRUFFAULT (F) *1907–1908*
Sté des Automobiles Truffault, Paris
   The Truffault was a belt-driven light car powered by a single-cylinder engine, probably a De Dion. Truffaults ran in the Coupe des Voiturettes races of 1907 and 1908, but without any distinction.   GNG

1928 TROJAN Apollo 10hp saloon. *Trojan Ltd*

1930 TROJAN Model RE 10hp Purley saloon. *Trojan Ltd*

1956 TROLL 700cc saloon. *Aftenposten, Oslo*

1915 TRUMBULL 13hp two-seater. *Neubauer Collection*

1947 TUCKER 6-cylinder sedan. *Henry Ford Museum, Dearborn, Mich.*

TRUMBULL (US) *1913–1915*
(1) American Cyclecar Co, Bridgeport, Conn. *1913–1914*
(2) Trumbull Motor Car Co, Bridgeport, Conn. *1915*

This make succeeded the American, made by the American Cyclecar Co of Detroit. The Trumbull was apparently superior to the typical cyclecar, having a water-cooled 4-cylinder engine of 1.7 litres. Friction transmission and double chain drive were used on the early models, but most Trumbulls had conventional transmission and rear axle.　　　　　　　GMN

TRUNER (GB) *1913*
Turner & Co, Willesden, London N.W.

The Truner was so called in order to avoid confusion with the Turner cars made at Wolverhampton. It was a cyclecar powered by an 8hp J.A.P. V-twin engine, with final chain drive to the offside rear wheel.　　　GNG

T.S.T. (GB) *1922*
This was a 3-wheeler steered from a side-car like the Seal. It had a single-cylinder Blackburne engine, a motor-cycle gearbox, and chain final drive.　　　GNG

TSUKUBA (J) *1935–c.1937*
Tokyo Jidosha Seizo Co Ltd, Tokyo

The Tsukuba was an unconventional light car powered by a 750cc V-4 sv engine driving the front wheels. It had a 3-speed gearbox, and was available in three body styles: two-seater, four-seater tourer and saloon. Only 50 cars were manufactured.　　　GNG

TUAR (F) *1913–1925*
A. Morin, Thouars, Deux-Sèvres

André Morin had been concerned with Decauville and Cornilleau et Ste-Beuve, but formed his own company in 1913 and chose this remote hill-top town. Orthodox light cars were assembled from proprietary components and decked with attractive bodies. Morin favoured 4-cylinder Chapuis-Dornier engines, in such sizes as 1,244cc, 1,495cc, 1,503cc and 1,821cc. Fivet (1,327cc and 1,496cc) and later C.I.M.E. (1,601cc 4-cylinder and 1,493cc 6-cylinder) engines were also used. A few cars were powered by Ruby, including a dainty racer with which Morin achieved some success at La Baule. Generally, the running gear was the cheapest that Malicet et Blin could supply, although some models employed a Gleason rear axle unit. Michelin disc wheels were mostly fitted, with D.F. as an alternative. In 1922 the firm had over 50 employees, but in 1925 the competition from popular makes from industrial areas finally proved too fierce, and production ceased at a total figure of about 800.　　　DF

TUCK (US) *1904–1905*
Tuck Petroleum Motor Co, Brooklyn, N.Y.

This car was designed to run on paraffin, and used a 4-cylinder water-cooled engine, of 1-litre capacity. No gearbox was used, as drive was direct, by shaft. The starting system operated by stored exhaust-gas pressure. No reverse gear was used, as it was claimed that the engine was reversible.　　　GMN

TUCKER (i) (US) *1900–1903*
William Tucker, San Jose, Calif.

The Tucker was a crude-looking car with a 2-cylinder air-cooled engine and artillery wheels. About 16 were made.　　　GMN

TUCKER (ii) (US) *1946–1948*
The Tucker Corp, Chicago, Ill.

Designed by the engineer Preston T. Tucker of Ypsilanti, Mich., this car progressed through a number of stages, beginning with the projected Tucker Torpedo sports and ending with the actual Tucker '48 sedan. Innovations were chiefly the work of Tucker and the former Auburn-Cord-Deusenberg stylist Alex Tremulis. Safety was stressed with disc brakes, padded dash, front passenger crash compartment and pop-out windscreen. The 3,600lb car was 5ft 0½in high, had independent suspension and a 10ft 8in wheel base.

Plans for a central steering wheel and front wings that turned with the wheels were shelved, but the three headlights were retained from the original Torpedo design. A flat opposed 9.6-litre engine and a rear wheel double torque direct drive system were also abandoned. The flat opposed 6-cylinder engine ultimately used was developed from a Franklin air-cooled model used on Bell helicopters. It was redesigned as a rear-mounted liquid-cooled sealed-system unit with a compression ratio of 7:1 hydraulic valve lifters and a separate exhaust leading from each cylinder. Advertised as a 150hp machine, the output proved to be somewhat greater.

Of the finished vehicles not all were exactly alike. Most contained a 4-speed manual Y-1 (Ypsilanti) transmission with a pre-selector or electric shift. A few were left with rebuilt Cord transmission, attached during the waiting period for the Y-1 to be finished, and some were built with the R-1 (Rice) Tuckermatic automatic transmission which had less than thirty basic parts. 49 examples were assembled in a former Dodge aircraft engine plant in Chicago before the company's demise. All too few Tuckers exist to prove what kind of performance could have been expected from the Model '48, but some rare units in the hands of private collectors are reported to be running well after many thousands of miles, with good fuel consumption figures and a maximum speed of 120mph.

After a costly court battle with the Securities Exchange Commission, in which he was charged with fraud and violations of its regulations, Tucker was vindicated in 1950. With much of his holdings wiped out, Tucker abandoned further plans until 1952, when he planned to build a small car in Brazil. Negotiations were still pending when Preston Tucker died in 1956.   BE

TUDHOPE (CDN) *1908–1913*

(1) Tudhope-McIntyre Co, Orillia, Ont. *1908–1909*
(2) Tudhope Motor Company Limited, Orillia, Ont. *1910–1913*

Several thousand automobiles were turned out by this firm, which had been making horse-drawn vehicles since 1865. In 1908 and 1909 the company built the Tudhope-McIntyre, a highwheeler using the U.S. McIntyre engine and available as a roadster, touring or pickup truck and available in 15 models. A flash fire destroyed the factory in 1909, and when a new one was finished it turned to production of the 1911 U.S. Everitt, though all the parts were made in Canada.

For 1912 the cars were updated and their name changed from Everitt to Tudhope, but sales lagged. The addition of electric lighting and a new streamlined six for 1913 did not help, and the company went bankrupt that summer.   HD

TUI *see* LEDA (ii)

TULSA (US) *1917–1923*

Tulsa Automobile Corp, Tulsa, Okla.

The Tulsa was one of the few cars built in Oklahoma. It used Herschell-Spillman 4- and 6-cylinder engines. Production was limited and ceased in 1922, cars remaining in stock being designated 1923 models.   KM

TUNG-FENG *see* DONG-FENG

TURBO (i) (CH) *1920–1921*

Automobilfabrik G.W. Müller, Oerlikon

The Turbo was an unconventional light car powered by an ohv 5-cylinder radial engine of 1½ litres' capacity, with air cooling by copper fins. The engine was front-mounted, and drive was by shaft to the rear axle. Body styles were an open two-seater or a four-seater saloon.   GNG

TURBO (ii) (D) *1923–1924*

Turbo Motoren AG, Stuttgart

The German Turbo cars were of similar design to the Swiss ones, being the work of G.W. Müller after he had abandoned production in his own country. They were made in two sizes: 6/25PS (1,540cc) and 8/32PS (1,980cc).   HON

TURCAT-MÉRY (F) *1898–1928*

Automobile Turcat-Méry SA, Marseilles

Léon Turcat and his brother-in-law Simon Méry carried out trials with examples of Panhards and Peugeots before starting work on their first experimental vehicle in 1896. This had tiller steering, a front-mounted horizontal 4-cylinder engine with coil ignition, chain drive, and pneumatic tyres. A 2.6-litre vertical 4 powered their 1899 Model A, which had a 5-speed gearbox and 2 reverse speeds, and this had given way by 1901 to a more conventional twin on Panhard lines with only 3 forward speeds. At this juncture the partners, who were short of working capital, signed an agreement with De Dietrich, under which they would be responsible for the design of cars for that firm; in effect the car on which De Dietrichs of Turcat-Méry type were based was a 16hp 4-cylinder with automatic inlet valves, side chain drive, and lt magneto ignition, capable of 50mph.

Subsequently parallel types were marketed by both firms, and in 1904 there were identical 12.8-litre De Dietrichs and Turcat-Mérys in the French Gordon Bennett Eliminating Trials, Rougier's example of the latter make being selected to represent France at Homburg; it finished 3rd in the actual race. The A.C.F. refused to countenance such duplication in 1905, in which year Turcat and Méry produced an interesting 6-wheeler, with interconnected suspension and chain drive to the centre pair of wheels, which was subsequently taken up by Lorraine-Dietrich. Their first six of 1907 retained lt ignition and chain drive, but was of L-head type. Engine capacity was 10.2 litres. The 1908 6.3-litre Type FM was also virtually a Lorraine-Dietrich, but this gave way to 2.6-litre and 3.3-litre shaft-driven cars in 1909. A Turcat-Méry won the first Monte Carlo Rally of all, in 1911. Conventional L-head monobloc 4-cylinder machines were made in the 1912–14 period, with thermo-syphon cooling, magneto ignition, 4-speed gearboxes, and bevel drive. Capacities were 2.6 litres, 3.3 litres, 4.1 litres, 4.7 litres and 6.3 litres. Splash lubrication and quadrant change were found on the smallest; the big Turcat-Mérys had pressure lubrication and elegant V-radiators, and the 35hp had the refinement of a bell as a warning against falling oil pressure.

Post-war production was concentrated on the '15/25', a long-stroke 3-litre of rather archaic design with fixed head, cone clutch and foot transmission brake, which cost £1,050 as a chassis in England. V-radiators were now standard. Finances were

1906 TUDHOPE-McINTYRE motor buggy.
Hugh Durnford

1924 TURBO(ii) 6/25PS two-seater. *Neubauer Collection*

1913 TURCAT-MÉRY 25hp tourer. Coachwork by Guffault. *Autocar*

1901 TURGAN-FOY 6hp tonneau. *The Veteran Car Club of Great Britain*

1908 TURICUM 10/12hp tourer. *Swiss Museum of Transport & Communications, Lucerne*

1922 TURNER(ii) 14/30hp all-weather tourer. *M.A. Harrison*

uncertain, and two reorganizations followed rapidly, the first in 1921 and the second in 1924. SV cars were still made in 1923, but there was also a very clean and advanced 2.8-litre ohc type with detachable head, dual coil ignition, plate clutch, and uncoupled 4-wheel brakes. This lasted only one season, for in 1924 Turcat-Méry came up with the UG-type, also an ohc model, but with fixed head, a capacity of 2.4 litres and proper coupled brakes, which survived until the end of production.

From 1926 onward the company had recourse to proprietary power units in a vain attempt to widen the make's appeal, starting with a 1.2-litre 7CV using the ohv C.I.M.E.-engine, and the S.C.A.P.-powered 1.6-litre Type VF, also ohv. In 1927 there were two small sv sixes using 1.2-litre and 1.7-litre C.I.M.E. engines, and even a 2.3-litre push-rod straight-8 using a S.C.A.P. unit. Operations ceased in 1928, and though a company under the control of Monnerot-Dumaine continued to list Turcat-Mérys up to 1933, this firm was merely offering parts and service, and disposing of unsold stocks of cars. MCS

TURGAN-FOY (F) 1899–1906
Turgan, Foy et Cie, Levallois-Perret, Seine

The first Turgan-Foy cars used the unusual Filtz engine, in which two horizontal pistons each drove a separate vertical crankshaft. These were geared to a central vertical shaft with a horizontal flywheel at the bottom, from which drive was by belt to a 4-speed gearbox. Final drive was by single or double chain. The engine originally developed 4½hp, later increased to 6 or 8hp, while 1901 models used shaft drive to the gearbox.

The Filtz design was dropped after 1902, and replaced by a range of conventional cars with 16 or 24hp 4-cylinder engines and shaft drive. 24 or 60hp chain-drive cars were offered in addition to a 20hp shaft-drive model in 1905, but the company was concentrating increasingly on commercial vehicles, both steam and petrol. These, and the later private cars, were generally known simply as Turgans, rather than Turgan-Foys. GNG

TURICUM (CH) 1904–1914
Automobilfabrik Turicum AG, Uster, Zürich

Designed and built by Martin Fischer, the prototype Turicum light car had a small single-cylinder air-cooled engine, final drive by long chain, and steering by two pedals. His second car retained the unusual steering, and introduced a feature which was to characterize the cars until the end of production: friction drive. The first production cars used wheel steering, but retained the air-cooled single-cylinder engine, friction transmission and chain final drive. The engine developed 7hp, and had square dimensions of 100 × 100mm (785cc). An unusual feature of these early Turicums was that the wheels had nine spokes. In 1908 4-cylinder water-cooled models were introduced, and at the end of that year, Martin Fischer left the company to make cars under his own name. A short-lived 2-cylinder car was made in 1909, and thereafter Turicum concentrated on fours ranging from a 10/12hp 1,608cc to a 16/20hp 2,613cc. GNG

TURNER (i) (US) 1900–1901
Turner Automobile Co, Philadelphia, Pa.

This company made very light voiturettes with bicycle-type tubular frames and rear-mounted engines. 1¼ and 3hp engines were used in the 3-wheelers, called Lilliputian and Gadabout, and a 3hp engine in the Runabout 4-wheeler. GNG

TURNER (ii) (GB) 1906–1907; 1911–1930
Turner's Motor Manufacturing Co, Ltd, Wolverhampton, Staffs.

One of the more interesting aspects of this company's operations is the diversity of machines they produced for other firms. Up to 1906 their staple product had been the Turner-Miesse steam car, but for the 1907 season only they brought out a 20/25hp Seymour-Turner petrol-car, made for Seymours of London. This was a conventional 4.1-litre, L-head 4-cylinder vehicle with ht magneto ignition, 4-speed gearbox, gate change, and shaft drive. Steam then engaged all their efforts again until 1911, when they introduced the 1,100cc V-twin Turner cyclecar with tubular frame, 2-speed constant-mesh gearbox and worm drive, and cycle-type wings.

A similar gearbox and transmission were used in the Ten of 1912, which had a 4-cylinder sv engine and sold for £200, while there was also a more conventional 2.1-litre bevel-driven Fifteen at £320.

After the demise of the steamers in 1913, the 10hp car came to the fore, now with 3 forward speeds; there was also a 4-speed sporting version with a V-radiator and the unusual combination of wire wheels and detachable rims, at £250. The sub-variants of this Ten were made for outside companies. The J.B., intended for sale in the Colonies by John Birch and Co, had a raised ground clearance and the sports car's wire wheels, while the Universal of 1914 (sometimes regarded as a make in its own right) was a standard chassis fitted with drophead coupé bodywork and electric lighting as standard, and retailing at £250 (or at £276 5s with a starter). A bigger 12/20hp 2.2-litre on similar lines (also listed in Universal form) was on the market by the outbreak of World War 1.

Turner's post-war private car production was on a very modest scale, and did not get under way again until 1922, though in the immediate post-1918 period the firm built Varley-Woods chassis for H.S. Motors Ltd of London. The Turners proper were still worm-drive 4-cylinder machines with sv monobloc engines; 1.8-litre models had fixed cylinder heads whereas those on the 2.3-litre cars were detachable, and 4-speed gearboxes were standard. In 1923 the smaller Turner was fitted with a 1½-litre sv Dorman engine with a 3-bearing crankshaft and detachable head, and at the same time bevel drive was adopted; also bevel-driven was a 2.1-litre Colonial model of 1924 with the ohv Meadows unit, which first supplemented and then supplanted the 14/30hp Turner.

After 1926 only the 12hp was made, but though front-wheel brakes were standardized for 1928, this was virtually the end. Even the buyers' guides ceased to quote the make after 1930. The company, however, remained active as manufacturers of components, and as late as 1954 they announced a complete fwd unit suitable for mini-buses. This used their own make of 1.4-litre, 2-cylinder, 2-stroke supercharged diesel engines, developing 37.5bhp. MCS

TURNER (iii) (GB) 1951–1966
Turner Sports Cars Ltd, Wolverhampton, Staffs.

John H. Turner produced an unsuccessful 500cc 4-cylinder Formula 3 engine, and experimented with larger units, before turning to sports car production. The recipe of a simple, straightforward tubular chassis with ifs, proprietary axle parts and lightweight body was usually adhered to. Early cars used a variety of engines – Ford Zephyr, Lea-Francis, Vauxhall, and so on, before the Austin A30 found favour, with the Coventry-Climax as a racing alternative. A few single-seaters were also made in the mid 'fifties. Tubular re-inforced fibreglass bodies became the recognized wear, and were sometimes part-stressed. Some models had torsion-bar irs; later on, Armstrong coil/damper units were used. The 950 open two-seater, with B.M.C. 'A' mechanical parts, was available from 1957 to 1965 in various forms; less long-lived models used the FWA Coventry-Climax and Ford 105E, 109E, and 116E engines, although Ford engines were used rather later than B.M.C. Most cars sold in Britain were in kit form, but the greater part of production was exported. DF

TURNER-MIESSE (GB) 1902–1913
Turner's Motor Manufacturing Co Ltd, Wolverhampton, Staffs.

This was the Belgian Miesse steamer built under licence in Britain, and it outlasted its prototype by at least seven years. The design featured a flash-type boiler mounted under the bonnet and a 3-cylinder single-acting engine; the burner could serve as a pilot. In appearance it resembled a petrol car of its period, with a De Dion-style bonnet, frontal condenser, armoured wood frame, and final drive by side chains. A 10hp model cost £430, and more powerful variants followed: a sixteen at £640 in 1904, when Turner acquired the Wulfruna cycle works, and a 20hp at £750 in 1906, when Turner-Miesses appeared with an angular bonnet with the condenser perched untidily in front. 1908 brought a big 30 with pressed-steel frame, single-chain drive, and a 'radiator' in the Mors style, while the firm entered the low-priced field with a shaft-driven 10hp two-seater, also steel-framed, at £295.

A year later there were a four-seater 10 and a bigger, shaft-driven 12, but Turner's acquisition of the Laurin-Klement agency showed the way their development was going, and from 1911 onwards petrol cars predominated, these being sold under the Turner name. Shaft-driven steam cars were offered for the last time in 1913, in 10hp, 15hp and 20hp ratings. MCS

TURRELL see ACCLES-TURRELL

T.V.D. (B) 1923–1925
Éts Thiriar et Van den Daele, Brussels

Announced in 1920, the T.V.D. did not go into production until 1922 or 1923. It was a conventional light car powered by 4-cylinder engines of 1,094cc or 1,496cc. It was a neat-looking, well-made little car, but the company failed through lack of capital. GNG

T.V.R. (GB) 1954 to date
(1) Layton Engineering, Blackpool, Lancs. 1954–1957
(2) Layton Sports Cars Ltd, Blackpool, Lancs. 1957–1962
(3) Grantura Engineering Ltd, Blackpool, Lancs. 1962–1963
(4) T.V.R. Cars Ltd, Blackpool, Lancs. 1964–1965
(5) T.V.R. Engineering Ltd, Blackpool, Lancs. 1965 to date

Trevor Wilkinson commenced production in the tubular chassis market, mainly for Ford components, before graduating to complete kits in 1957. The Mark I Grantura of this date was powered by Coventry-Climax or Ford 100E, and independently suspended by courtesy of Volkswagen. This model was sold in the United States as the Jomar. The Mark II of 1960 retained a similar brief two-seater fibreglass body, with Coventry-Climax 1,216cc, Ford 105E or M.G.A. engine. The Mark III, with a new tubular chassis designed by John Turner to incorporate double wishbone suspension, was introduced in 1962. This model was raced extensively, and earned the Freddie Dixon Trophy for T. Entwistle in 1963. The Ford V8-engined Griffith then appeared, and continued as a T.V.R. model after the Griffith American company had folded up. 1965 saw the Fiore-bodied Trident version of this car, later to be developed as a separate marque, based on the large Austin-Healey chassis. In 1966 the Mark IV GT was introduced, with the latest

c.1960 TURNER(iii) 948cc sports car. *Autosport*

1905 TURNER-MIESSE 16hp landaulette. *Autocar*

1954 T.V.R. (prototype) 1.2-litre coupé. *Autosport*

1966 T.V.R. 1600 coupé. *T.V.R. Engineering Ltd*

1910 TWOMBLY(ii) 40hp limousine. *Autocar*

1905 TWYFORD 10hp tourer. *Keith Marvin Collection*

1912 TYSELEY 8/10hp coupé. *Autocar*

1800S M.G.B. engine. In 1968 there was a new small model, the Tina, with Hillman Imp engine and Fiore bodywork. The 1800S was available with Ford Cortina GT engine, this model being known as the Vixen 1600. They were consistently successful in diverse forms of motor sport: Brian Hough, Rod Longton and Ted Worswick took four 'Modsports' Championships between 1970 and 1972 with V-6 and V-8 Tuscan models, Mike Day won the British 1970 Autocross Championship and 'Spotty' Smith the 1971 Shell Leader hill-climb Championship.

In 1971 the 2500M with Triumph engine was introduced with a new multi-tubular chassis that enabled a longer body to be used, and the opportunity was taken also to provide an estate version. In 1972 this chassis was further revised and applied to all models, the new 'M' series being available as the 1300 (Spitfire engine), 1600 (Cortina GT, as in the superseded 'Vixen'), 2500 (Triumph) and 3000 (Ford V-6); the last-named sold at £1,884 in basic or component form.   DF

TWENTIETH CENTURY *see* OWEN (i)

TWIN CITY (US) *1914*
Twin City Cyclecar Co, Minneapolis, Minn.

This cyclecar used an unusual 4-cylinder air-cooled engine with piston valves, producing 20hp at 2,000rpm. A friction transmission was used and suspension was by coil springs all round.   GMN

TWOMBLY (i) (US) *1903*
Twombly Motor Carriage Co, New York, N.Y.

The Twombly steamer used a 250psi boiler, at which pressure, it was claimed, the car could achieve 50mph. The 4-cylinder engine could be changed from single acting to compound. As a compound, engine output was 12hp, or 28hp as single-acting. An aluminium body was fitted, and touring or limousine styles were available at up to $3,000.   GMN

TWOMBLY (ii) (US) *1906–1911*
Twombly Motors Co, New York City, N.Y.

Apparently no connection with other makes of this name, this Twombly had a 40hp 6.4-litre flat-4 engine, and dashboard radiator. The engine was designed for easy removal for servicing, and the aluminium body was transformable from limousine to tourer.   GNG

TWOMBLY (iii) *1913–1915*
Twombly Car Corp, Nutley, N.J.

This make began as a cyclecar, and was actually manufactured by Driggs-Seabury. The last model was a light car for two passengers with a 4-cylinder L-head engine. With wire wheels and 3-speed transmission, the price was $660.   GMN

TWYFORD (US) *1902–1908*
Twyford Motor Car Co, Brookville, Pa.

The Twyford was a crudely engineered car with 4-wheel drive. It used 2-cylinder engines with a choice of 10 or 18hp. The drive was by shaft, with open bevel gears, and no differential. This five-seater with side-entrance was priced at $2,700.   GMN

TX (GB) *1970 to date*
Technical Exponents Ltd, Denham, Bucks.

The TX Tripper was a convertible four-seater sports car, a rare type at this date, though the cut-away sides of the fibreglass body gave something of a 'buggy' appearance. The chassis was a double backbone steel box section and running gear was mainly Triumph, with a choice of 1300, GT6, 2.5PI Triumph or 1600 Ford engines. The car was available complete or in component form.   DF

TYNE (GB) *1904*
W. Galloway & Co, Ltd, Gateshead, Co. Durham

Two models of Tyne car were advertised by W. Galloway & Company, but it is unlikely that they were the manufacturers. One model used a 6½hp single-cylinder engine, double chain drive, and cost £155 for a two-seater, while the larger model had a 12hp 2-cylinder engine, shaft drive and cost £275 for a four-seater tonneau.   GNG

TYSELEY (GB) *1912–1913*
(1) Tyseley Car Co, Tyseley, Birmingham
(2) Bowden Brake Co, Tyseley, Birmingham

The Tyseley appeared during the cyclecar boom, but was more like a proper light car than many of its contemporaries, and was even made in closed coupé form. It used an 8/10hp water-cooled 2-cylinder engine of the company's own make, a 2-speed gearbox and shaft drive.   GNG

T.Z. (E) *1956–1966*
Talleres Zaragoza, Zaragoza

This was an all-independently sprung small saloon powered by a 2-cylinder 350cc 2-stroke engine developing 18hp and driving the front wheels. Although the T.Z. was advertised for several years, very few were made.   JRV

U

U (A) 1919–1923
U-Wagen Werke Ing. Umann, Vienna

After a prototype with a 2-cylinder 480cc engine, a 4-cylinder cyclecar with a 760cc 7/18PS engine was produced, mostly with two-seater roadster bodies. This make participated in various national racing events. HON

U.2 (GB) 1959 to date
The Mercury Stable, Roade, Northamptonshire

These cars were designed by Arthur Mallock, a champion of low-cost racing. Based on light and simple tubular frames, the cars were easily adaptable for various racing classes. Starting with the 1,172cc Formula for Ford 10 engines, models also raced in Clubmans, Junior, and Formulae 2, 3 and Ford events. By 1966 some 50 had been made, and the marque was alone in some classes in continuing the front-engined layout. Notable competition successes included an international win at the Nürburgring in 1961, the 1,500cc Clubman's Championship in 1965, and over 50 wins of various kinds in 1966. The Mark 6R of 1967 and the 1969 Mark 10 were sold also as road cars, but most models were built as suitable for the various racing formulae. They achieved a virtual monopoly of the British Clubmans racing class, with further championship wins for Jeremy Lord (1968 and 1969), Andy Diamond (1969 1,000cc), Ray Mallock (1970 and 1971) and Geoff Friswell (1972). The front-engined cars were successful on occasion even in Formula Ford, in which the constructor's elder son Richard raced.

The 1972 range included the offset 9C Formula Ford car, the Mark 11B Clubmans, and the Mark 12 with De Dion rear end and disc brakes which could be obtained in Formula 3 trim. A Clubmans car, fully assembled and ready to race, cost £2,000 but production was centred mainly on kits, selling steadily at around 20 annually. DF

1972 U.2 1600 Clubman racing car. Geoff Friswell at the wheel. *Arthur Mallock*

UAZ (SU) 1961 to date
Ulyanovsk Automobile Works, Ulyanovsk

This factory makes the UAZ-469, a 4×4 cross-country vehicle based on the GAZ-69. Output of the 2.4-litre 4-cylinder engine is 75bhp. BE

UIRAPURU (BR) 1967–1968
Sociedad Tecnica de Veiculos SA, São Paulo

Introduced in 1965 under the name Brasinca, the Uirapuru was a sports car powered by a 4.3-litre Chevrolet V-8 engine. Convertible or GT coupé bodies were available. GNG

ULMANN (D) 1903
Edmund Ulmann, Berlin W

This firm distributed the Oldsmobile in Germany, but also produced their own 12hp car in limited numbers. HON

ULTIMA (F) 1912–1914
B. Bournay, Levallois-Perret, Seine

The Ultima was made in two models, a 10hp single-cylinder (954cc), and a 10/12hp 4-cylinder (2,120cc). Both models had friction transmission and chain final drive. GNG

ULTRAMOBIL (D) 1904–1908
Deutsche Ultramobil GmbH, Berlin-Halensee

This was the Oldsmobile 'curved dash' model made under licence. From 1904 to 1906 it was produced by the Fahrzeugfabrik Eisenach and after 1906 by W.A. Boese & Co of Berlin for the Ultramobil company. In 1906 a 2-cylinder front-engined model appeared. HON

ULTRAMOBILE (F) 1908
Voitures Ultramobile, Paris

The Ultramobile was a conventional light car, powered by a 6/12hp monobloc 4-cylinder engine. Only two forward speeds were provided, and the engine was said to be as flexible as a steam engine. Final drive was by shaft, and there were two wheelbases available, for two- and four-seater bodywork. Suspension was by long springs running the length of the frame, as on the Curved Dash Olds. This suggests that, like its German namesake, this make was of Oldsmobile origin. GNG

1900 UNDERBERG 3hp voiturette. *Geoffroy de Beaufort Collection*

UNDERBERG (F) 1899–1909
Underberg et Cie, Nantes, Loire-Inférieure

1912 UNIC 10/12hp coupé. *G.N. Georgano*

1922 UNIC 1.8-litre sporting four-seater. *Autocar*

1931 UNIC 15CV straight-8 coupé. *Omnia Photo;*
Lucien Loreille Collection

1934 UNIC U4 11CV 2-litre saloon. *Simca*
Industries

The first Underberg was a two-seater voiturette powered by a single-cylinder air-cooled 3hp Gaillardet engine mounted in front. By 1901 the range consisted of a 6/8hp twin, and 12/16 and 28/40hp fours. The latter was a large four-seater tonneau with chain drive, gilled-tube radiator and the general appearance of a Panhard. These cars and subsequent ones were often known under the name Salvator. For 1906 there were three 4-cylinder models, of 12, 16 and 24hp, all with chain drive, armoured wood frames and circular radiators. The 24hp model was listed up to 1909. GNG

UNIC (F) *1904–1939*
(1) Sté des Anciens Ets Georges Richard, Puteaux, Seine *1904–1914*
(2) SA des Automobiles Unic, Puteaux, Seine *1914–1939*

When in 1905 Georges Richard left the firm he had founded, he embarked on his second motor manufacturing career with what was intended to be a single-model policy – hence the name of his new car. However, his 10/12hp 2-cylinder machine was joined within a year by two additional fours. After this the make remained undistinguished. The most famous of the small fours was not a passenger car at all, but a taxi. The monobloc 12/14hp of 1908 was made for 20 years, and served on London streets for longer still. In 1909 there was a 4.1-litre 6-cylinder model. By 1914, three 4-cylinder cars were listed, of which the 10/12hp was best known.

The basic model of the 1920s was the 10CV Type L, a worthy, long-lived but uninteresting car with an 1,847cc sv engine and the modern feature of unit construction of engine and gearbox. It had front-wheel brakes from 1923. The Type L313 Sport, an 11CV, with a bigger bore and 2 litres, was added in that year. It had overhead valves, and was a good-looking 70mph fast tourer in the French tradition. It must have been one of the first cars anywhere to have horizontal bonnet louvres. In 1926, the 11CV was also listed in sv touring form; only cars of this rating were made, the company having temporarily reverted to their original policy. At this time, the company employed women road-testers, a rare but not unique practice.

Unic's penchant for unusual rear suspensions – the 10CV had used a combination of cantilevers and quarter-elliptics – was perpetuated on their straight-8 of 1928, which had transverse springs located above and below the axle. Engines were push-rod ohv units of 2,494cc or 2,650cc, there were four forward speeds, and brakes were servo-assisted; both types persisted until 1934, though the old 11CV had gone by 1932, and during the Depression years the company concentrated on commercial vehicles. New for 1934 was the U4, a 2-litre sv four with magneto ignition (used on Unics almost until the end), articulated-arm ifs and a double reduction back axle. It competed with the Berliet 944 and the new small Delage and was joined during the year by the U6, a 3-litre six on similar lines, available with a 4-speed Cotal electrically selected gearbox. This option was extended to the U4 in 1936, and in 1937, when traditional radiators gave way to fencer's mask grilles, both 4- and 6-cylinder Unics were available in sports cabriolet form with ohv. The U4D of 1938 with 2,150cc ohv engine, and an improved U6 survived until the outbreak of World War 2. Private-car production was not resumed in 1946, though Unic are still active in truck manufacture as an associate of Fiat. TRN

UNICAR *see* OPPERMAN

UNION (i) (US) *1902–1905*
Union Automobile Co, Union City, Ind.

This make was a small 2-cylinder car, with a single headlamp. The engine was either air- or water-cooled, with friction transmission and double chain drive. Models included both two- and five-seaters. GMN

UNION (ii) (US) *1911–1914*
Union Sales Co, Columbus, Ohio

The Union from Columbus was a conventional car with a 25hp 4-cylinder pair-cast engine, and 3-speed gearbox. Tourer and roadster models were available, at a price of $650. GNG

UNIPOWER (GB) *1966–1970*
(1) Universal Power Drives Ltd, Perivale, Middlesex *1966–1968*
(2) Unipower Cars, London N.W.10 *1968–1970*

The Unipower was a high quality small GT car, developed by Andrew Hedges and Tim Powell, and built by a firm specializing in forestry tractors. A smart fibreglass body was mounted on a multi-tubular space-frame chassis and fitted with all-independent suspension, with a B.M.C. Mini engine.

Up to the end of 1967, 50 road cars had been sold, as well as 5 competition machines. The car interests were transferred subsequently to a separate concern, but this venture did not prosper and only a dozen or so further cars were made. DF

UNIQUE (GB) *1916*
The Motor Carrier & Cycle Co, Clapham, London S.W.

The Unique cyclecar used an 8/10hp 2-cylinder engine of the company's own make, a 3-speed gearbox and shaft drive. The price was £165. GNG

UNIT (GB) *1920–1923*
Rotary Unit Co Ltd, Wooburn, Bucks.

After A.G. Grice left G.W.K., he continued his devotion to friction drive with a car to which he gave the uninspiring name of Unit No. 1. The G.W.K. had grown up, but with his Unit, Grice reverted to the older pattern he preferred. The Unit used a flat-twin air-cooled 1,100cc rear-mounted engine with chain drive. An otherwise similar, but water-cooled engine was also available. As with G.W.K., however, he was forced to compromise with modern taste. By 1921, the engine was at the front; by 1923, it had 4 water-cooled cylinders (Coventry-Climax), and even a differential. It could not compete with the quantity-produced light car and the make died.   TRN

UNITED (US) 1914
National United Service Co, Detroit, Mich.

The United cyclecar was a side-by-side two-seater. Its 4-cylinder, 1½-litre engine was water-cooled, and friction transmission with double chain drive were used. Its weight was 850lb and its price $395.   GMN

UNIVERSAL (i) (US) 1914
Universal Motor Co, Washington, Pa.

The Universal was a two-seater roadster with an 18hp 4-cylinder engine. It was classed as a light car and had a 3-speed transmission. Its price was $475.   GMN

UNIVERSAL (ii) see TURNER (ii)

UNIVERSITY see CONTINENTAL (ii)

UPTON (i) (US) 1900–1907
(1) Upton Machine Co, Beverly, Mass. 1900–1905
(2) Beverly Manufacturing Co, Beverly, Mass. 1905–1907

The first Upton was a light runabout powered by a 3½hp De Dion engine. It had chain drive to a 2-speed gearbox and single drive to the rear axle. The most interesting model was the Beverly of 1904 which had a large 4-cylinder engine, chain drive, and the unusual feature of headlamps which turned with the steering. The price was $4,000. This model was also made in Lebanon, Pa. as the Upton (ii).   GNG

UPTON (ii) (US) 1905–1906
(1) Upton Motor Co, Lebanon, Pa. 1905
(2) Lebanon Motor Works, Lebanon, Pa. 1905–1906

The 4-cylinder Upton was initially furnished with double chain drive, shaft drive being introduced in 1905. A five-seater tonneau was the only model offered. The bullet-shaped head lamps were connected to turn with the steering. Later models with 4.4-litre engines were priced at $2,500.   GMN

URBANUS see HAGEN

URECAR (GB) 1923
Urecar Motor Co, Bournemouth, Hampshire

This was a light car powered by an 9.8hp 4-cylinder Dorman engine. The 3-speed transmission was by dog clutches and chains.   GNG

URSUS (F) 1908
G. Menegault-Basset, Arcueil, Seine

The Ursus was one of a number of friction-driven light cars of its period. It was sold in two-seater form, and had an 8hp single-cylinder engine.   GNG

U.S. (US) 1908
U.S. Motor Car Co, Upper Sandusky, Ohio

This car was a small two-seater on a wheelbase of 8ft. Its 4-cylinder, 1.8-litre, air-cooled engine was mounted beneath the seat. The drive was through a 3-speed transmission and propeller shaft. The cost was $900.   GMN

U.S., BREVETS MATHIEU see MATHIEU

U.S. ELECTRIC (US) 1899–1901
U.S. Automobile Co, Attleboro, Mass.

This company made a small number of electric cars, mainly open two- and four-seaters.   GNG

U.S. LONG DISTANCE (US) 1901–1903
United States Long Distance Automobile Co, Jersey City, N.J.

This marque started life as a light runabout powered by a single-cylinder horizontal 7hp engine mounted under the seat, a 2-speed epicyclic gear and single chain final drive. In 1903 a 2-cylinder four-seater tonneau model appeared, and in the same year the name of company and car was changed to Standard (ii).   GNG

UTILE (GB) 1904
Utile Motor Manufacturing Co Ltd, Kew Gardens, Surrey

The Utile light car used an 8hp single-cylinder engine described as being 'of

1967 UNIPOWER 1,275cc GT coupé.
Universal Power Drives Ltd

1920 UNIT 8.9hp two-seater. *Autocar*

1905 UPTON(ii) 4-cylinder tourer. *Dr Alfred Lewerenz Collection*

1901 U.S. LONG DISTANCE 7hp runabout.
Kenneth Stauffer

1914 UTOPIAN two-seater 3-wheeler. *David Filsell Collection*

De Dion type'. It had 2 speeds but one was said to be sufficient for all normal running. Final drive was by shaft, and a two-seater body was fitted. GNG

UTILIS (F) *1923–1925*
Camille Lafarge, Paris 17e

The Utilis was a very light cyclecar made in single- and 2-cylinder form. In each case the dimensions were the same, 76mm × 76mm, giving a capacity of 344cc for the single, and 688cc for the twin. A 2-speed gearbox was used, and final drive was by belts. GNG

UTILITAS (D) *1920–1921*
Utilitas-Gesellschaft Ritzer & Co mbH, Berlin

This company began car production with cyclecars with single and 2-cylinder engines. Later models were a 4-cylinder 4/10PS tandem two-seater and a 4/14PS four-seater. The make was not widely sold. HON

UTILITY (US) *1921–1922*
Victor W. Pagé Motors Corp, Stamford, Conn.

Built by Major Victor W. Pagé, whose Aero-Type Four car carrying his name had already been produced, the Utility was an attempt to produce a car the size of the contemporary Ford or Chevrolet. The cars were equipped with disc or artillery wheels and bonnet louvres were confined to the rear of each side, as on the Ford. Models known to have been produced were a roadster, a touring car, a station or estate wagon and a small truck. KM

UTOPIAN (GB) *1914*
Utopian Motor Works, Leicester

The Utopian 3-wheeler was an unusual car with single front wheel, and steering by side tiller in the manner of some early steam cars. The 2-cylinder water-cooled engine was mounted under the seat. It was built for a local clergyman, and possibly only one was made, although the firm also made bicycles. GNG

V

VABIS (S) *1897–1915*
Vagnfabrik AB Södertälje, Södertälje

This firm was established in 1891 as a subsidiary of Surahammars Bruk, makers of railway carriages. The first car was made at Surahammar in 1897, and is sometimes known as the Surahammar. Designed by Gustaf Eriksson, it used paraffin fuel, and was unsuccessful, but the following year it was re-fitted with a 2-cylinder petrol engine with ignition by heated clay and ran satisfactorily.

Because of Eriksson's inventive mind, few of the early Vabis cars were alike, but design passed through the buggy stage to that of solid 4-cylinder, 2-litre touring cars, although some were larger. In 1911, after about 85 cars had been made, the firm amalgamated with Maskinfabriks AB Scania, but cars of Vabis name and design continued to be made until 1915. OB

VAGHI (I) *1920–1924*
(1) Ditta Ludovico Boltri di Mezzi, Ganna & Cia, Milan *1920–1922*
(2) Motovetturette Vaghi SA, Milan *1922–1924*

The Vaghi was a 3-wheeler with single front wheel and shaft-driven rear wheels, powered by a 970cc V-twin engine. A conventional 3-speed gearbox was used; capacity was increased to 1,100cc in 1923. The company's 4-wheeler design was taken over by S.A.M. after the Vaghi concern collapsed. MCS

VAGNON ET CANET (F) *1898–c.1900*
Vagnon et Canet, Lyons

This company announced in May 1898 that they would build cars of any design or power to order, and a very small number of machines were produced up to about 1900, as well as a few motor-cycles and trucks. LL

VAGOVA (F) *1924–c.1926*
Vereille et Godet, Levallois-Perret, Seine

The Vagova used a very small 6-cylinder engine of only 745cc, with an overhead camshaft and desmodromically operated valves. This unit developed 38/40bhp. The chassis was conventional, and the car was only made in competition form. One was entered for the 1924 200 Miles Race at Brooklands, but broke down in practice. A touring model, without the desmodromic valves, was shown at the 1925 Brussels Salon. GNG

VAILLANT (F) *1922–1924*
Cyclecars Vaillant, Lyons

The Vaillant was a cyclecar powered by a 5CV 4-cylinder Chapuis-Dornier engine. GNG

V.A.L. (GB) *1913–1914*
V.A.L. Motor Co Ltd, Birmingham

The V.A.L. cyclecar was powered by an 8.9hp Precision V-twin water-cooled engine. It used friction transmission and chain final drive. GNG

VALE (GB) *1932–1936*
Vale Engineering Co Ltd, Maida Vale, London W.9

The Vale, or Vale Special, was a low-built sports car originally powered by a modified 832cc Triumph engine. Priced at £192. 10s. they were nearly all two-seaters, although an occasional four known as the Tourette was offered in 1933. Vales never became really popular as they were too low for trials, and not fast enough for sports car racing, although road-holding was very good. In 1934 the company announced that they would install larger engines in existing cars, or supply complete new cars. These had Coventry-Climax units of 1,098cc (4 cylinders) or 1,476cc (6 cylinders), although at least one of the re-engined cars used a 1,242cc ohc Meadows engine. In 1935 a supercharged 6-cylinder racing car was built for Ian Connell, and Vale Engineering said that they would build replicas for £625. In all, 103 Vales were made. GNG

VALIANT *see* PLYMOUTH (ii)

VALKYRIE (i) (GB) *1900*
Springfield Cycle Co Ltd, Sandiacre, Notts.

The Valkyrie was a French-style voiturette powered by a 3⅓hp De Dion engine which was mounted in front under a small bonnet. It had a 3-speed gearbox and shaft drive. GNG

1910 VABIS Type G4 12hp tourer. *Scania-Vabis AB*

1935 VALE 10hp sports car. *W.E. Gray*

1899 VALLÉE 6hp racing car. *David Filsell Collection*

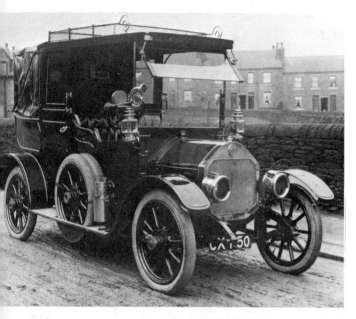

1910 VALVELESS 25hp landaulette. *David Brown Corporation*

1960 VANDEN PLAS 3.9-litre limousine. *British Motor Corporation*

VALKYRIE (ii) (US) *1967 to date*

Fiberfab, Division of Velocidad, Inc, Santa Clara, Calif.

Driven by a rear mounted V-8 of 450bhp, the Valkyrie GT sports car is a sleek two-seater of advanced design, priced at $12,000. A five speed Z-F transaxle enables the machine to attain speeds in excess of 180mph. The chassis is of steel tubing, suspension is independent and the brakes are 11.75in discs. A Simpson Drag parachute is used for primary braking at speeds over 140mph. Acceleration in fifth gear is 0–60mph in 3.9 seconds. The Valkyrie may be had in kit form with provision for use of Corvair parts if desired. Fiberfab also make fibreglass bodies for mounting on Volkswagen chassis. BE

VALLÉE (F) *1895–1901*

Sté des Automobiles Vallée, Le Mans, Sarthe

Vallée was a bicycle maker, and his first car made its appearance at the 1895 Salon du Cycle. It had a 4hp 2-cylinder horizontal engine, 4 speeds, chain final drive, and front wheels in a modified form of cycle forks. The headlamps turned in the direction of the steering, surely the first example of this rare practice. By 1898 a range of cars was being made with 2-cylinder engines of 3, 4½ or 7hp, belt drive to a countershaft, and chain final drive. Bodies ranged from a two-seater 'racer' to a six-seater brake. In 1899 appeared the curious racing car known as the 'Slipper' on account of its body shape. It had a 4-cylinder engine, still horizontal, of 110mm × 200mm (7,598cc). No gearbox was provided, the engine being thought sufficiently powerful and flexible to avoid the need for one. Final drive was by a single wide belt to the rear axle. Driven by Dr Lehwess, who later tried to drive a Panhard, 'Le Passe Partout', around the world, it competed in a number of events in 1899, its best result being 5th in the Paris-St Malo race. Later Vallées used 2- or 4-cylinder horizontal engines, but of smaller size than that of the Slipper. GNG

VALVELESS; LUCAS VALVELESS (GB) *1901–1914*

(1) Ralph Lucas, Blackheath, London S.E. *1901–1908*
(2) Valveless Cars Ltd, Huddersfield, Yorks. *1908–1914*

Ralph Lucas's first Valveless car appeared in 1901, and various experimental models were made during the next six years without any production being undertaken. The design was a vertical 2-cylinder 2-stroke with common combustion chamber, the crankshaft being placed transversely in the frame. 2 forward speeds were provided, reverse originally being obtained by reversing the engine, although an epicyclic reverse gear was later fitted. Final drive was by chain. Early models had the engine centrally-mounted, and no bonnet, but when the car first appeared at Olympia in 1907 it had a conventional bonnet, although the engine was still under the seats. At this Show it was exhibited by Crawshay-Williams Ltd of Ashtead, who had made cars under their own name a few years earlier, but in 1908 it was put into production by David Brown Ltd, being the first road vehicle venture of this famous firm. Called a 20hp, the production Valveless had the same design of engine, but it was now mounted under the bonnet with the crankshaft placed longitudinally, and had a 3-speed gearbox and shaft drive. In 1910 it was known as the 25hp, and was joined by a smaller 15hp model. At the 1911 Olympia Show they shared a stand with the David Brown-sponsored Dodson car, and in one list they were called the Dodson Valveless. They were made until 1914, the only alteration in the range being that the 25hp had its bore reduced and became a 20 (19.9hp RAC rating), but as well as Dodsons, David Brown were selling the Belgian S.A.V.A., and the Valveless became of only subsidiary importance. An excellent example of a 1910 Valveless survives in the National Motor Museum, Beaulieu. GNG

VAN (US) *1910–1911*

Van Motor Car Co, Grand Haven, Mich.

The Van 22 was 'the car for you', with an ohv 4-cylinder engine. It was a two-seater roadster with full elliptical springs for $850. GMN

VANDEN PLAS (GB) *1960 to date*

(1) Vanden Plas (England) 1923 Ltd, London N.W.9 *1960–1970*
(2) Austin-Morris Division, British Leyland Motor Corporation Ltd, London N.W.9 *1970 to date*

Originally the English offshoot of a Belgian coachbuilding house, this firm was associated in the inter-war period with open sporting bodywork on luxury chassis, such as Bentleys, but after World War 2 it became a subsidiary of Austin (ii), and was responsible for bodies on the luxury A 135 chassis of 1947–48. 'Custom' versions of the 6-cylinder A 105, were added in 1958, and in 1960 the Princess Austins became a separate make, distinguished from other B.M.C. cars by their luxurious interiors, and traditional radiator grilles with crown emblem. Initially the range consisted of long-wheelbase limousine developments of the original 1948 theme, plus a de luxe edition of Austin's 2.9 litre 6-cylinder saloon, but in 1964 these were joined by a variant of the Issigonis-designed front-wheel-drive 1100. In 1965 the middle member of the range grew up into the Princess R, a similar type of vehicle, but with a 3.9-litre ioe 6-cylinder 175bhp engine by Rolls-Royce and automatic transmission as standard. The small car became available with a 1,300cc engine in June 1967, this version being standardized nine months later, when the two big 6-cylinder types were discontinued. Vanden Plas, however, made the bodies for the limousine replacement, a 4.2-litre 6-cylinder Daimler. In 1973 only the 1300 4-door saloon carried the Vanden Plas name. MCS

VANDY (GB) *1920–1921*
Vandys Ltd, Notting Hill, London W.11

The Vandy was an assembled car using a large, slow-revving engine of American origin, and many American components. The engine was an sv 6-cylinder Rutenber unit of 3,772cc, and the design included dual ignition, a 4-speed gearbox and multi-plate clutch. The bodies were British made. The company was formed by Major Frank Vandervell and Lieut. Perry Vandervell of the C.A.V. Company, and the cars were assembled in the Pembridge Villas premises from which J.H. Bartlett sold sports cars in the 1930s. GNG

VAN GINK (NL) *1899–1900*
Van Gink, Otto Bultman & Co, Amsterdam

The Van Gink light car was powered by two 2½hp air-cooled engines mounted at the rear, which could be used together or separately. It had a tubular frame and four-seater body. The company also made bicycles under the name Hinde, which was sometimes applied to the cars. GNG

VANGUARD (US) *1972 to date*
Vanguard Vehicles, Inc, Kingston, N.Y.

The Vanguard Sport Coupé is a tiny electric car with a wheelbase of 5ft 8in. It has an aluminium frame and two-seater fibreglass body, and a claimed speed of 31mph. It is said to have a range of 40 to 60 miles including 84 stops and starts. GMN

VAN LANGENDONCK (B) *1901–1902*
Compagnie Générale d'Automobiles, Brussels

This light car used front-mounted 5hp De Dion or 8hp Buchet engines, with shaft drive to the rear axle. Body styles were two-seater or four-seater tonneaux. GNG

VANNOD (F) *1958*
L. Vannod, Neuilly, Seine

The Vannod was one of the last of the 'follies' for which the Paris Salon was once celebrated. Its 4 wheels were arranged in diamond pattern in the style of the Sunbeam-Mabley, both front and rear wheels steering. A 2-stroke Sachs engine drove the rear wheel by chain. The body was a three-seater, with the driver alone in front of the two passengers. GNG

VAN WAGONER *see* SYRACUSE

VAPOMOBILE (GB) *1902–1904*
Motor Construction Co Ltd, Nottingham

The Vapomobile was a light steam car very much on American lines, although the makers claimed that it was of entirely English construction, and much stronger than its American equivalent. One model, the 12hp, certainly used an American Mason engine; there were three models in all, the 5 and 7hp cars having tiller steering, and the 12hp wheel steering. GNG

VAR (A) *1924*
Gianni Varrone, Hard, Vorarlberg

The Var was a light car built in Austria by an Italian-Swiss engineer. It was of his own design and manufacture, and used a 300cc flat-twin two-stroke engine, wooden chassis frame, and body panels of imitation leather. Varrone could get no financial backing, and only one car was made, a 4-stroke engine being fitted later. GNG

VARLEY-WOODS (GB) *1918–1921*
(1) High Speed Tool Company Ltd, Acton, London W.3 *1918–191.*
(2) H.S. Motors Ltd, Acton, London W.3 *1919–1920*
(3) H.S. Motors Ltd, Wolverhampton *1919–1920*
(4) Turner's Motor Manufacturing Co Ltd, Wolverhampton *1919–1920*

The Varley-Woods was a typical 'assembled' car of the post-war period which when first announced sported a vee-radiatored torpedo body. It quickly acquired a flat-fronted Rolls-type radiator which, together with the rivets down its unpainted aluminium bonnet, gave it a distinguished appearance. Some handsome saloon coachwork was also offered on the standard chassis but the overall effect was marred by the use of Sankey artillery wheels.

The car was made for its sponsors by Turners of Wolverhampton, a separate factory being rented for assembly purposes. Although a Dorman engine was employed, it was not the dull side-valve unit more often encountered but possibly the most exciting engine they produced. Designated the KNO, it was a 69mm × 120mm 1,795cc unit with aluminium block and crankcase, iron liners and an ohc driving inclined ohv. (Seabrook Bros., Westwood and Dawson also used this unit.) From mid-1920 a 14.3hp Tylor engine was used.

Initially however, some cars were assembled in a disused laundry in Acton using

1920 VANDY 25hp all-weather tourer. *Autocar*

1958 VANNOD 200cc saloon. *Autosport*

1920 VARLEY-WOODS 14.3hp tourer. *Autocar*

1905 VAUXHALL 7/9hp 3-cylinder two-seater.
Vauxhall Motors Ltd

1913 VAUXHALL 30/98 sporting four-seater.
The Veteran Car Club of Great Britain

1925 VAUXHALL OE 30/98 coupé. Coachwork by
Grosvenor. *National Motor Museum*

1925 VAUXHALL 14/40 Princeton tourer.
Vauxhall Motors Ltd

French components acquired from the Storey Machine Tool Company of New Cross, by Ernest Vernon Varley Grossmith one of the directors of the company.

Grossmith, a member of the acting and perfumery family dropped his surname in 1919 and after an abortive attempt to manufacture a car called the Winchester with John Storey in the city of that name, joined forces with John Robert Woods, a Near East river trader (*à la* 'Africa Queen') to launch the Varley-Woods. Both were a good deal more colourful than the cars they produced, Varley having already tried his hand at canned soup, mouth-organ manufacture at Clapham (where he met Storey who owned a garage at Clapham Park) and government surplus. Woods, who returned to Lake Nyasa, was eaten by a lion, and the Varley-Woods folded when the landlord of the Lichfield St premises, backed by Turners, petitioned for the winding up of the company because of unpaid rent. A Receiver Manager was appointed in October 1920 and unsold stocks were still being offered in 1921.

MJWW

V.A.T.E. (F) *1908*
Voitures Automobiles de Transmission Electrique, Paris

The V.A.T.E. was a light car using a petrol-electric transmission. A 10hp 2-cylinder engine drove a combination dynamo and motor mounted in the flywheel, and power was taken by conventional shaft drive to the rear axle.

GNG

VAUXHALL (GB) *1903 to date*
(1) Vauxhall Iron Works Ltd, London *1903–1904*
(2) Vauxhall Iron Works Ltd, Luton, Beds. *1905–1906*
(3) Vauxhall and West Hydraulic Engineering Co Ltd, Luton, Beds. *1906–1907*
(4) Vauxhall Motors Ltd, Luton, Beds. *1907 to date*

This marine engineering concern's first cars were horizontal-engined single-cylinder runabouts in the American idiom with chain drive and tiller steering, rated at 6hp and selling for £150. In 1904, when 76 cars were sold, wheel steering and a reverse gear featured in the specification, and the singles were joined by 3-cylinder models of 1.4 and 2.4 litres' capacity, with mechanically-operated inlet valves and vestigial flutes on their bonnets. In 1905 the works were moved to Luton, and the first attempt at competitions was made with the entry in the Tourist Trophy of a 3-cylinder car with overdrive gearbox. The classic Vauxhall radiator with its flutes appeared on a 3.3-litre T-head 4-cylinder car introduced in 1906. This was followed by a smaller shaft-drive 12/16, still T-headed, and the Pomeroy-designed L-head 20hp, which gave 40bhp and won the 2,000 Mile Trial of 1908. Pomeroy's 4-cylinder cars were among the classic British designs of the next six years, boasting 5-bearing crankshafts and monobloc engines, and, from 1912, Hele-Shaw multi-plate clutches. In 1910 the first of the Prince Henry models with 3-litre engine won its spurs in the German Trials of that name: these round-nose sporting Vauxhalls later grew up into 4 litres' with 70bhp, capable of 75mph and selling for only £615 in 1913. The company's bread-and-butter car was the smaller and staider A type on similar lines, joined in 1913 by a 4-litre D type with close affinities to the Prince Henry, while the B-type, a 6-cylinder formal carriage with its cylinders cast in threes, was made in small numbers from 1910 onwards. A Linley preselective gearbox was listed as an option in 1911, in which year Vauxhall started racing in earnest. Already a 3-litre with single-seater streamlined bodywork had recorded 100.08mph over the flying kilometre, and cars were entered for the Coupe de l'Auto voiturette races of 1911, 1912 and 1913. These were followed by twin-ohc designs in 1914 for the French Grand Prix and the Tourist Trophy. The GP models' 4½-litre engines developed 130bhp. The prototype of Vauxhall's best known sporting model, the 30/98, appeared in 1913. Its capacity was 4½ litres and it was listed at £925 in 1915, though only 13 were made before the outbreak of World War 1.

D types were made at the rate of eight a week for the Fighting Services during the war years, and both this model and the E type 30/98 were available again in 1919 with full electrical equipment. The latter was one of the greatest of all fast tourers, offering superb flexibility and a top speed of over 80mph for £1,600, though brakes were never its strong suit. 1922 saw Vauxhall, like Sunbeam, offering a smaller and cheaper car, the 2.3-litre M type 14/40 with detachable head, 3-speed unit gearbox in place of the 4-speed separate type on the big cars, single-plate clutch and all brakes on the rear wheels (supplanting a foot transmission brake), at £750. The last serious competition Vauxhalls were a team of 3-litre twin ohc machines for the 1922 Tourist Trophy, which had 110bhp and air-pressure operated brakes, but could manage no better than a 3rd place. Both the D and E types acquired overhead valves in the summer of 1922, the latter emerging as the 120bhp OE which had 4-wheel brakes of rather dubious efficacy by 1923. Capacity of the engine was now 4.2 litres. Vauxhall sold 1,400 cars in 1924. 1925 14/40hp models had 4 forward speeds, but finances were uncertain, and the company was bought by General Motors in December of that year. 1926 Vauxhalls were still on traditional lines, the 14/40 acquiring front wheel brakes, and being supplemented by a new luxury 6-cylinder car, the S type with 3.9-litre single-sleeve valve engine and hydraulic brakes at £1,250. The 30/98 survived into 1927, also now with hydraulics: only about 600 of both types, the E and OE were made, and three-fifths of these were exported to Australia. The 14/40 in its last year could be had with a Wilson preselective gearbox. The first G.M. Vauxhall was introduced for 1928: this was a rather American-looking 20/60hp ohv six with coil ignition and central change, but still with a 4-speed box, at £475. This R type was steadily increased in capacity, ending its production run as the 3.3-litre T80 in 1932. A really inexpensive Vauxhall Six, the 2-litre Cadet at £280, was offered in 1931, in which year a range of Chevrolet-based Bedford trucks helped to boost Vauxhall Motors' overall sales. The Cadet pioneered synchromesh in Britain in 1932, a few months ahead of Rolls-Royce, but the need for smaller horsepower cars resulted in the introduction of a couple of light sixes of 12 and 14hp in the summer of 1933. These cars and their companion 2.4-litre and 3.2-litre Big Sixes of 1934 had Fisher no-draught ventilation, but boasted 4 forward speeds in place of the Cadet's 3. Prices of the smaller cars started at £195, and in 1935, in which year a record 25,000 Vauxhalls were sold, they also had General Motors' 'knee action' independent front suspension. In 1937 the Big Six gave way to a 3.2-litre, 80bhp 25 with independent front suspension and hydraulic brakes, selling for £298, and also available in long-chassis limousine form. All 1937 cars had stylized grilles in place of radiators, with headlamps attached to the shell, though the flutes survived until 1962. In 1938 came the 1.2-litre Ten with 3-speed gearbox and unitary construction, also made as a coupé with separate chassis, while the 25 now had a 3-speed box as well. Hydraulic brakes were standard on all models in 1939, in which year the 12/6 gave way to a unitary-construction 3-speed 4-cylinder model at £189, and the 14 also went over to unitary construction.

With the discontinuation of the 25 after World War 2, cars with separate chassis were no longer made for the home market, though certain export versions were thus made until 1954. Post-war production started with revised editions of the 1940 model Ten, Twelve, and Fourteen, but in 1948 a new model with bigger boot, a standardized hull, and steering-column change was introduced, with a choice of two long-stroke ohv engines – the Velox had a 54bhp 2.3-litre 6-cylinder unit, and the Wyvern the old 35bhp Twelve of 1.4 litres' capacity. Lowered and restyled versions with hypoid back axles were introduced for 1952, short-stroke engines replacing the earlier type during the season. These cars were in production until 1957 with relatively little change, though a de luxe 6-cylinder edition, the Cresta, appeared in 1955. A very American 1½-litre saloon, the Victor, with Chevrolet-like wrap-around windscreen and 3-speed all-synchromesh gearbox, was announced in 1957 at £729, and the 6-cylinder models received similar treatment in 1958. Though the styling was critically received, this was a record year for Vauxhall, with 114,177 cars sold. Overdrive was an option on the 1959 6-cylinder line, followed by automatic in 1960, while the flutes were gone from the 1962 Victor, a better-looking car with a 56bhp engine, and the choice of a 3- or 4-speed box. A faster twin-carburettor 71bhp version, the VX 4/90, had front disc brakes. The Velox and Cresta were restyled on similar lines in 1963, also with discs at the front, and power was increased in 1965, Victors having 1.6 litres and 70bhp, and the 6-cylinder engines being enlarged to 3.3 litres. 1964 produced a new small Vauxhall, the 1,057cc Viva which was almost identical with the German Opel Kadett. It sold for £566, but by 1967 had been replaced by the more attractive 1,159cc HB series, with such options as a 69bhp SL model and automatic transmission. The van-based Bedford Beagle estate car, however, retained the original HA shape into 1973. In 1966 there was a prestige version of the Cresta, the Viscount at £1,483, on which automatic transmission, power windows and a vinyl roof were standard.

A new phase in Vauxhall design was heralded in 1968 by an all-new Victor. Its 4-cylinder engines, of 1,599cc and 1,975cc, had 5-bearing crankshafts and belt-driven ohc, and also featured were 4-speed gearboxes, rack-and-pinion steering, and all-coil suspension with rigid axles at the rear. The costliest estate-car version used the 3.3-litre 6-cylinder engine, as did a new sports-compact introduced during the year, the Ventora saloon. Next to appear was a Viva GT, combining a Viva hull with 2-litre Victor mechanics and, in 1970, an updated version of the sporting VX 4/90. In 1971 came Vauxhall's answer to the best-selling Ford Capri, the Firenza coupé with front disc brakes and a choice of Viva or Victor engine. The former unit was enlarged to 1,256cc for 1972, and in the spring of that year came new, more elegant Victors and Ventoras, the fours now having 1.8-litre or 2.3-litre engines. Twin-carburettor editions of the latter now developed 122bhp. They were fitted to the Sport SL Firenza as well as to the VX 4/90, which came with overdrive as standard, and to the fiercest of the Viva family, retailing for £1,218 in 2-door saloon form. Top of the range was now the Ventora. The Cresta and Viscount, unchanged since 1966, disappeared in September 1972. Viva mechanical elements were used in the Grumett, a Uruguayan coupé-utility in the Australian-Japanese idiom, and also in a new light truck evolved in 1972 by the parent General Motors for sale in emergent countries. In 1972 models of the Viva/Firenza range with 2-litre ohc engines were sold under the name Pontiac Firenza by General Motors of Canada. MCS

VAUZELLE-MOREL (F) 1902

Emile Vauzelle, Morel et Cie, Paris 11e

The Vauzelle-Morel voiturette was powered by a 5hp Aster engine mounted under the seat, although it had a small sloping bonnet of De Dion pattern. Drive was via a 2-speed Bozier gear to the rear axle. GNG

VAZ (SU) 1969 to date

Volzhsky Automobilny Zavod, Togliattigrad

1935 VAUXHALL Big Six 27hp landaulette. Coachwork by Grosvenor. *National Motor Museum*

1949 VAUXHALL Velox L-type 2.3-litre saloon. *Vauxhall Motors Ltd*

1968 VAUXHALL Victor 2000 2-litre saloon. *Vauxhall Motors Ltd*

1973 VAUXHALL Firenza Sport SL 2.3-litre coupé. *Vauxhall Motors Ltd*

1972 VAZ 2101 1.2-litre saloon. *Satra Motors Ltd*

1901 VÉHEL 6/8hp tonneau. *Geoffroy de Beauffort Collection*

1926 VELIE Model 60 coupé. *Harrah's Automobile Collection*

Sold in some export markets under the Lada name, the VAZ is the outcome of an agreement signed between Fiat of Italy and the Soviet government in August 1966, under which the Italian concern provided the technical advice. The cars are made in a factory at Stavropol on the Volga (the town was renamed after the former Italian Communist leader Palmiro Togliatti). VAZ production was running at 700 units a day in December 1971, two years after the first pilot models were delivered. Structurally the VAZ is a modified Fiat 124, but its engine is a 1,198cc sohc 4-cylinder developing 62bhp, and a starting handle is standard equipment. It competes against the native Italian product in several European markets. A station wagon was added to the range early in 1972. MCS

V.C.S. *see* SCHILLING

V.E. (V.E.C.) (US) *1903–1905*
Vehicle Equipment Co, Long Island City, N.Y.
The V.E. electric was a three-seater with shaft drive. Its wheelbase was 7ft 10in and the tread an unusual 4ft 6in. This manufacturer was a large producer of electric commercial vehicles. GMN

VĚCHET (A) *1911–1913*
Automobilfabrik Věchet & Co, Nimburg
Two types of small cars with 2- and 4-cylinder engines were made. HON

VÉDRINE (F) *1904–c.1910*
La Voiture Electrique Védrine, Neuilly, Seine
This company were mainly coachbuilders whose work was found on Panhard-Levassor and other high-class cars of the day. However, they made a number of expensive electric cars of the usual brougham and landaulet fashion. They had single electric motors mounted just forward of the rear axle, and some had sharply dropped frames to allow for low entrance bodies. In 1906 their production was 1,500 vehicles, but this may have included coachwork on other chassis. GNG

VEE GEE (GB) *1913*
Vernon Gash & Co, Leeds, Yorks.
The Vee Gee was a cyclecar powered by an 8hp V-twin J.A.P. engine. Unlike many such machines it used a propeller-shaft and worm-driven rear axle. It had a tubular frame and was planned to sell at 110 guineas. GNG

VEERAC (US) *1913*
Veerac Motor Co, Anoka, Minn.
The name Veerac was a mnemonic for 'valveless, explosion every revolution, air-cooled'. This car with its 2-stroke engine, and air-cooling, was first proposed by Frank Merrill of New Jersey in 1905. Later he was chief engineer for the Veerac Motor Co. The original two-seater car had a 2-cylinder engine of 1.6 litres, planetary transmission and shaft drive. GMN

VÉHEL (F) *1899–1901*
M. et A. Dulac, Paris
The Véhel was made with vertical engines of 6 or 8hp (single- and 2-cylinders respectively), mounted at the front, 3-speed gearboxes, and chain final drive. They had sharply pointed bonnets, and were sold in England in 1901 under the name Torpedo. (No connection with the 1909 Lincolnshire car of the same name.) GNG

V.E.L. (F) *1947–1948*
Sté V.E.L., Paris 18e
This was a two-seater minicar with a 1CV single-cylinder Train engine driving the front wheels. It had a 3-speed gearbox, and a top speed of 40mph. GNG

VELIE (US) *1909–1928*
(1) The Velie Motor Vehicle Co, Moline, Ill. *1909–1916*
(2) The Velie Motor Corp, Moline, Ill. *1916–1928*
Velie were already well-known carriage builders when they launched their first car in May 1909. It was a conventional machine with a 30/35hp 4-cylinder engine made by the American & British Manufacturing Company of Bridgeport, Conn., who later made the luxurious Porter (ii) car. The Velie Corporation was backed by the John Deere Plow Company, and the cars were distributed through Deere dealers until 1915. By 1914 a range of two fours and a six was made, with power ratings from 25 to 34hp. From 1917 onwards Velie made sixes only, standardizing on Continental engines. One of the most striking Velies was the Sport Car of 1918, a four-seater with wire wheels and outside exhaust pipes. This was the only model with the 29hp engine, but the 25hp was supplied with a wide range of open and closed bodywork. In 1922 Velie began to make their own 6-cylinder engines, joined in 1927 by a straight-8 Lycoming. In 1928, the last year of production, there were three sixes, the Standard 50, the 6-66, and the 6-77, in addition to the 8-88 Lycoming developing 90bhp. 1929 models were announced but not built. However, the name survived in the town of Velie, Louisiana, a suburb of Shreveport. This obtained its name in 1916 because of the local popularity of Velie cars. GNG

VÉLOCAR see MOCHET

VELOCE (GB) *1909*

Veloce Ltd, Birmingham

Two models of the Veloce car were announced, an 18/24hp and a 24/26hp, both using 4-cylinder engines of their own design and manufacture, and shaft drive. They were intended for colonial use, so had good ground clearance and large radiators. In fact only one car was made, the 18/24. The company later made the well-known Velocette motor cycle. GNG

VELOMOBIL (D) *1905–1907*

(1) Motorfahrzeugfabrik Hermann Dettmann, Berlin *1905–1906*
(2) Velomobil-Kraftfahrzeugfabrik, Berlin *1906–1907*

The Velomobil was a 3-wheeled vehicle with one driven front wheel. Two- and three-seater bodies were available. HON

VELOREX (CS) *1958 to date*

VD Velorex, Solnice, Rychnov

The Velorex motor-cycle works built a 3-wheeler with tubular frame and imitation leather bonnet from 1958 to 1971. Power was provided by a 250 or 350cc Jawa engine. A prototype 4-wheeler was made in 1959, and production 4-wheelers with 350cc engines have been made since January 1972. GNG

VELOX (i) (GB) *1902–1904*

Velox Motor Co Ltd, Coventry, Warwickshire

Velox cars were originally built in part of the Parkside Works of the Amalgamated Tyre Company. The first model had a 10hp 2-cylinder Abeille engine, a 4-speed gearbox and shaft drive. For 1903 two models were made, a 10hp 4-cylinder with a Forman engine and the Miniature Velox, a very low two-seater powered by a 4½hp single-cylinder Aster engine. Both used shaft drive. A 20hp 4-cylinder car was added to the range late in 1903, but by then the company was wound up. Only 21 cars were completed, with 15 more in the course of construction at the time of the company's closure. GNG

VELOX (ii) (A) *1906–1910*

Prager Automobilfabrik 'Velox' GmbH, Prague-Carolinenthal

This firm produced one type of private car which was also extensively used as a taxicab. It had a single-cylinder 1,020cc 10hp engine. HON

VERA (US) *1912*

Vera Motor Car Co, Providence, R.I.

This was an imposing car with pleasing lines, in five-seater and seven-seater models. The engine was a 6-cylinder, T-head of 7 litres. GMN

VERITAS (D) *1948–1953*

(1) Veritas GmbH, Messkirch *1948–1949*
(2) Veritas Badische Automobilwerke GmbH, Rastatt *1949–1950*
(3) Veritas Automobilwerke GmbH, Nürburgring *1950–1953*

This firm was founded by former employees of B.M.W. with the intention of building sports cars based on the pre-war B.M.W. 328, using the 1,971cc 80bhp B.M.W. engine. In 1950 a new 1,988cc engine was developed and built by Heinkel which produced 100bhp. This new version was offered in Saturn coupé, Skorpion convertible, Komet sports car and Komet S sports racing car forms with the engine output developed to 150bhp. The Dyna-Veritas was a two-seater convertible using a 744cc opposed twin engine and front-drive components by Panhard. It was produced from 1950 until 1952, and carried Veritas-designed bodies built by Baur of Stuttgart. Financial difficulties forced the firm to close down in 1950, but it was re-established as Veritas Nürburgring by Ernst Loof. The 1,988cc Heinkel engines were also used for the new models, but the new company achieved no lasting success and production was abandoned. HON

VERMOREL (F) *1908–1930*

Etablissements V. Vermorel, Villefranche, Rhône

These makers of woodworking machinery were established in 1850 and were experimenting with motor cars as early as 1902, though production did not start until 1908. Early Vermorels were conventional 1.8-litre T-head machines with 4-speed gearboxes and three-quarter-elliptic rear suspension. 2.2-litre and 3.3-litre cars of this type were listed in 1912, but 1913 saw the beginning of a more modern trend with the introduction of new L-head monobloc models, the 1½-litre 8/10hp and the 2.8-litre 16/20. The bigger cars had V-radiators and were said to be capable of 72mph. A year later the last of the T-head models had been replaced by a 2.3-litre L-head 15/18, which reappeared after World War 1 in much the same guise. Also rather old-fashioned was the 1.7-litre 8/16CV of 1922, with its sv fixed-head engine, foot transmission brake, and cone clutch, though a dynamotor was fitted, the 4-speed gearbox had central change, and 4-wheel brakes were available. An ohv sports version with wire wheels was offered in 1923, and these two parallel models acquired full-pressure lubrication in 1925, and coupled brakes and plate

1962 VELOREX 350cc 3-wheeler. *G.N. Georgano*

1950 VERITAS Scorpion 2-litre sports car.
Lutz Becker

1912 VERMOREL 12/16hp two-seater. *George A. Oliver*

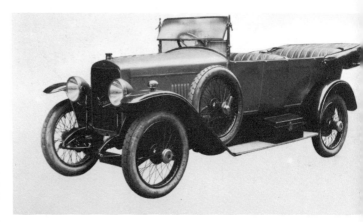

1921 VERMOREL 12hp tourer. *Autocar*

1930 VERMOREL Model AD 1.7-litre saloon.
Lucien Loreille Collection

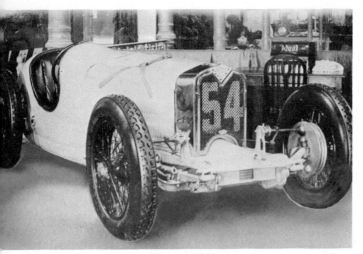

1928 VERNANDI 1½-litre V-8 racing car. *Lucien
Loreille Collection*

1960 VESPA 400 coupé. *National Motor Museum*

clutches a year later. 1924 saw an ohc 16/60hp 4-cylinder Vermorel with a 2.6-litre engine and detachable head, but it was clearly intended for formal coachwork with its 11ft 3in wheelbase. In 1927 the ZX type 1.7-litre car was still being made, and there was also an undistinguished 1,100cc sv 4-cylinder on conventional lines. The last of the Vermorels was the type AH3 of 1929, a straightforward ohv 2-litre 6-cylinder with 12-volt coil ignition, a 4-speed unit gearbox with central change, semi-elliptic springs, and spiral bevel final drive. The Etablissements Vermorel abandoned private-car manufacture in 1930.   MCS

VERNANDI (F) *1928–1929*
Naudillon, Garches, Seine-et-Oise

Only one prototype and two engines were made of the Vernandi racing car. Designed by the engineer Causan who had been responsible for some of the best designs of Bignan and La Licorne, it had a 1,494cc V-8 engine with overhead valves and two superchargers. A 2.9-litre V-16 was projected, but apparently never built.   GNG

VERNON (US) *1915–1920*
Vernon Automobile Corp, Mount Vernon, N.Y.

The Vernon's production was never large and was confined primarily to touring cars. It had an 8-cylinder engine of Vernon make, with a capacity of 2,750cc. Artillery wheels were standard, with wire wheels available as an option. An alternative name was Able Eight.   KM

VESPA (i) (I) *1913–1916*
G. Antonelli, Modena

This was a conventional light car with 1,460cc sv 4-cylinder engine and 3-speed gearbox. It was capable of 55mph and competed in minor Italian events of the period.   MCS

VESPA (ii) (F) *1958–1961*
Ateliers de Constructions de Motos et Accessoires, Fourchamboult, Nièvre

This was a minicar design by the Italian Piaggio aircraft firm, creators of the successful Vespa Scooter. Production however was undertaken entirely in the A.C.M.A. factory in France. It featured unitary construction, a rear-mounted 2-stroke vertical-twin air-cooled 400cc engine, 3-speed synchromesh gearbox, all round independent suspension, and hydraulic brakes. It was sold for the equivalent of £340, with a rolltop two-seater convertible body reminiscent of the original 500 Fiat. Better finished than most of the miniatures, and capable of 50mph, it lasted correspondingly longer.   MCS

VETTA VENTURA *see* APOLLO (iii)

V.H. (i) (VINING-HALLETT) *see* F.D. (i)

V.H. (ii) (E) *1961*
Pedro Vargas Hernandes, Villafranca de los Barros

The V.H. was a 3-wheeled minicar powered by a 400cc vertical-twin 2-stroke engine designed by the car's constructor. Production was intended, but only one car was made.   GNG

VIA (i) (GB) *1910*
Norburys Ltd, Manchester

Only one model of the Via was announced, a tourer with dashboard radiator of Renault lines, powered by a 27.5hp 6-cylinder engine.   GNG

VIA (ii) (H) *1921*
Villamos Autogyar Reszvenytarsasag, Budapest

This was a small electric car with tandem seating for two and a maximum speed of 25mph. Only a few were made.   GNG

VICEROY (GB) *1914–1915*
Viceroy Sidecar Co Ltd, New Basford, Nottingham

Made by a famous side-car company, the Viceroy was a light car powered by an 8/10hp 4-cylinder Chapuis-Dornier engine. It used shaft drive.   GNG

VICI (GB) *1906–1907*
Vici Motors Ltd, West Kilburn, London N.W.

The Vici car used a 12/16hp 4-cylinder engine, 3-speed gearbox and shaft drive. One ran in the 1906 Tourist Trophy Race, driven by one of the directors, R. Lascelles, but did not finish. It was said that future Vicis were to be all-British cars, but in order to complete the TT car in time, 'some Continental fittings were used'. In fact the TT car was probably the only one made. The company planned to acquire a factory at Walsall, but never did so.   GNG

VICKSTOW (GB) *1913–1914*
Vickers, Bristow & Co, London W.

This company listed a 4-cylinder car of just under 2 litres' capacity, but the factory location and details of the make are uncertain. GNG

VICTOR (i) (US) *1907–1911*
Victor Automobile Manufacturing Co, St Louis, Mo.

The Victor was a high-wheeler powered by a 2-stroke, single-cylinder water-cooled engine, rated at 12hp and driving through friction transmission. Seven different styles were offered with either solid rubber or pneumatic tyres. GMN

VICTOR (ii) (US) *1913–1914*
Victor Motor Car Co, Philadelphia, Pa.

The Victor cyclecar had a more substantial appearance than most cars of its class. The 2.2-litre, 4-cylinder engine was water-cooled and drove through a 3-speed gearbox and a shaft to the differential. Semi-elliptic springs were used. GMN

VICTOR (iii) (US) *1914–1915*
Richmond Cycle Car Manufacturing Co, Richmond, Va.

This two-seater cyclecar used a 2-cylinder, 13hp air-cooled De Luxe engine. The manufacturer was forced to get rid of the last of these cars at $245 each after the cyclecar boom ended. GMN

VICTOR (iv) (GB) *1914–1915*
(1) Victor Motors Ltd, Eynsford, Kent *1914–1915*
(2) Victor Cars Ltd, Ealing, London W. *1915*

Victor Motors Ltd had previously been the D.E.W. Engineering Company, makers of the Dew cyclecar, and the Victor was similar to the later Dews. It had a 10hp 965cc Precision engine and belt drive. The 4½hp Dew monocar was apparently not continued under the Victor name. In 1915 there was an 1,100cc 4-cylinder version, still belt-driven. GNG

VICTORIA (i) (D) *1900–1909; 1957–1958*
(1) Victoria Fahrradwerke vorm. Frankenberger & Ottenstein AG, Nuremberg *1900–1909*
(2) Victoria-Werke AG, Nuremberg *1957–1958*

The Victoria company were manufacturers of bicycles and motor cycles who introduced their first car in 1900. It was a single-cylinder voiturette, with either a 482cc, 4hp or a 596cc, 5hp engine. After 1905 two types were built with 2-cylinder engines of 804cc and 7hp, and 1,248cc and 10hp. During 1908–09 a 4-cylinder model with a 2,680cc, 20hp engine completed the range. After 1909 Victoria again concentrated on their highly respected motor cycles.

Victoria did not take up car manufacture again until 1955 when they co-operated with another firm in the Bayerische Autowerke and produced the Spatz. During 1957–58 this was marketed as the Victoria. It was a small car with 250cc rear engine developing 14bhp. Since 1958 Victoria has produced only motor cycles, and today forms part of the Zweirad-Union. HON

VICTORIA (ii) (E) *1905–1907*
SA Automobiles Victoria, Barcelona

This car was advertised locally and nationally from 1905 to 1907, but no details are available. There is no known connection with the later Madrid-built Victoria (iv). GNG

VICTORIA (iii) (GB) *1907*
Victoria Motor Works, Godalming, Surrey

This Victoria was an assembled car powered by a 10/12hp 4-cylinder Fafnir engine with overhead inlet valves. It had shaft drive, and the side-entrance tourer which was apparently the only body style, cost £300. GNG

VICTORIA (iv) (E) *1919–1923*
Talleres Franco Españoles, Madrid

Named in honour of Queen Victoria Eugenia of Spain, the Victoria was a well-designed small car using a 950cc ohv 4-cylinder engine, and 4-wheel brakes. Touring and sports models were made, and they won many prizes in local races. About 1,000 were made. In 1922 the patents were sold to Gwynne's Engineering Co to become the basis of the Gwynne Eight. JRV

VICTORIA COMBINATION *see* PARISIENNE

VICTORIAN (CDN) *1900*
Made in Hopewell, Nova Scotia, this was a primitive machine, powered by a petrol engine and resembling a crude Locomobile in appearance. It ran poorly and only one was built. HD

VICTRIX (i) (GB) *1902–c.1904*
Victrix Motor Car Works, Kendal, Westmorland

Most Victrix cars were advertised with 6 or 8hp De Dion engines, and it was probably an assembled light car like many of its period. 12hp 2-cylinder and 24hp 4-cylinder cars were also listed in 1903. GNG

1905 VICTORIA(i) 5PS voiturette. *Neubauer Collection*

*c.*1921 VICTORIA(iv) 950cc two-seaters. *J. Rodriguez-Viña*

1929 VIKING(iii) 4.3-litre V-8 sedan. *General Motors Corporation*

1901 VILAIN 6/8hp two-seater. Mons. Vilain at the wheel. *The Veteran Car Club of Great Britain*

c.1931 VILLARD 500cc drophead coupé. Coachwork by Felber. *Lucien Loreille Collection*

VICTRIX (ii) (I) *1911–1913*
Officine Meccaniche Torinesi, Turin

This company took over the licence-production of French Peugeots from the defunct Peugeot-Croizat firm in 1907, but latterly they made 695cc single-cylinder voiturettes with magneto ignition, three speeds, and shaft drive.　　　MCS

VICTRIX (iii) (F) *1921–c.1924*
Automobiles Victrix, Les Lilas, Seine

Little has been recorded about the post-World War 1 Victrix except that it had a 15hp 4-cylinder engine, and was available as a saloon, torpedo-tourer, landaulet, limousine, coupé, or delivery van.　　　GNG

VIKING (i) (US) *1908*
Viking Co, Boston, Mass.

The only known information about this make is that it was a five-seater touring car with a 10ft 6in wheelbase and a 40hp Rutenber engine. This car may have been manufactured in Maine but sold by the Boston company.　　　GMN

VIKING (ii) (GB) *1914*
Viking Motors Ltd, Coventry, Warwickshire

The British Viking was a light car powered by a 4-cylinder Mathis or Ballot engine. It had shaft drive, and Lanchester-type springs with long radius rods at the rear. The price was £160 for a two-seater.　　　GNG

VIKING (iii) (US) *1929–1930*
Olds Motor Works, Lansing, Mich.

By 1929, General Motors were making a remarkably complex range of cars, including ranges within ranges. Alongside the reliable Oldsmobile six, Lansing introduced a quite new model for a more expensive market, the Viking. In general, it bore a close resemblance to its more luxurious relative, the La Salle, of which it was intended to be a cheaper version, but its 4.3-litre, V-eight engine was unusual in that the chain-driven camshaft operated horizontal valves between the banks of cylinders. It developed 81bhp. The rationalization forced on American car manufacturers by the Depression killed the Viking after two seasons.　　　TRN

VILAIN (F) *1900–1902*
Vilain Frères, Paris 19e

Vilain cars used horizontal engines mounted either at the rear or, later, at the centre of the chassis. The first model had a 6/8hp 2-cylinder engine, friction-cone transmission and double chain final drive. 1902 models had 7 or 10hp single-cylinder centrally-mounted engines, and were sold in England under the name Motormobile. They boasted a special carburettor which was claimed to function equally well on petrol, paraffin, alcohol, or a mixture of any two of these fuels.　　　GNG

VILLARD (F) *1925–1935*
Sté des Automobiles Villard, Janville, Oise

The Villard was a late example of the cyclecar which had flourished in France a few years earlier. It was a 3-wheeler powered by a 345cc single-cylinder 2-stroke engine which drove the single front wheel via a 6-speed friction transmission and single chain. In two-seater touring form it was capable of 35mph, but a 50mph sports model was also available. In 1927 a few 4-wheelers were made. These also had chain drive to the front wheels, and a 500cc 2-cylinder engine. In 1931 a version with conventional gearbox and 500cc Chaise V-4 engine was made for export to America. The last private cars had similar transmission and 350cc ohc Chaise units. The 3-wheeler was made as a light delivery van, and probably more Villards were sold in this form than as private cars.　　　GNG

VINCKE (B) *1895–c.1905*
(1) Vincke & Delmer, Malines
(2) SA des Automobiles Nestor Vincke, Malines

Vincke and Delmer were the first firm to make cars for sale in Belgium, and the car which they exhibited at the 1895 Paris Salon was based on a Benz. Later models were large carriage-type vehicles of Panhard appearance, with 2-cylinder engines, solid tyres and electric ignition. Production was sporadic rather than regular, but a car with a 15hp front-mounted 4-cylinder engine and double chain drive was made in 1899. Later production was mainly of commercials, although a car was sold in England in 1903 known as the Vincke-Halcrow. It had a 9hp 2-cylinder Aster engine, and shaft drive.　　　GNG

VINDEC *see* ALLRIGHT

VINDELICA (D) *1899–c.1900*
Heinle und Wegelin, Oberhausen

This company were well-known bicycle makers who made a few light cars, sold in England under the name Liliput by the P.T.S. Company of Finsbury, London. They were two-seaters with 3½hp engines and 3 speeds.　　　GNG

VINET (F) *1900–c.1904*
Automobiles Vinet, Neuilly, Seine

Vinet were coachbuilders who introduced a voiturette in 1900. It was powered by a 3½hp De Dion engine, and had a tubular frame and belt drive. In the original drawing it had a pointed bonnet like the early Vauxhall, and the advanced feature of headlamps set into the bonnet, but this design was probably not built, as later photographs of the Vinet voiturette show it to have a large gilled-tube radiator and conventional bonnet. By 1902 Vinet were making larger cars with 12 or 16/20hp Aster engines (2- and 4-cylinder respectively), and double chain drive. They had low bonnets but in the closed models these were offset by very high limousine coachwork.   GNG

VINOT (F) *1901–1926*
(1) Vinot et Deguingand, Puteaux, Seine *1901–1926*
(2) Vinot et Deguingand, Nanterre, Seine *1919–1926*

More correctly designated the Vinot-Deguingand, this make was invariably known as plain Vinot once it had become firmly established. The first Vinots (sold in England under the name La Silencieuse) had 1½-litre vertical-twin aiv engines rated at 5½hp, coil ignition, pressed steel frames, and belt-and-chain transmission. An unusual feature which persisted for many years was the vertical gate gear change. By 1903 cars had conventional side-chain drive and armoured wood frames, an improved 10hp twin at 6,000fr being available alongside a pair of 4-cylinder cars (the 14hp 3.3-litre Type H and the 18hp Type F) with mechanically-operated side valves in a T-head, and a 4-speed gearbox. Other features included pump cooling, coil ignition, and sight-feed lubrication. Honeycomb radiators were introduced in 1905, when the pressed steel frame reappeared on the larger cars, and there was a 5.8-litre 30hp with dual ignition. A 3.3-litre 4-cylinder car finished 3rd in that year's Tourist Trophy. Steel frames were standardized in 1906, when a 6-cylinder model made its appearance; this was available in 6.5-litre form with pair-cast cylinders the following year, other regular features that season being exhaust-pressure fuel feed and ht magneto ignition. A 16/20hp 4-cylinder sold at £525, and shaft drive came to Vinot et Deguingand in 1908 with a L-head 10/14CV (sold as the 12/16 in Britain) of 2.1 litres' capacity. The 3.7-litre, now rated at 16/24hp, was also shaft-driven, and slowly live axles spread up the range, though as late as 1911 four chain-driven models were still listed.

In 1909 Vinot took over Gladiator, and from 1910 to 1920 two parallel and identical ranges were on offer, even the catalogued prices being the same. The only difference was that the 24hp of just over 4 litres (with shaft drive from 1909) remained peculiar to Vinot. In 1911 came a more modern monobloc 12hp with pressure lubrication, town-carriage versions being available with a double-reduction back axle. In 1912 the company took a brief interest in racing with some short-stroke 3-litres for the Coupe de l'Auto: these had overhead inlet valves and remarkably well streamlined tails in an era of slab tanks. The 1.7-litre Vinot (which sold for £280 in 1912) was offered without the famous vertical gate, but this feature was retained on the next type to go monobloc, a 15/20hp with the classic cylinder dimensions of 80mm × 130mm. 1914 Vinots were 4-cylinder cars with pressure-fed crankshafts, and came in 1.7-litre, 2.1-litre, 2.6-litre, and 4.2-litre sizes, all with wire wheels. The two smaller models had 3-speed gearboxes and pair-cast cylinders were retained on the big 25/30hp car at £745. Apart from full electrical equipment, the cars announced in 1919 resembled pre-war models, though inflation had pushed the price of the 4-speed 15/20 up from £465 to £915, and Vinot, like De Dion and Delaunay-Belleville, were not destined to recover their pre-war standing in the market. There were no Gladiators after 1920, but all Vinot could do in the way of a new model was the 11/25hp of 1921, an ohv 1.8-litre with aluminium pistons, straight bevel final drive, cone clutch, and 4-speed gearbox with right-hand *ball* change. Its price was £685, and a year later the old-established 15.9hp car acquired overhead valves as the Type BO. In 1924 the 1.8-litre, now rated at 12/25hp, was given front-wheel brakes, but Vinot were now in serious financial trouble, and few, if any cars, were made thereafter. The Nanterre works were acquired by Donnet, and the last traces of a once popular make were seen in 1928, now under the Deguingand name; this was a 2-stroke cyclecar from the drawing-board of the prolific Violet.   MCS

VIOLET-BOGEY (F) *1913–1914*
Marcel Violet, Paris

Although Marcel Violet became famous for his 2-stroke cyclecar designs, the first car to be associated with his name had a normal, if unusually sophisticated, 4-stroke engine. The Violet-Bogey cyclecar had a 2-cylinder, 1,100cc, water-cooled power unit with the advanced specifications of pressure lubrication, a crank-shaft carried on ball-bearings, and, to provide the power which these features permitted, exceptionally large overhead inlet valves, operated by a single push-and-pull rod from one camshaft. The outcome was 22bhp at a safe 2,400rpm, which made the Violet-Bogey a very fast machine indeed, and brought it success in competition before World War 1. The transmission, too, was un-usual, there being friction-disc primary drive. The final drive was normal, by chain to a differential-less axle.   TRN

1903 VINOT-DEGUINGAND 14hp tonneau.
Sussex Express & County Herald

1913 VINOT-DEGUINGAND 15/20 two-seater. Coachwork by Gill of Paddington. *Autocar*

1921 VINOT-DEGUINGAND 10hp tourer. *Autocar*

1913 VIOLET-BOGEY 1,100cc two-seater. *David Burgess Wise*

1912 VIVINUS 16/20hp limousine. *Geoffroy de Beauffort Collection*

1966 VIXEN(ii) Formula 4 racing car. Nick Britain at the wheel. *Autosport*

VIPEN (GB) 1898–c.1904
East Riding Cycle Co, Hull, Yorks.

Cars were sold by this company under the names Vipen and Holderness, but they were probably all imported machines. Early Vipens were heavy-looking vehicles on the lines of the Panhard or M.M.C., and in 1902 the firm were advertising a range of vehicles from a 1½hp motor cycle to a 12hp 2-cylinder car. In 1903 they were selling a four-seater tonneau on De Dion lines.　GNG

VIQUEOT (US) 1905
Viqueot Co, Long Island City, N.Y.

This car used a chassis built at Puteaux, France, with bodies fitted in America. Two 4-cylinder engines were available, of 28/32hp and 40/45hp. These had 3-speed transmission and double chain drive. The Viqueot Co was controlled by the Vehicle Equipment Co, of the same city, whose main business was commercial vehicles.　GMN

VIRATELLE (F) 1922–1924
Sté des Moteurs et Automobiles Viratelle, Lyons

Viratelle made motor cycles, and the few cyclecars produced made use of the motor-cycle engines and other components.　GNG

VIRGINIAN (US) 1911–1912
Richmond Iron Works, Richmond, Va.

The Virginian was a large car driven by a 50hp 4-cylinder engine of 6.4 litres. A four-seater roadster and a seven-seater touring car were available at $3,000.　GMN

VIRO (GB) 1970
Adnams Motors Ltd, Basingstoke, Hants.

A wedge-bodied Formula Ford single-seater was advertised briefly by this firm.　DF

VISTA (GB) 1969 to date
Asquith Bros (Engineers) Ltd, Staincliffe, Dewsbury, Yorks.

This firm made a handful of Formula Ford cars, notable for rear radiators and inboard rear suspension. The pointed-nosed Mark 2 was offered in 1970 at £900 as a kit. In 1972 a Formula 5000 car was also constructed on similar lines.　DF

VITTORIA (I) 1914–1915
Giorgio Ambrosini, Turin

The 3.2-litre Vittoria was a conventional 4-cylinder car with sv monobloc engine and 4-speed gearbox. Ambrosini made his own power units, but bought bodies and other components from outside suppliers.　MCS

VIVINUS (B) 1899–1912
Ateliers Vivinus SA, Schaerbeek, Brussels

When it first appeared, the little voiturette of Alexis Vivinus had a transversely-mounted, air-cooled single-cylinder engine, driving through belts that provided 2 forward speeds. This was a refined vehicle of its type and age, and easy to control. A 2-cylinder model that appeared in 1900 was fast as well, being capable of over 35mph. The Vivinus was very popular, not only in its native land but also in Britain, France and Germany, where it sold respectively as the New Orleans, the Georges Richard, and the De Dietrich. A second single, with a water-cooled De Dion engine, was apparently offered at the same time. A 7hp water-cooled vertical twin with a 3-speed gearbox and shaft drive brought the 2-cylinder design up to date in 1901, but in 1902 the Vivinus grew up into a modern 15/18hp 4-cylinder car with mechanically-operated inlet valves and shaft drive. From then on, a variety of completely conventional, conservative twins, fours and sixes was listed. By the time production ceased the twins and sixes had been dropped, and the range consisted of three 4-cylinder models, a 10/12hp, a 16/20hp and a 24/30hp.　TRN

VIXEN (i) (US) 1914
Davis Manufacturing Co, Milwaukee, Wisc.

This cyclecar used a water-cooled 4-cylinder engine with a friction transmission. The drive to the rear wheels was by chains. The front suspension was by double cantilever springs.

VIXEN (ii) (GB) 1966–c.1970
Vixen Racing Ltd, Cheshunt, Herts.

British Formula 4 racing was for a few years almost monopolized by Alec Bottoms' neat Vixen VB series of designs. Habitual winners included works driver Keith Norman in 1969, Bob Jarvis and Mike Wilds in 1970 and John Cavill in 1971. In 1972 hill-climbs D. Franklin's Huntsman-Vixen-Imp featured regularly in the class awards. Plans for production for other racing classes did not reach fruition.　DF

VOGTLAND (D) 1910–1912
Maschinen- und Automobilfabrik Endesfelder & Weiss, Plauen

Two models with 4-cylinder 6/12PS and 10/20PS engines were produced by this firm, available as two-, four- or six-seaters.　HON

VOGUE (US) *1917–1923*

Vogue Motor Car Co, Tiffin, Ohio

A typical assembled car, the Vogue was built for its first two years in the same factory as the Economy and the differentiation between the two makes and the two companies remains a mystery. The cars had a 9ft 11in wheelbase and, except for an 8-cylinder type, which was discontinued late in 1918, sixes with Continental and Herschell-Spillman engines were standard. Slanted louvres gave the cars a rakish appearance and wire wheels were available at extra cost. Prices ranged from $1,995 upwards. Several hundred were built in seven years of production. KM

VOISIN (F) *1919–1939*

SA des Aéroplanes G. Voisin, Issy-les-Moulineaux, Seine

Gabriel Voisin was first famous for his aircraft. He was one of the earliest and most important pioneers, claiming to have developed a practical aeroplane before the Wright brothers; the controversy still rages. Voisin was always a spectacular character, and so were his cars. However, like his aircraft, they were efficient machines as well. With the post-World War 1 depression in the aircraft industry, he entered motor manufacture by acquiring the rights in a Citroën model which was never made as such. This was the 18CV of 1918, which used a Knight double sleeve-valve engine. Sold as the Type C1 Voisin, it had 4 cylinders and a capacity of 4 litres. It was a fine car, and henceforth Voisin used only sleeve-valve engines, developed by himself to a high degree. The 4-litre had aluminium pistons, to permit higher engine speeds, and was eventually capable of 80mph. In spite of an excellent performance, the 4-litre was an immensely strong, refined and silent motor car − all characteristics of Voisins in general. A sports version was also offered, with 90bhp. The 4-litre was made until 1926. Alongside it, from 1921, was the smaller C4, an 8CV of 1¼ litres that was later enlarged to 10CV and 1½ litres. In its final form, the 10CV engine produced 44bhp at 4,000rpm − so much for the opponents of sleeve valves, who claimed that high revolutions could not be combined with reliability − and the car was capable of 70mph. It had Dewandre vacuum servo brakes, as had all Voisins from late 1925. The 10CV, too, survived in basic form until 1928. All the same, Voisin had to follow fashion in one respect, and introduced three 6-cylinder cars for 1927. The best-known was the 13CV, providing 2.3 litres, the first Knight-engined six to be sold in France. Even in normal form, this was a 66bhp, 75mph vehicle, but a sports model was also available. From 1928, this six, known as the Charmant, had alternative final-drive ratios for fast cruising.

Apart from sleeve valves, to which a number of famous manufacturers were wedded at the time, Voisin had three other enthusiasms that were considerably less common. One was truly easy gear-changing, which many makers sought, but few actually incorporated in their production cars. The Sensaud de Lavaud system of infinitely variable gears was applied in 1929 to the 10CV which, in the following year, had been superseded by a Cotal electric epicyclic gearbox. To this interest was related Voisin's fondness for multi-cylinder engines, which aimed at giving the utmost flexibility, thereby avoiding gear-changing altogether. He made a V-twelve luxury car as early as 1921. The layout was revived in 1930 for the Type C18 Diane. It was a 4.8-litre car with a 115bhp engine that needed only 3 forward speeds. The Simoun and Sirocco were two low chassis models with striking razor edge saloon and coupé bodies which were made in very small numbers in 1930. Identical except for their engines, the Simoun used a 5.8-litre six, and the Sirocco the V-12. The Diane was still listed for 1938. The other Voisins of the 1930s were sixes, the Charmant continuing to 1934.

Voisin had a reputation for putting into practice ideas which remained ideals for most manufacturers. For example, he was dedicated to weight reduction, and to this end produced notably light patent bodies whose only drawback was their extreme ugliness. Of wood and aluminium, they were entirely practical, being cheap to make, compact, and strong, as well as light. A 2-door, four-seater saloon body on the 10CV chassis weighed only 1,060lb, keeping the weight of the whole car down to 22cwt. The most unprepossessing were the convertibles and those with detachable hard tops. Because of their looks, the Voisins, with their maker's patent bodies, never sold well − a deplorable waste of well-directed ingenuity. However, fabric Weymann-type and other normal bodies were also supplied. From 1931 to 1934, some Imperia cars from Belgium were made under licence. In 1936 a most unusual car was made in the shape of the straight-12; this had two 3-litre, 6-cylinder engines in line, the rear part of the hindmost engine projecting into the driving compartment. 180bhp and 125mph were claimed, but the car was not put into production. The last Voisins, introduced in 1937, used the 6-cylinder 3½-litre Graham engine, though without the supercharger. These were not the work of Gabriel Voisin, but were made by a syndicate that had acquired the name. After World War 2, Voisin designed a car which was as complete a contrast to his former work as can be imagined − the Spanish-built Biscuter. TRN

VOLGA (SU) *1955 to date*

Zavod Imieni Molotova, Gorky

Although the Pobieda (M-20) sedan served the Russians well during the early post-war years, it was rather out of date by the 1950s. Thus it was that the Gorky

1923 VOISIN 18hp coupé de ville. *Autocar*

c.1932 VOISIN 4.8-litre V-12 saloon.
Automobielmuseum, Driebergen

1938 VOISIN 3½-litre drophead coupé. *Autocar*

1964 VOLGA 2½-litre saloon. *Thomson & Taylor (Brooklands) Ltd*

1937 VOLKSWAGEN(i) VW30 tourer. *Neubauer Collection*

1960 VOLKSWAGEN(i) 1200 saloon. *Volkswagenwerk AG*

1965 VOLKSWAGEN(i) 1600TL coupé. *Volkswagenwerk AG*

Works decided upon the Volga as the Pobieda's successor in 1955, both models being produced until assembly line conversion was completed in 1958.

Various modifications have been made through the years; several grille changes have been noted, and in 1959 there was an unsuccessful attempt to add an automatic transmission. The Volga is a sturdy 4-door sedan with a 2.5-litre 4-cylinder, ohv engine using wet cylinder liners and a 5-bearing crankshaft. A choice of power has been offered, varying from 70 to 97bhp depending on the year and model. In Belgium a Rover Diesel of 65bhp is installed by the firm of Sobimpex as an export option. As on the Moskvitch, the front seat folds back to make a bed.

A station wagon (M-22G) and an ambulance (M-22E) were built on the Volga chassis, and a good many sedans were made into taxis with a checkered strip painted along the door panels. In 1968 the Volga 24 appeared, with lower lines and a longer wheelbase. Output was up to 110bhp, and a 4-speed all-synchromesh gearbox with floor change was provided. It had supplanted the older type by 1971.

BE

VOLK (GB) *1895*

Volk's Electric Tramway, Brighton, Sussex

Magnus Volk, whose electric railway on Brighton seafront was the first of its kind open to the public, also built a few electric dogcarts in 1895. These were 3-wheelers, tiller steered and powered by batteries and a 1hp Immisch electric motor, said to have propelled them at 10mph.

Following a demonstration in Constantinople, Volk was successful in making a sale to the Sultan of Turkey, even though it is reported that the latter's slaves had to manhandle the car round the corners of the narrow paths of the palace courtyard.

MJWW

VOLKSWAGEN (i) (D) *1936 to date*

(1) Dr.ing.h.c.F. Porsche GmbH, Stuttgart *1936–1937*
(2) Gesellschaft zur Vorbereitung des Volkswagens, Berlin; Stadt des KdF-Wagens *1937–1938*
(3) Volkswagenwerk GmbH, Berlin Wolfsburg *1938–1960*
(4) Volkswagenwerk AG, Wolfsburg *1960 to date*

The development of the Volkswagen is closely linked with the name Ferdinand Porsche. After World War 1 he tried to realize one of his favourite schemes: a small economical car for a wide public. One of his attempts was the Austro-Daimler Sascha. He continued his efforts while working for Daimler-Benz at Stuttgart. His plan was brought a step nearer to fruition when he set up his own office at Stuttgart. There he designed small cars for Zündapp in 1932 with 5-cylinder radial engines, and for N.S.U. in 1933 with 4-cylinder horizontally opposed units. But neither Zündapp nor N.S.U. were able to invest vast sums during the Depression years and neither design was put into production, although a few prototypes were built.

In 1934 Porsche was directed by the Nazi government of the day to develop a small car and to build three prototypes. These prototypes were constructed by Porsche and his team in his own garage. They were ready in 1936 and the design became known as the VW3. Another series of 30 prototypes (VW30) was built in 1937 by Daimler-Benz and in Porsche's newly founded workshops at Stuttgart-Zuffenhausen, the site of the present Porsche works. In 1938 the final version, the VW38, was introduced. These types had 704 or 984cc air-cooled engines. Also in 1938 the foundation stone for the new factory was laid, and the name KdF-Wagen was officially adopted. KdF was the abbreviation for 'Kraft durch Freude' (Strength through Joy), the Nazi organization which sponsored and financed the development of the car, controlling it through its newly founded Gesellschaft zur Vorbereitung des Volkswagens.

In his Stuttgart workshops, Porsche built three streamlined, Volkswagen-based sports cars with tuned engines for the intended Berlin-Rome Race of 1939, but this event was cancelled as a result of the outbreak of World War 2. They can be regarded as the forerunners of the Porsche sports car which appeared after the war. Until 1939 no cars were available for the public and only prototypes existed. During the war the Volkswagen was built in various versions for the armed forces with an increased engine capacity of 1,131cc. The Jeep-type Kübelwagen and an amphibious car, the latter with 4-wheel drive, were produced in large numbers and were the first Volkswagens to become widely known. After the war the factory came under British control and a number of cars were assembled from parts. In 1945 a total of 1,785 cars was produced, this number being increased to 10.020 in 1946, all of them delivered to the British army. These private versions used the 1,131cc engine, developing 25bhp. In 1949 the factory was released from British control and returned to German administration.

The Volkswagen works themselves produced only the saloon version but several convertible versions were offered by various firms. The four-seater convertible by Karmann — one of Germany's oldest coach-building firms — and the Karmann-Ghia two-seater convertible and coupé versions became part of the official sales programme. The Volkswagen became known as a car which made no changes in body style although its technical details were constantly improved. In 1954 the engine was developed to 1,192cc and 30bhp and a further increase in engine output to 34bhp came in 1960. In 1961 the five millionth Volkswagen was produced. In the same year a new model was introduced, the 1500 with a 1,493cc 45bhp engine and new body, followed two years later by the 1500S developing 54bhp. 1965 saw the 'Beetle' VW with a 1,285cc, 40bhp engine and the introduction of another new model the 1600TL with a 1,584cc 54bhp engine. Since 1966 the Beetle has also been available with the 1,493 engine. The 1968 versions of the 1500 Beetle and 1600 were available with a selective automatic transmission; at the same time 12-volt electrics were standardized on all models save the basic 1200. In 1969 Volkswagen attempted to broaden their range with the 411, still an air-cooled flat-4, but now featuring unitary construction, McPherson strut ifs, and a new type of semi-trailing link irs already tried on 1600s. Its 1,679cc pushrod engine developed 68bhp, and it was sold as a 4-door saloon or estate car. The 1970 models could be had with fuel injection. Another new Volkswagen was the VW 181, an open jeep-type vehicle available in civilian or military guises. Sales that year were 1,621,197 units. Prices ranged from DM4,626 for a 1200 saloon up to DM8,755 for the most expensive 411.

The 411, however, did not prove a great commercial success, and for 1971 Volkswagen took advantage of their ownership of the Audi-N.S.U. combine to issue the latter firm's piston-engined Ro80 derivative, the K70, under their own imprint. This development smacked of heresy at Wolfsburg, for the new car had a vertical 5-bearing water-cooled 4-cylinder ohc engine mounted at the front and driving the front wheels. It came in 75bhp and 90bhp forms; other differences from the N.S.U. prototype were the 4-speed manual gearbox, a wheelbase 6½in shorter, and a far lower price – DM9,450 as against the DM17,300 asked for the Ro80. The Beetle was now available with a 60bhp 1,584cc engine and front disc brakes, McPherson strut front suspension being used on this version. During 1972 the firm began production of electrically-propelled light vans and Kombis. On 17 February 1972 the Beetle officially broke the Model-T Ford's record of 15,007,003 units of an individual model. The 1973 Beetles had panoramic windscreens, and came in 1.2-litre, 1.3-litre and 1.6-litre sizes, with disc brakes available on all but the 1200. At the same time the 411E with fuel injection was replaced by an improved 412E. The 1600 series, the Karmann-Ghia coupés and the K70 were continued, as was the open VW 181.

Volkswagen are currently manufactured or assembled in several foreign countries; in 1970 these overseas plants accounted for over 325,000 units. In 1963 Formula Vee was introduced, a poor man's racing formula using Volkswagen-based cars. The Beetle is also the recognized raw material for the beach buggy, a form of fun car offered by many small specialist concerns.   HON

VOLKSWAGEN (ii) (BR) *1968 to date*
Volkswagen do Brasil S.A., São Bernardo do Campo

Since 1968 this associate of the Volkswagenwerk has been building special Brazilian models alongside the regular Beetles and Karmann-Ghias. At first these were 4-door versions of the 1600, but in 1971 a fastback edition of this type was added to the range, and in 1972 came the SP series of fastback GT coupés with front disc brakes. The more powerful 1.7-litre SP2 version was credited with 100mph.   MCS

VOLKSWAGEN-PORSCHE (D) *1969 to date*
VW-Porsche Vertriebsgesellschaft mbH, Ludwigsburg

This car was unveiled at the 1969 Frankfurt Show as an inexpensive companion to the regular Porsche range: basic price was DM12,250 as against something over DM21,000 for a standard 911. Flat-4 and flat-6 engines of Porsche type, with capacities of 1,679cc and 1,991cc respectively, were mounted amidships, other features being electronic fuel injection, a 5-speed gearbox, all-disc brakes, pop-out headlamps and all-independent suspension. A semi-convertible body based on the Porsche Targa was standard. These models continued without basic change until 1973, when a 2-litre, 100bhp pushrod four replaced the 6-cylinder unit.   MCS

VOLPE (I) *1947–1949*
Anonima Lombarda Cabotaggio Aereo, Milan

The Volpe was a typical post-war minicar powered by a rear-mounted 125cc 2-cylinder 2-stroke engine. It developed 6bhp at 5,000rpm, and a speed of 47mph was claimed. The body was an open two-seater.   GNG

VOLPINI (I) *1954–1955; 1958–1959*
Milan

The Arzani-Volpini, based on a 1950 Maserati, had a brief and unhappy career as a Formula 1 car. With the advent of Formula Junior, a new car was offered, with tubular ladder frame and Fiat vital parts. For the considerably lightened 1959 version, a live coil-sprung axle replaced the previous independent rear end. Lorenzo Bandini achieved some competition success, but results were not sufficiently encouraging to justify further development. A Formula 3 car was also made.   DF

VOLTOR (F) *1922–1925*
Constructions Électrique Voltor, Sainte-Étienne, Loire

This company specialized in the manufacture of electric batteries and chargers, and made a few electric cars. In 1923 one of these made an endurance run between Sainte-Étienne and Avignon. The limited production of cars ceased in 1925, but a light electric van was shown at the 1939 Lyons Fair.   LL

1973 VOLKSWAGEN(i) 412 1.7-litre saloon.
Volkswagenwerk AG

1973 VOLKSWAGEN(i) K70 1.6-litre saloon.
Volkswagenwerk AG

1973 VOLKSWAGEN-PORSCHE 914 2-litre sports car.
VW-Porsche

1929 VOLVO PV651 3-litre saloon. *AB Volvo*

1936 VOLVO PV36 3.7-litre saloon. *AB Volvo*

1955 VOLVO PV444 1.4-litre saloon. *AB Volvo*

1973 VOLVO 145 2-litre estate car. *AB Volvo*

VOLUGRAFO (I) *1946–1948*
Volugrafo Officine Meccaniche, Turin

One of the smallest of the post-war minicars, the Volugrafo was powered by a rear-mounted motorcycle engine of 125cc. It had an open two-seater body with no doors, and the appearance was not unlike that of a fairground dodgem car.   GNG

VOLVO (S) *1927 to date*
AB Volvo, Gothenburg

The Volvo company was formed under the management of Assar Gabrielson with financial backing from the SKF ball-bearing firm. Their first product was the P.4, a 4-cylinder 1.9-litre car with an sv engine and a comparatively low output of 28bhp. However, it was well built, and sold well. A 3-litre 6-cylinder machine appeared in 1929, and during the 1930s Volvo evolved a range of solid family cars similar to contemporary Americans in appearance, one model being reminiscent of the Airflow Chrysler. The 1939 model, the PV60 with a 3.6-litre sv engine, was the culmination of this range and remained in production until after World War 2.

In 1944 company policy changed in favour of a small saloon with a 1.4-litre ohv engine developing 40bhp. This car, the PV444, was the first Volvo to sell in any numbers outside Scandinavia, and during the 1950s it rapidly established the company's reputation for good roadholding and fine quality construction. The specification included ifs, coil rear suspension, 3-speed gearbox and hydraulic brakes. Production did not cease until 1965, by which time the engine size had been increased to 1.8 litres, and power to 80bhp (Model 544). In 1956 the Model 122 appeared with the same engine as the 444 and a completely new 4-door saloon body. The 3-speed gearbox was retained until 1958, though the limited production sport roadster had a 5-speed box in 1956. The 122 won more friends for Volvo throughout the world, and was supplemented by the P.1800S, a sports coupé with a body built by Jensen of West Bromwich, and Girling disc brakes on the front wheels. The output of this engine was 115bhp, and top speed was over 110mph. Power units of this type were also used by Facel Vega and Marcos. For 1967 the 1.8-litre engine was installed in an entirely new model, the 144, noted for a safety-keyed structure with reinforced passenger compartment, telescopic steering column, and dual-circuit, 4-wheel disc brakes. Unique was the six-figure odometer. A full range of saloons and station wagons first supplemented and then supplanted the old 122 family, though this soldiered on until 1970.

All the 4-cylinder engines were enlarged to 2 litres in 1969, when there was a companion six, the conventional 3-litre 164 with a Vanden Plas Princess-style radiator grille, alternator ignition, and the choice of 4-speed manual gearbox (with or without overdrive) and automatic. Through-flow ventilation featured on 1970 Volvos, and Bosch fuel injection was standardized on the P1800 (it was available on all models by 1972). In this latter year the sports model was once again modified, emerging as a GT estate car in the Reliant manner, the coupé being discontinued a year later. Main improvements for 1973 concern new safety features such as revised controls and a deforming boss to the steering wheel.   OB

VOODOO (GB) *1972 to date*
Normandale Products, Long Itchington, Warwickshire

The Voodoo Tragonic was sponsored by David L. Trager-Lewis and designed by Geoff Neale and John Arnold. It was a GT coupé with square-tube space-frame and a fibreglass body only 2ft 11in high. Hillman Imp mechanical parts were used. Entry was via a hydraulically assisted front-hinged 'flip top'.   DF

VORAN (D) *1926–1928*
Voran Automobilbau AG, Berlin

Richard Bussien was a designer of small front-driven cars. His Voran 4/20PS and 5/30PS models with sv 4-cylinder Pluto engines were produced in limited numbers. The Voran company was acquired by N.A.G., the N.A.G.-Voran being the result of this merger.   HON

VOUSEMOI (F) *1904*
This car, whose name means 'you and I', was appropriately a two-seater. It used a 10hp 2-cylinder or 16/20hp 4-cylinder Gnome engine, a 3-speed gearbox, and shaft drive.   GNG

VOX (GB) *1912–1915*
Lloyd & Plaister Ltd, Wood Green, London N.

The Vox light car used a 750cc 2-cylinder 2-stroke engine designed by Harry Ricardo, who had built the Dolphin car which also made use of Lloyd & Plaister parts. The engine had one pumping cylinder and one working cylinder, the mixture being admitted to the latter by a leaf-spring valve. Final drive was by shaft. About 50 Voxes were made.   GNG

VULCAN (i) (GB) *1902–1928*
(1) Vulcan Motor Manufacturing and Engineering Co Ltd, Southport, Lancs. *1902–1906*
(2) Vulcan Motor and Engineering Co Ltd, Southport, Lancs. *1906–1928*

This firm was better known for commercial vehicles. Vulcan private cars stemmed from experiments conducted in the 1897–99 period by the brothers Thomas and Joseph Hampson. A belt-driven single-cylinder voiturette with lateral radiators was shown in 1902, being replaced a year later by a 6hp car with armoured wood frame, mechanically-operated inlet valves, and shaft drive. It was listed at only £105, and was soon followed by a 10hp twin, also T-headed but with a steel frame, selling for £200. 4-cylinder cars of 12 and 16hp, still modestly priced, were available in 1905, while the biggest 1906 models, with capacities of 3.1 and 5.2 litres, had gate change. No 2-cylinder models were catalogued after 1908, but a year previously Vulcan had joined the ranks of 6-cylinder manufacturers with a 4.8-litre T-headed machine featuring dual ignition and cone clutch, at £600 for a chassis. Unlike other makers, Vulcan retained their interest in this type, which had acquired a 4-speed box and had grown to 6 litres by 1908, and the 1909 range consisted of four 4-cylinder cars and the six, all shaft-driven and still with T-heads; the smallest Vulcan, rated at 12hp, had a 3-speed gearbox and worm drive. A new 3.6-litre six with unit gearbox and worm drive followed in 1911, along with an L-head 2.4-litre fifteen. Worm drive was standardized on the 1912 cars, when the bigger models had T-heads, and a 1.8-litre, 2-cylinder with an Aster engine was offered. All but the smallest model had detachable wheels as standard in 1913, and by the outbreak of World War 1 the company was well established with a range of solidly-built machines: a 2.4-litre 10/15, a 2.6-litre 15.9, and a 3-litre monobloc 15/20 at £375. All these had L-heads and bull-nose radiators, though the similarly styled six retained the older configuration. A 1½-litre Vulcanette with a 3-speed rear-axle gearbox and full electrical equipment was announced for 1915 but the war intervened.

After 1918 the company concentrated increasingly on trucks, and a brief association with the Harper Bean Group (1919–20) did no good to finances. Some odd experiments included a worm-drive 3½-litre V-8 tourer intended to sell for £625 (1919), and two models in 1922 with Howard sleeve-valve engines, a big 3.6-litre sports-touring four and a 10hp 1.4-litre flat-twin listed at £315. However, none of these reached the public, the regular Vulcan lines being a 1.8-litre ohv 12 and a 2.6-litre sv 16/20, both with Dorman engines. There was also a conservative 20hp model with the company's own 3.3-litre sv fixed-head engine and 4-speed separate gearbox, selling for £850 in 1921; by this time flat radiators were again being used. The Vulcan 20 was available to military order with full wireless equipment in 1923, in which year C.B. Wardman effected a liaison of Vulcan and Lea-Francis. The two companies pooled their dealer network, Vulcan became responsible for certain Lea-Francis power units and bodies, and Lea-Francis made gear and steering boxes for Vulcan. A 1½-litre sv Dorman-engined Vulcan 12 was listed at £295 in 1925, followed a year later by an ohv worm-driven derivative, also with Dorman engine, and looking very like a Lea-Francis. 4-wheel brakes were available in 1925 and standardized in 1926. Last of the line were the 14/40 and 16/60, with the disastrous twin ohc 6-cylinder engines of their own make. Short-chassis cars were worm-driven, but bevel drive was adopted for long-chassis versions. Vulcans wore artillery wheels, but were otherwise identical to their Lea-Francis counterparts which were made alongside them at Southport. Not many were made, and after 1928 only commercial vehicles were produced. The firm subsequently amalgamated with Tilling-Stevens and thus were absorbed into the Rootes Group after World War 2. Truck production ceased in 1953.

MCS

VULCAN (ii) (US) *1913–1914*

(1) Vulcan Motor Car Co, Painesville, Ohio *1913*
(2) Vulcan Manufacturing Co, Painesville, Ohio *1913–1914*

This car was a cleanly-designed light car with a 27hp 4-cylinder engine. A two-seater speedster on an 8ft 9in wheelbase with electric lights sold for $750. A five-seater version with the same engine, but on a longer wheelbase, cost $850. GMN

VULKAN (D) *1899–1905*

Vulkan Automobilgesellschaft mbH, Berlin SW 13

Electric cars were built by this firm to the designs of Robert Schwenke. HON

VULPÈS (F) *1905–c.1910*

(1) Automobiles Vulpès, Paris *1905–1907*
(2) Automobiles Vulpès, Clichy, Seine *1907–c.1910*

Vulpès cars were made in various models from an 8hp single-cylinder to a 30/40hp four. They were generally conventional in design, although the Janus engines used in some of the fours featured a transverse camshaft between the pair-cast cylinders. The voiturettes used De Dion engines, and competed regularly in voiturette races from 1905 to 1908 with some success. Their most successful driver was Barriaux who was also intended to drive the enormous 16.3-litre 4-cylinder car built for the 1906 Grand Prix. GNG

1912 VULCAN(i) 19.6hp two-seater. *Autocar*

1927 VULCAN(i) 16/60hp Gainsborough saloon. *Autocar*

1907 VULPÈS 4-cylinder tourer. *The Veteran Car Club of Great Britain*

1925 W.A.F. 15/45PS straight-8 tourer. *G.L. Hartner*

1906 WALKER(i) 10hp two-seater. *Floyd Clymer Publications*

1966 WALKER(ii) JW4 Formula 4 racing car. *Motorcycle*

WACO (US) 1915–1917
Western Automobile Co, Seattle, Wash.

The Waco was a very conventional 4-cylinder car made mainly in five-seater tourer form, and selling for $950. The engine was a 22.5hp G.B. & S. GNG

WADDINGTON (GB) 1903–1904
Waddington & Sons, Middlesbrough, Yorks.

The Waddington was a conventional car made in single- and twin-cylinder forms. The single had a 6½hp engine of De Dion type and a two-seater body, while the twin had a 10hp engine and a four-seater tonneau body. Both cars had shaft drive and sloping, De Dion-style bonnets. GNG

W.A.F. (A) 1910–1926
Wiener Automobil-Fabrik GmbH, Vienna X

W.A.F. took over the Bock & Hollender factory in 1910. Their range included 25hp and 35hp models. The 45hp 2.8-litre W.A.F. of 1914 was designed for the Alpine trial and was the best known of the pre-World War 1 models. After the war, 4-cylinder 40hp and 6-cylinder 70hp cars were produced. A 4-litre 8-cylinder car – Austria's first – was also introduced, but was built in limited numbers only. HON

WAGENHALS (US) 1913–1915
Wagenhals Motor Co, Detroit, Mich.

The Wagenhals was one of the few American 3-wheelers, and used an exceptionally large engine for such a type, of 4-cylinders and 24hp, carried under a bonnet which projected well in front of the front axle as in some commercial vehicles. Final drive was by chain to the single rear wheel. Wagenhals delivery vans were used by the U.S. Post Office; probably more of these were made than private cars. GNG

WAHL (US) 1913–1914
Wahl Motor Car Co, Detroit, Mich.

Wahl is the German word for 'choice' and it was with this idea that the manufacturer offered the customer a standard assembled car with a 4-cylinder 3.3-litre engine, 4-speed transmission and other components, at a reasonable price. The buyer then might attach his own nameplate to the car and, in effect, become an automobile 'manufacturer'. Five-seater touring and two-seater roadster models were made. KM

WAINER (I) 1959–1960
Milan

A rear-engined Formula Junior, using Fiat parts, was Gianfranco Mantovani's offering, at a price substantially less than many of its rivals. Before the more expensive and sophisticated designs gained the ascendancy, Manfredini gleaned one or two major wins. DF

WALCO (GB) 1905
W.A. Lloyd's Cycle Fittings Ltd, Birmingham

This company started making motor cycles in 1903, and announced a 3-wheeled car to be powered by a 4hp Stevens engine. Few, if any, were sold. GNG

WALCYCAR see WALL

WALDRON (US) 1909–1910
Waldron Runabout Manufacturing Co, Kankakee, Ill.

The Waldron was mechanically a simple car, with an opposed 2-cylinder engine under the body, a friction transmission and double chain drive. Three body types were offered. GMN

WALKER (i) (US) 1905–1906
Walker Motor Car Co, Detroit, Mich.

This car used 2-cylinder, 4-stroke engines of 4.1 litres, with a claimed output of 10hp. They had planetary transmissions and shaft drive. The two-seater runabout cost $600. GMN

WALKER (ii) (GB) 1965–1970
(1) Johnny Walker Racing, Wotton-under-Edge, Gloucestershire 1965–1967
(2) Johnny Walker (Developments) Ltd, Tetbury, Gloucestershire 1967–1970

Pioneers of Formula 4 racing, Johnny Walker Racing had produced nearly 30 cars by the end of 1966. These had multi-tubular chassis construction, with Armstrong spring/damper units and three-part fibreglass bodywork by Specialised Mouldings Ltd. This design progressed steadily to the Mark 6, an Imp-engined car made in 1970 which the works were still racing and developing during the 1972 season. The Costin-Walker, priced at £950 in 1969 ready for Imp engine installation or at £1,500 complete with Honda motor, did not attract buyers, despite advertised adaptability for Formulae 2 or Ford. There was also at that time a plan to market Frank Costin's Amigo GT. DF

WALKER & HUTTON (GB) 1902
Walker & Hutton, Scarborough, Yorks.

This was a light two-seater voiturette powered by a 4hp engine, and using belt drive. It probably never left the experimental stage. GNG

WALL (i) (US) 1901–1904
R.C. Wall Mfg Co, Philadelphia, Pa.

The Wall used a 3-cylinder engine rated at 9hp. Final drive was by double chains to the rear wheels. The five-seater tonneau sold at $1,500. GMN

WALL (ii) (GB) 1911–1915
A.W. Wall Ltd, Tyseley, Birmingham

The Wall was an unusual 3-wheeler with a two-seater body not unlike a sidecar, and steering by long tiller to the single front wheel. The engine was a 4/5hp single or 6hp 2-cylinder Precision which drove the rear wheels by shaft. Wheel steering was available as an alternative from March 1914. The company also made a J.A.P.-engined shaft-drive 4-wheeled cyclecar known as the Walcycar. The 3-wheeler was sometimes known as the Roc, after the Roc Motor Works where the cars were made. GNG

WALMOBIL (D) 1920
Maschinenfabrik Walter Loebel, Leipzig

This was a 3-wheeled single-seater with a 2-cylinder 3/7PS engine mounted above the single driven front wheel. HON

WALTER (i) (US) 1904–1909
(1) American Chocolate Machinery Co, New York, N.Y. 1904
(2) Walter Automobile Co, Trenton, N.J. 1905–1909

The Walter was an expensive and well-designed car. It was available with 30, 40 or 50hp 4-cylinder engines with overhead inlet valves. Open touring models and limousines were produced, ranging in price up to $5,700. These had sliding-gear transmissions with 3 forward speeds and shaft drive. The company is still in business today, making specialized trucks and fire engines. GMN

WALTER (ii) (A;CS) 1908–1936
Jos. Walter & spol., Jinonice

After building motor cycles and motor tricycles Walter started car production in 1908 with a 3-wheeler using V-twin engines of 500cc capacity, which was increased gradually to 1,250cc in later models. The engine was placed behind the single front wheel and transmission was by shaft to the rear axle. The first versions were open two-seaters; later closed four-seater bodies were also available. In 1912 the first 4-wheeled car was introduced: the WI with a 4-cylinder 14hp engine. This was followed by the WII and WIII with increased engine capacity and output. After World War 1 the WZ model with a 1,540cc engine was brought out, followed by the WIZ.

From 1928 the Walter range was based on a 4-bearing ohv six on British lines with cruciform-braced frame, magneto ignition, and hydraulic servo brakes. Capacity, originally 2,860cc, was increased to 3.3 litres in 1930, and sports versions had 95bhp, or 115bhp with the optional Cozette supercharger. Later models used a 4-speed synchromesh gearbox with Maybach overdrive. Between 1931 and 1933 the company also built a dozen Royals, vast prestige cars on Maybach lines with 5.9-litre ohv V-12 engines, twin carburettors, coil ignition, and Maybach's complex 8-speed *Doppelschnellgang* gearbox. Walter production was never large, and most of it was made up of licence-produced Fiats, many with local styling modifications. These comprised 1,438cc 514s, 995cc touring and sports 508s, and 2,516cc 521s in short- and long-chassis forms, these last being sold as Walter Lords. After 1936 the company concentrated on aero-engines. HON

WALTHAM (i) (US) 1898–1900
Waltham Automobil Co, Waltham, Mass.

The Waltham steamer was a typical New England runabout with a 2-cylinder engine, single chain drive and tiller steering. It was designed by John Piper and George Tinker, who built the prototype in the bicycle factory of the Waltham Manufacturing Company (*see* Waltham (ii)), although there was no financial connection between the two companies. GNG

WALTHAM (ii) (US) 1898–1908
Waltham Mfg Co, Waltham, Mass.

1912 WALL 6hp 3-wheeler. *M.A. Harrison*

1909 WALTER(ii) 7hp 3-wheeler. *Ing Adolf Babuška*

1929 WALTER(ii) 6B Super 3.3-litre saloon. *Ing Adolf Babuška*

1934 WALTER(ii) Regent 3.2-litre cabriolet. Coachwork by Sodomka. *Václav Petřík Collection*

1904 WALTHAM(ii) Orient Buckboard 4hp
runabout. *G.N. Georgano*

1931 WANDERER 10/50PS cabriolet. *Neubauer
Collection*

1936 WANDERER W25K 2-litre sports car.
Autocar

1914 WARNE 8hp cyclecar. *National Motor
Museum*

This company made an experimental electric runabout in 1898, but did not put it into production. Their first petrol-engined vehicles were motor cycles, tricycles and light runabouts powered by De Dion engines. In 1902 they introduced the Orient Buckboard, a very simple car consisting of two seats on a wooden platform, with a 4hp air-cooled engine geared to the rear axle, and, originally, only one speed. There were no springs, as the wooden platform was said to have enough resilience. The weight was 350lb and the price $375 (£94 10s in England).

Although the simple Buckboard was continued, more sophisticated cars were gradually introduced, including a four-seater version which in turn became a side-entrance tonneau. Wheel steering and small bonnets to cover the driver's feet appeared in 1904, although the engine was still at the back, and the Buckboard ancestry remained obvious.

In 1905 a completely new car appeared, known as the Waltham Orient. This had a 4-cylinder air-cooled 18/20hp engine mounted in front in the conventional manner, friction transmission and shaft drive. A slightly smaller 16hp model was also made. In 1908 Waltham merged with the C.H. Metz Company, and for the following year the cars were known as Metz.   GNG

WALTHAM (iii) (US) *1922*
Motor Manufacturers of Waltham Inc., Waltham, Mass.

Formerly makers of the Metz, the Waltham Motor Manufacturers, Inc., produced a car under their own name, but only during 1922. A Rutenberg 6-cylinder was used and prices began with the touring car at $2,450.   KM

WALWORTH (US) *1905–1906*
A.O. Walworth & Co, Chicago, Ill.

This car was powered by a 14hp 2-cylinder opposed engine. A five-seater tonneau with rear entrance had a wheelbase of 6ft 8in. A planetary transmission and shaft drive were used.   GMN

WANDERER (D) *1911–1939*
(1) Wanderer Fahrradwerke vorm. Winkelhofer & Jaenicke AG, Schönau *1911–1917*
(2) Wanderer-Werke AG, Siegmar *1917–1939*

This firm — like many others — started with bicycle manufacture; motor cycles followed and led the way to cars. Extensive experiments were undertaken. In 1905 the 2-cylinder Wanderermobil was ready, but it remained a prototype. Another — which is still in existence — is claimed to date from 1904.

It is reported by some sources that Ettore Bugatti offered a small car design to Wanderer in 1910 before starting manufacturing on his own. But Wanderer did not take over the Bugatti car, as their own designs were ready and they started production in 1911. Their first production model had a 4-cylinder 1,150cc, 5/12PS engine and a two-seater tandem body. This car was popularly known as the Püppchen (doll). Engine capacity was increased to 1,220cc in 1914 and the output raised to 5/15PS. Three- and four-seater versions were also available and this model was listed until 1922. Some 4-cylinder models in the 1½- and 2-litre range followed during the 1920s. A 6-cylinder model (the W11) with a 2,540cc 50bhp engine was built under licence by Martini of Switzerland. The W11 was also available in a sports version of 2,995cc and 65bhp. In addition to 4-cylinder models, a range of 6-cylinder cars was built during the 1930s which were based on a Porsche design. These had push-rod ohv engines, and later cars had swing-axle rear suspension.

A very sporty looking car appeared in 1936, the W25K (K for Kompressor). The 1,936cc engine with blower developed 85bhp and the car easily reached 93mph. However, it did not figure much in competitions and was produced in limited numbers only. After 1932 Wanderer was a member of the Auto Union. Their cars had a reputation for quality, finish and good performance although they were intended for workaday use. In the Auto Union catalogues they represented the 'upper middle-class'. Car production ceased at the outbreak of World War 2 in 1939, by which time two sv models, with all-round independent suspension, a 1.8-litre four and a 2.6-litre six, were being offered.   HON

WARD (i) (US) *1914–1916*
Ward Motor Vehicle Co, New York, N.Y.

The Ward electric was made as a closed four-seater, with 2 doors. The drive was by shaft and the manufacturer claimed 100 miles per charge. The body had an awkward and boxy appearance. It was priced at $2,100.   GMN

WARD (ii) (US) *1914*
Ward Cyclecar Co, Milwaukee, Wisc.

This cyclecar was made in two models, both two-seaters, on a wheelbase of 8ft 4in. One had an air-cooled, 2-cylinder engine of 1.1 litres, the other a water-cooled, 4-cylinder, 1.6-litre unit. Both models used friction transmission.   GMN

WARD LEONARD *see* KNICKERBOCKER

WARFIELD (GB) *1903*
Warfield Motor Car Co, Teddington, Middlesex

The Warfield company made engines for steam launches, and their car was a sideline which never went into production. It had a special design of flash boiler said to be capable of resisting a pressure of 3,000psi. GNG

WARNE (GB) *1913–1915*
Pearsall-Warne Ltd, Letchworth, Herts.

The Warne cyclecar was powered by an 8hp J.A.P. V-twin engine, and used belt drive. Although the engine was air-cooled the car had a dummy radiator which gave it a very neat appearance. The price was £99. GNG

WARREN (WARREN-DETROIT) (US) *1909–1914*
Warren Motor Car Co, Detroit, Mich.

This make was available in models with imaginative designations such as Pilgrim, Resolute and Woverine. These were furnished with 4- and 6-cylinder engines. Larger models, with a 6.2-litre 6-cylinder engine, were priced at $2,500. GMN

WARREN-LAMBERT (GB) *1912–1922*
(1) Warren-Lambert Engineering Co Ltd, Shepherds Bush, London W. *1912–1914*
(2) Warren-Lambert Engineering Co Ltd, Richmond, Surrey *1919–1922*

Originally known as the Lambert & West, this was a typical cyclecar, more comfortable than many, with a water-cooled Blumfield 2-cylinder engine and shaft drive. By 1914 a Dorman 4-cylinder engine was used, and production was about 25 cars per week. After World War 1 the firm restarted at Richmond using an Alpha 4-cylinder 1,330cc engine, and produced a striking super sports with a 1½-litre Coventry-Simplex engine and an enormous burnished copper exhaust pipe. The Warren-Lambert was always successful at hill-climbs, a 2-cylinder car defeating the notorious Nailsworth Ladder before the war, but supply difficulties forced it out of production in 1922. GNG

1921 WARREN-LAMBERT 10hp sports car. *Autocar*

WARSZAWA (PL) *1951–1972*
Fabryka Samochodow Osobowych, Warsaw

This was the Polish equivalent of the Russian Pobieda, built under licence from GAZ. At first a change in the grille design was virtually the only difference between the two cars and, in fact, until 1955 the Warszawa was partially Russian made, with a Polish chassis and suspension added to an imported body and engine.

Subsequently improvements were effected, Model 201 with 50bhp sv engine giving way to Model 202 with ohv and 70bhp. By 1965 the original fastback body had been replaced by the notchback style on the Warszawa 203, and the final series comprised the 223 saloon and 223K station wagon of 1970. Features included unitary construction and coil and coil-and-wishbone ifs. Taxi, ambulance and light commercial versions were also catalogued. The introduction of the Polski-Fiat range, also made by FSO, led to the gradual withdrawal of the Warszawa from production. BE

1902 WARTBURG(i) 15hp tonneau. *Neubauer Collection*

WARTBURG (i) (D) *1898–1904*
Fahrzeugfabrik Eisenach, Eisenach

This firm – a part of the Ehrhardt concern – started car production under the name of Eisenach. The name Wartburg was chosen for the Decauville Voiturelle built under licence. It was equipped with a rear-mounted 2-cylinder engine, either a 3½hp air-cooled or a 5hp water-cooled unit. This small car was quite popular and was produced in large numbers. Front-engined models were built after 1900. These were 2-cylinder cars of 5, 6, 8 and 10hp and 4-cylinder cars of 15, 30 and 45hp. In 1904 Ehrhardt left the firm and subsequent models were marketed as Dixis. Ehrhardt himself started car manufacture under his own name.

The Wartburg name was briefly revived by B.M.W. in 1930 for a sports version of their Austin Seven-based Dixi. HON

WARTBURG (ii) (D) *1956 to date*
VEB Automobilwerk Eisenach, Eisenach

The IFA model F9 was superseded by the Wartburg, which followed the same mechanical design, using a 3-cylinder 2-stroke engine and front drive, but had a new body. At first an 894cc engine of 40bhp was installed, also available with 50bhp for the sports version. Engine capacity was raised to 991cc (45bhp) in 1962. The Knight model, sold since 1967, had a restyled body, semi-trailing-arm rear suspension, and 13in wheels. The 1972 British price was only £719. HON

1967 WARTBURG(ii) Knight 1-litre saloon. *VEB Automobilwerk Eisenach*

WARWICK (i) (US) *1903–1904*
Warwick Cycle & Automobile Co, Springfield, Mass.

This four-seater, with its engine under the body, was built with either 2- or 3-cylinder power units. The cars had a reach frame, with a non-standard track, (4ft 6in) and the body was hinged at the rear for complete access to the mechanism. They were steered by tiller. GMN

WARWICK (ii) (GB) *1960–1962*
Bernard Rodger Developments Ltd, Colnbrook, Bucks.

The designer of the Peerless (ii) recommenced production on his own account of an improved version of this car, similar in all major respects, and with the same

1924 WASP(ii) 31hp rickshaw tourer. *Keith Marvin Collection*

1905 WATROUS 12hp tourer. *Dr Alfred Lewerenz Collection*

1907 POPE-WAVERLEY electric two-seater. *Museo dell'Automobile, Turin*

Triumph TR engine. Capital was limited, and although the Warwick was both lighter and more refined than the Peerless (ii), it eventually suffered the fate of its predecessor. A version powered by a 3½-litre Buick V-8 was tried in 1961.   DF

WASHINGTON (i) (US) *1909–1911*
(1) Carter Motor Car Corp, Washington, D.C. *1909–1910*
(2) Carter Motor Car Corp, Hyattsville, Md. *1910–1911*
    The Washington had up to five body types, most using a 4-cylinder engine. This power unit was water-cooled and had a capacity of 4.2 litres. A later model with a 4.6-litre engine was a $3,350 limousine. In 1909 a six, the 6-60, was introduced at $2,750. The company had previously made the Carter Twin Engine car.
          GMN

WASHINGTON (ii) (US) *1921–1924*
Washington Motor Co, Middletown, Ohio; Eaton, Ohio
    The Washington was a conventional assembled car made in touring and sedan versions. Prototypes of 1921 used 3.2-litre Falls engines, but production cars were powered by the 3.7-litre Continental Red Seal 7-R in 1922, and the 4-litre Continental Red Seal 8-R in 1923. A steam car was planned for 1924, but only one was completed. Not more than 35 Washingtons were made in all.   GNG

WASP (i) (GB) *1907–1908*
Thames Bank Wharf Motor Works, London
    The Wasp was a large car powered by a 50/60hp 6-cylinder Mutel engine, with pair-cast T-head cylinders, a 3-speed gearbox and shaft drive. Both phaeton and Pullman-limousine bodies were available, but the car was never put into production.   GNG

WASP (ii) (US) *1919–1925*
Martin-Wasp Corp, Bennington, Vt.
    Karl H. Martin, designer of the Wasp, had been a successful coachbuilder and was the designer of the Deering-Magnetic and the Kenworthy cars. Between 1919 and 1925, a total of 18 Wasps were constructed, with sharply pointed wings and custom-built rickshaw-type bodies, and costing between $5,500 and $10,000. Earlier models were 4-cylinder types with Wisconsin T-head engines; the later cars used a Continental 6 unit. The Wasp was the only car ever built in the United States, and perhaps in the world, which carried a St Christopher medal on its dashboard as standard equipment. This bronze medallion was also fabricated and cast by Martin.   KM

WATERLOO-DURYEA (US) *1904–1905*
Waterloo Motor Works, Waterloo, Iowa
    This was nearly identical with the original Duryea and was built under licence. Two-seater Phaetons had graceful Empire-inspired lines, peculiar to the Duryea of this period. The Duryea's folding front seat was not used in this car.   GMN

WATFORD (GB) *c.1959–c.1962*
Watford Sports Car Ltd, Watford, Herts.
    A typical kit-built car, the Watford was offered with an ifs tubular chassis to suit the side-valve Ford engines, and option of fibreglass bodies. The later version, sold as the Cheetah, was distinguished by independent suspension all round.   DF

WATLING (GB) *1959–1961*
Watling Cars, Parkstreet Village, St Albans, Herts.
    Watlings offered parts for the amateur builder, and particularly fibreglass bodies in two- and four-seater open and saloon styles. A tubular ladder chassis, with coil independent front suspension, was also available, in two different sizes to cover the most popular mechanical permutations.   DF

WATROUS (US) *1905–1907*
Watrous Automobile Co, Elmira, N.Y.
    The Watrous was made as either a five-seater, or as a two-seater runabout. Both were powered by a 12hp 2-cylinder engine, which drove through a planetary transmission. These were small cars, the runabout being on a 7ft 5in wheelbase, and priced at only $400. Later this firm confined their efforts to fire engines, Elmira now being the centre of this manufacture.   GMN

WATT (US) *1910*
Watt Motor Co, Detroit, Mich.
    The only model of this make was a five-seater touring car, powered by a 5.6-litre 6-cylinder engine with overhead valves. The price of this car was $1,850.   GMN

WATTEL-MORTIER (F) *1921*
    The Paris-built Wattel-Mortier used a 2,652cc 6-cylinder engine of the maker's own design, in which the crankshaft was made up in two pieces bolted together. It had a 3-speed gearbox and conventional chassis, apart from the front-wheel brakes which were still fairly rare at the time.   GNG

WAVERLEY (i) (US) *1898–1903; 1908–1914*
POPE-WAVERLEY *1903–1907*
(1) Indiana Bicycle Co, Indianapolis, Ind., *1898–1899*
(2) American Bicycle Co, Indianapolis, Ind. *1900–1901*
(3) International Motor Car Co, Indianapolis, Ind. *1901–1903*
(4) Waverley Dept., Pope Motor Car Co, Indianapolis, Ind. *1903–1907*
(5) Waverley Co, Indianapolis, Ind. *1908–1914*

The original Waverley electric was a two-seater with tiller steering and a single headlamp which sold for $850. During the Pope régime the line of models was expanded to include closed bodies, including a miniature limousine with a wheelbase of only 7ft 6in. After the failure of Pope, a large range of cars was marketed, with four different shaft-drive models in 1914, and similar in appearance to petrol cars. GMN

WAVERLEY (ii) (GB) *1901–1904*
(1) Scottish Motor Co, Edinburgh
(2) New Rossleigh Motor & Cycle Co, Ltd, Edinburgh

The Waverley from Scotland was one of the many British cars of the time that consisted of a De Dion engine in a home-produced chassis. A 9hp single-cylinder unit was used, in conjunction with a 3-speed gearbox. 'The Pride of the North' cost £280 in 1902. TRN

WAVERLEY (iii) (GB) *1910–1931*
(1) Light Cars Ltd, Willesden, London N.W. *1910–1915*
(2) Waverley Cars Ltd, London W.10 *1919–1931*

The London Waverley was a name which lasted a long time, but not many cars were made, and they never achieved any fame. The first were light cars with 9hp V-twin J.A.P. engines, and gearboxes in their back axles. Only one rear wheel was driven, so a differential was unnecessary. Initially, there were only 2 forward speeds; later there were 3. A 10hp 4-cylinder in-line unit supplemented the twin, and a 15hp was added. These engines were made by Chapuis-Dornier, and by 1913 were installed in conventional cars. In the 1920s the Waverley was generally a small to medium-sized assembled family car of no distinction, like so many of its contemporaries in Britain.

In 1919 the staple model was the Twelve. From the very beginning Waverley suspension was praised, but the Twelve's engine was rough and noisy. The same applied to the 10hp 1½-litre, current from 1922 and renamed the 11hp in 1924. Both engines were by Coventry-Simplex. Other units were made by Tylor. However, the new Twelve of 1924 was given a 1½-litre, single sleeve-valve engine of Burt-McCollum type, which overcame the main criticism. This model had front-wheel brakes. A new 16hp Coventry-Simplex-engined six appeared for 1925. It was also an improvement as far as silence and smoothness were concerned. In the same year, an odd ephemeral '£100 car' was shown. It was propelled by a rear-mounted flat-twin water-cooled engine of 900cc. Transmission was by friction disc, which provided 4 forward speeds. TRN

WAYNE (i) (US) *1904–1908*
Wayne Automobile Co, Detroit, Mich.

The Wayne line included as many as five models in a single year. These ranged from two-seaters with 2-cylinder engines, to 50hp cars of 4-cylinders. The smaller cars used planetary transmissions, and the larger models had 3-speed, selective gearboxes. This company was absorbed by the E.M.F. Co in 1908. GMN

WAYNE (ii) (US) *1905–1910*
Wayne Works, Richmond, Ind.

The earliest model of this make was a 2-cylinder, water-cooled runabout of 16hp. The later models were all powered by 4-cylinder, L-head engines. As late as 1910 one model had a progressive transmission and an air-cooled 4-cylinder engine. This manufacturer also made the Richmond (ii). GMN

WEARWELL; WOLF (GB) *1899–1905*
Wearwell Motor Carriage Co, Wolverhampton, Staffs.

The Wearwell was a voiturette with a 2-cylinder air-cooled engine mounted under the seat, not unlike a Decauville in appearance. It was announced at the end of 1899, but very few were made. The company later made motor cycles and tricars under the name Wolf. One of the latter had a coachbuilt body and an enclosed 6hp engine mounted between front and rear seats, so that it qualifies as a 3-wheeled car. A 7/8hp engine was used in 1905. GNG

WEBB (GB) *1922–1923*
V.P. Webb & Co Ltd, Stourport, Worcs.

The Webb was a conventional light car powered by a 9hp 4-cylinder Alpha engine, and using shaft drive to a spiral bevel rear axle. A four-seater body was standard, and the price was £265. GNG

WEBB JAY (US) *1908*
Webb Jay Motor Co, Chicago, Ill.

1915 WAVERLEY(iii) 10hp tourer. *G.N. Georgano*

1927 WAVERLEY(iii) 16/50hp saloon. *Autocar*

1922 WEBB 9hp four-seater. *Autocar*

This steamer was built as a single model, a five-seater touring car. Its 2-cylinder engine was a compound type with 3in and 6in diameter cylinders for high and low pressure steam. The stroke was 4in and the boiler operating pressure was 500psi. The car weighed 2,900lb and its price was $4,000.　　　　GMN

WEBER (CH) 1899–1906
J. Weber & Co, Uster, Zürich

The first cars built by this company were 3-wheelers made under licence from Egg & Egli, but in 1899 a 4-wheeler powered by a front-mounted 6/8hp single-cylinder vertical engine was produced. It had shaft drive. Their first production 4-wheeler, however, reversed all the contemporary trends, for it used a horizontal engine mounted at the rear, and the shaft drive was replaced by belts. The engine was a large single-cylinder unit of 145mm × 160mm giving a capacity of 2,510cc. Later an even larger engine was used. About 60 cars per year were sold for several years, but as design did not change, the cars became increasingly hard to sell.　　　　GNG

WEGMANN (D) 1925–1926
Waggonfabrik Wegmann & Co, Kassel

This railway carriage builder also introduced a small 4/20PS car with a 4-cylinder 1,016cc engine. It had a 3-speed gearbox and shaft drive. The body was an open three-seater.　　　　HON

WEICHELT (D) 1908
H. Weichelt, Automobil- und Motorenfabrik, Leipzig

Two voiturette-type models were offered, a 2-cylinder 10PS and a 4-cylinder 16PS. Both were available with water- or air-cooled engines.　　　　HON

WEIGEL (GB) 1906–1909
(1) Weigel Motors Ltd, London E.C. 1906–1907
(2) Weigel Motors Ltd, London W. 1907–1909

D.M. Weigel was the first managing director of Clément-Talbot Ltd. The cars bearing his own name were assembled vehicles, the design of which was variously attributed to Itala or Pipe, comments which invariably brought forth vigorous denials by Weigel in the motoring press. The Wilkinson Sword Company had a hand in finishing the chassis, while some bodies were made by the English branch of J. Rothschild et fils. The first model was a 40hp 4-cylinder car of identical cylinder dimensions to the Itala, which was to have been exhibited on the stand of the Ivanhoe Motor Company at the 1906 Olympia Show (see Mercury (i)). In 1907 the 40hp and a 25hp car were shown, and a 60hp 6-cylinder was also listed.

At the end of 1907 Weigel moved his works from Goswell Road in the City to Latimer Road in North Kensington. In 1907 and 1908 he entered a team of cars in the Grand Prix, using a straight-8 consisting of two 40hp engines coupled together, in 1907, and a 110hp four in 1908. In neither race did the Weigels last beyond the fifth lap. The 1909 range consisted of 20, 30 and 40hp fours, but at the end of that year the Weigel company was acquired by Crowdy Ltd, who made cars under their own name at the Latimer Road works.　　　　GNG

WEISE (D) 1932
Weise & Co GmbH, Berlin NO 55

After producing 3-wheeled vans this firm brought out a four-seater saloon. A single-cylinder 196cc 5bhp Rinne engine was used, mounted above the single driven front wheel. Later production was concentrated on 4-wheeled vans.　　　　HON

WEISS (D) 1902–1905
(1) Maschinenfabrik Otto Weiss & Co, Berlin NO 55 1902–1904
(2) Automobil- und Motorenfabrik vorm. Otto Weiss, Berlin NO 55 1904–1905

This firm produced friction-driven cars which were known under the name of Weiss-Herald, French Herald engines being used. The main types were equipped with 2-cylinder 10/14PS and 4-cylinder 10/12PS units. The friction-drive transmission was almost an exact copy of the Maurer system.　　　　HON

WEISS MANFRED (H) 1924–1930
Weiss Manfred Acel es Femmuvei R-T, Budapest

Products of the Weiss Manfred works ranged from household goods and bicycles to aircraft and munitions, and cars were never more than a sideline. Their first car had a 750cc 4-cylinder 2-stroke engine, enlarged in 1928 to 875cc. With one of these cars Victor Szmick finished second in the 1929 Monte Carlo Rally. Weiss Manfred also built their own bodies on Model A Ford chassis, but mainly trucks and taxicabs. From the end of World War 2 the factory was used for the manufacture of Csepel trucks, made under Steyr licence.　　　　GLH

WELCH (US) 1903–1911
(1) Chelsea Manufacturing Co, Chelsea, Mich. 1903–1904
(2) Welch Motor Car Co, Pontiac, Mich. 1904–1911
(3) Welch Motor Car Co, Detroit, Mich. 1909–1911

The Chelsea Manufacturing Company was a bicycle shop in which the Welch

1902 WEBER 12hp victoria. *Swiss Museum of Transport & Communications, Lucerne*

1908 WEIGEL 60hp limousine. Rothschild. *Autocar*

1927 WEISS MANFRED 750cc saloon. *G.L. Hartner*

brothers experimented with cars from 1901 to 1903. They showed their Welch Tourist for the first time at the 1903 Chicago Show. It had a 20hp 2-cylinder engine with the advanced features of overhead valves and hemispherical combustion chambers. A few were made at Chelsea before the Welch brothers set up their own factory at Pontiac. Here larger cars were made with 36hp 4-cylinder engines, and later, 6-cylinder engines of up to 75hp. With wheelbases of up to 11ft 6in they were among the largest cars of their time, and carried spacious limousine or tourer bodies. The hemispherical combustion chambers and overhead valves were retained, now operated by a single overhead camshaft.

In 1909 a new factory was set up at Detroit to make a smaller 4-cylinder car, known as the Welch-Detroit. A.B.C. Hardy, who had designed the Flint (i), was general manager at the Detroit plant, and in 1911, acting on instructions from General Motors, he removed the machinery from Detroit and Pontiac, and combined with the Rainier plant at Saginaw, Michigan to make the Marquette (i).

GNG

WEL-DOER (CDN) *1914*

Welker-Doerr Co, Berlin, Ont.

This was one of the few Canadian cyclecars. It had side-by-side seating for two persons. The 2-cylinder, air-cooled engine was quoted at 9–13hp. Drive was by friction transmission with belts to the rear wheels. Three-quarter elliptic springs were used all around. Only one car was produced before wartime shortages stopped production.

GMN

WELLER (GB) *1903*

Weller Brothers Ltd, West Norwood, London S.E.

The Weller car used a 20hp 4-cylinder engine, and double chain drive. An unusual feature was that engine and gearbox were mounted on an underframe separate from the chassis. They also made motor cycles, and advertised cars of 8, 10, and 15hp, but in fact only one car was made, the 20hp shown at the 1903 Crystal Palace Show. John Weller was later concerned with the founding of Autocarriers Ltd, who afterwards made the A.C. car.

GNG

WELLINGTON (GB) *1900–1901*

F.F. Wellington, London N.W.

As well as selling Phébus-Aster and other cars, Frank Wellington built a voiturette with a rear-mounted 2½hp air-cooled single-cylinder engine.

GNG

WENDAX (D) *1950–1951*

Wendax Fahrzeugbau, GmbH, Hamburg

This firm produced 3- and 4-wheeled vans in the 1930s and then started private-car manufacture in 1950. Their first version had a primitive transmission to the right-hand rear wheel, but their second model had front drive and a 2-cylinder 2-stroke 750cc Ilo engine. Production was limited, and ceased as a result of inadequate technical design and finish.

HON

WENKELMOBIL (D) *1904–1907*

Automobilwerke Schneider & Co, Berlin

This car, using friction drive, was designed by Max Wenkel, who built the first prototypes in Java; they were probably the first motor cars built in the Far East. The firm of Schneider & Co became interested in the design and started production in 1904. Various models were made, using single- or 2-cylinder air- or water-cooled engines placed either in the rear or in the front. During 1906–07 two types with single-cylinder 8hp and 10hp water-cooled engines were produced.

HON

WERBELL (GB) *1907–1909*

W. and E. Raikes-Bell, Dundee

The Werbell derived its name from its makers, the brothers William and Edward Raikes-bell. It was a conventional shaft-drive touring car powered by a 25hp 4-cylinder White & Poppe engine. About eight cars were made.

GNG

WERNER (F) *1906–1914*

Werner Frères et Cie, Billancourt, Seine

Werner were well-known makers of motor cycles, and came to car manufacture via tricars, first with handlebar, and later with wheel steering. Their first car appeared in 1906, and was a shaft-drive voiturette powered by a 7hp 2-cylinder engine. A 12/14hp 4-cylinder car was added the following year, and a light car with 1.3-litre 4-cylinder De Dion engine in 1909.

By 1913 4-cylinder cars of up to 20/30hp (4.1 litres) were made, with unusual sloping radiators. However, it was with single- and 2-cylinder cars that Werner made their name, especially the racing voiturette powered by the long-stroke De Dion single. They competed regularly in voiturette races from 1907 to 1909, their best result being 3rd place in the 1909 Catalan Cup.

GNG

WESEN (D) *c.1900*

Fahrzeugfabrik Wesen GmbH, Wesen bei Lindau

This company made a small number of *vis-à-vis* cars powered by 4½hp water-cooled engines. They also made lorries.

GNG

1909 WELCH Model 4-0 tourer. *Harrah's Automobile Collection*

1907 WERBELL 25hp tourer. *Museum of Transport, Glasgow*

1905 WENKELMOBIL 8PS voiturette. *Neubauer Collection*

1907 WEST-ASTER 14/16hp tourer. With the
Copper Queen of America. *J. S. Spicer*

1922 WESTCAR 11.9hp tourer. *M.J.
Worthington-Williams*

WESNIGK (D) *1920–1923*
Dipl. Ing. Erwin Wesnigk

The Wesnigk was a small aerodynamic 3-wheeler with a single driven rear wheel. Single-cylinder 1.8PS B.M.W. and 1.35PS Kühne engines were used.   HON

WEST & BURGETT (US) *1899*
William S. West-C.E. Burgett, Middleburg, N.Y.

Although its builders intended to start car production, the West & Burgett 2-cylinder steamer only appeared as a prototype. This wire-wheeled car resembled others of its type.   KM

WESTALL (GB) *1922*
Sidney C. Westall, London S.W.1

The Westall was a very light cyclecar powered by a single-cylinder 7hp engine of 865cc capacity. It was to have sold at the low price of £130 for a two-seater, but production never started.   GNG

WEST-ASTER; WEST (GB) *1904–1913*
(1) E.J. West & Co Ltd, Coventry, Warwickshire *1904–1913*
(2) West Ltd, Coventry, Warwickshire *1906–1908*

E.J. West had previously made the Progress car, and there was little change in design between the last Progress and the first Wests, which used the 10/12hp 2-cylinder Aster engine. A few of the early West cars had used White & Poppe engines, but when West Ltd was founded in 1906 they standardized on Asters, the cars generally being known as West-Asters. By 1908 a range of 2- and 4-cylinder cars from 10/12 to 35hp was being made, as well as delivery vans and taxis. A West-Aster taxi was the first British taxi to pass the Scotland Yard test for use in the London area. However, West Ltd went into receivership in May 1908, and production ceased.

The original company of E.J. West & Co Ltd continued in business as a maker of chassis for other firms, including Academy, Heron (i), Pilot (ii), Scout, and Singer (i). They also assembled one or two cars with 16hp White & Poppe engines in 1909. In 1911 they announced a friction-drive light car powered by a 7/9hp single-cylinder West engine, but this was not produced. In 1913 a new factory was taken to make the West cyclecar, powered by a 2-cylinder Chater-Lea engine. This went into production later in the year with a Precision engine, under the name Ranger.   GNG

WESTCAR (GB) *1922–1926*
Strode Engineering Works, Herne, Kent

The Westcar was a conventional, assembled family machine with a 4-cylinder, 11.9hp sv engine by Dorman and a radiator very like that of the Galloway and the Austin Twelve. It had a 4-speed gearbox. The unconventional Heron (ii) was manufactured by the same company, whose head was Major Charles Prescott-Westcar, O.B.E.   TRN

WESTCOTT (US) *1912–1925*
Westcott Motor Car Co, Richmond, Ind.; Springfield, Ohio

The Westcott Motor Co marketed a highly-regarded, assembled car, briefly at Richmond, Ind., and then at Springfield, Ohio. Continental 6-cylinder engines were used exclusively in Westcotts and several thousand units were produced through its years of production, although a peak of 1,850 in 1920 indicates that the cars were never common. Unlike many assembled cars of the period, Westcotts did not necessarily sell only in the area of manufacture, and the care with which they were made commanded a relatively high price through the years. A complete line of body styles was available.

After about 1920, Westcott concentrated on two models of different size (3.9 litres and 5 litres), but the reputation of the make depended on the larger car. In an unsuccessful attempt to remain active in a market dominated by larger corporations, Westcott introduced 4-wheel brakes and balloon tyres as standard equipment for its 1925 line, but that year proved to be the company's last.   KM

WESTFALIA (D) *1906–1914; 1911–1913*
Ramesohl & Schmidt AG, Oelde; Bielefeld

This firm was, and still is, a specialist builder of dairy apparatus. In 1906 car production was started using De Dion and Fafnir engines at first. After about 1909 their own engines were installed. In 1911 a new factory was built at Bielefeld and car production was concentrated here. At this time the range consisted of 6/16, 8/20, 10/25 and 12/30PS models. The Bielefeld factory was taken over by Hansa in 1913. The Westfalia 6/16 and 10/25PS were continued in the Oelde works until 1914.   HON

WESTFIELD (US) *1902–1903*
The C.G. Moore Manufacturing Co, Westfield, Mass.

This company made running gear and bodies ready to be fitted with engines, and also a few light steam- and petrol-engined complete cars. The steamer had a 6hp 2-cylinder engine, single chain drive and tiller steering, while the petrol car had a single-cylinder engine.   GNG

WESTINGHOUSE (F) *1904–1912*
Sté des Automobiles Westinghouse, Le Havre

Westinghouse cars were made by the French branch of the famous American Electrical Company. Introduced at the 1904 Paris Salon, they were conventional high quality cars with 4-cylinder pair-cast engines of 20/28 and 30/40hp, and double chain drive. Mostly provided with heavy touring or limousine coachwork, they were not sporting cars, although one was entered in the 1908 Four Inch Race. From 1908 to 1914 Westinghouse vehicles were made under licence in Hungary, commercial vehicles at first, and, from 1912, cars which were called Marta. By this time the smaller Westinghouse cars, the 16/20 and 20/30, had shaft drive, although the 35/40 retained chains.　　　　　　　　　　　　　GNG

WESTLAKE (GB) *1907*
Westlake Motor Syndicate Ltd, Maidenhead, Berks.

Designed by H.B. Lyon of Taplow, the Westlake had a 24hp 6-cylinder air-cooled engine with a 2-speed epicyclic gear and final drive by single chain. A water-cooled model was said to be available as well, but probably no more than one Westlake was made.　　　　　　　　　　　　　GNG

WESTMINSTER (GB) *1906–1908*
Westminster Motor Works Ltd, London S.W.

Westminster cars were assembled from various components, the 1906 model using a 10hp engine of French origin. Some cars sold under this name were 30/35hp Prunels with English coachwork.　　　　　　　　　　　　　GNG

WESTWOOD (GB) *1920–1926*
(1) Westwood Motor Co Ltd., Wigan, Lancs. *1920–1924*
(2) Westwood-Ince Ltd, Wigan, Lancs. *1924–1926*

The Westwood was a conventional assembled car powered by an 11.9hp ohv Dorman engine of 1,794cc capacity. In 1924 the company was reorganized and a 14hp Meadows engine of 2,121cc adopted. A striking sports model with pointed tail was offered on this chassis, but performance was not in keeping with appearance, and few were sold.　　　　　　　　　　　　　GNG

WETZIKON (CH) *1898*
Motorenfabrik Wetzikon AG, Wetzikon

This company made a heavy-looking four-seater car with a rear-mounted engine and chain final drive. It was designed by Franz Brozincevic who later made lorries under the names Franz and F.B.W., the latter still in production today.　　　　　GNG

WEYHER ET RICHEMOND (F) *1905–c.1910*
Automobiles Weyher et Richemond, Pantin, Seine

Although they made a steam fire-engine in 1903, Weyher et Richemond did not begin the manufacture of private cars until the end of 1905. Their first steam car had a tubular flash boiler of Serpollet design, and a 15hp 4-cylinder horizontally opposed engine based on Knoller-Friedmann patents. It also had 4-wheel brakes, but the makers soon dropped this feature, as they said the public did not like them. The cars had the appearance of petrol vehicles. For 1908 a range of petrol-engined cars was introduced. This consisted of three fours of 10/15, 16/20 and 28/32hp, and a 25/30hp six. Weyher et Richemond also built petrol cars called Labor. The steamers were sold in England under the name Rexer.　　　　　　GNG

W.F.S. (US) *1911–1913*
W.F.S. Motor Car Co, Philadelphia, Pa.

This obscure make offered at least five body styles, from a runabout to a five-seater limousine, on a standard chassis. The 4.9-litre, 4-cylinder engine had a drilled crankshaft for positive lubrication. Final drive was by shaft, and the gearbox was at the rear axle.　　　　　　　　　　　　　GMN

WHARTON (US) *1921–1922*
Wharton Motors Co, Dallas, Texas

The Wharton was an ambitious attempt by a Texas firm to market an 8-, a 6- and a 4-cylinder series of private cars in addition to a 4-wheel-drive truck and a tractor. Of its private cars, only a handful of the eights actually got on the road. These were imposing vehicles, using a Curtiss O.X.5 aero engine and with a price range from $3,450 for the tourer to $4,975 for the 'suburban' car. The four was planned to start at $1,450 and the six at $1,750.　　　　　　KM

WHEELER (US) *1900–1902*
Wheeler Automobile Manufacturing Co, Marlboro, Mass.

The Wheeler light car was powered by a single-cylinder De Dion engine, and had epicyclic gears and shaft drive. Only three were made.　　　　　GNG

WHERWELL (GB) *1920–1921*
Thompson & Son, Wherwell, Andover, Hampshire

The Wherwell cyclecar was powered by a 7hp Coventry-Victor flat-twin engine, and had friction transmission with chain final drive. Only three were made.　GNG

1914 WESTFALIA 6/16PS two-seater. *Neubauer Collection*

1906 WESTINGHOUSE 35/40hp landaulette-limousine. Coachwork by Kellner. *Lucien Loreille Collection*

1920 WESTWOOD 11.9hp coupé. *Autocar*

1901 WHITE(i) steam surrey. *National Motor Museum*

1909 WHITE(i) Model O 15hp steam tourer. *G.N. Georgano*

1913 WHITE(i) 30hp tourer. *Don McCray*

WHIPPET *see* WILLYS

WHITE (i) (US) *1900–1918*
(1) White Sewing Machine Co, Cleveland, Ohio *1900–1906*
(2) The White Co, Cleveland, Ohio *1906–1918*
    Rollin H. White of the Cleveland sewing-machine concern produced his first steamer in 1900. This was a light chain-drive stanhope with tiller steering and a simple 2-cylinder under-floor engine. It had an underslung frontal condenser, and 193 were sold in 1901, the first year of full production. This gave way in 1903 to a model with a front-mounted compound engine under a bonnet, condenser in the normal 'radiator' position, wheel steering, and shaft drive.
    These and subsequent Whites used a semi-flash type of boiler, and could run a hundred miles between fillings of water. Frames were of armoured wood, and a tonneau cost $2,000.
    The cars did well in early Glidden Tours, and racing versions, such as Webb Jay's Whistling Billy with an underslung frame, were also successful; this car covered a mile at 74.07mph. Theodore Roosevelt used a White during his tenure of the White House. 1905 Whites had a 2-speed back axle, and also a 'free engine' enabling the pumps to work without manual assistance when the car was stationary in traffic. 1906 was the best sales year, with 1,534 cars delivered, but steam-car production was held at over 1,000 a year to the end. By 1908, the company was offering two models, a 20hp Model L at $2,500, and the big seven-seater Model K with a 10ft 2in wheelbase at $3,700. Joy valve motion replaced the Stephenson link type on 1909 cars, which had both sets of brakes working on the rear wheels.
    Steamers continued to be listed into 1911, though the 1910 MM and OO were the last new models. For the 1910 season the company offered a $3\frac{1}{2}$-litre sv petrol car with a monobloc engine inspired by the Delahaye; the 4-speed gearbox had a geared-up top. This was joined in 1912 by a really big six rated at 60hp, and selling for $5,000, still with 4 forward speeds. Electric lighting and starting were added during the year, and these 4- and 6-cylinder Whites were continued until 1916.
    The 1917 models were 16-valve fours of over $6\frac{1}{2}$ litres' capacity, with magneto ignition, selling at $5,000 upwards.
    By this time the company was firmly established in the truck field, and after 1918 private cars were made to special order only, and in very small numbers. The last of these 'specials' was made in 1936.
    Rollin White was subsequently responsible for the Rollin car in 1923, while the firm also absorbed two truck-makers who had previously built private cars, Autocar and Reo.   MCS

WHITE (ii) (US) *1909*
George White Buggy Co, Rock Island, Ill.
    This was a high-wheel buggy, but the mounting of the engine at the front under a bonnet gave it more the appearance of an ordinary car than many of its kind. The engine was a 2-cylinder 12/14hp unit which drove via a 2-speed epicyclic gear and propeller shaft. Two- and four-seater bodies were available.   GNG

WHITE (iii) (US) *1914*
White Manufacturing Co, Waterloo, Iowa
    The White cyclecar used a 9hp ohv V-twin engine, and chain final drive.   GNG

WHITEHEAD (GB) *1920–1921*
Whitehead Light Cars, Bradford, Yorks.
    The Whitehead was powered by a 1,498cc Coventry-Simplex engine, and used a 3-speed Moss gearbox. It had transverse front suspension and, an unusual feature for its date, a wooden chassis. About 16 cars were made, all two- or four-seater tourers.   GNG

WHITEHEAD-THANET (GB) *1920–1921*
Amalgamated Motors Ltd, Ashtead, Surrey
    The Whitehead-Thanet scheme was one of the most ambitious of the post-World War 1 mass-production projects, but there is no evidence that even one car was made. The company was formed by A.J. Whitehead, who had made a fortune in aircraft during the war, and they planned to make 5,000 cars per month by the summer of 1920, rising to 100,000 per annum in 1921. Assembly was to be at Ashtead, and manufacture of parts not bought out at Richmond. The car was to have an American Chassis from the Gray Andrews Corp, and an English 16/20hp 4-cylinder engine. Coachwork was to be by F.J. Wraight of London S.W.11, who are sometimes listed as makers of the Thanet car.   GNG

WHITE STAR (US) *1909–1911*
(1) White Star Co, Atlanta, Ga. *1909*
(2) Atlanta Motor Car Co, Atlanta, Ga. *1910–1911*
    This vehicle was a two-seater buggy with large diameter wheels and solid rubber tyres. The 2-cylinder opposed engine developed 20hp. This was mounted beneath the seat and drove through a planetary transmission and double chains. A larger car with its engine under the bonnet was also made.   GMN

WHITGIFT (GB) *1913*

Croydon Central Motor Car Co Ltd, Croydon, Surrey

The Whitgift was a low-built cyclecar powered by an 8hp V-twin J.A.P. engine. It had friction transmission and chain drive to the offside rear wheel. GNG

WHITING (US) *1910–1912*

(1) Flint Motor Wagon Works, Flint, Mich. *1910*

(2) Whiting Motor Car Co, Flint, Mich. *1911–1912*

The Whiting was offered as a 20hp two-seater with a 2-speed gearbox, and as a 40hp five-seater with a 3-speed box. Both used 4-cylinder engines. Prices were $775 and $1,600 respectively. GMN

WHITING-GRANT *see* GRANT

WHITLOCK (GB) *1903–1932*

(1) Whitlock Automobile Co, London W.

(2) Lawton-Goodman Ltd, Cricklewood, London N.W.

The Whitlock Automobile Company of Holland Gate was an offshoot of Henry Whitlock & Company who had been coachbuilders since 1778. In 1903 they began selling cars called Whitlock-Century of 6½, 9, 12, and 16hp, but these were not made by them at all. In 1904 came the Whitlock-Aster which had an Aster engine and chassis with Whitlock body. These were made in various sizes such as 10/12 or 12/14hp 2-cylinder, and 18/22 or 24/30hp 4-cylinder models. The twins had armoured wood frames, and the fours pressed steel. A 12/14hp car ran in the the 1905 Tourist Trophy.

After 1906 no Whitlock cars were made until just before World War 1. By this time the Liverpool branch of Henry Whitlock had been taken over by J.A. Lawton-Goodman, and two models of 4-cylinder car were announced, a 12/16 and a 20/30hp. They were listed as Lawtons in 1914, and Whitlocks in 1915, but very few, if any, reached the public. No post-war cars were made until 1922, when a light car powered by a 4-cylinder 11hp Coventry-Climax engine appeared. From then on, all Whitlocks were made at Lawton-Goodman's works at Cricklewood. In 1924 a 6-cylinder car with a 16/50hp Coventry-Climax engine of 1,990cc was introduced and made with the fours for a few years. However, for 1927 and subsequent seasons Whitlocks standardized on the 6-cylinder 20/70 Meadows engine of 2,972cc, increased in 1928 to 3,301cc. The cars had Bentley-type radiators, although for the very last models this was replaced by a tall, flat radiator.

Whitlocks appeared regularly at Olympia until 1929, but very few cars of any model were actually sold. Some sources list the 20/70 until 1936, but it was certainly out of production by then. Lawton-Goodman Ltd are still in business as makers of specialized commercial vehicle bodywork. GNG

WHITNEY (i) (US) *1897–1900*

G.E. Whitney Motor Wagon Co, Boston, Mass.

George Whitney spent several years experimenting before a company was formed to make his steam cars, and few were in fact made under the Whitney name. A prototype was running in 1896, and Whitney was constantly experimenting with different designs during the company's lifetime. Most had vertical engines, but in at least one the engine was horizontal. After the Stanley brothers had sold their patents to Locomobile and Mobile, they began to make cars of Whitney pattern under the name Stanley-Whitney or McKay (from McKay sewing machines, a company owned by Frank E. Stanley). Brown Brothers of London sold the car in England as the Brown-Whitney from 1899 to 1900. The second prototype, with horizontal engine, survives today in England. GNG

WHITNEY (ii) (US) *1899–1905*

Whitney Machine Co, Brunswick, Maine

R.S. Whitney made only three cars during his six-year manufacturing period. The first two were conventional 2-cylinder steamers, a two-seater runabout and a four-seater surrey, but the last model, in 1905, showed some originality in having a front-mounted boiler and integral construction of body and chassis. GNG

WHITWOOD MONOCAR (GB) *1934–1936*

O.E.C. Ltd, Portsmouth, Hampshire

Made by a well-known motor cycle firm, the Whitwood was a tandem two-seater on 2 wheels, with small stabilizing wheels at either side. It had an all-enveloping body and wheel steering. Engines varied from a 150cc 2-stroke to a J.A.P. 1,000cc V-twin. Prices, according to engine size, were from £49 to £85. GNG

WHITWORTH *see* HAMMOND

WICHITA (US) *1914*

Wichita Falls Motor Co, Wichita Falls, Tex.

This 2-cylinder cyclecar used belt drive, and the front axle pivoted for steering. It was a tandem two-seater with a track of 3ft. Unusual features were bicycle mudguards for the front wheels, and a half steering wheel to allow clearance for the driver. GMN

1913 WHITGIFT 8hp cyclecar. *G.N. Georgano Collection*

1905 WHITLOCK-ASTER 12/14hp Tourist Trophy car. *Autocar*

1928 WHITLOCK 20/70hp drophead coupé. *Autocar*

1931 WIKOV 1½-litre streamline saloon.
Neubauer Collection

1904 WILKINSON-DE COSMO 24hp tonneau.
Wilkinson Sword Co Ltd

1972 WILLAM 123cc two-seater.
Crayford Auto Development Ltd

WICK (US) *1902–1903*

The Wick Co, Youngstown, Ohio

The Wick was a large, expensive car with a 30hp 4-cylinder engine of 5.6 litres' capacity. It carried coachwork by Quimby, one of America's finest coachbuilders, and was priced at $8,000.   GNG

WIGAN-BARLOW (GB) *1922–1923*

Wigan-Barlow Motors Ltd, Coventry, Warwickshire

The Wigan-Barlow was a conventional assembled car of which very few were made. Pilot models were made with 1,368cc Coventry-Simplex or 1,496cc Meadows 4-cylinder engines, and Wrigley rear axles.   GNG

WIIMA (SF) *1958*

The Wiima was the only example of a car designed and built in Finland. It was a two-seater minicar powered by a rear-mounted 500cc Fichtel & Sachs engine from Germany. Only prototypes were made.   GNG

WIKOV (CS) *1929–1936*

Wichterle & Kovarik as, Prostejov

One basic Wikov model, an ohc 4-cylinder made under Ansaldo licence, was built but engine capacities were raised steadily, starting with 1 litre and ending with 2 litres. In 1931 Wikov introduced a streamlined version, built to a Jaray design which was very advanced for that time. The 1½-litre two-seater sports car, derived from the standard model, also became well known. It was used in quite a number of sports events and was capable of about 85mph, and about 100mph with a blown engine. The last model was a 2-litre (1,960cc) which was much favoured for its performance. Engine output was 43bhp, and a maximum speed of about 68mph could be attained with a saloon body. A prototype 3½-litre straight-8, also Ansaldo-based, was built in 1933.   HON

WILBROOK (GB) *1913*

Brooks & Spencer, Levenshulme, Lancs.

The Wilbrook cyclecar had an 8hp V-twin J.A.P. engine, and belt final drive, but was unusual in having a four-seater body. It also had 4-wheel brakes.   GNG

WILCOX *see* WOLFE

WILES-THOMSON (AUS) *1947*

Wiles Manufacturing Co, Adelaide, S.A.

This was a light car intended for mass-production, but only two prototypes were made. It had a 7.2hp 2-cylinder 2-stroke engine, hydraulic brakes and integral construction open tourer body.   GNG

WILFORD (B) *1897–c.1901*

Ateliers de Construction Mécanique Ch. Wilford et fils, Tamise

The first Wilford was a high four-seater *vis-à-vis* with a single-cylinder horizontal heavy-oil engine, belt transmission and chain final drive. Various types of heavy-looking vehicles were made from 1897 to 1899, one of which was bought by the racing driver Baron de Caters. A Wilford covered a flying-kilometre at over 60mph in 1899, which was not far short of the Land Speed Record at the time. In 1900 smaller, front-engined cars were made – a 3hp with belt drive and a 6hp with chain drive.   GNG

WILKINSON (GB) *1903–1904; 1912–1913*

Wilkinson Sword Co Ltd, Acton, London W.

The first car to bear the name Wilkinson was a Belgian design, the de Cosmo. It had a 24hp 4-cylinder engine, a 3-speed gearbox and shaft drive, and was the first car designed by J. de Cosmo after he left F.N. to make cars on his own. It was to have been made by Wilkinson, but probably the few Wilkinson-de Cosmos that appeared were imported from Belgium. In 1907 there was a rumour that Wilkinson were to build the Mors car under licence, but nothing came of it.

In 1912 appeared the Wilkinson light car, powered by a 4-cylinder 7hp engine of 848cc. At £175 it was one of the most expensive light cars, and few were sold. However, it was the basis of the later Deemster.   GNG

WILLAM (F) *1969 to date*

Lambretta S.A.F.D., Paris

Very similar to the Italian Lawil, the Willam minicar, made in open (Farmer) and closed (City) forms is powered by a 123cc single-cylinder 2-stroke scooter engine developing 5.6bhp. Top speed is about 38mph.   MCS

WILLIAMS (i) (US) *1905*

W.L. Casaday Manufacturing Co, South Bend, Ind.

The Williams was a cleanly designed five-seater with an air-cooled flat 4-cylinder engine of 25hp. The bonnet was circular in cross-section and the same diameter (36in) as the tyres, a spare being mounted on the front. This car had an early example of a permanent windshield.   GMN

WILLIAMS (ii) *see* DE MARS

WILLIAMS (iii) (US) *1957–1968*
Williams Engine Co, Inc, Ambler, Pa.

Calvin C. Williams and his twin sons began experimenting with steam cars in 1940, and by 1957 were advertising that they would build complete cars, or convert petrol cars to steam power. At least one original car was built, using a flash boiler, 4-cylinder single-acting engine and fibreglass body. In 1966 they were offering a steam-converted Chevrolet Chevelle for $10,250, and received orders for nine of these, together with one for a Ford Fairlane from the Ford Motor Company. However, difficulties in obtaining small quantities of components at reasonable prices delayed the project, and rather than raise extra capital the Williams closed their business in late 1968.　　　　GNG

WILLIAMSON (GB) *1913–1916*
Williamson Motor Co Ltd, Coventry, Warwickshire

The Williamson 3-wheeler had an 8hp Douglas 2-cylinder engine, and chain drive to the single rear wheel. With a two-seater body, it was rather like the contemporary Morgan in appearance.　　　　GNG

WILLIS (GB) *1913*
Finchley Place Garage, London N.W.

The Willis cyclecar used an 8hp J.A.P. V-twin engine like many others of its kind, but it had an unusual transmission. Two chains gave a 2-speed drive to a countershaft, whence the rear wheels were driven by belts. The countershaft consisted of two tubes, one rotating inside the other, and this gave a differential effect not normally found on belt-driven machines.　　　　GNG

WILLMENT (GB) *1957–1959*
Willments Speed Shop, Twickenham, Middlesex

Deriving from the civil engineering firm of Willment Bros Ltd, Willments' automobile businesses made many one-offs at different times, and once planned to market a supercharged 750cc car. Their only production model used a tubular space frame, light alloy body, a Coventry-Climax FPF 1½-litre engine, and Willments' own transmission, incorporating a 5-speed gearbox. A 2-litre version of this purposeful sports car was also offered.　　　　DF

WILLS SAINTE CLAIRE (US) *1921–1927*
Wills Sainte Claire Co. Marysville, Mich.

The Wills Sainte Claire, so called after its devisor, Childe Harold Wills, who had helped to develop the Ford Model T and Lake Sainte Claire near his factory, was a beautifully made luxury car. From 1921 to 1924, it had a V-8 engine of 4.3 litres, with the advanced feature of two overhead camshafts (one to each bank of cylinders). In spite of this, it produced a modest 67bhp at 2,800rpm. However, considering the car's quality and specification, $2,475 in 1923 was not a high price. Such a figure was only possible with production of the order of 1,500 a year, which Wills Sainte Claire attained in 1923. In 1924, a long-stroke ohc engine, with 6 cylinders in line, replaced the V-8, and this model remained in production, with slight changes, until 1927.　　　　TRN

WILLYS (i) (US) *1909; 1916–1918; 1930–1963*
including **OVERLAND** *1903–1929; 1939.* **WILLYS-KNIGHT** *1914–1932*
(1) Standard Wheel Co, Terre Haute, Indiana *1903–1905*
(2) Overland Co, Indianapolis, Indiana *1905–1907*
(3) Willys-Overland Co, Toledo, Ohio *1908–1963*

These makes are inseparable, if only because of their confusing nomenclature. The original product of the Standard Wheel Co was a tiller-steered single-cylinder runabout with solid tyres which differed from most of its contemporaries in having its engine mounted in front under a real bonnet. It sold for $595. This had grown up by 1905 into a wheel-steered 1.3-litre twin, still with planetary transmission, and the company changed its style and moved to Indianapolis. Financial difficulties in 1907 brought John North Willys, an Elmira, N.Y. automobile dealer into the picture, and under his ownership a $1,250 4-cylinder model was produced, this having a pedal-controlled planetary transmission in the Ford manner, separately-cast cylinders, and a transaxle. There were two sixes in 1909, an Overland at $2,000, and the 45hp Willys costing $250 more. Both the Willys name and multi-cylinder engines disappeared in 1910, and production of 4-cylinder cars was concentrated in the old Pope factory at Toledo. During these years Willys continued to distribute the Marion, for which he had held an agency in the Elmira days. High-tension magneto ignition was used on the 1912 Overlands, which included a 3.2-litre 2-speed Model 58 at $850, a 3-speed version (Model 59) with conventional gearbox at $900, and two bigger 4s at $1,200 and $1,500 respectively. By 1914 Overland had moved into the ranks of the best-sellers with the 79 series at $950, a 4-litre car which helped to sell 80,000 that year. New also was the Willys-Knight with Knight double sleeve-valve 4-cylinder engine: this was in fact the former Edwards-Knight, which concern Willys had acquired, and early production was undertaken for Willys-Overland by Garford of Elyria, hitherto associated with the manufacture of cars

1925 WILLS SAINTE CLAIRE Six sedan.
Automobile Manufacturers' Association

1906 (WILLYS) OVERLAND Model 22 8hp two-seater.
Kaiser-Jeep Corporation

1926 (WILLYS) OVERLAND Whippet 2.2-litre tourer. *G.N. Georgano*

1933 WILLYS(i) 77 2.2-litre coupé. *Kaiser-Jeep Corporation*

1942 WILLYS(i) American 2.2-litre coupé. *Kaiser-Jeep Corporation*

1949 WILLYS(i) Jeepster 2.2-litre tourer. *Kaiser-Jeep Corporation*

1964 WILLYS(ii) Aero 2600 sedan. *Willys-Overland do Brasil SA*

for sale by Studebaker. 1915 saw a sv Overland 6 at $1,145, with the group moving up into second place behind Ford in the sales race. Willys-Knight, still a young make, was placed eighteenth: and in 1916 a second Willys 6, with 5-litre engine, joined the range, to remain there for three seasons. Willys-Knight had a V8 on a 10ft 5in wheelbase for $1,950 in 1917, but in 1919 4s only were being made, the classic L-head Overland having made its appearance at the low price of $495. The 4-cylinder Willys-Knight had 3.3-litre engines and sold around the $1,400 mark.

In 1920 Willys Overland Crossley Ltd was formed in England with works at Stockport: this was a subsidiary of Crossley Motors Ltd, and assembled cars for the British market. It originated nothing save a 1924 version of the Overland powered by a 1,802cc Morris-Oxford engine. Overlands continued to sell well in America, the Model-92 'Redbird' appearing in 1923 and helping to push the year's sales up to 196,000. Sixes were back in the programme for 1925, the Overland being a straightforward 3.3-litre sv machine selling for $895, while Willys-Knight's Model-66 had a 60bhp 3.9-litre unit and fwb, and cost $1,845. It supplanted the sleeve-valve 4s the following year, and 1926 also saw the first of Overland's 2.2-litre 4-cylinder 'Whippet' series, priced at $625: these repeated the success of the 1919 type. 'Whippets' had fwb in 1927, in which year a companion 2.4-litre 6 was listed, as well as a smaller and cheaper Model-70 Willys-Knight. This could be bought for only $1,145 in 1928 – a record year both for the group and for the Knight-engined machines, which found 55,000 customers. Other Willys-Overland products during this period were the Stearns-Knight and Falcon-Knight. The 'Whippet' was restyled for 1929, and the Willys range was now headed by a handsome Willys-Knight Great Six; this competed with the bigger Chryslers at $1,850. In 1930 the Willys name was once again seen on a 3.2-litre 6 and 4-litre straight-8, both sv: the former was made in small-bore 2.4-litre 'Palatine' form for the British market. The 'Whippet' was now a Willys rather than an Overland, and in 1931 the 4-cylinder cars were dropped. Sales also slumped, and the sleeve-valve Willys-Knights were allowed to die out with the 87bhp Model-66E of 1932. From 1933 to 1936 the company struggled through a receivership, making only a 2.2-litre sv 4, the Model 77, with some pretensions to aerodynamic shape and a low price of $445, but this was brought up to date in 1937 with new styling and synchromesh. It acquired hydraulic brakes in 1939, reverting briefly to the name of Overland: both name and styling were different again by 1941, when it went under the designation 'Willys-American', with roomier bodywork, hypoid final drive, and a list price of $705.

During World War 2, Willys-Overland, along with Ford, were responsible for series production of the famous 4 × 4 Bantam inspired 'Jeep', and Willys continued its manufacture to civilian account after the War, licences being sold to Hotchkiss in France and Mitsubishi in Japan among others. Station wagon and sports 4-seater versions with 2-wheel drive and 6-cylinder engines were added to the range. It was not until 1952, however, that the company again offered orthodox private cars, these being fairly small vehicles with either the well-established 4- or a 2.6-litre ioe 6, unitary construction, and coil-and-wishbone ifs, selling in the region of $1,750. An sv 6 was available in 1953, when 4-door sedans were offered alongside the 2-door type. 1953 also saw the purchase of the company by Kaiser, and the 'Aero' line was dropped in 1956, though development and production have continued in the Willys-Overland do Brasil factory at São Paulo. Activities at Toledo have centred round the 'Jeep' family. The firm's name was changed to Kaiser-Jeep Corporation in 1963. For subsequent products, see Jeep.   MCS

WILLYS (ii) (BR) *1958–1967*
Willys-Overland do Brasil SA, São Paulo

This offshoot of the American concern started to build Jeeps under licence in 1954, but private cars did not join the range until 1958, when the Jeep Station Wagon was offered as the Rural-Willys. A development of the 1955 Aero Willys sedan with 90bhp sv 6-cylinder engine was added in 1960: two years later this gave way to a completely restyled model with twin-carburettor 2.6-litre ioe engine selling for the equivalent of £1,425. Since 1959 the company has also built Renaults under licence, as well as a Willys Interlagos sports car (1961) based on the Alpine. A prototype GT car of their own design was exhibited in 1965. In 1967 the company merged with Ford do Brasil, who continued the Willys range.   MCS

WILSON (i) (GB) *1922–1923*
W. Wilson, Loughborough, Leics.

Two models of the Wilson were listed, both with 11.9hp engines of unspecified make, and varying wheelbases. W. Wilson was an engineer who had designed the Coltman car, but there is no evidence that cars of his own name ever went into production.   GNG

WILSON (ii) (GB) *1935–1936*
Partridge, Wilson & Co Ltd, Leicester

This company were makers of battery-electric delivery vans, who built an attractive electric coupé with petrol-car styling. The bodies were by Arthur Mulliner of Northampton, and the cars had a range of 40 miles per charge and a speed of 27mph. Only 40 were made, of which at least one survives, but this was a larger number than any other electric car made in Britain between the wars. Electric vans were made until 1954.   GNG

WILSON-PILCHER (GB) 1901–1907

(1) Wilson and Pilcher, London S.W. 1901–1903
(2) Sir W.G. Armstrong, Whitworth and Co Ltd, Newcastle upon Tyne 1904–1907

The Wilson-Pilcher was an advanced design featuring a horizontally-opposed engine with automatic inlet valves, an epicyclic constant-mesh gearbox (giving 4 speeds forward and reverse and a clutchless change), both axles located by radius rods, and helical bevel final drive. The 1.4-litre 4-cylinder prototype had its heads only water-cooled, but full water cooling was adopted on production cars, which had 2.4 litres and 9bhp: these units were mounted in front under a short bonnet, and the flywheel was frontally located. Capacity went up to 2.7 litres in 1903, by which time 40mph was claimed.

In 1904 production was undertaken by Armstrong-Whitworth. The Newcastle-built Wilson-Pilchers came in two models: the four at £735, and a 4-litre 'square' flat-six on similar lines selling at around the £900 mark, and rated at 18/24hp. Though these cars were still listed as late as 1907, that season brought the first of the conventional 4-cylinder T-headed Armstrong-Whitworths, and the end of the Wilson-Pilcher line.   MCS

WILTON (GB) 1912–1924

(1) Wilton Cycle & Motor Co Ltd, Victoria, London S.W. 1912–1914
(2) Wilton Cars Ltd, Clapham Junction, London S.W. 1914–1920
(3) Wilton Cars Ltd, Tooting, London S.W. 1921–1924

The prototype Wilton light car had a V-twin J.A.P. engine, and a Siddeley-Deasy type bonnet, but when it went into production in 1913 it had a 4-cylinder 9hp engine of Wilton's own make, and an ordinary bonnet with V-radiator. The post-war Wilton was a larger affair powered by an 11.9hp Meadows engine of 1,794cc, and using a worm rear axle. By 1923 the engine had been changed again, and was now an 11.9hp 1,496cc Dorman.   GNG

WIMHURST see PALLISER

WINCO (GB) 1913–1914

Stringer & Co, Sheffield, Yorks.

The Winco light car was designed by G. Bullock, a former L.G.O.C. draughtsman, and used a 9hp 2-cylinder engine of the company's own manufacture, and shaft drive. A streamlined version was raced at Brooklands in 1913 and 1914.   GNG

WINDHOFF (D) 1908–1914

Gebr. Windhoff Motoren- und Fahrzeugfabrik GmbH, Rheine

This firm produced automobile parts (engines, radiators, transmissions etc.) before starting to build their own cars. Two 4-cylinder and two 6-cylinder models appeared in 1908 with engine capacities ranging from 2,012cc to 6,125cc. From 1911, overhead inlet valves were used. Windhoff cars were of a high technical standard and good finish. They appeared in various trials, including the Prince Henry, which they finished quite satisfactorily, proving their design as sporting cars of high performance. The 6-cylinder 3.9-litre model in particular was among the best the best cars of its time. A variety of models, including 6/18PS 1½-litre and 10/30PS 2.6-litre fours, and the 15/40PS 3.9-litre six, was offered until 1914, when car production was discontinued because of the outbreak of World War 1.   HON

WINDSOR (i) (US) 1906

Windsor Automobile Co, Evansville, Ind.

The only model of this make was a five-seater tourer priced at $2,500. This car used a 6-cylinder, 30hp engine driving through a friction transmission with shaft drive to the rear axle. This later became the Simplicity made by Evansville Automobile Co.   GMN

WINDSOR (ii) (GB) 1924–1927

Jas. Bartle & Co, Ltd, London W.11

In terms of quality, the Windsor was one of the finest light cars produced in Britain during the 1920s. It was first offered for 1924, at a time when the most dangerous competitors were already well established, but its list of virtues was formidable. It was modern, with its efficient 10.4hp 1,353cc push-rod-ohv engine and excellent 4-wheel brakes. The engine was very neat and clean in outward appearance, and all mechanical parts, indeed the whole car, were beautifully made and finished. None of the mechanical parts was bought outside. The engine was smooth and quiet; unusual features of an ohv light-car engine at this date. The 4-speed gearbox, too, was a rarity in this class of car, and its ratios were well-spaced; 57mph was available in top gear, and 46 in third. Finally, the bodies were spacious, and sold with full equipment.

Unfortunately, all this cost a great deal – £400 – and for that money a much larger car of good quality and name could be bought, such as the new 14/45hp Talbot, shown at Olympia in 1926, for £5 less. Very few Windsors were made, for, as other manufacturers had found out, there was no market for a high-quality, expensive light car.   TRN

WINDSOR STEAM CAR see DETROIT STEAM CAR

1935 WILSON(ii) electric coupé. *Autocar*

1921 WILTON 11.9hp coupé. *M.J. Worthington-Williams*

1913 WINDHOFF 15/40PS tourer. *Neubauer Collection*

1926 WINDSOR 10/15hp sports car. *Autocar*

1920 WINGFIELD 23.8hp chassis. *Autocar*

1922 WING MIDGET single-seater roadster.
Keith Marvin Collection

1904 WINTON 30hp tourer. *G.N. Georgano
Collection*

1923 WINTON Model 40 34hp tourer. *Keith
Marvin Collection*

WINDSOR WHITE PRINCE *see* MOON

WINGFIELD (GB) *1909–1920*

Wingfield Motor Co, Norbury, London S.E.

The first Wingfield, an 18/23hp 4-cylinder car, appeared in 1909, but did not go into production. In 1912 the company was bought by Cars & Motor Sundries Ltd who planned to buy new premises near London, and make 250 cars per year. A wide range of Wingfields was listed for 1914, four 4-cylinder models from 10.4 to 25.6hp, and three sixes from 16.9 to 38.4hp. It is not certain how many, if any, of these were actually made, but in 1920 a 23.8hp six of 3,920cc was definitely built, at least as a prototype. It had pair-cast cylinders, a 4-speed gearbox, and fully floating bevel rear axle. It was priced at £750 for the chassis, and it was said that orders were then being taken, in January 1920. However, little was heard of the Wingfield after that.   GNG

WING MIDGET (US) *1922*

H.C. Wing & Sons, Greenfield, Mass.

The Wing Midget was a miniature single-seater car with the appearance of a scaled-down racing car of an earlier era. It had outside exhausts and double chain drive, and was advertised as being capable of 80mph, and 40 to 50mpg, though not, presumably at the same time.   GNG

WINNER (US) *1907*

Winner Motor Buggy Co, St Louis, Mo.

The Winner was a typical high-wheel buggy with tiller steering. At $300 it was one of the cheapest ever made.   GNG

WINNIPEG (CDN) *1921–1923*

Winnipeg Motor Cars Ltd, Winnipeg, Man.

'As Good as the Wheat' was the slogan of this car, which had a 4-cylinder Herschell-Spillman engine and a radiator guaranteed not to burst even if it froze in the bitter Prairie winter.   HD

WINSON (GB) *1920*

Messrs J. Winn, Rochdale, Lancs.

The Winson was one of many friction-driven cyclecars on the market during this period. Powered by either 8hp Precision or Blackburne engines, the cars boasted a novel fitting of the friction disc that gave a differential effect. Final drive was by silent chain to the rear axle.   MJWW

WINTER *see* W.W.

WINTHER (US) *1920–1923*

Winther Motors Inc, Division of Winter Motor Truck Co, Kenosha, Wisc.

A short-lived car produced by a truck concern, the Winther used a 6-cylinder Herschell-Spillman engine and did not differ much from other assembled cars, either in appearance or design. Probably less than 500 private cars were built in the four years of manufacture.   KM

WINTON (US) *1897–1924*

Winton Motor Carriage Co, Cleveland, Ohio

Alexander Winton, a Cleveland bicycle maker, built a 12hp twin-cylinder experimental car in 1897, which recorded 33.7mph over a mile. He produced his first vehicle for commercial sale the following year; this was a two-seater phaeton with a horizontal single-cylinder engine, 2-speed transmission, and laminated wood frame, listed at $1,000; 25 cars were sold in the first season, early customers including the Packard brothers.

The first of the Gordon Bennett Cup races in 1900 stemmed from a challenge issued by Winton to Fernand Charron, and the designer himself took part on a Benz-like vehicle with an enormous single cylinder of 3.8 litres' capacity, said to produce 14bhp. It failed to make any impression, but by 1901 Winton was producing a large horizontal-twin with its 2-speed gearbox mounted under the floor and alongside the engine. The bonnet was devoted to tankage, wheel steering was provided, and 40bhp was claimed. A Winton characteristic which persisted for several years was a variable-lift inlet valve actuated by compressed air, a medium to which Alexander Winton was addicted. A 15hp touring car on similar lines, with central chain drive, sold for $2,000 in 1902, increased to $2,500 in 1903, when nominal output went up to 20hp. One of these cars was used for Jackson's successful trans-Continental run; also in 1903 Winton made another bid for international racing laurels with his two Bullets. Both of these had in-line engines lying on their sides in the frame, and the inevitable pneumatic governor. Percy Owen's Gordon Bennett car was an 8½-litre four, but Winton himself drove an 80bhp eight of 17 litres' capacity, and with only a single forward speed. Both cars retired, though the Bullets later did fairly well in American sprint events.

Vertical 4-cylinder engines and conventionally-located gearboxes were the order of the day in 1905, and ht magneto ignition was also used, but 2 forward speeds were still deemed sufficient. Three types were marketed, ratings being 16, 24, and

40hp. The 5.8-litre Model K of 1906 retained the 2-speed box, but sliding-type transmissions were found in both of Winton's 1907 offerings, the 35hp 4-cylinder Model M, which had 4 speeds and a geared-up top, and the 7¾-litre Model XVI six, a 3-speed model. Two sixes were sold in 1909, the larger of the two having a capacity of over 9½ litres and a wheelbase of 10ft 10in. It cost $4,500, and Winton offered a compressed-air starter; by 1911 this was being used to pump up the tyres as well. Thereafter pair-cast sixes were standard and electric starting was adopted finally in 1915. No major changes occurred after 1920, when the earlier types gave way to the 5.7-litre Series 25 with a 4-speed gearbox.

Winton elected to abandon car manufacture in 1924 in favour of marine diesel engines, and the company is still active in this field as a Division of General Motors.

MCS

WISCO (US) 1910
Wisconsin Motor Car Co, Janesville, Wisc.

The Wisco chassis had a 4.7-litre 4-cylinder engine, with 3-speed selective transmission, on a wheelbase of 9ft 10in. Body styles were a four-seater tonneau and a five-seater tourer.

GMN

WITHERS (GB) 1906–1915
Withers Motors Ltd, London W.

Withers cars were assembled in small numbers in premises in the Edgware Road, where the company is still in business. The first models were a 12/14 and 20/22hp, both with Aster engines, and a 24/30hp which used a Barriquand et Marre engine. Up to about 1911 the engines used were mostly Asters, after which the firm standardized on White & Poppe units. These were available in 20, 25, 30 and 35/40hp models, but generally the cars were only completed to special order. Bodywork was entirely made by Withers at their own premises. At the 1913 Olympia Show Withers exhibited the Magic sleeve-valve car; this was built under Fischer patents, and was probably a Delaugère-Clayette.

GNG

WITTEKIND (D) 1922–1925
Wittekind Automobile GmbH, Berlin-Lichterfelde

This firm produced a small car with a 4/12PS or 5/15PS 4-cylinder engine and a two- or three-seater body; 6/18PS and 6/24PS versions were also available with four-seater bodies.

HON

WIZARD (US) 1921–1922
Wizard Automobile Co, Charlotte, N.C.

The Wizard was more of a plan than a reality although probably a few cars were actually produced. The Wizard Jr was a small roadster selling at $395, equipped with artillery wheels and planetary transmission, and powered by a 2-cylinder air-cooled V-type ohv engine. A planned 4-cylinder series failed to materialize.

KM

WM (PL) 1927–1928
Inz. Wladyslaw Mrajski, Warsaw

The WM was a co-operative project by Polish industry. Mrajski, a director of C.W.S., co-ordinated the work and seven other firms supplied components. A saloon and an open tourer were built, powered by a flat-twin, 4-stroke air-cooled engine. They could seat two adults and several children. A speed of 50mph was attained in successful road tests, but the WM project was abandoned after several years of work.

BE

WOLF see WEARWELL

WOLFE (US) 1907–1909
H.E. Wilcox Motor Car Co, Minneapolis, Minn.

The Wolfe was a five-seater on a 9ft wheelbase. Continental water-cooled or Carrico 4-cylinder air-cooled engines were used. These were of 3.3-litre capacity, and had overhead valves. The drive was by 3-speed selective transmission and double chains to the rear wheels. The car weighed 1,950lb and sold for $1,800. The company continued to build water-cooled cars under the name Wilcox until 1912, and trucks until 1928.

GMN

WOLSELEY (i) (GB) 1899–1906; 1911 to date
WOLSELEY-SIDDELEY (GB) 1904–1910
(1) Wolseley Sheep Shearing Machine Co, Ltd, Birmingham *1899–1901*
(2) Wolseley Tool and Motor Car Co, Ltd, Birmingham *1901–1914*
(3) Wolseley Motors Ltd, Birmingham *1914–1927*
(4) Wolseley Motors (1927) Ltd, Birmingham *1927–1948*
(5) Wolseley Motors (1927) Ltd, Cowley, Oxford *1949–1970*
(6) Austin-Morris Division, British Leyland Motor Corp Ltd, Cowley, Oxford *1970 to date*

The first prototype Wolseley was a 3-wheeler on Léon Bollée lines made by the company's General Manager, Herbert Austin, in 1896. It featured two horizontal cylinders and overhead camshaft. A second improved model was made in 1897, but production cars were based on the 3½-hp 4-wheeler of 1899, which competed successfully in the Thousand Miles' Trial of 1900. It had a single-cylinder horizontal

1907 WOLFE Model D 30hp tourer. *Clarion Larson*

1902 WOLSELEY 30hp Paris-Vienna racing car. Montague Grahame-White at the wheel. *National Motor Museum*

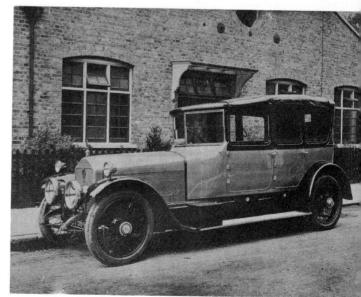
1920 WOLSELEY 30/40hp all-weather tourer. *The Veteran Car Club of Great Britain*

727

1920 WOLSELEY 15hp coupé de ville.
Coachwork by Thrupp & Maberly. *Autocar*

1932 WOLSELEY Viper 16hp saloon. *National
Motor Museum*

1935 WOLSELEY Hornet Special 14hp sports
car. *National Motor Museum*

1940 WOLSELEY Ten drophead coupé.
National Motor Museum

engine mounted at the front with the head pointing forward, automatic inlet valve, coil ignition, a wrap-round tubular radiator, 3 forward speeds, tiller steering, and belt primary and chain final drive, and formed the basis for the Austin-designed Wolseleys made under Vickers auspices for the next six years.

By 1901 wheel steering, artillery wheels and chain primary drive had been adopted, and the single, now rated at 5hp, could be bought for £260, while there was a 10hp 2.6-litre twin at £360, and a 4-cylinder racing model with 5-speed gearbox available to special order. Wolseley were already among the biggest British producers with 327 cars sold that year, increasing to 800 in 1903 and 3,000 by 1914, when they led the national industry. A 5.2-litre horizontal-four was listed in 1902, from which 52mph was claimed, and the twin-cylinder versions of 1905–06 had mechanically-operated inlet valves.

Austin supported racing energetically, entering 3- and 4-cylinder machines for the Paris-Vienna in 1902, while the big 11.9-litre flat-4 Beetles put up the best British performances in the Gordon Bennett Cup Races of 1904 and 1905. Queen Alexandra bought a Wolseley in 1904, but Austin's obstinate adherence to the horizontal engine was not appreciated by his directors, and he resigned in 1905 to form his own company. Already Wolseley were making a 3.3-litre vertical-engined 4-cylinder car to the designs of J.D. Siddeley (variously known as a Wolseley-Siddeley or Siddeley), and these versions dominated the range in 1906, though single- and twin-cylinder Wolseleys of the Austin era survived for one more season. 1906 Wolseley-Siddeleys were made with overhead inlet valves, and (in some cases) overdrive gearboxes, bigger models having oversquare engines, separately-cast cylinders, and chain drive, while the range embraced everything from a shaft-driven 12hp vertical-twin at £325 up to a touring version of Siddeley's 1905 Gordon Bennett Trials racer, a 15.7-litre machine listed at £1,250. Licence-production in Italy was initiated under the name of Wolsit. Thermo-syphon cooling was introduced on the Ten in 1907, in which year a shaft-driven version of the 5½-litre 4-cylinder 30 could be bought, as well as the company's first six, an 8½-litre 45 with dual ignition. L-head engines were standard in 1908, and 1909 saw the end of chain drive and the introduction of a smaller 24/30hp 6-cylinder. In 1910 came the very successful monobloc 2.2-litre 4-cylinder 12/16 with pressure lubrication and worm drive at £370. At the other end of the range was the big bevel-driven 6-cylinder 40/50 at £660 for a chassis.

Siddeley had gone to Deasy in 1909, and for 1911 the cars became plain Wolseleys once more. 1913 models had air-pressure fuel feed, the best seller being the 3.2-litre 16/20 with dual ignition at under £500. In this year an experimental gyrocar was made for the Russian inventor Count Schilovsky, while a worm-driven light car, the Stellite, was being made by a subsidiary company. The 1914 range consisted of the 16/20, and two sixes rated at 24/30 and 30/40, all with electric lighting and detachable wire wheels. The sixes had bevel drive, and came equipped with compressed-air starters, supplanted in 1919 by conventional electrical units.

Wolseley made the V-8 overhead-camshaft Hispano-Suiza aero engines during World War 1, and their first true post-war models featured both overhead camshafts and detachable heads, though a 3.9-litre sv six was made in various forms up to 1927. The 1.3-litre 10 had a rear-axle gearbox, quarter-elliptic springs, worm drive, and coil ignition, and replaced the Stellite; it cost £500, and there was a companion 2.6-litre ohc 15 with a conventionally-mounted gearbox. In 1921 Wolseley made 12,000 cars, and numerous types were offered in ensuing years, including aluminium-bodied sports versions of the 10 and 15, an austerity edition of the 10 two-seater, and a 7hp flat-twin at £295. In 1925 the 10 grew up into a four-seater 11/22, and the 15 was replaced by an sv 16/35, the last new side-valve Wolseley.

For 1927 the company offered a new 2-litre 16/45hp ohc Silent 6 with spiral bevel final drive and 4-speed gearbox, but in the meanwhile it had gone bankrupt, and had been acquired by Sir William Morris (Lord Nuffield). Under new management the ohc designs were developed as well as being adapted to the companion makes of Morris and M.G. New Wolseleys in 1928 were a coil-ignition 2.7-litre straight-8 at £750, and a 12/32hp 4-cylinder, also ohc, at £315. In 1929 there was a short-lived and very expensive 8-cylinder 32/90 and a more important 6-cylinder 21/60 which in export form boasted Budd welded all-steel bodywork and Lockheed hydraulic brakes, and was virtually a Wolseley edition of the Morris Isis which followed it in the 1930 season.

That year Wolseley pioneered the really cheap small six in England with the 1.3-litre Hornet; this shared the 21/60's hydraulics, and resembled a Morris Minor with two extra cylinders and an elongated bonnet. It offered remarkable flexibility for £185, and attracted a vast diversity of inexpensive special bodywork from such firms as E.W. (Eustace Watkins) and Swallow. Its 1931 stablemates were a 2-litre Viper with Morris styling at £285, and 6- and 8-cylinder versions of the 21/60, all with overhead camshafts. 1932 Hornets had a forward engine mounting allowing of roomy 4-door saloon bodywork without lengthening the wheelbase, while a twin-carburettor sports version, the Hornet Special, was marketed as a chassis only at £175.

In 1933 came the illuminated radiator badge, a Wolseley hallmark ever since, and 1934 cars had synchromesh, a roomy 1-litre 4-cylinder Nine at £179 joining the Hornet, now available with free wheel at £215. In 1935 there was a brief venture with preselector gearboxes and some new ohc 6-cylinder cars. The Nine gave way to the bigger Wasp, the Hornet grew up to 1.4 litres, and a 1.6-litre 14hp formed the basis for a 50bhp Hornet Special capable of nearly 80mph, but 1936 was the last year of overhead camshafts. Already the old 21/60 had been replaced by a range of ohv push-rod Super Sixes, virtually luxury 4-speed derivatives of the Series II Morris with easy-clean wheels and more luxurious equipment, and by the end of the year the 4-cylinder light cars had fallen into line with this theme. Last to go was the Fourteen which in June, 1936 reappeared as a push-rod 1.8-litre 14/56 selling for £265.

By 1939–40 a comprehensive range included a 1,140cc Ten (the mechanical components of Morris's Series-M mounted in a separate chassis), a 1½-litre 4-cylinder 12/48, and sixes of 14, 16, 18, 21, and 25hp, the last-mentioned version of the Super Six being also available as a sporting drophead coupé and a limousine. The 18hp model, introduced in 1937, was adopted by Scotland Yard and was the first Wolseley to win general favour with police forces, a connection that has continued with subsequent 6-cylinder models into the 1960s. A 1939 18/85 driven by Humfrey Symons broke the London-Cape record with a time of 31 days 22 hours despite falling through a bridge in the Congo.

A rather smaller range of similar Wolseleys went back into production in 1945, rounded out by an 8hp car which was a de luxe, ohv development of the Series-E Morris 8. For 1949 a removal to Cowley was accompanied by two entirely new models with unitary construction, and hypoid final drive: they were basically similar to the Morris Oxford and Six, though the smaller 4/50 had a 4-cylinder version of the ohc power unit common to the Morris and Wolseley Sixes. Coil-and-wishbone independent front suspension replaced the torsion-bar layout in the 1953 4/44, powered by a detuned version of the T-type M.G. engine, but the effect of the Nuffield-Austin merger was soon felt in a rationalization of design.

The first Austin-engined Wolseley was the 2.6-litre 6/90 of 1955, which shared a body with Riley's Pathfinder, and was available the following year with overdrive or automatic transmission, but 1958 brought an attractive compact 1½-litre saloon, the 1500, which was basically an expanded Morris Minor with rack-and-pinion steering and a close-ratio 4-speed gearbox. A Riley equivalent was also marketed, and B.M.C.'s Australian factory offered variants with Austin and Morris nameplates.

This was Wolseley's last individual effort, and subsequent models have been luxury editions of basic Austin/Morris themes, a Mini variant, the Hornet, making its appearance in 1962. A luxury 1100 variant appeared in 1966, evolving into a 1300 by 1968. A year earlier Wolseley had announced their 18-85 or de luxe 1800, though the Hornet had gone by 1969. In 1973 the 1300, the 18-85, and a 6-cylinder fwd 2200 were offered.   MCS

WOLSELEY (ii) *see* AUSTIN (iii)

WOLVERINE (i) (US) *1904–1906*
(1) Reid Manufacturing Co, Detroit, Mich. *1904–1905*
(2) Wolverine Automobile & Commercial Vehicle Co, Dundee, Mich. *1905–1906*
The Wolverine used 2-stroke, 2-cylinder engines of 10hp and 15hp. It was produced as a four-seater tonneau and a two-seater runabout. This make was superseded by the Craig-Toledo.   GMN

WOLVERINE (ii) **(WOLVERINE SPECIAL)** (US) *1917–1920*
Wolverine Motors Inc, Kalamazoo, Mich.
Announced in September 1917, the Wolverine was built in a single speedster model. A large amount of aluminium was used in its construction. It had a Rochester-Duesenberg 4-cylinder engine and a speed of 75mph was guaranteed. The Wolverine was equipped with wire wheels, a pointed radiator, bicycle mud-guards, step plates and a large 30 gallon petrol tank to the rear of the seat, as on the Stutz Bearcat. Its price was $3,000.   KM

WOLVERINE (iii) (US) *1927–1928*
Reo Motor Car Co, Lansing, Mich.
This Wolverine was in fact a smaller companion car to Reo's Flying Cloud models of 1927 and 1928, but was marketed as a make of its own and carried its individual radiator and hub-cap insignia. Introduced in April 1927, the car had a Continental 6-cylinder engine and artillery spoke wheels, and differed from the Flying Cloud in the grouping of its horizontal bonnet louvres. A 2-door and 4-door sedan and a two/four-seater cabriolet constituted the line.   KM

WONDER (US) *1917*
Wonder Motor Truck Co, Chicago, Ill.
This truck company made a touring car with a 22hp 4-cylinder engine, for one season only. It was of thoroughly conventional design and cost $800.   GNG

WOOD (US) *1902–1903*
Wood Vapour Vehicle Co, Brooklyn, N.Y.
The Wood was a light two-seater steam car powered by an 8hp 3-cylinder engine. A horizontal water-tube boiler was slung beneath the frame, and the price was $450, making it one of the cheapest steamers ever produced.   GNG

1965 WOLSELEY 6/110 2.9-litre saloon.
British Motor Corporation

1973 WOLSELEY 1300 saloon. *British Leyland Motor Corporation*

1927 WOLVERINE(iii) 25hp sedan. *Autocar*

1956 WOODILL Wildfire coupé. *Woodill Fibreglass Body Corporation*

1913 WOODROW 9hp sports car. *A.L. Butlin*

1914 WOODS Model 1334 electric brougham. *The Veteran Car Club of Great Britain*

WOODILL (US) *1952–1958*
Woodill Fibreglass Body Corp, Tustin, Calif.

The Wildfire was a sports car with a two-seater fibreglass body mounted on Willys running gear. The choice of power unit included Willys 90hp, Cadillac 300hp, and Ford V-8 engines. A Brushfire model was built for children (ages 6–12) and was equipped with a single-cylinder 3hp engine with one forward gear. The body design was the same as the Wildfire but scaled down to a 5ft 3in wheelbase.   BE

WOOD-LOCO (US) *1901–1902*
Wood-Loco Vehicle Co, Cohoes, N.Y.

Powered by a 2-cylinder horizontal 8hp steam engine, the Wood-Loco was available as a private car of buggy type, as a delivery van and as a ten-seater commercial vehicle. Very few Wood-Locos were built.   KM

WOODROW (GB) *1913–1915*
Woodrow & Co Ltd, Stockport, Cheshire

The Woodrow cyclecar was first made with an 8hp J.A.P. air-cooled V-twin engine, 3-speed gearbox and chain drive to a differential-equipped rear axle. A later model used a Precision water-cooled engine and shaft drive. The sports model had a rakish appearance, with sharply pointed V-radiator and streamlined body.   GNG

WOODRUFF (US) *1904*
Woodruff Automobile Co, Akron, Ohio

The Woodruff was not an attractive car, as it had a peculiar sloping bonnet. It had a 3-cylinder engine, and a 3-speed transmission with shaft-drive.   GMN

WOODS (US) *1899–1919*
Woods Motor Vehicle Co, Chicago, Ill.

The Woods Electric was one of the longest-lived American electric makes, although its sales never reached those of the Detroit, Baker or Milburn. The usual range of town cars was made, including a hansom cab, powered by a single 3hp motor mounted on the rear axle. In 1903 a four-seater tonneau was made complete with bonnet which made it look exactly like a petrol-engined car. Woods Electrics were expensive, with prices up to $4,500. The most interesting Woods was the Dual Power of 1917 onwards. This had a 12hp 4-cylinder Continental petrol engine as an auxiliary to the electric motor. Maximum speed was 20mph with the electric motor alone, or 35mph with both engines.   GNG

WOODS MOBILETTE (US) *1914–1916*
Woods Mobilette Co, Harvey, Ill.

The first prototype of the Woods Mobilette appeared in 1910, but production did not start until early 1914. It was a two-seater cyclecar with 12/14hp 4-cylinder engine and tandem seating. Although the prototypes were air cooled, all production Mobilettes used water-cooled engines. Staggered side-by-side seating appeared on 1916 models, with electric lighting and starting as optional extras. These were standardized on the models announced for 1917, but production did not continue beyond the end of 1916.   GNG

WOOLER (GB) *1920–1921*
Wooler Engineering Co, Ltd, Alperton, Middlesex

The Wooler, or Wooler Mule, was appropriately named, for it was a crude and strange device. In specification, it belonged rather to pre-1900 Scotland than to the teeming world of light cars and cyclecars of the post-World War 1 period. The engine was a horizontally-opposed twin, each cylinder having a single rotary valve. The latter were fed from a surface carburettor. There was belt drive to a worm-gear axle, the rear wheels being set close together in the manner of the Isetta. Changes of speed were effected by a hand wheel. There was coil-spring independent front suspension, the only feature that was neither primitive nor peculiar. Needless to say, this make did not last long.   TRN

WORLDMOBILE (US) *1928*
Service-Relay Motors Corp, Lima, Ohio

The Worldmobile was a large six-seater saloon powered by a 4½-litre sv Lycoming straight-8 engine. Service-Relay were truck builders and intended to put the Worldmobile into production, but only seven were made. One survives in Harrah's Automobile Collection.   GNG

WORTH (US) *1909–1910*
Worth Motor Car Manufacturing Co, Kankakee, Ill.

The Worth was a high-wheeler with a false bonnet in front, and the engine beneath the body. The only model, a two- or four-seater, was driven by an air-cooled, 2-cylinder engine. The drive was through a friction transmission and double chains to the rear wheels. The gross weight was 1,400lb.   GMN

WORTHINGTON BOLLÉE (US) *1904*
Worthington Automobile Co, New York, N.Y.

This was a slightly modified 24/32hp 4-cylinder Léon Bollée sold by the Worthington Company. In 1905 the company merged with the Berg Automobile Company, of Cleveland.　GNG

WORTHINGTON RUNABOUT (GB) *1909–1912*
Worthington Bros, Hythe, Kent

Only one Worthington Runabout was built, although development continued throughout the period shown. The car was originally powered by an 8hp horizontally-opposed twin engine built in Worthington's workshop, but this was replaced by an 8/9hp V-twin J.A.P. The transversely mounted engine drove by two chains to a countershaft, final drive being by belt. It was intended to sell the car at £90, but the company became involved in grandiose plans to built aircraft, and in the end nothing was seen of either aircraft or cars.　MJWW

WREN (AUS) *1969–1970*
Bill Reynolds, Melbourne

This was a typical Formula Ford racing car with multi-tube space-frame and colour-impregnated fibreglass body.　GNG

WRIGHT (i) (US) *1910*
Wright Motor Car Co, New Cumberland, Pa.

This was a conventional five-seater touring car powered by a 20hp 4-cylinder Waukesha engine. Only six were made.　GNG

WRIGHT (ii) (CDN) *1929*
Montreal, Que.

The rakish Wright Flexible Axle car was a final attempt to base a car on the excellent Wright-Fisher independent suspension system. It was built by Benjamin Wright, formerly of Wright-Fisher, whose suspension system was used in the U.S. Birmingham which was related to the Montreal-built Parker. Production believed limited to one touring car, which performed well but never had a chance.　HD

WRIGLEY (GB) *1913*
Wrigley & Co Ltd, Birmingham

The Wrigley cyclecar was powered by a 7/9hp 2-cylinder engine with the option of air or water cooling. It had a 2-speed gearbox on the rear axle. Very few were made, and the company concentrated on the manufacture of axles and gearboxes for other firms. In 1923 the Wrigley factory was bought by William Morris, and used for the manufacture of Morris Commercials.　GNG

W.S.C. (GB) *1914*
Wholesale Supply Co, Aberdeen

This was a cyclecar with an 8hp J.A.P. V-twin engine, friction transmission and belt final drive. It was sold through the Wholesale Supply Company, but the actual makers are unknown.　GNG

WUNDERLICH (D) *1902*
Motorenfabrik Carl Wunderlich, Berlin

This voiturette with a 2-cylinder proprietary engine was produced only for a short period.　HON

W.W. (GB) *1913–1914*
Winter & Co, Wandsworth, London S.W.

The W.W. (Winter of Wandsworth) light car was powered by an 8hp Precision V-twin engine, used a Chater-Lea gearbox and overhead worm rear axle. The 1914 model was known as the Winter, had a V-twin Blumfield engine, friction transmission and belt final drive.　GNG

WYNER (A) *1903–1905*
Michael A. Wyner, Vienna I

Wyner built various types with single-, 2, and 4-cylinder engines. Best known was his Populaire with a single-cylinder 8hp De Dion engine. After 1905 production was carried on by the Maschinen- und Waggonbau-Fabrik (*see* M.W.F.) and Wyner acted as sole sales representative.　HON

WYSS *see* BERNA

WYVERN (GB) *1913–1914*
Wyvern Light Car Co, Ltd, Twickenham, Middlesex

The Wyvern light car used a 10.5hp Chapuis-Dornier engine and shaft drive. It had a two-seater body and an attractive V-radiator not unlike that of a Métallurgique.　GNG

1917 WOODS Dual Power 12hp coupé. *Henry Ford Museum, Dearborn, Mich.*

1915 WOODS-MOBILETTE 12/14hp cyclecar. *Kenneth Stauffer*

1914 XENIA 13hp cyclecar. *The Veteran Car Club of Great Britain*

1922 XTRA 3¾hp 3-wheeler. *Autocar*

1905 YALE(i) 24/28hp tourer. *Keith Marvin Collection*

XENIA (US) *1914–1915*
Hawkins Cyclecar Co, Xenia, Ohio

This two-seater cyclecar was for a short time called the Hawkins. It had a V-twin air-cooled engine of 9/13hp. A 2-speed transmission with belt drive was used. GMN

XIAN-JIN (p); HSIEN-CHIN (wg) (PIONEER) (CHI) *c.1963 to date*
H'sin-Chin Mechanical Works, Chunking, Szechuan

A 6-cylinder saloon featuring a 95bhp engine, independent front suspension, and a top speed of 75mph. BE

XTRA (GB) *1922–1924*
Xtra Cars Ltd, Chertsey, Surrey

The Xtra cyclecar was really no more than a single-seater side-car mounted on a 3-wheeler chassis. The 3¾hp single-cylinder Villiers engine and 2-speed transmission were mounted on the rear wheel, and lighting was by acetylene. GNG

YAK (GB) *1969–1970*
Grantura Plastics Ltd, Blackpool, Lancs.

This was a light, general-purpose vehicle similar in conception to the B.M.C. Mini Moke, but with a one-piece fibreglass body. It was not supplied complete, but Mini components could be mounted easily. GNG

YAKOVLEV-FREZE (SU) *1896*
E.A. Yakovlev Works, St Petersburg

The pioneer of all Russian automobiles, the Yakovlev-Freze was a two-seater of rather crude construction with a single-cylinder 2hp rear engine. Power from the engine was transmitted to the differential by two rubber drive belts that could be lever-shifted on to discs of different diameters and engaged by a second lever. A split axle was linked with the rear wheels and road speed was estimated at over 13mph.

A winter modification was built with a slide device on the front and toothed chains on the rear wheels. The Y-F displayed at the 1896 Industrial Exhibition at Nijny-Novgorod caused considerable comment and acclaim according to news reports of the time. BE

YALE (i) (US) *1903–1907*
(1) Kirk Mfg Co, Toledo, Ohio *1903*
(2) Consolidated Mfg Co, Toledo, Ohio *1903–1907*

One model of the Yale, with a single-cylinder engine, remained virtually unchanged through the life of the make. There were also 2-cylinder and 4-cylinder models, the latter with a 24/28hp engine. The advertising slogan of the Yale was 'The Beau Brummell of the Road'. GMN

YALE (ii) (US) *1916–1918*
Saginaw Motor Car Co, Saginaw, Mich.

The Yale appeared only as an ivory and black seven-seater touring model. It had V-8 engine of 3.5 litres, with a 3-speed transmission. GMN

YALTA *see* ZAPOROZHETS

YAMATA (J) *1916*
Built in Osaka, this was one of the earliest Japanese 3-wheeled cars. It had two wheels in front, one in the rear. BE

YANK (US) *1950*
Custom Auto Works, San Diego, Calif.

The Yank was an assembled sports car using a 4-cylinder Willys engine and an aluminium two-seater body. A maximum speed of 78mph was claimed. GNG

YANKEE (US) *1910*
Yankee Motor Car Co, Chicago, Ill.

The Yankee was built as a high-wheeler with solid-rubber tyres, and as a two-seater Racy Roadster model with pneumatic Tyres. Both were powered by a 2-cylinder air-cooled engine, and both used a planetary transmission. GMN

YAXA (CH) *1912–1914*
Charles Baehni et Cie, Les Acacias, Geneva

The Yaxa derived its name from the phase 'il n'y a que ca' (it's the only one). It was designed by Charles Baehni who had worked with Charles-Edouard Henriod at Neuilly, and later was technical director of Martini. It had a 6/12hp 1,551cc monobloc 4-cylinder engine made by Zürcher of St Aubin (Zédel cars). A centrally placed gear-lever and hand-brake allowed for very modern-looking torpedo tourer bodywork. About 100 Yaxas were made in all, and they were available on the British market in 1913 and 1914.   GNG

Y.E.C. (GB) *1907–1908*
Yorkshire Engine Co, Sheffield, Yorks.

The Yorkshire Engine Company were locomotive builders who were commissioned to build a car for the British & Colonial Daimler-Mercedes Syndicate Ltd. About 50 cars were made, of exactly the same design as the 30hp Mercedes then being sold in England by the Mercedes Daimler Motor Co Ltd. The British & Colonial company paid royalties to Mercedes-Daimler for these 50 cars, and when they refused to continue to do so, a lawsuit not unnaturally arose. The decision went against British & Colonial, and they ordered no more cars from Y.E.C.   GNG

YENKO (US) *1965–1969*
Yenko Sportscars, Cannonsburg, Pa.

The Yenko Stinger was a Chevrolet Corvair Corsa 2-door coupé modified by Don Yenko for club racing. The normal 2.7-litre engine was bored out to 2.8 or 2.9 litres and various stages of tune were available. Jerry Thompson won the 1967 SCCA 'D' class production national championship in a Stinger. A total of 185 was made.
                                                                        GNG

YIMKIN (GB) *1959–1961*
Yimkin Engineering, London W.1

A.J.D. Sim claimed that the name chosen for his space-framed machines was Arabic for 'maybe'; however, notable wins were achieved in 1,172 Formula races. The Formula Junior version, with BMC parts, was less successful.   DF

YLN (RC) *1958 to date*
Yue Loong Motor Co Ltd, Taipei

A licence agreement with Nissan-Datsun of Japan allows the manufacture of their private cars and light commercials in Taiwan (Formosa), with some modification, under the YLN name; 60% of the parts are built by YLN and 40% purchased from Nissan. Yue Loong also built the Cony utility car during the 1960s, and a further agreement with the American Jeep Corporation enables them to make this range as well. In 1972–3 Yue Loong's private-car range embraced a Datsun Bluebird derivative, the YLN-706 with 1,299cc pushrod 4-cylinder engine, the YLN-751 station wagon with a similar engine, and a big 2-litre 4-cylinder saloon (YLN-801A) based on the Nissan-Datsun Cedric.   BE

YORK (i) (US) *1905–1907*
York Automobile Co, York, Pa.

The initial York model was a five-seater surrey, with very curving lines. It was powered by a 4-cylinder engine of 18/20hp, and had shaft drive. It is possible that this make may have been made as late as 1909.   GMN

YORK (ii) (D) *1922*
York Motoren AG, Plauen

A cyclecar with a V-twin engine was produced in limited numbers by this company.
                                                                        HON

YUE LOONG *see* YLN

1906 Y.E.C. 30hp chassis. *Yorkshire Engine Co*

1905 YORK(i) 18/20hp tourer. *Floyd Clymer Publications*

1930 Z Type Z9 1-litre tourer. *Neubauer Collection*

1936 Z Type Z6 750cc saloon. *Ing Adolf Babuška*

1967 ZAPOROZHETS 966B 887cc saloon. *Andrzej Rusinek*

Z

Z (i) (I) *1914–1915*
Zambon & Cia, Turin

The Italian Z was designed by Giuseppe Cravero, who had been responsible for the Florio car. Though a sports model was planned, World War 1 restricted Z's programme to a single type with 3,690cc sv monobloc 4-cylinder engine on classical lines.   MCS

Z (ii) (CS) *1924–1939*
Akciova spolecnost Československá zbrojovka, Brno

This ex-armaments factory — like many others — had to look for new business after World War 1. They started with a design by Novotny known as the Disk. It had a single-cylinder 2-stroke 600cc engine. The company became more widely known through their unorthodox competition cars, which also used 2-stroke engines. The most famous were the Z2 of 1929 and the Z13 of 1931. The Z2 had a 6-cylinder 1,100cc engine, with opposed pistons and a Roots blower, developing 60bhp. The most remarkable feature of the Z13 was its engine, an 8-cylinder 1,500cc unit with 4 parallel pairs of cylinders. Each pair of cylinders had two pistons, but one common combustion chamber. A Roots blower was also used for this engine and the output was 60bhp. The maximum speed of both models is reported to have been 95mph. Both versions were used mainly in Czech race meetings. During the 1930s some private cars were built, also equipped with 2-stroke engines. Best known were the 2-cylinder Z4, Z6 and Z9, and the 4-cylinder 1.5-litre Z5. The engine output of the Z5 was a remarkable 40bhp.   HON

ZAPOROZHETS (SU) *1960 to date*
Communard Works, Zaporozh, Melitopol

Containing a 887cc 27bhp air-cooled V-4 engine in the rear, this 2-door saloon is similar in layout to the Fiat 600. Construction problems are said to have been experienced with the Zaporozhets ZAZ-965 and this was replaced by an improved 966. Unitary construction is employed, suspension is independent and the car may be ordered with a centrifugal clutch if desired. In 1968 an export edition, known as the Yalta, was exhibited at Geneva; it had a 1-litre water-cooled Renault engine, but that year's home-market Zaporozhets featured enlarged and more powerful 1,196cc V-4s with synchromesh on bottom gear. The 1972 version of this model had a 50bhp unit.   BE

ZASTAVA (YU) *1954 to date*
Zavodi Crveni Zastava, Kragujevac

Zastava started by assembling or manufacturing Fiat cars under licence: 1400s, 1900s and 600s were the first types to appear, followed by the 1100, 1300 and 1500, the 124 and 125 (1968), and the Polski-Fiat 125P (1970). Since 1971 the firm has also been making the 101, a slightly modified version of the 1,116cc fwd 128 saloon.   MCS

ZEDDECO (F) *1905–1906*
The Zeddeco was an electric car powered by two Lohner motors, one mounted in each front wheel. This was the same system as used on the Lohner-Porsche cars.   GNG

ZÉDEL (F;CH) *1906–1923*
(1) Sté Française des Automobiles Zédel, Pontarlier, Doubs (France) *1906–1923*
(2) Fabrique de Moteurs et Machines Zédel, St Aubin, Neuchâtel (Switzerland) *1907–1908*

The name Zédel comes from those of the makers, Ernest Zürcher and Hermann Lüthi (Z.L.). Originally they made engines for motor cycles and tricycles at St Aubin. Car production was started on French soil to avoid customs duty, as France provided a much larger market than Switzerland. The first Zédel was a neat light car powered by a 4-cylinder 1,128cc monobloc engine, with multiple-plate clutch, shaft drive and a two-seater body. A few of these were made in Switzerland, together with the 10/12hp four-seater model which joined the range in 1908. A 16/18hp was added in 1909, and by 1912 there were three models, of which the largest was an 18hp 4-cylinder of 3,563cc. The post-war Zédel range consisted of two models, both 4-cylinder sv cars of no originality, with engines of 2,120cc and 3,168cc. In 1923 the company merged with Donnet. Production was transferred to Nanterre, and the cars sold under the name Donnet-Zédel.   GNG

ZEILLER ET FOURNIER (F) *1920–1924*
Automobiles Zeiller et Fournier, Levallois-Perret, Seine

The Zeiller et Fournier used an 1,131cc Ballot 4-cylinder engine, a 5-speed friction transmission and chain final drive. It was designed by the racing driver Charles Fournier, and was often known simply as Fournier. The 2-cylinder Train-engined cars made at the same time were apparently always called Fourniers.

GNG

ZENA (I) 1906–1908
Zena Fabbrica di Automobili SA, Genoa

A short-lived firm that was a casualty of the Agadir Crisis, Zena offered a wide range of types with sv engines and shaft drive – 6hp and 8hp singles, a 10hp four, a larger 14hp four with separate cylinders, and a 20hp six, the N3. MCS

ZENDIK (GB) 1913–1914
Zendik Cars Ltd, Kingston-on-Thames, Surrey

The Zendik cyclecar was powered by an 8hp Chater-Lea 2-cylinder engine. It had 2 speeds, with direct drive on top, and a chain reduction for bottom, while reverse was obtained by two friction wheels. Final drive was by overhead worm gearing on the rear axle. GNG

ZÉNIA (F) 1913–1924
Automobiles Zénia, Paris

The Zénia was powered by a 4-cylinder T-head engine of 3 litres' capacity. Two cars were entered in the 1913 Coupe de l'Auto but neither made the reputation of the company. The post-war Zénia used a smaller engine of 1,775cc, and seems to have made very little impression on the motoring world. GNG

ZÉNITH (F) 1910
M. Arnaud, Forcalquier

The Zénith was an 8hp single-cylinder voiturette using friction transmission. GNG

ZENT (US) 1902–1907
(1) Zent Automobile Manufacturing Co, Bellefontaine, Ohio 1902–1907
(2) Bellefontaine Automobile Co, Bellefontaine, Ohio 1907

The Zent was built in two- and five-seater models, with 2-, 3-, and 4-cylinder engines. The transmissions were of the planetary type, and the later models at least used shaft drive. The Zent was succeeded by the Bellefontaine. GMN

ZEPHYR (GB) 1919–1920
James, Talbot and Davidson Ltd, Lowestoft, Suffolk

The three men concerned with this company had all worked together at the Adams-Hewitt company before joining forces to make their own car. This had an 11.9hp 1,944cc push-rod ohv 4-cylinder engine, and a 4-speed gearbox. Conventional two- and four-seater bodies were provided, and the cars had a tall, narrow, V-radiator. They were shown at Olympia in 1919, and deliveries were promised for July 1920, but supply difficulties were very great at this time, and production never started. The firm made Zephyr pistons for some time, and the name survived on floats for fishermen until after World War 2. GNG

ZETA (i) (I) 1914–1915
Fratelli Zambelli, Piacenza

Zetas were orthodox cars with 4-cylinder sv monobloc engines. Only one chassis was marketed, but buyers had the choice of two engine sizes 1,131cc or 1,723cc) and three or four forward speeds. MCS

ZETA (ii) (AUS) 1964–1967
Lightburn and Co Ltd, Camden, South Australia

The Lightburn organization manufactures a diversity of products. In addition to assembling Alfa Romeos for the Australian market, it also makes concrete mixers, fibreglass boats, spin driers, washing machines, and wheelbarrows. The Zeta was a small utility vehicle with reinforced channel-steel frame, all-round independent suspension, and a reinforced plastic body with pressed-steel doors. Power was provided by a 324cc transverse-twin 2-stroke Villiers air-cooled engine driving the front wheels, and there was a 4-speed gearbox. Bodywork was in the station wagon style, though an open sports version was exhibited. MCS

ZETGELETTE (D) 1923
Zetge-Fahrzeug-Werk AG, Moys nr Görlitz

The Zetgelette was a small 3-wheeled two-seater vehicle with a 3PS 2-stroke D.K.W. engine mounted above the front wheel, which was driven by belt. HON

ZÉVACO (F) 1923–1925
SA des Voiturettes Cyclecars, Eaubonne, Seine-et-Oise

The Zévaco cyclecar was made in three versions, a 900cc twin with a Train engine, a 961cc four with a Chapuis-Dornier engine and a Ruby-powered four of 1,095cc. GNG

ZIEBEL (US) 1914–1915
A.C. Ziebel, Oshkosh, Wisc.

1923 ZÉDEL Model C16 12.1hp tourer. *Murray Beecroft*

1920 ZEILLER ET FOURNIER 8hp two-seater. *Autocar*

1964 ZIL 111G 6-litre limousine. *V/O Autoexport, Moscow*

1954 ZIM(ii) 3½-litre saloon. *V/O Autoexport, Moscow*

1909 ZIMMERMAN 12hp motor buggy. *Eugene Zimmerman*

1939 ZIS 101 5½-litre saloon. *Autocar*

The Ziebel cyclecar had two side-by-side seats. It was driven by a 4-cylinder, water-cooled Badger engine. Wheelbase was 8ft with track of 3ft 6in. GMN

ZIL (SU) *1956 to date*
Zavod Imieni Likhacheva, Moscow

The large Zil seven-seater limousine is the luxury car of Soviet Union and a continuation of the previous Zis series, built at the Likhachev factory, formerly known as the Stalin Works.

The Zil, as the Zis before it, is not generally available on the open market, for it is used largely by government officials. The cars are built to order by the government and no production figures have ever been published, but they are certainly quite limited, and thus very expensive units to produce. The factory turns out a variety of other products including trucks, bicycles and refrigerators and is the second largest factory in Russia.

In 1956 the name of the factory was changed from Stalin and the new Zil commenced with model 111. This series, like its predecessor, was largely Packard influenced with a frontal treatment much like the 1956 American car. Some 111-V tourers were built and a 112 sports is reported to have been made. The engine was a V-8 of 220bhp driving an automatic transmission with push button shift. Power assisted brakes and steering featured with other high grade appointments.

In 1963 the greatly revised 111-G was introduced with styling more like that of General Motors. A 6-litre V-8 of 230bhp at 4,200rpm is used, giving a reported maximum speed of 106mph.

A prototype Zil was shown in 1960 with six headlights and a mixture of Ford and General Motors ideas, but it never re-appeared and was apparently abandoned as too flamboyant. In 1970 a new limousine was announced. This 114 had razor-edged styling above the waistline, and was powered by a 7-litre V-8 engine. Air conditioning was standard. BE

ZIM (i) (F) *1922–1924*
Automobiles Zimmermann, Epernay, Marne

The Zim was a very small cyclecar made in single- and two-seater forms. It was powered by a single-cylinder Train engine of 344cc, and used chain drive. GNG

ZIM (ii) (GAZ M-12) (SU) *1950–1957*
Zavod Imieni Molotova, Gorky

Construction of the Zim provided a luxury sedan for those in the Soviet Union who did not quite rate a Zis. Some were also exported to Finland.

With an L-head, 94hp 6-cylinder engine, the car seated six in comfort and had a fairly handsome, rugged appearance comparable to some General Motors bodies of the time. A fluid drive coupling with a single dry-plate clutch and three speed gearbox made up the transmission assembly and a maximum speed of 80mph was attained. Additionally to the sedan, some Zims were built as ambulances and a few as touring cars but these seem to be rather rare.

The Andrei Lipgart design team that developed the Zim was also responsible for the Pobieda. BE

ZIMMERMAN (US) *1908–1914*
Zimmerman Manufacturing Co, Auburn, Ind.

The original model of this make was a high-wheeler with solid rubber tyres and a 12hp engine. In 1910, standard cars replaced the high-wheelers. The 1910 cars used 4-cylinder engines of 5.5 litres. The company was bought by Auburn (i) in 1911. The first 6-cylinder model was the Z-6 of 1912 with a 5.4-litre engine. During the last four years of manufacture, 4-cylinder engines were also used. GMN

ZIP (US) *1913–1914*
Zip Cyclecar Co, Davenport, Iowa

The Zip cyclecar carried two passengers, side by side. Its V-twin air-cooled engine delivered 10/14hp. A 6-bladed fan provided cooling. Friction transmission and belt drive were used. With sporting wire wheels, this cyclecar cost $395. GMN

ZIS (SU) *1936–1956*
Zavod Imieni Stalina, Moscow

As the luxury limousine of the Soviet Union, the Zis was limited to a few designs during its 20 year span, beginning with the Model 101 which had the general configuration of a large American sedan of the mid-1930s. Little was reported about the specifications of these cars, but it is known that the engine was strongly influenced by the Buick straight-8 and had an estimated capacity of 5.5 litres. Transmission was 3-speed with synchromesh, and suspension was by semi-elliptic springs at front and rear.

As the Stalin Works operated on a special order basis for the government, the cars were in reality custom made. It has been calculated that probably no more than two a day were turned out, implying a high production cost per unit. Zis cars were reserved for officials or professional men with high positions in the Soviet Union.

Trucks and some consumer goods actually accounted for most of the Stalin Works' production – and still do under the present management.

A general face-lifting was accomplished on the Model 102 introduced about 1940. This machine was built as an open touring car as well as a limousine and appeared frequently in Moscow parades.

The German invasion of 1941 interrupted Zis car manufacture, but it is reported that as early as 1942 plans were made for the post-war Model 110. This appeared at the end of 1945 and was very similar to the much admired Packard Series 180: Packard dies had been purchased from Briggs in Detroit by a Russian trade delegation, and these were skilfully adapted to the proposed 110, thereby greatly reducing the time required to bring out the new design.

The Model 110 had an 8-cylinder, 137bhp sv engine driving through a 3-speed synchromesh gearbox. Standard equipment included power windows and folding occasional seats. Maximum speed was about 90mph with a fuel consumption of 10mpg. Some tourers and a number of ambulances were built on the 110 chassis in addition to the limousines.

The factory had originally been called the AMO Works, producing model F-15 trucks, but was rebuilt and named after Stalin during the first Five Year Plan in 1928. In 1956, the ZIS factory was renamed Zavod Imieni Likhacheva in honour of Ivan A. Likhachev, the former director of the plant and a pioneer in experimental car construction after the Revolution. Apparently consideration was given to the manufacture of an 8-cylinder, seven-seater limousine called the Moskva during this transitional period, but this was built only as a prototype and abandoned.

Because of the change in factory name, the Zis became known as the Zil.

BE

ZÜNDAPP (D) 1956–1958
Zündapp-Werke GmbH, Nuremberg; Munich

Zündapp was one of the best known German manufacturers of motor cycles. A first attempt at car production was made in 1931 with a Porsche design, characterized by an air-cooled 5-cylinder radial engine and recognized today as one of the Volkswagen predecessors, but only a few prototypes were built. In 1956 Zündapp took a licence for a small Dornier-designed vehicle distinguished by *dos à dos* seating which inspired its name: Janus, after the Roman god who faced two ways. The 248cc single-cylinder 2-stroke engine was placed between the front and back seat. Production ceased in 1958 and Zündapp today builds only motor cycles. HON

ZUNDER (RA) 1960–1962
Industrias del Transporte Automotor srl, Rio Cuarto

The Zunder was a rear-engined saloon using a 1½-litre air-cooled flat-4 Porsche engine and Porsche-type suspension. The frame was tubular and the fibreglass coachwork resembled that of the contemporary Ford Anglia. A top speed of 87mph was claimed, but only about 200 were made. MCS

ZÜST; BRIXIA-ZÜST (I) 1905–1917
(1) Ing Roberto Züst Fabbrica Italiana di Automobili SA, Milan *1905–1911*
(2) Brixia-Züst SA, Brescia *1906–1911*
(3) Fabbrica Automobili Züst, Brescia *1912–1917*

The Swiss-born engineer Roberto Züst made turbines at Intra on Lake Maggiore and left his company to his sons on his death in 1897. There seem to have been some experiments with cars at the turn of the century, but serious manufacture did not begin until the establishment of the Milan works in 1905. The first Züsts were typical Italian interpretations of the Mercédès theme, with four pair-cast cylinders, lt magneto ignition, pressed-steel frame, 4-speed gate-change gearboxes and side-chain drive. There was, however, one big difference: what appeared to be a T-head engine was not, since on Züsts the second camshaft merely actuated the make-and-break. Two models were made at first, a 7.4-litre 28/45 and an 11.3-litre 40/50; these were joined by a smaller 5-litre car in 1908. Züsts of this type were still being marketed as late as 1913, and a 28/45 took 3rd place in the 1908 New York-Paris marathon.

In 1906 an associate company was set up in Brescia (the Latin name for the city was Brixia) to make more economical cars such as the 14/18hp Brixia-Züst with ht magneto ignition and shaft drive. Two years later they made a bid for the economy market with a 1.4-litre three-in-line rated at 10hp. Cylinders were cast monobloc, and this one had a true T-head; 150 examples of a 1½-litre development served as taxicabs in London in 1910. Meanwhile the Milan-built Züsts continued with little change until 1910 when a shaft-driven L-head 3-litre 16/20 was marketed, still with pair-cast cylinders. By this time the Brescia operation had been losing money for several years, and even a small 2.3-litre four made little impression. The two concerns were therefore merged at the end of 1911, and production concentrated at Brescia, where more developments of the 16/20 theme made their appearance. They came in 2.9-litre, 6.2-litre and 7.4-litre sizes, the biggest of the range having lightweight connecting rods and pistons, frontal and flywheel fans, and the options of Riley wire wheels and dual ignition. Monobloc engines and pear-shaped radiators *à la* Fiat were seen on the 4.7-litre S305 of 1913, a 60mph car with all its brakes on the rear wheels. Two years later the 2.9-litre 15/25 was updated in like fashion, but at the end of 1917 Züst sold out to the Officine Meccaniche. This firm continued production of S305s under the O.M. name. MCS

1950 ZIS 110 5.4-litre convertible. *V/O Autoexport, Moscow*

1956 ZÜNDAPP Janus 248cc saloon. *G.N. Georgano*

1960 ZUNDER 1500 saloon. *G.N. Georgano*

1908 ZÜST 1,495cc 3-cylinder tourer. *Museo dell'Automobile, Turin*

1958 ZWICKAU P70 684cc saloon. *G.N.*
Georgano

ZWICKAU (D) *1956–1959*
VEB Automobilwerk Zwickau, Zwickau

The IFA F8 was succeeded by the Zwickau P70 which had the same 684cc engine and front drive, but new bodywork: this type was the first mass-produced German car with a fibreglass body, and 25,000 were made. It was succeeded by the P50 in 1959, which is marketed as the Trabant.   HON

Glossary

A guide to the more frequently-used technical and general terms which may not be familiar to the present-day reader. No attempt has been made to give a complete glossary of the motorcar.

The definitions of body styles are very general, as there have been few standard definitions laid down, and these few have been frequently ignored by car makers and coachbuilders.

ALAM formula rating – *see* horsepower.

Automatic inlet valves (aiv). Inlet valves opened atmospherically, without any mechanical control. A primitive system, soon replaced by mechanical actuation (moiv).

Avant-train. A two-wheeled power unit consisting of engine, gearbox, final drive, steering wheel and other controls, which could be attached to a horse-drawn vehicle, or to enable various bodies to be used with the same engine. *Avant-train* units were the earliest examples of front-wheel drive, but were outmoded soon after 1900. Electric as well as petrol engines were used.

Belt drive. A system whereby the final drive is conveyed from countershaft to rear axle by leather belts.

bhp – *see* horse power.

Bialbero. Twin overhead camshafts.

Blower – *see* supercharger.

Brake – *see* shooting brake.

Cabriolet – *see* drophead coupé.

Cardan (shaft). The driving shaft which conveys power from gearbox to rear axle. More usually known as the propeller shaft, the word was widely used in France (transmission à cardan) in early days to distinguish shaft drive from chain drive. The principle is said to have been invented by the Italian philosopher, Girolamo Cardano (1501–1576).

Chain drive. A system whereby the final drive is conveyed from countershaft to the wheels by chains. Double chain drive was widely used on powerful cars until about 1908, but could still be found on some old fashioned machines as late as 1914. Indeed Frazer Nash used three chains, one for each forward speed, as late as 1939. A number of light cars used centrally-mounted single chain drive to a live axle.

Convertible (orig. convertible sedan or convertible coupé). Any car with folding roof and wind up windows; the term is largely found in American usage, and dates only from the early 1930s. In the 1950s the term 'hard-top convertible' came into use, meaning a style resembling a convertible, but whose roof could not, in fact, be folded.

Coupé de ville. A body style in which the passenger compartment was closed, but the driver was exposed to the weather, although from the 1920s onward a sliding roof was often provided. The sedanca de ville was a similar style, although often with four windows in the passenger compartment, whereas the coupé de ville had two windows and closed panels with imitation hood irons. Some 'de ville' bodies had folding rear quarters as in the landaulette. In America they were more often known as town cars.

CV – *see* horsepower.

Cyclecar. A simple light car whose design owed much to motorcycle practice, of which a large variety were made from 1912 until about 1922. The typical cyclecar had an engine of less than four cylinders, often air-cooled, with final drive by belts or chains. Cyclecars flourished in England, France and the United States, but disappeared with the coming of mass-produced 'genuine light cars' such as the Austin Seven and Citroën 5CV.

De Dion axle. A system of final drive in which the rear axle is 'dead', or separate from the driving shafts. The drive is transmitted by independent, universally-jointed half shafts. The system was first used on the De Dion-Bouton steamers of the 1890s, but was abandoned by the firm after 1914. It is, however, used on a number of modern sports cars.

Dickey (US : Rumble seat). A folding seat for two passengers, used to increase the carrying capacity of an ordinary two-seater car. These were sometimes referred to as 'two/four seaters'.

Dos-à-dos. A four-seater car in which the passengers sat back to back. Seldom seen after about 1900, this layout was revived briefly in the Zündapp Janus of 1956.

Drophead coupé. A body style incorporating a folding roof and wind-up windows, in its most typical form a two-door, four-seater, although some were two-seaters. An alternative name was cabriolet, which was especially used in Germany for this style.

Epicyclic gearbox. A form of gear in which small pinions (planetary pinions) revolve around a central, or sun gear, and mesh with an outer ring gear, or annulus. Best known for their use in the Ford Model T, epicyclic gearboxes were found in a wide variety of early American cars. In America they are known as planetary transmissions.

Estate car – *see* shooting brake.

Fast and loose pulleys. A system of transmission in which the countershaft carried a loose pulley for neutral, and two fixed pulleys meshing with spur gears of different ratios on the axle. Moving a belt from loose to fixed pulley provided a clutch action. The system was used on early Benz, New Orleans, and other cars.

F-head. Cylinder head design incorporating overhead inlet and side exhaust valves. Also known as inlet-over-exhaust, or ioe. *See also* L-head, T-head.

Friction transmission. A system of transmission using two discs in contact at right angles. Variation in gear ratio was obtained by sliding the edge of one disc across the face of the other. This theoretically provided an infinitely variable ratio, although in some systems there were a limited number of positions for the sliding disc.

High-wheeler. A simple car with the appearance of a motorized buggy which enjoyed a brief period of popularity in the United States and Canada, between 1907 and 1912. Over 70 firms built high-wheelers, the best-known being Holsman, International and Sears.

Horsepower (hp, bhp, CV, PS). The unit used for measuring the power output of the engine, defined mechanically as 33,000 foot-pounds per minute. Up to about 1910 the horsepower quoted by makers was meant to correspond to the actual output, though often used with more optimism than accuracy. Sometimes a double figure would be quoted such as 10/12 or 24/30; here the first figure represented the power developed at 1,000 rpm, while the second was the power developed at the engine's maximum speed. In 1904 the Automobile Club of Great Britain & Ireland's rating (the RAC rating from 1907 onwards) of horsepower was introduced, calculated on the bore of the engine only, and as engine efficiency improved, the discrepancy between rated and actual horsepower grew. Thus by the mid-1920s a car might be described as a 12/50 or a 14/40, where the first figure was the rated hp, and the second the actual horsepower developed at maximum revs. RAC ratings were widely used until after World War 2, but when taxation by horsepower was abandoned in January, 1948, manufacturers soon ceased to describe their cars as Eights or Tens.

The American ALAM (later NACC) horsepower rating followed the British system of calculation on the cylinder bore alone, but French (CV) and German (PS) ratings were based on different formulae, with the result that a 15hp British car might be called an 11CV in France and a 9PS in Germany. The French rating was introduced in 1912, and the German at about the same time. Prior to this, the terms CV and PS were used to denote actual brake horsepower. Today horsepower rating has largely been abandoned; engine capacity is indicated in litres, and power in developed or brake horsepower (bhp).

Hot-tube ignition. An early system in which the mixture was ignited by a small platinum tube, open at its inner end, which was screwed into the cylinder head. The outer, closed end was heated to red heat by a small, petrol-fed burner, and when the mixture passed into the tube, it ignited. The system was outdated by 1900, though some firms continued to fit tubes as an auxiliary to electric ignition.

Inlet over exhaust valves – *see* F-head.

Landau. A body style with a folding roof in two parts, so that it could be half open at front or back, or entirely open. The term was used for horsedrawn carriages, but seldom applied to motorcars.

Landaulet (or **landaulette**). A closed car, the rear portion of which could be opened in fine weather.

L-head. Cylinder head design in which inlet and exhaust valves are mounted on one side of the engine. It was the most commonly used design for all but high performance engines, from about 1910 until after World War 2. Also known as side valves (sv). *See* T-head.

Limousine. A closed car with glass division between driver and the passenger compartment.

Live axle. An axle which transmits power, as opposed to a dead axle, where the power is either carried by separate half shafts (*see* De Dion axle) or by side chains.

Mechanically operated inlet valves (moiv) – *see* automatic inlet valves.

Monocar. Single-seater car. The expression is never used for racing cars, most of which have been single-seaters since the late 1920s (these are sometimes known as Monopostos), but for the ultra-light single-seater cyclecars of the 1912 to 1915 period.

Motor buggy – *see* high-wheeler.

Overhead valve. Cylinder-head design in which the valves are mounted above the combustion chamber, either horizontally, or inclined at an angle. Generally abbreviated to ohv.

Over-square. An engine in which the cylinder bore is greater than the stroke (eg 110mm × 100mm). A 'square' engine is one in which bore and stroke are identical (eg 100mm × 100mm).

Phaeton. An early word for an open car, especially used in the term double phaeton which was a four- or five-seater tourer. One with three rows of seats was a triple phaeton. The term was also applied to some American four-door convertible sedans of the 1920s and 1930s. See also *Roi des Belges*.

Planetary transmission – *see* epicyclic gearbox.

PS – *see* horsepower.

R.A.C. rating – *see* horsepower.

Roadster. A two-seater open car of sporting appearance.

Roi des Belges. A luxurious style of open touring car, named after King Leopold II of Belgium. The style is said to have been suggested to the King by his mistress Cléo de Mérode. The style was sometimes known as the Tulip Phaeton.

Rotary valves. Valves contained in the cylinder head whose rotary motion allows the passage of mixture and exhaust gases at the appropriate times.

Rumble seat – *see* dickey.

Runabout. A general term for a light two-seater car of the early 1900s, especially those made in America.

Saloon (US: Sedan). A closed car for four or more passengers, with either two or four doors. Sports saloon is a loose term for a high-performance version, generally with only two doors.

Sedanca de ville – *see* coupé de ville.

Selective transmission. The conventional transmission in which any gear may be selected at will, in distinction to the earlier progressive transmission in which the gears had to be selected in order.

Shooting brake, brake, estate car, station bus, station wagon. The original brake or shooting brake was similar to the wagonette, and was used on large estates for carrying members of shooting parties. The station bus was used for conveying guests and servants, and was usually a closed vehicle whereas early brakes were open. After World War 1 both types declined in use, but the names were reincarnated in the wood-panelled station wagon which American manufacturers began to offer as part of their ranges in the 1930s. By 1941 all the popular makers were listing station wagons, and the fashion spread to Europe, where the name estate car was more often used, after World War 2.

Side valves. Cylinder-head design in which the valves are mounted at the side of the combustion chamber. They may be side-by-side (L-head), or on opposite sides of the engine (T-head). The usual abbreviation, sv, applies to the L-head design, the rarer T-head design being specifically mentioned.

Sleeve valves. Metal sleeves placed between the piston and the cylinder wall. When moved up and down, holes in them coincide to provide passage for gases at the correct times.

Spyder. A light two-seater car, sometimes with a precarious looking third seat behind, used in the early years of the century. In the 1950s the word was revived by some Italian manufacturers for an open two-seater sports car.

'Square' engine – *see* over-square.

Station bus, station wagon – *see* shooting brake.

Supercharger (colloquially, 'blower'). A compressor fitted to an engine to force the mixture into the cylinders at a pressure greater than that of the atmosphere. First seen on the 1908 Chadwick, the supercharger was widely used on sports and racing cars between the wars, and on Formula 1 racing cars up to 1954.

Surrey. An open four-seater car, often with a fringed top.

T-head. Cylinder head design in which inlet valves are mounted on one side of the engine, and exhaust valves on the other. Two camshafts were needed, and in order to make do with only one, the side by side or L-head design was developed, and the T-head was outmoded after about 1910.

Tonneau. Strictly speaking, a four-seater car in which access to the rear seats was by a door at the rear of the body. This layout was used up to about 1904, after which longer wheelbases enabled doors to be mounted at the sides. This design was sometimes called the side-entrance tonneau, but in this book we are calling all side-entrance open cars tourers.

Torpedo (or **torpedo tourer**). An open touring car with an unbroken line from bonnet to windscreen, and from windscreen right through to the back of the car, the seats being flush with the body sides. Bodies of this design began to appear in about 1910, and by 1920 were taken for granted, so the name torpedo was usually dropped in favour of tourer. However, French manufacturers continued to call their tourers 'torpédos' until 1930, and the term was used in Italy later still.

Tourer. An open car with seats for four or more passengers. Early tourers had no weather protection at the sides, later ones being provided with detachable side-screens and curtains. Those with wind-up or fixed windows were more often called all-weather tourers. After about 1930 the mass-produced closed car replaced the tourer as the most popular type, and the average manufacturer soon abandoned the production of tourers.

Town car – *see* coupé de ville.

Trembler-coil ignition. Ignition by induction coil and electromagnetic vibrator which broke the primary circuit and induced the high-tension current in the secondary windings. Used by Benz and many other pioneers, but superseded by the De Dion-Bouton patent contact breaker, invented by Georges Bouton in 1895.

Victoria. A two-seater open car, often with a large, folding hood. More frequently applied to horsedrawn carriages, the word was seldom used for cars after 1900.

Vis-à-vis. A four-seater car in which two passengers sat facing the driver.

Voiture Légère. Light car; a term used to describe racing cars falling between the heavy car class and the voiturettes. In the early town-to-town races, *voitures légères* were confined to a weight limit of 650kg, while from 1911 to 1914 there was an engine capacity limit of 3 litres. The term was never used widely to describe production cars.

Voiturette. A French term for a light car, initially used by Léon Bollée for his 3-wheeler of 1895, but soon applied by manufacturers and journalists to any small car. The voiturette class in racing has had various definitions: up to 1905, a weight limit of 400kg; 1906–1910 a limited bore varying with the number of cylinders; 1921–1925, a capacity limit of 1500cc. After 1925 the term was used only loosely for small racing cars, and not for production cars at all.

V-radiator. A honeycomb radiator coming to a more or less sharp point. The first production car to use the design was probably the Métallurgique in 1907, and by 1914 a large number of makes had V-radiators. They were especially popular in Germany, and from 1919 to 1923 there was hardly a single German or Austrian car without a V-radiator. They should not be confused with the V-shaped grille found on many cars of the later 1930s, whose flamboyant design concealed an ordinary flat radiator behind.

Waggonette. A large car usually for six or more passengers, in which the rear seats faced each other. Entrance was at the rear, and the vehicles were usually open. *See also* shooting brake.

Personalities

Component Manufacturers; Agents